The Public Image of Henry Ford

As mechanics work on a Model K, Henry Ford, in goggles, awaits his chance to lower the world's speed record for the mile on the sands of Cape May, New Jersey. At left is Gaston Plantiff, the Ford Company's New York branch manager.

The Public Image of
HENRY FORD

An American Folk Hero

and His Company

by David L. Lewis

UNIVERSITY OF MICHIGAN

Wayne State University Press, Detroit, 1976

Library of Congress Cataloging in Publication Data

Lewis, David Lanier, 1927–
    The public image of Henry Ford.

    Includes bibliographical references and index.
        1. Ford, Henry, 1863–1947. 2. Ford Motor Company.
    3. Automobile industry and trade—United States—History.
    I. Title.
    HD9710.U52L49   338.7'62'62920924   [B]   76–807
    ISBN 0–8143–1553–4

Second Printing, November 1976

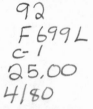
    All photographs were furnished Courtesy of the Ford Archives, Henry Ford Museum, Dearborn, Michigan, except those carrying an acknowledgment to another source.

To Yuri

Contents

Acknowledgments

The resources of the Ford Archives, a part of the Henry Ford Museum, have been invaluable in researching this book; and I am deeply indebted to the Archives' director, Henry E. Edmunds, and archivists Winthrop Sears, Jr., and David R. Crippen for their cooperation and assistance over a span of two decades. Special thanks is owed James J. Bradley, curator of the National Automotive History Collection of the Detroit Public Library for his courtesies; Sidney Fine, Andrew Dickson White Professor of History, University of Michigan, for his counsel and editorial assistance; Philip Slomovitz of the *Jewish News* for his advice; and two late Ford advertising/public relations executives, Fred L. Black and A. R. Barbier, each of whom reviewed large portions of the manuscript. I am very grateful for the editorial guidance provided by editors Faith Schmidt and Elaine P. Halperin of the Wayne State University Press and for the continuing encouragement offered by former Press directors Harold A. Basilius and Herbert M. Schueller and current associate director Richard R. Kinney. A heartfelt thank-you also is due my wife, Yuri, who made it possible for me to devote the necessary time to this work, and typed and proofread the manuscript.

David L. Lewis
Ann Arbor, June 1975

Introduction

Henry Ford, one of the world's best-known industrialists, wielded an extraordinary influence on the American scene. His Model T, mass production methods, and wage-price theories revolutionized American industry and reverberated around the world. An indigenous folk hero, Ford appealed to millions of his countrymen because, in their view, he succeeded through his own creativeness and hard work and by supplying a product to meet the public's desires rather than by manipulating money or people. He also was admired, despite his great wealth, for having retained the common touch. Asked on his fiftieth birthday to cite the greatest handicap of the rich, he replied, "For me, it was when Mrs. Ford stopped cooking." Regarded as an industrial superman and believed by many to typify American civilization and genius, he reminded people of an earlier, simpler society.

Ford was a late starter; life for him began at forty. Born in 1863, he was unknown outside of Detroit until 1901, when his racing exploits placed his name on sports pages. He made two false starts as an auto manufacturer before founding the Ford Motor Company in 1903. Within a decade he had acquired wealth, had become the auto industry's dominant figure, and gained a measure of national prominence. In 1914, at age fifty-one, he became an overnight international celebrity by more than doubling the wages of most of his workers. Ford's prime extended into his late sixties, and perhaps would have lasted longer had it not been for the great depression of the 1930s. Even so, the auto maker remained vigorous and continued to guide and personify his company even in his eighties.

Controversial, paradoxical, colorful, Henry Ford was an enigma, endlessly fascinating. An idealistic pioneer in some respects, he was a cynical reactionary in others. He had a selfish, mean, even cruel streak, yet often was generous, kindly, and compassionate. He was ignorant, narrow-minded, and stubborn, yet at times he displayed remarkable insight, vision, open-mindedness, and flexibility. His chameleon-like, mercurial personality kept his associates on edge, so unpredictable was his behavior. "History," he proclaimed, "is more or less bunk," and he went on to build a depository of Americana. He constructed the world's biggest factory, yet found delight in building waterpower plants that employed as few as eleven workers. Highly sympathetic toward blacks, he was known as a persecutor of Jews. He did not believe in organized charity, yet gave millions to good works. The list can go on and on. How, one must ask himself, did such a man rise to the heights?

Ford had several outstanding qualities: native intelligence and common sense, even though the latter occasionally failed him; an intuitive mind which leaped beyond the present, and a special engineering talent that combined creativity with practicality; a remarkable memory, a missionary's zeal, and a lifelong capacity for hard work, especially thinking, which he termed "the hardest work there is." He shunned the conventional vices, although circumstantial evidence suggests that he had a brief, intense extramarital relationship during the early 1920s. Ford also had, or made, his share of good luck. His entry into auto making and the introduction of his Model T were perfectly timed. He was teamed, by accident, with James Couzens, who contributed as much as Ford to the Ford Company's early success.

Finally, he married a woman who understood and complemented him. Clara Bryant, like Henry, was reared on a farm in the Dearborn area. Three years younger than her husband, she was convinced from the time they were married in 1888 that her husband would accomplish something notable. Ford called her "The Believer." Henry's sweetheart in springtime, his nurse during the autumnal years, his companion in all seasons, Clara encouraged and stood by her husband for fifty-nine years. She intervened in company affairs on only two occasions. In 1941, when Ford threatened to shut down his company rather than sign a labor contract, she threatened to leave him if he did not immediately settle with his workers. He did. In 1945, she labored to convince her eighty-two-year-old husband that the time had come to transfer the presidency to his grandson. Henry again gave way. Clara could not prevent her husband's frequent harsh treatment of their only son, Edsel, but she deeply resented it.

Edsel Ford, born in 1893, grew up with the Ford Company. He was named president of the firm in 1918, but remained in his father's shadow. Competent and respected, he gradually gained responsibility for styling, sales, and advertising (but never for labor relations, engineering, or manufacturing). In the 1930s the company would have benefited greatly had Edsel been allowed to assume his aging father's mantle. Edsel and his wife, Eleanor Clay, born in 1896 into a socially prominent Detroit family, had four children between 1917 and 1925—Henry II, Benson, Josephine, and William Clay. Henry II has successfully administered the company since 1945; his son, Edsel II, born in 1948, is being groomed for the presidency as of this writing.

Since 1952 I have read and thought a great deal about Henry Ford, published more than a million words about him, exclusive of this book, and visited all of his familiar haunts. I probably know more about Ford's life and work than any other writer. But I cannot say that I have completely sorted him out; nor am I sure that I shall fully understand him. But it is time to set down what I know.

Readers can start this book at the beginning, and move chronologically through the Ford saga. Or they can quickly capture the flavor of Ford's prime of life and his company's public relations by sampling such chapters as "The Five-Dollar Day," "Peace Crusade," "Genius-Ignoramus," "Flivver Public Relations," "Farewell, My Lovely" (Model T), and "Folk Hero."

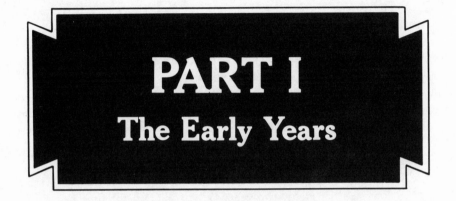

PART I
The Early Years

Chapter 1
Racing for Recognition

1

William H. Vanderbilt had had enough. The crack train his New York Central was running between New York and Chicago was losing money, and, he told reporters, it was going to be withdrawn. "But," a journalist asked, "how about the public?" Vanderbilt thereupon snapped the dictum that has come to be regarded as characteristic of the American business community between 1865 and 1900: "The public be damned." [1]

Big business public relations during this period could be characterized by a second doctrine: the less the public knew of business operations, the more efficient and profitable these operations would be. This policy so permeated business thinking that the greater the public interest, the more determined the industry was to keep its activities secret. [2]

Shortly before the emergence of more enlightened public relations another fledgling business, the automobile industry—destined in less than three decades to take first rank among manufacturers—clattered onto the American stage. From the start of the auto industry in the mid-1890s most manufacturers engaged in contests, participated in exhibitions, sought press publicity, prepared promotional literature, and bought advertising space. The Ford Motor Company, organized in 1903, was caught up and carried along with these sales-promotion ventures. Within a half-dozen years, it was a leading exponent of most of them; within a decade it had introduced several new promotional techniques (including owners' clubs, radical pricing policies, and motion pictures) which spurred the sale of autos and added a new dimension to public relations. [3]

Of the various promotional activities in which auto makers were engaged during the early years, racing was by far the most important. Cars quickly proved themselves speedier than the bicycle or the horse and just as quickly appealed to the public as a racing vehicle. As Henry Ford later pointed out, "When it was found that an automobile really could go and several makers started to put out cars, the immediate query was as to which would go fastest. . . . Therefore . . . we had to race." [4] Successful participation was the surest way to receive widespread and favorable attention in the trade and daily press. Men who built "home made" automobiles and who hoped to organize companies—among them Henry Ford, Alexander Winton, the Stanley twins, George N. Pierce, James Packard, and Louis Chevrolet—entered contests to obtain recognition and the financial backing that could accompany such recognition. Established manufacturers raced for the sales advantages that victories would bring; from 1895 on major racing victories were trumpeted by newspapers across the land.[5]

Ford was not the first auto maker to make a name for himself in racing. The first manufacturers to achieve national reputations by racing were the Duryea brothers, Charles E. and J. Frank.

At America's first automobile race, run over a fifty-two mile course in the Chicago area on Thanksgiving Day, 1895, six cars started. One of the Duryeas' vehicles, whose speed averaged 6.66 miles per hour, was the first across the finish line. The achievement was noteworthy, and for the first time an automotive story was heralded widely by the nation's press. *Horseless Age,* America's first automotive publication, which made its debut the month of the race, alone devoted five pages to the event.[6]

A Duryea vehicle also won America's second race, over a New York City to Irvington-on-the-Hudson course, on Memorial Day, 1896. The same machine scored six victories in thirteen starts at the first track races in the United States, at Narragansett Park, Rhode Island, in September 1896. To these triumphs the Duryea added a victory in the first English auto contest, a London-to-Brighton run held in November 1896. By the close of 1896 the Duryea was easily the best known of America's cars and the Duryea brothers had achieved nationwide prominence.[7]

The Duryeas' premier position was short-lived. In 1897, a year before the Duryea brothers parted and their car was taken over by the National Motor Carriage Company, the nationally known Pope Manufacturing Company, then the world's largest manufacturer of bicycles, placed the Columbia motor carriage on the auto market. *Horseless Age,* delighted with the prestige the Pope organization brought to the auto industry, devoted an unprecedented four pages, including three photographs and four sketches, to the Columbia's debut. Within two years the Pope Company, in association with the Electric Vehicle Company, ranked as the nation's leading and best known auto producer.[8]

Pope's chief competitor was Alexander Winton. Unlike Colonel Albert A. Pope, who (largely on the strength of his bicycle reputation) was the only auto manufacturer to be listed in the first (1899) edition of *Who's Who in America,* Winton was an unknown bicyclemaker when he turned to horseless carriages. This deficiency was soon overcome, however, as Winton was easily the most publicity-conscious manufacturer of the early automotive era. Before he had formed his company in March 1897, he had wheedled *Horseless Age* out of a three-quarter-page photo-feature and was distributing circulars describing his experimental work.[9] From 1897 to 1900 virtually every issue of *Horseless Age* contained at least one Winton-supplied tidbit.

Two months after organizing his firm the aggressive young Clevelander set a speed record for the mile. He soon became one of the best known auto manufacturers in the country and quickly emerged as America's outstanding racer. From 1897 until the rise of Barney Oldfield in 1903 he was regarded as the nation's racing champion and the man whom aspirants to that title had to beat.[10] Among Winton's challengers was a self-made Detroit engineer named Henry Ford.

2

In the winter of 1895-96, while Winton and Colonel Pope were still primarily concerned with bicycles and the Duryea brothers were basking in the glory of their Chicago triumph, thirty-two-year-old Henry Ford was struggling to build his first car. Less than a week after the Duryeas had won their second race on Memorial Day, 1896, Ford drove his "quadricycle," as he called his first vehicle, through the streets of Detroit. The initial run of the little car was not reported in the local newspapers. Unlike Charles B. King, who in March 1896 became the first person to drive a motor vehicle in Detroit, Ford had not announced a public demonstration. Unlike Winton, he did not rush a photograph and description of his car to *Horseless Age*. [11]

Ford sold his first vehicle and then turned to building a second. The work went slowly, and it was carried on in a publicity vacuum. The first allusion to Ford in an automotive connection was in the November 1898 edition of *Horseless Age,* under the heading "Minor Mention":

> Henry Ford, of Detroit, Mich., chief engineer of the Edison Electric Light Co. of that city, has built a number of gasolene vehicles which are said to have been successfully operated. He is reported to be financially supported by several prominent men of the city, who intend to manufacture the Ford vehicle. From Mr. Ford himself no information can be gleaned regarding his vehicles or his plans for their manufacture. [12]

Ford's second car (the *Horseless Age* item had overstated the number built) became operable in the summer of 1899 and led to Ford's first press interview and a complimentary photo-feature in the July 29 edition of the *Detroit Journal*. A week later, largely on the strength of a successful demonstration given by Ford to a wealthy Detroit lumberman, the Detroit Automobile Company was organized. Ford was given a small share of stock in the concern and became its superintendent. [13] The company's secretary supervised relations with the press. Ford, staying close to the shop, received only one brief mention in news stories during the last half of 1899. [14]

In early February 1900, Ford gave a demonstration of his car's capabilities to a *Detroit News–Tribune* reporter. Normally shy with strangers, Ford was at home behind the tiller, and he proved as loquacious as an auto drummer. The resultant rollicking three-column story, headlined SWIFTER THAN A RACE-HORSE IT FLEW OVER THE ICY STREETS, provides the first inkling that Ford would one day have an easy way with reporters. [15]

Whatever their virtues, the cars produced by the Detroit Automobile Company did not sell. Apparently Ford wanted to improve the model, but the company's stockholders vetoed the suggestion. The firm ground slowly to a halt in late 1900. [16]

Ford and his assistants spent the spring and summer of 1901 building a racer. By fall a trim, light, twenty-six horsepower machine was ready. Its first test came at the Grosse Pointe race track, near Detroit, on October 10, 1901. Several of the nation's outstanding drivers, including Winton, were on hand. Ford's machine was entered in the ten-mile sweepstakes event, in which Winton was heavily favored. The champion's sales manager, Charles B. Shanks, was so confident of his employer's victory that he had picked as the prize a beautiful punch bowl which he thought would look well in the bay window of the Winton dining room.

Winton and Ford were the only starters in the main event, a third competitor, William N. Murray, Pittsburgh millionaire and owner of one of the fastest cars in the country, having withdrawn because of mechanical difficulties. Winton was on the inside, and his deftness in rounding curves (Ford shut off power and ran wide on each curve) enabled him to open up a lead of a fifth of a mile at the three-mile mark. Midway through the race Ford picked up lost ground on the straightaways, and on the sixth lap improved his position perceptibly. As the crowd urged Ford on, Winton began to have trouble with overheated bearings. Shanks, who was riding with him, drenched the bearings with oil, but to no avail. Ford shot ahead on the eighth lap and swept across the finish line well ahead of the faltering champion.[17]

That Ford entered his untried machine in a race against such formidable competition showed his confidence in his car; its victory showed that his confidence was not misplaced. Immediately after the contest Ford declared that he was finished with racing. At the same time he announced conviction that his machine, which had an average speed of 43.5 miles per hour in the race, was capable of a mile a minute and that he would try for that record.[18]

The victory over Winton brought Ford nationwide publicity, for his name appeared on the sports pages of many newspapers.[19] It also provided the impetus for the formation of a new company. A number of prominent Detroiters, including several old Detroit Automobile Company stockholders, had seen the triumph and were fired by the commercial possibilities of the Ford machine. They organized the Henry Ford Company (the name itself being a tribute to Ford's newly won reputation) on November 30, 1901. Ford was given a sixth share in the firm and the post of chief engineer.[20]

Meanwhile, Ford had forgotten, or changed his mind about, his decision to quit racing. Indeed, he was soon ready to devote all of his time to the sport. This change in plans apparently stemmed from Ford's dissatisfaction with the relatively small profit that he stood to gain from the company and high expectations of what he could win on the track. Ford's "racing fever" affliction is evident in a letter he wrote to a brother-in-law concerning a challenge he was issuing to the French champion, Henri Fournier.

> If I can bring Mr. Fournier in line there is a barrel of money in this business. . . . I don't see why he won't fall in line if he don't I will challenge him untill I am black in the face. . . . My Company will kick about me following racing, but they will get the Advertising and I expect to make $ where I can't make ¢ at Manufacturing.

Ford's preoccupation with racing quickly produced friction between him and the company's other stockholders and executives. Ford left the company after only three months, on March 10, 1902, having been given $900 and the uncompleted drawings for a new racing car. The company agreed to discontinue the use of his name.[21]

By early May, Ford had joined forces with Tom Cooper, a former bicycle champion who also had racing fever. With Cooper's money and Ford's know-how, the two men were able to build two eighty-horsepower monsters, the Arrow and the 999, the latter car being named after a record-breaking New York Central train. "There was only one seat," Ford recalled later. "One life to a car was enough. I tried out the cars. Cooper tried out the cars. We let them out at full speed. . . . Going over Niagara Falls would have been but a pastime after a ride in one of them." Neither Ford nor Cooper had the nerve to drive the racers in competition. Cooper, however, said that he knew a man "who lived on speed, that nothing could go too fast for him." A wire to Salt Lake City brought on Barney Oldfield, then a professional bicycle rider. Oldfield had never driven a car, but said that he would try anything once. He learned quickly, and proved fearless.[22]

Oldfield was primed for the five-mile Manufacturers' Challenge Cup, which was held at the Grosse Pointe track on October 25, 1902. Four drivers started, Winton and Shanks among them. Oldfield opened up the 999 immediately, was never headed, and defeated runner-up Shanks by a lap. The time was 5 minutes, 28 seconds, not quite the mile-a-minute record Ford had said he would aim for a year earlier, but nonetheless an American record. Once again Ford's name resounded in the press. The event launched Oldfield on his career as one of America's greatest race drivers. It also marked the end of Ford's preoccupation with racing. For purposes of advertising he would set a world's speed record two years later, and his cars would race until 1912; but now he was able to turn to his life's work, "putting a 'family horse' on the market."[23]

On August 20, 1902, Ford and Alexander T. Malcomson, a Detroit coal dealer, had signed an agreement to develop a commercial automobile. Only a portion of Ford's time, however, was devoted to the Malcomson car between August and October. Then came Oldfield's victory, and on the wave of enthusiasm and publicity created by this triumph, Ford and his assistants bent to the task of completing a prototype for a commercial vehicle. In November the partners carried their formal agreement a step further by organizing The Ford & Malcomson Company, Ltd., and offering shares for sale. By June 1903, ten investors had joined them, and on June 16, 1903, the Ford Motor Company was incorporated with a paid-in capital of $28,000. Henry Ford, who contributed his patents, his engine, and his knowledge to the new company was awarded a 25.5 percent interest in the firm.[24]

Chapter 2
Springtime for Henry

1

The Ford Motor Company was launched with a minimum of fanfare, having made no apparent attempt to obtain publicity for itself or the car, the Model A, that it was placing on the market. Detroit's three daily newspapers were unaware of the firm's incorporation until three days after the event, and then they buried brief stories about the company on their back pages. *Horseless Age* devoted a few lines to a rumor that the "Ford Automobile Company will build a factory at Pontiac." *Motor Age* in one paragraph told its readers the company would place a Fordmobile on the market. *Cycle and Automobile Trade Journal* ran a longer and more factual story, since by coincidence its June 1903 edition featured the automotive industry in Detroit. *Automobile* and *Automobile Topics* ignored the event.[1]

Even if the company had tried to obtain lengthy press notices it is doubtful that it would have received them. Ford was but one of fifteen Michigan companies and one of eighty-eight American firms introducing automobiles in 1903, and neither the amount of its capitalization nor its prospects for success were out of the ordinary.[2]

The Ford Motor Company was not, however, to remain commonplace for long. From the outset it could be distinguished from most of the auto class of 1903—and indeed from many of the established companies in the industry—in that it made money. A total of $36,957 was netted within the first three and a half months; a 10 percent dividend was paid on November 21. The flow of dividends would continue unabated for twenty-three years, much of the time at a phenomenal rate. In 1903, however, the new company's profit structure was overshadowed by its legal entanglements. Ford was made the target of litigation whose outcome would affect the pocketbook of everyone who made, sold, or bought an automobile in America.[3]

The celebrated Selden patent suit proved to be the first in a series of events—some related to the auto business, some not—which strongly influenced public attitudes toward Henry Ford and the Ford Motor Company. Indeed, these extracurricular activities probably did as much, perhaps more, to shape Ford's public relations than all the company's formal efforts to win and maintain public favor.

The Selden suit was filed on October 22, 1903, by George B. Selden, a Rochester, New York, attorney, and the Electric Vehicle Company. Selden had filed a patent application in 1879 for a road vehicle he had designed but never actually built. For sixteen years he delayed issuance of the patent by filing additions and changes. His claims were valueless, of course, until an auto industry had developed. Finally, in November 1895 the attorney obtained a patent for a "road-carriage," covering all gasoline-powered vehicles designed since 1879 and manufactured, sold, or used in the United States in the seventeen-year period ending in 1912. In 1899

Selden assigned the patent to the Columbia & Electric Vehicle Company (reorganized as the Electric Vehicle Company in 1900) for $10,000 and a percentage of whatever royalties could be collected. Suits were filed against five automobile firms, including the Winton Motor Carriage Company, in 1900 the nation's largest auto producer. By March 1903 all the defendants had been intimidated into acknowledging the validity of the patent and negotiating settlements. Ten auto manufacturers, believing further resistance useless, made a deal with the Electric Vehicle Company to organize a patent-pooling combination called the Association of Licensed Automobile Manufacturers (ALAM). The association's members, totaling twenty-six by the summer of 1903, agreed to pay to the Electric Vehicle Company a royalty of 1.25 percent of the price of each car sold. The company sent one-fifth of the fees to Selden, turned over two-fifths to the ALAM, and kept two-fifths for itself. The association was given the privilege of selecting the manufacturers to be licensed under the patent and those to be sued. The latter, presumably, would be put out of business.[4]

In February and again in June or July 1903, Henry Ford and his associates approached the acting president of the ALAM concerning the possibility of obtaining a license for their fledgling company. They were rebuffed, the ALAM executive expressing a lack of confidence in Ford's ability to meet the association's manufacturing standards and to qualify as a creditable member of the auto industry.[5] The rejection of Ford was followed by an advertisement in the *Detroit News* that characterized the twenty-six licensees as "the pioneers of the industry" and warned the makers, sellers, and buyers of unlicensed cars that they would be liable to prosecution for patent infringement. The Ford Motor Company defiantly rebutted this ad two days later in the *Detroit Free Press* and promised protection against suits that might be leveled against its dealers and purchasers. "Our Mr. Ford made the first Gasoline Automobile in Detroit and the third in the United States," the firm's advertisement inaccurately proclaimed. "Our Mr. Ford also built the famous '999' Gasoline Automobile, which was driven by Barney Oldfield in New York on July 25, 1903, a mile in 55 4/5 seconds, on a circular track, which is the world's record. Mr. Ford, driving his own machine, beat Mr. Winton at Grosse Pointe track in 1901. We have always been winners."[6]

The ALAM ignored this blast and continued to advertise and to issue bulletins assuring the industry and the public that it would eliminate irresponsible firms and otherwise "stabilize" the automobile business. Ford matched the ALAM advertisement for advertisement, and quickly took the lead among independent firms in opposing the licensed group. The company's aggressiveness eventually assumed the proportions of a challenge, leaving but one way out for the patent-holders. They had to go to court or be laughed out of the industry.[7]

The patent battle was to have an interest transcending the industry. The rising tide of Progressivism and its hostility to special privilege loomed in the background. Many newspapers and virtually all mass-circulation magazines featured detailed, indignant articles describing how some "trust" or company overcharged the public, fleeced its stockholders, or corrupted politics.[8] Now, as the manufacture of motor cars began to promise large profits, the Electric Vehicle Company and the ALAM, said to represent resources of $70,000,000, were attacking an automobile company which had just started operations with a working capital of $28,000. The public relations implications of this situation were not lost on Henry Ford, who stated that "he would give the 'trust' $1,000 if they would advertise his business by commencing suit against him."[9]

The treatment by the press and the public's view of the suit fully vindicated Ford's sense of advertising values. News stories alluded to the ALAM as the "automobile trust," and many contemporary motorists believed that every time Selden added his royalty to the purchase price they were being "flimflammed, cheated, and robbed." Henry Ford and the Ford Motor Company, on the other hand, were frequently pictured as underdogs fighting for their very lives—and for every prospective car buyer as well.[10] The company's anti-ALAM advertising consistently referred to the association as a trust. Product advertising emphasized that Ford cars could be bought for less because purchasers did not have to pay a "patent royalty."[11] Company dealers also attacked the ALAM. John Wanamaker, the New York and Philadelphia agent, declared in full-page ads: "The Ford Motor Car cannot be beaten by the Trust, in competition; so they have erected a scarecrow to frighten the buying public. . . . Of course, the Trust doesn't expect the noise of the tom-toms and its straw-stuffed scarecrows to frighten John Wanamaker. . . . When you buy a Ford Motor Car from John Wanamaker, you are guaranteed against any trouble with the trust."[12]

The powerful Wanamaker, who held Ford franchises until August 1905, proved to be the company's strongest ally in the early struggle against the Seldenites. For the public, the name of Wanamaker carried all the prestige the name of Ford lacked. The merchant-capitalist's vigorous defense of the Ford position and his attack on the Selden group helped Ford to compete successfully against licensed manufacturers in the east.[13]

The Selden case was a suit in equity, and once under way, it was conducted in a routine and undramatic fashion. The evidence was highly technical. There were no exciting courtroom scenes to provide headlines. For several years after the initial propaganda barrages, only sporadic reports on the suit's progress appeared in the general and even the trade press.[14] Ford's attorney was partly responsible for the news blackout. For several years he refused to permit the company to furnish information to the press—even when publications requested signed articles—for fear of supplying legal ammunition to the Seldenites.[15] The principal source of anti-Selden propaganda, therefore, was a trade group, the American Motor Car Manufacturers' Association (AMCMA), established in 1905 by Ford and nineteen other unlicensed firms. This organization's press bureau effectively counteracted the propagandizing activities of the ALAM and its member companies.[16] By 1907 all the evidence had been submitted to the court, and the Ford Company felt free to supplement the bureau's efforts. Both the anti-Selden and the Selden forces began "to fire hot shot into the ranks of the enemy through the public press" in an all-out effort to curry public favor.[17] The fireworks centered around the main exhibits presented during the trial. The Seldenites had constructed a motor buggy to demonstrate that a car built in accordance with the patent's specifications would run. The defense in turn had built a machine with an engine resembling one patented by an Englishman in 1869 to refute

Selden's claims to originality. The cars were demonstrated to reporters, after which each side praised its car and deprecated its opponent's. In a typical exchange in *Motor Age* (which pointed out that it was running both stories "just as received so the dear reader may take his choice") the Selden group said that its car "was reversed, turned around and backed up several times, much to the surprise and humiliation of those who have belittled the work." The adjacent Ford version said that its car traveled four times as far and as fast "as what has been termed the Selden machine," and offered to race the Selden car over fifty miles, giving it a forty-five-mile head start. Ford also said that the Selden buggy started only when facing downhill and that it always had to be pushed to that position.[18]

After these and similar outbursts, the case remained in limbo for two years. The decision of the federal district court at New York, handed down on September 15, 1909, decreed that every manufacturer, importer, and user of unlicensed cars infringed on Selden's patent and was subject to the consequent penalties. Ford immediately decided to appeal. His resoluteness was not shared by the majority of his AMCMA colleagues. Within a month eight of the organization's forty-three members defected to the ALAM; in January the AMCMA's general manager, Alfred Reeves, accepted a similar post with the rival group; in February 1910, with thirty of its members now in the licensed camp, the independent association folded. For all practical purposes Ford now stood alone against the industry. By this time, however, the company was a king-sized adversary. With assets of $6,000,000, it was the largest firm in Detroit. Conversely, the Electric Vehicle Company had gone bankrupt during the panic of 1907, and its affairs and the role of complainant in the suit were assumed in 1909 by the Columbia Motor Car Company. Still the combined assets of the ALAM members were many times greater than Ford's.[19]

In February 1910, the ALAM launched a nationwide advertising campaign "to educate the public" against the folly of buying an unlicensed vehicle. As in 1903 Ford took his case to the public:

> I have been notified in the press through the country that the A.L.A.M. is to wage war against what it sees fit to designate as 'unrecognized' motor cars, to educate the public against buying them, and the stockholders of unlicensed companies against making them. . . . I am willing to trust our case to the courts or to the public, and leave it to them to decide whether the motives of the A.L.A.M. are as it would have you believe. The public knows that all this campaign of education and all this expenditure of money for advertising is for the benefit of the seventy-two varieties [the number of companies in the A.L.A.M.], not for the benefit of the public, just as this same public knows that I am not building cars for the benefit of the public and that we are not conducting our campaign of publicity for the benefit of the public, but for the benefit of the Ford Motor Co. . . . It is said everyone has his price, but I can assure you that while I am at the head of the Ford Motor Company, there will be no price that would induce me to permit my name to be added to those of the seventy-two varieties.[20]

"The patent," Ford added, was "a freak among alleged inventions," and he offered a bond to each buyer, backed by the $12,000,000 assets of the company and its bonding company.[21] To the *Detroit Free Press,* which echoed the sentiments of many of its readers, Ford's stand was heroic. "There's a man for you, a man of backbone," declared an editorial entitled, "Ford the Fighter." "Of the case behind him, the lawyers are more able to talk, but as a human figure he presents a spectacle to win the applause of all men with red blood; for this world dearly loves the fighting man, and needs him, too, if we are to go forward." [22]

The appellate court's decision was handed down on January 9, 1911. This time the victory went to Ford, and it was total. Dozens of telegrams and letters poured into the Ford offices, many from opponents as well as from friends. Every automobile man in the country had the name "Ford" on his lips. [23] The story was given generous treatment in most papers in the country, and Ford, for the first time in his life, was front-page news in the Detroit and in the trade press. He was lauded on all sides as a giant-killer, as a symbol of revolt against monopoly, and as a magnificent individualist. [24] The victory was of tremendous advertising value. Ford later said (and James Couzens, the company's secretary, and Norval A. Hawkins, the sales manager, agreed) that no one factor publicized the company and its products as effectively as the Selden suit. [25]

The suit became one of the four or five foundation stones upon which Ford's reputation was built. The publicity which Ford received during and at the conclusion of the case was but the beginning. In later years every biography of Henry Ford and virtually every history of the automobile industry was to comment on the suit in terms highly favorable to Ford. Innumerable newspaper and magazine sketches would contain similar references. Ford's publicists recognized the public relations value of the suit, and in later years company advertisements and radio commercials pointed with pride to Ford's role in "liberating an industry." [26]

Couzens, who was as pugnacious as Ford was stubborn, perhaps deserves equal credit with Ford in pressing the Selden suit to a victorious conclusion. Opposed to the ALAM from the outset, he never wavered in his determination to fight the case to the finish. Couzens also wrote or signed most of the early anti-Selden advertising and publicity. But he received little general recognition—either in 1911 or in later years—for his contribution to the Ford victory. [27]

2

When the Selden suit was filed in 1903, Henry Ford was unknown except to followers of automobile racing, his small company had dubious prospects, and his car had scarcely created a ripple on the automotive scene. Eight years later, with the victory over the ALAM behind him, Ford was one of the best known of the country's auto manufacturers, his company the largest in the industry, and his car bobbed over roads in every civilized quarter of the globe. [28] The Selden suit had figured prominently in Ford's drive for leadership, but of even greater importance were Ford and his company's sales-promotion ventures. Of these, by far the most important was racing—the activity which had brought Ford financial backing and launched the company in the first place. [29]

Shortly before Oldfield's October 1902 victory in the Manufacturers' Challenge Cup, Ford sold the 999 to Tom Cooper. Oldfield continued to race that vehicle until the fall of 1903 and set numerous track and world records. As the designer of the 999 (after the sale usually referred to as the Ford-Cooper racer), Ford was frequently mentioned in press accounts of the daredevil's triumphs.[30] In fact, in the most important article to appear on the racer, in the January 17, 1903, edition of *Scientific American,* it was Ford—not owner Cooper or driver Oldfield—who was pictured with the vehicle and who received the lion's share of the publicity.[31]

Ford himself did not race during 1903, nor did anyone drive under his colors. In January 1904, however, he returned to competition to advertise a new four-cylinder touring car, the Model B, which he was placing on the market. A spectacular stroke was needed to give the $2,000 car a nationwide reputation, and Ford announced that he would break the world's record for the mile with an engine practically identical with that of the Model B. The test was to be made on the cinder-covered ice of Lake St. Clair, northeast of Detroit. On January 9 Ford unofficially raced the distance in thirty-six seconds, ten full seconds under the world's record. On January 12, with official timers on hand he repeated the run in thirty-nine and two-fifths seconds (91.37 miles per hour). The run, said the *Detroit Tribune,* was "the wildest ride in the history of automobiling. . . . Humped over his steering wheel, the tremendous speed throwing the machine in zigzag fashion across the fifteen-foot roadway, Ford was taking chances that no man, not even that specialist in averted suicide, Barney Oldfield, had dared to tempt."[32] Ford was very much aware of the dangers, but, as he wrote later, having come this far, there seemed no way out:

> The ice seemed smooth enough, so smooth that if I had called off the trial we should have secured an immense amount of the wrong kind of advertising, but instead of being smooth, that ice was seamed with fissures which I knew were going to mean trouble the moment I got up speed. But there was nothing to do but go through with the trial, and I let the old "Arrow" out. At every fissure the car leaped into the air. I never knew how it was coming down. When I wasn't in the air, I was skidding, but somehow I stayed top side up and on the course, making a record that went all over the world.[33]

Automobile men everywhere were astounded by Ford's mark, which was regarded as "so sensational that even the most enthusiastic supporters of American speed machines admitted that they would like to see further proof before accepting the figures." Under the headline "Ford's Mile Raises the Dander of the Track Champion," the *Detroit Tribune* pictured Barney Oldfield as green with envy. Dominique Lamberjack, the French champion, flatly stated that the time was an impossibility.[34] A Detroit newspaper, after thoroughly considering the question, decided that it was unlikely that any car would ever travel a faster mile. Eastern officials of the American Automobile Association discounted wire reports and insisted on seeing affidavits signed by the six timers and two surveyors before admitting the time was possible. The association's chairman also said that if the time were authentic the record would be placed in a special "made on ice" category, a view which incurred the wrath of

Detroit newspapers.[35] On January 20, 1904, Ford's record was made official. Seven days later William K. Vanderbilt, on the sands of Ormond Beach, Florida, eclipsed Ford's mark with a run of thirty-nine seconds flat.[36]

The Model B profited but little, however, from Ford's daring exploit and the resultant controversy. The press persisted in calling the rebuilt Arrow the 999, even though Ford visited the sports desk of each Detroit newspaper to see that the Model B received its full due. The racer itself was shipped express to New York, where it was a feature attraction of the Madison Square Garden auto show. It then toured the South under the aegis of promoters to whom it had been sold.[37]

Ford appears to have raced no more during 1904. In a new racing car the following year, however, he attempted to regain the mile record on the beach at Cape May, New Jersey, but he could not break forty-one seconds. The car was rebuilt, and in 1906 Ford announced that it would do a mile in thirty seconds. Despite this claim, the car failed to better forty seconds in exhibitions at Ormond Beach.[38]

Meanwhile the company was receiving considerable publicity from its racers' success on midwestern and eastern tracks. The firm entered the lists in 1904, and that year a daring mechanic, Frank Kulick, set light-car records for one, three, four, and five miles which stood for more than half-a-dozen years.[39] Between 1904 and 1907 Ford racers proved themselves almost invincible in their class and frequently won contests with larger vehicles in open competition.[40] Probably the most publicized Ford victory was a twenty-four-hour speed-endurance contest won by Kulick and a codriver over eight other cars at the Michigan State Fair Grounds in mid-1907. Ford advertisements called the race "the swiftest, maddest driving ever witnessed" and claimed world's records for distances covered in one, eight, and twenty-four hours.[41] The company also promoted races among its test drivers and Ford owners on a private track in Highland Park, Michigan, in 1907. Contests were held on alternate Saturdays and proved popular drawing cards for Detroit area motorists.[42]

Although racing enjoyed wide popularity through most of the pre-World War I period, it became the target for considerable criticism between 1905 and 1907. Accidents had become commonplace, and in 1907, six drivers were killed. The complaint was voiced that there were so many winners in race programs—which usually were broken down into seven or eight classifications determined by horsepower, weight, and price—that the gold medals awarded were a farce. Racing, some claimed, was valueless to the industry; the public was more interested in the sound construction of cars than in speed records.[43] *Motor Age* boycotted racing stories for a time, and other publications strongly urged that speed racing be replaced by hill climbs and reliability and economy runs.[44]

Henry Ford and the Ford Company abandoned racing in the fall of 1907, the manufacturer for good, the firm for almost two years. Kulick, while tuning a new racer, went off the Michigan State Fair track at full speed, narrowly escaping death. Ford, shaken by the accident, declared that until the industry could agree on limiting the speed and power of racing vehicles, he and his company would forego the sport. Ford suggested that maximum cylinder displacement be restricted to 250 cubic inches as a way to permit engineers to show the superiority of their designs and to bring about sane racing.[45] Ford's suggestion fell flat, however, and racers with up to 600 inches' displacement continued to ply American tracks. Similarly, with the exception of Barney Oldfield and the Locomobile and Thomas companies, most of the other leading drivers and sponsors of racing cars continued to enter contests.[46]

Ford apparently had another reason for quitting racing: his cars had virtually run out of competition in their own low-price, light-weight racing classification. In explaining the decision to quit racing, the *Ford Times* could grumble with considerable justification, "After we had beaten all the one and two-lungers and other low-priced cars, what good would the victory do us?"[47]

Nonetheless Ford's decision was sharply criticized by his dealers, who in their advertising had relied heavily on the racing prowess of the Ford car.[48] Since 1904 many dealers had entered contests themselves. Now they felt the need to intensify their efforts in order to keep pace with the competition. The *Ford Times,* fully aware of the promotional value of racing, sympathetically chronicled all Ford victories so that dealers could list them in their advertisements. The publication also devoted considerable attention to Ford's European racing triumphs (overseas branches were not bound by the parent company's policy).[49]

While Ford was publicizing his cars by racing, he was also advertising his products in newspapers, trade journals, and a few national magazines. Advertising was bought, in fact, four months before there was a Ford Motor Company. Alexander Malcomson, Henry Ford's chief backer, took space in trade papers in February 1903, to announce "The Fordmobile," to be made by the Fordmobile Company, Ltd. Neither the company nor the product came into existence, although the ads did result in some C.O.D. orders which encouraged at least one Detroiter to invest in the future Ford Motor Company.[50]

Ford's advertising was conventional throughout the early years, the company taking its cue from its competitors. Most early automobile advertising either sought to convince the public that the particular company was not selling experiments and could make deliveries or that the particular product had a wide range of desirable qualities. The 1895 Racine was said to offer "speed, safety, comfort and economy." The 1899 Oakman promised freedom from odor, speed at will, economy, simplicity, durability, practicality, and attractiveness. Locomobile's steamer of the same year was advertised as the ultimate in reliability, safety, comfort, simplicity, speed, and low cost.[51]

Great importance was attached to advertising slogans. Manufacturers constantly experimented with slogans, trying to settle on one which would capture the public's fancy. Although most slogans lasted only one season, some were used for several years, and one, "Ask the Man Who Owns One," originated by Packard in 1901, was used continuously until 1956. Trademarks began to be featured in advertising and promotional literature about 1908 or 1909. Three-fourths of the manufacturers also placed metallic trademarks on the radiators of their cars at this time.[52]

From 1903 until the spring of 1907 the Ford Company had no advertising department or staff. Business Manager James Couzens had direct charge of advertising, along with sales, bookkeeping, shipping, and other duties. Couzens's first advertisement was straightforward and in keeping with the general practice of claiming one's car to be superior to all others. Headlined BOSS OF THE ROAD the

The red brick shed behind 58 Bagley Avenue, Detroit, in which Henry Ford built his first car in 1896. Since the doorways were too narrow to permit the car's removal, Ford applied an ax to one. The shed now stands in Greenfield Village.

Henry Ford and his 1896 quadricycle.

Barney Oldfield, Henry Ford, and the 999 in the winter of 1902–03. (Courtesy of the Ford Motor Company.)

Henry Ford at the wheel of the 999 on January 12, 1904, the day he set a world's speed record for the mile.

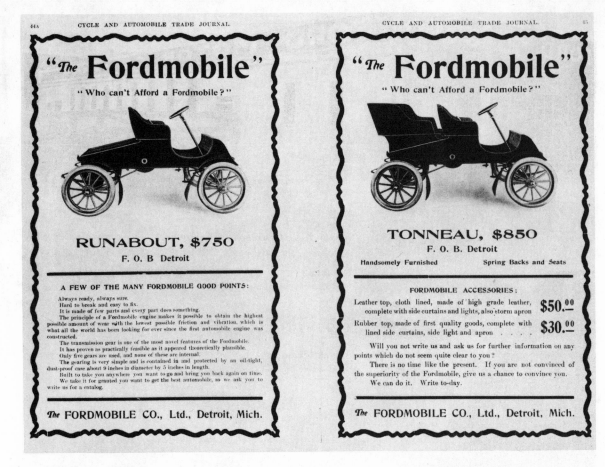

Neither the "Fordmobile" nor "The Fordmobile Co., Ltd.," which were advertised in February 1903, came into existence. But the advertisements encouraged investment in the future Ford Motor Company.

An advertisement which trumpets Henry Ford's record-setting mile run on ice.

Ford Motor Company's first plant on Mack Avenue, Detroit, as it looked at the time of the firm's organization.

Ford's famous advertising slogan, introduced in 1907, featured in an electric spectacular atop a Detroit building in 1915.

A 1910 advertisement which attempts to pass off the Model T as a car for the carriage trade.

Ford's entries in the New York-to-Seattle race of 1909 pause briefly on the main drag of Goodland, Kansas.

Henry Ford in a moment of glory—the finish of the New York-to-Seattle race of 1909. Behind the wheel of winning Ford No. 2 (later disqualified) is Bert Scott; at his side is C. J. Smith.

Henry Ford seated in a Ford-powered racer at the Indianapolis Speedway in 1924; a similar vehicle finished fifth in the 1923 classic. Barney Oldfield, with cigar, stands behind the wheel; Edsel Ford is second to the right of Oldfield.

A 1911 Model T being driven up the steps of the Tennessee state capitol.

A Ford-sponsored song played at President William Howard Taft's inaugural ball in 1909.

A popular 1914 song, one of dozens written about the Model T during the 'teens and 'twenties.

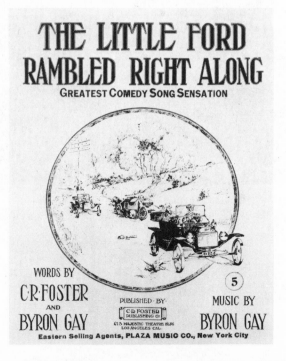

Part of a day's production of Model Ts at the Highland Park plant in 1913.

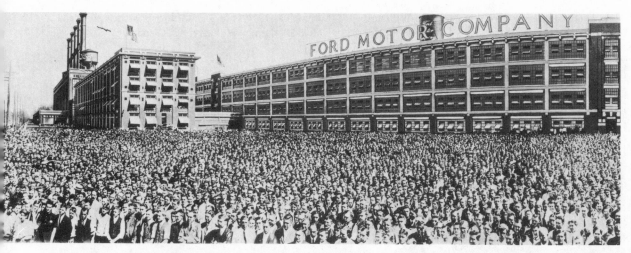

Twelve thousand Highland Park plant employees in 1913. The photo was said to
be the most expensive ever taken since all the workers were paid while posing.

Model T owners pause during a 1912 auto parade sponsored by Ford's Hooper, Nebraska, dealer.

Farmers' dollars are big dollars—because they are hard earned dollars. It is because the American farmer is ever a careful and painstaking buyer that he is today the happy and proud possessor of more than half the Ford cars in existence.

75,000 Ford cars already sold this season—one-third of America's product. Five passenger touring car—torpedo runabout—delivery car—town car. Get Catalog from Ford Motor Company, Detroit, Mich.

A 1912 Ford advertisement featuring the company's "winged pyramid" trademark and a sales pitch to farmers.

ad read: "This new light touring car fills the demand for an automobile between a runabout and a heavy touring car. It is positively the most perfect machine on the market, having overcome all draw-backs such as smell, noise, jolt, etc., common to all other makes of Auto Carriages. It is so simple that a boy of 15 can run it. For beauty of finish it is unequaled."[53] Copy themes changed constantly, but in general the emphasis was on utility, simplicity, initial low cost, durability—and contest victories.[54] For a decade after 1907 considerable stress was placed on the use of vanadium steel, which Ford introduced in American automobiles that year.[55]

Two advertising agencies were retained by the company during 1903–4. The Chas. H. Fuller Advertising Agency bought approximately $1,000 worth of space during the last half of 1903. O. J. Mulford Advertising Co., one of the oldest and most prominent agencies in Detroit, served the company from July 1903 to at least September 1904, placing more than $12,500 worth of advertising during that time.[56] The company, which from the outset had also bought space directly from publications, apparently placed all of its own advertising for a number of years after 1904.[57]

Through September 1904 the company spent an average of $1,600 a month on advertising, including exhibitions and racing, a small amount compared to the six-figure sums spent annually on space advertising alone by more than a dozen auto manufacturers. During the fiscal year ending September 30, 1905, a total of $39,513 was spent for newspaper and periodical space. An appropriation of $50,000—for all kinds of advertising—was made for the fiscal year beginning October 1, 1905.[58] Figures are not available for later years, but an analysis of the media used by Ford during this period indicates that space expenditures never reached this amount. In some years it probably was considerably less. From 1906 to 1908, for example, Ford usually bought only one twenty-seventh or one-thirtieth of a page in trade journals. Full-page advertisements were rare, and even one-quarter- and one-third-page ads were uncommon.[59]

The "small space" policy found a warm advocate in E. LeRoy Pelletier, Ford's first advertising manager. According to *Motor World,* Pelletier was "a brilliant, plausible, rapid-fire conversationalist . . . a clever writer . . . and resourceful far, far beyond the average." The magazine added that "in the art of 'putting them over' he has few peers. Even the great Barnum himself would have found him a valuable assistant." Pelletier had used his talents as an advance agent for a circus and as a *New York Times* correspondent in the Klondike, where he prospected, promoted a telephone line between Dawson and Nome, established the region's first daily newspaper, and operated a real estate firm.[60] He returned to the United States in 1901 to build a motor sled with which he hoped to conquer the North Pole. Locating in Jamestown, New York, he turned to more practical matters and designed an air-cooled automobile, the Duquesne.

After serving for several years as president of the Duquesne firm, Pelletier in 1905 joined Ford Motor Company in an engineering capacity.[61] His promotional talents were recognized, and by the spring of 1907 he had relieved Couzens of direct responsibility for advertising.[62] He replaced Couzens's type-filled hard-selling advertisements with light and breezy copy that used a maximum of white space. "Light, Limber, and Tough as a Hickory Withe," went one of Pelletier's ads, "the Ford

4-cylinder Runabout ($600) Will Withstand More Rough Usage . . . Than Any Other Motor Car Made—Bar None.''[63]

It was Pelletier who promoted the races among Ford's test drivers and Ford owners at the company's Highland Park mile track, a stunt which, *Motor Age* declared, ''will make him the despair of all other press agents.'' Either he or the company's traffic manager, W. S. Hogue, originated the slogan ''Watch the Fords Go By,'' which was featured off and on in company advertising from 1907 until the early 1940s. The *Ford Times,* after Pelletier's departure, credited the phrase to Hogue, who was said to have shouted it at a race in which Fords were whizzing by the competition.[64] In any event, Pelletier popularized the slogan with the following kind of advertising:

WATCH THE FORDS GO BY

Today there are 8,833 of those wonderful Ford Runabouts on the road. Perhaps we shouldn't refer to it but after all there's a lot of human nature even in business, and we can't resist the temptation to compare conditions of a year ago with present ones. Then there were those who criticized the Ford policy and discounted the Ford promise to build 10,000 cars.

WATCH THE FORDS GO BY[65]

Pelletier's efforts, in turn, inspired the following verse, recited at a 1907 auto show:

> As manager of auto shows,
> Roy Pelletier ranks high,
> But his hobby's writing auto ads,
> Like Watch the Fords Go By.

The slogan was a familiar sight on many of the ''all-Ford'' trains which puffed out of Detroit to all parts of the country. It also was featured on a mammoth electric display erected on the top of Detroit's Temple Theater in 1908. Other Ford slogans and the company's ''winged pyramid'' trademark shoved aside ''Watch the Fords'' within a few years,[66] but the phrase was dusted off from time to time and became, with Packard's ''Ask the Man Who Owns One,'' one of the two best-known automobile slogans of all times. There have been numerous ''take-offs'' on the slogan over the years. J. T. Flynn wrote an article, ''Watch the Ford Myths Go By,'' for *New Republic* in 1937. Al Pearce, appearing for Ford on radio the same year, called his show ''Watch the Fun Go By.'' Ford's World War II newscast was entitled ''Watch the World Go By.'' A 1940 cartoon showing Henry and Edsel Ford whizzing by John L. Lewis was captioned ''Watch the Fords Go By,'' as was a 1944 editorial which equated Henry Ford's 1942 and 1944 predictions that the war would end in a few months with his 1931 statement that ''prosperity is here, but only a few realize it.'' *Broadcasting-Television* made use of the slogan in a 1949 article, ''Watch the UN Go By!,'' on the Ford Company's sponsorship of United Nations telecasts. The slogan also served as the headline over a 1963 *Newsweek* story on Henry Ford II's luxurious new yacht, and found expression in the form of ''Watch the Fords Go Back'' in a 1972 *Business Week* article on the Ford Company's recall of faulty cars.[67]

Pelletier left the company in December 1907, after less than a year as advertising manager, "to broaden his business connections."[68] He later said he had been fired, but he gave no reason.[69] His successor was Robert Walsh, who after a few months at the advertising helm was replaced by H. B. Harper, to whom Walsh became an assistant.[70]

Just as the Ford Company's advertising received minimal and unimaginative attention during the early years, the firm's press relations similarly were handled on a sporadic, informal basis. In contrast, many other auto makers assiduously courted the press. Colonel Albert A. Pope staged the industry's first press preview when he introduced the Columbia in 1897, and the practice of inviting journalists to inspect and ride in new models was quickly adopted by several other manufacturers. Oldsmobile around the turn of the century solicited the favor of auto editors by financing their national publication, *Goop Talk*. Other companies wooed the press at automobile shows. Private parties sometimes ran to $200 a plate, "with charming and acquiescent partners for the occasion."[71]

Auto companies's publicity men bombarded the press with news stories and photographs. The business manager of the *New York World* complained that the industry sent a page of "tripe" to his paper each day. The auto editor of the *San Francisco Chronicle* noted that when news was slow he could always turn to a two-foot high stack of "press agent stuff."[72]

When cars were a novelty, the daily press liberally reported automotive activities. As automobiles became more commonplace, however, resistance stiffened. In 1908 the *Chicago Tribune* went to the extreme of not mentioning the name of any motor car in its columns. Only when auto manufacturers and dealers had cancelled $200,000 worth of advertising was the policy rescinded. Similar business considerations and the fact that automobiles *were* news prevented many newspapers from supporting a stand by the American Newspaper Publishers Association against all automotive publicity. The ANPA was more successful in influencing syndicated news organizations. The Associated Press, the nation's leading purveyor of news, bent over backwards for many years to keep automotive stories off the wires.[73]

In the absence of a press specialist between 1903 and 1908 (except for Pelletier in 1907), the Ford Company's principal officers assumed responsibility for the home office's press relations. Couzens occasionally issued statements to the press, and from time to time he or Ford was interviewed, usually in connection with the Selden suit, racing, or production figures. Neither Couzens nor Ford called a press conference during the early years, and their interviews occurred most frequently at race tracks and auto shows. Very little product publicity was placed in the Detroit press prior to the 1906 introduction of the Model N, and only a trifle more was published during the next two years.[74] The company even farmed out its photographic work until 1908.[75]

Branch managers were responsible for public relations activities in their respective territories. The New York manager, Gaston Plantiff, described as "a rounder in getting around people," was particularly adept in entertaining the press and other company guests. Tom Hay, of Chicago, had the foresight to hire Chris Sinsabaugh—who simultaneously was editor of *Motor Age* and auto editor of the

Chicago Tribune and the *Chicago Daily News*—to prepare and place publicity for his branch.[76]

Although the Ford Company treated advertising and press relations like stepchildren during the early years, it paid very close attention to building and maintaining good customer relations. Many other companies also devoted continuing attention to customers, for it was recognized that the ease and speed with which motorists could secure repair parts and services was a vital element in selling cars and maintaining goodwill. The more public relations-conscious firms consequently insisted that their dealerships and branch offices be well equipped, and also dispatched factory mechanics to customers in difficulty.[77]

Before establishing branches and dealerships throughout the country, the Ford Company sent out "missionary mechanics" to aid and appease complaining customers.[78] Later, under the watchful eye of Sales Manager Norval Hawkins, dealers had to provide top-notch service facilities in order to obtain and retain franchises. Clean, neat places of business, pleasing show windows, and attractive cars for demonstrations were required. Branch roadmen took photographs of dealerships, inside and out, to satisfy the home office that its conditions were being met. Snapshots were taken of dealers and their salesmen to insure their correct and businesslike appearance. Roadmen kept a constant watch over dealers' financial positions and their standing in the community, comparing them with dealers serving other companies.[79]

Dealers were instructed to separate repair garages and stockrooms from the sales and display room, so that prospective customers would not see Fords being ripped apart for repairs or hear irate owners complain about their cars. Chains could not be advertised in dealerships for fear of suggesting the possibility of breakdowns. At least one branch ordered that malfunctioning cars be towed through city streets only after nightfall, so as to reduce the impact of this "very bad advertisement." Nobody, including customers and visitors, was permitted to smoke in Ford branches. Tipping was not tolerated, and acceptance of a gratuity brought instant dismissal. Fresh, clean signs—not faded or soiled ones which "invite breaking of rules"—had to be posted prominently throughout the premises.[80] Strong efforts were made to induce dealers to buy standardized Ford letterheads and outdoor and window signs.[81] Couzens and Hawkins frequently lectured factory, branch, and dealer personnel to be on their best business behavior at all times, to answer letters promptly, and to "see callers right off."[82]

The concern with customer relations was well founded, for within less than a decade of its incorporation Ford's vast branch and dealer network brought more representatives into contact with the public than did any other automobile or manufacturing company. In fact, Ford probably had more sales outlets (7,000) and personnel than the rest of the automobile industry combined.[83] Obviously, the policies and practices of an enterprise of such proportions would have a considerable bearing upon the company's relations with the public.

Following the pattern of older companies, Ford participated extensively in auto shows during its early years. Starting as mere appendages to bicycle exhibits before the turn of the century, auto exhibits had graduated to full-scale independent auto shows by 1900, when thirty-four models were displayed at Madison Square

Garden. From 1901 on, "national" auto shows were held annually in New York and Chicago, and lesser shows were held in most other large cities.[84]

The Ford Company's vehicles appeared in auto shows in New York, Chicago, and five lesser cities in early 1904.[85] From 1905 to 1910 the company exhibited under the auspices of the AMCMA in New York; in other cities Ford vehicles were displayed at combined AMCMA-ALAM shows. After the rival organizations folded in 1911, Ford refused to exhibit in New York under the aegis of successor associations. He maintained this policy until 1940. The company exhibited at trade association auto shows outside New York in 1911–12 and then began introducing its new models at private showings in New York and other key cities.[86]

Numerous nonautomotive shows and expositions also attracted the company during its early years. Three cars were displayed in 1904 at the Louisiana Purchase Exposition in St. Louis. Cut-out chassis and engines operated by electricity were featured at industrial shows several years later.[87] Henry Ford's personal interest in rural folk was reflected by the exhibition of tractor engines at state fairs in 1909–10 and of Model T's at the New York Land Show (for farmers) in 1911–12.[88]

The Ford Motor Company was a latecomer to the automotive field compared to many of its principal competitors. But by 1908 it had produced eight models—A, B, C, F, K, N, R, and S—and despite the legal complications of the Selden suit and several years of sporadic and unimaginative advertising and press relations, had firmly carved a niche for itself in the industry. In the fiscal year ending July 31, 1908, the company sold 6,398 cars; in the fifteen months ending December 31, 1908, it netted $1,145,392.48. It was among the industry's "Big Four" in sales, and was perhaps four rungs from the top of the profit ladder.[89] When the Ford Company introduced its ninth model, the Model T, in October 1908, its competition was still formidable, and the dark cloud of the Selden suit hung ominously on the horizon. But with the Model T, Ford abruptly left the pack. The company was to dominate sales for the next eighteen years and to produce more than half the industry's output in 1918–19 and from 1921 to 1925. Profits were correspondingly great, and from 1911–15 and in 1918 and 1921 the company earned more than the rest of the industry combined.[90]

As the company gained in stature, it began to acquire a more sophisticated public relations outlook. For the first time, beginning in 1908, conscious efforts were made to obtain publicity on matters other than the Selden suit or contests. Press-relations activities were formalized, a spritely magazine for members of the Ford organization was introduced, a wide variety of promotional literature was prepared, a Ford song was commissioned, and plant tours were organized. The company also encouraged the organization of Ford owners' clubs, showed an interest in legislation affecting the industry, and began to systematize and broaden its advertising. In short, the company's public relations and advertising were coming into their own.

Two or three years after 1908, the broadening stream of public relations and promotional activities helped make the Ford Motor Company and its product better known to the general public than any other automobile firm or car. Within another two years—by 1913—the company was regarded as one of the outstanding business institutions in the country. Its leading owner-executive, Henry Ford, had become the motor world's commanding figure and one of America's leading industrialists.

Chapter 3
Birth of the Model T

1

On March 18, 1908, advance catalogs describing the Model T were sent to Ford dealers throughout the nation. They evoked an immediate and enthusiastic response. "We must say it is almost too good to be true," a Detroit dealer wrote the company, "and we have rubbed our eyes several times to make sure we were not dreaming." "It is without doubt the greatest creation in automobiles ever placed before a people," averred a Pennsylvania agent, "and it means that this circular alone will flood your factory with orders." Several dealers told the company they were hiding the advance catalogs, because they feared that it would be impossible to sell older models on hand if word of the Model T's improvements got out. "We have carefully hidden the sheets away and locked the drawer, throwing the key down the cold-air shaft," declared an Illinois agent.[1]

Introduced on October 1, 1908, the Model T had several attention-getting innovations. The steering apparatus was on the left, a feature with such far-reaching consequences that within a few years every automobile manufacturer in the United States followed suit. The entire power-plant and transmission were completely enclosed. The T's four cylinders were cast in one solid block and there were only two semi-elliptic springs. In addition the T borrowed from its predecessors, Models N, R, and S, three-point suspension, vanadium steel, and a planetary transmission. These mechanical features, plus the fact that the new car was to sell for only $825 and up, gave the company considerable justification for claiming, "No car under $2000 offers more, and no car over $2000 offers more except in trimmings." In the T, as Allan Nevins and Frank Ernest Hill have pointed out, the company "had an Aladdin's lamp which needed but to be rubbed vigorously to produce a long career of industrial growth, fame, and prosperity."[2]

The "rubbing" applied to the Model T at the time of its introduction was perhaps the most energetic any American manufacturer had yet applied to a new product.[3] News releases, photographs, and sketches were sent to the press on an unprecedented scale, and the response proved commensurate with the effort. *Horseless Age* and *Motor Age* each published eight photographs or diagrams of the car, along with highly complimentary stories. *Motor World* ran four large photographs of the T, calling it "a credit to the genius of Henry Ford."[4] A record amount of literature was sent to dealers, who unleashed a torrent of orders by mail, telegraph, telephone, and personal visits. Branch managers, called to Detroit in September, demanded 15,000 cars for branch store requirements alone. Immediately thereafter advertisements appeared in the trade journals, prompting a flow of urgent orders from general dealers. Ads were also placed in the national weekly magazines. "If we were flattered by the reception the trade tendered the T,'' stated the company's employee-dealer magazine, the *Ford Times*, ''and surely no announcement ever received so glorious an acknowledgment, . . . much more were we elated by the response from the consumer. The 'ad' [in the national magazines] appeared on Friday; Saturday's mail brought nearly 1,000 inquiries. Monday's response swamped our mail clerks and by Tuesday night the office was well nigh inundated. There isn't a state in the Union that has not registered its approval of the Model T and the Ford Policy.''[5] Branches and local agencies also beat the drums as never before, buying unusually large amounts of newspaper space to advertise the new vehicle. Some Middle Atlantic and New England branches even took half-page ads in local papers to boom the company's exhibit at the New York auto show.[6]

Once loosed, the cataract of orders flowed unchecked. In the fall of 1908 demand ran so far ahead of production that the company could insist that it would supply T's only to those dealers who had sold all of the previous models on hand. Such ''rationing'' was unprecedented in the automobile business. By May 1, 1909, sales were so far ahead of production that the company stopped taking orders for nine weeks. Model T sales literally skyrocketed for a decade, some years showing more than a 100 percent increase over the year before. America's involvement in World War I broke the upward spiral from 1917 to 1919, but then came the T's heyday—six years in which domestic sales passed the million mark, and one in which they topped two million.[7]

On the eve of World War I, the Model T was selling at the rate of 250,000 per year, and it had attained a worldwide reputation enjoyed by no other car. ''While the constitution may follow the flag, or the flag the constitution, all depending on the viewpoint with reference to the foreign policy of the United States,'' reported the *Indianapolis Star,* ''the Ford Motor Company has beaten out both the flag and the constitution in carrying civilization into the wild places of the world.''[8] Twenty Model T's were used in the construction of the Amur River Railroad in Siberia; thirty Indian princes rode in Model T's, interspersed with elephants, camels, and horses, at the Delhi coronation of King George V; a Model T was delivered to the Tasha Lama of Urga, after a seven hundred-mile trip across the Gobi desert; the car sold briskly among tea planters in Ceylon; a T won the Johannesburg-Bereeniging race in South Africa; and French troops used T's in pursuit of brigands in Morocco.[9] By mid-1914, more than 550,000 Model T's were on the roads of the world, traveling ten million miles daily. ''A car that is seen as often as the Ford must be right,'' the *Ford Times* declared with some justification, ''or its very presence would kill it.''[10]

The vehicle's prodigious numbers were, in fact, an advertising asset. Every car bore the name ''Ford'' in bold script on the radiator, and, quite apart from that fact, the distinctive design of the Model T made it recognizable a half-mile away.[11] In a day when every automobile purchase and virtually all out-of-town trips were reported in the ''personals'' section of small-town newspapers, Fords naturally were mentioned thousands of times. ''W. H. Judd is now riding around in a new Ford car, which he recently purchased. These are a very neat little car. . . .'' ''Our genial and efficient mail carrier now delivers the mail on his route in a stylish and comfortable runabout of the Ford make whenever the conditions of the roads will permit.'' ''R. E. Rice is sporting a fine Ford runabout which he purchased from Agent Fred Scott of

Coalton." "Mr. and Mrs. John Inglebrecht and children, of near Jefferson City, drove over to Eldon Saturday in their Ford to visit Mr. and Mrs. R. J. Rush." Sometimes the publicity backfired: the *Elgin* (Illinois) *Courier* reported that "The funeral of William Kiel, who was killed last Friday from being tipped in the Ford automobile, which he and Joe Seyle were driving, was held Sunday."[12]

From 1908 to 1914 the Ford Company made a vigorous, if losing, effort to establish the indomitable little rattletrap as a prestige car. Ford press releases boasted of English aristocrats who owned Fords, and stories appeared around the country under such headlines as " 'Swells' Own Fords" and "Breaks into Society." The *Ford Times* pointed out that two Russian grand dukes and nineteen princes owned Fords, and that President Wilson had bought one for use at his summer home. Ford publicists arranged for Eddie Foy, Billie Burke, and Henrietta Crossman to be photographed in Fords for testimonial purposes. Similarly, dealers were asked to furnish pictures of well-known customers and their cars, against a background of "fine-looking residences."[13]

But in the long run, the prestige campaign was doomed to fail. Henry Ford was not, in point of fact, building automobiles for the elite. "I will build a motor car for the great multitude," he stated early in his career, ". . . constructed of the best materials, by the best men to be hired, after the simplest designs that modern engineering can devise . . . so low in price that no man making a good salary will be unable to own one—and enjoy with his family the blessing of hours of pleasure in God's great open spaces." In view of the times and the embryonic state of the auto market, Ford could not have conceived a more intelligent marketing approach, nor could he have communicated a more appealing message to the consumer public.[14] The Model T was, of course, the practical embodiment of Ford's vision. It was designed primarily for farm and family use. Utility, not stylish beauty, was its hallmark.[15] As the car of the common man, the Model T could not hope to achieve the kind of prestige which the Ford Company had in mind; in fact, after 1914 it became the butt of thousands of jokes which echoed around the nation. Finally, the inexpensiveness of the T—and particularly the annual price reductions starting in 1910—subverted the company's efforts to sell the car on the basis of snob appeal.[16]

Price cuts, to Henry Ford, were by far the most important element in merchandising the Model T. The manufacturer often said that he gained 1,000 new customers for every dollar the car was reduced in price. By 1912–13, he was so strongly convinced of the relative importance of price cuts that he began vetoing carefully worked out sales and promotion campaigns approved by James Couzens, who, until this time, had reigned supreme over the company's nonproduction affairs.[17]

Until America's entry into World War I, Ford could support his pricing theories by relating T prices to mounting sales figures and by pointing out that his company—in spite of prodigious increases in production—could scarcely meet the demand for its cars (note, however, that the price decreases did not start until the T's second year).[18]

The price cuts were generously reported in newspapers and magazines. Wire services, which rarely carried automotive news, flashed stories highly favorable to Ford following the 1912 and 1913 price reductions. *Harper's Weekly,* after weighing

Fiscal Year	Price (touring car)	Total Sales
1907–8	$850	6,398
1908–9	950	10,607
1909–10	780	18,664
1910–11	690	34,528
1911–12	600	78,440
1912–13	550	168,304
1913–14	490	248,307
1914–15 (10 months)*	440	221,805
1915–16	360	472,350

*Ford changed the end of its fiscal year from September 30 to July 31 in 1915, hence the ten-month figure for 1914–15. The company sold 308,213 cars between July 31, 1914, and August 1, 1915, according to figures released by the firm at the close of a year-long sales promotion event.

the contribution of the price cuts to the T's success, agreed that Ford "has thought out the best advertisement, and made the deepest, most sensational appeal to human nature he could have made."[19]

2

In addition to price cuts, Ford also promoted his vehicle by more conventional means, including the activity he knew and liked best—racing. Eager to demonstrate the Model T's sturdy dependability, and urged on by "a thousand dealers and a host of Ford enthusiasts," the manufacturer, when invited in the spring of 1909 to compete in a New York-to-Seattle race, rescinded the ban he had imposed on racing in 1907.[20] Robert Guggenheim, the mining magnate, who arranged the race to help boom the Alaska-Yukon-Pacific Exposition, imposed rigid requirements on the competitors. Cars had to check in at thirty points; they could obtain new parts only in Chicago and Cheyenne; and they were forbidden to travel on railroad tracks. Fourteen vehicles had entered the contest, but only five—two Fords, an Acme, a Shawmut, and an Italia— responded to the starting gun. Both Fords reached St. Louis two hours ahead of the nearest rival, and remained together in the van until reaching Idaho. Then Ford No. 1, driven by Kulick and H. B. Harper, the company's advertising manager, forged ahead with a nine-hour lead. However, because of misdirections from ignorant pilots, they twice became lost and fell one-and-a-half days behind. In the meantime Ford No. 2 headed straight for Seattle, arriving at the exposition amid the cheers of 200,000 persons. The trip had taken twenty-two days and fifty-five minutes. The Shawmut arrived seventeen hours later, followed several hours later by Ford No. 1. The Acme reached Seattle a week later; the Italia had been withdrawn at Cheyenne.[21]

The race was widely reported in the press, and the company and its dealers sought to capitalize on the public's interest. Harper's booklet, *The Story of the Race,* was distributed in tens of thousands to dealers. A large-scale newspaper and magazine advertising campaign trumpeted the achievement and flailed the many manufacturers who refused to enter the contest.[22] The winning car was displayed at hundreds of dealerships during a 6,000-mile swing from Seattle to Los Angeles to New York, reaching the latter city in time to be exhibited at the Hudson-Fulton celebration.[23]

The boom of Ford's victory drums was soon silenced. Five months after the race, the judges discovered that the crewmen of Ford No. 2 had violated the rules by changing the engine during part of the run. First prize was taken from the Ford and awarded to the Shawmut.[24] At this stage, the Ford Company may have felt that only the moral victory had been lost; the propaganda hay had been lofted long before.

Ford "re-enacted" the race for publicity purposes in 1959. A 1909 Ford stopped in eighty-five cities along the route and was seen by tens of thousands of people. William Clay Ford, a company vice-president and youngest grandson of Henry Ford, greeted the car and escorting vehicles at the site of the Seattle World's Fair of 1962. According to the company's northeast regional office, which had major responsibility for the re-enactment, the promotion was "the most important and successful program carried out by this office in recent years." None of Ford's press releases, nor a film of the expedition, released in 1962, made any mention of the disqualification of the original Ford "winner."[25]

Following its dramatic re-entry into racing in 1909, the company resumed full-scale racing in the summer of 1910.[26] Dealers were delighted, and within a few months many were reporting that the return to competition was greatly stimulating sales. Kulick again became a consistent winner, *Motor Age* ranking him as one of America's top drivers during 1910–11.[27] Two other drivers helped the Ford cause: R. P. Rice, manager of the Seattle branch, dominated northwest tracks and held the Seattle-to-Portland road record from 1910 to 1912, and E. Roger Stearns, a Los Angeles dealer, who was California's No. 1 driver in 1910, defeating Barney Oldfield (who by then had also resumed racing) and other leading professionals that year.[28]

Model T's sometimes were discriminated against in races because of their low weight-to-power ratio and their low price. In certain meets the 950-pound Ford, in order to compete with the heavier, higher-powered cars whose defeat would count for something, would have had to carry several hundreds of pounds of dead weight and to raise its price many hundreds of dollars to conform to classification requirements. On principle Henry Ford refused to bow to such demands, for he regarded the T's lightness and low cost as its chief attributes.[29] In the contests open to the little twenty-horsepower stock chassis, it proved a match for the heaviest, most powerful vehicles in the land.[30] The company, as a matter of fact, was supremely confident that Kulick, "The Pride of the Company," could defeat anyone. When rain postponed an exhibition between Kulick and Barney Oldfield and his specially built two-hundred-horsepower Benz, the *Ford Times* was keenly disappointed that "such is fate, and the honors that would have come to Ford were postponed for another meeting."[31]

Kulick and the company bowed out of track racing at the Michigan State Fair in September 1911. In an exhibition mile the Ford driver defeated some of racing's biggest names and broke the track record in the process. Immediately after the achievement a delighted Henry Ford pressed a $1,000 bill in Kulick's hands.[32]

The victory marked Kulick's last appearance on a race track. He figured in two more outstanding sporting events, however, before his final retirement from competition. In January 1912 he drove 999 the Second a mile in thirty-three and two-fifth seconds on the ice of Lake St. Clair. The time was the fastest on ice since Henry Ford's 1904 effort.[33] During the summer of 1912 Kulick made "the automobile world stand aghast" as he won the celebrated Algonquin (Illinois) Hill Climb in record-breaking time. His performance so embarrassed big-car manufacturers that in 1913 none would enter the contest unless Kulick and his machine were barred. But a boycott of the classic was avoided when it was announced that Kulick and the Ford Company were finished with competition.[34]

Kulick's departure from the Ford organization in 1927 provides a good example of Henry Ford's callousness toward men who had helped to build his firm. For some obscure reason—perhaps because of the company's financial problems during the Model T-Model A changeover period—Kulick was dismissed. He appealed to Henry Ford, who indirectly sent him to his hatchet man, Harry Bennett. Kulick was asked to repair a car engine, did so, and delivered the automobile to Bennett. The latter told Kulick the engine was still noisy and asked him to lie on the running board and listen through the hood. Bennett then sped out of the Ford gate so rapidly that Kulick was thrown off. Bennett drove back into the plant, leaving Kulick outside. When Kulick tried to re-enter, Bennett's thugs barred the way. Kulick entered the construction business in Detroit and invested in real estate; in 1946 he was reported as being "comfortably off."[35]

The Ford Company did not sponsor a racing entry again until 1935. Its dealers, with a few exceptions, also abandoned racing between 1912 and the mid-1930s.[36] Private owners and auto accessory firms, however, entered Model T's in hundreds of races in the 'teens and 1920s. During this period Ford racers, particularly the so-called Fronty-Fords—equipped with the powerful Frontenac cylinder head—dominated the country's small town dirt tracks. In 1923, three Fronty-Fords qualified for America's premier race, the Indianapolis Speedway 500-mile Memorial Day classic. To the delight of race referee Henry Ford and to the surprise of the racing fraternity, each of the T's was still running at the finish of the gruelling contest. The fastest of them, averaging 82.58 miles per hour, captured fifth place—an exceptionally good showing for an inexpensive modified stock car. After the introduction of the Model A in 1927, the machine-gun blast of the racing Fords was heard less often, although T's continued to compete on dirt tracks into the 1930s.[37]

Between 1905 and 1910, while the racing craze was undergoing criticism, milder forms of competition gained favor. Countless hill climbs, reliability-endurance runs, and economy tests were conducted in the pre-1913 period, and the Ford Company participated in hundreds of them. The company's earlier models seem to have avoided this sort of competition, but Models S and N, both built between 1906 and 1908, were successful in many contests. The *Ford Times* boasted that these models had won every hill climb in which they had been entered and suggested that such contests should be limited to one class, "Fords."[38]

The Model T proved much superior to the S and N, and certainly on a pound-for-pound basis there is considerable evidence to support the *Ford Times's* contention that it was "the greatest hill climber ever built." The car had no real competition in the low-price classification and carried off honors time and time again in climbs against the most expensive and powerful of automobiles.[39]

During the hill-climbing era virtually every navigable summit in the country was scaled, some with a monotonous frequency. A victory in one of the more important climbs definitely boosted a car's prestige. The Ford Company, consequently, focused on the "name" contests—especially the Algonquin, where notable victories were scored from 1910 to 1912. Meantime, dealers and owners carried the Ford banner into innumerable minor competitions.[40]

Some dealers were so eager to demonstrate the car's capabilities that they advertised for competition. A typical notice was posted by a Columbia, South Carolina, agent: "CHALLENGE Regardless of price, and including Steamers, July 5th, '09, The Ford Model T cleaned up every automobile sold in Columbia in a Hill Climb. If you want to make a little more sport for Labor Day, the Ford is ready." Between contests many dealers drove their Fords up and down the sides of a variety of near-perpendicular surfaces.[41] A Model T climbed Ben Nevis in 1911, receiving widespread publicity in Great Britain and the United States.[42] Before thousands of spectators, the company's Nashville dealer drove his car up the sixty-six steps of the Tennessee capitol building. The Duluth agent covered a $100 bet by climbing up three flights of courthouse steps, and a Los Angeles dealer used dynamite to blast his way in and out of the Grand Canyon.[43]

Of all of the Ford's climbing exploits, none was more publicized than a flivver's victory in the fourth annual world's championship hill-climbing contest, held on Pikes Peak in 1922. The triumph had rags-to-riches overtones worthy of the T. Owner and driver of the winning car was a twenty-one-year-old small-town Nebraskan, Noel E. Bullock, who had driven up the mountain only once before the race. The car itself, named "Old Liz," unpainted and hoodless, had been "home brewed" by the impecunious youth. Before the race the Ford entry had been publicly ridiculed by several drivers, who had called it a "tin can" and a "cross between a kiddie-kar and a pushmobile." Yet the T, competing against the "elite [drivers] of road racing" and "many of the highest-priced cars . . . in America" flashed to the top the winner. The Tin Lizzie's "spectacular performance" was reported in virtually every daily newspaper in the country.[44]

The Ford Company never worked up quite the enthusiasm for reliability-endurance runs that it did for racing and hill climbs. Perhaps it regarded the former as being too tame. "Endurance runs," complained the *Ford Times,* "are that only in name; in actuality they are joy rides that accomplish nothing except a holiday for the contestants and advertising orders for the newspapers." The publication also complained that many of the contestants who finished with perfect scores had cheated, and suggested that each car should be equipped "with a moving picture machine and a talking machine to see what the driver and observer are up to."[45] Misgivings notwithstanding, during the period 1907–12 the company, some of its branches, and many of its dealers participated in hundreds of contests. Fords were frequent winners in their classification and occasionally showed up well in the sweepstakes competition of important tours.[46] A Model T finished second in the 1910 Munsey Tour, and a team of three Fords ranked fourth, ahead of the Cadillac, Marathon, and Flanders in the prestigious Glidden Tour in 1911. Perhaps the T's greatest victory came in Russia, where it was the only one of forty-five European and two American cars to receive a perfect score in a 1,954-mile test conducted by the Imperial War Department. Czar Nicholas II personally inspected the winning T and recommended Fords for the Russian army.[47]

Ford dealers often conducted special endurance tests and stunts to show that their cars could withstand the roughest kind of treatment. A Rochester, New York, dealer annually sponsored January tours of Ford cars over hundreds of miles of snow-covered roads.[48] Other dealers loaded Model T's with a dozen or so persons for a "parade" down Main Street. This stunt reached its climax in 1911 when a flivver carrying thirty-four boys weighing 3,492 pounds was driven around Payne, Ohio.[49]

A Wichita dealer started a craze by introducing autopolo, played with two Model T chassis as field cars and two touring cars as goal-tenders. "Endurance runs, speed races, hill climbs and all other contests are mere parlor games in comparison," the enthusiastic agent assured the company. The Wichita team staged exhibitions all over the country, concluding its tour with a match in Madison Square Garden.[50]

The promotional value of hill climbs and reliability runs underwent a slow decline between 1910 and 1913, then rapidly fell off as cars became powerful enough to whisk up almost any hill and easily cover routes between distant points. Economy runs, although they have survived to the present, were never as popular as other contests during the early years, and Fords were entered in only a handful of them. Winning performances in these runs were based on a fuel-to-weight ratio, which the company regarded as discriminatory toward its light, economical car. Ford's recommendation that weight should not be a criterion in economy runs elicited no response among contest sponsors.[51]

Ford's successful participation in racing and the more practical forms of competition convinced many motorists that the Model T was spirited, dependable, and economical to operate and helped to push Ford into the forefront of the automotive field. While engaging in these contests the company undertook several new sales promotion ventures, including an extensive publications program, a more systematized press relations operation, song promotion, plant tours, and owners' clubs. These activities came increasingly to the fore as the importance of contests diminished.

3

The company entered the publishing field in April 1908, a few months before the Model T's debut, by launching the *Ford Times*. Although the *Ford Times* acquired within a few years the largest circulation of any industrial publication in the country, it was a relative latecomer among magazines published by auto companies. Olds Motor Works and the Winton Motor Carriage Company introduced the industry's first house organs at the turn of the century and at least a dozen manufacturers issued such magazines by 1908.[52] Begun at the suggestion of Sales Manager Norval Hawkins, the

Ford Times was edited initially by H. B. Harper, who succeeded Robert Walsh as advertising manager early in 1908, Walsh remaining as Harper's assistant. At first the *Ford Times* was a semimonthly sixteen-to-forty page slick for Ford home office and branch personnel and for dealers and their employees. It reported a wide variety of developments at the factory and in the field—news of car design and production, participation in contests, stunts, personnel shifts, new agencies, employee bowling scores, and so on. In addition it provided an almost endless supply of sales hints, promotion ideas, buyer testimonials, sample advertisements, exhortations to better business methods, and sermonettes on self-confidence, optimism, and enterprise. Harper and Walsh wrote most of the copy, but articles occasionally were supplied by Hawkins, Couzens, other executives, and outsiders. Branch managers and dealers were constantly asked to contribute, and almost as frequently were reprimanded for not doing so.[53] By early 1910 the magazine was reprinted in French, Spanish, Portuguese, and Russian, and, on the basis of being sent to 2,100 dealerships around the world, claimed the widest geographical circulation of any American publication.[54]

After editor Harper's promotion to the export managership in June 1910, the magazine adopted several new policies. Starting in September 1910, copies were mailed to Ford owners and prospective customers as well as to Ford dealers and their employees. The magazine was enlarged and changed from semimonthly to monthly publication status in January 1911, and three months later it began accepting advertisements from accessories manufacturers.[55] These changes were accompanied by an improved physical layout and a revised editorial format. Covers were illustrated in four colors; inside pages in two. Halftones showed a marked improvement over earlier editions. Although four pages in each issue were devoted to product photographs and information, the magazine was no longer as overtly "commercial." Considerable travel information was provided, and such features as "Owners' Experiences," "Hints to Users," and "Good Roads" became a regular part of the publication. Outsiders contributed articles more frequently. By mid-1914 the transformation was complete: the internal-external house organ had become a publication aimed at "the automobile public in general—and to Ford owners in particular."[56] During most of this transition period (June 1910-January 1913 and October 1913-July 1914), the *Ford Times* was prepared by the advertising staff. From January until October 1913, a dynamic Chicago advertising man, Glen Buck, whose agency had been retained by the company since early 1912, held the editorship. A native of Grand Rapids, Michigan, Buck was a former country editor and advertising manager of the Buck Stove and Range Company. He spiced the *Ford Times* with scores of pithy "Glen Buck-Isms," innumerable illustrations of the "winged pyramid" trademark he had designed for the company, and dozens of parables with a sales message.[57] Charles A. Brownell was appointed editor of the *Ford Times* in August 1914,[58] and served at the same time as Ford's advertising manager and Henry Ford's "spokesman, orator, herald, and . . . interpreter." Under Brownell's conservative supervision, the magazine was less lively and somewhat less interesting. Greater emphasis was placed on product- and company-related articles, on the Model T's power plant, transmission, and spark plugs, the company's branch plants and its English

Language School, profit-sharing, and so on. Beginning in 1915, at Ford's behest, pacifist articles—decidedly out of place in a sales magazine—were published in many issues.[59]

By January 1916, the *Ford Times,* which was offered free of charge, had a circulation of 400,000. Reflecting the rapid increase in the number of Model T owners, the circulation stood at 600,000 in early 1917. Apparently there was a huge backlog of unfilled requests, for circulation zoomed from 600,000 to 900,000 when the magazine acquired additional press facilities in March 1917. At this point the *Ford Times* announced that it had one of the largest circulations of any periodical in the country and soon would pass the million mark. But it was not to attain this goal, for America's entry into World War I prompted the company to announce the magazine's suspension in April 1917.[60]

The *Ford Times* was by no means the only literature that the company furnished to the public. Even in the pre–Model T period, sales booklets were prepared specifically for doctors, salesmen, and lawyers.[61] With the advent of the Model T, additional literature was written for taxicab companies, motor freight concerns, and the feminine trade. Pamphlets also were prepared on the Ford factory, vanadium steel, tires, the T's ignition system, and so on. Standard- and pocket-sized catalogs and attractive souvenir booklets were printed in English, Russian, Spanish, French, and Dutch. Some of the literature was prepared by outside writers. Irvin S. Cobb, for example, received $500 for writing ''Six Talks by the Jolly Fat Chauffeur with the Double Chin.''[62]

The Ford Company claimed that its advertising literature was ''the most elaborate and instructive series'' ever prepared for automobile prospects and insisted that it be used to full advantage. ''Throw away that old stuff and order new literature!'' exclaimed the *Ford Times.* Hawkins was even more explicit:

> The aggressive and successful dealer does not allow his advertising literature to pile up in his office on desks or shelves, but keeps it in motion . . . alive, burning, blazing all the time. . . . The trade literature sent out by the Ford Motor Company to its Branches, Dealers and Sub-Dealers is not the result of idle guessing, not because of any philanthropic desire to put some pleasing playthings in the hands of the Ford trade. No—it [is] a most serious sort of business; it is arming the trade to do business in the largest possible measure; it is literally baptizing civilization with the name FORD, and the merits of Ford cars. . . . Therefore we have an interest at stake in keeping this literature going out.

Hawkins's exhortations must have borne fruit, for even before annual sales reached the 200,000 mark, Ford branches and dealers each year distributed more than five times that number of catalogs alone.[63]

The home office was not the only source of Ford literature. A number of dealers published booklets about their agencies, and one of them, J. G. Lightner, of Odessa, Missouri, distributed a wide variety of maps and brochures to all motorists passing through his hometown.[64] A Milwaukee publishing house started a magazine entitled the *Fordowner* which circulated nationally. This monthly promoted camaraderie among Model T owners in the same way that vintage and sports car publications encourage fraternal feeling among certain contemporary motorists. Introduced in 1914, the *Fordowner* contained a full range of technical "how to do it" articles, touring and driving tips, news of the Ford Motor Company, the latest Ford jokes, and even fiction with such titles as "Fords and Romance."[65] The magazine must have been very profitable during the Model T's heyday. In its peak year, 1920, paid monthly circulation (one dollar a year or ten cents a copy) exceeded 42,000; and, on the average, 264 accessory manufacturers advertised in each edition. That year the title was changed to *Ford Owner and Dealer,* indicating a trend toward a technical and service publication.[66] In 1925 the magazine was retitled *Ford Dealer and Owner,* and beginning in 1926, when its name was again changed—to *Ford Dealer and Service Field*—the publication was prepared expressly for dealers.[67]

Just as the Ford Company adopted a more sophisticated approach to promotional literature, it also broadened the scope of its press relations activities starting in 1908. In the early days of the company, the firm's press relations efforts were largely confined to the Selden suit and to contests. Few statements were issued to the press, Couzens and Ford were interviewed only sporadically, and little effort was made to obtain product publicity. This situation changed after 1908. News releases on a wide variety of subjects—production and sales, a decision to paint all cars Brewster green, price cuts, the amounts of hide, steel, and cocoa matting used in Model T's, unusual jobs performed by Highland Park employees, branch plant expansion, and so on—were sent directly to the metropolitan press, or, as was usual in dealing with small city papers, to branch managers who forwarded them to dealers for placement. Some of these stories were virtual reprints from the *Ford Times* (which itself was sent to leading newspapers and frequently quoted by them), while others were prepared independently of the magazine. Thus, by 1908, Ford had joined the many other manufacturers who during the first decade of the century had come to recognize the value of supplying news to the press.

News releases, as a matter of routine, were tailored for hometown consumption. Sometimes the local angle was stressed in specially written leads, but more often general stories contained blank spaces in which the branch manager or dealer could insert his own name, business title, and localized data. Releases regularly were sent to all newspapers on Ford's advertising schedule on the usually correct assumption that they would be given special consideration by this segment of the press. Some papers in which Ford did not advertise also were occasionally serviced, and the response even here was gratifying.[68]

In addition to preparing routine stories, the publicity staff exercised considerable ingenuity in associating the Model T with current events. For instance, when trouble with Mexico was anticipated in 1913, the publicists recommended that every American battleship be equipped with T's to enable the Marines "to charge on Mexico City from Vera Cruz in record time." The idea was hailed in metropolitan papers all over the country.[69] The company's board of directors also appointed one of its members to arrange for a Ford to be the first automobile to pass through the Panama Canal.[70] The mission must have been unsuccessful, for the company never published an account of any such achievement.

Following another industry pattern, the Ford Company also sought to promote its sales with song. Probably the first car to get a melodious sales lift was the Mobile steamer, which was rolled on stage to the accompaniment of "My Mobile Gal" in the

1903 musical, *The Belle of Bohemia*. After Gus Edwards's and Vincent Bryan's 1905 hit, "In My Merry Oldsmobile," gave the Oldsmobile a tremendous amount of valuable advertising, all motor manufacturers hoped for a song which would publicize their product, and many of them commissioned composers for this purpose.[71] In early 1908 Ford joined the rush to Tin Pan Alley, commissioning song writer Harry H. Zickel to prepare a "catchy thing" which would have everyone "clamoring for copies, whistling the air and dancing to its spritely measures." Zickel responded with the "Ford March & Two-Step," sheet copies of which were distributed by the company to every prominent band and orchestra in the United States and Canada and to all Ford dealers. "We want it in every home where there is a piano," declared the *Ford Times*. "It is not too advertisy and is something that will, by its own merit, remain on the piano instead of being consigned to the bottom of the music cabinet. Piano owners are possible car owners—their guests equally so, and with a piece of music so attractively gotten up and containing such genuine worth, the advertising feature cannot be other than one of *immense profit*." Many dealers shared the magazine's enthusiasm. Ordering 100 copies, a Milwaukee dealer explained, "My wife plays it beautifully and she says that it is a perfect dream." Although the song never achieved the widespread popularity of "In My Merry Oldsmobile," it became sufficiently popular to be arranged for automatic piano players and to be recorded for the Victor Talking Machine Company by Arthur Pryor's band. Its finest hour was at the President's Inaugural Ball of 1909, when 350-pound William Howard Taft and his entourage pranced to its stirring beat. The *Ford Times* reported that the inclusion of the march on the ball's program generated a heavy demand for copies, a claim which appears a trifle hollow inasmuch as the song was soon forgotten.[72]

Although the Ford Motor Company commissioned no more songs during this period, composers, hoping to emulate Gus Edwards's success, turned out more than three-score melodic tributes to the Model T.[73] One of the compositions, "The Little Ford Rambled Right Along," written in 1914, achieved considerable popularity.[74] Many of the tunes attempted to capitalize on Model T jokes. Typical of such titles were "I Didn't Raise My Ford To Be a Jitney," "It's a Rambling Flivver," and "Let's Take a Ride on the Jitney Bus." Others had a romantic flavor. "The Packard and the Ford" suggested that Mr. Packard and Miss Flivverette marry and give birth to a Buick, and "The Scandal of Little Lizzie Ford" depicted a demure T garaged with a rakish, low-slung sports car. "On the Old Back Seat of the Henry Ford" promised that the moon would smile on couples spooning in flivvers.[75]

The Model T even inspired a fantasia, "Flivver Ten Million," which "created a furore" when performed by the Boston Symphony Orchestra and was responsible for an attendance record at New York's City College Stadium when played by the New York Philharmonic Orchestra. Written by T. S. Converse, a professor of music at Harvard, the fourteen-minute "joyous epic" described the assembling of the ten millionth Model T (announced by a motor horn, full blast) and followed its wandering across the country. After a necking party and a joy ride, interrupted by a collision, " 'Phoenix Americanus,' " according to the program note, "righted and shaken, proceeds on his way with redoubled energy, typical of the indomitable spirit of America." At first Serge Koussevitzky, conductor of the Boston

Symphony Orchestra, protested against some of the honks, rattles, squeaks, and crashes in the score, but Converse insisted that they were essential to his art. The composer's judgment was upheld by favorable reviews in the *Boston Transcript* and the *New York Times*.[76] The final Model T songs were inspired by the car's demise in 1927. "Henry's Made a Lady Out of Lizzie," which of course alluded to the new Model A, and "Poor Lizzie, What'll Become of You Now?" were typical of the nostalgic compositions of this period.[77]

Another source of publicity for the Model T and the Ford Company in the post-1908 period was the mammoth Highland Park plant, located in Highland Park, Michigan, a community of 4,120 population surrounded by the city of Detroit. The plant was designed and built by America's greatest industrial architect, Detroiter Albert Kahn and was the world's largest auto factory, Michigan's biggest building under one roof, and the most artistic factory of its day—in architecture, shining cleanliness, and harmonic arrangement. Eight hundred and sixty-five feet long and seventy-five feet wide, the four-story building had more than 50,000 square feet of glass, a feature which led some to call it the "Crystal Palace."[78] The company's publicity staff spared little effort to inform the press that the factory was "the wonder of the automobile world," the "largest single manufacturing institution in the world," and that it maintained the "largest machine shop in the world." A photograph of 12,000 of the 16,000 workmen was taken in front of the factory, and many newspapers ran six-column cuts accompanied by stories stating that the picture was the "largest specially posed photo ever taken, and [is] far and away the most expensive, considering the employees' time and loss of production."[79]

As time went on, the plant's size (a complex of buildings, including a foundry, covered sixty acres by 1913) evoked less interest than the production feats taking place therein. To the *Boston News Bureau,* the factory's output in 1912 was "remarkable" and in 1913 was "simply phenomenal."[80] Automobile executives, realizing that size alone could not account for the prodigious production, hastened to Highland Park to examine the techniques which made such volume possible. They were generous in their praise. Karl Neumaier, general manager of Germany's famed Benz Company, told the press, "The Ford plant is the most remarkable in the world; it is the very best in equipment and method"; and Louis Renault, head of the French firm bearing his name, declared that the plant was "the best organized in the country" and that he was "very much impressed by the ingenuity displayed in the manufacturing of cars."[81]

The experts found full agreement among Ford publicists, whose steady flow of news releases dramatized the factory's productivity and "special machinery." Such headlines as "Figures on Ford Production Amaze" became commonplace. The statement in one Ford handout that "thousands of columns have been written about how mammoth production has been accomplished in the parent plant of the Ford Motor Company" was made all the more credible by being published in scores of newspapers.[82] Those papers which were not disposed to take the company at its word still found the plant's productivity newsworthy enough to warrant space. "We can quote authorities and not advertising sharps," stated the *Peoria* (Illinois) *Transcript.* "The *American Machinist* comes out boldly in a special series of articles and proves that the achievment of Henry Ford as wholesale producer of automobiles amounts to one complete car every forty seconds by the clock."[83] Ford's assembling techniques gained more fame in 1913 when they were featured in a nationally distributed newsreel, believed to be the first ever made in an industrial plant.[84] Thus the Highland Park plant and the stirrings of mass production brought Ford to the public's attention even before the introduction of his radical five-dollar-day wage policy focused immediate and lasting worldwide attention on him and his organization.

In the wake of the five-dollar day—which overnight more than doubled Ford workers' pay—scores of newspaper and magazine writers swarmed to Highland Park. Their impressions were all the more vivid in that the factory was very likely the first of any kind that many of them had ever seen. Gaping at the smooth-flowing assembly lines, the writers used such adjectives as "miraculous," "phenomenal," "revolutionary," "epochal," and "world-shaking" in attempting to describe the process. Syndicated stories on how "Ford cars grow up by magic methods" appeared in hundreds of newspapers throughout the nation.[85]

Mass production, believed by some observers to be "the greatest of the achievements associated with Ford and his company," received a tremendous amount of publicity for a decade after 1914. To a worldwide public Henry Ford became the incarnate symbol of the process.[86] As such, he was a messiah to many who were impressed by quantity production, bigness, and the higher standard of living which mass production made possible. Conversely, he was a devil to the minority who deplored the triumph of the machine over the individual and who found no solace in huge industrial operations and uniformity of product.[87]

Responding to the Highland Park plant's widespread publicity, engineering societies, business organizations, and dealer groups visited the plant as early as 1910 to see the "magic methods" about which they had read and heard. Two years later the *Ford Times* reported that "the reception business is being systematized and soon will be able to handle four or five crowds a day."[88] A twenty-five to thirty-man guide corps was organized, and a concerted effort was made to encourage visits to the plant. The promotional efforts evidently were successful, the *Christian Science Monitor* reporting that "the competent corps of guides" had escorted "thousands of persons" through the plant in 1912.[89] In the early spring of 1914 an average of 150 guests visited the plant daily. By this time the company's newly organized Motion Picture Department also was filming visiting celebrities to provide exclusive material for the company's newsreel, the Ford Animated Weekly.[90]

After the announcement of the five-dollar day, the plant became "a national landmark and a new Niagara Falls," a place to be seen by every visitor to Detroit. William Howard Taft thought the plant "wonderful, wonderful," and Roger W. Babson, president of Babson Statistical Organization, said his visit was as a pilgrimage to a shrine. His view was shared by William Bausch, head of Bausch & Lomb Company, Rochester, New York, who, with nineteen business friends, traveled the 320 miles to Michigan solely to go through the Ford factory. During 1915, approximately 100,000 persons visited the plant, and this figure was more than doubled two years later.[91]

More praise came Ford's way when the company began building branch assembly plants around the country. Until after World War I, Ford was the only auto firm with sufficient output to make regional assembly operations economically sound. By the summer of 1912, assembly plants were in operation in Kansas City, Long Island City, and Buffalo, and similar facilities soon were added in more than a dozen other centers of population. As might be expected, wherever plants were built, the payrolls delighted employees, bankers, merchants, and politicians, and newspapers went out of their way to provide complimentary publicity.[92] When the Oklahoma City facility was opened in 1916, for example, the mayor declared a holiday, the *Daily Oklahoman* devoted almost an entire issue to the new installation, and more than 100 merchants bought twelve pages of welcoming advertising in that newspaper. At least 3,000 townspeople were at the factory—one of the largest in the state—to see the first car come off the final line. At noon the Oklahoma City Chamber of Commerce and the company played host to 5,000 Ford dealers and guests, and in the afternoon more than 2,300 Model T's, including the 175 assembled that day, paraded through the streets.[93] Ford's assembly branches also received visitors, and in 1916 the Omaha and Minneapolis plants each welcomed more than 20,000 guests.[94]

Goodwill in the field was also generated and maintained by the sponsorship of innumerable Ford owners clubs by branch sales offices and dealers. The first organization of this kind—in fact, the first club formed by the owners of any one make of car—was organized in St. Louis in mid-1908, after a group of Ford owners had broached the idea to the local manager. The official asked the city's 300 "Fordists" to be his guests at a nearby resort, where a club was organized, membership and tourist committees appointed, and an identifying radiator emblem selected. Runs of up to 150 miles were planned for summer and fall Sunday afternoons. The *Ford Times,* advised of these arrangements, found "the idea to be an excellent one, for it promotes sociability among members, boosts the automobile generally, and assists in FORD sales in particular."[95]

Taking their cue from the St. Louis branch, Ford branches and dealers during the next few years organized owners' clubs in hundreds of American communities. On Sundays and holidays long lines of Model T's clattered along dusty roads all over the nation, ostentatiously parading through villages on the route, then stopping at a park or grove where contests were held after a potluck picnic lunch. The club's sponsor usually provided free lemonade and coffee and offered prizes for the contests, which ranged from fifty-yard dashes for girls and bald-headed men to hill climbs and "eccentric Model T stunts." Some of the sociability runs and picnics brought hundreds of Model T's and thousands of people together.[96] Perhaps the largest of these events occurred in Milwaukee, where 1,200 T's paraded through the streets in 1914, and at Hillsdale, Michigan, where more than 5,000 Ford owners and members of their families attended a picnic in 1916.[97] In addition to organizing social activities, some of the Ford owners' clubs were chartered to conduct cooperative buying and manufacturing operations. The Denver Ford Touring Club sought to obtain "more reasonable prices by the purchasing of tires, gas, oil, and accessories," and Toledo Ford owners formed a cooperative company to manufacture tires and tubes exclusively for Model T's.[98]

During the 1908–13 period the Ford Company also tentatively expressed an interest in federal and state legislation affecting automobiles. In 1908 the board of directors appropriated $2,000 "to aid in securing a good roads law such as is being promoted by the National Good Roads Financial Committee," and in 1913 Hawkins urged all New York auto dealers to urge their state legislators to vote against insurance bills advocated by a number of indemnity insurance firms.[99]

The company, or more accurately, Henry Ford was also greatly concerned with legislation affecting birds. Ford was one of the nation's leading bird fanciers, maintaining by 1911 a 2,150-acre wildlife preserve in Dearborn, Michigan.[100] It was natural for him to become interested in a federal bill designed to protect migratory birds. The Weeks-McLean Migratory Bird Bill had languished in Congress from 1909 to 1912, but in December 1912 Ford decided to throw his full weight behind the proposal in an effort to obtain passage in 1913. Glen Buck, a prominent member of the Audubon Society and a personal friend of the naturalist John Burroughs, whom Ford greatly admired, was enlisted to push the measure through Congress "even if it costs $100,000." Buck rallied wildlife societies, schoolchildren, and the Boy Scouts to the cause and sent telegrams to all state game wardens, Ford dealers, banks with which Ford did business, and "every prominent man and institution in America" to urge them to wire their congressmen to support the measure. He also "worked untiringly night and day lining up all the newspapermen" and thus obtained a flood of publicity about birds. Ford personally requested Thomas A. Edison "to give an interview to some good newspaperman urging immediate passage," and asked John D. Rockefeller to discuss the matter with the House speaker, Champ Clark, and other congressmen. The bill passed the Senate with ease. In the House, however, it bogged down until Buck managed to have it attached as a rider to a "must" piece of legislation, the agriculture appropriation bill.[101]

Although there is little question that Ford's primary interest in the bill was not self-serving, his concern did pay—and perhaps not unexpectedly—bountiful dividends in publicity. As with the Selden suit, the contemporary publicity was but the beginning. During the first months following the five-dollar day, when a great number of articles were introducing Ford to the public, much mention was made of his regard for birds and his all-out fight for the Weeks-McLean Bill. Although this aspect of the manufacturer's life received less attention in later years, whenever the subject was mentioned, it was discussed in terms flattering to Ford.[102]

The Ford Company was perhaps unique among automobile firms in its formalized approach to market research during the pre-World War I period. Ford first surveyed public opinion early in 1912, when 1,000 Model T owners (a sample of 1 percent) were asked, "Just what reason or reasons were foremost in your choice of a Ford car?" Twelve respondents indicated that low price was the primary reason, 38 pointed to the sound ignition system, 108 referred to the low maintenance cost, and 842 reported they had made the purchase on the recommendation of other owners. The same question was asked in a poll of 2,000 Ford owners in the fall of 1912, but records of the results are not extant.[103] During this period the company also attempted to obtain specific market data from each of its branch managers:

> We want to know [Norval Hawkins wrote to the branch managers on June 31, 1914] what sections are dependent upon farming and the kinds of crops

raised; what sections depend upon manufacturing and principal kinds; mining, lumber, etc., and the actual reasons for increased prosperity, normal business or financial depression, whichever may be the case, so that we can have our finger on actual trade conditions and the reasons why . . . so that should there be bumper crops or crop failures, strikes or bank failures, political upheavals, reduced tariffs, or anything affecting the industries, commercial or farming, we will be in a better position to know what to expect from your Branch territory and to measure your results, present and prospective.[104]

The company, unfortunately, soon discontinued its pioneering in market research. The statement, "The public can have any color it wants so long as it's black," if not actually made by Henry Ford, at least expressed his attitude regarding the opinions of customers during the years the Model T dominated the auto market. The industrialist bowed to an obvious consumer demand for multicolored and balloon-tired cars during the mid-1920s, but not until the 1940s did his company again conduct surveys of public opinion.[105]

Between 1908 and 1913, perhaps with an eye toward the rapidly increasing sums spent annually on advertising by other auto companies (the industry's first $1,000,000 appropriation was made by General Motors in 1910), Ford adopted new advertising policies and made several personnel and agency changes. The company sought to coordinate factory and dealer advertising. Dealers were asked to copy sample ads in the *Ford Times* "so that everybody stands equally strong and on the same footing with no chance for disagreement or misunderstanding." They also were asked to coordinate their local schedules closely with the company's national advertising campaigns. Finally, they were expected to advertise with consistency. If at times a brisk demand left them without automobiles to sell, they were told to buy space for "good will" purposes.[106] This stipulation, paradoxically, was of the "You do as I say, not as I do" variety, for the home office repeatedly suspended advertising when sales ran ahead of production. "When Ford is sold out," wrote Harper in 1910, "the advertising manager gets instructions to stop advertising, and he stops, though several score or more salesmen of space spend a lot of time arguing the foolishness of such a policy."[107]

This practice meant that the amount of money spent on advertising varied widely, not only from year to year, but from month to month. Buck indicated that one of the reasons he left Ford was that he never knew from one month to the next whether his appropriation would be $5,000, $8,000, or $30,000.[108] Ford's annual advertising volume ranged from a reported $25,000 in 1908 to an estimated $400,000 in 1913.[109] After 1913 expenditures dwindled very rapidly and were halted entirely in 1917. During these years most other automobile companies substantially increased their advertising appropriations. In 1915, notwithstanding the insignificant contribution made by Ford—which that year outsold the next six leading auto makers combined—the auto industry passed the food industry to become the nation's largest advertiser.[110]

The company's ideas about the most effective size of advertisements also differed greatly from time to time. It will be recalled that in 1906–7 small-space ads, many of them only one twenty-seventh or one-thirtieth of a page, were in vogue. From 1908 until mid-1912, conventional one-eighth of a page to full-page ads were used. Then the company reverted to tiny ads, many of them consisting of only twenty to thirty words of copy. With some exceptions, Ford advertisements were small from 1912 until 1917. Charles A. Brownell, Ford's advertising manager from 1914 to 1921, summed up the company's view on space requirements when he told the Cincinnati Advertisers Club, "People either read ads or they don't, and if they do read them, smaller space is just as productive of sales as larger."[111]

As in pre-1908 days, Ford copy frequently referred to the Model T's sturdiness, simplicity of operation and maintenance, use of vanadium steel, and lightness. Primary emphasis, however, was now placed on price appeal,[112] and, from early 1912, the company's "winged pyramid" trademark. The trademark, described by Buck as "a happy combination of two of the oldest Egyptian symbols—the pyramid symbolizing strength and stability—the scarab wings symbolizing lightness and grace," virtually permeated the Ford organization for several years. "Here is the new sun of the Ford advertising system," rhapsodized Buck in one of many articles extolling the trademark. "It shall be the 'blazing flag' around which the Ford forces shall rally." More than half the space of some Ford ads were devoted to reproductions of the trademark. Dealers were ordered to have it painted on their sales windows and were strongly urged to use trademarked letterheads. After October 1912 the number plates on all Model T's bore the emblem. Within a year of its introduction, the trademark, according to one latter-day expert, was "widely established all over the world" and was of "enormous value" to the company. It was used consistently until late 1916, when for some reason the company's Operating Committee questioned whether it should be continued. This body referred the question to Henry Ford, who, according to Ernest G. Liebold, the manufacturer's secretary, abolished the trademark after being told that "scarab" is another name for dung beetle.[113]

The 1908–13 period also saw a number of personnel changes. When Advertising Manager Harper was promoted in June 1910 to the export managership, with headquarters in New York,[114] the company named no successor, and the post remained vacant for two-and-a-half years. Ford advertising was handled by a New York advertising agency, the J. Walter Thompson Company, in late 1910 and 1911.[115] The manager of this agency's Detroit office, established in 1908, was Charles A. Brownell, who had been the head of his own Detroit agency since 1897. By 1908 Brownell was, according to the *Detroit News–Tribune,* a nationally known advertising figure, having "pioneered many advances in advertising methods."[116] As J. Walter Thompson's Ford account executive, Brownell supervised advertising, gave inspirational addresses at numerous dealer "rouser" meetings, and was responsible for some of the company's press relations activities.[117]

Early in 1912 Brownell and the J. Walter Thompson Company were replaced by Glen Buck, who serviced the Ford account out of Chicago for a year. When Buck was working on the Weeks-McLean Bill in December 1912 and January 1913, his energetic resourcefulness impressed Henry Ford, who suggested to Couzens that he be invited to join the company as advertising manager and editor of the *Ford Times*.[118] Buck sailed into both jobs with missionary zeal, performing each in a highly creditable manner, but his aggressive nature soon brought him into conflict with Ernest G. Liebold, Henry Ford's strong-willed secretary. Relations between the two men were strained to the breaking point when Ford ordered that page proofs be submitted to the secretary for approval. Buck's reaction was, ''I'll give Mr. Ford the proofs. I won't give them to you [Liebold].'' Ford was annoyed by the situation, and Buck, for his part, was unhappy with the manufacturer's diffidence toward advertising and with his erratic policies. Matters reached the boiling point in October 1913 when Buck resigned and then threatened to sue the company for a bonus that he claimed was due him. The advertising managership remained vacant until Brownell's appointment ten months later.[119]

The frequent changes in advertising policies and personnel and the zeal with which the Ford Company launched and pursued its varied public relations programs during the five years after 1908 suggest a restless, dynamic organization seeking to measure up to its newly-acquired status as America's No. 1 auto maker. Before 1908 Ford's sales-promotion efforts were directly tied to its cars: models were shown at exhibits, entered in races, and described in advertisements. These promotional techniques were continued in later years, but from 1908 the company placed as much emphasis on public relations activities that publicized the company—and indirectly the Model T—as on the Model T itself. Thus Ford not only displayed its car at exhibits and race tracks and in advertisements; it also called the public's attention—through news releases, a magazine, and plant tours—to the company and the factories which made the Model T. The company's solidly established dealer organization was made a vital part of these activities, especially in fostering the novel owners' club idea. And if these varied programs were not enough to make the public take notice of the Ford Company and its car, there were always Henry Ford's annual price cuts—which the industrialist correctly regarded as the best public relations technique of them all.

Just as Henry Ford's views on pricing suggested that the manufacturer would not confine himself to orthodox business practices, his concern with principles in the Selden suit and his support of the Weeks-McLean Bird Bill suggested that he was not likely to limit his future activities to building cars—and that his reputation might be based on more than successfully administering an auto company. These forays also served notice that in Henry Ford the automobile industry had produced a man who would not be an imitator, who would drive vigorously toward his objectives, and who, at least for a time, would be guided by high-minded and idealistic motives.

```
┌─────────────────────────────────┐
│          Chapter 4              │
│          On the Eve             │
└─────────────────────────────────┘
```

The year 1914 marks a decided turning point in the public relations status of Henry Ford and the Ford Motor Company. Before that year Ford was known only as one of the nation's more prominent industrialists. From 1914 until his death in 1947, he was easily the world's best-known manufacturer. His company, similarly, enjoyed a considerable reputation prior to 1914; however, from there on it was the best-known business enterprise on the face of the globe.

Most of the thirty-two biographers of Henry Ford, noting that the executive was not listed in the 1913 edition of *Who's Who in America* and that neither he nor his firm is cited in 1913 by the *New York Times Index* or the *Readers' Guide to Periodical Literature,* have assumed that both Ford and the Ford Motor Company were relatively little known before 1914.[1] This view is not without some substance when one compares the publicity given to Ford before 1914 with that which he received after that date. But it underestimates the impact which Ford and his company had made during the years prior to 1914. *Who's Who* ignored not only Ford but virtually everyone else in the automobile industry as well. Only two persons concerned with motor car manufacturing, Colonel Pope and J. M. Studebaker, were listed in *Who's Who* prior to the 1912–13 edition, and neither gained admittance on the strength of his auto activities. Colonel Pope was the world's leading bicycle manufacturer; Studebaker was the world's largest maker of wagons. In its 1912–13 edition, the directory listed 18,794 persons, and only five auto manufacturers were among them. A second Studebaker was cited, as was Hugh Chalmers, who had earned his reputation as vice-president of the National Cash Register Company. The only old-line automobile men listed were Alexander Winton and Elwood Haynes.[2] (Colonel Pope died in 1909.)

The omission of Ford's name drew fire from several quarters. "One will look in vain for his biography in the pages of 'Who's Who,' for that usually reliable publication contains no mention of him," observed the *San Antonio Light* in 1913. After the announcement of the five-dollar day, the *Roanoke News* found it "hardly credible that a man who has built up one of the largest industries in America, a man who employs nearly 30,000 men and women, a man who pays today the third largest income tax of any man in the world, should not have his name mentioned in the ordinary reference books containing biographies of the 'men of the day.' "[3]

The fact that the *New York Times Index* for 1913 did not list Henry Ford or the company also fails to tell a full story. Many writers incorrectly assume that since Ford was not listed in the 1913 *Index,* which was the first *Times* index prepared, the *Times* had not found him worthy of comment in prior years. Actually, the *Times* carried several stories on Ford before 1913. Also, this newspaper, a conservative organ with relatively high demand on its news space, published comparatively little of the "lighter" feature material which appealed to many other newspapers. There were numerous syndicated stories on such matters as Ford's wealth, his farming and wildlife interests, his views on the auto industry, the company's plants, and its production plans which were ignored by the *Times* but were published in scores of metropolitan papers all over the country. Similarly, although the *Readers' Guide to Periodical Literature* lists no articles on Ford in 1913, the *Industrial Arts Index* for that year cites three stories about the company. Only five other firms—U.S. Steel, which was battling a dissolution suit, and four Class I railroads—received more attention in the publications examined by the *Index* in 1913.[4]

The view that Henry Ford and the Ford Company were hardly known prior to 1914 scarcely does justice to the amount of publicity that Ford and the company had received or to the degree of fame that publicity had brought them by that time. This is particularly true of the company, which before 1914 (in contrast to later years) received more publicity and was better known than its principal owner and chief executive.[5]

The company, as a matter of fact, had become a well-known member of the automobile industry within a few years of its founding. As early as 1905, *Horseless Age* referred to Ford as "one of the largest and best-known manufacturers" in the industry. By 1910–11 the company (and the Model T) was "in the public eye in a large way," receiving more publicity than any other auto firm.[6] As if in recognition of the increasing attention paid to it by the press, the company in 1911 began compiling the first of the 167 press clipbooks it was to fill during the next thirty-six years. In partial contrast to later years, all of the publicity before 1914 could be classified as favorable or routinely neutral. Probably the only instances in which the company was the subject of controversy were the discussions of its ability to produce the 35,000, 75,000, or 200,000 cars that it scheduled in advance for 1911, 1912, and 1913. Ford executives were irritated by the occasional rumors that the company was to be sold to Studebaker, Standard Oil Company of California, or some other firm or that Model T's were to be sold three for $1,000 on a given date, but such stories were less damaging than annoying. Indeed, they did much to advertise the high value which other firms placed upon the Ford Company and the Model T's volume production and low cost.[7]

By 1913 the sizable volume of publicity received by the company had, according to the *New York Herald,* earned Ford "a world-wide reputation for the enormous number of cars it manufactures, the size of its main plant in Detroit, and the number of its assembling plants and branches scattered over the globe." The company was "the largest and most widely known motor car company in the world in 1913 . . . and had acquired valuable good will, had an extraordinary reputation, and stood in a class by itself," according to a well-buttressed court opinion handed down in 1928. A year earlier, a group of investment bankers described the company as having in 1913 "as splendid a reputation as any industrial company could possibly have for the efficiency of its methods, its financial strength, its management and the quantity of its product." To an Irish writer, in 1912, the firm was "a great state, perfect in every particular—the nearest that anything on the face of the earth has got to Utopia.'' To the *Detroit Times,* Ford, on its tenth anniversary, was the ''Eighth Wonder of the World'' and the ''industrial marvel of the age.''[8]

If not as well known as the company in 1913, Henry Ford had, by that time, become the commanding figure in the automobile industry and was ranked as one of America's leading industrialists. Ford's reputation was, of course, largely tied to the company's public standing and tended to run parallel with it. Thus in 1903 he was known to the local press as ''a promising Detroit chauffeur'' and as ''the builder of the famous 'No. 999.' '' By 1905 he had gained enough hometown prestige to be included in a *Detroit Free Press* biographical series, ''Detroit Captains of Industry.'' A year later he had attained sufficient stature in the trade to be included in a group sketch of seventeen of the leading automobile personalities attending the Chicago Auto Show and to be ranked by *Motor Age* as one of America's fifteen leading automobile men.[9]

As the company became pre-eminent in the industry, Ford's stature grew commensurately. Historians expressed interest in his early contributions to the industry.[10] The New York press sought to replace the ''haphazard pictures [of Ford] in their respective biographical libraries . . . with really good likenesses.'' A New York photographic studio asked if it could include Ford's portrait in its ''Gallery of Eminent Americans.'' The manufacturer was one of 400 ''Prominent American Gentlemen'' invited to submit his photograph in behalf of a ''scientific effort'' to devise a composite portrait of the ''Typical American.'' On the eve of the five-dollar day, Ford was ''undoubtedly the biggest single figure in the automobile world'' and was one of the nation's more prominent industrialists. ''His life story,'' reported the *Grand Rapids* (Michigan) *Herald,* ''reads like a fairy tale that rotates around Aladdin's lamp. . . . He is a mighty unique figure and one of the most interesting men in the world.''[11]

That Ford was spoken of in such terms was probably due to a conscious, decade-long build-up campaign directed by Couzens, who had charge of the company's advertising in the pre-1914 period.[12] Several circumstances made it expedient to enhance Ford's reputation. He was, in 1903, the only member of the group that formed the Ford Motor Company who had any sort of automotive reputation. Members of the firm readily recognized the distinction Ford had attained as a designer of racing cars by affixing his name to the motor company they organized. It naturally followed that advertisements would place heavy emphasis on ''the same genius which conceived the world's record maker—the '999.' '' When the Selden forces began threatening the company, it was not enough to proclaim Ford as an eminent designer. To counteract Selden's claims, it was necessary to publicize Ford as a pioneer and inventor as well. Thus, such statements as ''Our Mr. Ford made the first Gasoline Automobile in Detroit and the third in the United States'' (both claims, incidentally, untrue) appeared in many ads.[13]

Aside from the need to launch the company on Ford's reputation and the demands posed by the patent struggle, it was standard business procedure in an era when an automobile's soundness could not be taken for granted for a company to emphasize the accomplishments and reputation of the chief engineer. The Hupp Company, for example, gave great prominence in its ads to E. A. Nelson, and Hudson devoted its 1912 advertising campaign to extolling the talents of Howard E. Coffin and his staff.[14] It was also common for the presidents of auto companies to be featured in advertisements. Indeed, many of them, unlike Ford (who had been elected president of the Ford Company in July 1906),[15] wrote and/or signed advertising copy themselves. "It has always been my ambition to build one of the world's best cars," wrote E. R. Thomas in a 1905 advertisement, "and I have done it!" Even more convinced of his personal triumph, R. E. Olds asserted in 1913, "I have seen the factory swamped, and men paying a bonus to get my latest creation. But Reo the Fifth . . . embodies the final results of my 25 years of experience. . . . There is no probability that we shall ever see a materially better car. The years can bring only minor changes." John North Willys, though he did not write first-person copy, permitted Willys-Overland ads to refer to him as "a man of wonderful breadth and attainment" and to state that "it is absolutely essential that the reader understand this personality to realize fully the character and standard of the product which he controls."[16]

Amidst the grandiose claims of competitors it was not out of place for Couzens to refer to Ford as the "foremost designer of gasolene motor cars in the United States" and as "America's master builder of automobiles" and to state that "just the imprint 'Ford' on a car has acquired a value equivalent to the name Sterling on silver." The company sometimes went a step beyond: "Henry Ford has been the greatest factor in the development of the automobile industry, greater than any other man in the world," stated a 1910 advertisement. A week later another ad proclaimed, "He is as well known in Europe as in America [and] stands out independent and alone, clear and strong, as the most dominant factor in the automobile industry of today."[17]

There is no evidence to suggest that Ford wanted to be featured in company advertising or, for that matter, that he sought personal publicity from the time of his early racing days—when it was a financial necessity—until after the five-dollar day. In fact, and in direct contrast to later years, Ford was quite willing to share credit for the company's achievements. The *Ford Times* in 1908 gave C. H. Wills equal credit with Ford for having designed and built the 999 and noted that he "directs the entire working of the manufacturing department." Three years later the magazine placed Ford's and Wills's photographs side by side, over the caption, "Mr. Henry Ford and Mr. C. H. Wills, the two men who have developed the Ford car." On several occasions the *Ford Times* acknowledged Couzens's great contribution to the company's success and in some years devoted almost as much space to him as to Ford.[18]

An indifference to publicity is revealed by Ford's avoidance of the press. The secretary of the Detroit Board of Commerce, exasperated after trying for weeks to obtain an interview with Ford for a member of his staff, wrote the manufacturer's office that "it is a pity that the leading exponent of the auto industry would not cooperate with our magazine," and he noted that Ford was the only industrial leader in Detroit who had failed to do so. Ford's special interest in tractors led him, however, to make exceptions for the agricultural press. Requests for photographs, information, or interviews concerning the tractor project invariably received an immediate and affirmative response.[19]

When reporters did manage to reach Ford, they found an individualist with a flair that made for lively copy. To a writer for *Motor Age* who commented that $1,000 was too low a price for the landaulet taxicab which the company had in mind, Ford displayed a little of what the press was already beginning to call his highly independent philosophy by snapping, "That's all it's worth!" Newspapers delighted in his "bubbling optimism." "He says 'We are going to build 25,000 Fords' with the same easy assurance that he would tell you the new car is larger and better than its predecessor," snickered a skeptical *Detroit News*. Ford's statement that 1,300-pound autos would be reduced in weight to 500 pounds and that "eventually cars will go 150 to 200 mph, but there will be no room for them" also produced a rash of merry headlines. Ford's victory against the Seldenites, his ability to meet "fantastic" production schedules, and his constant lowering of Model T prices strengthened his reputation for predicting—and sometimes accomplishing—the unexpected. Newspapers frequently asked the question, "What will Henry Ford do next?" and Ford publicists were quick to encourage speculation. "Be assured," one of them told the *Chicago Post*, "that whatever move may be contemplated or consummated by the industry, Mr. Ford always has something up his sleeve."[20]

Ford's indifference to interviews and his shyness gave him a reputation for modesty. He made every effort to avoid the limelight, and was visibly embarrassed when his name was as much as mentioned at a public gathering. Eulogized by Charles M. Schwab at a Detroit banquet in 1913, Ford "slid down in his chair, and before Schwab had finished, had completed a vanishing act... almost under the table." "Out of deference to Mr. Ford's modesty and dislike for display," according to the *Detroit Times,* the company did not publicly celebrate its tenth anniversary. Other newspapers also paid tribute to Ford's retiring nature, as the following *New York Sun* headline indicates: "Modest Henry Ford, Great Mechanical Genius, Inventor of Ford Automobile and First Gasolene Engine, Employs More Than 15,000 Men."[21]

If Ford shrank from mere appearances in public, he fairly trembled at the thought of speaking on formal occasions. There is no record, in fact, that he addressed a group before 1915, when he was fifty-two years of age. In a letter typical of many, Ford's secretary, F. L. Klingensmith, wrote to the Engineering Society of the University of Michigan in 1909, that "Mr. Ford absolutely declines, and has on hundreds of other occasions, to appear before a class or before any sort of gathering of strangers. If you were in his office or his work shop, however, he could probably give you some ideas and some information that might be very attractive to you." The letter not only illustrates Ford's lifelong aversion to speaking before public groups but hints at his willingness and ability to meet people informally. "He was a very good speaker with two or three people, just sitting around a table," recalled Fred L. Black, a close associate of Ford from 1918 until 1942, "but with half a dozen or more he became very retiring and could not express himself as freely." Once on a visit to the Oliver Chilled Plow Works, in South Bend, Indiana, Ford stumbled in on a sales meeting by mistake. Asked to say a few words, he panicked, mumbled a dozen incoherent sounds, and fled from the room. The manufacturer was frank about his inability to make a speech. "I can hire someone to talk for me that knows how," he said. "That talking is a gift. I'm glad I never acquired it."[22]

Ford spoke to groups unfamiliar to him only sixteen times in his life. Four of these occasions were radio addresses, and two were talks to dealers over the telephone. He was fond of telling people that the first speech he ever gave was at Sing Sing, where he began by saying, "I'm glad to see you all here." His second speech, according to the *Chicago American,* was made at a 1915 banquet celebrating the production of the one millionth Ford. The manufacturer rose, said, "Gentlemen, a million of anything is a great many," and sat down. Ford's third speech was delivered November 26, 1915, at a mass meeting of pacifists in the Belasco Theatre, in Washington. Ford sat on the platform, while two women addressed the audience. Finally there were calls: "We want Ford!" Terrified, Ford whispered to an aide, "You say it for me." The aide urged him to say a few words. Finally Ford cried out, "Out of the trenches by Christmas, never to return!" and darted off the stage as if the applause were a pursuing monster.[23]

Ford did a little better when speaking to schoolchildren or when reading from a text. Even so, while speaking in 1934 at the dedication of a monument to William Holmes McGuffey, he became so flustered that he omitted three-fourths of his prepared address. His speeches invariably were brief. He spoke thirty-one words at a dinner given in his honor in 1928 by the American Society of London. In delivering the "major" address before the American Newspaper Publishers Association in 1938, all he had to say was, "We are all on the spot. Stick to your guns, and I will help you, with the assistance of my son, all I can. Thank you." The longest address he ever made consisted of 486 words, delivered in 1939 on "Ford Day" at the New York World's Fair.[24]

Ford could write no better than he could speak, but it was a simple matter for ghostwriters to prepare material for his signature. The first article prepared in his name, a description of the Model N, appeared in a Detroit newspaper under the title, "Henry Ford's Own Story of the Automobile Trade's 1906 Sensation." A more ambitious effort was a piece on the uses of vanadium steel prepared in 1907 for *Harper's Weekly.*[25] During the next few years several other stories, dealing with such subjects as the history and future of the automobile and the struggle of American motor car manufacturers for overseas recognition, were signed by Ford. Ghostwriters almost certainly based their articles on Ford's thoughts, but sometimes they soared to heights of grandiloquence which must have seemed incongruous to anyone familiar with the manufacturer. It is plausible to question, for example, whether Ford would have used, or even was familiar with, one or two words in such a statement as "When I look toward the future and perceive what it holds for the automobile industry, my eyes are dazzled by its radiant portent."[26]

However out of character the expression may be, the prediction it makes was to be borne out by events. Had Ford seen in a crystal ball what his own and his company's future was to be, his eyes might well have been "dazzled by its radiant portent." The next year would find the shy auto maker transformed into one of the most exciting and best publicized figures in American history. The next half-dozen years would find him well on the way to becoming one of the nation's greatest folk heroes.

PART II
America Discovers Ford
(1914-19)

Chapter 5
The Five-Dollar Day

In 1913, the Ford Motor Company distributed $11,200,000 in dividends among its twelve stockholders and several hundred thousand dollars in bonuses to a select list of employees. On August 1 of that year, the company for the fourth time in three years substantially reduced prices on the Model T. Ford and Couzens became colossally rich, paid executives higher salaries and bonuses, and gave the public ever cheaper cars. This led them to ask themselves: "What of our workers?"[1]

Concern over this question produced certain labor reforms in 1913. The company's chaotic wage structure was overhauled after a thorough evaluation of jobs. Employee efficiency was rewarded with pay increases. Action was taken to protect employees from arbitrary or discriminatory conduct by foremen. On October 1, 1913, every worker received a wage boost—the increase for all employees averaging 13 percent. The pay increase provided a minimum daily wage of $2.34, a scale as good as or better than any of Ford's competitors.[2] This minimum was soon dwarfed, however, by the five-dollar day which the company inaugurated early in 1914.

Was it Ford or Couzens who was primarily responsible for the five-dollar day? The evidence conflicts. Charles E. Sorensen, a Ford production executive, states that Ford originated the plan and then obtained Couzens's acceptance of it. "I've thought about that five-dollar plan all night," Ford reportedly told Sorensen. "I'll have to tell Couzens about it. . . . He will support it if he makes the announcement and gets the publicity that goes with it." Ford was pictured as having no doubt that Couzens would fall into line, because of the latter's "growing appetite for personal publicity" and "a heightened interest in public affairs which was drawing him into local politics." After Ford obtained Couzens's agreement, according to Sorensen, the vice-president remarked, "I want to be governor of Michigan, and this will help elect me."

On the other hand, E. G. Pipp, a confidant of Henry Ford from 1914 to 1920, states that it was Couzens who "sold" the five-dollar day plan to Ford. "A straight five-dollar wage," Couzens reputedly told Ford, "will be the greatest advertisement any automobile concern ever had." "Couzens," Pipp adds, "did not have to say that twice to Ford." Of the two views, Pipp's version is the more credible, both in the light of the company's long-standing policy to focus public attention on Ford and in view of statements and actions by Ford and Couzens during the post-announcement period. In any event, both men, who together owned 69.5 percent of the Ford Company's stock, supported the plan at the January 5, 1914, board meeting at which it was adopted.[3]

Following the board's action, three Detroit newspapers, the *Free Press, News,* and *Journal,* were told that there was a story for them at the Ford plant. An hour or so later, reporters were shown into Couzens's office. Ford stood by a window, while Couzens read a two-page statement to the newsmen:

> The Ford Motor Co., the greatest and most successful automobile manufacturing company in the world, will, on Jan. 12, inaugurate the greatest revolution in the matter of rewards for its workers ever known to the industrial world.
>
> At one stroke it will reduce the hours of labor from nine to eight, and add to every man's pay a share of the profits of the house. The smallest amount to be received by a man 22 years old and upwards will be $5 per day. . . .
>
> Instead of waiting until the end of the year to make a distribution of profits among their employees in one bonus sum, Mr. Ford and Mr. Couzens have estimated the year's prospective business and have decided upon what they feel will be a safe amount to award the workers. This will be spread over the whole year and paid on the regular semi-monthly pay days.
>
> In order that the young man from 18 to 22 years of age may be entitled to a share in the profits he must show himself sober, saving, steady, industrious and must satisfy the superintendent and staff that his money will not be wasted in riotous living.
>
> . . . It is estimated that over $10,000,000 will be thus distributed over and above the regular wages of the men.[4]

The announcement, made in the midst of a mild worldwide depression, was immediately flashed to every corner of the globe. Forty years later the *London Economist* called the proclamation "the most dramatic event in the history of wages." In 1959 the distinguished French intellectual, Father R. L. Bruckberger, went further: "How I wish I could find words to impress the reader with the importance of that decision of the five-dollar day! . . . Let me speak plainly: I consider that what Henry Ford accomplished [in] 1914 contributed far more to the emancipation of workers than the October Revolution of 1917. . . . He took the worker out of the class of the 'wage-earning proletariat' to which Ricardo and Marx had relegated him and . . . made every worker a potential customer."[5]

Although Henry Ford and James Couzens regarded the five-dollar day as "the greatest revolution in the matter of rewards for . . . workers ever known" and were aware that the plan would be of great advertising value, they vastly underestimated the immediate impact the plan would have upon the world, much less the homage of latter-day commentators. Realizing, of course, that the scheme would be of much interest to Detroiters, they summoned representatives of the Detroit daily press to the conference at which the announcement was made. However, similar invitations were not extended to the Detroit offices of the wire services or to the local correspondents of the eastern newspapers, nor was there any attempt to publicize the plan independently of the press conference.[6]

The announcement was easily the biggest news story to have originated in Detroit up to 1914.[7] The statement was read in mid-morning, and by noon cablegrams and telegrams from wire services and newspapers were pouring into Detroit from around the earth. By the following morning, every daily newspaper in the United States and thousands of newspapers abroad had carried the story. The American public, which had been debating Francisco Villa's rout of the Federalists in Mexico, Mrs. Pankhurst's visit to the United States, the marriage of President Woodrow

Wilson's daughter, the New York New Haven & Hartford Railroad's suspension of dividends for the first time in forty years, and Ty Cobb's possible desertion to the Federal League, dropped all these matters to discuss the five-dollar day and the man considered wholly responsible for it, Henry Ford. In seven days' time the press of New York City alone devoted fifty-two columns—most of it front-page news—to the profit-sharing plan and to Ford. Nationally, according to Charles A. Brownell, the story received "more than 2,000,000 lines of favorable advertising on the front page of newspapers and thousands and thousands of editorial endorsements." The seven weeks following the announcement produced enough profit-sharing stories to fill more than 1,100 pages in Ford's clipbooks—and this was probably only a small fraction of the total number of newspaper and magazine articles.[8]

To many newspapers, the five-dollar day was an economic second coming. The *Cleveland Plain Dealer* reported editorially that the announcement "shot like a blinding rocket through the dark clouds of the present industrial depression"; the *New York Sun* described it as "a bolt out of the blue sky flashing its way across the continent and far beyond"; and the *New York Herald* called it "an epoch in the world's industrial history." Most newspapers, according to a press analysis by the *Toledo Blade,* also regarded the plan as a "lordly gift" to the Ford workers. The *New York Evening Post* credited the company with "a magnificent act of generosity"; the *New York World* called Ford "an inspired millionaire"; and the *Algonac* (Michigan) *Courier* ran the headline, "God Bless Henry Ford of the Ford Motor Company," over a story which referred to the manufacturer as "one of God's noblemen."[9]

Cartoonists had a field day in depicting the newly acquired opulence of Ford employees. Mutt told Jeff he was going to work *one* of those five-dollar days. A belligerent farm boy was pictured as telling his nonplussed father that he was going to Detroit unless he got five dollars for each eight hours of work on the farm. Ford's employment gates were shown swarming with small boys wearing false whiskers in an attempt to appear twenty-two years of age, of women trying to masquerade as men, and of college-bred professional men offering to furnish their own brooms if allowed to sweep the factory's floors. Ford employees were shown hailing their chauffeur-driven limousines as they emerged from the plant or as plutocratic figures, complete with opera hats, cigars, and fur-lined coats, lining up at the company's pay windows with cavernous satchel bags. A cartoon by H. T. Webster pictured a prosperous looking gentleman telling his chauffeur: "Hawkins, will you step over to the pay window and get my wages? I quite overlooked the matter last week."[10]

The financial and conservative press, on the other hand, was far from enthusiastic about the plan. The *Wall Street Journal,* in warning that the scheme would lead to "material, financial, and factory disorganization," declared that Ford "has in his social endeavor committed economic blunders, if not crimes" and they "may return to plague him and the industry he represents, as well as organized society." The *New York Times* expected "serious disturbances" to follow from a policy which was "distinctly Utopian and dead against all experience," and the *Pittsburgh Gazette–Times* denounced the plan as a "demoralizing scheme."[11]

Industrial leaders were equally dismayed. The general manager of the Erie City Iron Works called the plan "the most foolish thing ever attempted in the industrial world'' and added that ''such a move can only result in unrest among the laboring classes.'' The president of the Pittsburgh Plate Glass Company declared that if other employers were to follow Ford's lead, ''it would mean the ruin of all business in this country'' and that ''Ford himself will surely find that he cannot afford to pay $5 a day.'' Ford's automotive colleagues were also displeased, for no one's average daily wage rate was as high as $2.50; and all anticipated labor unrest in the wake of Ford's wage hike. Hugh Chalmers said that Ford should have consulted the other manufacturers before announcing the plan, Windsor T. White believed the scheme ''an economic mistake,'' and J. J. Cole stated, ''If Ford wants to amuse himself, all right. He can afford it. Others can't.''[12]

While the business community lamented, the press speculated endlessly on the value of the publicity accompanying the five-dollar day. The *Everett* (Washington) *Tribune* set the figure at $5,000,000; the *New York Times, Boston News Bureau,* and *Printers' Ink* at $10,000,000; and the *Syracuse Journal* at $20,000,000. The *Philadelphia Telegram* simply stated that the event was ''the best piece of advertising in the history of industrial publicity,'' while the *Menominee* (Michigan) *Herald–Leader* reported that every editor in the country ''had a free car coming without any further payment.'' Newspapers also pointed out that even if Ford had invested many millions of dollars in space advertising, front page columns would not have been available to him, nor would paid advertisements have had the same impact on the public as did banner headlines and lead editorials.[13]

Very few papers begrudged Ford the publicity windfall. ''A smashing good advertisement,'' declared the *Burlington* (Iowa) *Hawkeye,* ''and would not the employees of other establishments be happy if their employers could afford that sort of advertising and then did it.'' The *Marshalltown* (Iowa) *Republican* echoed this sentiment: ''Perhaps Mr. Ford will get a great deal of advertising out of his gifts. If so he is welcome to it. And the welcome holds to other successful men and corporations who incline to follow his example.''[14] Some newspapers were so impressed that they made a special point of publicizing the Model T. The *East Boston* (Massachusetts) *Free Press* suggested that ''When you see his [Ford's] modest little car running by, take your hat off,'' and the *Cleveland News* ran a large photograph of a Model T touring car under the headline, ''The Car Humanitarian Henry Ford's Making.'' Although Ford and Couzens had estimated the annual cost of the profit-sharing plan at $10,000,000, the outlay in 1914 was only $5,838,929.80. As advertising for the company and as a means of winning the goodwill of the American people, the innovation was obviously worth much more.[15]

If, as Nevins and Hill have estimated, 90 percent of newspaper comment regarding the plan was favorable, much of it ecstatic, the general public was almost unanimous in its approval. A few people feared that such big wages would go to the workers' heads and harm them, but most Americans disdained that cynical view. Plain people lauded the plan in letters to newspapers; and labor leaders, sociologists, ministers, politicians, and even many industrialists hailed the innovation in the most glowing terms. Wage earners found Ford's scheme a source of hope and inspiration. Detroit became in 1914 what California had been in 1849, the end of the rainbow. An estimated 10,000 men gathered at the Ford employment office the day after the announcement, and throngs of 4,000 to 15,000 camped at the Ford gates during the following week. Unfortunately, 10,000 of these job hunters, upon being told there was no work available for them, rioted in near zero weather on January 12. City policemen turned fire hoses on them, soaking 3,000 before the crowd was dispersed. To the considerable embarrassment of the Ford Company, this incident received nationwide publicity.[16]

The profit-sharing announcement brought a deluge of mail. "It rained letters; it poured letters. Letters came by dozens, by grosses, by hundreds, yes, and almost literally by thousands," declared the *Ford Times*. Fourteen thousand letters were directed to the company's employment office within one week of the announcement. Seven weeks later, an average of 500 letters a day—virtually all of them addressed to Henry Ford—poured into the company's mail room from job applicants and persons offering congratulations or seeking additional information on the plan.[17]

It was natural for letter writers to address their missives directly to Henry Ford, for within twenty-four hours of the announcement practically the entire press and the public credited him personally with responsibility for the five-dollar day. Couzens received as much play as Ford in the Detroit newspapers on January 5, but the out-of-town press, aside from those papers which ran only the announcement itself, gave Couzens much less attention than the company's president. Couzens, it is clear, deliberately abdicated the limelight in Ford's favor. On the day of the announcement he told the United Press, "Henry Ford is the originator of the plan. He believes there has been too big a division between capital and labor and labor has not shared to the extent it should." The lead on the news service's initial story read, accordingly, "Henry Ford, head of the Ford Motor Company, announced today one of the most remarkable business moves of his entire remarkable career." Couzens entrained for the New York automobile show on the evening of January 5, a few hours after the momentous announcement. Although beseiged by more than 100 newsmen while in New York, he refused to supply them with any new information. Couzens had little regard for the press. Once when a reporter approached the executive at a hotel to get material for a story that would publicize the company, Couzens snubbed him: "Newspapermen! Nothing to say." For years the possibly apocryphal story was circulated that Couzens, angered over a *Detroit News* story on Ford jokes, had written the editor of that newspaper: "Sir: I hereby forbid you ever again to mention the name of the Ford Motor Company in your publication."[18]

In any event, Couzens returned to Detroit on January 9 and left five days later for a secluded and lengthy vacation in California. Thereafter he dropped so completely out of sight that it is difficult to find his name in any newspaper outside Detroit until his resignation from the company in the fall of 1915. The 1914 *New York Times Index*, for instance, after mistakenly listing him as, "COUZENS, George," merely says "see Ford, Henry." In the periodical press, Couzens's name was mentioned in only one of the major stories on the profit-sharing plan, and that article simply recalled that it was in Couzens's office that the announcement was made.[19]

Henry Ford, on the other hand, basked in the publicity spotlight from the day of the announcement. Remaining in Detroit until the evening of January 7, he "extended his congratulations to the press" for doing a fine job of explaining the profit-sharing plan, and then he boarded a train for the New York auto show. Arriving at the Belmont Hotel on January 8, Ford briefly went unnoticed. When word leaked, however, that *the* Henry Ford was at the hotel, the management had to employ an extra squad of house detectives to protect him from the bellboys, doormen, waiters, and hundreds of other persons who beseiged him in hallways, elevators, and stairways. Each time he crossed the lobby he had to elbow his way through the crowd of reporters, photographers, and movie cameramen stationed there. On one occasion pandemonium broke loose, with photographers breaking down palm trees and movie cameramen digging their tripods into marble-topped tables in an effort to get unobstructed shots of the manufacturer. Through it all Ford's "benign, sweet smile never relaxed," and his "smooth, modulated voice" was never raised in anger. "He submitted to interviews," noted one newspaper, "as if they were a pleasure." Ford was indeed a model of cooperativeness, and his apparent modesty and simplicity won over every cynical newsman whom he met.[20]

Capitalizing on the press's interest, Ford exhibited considerable talent in generating publicity beyond that which would have been given him as a matter of routine. On January 9, four days after the five-dollar-day announcement, Ford told reporters, "I think it is a disgrace to die rich." The statement appeared under multicolumn headlines throughout the country. No sooner had the ink dried on the story than Ford sent the reporters rushing for telephones again by saying, "Goodwill is about the only fact there is in life. With it a man can do and win almost anything. Without it he is practically powerless." Later in the same day Ford generated a third nationwide story by telling of his reply to the New York barber, who, not suspecting that the industrialist was in his shop, had observed that the five-dollar plan looked pretty fishy to him. "I work out in Detroit too, right in the Ford works," Ford told the reporters he had replied to the barber, "and I know Ford well enough to know that he will put the plan through."[21]

After three days of being lionized in New York, Ford headed west, accompanied by a large contingent of the eastern press. This advance guard was reinforced during the next few weeks by "a trainload of staff correspondents, star reporters, magazine writers, and experts on human interest," who had come to Detroit to report on Ford on his stamping ground. As Charles Merz points out:

> Ford had to be caught at work and at play, caught on the steps of his plant, caught on the porch of his house, caught at the wheel of the first Ford, caught at the wheel of the last Ford, caught shaking hands with an old neighbor on his farm, and caught in a moment of leisure playing with his dogs; and if he had no dogs the photographers were ready to supply them. For the great news machine was in full motion now, and the presses panted for more copy.[22]

The conservative *New York Times* ran thirty-five stories on Ford within ninety days of the profit-sharing announcements, and no fewer than fourteen magazines carried biographies of the manufacturer during 1914. Biographical sketches of Ford appeared in thousands of newspapers, frequently running under eight-column streamers and filling entire pages. Many newspapers added a new feature, "Some Maxims of Head of the Ford Motor Co.," to their columns, while other papers urged their readers to send to Ford signed "coupons" reading, "Here's to you! If there were more Henry Fords in the ranks of capital there would be fewer Calumets!'' (a bitter copper strike had occurred in Calumet, Michigan in 1913–14).[23]

The ''ocean of publicity'' made Ford the best-known manufacturer in the world by mid-1914. One newspaper even predicted as early as January 10, 1914, that Ford would become ''one of the best-known men that America has ever produced,'' and that his name would ''be famous until the sun takes its first chill.''[24] As stories on the manufacturer multiplied, a Ford image—an incomplete one to be sure—began to impress itself upon the public consciousness. In some ways the picture was distorted and yielded to revision in later years; in other respects fancy and fact were combined to form legends which were to span Ford's lifetime and to be of incalculable benefit to the manufacturer and his company.

The press agents who dramatized the legends in later years had no part in shaping the Ford image in 1914, the opinions of certain biographers notwithstanding. Indeed, Ford had less need for press agents in the year of the five-dollar day than he did for protection from the horde of newsmen who were trying by every conceivable means to interview him. The legends were, in point of fact, started by a press which was fanatically eager to print something, anything, about Ford and which wanted to cast him in a mold befitting a man who had just offered an alleged $10,000,000 to his employees.[25]

Ford, according to the vast majority of newspapers and magazines, was shy, modest, sincere, and simple, ''a rich man with a poor man's tastes,'' who had retained old-fashioned American virtues as he struggled from humble beginnings to the presidency of the largest automobile company on earth and the third largest income in the world. He was a fighter, as witness his role in the Selden suit, yet he was a gentle man who loved birds and who attributed his success to his wife's moral support. His mind and his pocketbook, unlike those of many millionaires, were open to the public. When a Chicago reporter asked Ford for the company's sales and profits figures from 1903 to 1914, the firm's treasurer, taking an attitude common in the business community at that time, protested that they had never been published and should remain confidential. ''Shucks,'' replied Ford, ''there's nothing to conceal here, and this young man wants the information.''[26]

Above all, an image of Ford as a man ''who has declined to forget that the distance between overalls and broadcloth is very short'' and as the greatest friend, bar none, of the American working man was imprinted on the minds of wage earners and of the rest of the American public. This facet of Ford's character, quite accurate in 1914, gradually eroded; by the 1930s it was no longer true. Still, on the basis of the never-forgotten five-dollar day (followed by an uneventful six-dollar day in 1919 and a dramatic seven-dollar day in 1929), the public believed for a generation that Ford's men were ''the highest paid and the best treated in the world, and that his shops, since 1914, had been the model of the factory system.''[27]

This view, expressed by one of Ford's bitterest critics, is substantiated by several public opinion polls taken between 1937 and 1941. In a survey published in May 1937—the month in which the famed ''Battle of the Overpass'' between Ford's plant police and the UAW-CIO took place—the Curtis Publishing Company found that 59.1 percent of Americans believed the Ford Company treated its labor better than any other firm. Second-rated Bell Telephone Company received only a 14.1 percent response, third-place General Motors Corporation, 6.3 percent. In 1940—by which time the National Labor Relations Board had adjudged the Ford Company guilty of engaging in unfair labor practices in nine of its plants—a *Fortune* survey of laboring men and women found that 73.6 percent of the respondents believed that Henry Ford was among those Americans who were "helpful to labor." Senator Robert F. Wagner received only a 51.8 percent response; William Green, 49.7 percent; and Secretary of Labor Frances Perkins, 43.4 percent. Among those persons considered "harmful to labor," Ford's 12.3 percent vote was topped by John L. Lewis's 44.6 percent, Secretary Perkins's 19.4 percent, and Green's 18.2 percent. In March 1941, as the Ford Company girded for a showdown with the UAW-CIO, the American Institute of Public Opinion discovered that Americans upheld by a two-to-one margin Ford's refusal to recognize unions in his plants.[28]

The publicity surrounding the five-dollar day not only affected the public's attitude toward Ford, it was also instrumental in changing the manufacturer's opinion of himself. Ford's modesty became a thing of the past. During the six months following the wage announcement he still found it easy, for example, to say, "I pass that one" or just shake his head to hundreds of extraneous questions which newsmen felt constrained to ask him. But as the questions and requests for interviews continued, as the bundles of admiring mail mounted, and as Ford's reputation burgeoned, the manufacturer began to accept the tacit implication that his was a wisdom extending beyond mere Model T's, mass production, and labor relations. Without awe or misgiving, he took a public position on the gold standard, the single tax, capital punishment, General Carranza, the causes of war, foreign trade, railroads, alcohol, and the theory of evolution. He had, it seemed, a ready solution for virtually every problem, the panacea often requiring no more than a single sentence for its expression.[29]

Ford's shyness and bumbling inarticulateness concealed the change. Many publications were unaware that the manufacturer was no longer the genuinely modest man whom they discovered in January 1914. The *Detroit Journal* told its readers in July 1914 that Ford was "the most modest man in the world," and the *Detroit Tribune* in January 1915 noted how "the modest, self-effacing, nervous Mr. Ford," when appearing before the U.S. Commission on Industrial Relations, requested Chairman Thomas J. Walsh to read for him "the remarkable document in which were set down the achievements of a year at the Ford works." During the same month, the editor of the *Gloversville* (New York) *Republic,* in noting that Ford was "one of the greatest benefactors of the race," added, "the fact that this modest mechanic-millionaire doesn't know he is a great man makes him all the greater. He is not a dominant or compelling personality; he is one of the most shrinking persons I have ever met, embarrassed almost to speechlessness by a word of praise."[30]

As Ford almost indiscernibly began to shed his modesty, he developed an insatiable appetite for headlines. No other Ford executive was allowed to share them. "After the name of Henry Ford became a household word," observes Charles E. Sorensen in his autobiography, "men in the Ford Motor Company who might temporarily get more publicity than he did aroused his jealousy, and one by one they were purged.'' Sorensen, a Ford manufacturing official for forty years, recalls one occasion when, in Ford's presence, Arthur Brisbane directed to Sorensen numerous questions about a particular factory operation. ''Suddenly the atmosphere got very chilly,'' says Sorensen. ''I sensed the reason and abruptly left for the plant.''[31] Many Ford executives, including Sorensen, were fired because they were too highly regarded by the public or because they made the mistake of projecting themselves into news stories. The wise Ford official, wrote Dean Samuel S. Marquis, when handed ''bouquets'' for an achievement, hastily ''tossed them over to Henry, and when there was no one around explained to him what it was all about. And,'' added the Dean, ''Henry kept the flowers.''[32]

Chapter 6
Peace Crusade

Throughout the last thirty-five years of his life, Henry Ford embarked upon a series of crusades which had little or no relation to the automobile industry. At one time or another he was saving birds, proclaiming that every criminal was "an inveterate cigarette-smoker," exposing a fictitious character called the "international Jew," attempting to convince a jazz-mad generation that the Virginia Reel was more fun than the Charleston, or insisting that "wheat is the divine food."[1] Some of Ford's campaigns made little impression upon the public. Others, however, captured the nation's imagination for a brief time, and still others influenced the attitudes of certain groups for long periods.

Of Ford's various crusades, none created more excitement than his pacifist campaign, of which the climax was the voyage of the so-called peace ship. This expedition, which once again focused the eyes of the world upon Ford, proved at once to be his greatest personal disaster and one of the principal reasons for his popularity with the masses.

The first hint of Ford's pacifist views came in the February 1915 edition of the *Ford Times,* which published, in deference to the manufacturer's wishes, George Washington's valedictory warning against foreign entanglements. A few months later, Ford, brooding over the European war and the domestic preparedness issue, declared that the 1,153 men and women lost at sea when the *Lusitania* was torpedoed "were fools to go on that boat." In August 1915, in conversation with a twenty-five-year-old *Detroit Free Press* reporter, Theodore Delavigne, Ford chanced to remark that he would "give everything I possess" if he could stop the war and prevent the amassing of arms in America. "You mean that, Mr. Ford?" asked Delavigne. "Yes sir, in heaven's name, I do," replied the manufacturer, who then authorized Delavigne to give expression to his views.[2]

Delavigne, first as a *Free Press* reporter and later as Ford's "peace secretary," wrote numerous antipreparedness articles which appeared in newspapers all over the country under the industrialist's signature. Declaring that he would not let cars leave his plant if he thought they would be used for warfare, Ford announced that he would inaugurate a "world-wide campaign for universal peace." The campaign, to be supported by a Ford-endowed $1,000,000 fund, was to show the benefits of peace and the horrors of war. Part of the sum was to be awarded as prize money to the author who could best describe the ravages of war over the span of recorded history.[3]

Ford's views naturally were welcomed by those segments of the press which agreed with them, but were strongly criticized by militant publications, which dismissed the Detroit industrialist's crusade as "only an advertising scheme."

"When under the guise of a peace advocate, a man attempts to sell automobiles by referring to the men who wear the United States uniform as 'sloths and lunatics,' " reported the *Army and Navy Journal*, "he is surely going too far ... evidently he thinks that the millennium will be at hand when everybody owns a Ford." The manufacturer was undaunted by the hostile publicity. "The more criticism that comes the better," he declared. "By criticism I get my education."[4]

Couzens did not share Ford's enthusiasm for criticism. Moreover, he was indignant when Ford's tirades and antipreparedness editorials and cartoons were ordered published in the *Ford Times*. A showdown between the two men occurred when Couzens, who, through Hawkins and Brownell, had exercised supervisory control over the *Ford Times*, told Ford that he had suppressed two pacifist items scheduled for the October edition. Ford told Couzens the copy was going to be published. Couzens angrily quit, issuing a statement saying that he had resigned because of Ford's views on peace, on the Allies' war loan, and on national preparedness.

Actually, Ford—who probably longed for complete control of the Ford organization—seems to have seized upon this dispute as a way of easing the strong-willed Couzens out of the company's management. Couzens retained his company directorship, but without his restraining hand in active administration Ford was free to press his peace campaign with intensified fervor.[5] Within six weeks he emerged as the world's most publicized advocate of peace.

Since August 1915 Ford's pacifist sentiments, coupled with an awareness of the resources which he could bring to bear in their behalf, had been spurring the imagination of peace advocates the world over. Two of them, Rosika Schwimmer, a Hungarian author and lecturer, and Louis P. Lochner, a former secretary of the International Federation of Students, arrived in Detroit in November 1915 to present to Ford a plan whereby President Wilson might call a peace conference at Washington, at which representatives of neutral nations would appoint a commission to work unremittingly ("continuous mediation") for a peace acceptable to all belligerents. Through Edwin G. Pipp, managing editor of the *Detroit News* and at this time Ford's informal public relations counselor, the pair obtained an invitation to Ford's home. The manufacturer and his wife warmly supported the idea of continuous mediation and agreed to Lochner's suggestion that Ford seek an interview with Wilson at which he would offer to maintain an official commission abroad until Congress could make an appropriation; failing this, he could support an unofficial body which would perform comparable work.

Ford and Lochner entrained for New York the following day, November 20, the industrialist aglow with plans for publicizing the venture. "Whatever we decide to do," he declared, "New York is the place for starting it." Maxims rolled from his tongue: "Men sitting around a table, not men dying in a trench, will finally settle the differences." He watched Lochner closely, and if he detected a favorable response he would say, "Make a note of that; we'll give that to the boys when we get to New York." At a luncheon with peace advocates on November 21, plans were drawn up for sending the proposed American mediation group abroad. "Why not a special ship to take the delegates over?" Lochner half jestingly suggested. Ford, perhaps sensing the publicity possibilities in such a dramatic maneuver, was immediately responsive. By evening he had chartered a "peace ship," the Scandinavian-American liner, *Oscar II*.[6]

On the following day, November 22, Ford visited the White House. Wilson was friendly but refused to endorse Ford's proposal. Undaunted, the manufacturer was back in New York the next morning to announce his plans at a press conference. Forty newsmen were on hand, and Ford developed stage fright. "Nothing could have been more naive or pathetic" than Ford's attempt to communicate with the press on this occasion, the noted liberal editor, Oswald Garrison Villard, a spectator, wrote four years later.

"Well, boys, I've got the ship," Ford began.

"What ship, Mr. Ford?"

"Why the *Oscar II*."

"Well, what are you going to do with her?"

"We're going to stop the war."

"Going to stop the war?"

"Yes, we're going to get the boys out of the trenches by Christmas."

"But how are you going to do it?"

"Oh, you'll see."

"Where are you going?"

"I don't know."

"What country will you head for?"

"I don't know."

"But what makes you think you can put it over?"

"Oh, we have had assurances."

Ford went on to explain that the *Oscar II* would have on board the most influential peace advocates in the country, including Jane Addams, John Wanamaker, and Thomas Edison. It would also sail with "the longest gun in the world—the Marconi." The press conference was page one news in New York and across the nation.[7]

Most of the nation's press gave scant attention to the announced purpose of the voyage, to transport American peace delegates to Europe, where they would help form a commission for continuous mediation. As one observer later pointed out: "Give any newspaper editor his choice between a distant plan for a neutral agency and an immediate boatload of determined pilgrims sailing out into a submarine-infested sea in a bold effort to put an end to a war in Europe, and there is no doubt which half of the news would dominate the story." Consequently, newspapers played up the ship, its passengers, Ford's millions and motives, rather than the peace mission. Some newspapers and observers regarded the voyage as a Ford-inspired advertising scheme and agreed with Billy Sunday that "Henry has P. T. Barnum skinned a mile." The majority of the press, however, credited Ford with being sincere and well-meaning, but, with few exceptions, added or implied that he was a buffoon as well.[8]

The combination of ridicule from many quarters, the suddenness of the ship's departure, and disagreement over the means, if not the ends, of seeking peace brought polite refusals from most of the 115 distinguished Americans who had been invited to

Left to right, Detroit banker William Livingston, President William Howard Taft, and Henry Ford in Ford's Highland Park, Michigan, office in 1915. Thomas A. Edison's picture hangs on the wall.

Scottish comedian Harry Lauder posing for Model T publicists in 1914.

A cartoonist's view of Ford's profit-sharing plan (five-dollar day), 1914.

Suggested for the automobile company that proposes to divide $10,000,000 among its men in profit sharing.

Reaction of farm boy to Henry Ford's five-dollar day, 1914.

FORD'S PROFIT-SHARING EXPERIMENT

The Germs of Socialism

Many differences separated the Ford Company's second-in-command, James Couzens, left, and Henry Ford when this picture was taken in 1915.

Top, Henry Ford waves to cheering crowd as his peace ship departs; bottom, Clara and Edsel Ford, right, bid farewell to the head of the family.

Henry Ford, left, and Capt. J. W. Hempel, right, as the peace ship embarks for Europe. (*Detroit News* photo.)

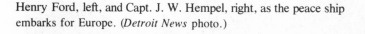

Henry Ford's peace ship, *Oscar II,* being nudged from its Hoboken, New Jersey, pier on December 5, 1915.

Henry Ford's World War I "flivver tank."

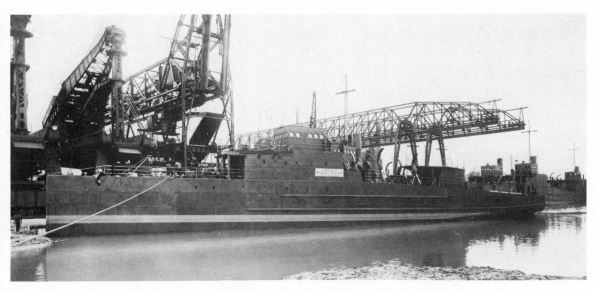

"Eagle boat" No. 49, built in ten days in 1919.

A cartoon links Ford's $1,000,000 libel suit against the *Chicago Tribune* with a Model T owner's opinion of a balky Tin Lizzie.

One of 308,213 rebate checks sent to purchasers of Model Ts between August 1, 1914, and July 31, 1915.

The Ford Motor Company band on tour in Hamilton, Ontario, in 1913. Henry Ford's personal secretary, Ernest G. Liebold, who managed the band, is at far left, in straw hat. Band Director H. G. Phillip, baton in hand, is at far right.

A mobile Ford newsreel camera crew shows off its equipment in front of the Highland Park plant in 1914.

make the trip. Edison, Wanamaker, John Burroughs, Luther Burbank, William Howard Taft, William Jennings Bryan, David Starr Jordan, Colonel Edward M. House, James Cardinal Gibbons, Louis Brandeis, Morris Hillquit, were among those who sent their regrets. However, many who declined sent heartening messages and stood by Ford during the ordeal ahead. Only a handful of public figures accepted invitations, among them, S. S. McClure, the magazine publisher, Governor Louis B. Hanna of North Dakota, Judge Ben Lindsey, and Jane Addams (who was unable to sail because of illness). The vast majority of the delegates were unknowns— ministers, feminists, socialists, single-taxers, lecturers, and college students—many of whom later admitted that they went along "for the ride." About half of the passengers were newsmen, as every writer "who saw in the affair a chance to make some sensational 'feature copy' applied for a berth." Ford was delighted to have the fifty-four press representatives aboard, and he expressed willingness to let the success or failure of the expedition hinge on their reaction to the voyage.[9]

At the Hoboken, New Jersey, dock, a crowd estimated at 15,000 gathered for the sailing "amid scenes so remarkably extravagant," according to the *Philadelphia North American,* "as to be almost beyond belief." Germans cheered for the Fatherland, British and French for the Allies, and one of the peace delegates, Lloyd M. Bingham, "like the interlocutor in a minstrel show," called for three cheers for many of the delegates and dignitaries, including Bryan and Edison, who had come to see the Ford party off for Norway. On board, Bryan acted as a witness at the marriage of the "tramp poet," Berton Braley, and Miss Marion Rubicam. The reporters described the episode as being fully in the spirit of the cruise, pointing out that the presiding clergyman read the ceremony "in a quavering, yet not unmusical voice" in the darkened "saloon" in which a photographer's flash equipment served as the altar light. The fact that the parson had married a couple with a New York license aboard a ship tied up at a New Jersey pier only added to the press's merriment. Fully as much mirth was created by a squirrel dispatched to Ford by a prankster who had written "To good ship Nutty" on the animal's cage. In a final touch of the mad circus atmosphere, as the ship swung into the river, a figure leaped from the pier and swam stoutly after it. Rescued, he announced himself as "Mr. Zero," and exclaimed, "Don't think I was trying to reach that ship. I was swimming to reach public opinion. War must cease."[10]

The departure provided cartoonists with themes aplenty for the next few weeks. Mutt and Jeff "sailed" with the expedition on the comic pages of newspapers all over America. Squirrels driving miniature Model T's were shown on the pier waving good-bye to their compatriot on board and making such cracks as "Barnum was right" and "Some grape juice gathering." Other cartoons showed ragged bums boarding the ship with the question, "Is my berth made up?" and a jibbering idiot dressed in a clown suit and nautical cap who, when asked by his guard if he intended to sail on the peace ship, replied, "I hope you don't think I'm crazy, do you!" Scores of cartoons pictured Ford as a Don Quixote at the wheel of a tiny Model T or a "flivverboat," charging a huge war machine. Cartoons often were tied to the Ford joke, then at the height of its popularity. Model T's, for example, were shown strewing nuts and bolts over shell-pocked fields under the caption "Ford to Advertise America on the Battlefields of Europe."[11]

Most of the fifty-four newsmen on board the *Oscar II* frankly looked upon the voyage "as a foolish exploit of an ultra-rich idealist" and were bent on satirizing the expedition and its passengers to the fullest. They organized the Viking Press Club, whose insignia was a nut bound upon the brow and whose handclasp was "a violent and horrified clasp of the hand on the forehead"; the club held three scheduled meetings a day at its "headquarters," the ship's bar. The reporters established a daily newspaper, the *Argosy*, and easily became the "most felt" group on board.[12]

News was comparatively meager the first four days at sea, but on December 9 the routine was broken by a rift within the peace party. The dissension centered around President Wilson's message to Congress, a plea for preparedness. The President's views were denounced by the majority of the peace delegates, but a number of others, including McClure, Governor Hanna, and Judge Lindsey, voiced approval. The two factions fell to denouncing each other, with Lochner declaring that anyone who accepted Ford's invitation and yet refused to denounce preparedness "came for a free ride." The reporters welcomed the dissension with undisguised glee, magnifying it out of all proportion. "Thank heaven," they were quoted, "at last a story has broken." Throughout the world the press carried blow-by-blow descriptions of the quarrel, and once again the cartoonists had a field day. The *Oscar II* was depicted as the scene of pitched battles involving squirrels and peace doves; the French and German armies were pictured as fleeing the trenches for fear of being trampled in the rioting of the approaching pilgrims; and German zeppelins were shown looking down on the scene and saying to one another, "Turn around and go back. It's not safe here." Speaking for a majority of the nation's newspapers, the *Troy* (New York) *Record* observed: "The only way that harmony can be insured aboard the peace ship is by chartering a vessel for each member of the party and then keeping them a mile apart."[13]

As the press contingent made a mockery of the voyage, relations between newsmen and the delegates deteriorated from mutual suspicion to outright hostility. To the delegates, the newsmen were "the snakes in our palm garden" and the "most conscienceless liars as ever scuttled a ship or cut a throat." A number of delegates sought to have the newsmen expelled from the peace party at Oslo, but McClure, explaining that they would tag along anyway, prevented a complete break between the two groups. For their part, the reporters characterized most of the delegates as "nuts, fools, and maniacs."[14]

The press was particularly antagonistic toward Mrs. Schwimmer, who was accused of having organized an espionage system on board and of being uncommunicative with the press. The reporters' ire was aroused particularly by Mrs. Schwimmer's refusal to discuss allegedly important "mediation documents" in her possession. On December 15, Katherine Leckie, the peace ship's official press-relations officer and a warm supporter of Mrs. Schwimmer, arranged a conciliatory meeting between the reporters and the pacifist, at which the celebrated documents were to be displayed. As Mrs. Schwimmer entered the conference room, the journalists applauded heavily. "Do not be insincere!" she snapped in a voice low and thick with anger, effectively quashing any goodwill. She completed the job by accusing the reporters of telling Ford that she listened at keyholes.[15]

Among the peace pilgrims, only Ford was spared the blanket condemnation of the newsmen. Cynical and antagonistic toward the manufacturer when they boarded the ship, the reporters without exception were won over by his sincerity and friendliness. "I came to make fun of the whole thing," said one reporter, "but my editor is going to have the surprise of his life. I tell you I believe in Henry Ford and I'm going to say so even if I lose my job for it." Another stated: "My chief told me to do satirical stuff—more of the kind we put over the week we sailed. I'm not going to do it. I can't after seeing Henry Ford's face." A midwestern editor, who, when he first met Ford, saw "a suggestion of a foxy look in his face," within a few days found only "a look of goodness, of genuineness, of sincerity." On the seventh day of the voyage the press corps met in solemn session with the view of extricating Ford from the debacle surrounding him. "The men are going to see Henry Ford through on this deal," wired the *New York Tribune*'s representative, "no matter what happens to the party. That is exactly where the distinction lies. Ford is a white man—and most emphatically sincere. We ought to know, we lived with him. And we are not hypnotized."[16]

The ship docked at Oslo on December 18. A discouraged and cold-ridden Ford disembarked, but did not appear in public during the five days he was in Norway. On December 22 he called in the press of the city, but to the newsmen's surprise he discussed not mediation but his new tractor. He pointed out that his invention was unpatented and that he would try to convince the armament makers that they could realize a greater profit by manufacturing tractors than by making guns. The reporters were mystified. "He must be a very great man who permits himself to utter such foolishness," pondered one of them. Ford surreptitiously left the peace expedition the next day and boarded an America-bound ship at Bergen. His departure grieved his fellow pilgrims, who nonetheless—in league with the representatives of five other neutral nations—formed the Neutral Conference for Continuous Mediation. This group, financed by Ford, met at The Hague in continuous session until February 1917, when the hopelessness of attaining peace became apparent to the industrialist.[17]

Meanwhile, Ford must have been most agreeably surprised at the reception accorded him upon his return to America. The *Saginaw* (Michigan) *Herald* expressed the view of most of the nation's press:

> He had sailed away a short time before one of the most ridiculed men of his generation; he sailed back into an atmosphere of sympathy. In the meantime, his expedition had appealed to the imagination of his countrymen. The very hopelessness of the task he had attempted commanded a sort of respect. "God's Fool," the *Springfield Republican* calls him, striking in those two words perhaps the keynote of the comment of the majority of the journals of this country. . . .
>
> It is a curious turn in sentiment. The Ford expedition is no less ridiculous than it was—indeed it is in some ways even more absurd than had been anticipated—but the point of view has changed. Men see now Ford the dreamer, the idealist, and see him, too, touched with pathos in the unexpectedly

bad success of his expedition and his own illness. Mr. Ford stands before the people now very much like the farmer who stood on the railroad track and defied the train; they do not respect his judgment, but they admire his nerve and extend him sympathy.

The *New York American,* which admitted that it had "caricatured, lampooned, ridiculed, and vituperated" Ford unmercifully, published an editorial entitled, "Henry Ford Deserves Respect, Not Ridicule." "No matter if he failed," stated the *American,* "he at least TRIED. Had every citizen of the United States, including the President and his Cabinet and the members of Congress, put forth one-tenth the individual effort that Henry Ford put forth, THE BOYS WOULD HAVE BEEN OUT OF THE TRENCHES BY CHRISTMAS."[18]

As for Detroit, it was "waiting with open arms" for the crusader. "For once the wand has failed," wrote a special writer sent to Detroit by the *New York Tribune,* "but to the city which remembers how he looked in overalls its wielder is still the same old miracle man. If the boys choose to spend a dismal Christmas in the trenches, that—says Detroit—is because there's something the matter with the boys. The first fly visible to the local eye yet has to light on Henry."[19]

Over the long run, the peace expedition—despite the ridicule which the press heaped upon it in November and December 1915—undoubtedly popularized Ford among the masses. "The day the ship sailed, the common people of the world gave Ford their hearts—and have never recalled them," wrote a Ford biographer in the early 1920s. "From that day to this, malignant criticism of Ford has been, so far as the common people are concerned, like a tallow arrow fired at a stone wall." The respect which many Americans had for Ford's idealism unquestionably contributed to the industrialist's amazing strength as a senatorial candidate in 1918 and to the persistent Ford-for-President talk between 1916 and 1924.[20]

Ford also received more immediate and practical gains from the expedition. Although he doubtless did not charter the peace ship to advertise himself or his car (Model T orders ran ahead of production during nearly all of 1915), the voyage publicized both. When Liebold told him that the total costs were $465,000, the idealist-turned-canny-businessman remarked: "Well, we got a million dollars worth of advertising out of it, and a hell of a lot of experience." He later claimed that he had discovered potential markets for his tractor and that the peace ship, which had made the name "Ford" a household word all over Europe, had enabled the company to break into the postwar Continental market at only one-twentieth of what it would have otherwise cost.[21]

Ford's opposition to war and preparedness did not stop with the peace ship and the Neutral Conference for Continuous Mediation. Less than two months after leaving the peace delegates in Norway, he denounced the preparedness program then before Congress in press releases and "educational news plates" sent to 12,000 small daily and weekly newspapers. During the same month, Ford placed full page antipreparedness advertisements in forty metropolitan newspapers and a dozen farm and home periodicals. The advertising campaign was conducted with increasing intensity throughout the spring of 1916, eventually reaching more than 250 of the nation's largest newspapers and savagely attacking naval and military bills pending before

Congress and those organizations considered to be in collusion with the "munitions interests."[22]

Two lawsuits developed out of the campaign. The Navy League, one of the organizations which Ford accused of being associated with munitions makers, sued him in May 1916 for $100,000. The Vitagraph Company of America, producer of *The Battle Cry of Peace,* asked $1,000,000 damages in August 1916 as compensation for Ford's accusation that the film was inspired by Hudson Maxim, "a manufacturer of munitions, in the interest of munitions manufacturers." Ford claimed that the suits were filed for advertising purposes, while the plaintiffs accused the industrialist of having conducted his antipreparedness campaign for the same reason. A number of newspapers agreed with the plaintiffs, the *Evansville* (Indiana) *Courier* pointing out that Ford "could lose the cases by default and come out a winner. He'll get a million dollars worth of publicity out of them." Actually, neither case was fought to a finish, for when diplomatic relations with Germany were severed on February 3, 1917, and two days later Ford declared that "[I] will place our factory at the disposal of the United States government and will operate without one cent of profit," the unhappy plaintiffs found themselves suing the most popular private citizen in America. The suits were quietly dropped.[23]

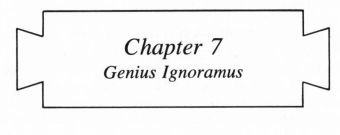

Chapter 7
Genius Ignoramus

1

Henry Ford remained a pacifist during World War I, but was now a "fighting pacifist." In addition to his plants, he offered to contribute his time to the war effort and "to work harder than ever before." He also announced that his factories could build 1,000 small submarines and 3,000 motors each day. The pronouncement was seized upon by the press, which, as it was to do throughout the war, dramatized Ford as a symbol of mass production and of the company's productive capacities.[1]

Ford never denied that he possessed the industrial magic attributed to him; rather he continually proposed ways, some of them highly unorthodox, of using it. The submarine he wanted to build, for example, would have carried only one man, who was to guide the midget vessel to the side of an enemy ship and then, by means of a pole, to attach a "pill-bomb" to the victim's hull. The navy was unimpressed with Ford's offer, but its rejection did not deter the manufacturer from proclaiming in August 1917, that he intended to turn out airplanes on a moving assembly line. Twenty-three years later Franklin D. Roosevelt was ridiculed for proposing to build 50,000 airplanes in a year; Ford outdid him three to one, proposing to manufacture 150,000. He asked the manager of his British plant to send him a captured German fighter to help him set a design and began publicizing his idea in the United States. However, he failed to convince the government that he could build airplanes as rapidly as motor cars, and the idea was abandoned.[2]

Ford next announced that he could build 1,000 two-man tanks a day. The army was interested and called for a demonstration in a trench-strewn field. The "flivver tanks," as the press dubbed them, performed creditably except that they occasionally became stuck nose-up in the trenches. "What are you going to do about that?" inquired an officer. "We'll have so many of them," replied Ford, "that we'll use stranded tanks to make a crossing for the following army." The army, apparently convinced, ordered 15,000 of the tanks, but the war ended before any had been shipped to Europe.[3]

The Ford war work which, when announced, most "amazed the public" paradoxically was not sought by the manufacturer. The so-called Eagle submarine patrol boats, although conceived in a conversation among Ford, Liebold, and Edward N. Hurley, chairman of the U. S. Shipping Board, originally were to have been built at naval or commercial shipyards. However, since none of these facilities was available for the work in early 1918, the contract was awarded to Ford. The industrialist characteristically planned to turn the submarine chasers out as factory products, using mass-production techniques. He was supremely confident that he could meet the challenge and accepted a contract to build 100 of the vessels, the first to be delivered by August 1, ten in the ensuing month, twenty in the next, and twenty-five or more each month thereafter. An immense assembly building was rapidly constructed on the site of the company's present River Rouge plant, in Dearborn, Michigan (the ships were to be sent to the Atlantic coast via the Rouge River, Lakes Erie and Ontario, and the St. Lawrence River). On May 7, 1918, the keel of the first boat was laid; on July 10 the first Eagle was launched. The optimism of Ford and of Secretary of the Navy Josephus Daniels, who prophesied that the Ford Company would shatter all previous shipbuilding records, seemed fully warranted. Ten thousand Ford employees marched down the streets of Highland Park, waving banners, "An Eagle a Day Keeps the Kaiser Away," and under the headline, "Warships While You Wait," the *New York Times* reported that the ships were being "hatched like flivvers."[4]

Unfortunately, the congratulatory notes were premature. After producing the first Eagle on schedule, the Ford organization never came within sight of the remainder of its goals. The company appears to have dispatched only seven boats for the Atlantic coast before Armistice Day, and only two of these had actually reached the ocean by that date. Ford did not really get into mass production (two boats a week) until January 1919. The sixtieth and final boat under the reduced contract was not built until May 1919. The Eagle boat operation briefly came under challenge in January 1919, when Senator Henry Cabot Lodge, acting upon an adverse commentary in the *Daily Iron Trade and Metal Market Report,* called for an investigation. However, at the hearings naval officials defended the boats as a necessary experiment, and as well made, and Ford profits proved to have been modest.[5]

Henry Ford's grandstanding and the Ford Company's difficulties with the Eagle boat project notwithstanding, the firm did make a substantial contribution to the American war effort. Six thousand ambulances and 33,000 cars and trucks were supplied to the American and Allied forces at a 15 percent price discount. Seven thousand tractors were sold at cost—$750—to Britain, and 27,167 more were sold at the same price to American distributors, who, in turn, were asked by Ford to sell them to farmers without profit. The company's prompt response to Britain's request for the farm vehicles was particularly gratifying to Ford of England, which had been the target of much ill-directed abuse from the British press during Ford's pacifist campaign of 1915. The company also produced steel helmets, caissons, submarine detectors for the British navy, and light-weight armor plate for tanks, and it designed a robot airplane bomb which anticipated the V-1.[6]

The company's outstanding production achievement centered around the Liberty airplane engine. In response to a plea from the army, Ford's engineers first designed a machine tool which cut the cost of the engine's cylinders from $24.00 to $8.25. The army then asked Ford to make cylinders for the motors, which were manufactured at Packard, Lincoln, and Nordyke & Marmon. The company produced 415,377 cylinders. Finally, the Ford organization was given a contract for 5,000 complete engines. Establishing a partial assembly-line operation, the Ford Company within five months had attained the impressive output of seventy-five engines daily.

The company produced 3,940 of the motors before the contract was cancelled at war's end.[7]

The Model T earned special praise during the war and was cited for "gallantry in action" in a number of battlefield dispatches. Ten machine-gun-laden T's were used to drive Germans from an entrenched position on the Marne, and the sturdy little car was the only vehicle that could get through to wounded men during the first five days of fighting in the Argonne Forest. By providing motive power for flat boats, the T saved a detachment of British soldiers from starvation in Africa. General Edmund Allenby attributed the success of the Palestine campaign to "Egyptian laborers, camels, and Ford cars." According to Lowell Thomas, then lecturing on the Middle Eastern campaign, Allenby rode in a Rolls-Royce, but always had a Ford on hand as a kind of insurance.

"Hunka Tin," a parody on Kipling's "Gunga Din," brought down vaudeville houses after its publication in the *American Field Service Bulletin,* and was used in Ford dealers' advertising all over the country. Cited by *Printers' Ink* as the most effective product advertising to emerge from the war, the poem concluded with a rattling stanza fully worthy of its subject:

> Yes, Tin, Tin, Tin,
> You exasperating puzzle, Hunka Tin,
> I've abused you and I've flayed you,
> But, by Henry Ford who made you,
> You are better than a Packard, Hunka Tin.[8]

On the home front, the company subscribed heavily to Liberty Loan and Red Cross drives, donating $500,000 worth of ambulances to the charitable organization on one occasion. Ford also produced several films in behalf of the Liberty Loan and Red Cross campaigns. One of them, *How and Why Liberty Bonds Are Made,* was so highly regarded by the government that it scrapped its own film on this subject in favor of the Ford production, which subsequently was shown in 5,000 American theaters. In addition, the company produced films on its war work (*The Truth about the Liberty Motor, The Story of the "Ford Eagle"*), on military training (*The Making of a Man-O-Warsman, Training Officers for Our National Army*), and on the activities of the various services (*Heroes of the Coast Guard, The Eyes of the Allies*). These films usually were sent to a minimum of 4,000 theaters by the film distributor firms which served the company during the war.[9]

Ford executives accepted a number of high-level government assignments during the war. Henry Ford served on the U.S. Shipping Board and National War Savings Committee and as an arbitrator for the War Labor Board. John R. Lee, the company's Washington representative, served as an advisor to the War Industries Board, and Norval Hawkins took a leave of absence to serve as a transportation consultant to the army's Ordnance Department.[10]

Everything considered, Henry Ford (and the Ford Company) enjoyed splendid relations with the public throughout most of World War I. The industrialist's patriotism and the exigencies of war silenced those who had criticized Ford's pacifist views in 1915 and 1916. The manufacturer's bold plans to build prodigious numbers of submarines, tanks, airplanes, and ships—even though they bore little practical fruit—were vigorously applauded by a press and a people which fervently wanted to believe and did believe that Ford could perform production miracles. He was frequently called "Germany's greatest individual enemy" and "the civilian who is more important to the conduct of the war than any other in the world." Ford's statements "were read with as close attention as was given to the words of Wilson or Roosevelt" by many persons, and the industrialist undoubtedly received more wartime press attention than any other private American citizen. "Barnum, that so-called prince of press agents, even at his best was a child in the matter of securing free advertising in comparison with Ford," said an automobile trade journal, and the *Philadelphia North American* declared that Ford, Wilson, and Theodore Roosevelt "gained so much more publicity than any others that they constituted a class by themselves."[11] The unwillingness of Henry Ford, John Dodge, and other auto manufacturers to comply with the War Industries Board's requests to curtail civilian car output in favor of defense production was little publicized. The auto makers fell into line only after Bernard M. Baruch, head of the board, in the summer of 1918 threatened to commandeer their coal and steel supplies and halt rail shipments to and from their plants if they did not submit to his directives.

Perhaps no aspect of Ford's war record generated more publicity and goodwill for the industrialist and his firm than his oft-repeated promise to return all war profits to the government. His failure to do so went unnoticed until 1922, when one of Ford's biographers erroneously stated that the manufacturer had handed over $29,000,000—allegedly the total amount of his war profits—to the government. Andrew W. Mellon, Secretary of the Treasury, thereupon wrote to Ford, remarking that the Treasury knew nothing of the return of any Ford profits. Ford then agreed to cooperate with a Treasury agent to determine the exact amount he was "liable" to the government. Actually, the industrialist's war profits never approached $29,000,000. The company's war profits totalled $8,151,119.31, and when taxes had been deducted stood at $4,357,484.97, Ford's own share (58.5 percent) amounting to $2,483,766.43. After the deduction of personal income taxes Ford was left with profits of only $926,780.46.[12]

However, the industrialist never paid this or any other sum into the Treasury. His failure to do so received little attention, and, curiously, biographers and Ford publicists have repeatedly stated that Ford was the "only rich man of note who . . . refused to coin money out of the blood of nations." As late as 1938, the *Ford News* declared that Ford had made good on his wartime promise, and in 1941 the company's Cincinnati branch manager suggested to the general sales manager that the story of "Ford's refusal to accept personal profit from war work" ought to be given the widest publicity. The myth of the rebated war profits thus persisted for a generation even among Ford publicists and officials. As for the public, as Roger Burlingame points out, the fact that Ford *intended* to pay back the profits was quite enough; only a "carping critic" would have taken him to task for "forgetting" to do so.[13]

2

On February 5, 1914, one month to the day of Ford's epochal wage announcement, Henry Ford was endorsed as a candidate for governor at a mass meeting of the Bull Moose Progressives in Calhoun County, Michigan. Three months later, as the manufacturer was rejecting a similar endorsement by the Progressives' statewide executive committee, a movement was started by Michigan's secretary of state, attorney general, and land commissioner to promote Ford for the Republican vice presidential nomination in 1916.[14] So rapidly had the magic aura and the publicity surrounding Ford's name attracted the politicians.

In April 1915, the *Pasadena News* suggested that the Republicans nominate Ford for president in 1916. "Well," observed the *New York Herald,* "one manifest advantage of Mr. Ford's nomination would be that the Republican National Committee could conduct its campaign without calling in the services of its publicity bureau." The *Bemidji* (Minnesota) *Herald,* as the *Oscar II* neared Norway, declared itself for Ford for president, remarking that his election would mean "Peace, Progress, Prosperity for ALL Americans and for the WORLD AT LARGE."[15]

After Wilson had demanded that Congress strengthen his hand by measures to arm the country, many pacifists turned toward Ford as the symbol of their hopes. Popular petitions put him on the presidential-preference ballot of the Republican Party in Michigan. Ford dismissed the movement as a joke, but early in April he defeated the politically insignificant Senator William Alden Smith, 83,057 to 77,872. Two weeks later, despite emphatic public statements that he was not a presidential candidate, Ford came close to a victory over Senator Albert B. Cummins of Iowa in the Nebraska preferential primary. The Eastern press, representing an area with strong sentiments for militarism and military preparedness, began, according to the *Detroit News,* "to take Mr. Ford very, very seriously." When in May the *St. Louis Times* conducted a poll on candidates for the presidency, Ford stood at the top of the list, and in the Ohio preferential primary some 5,000 voters wrote his name on their ballots. At the Republican National Convention in 1916, Ford received thirty-two votes on the first ballot but lost this support on the second vote.[16]

Both as a pacifist and an admirer of the President, Ford supported Wilson in 1916. On July 10, after a Detroit speech, the President visited Highland Park, where 30,000 Ford workers were permitted to leave their machines to greet him with "ear-splitting cheers" and huge banners reading, "Hats Off to Woodrow Wilson, the President Who Kept Us Out of War." Ford's enthusiasm for the President encouraged Democratic leaders to apply to him for a large campaign gift. He refused to contribute to the war chest, but agreed to finance a personally conducted advertising campaign in Wilson's behalf. Ford-signed half-page and full-page ads in Wilson's behalf appeared in 500 metropolitan papers before the end of October. The ads were largely concentrated in New York, New Jersey, Illinois, Indiana, California, and other closely fought states. Altogether, Ford spent $58,800 for the cause (and, characteristically, was credited with having expended amounts ranging from $100,000 to $250,000 by most of the nation's press). Perhaps even more important than the advertising were

Ford's enthusiastic pro-Wilson interviews, aimed particularly at workers and farmers, and widely reprinted. When Wilson, carrying California by less than 4,000 votes, was re-elected, Ford could have claimed (although he did not) with some justification that his influence had shaped the decision of 2,000 Californians and had thus kept Wilson in the White House.[17]

In 1918 the President, impressed with Ford's tremendous wartime popularity and knowing that the manufacturer was the only ''Wilson and League of Nations'' man capable of being elected to the U. S. Senate from traditionally Republican Michigan, pleaded with Ford to enter the race. The industrialist reluctantly agreed to run, adopting the attitude, ''If they want to elect me let them do so, but I won't make a penny's investment.'' As a nominal nonpartisan independent, Ford was entered in both the Democratic and Republican primaries. Most Democratic papers, identifying Ford with Wilson, were enthusiastic about his candidacy. The Republican and independent press, however, was tartly critical. The *New York Times* remarked that for all of his amiability, he lacked the type of mind needed to grasp national or international problems, his election ''would create a vacancy in both the Senate and in the automobile business, and from the latter Mr. Ford cannot be spared.'' The Senate, grumbled the *Grand Rapids Herald,* made laws, not Lizzies, and the *Detroit Saturday Night* acidly declared that Ford had not known what the war was about until it began. The half dozen leading candidates for the vacant seat were, of course, as little pleased, and one of them, former Michigan governor Chase S. Osborn, on the very day Ford announced his candidacy, handed the press a list of fifteen vitriolic reasons why Ford ''was not a fit person for United States senator.''[18]

Ford was virtually without competition in the Democratic primary. The GOP regulars, however, closed ranks behind Truman H. Newberry, a former Secretary of the Navy and wartime lieutenant-commander, while some resolute Bull Moose veterans clung to Osborn. Newberry spared no effort to win, making speeches, mobilizing the party press, and spending $176,568 on his campaign, mostly for advertising and publicity. Ford, on the other hand, made no speeches, gave out no statements beyond a declaration for woman suffrage, and spent not a cent. The result was all but inevitable: Newberry carried the primary by a vote of 114,963 against Ford's 71,800, and Osborn's 47,100. In the Democratic balloting, however, Ford defeated his nearest opponent by nearly a four-to-one margin.

The general campaign was a repetition of the primary. Ford again announced that he would not conduct an active campaign, and except for a number of booklets, financed by Harvey S. Firestone and other friends of Ford and written by Edwin G. Pipp, he did virtually nothing to advance his candidacy. The Newberry forces continued to spend money lavishly, conducting a hard-hitting campaign on the theme of Americanism. They placed special emphasis on Edsel Ford's draft deferment. Henry was more successful, sneered one Republican newspaper, in keeping his boy out of the trenches than in getting other boys out by Christmas. ''Why not send the indispensable Edsel to the Senate?'' asked another. A cartoon in the *Grand Rapids Press* showed Quentin Roosevelt's grave and the younger Ford with a golf club in hand. In answering these gibes, Ford took full responsibility for retaining Edsel at Highland Park and remarked that if Edsel did serve he would be found ''fighting, and not sticking his spurs into a mahogany desk in Washington,'' an obvious slap at Newberry's son, who was an army officer stationed in Washington during the war.[19]

On Sunday, November 3, two days before the general election, the Republican State Central Committee played its trump card, a full-page ad in the *Detroit Free Press* implying that Ford was a "Hun-lover" and harbored German aliens and sympathizers in his Highland Park plant. The committee pointed particularly to German-born Carl Emde, who had charge of tool design and drafting on the Liberty airplane engine. "If Carl Emde wishes to make plans and photographs of the Ford plant or the Liberty motor for use by enemies of the United States," the ad pointed out, "Henry Ford is willing to give him the chance to do it." The fact that Emde was an American citizen, had worked for the Ford Company since 1908, and had helped to improve the Liberty motor at a savings of $345,000 a month to the government was swept aside.

Pipp had a rebuttal ready for Ford's signature on Monday morning, but it missed the state editions of the Detroit papers and most outstate dailies because the manufacturer insisted on assuring Emde of his support before issuing the statement. The original charge meanwhile echoed throughout the state in the Monday editions of unfriendly newspapers. Consequently, many thousands of voters went to the polls on Tuesday aware of the accusations, but not the defense. The delay perhaps cost Ford the election. He received 212,751 ballots to Newberry's 217,088. A change of fewer than 2,200 votes thus would have sent the manufacturer to Capitol Hill. Pipp estimated that the failure to reach outstate voters before the polls opened cost Ford 10,000 votes. By the time Emde's name had been cleared of the guilt-by-association charges, Ford had lost the first and only major political office he would seek.[20]

3

In 1916–17, Henry Ford was involved in a lawsuit with two of the company's stockholders, John F. and Horace Dodge. The statements that Ford made in and out of court during the period of this suit were widely publicized and did much to brighten his image as an American folk hero.

The suit originated with Ford's plan, conceived in 1915 and early 1916, to double the size of the Highland Park plant, to construct a blast furnace and a foundry ten miles away on the Rouge River, and to suspend all but nominal dividends (that is, 5 percent per month on the ridiculously low book capitalization of $2,000,000) until the indefinite date of the expansion program's completion. Ford believed that he had to increase his productive capacity and output, or risk falling behind rapidly growing competitors in the low-priced field. He was indifferent to the Dodges' medium-priced car, introduced in 1913. But the Dodges, who between them owned 10 percent of the Ford Company's stock, were thoroughly alarmed by Ford's plan. They had used several millions of dollars of Ford profits to launch their car, and they were counting upon the continued flow of impressive Ford dividends to expand production. They remonstrated with Henry, who in August 1916 replied that the company, in addition to withholding special dividends, would plow back into the business $58,000,000 of accumulated profits. The same month, Ford slashed prices on the Model T an average of $66.00. To the Dodges, the price cuts added insult to injury. The Ford Company had been able to sell all the cars it could make. Simple arithmetic showed that at one sweep Ford had skimmed about $40,000,000 of profits from company income. The Dodges felt that he might as well have thrown the money away. They filed suit against the Ford Motor Company and Henry Ford, asking that the defendants distribute as dividends 75 percent of the company's cash surplus, or about $39,000,000. Simultaneously, they obtained a court restraining order which forbade the use of company funds for plant expansion.

Characteristically, Ford at once took his case to the public, declaring in an interview published in the *Detroit News* that his only aims in life were to enable "a large number of people to buy and enjoy the use of a car" and to give "a larger number of men employment at good wages." "And let me say right here," he continued, "that I do not believe that we should make such an awful profit on our cars. A reasonable profit is right, but not too much. So it has been my policy to force the price of the car down as fast as production would permit, and give the benefits to users and laborers." Such statements, probably unprecedented in the business world, astonished and delighted the American public. In subsequent interviews Ford hammered home this theme, pointing out, "We could easily have maintained our price for this year and cleaned up from sixty to seventy-five millions; but I don't think it would have been right to do so; so we cut our prices and are now clearing from $1,500,000 to $2,500,000 a month, which is all any firm ought to make, maybe more—unless, as I said, the money is to be used in expansion. I have been fighting to hold down income right along. A man is not a success unless he can pay good wages and clear something for himself, but I think these wages should be paid without taking them out of the public."[21]

Once on the witness stand, Ford gave answers which—if their purpose was to please the public—could not have been better written by any public relations expert in the land.

"Now," said Elliott G. Stevenson, the Dodges' truculent attorney, "I will ask you again, do you still think that those profits were 'awful profits?' "

"Well, I guess I do, yes," replied Ford.

"And for that reason you were not satisfied to continue to make such awful profits?" the lawyer inquired.

"We don't seem to be able to keep the profits down," apologized Ford.

"...Are you trying to keep them down? What is the Ford Motor Company organized for except profits, will you tell me, Mr. Ford?"

"Organized to do as much good as we can, everywhere, for everybody concerned."

The dumbfounded attorney quit for the day. However, in his need to prove that a business firm's primary responsibility is to its stockholders, he returned to the attack. "What," he asked Ford, "is the purpose of the [Ford] company?"

"To do as much as possible for everybody concerned," responded Ford, "to make money and use it, give employment, and send out the car where the people can use it . . . and incidentally to make money. . . . Business is a service not a bonanza."

"Incidentally make money?" queried the attorney.

"Yes, sir."

"But your controlling feature . . . is to employ a great army of men at high wages, to reduce the selling price of your car, so that a lot of people can buy it at a cheap price, and give everybody a car that wants one."

"If you give all that," replied Ford, who must have felt that Stevenson had admirably stated his policies, "the money will fall into your hands; you can't get out of it."[22]

The Dodges, although they scarcely could convince the public that Ford's theories were dangerous, did make an impression upon the state circuit court that tried the case. In October 1917 the Ford Company was ordered to give up most of its Rouge expansion plans, on the narrow ground that it exceeded the powers expressly granted the firm in its charter, and to declare a special dividend of $19,275,385. Henry Ford appealed. In February 1919 a state superior court held that the Ford Company could go forward with its Rouge plans, but had to pay the dividend recommended by the lower court. The bench, wagging a reproving finger at Henry Ford, noted that "it is not within the powers of a corporation to shape and conduct a company's affairs for the merely incidental benefit of shareholders and for the primary purpose of benefiting others." The wage-earning, car-buying public could hardly have been expected to agree with this portion of the judge's opinion.[23]

Ford's well-publicized views were enthusiastically received by millions of people. Many of his statements were, in a sense, "frosting" on the five-dollar-day and peace-ship cakes, and they served immeasurably to identify the industrialist with the best interests of the common man. Ford, the average man reasoned, was on their side; indeed, was one of them. The fact that he was a multimillionaire and the president of a huge corporation was beside the point; he had consistently defied the rules of the game to prove he was for the little man rather than for "bloated" stockholders. The press was similarly taken with Ford's earnest and well-meaning testimony. "If only as an inspiration to humanity," the *Detroit Journal* typically observed, "his performance is worth the price."[24]

The Dodge suit itself attracted little attention at the time of its settlement in 1919. But the testimony and interviews which Ford gave during the course of the suit, particularly his statements expressing concern for the workingman and the automobile consumer, have been quoted in the press and in books on many occasions ever since. When President Kennedy attacked United States Steel Corporation for raising prices in April 1962, Drew Pearson's syndicated column quoted Ford's testimony and suggested that the steel company's executives read it to determine "whether profits or prices should come first." Father R. L. Bruckberger, commenting in 1959 on Ford's remarks quoted above, suggested that "in all the world's universities all young people seeking some knowledge of political economy should be required to learn this remarkable dialogue by heart. It is as important in economics as the Declaration of Independence is in politics. . . . Indeed, this fantastic dialogue should be looked upon as the businessman's Hippocratic Oath." The French priest, who holds that the trial demonstrated that the capitalist economic system as described by Adam Smith, Ricardo, and Marx "was not only obsolete but absurd and unsuited to America,'' concludes that the case itself "should be as celebrated in political economy as the trial of Socrates in philosophy or that of Galileo in astronomy" and that historians "may well decide that it was the most extraordinary trial of the century."[25] The Dodge suit, like the peace ship, was, in the narrow sense, a defeat for Ford. But the industrialist, as 58.5 percent owner of the company, pocketed the greater part of the dividends distributed. Moreover, to a man seeking credit as a public benefactor—and Ford's desire to be a hero to millions strongly motivated his fight to the finish—the suit served as an excellent forum for publicity, and thus made an important contribution to the Ford legend.

4

Even before the Dodge brothers had filed suit against him, Ford had publicly equated stockholders with parasites—people who "gave nothing but money to an enterprise." The Dodge suit strengthened this conviction and hardened Ford in his resolve to rid himself of those whom he considered to be "drones."[26]

While waiting for his appeal in the Dodge suit to come before the superior court, Ford took his first step. On December 30, 1918, he submitted his resignation, effective the following day, as president of the Ford Motor Company "to devote my time to building up other organizations with which I am connected." Edsel was elected president; his father retained his seat on the board of directors. If the unexpected move did not create a stir comparable to the assassination of the President, as one Ford biographer later averred, it did cause the press to produce its biggest, blackest type and startled both automotive circles and the lay public. What did it mean? For two months there was no answer, and then Ford launched a campaign of psychological warfare against other Ford Company shareholders. Within four months he and his immediate family had bought out the other stockholders and were in sole possession of the firm.

To soften up his fellow shareholders for a purchase bid, Ford, in California, where he was vacationing, told a Los Angeles reporter that it was his intention to build a new and better car which would undersell the Model T (whose average price was $466) by $100 to $200. The new vehicle was to be built and marketed by a concern other than the Ford Motor Company. He explained that the recent Dodge suit decision had been responsible for his astounding plan. His only recourse was "to get out, design a new car," and win anew his freedom to operate according to his judgment. The old company? "Why, I don't know exactly what will become of that," the industrialist said vaguely. The story was, of course, page-one news in almost every daily newspaper in the country.[27]

With scores of reporters camping on the doorstep of his vacation quarters, Ford provided sensation after sensation. "The present Ford Motor Company employees number about 50,000 in the actual manufacture of its cars. Our new company will have four or five times that number." Again, "The new car is well advanced, for I have been working on it while resting in California." Still again, "For our new project we are already looking about for waterpower sites. . . . We shall have a plant on this coast and all over the country. In fact, we propose to dot the whole world with our factories." Chambers of commerce in virtually every American city on a water site went into a tizzy. Fifty-one of the commercial organizations immediately wired Ford that they knew of just the kind of place that he had in mind. Many newspapers carried glowing editorials, dutifully sent to Ford, on why the city in which they published was an eminently well-qualified location for a Ford plant.[28]

Meanwhile, back in Highland Park, Liebold "admitted" that his employer was contemplating selling his Ford stock to General Motors. Speculation mounted as to what Ford would do next. One of the wire services reported that Harvey Firestone would be Ford's partner in a $200,000,000 company which was to manufacture the new car. *Printers' Ink* speculated that the new vehicle would be called the "Flivv Junior," while the *Washington Herald* was sure it would be named the "Flivverette."

Within two weeks the loose comment had gotten out of hand, and many Ford dealers began to panic. Edsel was forced to write them a soothing letter. "A large majority of the reports afloat are greatly distorted and exaggerated," he stated. "A new car may be manufactured, but . . . [it] could not possibly be designed, tested out, manufactured and marketed in quantities under two or three years' time." He admonished the dealers to stop worrying about the new car and get busy selling Model T's.[29]

Ford's fellow stockholders were worried. The Dodge brothers ironically insisted that "Henry Ford is under contract to the Ford Motor Company and he will not be allowed to leave the firm and start a competitive business." Ford, speaking through Liebold, replied: "The Ford Motor Company has no mortgage upon Mr. Ford's body, soul, or brains. He is a free agent." The shareholders, concerned lest Ford actually carry out his threat to form a new company and thereby depress the value of their holdings, were thus prepared for the calls they began to receive from financial agents acting secretly in Ford's behalf. The representatives initially offered $7,500 for each of the 8,300 outstanding shares, but finally agreed to pay $12,500 per share (except to Couzens, who held out for $13,000)—a good price considering the reigning uncertainty over the company's future. The transaction, completed in July 1919, cost Ford $105,820,894.57. Although he had had to borrow $60,000,000 to complete the purchase, Ford knew that the shares were bought at a reasonable price. When his stock-purchasing emissaries told him that their mission had been accomplished, he "danced a jig all around the room."[30]

Ford immediately abandoned plans (assuming he ever really had any) for the rival to the Model T and thus drew down the curtain on "the most adroit sleight-of-hand performance of his entire career." "Foxy" Ford, one historian observed, would have more than held his own in the company of Daniel Drew, Jay Gould, or Cornelius Vanderbilt.[31]

5

Henry Ford was just getting the stockholder situation under control when another troublesome chicken came home to roost. As Ford's financial agents were completing their stock-purchase errands, a trial began in a small Michigan town which once again was to bring the auto magnate before the public eye—but in a rather different light than in the past. The liberator of an industry in the Selden suit, the seeker of peace on the *Oscar II,* the fighting pacifist of World War I, the champion of the "little man" in the profit-sharing plan and the Dodge suit, was now cast in a defensive role. The easy targets—"monopolists," war, foreign aggressors, the "munitions interests," stockholding "drones"— were gone. In their place was a newspaper defending its right to "free speech."

Ford's million-dollar libel suit against the *Chicago Tribune* played an important part in molding the image which the public held of the manufacturer during the last two-and-a-half decades of his career. The suit grew out of an editorial in the *Tribune,* which in June 1916 was asking large employers whether they would give financial aid to workers mobilized for National Guard duty along the Mexican border because of Pancho Villa's attack on Columbus, New Mexico. When the *Tribune* called Frank Klingensmith, by then the Ford Company's treasurer, he erroneously replied in the negative. The newspaper promptly published an editorial entitled, "Ford is an Anarchist," suggesting that Ford move his factories to Mexico. It added that if the manufacturer continued to deny aid to Guardsmen, "he will reveal himself not merely as an ignorant idealist, but as an anarchistic enemy of the nation." Ford demanded a retraction. When the *Tribune*'s publisher, Colonel Robert R. McCormick, insolently rejected his request, Ford filed a libel suit.[32]

In general, the press—which was very concerned with the legal implications of the case—felt that Ford erred in his resolve to take the *Tribune* to court. Many newspapers believed that as a public figure he should reconcile himself to attacks, especially since, in the opinion of certain of these papers, the *Tribune*'s accusations were not without justification. Typifying this view, the *Washington* (Indiana) *Herald* observed that the Chicago paper's editorial was incisively brilliant, except that it failed to call Ford "a pale, green ass."[33]

Two-and-a-half years were spent in preliminary wrangling, including two changes of venue, before the case finally came to trial on May 12, 1919, in Mount Clemens, Michigan, a small health spa located twenty-two miles northeast of Detroit. The suit had attracted nationwide attention, and nearly fifty newsmen, representing leading journals and news agencies, were on hand to cover the proceedings.

Ford was greatly concerned about the ability of the press to be objective during the trial. He felt that the country papers would be inclined to present his story sympathetically, but, of course, none of them was represented in Mount Clemens and comparatively few of them had direct access to wire copy. His chief worry was the metropolitan newspapers, which, he reasoned, would be prejudiced against him because one of their number was involved in a case which conceivably could curtail freedom of the press. He also believed that "powerful enemies" who resented "his strong stand against the exploitation of labor for the benefit of speculative capitalists" would apply pressure on the metropolitan press to use the trial as an excuse to discredit his policies in general.[34]

To protect his interests, Ford decided to have a national news agency of his own during the course of the trial. He instructed Liebold and Fred L. Black, business manager of the *Dearborn Independent,* a Ford-owned weekly newspaper, to establish such a service, with headquarters in Mount Clemens.[35] Nationwide newspaper lists were quickly obtained, distribution facilities were arranged, and an outstanding staff was built around a half-dozen veteran newsmen borrowed from the *Independent* and recruited from metropolitan newspapers. E. G. Pipp, who then was editor of the *Independent,* briefly gave editorial direction to the agency, called the "Mount Clemens News Bureau." He was succeeded by D. D. Martin, a member of the *Independent*'s editorial staff, who had previously worked for Pipp on the *Detroit News.* William J. Cameron, who for a generation was to play a notable role in publicizing Henry Ford and the Ford Motor Company, was the bureau's chief writer.[36]

Cameron, a brilliant forty-year-old Canadian, had worked on the *Detroit News* as a reporter and editorial writer from 1904 to 1918. On the *News,* where he established a reputation as one of the best newspaper writers in America, he had written an editorial, "Don't Die on Third"—an exhortation to get to home plate on any undertaking—which perhaps was reprinted more often than any other editorial. Pipp, who said that he would "be lost without Billy Cameron," had lured the writer from the *News* shortly after assuming the *Independent*'s editorial reins in late 1918.[37]

The Mount Clemens News Bureau occupied one entire floor of a commercial building across the street from the courthouse. The editor's office resembled a staff headquarters behind a battlefront. On one wall hung a huge map of the United States, bristling with colored pins. More than 12,500 blue pins represented newspapers which were favorable to Ford; 397 yellow pins indicated hostile publications. At the height of the trial, the bureau distributed column-length "boilerplate" of the day's proceedings to 260 daily newspapers and 2,507 weeklies, each of which had responded affirmatively to Ford's offer to provide this service free of charge. The company spared no expense in rushing the plate to newspapers at the earliest possible moment. Dispatches were wired each afternoon to newly organized distribution points in twelve strategically located cities, where plates were cast and forwarded to newspapers in time for the next day's editions. In addition, the bureau mailed reports and special feature stories on the trial to more than 13,000 daily and weekly newspapers throughout the country. All told, Ford spent $50,089.48 in financing the bureau's activities, including $20,211.50 for plates.[38]

The bureau repeatedly assured its subscribers that the material furnished them was not propaganda. "If we have any propaganda," the agency informed editors, "it will be sent out as advertising matter and paid for. This service is straight court testimony, without editorial bias." The bureau, however, did not fully live up to its promises. The reports frequently contained comment other than straight court testimony. Furthermore, when Henry Ford was on the stand, the bulletins consistently underplayed the industrialist's ignorance. For example, when Ford said Benedict Arnold was a writer, a statement which appeared on front pages throughout the country, all the bureau reported was: "Later in the examination the name of Benedict Arnold arose, which name Mr. Ford confused with that of an author, a mistake of which *Tribune* counsel endeavored to make capital, but it came to nothing." By the same token, when Ford said the word "ballyhoo" meant "blackguard," the bureau said only: "A humorous interval came about through the use of the innocent word 'ballyhoo' which appeared in some peace literature."[39]

Ford often told reporters that one of the reasons he had brought suit against the

Tribune was "to educate people." He undoubtedly looked forward to expounding his views, as he had during the Dodge suit, before an appreciative nationwide audience. However, he failed to take into account one important consideration. During the Dodge suit he was on "home ground"; the testimony centered around the Ford Motor Company, a subject on which Ford frequently was the best-informed man in the courtroom. In the *Tribune* case, however, the newspaper's attorneys, seeking to prove that Ford was every whit the "ignorant idealist" which the offending editorial had said he was, ranged far afield in their questioning to show that the manufacturer was one of the least well-informed national figures in the country. On cross-examination, Ford could not say when the United States was created, nor did he know when the American Revolution was fought (he ventured the year 1812). Led into definitions, he answered like a truant schoolboy. A mobile army was "a large army, mobilized"; the Monroe Doctrine was "a big-brother act"; anarchy was "overthrowing the government and throwing bombs." Delighted newspaper cartoonists showed Ford standing in a corner with a dunce cap on his head or writing on the blackboard a thousand times, "Benedict Arnold was a traitor." The *Cincinnati Times-Star* offered an opinion typical in press circles, that "a little education along historical lines may be good even for an idealist."

The case dragged on through most of the summer of 1919. Tired reporters coined a phrase: "Out of Mount Clemens by Christmas." Finally, on August 14, the case went to the jury which was composed of ten active farmers, one retired farmer, and one roadbuilder. The jury apparently could not bring itself to admit that the producer of more than two million automobiles was an ignoramus. Similarly, the jurymen (one of whom had testified that he owned a Model T and insisted that "this would not prejudice me against Mr. Ford") could not believe that a man who was well on the way to becoming the nation's richest citizen was an anarchist. On the other hand, the jury did not think that their peer had suffered financially from the *Tribune*'s editorial. The newspaper, therefore, was found guilty of libel and fined six cents. Both Ford and the *Tribune* claimed victory and vindication.[40]

Some publications, in summing up the case, expressed the opinion that Ford had lost a great deal more than he had gained in taking the *Tribune* to court. The *New York Times,* observing that Ford had been subjected to a severe examination of his intellectual horizons, remarked, "He has not received a pass degree." The *New York Tribune* concluded that Ford was "deliciously naive and omniscient and preposterous," and the *Sioux City* (Iowa) *Journal* regarded Ford "as a man with a vision distorted and limited by his lack of information." Perhaps the feeling of judicious men was best summed up by the *Nation,* which sadly reported that the veil of glamour which had gathered about the miracle-working industrialist had in great part been torn away:

> Now the mystery is finally dispelled. Henry Ford is a Yankee mechanic, pure and simple; quite uneducated . . . but with naturally good instincts and some sagacity. . . . He has achieved wealth but not greatness; he cannot rise above the defects of education, at least as to public matters.
>
> So the unveiling of Mr. Ford has much of the pitiful about it, if not of the tragic. We would rather have had the curtain drawn, the popular ideal unshattered.[41]

Although many educated people had been disillusioned, Ford's performance on the witness stand produced quite the opposite reaction among millions of common folk. Many Americans would have been no more successful in defining "a mobile army," "the Monroe Doctrine," or "anarchy" than Ford. Many more would have admitted, as the industrialist had on the stand, that it was difficult for them to read. Ford's statement, "History is bunk," struck a responsive chord in the hearts of countless ex-schoolboys who had the same belief but lacked the ability to express it as tersely as Ford. Plain people of the kind who had approved of Andrew Jackson's bad grammar, Abraham Lincoln's backwoods stories, and William McKinley's tobacco chewing, and who had appreciated Grover Cleveland for the enemies he had made, liked Ford all the better because he did not have all the answers and had been ridiculed at the hands of the generally disliked *Chicago Tribune*. The manufacturer thus vindicated the ignorance of the untutored among his countrymen, thousands of whom responded to the Hearst papers' suggestion that they send to Ford signed coupons reading, "Dear Ford: I am glad to have you for a fellow citizen and I wish we had more of your brand of (anarchism), if that is what it is." The view of such people perhaps was best expressed by the *Ohio State Journal,* which, after admitting that the industrialist was ignorant, remarked, "We sort of like old Henry Ford, anyway." The *Cleveland Plain Dealer* subscribed to this view and added: "What he thinks about history does not matter so long as he confines himself to the manufacture of hardy little vehicles."[42]

Meanwhile, Ford had been greatly pleased by the thousands of columns of favorable publicity which the Mount Clemens News Bureau had obtained for him during the course of the trial, and on July 21 he announced that the agency would be maintained permanently. His objectives were twofold: (1) to provide the nation's press, particularly small papers, with free and "independent" news coverage of events of national significance; and (2) to publicize himself and the Ford Motor Company.[43]

The bureau carried out only one assignment in furtherance of its first objective—coverage of President Wilson's nationwide speaking tour in behalf of the League of Nations. Arrangements were made for Joseph J. O'Neill, who had been borrowed and then hired from the *New York World* to assist the bureau during the *Tribune* trial, to be among the twenty correspondents assigned to the President's train. O'Neill's dispatches, which reflected Ford's enthusiastic support of the league, were sent in plate form to 5,500 newspapers, including 500 dailies, and were read by more than one-fourth of the American population. The campaign cost Ford $33,544.84.[44]

After the conclusion of the league campaign, the agency, renamed the Independent News Bureau, placed its entire emphasis on publicizing Henry Ford and the Ford Company and its subsidiaries. A wide variety of news and feature articles were readied for general distribution, and, in response to requests from individual newspapers and magazines, a number of articles were prepared for Ford's signature. The bureau also wrote articles for the *Dearborn Independent,* some of which appeared under Liebold's signature.[45]

By the end of 1919, however, the bureau, despite its success in placing articles on Ford and the company, seems to have lost Henry Ford's interest and support.

Perhaps Ford believed that the *Dearborn Independent,* for which he had grandiose plans, would be a sufficient means of focusing attention on the national events in which he was interested. Too, he might have felt that he did not need a staff of publicists, for he had no difficulty in generating news at any time he wished. In any event, he was no longer willing to underwrite all the bureau's expenses; to continue, the agency had to obtain some revenue from its clientele. The bureau's plate service, hitherto free and therefore welcomed by thousands of impecunious country papers, was now offered for sale at seventy-five cents a column. Although the price was competitive with prices charged by leading suppliers of plate materials, the offer fell upon thousands of deaf journalistic ears. Only three newspapers subscribed to the service. The bureau folded in February 1920.[46]

It was unfortunate that Ford did not maintain the bureau, without the plate expense, on a permanent basis. Had he done so and had he also adopted the policies proposed for the agency by its editorial director, D. D. Martin, he would have had at his service a press relations unit which was years ahead of its time. Martin advocated the organization of the bureau along the lines of a daily newspaper's staff, with the editor assigning reporters to various beats: Highland Park, the Rouge, the tractor plant in Dearborn, the Dearborn Realty & Construction Company (established by Ford to build houses for employees), and other Ford operations. The bureau, in Martin's view was to be the "fountainhead of Ford publicity," the one organization within the company that would disseminate news and to which outside newsmen would automatically be referred for information. Detailed plans were drawn up to distribute news stories and photographs simultaneously on a national basis, to obtain maximum publicity by using follow-up stories after most initial news releases, and to establish a clipping-analysis unit, which would report continuously on the attitude toward Ford of every newspaper and magazine in America. Martin also suggested that the bureau should be directly accountable to one top-level Ford official. Finally, the editor suggested that the agency should "quietly direct the course of publicity" concerning the company's young president, Edsel Ford. "Whether the treatment which he receives is favorable or unfavorable," Martin predicted, "will depend to a large extent upon . . . this direction."

Although Martin's recommendations were swept away early in 1920, they were vindicated a generation later. Steve Hannagan, when asked to organize a "Ford News Bureau" in 1942, incorporated many features of Martin's prospectus.[47]

6

If the Mount Clemens trial showed that a genius can be an ignoramus, the sleight-of-hand performance of Henry Ford during the depression of 1920–21 demonstrated that an ignoramus can be a genius.

Because of curtailed production for civilians during 1917 and 1918, the automobile industry anticipated unprecedented prosperity during the postwar era. Large-scale civilian production was resumed in early 1919, and the demand for virtually all automobiles exceeded output well into 1920. The Ford Motor Company, which had sold from one-third to one-half of America's cars during the prewar and war years, remained in the van, building a record-breaking 750,000 units (40 percent of the national production) in 1919.

Unfortunately, various economic forces were combining to check the tide of production and sales. The postwar prosperity of the nation was largely the result of artificial factors: private spending of war savings, government spending, a low discount rate, and a temporarily large European market. These props either diminished in importance or disappeared by mid-1920, when a weakening of the automobile market accurately reflected the economic situation of the country.[48]

Henry Ford observed these developments with concern, for he had special reasons for wanting to maintain production and income. His financial situation was delicate, for he needed $25,000,000 by April 1921 to pay off the $60,000,000 loan he had negotiated in 1919 to obtain ownership of the firm. Furthermore, he owed from $18,000,000 to $30,000,000 in taxes, and he was determined to distribute a $7,000,000 bonus to his employees in January 1921. In the fall of 1920 the company—having spent more than $75,000,000 on expansion between 1917 and 1920 and having distributed $20,000,000 in dividends as a result of the Dodge suit—had only $20,000,000 in cash to meet its obligations.

The situation had become menacing by the late summer of 1920. Model T sales were falling off, yet the cost of raw materials remained high. To maintain production and income, some kind of wizardry was needed. Ford decided to follow a familiar formula—to reduce prices, so drastically that the automobile industry would be shaken and the nation startled. Over the objections of his leading executives, he instituted price cuts on September 21 ranging from $105 to $180 on his five models (which had been priced from $525 to $975). The reductions, averaging $148, in percentage terms were the largest in the history of the industry.

Ford justifiably regarded the price rollback as a frontal attack on inflation, which at the time was a matter of great concern to many Americans. "The war is over," Ford was quoted in the news release announcing the reductions, "and it is time war prices were over. . . . We must of course take a temporary loss because of the stock of materials on hand, bought at inflated prices . . . but we take it willingly in order to bring about a going state of business throughout the country. . . . Now is the time to call a halt on war methods, war prices, war profiteering, and war greed."[49]

The announcement was front-page news in virtually every newspaper in the country. Not untypically, the *San Francisco Call* gave the story a three-inch blackface banner, while the *Sidney* (Delaware) *Record*'s three-deck headline read, "Henry Fires a Bomb," "Just Like Him," "The Ford Is the Thing and Everybody Can Afford to Buy a Ford." Editorial comment on the reduction was among the most favorable of Ford's career. Scores of newspapers, writing on the theme, "Henry Ford has performed another big thing for humanity," linked the announcement to the five-dollar day, the company's labor policies, the 1915 price rebate, and the peace ship. Several papers suggested that the industrialist—since he alone had demonstrated the courage and ability to give the people relief from inflation—should be made general manager of the nation. Other editorials took the form of open letters to Ford, in which the manufacturer received the most lavish praise. Under a forty-eight-point headline titled, "IN APPRECIATION," the *Denver Post* offered the following eulogy:

> Henry Ford—the more the American people see of you, the better they like you. You wear well. . . . How does it happen that you are big enough and generous enough and just enough to give back to the people, your customers whose orders are in, fifty millions of dollars, and at the same time, how does it happen that you are generous enough and big enough and humane enough to continue to pay your workmen their usual wages, without one cent's reduction?
>   . . . We are glad that your name is the plain simple name of Henry Ford; that you were a plain industrious, ambitious laborer in early life; that you started life with nothing but a clean heart, a clean mind, an ambition to work, a hope to succeed, and a desire to give good and efficient service for the pay received. And, from this humble start, you have become one of the world's richest men, and it has not spoiled you a bit—just the same Henry Ford—the same honest, sincere man with the same clear brain; with the same clean heart; with the same desire to do justice to all and be generous to all.
>   As you were a good workman in the early days, you are easily one of the best, if not the best, citizen in the United States.
>   Your life; your character; and your achievements should be an inspiration to every laboring man; to every good American citizen; and to every rich man and capitalist in the country—plain, simple, good-hearted, just, generous Henry Ford!
>   The American people love such characters as you. Men like you are a blessing to the world.[50]

Many publications congratulated Ford on his clever timing. "Henry Ford is the shrewdest advertiser in America," declared a Baltimore financial magazine, "for he is always able to use the psychological moment for an advertising campaign which forces every paper in the country, just as the *Manufacturers' Record* is now doing, to discuss his schemes." "The master psychologist has spoken," reported a San Francisco newspaper, "and an advertisement that could not have been bought with all his millions has spread instantly to the uttermost ends of the earth . . . everybody everywhere with an automobile pocketbook will praise Henry Ford, praise the merits of the Ford car and spread the BILLION DOLLAR ADVERTISEMENT that will maintain the Ford factories at the highest pitch of activity while rival plants may be reducing their forces because of gradually decreasing demand."

> Whatever his ignorance of history [said the *Arkansas Democrat*], Ford, as a spotlight artist and consummate master of the increasingly difficult work of prying the newspapers loose from vast gobs of free publicity, stands without a peer in the industrial life of America. . . . In his latest "scoop" Mr. Ford saw deflation coming a mile off. He saw that the market break was inevitable . . . instead of sulking about it, and fighting it off, and camouflaging about it, he ran to meet it. He got there first, gladly, cheerfully, explosively, and he "busted" the story. . . . Publicity, free publicity of the rare kind that cannot be bought, on front page, in editorial, in paragraph, in cartoon, and in joke, came in vast wagonloads to the Ford door. The flivver had again set the pace. . . . Mr. Ford got the inflation and some free advertising. The rest of the boys are getting the deflation.[51]

The "rest of the boys" in the automobile industry were, with few exceptions, incensed over Ford's precipitate action. "According to the industry," reported a Michigan financial journal, "Mr. Ford has accomplished his purpose and his press agent has earned a material increase in pay. It was very clever publicity, manufacturers declare, the cost of which will be paid by the industry as a whole. This, they charge, is Ford's way of doing things." One group of car makers, including Dodge, Maxwell-Chalmers, Hupp, Hudson, Essex, Paige, and General Motors, conferred in Detroit and solemnly announced that prices should not be lowered because buyers would then expect further reductions, and all buying would cease. Such statements only made Ford's halo glow all the brighter. Despite great reluctance to lower prices, a number of firms, led by Franklin, Studebaker, and Willys-Overland, found it expedient to follow Ford's lead. By October 9, twenty-three auto companies had lowered prices, and twenty-eight had not. "It was said that we were disturbing conditions," Ford remarked later. "That is exactly what we were trying to do."[52]

For a time it appeared that Ford's pricing strategy might succeed. The company immediately exerted pressure on parts makers and suppliers of raw materials and obtained price reductions, although the reductions were not proportionate to the lowered prices of cars. In addition, more than 100,000 Model T's were sold in October. In November, however, sales were off approximately 10 percent, and in December they sank to less than 50 percent of the November figure. As the nation's will and power to buy disintegrated, the remainder of the automobile industry also floundered in the doldrums. Ford had failed in his plan to maintain production at a loss and to sustain consumer demand by low prices until the costs of raw materials fell and profits were again possible.

The company produced 78,000 cars—some 35,000 more than dealers could sell—during the first twenty-four days of December, then closed its plants "for inventory," promising to reopen on January 5, 1921. In late December officials were forced to announce that a "lack of orders" and "general financial and business conditions" made it necessary to keep operations suspended indefinitely. During the hiatus, which lasted until February 1, Ford moved rapidly to cut his losses. He stripped his production and office forces to a skeletal crew of managers and superintendents (discharging, in the process, some of his most capable lieutenants, including Klingensmith, Knudsen, and Brownell) and relentlessly collected and sold all useless or surplus material and machinery.[53]

Meanwhile, rumors that Ford was in financial straits circulated throughout the nation. It was variously reported that Wall Street intended to foreclose on Ford and bring him to his knees; that the industrialist was besieged by bankers who were eager to supply him with capital; that General Motors would obtain financial control of the Ford Company; and that Ford refused to part with a share of stock, come what may. "Henry Ford has reached his limit," the Dow-Jones Financial Ticker Service informed its clients. "It is beyond the powers of any one man to raise money and carry forward single-handed the manifold enterprises in which he has started." Many newspapers dramatized the situation. In red ink, the *Denver Post* splashed across its front page the headline, "FORD BATTLES WALL STREET TO KEEP CONTROL OF PROPERTY."

Many people became genuinely alarmed at Ford's plight, and some of them sent to the manufacturer contributions and offers of assistance. The offers came from a wide variety of persons, ranging from the Detroit woman who wanted to loan him a few dollars to a fellow industrialist who tendered several millions. Model T owners "rallied like bees" to a suggestion by the chief of the Columbus, Ohio, Western Union bureau that each lend Ford $100 to tide him over. Edison told the *New York Sun* that the American people would loan Ford $100,000,000 any time he made his needs known to them.[54]

Ford returned the unsolicited contributions, declined all offers of aid, and on February 1 told the press that he was not in the market for a loan. On the same day, 15,000 men reported for work at the Highland Park plant, and a number of assembly plants around the country began producing cars from stocks on hand. The February output, 35,000 units—along with 30,000 unconsigned cars produced in late 1920— was immediately shipped to dealers. The agents, as was the practice in the industry, were required to pay for the cars upon arrival. Many dealers protested against the consignments, but in the last resort each had to pay for them or forfeit his franchise. In most instances the dealers went to their bankers, got the money needed, and gradually saw demand overtake the excess supply. Ford, instead of borrowing money himself, had compelled his dealers to borrow for him. In addition, the company saved or procured $42,600,000 by cutting down inventory, cashing Liberty bonds, selling by-products, and collecting dividends from foreign operations. By April Ford had paid his debts in full and had cash on hand.[55]

The full story of how Ford had "outwitted the bankers" and "paid his way out" was published under James Sweinhart's byline in the *Detroit News* on July 22, 1921. This lengthy interview, cited by one of Ford's biographers as "the most successful publicity stunt of his career," was reprinted in almost every American newspaper and news magazine. It was also the subject of scores of editorials which credited the industrialist with the powers of a financial magician and with having devised "the most brilliant piece of administrative strategy that has thus far marked [his] career." Almost invariably, the articles clothed Wall Street in the dress of Goliath and Ford in the garb of David, a comparison which, of course, enhanced Ford's knight-errantry all the more among millions of people. The fact that the manufacturer had ruthlessly fired long-term employees and had forced dealers to accept cars at a time when many of them also were in financial straits seemed to have made little impression on the public. Indeed, as the *Nation*'s editor, Oswald Garrison Villard, pointed out, it was enough for the people that Ford, "being rich, still hates Wall Street . . . and they do not mind if he frequently turns a trick for which they would denounce any well-known Wall Street operator." In the spring and summer of 1921, with a "victory over the bankers" behind him, with his cars being produced and sold at a record-breaking rate, Ford's stature as a folk hero had reached a new high.[56]

Chapter 8
Flivver Public Relations

1

The five-dollar day, the peace ship, the Dodge and *Tribune* suits, the Ford senatorial campaign, and the company's war record—these events undoubtedly did more to determine the public's attitude toward Henry Ford and the Ford Motor Company between 1914 and 1919 than all of the firm's formal public relations efforts during this period. Nevertheless, the Ford Company's sales and advertising staff continued to publicize the Model T and its manufacturer along conventional public relations lines, and, in a few instances, ventured onto uncharted sales-promotional paths as well.

One of the most striking sales promotion events in business history was Ford's offer of July 31, 1914, to rebate between $40.00 and $60.00 to each purchaser of a Model T should sales exceed 300,000 units during the following year. Coupled with the offer was a price reduction of $60.00 on each Model T and a promise not to cut prices again until August 1, 1915.[1]

Rather surprisingly, in view of the company's oft-demonstrated press-relations acumen, the proposed refund was announced at one of the least propitious times imaginable—the start of World War I. Metropolitan newspapers everywhere, and particularly on the eastern seaboard, relegated the Ford announcement to a back page, while they devoted their front pages to the outbreak of hostilities in Serbia and the Kaiser's ultimatum to Russia. The *New York Times,* in an editorial entitled, "Well Devised But Ill Timed," apologized for its page-five treatment of the announcement, conceding that the offer deserved as much publicity as the five-dollar day. "Ford's mistake is rather serious," the *Times* pointed out, "for cutting prices to customers would not excite the bitter criticism that a huge jump in wages did."[2]

The announcement did appear, nonetheless, in virtually every newspaper in the nation, and in the smaller dailies and country weeklies it received rave notices. To the *Jackson* (Michigan) *Press,* the rebate was "the most tremendous retail buyers profit-sharing plan ever known in the history of the world of salesmanship and one of the wisest selling plans ever devised by man," and to the *New Castle* (Pennsylvania) *Herald,* it was "one of the greatest events in mechanical history." The *San Antonio Light* said that the competition had been "stunned" by the "amazing purchaser's profit-sharing scheme," and the *Detroit Free Press* reported that the people had been "lifted off their feet" by the announcement. The *Butte Miner* declared that groups of Montanans had banded together to buy Fords and were pressuring their friends to "protect" their investments. This sort of chain reaction was, of course, what Norval Hawkins anticipated when he proposed the refund to Henry Ford, and in many communities during the rebate year the best Model T salesmen were persons who had bought Fords after August 1, 1914.[3]

On August 1, 1915, the company announced that it had sold 308,213 automobiles during the previous year, and set the amount to be refunded to each buyer at $50.00, or about 9 percent of the average purchase price. "Profit-sharing" checks totaling $15,410,650 thus were mailed into virtually every American hamlet, town, and city during the next few months. Many newspapers, acknowledging that the rebate offer "was a game in which Ford had everything to win and nothing to lose," [except the refunds] congratulated the company on its "sales-promotion genius" and its customers on their good fortune in climbing aboard the "rebate wagon." The checks, later called "the most virile crop of good will seeds ever planted," naturally made hundreds of thousands of friends for the Model T, Henry Ford, and the Ford Motor Company.[4]

2

Four months before the rebate proposal was announced the Ford Motor Company embarked upon a program, which, if not as spectacular as sharing profits with customers, was no less imaginative and bold for its day: motion-picture production and distribution. The Ford organization was the first American business firm to organize a motion-picture department. It was the only company in the country to maintain such an operation until 1916, when the General Electric Company established a film-producing unit.[5]

Henry Ford was introduced to motion-picture production in mid-1913, when a commercial organization filmed operations in the Highland Park plant, including a scene showing the industrialist testing a huge gas engine. Intrigued, the manufacturer bought a moving-picture camera in September 1913, and began recording assembly processes in the company's various plants. Four months later Ford discussed films with two men, Thomas Edison and Judge Lindsey, who were confident that motion pictures could be used as educational devices. The upshot was that in April 1914 Ford marched into the company's Advertising Department, surveyed the staff, turned to young Ambrose Jewett, and said, "Start a moving-picture department for me." Jewett hastily recruited a staff from various departments of the company and by mid-summer had produced Ford's first film, *How Henry Ford Makes One Thousand Cars a Day.*[6]

No expense was spared in equipping and staffing the newly established Motion Picture Department. By the fall of 1914 the company's equipment and laboratories (which were operated on an assembly-line basis) were judged to be the equal of any motion-picture studio in the country. The staff of twenty-four persons included a half-dozen cameramen, whose assignments sent them ranging into every part of the civilized world.[7] Until 1916 the department's principal production was the Ford Animated Weekly, a ten- to fifteen-minute newsreel. A typical reel showed a fire, a race, German liners in the Hudson, John McGraw lecturing the Giants, pelicans in the Everglades, cars trying out a new rotary traffic system, and a trip through San Francisco's Chinatown. A Model T occasionally flitted through a scene, and subtitles were shown on a simulated T radiator. Otherwise there were no commercials. The newsreel was offered without charge to theaters and each week was viewed by more than 3,000,000 persons in 2,000 movie houses. The company estimated that the film was seen each week by 11.3 percent of the nation's movie audience, "a distribution, stated the *Ford Times,* "that any of the great exchanges might envy." Advertising men were agreed that the Ford newsreels were an excellent investment. "The viewer is entertained so interestingly," reported *Editor & Publisher,* "that he forgets that he is witnessing one of the cleverest advertising plans of these times."[8]

But the newsreels had one important drawback: by their very nature they were soon obsolete. This feature led Henry Ford to suggest in late 1916 that the department devote its attention to historical and educational films. The Ford Educational Weekly, believed to be the nation's first series of historical, geographical, travel, and educational films, was at first greeted with derision by producers and theater managers. "None of this dry, educational stuff for audiences," they were quoted as saying by the *Detroit News.* "Give 'em action, give 'em thrills, give 'em romance." Ford agreed that people did not want sterile educational films, but he insisted that the topics he had in mind would be fully as interesting as custard pie battles and the perils of Pauline. He was proved right week after week as such films as *Historical Boston, Canadian Rockies, Story of a Grain of Wheat, Petrified Forests of Arizona, Congo Basket-making, Harvesting Ice on the Hudson,* and *A Visit with Luther Burbank* proved to be as big drawing cards as the regular features. These films, like the newsreels which preceded them, were noncommercial, except for the line on the title frame, "Distributed by the Ford Motor Company." The Educational Weeklies were offered free to theaters until mid-1919, when the company asked exhibitors to pay twenty-five cents per film or a flat fee of one dollar a month to cover distribution costs.[9]

From 1917 to 1920 the Ford feature was shown each week in a minimum of 4,000 theaters and was seen by 5,000,000 persons, or one-seventh of the nation's weekly motion-picture audience. In addition, Ford films were given subtitles in eleven foreign languages and were shown in thousands of theaters outside the United States. By 1918 the Ford Company was the largest motion-picture distributor on earth. More than $600,000 was spent annually on film production and distribution, a phenomenal amount for its day and a figure which compares very favorably with present-day motion-picture budgets of the largest corporations.[10]

From 1916 to 1918 Ford films were distributed by "independent" picture exchanges. In late 1918 Ford engaged the Goldwyn Distributing Corporation to circulate the Educational Weekly among at least 7,000 theaters. By late 1919 the Goldwyn organization built circulation to a high-water mark of 5,238 theaters, but opposition from theater owners developed in mid-1920, when Ford adopted a policy of charging theaters one dollar a week to show the Ford feature. The fee was substantially less than prices charged by producers of comparable films, but exhibitors and trade publications howled. Although they had lauded Ford films when they were free (except for the distribution charge), they now complained that the company was impudent to expect the theaters to pay for "a clever form of subtle, indirect advertising." As a distressed Motion Picture Department staff member wrote Henry Ford two years later, "Good will vanished when Ford started to charge for the films."[11]

In addition, Ford films were banned in many theaters following attacks on Jews by Ford's magazine, the *Dearborn Independent,* starting in May 1920. In a series of ninety-two articles sanctioned by Ford, the *Independent* blamed Jews for many of the world's problems. The powerful Motion Picture Theatre Owners of New York State was only one of a number of trade associations which condemned the Ford series "on the ground that it foments racial animosity." Although there is no evidence that any of the Ford films contained anti-Semitic propaganda, the resentment created by the *Independent*'s tirade, accompanied by the opposition to the fee asked for the Weeklies, caused the company's film circulation to dwindle rapidly to 1,300 theaters by August 1920. The Educational Weekly was cancelled in December 1921 because of lack of interest on the part of theater managers.[12]

Meanwhile the company had introduced another film series, the Ford Educational Library, a collection of films for elementary, high school, and college level instructional use. Special films were prepared for a number of educational fields, including transportation, industry, agriculture, geography, geology, physics, medicine, zoology, safety, history, and civics. A committee of college professors aided in the selection of subjects to be filmed and edited certain productions. The films were sold to educational institutions for five cents per foot or rented for fifty cents a day per reel. More than fifty films were produced for the Educational Library between 1920 and 1925, and fifty-five Educational Weekly films were added to the Library when the older series became defunct.[13]

The Ford Motor Company aggressively promoted the Educational Library by advertising in national educational magazines, conducting direct mail campaigns among faculty members and school administrators, and enlisting dealers to establish local film libraries and to encourage the use of the films in their communities. Individual films and the program as a whole received considerable praise from the press and from such leaders of the motion picture industry as Will Hays, president of the Motion Picture Producers and Distributors Association of America.[14]

The Library, however, never received the widespread support of educational institutions, and only 100 films (valued at $3,750) were sold during the first three years of the program's operation. Perhaps too few schools, particularly the elementary and high schools, had the facilities to show movies. In addition, the purchase or rental of films was expensive, and it was made more so in 1922, when the purchase price was set at $50.00 per film and the rental rate was increased from $2.50 per week to $4.25 per week. C. R. Frede, who had replaced Jewett as head of the Department of Photography (successor to the Motion Picture Department) in 1919, naively thought that the financial problem could be solved if students sold copies of the *Dearborn Independent* or paid a ten-cent admission fee for each Ford movie they saw. Frede's plan was a failure, and by mid-1923 it had become apparent that the Educational Library would not be a successful business proposition. The company consequently discontinued active promotion of the program in late 1923, although the library continued in name until 1925. A number of its films continued to be made available, rent-free, throughout the 1920s.[15]

Some Ford executives probably cheered the discontinuance of the Educational Library. The company's Moving Picture Committee (composed of four branch managers and Jewett), the Executive Committee (which included the company's top-ranking executives), and most branch managers had, to be sure, enthusiastically supported the Animated Weekly and the Educational Weekly; but such men as P. E. Martin, head of manufacturing, and Hubert E. Hartman, assistant secretary and general attorney, both of whom at one time had charge of the Educational Library, "ranted and criticized" that program for not providing more direct advertising. "It doesn't help the sale of Ford cars," asserted Martin, who intimated early in 1921 that he would have abolished the program were it not for Henry Ford's "different" ideas on the subject.[16]

Ford management was agreed, however, that sales-promotion films were of definite value to the company. The first such films, *Keep the Boy on the Farm* and *Farm with a Fordson,* produced in 1920, were enthusiastically received by branch managers and dealers throughout the country. They were followed by nine additional tractor films during the next decade. Between 1921 and 1930 Ford also produced more than a score of films on other phases of the company's activities, ranging from the *Ford Way of Coal Mining* and the *Ford Way of Railroading* to *Romance of Making a Modern Magazine,* a *Dearborn Independent* promotion, and *Golden Opportunity,* which advertised the company's car purchase savings plan. The most sophisticated of the sales-promotion films was *The Ford Age,* an hour-long survey of Ford's mining, lumbering, and manufacturing operations, which was billed as "the highest attainment of the motion-picture photographer's art."[17]

Like Ford's earlier film ventures, the sales-promotion films attracted large audiences. They were shown to as many as 2,500,000 people a month during the mid-1920s, and monthly attendance always exceeded one million from April through October. Films were shown at a great variety of places: dealers' showrooms, churches, fraternal lodges, schools, recreation halls, luncheon clubs, county fairs, city parks, in the homes of prospective purchasers of Ford cars, and—in many small towns—on the side of a billboard or building.[18]

Ford films broke the monotony in the lives of many rural folk, who jounced into villages in their Model T's by the tens of thousands on the night of the week the "flickers" were to be shown. A Ford sales representative reported that in Pound, Wisconsin, a village of 400 population, more than 2,000 persons from the area saw sales films at the Ford dealership every Wednesday night. In Bridgeboro, New Jersey, a Ford agent showed films to an eager audience of 1,800 to 2,000 farmers every week in a grove near the dealership. Many of the branches and dealers kept specially-equipped Model T's and projectionists on the road showing sales-promotion films. "We've given more than 40 shows with an average of 200 to 250 on hand," reported the dealer at Silsbee, Texas, "and are creating good will by the bushel." Ford films were the first and only motion pictures many people had ever seen, a number of dealers reported. Especially strong emphasis was placed on reaching youthful audiences. Exhorting dealers to get the films into schools and recreation halls, a Ford publication pointed out that "Ford products will enjoy an immense advantage with the child or youth when he reaches the purchasing age if he is exposed to Ford films now."[19]

The Ford Motor Company was one of the first companies in the country to produce sales-promotion films with sound, recording the dialog on discs in as many as sixteen languages. The "talkies" were widely circulated until early 1931, when the novelty wore off. A year later the sound-on-film recording technique, ten times more costly than sound-on-disc, made the latter process obsolete. Ford, in the throes of the worst sales year in its history, decided to abandon its motion-picture laboratories. Until 1952, when a Motion Picture Department was re-established, Ford films were produced on a contract basis by outside agencies.[20]

3

Ford's foresight in producing films at an early date was matched by its initiative in presenting a striking demonstration of the mass assembly of automobiles at San Francisco's Panama-Pacific Exposition in 1915. The company, hoping to unveil this novel demonstration at the Michigan State Fair of 1914, constructed a building on the fairgrounds for this purpose. For some unexplained reason, perhaps because the technical problems were too numerous to be solved in the two months allocated for getting the building and equipment in order, the exhibition did not materialize. At the Panama-Pacific Exposition, from eighteen to twenty-five cars were produced during the three-hour period that the line functioned each day. The exhibit, easily the most popular industrial demonstration at the fair, received nation-wide publicity and was viewed by huge crowds. In recognition of its contribution to the success of the exposition, the exhibit was awarded a special gold medal by the fair's management.[21]

In addition to the assembly exhibit, Ford's Motion Picture Department showed films to thousands of spectators, and the Sociological Department demonstrated, by means of a "before and after" model village, the way in which the five-dollar day had improved the living standards of Ford employees. The three exhibits, which, according to the *New York Herald,* placed Ford "more in evidence" at the fair than any other company, were a reflection of Henry Ford's personal interest in fairs. In 1893 he had attended the World's Columbian Exposition in Chicago, where he saw an exhibit of a fire-fighting pump powered by a two-cylinder engine which convinced him that he could build a similar-type gasoline motor to provide motive power for a buggy. This experience deeply impressed Ford and undoubtedly contributed to the decisions which consistently made his company, from 1915 to 1940, one of the largest exhibitors at world's fairs and other leading expositions. Ford's displays, as might be expected, largely consisted of educational features. "If we do a good educational job," Ford told his associates, "who knows what effect it may have on some of these young people who come here? It may do something that will have great effect on the economy of the country."[22]

The educational approach which characterized Ford's films and exhibits was also carried out musically. Three years after introducing the "Ford March & Two-Step," the Ford Company, in 1911, organized a sixty-piece concert band at the Highland Park plant. This musical group frequently headed parades and played concerts before thousands of people at civic celebrations and fairs throughout the Midwest and Ontario. On a number of occasions the band toured Michigan and Ontario with organizations advocating good roads. In 1915, in conjunction with a week-long appearance at the San Francisco Fair, the Ford musicians toured eighteen midwestern and western states. On this trip the band gave concerts in twenty Ford branch plants and at scores of whistle-stops. Fargo, North Dakota, declared a civic holiday in honor of the band's appearance, and more than half of the city's 18,000 people attended a concert there. Four thousand people gathered around the Ford train in Butte, Montana, for a brief performance, and 35,000 people attended an outdoor concert in Seattle, the largest audience ever to attend a musical performance in that city. The band drew 25,000 persons at Portland, also a record-breaking audience, and played before 40,000 persons in Omaha. Altogether, the musicians entertained 350,000 persons while on the tour, exclusive of the large audiences at the San Francisco Fair. The Highland Park band also presented a concert series for Ford's Detroit-area employees, their families and friends during the 1920s and frequently broadcast over local radio stations.[23]

Encouraged by the success of the Highland Park band, most of Ford's branch plants also formed bands between 1915 and 1920. These units made numerous public appearances in their local areas. In the Detroit area several musical units supplemented the Highland Park band. The Ford Hawaiian Quintette, which Henry Ford "discovered" at the San Francisco Fair, was placed on the Ford payroll in 1915 and performed at many company and noncompany social gatherings. Bands were organized at three of the factories making up the new Rouge industrial complex. One of them, the Ford Eagle Builders' Saxophone Band, was formed in 1920 by Harry H. Bennett, an ex-sailor and former artist for Ford's Motion Picture Department who was responsible for plant protection at the Rouge. Bennett's star rose slowly but steadily, and from the mid-1930s, as Henry Ford's "personal man," he was to play a leading role in shaping the policies of the Ford Company.[24]

4

Several of the Ford Company's public relations policies and programs were shaped by Henry Ford's personal motto, "Help the Other Fellow," which was widely publicized and put into practice by the Ford organization during the half-dozen years after 1914. "Helping the other fellow," in Ford's view, did not mean that a destitute or handicapped person should be aided by conventional forms of charity. In fact, the industrialist regarded almost any kind of organized "alms-giving" as a dangerous crutch that, instead of helping a man to walk, would eventually destroy him. Consequently, he gave little or no money to organized charitable groups, and his company spent infinitesimal sums—ranging from $5,000 in 1912, 1914, and 1915 to $18,703.01 in 1918—for conventional philanthropic purposes.[25]

The way to help men, Ford believed with fervor, was to provide an opportunity for men to help themselves. This attitude was reflected in the industrialist's enlightened labor policies (including the five-dollar day) and humanitarian activities.

When the five-dollar-day plan went into operation, an order was issued to the employment office that no job hunter should be rejected because of his physical condition unless he was suffering from a contagious disease. In 1919, after a five-year trial of this policy, the company employed 9,563 persons with some kind of handicap—19.8 percent of all employees. One had lost both hands; four, both legs or feet; four more were totally blind; 123 had lost one hand or arm; 460 had only one good eye; thirty-seven were deaf and dumb; sixty were epileptics; 1,560 had hernias. Even men with mental illnesses were given safe jobs and ex-prostitutes were placed in departments where visitors were not allowed. Ford also employed from 400 to 600 ex-convicts, many of them parolees, during the 1914–20 period.[26]

Ford's liberal employment policies worked well, despite protestations on many sides. They also generated a great deal of favorable publicity for the company. When Henry Ford gave a job to a young Philadelphian who had forged the name, "Henry F. Ford, Jr.," to a $15.00 check, most of the nation's newspapers noted the manufacturer's generosity and recorded the relieved youngster's remark: "God bless Henry Ford for giving me another chance. . . . I will make good." The nation "fairly gasped" when Ford, appearing before the U.S. Commission on Industrial Relations, "guaranteed to take every prisoner out of Sing Sing and make a man of him." "Henry Ford," declared the *San Francisco Star* in an editorial typical of many, "is a businessman with a heart." Inevitably there were critics who carped that Ford's employment policies were a publicity trick arranged to cover dark abuses. An even greater number of commentators, however, were quick to retort that even if this were true, such policies benefited society.[27]

In 1914 Ford opened an English Language School at the Highland Park plant. In two years the school had an enrollment of 2,500 foreign- and native-born employees. Semiannual graduation ceremonies, in which more than thirty nationalities were represented, were held before thousands of spectators and were widely publicized in the Detroit press. In 1916 the industrialist started the Henry Ford Trade School, open to indigent teen-age boys who wished to acquire a trade. Begun with an enrollment of six youngsters, the school had a student body of 2,750 within a dozen years. The institution was often mentioned in news stories.[28]

The Henry Ford Hospital, on which the industrialist spent $11,167,024 in construction costs and subsidies between 1914 and 1926, belied Ford's oft-expressed opinion that he would have nothing to do with "organized charity"—at least when it was organized by somebody else. When a public campaign for building funds bogged down in 1914, Ford assumed full responsibility for financing construction of the hospital—even to the point of reimbursing the original donors the $600,000 they had contributed. After its completion Ford assumed responsibility for administering the institution and worked out a type of hospital different from that which had originally been contemplated. The institution was "closed"; that is, although any doctor could bring patients to the hospital, once inside, they could be treated only by staff physicians and surgeons. Furthermore, laborers and millionaires were charged the same amount for the same service.[29]

The Ford Hospital at once incurred the displeasure of the Detroit area medical fraternity, which for a time refused to admit Ford's physicians to the local medical association and complained of "unethical publicity." There perhaps was substance to the publicity charge, for Ford believed that the profession made a fetish of withholding information that belonged to the public and felt that news should be supplied about a hospital just as news was supplied about a factory. Accordingly, the public was told that in the sound-conscious Ford Hospital "doors close without as much as a click, signals flash but are not heard, elevators glide up and down noiselessly, and the noiseless typewriter is standard." News releases stated that "a volume could be written on the X-ray department only" and that the hospital had a machine "by which the air a person breathes can be measured and analyzed and the exact amount of oxygen absorbed determined." Ordinary instruments such as stethoscopes and microtomes—found in any well-conducted hospital—were glorified to the edification of the public. Many thought that Henry Ford had manned his hospital with medical geniuses and had installed marvelous and intricate equipment. The fact that Ford permitted certain of his bedridden employees to earn regular wages by screwing nuts on bolts by hand naturally created a stir and prompted innumerable rumors and jokes. The Ford Hospital was one of the best publicized medical institutions in America during the 'teens and 1920s, and it contributed considerably to Ford's worldwide reputation as a humanitarian.[30]

5

Another type of Ford publicity, one of the most unorthodox and certainly one of the most valuable, was the Ford joke, which flourished during much of the period in which the Model T was made. It is impossible to determine exactly the origins of the Ford joke. It may have been an offspring of the "automobile joke," which was a stock-in-trade of vaudeville performers after 1902. The Essex, the Saxon, and even the high-priced Pierce-Arrow were among the targets of comedians during the early automobile period. One gag that always brought a laugh at the Franklin's expense was the description of a buck-toothed girl: "She wouldn't be so bad-looking only she's got Franklin teeth—they're 'air-cooled.' "[31]

Another view, shared by Charles A. Brownell and a Wisconsin editor, was that the jokes were started "in the early days of the company" by competitors. "It's not a car," rival salesmen allegedly told potential buyers, "it's just a Ford." Credence is given this opinion by some of the company's 1907 advertising. "The Ford 4-cylinder ($600) runabout owes half its unparalleled popularity to the misrepresentation of jealous rivals," stated one advertisement, while another remarked: "Had you ever noticed that it is a weakness inherent in disciples to disparage their leader? Some makers affect to discount the achievements of FORD." Vanadium steel was criticized by many manufacturers, who, until the alloy was adopted as armor plating on American warships, predicted that Ford's "flimsy contraption" would soon fall apart. Some auto manufacturers carried on an organized "mud-slinging propaganda campaign" against the Model T. "The best wits were hired to write the material," averred the *Ft. Atkinson* (Wisconsin) *Union,* "and many were the editors who were caught by it. It came in a blank envelope, apparently from nowhere, and usually had concealed somewhere a thrust at the 'Tin Lizzie,' coupled with a cute story."[32]

Perhaps another source of the Ford joke was the Ford owner himself. Professor B. A. Botkin believed that the quips and gibes originated in the self-consciousness of the Ford owner, who, out of the desire to forestall or avert criticism, resorted to "the psychology of the defense mechanism." By joking about the car's smallness, its low price, and so on, the Ford owner "could laugh off any joshing the owner of a bigger and higher-priced car might be disposed to give him."[33]

The Model T itself, because of its very cheapness, versatility, and toughness, must have encouraged many Ford jokes. Almost everyone knew that more than half of the pieces that made up the Ford engine sold for ten cents or less. News stories frequently told of a stationary Model T providing power for motors which did everything from running newspaper presses and telephone exchanges to pumping water and exterminating gophers. The car's toughness was also widely discussed. A Texan had to abandon his T to escape Mexican bandits, who hacked and burned the car until it was a wreck. However, the owner returned and was able to drive the T away. Another Ford, although buried for six years in the muck of a California river bed, still had gas in the tank and ran "as good as new" after starting wires were installed. Still another true story concerned the Ford whose engine had been removed to pump water and whose body was drawn by a burro. The moral, as the press was quick to point out, was: "You may dissect a Ford, but you cannot kill it."[34]

Such stories made the public feel that almost anything was possible for a Model T—hence the countless jokes which, though bordering on the ridiculous, had a trace of plausibility about them. No doubt many of the people who invented or repeated Model T jokes fully shared the opinion expressed by Ida Tarbell in 1915: "I have never in all the world . . . seen so much to cause me to laugh and weep, to wonder and rejoice, as I have at the Ford."[35]

Advertisements of many Ford accessory manufacturers also generated Ford jokes. Whereas the Ford Company's advertisements proclaimed the Model T to be as flawless as any car made, gadget and accessory firms catering to T owners spent huge sums to convince the public that the car was far from perfect and that much better performing, easier riding, more powerful, and more economical Fords could be had by purchasing their devices. Ford owners were told that their cars drove like trucks and that a shock absorber would make them ride like Pullmans. They were assured that in buying a $2.50 crankcase support they would actually save $20.00, for otherwise the crankcase would surely break and entail a $22.50 repair bill. The difficulty of starting a Model T was emphasized in advertisements which suggested that old-fashioned blow torches should be replaced by special firetraps built into the intake manifold. Finally, every potential rattle in the Model T was publicized by the "anti-rattler" accessory firms, which marketed devices that fastened down offending Model T parts. Of course, like the offending parts of the T, the anti-rattlers themselves eventually worked loose and added to the clatter. It is doubtful that any industrial product in American history ever had its real and imaginary shortcomings so thoroughly advertised as had the Model T. That such publicity should inspire and add fuel to the Ford joke craze is hardly surprising.[36]

During their heyday, 1914 to 1920, Ford jokes were as much a part of everyday conversation as shop talk, sports gossip, or interest in the weather and were as commonly voiced over a glass of tea at a church social as over a glass of beer at the corner saloon. To vaudeville monologists they were the staff of life, to toastmasters a rock of refuge in time of need. Salesmen opened solicitations with them, clergymen pointed sermons with them, and physicians carried them as part of their pharmacopoeia of cheer. For half a dozen years, Ford jokes were fully as universal and innumerable as America's time-honored mother-in-law, Pat and Mike, and farmer's daughter jokes.[37]

Scores of Ford joke books, some of which sold in the tens of thousands, were published between 1915 and 1920. Most of them were cheap paperbacks hawked for five, ten, or fifteen cents. Some, however, featured contributions by the nation's leading humorists and cartoonists, including Ring Lardner, Irvin S. Cobb, Bud Fisher, Chic Jackson, and H. T. Webster.[38]

Ford jokes followed several patterns. Perhaps the most numerous were those whose point derived from the Model T's diminutiveness: postmen were reportedly concerned over the rumor that T's were to be delivered by mail; the garbage collector complained of the difficulty of sorting dead cats, broken bottles, and Fords; a patron of a large department store who asked for tires for his T was cheerfully directed to the "Rubber Band Department." The Model T's loose-jointed qualities inspired innumerable "rattle and shake" jokes: Henry Ford reputedly was a better evangelist than Billy Sunday because he had shaken hell out of more people than Sunday ever saw; a Ford owner, asked if his car always made a racket, innocently replied, "Oh no, only when it's running."[39]

The general belief that Fords were made wholly of tin provided the theme for the "Tin Lizzie" jokes: "What time is it when one Ford follows another? Tin after tin"; the Ford Company planned to produce cars without doors, but would furnish can openers; a man hitched his dog to his balky flivver and then was arrested for tying a tin can to a dog; a farmer, knowing that the Ford Company needed lots of tin, shipped a battered tin roof to Detroit, and later received a letter stating, "While your car was an exceptionally bad wreck, we shall be able to complete repairs and return it by the first of the week." Another type of joke referred to the T's social inferiority: "Why is a Ford like a bathtub? Because you hate to be seen in one"; a Ford reportedly ran over a chicken, which got up saying, "cheep, cheep, cheep"; Henry Ford, when offered $1.50 after repairing a farmer's stalled car, refused, saying that he had all the money he wanted. "You're a liar," retorted the farmer, "because if you had plenty of money you'd take some of it and buy yourself an 'automobile.' "[40]

Counterbalancing the Ford jokes which cast aspersions upon the Model T were those which were testimonials to the car's sturdy dependability: a man wanted to have his Ford buried with him, for it had always gotten him out of every hole he had ever been in; owners of Cadillacs, Pierce-Arrows, and Packards carried Fords in their tool boxes to pull the big cars out of the mire when they bogged down; a Ford was like a motion to adjourn—because it was always in order; a Model T left the assembly plant without an engine, but ran for a month anyway—on its reputation.

Other Ford jokes—inspired by mass production, the five-dollar day, the fifty-dollar rebate, and other departures from convention—complimented the Ford Company. In order to avoid fire risks, according to one story, the company was shipping its cars in crates of asbestos, since each came from the assembly line so fast that the metal was still smoking; although two flies could "manufacture" 48,876,552,154 new flies in six months, they did not have anything on two Ford factories; a worker on the Ford assembly line dropped his wrench, and before he could pick it up twenty Model T's had passed by him; the company planned to retail its cars at grocery stores and would paint them yellow, rather than black, so that they could be hung outside and sold in bunches like bananas.[41]

Most Ford owners enjoyed hearing Ford jokes and were among the more inveterate spinners of them. Even if some of the puns rubbed them the wrong way, "they could," as one of the Ford joke books pointed out, "always pat their pocketbook, let in the clutch, and ride serenely on their way, proud of their possession and confident of their good judgment." There were, however, Ford owners who never reconciled themselves to the incessant jesting. In 1920 a long-suffering Englishman, in a widely reprinted letter to a British motor publication, expressed the anguish that this dissident minority had experienced over the years:

> In our opinion it is quite time that we Fordists should strongly protest against the jokes and insults which have been hurled at us. . . . For years we have been the stock joke of the vermillion proboscis tinted "comedian"; sneered at by the nut whose sole ambition in life soared to the height of his socks matching his coachwork, and the glossiness of his hair equaling a seal emerging from the water; held in contempt by the chauffeur of a big "six," doubtless because a Ford has passed him on the hill; treated with brusqueness by many a garage man—such has been the experience of most of us.
>
> I took delivery of my earliest Ford ten years ago and at the first garage at which I stopped I was strongly advised to have fitted a tray under the chassis. Innocently I asked the reason. "So that it will pick up the nuts," came the reply. I have lost count of the number of times people have told me that they would not be found dead on a Ford.
>
> But what angers me most is when we are classed as a God-forsaken, poverty-stricken lot. "He has to put up with a Ford because he cannot spring enough to buy a car." That is what I frequently hear. Could anything be more insulting? Could anything be more remote from the truth?
>
> Many a Fordist could buy up a majority of these revilers; many a Fordist is their intellectual superior; many a Fordist possesses more gentleness and character. Therefore, should these lines reach the eye of a Ford scoffer, I will tell him plainly that he is a snob. And a snob of the worst order.[42]

A special form of Ford joke was the Lizzie Label, which, painted on flivvers, was at its height during the early and mid-1920s. The Lizzie Label flourished particularly in college communities, especially the homes of state universities, normal schools, and agricultural colleges, which recruited the small-town smart aleck and country clown and were abundantly supplied with dilapidated Model T's. The exact origin of the Lizzie Label is obscure, but Professor B. A. Botkin, who made a detailed study of the subject, believes that they were greatly popularized by *Judge,* a widely-quoted satirical weekly, which raised the folk product to the dignity of humorous literature by paying five dollars for the best of them.

Like Ford jokes, Lizzie Labels had certain discernible patterns. Many of them were borrowed quotations, such as "Abandon hope, all ye who enter in" and "I do not choose to run." Others were familiar sayings: "Barnum was right," "Our boozem friend," "The answer to a maiden's prayer." One category parodied song, play, and movie titles and advertising slogans: "I ain't got no body" (on stripdowns), "I wonder how I look when I'm asleep," "Instead of a treat," "Made walking a pleasure." Some were in the form of notices: "Girls wanted—apply at side door," "Quiet please, violent ward" (on hood), "Night calls by appointment only." Another theme was the wisecrack: "Follow us, farmer, for haywire," "Welcome blondes, six to sixty," "You may pass me, bigboy, but I'm paid for," "Heck of the Resperus." Sex was perhaps the most prevalent Lizzie Label theme: "Girls, watch your step-ins," "Chickens' coop," and "For fastidious flappers" were among the least crude of the innumerable labels with sexual connotations.[43]

Advertising men constantly were asked whether the Ford joke helped or hindered Model T sales. Until the early 1920s most of them agreed that "every knock was a boost" and that unquestionably the publicity made the car all the more popular. When asked to place a valuation on the company's stock as of 1913, a New York investment banker testified in 1927 that the jokes were "an important asset" of the firm and that any manufacturer, if he had a sense of humor, would have welcomed them. Many newspaper editorials echoed this view. "The jokes were capitalized by Henry Ford," observed the *New York Times,* "and millions of dollars fell into the hands of the man who was the object of all the raillery." The industrialist was delighted with the jokes, and, according to Brownell, told more of them than any man in the country (his favorite was the one about the man who wanted to have his T buried with him, so that he could get out of the hole). Some publications, knowing that Ford had a fresh joke for every reporter who came into view, even credited him with having concocted the best of them during his leisure moments. Toastmasters invariably bantered the Model T at banquets at which Ford was a guest, and no one enjoyed the witticisms more than the industrialist. He did not, however, as rumor often had it, subsidize the publication of Ford joke books, although he often made a considerable show of buying them from hawkers. "The jokes about my car sure help to popularize it," Ford once remarked. "I hope they never end."[44]

After the early 1920s, however, as the Chevrolet, Dodge, Hudson-Essex, and Willys-Overland moved rapidly to the fore and the Model T became an anachronism, the Ford joke boomeranged too frequently to be considered an asset. Now Ford owners realized that their critics were in dead earnest and fewer of them could laugh it off when someone asked, "Why is a Model T like an affinity?" [*affinity* was often used as a synonym for *mistress* in the 1920s] and volunteered the reply, "Because you hate to be seen on the streets with one." The nationwide Keith-Albee vaude-ville organization, perhaps the country's leading arbiter of street-corner humor, issued a mandate that Ford jokes, because they were not funny anymore, were to be barred from the stage. Advertising experts also sensed the change and suggested that Ford ought to advertise "to give the T prestige and to take the joke out of the car." A number of Ford executives, including Edsel Ford, agreed, and in 1923 the company resumed advertising on a massive scale, aggressively publicizing the T as "a quality product" with "a high social standing."[45]

For practical purposes the Ford joke died with the Model T. The Model A, introduced in December 1927, was too highly regarded stylistically and mechanically to lend itself to humor. "With her," observed the *New York Sun,* "he who goes to josh remains to praise." The Ford joke has never completely died out, however. In 1953, an owner of a 1908 Model T was fined for speeding. His widely publicized courtroom comment was in keeping with the Lizzie tradition: "It was only hitting on three. If it had been hitting on all four I doubt if you would have caught me."[46]

6

In the realm of paid advertising, for nearly a decade after 1914 the Ford Company—following a policy established in 1910—related expenditures (or the absence of them) directly to the number of Model T orders in hand. Thus on February 13, 1915, Brownell, echoing Harper's views of five years' before, wrote to branch managers, "Today, we have instructed our advertising agency to wire immediate discontinuance of all Ford advertising. This is done because we are now from 40,000 to 50,000 cars behind orders, and it is simply a waste to continue advertising when production is behind." Similar messages went to the branches in May and November 1915. National magazines were virtually dropped from the advertising schedule after 1914, and motor magazines were omitted starting in 1916. That year, the company spent only $6,000 on paid advertising, virtually all of it for tiny newspaper ads.[47]

In early 1917 the company discontinued paid advertising and bought not a line of space (except in behalf of tractors and Lincoln cars) until 1923. Henry Ford's attitude toward paid advertising was perhaps the primary reason for this policy. Like many manufacturers with a mechanical background, including John Dodge and Walter P. Chrysler, Ford felt that most advertising was unnecessary. He conceded that advertising was "absolutely essential to introduce good, useful things," but argued that it was "an economic waste" for products already on the market. "If you really have a good thing," the manufacturer often pointed out, "it will advertise itself." He also liked to say that "our best advertising is free advertising" and that he would rather have a news story on the front page than a paid campaign. Advertising men found themselves at a loss to refute Ford on this point, for, as *Printers' Ink* lamented in 1926, the manufacturer had for years found it "a simple matter to break into the front pages of newspapers almost at will." Of course, it was a moot question how helpful Ford's personal publicity was in selling cars. *Printers' Ink,* whose view naturally was not a detached one, believed that such publicity was largely worthless, for it "does not tell the full story of the Ford car to buyers" or "firmly fix it in the consciousness of the buying public." Other authorities, however, were convinced that the Model T profited from the industrialist's publicity and, indeed, owed a considerable portion of its success to the fact that the name "Ford" was constantly appearing in headlines.[48]

Ford himself had tremendous respect for the power of the press, and he had a marvelous aptitude for harnessing that power. At the time of the five-dollar day he remarked, "I am setting an example and trusting to the newspapers to do the rest. Publicity is the greatest power in the world." Just before the peace ship sailed, he told reporters, "I pin my faith in the press of the United States. . . . I have made it a point in all my dealings to take the public into my confidence through the newspapers." As he launched his advertising campaign for President Wilson in 1916, he told the press, "I am going to use you fellows—I mean you newspapermen—and the newspapers. I am strong for printers' ink. You can do almost anything with publicity." And again in 1925, following the first commercial flight of his trimotor airplane: "We are going to take the public into our confidence in this thing. It's so big that everybody will be interested." Such statements indicate that Ford was much impressed with the importance of the printed word and placed heavy reliance on publicity in attaining his objectives, whether sympathy for a peace expedition or sale of an automobile.[49]

The chief reason that the company could afford to forego advertising for six years was the strong demand for the Model T during this period. The T enjoyed a seller's market even before America entered World War I, and production cutbacks during the conflict contributed to a shortage of Fords well into 1920. Sales fell off rather alarmingly during the winter of 1920–21, but bounced back so vigorously in the spring of 1921 that the company had to strain its productive capacity for two years in order to meet the unprecedented demand. The situation was embarrassing to advertising men, "some of whom," said *Printers' Ink,* "would have felt inclined to chip in if Ford had passed the hat, just to get away from the task of trying to answer reactionaries who pointed to Ford's nonadvertising success."[50]

The fact was, however, that although the Ford Company did not advertise, its dealers did. Indeed, the mercurial Henry Ford, despite his protestations that advertising was "an economic waste" (at least for the Ford Motor Company when demand was high) required dealers to advertise under the terms of their contracts. For many years the agents had placed their advertising on an individual basis, but in late 1916, at the company's suggestion, they began "clubbing together" in the larger cities. Full-page ads, listing dealers' names at the bottom of the page, appeared in metropolitan newspapers. The expense was prorated according to the number of cars sold by each agent. A number of dealers balked at this policy, claiming that Ford was using them "to pay its bills." Others, because they thought the investment was sensible as well as necessary, went along without objection. From 1917 to 1923 dealers advertised at the annual rate of $3,000,000, a figure which, in the company's view, placed Ford among the nation's largest advertisers. Strictly speaking, the company itself spent only a few thousand dollars a year to supply matrices and electrotypes to dealers who would use them.[51]

Ordinarily the company did not concern itself with the dealers' choice of media or copy appeals. Ford did insist, however, that its trademarked signature, the famous Ford script which had served the company continuously from 1903, should be used in all advertising. Also, the parent firm strongly reprimanded dealers who resorted to unfair types of advertising. Referring to an advertisement which showed a competitor's broken down car over the caption, ''Sell it and buy a Ford,'' Brownell angrily told the branch managers, ''This is an unwholesome type of advertising which has long since been taboo, and we certainly feel that Ford dealers have enough good things to say about our cars without knocking the other fellow.''[52]

The Ford Company retained two advertising agencies between 1914 and 1917. The MacManus Company, which later conducted memorable campaigns for Dodge, Cadillac, Maxwell, and Chrysler, served Ford in 1914; and Power, Alexander & Jenkins Advertising Agency was retained for the next two years. Brownell served as Ford's advertising manager from August 1914 until December 1920, although after 1916 his chief responsibilities were publications and sales promotion. Brownell was among the first of the Ford executives to be fired in the ''purge'' accompanying the sales slump of 1920–21.[53] The cause of his dismissal is not altogether clear. His ability was never questioned and he was exceptionally popular among company associates and dealers, all of whom affectionately called him ''Dad.'' Furthermore, he was sincerely devoted to Henry Ford and his ideals of service. ''No man ever had a greater admiration for Mr. Ford,'' observed Dean Marquis, ''no one ever had more faith in him.''[54] Between January 1921 and August 1923, when a new manager and an agency were appointed, direct responsibility for the company's advertising was assumed by William A. Ryan, who had replaced Norval Hawkins as sales manager in late 1918.[55]

7

If the Ford Company's advertising policies were perhaps more erratic, its advertising expenditures more parsimonious than those of any other major consumer firm during the 'teens, its public relations policies were more advanced and its programs more expensive than those of other concerns. Moreover, Ford's public relations activities probably reached more people than did those of other firms. The company's $50.00 rebate personally affected hundreds of thousands of Americans; its films, publications, exhibits, and band concerts reached many millions more. In addition, a torrent of publicity—ranging from articles on the labor and consumer profit-sharing plans and the company's net income to stories on the Model T and on Henry Ford—acquainted vast number of Americans with the Ford organization and its ubiquitous product.

In fact, the Ford Company was the best publicized business firm in the country in the half-dozen years following the introduction of the five-dollar day. In the periodical press the company received more than twice as much publicity as any other business institution; more than the rest of the automobile industry plus United States Steel, General Electric, Du Pont, American Telephone and Telegraph, and Standard Oil of New Jersey combined.

Newspapers undoubtedly gave the Ford Company a comparable amount of attention. Even the *New York Times,* with its relatively greater interest in New York-based companies, gave Ford more publicity than any other business organization except the New York Central and Pennsylvania railroads and United States Steel. Furthermore, Ford's publicity, in contrast, for example, to the space devoted to Big Steel's dissolution hearings or the New York Central's troubles over hauling rights and taxes, was almost all favorable. Within a few years after 1914 this publicity had given the auto firm a reputation "as the greatest single enterprise yet reared on the face of the globe." [56] Even so, the Ford Company's fame did not reach its zenith until the 1920s, when the firm's reputation and prestige attained heights perhaps never before or since equaled by a business institution.

8

During the half-dozen years after 1914, Henry Ford was one of the most publicized individuals in the world. In Great Britain, where he received even more publicity than W. E. "Pussyfoot" Johnson, the celebrated prohibitionist, Ford was dubbed "Henry the Conqueror" by the London press. South Africans knew more about him than about any other American, and a group of large landowners in that country predicted he could become "czar of South Africa" within five years should he wish to take up residence there. In America, only four persons, Woodrow Wilson, Charles Evans Hughes, William Jennings Bryan, and Theodore Roosevelt, received more press attention than Ford during the period from 1914 to 1920. The industrialist got twice as much publicity as John D. Rockefeller, Sr., and John D. Rockefeller, Jr., who, next to Ford, were America's best-publicized businessmen, and he received five times as much publicity as either Mary Pickford or Charlie Chaplin, the nation's best-known entertainers. [57]

Everything that Ford did or said was news. Reporters and writers lounged outside his office door, camped at the gates of his estate, and swarmed about him during his travels. In 1920, a relatively poor year for Ford publicity, more than 150 newsmen formally sought to interview the manufacturer. Only a handful were successful; after 1914, except when Ford himself wanted to generate publicity for a special purpose, he was virtually inaccessible to most newsmen. The occasional reporter who by stealth or sheer good luck happened to stumble into an interview with Ford often devoted as much space to telling how he obtained the interview as to the content of the discussion itself. [58]

The buffer between Ford and the press was Ernest Liebold, whom newsmen disliked as much for the way he said "No!" to their entreaties as for the fact that he said it at all. Occasionally Liebold showed a friendly side to newsmen, some of whom he took the trouble to thank for articles which he regarded as especially complimentary to Ford. For the most part, however, the secretary, described by associates as a Prussian type, antagonized the press with his brusque heavy-handedness. Newsmen reciprocated Liebold's treatment of them and magnified his every real or imagined mistake in an attempt to embarrass him. Apparently they succeeded, for in 1921 Liebold was sufficiently exasperated to confide to a friend, "I have long ago learned that one cannot associate with newspapermen without being stung. It has happened so often with me that I find no further enjoyment in their company." [59]

Ford, for his part, was aware of the way Liebold treated the press and approved of it. "When you hire a watchdog," he told one employee who remonstrated that Liebold was alienating the press, "you don't hire him to like everybody that comes to the gate." Ford, in addition, was himself wary of reporters. "They're all a bunch of skunks," he once told an aide, "and you know what happens to people who play with skunks." Thus Liebold was only carrying out Ford's wishes. "People who do not understand," observed Dean Marquis, "blame [Liebold] for making this man of the people so inaccessible. But his secretary is to be praised for the thoroughness with which he does the work assigned him. A Chesterfield might suggest that which here and there would add grace and charm to the manner in which the job is handled but he certainly could do nothing to raise the present standard of efficiency.[60]

Liebold was virtually the only person authorized to arrange interviews for Ford until about 1920. By this time, however, a number of extracurricular assignments, including supervision of the Henry Ford Hospital, the *Dearborn Independent,* a housing development for Ford employees, and the purchase of a railroad, mines, forests, and hydroelectric sites, made it impossible for Liebold to devote as much attention to Ford's personal press relations as he had in earlier years. At the same time, William J. Cameron, who had become well acquainted with Ford and his views through authorship of "Mr. Ford's Own Page" in the *Dearborn Independent,* assumed an increasingly important role as the manufacturer's press relations representative, arranging for and sitting in on interviews and clearing manuscripts. By the mid-1920s, Cameron tacitly had complete charge of Ford's personal public relations, which meant, of course, that indirectly he had a considerable influence on the company's public relations policies as well.[61]

Ford did not, however, allow aides to arrange all his interviews with newsmen. From the time he achieved national fame until the end of his career, Henry Ford had certain favorites among the press corps, men and women to whom he generally was accessible and to whom he gave exclusive stories. Many of them were in his good graces for only a few months or a few years, while others were held in high esteem for two or three decades. The first of "Ford's white-haired boys," as they were known in Detroit press circles, were Ralph L. Yonker of the *Detroit Journal* and Theodore Delavigne of the *Detroit Free Press.* Yonker became acquainted with Ford in 1914 when he called at the manufacturer's home for a story. Told by a servant that Ford was not at home, the reporter turned away, only to be called back by Ford himself. After a stroll in the garden, the unpredictable Ford gave Yonker his unlisted telephone number. For months the *Journal* reporter was the one man in Detroit's newspaper row who could reach Ford directly at any time. Delavigne became well acquainted with Ford during the industrialist's 1915 pacifist campaign and resigned from the *Free Press* to become Ford's peace propagandist.[62]

Among Detroit's newspaper executives, Ford was most friendly with Edwin Pipp, editor of the *Detroit News,* who served as the manufacturer's informal public relations counselor during much of the period between 1915 and 1918. Two New York newspaper executives, Edward A. Rumely, of the *Evening Mail,* and Arthur Brisbane, editorial head of the Hearst organization, also were close to the industrialist. Ford first knew Rumely as an inventor and head of a private preparatory school in Indiana in 1909–10. Rumely acquired the *Mail* in 1915, and for several years thereafter Ford gave him exclusive stories and authorized him to release announcements to the New York press.[63] In 1916 Rumely introduced Ford to Brisbane, who undoubtedly did more to enhance Ford's popularity among the masses than any other newspaperman. The editor's column, "Today," appearing in all the Hearst newspapers and read by one-third of the American population, spoke again and again of Ford in the most favorable terms. Brisbane sincerely thought that Ford was flawless, except for his anti-Semitic views, which Brisbane deplored. The editor, in his column and on the lecture platform frequently referred to Ford, along with Washington and Lincoln, as "one of the three most useful men in American history." Insisting that Ford "is trusted more than any other man in the United States, and has more friends and followers," Brisbane also expressed the view that the manufacturer should be elected to the presidency.[64]

Of course, Brisbane's high regard for Ford and the favors he extended the manufacturer were not altogether without reciprocation. Ford often boosted Brisbane's prestige with such statements as "Brisbane is a great writer. Everybody ought to read his column. He writes what I like to read." The manufacturer also gave the Hearst official exclusive material whenever he came to Dearborn. The mere fact that Brisbane could interview Ford almost at will (although he was careful not to overextend his welcome) was of considerable worth to the Hearst organization, particularly during the 1920s, when an interview with Ford often had as much news value as a talk with the President. The industrialist also directed extra advertising into newspapers which Brisbane managed, gave buses and cars to the editor, and occasionally provided manpower for his farm.[65]

During the late 'teens, the 1920s, and the early 1930s, two Detroit reporters, William C. Richards of the *Free Press* and James Sweinhart of the *News,* were Ford favorites. For years Ford would see one of them one day, the other the next day, and to each he might give an exclusive story which he would not mention to the other. In his excellent biography, *The Last Billionaire: Henry Ford,* Richards bewailed the insecurity of reporters assigned to the Ford beat: "A little pompous in my nearness to the fountainhead, I imagined that I was riding some of the clouds with him [Ford], but they were filmy and insubstantial—and my edge always gave way, of course, tumbling me back to earth to watch Mr. Ford float by . . . no reporter ever could be sure of waking in the morning and not finding that a rival had skinned the pants off him." Richards resigned from the *Free Press* to enter the advertising business in 1935, and Sweinhart left the *News* a year earlier to join N. W. Ayer & Son, Inc., Ford's advertising agency. While with Ayer, Sweinhart wrote booklets, briefly edited the *Ford Almanac* (a sales-promotion brochure prepared for farmers), and saw to it that Cameron, the commentator on the Ford Sunday Evening Hour, was sober enough to go on the air every week. Sweinhart switched from Ayer to McCann-Erickson, Inc., when the latter agency assumed responsibility for the Sunday Evening Hour late in 1940. After the program was canceled in 1942, he returned to the *News.*[66]

Among the news-service executives closest to Ford were Karl A. Bickel, general news manager and later president of the United Press, and David J. Wilkie, automotive editor of the Associated Press. Bickel, who was based in New York, was for many years the only United Press representative who was able to get along with Liebold. Half a dozen United Press reporters were assigned to the Ford beat; but Liebold sent them packing, one after another. "It just seems we have never been able to get together," Liebold explained to Bickel, who despite repeated protests against what he considered discrimination against his men, never got a better reason for Liebold's attitude toward them. Bickel, consequently, had to devote a good deal of his own time to covering Ford's activities, and for a number of years his correspondence with Henry Ford's office was greater than Ford's correspondence with the rest of the press combined. Wilkie, who began interviewing Ford as early as 1923, was given a number of exclusive stories in the early 1940s, a fact which caused considerable anguish among United Press and International News Service news executives.[67]

Ford's favorite newspaperwoman was Anne O'Hare McCormick, of the *New York Times,* who interviewed the manufacturer a number of times and whose stories occasionally inspired Ford to send her congratulatory letters. The press favorite who stood highest in Ford's esteem during the last few years of his career was Merrill C. Meigs, a long-time Hearst executive, who had been introduced to Ford by Brisbane in 1931. Ford and Meigs shared a common interest in antiquarian and agricultural pursuits, and during World War II Meigs's status with Ford was such that he was one of the few persons privileged to enter the company's executive dining room as an uninvited guest.[68]

Most of Ford's publicity did not, of course, emanate from his press favorites; it was prepared by reporters and editors who seldom, if ever, interviewed him. To the new messiah, never standing still for his halo, it did not matter where the publicity came from—as long as it came.

PART III
The High Plateau (1920-32)

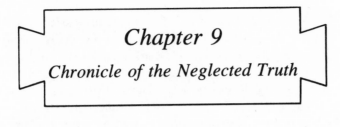

Chapter 9
Chronicle of the Neglected Truth

1

From 1919 to 1927 Henry Ford published a weekly magazine, the *Dearborn Independent*. During most of this period the *Independent*'s nationwide circulation exceeded a quarter of a million; from 1923 to 1927 it topped the half-million mark.[1] The publication disseminated among this considerable body of Americans many of Ford's views—most notoriously, his anti-Semitism. The *Independent*'s attacks on Jews have cost the Ford Company untold millions of dollars worth of sales, and have been a source of embarrassment to the firm and one of its leading public relations problems for several decades.

Two considerations motivated Ford to publish a personal journal. In the first place, the criticism given the five-dollar day, the ridicule showered upon the peace ship, and the denunciation of his pacifism by the *Chicago Tribune* and other militant sheets had caused him to think of creating his own editorial organ, even before the United States entered the war. The bitter allegations leveled against Ford during the 1918 senatorial campaign, particularly the attacks on his son, Edsel, strengthened the industrialist's desire for a defense agency against that part of the press which he believed was bent on misinterpreting his opinions and attitudes. Secondly, Ford thought that he had something important to say. "I am very much interested in the future, not only of my own country, but of the whole world," he stated when announcing his publishing plans, "and I have definite ideas and ideals that I believe are practical for the good of all, and intend giving them to the public without having them garbled, distorted, or misrepresented."

Late in 1918 Ford purchased the *Dearborn Independent,* a typical country newspaper, and installed E. G. Pipp and Fred L. Black, with whom Ford had discussed his journalistic plans in 1916, as editor and business manager, respectively. Pipp had an understanding with Ford that he would have complete editorial control of the magazine, with one exception: Liebold, who was named general manager of the publication, was to have responsibility for "Mr. Ford's Own Page," a weekly feature on which Ford would collaborate with William J. Cameron.[2]

The announcement of Ford's publishing intentions evoked wide comment. A number of newspapers could not restrain themselves from remarking that "as a newspaperman Ford will be a great manufacturer of flivvers," but the majority of press observers expressed approval of Ford's publishing venture. The *Detroit Times* typically commented: "Move over please, and make a place for Henry Ford on the editorial tripod. The new volunteer is thrice welcome. If he does as much good with his journal of civilization as he has with his factories, bank, school, farm, and hospital, the world will be better for his 'hunch' that he ought to have a newspaper.'' Several trade organs also predicted that ''Mr. Ford's genius may be counted upon to show itself'' in the advertising, printing, and distribution aspects of the new venture.[3]

The first issue of the *Independent* under Ford's auspices appeared on January 11, 1919, sixteen large pages of calendered paper, five cents a copy, a dollar a year. In appearance it was a weak, hybrid adaptation of the *Saturday Evening Post, Collier's,* and *Harper's Weekly;* its numerous illustrations tended to be muddy; its layout was crowded. There was no advertising, as Ford did not want to take a chance on having his journal influenced in any way by commercial considerations, nor did he care to advertise products to which he was opposed (tobacco, alcohol) or whose value was questionable (patent medicines). The publication was not a medium for publicizing the Ford enterprises; in fact, much to the regret of Pipp and other staff members who looked upon Ford stories as circulation builders, the industrialist insisted that the magazine scrupulously avoid comment on himself or the company. Editorially, the *Independent,* with its antiprofiteer, antimonopoly, antireactionary articles (it was a staunch supporter of Wilsonian ideals of postwar reconstruction at home and abroad), had the flavor of a muckraking periodical ten years after muckraking went out of fashion.[4]

Scores of newspapers and magazines commented on the *Independent*'s debut. A few publications, notably those which had made arrangements with Ford and Pipp to republish certain articles, were favorably disposed toward the weekly. Most press reviews, however, described the *Independent* as dull; ''as tranquil as a peace ship upon a painted ocean . . . the *Oscar II* of the becalmed journalistic main.'' Commentators inevitably compared the enterprise with what the publisher had accomplished in other realms. ''He has led always,'' reported the *Detroit Times,* ''but he is not now a pathfinder; he is just a humble follower. The role doesn't fit the genius of Ford.''[5]

Despite Ford's earlier announcement that he was willing to spend $10,000,000, if need be, to finance the publication, a number of editors humorously dismissed the magazine as another of Ford's whims. ''It is not true,'' reported the *New York Herald,* ''that old Ford parts or tires will be accepted as payment for subscriptions.'' Noting that the publication's offices and plants were located in Ford's tractor factory, the *Detroit Times* referred to the magazine as ''the best periodical ever turned out by a tractor plant,'' and another Detroit publication called it the ''Weekly Flivver'' and the ''tin weekly'' of journalism. ''It has already served a humane purpose,'' added the editor of the *Detroit Times,* ''in making it possible for Editor Pipp to conduct a fresh air experiment for the benefit of a portion of the Detroit News staff . . . the ozone is sweet where rolls the Rouge, and there is no such advertising in the Dearborn Independent as the News workers were thrown in contact with, often before they had time to adjust their gas masks. Whatever betides journalistically in Dearborn, it is a beautiful back-to-unblemished-nature adventure for the staff.''[6]

''Mr. Ford's Own Page,'' a collection of epigrams and articles based on such views of the industrialist as, ''Opportunity will not overlook you because you wear overalls,'' ''Any place is a good place to start from,'' ''We are in great need of new developments in industry to-day,'' and ''The man who sees is master,'' brought mixed reviews. *Life* thought the page "very good reading, interesting, agreeable and considerably wise" and predicted that Ford with his personal contribution "could carry his paper on his own shoulders"; but most editors were unimpressed with Ford's efforts, dismissing his epigrams, which were nationally syndicated for a time, as "trite truths."[7]

On the strength of the publicity surrounding the new venture, the *Independent* had between 40,000 and 50,000 subscriptions before publication of its first edition. Even so, and in spite of a series of vigorous promotional efforts, including solicitation of new Ford employees and all persons listed in the telephone books of several metropolitan centers, circulation increased only to 56,688 during the first year of publication. Ford's loss for this year was $284,000. The colorless magazine continued to lose ground during early 1920, its circulation dipping to 26,000 by March 13.[8]

By the fall of 1919 it had become evident to the staff that major changes would have to be made in the magazine's editorial policy if it were to become a journalistic force. However, only Joseph J. O'Neill, ex-member of the Mount Clemens News Bureau, offered a striking alternative to the status quo. Pipp, who believed that the solution to the *Independent*'s problem lay in serving to the public "fiction in large quantities and information in small quantities," proposed to sponsor a fiction contest. Liberal prizes were to be offered and two of the better stories were to be published in each week's edition. The proposal, which hardly seemed imaginative enough to have turned the magazine into a best-seller, was turned down by Liebold, who at this time was opposed to "outside" contributors. A staff conference on the subject of editorial content produced only the recommendation that the magazine "keep in the closest sort of touch with the great national and international events of the day."[9]

O'Neill, on the other hand, after "a careful and exhaustive study of the reasons the *Independent* is not a success," prepared a fourteen-page report which was full of constructive criticism. He correctly pointed out that the publication lacked plan, coherence, and force; that it stood for little. Henry Ford's name was not emphasized, he complained, the staff lacked cooperation, the headlines were dull, the fiction lackluster, there were no big name writers, and the foreign correspondence was of mediocre quality. Above all, he was displeased with the publication's failure to live up to its promise to be "fearless and independent," to be "the chronicler of the neglected truth." Pointing out that the *Independent*'s antiadvertising policy and Ford's financial backing offered the publication a unique opportunity for crusading, O'Neill again and again insisted that the magazine should "find an evil to attack, go after it and stay after it . . . name names, and tell actual facts." He added: "PUSSY-FOOTING and being afraid to hurt people will keep us just where we are if not send us further down the ladder. . . . If we get and print the right sort of stuff, ONE SINGLE SERIES may make us known to millions. A succession of series of FEARLESS, TRUTHFUL, INTERESTING, PLAIN-SPOKEN articles, if properly handled . . . will make a lasting reputation. . . . LET'S HAVE SOME SENSATIONALISM." O'Neill conceded that crusading might offend some people. "But shouldn't we offend people?" he asked. "If we are going to tell only *pleasant* truths, we might as well consolidate with the *Christian Herald*. If this magazine is ever going to get anywhere at all, it will have to FIGHT.''[10]

2

O'Neill's report furnished the format, if not the subject matter, for the notorious ninety-one-week anti-Semitic campaign launched by the *Independent* on May 22, 1920. As to what moved the magazine to single out Jews for attack, there are a number of theories. One thesis, vigorously maintained by Pipp and supported by Black, is that anti-Semitic feeling was subtly implanted in Ford's mind by Liebold. ''I am sure that if Mr. Ford were put on the witness stand,'' wrote Pipp in 1921, ''he could not tell to save his life just when and how he started against the Jews. I am sure that Liebold could tell.'' Black, in his reminiscences, observes that Liebold ''did have a fertile field to work on, but if I were to put the number one blame on anyone, I would put it on Liebold.'' Unquestionably, Liebold was viciously anti-Semitic, as attested by dozens of his letters in the Ford Archives.[11]

Another powerful influence on Ford may have been exerted by his close friend, Thomas Edison, whose letters to Ford and Liebold show a distinct anti-Semitic bias and approval of the *Independent* series. Others felt that Cameron, a member of a religious sect called the British Israelites whose members believed themselves descendants of the Lost Tribes, might have looked with disfavor on ''other Israelites'' and strengthened Ford's own prejudice. This speculation, however, was emphatically denied by Pipp; it is made more improbable by Cameron's kindly disposition and outlook and his role of interpreter rather than instigator of Ford ideas.[12]

Ford's own attitudes toward Jews undoubtedly were shaped by boyhood influences, for, as Nevins and Hill point out, in rural communities where the only Jew ever seen was a roving peddler, where Christian and Jew were antithetical terms, and where such images as Shylock and Fagin were traditional, parochialism bred strange distortions of view. In many ways Ford remained true to the fundamentalist moral dogmas of his youth, the prejudices of the older American stock, and the prescriptions which he had heard the Populists expound during the 1890s. His anti-Semitism had more of loutishness about it than of deep-seated bigotry or malice. Moreover, Ford's very ignorance made it relatively easy for him to conclude, as he did, that an ''international Jewish banking power'' had started the war and kept it going, that Jews were plotting ''to destroy Christian civilization,'' and that most Jews were ''mere hucksters, traders who don't want to produce, but to make something out of what somebody else produces.'' While protesting that most Jews were not producers, the auto king employed thousands of Jewish laborers in his plants; ''we see that they work too,'' he told a reporter, ''and that they don't get into the office.''

In making harsh accusations against the Jew, the magnate referred less to race or religion than to certain traits which he abhorred and for which the term ''Jew'' seemed convenient. He would conceivably have called J. P. Morgan an ''international Jew.'' He did call some of Morgan's Gentile associates ''Jews.'' Ford sincerely believed that in exposing "the international Jew's" attempt to disrupt Gentile life by war and revolt—and thus finally gaining world control of politics, commerce, and finance—he was performing a great service to mankind. Ford felt that "good" Jews should rejoice in the exposé of the "international" element; although his secretary acknowledged that "it is possible that all Jews may temporarily feel the sting" of the *Independent*'s campaign.[13]

In truth, discussion of that mythical creature, the international Jew, could under no circumstances be "fair, temperate, and judicial," as certain Ford officials declared it to be. Pipp indignantly resigned the editorship of the *Independent* in April 1920. Cameron, assigned by Ford and Liebold to amass a body of information about Jews, undertook his assignment disgustedly, and in his initial report told "what a wonderful race they were, and how little he had known of their history, and what a magnificent history it was." Yet Cameron, who replaced Pipp in the editor's chair, was either unable or did not try to dissuade Ford from launching the attack. Rather, according to one observer, he bent to the demands of his employer "with the same pseudo-enthusiasm of an advertising man suddenly called upon to promote a tooth-paste no different than a hundred others. It was an assignment." In time, however, he apparently came to believe much of the anti-Semitic material which he wrote or which crossed his desk.[14]

The campaign of defamation, "the first systematic anti-Jewish agitation in the United States," was preposterous from almost any standpoint. Certainly, for its spirit of enterprise, for marvel of invention, and for effrontery, the series of articles had no parallel in all the literature of anti-Semitism. The *Independent* actually revived that hoary forgery, *The Protocols of the Wise Men of Zion,* which contended that Jews everywhere were conspiring to attain world domination. A flavor of outraged rural puritanism pervaded many of the charges. Jewish interests were held responsible for a decline in public and private morals, for intemperance, for high rents, short skirts, rolled stockings, cheap movies, vulgar Broadway shows, gambling, jazz, scarlet fiction, flashy jewelry, night clubs, and so on. Ridiculous charges were leveled against many prominent Jews. Bernard M. Baruch, for example, was proclaimed the "pro-consul of Judah in America," a "Jew of Super-Power," the head of a dictatorial conspiracy. Asked by newsmen what he had to say about the charges, Baruch, tongue-in-cheek, replied, "Now boys, you wouldn't expect me to deny them would you?"[15]

Jews and Jewish newspapers were, of course, baffled by the attacks. Some of them, expressing their admiration of Ford and his product, asked the manufacturer what it was all about. Some of the papers tolerantly suggested in their editorials that Ford was not aware of the onslaught, or that if he was, he was misinformed. A number of editors volunteered to meet with Ford or his representatives to clear up the misunderstanding. Such proposals were slapped down by Liebold, who told the editors that they themselves were misinformed, and that they should continue to follow the *Independent*'s articles so as to "get a new light on the Jewish situation." He added that "all fair-minded Jews must help rid the world of the peril which threatens."[16]

The general press, except for the Hearst papers, which published Arthur

Brisbane's column, largely ignored the *Independent*'s tirades. In fact, an *Independent* staff member concerned with circulation building complained that newspapers and magazines were "maintaining what may be termed a 'conspiracy of silence' insofar as mention of The Dearborn Independent's series . . . is concerned." However, of those papers which did refer to the attacks, all but one, the tiny *Redford* (Michigan) *Record*, spoke critically of Ford's anti-Semitism.[17]

The series of articles naturally produced a reaction against the *Independent* and the Ford car among Jews and their friends. Although the American Jewish Committee maintained that counterattacks "would only serve to give publicity to these articles which they otherwise would not have," many persons called for a Congressional investigation of and libel suits and demonstrations against the weekly, plus a boycott of the Ford car. In some instances extremists threatened or assaulted the magazine's salesmen. Petty riots took place in Pittsburgh and Toledo. Newsstand sales in New York were so impeded by interference that Ford found it necessary to obtain an injunction. In Boston, in the summer of 1921 the police tried to stop sales, but, being unsure of their legal ground, soon desisted. In Cincinnati vigorous protests from citizens prompted the city council to establish a press censorship. Public libraries in Paterson, New Jersey, and Hartford, Connecticut, barred the *Independent* from their tables. Mass meetings in various cities denounced Ford, and a resolution of protest was introduced in Congress. Representatives of almost all national Jewish organizations and religious bodies issued a common declaration deploring the campaign. One hundred and nineteen widely known Christians, including Woodrow Wilson, William Howard Taft, and William Cardinal O'Connell, called upon Ford to halt his "vicious propaganda." The theatrical producer Morris Gest filed a $5,000,000 libel suit against Ford, soon dropped, while journalist Herman Bernstein, accused by Ford of having told him about the activities of the "international Jew" when aboard the peace ship, brought a $200,000 damage suit against the industrialist. Hartford Jews, when arranging a 400-car parade in honor of Dr. Chaim Weizmann and Albert Einstein, gained nationwide publicity by ordering "Positively no Ford machines permitted in line."[18]

Although no Jewish organizations or groups formally declared a boycott on the Model T, many Jewish firms and individuals ceased buying Fords. So did some Gentile firms doing business with Jewish concerns and dependent on their goodwill. Branch managers and dealers, particularly those in cities with large Jewish populations, complained bitterly of the sales resistance and the economic pressures which the *Independent*'s campaign had brought down upon them. The manager of the second-ranking dealership in the New York branch, in protesting that the anti-Jewish articles had hurt his business, suggested that if Ford would put the money spent on the weekly into making better cars, everybody would be happier. Some dealers were threatened with eviction by Jewish landlords. Little consolation was offered them by Liebold, who in reply to the Virginia, Minnesota, agent's plea for discontinuance of the articles, suggested that dealers should own their own buildings so as to place themselves beyond the exertion of such pressure. Ford similarly was unmoved by protests from dealers and from his Sales Department. His stock answer to them was, "If they want our product, they'll buy it."[19]

It is difficult to determine the number of sales the informal Jewish boycott cost the Ford Company during the period 1920–22. We have seen that there was a sharp drop in sales during the last half of 1920, but this decrease was caused by a decline in the state of the economy and was general throughout the automobile industry. Then, as the economy improved, Ford sales reached new highs in 1921, 1922, and 1923. Unquestionably, some Jewish fleet owners and individuals condemned Ford, but still bought his products. As Will Rogers pointed out, the boycott "may not be a complete success yet—but it will be as soon as someone learns how to make a cheaper car." At this stage the Model T definitely was a better buy than any competing make. Ford, however, was to learn during his second anti-Semitic campaign, waged during the mid-1920s, that the aging Model T no longer could afford him the luxury of complacency about boycotts.[20]

As impulsively as he had begun the series Ford ordered it discontinued in January 1922. The reasons for Ford's decision are not altogether clear. Pipp stated that the order was issued following a long conference that Ford had with Gaston Plantiff, in which the New York manager impressed on the manufacturer the difficulty of selling Fords in centers of Jewish population. Nevins and Hill suggest that Edsel, who had been deeply pained by the series, may have prevailed upon his father to stop the campaign. President Harding, after an appeal by Louis Marshall, president of the American Jewish Committee, privately asked Ford—through his friend, Judson C. Welliver—to halt the attacks. There were also reports, according to Nevins and Hill, that Harding had enlisted the aid of two men, Edison and Brisbane, who had special influence with the industrialist. Brisbane did, in fact, repeatedly ask Ford to discontinue the campaign. Finally, if Upton Sinclair may be believed, Ford was swayed by William Fox, president of Fox Film Corporation, who threatened to show choice footage of Model T accidents in his newsreels, if the industrialist persisted in attacking the character of Jewish film executives and their motion pictures. In any event Ford called off the campaign, although in doing so he retracted nothing, and indeed, later boasted that his articles had opened the minds of Americans to possible evils.[21]

3

The anti-Semitic articles had little lasting effect on the *Independent*'s circulation. Both Pipp and Black believed that the stories increased circulation for a few months, then did not affect it materially one way or another. Actually, the *Independent*'s circulation depended chiefly on semicompulsory subscription campaigns conducted by dealers. Thus, circulation figures varied tremendously within short spans of time, depending on when a subscription drive was conducted throughout the dealer organization.[22]

Most dealers bitterly resented having to solicit subscriptions for the *Independent,* but they had no choice. Agents were summarily informed that the magazine was a Ford product, and that it should be as aggressively merchandised as Model T cars and trucks. Many dealers conscientiously tried to sell the magazine, but often the sales quotas assigned to them could be met only by sending prepaid subscriptions to persons whose names were selected at random from a telephone book, to all service club members in their locale, and so on. This forced circulation naturally was of dubious value to the *Independent;* and often, when the magazine was received by Jews and others unsympathetic to the publication's views, cancellations would be accompanied by caustic letters to dealers and to the Ford Company.[23]

A number of promotional schemes were tested by the *Independent*'s staff in an effort to build circulation. Two sales-promotion films, *The Dearborn Independent* and *Romance of Making a Modern Magazine,* were widely shown by dealers, who distributed free copies of the publication at exhibitions of these and other company films. The *Independent* maintained display booths at a number of state fairs and expositions. Both full-time solicitors and part-time salesmen were employed, and the *Independent* even tried to enlist schoolchildren and church organizations to sell the magazine. Service fees were paid to newsstand operators (the *Independent*'s five-cent price discouraged most newsstands from handling the publication) in return for merely stocking the weekly. Still, the great bulk of circulation was obtained through the Ford dealer organization, street sales averaging only .009 percent of the total.[24]

Although the *Independent*'s circulation averaged 650,000 during 1924 and 1925 and the annual subscription price was raised from a dollar to a dollar and fifty cents in 1925, the publication steadily lost money. Total losses incurred by the weekly over its eight-year history were $4,795,000, no small sum even for Ford. In an effort to alleviate the financial drain, in October 1925 the *Independent* began to accept advertising. At the same time, the weekly was enlarged from thirty-two pages (it had graduated in size from sixteen pages in May 1925) to forty-eight pages and was given a new format, covers in color, and improved illustrations. The editorial content had improved steadily from 1920, when arrangements were made with free-lance writers in various sections of the country to represent the *Independent* on an assignment basis and the magazine began to buy articles from newspaper and magazine staff members.

Starting in 1925, the *Independent* purchased articles and poetry from "name" writers such as Edwin Markham, Robert Frost, Hugh Walpole, Hamlin Garland, Carl Sandburg, and Booth Tarkington. Perhaps the most prolific outside contributor to the *Independent* was Allan Benson, Socialist candidate for president in 1916, who between 1924 and 1926 sold fifty-seven stories to the magazine for as much as $500 apiece (the magazine's top rate).[25]

From 1922 to 1924 the *Independent*'s criticism of Jewish people was only sporadic, like its criticism of arms-makers, bankers, bootleggers, Wall Street, and Hollywood. However, during this period other products of Ford's anti-Semitism were at work. Between 1920 and 1922 Ford arranged for the publication of four brochures, each containing a score or more of the ninety-one articles in the *Independent,* as well as for a more comprehensive compilation of these articles entitled, *The International Jew.* More than 3,000 of these publications were sent gratuitously to friends and acquaintances of Henry Ford and to *Dearborn Independent* readers who had written to the newspaper about its anti-Semitic articles. Moreover, *The International Jew* was translated into most European languages by foreign anti-Semites, chief of whom was

Theodor Fritsch, editor of the Leipzig publication *Der Hammer*. It was eagerly seized upon by the nationalist, reactionary, and other groups from France to Russia. The booklets undoubtedly influenced many readers, all the more because they carried the imprint, not of a crackpot publisher in an alleyway, but of one of the most famous and successful men in the world. Baldur von Schirach, leader of the Hitler youth movement, declared at the postwar Nuremburg war crimes trials that he had become an anti-Semite at the age of seventeen after reading *The Eternal Jew* (the German title of the brochures). "You have no idea what a great influence this book had on the thinking of German youth," von Schirach said. "The younger generation looked with envy to the symbols of success and prosperity like Henry Ford, and if he said the Jews were to blame, why naturally we believed him." A prominent Jewish attorney, after completing a world tour in the mid-1920s, stated that he had seen the brochures in the "most remote corners of the earth." "But for the authority of the Ford name," he maintained, "they would have never seen the light of day and would have been quite harmless if they had. With that magic name they spread like wildfire and became the Bible of every anti-Semite."[26]

In America, Ford was widely criticized for his role in encouraging anti-Semitism abroad. Norman Hapgood, writing for *Hearst's International Magazine,* reported that Ford had been "sold his anti-Jewish mania" by a czarist pogrom-maker and that the industrialist was a tool of Russian imperialists who sought the restoration of the Romanoffs. Ford's picture was said to be on display in a place of honor at the headquarters of the German National Socialist Party, and the manufacturer was reported to be financing the Hitler movement. Hitler denied receiving funds from Ford; in fact his agent reported that, "if I had been trying to sell Mr. Ford a wooden nutmeg, he couldn't have shown less interest in [our] proposition." Although denied Ford funds, Hitler acknowledged that "the struggle of international Jewish finance against Ford . . . has only strengthened the sympathies of the National Socialist Party for Ford and has given the broadest circulation to his book, *The International Jew*." Hitler's ravings and public speeches against Jews frequently were based on Ford's anti-Semitic literature. Ford, moreover, was the only American mentioned in the American edition of Hitler's *Mein Kampf*. Insisting that Jews were "increasingly the controlling masters" of American labor, Hitler noted that "one great man, Ford, to their exasperation still holds out independently." Hitler also repeated several of the *Independent*'s charges against Jews.[27]

In April 1924 the *Independent* launched its second series of anti-Semitic articles under the general title, "Jewish Exploitation of Farmer Organizations." The articles dealt in large part with the activities of Aaron Sapiro, a prominent Chicago attorney who, as a counselor in farm economics, had written a standard contract binding growers in a cooperative marketing arrangement and had done much to promote this arrangement. For some time Sapiro had been laboring to draw deeply discontented midwestern farmers into a vast new wheat-marketing organization. Among the numerous friends of this organization were Bernard M. Baruch, Julius Rosenwald, Otto Kahn, and Eugene Meyer. The *Independent* promptly concluded that a Jewish group was trying to obtain control of American wheat farming. The subsequent attacks were laced with offensive references to "Jewish combinations," "international banking rings," and "Jewish international bankers"; Sapiro, specif-ically, was accused of cheating his clients. The upshot was a million-dollar suit by Sapiro against Henry Ford (not the *Independent*) for defamation of character.

The widely publicized suit came to trial in Detroit in March 1927; the chief issue: the responsibility of Ford for the libelous matter. Editor Cameron took the stand as Ford's chief witness. Testifying for five days, and maintaining perfect aplomb under severe cross-examination, Cameron declared that he had the sole responsibility for whatever the *Independent* had published; that he had never discussed with Ford any article on any Jew, had never sent Ford an advance copy of the weekly, and had never even seen Ford read a copy. The defense, in short, took the position that Ford had given Cameron and his staff a free hand in shaping policy and had simply been an innocent bystander. The question of *Independent* General Manager Liebold's rela-tions with the staff and with Ford was not explored.[28]

It was unquestionably true that Ford had paid less and less attention to the *Independent* as the years elapsed. But it was obvious that he bore the ultimate and direct responsibility for the articles on Jews and on Sapiro. Indeed, on any number of occasions, Liebold and Cameron and the *Independent*'s promotional literature boasted that "the Dearborn Independent is Henry Ford's own paper and he authorizes every statement occurring therein," and that "the paper has the personal assistance of Mr. Ford's guidance and instruction and the benefit of his keen foresight and experience." "We never step out on any unusual program without first getting his guidance," Cameron told a Ford branch managers' convention in 1924.[29]

Haunted by memories of Mount Clemens, Ford was naturally reluctant to testify. He was spared the agony by two dramatic events, an automobile accident and a grave blunder by a juror. On the day before Ford was to appear, a coupe he was driving was sideswiped and forced down a fifteen-foot bank near the River Rouge, where it struck a tree. The sixty-three-year-old Ford, badly shaken, bleeding, and half-dazed, staggered to the gatehouse of his estate, whence two days later he was removed to the Ford Hospital.[30]

The accident was reported on the front page of virtually every newspaper in the country, and initial reports were highly sensationalized. Streamers shouted, "HENRY FORD NEAR DEATH IN AUTOMOBILE CRASH," "PLOT TO AS-SASSINATE FORD SEEN," and "FORD INJURED BY ASSASSINS: HURLED OVER RIVER BANK IN CAR." The *New York Graphic* carried a composograph (imagined photograph) of Ford, the first and only such portrait of the manufacturer, which showed the industrialist, his head about two sizes too large for his body, "bearing up bravely under intense pain" as he "underwent the knife of a high-priced surgeon," with presumably lower-priced surgeons and nurses hovering in the back-ground. Cameron quickly issued a statement denying any foul play and reporting Ford's speedy recovery. The manufacturer, in fact, did not undergo an operation and left the hospital after only two days.[31]

The juror's blunder, an accusation by a woman on the panel that Ford's counsel showed excessive anxiety to keep the case from going to the jury, resulted in the declaration of a mistrial in April 1927 and adjournment of the case for six months. This decision gave Ford an opportunity to settle the case out of court, and on July 7, he published a personal apology to Sapiro and a formal retraction of all his past attacks on the Jewish people. He appears to have acted on his own initiative; certainly Liebold, Cameron, and the defense attorneys were taken by surprise.

No doubt Ford's motives in issuing the public apology were complex. His company was in the midst of the critical changeover from the Model T to the Model A, and he unquestionably knew that many branch managers and dealers were complaining that Jewish hostility hurt business. Many individual Jews and Jewish fleet owners and a number of Gentile fleet operators, in response to the insistence of Jewish financial backers, now found in the Chevrolet, Dodge, and Willys-Overland quite practical alternatives to the outmoded Model T. The Sapiro suit also may have brought home to Ford's well-insulated mind the volume and force of the public criticism of his obnoxious campaign. Moreover, Ford may well have been genuinely frightened over the prospect of going on the witness stand in front of 118,000,000 Americans.[32]

In any event, details of a retraction were worked out by two of Ford's friends, Joseph A. Palma and Earl J. Davis, and two prominent Jews, Louis Marshall and former Congressman Nathan D. Perlman. Marshall wrote the retraction, which, he hoped, would not only serve as an apology to Jews, but would also make the industrialist appear ridiculous. "If I had his money," the Jewish leader wrote a former law partner, "I would not [make] such a humiliating statement for one hundred million dollars." To Marshall's astonishment, the industrialist signed the retraction without changing a letter. Ford was, in fact, willing to sign *any* statement to make peace with the Jews. "I don't care how bad [the apology] is," he told a protesting Bennett, "just settle this thing up . . . the worse they make it, the better." The retraction, said by the *American Hebrew* to be the first public recantation of anti-Semitism in history, was issued at Ford's request through Brisbane:

> For some time past I have given consideration to the series of articles concerning Jews which since 1920 have appeared in the *Dearborn Independent*. Some of them have been reprinted in pamphlet form under the title "The International Jew." Although public publications are my property, it goes without saying that in the multitude of my activities it has been impossible for me to devote personal attention to their management or to keep informed as to their contents. It has therefore inevitably followed that the conduct and policies of [my] publications had to be delegated to men whom I placed in charge of them and upon whom I relied implicitly.
>
> To my great regret I have learned that Jews generally, and particularly those of this country, not only resent these publications as promoting anti-Semitism, but regard me as their enemy. Trusted friends with whom I have conferred recently have assured me in all sincerity that in their opinion the character of the charges and insinuations made against the Jews, both individually and collectively, contained in many of the articles which have been circulated periodically in the *Dearborn Independent,* and have been reprinted in the pamphlets mentioned, justifies the righteous indignation entertained by Jews everywhere toward me because of the mental anguish occasioned by the unprovoked reflections made upon them.
>
> This has led me to direct my personal attention to the subject, in order to ascertain the exact nature of these articles. As a result of this survey I confess I am deeply mortified that this journal, which is intended to be constructive and

not destructive, has been made the medium for resurrecting exploded fictions, for giving currency to the so-called Protocols of the Wise Men of Zion, which have been demonstrated, as I learn, to be gross forgeries, and for contending that the Jews have been engaged in a conspiracy to control the capital and the industries of the world, besides laying at their door many offenses against decency, public order, and good morals.

Had I appreciated even the general nature, to say nothing of the details, of these utterances, I would have forbidden their circulation without a moment's hesitation. . . . I deem it my duty as an honorable man to make amends for the wrong done to the Jews as fellow-men and brothers, by asking their forgiveness for the harm that I have unintentionally committed, by retracting so far as lies within my power the offensive charges laid at their door by these publications, and by giving them the unqualified assurance that henceforth they may look to me for friendship and good will.[33]

In addition, Ford promised that he would publish no more offensive articles and agreed to withdraw *The International Jew* from the book market. Out-of-court settlements were made with Sapiro and Bernstein. Ford also discharged Liebold from the general managership of the *Independent* and Cameron from his editorial post, though both remained in his employ. Ford had decided as early as the spring of 1927 to suspend the weekly, having instructed Black at that time to work out a liquidation plan. The paper stopped accepting subscriptions in July, and Ford—in answer to Brisbane's Hearst-backed offer of $1,000,000 for the property—stated that he was going to convert the *Independent* into a house organ. However, the magazine was suspended permanently in December 1927.[34]

From a public relations standpoint, Ford's retraction, albeit humiliating, scored heavily in his favor. To be sure, nobody was taken in by his professed ignorance of the existence of the *Independent*'s anti-Semitic articles. Many Gentiles wrote Ford that he had "turned yellow," "was built on the jelly-fish order," "was a pitiful quitter," and had "sold [his] birthright for a mess of porridge," while an equal number of them congratulated Ford on his retraction. Four-fifths of the hundreds of letters addressed to Ford in July 1927 were from Jews, and almost without exception they praised the industrialist for his "courageous and manly statement" and his "breadth of character and broadmindedness." The attitude of the great majority of these correspondents is typified by a letter from a New York rabbi:

I am deeply touched by your statement published in to-day's papers. Since I had the occasion to learn of your humane and generous treatment of your employees, I couldn't conceive how a man with so fine a character could promote animosity towards a whole people, and I am therefore inclined to believe that your statement was made wholeheartedly and most sincerely. I am happy that the ill-feeling of my brethren will henceforth cease toward a man who has done so much for the country beloved by all of us. . . .

You may be proud for possessing the courage and the righteousness to confess publicly your error and to my people belongs the honor of forgiving a man who caused them so much pain and humiliation.[35]

Most Jewish publications also accepted Ford's apology. Some metropolitan dailies, however, gagged on the manufacturer's plea in extenuation. "Nobody but Mr. Ford," said the *New York Herald Tribune,* "could be ignorant of a major policy of his own newspaper. Nobody but Mr. Ford could be unaware of the national and international repercussions of this policy of anti-Semitism." "He phrases his statement," stated the *New York Times,* "as if his attention had 'recently' been drawn to the grievous wrong which he had done. The fact is, of course, that for several years he has had the matter brought to his notice, both privately and publicly. Till now he has remained unyielding." But most publications regarded the apology as "handsome" and "courageous" and rejoiced that it "healed a sore spot in national life." "The pity is," said the *Atlanta Constitution,* "the retraction was not made long ago."[36]

Tin Pan Alley cashed in on Ford's apology. "Since Henry Ford Apologized to Me" briefly achieved popularity on the strength of these lyrics, written by the future theatrical producer, Billy Rose:

> I was sad and I was blue
> But now I'm just as good as you
> Since Hen-ry Ford a-pol-o-gized to me
> I've thrown a-way my lit-tle Che-vro-let
> And bought my-self a Ford Cou-pe
> I told the Sup-'rin-ten-dent that
> the Dearborn In-de-pen-dent
> Does-n't have to hang up where it used to be
> I'm glad he changed his point of view
> And I even like Edsel too,
> Since Hen-ry Ford a-pol-o-gized to me
> My mother says she'll feed him if he calls
> 'Ge-fil-te-fish' and Mat-zah balls
> And if he runs for President
> I would-n't charge a sin-gle cent
> I'll cast my bal-lot ab-so-lute-ly free
> Since Hen-ry Ford a-pol-o-gized to me.

4

For half-a-dozen years after 1927, Ford enjoyed excellent relations with the Jewish public. The *Dearborn Independent* was defunct; *The International Jew* was dormant. Furthermore, the Ford Company and the industrialist went out of their way to heal the breach. During the introductory campaign for the Model A in December 1927, approximately 12 percent of the $1,300,000 advertising appropriation went to Jewish newspapers; no other "minority" newspapers were used. Ford found time to attend a number of testimonial dinners in behalf of prominent Jews and Jewish fund-raising banquets. On one such occasion, at the mere mention of his name by one of the preliminary speakers, the entire gathering—2,000 guests—stood and cheered the manufacturer for a full minute. The magnate also called at the New York office of Louis Marshall and expressed readiness to do anything that Marshall might suggest to "minimize the evil that has been done." During the conference Ford offered the

Jewish leader a Model A, which, at the time (January 1928) was in tremendous demand. "I respectfully *declined,*" the Jewish leader wrote his son, "informing [Ford] of my devotion to pedestrian locomotion."[37]

The honeymoon ended in the early 1930s, when copies of *The International Jew,* often with Ford's name on the title page or with his photograph inside, began turning up in large numbers throughout Europe and South America, and when Ford's anti-Semitic past was thoroughly aired by a Congressional committee investigating Nazi propaganda in the United States.[38]

The International Jew was published in Barcelona, Pôrto Alegre, Brazil, and Leipzig. The Brazilians inquired of Ford in 1932 whether they might buy the translation rights. Liebold assured them that permission to publish was unnecessary "since the book has not been copyrighted in this country" (a correct statement). He made no mention of Ford's 1927 public apology to the Jews or his simultaneous letter to the German publishers of *The International Jew,* demanding that publication of the volume be discontinued. The Brazilians, correctly assuming that Liebold had given the green light, printed 5,000 copies of the book from the German translation and displayed Ford's name prominently on the front cover.

This fact was brought to Ford's attention (assuming that Liebold showed his employer the letter) by Rabbi Leo M. Franklin, Detroit's leading rabbi and in years past one of Ford's closest friends, who asked the industrialist to cable the American consul in Brazil to halt publication. A month later Liebold sent a flabby letter to Ford's Brazilian manager, requesting "whatever facts you are able to secure in connection with this report and what the circumstances are warranting this publication." The manager checked with the publisher, was shown Liebold's letter of virtual approval, and tartly replied that after seeing the letter he "felt it unnecessary to investigate further." Liebold then (three months after receiving Franklin's letter) blandly informed the rabbi that he had not replied sooner because he had no knowledge of the book. At the same time Liebold wrote to the company's Brazilian manager, telling him to request that the publisher discontinue the use of Ford's name in the book. The publisher agreed to insert a note in future editions disavowing Ford's authorship.[39]

Liebold reacted in much the same way regarding German publication of the book, although, of course, in that country it is doubtful whether any amount of pressure from Ford would have stopped publication of the volume or the use of the automobile manufacturer's name. Answering one of Liebold's routine complaints, the manager of Ford of Germany, Edmund C. Heine (an American citizen), explained that *The International Jew* had government backing and was an important factor in educating the nation "to understand the Jewish problem as it should be understood." Heine further pointed out that Fritsch, who insisted that "it is Henry Ford's book about World Judaism which hits the Jews most severely," would not relinquish his "publication rights." Liebold cooed in reply: "We understand the matter perfectly and this thoroughly answers our recent inquiry." By late 1933, Fritsch had published twenty-nine editions of *The International Jew,* each of which carried Ford's name on the title page and lauded Ford in the preface for the "great service" that he had done America and the world by attacking the Jews.[40]

Copies of the German edition of the book as well as English-language reprints of articles from the *Dearborn Independent* were widely distributed in the United States by the German-American Bund, Rev. Gerald B. Winrod's Defenders of the Faith, and William Dudley Pelley's Silver Shirts of America. Alarmed, Rabbi Franklin, in August 1933, suggested that Ford publicly restate his 1927 position so as to make it clear to German and other publishers that his repudiation of the *Independent*'s articles and *The International Jew* was sincere. In conversation, Ford agreed to sign a letter to this effect, to be prepared by Franklin. However, when the letter was presented to him he refused, without giving a reason, to affix his signature. He did, however, tell the rabbi that he had not changed his attitude, as expressed in the 1927 apology, and that anyone attributing anti-Semitic views to him did so without his authority and with his "definite disapproval." In January 1937, Ford issued a statement to the *Detroit Jewish Chronicle,* "disavowing any connection whatsoever with the publication in Germany of the book known as *The International Jew.*" Issued at a time when publication of that book was not a topic of general currency, the statement did not receive any attention in the daily press. [41]

If renewed publication of *The International Jew* led the Jewish community to question Ford's sentiments, publicity which linked the magnate's name to the Nazi Party and leading figures in Germany contributed equally to a deterioration of his relations with Jews. In 1933 a congressional committee investigated reports that the industrialist had contributed heavily to Nazi coffers in return for Hitler's promise to reprint the *Independent*'s articles. Ford also was reported to have paid $300,000 to Prince Louis Ferdinand, second grandson of the deposed kaiser, during the two-and-a-half-year period when the young nobleman was employed by Ford as a salesman in Argentina and production trainee at the Rouge. Ford officials admitted that the company had been solicited by the Nazis, but they emphatically denied that any contributions had been made. A company spokesman also declared that the use of Ford's name on Nazi propaganda was unauthorized and that Louis Ferdinand received only regular wages during his employment by the company. Although the committee accepted the refutations, the widely publicized charges, when set against Ford's anti-Semitic background and the concurrent circulation of *The International Jew,* were enough reason for many Jews to suspect the manufacturer of duplicity. [42]

Jewish fears appeared to be justified in mid-1938 when Ford, on his seventy-fifth birthday, accepted the Grand Cross of the Supreme Order of the German Eagle, the highest honor the Reich could then bestow upon a foreigner. Ford was the first American and the fourth person (Mussolini was another) to receive the award, created by Hitler himself in 1937. The decoration was bestowed in Ford's office by Consul Karl Kapp, of Cleveland, with Consul Fritz Hailer, of Detroit, and Liebold and Cameron in attendance. The citation accompanying the medal (offered "in recognition of [Ford's] pioneering in making motor cars available for the masses") was read by Kapp at Ford's birthday dinner, attended by 1,500 prominent Detroiters. Hitler's personal congratulations were simultaneously extended to Ford. [43]

Attacked by the leftist press, prominent Jews, and Harold L. Ickes, secretary of the interior, Ford declined to comment on why he had accepted the decoration. Liebold, who himself received the Order of Merit of the German Eagle, First Class, in

September, only six weeks after Ford accepted the Grand Cross, very possibly influenced Ford. In reply to Ford's critics, Liebold pointed out that the company employed 3,500 Germans and marketed 15,000 cars annually in Germany. "For a nation of 70,000,000 to recognize the achievements of a man in another land seems to be an honor which cannot be disregarded or ignored. We have interests, physical, financial, and moral, which have taken many years to establish, and consequently such foundations cannot be uprooted overnight to comply with propaganda intended to arouse American sympathy."

Of course, a recommendation from Liebold would have meant nothing had not Ford himself been receptive to the idea of accepting the award. Harry Bennett attributed the manufacturer's decision to a combination of ignorance, mulishness, and a desire to anger President Roosevelt (with whom Ford was at odds). Perhaps closest to the truth was Oswald Garrison Villard, who observed: "I honestly do not think that Mr. Ford has the mentality to understand the significance of actions like that . . . a boy of 12 would do better. . . . I do not believe he ever thought there could be another side to accepting the decoration from Hitler. He has a Ford factory in Germany and employs a lot of German labor and so I have no doubt it seemed to him just a pleasant gesture, quite harmless."[44]

Outside of the leftist press, relatively little publicity was given Ford's acceptance of the award. Several newspapers carried a photograph of Ford, wearing the wide sash of the order, standing at attention as Kapp attached a cross and star to the cloth. Most newspapers tended to play down the event. Rather surprisingly, the general press seems to have expressed no editorial comment whatever.[45]

Nonetheless, the award made a vivid impression on American Jewry. Eddie Cantor sounded the first note of scorn, telling a women's Zionist organization that Ford "is a damn fool for permitting the world's greatest gangster to give him a citation." The entertainer added, "I question Mr. Ford's Americanism and I question his Christianity. The more men like Ford we have, the more we must organize and fight." The National Encampment Committee of the Jewish War Veterans of the United States, which had gathered in Detroit to plan for the organization's forthcoming Detroit convention, declined Edsel Ford's offer to supply seventy-five autos for delegates. The group urged Henry Ford to repudiate the decoration, saying that his acceptance of the award implied "endorsement of the German-American Bund and their subversive un-American activities and other anti-democratic groups subsidized here by Nazi funds."[46]

Others joined the attack on Ford. Professor Clyde R. Miller, director of the Institute for Propaganda Analysis, declared that acceptance of German decorations by Ford and Charles A. Lindbergh "expressed approval of the Nazi government," and suggested that they be returned. The sharpest blast was delivered by Ickes, who, before the Cleveland Zionist Society, orally horsewhipped Ford and other Americans "who obsequiously have accepted tokens of contemptuous distinction at a time when the bestower of them counts that day lost when he can commit no new crime against humanity." This statement received worldwide publicity and prompted the German government to attempt to deliver a sharp protest to the State Department. The note was abruptly rejected. Privately, Ford was unmoved by the criticism, telling an associate: "They [the Germans] sent me this ribbon band. They [the critics] told me to return it or else I'm not an American. I'm going to keep it!"[47]

However, in December 1938, Ford, after a conference with Rabbi Franklin, permitted the latter to issue a statement which denied that Ford's acceptance of a medal "from the German people . . . involved any sympathy on my part with Nazism." He expressed the view that the German people were "not in sympathy with their rulers in their anti-Jewish policies, which is the work of a few war-makers at the top." "Those who have known me for many years," Ford added, "realize that anything that breeds hate is repulsive to me." The manufacturer also said that he believed that the United States must continue to maintain its traditional role as a haven for the oppressed and promised to do everything within his power to give oppressed Jews an opportunity to rebuild their lives in America.[48]

The statement, which naturally was welcomed by the Jewish press and various liberal organizations, lost some of its effectiveness when it was attacked by Father Charles E. Coughlin, the anti-Semitic priest of Royal Oak, Michigan, and muddied by Harry Bennett, Ford's chief aide. Coughlin, in his weekly radio address, charged that Franklin was the author of a "totally inaccurate" statement attributed to Ford and that the industrialist, far from condemning Nazi persecution, actually had said that he believed there was little or no persecution in Germany, and that if there was "it was not due to the German government, but to the war-mongers, the international bankers." Coughlin substantiated these charges by quoting a signed statement given to *Social Justice,* his weekly magazine, by Bennett, speaking "officially for the Ford Motor Co., and in the presence of Mr. Ford." Bennett, who had arranged the Ford-Franklin meeting, talked on all sides of the matter. He admitted that he and Ford had authorized a statement written by Franklin, that they had agreed to change this statement from third to first person, and that they had authorized the revision and its release to the newspapers. At the same time he said that he had signed the statement to which Coughlin referred and that the priest's remarks regarding this statement were "virtually correct." Bennett, an old hand at duplicity, denied that he had told *Social Justice* that the Ford statement was "totally inaccurate"; rather he had told it that "it was not totally inaccurate."[49]

The *Detroit Free Press* rushed to Franklin's defense, pointing out that he and Ford had been friends for many years, "and the Doctor's reputation and standing in this community is such that when he issued the statement, and said that that it was authorized by Henry Ford, no newspaper in this city had any reason to question it. Nor have they now." The *Free Press* assured its readers that the Ford statement was an exact copy of the one prepared by Franklin and authorized by Ford, adding that Coughlin was not to be taken seriously as he attacked the Jewish people every week and had a "congenital inability to tell the truth." Coughlin thereupon sued the *Free Press* for $4,000,000. The newspaper answered the charge by preparing seventy pages of direct and conflicting statements made by the priest, who hastily dropped the suit. Bennett also backtracked quickly, stating that "Father Coughlin crossed me up. I am going to get in touch with him and tell him so. The statement as published was accurate and expresses Mr. Ford's sentiments."[50]

Criticism of Ford's alleged Nazi sympathies and his anti-Semitism mounted as Europe was plunged into war and as Americans became increasingly conscious of the German menace. The employment of Fritz Kuhn, leader of the German-American Bund, as a laboratory technician by the Henry Ford Hospital and the Ford Company between 1928 to 1937 was repeatedly mentioned in the press. Leftist publications tried to link Kuhn and Cameron as fellow conspirators, even to the point of publishing a forged letter in which the fluent Cameron allegedly told Kuhn:

> Several inquiries were made to our Personnel Department by reporters from New York newspapers, (by phone) asking whether or not, you are employed by our organization as a chemist, at each and every instance, we denied knowing you. Some important matters came up, which have to be cleared away before I can leave for New York, but you can look for me by the first of the month, at that time we will outline our next move. H. is in Florida, but keeps his eyes and ears open.[51]

Another barrage of unfavorable publicity fell on Ford in 1941 when Edmund C. Heine, ex-manager of his German operations, was tried and convicted on espionage charges in the Federal District Court in Brooklyn. Earlier the same year, in a complaint filed in the Federal District Court in San Francisco against German Consul-General Fritz Wiedemann, Ford was accused of working with Wiedemann and Lindbergh "to lull the nation into a false sense of security." In an open letter to the Army and Navy Departments, the UAW-CIO, which had reasons of its own for attacking Ford, demanded in 1940 that the heads of the two services investigate the "Nazi sympathies" of the Ford Company. The union also insisted that Edsel Ford resign his directorship and sell his interest in General Analine and Film Corporation, the American subsidiary of the German dye-and-chemical trust. The younger Ford complied with these demands in 1941, at a heavy financial loss to himself. Ford's name was frequently linked with the Ku Klux Klan, which, without Ford's permission, was reprinting Ford ads on Americanism in its publication, *The Fiery Cross,* and circulating copies of *The International Jew.* Finally, Ford was attacked by a number of American intellectuals, among them Robert E. Sherwood, twice a Pulitzer prize-winner, who, in a radio message broadcast throughout the British Empire, denounced Ford and Lindbergh as "bootlickers of Hitler."[52]

Ford had no one but himself to blame for some of the abuse which was heaped upon him. His willingness in 1940 to become a godfather to Louis Ferdinand's second son might be ascribed to personal attachment, but some of his public statements gave gratuitous confirmation to the allegations against him. When, in late August 1939, he was asked his opinion of Hitler, he replied, "I don't know Hitler personally, but at least Germany keeps its people at work. . . . Apparently England's reason for going to war is that she doesn't make enough use of her land." The manufacturer also voiced strong anti-Semitic statements to newsmen. In June 1940 he told David J. Wilkie of the Associated Press that "international Jewish bankers" were responsible for the war. "He would propound ideas about the Jews and about the press that left one speechless," wrote a reporter for the *Manchester Guardian* who interviewed Ford in 1941. "The best he would say about the Jews was that you couldn't do without them. The Gentiles wouldn't work if the Jews weren't here."[53]

During the late 1930s the combined weight of the anti-Semitic and pro-Nazi accusations against Henry Ford began to trouble officials of the Ford Company, who reasoned that declining sales in certain areas of the country were attributable to "an active and effective boycott" of Ford products by Jews and other Americans unsympathetic to the industrialist's views. The sales slump was particularly acute in the company's eastern [sales] region, which had the largest Jewish population in the nation. That region's manager, W. K. Edmunds, wrote in 1944: "Mr. Edsel Ford understood this situation thoroughly, and just prior to the time we discontinued making automobiles, he had allotted us a special fund [approximately $50,000] to be used for sales promotion and advertising in this area to improve our sales and counteract the existing antagonism." A company-conducted investigation also revealed that, in Hollywood, "Jewish interests . . . agreed to ban all Ford units from their studio lots and forbade employees and stars to buy Ford products." The report added, "A few stars are in a position to disregard the order, but many sales are being lost."[54]

Other surveys also emphasized the seriousness of the situation. A poll conducted for Ford in 1940 by Maxon, Inc., one of the company's advertising agencies, revealed that an astonishing 80.3 percent of the American male public had heard that Ford was anti-Semitic. Another Maxon survey, conducted in late 1942, substantiated the earlier figure by showing that 78.6 percent of American men knew of Ford's racial prejudices. As the *Jackson* (Mississippi) *News* reported in 1941, "millions of persons regarded Henry Ford as an implacable enemy of the Jewish race." In 1944, Elmo Roper, after sampling the American public in Ford's behalf, drew the inescapable conclusion that Henry Ford had alienated Jews to such an extent that they had virtually stopped buying Ford products several years prior to World War II.[55]

Henry Ford was unimpressed by the magnitude of the problem; indeed he refused to admit the existence of any sort of boycott, even after sales officials showed him figures and charts which could lead to no other conclusion. Shortly after America's entry into the war, however, Ford, in a burst of patriotism, undertook to close the wide gulf which now separated him from the Jewish public. Following a meeting with Richard E. Gutstadt, national director of the Anti-Defamation League of B'nai B'rith, the industrialist issued a nationally publicized statement intended "in our present national and international emergency" to "clarify some general misconceptions concerning my attitude toward my fellow-citizens of Jewish faith." Ford stated that he did not subscribe to or support any agitation which promoted antagonism against Jews and that he considered the "hate-mongering prevalent for some time in this country against the Jews of distinct disservice to our country, and to the peace and welfare of humanity." Regarding reprints of the *Dearborn Independent*'s articles, Ford insisted that he had sanctioned no one to use his name as the sponsor or author of such publications.[56]

Ford's statement brought to a close his generation-long effort to explain his attitude toward Jews. His prejudices were born of ignorance, but after consideration he came to believe in their validity. On various occasions he apologized to Jews or "clarified" his stand toward them. But his apologies were self-serving; his anti-

Semitic beliefs remained with him to the end. Ford's anti-Semitism was the darkest blot on his career.

At the time Ford issued his 1942 statement, the Ford Company's attorneys finally brought strong pressure to bear on publishers and distributors of *The International Jew*. The Ku Klux Klan was threatened with a lawsuit if it did not stop printing and circulating the book with Ford's name thereon. The Klan's Imperial Wizard, J. A. Colescott, thereupon informed the company that his organization was complying with its request. Letters also were sent to the governments of Mexico, Argentina, Peru, Chile, and other Latin American countries, asking them to take measures to suppress the circulation of the volume. *The International Jew* continued to circulate in Latin American countries until 1944. By 1945, however, the Anti-Defamation League could report that no Ford-related anti-Semitic literature was to be found in bookstores or libraries of the ten Latin American countries which it had investigated. "This improved situation," noted the league, "develops from the direct efforts of the Ford Company."[57]

5

The formidable task of rebuilding and maintaining good relations with the Jewish public lay ahead for the Ford Company. Starting in 1941 with the special appropriation by Edsel Ford, the company annually budgeted large sums for product and institutional advertising in the Jewish press. In 1943 the company spent $83,709.72 in Jewish publications. This amount, almost nine times greater than annual expenditures in such media between 1935 and 1940, was all the more significant in that during the war Ford had nothing to sell except prestige. Breakdowns of the company's postwar advertising appropriations do not show the amounts expended for advertising in Jewish newspapers. Undoubtedly the sums were considerable, however, as correspondence shows that the company spent as much as $11,117 for just one institutional ad running simultaneously in sixty-four Yiddish and Anglo-Jewish (English language) newspapers across the country. The list of publications in which the Ford advertisements appeared was prepared, at Ford's request, by Nathan H. Seidman, president of the Inter-Racial Press of America, Inc. Seidman, on dozens of occasions starting in 1941, also sent Ford Motor Company news releases to Jewish editors, with a personal request that they publish them in their newspapers.[58]

A number of Ford officials, led by Henry Ford II, Henry Ford's grandson—who was elected to a vice-presidency of the company in 1944 and to the presidency in September 1945—made personal efforts to improve the firm's relationship with the Jewish public. In 1946 the youthful president addressed the Community Committee of New York in behalf of the United Jewish Appeal. Two years later he was awarded a certificate by the National Conference of Christians and Jews (NCCJ) for his contribution to brotherhood. In 1951 Henry II, while serving as chairman of the NCCJ's first national special gifts campaign, was responsible for a Ford Motor Company gift of $1,000,000 to the conference for a national headquarters building in New York. The same year he was awarded an America's Democratic Legacy Award—presented annually by the Anti-Defamation League, the civil rights arm of B'nai B'rith—for "distinguished contributions to the American heritage of freedom."[59]

Benson Ford, a second grandson of Henry Ford, served as Protestant national co-chairman of the NCCJ from 1951 through 1954 and was chairman of the organization's national special gifts campaign in 1953–54. John S. Bugas, the Ford Company's vice-president-industrial relations, became a director of the NCCJ in 1947 and made several public appearances that year in support of the conference. William Clay Ford, the youngest of Ford's grandsons, and Ernest R. Breech, executive vice-president of the company, also served on boards and committees of Jewish organizations during the immediate postwar period. Breech was awarded a NCCJ brotherhood award in 1953. In 1956 Ford's board of directors took a step unprecedented in company annals, naming a Jew, able Wall Street investment banker Sidney J. Weinberg, to a directorship.[60]

Shortly after Bugas joined Ford in 1944, the company retained a Jewish friend, Detroit attorney Alfred A. May, a fellow alumnus of the Federal Bureau of Investigation, to advise the firm on its relations with the Jewish community. For three decades May's recommendations have played an important part in many of Ford's decisions affecting Jews—from lending courtesy cars to Jewish organizations, advertising in Jewish newspapers and banquet programs, and framing a reply to charges that the company underemploys Jews to deciding how much money should be given Jewish causes and determining the degree and kind of assistance to be extended to the State of Israel and Israeli institutions. Most of May's work has been conducted behind the scenes. He advises; Ford acts. Occasionally, however, May negotiates directly with Jewish organizations in Ford's behalf. But because many leading Jews have come to regard the attorney as an apologist for the Ford Company, his influence within the Jewish community has declined over the years. In the late 1940s, the Ford Company also retained rabbis in Detroit, Chicago, New York, and other large centers of Jewish population to assist in overcoming its reputation for anti-Semitism.[61]

Since 1944 Ford has been repeatedly embarrassed by the circulation of anti-Semitic literature linked to Henry Ford and occasionally by efforts to honor the founder's memory. In 1947 Henry II found it necessary to declare publicly that *The International Jew* and a second book, *Henry Ford and the Jews,* then being circulated by rabble-rouser Gerald L.K. Smith, was "entirely without the sanction, authorization or approval of Mr. Henry Ford, the Ford Motor Company or [myself]." Taking note of the disavowal, the *Canadian Jewish Review* observed, "He was doing something which he probably will be called on to do at intervals during his whole life because his grandfather unloosed an evil which will not be cleaned up in the grandson's time." The dimensions of that "evil," as far as the Jewish public was concerned, was re-emphasized in a nationwide survey conducted by Elmo Roper in 1948. The general public, when asked which American company it "would least have liked to see go out of business," gave Ford the nod by a comfortable margin over any other firm (one in three respondents cited Ford). However, a similar sentiment was expressed by only one-eighth of the Jewish public, one-third of which named Ford's chief competitor, General Motors, as the nation's most indispensable business institution. Subsequent Ford-sponsored surveys among New York Jews revealed a "substantial residue of ill feeling" toward the firm and Ford, Mercury, and Lincoln cars.[62]

In 1964 the *Thunderbolt,* organ of the National States Rights Party, serialized many of the *Dearborn Independent's* anti-Jewish articles, running Ford's by-line and official company picture with each. That same year, Gerald L.K. Smith proudly announced that "a new popular edition of Mr. Ford's 'International Jew' " was available "in bulk quantities." The Anti-Defamation League of B'nai B'rith asked the Ford Company to stop Smith from reprinting and circulating the tract. Since the literature was not copyrighted, the firm expressed its inability to intervene. In 1966 Smith, correctly claiming that Henry Ford never changed his original opinion of Jews, serialized *The International Jew* in his magazine, *The Cross and the Flag,* and re-offered for sale bound copies of *The International Jew.*

Articles in *The International Jew* were revived again in 1972 in a book, *None Dare Call It Conspiracy,* which was distributed free on a massive scale by the John Birch Society. Neo-Nazi publishers and other anti-Semites including Arab organizations have repeatedly reissued *The Protocols of the Wise Men of Zion.* The reprints and literature promoting them usually state that the documents were endorsed and previously published by Henry Ford. Jewish reference works provide no comfort to Ford's memory. Some of them simply say "Ford, Henry, see ANTI-SEMITISM," then describe him as "one of the first to undertake anti-Jewish agitation in the U.S." or as a purveyor of "strong anti-Semitic propaganda by means of his newspaper the *Dearborn Independent.*"[63]

The editor of the *Jewish News,* voice of Michigan Jewry, protested vehemently in 1963 against Detroit Mayor Jerome Cavanagh's proposal to name a civic plaza for Ford. The newspaper also censured two Jews, one of them Michigan's senior reform rabbi, Leon Fram, for accepting membership on the Henry Ford Centennial Committee of Detroit. Jewish publications denounced even more forcefully the [unsuccessful] efforts of Michiganians to induce the United States Post Office Department to issue a stamp in 1963 in commemoration of the 100th anniversary of Ford's birth. "We may as well," thundered the newspaper, "think in terms of issuing a stamp in honor of [Jew haters] Pobedonostzev or Krushevan or Torquemadea [or] Hitler." In 1968, when the Post Office issued a twelve-cent Ford stamp as part of its prominent American series, the *Jewish News* again insisted that "the bigotry in [Ford's] record should rule out such an honor."[64]

Conscious that a special, sustained effort was necessary to regain the goodwill of Jews, the Ford Company has cooperated more fully with Jewish organizations and done more for world Jewry than any other American firm during the past three decades. Aside from its $1,000,000 gift for a NCCJ building, the company has made substantial donations to Yeshiva University and the Albert Einstein Medical Center (attached to Yeshiva) and contributed generously each year to national Jewish organizations and causes. The contributions for years have been made without fanfare, the company not wishing to publicize among the general public its largess to the Jewish community. Conversely, the firm has gone out of its way to acquaint the

Jewish public of its special interest in Jewish affairs. When, for example, Max Fisher, of Detroit, was named general chairman of the United Jewish Appeal's 1965 campaign, Ford was the sole industrial firm to extend congratulations by means of a paid advertisement in the Motor City's Jewish newspaper.[65]

Ford also has taken extraordinary care to avoid any misunderstanding with the Jewish community. When the 1949 Ford was introduced at the time of the Arab-Israeli conflict in 1948, one of the car's colors was called "Arabian Green." A number of dealers, fearful of offending their Jewish customers, asked the company to reconsider the name. "In a flash ... the company scrapped all kinds of already printed promotion material and changed the name to 'Meadowbrook Green.' " When the Anti-Defamation League charged in 1963 that there was a "serious underutilization" of Jews in white-collar positions within the auto industry, Chrysler and General Motors withheld public comment. Ford, however, immediately issued a public denial of the charges as they applied to the Ford organization—and the next day flew four officials, headed by Allen W. Merrell, vice-president—civic and governmental affairs, to New York to confer with Arnold Forster, the League's general counsel and civil rights director. Following the meeting, which Forster described as a "happy" one, the civil rights leader contrasted the Dearborn company's prompt response to Chrysler's and General Motors' dilatory replies.[66]

To the new and unstable State of Israel, Ford in 1949 extended the most liberal credit terms ever offered to a buyer of Ford trucks. During the 1950s the company began exporting passenger cars to Israel from the United States, England, and Germany. The thirteen-member Arab League, which in 1951 set up a Boycott Office to monitor and blacklist firms doing business with Israel, protested Ford's cooperation with the Jewish state, but stopped short of declaring a boycott of the company's products. The Arab League also expressed disapproval of the Ford Company's gifts of funds and equipment to Israel's Weizmann Institute of Science, Hebrew University, and Technion and Henry Ford II's personal gifts to the United Jewish Appeal. Executives of Ford Overseas Automotive Operations (OAO) which administered an assembly plant in Alexandria, Egypt, a dealer assembly operation in Casablanca, Morocco, and dealerships throughout the Arab world—representing a company-dealer investment of $60,000,000—pleaded with Henry II to soft-pedal his personal contributions to Jewish causes and requested permission for the company to donate an equal sum to the United Nations Relief and Works Agency for Palestine Refugees. The OAO officials also asked Henry II to resist mounting pressure from American Jewish and Israeli leaders to set up a dealer assembly plant for trucks and tractors in Israel. The company, argued the executives, outsold all rivals in the Arab world, and should not sacrifice annual sales of 20,000 to 22,000 units for one-tenth that number of Israeli sales. Henry II endorsed a matching company donation to the refugee agency, a gift which was publicized in Arab nations, but not in the United States, for fear of offending American Jews. Henry II insisted, however, on pushing ahead with plans for Israeli expansion, and sent technicians to the Jewish state to start up a dealer assembly plant for knocked-down vehicles. "Ford," a spokesman for an American Jewish organization said later, "was thinking of the market in Brooklyn, not Tel

Aviv.'' Henry II's decision to expand in Israel, in the face of Arab threats, evoked hundreds of letters of appreciation from Jews around the world and a barrage of favorable editorials in the Jewish press.[67]

Although committed to Israeli expansion, the company tried vainly to appease the Arab League, offering, according to the Jewish Telegraphic Agency [a worldwide Jewish press service] to export cars and trucks from Egypt to help that country earn foreign currency. Ford also declared that it would not invest ''one cent in operations inside Israel,'' and claimed that its expansion was more a matter of degree than of principle. The firm noted that its trucks had always been shipped to Israel in a semi-knocked-down state to save on transport costs; its Israeli dealer had always assembled parts. The dealer, said the company, now wanted to assemble completely knocked-down units to avoid payment of a new Israeli tax of 180 percent on fully assembled imports.[68]

Ford's plea was rejected by the league, which on November 20, 1966, declared a boycott of Ford vehicles and Ford-Philco television receivers, re-frigerators, and air conditioners—a ban which remains in effect as of 1976 and shows no sign of being rescinded. Ford's Egyptian plant and Moroccan facility, financed by Moroccans, were closed; and its dealers, unable to obtain new vehicles and parts, were phased out. The company lost an estimated $200,000,000 in sales during the first three years of the boycott, according to Mohammed Mahjoub, commissioner-general of the Boycott Office. In contrast, General Motors, which had exported cars and trucks to Israel since the late 1940s and privately informed Arab leaders that it had no intention of establishing an assembly operation in Israel, went on to increase its sales to Arab countries. In 1974 General Motors sold approximately 2,000 cars and trucks in Israel, approximately 30,000 in Arab states. That year the big auto maker announced that newly formed General Motors Saudi Arabia Ltd., 60 percent owned by General Motors, 40 percent owned by private Saudi interests, would begin pro-ducing Chevrolets and GMC commercial vehicles near Jedda in late 1976.[69]

Henry Ford II never wavered in his decision to forsake the increasingly lucrative Arab market for Israel, and American Jewry. In 1967, he permitted his company to accept an award of merit from the American-Israel Chamber of Commerce and Industry for its decision to assemble vehicles in Israel. ''That is all we need,'' a Ford overseas executive groaned at the time. Three years later Henry II told a delegation of Jewish visitors to his office that his only regret over his decision was ''the harm imposed on Ford's Arab dealers who were innocent victims.'' In 1972, Ford visited his company's Nazareth assembly plant, whose 1,200 employees built commercial vehicles and the Escort car. ''I have been a friend of Israel for many years,'' Henry II told Transport Minister Shimon Peres, ''and after my visit here, I am even a bigger friend.''

The boycott of Ford took on a new dimension in 1975, when Henry II visited London's money market in search of Arab financing for Detroit's Ford Company-sponsored Renaissance Center, a huge hotel-office-apartment complex. The Arabs, pointing to the inclusion of Ford's name on their blacklist, summarily rejected the company chairman's appeal. The Ford Company subsequently put up the money to permit Center construction to proceed.[70]

Where does the Ford Company now stand with American Jewry? Most older Jews have not forgotten, and many have not forgiven, Henry Ford for his anti-Semitic braying. Some elderly Jews will not buy a Ford vehicle because of Ford's anti-Semitism, and are critical of Jews who purchase Ford cars. "Time heals all wounds," said a Jewish leader, "but some remain for ages. I have owned cars for many years but just cannot allow myself to buy a Ford." Some older Jews also show copies of the *Dearborn Independent* and dog-eared editions of *The International Jew* to their children and grandchildren; others buy newer editions of the booklet for the same purpose. One of the author's Jewish students said in 1967 that his New York grandparents threatened to disinherit him if he bought a Ford car or Ford stock; to do so, they said, would be to "trade with the enemy." Another Jewish student the same year inquired of his "usually mild-mannered" father about Ford's anti-Semitism. The father, a Brooklynite, replied: "You ask about my attitude toward Ford. I did have an unlimited hatred of *the* Henry Ford—that old ignorant hating bastard, who, in my mind, was a vastly overrated genius who cheated some of his early associates and by his conduct must have helped drive some of them to untimely graves, including his own son. But, certainly the grandsons have given every indication of being enlightened, of making every effort to atone for the sins of that contemptible old bastard ignoramus. You must have gathered that I didn't like him."[71]

Almost all Jews, however, including those who have neither forgotten nor forgiven Henry Ford, are gratified by the friendliness and generosity of the Ford family and the Ford Company toward the Jewish community since the late 1940s. "The grandchildren, and Mrs. Edsel too," observed the head of a large Jewish welfare organization, "are just fine, just wonderful." "It would be difficult to find a family which is so completely free of racial or religious prejudice as the Ford family," echoed a prominent Detroit rabbi. "The new generation of Fords," declared an influential Jewish editor in 1970, "looks back at the era of their grandfather with a sense of deep regret, rejecting whatever smacked of prejudice and of anti-Semitism. The Liebold-Cameron-Bennett chapter of bigotry is treated with contempt." Because of the Ford Company's acts of atonement, most Jews, according to an official of the Anti-Defamation League, base decisions on whether or not to buy a Ford car on the merits of the product rather than on their estimate of the company or its founder. A few Jews, according to the welfare executive, are sufficiently grateful for the Ford family's and Ford Company's contributions to Jewry, to be biased in favor of Ford cars.[72]

That Ford products are no longer discriminated against by many Jews may be regarded as highly gratifying progress in Ford's campaign to regain the goodwill of the Jewish community. If, in time, through the company's good works, large numbers of Jews come to look upon Ford as a firm sympathetic to them—and for that reason include a Ford car in their future—Henry Ford II and his associates may well congratulate themselves on having conducted an exceptionally intelligent and mutually beneficial long-range public relations program.

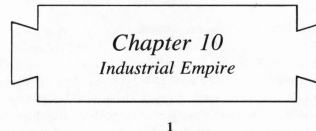

Chapter 10
Industrial Empire

1

During the 1920s Henry Ford developed America's first vertically integrated, yet highly diversified industrial empire. His company mined coal, iron ore, and lead; owned timber lands, sawmills, dry kilns, a wood distillation plant, a rubber plantation, and a series of "village industries"; operated a railroad, blast furnaces, coke ovens, foundries, steel mills, and lake and ocean fleets; produced glass, artificial leather, textiles, gauges, paper, and cement; built airplanes; farmed 10,000 acres; and made Model T's, Lincolns, and the Fordson tractor. In addition, it prospected for oil, bought dolomite lands with the production of magnesium in mind, took steps to produce abrasives, bought acreage in the Everglades with the intent of planting rubber trees, and experimented with the development of power by burning coal at the mine and making charcoal iron. These multifarious activities received wide attention during the 1920s and contributed importantly to the public's belief that Henry Ford had a daring and highly original mind, virtually unique technical skills, and a never ceasing desire to serve mankind.[1]

The cornerstone of the sprawling Ford organization, until the mid-1920s, was the Highland Park plant. Attaining a peak employment of 68,285 in 1924, the factory for fifteen years was ranked as the world's largest automobile plant. This fact, coupled with Highland Park's fame as the "birthplace of mass production," created a steady flow of plant publicity and enabled the factory from 1912 to 1927 to attract more visitors than any other industrial institution in the country. An average of 124,000 guests toured the plant annually between 1922 and 1927, with the highest figure, 156,707, being recorded in 1925. By comparison, the second most visited plant in the Detroit area, the Dodge factory, drew only 50,000 persons during its best year, 1927.[2]

In 1925 the burgeoning Rouge plant eclipsed the Highland Park factory in total employment. Two years later, when the company started to produce the Model A, Highland Park's final assembly line was transferred to the Rouge. Thereafter the older factory lost its popularity with the public. From 1928, when space was leased to the Briggs Body Corporation, the number of Ford employees at Highland Park also declined rapidly. The plant had but 30,507 Ford workers in 1928 and only 18,231 in 1929.[3]

The Rouge first attracted attention during the late 'teens, when the Dodge brothers took Henry Ford to court in an effort to thwart his plans to build blast furnaces and other manufacturing facilities at the Dearborn site. There was little building activity at the Rouge, however, until 1918, when the B Building was hastily erected for the construction of Eagle boats. This structure was converted into a body-making plant in 1919, and during the next few years was rapidly surrounded by an industrial complex designed to transform raw materials into finished products within a matter of hours. Coke ovens went into operation in late 1919; a sawmill, designed to prepare wood for body-making, began to function in early 1920; and Blast Furnace A was "blown in" in May of that same year. The latter event was celebrated with a drama worthy of the launching of an ocean liner. A pile of cordwood and coke was placed in the furnace, and Henry Ford II, Edsel's oldest child, was designated to light it. "The fun of playing with matches," reported the *Detroit News,* "was almost too much for Henry II, who is only three years old, and he had some difficulty, but with his grandfather's aid the blaze was started and then he sat perched on grandfather's shoulder while everyone cheered."

In early 1921 the Ford Company began producing tractors in the B Building, and in the same year the Rouge foundry and the power plant, both the largest units of their kind in the world, came into operation. Although at this stage the Rouge was little more than a third finished, it became the subject of several news stories. Predictions were made that the industrial concentration eventually would surpass Krupp's Essen works in size, and thereby become the largest single-company manufacturing complex on earth. Articles also pointed out that the Rouge, upon completion, would bring together for the first time in the history of metalworking the three great divisions of steel making—furnace, foundry, and mills.[4]

By 1924 the Rouge had 42,000 workers; by 1925, 58,000; by 1926, 75,000; and by 1929 more than 103,000. In 1926, still short of completion (for it was being expanded as late as 1937–38), the complex sprawled over 1,115 acres. Ninety-three separate structures stood on the site, twenty-three of which were classified as "main buildings"; there were 160 acres of floor space; railroad trackage covered ninety-three miles and conveyers, twenty-seven. By the mid-1920s, the Rouge was easily the greatest industrial domain in the world.

The complex was also without parallel in sheer mechanical efficiency. Ford had set out to build a maze of plants which would afford continuous, integrated manufacturing processes. The Rouge brilliantly realized this dream. A leading technical writer described the total effect upon the visitor as follows: "He sees these units not only in their impressive individual and astounding collective magnitude, *but he also sees each unit as the part of a huge machine*—he sees each unit as a carefully designed gear which meshes with other gears and operates in synchronism with them, the whole forming one huge, perfectly-timed, smoothly operating industrial machine of almost unbelievable efficiency." Ford publicists delighted in illustrating the Rouge's manufacturing prowess by pointing out that iron ore was melted, molded, and converted into a finished motor traveling along the final assembly line in only thirty-three hours. In the 1930s the time span was reduced to twenty-eight hours.[5]

The Rouge probably was the most publicized plant in the United States during the 1920s. Many of the news stories were generated by the Ford Company, which annually sent out dozens of news releases extolling the factory. As early as 1924 one press release proclaimed that "the River Rouge plant of the Ford Motor Company, as yet scarcely half completed, today stands as the greatest industrial marvel in the world . . . exceeding in magnitude and achievement any industrial project ever before attempted."[6]

The publicity helped the Rouge to supersede the Highland Park plant as America's most visited factory. The Rouge drew only 15,000 visitors in 1924, 24,797 in 1925, 40,782 in 1926, and less than 50,000 in 1927. In 1929 the number of tourists swelled to 121,811, a record figure which was unbroken until 1936, when 132,507 people visited the plant. In 1939 the Rouge played host to 163,188 persons, a total exceeded only by Highland Park's 200,000 visitors in 1917. The newer factory's highest prewar attendance figure, 166,519, was set in 1940.

Visitors perhaps were most impressed by the Rouge's panoramic vastness, for no other embodiment of the industrial revolution was (and is) more commanding or more overpowering. "In the eyes of many a spectator," observed one writer, "this monument of Ford is more awesome than the mightiest sights of nature for the reason that it is man-made. It looks like the ultimate, even in an age that is accustomed to feast on the big and the spectacular." Its cleanliness was as impressive as its size. Ford's plants had always been among the neatest and trimmest in the country; and the route over which Rouge tourists were taken was always kept "as spotless as a Dutch kitchen."[7]

2

In striking contrast to the Rouge's vastness were Ford's village industries. During the late 'teens the industrialist, probably with Thomas Edison's active encouragement, conceived a plan to dot many of America's rivers with small water-driven factories which would offer employment to farmers during the winter. The city, Ford pointed out, had been a mistake. It meant high land costs, high taxes, poor housing, and congested transportation. The country, in contrast, was an area of hope. "Factory and farm should have been organized as adjuncts one of the other, and not as competitors," Ford declared. "With one foot in industry and one foot in agriculture, America is safe."

In 1919 plant sites were acquired on two small Michigan rivers, the Miami River in Ohio, and the Hudson in New York. The first rural production center, a reconverted mill at Northville, Michigan, twelve miles up the Rouge River from Dearborn, began making valves in early 1920. By 1925 nine hydroelectric plants were in operation. Some of these factories were truly "village industries," employing only a dozen to three or four dozen workers. Others were sizable. The Flat Rock plant, on Michigan's Huron River, employed 500 men and made 500,000 headlights per month. The Green Island facility, utilizing a government-built dam on the Hudson, generated 10,000 horsepower and employed 1,000 men. Larger still was the Hamilton factory on the Miami River, which had a work force of 2,500.[8]

The village industries were consistently publicized by the Ford Company, as Henry Ford—hopeful that his experiment would foster sweeping changes in society—sought to focus as much attention on his factory-farm philosophy as possible. In addition to Ford's many public statements on the subject and the news releases sent out by the company, a number of institutional advertisements and speeches by

Ford executives (including talks by William J. Cameron on the Ford Sunday Evening Hour) dealt with the village-industry idea.[9]

During the early 1920s, particularly, the hydroelectric plants were the objects of wide discussion, often in connection with rumors that Ford was considering locating a small factory in this or that town. "Let Ford visit any place," observed the *Elyria* (Ohio) *Telegram* in 1921, "and immediately there is a story flashed over the wires that he is visiting that locality looking over sites.... For the past few years there have been more communities in the country which were supposed to be under the watchful and guardian eye of Henry Ford to upbuild and advance their interests than could comfortably be counted over on both hands several times." The Ford Company's clipbooks amply bear out this observation. During a twelve-month period in 1922–23, Ford was variously reported to be scouting Wisconsin's Kickapoo River with an eye toward manufacturing zinc to be used in making tires and galvanized fencing; to be seeking a site for a Lincoln plant in Buffalo; to be contemplating a $3,000,000 factory in Walden, New York; to be interested in making tires in Noblesville, Indiana; and to be thinking of locating small plants in New London, Connecticut; Alexandria, Indiana; and southern Illinois.[10]

The village industries were not a financial success, but Ford, breaking ground, did not count what he spent. In fact, between 1935 and 1941 he established a dozen additional hydroelectric plants on small Michigan streams. Making such parts as cigarette lighters, carburetors, horns, and ignition coils, the factories employed 2,460 persons in 1939.[11]

Although not really a panacea for factory worker or farmer, the village-industry plan did influence industrial planners in three countries during the mid-1930s. The governor of East Prussia advocated the scattering of small plants over his province. Each factory was to be the nucleus of a village and each working family therein was to be given a plot of land nearby. *Le Temps* of Paris reported that Ford's idea had inspired Marshall Pétain to incorporate in a defense program submitted to the French general staff a provision for setting up small factories throughout France. Finally, Harry L. Hopkins, director of the Federal Emergency Relief Administration, acknowledged indebtedness to Ford for his plan to remove hundreds of thousands of unemployed city laborers to small communities where "they would be able to support themselves partly by factory work and partly by farming on a minor scale." "It would be a good thing for America," stated Hopkins, "if large cities disappeared and their industries were scattered in a thousand smaller communities."[12]

3

Two important elements in Ford's empire were raw materials and transportation facilities. In 1920 the manufacturer purchased more than 360,000 acres of forest and an iron mine in northern Michigan. Within the next few years, he built lumber camps and sawmills and bought dock facilities at two places on the southern shore of Lake Superior, acquiring in the process a town, 400,000 additional acres of forest, towing outfits, tugs, and scows. Later he bought 2,200 additional acres of northern Michigan ore-bearing land and opened a second iron mine.

In July 1920, just before buying the first large timber tract, Ford bought two coal mines in Kentucky. A few months later he bought a mine in West Virginia. These mines could have supplied sufficient fuel, if worked at full capacity, for the chief Ford factories and Ford's newly acquired railroad. However, after a nationwide coal strike created a fuel shortage which closed Ford plants for five days in September 1922, the company bought three additional groups of mines in Kentucky and West Virginia to safeguard its coal supply.[13]

This shutdown gave Ford a magnificent opportunity to appear as the champion of the consumer. "This coal shortage has not come about naturally," he declared. "It has been brought about artificially by the Wall Street interests that own the railroads and coal mines." He further claimed that "coal bootleggers" had offered "to steal coal from men, women and children" and sell it to him at inflated prices. "I am going to shut down," he told reporters, "because I will not pay graft to get coal. . . . It is all a conspiracy to fleece the public." Secretary of Commerce Herbert Hoover, when pressed for a statement on Ford's shutdown, suggested that Ford could stay open if he would pay the going price for coal, $6.50 a ton (Ford was willing to pay $4.50). Ford lashed out at Hoover, stating that it would be unfair to ordinary consumers to permit himself "to be held up" for coal—even though he personally could afford to pay the operators' "exorbitant prices."[14]

Ford's stand was frequently compared with his price rollback of 1920, and once again he emerged a knight in shining armor, battling the vested interests in behalf of the people. "Give us a few more Fords and less Hoovers and this U.S.A. will be much better off," the *Sacramento Leader* editorialized. Noting that Ford was reaping a harvest of nationwide publicity, the *Modesto* (California) *Herald* reported: "He is performing a valuable public service. From this standpoint, Henry Ford . . . may well be generously accorded all the free advertising that headlines may carry." The publicity also helped Ford in a material way, for within a week of his shutdown he was able to buy all the coal he wanted for $4.50 a ton. Several publications could not refrain from congratulating the industrialist on the way he "manipulated the newspapers so as to get several kinds of favorable advertising." "Could anybody else," asked the *Detroit Saturday Night,* "out of a simple coal situation get so many free rides in the press?"[15]

Two months after the coal crisis Ford announced that he would start selling coal from his mines directly to the public. The International News Service regarded this move as "Ford's first step in his fight to break the grip of the coal trust on the public." Actually, Ford's coal resources were of such size that he found it necessary to place as much as one-quarter of his output on the open market. Nonetheless, this step, together with the well publicized improvement of working conditions and wages in Ford-owned mines, gave the industrialist something of a reputation as a coal mining expert. Senator Robert F. Wagner suggested in 1928 that Ford should be consulted by a Senate committee then endeavoring to frame legislation to help cure the coal industry's ills. Expressing great faith in Ford's mining knowledge, the

Providence News "devoutly hoped" that the industrialist would appear before the committee "and tell it what he knows about running a coal mine."[16]

4

One of the fields in which Ford invested most heavily and, in the long run, least successfully was rubber production. The industrialist became interested in this raw material in 1922, when the British, whose Ceylonese and Malayan plantations supplied two-thirds of all crude rubber, approved a restriction scheme which seemed likely to raise the crude-rubber bill of the United States by tens of millions of dollars annually. Harvey S. Firestone took a militant stand against the plan and persuaded Ford and Edison to experiment with trees, vines, and plants containing rubber in an attempt to create a domestic rubber supply. At the same time the trio undertook to find suitable places in Latin America, Africa, and the Philippines for establishing American-controlled plantations.

Edison, whose laboratories conducted the research on the local plants, was unable to produce a satisfactory substitute for rubber. Firestone and Ford were therefore forced to look overseas. Firestone turned to Liberia, but Ford, whose wealth and industrial accomplishments had prompted the Brazilian government to offer special inducements to him should he develop a Brazilian plantation, bought a 2,500,000-acre tract on the Tapajós River (a main tributary of the Amazon) in 1927. Planting and cultivating of rubber seedlings began in 1928, and although the mortality rate of the trees was high for a number of years, the Ford plantation (Fordlandia) contained 3,651,500 trees by 1941.

Early in World War II the company's Brazilian holdings received a considerable amount of publicity, as the nation hopefully looked to Ford for some of its rubber needs. However, Ford's first harvest, in 1942, yielded only 750 tons of creamed latex—only a fraction of America's requirements. By 1950 a yield of 7,500 tons was expected, with an eventual goal of 38,000 tons, the amount required yearly by the Ford Company. In 1945 the plantation still needed financing, even though an estimated $20,000,000 had been poured into the venture. By that time adverse Brazilian labor legislation and the development of artificial rubber during World War II were adding to the plantation's troubles. In December 1945, the company sold its holdings to the Brazilian government.[17]

5

Ford entered nonautomotive transportation with the purchase of the Detroit, Toledo & Ironton Railroad in 1920. This railroad had been in and out of receivership since its construction in 1874, had never paid a dividend, and for the year 1920 showed a deficit of $1,896,523. Many railroad men and business experts regarded the $5,000,000 purchase with sardonic amusement. Some called it the T.L.R.R. (the Tin

Lizzie Railroad); others grimly remarked that Ford had found a bottomless hole into which to pour his money.[18]

Railway Age, on the other hand, while admitting that the purchase "will supply material for every paragrapher and jokesmith on every newspaper in the country," declared that the purchase was sound. This publication saw in the D.T.& I. what Ford had seen and others had not—that it would permit Ford to ship his Kentucky coal northward in record time; that it could speed automotive shipments from the Rouge southward; that it crossed all the northern east-west trunk lines, and to the south connected with the Baltimore & Ohio, the Chesapeake & Ohio, and the Norfolk & Western. With the D.T.& I., Ford need have no fear that motor vehicles or automotive parts would pile up at the Rouge for lack of rail transportation.

When purchased, the railroad was in a precarious position. Its 465 miles of roadbed were defective, its rails light and badly worn, its locomotives and cars inadequate in number and in poor condition, its stations and shops in disrepair, and the morale of its employees low. Ford, who was determined to exhibit a "showcase railroad," announced a program of improvement requiring from $10,000,000 to $20,000,000. Fifty-six-pound rails were replaced with eighty-five-pound stock; the roadbed was put in order; ten new locomotives and 800 new freight cars were acquired; and stations and shops were repaired. The number of employees was slashed from 2,760 to 1,650. Ford's minimum wage of six dollars a day was introduced, which meant higher pay for most employees. The cost of operation was drastically reduced, the amount of traffic increased, and the employees' morale soared. In October 1921, the road was the only one not affected by a nationwide strike. The president of the Switchmen's Union of North America stated that D.T.& I. men would not affiliate with the brotherhoods because of their favorable treatment by Ford.[19]

In mid-1921 Ford announced a 20 percent reduction in freight rates, a move which made the industrialist "about as popular as a snake with the other railroad executives of the country." The reduction was held up for a year by the Interstate Commerce Commission, which paid for its dilatoriness by a blast from a sizable segment of the press. Conversely, Ford, whose railroad brought profits of $1,417,036 in 1923 and $1,719,290 in 1924, received warm praise from many newspapers and was regarded by many as a "railroad genius." The fruit-growers of Oceana County, Michigan, even petitioned President Harding to have the government buy up the nation's railroads and place them under Ford's general managership.[20]

Undoubtedly, as rival railroad executives asserted, the D.T.& I.'s gains were partly due to company traffic. "Henry Ford, the shipper, gives his freight to Henry Ford, the railroad man," stated one critic. Yet, as Oswald Garrison Villard observed, there is no doubt that, coming to railroading with a fresh mind and freedom from the methods of the older railway corporations, Ford had put new life and efficiency into what had been a dead, or nearly dead, artery of traffic. His men also worked hard to obtain freight from competing railroads and were quite successful in doing so.[21]

Ford was continually annoyed by the regulations of the Interstate Commerce Commission and the need to comply with federal law (he was fined $20,000 in 1928 for failure to charge demurrage on certain shipments to the Rouge, in violation of federal legislation governing railroad rebates). Rather than "share" control of his railroad with the government, Ford decided to sell. "I learned you could own a railroad, but you couldn't run it," he told an associate, "The Interstate Commerce Commission did that for you." In 1929 the Pennroad Corporation (associated with the Pennsylvania Railroad) bought the D.T.& I. for $36,000,000. This figure was more than seven times what Ford had paid for the road nine years before, a handsome profit even when set against the $8,000,000 the magnate had spent on improvements for the facility. In addition, the road had earned rich dividends for Ford from 1923 through 1926, these ceasing in 1927 when the gestation of Model A cut down traffic and caused a deficit of $134,000.[22] When Ford retired from railroading in 1929, he could look back on his experience as a rewarding one. He had made money in operating his railroad, sold at a profit (just in time to escape the depression), and reaped a harvest of publicity which enhanced his reputation as the world's leading industrialist.

6

Ford entered the shipping field in 1924, when he bought two ocean vessels, the *Oneida* and *Onondaga,* and converted them into lake carriers, and built two lakers, the *Henry Ford II* and the *Benson Ford.* Six hundred-and-twelve feet in length, sixty-two in beam, and thirty-two in depth, the *Henry Ford II* and the *Benson Ford,* with carrying capacities of 11,750 and 12,000 gross tons, respectively, were exceeded in capacity by only eighteen vessels operating on the Great Lakes during the 1920s. The ships, with speeds up to fourteen knots, were used chiefly to carry Ford coal from Toledo to Lake Superior ports and to haul iron ore (some of it mined by Ford) from northern Michigan and Minnesota to the huge plant on the River Rouge. A dozen vessels soon were added to the fleet, among them three large lakers, two smaller vessels for lake and barge canal traffic to New York, and six barges. By 1929 Ford had a fleet of twenty-one carriers, barges, and tugs on the Great Lakes; in terms of both number of vessels in service and fleet capacity, he consistently ranked among the top twenty lake shippers from the mid-1920s until the start of World War II.[23]

Ocean shipping also beckoned. In 1925 several of Ford's vessels were assigned to European and South American service. Immediately there was speculation to the effect that Ford's plunge into sea transportation would "revolutionize the shipping world." Arthur Brisbane, noting that Americans had been unable to compete successfully with foreign fleets, predicted that Ford, if anyone, could show his countrymen the way to profitable shipping operations. Characteristically, Ford did raise the wages of his seamen to a level 50 to 100 percent higher than the prevailing rates, thereby provoking "the greatest sensation American shipping circles have known in recent years." On the Great Lakes, Ford had been able to force other lines to liberalize their carrying practices (for example, they finally agreed to handle unboxed motors and parts as well as boxed goods), and to reduce their rates, while operating the *Henry Ford II* and the *Benson Ford* at a profit ($887,810 during the period 1925–1929).[24] But Ford's stake in ocean transportation was too small to have much of an impact on the industry.

Ford also received considerable publicity when he bought 199 steel vessels for scrappage in 1925. The government-owned ships, built during the war, were towed from Atlantic ports to the Rouge. Ford paid only $1,697,470 for them, less than 2 percent of their original cost. He made a profit of nearly $5,000,000 on the transaction, a fact which added to his reputation as a "financial genius."[25]

7

Although Ford was a latecomer to the older, better-established forms of transportation, making his entry into railroading and shipping in the early 1920s, his interest in air transportation began almost with the first trial flights. In 1908 or 1909, after the flights of the Wright brothers for the army and the advent of Glenn Curtiss and others had stirred the imagination of the nation, Henry and Edsel Ford began to take notice. Prodded by Edsel and a twenty-year-old employee, Charles Van Auken, the senior Ford permitted Van Auken to build an experimental plane using a Model T engine for motive power. The craft, completed in 1910, was tested on a plank runway laid out on a gentle slope on the Ford farm in Dearborn. On its test runs it would rise to a height of about six feet and then drop. During one test the crankshaft broke, and the plane was blown into a tree, causing mild injuries to the pilot, Van Auken. Ford then stopped the trials, but continued to watch aeronautical progress closely, particularly after his company began the manufacture of Liberty motors during the war. In 1920 he toyed with the idea of building dirigibles, and after conferring in Detroit with representatives of the Zeppelin firm, he sent an employee, William B. Mayo, to Europe to study dirigible construction techniques. The Zeppelin negotiations came to naught, but Ford was sufficiently impressed with the future of aviation to predict that airships combining the features of rigid dirigibles and the airplane would be spanning the Atlantic by 1925.[26]

In 1922 Henry and Edsel Ford and Mayo joined 125 other Michiganians who invested $1,000 each in the newly formed Stout Metal Airplane Company, headed by William B. Stout, an ingenious promoter and engineer with bold ideas in the field of aviation. Stout built a commercially feasible aluminum monoplane, but his plans for launching an air freight service were frustrated by the lack of a good landing field in the Detroit area. In mid-1924 he appealed to Henry Ford to build an airport. The manufacturer responded by constructing in Dearborn what was then one of the world's finest air installations, with paved runways; passenger, mail, and freight facilities; ample hangar space for visiting planes; and parts and shop service. The industrialist extended a public invitation to all flyers—army, navy, marine, or private—to use the field. For a number of years it was one of the busiest air terminals on earth.

Ford also built a factory for Stout, and in early 1925 he proposed to purchase the Stout Metal Airplane Company by paying each co-owner twice the amount of his original investment. Ford's bid for Stout's company was accompanied by widespread publicity. To many it meant that aviation had now come of age. The *Detroit Times* remarked that "if the Fords, father and son, undertake the building of all-metal

Covers of two Ford joke books.

One of numerous Model T postcards sold in the 'teens and
'twenties.

One of Henry Ford's favorite journalists, Hearst editor Arthur Brisbane, standing, and the auto maker at a 1930 dinner. (United Press International photo.)

Rabbi Leo M. Franklin of Detroit's Temple Beth-El, left, and Henry Ford.

Henry Ford receives the Grand Cross of the German Eagle in 1938 from Fritz Hailer, left, German consul in Detroit, and Karl Kapp, German consul in Cleveland. (*Detroit Free Press* photo.)

The Rouge plant, world's largest single-company industrial concentration, about 1928, showing iron ore carriers in the northern end of the slip at the right and storage bins at the left of the slip. Further left are the blast furnaces, foundry, and power plant (tall chimneys).

Henry Ford inspects a gleaming locomotive of his Detroit, Toledo & Ironton Railroad, 1921.

Henry Ford, coat askew, watches company mail being loaded into Stout Transport's *Maiden Dearborn* in April 1925. Edsel Ford stands to the right of his father, Clara Ford is third from left. William B. Stout is mostly hidden by Henry Ford.

Henry Ford greets Charles A. Lindbergh in Dearborn on August 11, 1927. Ford took his first flight with the Lone Eagle.

A bird imitator and his wife performing on Henry Ford's pioneer radio station, WWI, Dearborn.

The Ford Company's 1923 Model T advertising emphasized low, low prices.

A 1924 Model T coupe.

airplanes in quantity production, one great problem will be solved." Arthur Brisbane declared that "the Fords have the power, knowledge, industrial genius, and money to put this nation ahead of all others in air defense. Let them do that, and their fame will outlast the memory of war."[27]

The Stout organization was not formally incorporated into the Ford Motor Company until August 1925, but for several months prior to this time Ford had been active in new aviation ventures. On April 13 he inaugurated a Detroit-Chicago air freight service, the nation's first commercial airline. The event was hailed by newspapers the country over. Editorials predicted that flying Fords soon would blacken the sky and cartoons showed the air filled with "flying flivvers." The publicity apparently strengthened Henry Ford's resolve to move into aviation in earnest: "It's so big that everybody will be interested. . . . Up to the present I haven't taken any particular charge of this flying business. I left it to Edsel. . . . But now that the product is ready to be used I am more interested than ever. It's a great proposition and I feel it is now or never to get a hold of commercial flying and make a success of it."[28]

Ford now entered aviation in earnest. On July 1, 1925, he inaugurated Detroit-Cleveland air service, and seven-and-a-half months later the company was awarded government contracts to carry the mails between Detroit and Chicago and Detroit and Cleveland. In the meantime, the Ford plane received wide recognition because of its performance in the first National Air Reliability Tour, initiated in 1925 by the Detroit Aviation Society. Sixteen aircraft entered the 1,900-mile contest, which originated and ended at the Ford airport. A Ford air transport demonstrated the greatest speed, a little more than 100 miles an hour. Henry Ford personally greeted each incoming flier, before a crowd of 35,000 people. The contest was front-page news in most of the daily press for six days, and the two Fords (Edsel provided a trophy to each pilot who finished) and their entry received a good deal of press attention. On the strength of the victory and attendant publicity the first commercial sale of a Ford plane was made. The buyer, the John Wanamaker Company, promptly displayed the plane in its New York show window, opened an "Airplane Department," and placed a $25,000 price tag on its line of Ford merchandise.[29]

The National Air Reliability Tour, often cited by the press as the Ford Reliability Tour, became a yearly event. A number of Ford victories, coupled with the fact that the contests always started and ended in Dearborn, gave the Fords and their Aircraft Division, as it was now called, a great deal of publicity. The 1929 tour, for example, generated more than 30,000 news stories, with the name "Ford" mentioned in all of them. Moreover, as many as 150,000 persons gathered at the Ford airport for the start of the competition.[30]

Although these aviation activities were primarily identified with Henry Ford, they also focused attention on Edsel Ford. In fact, Edsel's interest in aviation brought him more attention from the press during the half-dozen years after 1924 than at any other period of his career. Many people probably first learned of Henry Ford's son when they read newspaper accounts of the company's aviation ventures and items on reliability races and exploratory expeditions (Edsel gave financial support to Richard E. Byrd and Floyd Bennett for their 1926 flight over the North Pole, and he

was the chief instigator and financial backer of Byrd's 1929 antarctic air expedition).
No doubt many Americans were more aware of Edsel Ford the aviation enthusiast
than they were of Edsel Ford the president of the Ford Motor Company.[31]

In March 1926, the Fords announced that henceforth they would build only
multimotored airplanes—a somewhat astonishing declaration, since there were then
fewer than a half-dozen such craft in the entire country. The new plane, the famous
Ford trimotor, had a wing spread of seventy feet, carried eight passengers, and
provided separate space for freight. It was the largest multimotored type designed for
commercial use up until then. The trimotor found a ready acceptance among such
customers as the army and navy, Standard Oil Company, Royal Typewriter Company, Pan American Airways, Northwest Airlines, and Transcontinental Air Transport (the forerunner of Trans World Airlines). Sales in 1928 totaled thirty-six, a large
number for that day, and reached their peak, eighty-six, in 1929. During these years
Ford was probably the largest manufacturer of commercial planes in the world.

Ford also built a number of other planes. One was the forty-horsepower
"flivver plane," which weighed only 350 pounds. It had a wing span of only
twenty-two feet, and was a mere fifteen feet long. Introduced in mid-1926, the plane
at one time held the world's endurance record for small airplanes (986 miles). Henry
Ford became hostile to this model when a popular company pilot lost his life in one,
and in late 1928 he shelved the plane "until the public becomes more air-minded."
Ford next turned to the construction of an air behemoth. The 14-AT, the largest commercial land plane built in America before 1945, was designed to carry six tons of
freight or fifty-eight passengers. Flight tests were to have been conducted in 1932,
but the craft, which Ford saddled with heavy water-cooled motors, never left the
ground. The company also built a multiengined bomber, patterned after the trimotor,
which was flight-tested at Wright Field in 1931.[32]

In an effort to make Americans more air-travel minded, the Ford Company
launched a memorable series of institutional aviation advertising in 1927. The
campaign, which ran in national magazines, was the first to try to sell air transportation to the general public. Copy and illustrations were rich and visionary. The first ad,
entitled "Lift Up Your Eyes," showed a farm family looking and pointing skyward as
the shadow of an airplane crossed its lawn. Other ads spoke of the "golden path-
ways" that led across the "fenceless sky" and the mercy missions that planes could
perform "after levees melt away or blizzards cover city and country." Although the
advertising referred to Ford's experiments, flights, and air routes, it did not allude to
the availability of the company's aviation products. The series, which was put into
book form and sent to one thousand aviation executives and leading Americans, was
favorably received. "His [Ford's] advertising has done more to popularize flying
among the reading public," commented the *Aero Digest* in 1928, "than all the stunts
that ever have been stunted." The Harvard Graduate School of Business Administration awarded the campaign a $1,000 Bok Prize "for meritorious accomplishment in
the advertising field." Two decades later "Lift Up Your Eyes" was named by a
leading advertising executive as one of the "100 greatest advertisements."[33]

Henry Ford's aviation activity was cut short by the depression. Sales dropped
to twenty-six in 1930, twenty-one in 1931, and only three in 1932. By that time

the manufacturer's aviation venture had accumulated a total operating deficit of $5,627,996, while expenditures (plant, equipment, and losses) totalled $10,396,825. In addition, the parent company was struggling through one of the worst years, financially, in its history. Under the circumstances, Ford lost his enthusiasm for airplanes and decided to abandon what had become an unprofitable side activity.[34]

8

Another twentieth-century invention in which Henry Ford took an early interest, but also abandoned when expenses outweighed the return, was the radio. The magnate first expressed interest in this new form of communication in September 1919, when he hailed Fred L. Black as the latter strode past Ford's office:

"Say, Fred, what do you know about wireless [radio]?"

"I don't know anything, Mr. Ford. Just the stories published in the newspapers."

"Well, I think it would be a damned good time to learn. You make me one of these wireless receiving outfits."

Black left Ford wondering if he should offer his resignation or try to build the set, "because Ford might as well have told me to make a rocket to go to the moon, for what I knew about wireless at that time." However, after reading about the subject and attending a night course for wireless operators at a Detroit high school, Black, assisted by a Ford employee who had had radio experience in the Army Signal Corps, built a set. He also investigated the relative advantages of the several types of broadcasting equipment available at the time and reported that it would be possible to set up intracompany radio communications any time after October 1, 1919, when the government was to lift its ban on radio transmitting.[35]

Ford soon put his wireless apparatus to practical use: in August 1920, the company began transmitting messages among its plants in Dearborn and Northville, Michigan, and Henry Ford's yacht, the *Sialia*. The Flat Rock, Michigan, plant and the divisional offices of Ford's railroad, the Detroit, Toledo & Ironton, at Springfield, Ohio, were added to the intracompany network by February 1922. By early 1925 the company had installed radio equipment on its fleet of lake and ocean vessels, at its timber operations in northern Michigan, and at Jackson, Ohio, a D.T.& I. checkpoint. The chain of stations, according to the *Detroit News,* "put Ford far in the lead in the U.S. in the use of radio-telegraph in industry and commerce."[36]

Alert to opportunities, Ford extended the use of the wireless outside his company. In March 1922, the magnate was granted permission by the government to make public broadcasts over the Dearborn station (KDEN on the Intra-Ford network), using the call letters WWI. A flurry of publicity accompanied the announcement, the United Press reporting that Ford was "going to tell 'flivver' owners of the intricate methods of their operation by wireless phone." Later in the year the daily press reported that Ford planned to establish 400 radio stations throughout the United States "for business and political purposes" and "to communicate to people without recourse to newspapers."[37]

If Ford ever had such grandiose plans, he did not act on them. He beamed broadcasts to the public over only one 250-watt station, WWI, and it was on the air only one or two hours each Wednesday evening. Black and Ben R. Donaldson, who had charge of mailing for the *Dearborn Independent,* were responsible for programming. As with the *Independent,* there was no attempt to publicize Henry Ford or the Ford Motor Company. A typical program included a talk, a couple of dramatic readings, and several musical numbers. Talks on health ("Boils," "Shoes and Feet," "Breathing," etc.) were prepared by physicians of the Henry Ford Hospital and read either by the author or, if he had a poor voice, by Black. Occasionally such subjects as "Steel," "Cotton," or "Wood" were discussed by Ford engineers or essays on such topics as "The Rediscovery of a Small Town" and "The Christmas Story" were read by William J. Cameron. In fact, Cameron, who during the 1930s became nationally known as the commentator on the Ford Sunday Evening Hour, patterned his Hour talks on those he had delivered over WWI. The readings and musical selections, for the most part, were presented by Ford employees and their families and by residents of the Dearborn area. Most of the performers, in those early days of radio, would have been delighted to entertain without remuneration. However, in deference to Ford's view that if somebody did something, he should be paid for it, the station did pay its talent, and in so doing was one of the first stations in the country to reward entertainers.[38]

During the mid-1920s Ford's experiment in public broadcasting began to lose its luster. Radio had begun to achieve a certain degree of sophistication, while WWI continued to operate with the same wattage and under much the same conditions as it had when it went on the air in May 1922. Like the Model T, the station—because it stood still—began to fall behind competitively. WWI was invited to join one of the newly organized radio networks, but Ford, fearing that it might lose its independence, turned down the bid. He also refused to sell time to advertisers, lest the station should have to accept political speeches with which he might not agree. He was also concerned about having to police all the advertising, pointing out that if people did not, for example, like some soap that was advertised they would be inclined to blame Ford rather than the soap manufacturer. Black, who felt that it was inappropriate for an enterprise of the Ford Company's stature to operate a second-class station in the Detroit area, told Ford that it would be necessary to spend a quarter of a million dollars to make WWI competitive with the *Detroit News*'s WWJ and the *Detroit Free Press*'s WJR. Ford pondered the matter for a couple of months and then informed Black that WWI would be abandoned. Broadcasting was discontinued in early February 1926.[39]

9

Two consumer products, the Fordson tractor and the Lincoln automobile, figured prominently in Henry Ford's expansion plans of the 'teens and 1920s. Ford had begun experimenting with working models of tractors as early as 1907. By 1915 he was sufficiently satisfied with his machine to permit it to be demonstrated publicly in Dearborn and at the Michigan State Fair (held in Detroit). Gasoline tractors were not a novelty during this period; 26,670 of them were produced in the United States in 1916, and a number of the companies that produced them—including International Harvester, Emerson, Case, Moline, Little Giant, and Rock Island—had been in the field for a half-dozen years or more. Yet, the Ford machine, on the strength of Henry Ford's automotive reputation, at once became "the best advertised tractor in the world."[40]

Demonstration models of Ford's vehicle were widely exhibited at fairs during 1916. Henry and Edsel Ford and Charles E. Sorensen attended several of the expositions, the elder Ford sometimes taking along an Animated Weekly cameraman and his Hawaiian quintet. Although frequently pressed to place his machine in production, the industrialist, who was not entirely satisfied with its performance, steadfastly refused to do so.[41]

In mid-1917, however, Ford's hand was forced. The tractor shortage was acute. The British government, after testing the American machine, urgently requested delivery of 6,000 units (a figure equal to almost one-sixth of the world's tractor production in 1916) for the quick expansion of cultivated acreage in the United Kingdom. Ford still was reluctant to go into production, preferring to work on his vehicle until it was "right." However, after Viscount Northcliffe, head of a permanent British mission in the United States, personally pleaded with Ford to start production at once, the manufacturer acquiesced. His tractor company, Henry Ford & Son, which had been organized on July 27, 1917, quickly built a plant in Dearborn and by the end of the year had completed 254 machines. Production rose rapidly thereafter, and by April 1918, the entire British order, raised to 7,000, had been delivered. The British government was grateful to Ford for his assistance, and its Munitions Department, in thanking Ford of England for its role in assembling the machines, stated that without them "the food crisis would in all probability not have been surmounted."[42]

Ford next turned to the tractor-starved American market, where he accepted orders from distributors appointed by state governors to sell tractors on a priority basis. By June 1918, he had made 5,067 American sales at the cost price of $750 and had 13,463 orders on hand. By year's end 34,167 tractors had been produced and sold; Ford had vaulted past International Harvester, which itself had increased production by 36 percent—to become the world's largest tractor manufacturer.[43]

Ford tractor production was boosted to 57,290 in 1919 and to 70,955—which constituted 35 percent of America's tractor output—in 1920. International Harvester, for all of its tractor experience, was unable to stave off the Ford challenge, and General Motors, which had launched the Samson tractor in 1918, closed out its entry in October 1922 with a $33,000,000 loss. Moreover, Henry Ford & Son had sold its machines without entailing any advertising or promotional expense. Indeed, its attitude toward advertising in March 1920 was, "Why cultivate a demand for something you cannot supply? We could sell 25,000 tractors tomorrow if we had them." Distributors, similarly, were told "not to run wild on this subject of tractor advertising." To emphasize the point, dealers were required to pay for any electrotypes and folders which they chose to use in their sales-promotion activity. By the same token Henry Ford & Son gave little encouragement to the independently published *Fordson Farmer,* a monthly magazine which, starting in 1919, was bought and used by many distributors as a promotion piece.[44]

Henry Ford & Son was acquired by the Ford Motor Company in mid-1920, about the time the postwar agricultural prosperity began to fade. As a result the Ford Company soon found itself faced with a buyer's market and the need to promote its product vigorously. Ford dealers (who were added to the Henry Ford & Son distributing organization) were quickly supplied with free electros and advertising copy and told to buy space forthwith. Sales-promotion films and special literature were distributed throughout the dealer network. Plans were made to publish a tractor magazine with a format similar to that of the old *Ford Times,* but these plans were subsequently shelved in favor of the idea of closer cooperation with the *Fordson Farmer.* The tractor was put through its paces on a model farm set up at the Michigan State Fair; it was exhibited at numerous farm-implement and auto shows throughout the country; and it successfully competed in several important plowing contests. In January 1921, the company also reduced the price of the Fordson from $790 to $625, a figure below the cost of producing it, in an effort to expand output, lower per-unit costs, and earn long-term profitability.[45]

Despite these considerable efforts to promote its product the Ford Company could not buck the depressed state of agriculture. The company remained the nation's leading tractor manufacturer in 1921, but it produced only 36,781 units, a little more than half of the previous year's production. The company's cause was not helped by the well-earned reputation the Fordson had acquired for rearing up and toppling over when under stress. This bucking trait became so common that one farm journal suggested that the manufacturer ought to inscribe each machine with a warning in red paint: ''Prepare to Meet Thy God.'' Another magazine ran a list of the names of 136 persons who had been killed or maimed on a Fordson. For several years the Ford organization studiously ignored complaints about the Fordson. When Arthur Brisbane wrote Liebold that three Long Island farmers had been killed on the Fordson and suggested remedial action, the latter replied that such information ''seems to have been given out as organized propaganda throughout the country . . . we have paid but little attention to it as we have only 53,000 or 54,000 tractors in use.'' Finally, after hundreds of fatalities and manglings, the Ford management introduced several safety devices, including fenders with rear extensions designed to hit the ground before the tractor could flip over.[46]

Sales promotion, product improvement, and a substantial price cut notwithstanding, the tractor inventory mounted. In February 1922 the company acted: Fordson prices were reduced from $625 to $395. Alexander Legge, president of International Harvester, could scarcely believe his ears: ''What? How much? Well, I'll be. . . . Damn it all—meet him! and make it good. We'll throw in a plow as well!'' Even so, the cheapest Harvester tractor, formerly priced at $900, sold for $670. Ford, in order to increase production to the point where his new price would show a profit, announced shortly after the price reduction an all-out campaign to sell the tractor to construction and industrial firms and to municipalities. An ''industrial'' line of tractor implements, ranging from road-grading attachments and street-sweepers to hoists and cranes, was added to Ford dealers' stocks. The *Ford News* boasted that the Fordson had 1,700 potential uses.[47]

Many of the thirty-four Ford sales branches promoted "Fordson Industrial Parades," in which several score rubber-tired tractors hauled power equipment through metropolitan streets or around an entire state. On the statewide tours, demonstrations of the apparatus were given in most cities and towns along the route. In certain of these ventures other companies, among them the Oliver Chilled Plow Works, Goodyear Tire and Rubber Company, and Standard Oil Company (California), were associated with Ford.[48]

All of the company's sales branches staged "Ford Industrial Expositions" during 1922. Special efforts were made to have contractors, real-estate men, state and city officials, and express and railway executives attend the shows. Audiences usually would see thirty-five to forty Fordsons churning about, demonstrating as many as seventy-five pieces of equipment. The shows, which ran from one day to two weeks, drew large crowds, often averaging 25,000 daily. In addition Fordson dealers exhibited and demonstrated their wares at virtually every industrial exposition and state and county fair in the nation. Sales-promotion films entertained thousands of foot-weary persons in spacious Ford rest tents, which were lighted and ventilated by Fordson-supplied power. The Ford Band performed at a number of the more important exhibitions, and occasionally WWI's Wednesday evening "radio concert" would be beamed into the display area.[49]

The Ford Motor Company produced 68,985 tractors in 1922, and then raised its output to a record-breaking 101,898 in 1923. A number of these tractors were bought by the Soviet Union, which accepted delivery of 24,600 of the machines between 1920 and 1926. In America, sales were aided by the company's first national tractor advertising, launched in 1923. Ads were placed in twenty-nine national and regional farm publications. By 1925 a total of 7 percent of Ford's overall advertising appropriation was being spent in farm journals. Another 2 percent was used to advertise tractors and trucks in industrially oriented trade periodicals. The advertising appropriation, it should be noted, was provided by Ford dealers, who, starting in September 1923, were assessed $3.00 at the time of delivery of each Ford car and truck, Lincoln, and Fordson. This levy was discontinued (except for the assessment on the Lincoln) in mid-1926, and for a year the company ran no national tractor advertising. In the meantime, Ford had taken over and discontinued the *Fordson Farmer* (its publisher, Norton T. Brotherton, had become the company's advertising manager), and from 1923 to 1926 published *Fordson Magazine* for farmers and *Power & Haulage* for the industrial and municipal market. Offered free of charge, the two publications had a combined circulation of 300,000 in 1924.[50]

The company produced a record 104,168 machines in 1925 and maintained its ranking as America's number-one tractor manufacturer through 1926. In 1927, however, the company's production was exceeded by that of International Harvester. The implement firm had adopted a policy of challenging Fordson dealers to a tractor duel on every possible occasion. The Fordson, once a match for any rival, now frequently bowed to its arch-competitor's more powerful machine. Other tractor manufacturers also proved increasingly competitive. In February 1928 Ford decided to abandon tractor manufacturing in the United States. The Rouge's production machinery was shipped to the company's plant in Cork, Ireland, which offered the advantages of lower labor costs and proximity to European markets. Although the Cork factory exported a few machines to America during the 1930s, Ford was not a factor in the domestic tractor industry during this period.[51]

10

In the early 1920s, with his reputation secure in the tractor business, Ford embarked on another commercial venture: big-car manufacturing. Ford did not develop a big car, but bought a going concern, the Lincoln Motor Company. Lincoln had been organized in 1917 by Henry M. Leland and his son, Wilfred, to produce Liberty engines. The firm turned to automobile manufacturing after the war. Unfortunately, its product did not reach the market until September 1920, by which time auto sales already had begun to decline from postwar levels. The Lelands' car, selling in the $5,000 to $6,000 range, thus was handicapped from the outset. Furthermore, the vehicle, which was mechanically one of the soundest autos made in America, lacked style. Sales totaled only 752 in 1920, and the firm proved unable to produce and sell vehicles at a profitable level during 1921. Late that year the Lincoln Company faced bankruptcy.

Ford stepped into the breach. In December 1921, the auto king, after consultation with the Lelands, agreed to purchase the Lincoln firm at the receiver's sale set for February 4, 1922. At once news stories began to romanticize the transaction. The elder Leland, at seventy-eight, was one of America's most distinguished engineers. He had been an executive in the Brown and Sharpe plant in Providence, and had evolved the precision methods which made possible the Columbia chainless bicycle; in addition, he had manufactured engines for Oldsmobile, served as head of the Cadillac Company (successor to the Henry Ford Company) from 1902 to 1908, and had been general manager of General Motors' Cadillac Division from 1908 until 1917. Moreover, he had won acclaim as a Detroit civic leader. In "saving" this man's property (for Ford had told Leland, "You run it for me"), the purchaser was widely heralded as a good samaritan. A *Detroit News* cartoon, bearing the caption "Courtesy of the Road" and showing a flivver pulling a Lincoln out of the mire, typified the view of most Detroiters toward the transaction. Ford, indeed, encouraged this attitude by calling Leland "one of the greatest motorcar men in America" and asserting that "it would be a stain against the motor car industry and against Detroit to permit outsiders to secure control of the Lincoln plant merely because the Lelands have been caught in a pinch." The day of the sale was a festive occasion. Ford made the only bid, $8,000,000, and the Ford Band struck up "Hail to the Chief" as friends extended congratulations to the participants in this "marriage of volume and precision manufacturing."[52]

The honeymoon, however, was short-lived. From the outset the Lelands clashed with Ford executives delegated to work with them. Both sides apparently were at fault, the Lelands in demanding what would appear to be undue autonomy, the Ford people in assuming what would appear to be the Lelands' prerogatives. In any event, by May matters had reached the breaking point; in June Ford ordered Wilfred Leland out of the plant. Both Lelands then tendered their resignations. Newspapers in Detroit largely sided with Leland. Headlines such as "Motor King Broke His Vows to 'Old Man' " gave Ford as poor a press as he had yet experienced in his hometown.[53]

Ford, however, recovered most of the lost ground in March 1923, when he completed payments of $4,018,699.21 to the more than 900 creditors and seven directors (who had endorsed notes) of the Lincoln Company. Ford asserted that the act was voluntary; on the other hand, *Pipp's Weekly*, which supported the Lelands in their struggle against Ford, claimed that the payments were in keeping with the purchaser's oral pledge to liquidate the Lincoln Company's indebtedness. In any event Ford was widely lauded for his "generous and unusual action," inasmuch as he was popularly represented as having "no obligation, either legal or moral, to pay the debts of the old company." *Automotive Industries* reported that Ford's deed "has gained for him the esteem of the whole industry." Ford's admirers, obviously encouraged by the industrialist himself, extolled his act in newspapers, magazines, and books, often with startling exaggerations.[54]

The Lelands next began to press for the payment of the Lincoln's original stockholders, claiming that Ford had similarly pledged himself to compensate this group for their interest in the former Lincoln Motor Company. Ford, however, took no action, and in 1927, 1,800 of the Lincoln's stockholders, led by the Lelands, sought redress in court. The case was fought to the Michigan Supreme Court, which in 1931 ruled in Ford's favor. Henry M. Leland, who died the following year, notified the stockholders that he had exhausted all possible efforts in their behalf.[55]

The Lelands' early fears that the Ford organization might lower the high standards that they had set for the Lincoln proved groundless. On the contrary, the car's mechanical efficiency was maintained and its styling—for which Edsel Ford assumed responsibility—was considerably improved. Moreover, starting in 1922 the Ford Company conducted a continuous campaign to publicize and advertise the Lincoln as a car of the highest quality. At auto shows and in hotel settings Lincoln exhibits (frequently called the Lincoln Salon Petite) strove to create "snob appeal" for the car. "Guests," many of whom had been sent engraved invitations, were greeted by "doormen and other attendants appropriately uniformed and carefully schooled in the proprieties." They were then escorted to the Lincoln display, "a picture of exquisite appointments, floral decorations, and perfumed fountains, further enhanced through artistic lighting effects." "Charmingly costumed" pages and tuxedo-clad salesmen, each of whom wore a white carnation, were on hand to serve the guests, while liveried drivers awaited without to demonstrate the "chauffeur-driven equipage."[56]

Lincoln advertising, similarly, centered around a prestige-building theme. At first Ford tried to persuade its dealers (who of course were enlisted as Lincoln agents) to carry the advertising load, as they had done for the Model T ever since 1917. Those dealers who bought Lincoln advertising, however, tended to do so at the expense of Model T space. The company protested that agents should have separate appropriations for Lincoln advertising. Then, realizing that hit-or-miss local newspaper advertising would not achieve the desired results, the home office elected early in 1923 to conduct its own national advertising campaign. The ad appropriation, Ford's first in half-a-dozen years, was directed mostly to ten "class" publications, among them *Vogue, Vanity Fair, Town & Country, Spur,* and *Motor Life.* Later that year the magazine campaign was supplemented with advertising in fifty selected metropolitan newspapers.[57]

During 1923 and 1924 the company spent more than $400,000 on Lincoln advertising. Since the $3.00 assessment against each Lincoln delivery brought a total of only approximately $35,000, big-car advertising was heavily subsidized by the levies made on the Model T and the Fordson. Dealers who sold relatively few Lincolns—and of course these dealers were in the majority—were bitter about the transfer of funds. The company recognized their complaints, and after 1924 separated the Ford and Lincoln advertising accounts. The Brotherton Company, of Detroit, was the Lincoln's advertising agency during 1922 and 1923. The account was handled by McKinney, Marsh, & Cushing, Inc., of Detroit, from 1924 through 1926.[58]

Aside from space advertising, the Lincoln's leading sales-promotion medium was a monthly motoring publication, *Lincoln.* The magazine, introduced by Brotherton in December 1922, was designed to appeal to "people of taste and culture" and contained little of the "hard selling" copy that had been featured in the old *Ford Times.* The periodical was sent to Lincoln owners and prospective buyers, as well as to "many of the finest clubs" in the country. Circulation stood at 70,000 in January 1924, three months after Ford had taken over Brotherton's role as publisher.

The Lincoln was not an outstanding sales success. On the average, 7,000 cars were retailed annually between 1922 and 1930. Packard and Cadillac, competing at the same price level, outsold the Lincoln more than three to one, while the Pierce-Arrow, selling at a considerably higher price, marketed almost as many units as Ford's big-car entry.[59]

11

As Henry Ford extracted natural resources, wove a transportation network, pushed on to new frontiers in manufacturing, and placed new products on the market, he became a superman to millions of people. The Nebraska Senate voted to invite him to come to Nebraska to develop its waterpower resources; the New York State Waterways Association asked him to use his influence with Congress to see that the Hudson was properly developed from Albany to Troy; and an Alabama congressman asked him to buy enough cotton to stabilize the market. The Chinese government asked Ford to become its economic adviser; Germany's finance minister said his country would welcome him as an "economic dictator"; a group of German businessmen suggested that he should become their nation's kaiser; and one wing of Polish monarchists wanted Ford to assume their country's throne.[60]

Rumors fed upon the belief that nothing seemed impossible to Ford. It was reported that he would spend $100,000,000 to harness the Bay of Fundy's tides; that he would invest $120,000,000 to produce motion pictures in behalf of Blue Sundays and anti-Semitism; that he had offered to buy and scrap the entire French navy; and that he was willing to assume the whole German loan of $200,000,000 under the Dawes Plan. He planned, it was rumored, to open a string of banks for common people; he intended to establish a nationwide insurance company; he would pay $1,000,000 to anyone who could tell him how to reduce the cost of making the Model T by a dime; and he had learned to make trolley cars run on straw, to make leather out of gunpowder, and to manufacture cars out of cotton, stamping them as a baker might cut doughnuts. He was, newspapers reported, negotiating to buy the Dunlop Tire Company of Buffalo, the Victory plant at Squantum, Massachusetts, and a half-dozen railroads in every section of the country. The stock of New York's National City Bank rose fifteen points on the report that Ford was to become a director; the stock of the Gulf States Steel Company dropped twenty points on the news that Ford was not interested in buying it.[61]

Along with the publicity which accompanied pleas for Ford's assistance and rumors of his impending activities was much serious discussion of his expanding industrial empire. As early as 1920 the press began to discuss Ford's plan "to make his industry self-contained," and during the next six or seven years much attention was focused on the manufacturer's efforts to build a vertically integrated organization. Virtually all of the comment was complimentary. Arthur Pound, writing in the *Atlantic Monthly* in 1924, reported that the Ford Company, "from the standpoint of industrial security and efficiency, [is] in a class by itself." The *New York Times,* surveying the greater company in 1927, remarked, "Never before have so many industries been so admirably integrated."[62]

Such statements must have been gratifying to Henry and Edsel Ford and their advertising and publicity staffs, for they went to great effort during the 1920s to inform the public of how the Ford organization had brought about the "stabilization of costs and prices through the control of raw materials and the elimination of many middle profits." This concept was conveyed to consumers by a number of media, including dozens of press releases, a book (*The Ford Industries*), a three-reel film (*The Ford Age*), a number of exhibitions, and a national institutional advertising campaign.

The Ford Industries was published in several editions, one of which ran to 160 pages and carried 350 illustrations. The book was sent to all of America's public and college/university libraries, to most newspapers, and to many bankers, public officials, and businessmen. *The Ford Age,* which surveyed the Ford empire from mine and forest through to the finished product, was a feature attraction in scores of theaters throughout the country.[63]

The exhibitions, commonly titled "Transformation of Materials," or "Outline of Industry," used working models, panoramic canvases, and the actual manufacture of auto and tractor parts to convey the idea of the company's integrated operations. Staged at fairs, exhibition halls, and branch buildings, the displays also featured scores of Model T's, Lincolns, and Fordsons, as well as D.T.& I. locomotives and Ford trimotors. The largest of these exhibitions, in fact "one of the most comprehensive shows ever attempted by a single producer," was the Ford Industrial

Exposition, held in Madison Square Garden in 1928. This one-week show drew 1,052,842 visitors, a figure which impressed even Tex Rickard, the Garden's impressario. "I wouldn't have believed it if I hadn't seen it myself," Rickard remarked. "It breaks all records. Never in my memory has there been [an indoor event] to compare with it." (Thirty-four years later the Automobile Manufacturer Association's nine-day National Automobile Show—one of the most costly and spectacular auto shows ever held—drew but 1,147,742 people to Detroit's Cobo Hall.)[64]

Thousands of New Yorkers strained police lines when Henry Ford and Thomas Edison attended the exposition on opening day. The pair held one of the best-attended press conferences ever staged in New York, and among other things announced that they were thinking of going to South America by air. The interview was given nationwide publicity and drew attention from the National Automobile Show, which was being held simultaneously in New York. Complaining that Ford was "deliberately hogging the limelight" and that his exposition had received three times as much publicity as the national show, the *Detroit Saturday Night* grumbled that the latter's publicists "could have chartered an airship, powered with an engine embracing the principle of perpetual motion, chucked in Sloan, Willys, Durant, Erskine, and Chrysler . . . and still they would have played second fiddle to the announcement, 'Ford and Edison to Fly to S.A.' " After its New York triumph, the Ford Industrial Exposition moved to Chicago, where it was visited by more than 400,000 persons.[65]

The company also prominently displayed its tractors, airplanes, and by-products at its own "national" auto shows, held in the Broadway quarters of the New York branch. During the mid-1920s an average of 65,000 persons annually looked over the various products, saw Ford motion pictures, and listened to Henry Ford's Old Fashioned Dance Orchestra. Finally, six Ford Road Shows, designed to tell the story of the Ford organization to small-town and rural people, toured the United States, Mexico, and Cuba in 1930 and 1931. Exhibition tents were set up in 634 communities, and the company's products and a sound motion picture, *A Trip Thru the Rouge Plants,* were shown to more than 4,000,000 persons.[66]

In 1924 and 1925 the Ford Company, apparently at the instigation of Edsel Ford, ran a nationwide institutional advertising campaign to familiarize the public with its industrial complex. One of Edsel's friends, Wetmore Hodges, secretary of the American Radiator Company, questioned whether such advertising might not lead the public to think of Ford as it thought of United States Steel, Armour and Company, and Standard Oil, "of swollen size and profits, and therefore monopoly." Edsel replied that he was "not concerned regarding the possibility of a kick-back in the minds of the public regarding the size and resources of our institution," adding that the company's "one profit" advertisements would serve "to create goodwill and favorable reaction in the minds of the reader." The younger Ford was right. The ads, appearing twice monthly on double pages of the *Saturday Evening Post* and *Country Gentleman* and from time to time in forty-eight metropolitan newspapers, evoked only favorable response from the press. Indeed, *Printers' Ink* thought that the frankness with which Ford advertised his many-sided organization was its best protection against popular attack.

In 1931 the company conducted another institutional advertising campaign in an effort to depict the worldwide Ford organization's contribution to human progress. The advertisements, which featured paintings by some of America's leading illustrators, were widely acclaimed both for their artistic merit and because they were "so different from anything that has been run in the past."[67]

If Henry Ford's paid efforts to familiarize the public with his integrated operations were noted by millions of people, the free publicity which accompanied his manifold activities undoubtedly reached an even greater number of his countrymen. Newspaper and magazine cartoons often showed him as a "Colossus of Transportation," surrounded by ships, planes, trains, cars, and tractors, or spinning the world by means of power supplied by his products. "Whatever Mr. Ford does with the airplane, the tractor, the automobile," stated the *New York World,* "whatever he does in scrapping shipping and running railways, he has the public watching him." In fact, as Oswald Garrison Villard pointed out, the industrialist had so "affected the imaginations of his fellow men" that they virtually cheered for him. Citing Ford's acquisition of a valuable waterpower site in Minneapolis-St. Paul, Villard observed, "In anybody else this would have been denounced as a 'grab' and a 'steal' deserving of the utmost public condemnation." For Ford, however, there was only applause.[68]

Ford in the Rouge, Ford in Brazil, Ford on the D.T.&I., Ford on the Great Lakes or at the Dearborn airport, was Ford in a succession of creative phases. No one, as Nevins and Hill suggest, can follow these activities without recognizing the daring and flexibility of the manufacturer's mind. It did not matter that he fell short of the goals he set himself. He accomplished enough to command respect and to foster through his projects a widespread belief in his originality, his technical skills, and his will to serve the public. He also achieved a chuckling popular enthusiasm for his work. "Henry showed them," his admirers could say with considerable justification, whether of lumbering, railroads, village industries, ships, or airplanes.

Financially, a number of these forays into strange fields—notably the rubber and airplane adventures—brought heavy losses. Others were profitable. To his credit, Ford usually did not care. He was more concerned with what could be accomplished.[69]

Chapter 11
Farewell, My Lovely

During the period 1921–26 the Ford Motor Company sold more than half of the automobiles and trucks marketed in the United States. The best sales year in the firm's history before 1955 occurred in 1923 when more than two million Model T's were sold. Paradoxically, however, from 1923 to 1926, when the Model T recorded its largest sales, it was rapidly approaching obsolescence.

The T's greatest competitive assets, its reputation for utility and its low price, had served it well in an era of poor roads and unsophisticated yet high-priced competition. But during the mid-1920s, as hard-surfaced highways fanned across the nation and mechanically sound cars became commonplace, the T's selling points began to lose their significance. Furthermore, although Ford had cut prices $100 between 1922 and 1926, Chevrolet had slashed prices $140, Overland $300, Maxwell (Chrysler) $490, and Dodge $890 during the same period.

More important, public tastes, because of increased affluence and new values, were changing. Prospective car buyers—especially the women who had come to play a leading role in purchases—increasingly became style-conscious and demanded more conveniences and comforts. Many men insisted on the latest mechanical innovations and additional speed and power. The Model T had little style, and conveniences and mechanical improvements, if they could be had at all, cost extra. Times were changing, but the T was not.[1]

A number of manufacturers, sensing the shifting attitudes, rose to the challenge with extensive consumer research programs. General Motors surveyed hundreds of thousands of motorists to find out what they liked and did not like about their cars, and then skillfully designed and effectively promoted its new models accordingly. Noting Ford's inactivity in research, one magazine correctly surmised, "It is difficult to imagine Henry Ford asking one motorist for advice, let alone taking it." Ford, who perhaps was the only auto manufacturer to conduct formal market studies before World War I and whose views were so attuned to the public's needs of an earlier period, stubbornly ignored the winds of change.[2]

But even Ford could not ignore the sales figures. From 1924 to 1925 his unit sales dropped from 1,870,000 to 1,675,000 while Chevrolet advanced from 280,000 to 470,000. In 1925 the T received a face-lifting, including larger fenders and nickel-plated radiators. Touched up in gunmetal blue, highland green, phoenix brown, and fawn gray and resembling a renovated but prim spinster on her last fling, the Tin Lizzie sallied forth to meet the competition.

Colors and minor alterations made no difference. Neither did Ford's trumps, two 1926 price cuts; for the first time in Model T history price reductions failed to stimulate sales. Ford's 1926 deliveries were almost 400,000 units below the 1925 figure. In the meanwhile Chevrolet gained an additional 260,000 customers, and Dodge and Buick, the third- and fourth-ranked makes, made sales gains of 22 and 39 percent respectively.[3]

For a three-year period, 1923–26, Ford attempted to meet the challenge with large-scale advertising. Between 1917 and 1923, when the company did no space advertising, dealers had found it necessary to advertise, and those in the larger cities had "clubbed together" to conduct newspaper and billboard campaigns, spending an estimated $3,000,000 annually. This system, however, did not permit national campaigns and left much to be desired in the way of evenness of distribution and uniformity of sales appeals. The result was that in August 1923, after a conference of branch managers on the question, Edsel Ford announced the re-establishment of an Advertising Department.[4]

Norton T. Brotherton was named advertising manager, and his company, the Brotherton Advertising Agency, of Detroit, received the Ford account. An assessment of $3.00 was levied on each car, truck, and tractor delivered to dealers. With total Ford sales running at the yearly rate of 2,200,000 units, advertising expenditures were expected to approach $7,000,000 annually. Of this amount, two-thirds was to be spent on local media (newspapers, billboards, and streetcars), the remainder on national publications. The dealer was relieved of any responsibility for advertising.

One-twelfth of the total advertising budget was scheduled for women's and "prestige" magazines. Thus the Advertising Department realized, even though Henry Ford did not, that "pride, vanity, and a desire for something more impressive" were strong factors in determining sales, and sought to surround the T with "an atmosphere of 'Pride of Ownership' . . . of class and quality." Like prewar attempts to establish the Model T as a prestige car, this campaign met with little success. In fact, during the mid-1920s the Ford probably evoked less pride of ownership among women and prestige-conscious men than any car on the market.[5]

Dealers began to complain. The chief objection to the new advertising scheme was the elimination of all individual agents' names and of their special copy. The company explained that such information did not increase sales, and it continued, except in single-dealer localities, to sign the ads: "See the Nearest Authorized Ford Dealer." The agents also charged that the plan was inequitable, often ill-timed, and badly adjusted to local conditions. The district supervisor who covered North Carolina wrote Edsel Ford early in 1924 that his agents were "very much dissatisfied." Realizing "how much money Dealers have been paying for advertising and how little they have been receiving," the supervisor could readily understand their attitude.[6]

Three weeks later the company instructed each branch manager to appoint an advertising representative for his territory. These men were to calm dissident dealers, help plan and supervise advertising, place press releases from the home office, and prepare local news stories. The newly appointed branch advertising managers no doubt mollified many agents, but the company-dealer relationship continued to pose a problem. In 1925 and again in 1926 the company sent directives to the branch advertising managers to promote better understanding among dealers regarding the benefits derived from the parent firm's advertising. Technically, the Ford advertisements earned warm praise. *Printers' Ink* reported: "By artistic handling, by perfectly groomed compositions, by illustrations which are as fine as anything for a product selling for ten times as much . . . the advertising surrounds the Ford with an atmosphere of real worthiness."[7]

Norton Brotherton and his agency were dismissed in January 1924, after Brotherton, a heavy drinker, had encountered Harvey Firestone aboard a train. Firestone told Henry Ford that the intoxicated Brotherton had made an ass of himself and had shouted to anyone who would listen that he handled Ford's advertising. In any event, effective January 31, 1924, McKinney, Marsh & Cushing received the Ford account and W. W. Mitchell, formerly manager of the Atlanta branch, was given charge of all advertising, publicity, and sales-promotion literature. Other than the fact that "Henry Ford liked him," Mitchell apparently had little to recommend him for his new position. The Atlantan knew next to nothing about advertising, according to an associate, A. Roy Barbier, and he "had difficulties with the English language." Perhaps these very deficiencies appealed to Ford, who prided himself on having successfully introduced other employees to occupations seemingly inappropriate for them. The experiment with Mitchell came to naught, however, as the Atlantan died eight months after his Dearborn appointment. Mitchell's duties were assumed by Barbier, who, after four years in Lincoln's Advertising Department, had joined the parent firm's advertising staff in early 1924.[8]

Ford was one of the nation's biggest advertisers during the mid-1920s, spending $14,833,303 between September 1923, and October 1926. However, Henry Ford's basic dislike of advertising reasserted itself in June 1926, when he ordered the dealer assessment discontinued and told the dealers to arrange for their own advertising. Meanwhile, the company had been cutting back the advertising outlay, spending only half as much in May as in April, and halving the May figure in June. The $47,000 remaining in the advertising fund on July 1 was spent within the next four months, and the parent company bought no more space until the Model A's introduction late in 1927.[9]

Two factors reinforced Ford's decision to abandon advertising. Sagging sales plus large space expenditures in early 1926 had left the advertising fund with a temporary deficit of $257,828. Hearing this, Ford ordered that all advertising should cease until the levy (which in January 1926 had been reduced to $2.50 per unit) on future sales had eliminated the outstanding indebtedness. Moreover, the company ran into a barrage of criticism when it discontinued billboard advertising without consulting the dealers. Ford was irked by this criticism and announced that he was through with the "cooperative" advertising plan.[10]

After Ford discontinued the dealer assessment, dealers in many metropolitan areas again banded together, retained advertising agencies, and launched citywide advertising campaigns. Most of these dealer associations assessed their members $2.00 for each car they sold. Individual and rural dealers were aided considerably by McKinney, Marsh & Cushing, which, on its own initiative, made available to them an advertising service in the form of sample ads, mats, and electros.[11]

By the spring and early summer of 1926 it was becoming apparent to virtually everyone in the Ford organization, except Henry Ford and one or two other executives who were wearing blinders, that the Model T was failing competitively. Despite an improved auto market, Model T sales during April–June 1926 dropped 154,000 from the comparable period in 1925. These figures did not escape the notice of the press, which, taking stock of Chevrolet's 33 percent increase in sales and its plan to expand productive capacity to one million units per year by 1927, observed that the Model T's dominance was being seriously threatened for the first time in almost two decades.[12]

Speculation immediately began as to how Ford would meet the challenge. First reports predicted that he would replace the four-cylinder T with a six-cylinder auto. When the manufacturer denied this, it was rumored that the company's next model would be a "Sheik Car" designed to satisfy feminine demands for a more stylish vehicle. Again Ford issued a denial, remarking that he already had given the Model T colors and a nickel-plated hood. "Yes," a New York dealer was quoted, "you can paint up a barn, but it will still be a barn and not a parlor." Throughout the remainder of the year and into 1927 the rumors mounted: Ford would replace the Model T's planetary transmission with a selective gear shift; he would add a fourth speed; he would adopt a new carburetor permitting thirty miles to the gallon; he would produce an eight-cylinder model to sell below $1,000; he would enter the medium-price field with a car to be named the Edison; he would build a super-flivver, a two-cylinder car with as much power as a four. Invariably Ford was asked to comment on the latest rumor, and invariably he denied it and reiterated his determination to keep the Model T.[13]

Ford's overt stubbornness concealed an intense concern with public attitudes toward his product. When one of his men returned from a tour of the country, Ford asked: "Well, what did you see? What did the people say?" The employee replied: "The Chevrolet is making tremendous gains. Its dealers are disparaging the Ford, and especially the planetary transmission." He remarked also that customers grumbled over Model T peculiarities. "Is that what they are saying?" mused Ford, who obviously had been given food for thought. He also looked for an explanation. "I think we'll have good times if we don't do too much advertising," he stated in mid-1926. "A good thing will sell itself. . . . You've just got to let people know where to get it, and that's all." In December 1926, his perplexed mood was reflected in some wistful remarks he made about public taste. "I sometimes wonder if we have not lost our buying sense and fallen under the spell of salesmanship," he told an interviewer. "The American of a generation ago was a shrewd buyer. He knew values in terms of utility and dollars. But nowadays the American people seem to listen and be sold; that is, they do not buy."[14]

In mid-February, for the first time, Ford did not deny that he would have to place a new car on the market. He admitted that he was giving some thought to that vehicle but refused to name an introductory date, claiming that "a statement at this time on the matter . . . might do serious injury to my competitors." A new crop of rumors at once swept the nation. By early spring it was commonly assumed that a fresh model with higher speed and a standard gearshift would appear soon; some said in late June. But no authoritative announcement appeared. Competitors complained that Ford's refusal to speak had brought on a mild buyers' strike, as customers would not make decisions until they saw what Ford planned to offer them. "The result is getting on everyone's nerves," said an Ohio newspaper, "as Ford himself probably realizes."[15]

The first definite news of the T's discontinuance came on May 18, when a Detroit police official appeared before the Detroit Common Council to request the immediate purchase of 111 Model T's for the police scout fleet. An "authoritative source," he declared, had informed him that the company would abandon the T on May 28 and begin producing a new gear-shift car on July 1. This source turned out to be a local Ford agency handling the fleet sale. Confronted with this piece of intelligence, William J. Cameron, as company spokesman, emphatically denied any impending change in the Ford product and added that "we get more information about the plans of the company from the outside than we do from within." Few newspapers let the matter rest, for, as the *Baltimore Sun* stated on May 22, "The public is burning with curiosity. What will it look like? How fast will it travel? What equipment will it carry? . . . Will he still undersell his competitors? All of these are questions heard every day in all quarters of the United States."[16]

Even as he continued to oppose any change, Ford gave in. On the evening of May 25, 1927, the Ford Motor Company announced that it would build a new car. The story was front-page news in every newspaper in the country. Information supplied by the company about the new car was meager. It was to have speed, style, flexibility, and control in traffic; there was to be nothing quite like it in quality and in price; it would cost more to manufacture, but it would be more economical to operate. The company wired branch managers and dealers not to furnish any other information to the press or their employees, "FOR THE PREMATURE ANNOUNCEMENT OF FURTHER DETAILS WILL DETRACT FROM FORCE OF LATER PUBLICITY."[17]

During the afternoon of May 26, 1927, the fifteen millionth Model T rolled off the Highland Park assembly line. The occasion was appropriately simple. There were no bands, no bunting, no speeches. With Edsel at the wheel, and his father beside him, the automobile headed a motor procession of company officials and fifteen reporters and cameramen to the Dearborn Engineering Laboratory. On the plaza in front of the building, under gray skies, were Ford's first automobile and the first Model T. For the benefit of motion-picture cameramen, Henry Ford drove both of the older cars around the plaza. The ceremony was over.[18]

Most of the nation's newspapers and magazines commented editorially on the Model T's demise. There were, as the *Louisville Times* predicted, "acres of humorous writing devoted . . . to 'hunky Elizabeth, chunky Elizabeth, spunky Elizabeth Ford.' " The *Baltimore Sun*, for example, remarked, "Since the Model T makes as much noise as any 10 other cars and the new Ford cannot possibly be noisier than the old, life will be pleasanter, we will all live longer, and this may be more important than getting the boys out of the trenches by Christmas."

The majority of the press, however, regarded the occasion as momentous and treated it in a sentimental fashion. To the *New York Herald Tribune*, the T's passing was "The End of an Epoch"; in the view of the *Dayton News* a "world institution" was being "Retired with Honors." The *Roanoke News* spoke for many: "It will be long before America loses its affectionate, if somewhat apologetic, remembrance of the car that first put us on wheels. We probably wouldn't admit it to anyone, but deep in our hearts we love every rattle in its body.''[19]

There were many who were reluctant to see the Model T—which had had a longer life than any car save the expensive Rolls-Royce Silver Ghost (1907–27)—go out of production. Arthur Brisbane, adding a new Ford sedan and Ford truck to the several of each he already possessed, telegraphed Ford that he should keep one plant running indefinitely to make 500,000 Model T's a year; for, he thought, they could easily be sold at increased prices by mail order. A Ford dealer in Newark, ''believing in the great merit of the Model T and the continued demand for same,'' sought to arrange for its manufacture and/or assembly in New Jersey. Newark citizens, he assured Ford, would finance the proposition. On the morrow of Ford's announcement, countless owners began to take better care of their Tin Lizzies, anxious to prolong their lives. One elderly lady of means in Montclair, New Jersey, purchased and stored away seven new Model T's so that she would not be without one during the remainder of her life. A Toledo man bought six of the cars, finally wearing out the last of them in 1967.[20]

The perspective of time only served to increase affection and respect for ''the first log cabin of the Motor Age.'' Archibald Henderson, writing in 1930, not untypically declared that the Model T had performed a service to the people ''greater by far than that of the telegraph, the telephone, rural free delivery, the phonograph, the radio, or electric light and power.'' E. B. White and Richard Lee Strout, in their classic 1936 epitaph, ''Farewell, My Lovely,'' said of the machine, ''it was hard-working, commonplace, heroic . . . the miracle God had wrought. And it was patently the sort of thing that could only happen once.'' To Philip Van Doren Stern, writing in 1955, the Model T ''was, as no car before or since has been, truly the people's car . . . part of the fabric of American life, celebrated in song and legend and folklore.'' In 1959 *Fortune* reported that 100 of the world's leading designers, architects, and design teachers ranked the T as the eighty-second ''best designed mass-produced product of modern times'' (higher than all other Ford cars except the 1940 Lincoln Continental, which ranked sixth, and the 1955 Thunderbird, rated forty-first). In 1974 the T was voted ''the world's greatest motorcar'' by readers of *Motor Trend*.[21] That the T helped to change America's psychology, manners, and mores as well as the national economy cannot be questioned. No other single machine did so much to induce people of provincial mind to begin thinking in regional and national terms; none did so much to knit together different parts of the county, the state, and the country.

Ford produced 15,007,033 Model T's in the United States through May 31, a figure and date often cited in T literature as representing total output and the end of production. But the company assembled 477,748 additional T's during the summer of 1927; and Ford of Canada had built another 747,259 Tin Lizzies, Ford of England an estimated 250,000. For several decades automotive historians and journalists believed that the T's production mark would stand unchallenged. ''No other model was ever produced in such numbers,'' typically declared Allan Nevins and Frank Ernest

Hill in 1957 in their authoritative *Ford: Expansion and Challenge 1915–1933,* "and it is safe to say that on this score alone its record will never be matched." But Germany's Volkswagen, amid much fanfare, produced its 15,007,034th Model 1200 (the "beetle") on February 17, 1972, and smashed the T's worldwide production record the following year. For decades, the Lizzie shared honors with the Rolls-Royce Silver Ghost as the car with the longest life-span. During the 1960s and 1970s, however, several European models, including Volkswagen's 1200, Volvo's PV444, Citroen's 2CV, and Fiat's 1100, exceeded the T's production run.[22]

Ford's millions of T's proved as durable as flivver jokes and legend would have them be. In March 1927, nearly nineteen years after the first one was made, 11,325,521 Lizzies were registered in the United States. T's, despite their cheapness, lasted longer on the average (eight years) than other cars (6.3 years) because of the low cost of replacement parts, the ease in which owners could make repairs, and the accessibility of Ford dealerships. The number of T's declined rapidly with the cessation of production, but in late 1931 5,432,000 Lizzies still plied the nation's highways; in 1941, an estimated 600,000 to 800,000. In 1948, when R. L. Polk and Company made the last actual count of T's, 73,111 cars and trucks were registered. Many additional T's were unlicensed, stored in garages and farm buildings, or rusticating where they had stopped running years before (the author's 1921 Model T touring car, for example, was found in a corncrib in Nebraska). The Ford Company in 1953 estimated the number of extant flivvers at 100,000; in 1971 automotive historian Leslie R. Henry, taking into account subsequent large-scale T restoration, put the number of survivors at 300,000. "If an antique buff finds a 'T' frame with a serial number on it," he noted, "he's got enough to start building a car." Many of the T's 4,830 parts and some accessories are readily available from old-car parts houses. Some of the items are original, others newly made by entrepreneurs responding to a steady demand. The Sears, Roebuck catalog, which once devoted more space to T parts and gadgets than to men's clothing, still advertised T engine gaskets in 1975, perhaps for sentimental rather than business reasons. Today, every restored or restorable Model T sells for many times its original purchase price; even "basket cases" cost more than they did when initially sold. A few T's remain in daily service, especially in car-starved Latin American countries; and those in America invariably make headlines when stolen or involved in an accident.[23]

Two international organizations serve Model T owners: the Model T Ford Club International, founded in 1952 and one of the oldest old-car marque groups, and the Model T Ford Club of America, started in 1966. The Ford Club International, headquartered in Chicago, has twenty-six chapters whose members own more than 10,000 T's. The Ford Club of America has fifty-four chapters and 6,000 members, many of whom also own more than one Lizzie. Both organizations publish bi-monthly magazines which add steadily to knowledge and lore about the flivver. Virtually every old-car museum in the country—and there were seventy of them in 1975—displays at least one Model T. Harrah's Automobile Collection, in Reno, has the world's largest T collection—fifty-two cars and trucks representing each model year. The Henry Ford Museum displays one of the first T's, the 15,000,000th T, and several historically significant flivvers. Several individuals also have impressive T collections, and one of them, Cecil Church, of Harrisburg, Illinois, houses his vehicles in a wooden replica of an early Ford dealership.[24]

To this day the Model T continues to generate considerable attention. Since 1948 the car has been given full-length chapter treatment in at least fifteen volumes; and has been the subject of seven nonfiction and six fiction books, plus dozens of reprints of Ford Company owner and service manuals, parts catalogs, and sales brochures. In 1953, when the Tin Lizzie was a focal point of the Ford Company's fiftieth anniversary celebration, it received more press play than any car on the market. It was heavily publicized again in 1958, when the company marked the fiftieth anniversary of the T's introduction, and in 1963, when Ford beat publicity drums during the centennial of its founder's birth. In 1968, the firm's News Department, weary of paying for so many T articles, instructed its clipping agencies to stop forwarding them.[25]

The company occasionally uses the Model T in its advertising. In 1963 the firm's Autolite Division featured a 1914 flivver in its advertisements, claiming that the old car's economy of operation was improved with the use of Autolite replacement parts. In the early 1970s the company conducted a campaign which compared its new minicar, the Pinto, to the T. "The Pinto," declared ads signed by Henry Ford II, "is the new Model T. The first Model T stood for sensible, simple motoring; it was 'lively and easy to handle and fun to drive,' and this new version of the Model T stands for the same things." The new car, added Henry II, would be available in "Model T Black." This campaign's thousands of television commercials showed a Model T being overtaken on the highway by its successor, the Model A, and a Pinto. Volkswagen, Audi, and other auto and nonauto firms also have featured the T in their advertising, invariably complimenting the flivver, and, in effect, saying "me too."[26]

Much latter-day comment on the T relates the car to antiques and out-of-date programs and thinking, for the term "Model T" has become synonymous with old-fashionedness. Thus in 1963 *Life* described the navy's antiquated rescue vessel, *Skylark,* as a "small, prim, old-fashioned ship looking like a Model T"; the *New York Journal-American* criticized the nation's " 'Model T' highway program"; Michigan Governor George Romney compared his state's fifty-five-year-old constitution to a "broken-down Tin Lizzie"; and Vassar College's British-born president said "the American mind chugs along like a Model T—persevering and rugged, but without much grace." In 1964, United Auto Workers President Walter Reuther vowed not to accept a "Model T labor contract"; *Advertising Age* described the Ford Company's advertising campaigns as being "as bumpy as an old Model T"; and the *Insider's Newsletter,* in an article on dairying, noted that the "milk pail is as out of date as the Model T." In 1968, *Time* compared the Ohio State University football team's new "Apollo 8" attack to its old "Model T" offense. In 1971, the chief justice of the Michigan Supreme Court described the state's judicial system as "a lurching Model T," after which the *Detroit News* declared that the state's supreme court was "a Model T, too." After Gerald R. Ford described himself as "a Ford, not a Lincoln" when sworn in as vice-president in December 1973, dozens of cartoonists pictured him at the wheel of a Model T, or as a Model T labeled "Ford." Many journalists subsequently compared the President to a Model T, as well as to an Edsel, Thunderbird, a Maverick, and other Ford products.[27]

The T's name also is frequently invoked when durable, inexpensive, or widely-accepted products are discussed. Persian lamb has been called "one of the great 'Model T's' of the fur industry, seemingly fashionable forever." Douglas Aircraft's DC-3 and Ford's trimotor airplane often are referred to as "the Model T of the air" or "the Model T of aircraft." Caterpillar's basic tractor has been described as "the Model T of its business," the navy bathyscaphe, *Trieste*, "the Model T of the bathyscaphe," the Birney car as "transit's Model T," the Atwater Kent as the "Model T of radios," the Coinola Style A as "the 'Model T' of coin-operated pianos," and the Kodak camera as "the Model T of cameradom."[28]

Nowadays ownership of a Model T, especially a brass-mounted T, is positively stylish, much more so than at any time in the past. Many old-car buffs would own no other antique vehicle; others go to inordinate lengths to obtain a model similar to one they knew as young adults or children. The Model T, perhaps more than any other relic, also has a special niche in American hearts. Most older citizens had their first experience in automobiling when they rode in or drove a flivver. Today, the sight of a T bobbing along the street warms them like a ray of sunshine. They smile, and some yell "get a horse!" When the car is pulled over to the curb, they reminisce about the "good old days" and perhaps recall a Ford joke or two. If invited to take a spin, they immediately perch themselves upon a seat. When invited to drive, many accept, eager to prove that they remember how to manipulate the T's pedals and levers. Younger people are similarly amused by the sight of a T passing by, often shouting above the clatter, "what is it?" Thus the T's legacy—a mixture of folk legend and nostalgic affection tinged with humor—continues to build and maintain goodwill for the Ford Company.

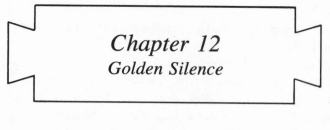

Chapter 12
Golden Silence

1

The worldwide interest and publicity which accompanied the advent of Henry Ford's new car, the Model A, was without precedent in the annals of business. During the Model A's six-month gestation period hundreds of reporters and writers stood on tiptoe to get a peek at what was going on in Ford's engineering shops; begged, bought, or stole any scrap of information or photograph that might conceivably have to do with the new product; and wrote literally tens of thousands of speculative columns about it. Even in a decade which saw Lindbergh's flight, the Scopes "monkey" trial, the Hall-Mills murder case, the execution of Sacco and Vanzetti, and two Dempsey-Tunney bouts, the Model A emerged as one of the two or three biggest news stories.[1]

So much curiosity was largely a tribute to the magical aura of Henry Ford's name and the sturdy reputation of the Model T. The question, "Can Ford create a new car that will do as much for America as the Model T?" was on millions of lips. Most people were agreed that Ford would produce a superior product. Yet, as his assembly lines remained idle month after month and as the Chevrolet steadily expanded its sales, another great question was posed: "Can Henry Ford regain pre-eminence in the automotive field?" The world waited with ever-increasing suspense for the answers to these questions.[2]

For the first few weeks after the May 25 new-car announcement there was relatively little press speculation concerning Ford's activities. The industrialist had promised a "complete description" of the new model "within a few weeks," and the press seemed willing to await Ford's pleasure. Then, on June 22, someone filched a series of advertisements from the offices of N. W. Ayer & Son, Ford's newly-appointed advertising agency. The ads were placed in the hands of the New York News Bureau, which promptly released a detailed description of the vehicle shown in the ads. In the meantime the mortified Ayer organization had telegraphed every newspaper in the United States and Canada that the "preliminary and experimental" advertisements were based on "fictitious and imaginative" specifications and begged editors to ignore the New York story. Most newspapers complied with Ayer's request, but many were so taken with the unusual character of the agency's wire that they published it in full and a day or two later offered editorial comment.[3]

A number of newspapers thought the theft and the telegram might have been "trumped up" for publicity purposes. "Talk about 'smoking up' interest in a prize fight or a football game," declared the *Marietta* (Ohio) *Times,* "this new Ford car has been carried along until it has already been given millions of dollars' worth of free advertising." Ayer's advertisements were, however, as "preliminary" as represented. More than a score of experimental cars were being tested by the company in

June, and a firm decision on the vehicle which was to be the Model A was not reached until August.[4]

From late June until the Model A's debut in December there was not a week—indeed, not a day in some weeks—in which fresh stories about the new car were not circulated around the country. The car was to have twelve cylinders; the car was to be a solar-energized electric, a teardrop, a pocket Diesel; the car's delay was due to Ford's inability to produce a vehicle with two fewer parts than the Model T; the car was a secret disappointment and Ford was in despair; the car was a dazzling success that would put Chevrolet in the shade. Cartoonists thrived on the subject: the new model was pictured with seventeen cylinders; as a collapsible car that could be parked on the sidewalk and disguised as a trash can; with gold radiator ornaments and door handles; with long ears on each side, so that no other car could pass it, and so on. The Ford joke briefly made a comeback: St. Peter, it was said, was stopping all Detroiters as they applied at the pearly gates and promised to admit anyone who could describe the new Ford.[5]

Illustrations of the new car also were much in demand; and in addition to the scores of press photographers who made their way to Dearborn, "a lurking army" of amateur cameramen besieged Ford plants with the stealth of spies assigned to chart an enemy's fortifications. Innumerable cars were snapped as they went in and out of the company's gates, and dozens of photographs—most of them blurred—were sold to newspapers and magazines. Of all the published photographs of the new Ford, only two were authentic. A representative of *Automotive Daily News,* while roaming through a Detroit printing plant, picked off the floor a scuffed and dirtied sales-promotion folder which contained a picture of the Model A. His journal published the illustration the next day, but refused to sell prints to the clamoring wire services and metropolitan papers. Shortly afterward a reporter on the *Brighton* (Michigan) *Argus* stumbled upon the new Ford parked outside a restaurant in his town. His photographs immediately were published throughout the country—even by papers which were skeptical of their authenticity—in "extras" and under eight-column banners.

The six-month "now-you-see-it, now-you-don't" procession of stories and pictures followed a pattern which, as the *New York World* pointed out, was very much in Ford's best interests:

> It is rumored that the car will be a six. A startled country rubs its eyes. The rumor is contradicted. It is rumored that the famous hood [of the Model T] will undergo a change and that the time-honored radiator is to have its face lifted. This rumor too is contradicted. But pictures purporting to represent the new-model car in action and at rest are smuggled to the press, debated by the nation, disavowed by the Ford Company, replaced by other pictures which in turn are half-confirmed, debated, disavowed—and the car-that-is-to-be remains consistently on the front pages of the newspapers.[6]

All this mystery and suspense was greatly dramatized by the Ford Company's "golden silence." No statement on the vehicle was issued between May 25 and August 10, when Edsel Ford made a simple announcement: "The new Ford automobile is an accomplished fact. The engineering problems affecting its design and equipment and affecting also its manufacture have all been solved. . . . The tests already made show it is faster, smoother, more rugged and more flexible than we had hoped for in the early stages of designing.'' The revelation was, of course, page-one news.

The press, though unhappy about the dearth of official information, could not but admire the way Ford was conducting his build-up campaign. ''In saying nothing,'' observed the *Washington Post,* ''he gains many times the amount of publicity that other manufacturers would receive through reams of prepared statements. What the new Ford car will be like, no one is able to say with even the slightest semblance of authority. Yet nearly everyone has a plausible story to offer, many of which are accorded columns of space.'' The *Elyria* (Ohio) *Telegram,* bewildered at the flood of contradictory reports coming over its wires, resolutely decided to publish all of them: ''We feel ourselves going sixty-five miles an hour, using a gallon of gasoline for each thirty-five miles, and are concluding that it is going to be cheaper to go than to stay.''[7]

From August 10 until October 11 the Ford Company again made no mention of its product. On the latter date, Edsel revealed that the new vehicle would begin to roll off the assembly line within a few days. He also said that dealers had received down payments for 125,000 of the automobiles. Many newspapers were staggered by the figure. The *Rochester* (New York) *Times-Union* wondered ''if ever in the history of trade the dollars and cents value of a reputation was more strikingly demonstrated''; the *Lynn* (Massachusetts) *Telegram-News* said that the orders represented ''a demonstration of faith and confidence in Ford which has no precedent in world history.''[8]

The next Ford announcement was made on November 25, when banner headlines proclaimed that the new car would be given its first public showing on December 2. On November 26 the company released a photograph showing Henry Ford wielding a hammer and die as he stamped ''No. 1'' on the motor block of the first car. The photograph showed nothing of the vehicle except a portion of the engine, yet it was reprinted everywhere.[9]

In the meantime, Ford was grappling with the Herculean task of getting the new vehicle into production. It was almost as if the Panama Canal had been closed by earthquake in a time of international tension, forcing the swift completion of a Nicaraguan waterway in its stead. Forty thousand highly specialized machines that were incapable of producing anything except the Model T were thrown out, and the mechanism of the Ford plants was rebuilt from the ground up. The retooling of the Rouge complex and the concurrent overhauling of thirty-four domestic assembly plants, twelve overseas factories, and scores of suppliers' shops constituted an unparalleled changeover. Large-scale production of various components began in mid-October, and on October 21 the first car was assembled. By November 1 approximately twenty cars a day were being produced.[10]

By that time many of the company's dealers were in dire straits. Their showrooms had been empty for many months. By the thousands, in May, they had bravely displayed window posters imploring ''Wait for the new Ford!'' As the summer wore on they put up other signs: ''Wait for the new Ford cars—Speed, Pick-up, Flexibility, Beauty, Comfort—Coming Soon.'' Yet all too often by late summer the windows were dusty, the posters flyspecked, the general premises forlorn. Under the circumstances Ford could give his dealers little encouragement. A folder containing a number of press items relating to the May new-car announcement was sent to dealers in June. Occasionally there were attempts to explain to the hard-pressed dealers the reasons for the long delay: Ford's "persistent passion for improvement," the inability of suppliers to meet company demands, the long running start to stock up the assembly plants, and so on. Also, Sales Manager William A. Ryan, whom agents universally despised, was replaced by the more considerate Fred L. Rockelman, formerly traffic manager of the D.T.& I.[11]

Dealers also may have derived some comfort from the realization that their competitors were not able to appropriate the normal Ford market during the changeover period. The Chevrolet's 1927 sales increase, for example, was only about one-fifth of Ford's decrease. Industrywide, there were approximately 1,000,000 fewer passenger cars sold in 1927 than in 1926, a reduction attributable solely to the Model T's demise. Many Model T owners were deferring the purchase of a new car until the new Ford model appeared, and many prospective buyers who normally would have been attracted to other makes were postponing a decision until after they had seen what Ford was bringing out. A number of bankers, economists, and editors attributed a mild economic recession to this wait-and-see attitude, a not unreasonable assumption in that the auto industry at this time consumed 18 percent of the nation's iron and steel supply, 85 percent of its rubber, 75 percent of its plate glass, 28 percent of its nickel, 27 percent of its aluminum, and so on.[12]

Even before abandoning the Model T, Henry Ford had committed himself to a large-scale introductory and continuing advertising campaign in behalf of the new car. "They kept at me about it," he told a writer in 1927, "until I was sick of the subject. At last I said, 'All right. If you have to have that kind of doctor, get the best one you can find.' " Actually, as has been shown, Ford was not averse to advertising a new product, and in the case of the Model A he felt it altogether necessary "to tell people how to take care of it, and get the most out of it."[13] On the other hand, his decision to continue advertising beyond the introductory campaign undoubtedly was made with considerable reluctance.

During the spring of 1927 four or five advertising agencies submitted presentations for the Ford account, and in early June the retention of N. W. Ayer & Son was announced. Founded in Philadelphia in 1869, Ayer was then, as now, the oldest continuing advertising firm in the country, having as many advertising "firsts" to its credit as Ford had manufacturing "firsts." Fred L. Black was designated by Henry Ford to take charge of the company's advertising function, and was instructed to ask A. Roy Barbier to serve as his assistant. Black and Barbier soon recruited new personnel and began shaping advertising policy with Edsel Ford, to whom they reported for the next six years.[14]

During the Model T–Model A interregnum the company and its agency planned an introductory advertising campaign which "for sheer size of appropriation and breadth of coverage" dwarfed any previous effort of its kind ever conducted in America. For five straight days, from Monday, November 28, through Friday, December 2, full-page advertisements were run in all of the nation's 2,000 English-language daily newspapers. The ads cost the company $1,300,000. In addition, groups of dealers and individual agents bought $400,000 worth of space during this introductory period. The first ad, signed by Henry Ford, discussed the new car only in general terms. The second and third ads promised that the vehicle would sell at a low price and disclosed mechanical specifications. The fourth ad, published on the eve of the public showing, supplied, at long last, a photograph of the Model A and quoted its prices. The fifth advertisement summarized the four previous ads.[15]

This advertising series, cited by the president of the Advertising Club of New York as "the most soundly coordinated advertising campaign in America's advertising history," admirably maintained the suspense that had been built up during the preceding six months. The ads certainly were among the most widely discussed in advertising annals; as many commentators pointed out, "everyone who can read is reading them." In fact, it is probably safe to say that many newspapers would have run the ads free of charge—particularly the climactical fourth advertisement—so great was the public's interest in their revelations. As it was, virtually every paper in the country reproduced the advertising copy (including mechanical specifications) and photographs on its front page. Many newspapers published "extras" during the introductory week, and many more stepped up their press runs to meet the heavy demand for copies.[16]

On November 30 a press preview of the new model was held in Dearborn, and on the following day a private showing for 7,000 of New York's elite was staged in the Empire Room of the Waldorf-Astoria. Then, on December 2, the doors were thrown open to the public showrooms, convention halls, and assembly plants where the Model A was on display.[17]

Ten thousand people stormed Detroit's Convention Hall at the 10 A.M. opening hour; by nightfall 114,849 persons had filed by the new car. Five hundred people gathered at 3:00 P.M. outside Ford's main showroom in New York, trying to peek through cracks in the whitewashed windows. By 9:00 P.M. the street (Broadway) was so jammed that the police had to intervene, and in desperation that afternoon Ford's New York manager hired Madison Square Garden. A total of 1,250,000 New Yorkers saw the Model A during the first five days of its showing. The *New York World* declared that "excitement could hardly have been greater had Pah-Wah, the sacred white elephant of Burma, elected to sit for seven days on the flagpole of the Woolworth Building." The *New York Sun* observed that "it was just exactly as if Mr. Mellon had thrown open the doors of the Sub-Treasury and invited folks to help him count the gold reserve; or as if Mr. Ziegfeld had paraded down Broadway at the head of his Follies girls."[18]

Other cities were in a similar state of excitement. Denver, it was reported, had not been in such a frenzy since its Mint was robbed years before; mounted police had to be called out to control the Cleveland crowds; people trampled over one another to get close to the car in Kansas City's Convention Hall; extra editions of Dallas newspapers declared the event "the greatest since the signing of the armistice"; and a New Orleans paper reported that "every person [in the New Orleans area] . . . including businessmen, truck farmers, housewives, jellybeans and flappers, pressed forward to see the new Fords." Because there were not enough Model A's to supply each dealer, Ford representatives whisked cars from town to town so that they might be exhibited for an hour or so in each community.

In towns where no Fords were placed on display, the populace saw movies of the car or gawked at photographs. More than ten million persons, 8.5 percent of the nation's population, saw the actual car within the first thirty-six hours of its showing. Within less than a week, more than twenty-five million Americans had seen the new vehicle. Overseas, special trains were run to London for thousands eager to view the car; Berlin police had to fight back the throngs outside the exhibition rooms; and 150,000 Spaniards attended the Madrid showing. Never in the world's history had a vehicle aroused such excitement.[19]

The Model A, fortunately, lived up to, perhaps even exceeded, expectations. "Even the most godless scoffer," reported the *New York World* "must have realized that the magnum opus thus offered for sale was worth all the commotion it was causing." Automotive experts were complimentary, competing manufacturers envious, and each Ford dealer, according to the *New York Times,* was so pleased that "if stroked gently he would purr." Most important, the general public pronounced the car a success.[20]

The motor, combining strength with lightness and quietness, was unexcelled by any other motor product in the moderate-price class. In the use of safety glass in the windshield, the Model A was in advance of all other low or medium-priced cars. The body satisfied all but the most fastidious, for if it was not superior to those of the Chevrolet and other low-priced cars, it was their equal. Furthermore, people were astonished to find that the prices—ranging from $495 to $570—were held close to the Model T level and decidedly below that of the Chevrolet. Altogether, the Model A was a superior car for its price.[21]

Some 400,000 orders for the vehicle went on the company's books in less than a fortnight after its debut. By January 10, 1928, 727,000 cars were sold. Unhappily, the company could meet but a fraction of the demand. Production had been raised only to 125–140 vehicles a day by New Year's, and not until February was each dealer furnished with at least one sample car of most types in the Model A line. Little by little, however, the battle of production was being won. By mid-year daily output exceeded 4,000, and by year's end almost 800,000 vehicles had been assembled. Nonetheless, Chevrolet, by building more than a million units in 1928, outsold Ford to maintain the supremacy it had won in 1927.[22]

As the press filled its columns with lavish praise for the Model A, it also devoted many editorials to adulatory comment on Henry Ford. The industrialist naturally—and correctly—was given the major credit for the excellence of his product, and the amount of publicity on this theme alone perhaps raised his personal prestige to an all-time high during December 1927. In addition, the journalistic and advertising fraternity almost ran out of adjectives in complimenting Ford on his "strategy" in building up and introducing the Model A. The *Danville* (Virginia) *Bee* called the performance "the most amazing publicity coup of modern times"; the *Charleston* (West Virginia) *Gazette* termed it "the greatest publicity stunt of all time"; and the *New York World* commended it as "the perfect bit of salesmanship of all ages" and suggested that, as a classic, it was to its field as Spinoza's *Ethics* was to philosophy. To the *Newark News,* Ford was "the greatest showman in American business"; to the *Springfield* (Massachusetts) *Union,* he was "the master showman of all times"; and to the *Staunton* (Virginia) *Leader,* he was "the greatest advertising artist in the world."[23]

For years newspapers had compared Ford's genius for publicity favorably with that of P. T. Barnum, Theodore Roosevelt, Andrew Carnegie, Billy Sunday, and others; now all of Ford's rival publicists were denounced as "pikers" not fit to hold his hat. "Had the talents of the late P. T. Barnum, the brothers Ringling, and Tex Rickard been united in one grand effort," observed one writer, "it is doubtful whether they could have brought to pass any such spectacle as that of Friday, December 2." Editors who all their lives had fought to keep the names of products and companies out of their columns admitted that they had been beaten and gave a few sticks of type to "the most arrant space poacher in the world" and to his car. The *Nation,* previously one of Ford's severest critics, capped the laudatory comment by placing Ford on its "Honor Roll of 1927" for "teaching the advertising experts what national advertising can be." The industrialist was the only businessman on the thirty-eight-man list, which usually was restricted to public servants and men of letters and the arts.[24]

Actually, Ford was probably amazed by the public's tremendous interest in his automobile. There is no evidence to suggest that in May or June 1927, the manufacturer had conceived a master plan to withhold all information about the car and thereby create an atmosphere of mystery and suspense. On the contrary, he probably was sincere when he promised on May 25 to announce specifications of the new vehicle within a few weeks; he simply did not have anything to say after those few weeks had expired. Indeed, he could not point to *the* car which he was going to build until early August. The theft of the Ayer material dramatically revealed to Ford the full extent of the general interest in his new product, and undoubtedly the industrialist noted that from that point on newspapers gave their readers every scrap of news and misinformation they could obtain. Ford was far too able a publicist not to sense that the press would speculate endlessly if left to its own devices and that he could take full advantage of the situation by saying nothing. Therein lay a great part of Ford's "genius," as far as the Model A campaign was concerned.[25]

After the Model A's debut the Ford Motor Company made a conscious effort to put the new car into the "best garages," in accordance with the idea, "If you can sell the classes, the masses will follow." Priorities for acquiring the model were granted to select individuals—among them Princess Ileana of Rumania, Douglas Fairbanks and Mary Pickford, Franklin D. Roosevelt, and Carl Sandburg—and the Ford Company widely heralded their purchases. Display advertising usually showed the car in a "smart" setting: in front of a country club, skimming along the water's edge at a regatta, or bathed in Miami moonlight. The appeal succeeded. Whereas the Model T had failed all efforts at glamorization, the Model A quickly became a prestige car. "The Ford car is now positively fashionable," Arthur Brisbane remarked in the fall of 1928. "Everybody who has one is proud of it."[26]

The demand for Model A's, unsatisfied during 1928, continued to be heavy throughout 1929. Total output for the latter year was 1,851,092 units, the largest for the Ford Motor Company since 1925. Sales, as distinguished from factory production, came to 1,710,734 vehicles. In taking 34 percent of the market the company had outdistanced Chevrolet by approximately 400,000 units. Because of the solid merits of the Model A, the Ford Company weathered the first phase of the depression better than its competitors. In 1930 Ford's car outsold the entire line of General Motors by about 300,000 units. During 1929 and 1930 Ford's profits (after taxes) exceeded $131,000,000, a sum which more than offset the $101,000,000 lost during 1927 and 1928.

In 1931, however, the depression caught up with the Ford Company. Only 619,757 Model A's were sold that year, little more than half of the number marketed in 1930, and Ford lost $31,181,000. During the same year, General Motors, paced by a new and larger Chevrolet, netted $94,769,000, while the aggressive Chrysler Corporation, whose 1931 Plymouth had attracted wide attention, showed sales and profit increases over 1930. The Model A, which now sold for only $55.00 to $75.00 less than its principal rivals, which had been doing some price cutting on their own, began to experience the same disfavor which had overtaken the Model T before it. By 1931 it was clear that Ford would soon have to bring out a new model, one embodying advances over both the new Chevrolet and the new Plymouth. Henry Ford undoubtedly was shaken by this realization, for during the late 1920s he was of the opinion—based on the unparalleled reception given the Model A—that the car would serve the public as long as the Model T had. Faced with a critical situation, however, Ford never lacked nerve. In August 1931, he shut down production of the A "indefinitely."[27]

Like the Model T, the Model A continues to ply the nation's highways and to have many ardent admirers. Some auto historians and many old-car enthusiasts, in fact, believe that the A—pound for pound, dollar for dollar—is the best car ever built. Of the 4,320,446 A's produced in the United States, more than 300,000 were extant in 1963. Hundreds were licensed for daily service, but most were owned by old-car enthusiasts. Two rapidly growing nationwide organizations serve A hobbyists, the Model A Restorers Club (MARC) and the Model A Ford Club of America (MAFCA). MARC, founded in 1952, has headquarters in Dearborn. It had ninety-seven chapters and more than 5,500 members in 1975. MAFCA, established in 1955, is based in Pomona, California. The largest of the single-car clubs, MAFCA had 209 chapters and 11,600 members in 1975. Both clubs publish bimonthly magazines dedicated to A lore and restoration, and each sponsors well-publicized regional and national rallies. After attending a national meet, a writer typically rhapsodized, "The lump in my throat was so big I had to unbutton my collar. It was like stumbling on your old school sweetheart after a quarter-century lapse and finding her still slender and sweet, young in heart and fun to know and—can such things be?—lovely beyond recall." The A, like the T, has been featured in Ford (Pinto car) and Volkswagen advertisements, and is a staple of almost every old-car museum. Parts for A's are still easily obtainable, not only from old-car parts houses, but from "junkers" as well. The A, if not as highly publicized as the T, remains newsworthy; and since 1959 has been the subject of six full-length books. The car has even made a comeback of sorts; Glassic Industries, Inc., of West Palm Beach, Florida, in 1966 began producing full-scale fiberglass 1928-styled A's, priced at $7,595 in 1973.[28]

2

For some months after stopping production of the Model A, Henry Ford wavered between the manufacture of an improved four-cylinder Model A, a new six-cylinder car, or a new eight-cylinder model. The improved A actually went into production during the fall of 1931, but on December 7 the industrialist decided that his "corking good 'four' . . . was not the new effort which the public is expecting," and that he would produce an automobile featuring an eight-cylinder V-shaped motor.[29]

No one outside of Ford's inner circle really knew what the company intended to do. Ford, profiting from his experience with the Model A's introduction, revealed nothing to the press. Once again, although on a lesser scale, the formula of silence worked. Speculation on the new car was rampant during December 1931 and January 1932. "In all quarters there is gossip and prophecy," the *New York Post* reported in early January, "and lately the rumors have been coming so fast that many suspect a rumor-for-the-week idea has been launched." Press and amateur photographers armed with telephoto lens-equipped cameras stalked Dearborn, and *Automotive Daily News* again scored when a shot of an authentic V-8 appeared in its pages. Detroit's Hollywood Theater obtained forty feet of V-8 movie film from a cameraman who had spent weeks in the brush along roads on which the new car was tested. Apprised of the film, excited newsreel companies offered to "pay handsomely" for it. The Ford Company hastily announced that it would "match the top offer." The theater surrendered the film to the company in exchange for a coveted opportunity to exhibit a V-8 in its lobby on the day of its first public showing.[30]

On February 11 Ford permitted James Sweinhart of the *Detroit News* to announce that the company would build both a V-8 and an improved four-cylinder car (Model B). The *News* set the whole story in large boldface type, and virtually every paper in the country reprinted the article on its front page. Again, there were many editorials congratulating the industrialist on the skill with which he was conducting the introductory campaign. "Just enough news to tickle the public appetite," stated the *Cleveland Plain Dealer*, "but not too much. Henry Ford is still the master of merchandising showmanship. He still has thrust upon him the publicity which his rivals tumble over each other to get."[31]

In late February Ford generated another nationwide story by announcing through Sweinhart that he expected to build 1,500,000 of the new cars during 1932 and would employ well over 100,000 men and spend $300,000,000 on raw materials and parts in their manufacture. The announcement, coming as it did at the nadir of the depression, cheered millions of people and inspired widespread editorial comment. Many papers felt that Ford's program would "start a wave of industrial revival which, to greater or lesser degree, will be felt the whole world around." The industrialist, said a Massachusetts paper, is "an American Moses leading his people out of the Land of Depression Bondage into a new economic Land of Promise."[32]

The public demonstrated anew its faith in Ford by placing deposits on orders for more than 100,000 of the new vehicles (three-fourths of them for the V-8) by March 5. Another 100,000 orders came in within a few days of the public introduction of the new models on March 31. Full details of the V-8 were first revealed in full-page advertisements in 2,000 American and Canadian newspapers on March 29. Two days later a second full-page ad appeared in 200 newspapers of 200 metropolitan centers. In addition, film clips on the new car, entitled "Ford Starts Prosperity Drive," were shown free in approximately 6,000 theaters, including all those serviced by Pathé News. Ford made 4,000 prints available for these showings, the largest film release on record for an industrial subject.[33]

More than 5,500,000 persons visited Ford showrooms on the first day of the public showing (55 percent of the number of people who viewed the Model A within thirty-six hours of its introduction) and they were pleased with what they saw. The V-8, priced from $460 to $650, was agreeably streamlined, and was far more comfortable than its predecessor. It also offered an engine which, because of its quick acceleration, endeared itself to every motorist with a yen for a fast getaway, including public enemy No. 1 John Dillinger, and Clyde Barrow of Bonnie and Clyde fame. "Hello Old Pal," Dillinger wrote Henry Ford while racing from one bank hold up to another in 1934, "You have a wonderful car. It's a treat to drive one. Your slogan should be drive a Ford and watch the other cars fall behind you. I can make any other car take a Ford's dust. Bye-bye." "While I have still got breath in my lungs," Barrow wrote Ford from Tulsa in 1934, "I will tell you what a dandy car you make. I have drove Fords exclusively when I could get away with one. For sustained speed and freedom from trouble the Ford has got ever other car skinned and even if my business hasn't been strictly legal it don't hurt anything to tell you what a fine car you got in the V8." Unfortunately, the same engine which enabled lead-footed motorists to leave other cars in the ruck required inordinate amounts of oil after 1,000 miles of driving, and was responsible for Ford's most serious product public relations problem during the 1930s. A 1934 survey of 10,005 Ford owners revealed that in 39 percent of the cars two or more quarts of oil had to be added between each 1,000-mile change. Indeed, some V-8's devoured a quart of oil every fifty miles. Tens of thousands of Ford owners naturally complained. The problem was corrected during the mid-1930s, but not before the V-8 had acquired a nationwide reputation as an "oil burner."[34]

Despite its auspicious introduction, the V-8 could not wrest sales leadership from the Chevrolet in 1932 or 1933. Ford sales amounted to little more than 800,000 units for both years combined, and the company lost another $88,000,000 during this period. In 1934, however, Ford produced more than a million units, outsold the Chevrolet, and returned a modest profit.

The years between 1926, the last calendar year in which the Model T led the field, and 1934 marked the end of an automotive era. Despite the initial acclaim for the Model A, the Model B, and the V-8, none of the T's successors was able to capture the public's fancy as had the Lizzie. By the early 1930s it was apparent to everyone at the Ford Company, even to Henry Ford, that the salad days of the 'teens and 1920s were gone. Successive challenges to the upstart Chevrolet in 1927 and to the Chevrolet and fast-rising Plymouth in 1932 kept the Ford Company very much in the race. But its new products, unlike their predecessor of an earlier generation, could not sweep the heightened competition aside. By the early 1930s the Ford Motor Company was no longer *the* company in the automobile industry; rather, it was merely *one* of the "Big Three" firms destined to dominate the American auto market.[35]

The varying fortunes of the Ford Company and its products during the 1920s and early 1930s were paralleled by diverse approaches to the firm's formal public relations activities and programs.

In the realm of press relations, the vast majority of news stories which concerned the Ford organization during the 1920s and early 1930s, just as they had during the 'teens, were originated independently of the firm's publicists. However, a comparison of the company's news releases with clippings which appeared in hundreds of different newspapers shows clearly that a considerable amount of publicity was generated by Ford's press relations staff.

From Charles A. Brownell's departure in late 1920 until early 1923, the Sales Department issued news releases to the press on a sporadic, infrequent basis. Most of the stories were concerned with production and sales figures, although a few discussed mechanical refinements which had been made on the Model T. In March 1923, the company announced a policy of supplying dealers with "frequent and regular" news items on a variety of topics, including "Ford business in general, improvements in Ford products, expansion of our manufacturing facilities, as well as methods in the building of Ford products." Agents were urged to submit this copy to newspapers from which they were buying space, for, in the company's view, "with the amount of advertising our dealers are running, there is no reason why the newspapers should not be willing and glad to carry these stories." The company's roadmen were instructed to see that agents made suitable publicity arrangements with local publishers and to report on the amount of publicity obtained in each territory. In addition to placing publicity through the dealers, the company sent news stories directly to the press and had its branches distribute copy to metropolitan newspapers within their districts.[36]

Starting in early 1924, when each branch appointed an advertising representative, distribution of press materials was handled by this individual. The representative was ordered "to cultivate the newspapers in his territory, and to acquaint them not only with the Ford Motor Company but [with] the fact that the stories we release usually have exceptional reader interest." A number of the men "complied" with excessive zeal, and the company admonished them, alleging that their activities had "resulted in very unfavorable comments by the Press regarding Ford publicity methods." Acknowledging that "many publishers have their own policies with reference to the use of news stories," the company warned that "under no circumstances should threats or attempts to curtail advertising be made in an effort to club the publisher into using our news stories."[37]

During the early and mid-1920s Ford's news stories were prepared by three publicists working within the Sales Department, except for the five-month period in 1923–24 when the Brotherton Company had charge of the publicity function. The publicity men, all ex-newspapermen, wrote highly professional copy until about 1925, when a noticeable deterioration set in. One story, for example, which was to be sent to hometown newspapers while dealers were visiting the Rouge, contained the sentence, "I felt like little Alice in Wonderland, walking around in the midst of that tremendous enterprise." Other stories were so poorly constructed that they might have been written by amateurs. It is quite possible that Edsel Ford's assistant, John Crawford, was partly responsible for the lowered standards. All publicity had to be cleared through this former tractor-plant executive, and, according to one of the publicists who submitted stories to him, Crawford "often would in blissful ignorance blue pencil news of genuine reader interest right out." In time, the publicist adds, the staff "by mutual agreement wrote publicity stories not for news value and public interest but to please Crawford."[38]

Although the company relied chiefly on the press relations function as a means of drawing gratuitous attention to itself, it also sought publicity by heralding "milestone" cars, sponsoring plant open houses, and promoting small-town Ford Days.

Much to the company's chagrin, for it had hoped to "sound the loud timbrel," the production of the millionth Ford, which rolled off an assembly line in September 1915, went unnoticed. "With twenty-five assembly plants . . . and with a big factory in Detroit assembling so many Ford cars a day," the *Ford Times* lamented, "we passed the million mark without knowing it." The second through nine millionth car similarly went out into the world unheralded. The ten millionth Ford, however, completed at Highland Park in June 1924, led Ford-inspired parades through most of the towns and cities along the Lincoln Highway (New York to San Francisco) and U.S.66 (Los Angeles to Chicago). Several million people saw the vehicle, which was "greeted" by the governors and mayors of nearly all the states and communities through which it passed. A motion picture of the tour, *Fording the Lincoln Highway,* was widely exhibited during the mid-1920s.[39]

The eleven millionth car was presented to the Prince of Wales during his visit to Highland Park in late 1924. The assembly of the fifteen millionth Model T, as previously mentioned, coincided with the announcement of the T's discontinuance. The twenty millionth Ford, driven off the assembly line at Edgewater, New Jersey, by Henry Ford, toured the nation in 1931 much in the manner of the ten millionth vehicle's trip. In order to generate additional publicity, arrangements were made for each state through which the car passed to award the vehicle License No. 20 000 000. Dealers also set up innumerable receptions at which gifts, ranging from rattlesnake skins and beehives to peace pipes and limestone tablets, were presented to the milestone car's drivers.[40]

The company's branch assembly plants had long been open to visitors, but for the first time, during 1926 and 1927, an aggressive nationwide effort was made to get townspeople to visit Ford installations. Each of the thirty-odd assembly plants held a week-long "open house," during which visitors were guided through the premises by employees and dealers and their salesmen.[41]

Ford Days were held in hundreds of small communities throughout the country from 1921 to 1931. Local merchants, at the instigation of the local Ford dealer, would invite every owner or driver of a Ford in the surrounding area to come into town on a certain day. Special bargains were offered by all places of business, and a carnival atmosphere prevailed as Main Street was taken over for parades, band concerts, vaudeville performances, dancing, queen crownings, and Model T and athletic contests. Prizes were liberally awarded to contest winners and to owners of the cars carrying the biggest load of farm produce, the most eggs, the most children, the five prettiest girls, and so on. Model T owners turned up by the thousands, and virtually took over some towns, inasmuch as drivers of other cars were usually fined if they appeared on the streets with their vehicles. Nearly all of the 1,300 Fords in Appanoose County, Iowa, invaded Centerville in 1922; more than 15,000 Ford owners and members of their families spent the day in Opelousas, Louisiana, the same year; and 20,000 persons bought more than $200,000 worth of goods on Ford Day in 1931 at Chickasha, Oklahoma.[42]

Although Ford Days were still going strong in 1931, as attested by items in the *Ford News* and the company's detailed exhortations to branch managers to spread the idea to all communities within their jurisdiction, they seem to have died out quite suddenly thereafter. Perhaps depressed business conditions dampened the enthusiasm of many Ford dealers and their fellow merchants. Even more important, as the proportion of Ford owners shrank during the late 1920s and early 1930s, there undoubtedly was less justification for a Ford Day for Ford owners within the various communities.[43]

The demise of the Ford Day served notice that for the first time in two decades the Ford was no longer *the* car in small-town America. Increasing numbers of motorists were looking beyond the Model A to meet their needs. Sophisticated General Motors and hungry Chrysler were ready to serve them, and to put an end to Ford's long-time dominance of the industry.

Chapter 13
Folk Hero

1

Throughout the 1920s the Ford Motor Company received more publicity and had greater prestige than any other business institution in America. The company's acclaim did not stem entirely from its size, its wealth, its importance on the nation's economic scene, or even its product. Of far more importance to Ford's reputation than bricks and mortar and balance sheets were the ideals for which it stood or with which it was associated. The average citizen was far less likely to think of the Ford Company as a huge manufacturing concern than he was to think of the efficient mass production techniques, enlightened labor policies, and price reductions which had become the firm's hallmarks. In contrast, many other large corporations immediately brought to the public's mind an image of stock markets, high profits, and, in some instances, of monopolies.[1]

Although no representative survey of public attitudes toward large corporations was taken during the 1920s (when the Ford Company's prestige was at an all-time high), an indication of the public's attitude toward Ford can perhaps be seen in the results of a nationwide sample conducted by the Curtis Publishing Company in 1937. Respondents were asked to rate twelve of the country's leading corporations as to their labor and pricing policies, the excellence of their research and new products, their profit structure, importance, and concern for the public interest. The opinions reflected in this survey testify to the solidity with which the Ford Company's reputation—particularly in the labor and pricing spheres—had been established in the 'teens and 1920s. Even though it had not "made news" in the labor or pricing areas for eight years, the company was given top ranking in both categories.

Ford's labor policies were judged superior to those of any other corporation by two-thirds of the respondents. Bell Telephone was ranked second by a mere one-eighth of the interviewees. In the pricing sphere, more than two-fifths of the people surveyed rated Ford first. Bell and General Motors, which vied for runner-up honors in this category, were named by fewer than 10 percent of the respondents.

Ford also fared well in other areas of this survey. Only the Bell Company was believed by more people to be operating in the public's best interest, and the Ford organization stood in the upper half in both the research and new product categories. Similarly, Ford did *not* receive the dubious distinction of being named among the leading profit makers. All categories of the poll considered, Ford's reputation and prestige among the American public in 1937 was exceeded only by General Electric and Bell. General Motors was rated about even with Ford, and only Du Pont among the other firms (Goodyear, International Harvester, United States Steel, Bethlehem

Steel, Republic Steel, Westinghouse, and Union Carbide) could be considered a strong challenger to the "Big Four."[2]

These findings were corroborated in large degree by the findings of the Link Audit, which, starting in November 1937, conducted semiannual nationwide surveys to determine the relative public relations standing of eight major companies. The initial sample placed General Electric first, General Motors second, Westinghouse third, and Ford fourth (Bell was not a client). In the second division of this survey were Du Pont, Standard Oil of New Jersey, United States Steel, and United States Rubber. Ford's first-division showing was achieved despite its exceedingly poor relations with employees in 1937 (the Rouge plant's widely publicized "Battle of the Overpass"—in which unionists were beaten by Ford thugs—occurred in May of that year) and having paved the way for price advances throughout the automobile industry by unexpectedly hiking prices $15 to $35 on its models in August 1937.[3]

During the 1920s the press and such business analysts as Clarence W. Barron, B. C. Forbes, and Roger Babson, discussed the Ford Company in the most laudatory terms. During a month-long period in 1927, a dozen of the nation's leading financiers, testifying as expert witnesses in a tax appeal made by Ford's former stockholders, praised the company at sufficient length to fill whole pages of the daily press. Ford management was described by Paul Clay, vice-president of Moody Investment Service, as "the most skilled and efficient that I have ever observed in the records of any company." John W. Prentiss, a partner in the banking and brokerage firm Hornblower & Weeks, pictured Ford as "the best motor company in the world, which it has always been and always will be." Prentiss backed up his words by offering Henry Ford $1,000,000,000 for his company on three occasions. He predicted that the firm's stock, if placed before the public, would sell "like wildfire" for upwards of $1,250,000,000.[4]

As to sheer *volume* of publicity, Ford was the subject of more articles in the general periodical press than the ten next most publicized firms combined. United States Steel, the second most publicized, was discussed in only one-fourth as many articles as Ford. In the journals surveyed by the *Industrial Arts Index,* the Ford Company received more than twice as much publicity as any other firm. In the daily press Ford undoubtedly fared altogether as well as it did in general and specialized periodicals. The *New York Times,* during the ten years ending in 1930, published an average of 101 stories per year on the Ford Company. Except for the three major railroads serving New York City, no other company averaged more than thirty stories a year. Unquestionably the hinterland press, which had no interest in the number of commuters carried each month by the New York Central or the promotion of a United States Steel official, gave a much greater amount of publicity to Dearborn-based Ford than did the *New York Times.* Abroad, the Ford Company was the only business institution which was consistently publicized. During some years Ford received more press attention than the next dozen most publicized firms combined, including such foreign and international giants as Krupp, Imperial Chemical, Standard Oil Company (New Jersey), Royal Dutch Shell, and Unilever. A number of Ford's overseas plants also were well publicized in the nations in which they were located.[5]

2

Well publicized as it was, the Ford Motor Company stood in the shadow of its founder throughout the 1920s. The company's reputation during this period rested on Henry Ford's personality and character; undoubtedly the firm's greatest asset was the vast amount of goodwill which the industrialist enjoyed among the masses. Good deeds were, of course, the foundations upon which the magnate's fame and prestige were built. "Telling," however, was almost as important as "doing" in molding the Ford image; and, in placing himself in the public eye (albeit, as some of his critics said, "like a cinder"), Ford had no peer.[6]

An analysis of the *New York Times Index,* the *Readers' Guide to Periodical Literature,* and the *Industrial Arts Index* makes it very clear that Ford received more publicity during the 1920s than any other American except Calvin Coolidge; and Coolidge received a bigger press only because he occupied the presidency nearly two-thirds of this time. (As vice-president, Coolidge received only one-sixth as much attention as Ford.) Presidents Harding and Hoover, when in office, received more publicity than Ford, as did Charles Evans Hughes during part of the period he served as secretary of state. However, Harding was President less than two-and-a-half years and Hoover received widespread publicity only during the last two years of the decade. Thus Ford—whose "unrelenting, unremitting publicity," as one newspaper pointed out, "flows on as smooth as oil"—received more attention than Harding or Hoover during the ten-year span under consideration.

Other than the four above-named men, no one in America even approached Ford in press play. The best publicized industrialists, Elbert H. Gary, Charles M. Schwab, and the Rockefellers, Sr. and Jr., received less than one-fifth of the space accorded to Ford. The most publicized entertainers, Will Rogers and Charlie Chaplin, obtained less than one-twelfth of the manufacturer's publicity. Abroad, during the 1920s, only premiers, presidents, and dictators of the Great Powers (Great Britain, Germany, France, the United States, China, Italy, and the U.S.S.R.) and India received as much worldwide attention as Ford. Not even such internationally known figures as Thomas Edison and the Prince of Wales were as well publicized as the man from Dearborn; no other industrialist even came close.

Just how much publicity, then, did Ford receive? The conservative *New York Times,* which omitted many of the reports and rumors concerning Ford, ran an average of 145 stories per year on the industrialist throughout the 1920s. The general periodical press ran an average of twenty-one articles a year on Ford, and the specialized trade press added many more. Ford received so much publicity in Detroit that one of the daily newspapers sometimes ran a two-column index on its front page entitled, "What the World Is Doing to FORD Today." An analysis of the *Detroit Free Press* for 1922, when Ford received less than half as much publicity as in 1923 or 1927, showed that the industrialist was featured in an average of thirty-four stories per month.[7]

The Detroit papers probably gave Ford fuller treatment than he received elsewhere. Even so, as Arthur Pound pointed out, in newspaper morgues all over the country "the envelope [labeled] 'Ford, Henry' bulks larger than that devoted to any other private citizen." In 1923 the Associated Advertising Clubs of the World, in convention at Atlantic City, voted Ford the "best advertised individual in America, though at least 99 percent of his publicity comes to him without his lifting a finger to seek it." A rival auto manufacturer, addessing this same meeting, said that motor vehicle advertisers could be divided into two classes, "those who pay real coin of the realm for space and Henry Ford." In 1927 a Virginia newspaper echoed this view, remarking with considerable truth that "for many years it has been a dull day in which Ford has not been in the news columns of the 14,000 newspapers of the United States."[8]

Almost all of the nation's editors, even those who were rabidly opposed to giving a businessman "free advertising," acknowledged that Ford was so extraordinarily newsworthy that he could not be ignored. As Gerald Stanley Lee, writing in *Everybody's Magazine* in 1916, pointed out: "Ford is news. He comes under the head of news columns and of editorial matter. He is a part of what we pay our two cents for. . . . Mr. Ford is not getting for nothing out of the papers what other people would have to pay for. What Mr. Ford is getting other people could not get by paying for it. . . . Everybody has to advertise Henry Ford whether they want to or not." Journalistic trade papers frequently admonished their readers to stop giving Ford so much free space, but their advice largely went unheeded. A Massachusetts editor who ran an editorial on Ford's aviation activities consoled himself by stating, "Henry Ford gets so much free advertising that a little more will make little difference one way or another." A Tennessee paper, at the bottom of a column-length editorial praising Ford and the Model T, advised its readers, "No, Geraldine, this is not an advertisement of Ford cars."[9]

The *Detroit Saturday Night,* in analyzing the public's insatiable appetite for Ford news, concluded that almost everyone had "Ford-osis":

> It's on the brain and in the blood of the American people. They gobble the Ford stuff, and never stop to reason whether they like it, or whether it has any real merit in it. . . . You may hear him confess that he doesn't know who this fellow Benedict Arnold was, and still you would like to get his personal viewpoints on facts of American history. . . . Some of his words and acts, if spoken and done by any other man, would strike you as being more or less silly. Yet, under the spell of Ford-osis, you would hail them as matters of boundless consequence, and you would be the first to snatch from the fingers of a screaming newsboy the edition that breaks this news to the world.

In any event, the public's interest in Ford and his capacity for satisfying that interest made the industrialist "the most widely discussed man of his time." A number of newspapers and writers went further, and stated that, "No man *of any period* was ever in so many mouths in his lifetime as Henry Ford."[10]

In an attempt to satisfy the public's interest in Ford, a small library grew up about the industrialist. The first biographical sketch of Ford, written by Elbert Hubbard, author of the widely read *A Message to Garcia,* appeared in 1913. It was followed in 1917 by *Henry Ford's Own Story,* a collection of inaccurate articles written by a young Western writer, Rose Wilder Lane, and published in the *San*

Francisco Bulletin in 1915–16. A third book on Ford, *What Henry Ford Is Doing,* a hodgepodge of sayings, clippings, and hearsay compiled by Frank Bonville, a Seattle crank, appeared in 1920.[11]

After Ford achieved worldwide fame in 1914, many journalists naturally sought to write his biography. Foremost among them was Edward A. Rumely, of the *New York Evening Mail,* who proposed to have two ghostwriters prepare a book under his supervision. Liebold repeatedly put Rumely and others off by claiming that Ford found interviews "more or less burdensome" or that the manufacturer intended to write an autobiography "in order that it might be correct."[12] Despite the difficulties, five writers did gain access to him and published biographies during 1922 and 1923. During that time, two persons who had worked closely with Ford for a number of years also brought out volumes about the auto king. This spate of books on Ford, the largest number within any comparable period during his lifetime, elicited the remark of a Detroit publication that "one of the Ford jokes of the near future will probably be to the effect that a newspaper man has been found who hasn't written a book about Dearborn's leading citizen."[13]

Of the seven books published in 1922 and 1923, three were extremely eulogistic: Sarah T. Bushnell's *The Truth About Henry Ford,* Rev. William R. Stidger's *Henry Ford: The Man and His Motives,* and James Martin Miller's *The Amazing Story of Henry Ford: The Ideal American and the World's Most Famous Private Citizen.* Allan L. Benson's *The New Henry Ford,* though factually weak and cursory, was reasonably objective; and Dean Samuel S. Marquis's *Henry Ford: An Interpretation* stands even today as one of the finest and most dispassionate character studies of Ford ever written. E. G. Pipp's *The Real Henry Ford* was a scathing attack on the industrialist, largely inspired by the fear that he might become politically successful. None of these six books seems to have been widely circulated or to have made much of an impression on the general public. The volumes by Marquis and Pipp were, in fact, never available to the public in large numbers, for the Ford organization was fairly successful in buying up and suppressing them.[14]

The seventh book published on Ford during 1922–23 was *My Life and Work,* which sold all over the globe and did more to spread Ford's ideas and contribute to his fame than any other single volume. It was written for Ford by Samuel Crowther, a versatile journalist and something of an economist. He combined material from "Mr. Ford's Own Page" in the *Dearborn Independent* with relatively sparse data obtained during Ford interviews to produce assorted sketches of the manufacturer's life and a discussion of his philosophy of industry. Translated into twelve languages and Braille, the book was acclaimed throughout the world. It was a bestseller in Germany for months, outdistancing all works of fiction, and was reported to have been read by nearly every English manufacturer. The Russians, after making sixty omissions and changes in the copy and adding an introduction which stated that "Fordism is a system the principles of which have been known for long, [having been] laid down by Marx," used the book as a text in universities and technical schools.[15]

The resounding success of *My Life and Work* made sequels inevitable, and in 1926 Crowther collaborated with Ford to produce *Today and Tomorrow;* in 1930 they brought out *Moving Forward*. These books, which are largely concerned with Ford's economic theories, were translated into a half-dozen languages and sold throughout most of the world.[16]

Ford's name also appeared on the title page of three other volumes during the 1920s. Two of them, *Ford Ideals: Being a Selection from "Mr. Ford's Page" in the Dearborn Independent* (1926) and *My Philosophy of Industry* (actually written by Fay Leone Faurote, a well-known technical writer), had limited sales. Demand, however, for the third book, *Good Morning: After a Sleep of 25 Years, Old Fashioned Dancing Is Being Revived by Mr. and Mrs. Henry Ford* (1926), quickly exhausted a printing of 50,000 copies. The Fords' dance guide, reflecting an effort to popularize early American dancing, was adopted by many dancing masters as the standard work in its field. The book was in its fourth edition in 1943.[17]

Among the remaining books which concerned themselves with Ford during the middle and late 1920s, perhaps the one most widely read was Charles Merz's *And Then Came Ford* (1929). Well-written, one of the few books to discuss Ford's impact on the American scene in a detached and objective manner, it deserved the excellent reviews and wide popular support it received. Another objective and revealing book written on Ford during this period was E. G. Pipp's *Henry Ford: Both Sides of Him,* which achieved only modest sales.

Among the adulatory biographies which appeared during the middle and late 1920s were J. G. de Roulhac Hamilton's *Henry Ford: The Man, the Worker, the Citizen* (1927), William A. Simonds's *Henry Ford Motor Genius* (1929), and Ralph Waldo Trine's *The Power That Wins*. A slashing denunciation of the manufacturer's personnel policies was written by Walter M. Cunningham, a disgruntled former Ford employee, whose *"J8" : A Chronicle of the Neglected Truth* attributed the fluctuations of the American economy to the Ford Company's failure to adopt the author's "Golden Key," a plan to stabilize employment and provide a fair living wage. Cunningham's book was not reviewed by the general press.[18]

All in all, fifteen books on the life and work of Ford appeared during the 1920s. No other American of the period received so much attention in book form. In addition, full chapters were devoted to Ford in at least fourteen volumes dealing with world leaders, prominent Americans, and leading businessmen of the day.[19]

3

The plethora of articles and books about Henry Ford made him the most widely discussed man of his time. The origins of Ford's publicity were diverse, but most of the attention showered upon him can be traced to three major sources: the Ford Motor Company, Henry Ford himself, and the newsmen who, when the company or the man failed to provide them with "Ford news," nursed and magnified every crumb relating to the magnate they could uncover. The line between the publicity generated by Henry Ford and the news stories prepared by journalists famished for Ford items is a thin one, for, even though the most ordinary of Ford's activities and utterances commanded national attention, it is difficult to say which of these were due to the attention and which occurred despite it.

Although the firm's publicists aggressively and successfully publicized Ford in news releases, advertising, films, and other media, they played relatively little part in projecting the manufacturer onto the public stage. Of far more importance in presenting Henry Ford favorably was Henry Ford himself, who, as "one of the most skillful and avid self-advertisers of the century," all but instinctively fashioned the Ford image with its attendant myths and legends. As Fred L. Black points out in his illuminating reminiscences:

> Whatever they say about Cameron, or about me, or about anybody else, and what *we* did for Mr. Ford—and a lot of people got the idea that he had very astute and smart public relations men or press men—actually, Henry Ford was the top guy as far as creating situations that resulted in some of the top stories.... Nobody made Henry Ford from a publicity standpoint except himself; Cameron or any of the rest of us just merely *helped*.
>
> Any Ford legend would start with the boss himself, and it was nursed along by the newspapermen, rather than engineered by any staff at Ford's. This idea that Henry Ford was an ignoramus, and had his smartness due to his public relations men who engineered all his stuff, is *absolutely untrue*.
>
> It was a strange combination; he was a very shy man with this amazing sense of publicity values.[20]

Ford had several formulas for generating news. The *New York Times,* as early as 1914, cited two of them: "One is to do things nobody else does, which makes news that must be printed, and the other is to do familiar things in unfamiliar ways, and that also makes news of the same sort." In both of these spheres, the *Times* added, "he has a real talent—why not be generous and say a real genius." The newspaper was quite right, for again and again Ford did or said the unexpected or "dressed up" the commonplace. The five-dollar day, the dramatic price cuts, the peace ship, the statements made during the Dodge suit, the maneuvering to meet financial obligations during the postwar recession—all defied convention. So did Ford's introduction in 1926 of a five-day week for six days' pay, the announcement of a seven-dollar wage minimum after the stock market collapsed in 1929, the militant stand against the National Industrial Recovery Act in 1933 and 1934, and the acceptance of Hitler's medal. Any one of these actions, had they been taken by an industrialist other than Ford, would have been newsworthy. But with few exceptions only Ford took them, and this fact, coupled with the magic of the Ford name, led most news media to devote inordinate attention to them.[21]

Ford's unconventionality was not reserved solely for announcements and activities on the grand scale; it found expression on lesser occasions as well. At times, insisted one of Ford's long-time press favorites, William C. Richards, the industrialist deliberately leaned toward the eccentric in order to arouse comment. When Richards asked Ford why he was wearing a bandage on his ankle, the magnate replied that he had been injured playing football with children. Richards knew that Ford had not been playing football with children, but had to admit that the report of an injury on the gridiron at seventy-one was more dramatic than the truth that he had a common blister. On one of Ford's birthdays, Richards noted that the industrialist was wearing an old shoe that was not a mate of the other. Had he hurt his foot? Not at all, he said. Every birthday he put on an old shoe to remind him that he had once been poor and that there was no insurance he would not be poor again unless he watched his step. Knowing Ford, Richards surmised that the manufacturer probably had put on the wrong shoe in the dark, but with a little imagination had fabricated a story that the press could use. Similarly, Ford let word get about that he wore a red tie when he was fighting mad. Asked by Richards if this were true, he replied, "That's right. Makes me feel spunky. I put it on to match my temper." Richards, who could find no relationship between Ford's tie and his temper, concluded that the Dearbornite had concocted the myth for publicity purposes.

Found skating on the pond at the Wayside Inn in 1926, the industrialist told reporters and photographers that he had made his skates from a flivver axle. True or not, the majority of the nation's newspapers carried stories and photographs of the "flivver skates" and their owner. In 1920, putting forward his gasoline-powered streetcar, he challenged—through the press—the Michigan Central's fastest train, the Wolverine, to a race between Detroit and Chicago. He had no intention of pitting his vehicle against the Wolverine, but the challenge naturally received widespread publicity. In 1928, rather than have Thomas Edison simply turn over a shovelful of earth at ground-breaking ceremonies for his museum, the industrialist had the aged inventor climb atop a ten-foot high concrete block, and sign his name, leave his footprints, and imbed the late Luther Burbank's spade in the damp surface. The press play was much more satisfactory than if the conventional shovelful of earth had been dug.[22]

Ford delighted in generating news through the use of startling statements. It was less important, as we have seen, that a thing be true than that it be exciting. "He would advance outrageous propositions," reported a *Manchester Guardian* correspondent, "then sit back to see how you took them." If the effect was satisfactory, Ford would let his statement stand, and frequently would repeat it before a larger audience. Thus on various occasions Ford told newsmen that "this globe has been inhabited millions of times, by civilizations having airplanes, automobiles, radio, and other scientific equipment of the modern era"; that an acre of potatoes is capable of producing enough alcohol in one year to drive the machinery necessary to cultivate the field for 100 years; that all the art in the world is not worth five cents; that Gene Tunney should become a preacher; that George Washington's 200-year-old clock was one second slow; that he would conduct a nationwide advertising campaign to boost the pay of Supreme Court judges to $75,000 a year; that he had never made a mistake; that "there are only two things in the Book [the Bible] worth a damn"; and that he intended to turn all of his industrial interests over to Edsel and dedicate the remainder of his life to an economic research institution which he would endow with $100,000,000.[23]

Some of Ford's startling statements were so newsworthy that he used them again and again. In 1919 he advocated the elimination of horses, cows, and pigs. "The world would be better off without meat," he said. "It's 75 percent ashes, anyway. Milk can be manufactured chemically. Every animal used on the farm these days is a waste of time." A furore ensued, with many prominent persons, among them the naturalist John Burroughs, claiming that horses, cows, and pigs *were* needed. In 1921 Ford announced that "the cow is the crudest machine in the world" and that scientific food should take the place of milk. He added that the horse was nothing but a "twelve hundred-pound 'hay motor' of one horse power." Dr. E. V. McCollum, of Johns Hopkins Hospital, one of the leading authorities on food values in the United States, retorted that "Henry Ford knows about as much about food as he knew about history when they had him on the witness stand." On the other hand, Dr. Earl B. Carr, of Melrose, Massachusetts, reported that he had developed a synthetic milk made of oats, peanuts, water, and salt.[24]

In 1925 Ford attacked the cow anew, and again doctors, scientists, and authorities on animal husbandry debated the industrialist's views in the press. Following the usual pattern, the news stories left in their wake scores of serious editorials and humorous feature articles and cartoons. In the latter, Model T's were shown cavorting in pastures or being "milked," and cows, looking over the fence at Model T's equipped with horns, a tail, and an udder, were represented as saying, "That's a lot of bull." In 1927 Ford announced that chickens, as well as cows and pigs, must disappear from the barnyard. Foreshadowing the current health food fad, he added that he soon would produce a cracker made of oatmeal, wheat germ, four pecans, olive oil, water, and baking powder which would suffice in their stead. In 1939 Ford incurred the wrath of the organized butchers of America by declaring that mutton should be replaced by foods made from the soybean. In March 1944, the industrialist for the last time sounded the death knell for the cow. His prediction that "in another five years there shouldn't be any use for cows" (the soybean would replace them) was heralded throughout the country. Although Ford's prediction was not borne out by events, the search for cowless milk has continued. A group of vegetarian-sponsored English scientists announced in 1962 that by mixing nettles, grass, leaves, and cast-off cabbage stems they had managed to come up with a nutritious liquid that retained only a trifling of greenish color. "But before this milk by the kindness of humus is ready for the waiting world," observed *Life,* "one more obstacle awaits: it still doesn't taste like milk."[25]

In 1919 Ford horrified the banking community and many thrifty Americans by saying that saving was an overpraised virtue. "Frankly, I do not believe in bank accounts for boys," he said. "It's all very nice to save up for a rainy day when you grow old, but boys should invest in a mechanism if they have a mechanical bent and invest in good books if they like to read." The advice created sufficient publicity for Ford to instruct his advertising men four years later to change the company's advertising slogan, "Buy a Ford—SAVE the Difference," to "Buy a Ford—SPEND the Difference." There was, however, little editorial comment on the switch. Trying again, Ford in 1928 told an Associated Press reporter that "No successful boy ever saved any money. They spent as fast as they could to improve themselves." An intense pro and con discussion of Ford's theory raged in the press. James H. West, head of the Boy Scouts, warned that Ford was "spreading pernicious doctrine," and John D. Rockefeller and John N. Willys said that no young man could succeed unless he was thrifty and saved. The *Detroit Free Press* and the *Chicago Evening Post* advised boys not to take Ford's statement seriously, while the *New York Herald Tribune, Providence Journal, New York Evening Post,* and *Asheville Citizen* argued that the industrialist's plan had some merit. "What," asked the *Jersey City Journal,* "is a poor boy to do now?"[26]

Another of Ford's publicity stand-bys was the "busted billionaire" act, whose script appeared to be written especially for reporters. In 1929 the industrialist had to borrow two cents in order to buy a commemorative Edison stamp at a Jubilee of Light celebration in Atlantic City. A few weeks later he engineered another national wire story by sending the lender a two-cent check. In 1933 the *New York Times* informed its readers that "at the moment [Ford] has in his pocket just a $1.00 bill, and it is all he has carried for months." The bill, the *Times* added, had been presented to Ford by an appreciative youth to whom Ford had given a job. In 1934, at Gettysburg, Ford found himself without funds after he had accepted a twenty-five cent pamphlet from a vendor. His statement, "I haven't any money," made the nation smile. In 1939, H. T. Webster, who was inspired by another of Ford's financially embarrassing moments, drew one of his famous "The Thrill That Comes Once in a Lifetime" cartoons, showing the manufacturer standing next to a phone booth and asking a youngster, "Could you lend me a nickel?"[27]

Responding with a fine ear to the publicity implications, Ford avoided interviews and issued only the barest information at times when the press was speculating widely and the public was burning with curiosity about his next move. The Model A and V-8 introductory campaigns were excellent examples of this technique. Similarly, as newspapers and magazines carried thousands of columns of conjecture about Ford's chances for a presidential nomination in 1924, the industrialist maintained a virtually complete silence on political matters for two years, then endorsed Coolidge in December 1923. "He was willing to go along with it [the presidential boom] as a business proposition, thinking it a good advertising influence," recalled one of Ford's secretaries, "but he became scared [that] it would get out of hand and might amount to something." A number of publications suspected Ford's motive in permitting his "campaign" to gather a limited head of steam. "Every little movement," observed a Detroit magazine, "is supposed to have a meaning all its own." Another publication commented, "Whether Mr. Ford ever wins the presidency or not, this world-wide comment on his political possibilities isn't hurting the sale of Ford products in the least."[28]

Ford also had little to say for many months during his impasse with the National Recovery Administration (NRA). In mid-July 1933, as auto manufacturers were working on a proposed code for the industry, Ford spoke with tolerance of the NRA and offered warm praise to its administrator, General Hugh S. Johnson. But he refused to sign the code. Reports as to what Ford would or would not do were rampant, and Johnson repeatedly fanned the flames with statements on what the government intended to do and what the people might do to "crack down" on the recalcitrant manufacturer. Ford, on the other hand, did not issue a statement regarding the NRA from August until late October, and did not permit himself to be interviewed on the subject from July until January 1934. The industrialist's strategy, if it was designed to generate speculation, could scarcely have been more effective. As the *Louisville Times* pointed out in August 1933:

> Not since the international public waited two years to see what the Model T's successor would be, has Henry Ford had the public as much interested in his next step as it is today.
> The question now is whether he will sign the code of the automobile industry or go it alone, and "go it one better."
> While everyone guesses, Mr. Ford—lets everyone guess.

Even after it became quite clear that the industrialist had no intention of signing the code (the deadline was September 5), speculation continued, especially during the fall of 1933, as to what Ford proposed to do. As it turned out, he did very little except to spar occasionally with Johnson and to fight a rearguard action (waged mostly by Ford dealers) against the administration's boycott of the company's products.[29]

One of Henry Ford's chief press relations attributes was his winning way with newsmen. William J. Cameron's statement, "No newspaperman who has met Mr. Ford has ever gone away and 'knocked' him," was true with few exceptions. Access to Ford was difficult, but once a reporter was closeted with the manufacturer he was met with such "old-shoe" friendliness and openness that he almost invariably found himself more in sympathy with the interviewee and many of his ideas than he had been before the meeting had taken place.[30]

Ford also shone at press conferences (the big, formal meeting announcing the peace ship was an exception). "There were times when the press didn't pull punches," recalled Fred L. Black. "They'd ask him the *damnedest* questions . . . but he was very adept at side-stepping." Newsmen were appreciative of Ford's deftness. After a session with forty reporters and cameramen upon Ford's return from Europe in 1930, one wire association correspondent reported, "He had all the aces. He had won all the honors against the quiz experts of the quayside." Ford also was unlikely to "think out loud" at press conferences, realizing that whimsical and potentially embarrassing remarks would be difficult to deny once made before a large audience.

In the presence of one or two reporters, Ford said almost anything that came to his mind. Occasionally, after an interview was concluded, he had second thoughts about an indiscreet remark and asked an aide to request the interviewer to ignore it. Much more frequently, however, the elimination of the foolish or tactless statement was handled by William J. Cameron. From the early 1920s until the early 1940s, Cameron was Ford's chief press interpreter. He arranged most of the manufacturer's interviews, sat in (and helped to steer) most of them, and edited the resultant drafts and manuscripts.[31]

Cameron was more than a censor, for without his assistance, interviewers often found it difficult, if not impossible, to understand the meaning of much of what Ford said. The manufacturer often spoke in epigrammatic "telegrams" and parables which were quite incomprehensible without an intimate knowledge of his mind. A Toronto reporter who interviewed Ford in Cameron's absence, wrote the industrialist after his return home, "I am still groping around in a haze in most of the things we talked about and I should like very much to talk to you again, for my own education if for nothing else." A writer for the *New Republic* felt similarly frustrated: "Henry Ford's mind is an oyster; I failed utterly to open it."

Cameron, however, having spent a great deal of time in conversation with Ford, acquired the ability virtually to read the manufacturer's mind. Often he broke into Ford's conversation with, "What Mr. Ford means is—" and then proceeded to expound on Ford's views. The manufacturer, as he listened to the flawless presentation of his ideas, would nod pleasantly. Never, so far as his associates knew, did Ford repudiate his aide's comments.

In Cameron's absence, Fred L. Black or one of Ford's secretaries sometimes sat in on Ford's interviews. Black had an excellent understanding of Ford's mind, and was able to interpret his views much as Cameron did. The secretaries, however, were frightened by the responsibility of "censoring" Ford's conversation. "I would sit there sometimes, holding my seat in holy horror," said Harold M. Cordell, who recalled that on several occasions he had fled down a hallway to get Cameron or Black to join a meeting.[32]

Occasionally Ford seemed to tire of the censorship and would, when on a holiday at the Wayside Inn, near Boston, or at his Georgia plantation, call in the reporters. "Well, I haven't anybody to censor me," he would say with a pixy-like smile, "I can talk freely." The industrialist was as good as his word. In 1928, in one interview, he told Boston reporters that the army and navy should enforce Prohibition; that fruit, starch, and proteins should be eaten separately; that "somewhere there is a Master Mind which sends brain waves or messages to us—the Brain of Mankind, the Brain of the Earth"; that sex did not make the world go around; that the coming generation was too intelligent for another world war; that both Al Smith and Herbert Hoover were good for business. Ford found time in the same interview to discuss airplanes, rubber plants, farming, and the New Bedford textile industry's troubles.[33]

Ford expounded at similar length at the Wayside Inn on a number of other occasions, and it was there in 1939 that he praised Germany and criticized England when discussing the possible outbreak of war. The manufacturer's Georgia press conferences, held once every year or two between 1937 and 1944, also were eventful. In 1941 he told reporters that the United States should give England and Germany "the tools to keep on fighting until they both collapse." In 1944 the Georgia plantation was the originating point of Ford's final attack on the much-maligned cow. This interview marked one of the last occasions on which the magnate issued the kind of statement designed to excite or stun his fellowmen. After 1944, suffering from mental difficulties and subject to family censorship, the most interviewed private citizen of his time spoke to the press only through the Ford News Bureau.[34]

4

If a good deal of Henry Ford's publicity was drummed up by the Ford Company, and an even greater amount was engineered by the industrialist himself, the bulk of it was nonetheless a windfall. The largest number of stories in the Ford clipbooks are reports of the auto magnate's day-to-day activities. These of course included his multifarious business interests. However, he commonly expended fully as much time and energy on extracurricular activities (ranging from camping trips with Thomas Edison, John Burroughs, and Harvey Firestone to a variety of antiquarian interests and dietary experiments), which recieved an astonishing amount of attention.

The camping trips, which were initiated in 1918 to enable Ford and his "vagabond" friends to find quietude in the semi-wilderness, were chaperoned by newsmen and photographers who reported each camper's every move and hung on his every utterance. Almost all of the theaters in the country showed Ford, Edison, and Burroughs engaging in high-kicking, stair-jumping, sprinting, tree-chopping, and tree-climbing contests. Headlines blazoned, "Millions of Dollars Worth of Brains Off on a Vacation," "Genius to Sleep under Stars," "Kings of Industry and Inventor Paid City Visit," and "Henry Ford Demonstrates He's Not Afraid of Work; Repairs His Damaged Car"; and columns were filled with stories and trivia about the famous quartet. The *Chicago Tribune*, still smarting from the Ford-*Tribune* trial, was perhaps the only paper in the country to take issue with the United Press's news judgment in sending the following comments over the wire in 1921:

"Do you think Mr. Harding can put this disarmament program over?" Ford is said to have asked Edison.

"I think it will depend upon money. If Harding can keep them from getting the money he'll succeed with his program."

"The common people around the world will back him on that," interposed Mr. Ford—the man who envisaged the peace ship.

Mr. Firestone contributed his fear that Mr. Harding is going to meet subtle opposition, at which Mr. Edison said slowly, "The motives of men are unfathomable," and Mr. Ford brought the curtain down on this memorable occasion with, "Humph, you said it."[35]

The last camping expedition took place in 1924. "The trips were good fun," Ford wrote in *My Life and Work,* "except that they began to attract too much attention." Ford's statement, however, belied his interest in the publicity received by the group. In 1918, for example, he requested that a typewritten report, containing verbatim news stories from all papers in the six states through which the party traveled, be prepared for his perusal. Similarly, it is difficult to believe that many of the contests and hi-jinks in which the aging vagabonds participated were not staged for the benefit of the nearby reporters and photographers (Edison, incidentally, was also a top-notch publicist). As Charles E. Sorensen wrote in *My Forty Years with Ford:* "With squads of newswriters and platoons of cameramen to report and film the posed nature studies of the four eminent campers, these well-equipped excursions . . . were as private and secluded as a Hollywood opening, and Ford appreciated the publicity."[36]

The camping trips were publicized only a few weeks each year. Ford's antiquarian interests, on the other hand, created news stories the year around; and throughout the 1920s, as the *Chicago Journal* pointed out, "it was a queer day" when the manufacturer's antique collection or his concern for McGuffey's Readers, ancient inns, old-fashioned dancing, and old-time fiddlers was not mentioned in the daily press.

Ford first expressed an interest in building a historical museum on his way home from the *Tribune* trial in 1919. Reiterating his "history [in books] is bunk" philosophy to E. G. Liebold, the industrialist added, "You know, I'm going to prove that.... I'm going to start a museum. We are going to show just what actually happened in years gone by." The industrialist subsequently began to collect antiques and farm implements on his camping trips, and a few years later instructed his staff to start a systematic collection of "nearly all of the articles that have been used in this country since its settling." The press, showing its customary interest in anything concerning Ford, reported almost every acquisition and also commented on dozens of rumored purchases. The stories usually were brief, except when Ford made a major acquisition, such as "King Henry VIII's love nest" or Longfellow's famous smithy, or unsuccessfully tried to buy Frederick the Great's flute or an historic London church, or was rumored to be shopping for the Chinese imperial treasures. Nonetheless, the total amount of publicity obtained from the purchases and near-purchases was impressive.[37]

In 1927 Ford announced his intention to build an "industrial museum" in Dearborn for his collection. The following year he revealed plans to supplement the museum with an early "American village," where he would exhibit buildings representing several stages of American life or associated with important events and persons.

The museum and village, although not ready for exhibition, were dedicated by President Hoover on October 21, 1929, at a celebration of the fiftieth anniversary of the discovery of the electric light. Hundreds of notables attended the ceremonies, including Madame Curie, Orville Wright, Charles M. Schwab, Gerard Swope, Otto H. Kahn, Owen D. Young, Henry Morgenthau, Secretary of War James W. Good, Will Rogers, Will Hays, Julius Rosenwald, James W. Gerard, and Jane Addams.

The high point of the occasion was Thomas Edison's re-enactment of his invention of the incandescent lamp. The inventor's laboratories, machine shop, and library had been moved from Menlo Park, New Jersey, for preservation in Greenfield Village (as the area was called), and thus lent authenticity to the scene. As the guests sat in darkness in Independence Hall (as the museum was called at the time), Edison re-enacted his invention in the presence of his wife, President and Mrs. Hoover, Henry and Clara Ford, and one of his surviving assistants. At the moment the experiment was completed, the lights in the museum and in the homes of the millions of persons who were observing the anniversary were switched on. Later, at the banquet, Edison spoke briefly over an international radio network.[38]

The event naturally received worldwide publicity. The press was handled by Cameron and Edward L. Bernays, a publicist who had been retained by General Electric to dramatize "Light's Golden Jubilee" during 1929. In later years many writers, in discussing the jubilee (which has become a "public relations classic"), have greatly magnified Bernays's role in the Dearborn celebration (the jubilee's

climax). Stanley Walker, citing Bernays's showmanship, makes the following astonishing observation in his book, *City Editor:*

> There was, for example, Light's Golden Jubilee. The story of Edison's
> invention was retold. To Dearborn went Edison, Henry Ford, and even the
> President of the United States, as well as a great crowd of other important
> figures. It was not Mr. Ford's show, or Edison's, or even the President's. It was
> simply a publicity stunt pulled off by Bernays, representing powerful and rich
> interests, to exploit the uses of electric light. Newspaper editors who might
> have understood this may have felt sad, but what could they do about it—with
> the President making a speech and all those important persons there?

Other authors have claimed that Bernays arranged for Ford to reconstruct
Edison's birthplace and laboratory, for the President to preside at the dedication, and
for Edison to re-enact his invention. Actually, Bernays only helped to handle the
press, and, in fact, he would have had nothing to do with the Dearborn celebration had
not Ford, who had obtained Edison's promise to attend the dedication of the village on
October 21, permitted General Electric to tie in the jubilee with the Ford ceremony. It
was Ford's show, and it was he who issued the invitations to the prominent guests. As
for the reconstruction of the Edison buildings, that project was begun before anyone
in Dearborn had ever heard of Bernays. The publicist, as a matter of fact, incurred
Ford's wrath after the dedicatory party arrived in Dearborn because he tried repeatedly to inject himself into a group picture with Hoover, Edison, and the host. Ford
took Fred Black aside and told him to "get Bernays the hell out of here or I'll have
Harry Bennett's men throw him over the fence." Black told Bernays of Ford's threat,
and the publicist moved out of camera range.[39]

Several years before Ford announced his intention to build a museum and
village in Dearborn, he undertook two other historical projects: the restoration of the
Wayside Inn at South Sudbury, Massachusetts, and the Botsford Tavern, sixteen
miles northwest of Detroit. The refurbishing of the Botsford Inn, where Henry and
Clara Ford had danced in the 1880s, brought Ford little publicity outside Detroit; but
the New England hostelry, built in 1702 and said to be the oldest inn in the United
States, was well known as the tavern celebrated by Longfellow in his *Tales of a
Wayside Inn*. Ford bought the property in 1923 and originally planned to make it the
center of a "Pilgrim Village." Abandoning this plan, he remodeled and refurnished
the building and re-established on former sites a gristmill, a sawmill, and a blacksmith
shop similar to those that had operated in colonial days. He also built at his own
expense ($280,000) a well publicized mile of highway to reroute traffic on the Boston
Post Road away from the inn.[40]

Perhaps the most publicized of Ford's ventures at the Wayside Inn, however,
was his purchase of the nearby little red schoolhouse allegedly attended by Mary of
"Mary Had a Little Lamb" fame. On the day the school was reopened, Ford occupied
a seat in the first row, holding a lamb on a tether. When the manufacturer left at
recess, the lamb, as almost every newspaper in the country reported pictorially,
followed him. A spirited controversy later broke out as to the authorship of the poem
which celebrated Mary and the lamb, and as to whether or not Mary was imaginary

and her pet "a paper lamb." Ford was untroubled, and probably laughed as much as anyone when he read the following poem, written by a granddaughter of Mrs. Sarah Hale, alleged authoress of "Mary Had a Little Lamb," and published in the *New York Times:*

> Sweet Mary long has passed away,
> The poet, too, is dead.
> The children no more laugh and play,
> Afar they all have fled.
> At teacher's cold, unfeeling words
> The lamb no more can quivver,
> But still the gentle creature serves
> To advertise a flivver. [41]

Ford's interest in old-fashioned dancing and country fiddlers created more publicity for the industrialist during 1925 and 1926 than any of his other activities except aviation. Ford and his wife had organized old-fashioned dances even before World War I, but their interest in this type of recreation seems to have strengthened after the purchase of the Wayside Inn. Here in 1923 the Fords organized square dances as part of the regular program. Two years later the industrialist announced that he would lead a crusade to bring old-fashioned dances back into public favor. Organizing an "orchestra," consisting of a violinist, a cymbalist, and dulcimer and sousaphone players, he enrolled 300 friends and Ford executives and their wives into classes taught by his Wayside Inn dancing master, Benjamin B. Lovett. The announcement was, of course, gleefully publicized. In an article entitled, "Just a Reel at Twilight When Your Flask Is Low," the *Cincinnati Times-Star* typically reported that "it looks like it will be a big summer for grandma." [42]

To publicize his hobby, Ford invited 200 Ohio and Michigan dancing instructors to Dearborn to learn the schottische, Virginia reel, varsovienne (Ford's favorite), gavotte, ripple, minuet, and other almost forgotten steps which had been popular in Ford's youth. He also arranged for his orchestra to play old-fashioned dance music over a nationwide network of radio stations during the public showings of his new cars in January 1926, and January 1927. Hundreds of dealers set up loudspeakers in their showrooms and invited townspeople to dance to the music. In some communities 25 percent of the local populace attended the parties. In addition, the industrialist made arrangements for Lovett to teach dancing to Dearborn's schoolchildren. After the instruction had begun, 200 parents petitioned the school board to stop the dances, claiming that they were immoral. Amid nationwide clamor, a jury of 500 parents saw twenty-five student couples demonstrate the steps, and voted to have them continued. [43]

Old-fashioned dancing quickly became the rage throughout the country. Newspapers carried detailed instructions on the steps, often accompanying them with illustrations covering an entire page. Thirty-four institutions of higher learning, including Radcliffe College, Stephens College, Temple University, and the Universities of Michigan, North Carolina, and Georgia, added early American dancing to their curricula; and Ford sent Lovett on a junket to supervise the new classes. In the fall of

1926, the American National Association of Masters of Dancing, in convention in New York, announced that "the Charleston is dying, the Black Bottom can never be king, and during the past year there has been a great revival in old-time dancing." Henry Ford was credited with the renewed interest in the old steps. [44]

Another entertainment of earlier, less sophisticated days which Ford revived was old-time fiddling. The industrialist himself liked to fiddle, and in the private laboratory adjacent to his home often would play on a Stradivarius violin valued at $75,000 "Turkey in the Straw" and other favorite tunes. To his chagrin, however, he never learned to play well, and he found it quite impossible to dance a jig as he performed. Thus he was delighted when he discovered eighty-year-old Jep Bisbee, who combined both of these talents, at a dance in Traverse City, Michigan, in 1923.

Ford gave Bisbee a sedan and a miniature gold violin set with diamonds, and sent him to East Orange, New Jersey, in his private railroad car so that Edison could film his performance for posterity. For two years, Bisbee, who raised his fee from $3.00 to $35.00 a night on the strength of Ford's endorsement, was the nation's best known country fiddler. He was crowned "King of Old-time Fiddlers" after he had outplayed fifteen other hoary backwoodsmen to win the "Henry Ford Gold Cup" at a well-publicized Detroit contest. Jep, however, was quickly relegated to the wings when Ford's next "discovery," a Norway, Maine, snowshoe-maker, fiddled onto the national stage. Mellie Dunham, in fact, probably obtained more publicity in the months of December 1925, and January 1926, than Fritz Kreisler, Jascha Heifetz, and Mischa Elman received in any ten-year period of their careers. Even Ford stood on the edge of Dunham's spotlight, and for once he was content to do so. [45]

The seventy-two-year-old Dunham, who had the bewhiskered appearance of a Santa Claus, came to Ford's attention when he won a statewide fiddling contest in Lewiston, Maine, in the fall of 1925. The manufacturer immediately invited Dunham to play at one of his Dearborn dancing parties. Dunham, busily making snowshoes, ignored the letter for several days, thinking it was another order for his handiwork. After opening the missive, he replied that he could not get away for a while because he had to split kindling and patch the barn roof in addition to his regular work. The *Norway* (Maine) *Advertiser* learned of the invitation, published the exchange of letters, and the following day "every press association, every newspaper in the country thereupon shouted the news that Ford had a new favorite." The governor of Maine dispatched a press agent to Norway, and Mellie was prevailed upon to accept Ford's invitation. [46]

Dunham left Norway amid the biggest celebration in the town's history. Stores and schools were closed and the citizenry paraded behind Mellie, a brass band, and a police escort to the railroad station, where Governor Ralph O. Brewster and his staff conducted farewell festivities. Dunham was brimming with quotable quotes, many of them probably supplied by the press agent who accompanied him to Dearborn: "I only went west once before, to Berlin, New Hampshire"; "We're carrying coffee along because we don't know whether the coffee in Detroit will be good"; "I always thought I could make as good snowshoes as anyone else. But I never thought I would take my place in Maine's musical world with such noted artists as Nordica and Emma Eames." During the train journey through Maine, New

Hampshire, Quebec, and Ontario, the fiddler was hailed at every whistle-stop, and the press contingent accompanying him kept the news wires humming—with Ford's name prominently mentioned in each story.[47]

On December 11, 1925, Dunham played "Pop Goes the Weasel," "Weevily Wheat," "Speed the Plough," "Fisher's Hornpipe," "Old Zip Coon," and other melodies at Ford's dancing party. The event, attended by a large number of Detroit, New York, Boston, and wire service reporters and photographers, probably was the best publicized dance in the nation's history. On the following day, Dunham, using Ford's Stradivarius, gave "the most extraordinary recital in the history of music in America." The fiddler then entrained for New York, where, after remarking, "I came to make some money and I make no bones about it, since me and Ma have had honor enough," he signed a $500-a-week contract with the Keith-Albee vaudeville circuit. Dunham fiddled throughout the United States and Canada for seventeen months, at times receiving as much as $1,500 a week for his services.[48]

In the meantime, dozens of fiddlers throughout the country, including John J. Wilder, President Coolidge's eighty-year-old uncle, came forward to claim they "didn't figure Mellie Dunham was so much of a fiddler," and to challenge him (and Kreisler, Heifetz, Elman, Bisbee, et al.) to a playdown. Many of the challengers, including Coolidge's uncle, went into vaudeville, as the nation was swept by a fiddling craze. Contests were held in hundreds of communities throughout the country, and Ford offered a loving cup to many of the winners. Sheet music and song books featuring old-time tunes became best sellers in music shops, and stores handling violins and old-fashioned guitars reported a boom in sales. Horseshoe pitching, woodchopping, marble shooting, and other contests which smacked of the "good old days" sprang up on every side. As he contemplated what he and his fiddlers had wrought, Ford had every reason to be pleased. After the spring of 1926, however, the fiddling and the old-fashioned dancing crazes lost their popularity. Ford himself was not deterred, and continued to hold old-fashioned parties in Dearborn until the early 1940s.[49]

Although the public responded enthusiastically to Ford's ideas on music and dancing, it steadfastly declined to accept his views on dieting, health, longevity, and reincarnation. Nonetheless, the industrialist's ideas on these subjects made news for more than a quarter-century. Many of Ford's statements undoubtedly were sincere; for he was convinced that he knew how people could live so as to improve and conserve their health, and he fervently believed in reincarnation. However, the magnate's flair for publicity probably prompted him to express certain of his "views" solely for newspaper consumption.

Ford had two general recipes for health: first, the avoidance of "poisons" such as cigarettes, chewing tobacco, liquor, rich foods, and overeating in general; and second, the use of wholesome and particularly of nutritive foods. Smoking was not sanctioned in Ford's plants until after his retirement. As for alcohol, the motor magnate announced in 1929 that "if booze ever comes back to the United States, I am through with manufacturing." The statement was vigorously debated throughout the country, with most of the nation's press criticizing Ford's attitude. The *Asbury Park*

(New Jersey) *Press* simply remarked, "The Detroit oracle accomplished his purpose. The story made the front page."

For years Ford claimed that Dearborn was dry and that no one who worked for him touched a drop: "We watch them as they come in. We smell their breaths." Actually, Dearborn was wide open, and in 1930 a *New York World* reporter counted fourteen speakeasies in one block within sight of the Ford gates. As for smelling the employees' breath, the *World* pointed out that 100,000 men passed through the gates daily. The story was reprinted all over the country. When Prohibition was repealed in 1933, many newspapers recalled Ford's earlier statements about closing his factories. Ford replied that Americans had profited by Prohibition, and that the government would find ways to deal with the liquor problem. Simultaneously, businessman Ford served beer to newsmen who attended a luncheon at his new-car press preview.[50]

The industrialist's well publicized dietary fancies varied almost from year to year. In 1920 he ate only stale bread; in 1922 he claimed that "chicken is fit only for hawks"; in 1925 he said that starches and sweets were irreconcilable in the human system; in 1926 he regarded carrots as a cure-all, and ate a well publicized dinner consisting of fourteen carrot dishes; the same year he declared he was off fried salt pork and boiled potatoes; in 1929 he decided that people should not eat anything until 1:00 P.M.; during the 1930s he advocated soybeans as a panacea, ate meals consisting of only soybean derivatives, and developed a vile-tasting soybean biscuit which he pressed upon his friends; during the 1940s, wheat became the "divine food," containing everything a man needed to remain healthy and live long.

When, as sometimes happened, Ford's theories were demolished by experiments, he would forget them and move on to new ones. At one point the industrialist contended that tiny sugar crystals acted like knives on human tissue. To prove his theory he put sugar crystals under a magnifying glass that he carried with him. "Yes, Mr. Ford, but look at this," said an employee as he put a drop of water on the crystals. They dissolved at once, to Ford's annoyance. The manufacturer was cured of his wheat diet by an experiment on hogs. One litter was fed nothing but wheat grains for a week; another ordinary garbage. A few weeks later the "wheat" hogs were almost dead; the "garbage" ones were in normal health. Wheat was no longer the "divine food."[51]

Ford frequently predicted that he would live to be 100 years old, and said that anyone would "live to 125 or 150 if he would keep the carbon out of his system." His prescription for longevity included exercise, and his photograph appeared frequently in the newspapers as he jogged along on foot or pedalled a bicycle. Ford challenged scores of people, particularly reporters, to footraces, and only the most fleet-footed could stay with him over 100 yards. The manufacturer was still racing when he was eighty years old. In 1943, after forty-six-year-old Drew Pearson questioned whether the government might not have to take over the Ford Company because of Ford's failing health, the manufacturer, who only a few days before had bested several colleagues in a seventy-five yard dash, defended his physical condition and vowed, "I can lick him in any contest he suggests."[52]

Pearson, admitting that "the last time I saw Henry Ford I confess that he looked like a formidable adversary," accepted the challenge—"with any vehicle, foot, bicycle, or Model T Ford." The proposed contest quickly captured the public's imagination. Many newspapers and magazines ran photographs of Ford and Pearson "training" on bicycles. Sentiment was overwhelmingly in Ford's favor. The *Detroit Free Press* suggested that if Pearson remained unsatisfied after Ford had beaten him in a footrace, bicycle, or jumping contest, the industrialist would administer full satisfaction with "a good sound old-fashioned thrashing." Dr. Roy McClure, Ford's physician, voiced strong support for the motor magnate: "He can outwalk, outrun and outjump a fellow like Pearson any day in the week. . . . I doubt if Pearson could match him in any complete physical examination, to say nothing of the head." Many cities offered to stage the contest to kick off bond drives and Red Cross or United Service Organization campaigns. Finally, Pearson, in a move for peace, backed down: "Henry Ford has certainly convinced me, and, I am sure, the Government, that despite his 80 years no one needs to worry about the energetic way he is running his war plants. My hat's off to him for his spunk."[53]

Ford frequently stated his belief in reincarnation to the press. He claimed that he had accepted the theory as a young man, after reading a book entitled, *A Short View of Great Questions,* by Orlando J. Smith. As proof of the validity of his thesis, Ford would cite a chicken's behavior: "When the automobile was new and one of them came down the road, a chicken would run straight for home—and usually be killed. But today when a car comes along, a chicken will run for the nearest side of the road. That chicken has been hit in the ass in a previous life." This view and Ford's insistence that the body had a "queen cell" which could never be destroyed naturally astounded many listeners. On the other hand, Ford often was quoted in the press regarding his religious activities and his belief in God and in Jesus Christ.[54]

5

Henry Ford had no personal connection whatever with a great body of the publicity which he received during the 1920s. Rumors could be expected to abound during certain periods in Ford's life, as, for example, when he purportedly was seeking waterpower sites for his "new" company or during the Model A's gestation. The fact was, however, that Ford was so much on the public's mind that many newspapers and people seemed to identify the industrialist with the latest news development. Of course, once someone had started a rumor about Ford, nobody dared to spike it, for no matter how ridiculous the story might have appeared, it could possibly have been based on fact. Who could readily say, for example, that Ford had not offered Charles Lindbergh the general managership of his airplane factory, or Bulgaria a $5,000,000 loan in return for an auto plant concession; that he would not build 155 miles of highway in Egypt in return for duty-free admission of his cars; that he would not buy Jacob Ruppert's home on the Hudson; that Metro-Goldwyn-Mayer would not produce his film biography; that he would not sell cars for $100 on the day that Virginia went dry; that he was not taking instructions from a Catholic prelate; and that he would not give a free car to any woman bearing eleven or more children? After all, Ford had introduced a five-dollar minimum wage, rebated $50.00 to his customers, chartered a peace ship, "turned over" to the government all of his war profits, converted a derelict railroad into a profitable enterprise, and promised to build 50,000 airplanes in a year and to devise a food which would eliminate cows, pigs, sheep, and chickens![55]

Another important bloc of Ford news stories concerned the industrialist's wealth. In a civilization in which the checkbook is reputedly mightier than either pen or sword, the crude fact that Henry Ford was considered by many to be the world's richest individual made him, as well, one of the globe's most fascinating figures. Widespread discussion of Ford's wealth thus coincided with the discovery in January 1914, that his company was so affluent that it could afford to "give away" $10,000,000:

> In days agone, [wrote Elbert Hubbard in 1914] when conversation lagged and languished, some one always turned to the topic of Arthur Brisbane's salary.
>
> Nowadays the theme is Henry Ford. You hear it in barber shops, bar rooms, smoking rooms, ad clubs, Sunday schools, sewing circles.
>
> But while it is a fact that you can lie about Arthur Brisbane's salary, yet you cannot qualify for the Ananias club by talking about Henry Ford's income. . . . Brisbane draws a salary of $100,000 a year.
>
> Henry Ford's income is about 'steen million dollars a year. This is more than Eva Tanguay gets. It is more than I made in vaudeville. Also, it is more than any vaudeville artist ever said he was offered.[56]

During the 'teens and 1920s scores of journalists, especially financial writers such as B. C. Forbes and Roger W. Babson, took it upon themselves to rank the ten, or twenty, or fifty wealthiest men in the country, in the world, or in the history of the world. Almost everyone conceded Ford the No. 1 spot as far as current income was concerned. There were, however, varying opinions as to whether Ford, John D. Rockefeller, or an occasional outsider such as Andrew W. Mellon, Sir Basil Zaharoff, the Nizam of Hyderabad, or the Aga Khan, had the greatest fortune. The usual pattern was for one authority to publish a list and then for it to be attacked by other authorities who presented their own lists. On other occasions writers occupied themselves with lists of what Ford could do with all of his money: acquire the wheat, oats, potato, and tobacco crops of the United States for 1925; pay for Canada's imports in 1926; buy control of General Motors, United States Steel, and of the New York Central combined; purchase Guatemala, Honduras, and Haiti put together; buy up Great Britain's seventeen wealthiest men, and so on.[57]

Many of the articles spoke in very complimentary terms about how Ford acquired his wealth, and congratulated him on making "so much money in so short a time and in so clean a manner . . . in a free, open, unprotected, and competitive field." Far from resenting Ford's wealth, writers and the public felt that it was but "the reward of a poor man with vision and determination, who pays good wages, who lowers his price instead of cheapening his product, who fought and defeated Wall Street . . . and who is the only man in the history of the U.S. who had defied the big corporations and made them like it." In contrast, the Rockefellers, the Du Ponts, Zaharoff, and others frequently were castigated for "extorting their wealth through monopoly, from the wrecks of smaller businesses, and along paths of war."[58]

Just as Ford had no direct connection with the many stories about his wealth, so he had nothing to do with the large number of articles based on "greatest man" polls and selections in which he figured prominently for many years. The first such survey which mentioned the manufacturer was taken in March 1914, when the editor of the *Detroit News* asked the twenty-four members of his editorial staff to rank the "world's greatest living men." Thomas Edison headed the list, followed by Theodore Roosevelt and Guglielmo Marconi. Ford ranked only fifteenth.

Few polls and selections of "greatest men" were apparently taken during the 'teens, but during the 1920s a score or more such lists usually turned up in syndicated stories every year. Ford ranked high in nearly all of them. In 1922 he was named as the second greatest living American (after Woodrow Wilson) by readers of the *Denver News;* in 1923 he was cited as "the greatest business wizard of history" by Charles R. Flint; in 1924 he was ranked by President M. L. Burton of the University of Michigan with Theodore Roosevelt, Orville Wright, and Edison as one of the four greatest men of the twentieth century, and in the same year he was named the world's third greatest man (after Roosevelt and Edison) by readers of the *Detroit News*. In 1926 the industrialist placed second to Benito Mussolini in a worldwide YMCA poll to determine the greatest living men in the world. During the same year America's police chiefs voted Ford ahead of Mussolini as the greatest living man, and a business magazine's readership gave twice as many votes to Ford as to any other person in balloting on the men whom they felt had made the greatest contribution to the development of business since 1900.[59]

In 1927 Ford was ranked second to Edison as the greatest living man by twenty-five professors of the College of the City of New York, and he was named with Charles A. Lindbergh as one of the two most important news figures on earth by Northwestern University journalism students. Belleville, New Jersey, schoolboys, when asked in 1928, "Who would you like to be if you were not yourself?" placed only Lindbergh and Coolidge ahead of Ford. During the same year, a group of twelve prominent Americans, when asked by Dr. Archibald Henderson to select twelve living immortals, placed Ford fifth behind Edison, Mussolini, Albert Einstein, and George Bernard Shaw.[60]

Abroad, Ford was more highly regarded than any other American. It is almost impossible to overestimate his reputation among foreign businessmen as the apostle of mass production, and the common people in all civilized countries looked with great favor upon his labor and pricing policies, as well as upon the ubiquitous Model T. In the Soviet Union, for example, only Lenin, Trotsky, and Kalinin were better known to the masses than Ford, and only Lenin ranked higher in their estimation.[61]

6

On November 21, 1929, a little less than a month after the great stock market crash, President Hoover convoked a White House conference of business leaders to discuss solutions to the worsening economic situation and to provide a sounding board for an expression of confidence in the nation's future. The event, bringing together such men as Henry Ford, Owen D. Young, Alfred P. Sloan, Jr., Pierre du

Pont, Myron C. Taylor, Julius Rosenwald, Walter Teagle, and Secretary of the Treasury Andrew W. Mellon, naturally aroused nationwide interest, and more than fifty newsmen were gathered to report the proceedings.

The meeting broke up at 1:30 P.M., and the conferees, as they trickled through the lobby, were bombarded with questions. The magnates, having been informed that Hoover would issue a report on the conference later in the afternoon, shrugged aside the press with "no comment" and went on their way. Then Ford walked briskly down the lane of reporters, fumbled in an inside coat pocket, withdrew four copies of a lengthy typewritten statement, and, without pausing, shoved them indiscriminately at the "wildly scrambling" newsmen. "Nearly everything in the country is too high priced," the announcement stated. "The only thing that should be high priced is the man who works." Ford suggested that industry could defeat the depression by increasing the general wage level, and although he did not say that he intended to raise his own employees' pay, the implication was not lost upon the reporters, who swamped Washington's telegraph offices for an hour as they rushed the statement to their publications.[62]

At 2:30 P.M. Ford returned to the White House, spent fifteen minutes with Hoover, and created "a second exhibition of reportorial turmoil" by announcing that he had told the President that he intended to raise the wages of every Ford Motor Company employee. The announcement reverberated around the world, creating "a sensation almost rivaling the five-dollar day announcement fifteen years earlier." Ford had, as one newspaper pointed out, "stolen President Hoover's industrial conference . . . body, boots and breeches," and in doing so received some of the most favorable publicity of his career.[63]

The seven-dollar-day wage minimum which the company introduced on December 1, 1929, was part of Ford's overall plan for bolstering consumer confidence. He also lowered prices $5.00 to $35.00 on the Model A in November 1929 and announced a $25,000,000 program of plant expansion in early 1930. The industrialist found few emulators (except in the price-cutting sphere), however, and his scheme failed utterly to halt the onrushing tide of depression. Ford doggedly kept his "prosperity dollar" in effect for almost two years, then quietly reduced his base pay to $6.00 a day in October 1931.[64]

The Ford Company was not greatly affected during the first year of the depression, earning a profit of $40,000,000 in 1930. This comparative immunity to "hard times" perhaps explains some of the statements which, in 1930 and 1931, bewildered and shocked those who saw all around them the full impact of depression. "We are better off today than we have been for three or four years past," the manufacturer declared in August 1930. "It was a mighty good thing for the nation that the condition which we misnamed 'prosperity' could not last." In October 1930, Ford announced that "the depression is a good thing," and in March 1931, he added that "the average man won't really do a day's work unless he is caught and cannot get out of it" and that "these are really good times, but only a few know it."[65]

Ford also offered his countrymen advice in a series of three "open letters" published as advertisements in 200 daily newspapers in mid-1932. In the first of the letters he advocated the cultivation of family gardens; in the second he described the "self-help" rehabilitation program he had launched in Inkster, Michigan, a community with many unemployed Rouge workers; and in the third he advanced his village industries ("one foot on the land and another foot on industry . . . America is safe") theory.[66]

The ads appeared out of touch with reality to many readers. Calling Ford's statements "meaningless platitudes," a Louisianian wrote to an auto magazine that "for people who live in cities to be keeping one foot in industry and the other in land would be an acrobatic stunt quite impossible. Are farmers *really* going to permit indigent city folk to camp in their fields; and if they do, how do they live until the crop matures?" Will Rogers suggested that since "most people got no room for a garden what Mr. Ford will do is put out a car with a garden in it. Then you hoe as you go."

A number of newspapers read in the letters "a confession of Ford's failure to meet the depression's problems." The fact that he, "the greatest industrialist of his age, cannot care for his own employees, but must put them to work cleaning up backyards and roads of a town and working gardens" indicated all too clearly that the manufacturer had no magic formula for the depths of unemployment. "Something has happened to Ford," declared Anne O'Hare McCormick in the *New York Times,* "and perhaps through him to the America which he represents." Mrs. McCormick's observation was perceptive, for, as the depression closed in on the Ford Company in 1931 and 1932 the industrialist's silence was notable—especially for a man who normally had hair-trigger opinions on any subject. A journalist remarked to Cameron: "He thought he had the answer to depression. Now how does he take it?" Cameron replied, "I don't know. He doesn't talk about it much. It's so terrible that I believe he doesn't dare let himself think about it."[67]

Henry Ford, on Olympus for nearly a score of years, finally had wandered off the "high plateau." The public's attitude toward him and his company would never be quite the same again.

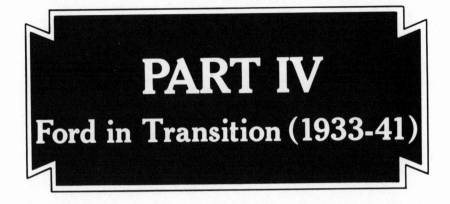

PART IV
Ford in Transition (1933-41)

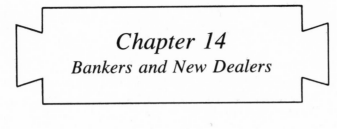

Chapter 14
Bankers and New Dealers

1

Henry Ford's career after 1932 was anticlimactic. Although the industrialist loomed large on the American scene on several occasions after that date, he had considerably less impact during the decade after 1932 than during the previous two decades. The break in the manufacturer's forward momentum can be attributed to at least two factors. One was his age; in 1933 he was seventy, albeit a very active seventy. Of more importance, however, was the depression, which not only checked the flow of Ford's profits, but also ruled out any opportunity to expand his organization. Indeed, the company's heavy losses during the early 1930s led to a severe retrenchment in 1933 which included mass layoffs of hourly and salaried personnel, discontinuance of all product advertising for almost a year, and divestiture of the Airplane Division and other properties.[1]

General Motors and Chrysler, on the other hand, although adversely affected during the 1931–33 period, were able to earn profits and to increase their share of the auto market at the expense of Ford and the "independent" companies. General Motors assumed sales leadership in 1931, a position it has never relinquished. Chrysler, after moving into second place in sales in 1933, then narrowly trailing Ford for two years, regained the runner-up position in 1936, holding this spot until 1950. Ford's relegation to the third-ranking position in the automobile industry, after having been the sales leader for twenty years, unquestionably contributed to the gradual erosion of his former prestige. A "superman," after all, has to lead the field, preferably by a wide margin.[2]

Ford's drive and his attitude—very probably affected by his age, the depression, and his loss of sales supremacy—also changed appreciably during 1932–33. After building his "last mechanical triumph," the V-8, in late 1931 and early 1932, the industrialist's interest in the company's products and in its day-to-day affairs gradually abated. His 1933 statement, "The Rouge is no fun any more," was indicative of his attitude toward his business activities in general. On the other hand his "hobbies"—the Edison Institute (Greenfield Village and the Henry Ford Museum), the "village industries," soybean and plastics experimentation, the Ford schools, and tractor development—increasingly absorbed him. These projects, although not unimportant, fell far short of the numerous bold and exciting ventures in which Ford had been engaged during the previous decade.[3]

2

Ford's hobbies and his company's formal public relations efforts were to play a part in shaping public attitudes toward him during the decade between 1932 and 1941. But of far more importance in determining the motor magnate's reputation was his reaction to the tide of events which affected him and his company in this period: his role in the Detroit banking crisis of 1933; his refusal to cooperate with the New Deal; his response to industrial unionism; his philosophy of isolationism.

Ford's role in the Detroit banking crisis, which foreshadowed the national bank moratorium of 1933, was one of the most controversial of his entire career. In later years biographers friendly to the industrialist absolved him of blame for the crisis. Other authors criticized him severely for not cooperating with the Reconstruction Finance Corporation (RFC) and officials of the stricken banks (whose reckless speculation, all students of the subject agree, was primarily responsible for the financial crisis).[4]

The Detroit banking collapse was triggered by the illiquidity in late January 1933 of the Union Guardian Trust Company, one of the larger units of the Guardian Detroit Union Group, Inc., which with another holding company, the Detroit Bankers Company, Inc., controlled more than 93 percent of the banking resources of Detroit. Edsel Ford was a director of the Guardian Detroit Union Group, Inc., and of several of its banks. The Fords, father and son, had funds deposited with both chains.[5]

Needing cash to remain in business, the Union Guardian Trust Company, which had already borrowed heavily from the RFC, Edsel Ford, and the Ford Company, turned to its parent company for additional aid. The parent organization's response was a request to the RFC for a loan of $50,000,000. After appraising the group's assets, the government agency agreed to furnish part of this amount if large depositors would guarantee the remainder. Henry and Edsel Ford and officers of General Motors and Chrysler, also large depositors, expressed willingness to cooperate. Acting on this information, President Hoover met with Michigan's two senators (one of whom was James Couzens, Ford's former business associate), the secretary of the treasury, and the head of the RFC to discuss the Guardian group's problems. Couzens, it developed, was under the impression that the purpose of the conference was to put through the requested RFC loan, which, in view of the tangled financial situation, he correctly thought would be a misuse of public funds. Actually, the conference was called to find a substitute for a loan. But acting on the misunderstanding, Couzens denounced the loan he *thought* was being proposed, emotionally declaring that he would "shout against it from the rooftops" if it were made. He also rejected a plea by the President to use his personal wealth in an effort to prop up the Union Guardian Trust Company, saying that the institution was "Ford's business."[6]

The Guardian group next turned to Ford for assistance. The manufacturer, whose son and company had supplied $9,500,000 to the group between 1930–32 and now was resentful of Couzens's attitude and sour on the RFC, refused. In fact, he withdrew his earlier commitment to cooperate with the hard-pressed bankers. Upon hearing this, General Motors and Chrysler also rescinded their earlier offer to help.

Couzens, after reappraising the now desperate situation, offered, if Ford would do the same, to put up at least $6,900,000 of his personal fortune as collateral to make possible an RFC loan to the trust company. Ford refused. It was apparent that the Union Guardian Trust Company would fail without immediate financial assistance and that its failure would bring about a collapse of Detroit's banking structure. In an effort to forestall this eventuality, Governor William A. Comstock in the early hours of February 14 declared an eight-day bank holiday, later extended. The governor also informed the press that Ford had refused to cooperate with General Motors and Chrysler in an effort to stave off the crisis. Later that day he repudiated his accusation, pointing out that he had "misunderstood the facts."[7]

At this point everybody tried to place the blame on everybody else. President Hoover blamed the bank holiday on Comstock for having "yielded to panic" and on President-elect Roosevelt for undermining "public confidence"; bankers placed the blame on "general conditions," ignoring the fact that some of their number had been motivated by "manipulation, greed, and dishonesty"; and other observers pointed to the RFC, the Senate Finance Committee's inquiry into Wall Street, the Communists, Father Charles E. Coughlin (because of speeches he had made attacking Detroit bankers), and the *Detroit Times* (because it had devoted a good deal of space to Coughlin's speeches). Of all the scapegoats, however, Couzens received the most criticism. It was said that the Detroit banks could have been saved by an RFC loan had not the senator blocked the aid, and that Couzens had balked because he hated Henry Ford and all other rich Detroiters. Harry Barnard, Couzens's biographer, later refuted this thesis and asserted that "if any one person forced the bank holiday this person was, not Couzens, but Henry Ford." Barnard's findings, however, came much too late to prevent Couzens's public reputation from sinking to an all-time low in 1933.[8]

In contrast to Couzens, Ford, at one stage of the crisis, received some of the most adulatory comment of his career. On February 26, the industrialist and his son dramatically offered to provide the private capital required—estimated at $11,000,000—to create two new banks to take over the liquid assets of the Guardian National Bank of Commerce (an affiliate of the Guardian group) and the First National Bank of Detroit (a mainstay of the Detroit Bankers group). Reserving the right to select the management of the new institutions, Ford announced that there was to be an immediate payoff of 30 percent to depositors of the "old" banks; that the institutions would be "for the people"; that loans would be made for "productive and not speculative purposes"; and that interest would be reduced or eliminated. When it was suggested that Wall Streeters might put money into the Ford pot, he flared: "I'll not put a nickel in it if they're in—not a nickel!"[9]

Ford's announcement excited the country. Newspapers declared in eight-column banner headlines, "Ford Springs to Defend His Native Soil," "Wins New Battle with Wall Street," and "Ford to the Rescue!" The press pictured Ford as "throwing his fortune into the breech. . . [as he] stepped forward to the aid of his home city," and as having "at a single stroke cut the Gordian knot of Detroit's confused and paralyzed banking situation." The *Christian Science Monitor* concluded that Ford was working out a bank code based on the Ten Commandments. Frank Vanderlip, ex-president of the National City Bank of New York, told the New

York Economic Forum that "we are going to learn a banking lesson from that great industrialist, Mr. Ford. To judge from his principles ... his advent into banking might offer him an opportunity to make a greater contribution to society than his Model T." The announcement also set off a new round of Ford jokes. "Every time Detroit outgrows Henry Ford," quipped Will Rogers, "he has to go in and save 'em again. He is going to have a bank where you can leave your money, and come back and find it before the banker does." Ford's money, so the jokes went, would zip about on endless conveyors tended by his banks' vice-presidents; his coins would pass through polishing machines and come out gleaming with Ford neatness.[10]

Detroiters believed that the Ford offer heralded the end of the banking crisis. Many people publicly commended the elder Ford. Alvan Macauley, president of Packard Motor Car Company, asserted that "of all the splendid things Ford has done for Detroit, [this] is probably the biggest ... the citizens of Detroit owe him a great debt of gratitude"; Judge Harry J. Dingeman, presiding circuit judge of Michigan, looked upon Ford as "the savior of the city"; and Howard J. Harvey, president of the Detroit Business Pioneers, regarded Ford's "magnificent contribution to the security of all Detroit ... as an historic thrill." Four thousand Dearbornites expressed their gratitude to and faith in Ford by marching through their city's streets waving "BANK WITH HANK" banners. The attitude of most Detroiters was summed up by Malcolm Bingay of the *Detroit Free Press:*

> Every dime will be shiny
> And every penny bright;
> For Uncle Henry's a banker
> And things will be all right.

Even the bankers who were to be displaced under the new scheme at first greeted the Ford plan with satisfaction, issuing a joint statement that it was "generous and public-spirited."[11]

On second thought, among the directly concerned, only the depositors were happy with the Ford solution. The bankers did not look forward to being squeezed out of the banking business, and they gagged at Ford's financial ideas. Other automobile companies were not pleased with the prospect of Ford's domination of the Detroit banking scene. Couzens and the RFC began to doubt whether a RFC loan upon which the Ford plan hinged should be made to the new banks. The upshot was that the bankers informed Ford on February 28 that his plan was unacceptable. In reporting the decision, the press, apparently baffled, made no editorial comment for or against the Ford offer. On March 24, General Motors and the RFC established a new institution, the National Bank of Detroit. This concern took over most of the liquid assets of the First National Bank and the Guardian National Bank of Commerce, neither of which reopened. On August 10, the Fords, without government assistance, opened a second bank, the Manufacturers National Bank of Detroit. Both of the new institutions prospered.[12]

The banking crisis was thoroughly aired at a one-man grand jury investigation conducted in Detroit in 1933 and by the Sub-Committee on Stock Exchange Practices of the Senate Committee on Banking and Currency during the following year. Ford's role in the crisis was given relatively little attention in the grand-jury investigation, but in the Senate's inquiry, the industrialist was criticized by a number of bankers. Couzens, who received an extremely unfavorable press during the grand-jury investigation, redeemed his battered reputation somewhat during the Senate inquiry.[13]

After the crisis had passed, the Ford Company made available to its dealers a booklet entitled, *The Truth about Henry Ford and the Banking Situation.* The brochure pointed out that "Mr. Ford is not a banker . . . but he did exert every effort over months to save other people, who, like himself, were merely depositors in the banks." This thesis seems to have found acceptance with many people who, while confused by the complexities, charges, and countercharges of the banking crisis, did recognize that Ford had championed depositors with a dramatic offer that he had been prepared to carry through. To many observers, recalling the industrialist's attack on the Selden "trust," his five-dollar day (which shocked numerous business groups), and his rejection of bank loans during the slump of 1920–21, Ford had revealed himself as ready once again to deal with "the interests" of the common folk.[14]

3

Hard on the heels of the banking crisis came another backlash from the disrupted depression economy. On this occasion Ford's opposition to one of the major recovery programs of the Roosevelt Administration made him a storm center of controversy and brought down on his head, for the first time in his career, vociferous criticism of his policies from a sizable portion of the nation's press and the American public.

The controversy grew out of enactment of the National Industrial Recovery Act (NIRA) signed into law in June 1933. This emergency measure declared that codes of fair competition—which generally were to deal with rates of pay, hours of work, working conditions, and the fixing of prices—were to be drafted for the various industries of the country. Any industry which failed to present an acceptable code would have one handed it by the administration. To balance concessions to businessmen, the famous Section 7A of the act proclaimed the right of employees to organize and to engage in collective bargaining free from employer interference.[15]

The automobile industry had little enthusiasm for submitting a code to the administration. Auto firms did not need legalized price-fixing, since they had neither cutthroat price competition nor overproduction. In addition, Section 7A was repugnant to firms that had long united to maintain the open shop. But sensing that public opinion firmly supported the NIRA, the companies comprising the National Automobile Chamber of Commerce (NACC) drafted a code, which was approved by the President on August 26. Although a representative of the Ford Company assisted the NACC in drawing up the code, Henry Ford refused to sign the document. The auto magnate balked because of his belief that the code would threaten the open shop that prevailed in his plants and because he feared that to sign it would be to surrender control of his business. He also argued that his company already exceeded the code's requirements regarding wages, hours of labor, and working conditions. "If we tried to live up to it," the industrialist told reporters, "we would have to live down to it."

Finally, Ford was suspicious of the NACC. The chamber had succeeded the Association of Licensed Automobile Manufacturers, which had tried to enforce the Selden patent. Ford had never joined the organization, and he did not now intend to come under its jurisdiction.[16]

During the summer of 1933, the administrator of the National Recovery Administration (NRA), Hugh S. ("Old Ironpants") Johnson, a blunt retired cavalry brigadier general who had administered the Selective Service Law in World War I, spared no effort to gain Ford's support. Winning Ford's cooperation was important. The Dearbornite controlled almost a quarter of the industry's production. Also, as a widely-admired business leader, Ford, if he went along with Johnson, might influence other businessmen to support the NIRA. In late June the general secretly flew to Dearborn and explained to Henry and Edsel the purposes and character of the act. He believed he had won the elder Ford's cooperation. Events soon proved him wrong. By the end of July, Ford was the only important manufacturer in the auto industry who had not signed the code.[17]

For several weeks prior to September 5, when the auto code became effective, many publications, as they often had in the past, suspected that Ford was "going it alone" and keeping his plans to himself for publicity purposes. "Mr. Ford's talents as a manufacturer and distributor," editorialized the *Louisville Times,* "are matched, or surpassed by his genius for keeping the public's eyes focused upon his course." The *Springfield* (Illinois) *State-Journal* observed that "our curiosity and the sweating of General Johnson' serve to keep Mr. Ford and his motor cars in the minds of the public," while the *New York Daily News* suggested that "the world's greatest press agent . . . is putting on this fight for the free publicity it will bring him, intending to sign the auto code a couple of eye-twinklings before the zero hour." Scores of rumors about what Ford might do spread through the country in the wake of the manufacturer's refusal to discuss his plans. Much of the speculation was to the effect that he would announce a "spectacular go-it-alone plan" which would include his own business code.[18]

In the meantime pressure was building up on many sides to induce Ford to sign the industry document. The governors of Maine and Pennsylvania announced that their states would not buy from nonsigners; the state purchasing agent of Tennessee vowed not to buy Ford products "until Henry Ford gets under the NRA." Johnson, when asked at an August 29 press conference if he intended to "crack down" on Ford, replied: "I think maybe the American people will crack down on him when the Blue Eagle is on other cars and he does not have one." Many Americans, though they appreciated Ford's apprehension and believed that he was "living up" to the code, were sympathetic to Johnson's viewpoint. Ford, they reasoned, should "get in line" with the business community to help the President pull the country out of the depression. In an editorial typifying this view, the *Brooklyn Eagle* questioned whether any one man "should regard himself as big enough to oppose the Federal Government or to hold himself aloof from a movement which has the support of the American people." *News-Week* professed astonishment that Ford "should stand out even for a day in opposition to [this] great united movement." Even Arthur Brisbane, who almost always approved of Ford's views, warned the manufacturer that he was making a mistake "when there is no actual principle involved except that of independence which we all have to yield to in wartime . . . to go against the Government of the United States and a whirlwind of sentimental emotion." The *Philadelphia Record* echoed this view. "The public," it asserted, "will not appreciate egoistic attempts to grab the spotlight at the expense of the wholehearted cooperation demanded by the NRA."[19]

The unfavorable sales implications of Ford's failure to sign the code also attracted considerable attention. "A leading competitor," an administration official admonished, "has decided to issue cars with a blue eagle etched on the windshield. This will give Ford something to think about." This opinion was restated graphically by a *New York Post* cartoon which showed Ford cutting off his nose with a scissors labeled "non-participation." The president of the Ford Owners Alliance, which claimed 200,000 members, wrote on September 1, 1933, that all members would soon display windshield stickers stating, "My last Ford supports NRA." Chevrolet and Chrysler Corporation fanned the anti-Ford sentiment by proclaiming in full-page advertisements that they were "proud and glad to do our part" in promoting recovery and that "the Blue Eagle flies from every flagstaff of Detroit's outstanding manufacturer." Ford Motor Company executives, most of whom were frightened by the mounting criticism, urged Ford to sign. The auto king was unruffled. "Hell," he said of the Blue Eagle, "that Roosevelt buzzard. I wouldn't put it on the car."[20]

At the same time many persons and newspapers sprang to Ford's defense. Senator Thomas D. Schall, of Minnesota, denounced the administration for trying "to put a Baruch-Johnson code over a man of the standing of Henry Ford, who led the way to the maximum wage scale." Brisbane, in his daily column, suggested that "a wise Administration will remember that everybody in Washington would have to grow considerably to be knee-high to Henry Ford, among the most distinguished and useful Americans and benefactors of United States industry and public." Ford also drew considerable praise from many persons who saw him as a symbol of opposition to government regulation and to the New Deal. "I observe from letters to the various editors," stated Heywood Broun, an antagonist of Ford, "that the position of the Marquis of Model T is likely to receive a large amount of popular support." Many businessmen, especially those in the auto industry, looked to Ford as their champion. "He has become," observed the *New York Times,* "the bright and shining knight of the motor capital."[21]

As long as Ford *complied* with the auto code, there was little the government could do to chastise him other than to refuse to award government contracts to the Ford Company or to its dealers, and to urge the public not to buy Ford vehicles. After September 5, Johnson and other administration officials, including the President, frequently suggested that the public should boycott Ford products. That many of Ford's dealers had signed the dealers' code was, to the administration, beside the point. "To let Mr. Ford escape the consequences of this Act because his dealer has a Blue Eagle," said Johnson, "would be to allow a billion dollar corporation hide behind the skirts of a thirty thousand dollar company." Concurring, the President declared, "It is the article rather than the person you buy it through . . . we have got to eliminate the purchase of Ford cars."[22]

Meanwhile, Ford took two actions which were designed at least in part to offset public criticism of his attitude toward the code. On September 5 he announced that his employees would receive wage increases ranging from forty cents to one dollar a day. Ten days later the company made it known that employment would be given to 5,000 Wayne County veterans. Neither action had any great public relations impact. Other auto manufacturers had already increased wages by a comparable or greater amount, and the hiring of veterans brought prompt charges from unemployed Ford workers who were also veterans that they were being discriminated against. In early November the company fared no better in a skirmish with Johnson growing out of Ford's compliance with an auto code stipulation that hours of work were to be limited to an average of thirty-five per week. Announcing that 9,000 Rouge workers (who heretofore had been working a forty-hour week) would be laid off for a week, the company petulantly told newspapers that it was taking the step "in compliance with the new prohibition against work in this country." Johnson hastily offered to exempt Ford from the work week requirement at issue. But Ford refused to discuss the offer. Johnson thereupon accused Ford of exercising "the most ruthless economic dictatorship of our time." That part of the press which commented on the exchange expressed disgust. "The Johnson-Ford performance is silly," stated the *Durham* (North Carolina) *Herald,* "and it's about time that Johnson and Ford stopped playing to the galleries." The *Akron Beacon-Journal* focused its ire on Ford: "His act is as childish as it is deplorable."[23]

The dispute between the administration and Ford attracted relatively little attention during the several weeks between late September and late October. On October 27, however, Johnson declared that if the Ford Company did not submit the wages and hours data required of it by the auto code, he would bring this fact to the attention of the attorney general. This moved Ford to break his lengthy silence. In a statement prepared by Cameron, the company declared that "Mr. Johnson's vocabulary has got him down again. Before assuming the airs of a dictator he should fortify himself with evidence that Henry Ford has refused compliance with Government requirements. The public has known the Ford Motor Company for thirty years and is not dependent on Mr. Johnson for information concerning it. . . . We suggest a code of fair publicity for Mr. Johnson's interviews." Johnson retorted that he had not said that he had evidence of any Ford violation of the code, but that Edsel had told him that the company would not "submit" to a code that required collective bargaining. In any event, Johnson said, Ford was not eligible to receive government contracts. Counterattacking, Cameron stated that Ford had *complied* with the code in every respect. By refusing to award contracts to Ford dealers, he added, Johnson was simply proposing to injure the taxpayer by having the federal government pay higher prices for motor vehicles produced by companies that paid lower wages than Ford did: "Johnson is not boycotting us. He is boycotting 5,300 American manufacturers [Ford dealers who had signed the code] who cooperate with Johnson. . . . Failing to induce the American people to demean themselves by boycotting decent industry, he seems to have hopes of better success with the government." Johnson, after this exchange of verbal blows, traded his Lincoln for a Cadillac. Many newspapers concluded that Ford had won this skirmish. "One cannot withhold a certain admiration of the statement in its own behalf of the Ford Company,'' editorialized the *New York Times*. "There can be little doubt that many large manufacturers, uncertain about their treatment by Government officials, will feel like echoing the caustic remarks of the Ford Company."[24]

Two weeks later Ford won another round with Johnson when the comptroller-general, who, as an agent of Congress had the last word regarding the legality of government contracts, ruled (contrary to Johnson's judgment) that nothing in the NIRA or the auto code required a company to sign a code or even to indicate its intent to comply in order to receive government contracts. Since the NRA acknowledged that Ford was complying with the auto code, the ruling opened the way to awarding government contracts to the company's dealers. On December 1, a Ford dealer received a contract for more than 700 trucks from the secretary of agriculture, prompting the *Cleveland Plain Dealer* to remark that Johnson's threat to ''crack down'' on Ford ''is now laid on the shelf with other militant slogans that didn't work.'' Other government awards followed, and by March 1, 1934, approximately $1,000,000 in government contracts had been granted to Ford dealers.[25]

The contest between Ford and the NRA was not over, however, for on March 14, 1934, the President issued an executive order which required the Ford Company to sign a certificate of compliance with the auto code if its dealers were to receive government contracts. Ford stubbornly refused to sign such a certificate, and since the comptroller-general accepted the provisions of the executive order, Ford bids were rejected. For several months Chevrolet virtually monopolized the government's purchase of small cars and trucks. But in the fall of 1934 government agencies resumed the purchase of Ford cars. Johnson chose not to make an issue of their purchasing policies. By early 1935 the government was buying vehicles on a large scale from Ford dealers.[26]

Although Henry Ford was heavily criticized for his attitude toward the NRA during August and September 1933, the tide of public opinion, as the stalemate continued, began to run heavily in his favor. ''The cheering and marching for NRA,'' said *Business Week* in October 1933, ''seems to have generated little if any public resentment against Mr. Ford.'' The magazine added that a newsreel's fleeting shot of Henry Ford, which followed several hundred feet of film on General Johnson and NRA activities, elicited applause in the theaters where it was shown. Johnson, who underestimated the public's deep-seated admiration for Ford, ''the symbol of individualism, high wages and short hours,'' was, in the opinion of some observers, largely responsible for the shift in the public attitude. Using ''strong-arm action which might be construed as persecution in behalf of a technicality,'' he tended to make a martyr of the industrialist. ''It is but stating a fact,'' said the *New York Times* in November, ''that General Johnson 'got mad' [at Ford]. When he found that the man whom he had intended for a drum-major's part would not even play the piccolo, the General boiled over.'' Many people, even if they disagreed with Ford's attitude toward the code, resented Johnson's angry blasts at a man they otherwise respected.[27]

Moreover, the boycott declared against Ford vehicles by the federal government and several state governments, although depriving Ford of the opportunity of gaining his share of several million dollars of business, was not supported by the automobile buying public. It appeared that the nation's motorists agreed with Will Rogers when he remarked, "you can take the rouge from the female lips, the cigarette from the raised hands, the hot dog from the tourist's greasy paw, but when you start jerking the Fords out from under the traveling public you are monkeying with the very fundamentals of American life." Whereas in 1933 the Ford Company had suffered a net loss of $7,888,718 after taxes and accounted for only 21.5 percent of the total new passenger car and truck registrations in the United States, in 1934 it made a profit of $21,362,111 after taxes and increased its percentage of registrations to 28.8. Ford triumphantly announced on November 1, 1934, that the depression was over for him and that this would be true of the nation as a whole "if American industrialists would just forget these alphabet schemes and take hold of their industries and run them with good, sound American business sense."[28]

Ford's joust with the NRA did much to enhance his reputation as a "rugged individualist." Many publications expounded on this aspect of Ford's character, and recalled at length his role in the Selden patent suit, the five-dollar and seven-dollar days, the "evasion" of the bankers in 1921, and so on. Ford was the only major businessman who had the will and the courage to stand against the NRA. "But for the Ford Motor Company," commented journalist Garet Garrett, "it would have to be written that the surrender of American business to government was unanimous, complete and unconditional." The stubborn auto king no doubt felt that his refusal to sign the auto code was fully vindicated when the Supreme Court unanimously declared the NIRA unconstitutional on May 27, 1935.[29]

Chapter 15
Labor Relations

Perceptive observers, noting that Ford was the one major businessman who had publicly stood up to the NRA, were not surprised when he put up a stiffer fight against organized labor than anyone else on the industrial horizon. Thus the fat was in the fire when employees at the company's Chester, Pennsylvania, and Edgewater, New Jersey, assembly plants walked off the job in September 1933. Protesting against wage and working conditions, they promptly affiliated with the American Federation of Labor. The union locals at the two plants had hoped that Section 7A of the NIRA would facilitate their attempts to organize the plants' employees and to engage in collective bargaining. Ford, however, refused to recognize either local. In fact, by closing the struck plants and then refusing to reinstate active unionists, the company succeeded in crushing the organized labor movement at Chester and Edgewater within a few months. The NRA's Compliance Board recommended that the company be prosecuted for alleged violation of Section 7A on the grounds that Ford employees were interfered with in their efforts to organize. The Justice Department, which had responsibility for pressing a suit, did not think the evidence against the company was strong enough to proceed. But the evidence did clearly indicate that automobile workers, should they attempt to bring unionism to the plants of the Ford Motor Company would face determined opposition.[1]

— Ford was but one of many manufacturers opposing organized labor and seeking to circumvent the labor provisions of the NIRA. In the auto industry, virtually all firms except Ford established company unions to stave off the threat of outside organization. A number of auto makers, including Ford and the other members of the Big Three, General Motors and Chrysler, also made extensive use of labor spies and private policemen in their efforts to keep workers from organizing. As far as the collective bargaining stipulation of Section 7A was concerned, no great moral distinction can be drawn between Ford and the other auto makers. While Ford impudently flouted it, other manufacturers quietly buried it. On the whole, efforts of the AFL and the so-called independent auto unions met with scant success during the NIRA period. Some of the smaller auto makers and parts companies, which were in a precarious financial position, made concessions to organized labor, but General Motors and Chrysler yielded little, and Ford nothing.[2]

In 1935, however, two events occurred which were to have a vital bearing on the organization of the auto industry. One was passage in July of the National Labor Relations Act (the Wagner Act) and the establishment of the National Labor Relations Board (NLRB) to administer the statute. In passing the act, Congress insured the right of all employees to self-organization and to engage in collective bargaining and other activities for mutual aid and protection. Stern penalties were provided for violators of the act. The second event was the formation in the fall of the Committee for Industrial Organization, later the Congress of Industrial Organizations (CIO), by John L. Lewis, president of the United Mine Workers, and others representing the industrial union bloc in the AFL. The United Automobile Workers (UAW), at odds with the AFL over the selection of its officers and the limitations on its jurisdiction, affiliated with the CIO in mid-1936. Homer Martin, an ex-Baptist minister and "gifted agitator," was president of the UAW; Walter Reuther, an ex-Ford foreman, was a member of the union's executive board.[3]

The UAW spent most of 1936 preparing for an invasion of the auto industry. General Motors was struck in December 1936, and, after six weeks of turmoil, agreed to recognize the UAW as bargaining agent for its members only. The union next turned to Chrysler, which capitulated on April 6. Outside the auto industry, United States Steel, General Electric, and other industrial giants fell before the CIO. But the new federation was stopped short by the resistance of a number of companies, including the members of Little Steel (of which Bethlehem Steel and Republic Steel were the most important firms), Westinghouse—and the Ford Motor Company.[4]

By 1937, labor practices at Ford plants were a far cry from the enlightened policies which gained the company its enviable labor-relations reputation in the years following the introduction of the five-dollar day and the establishment of the Sociological Department, created to advise employees on constructive ways to spend their higher wages. Ford's vaunted "high wages" were a myth; both General Motors and Chrysler paid their workers more. In addition, wages were uneven among employees performing similar tasks. The speed-up, stretch-out (assignment of a greater number of machines to each man), "driving" tactics by harsh foremen, and inequitable patterns of hiring and firing were only a few of the abuses to which employees were subjected. Ford's labor policies were enforced by the Service Department, variously and aptly described as "a standing army unique in America," the "O.G.P.U. of the Ford organization," and the "largest privately owned secret service force in existence." Many of the department's employees were thugs and ex-convicts. "They're a lot of tough bastards," the head of the Service Department, Harry Bennett, said of them, "but every goddam one of them's a gentleman." His "gentlemen," who knew why they had been hired, constantly harassed employees suspected of union sympathies, and sometimes beat them as well.[5]

Relatively few people outside the Detroit area were familiar with the way in which Ford's labor practices had deteriorated over the years. References in the press to the company's labor policies were, with very few exceptions, highly favorable. The most notable of these exceptions was a review of Ford's labor practices by Oswald Garrison Villard in an April 1937, issue of the *Nation*. "To tell the truth about Henry Ford," commented the editor, "one has to be a bit brutal"; Villard supplied the details and gave the manufacturer a "Z" on his labor report card.[6]

Henry Ford spoke out in defense of his labor record on many occasions. When the constitutionality of the Wagner Act was upheld in April 1937, for example, he told reporters, "We have had the spirit of the Wagner Act in effect 20 years. I would be ashamed to have any one tell me conditions and pay were wrong. That part of the job was started 20 years ago.'' Encouraged by the public's growing apprehension over the power of labor, Ford also made no secret of his dislike for unions: "A good mechanic and a skilled workman don't need a union. . . . I advise them it's foolish to join one"; union organizing would fail "because our workers won't stand for it, I won't stand for it, and the public won't stand for it." In April 1937, Ford told Edsel and Charles E. Sorensen how he would deal with the union threat. None of the three was to meet with any union officials, and Edsel and the manufacturing executive were not to discuss labor matters with anyone. Harry Bennett, head of the Service Department, was designated to "handle" the unions. His assignment was to stave off union organization and to avoid any sort of working arrangement with union members. The Wagner Act was to be defeated by evasion and delay.[7]

A fiction writer would be hard put to devise a more picaresque or colorful character than the man Ford had designated to handle the "union problem." An ex-sailor and amateur pugilist, alternately charming and ruthless, Bennett had joined the Ford Company in 1915 as an artist in the Motion Picture Department. He began his upward rise in 1919, when, after transfer to a supervisory post on the Eagle boat job, he was assigned various special tasks by Henry Ford. Proud of these assignments, Bennett executed them promptly and efficiently. In 1921 he was placed in charge of the Rouge's Service Department, which at that time was responsible only for protection of the plant. During the next decade Bennett's department gradually assumed full control over all personnel matters, including spying upon workers. By the early 1930s the service chief was one of the most powerful men at the Rouge, and his star, unlike that of Charles E. Sorensen and other veteran executives, was still rising.

The source of Bennett's power was his special relation with Henry Ford. Although the reasons why Bennett's ascendancy grew are complex, four seem of salient importance. First, Bennett did anything Ford told him to do, without question and with dispatch. Second, Bennett, beginning in the early 1920s, had an open relationship with the Detroit underworld which supposedly gave him the capacity to protect Henry Ford and his family from criminal molestation. Bennett's vigilance against the molestation of the Ford family—particularly the kidnapping of Edsel's children—is a cloudy subject and may or may not have been an important function; but Ford thought it was.

A third factor which gave Bennett and his department a larger role in plant affairs was the spread of discontent in the nation's factories during the early 1930s. Whether or not the danger of disturbances or sabotage was increasing, many industrialists believed it was and took precautions. Ford was among them. Finally, the psychological element was important. Ford had long tried to remold his son in his own image; he had failed. In Bennett, the magnate found many of the hard-nosed traits and attitudes he had vainly tried to implant in Edsel, and in time he gave the cocky ex-sailor a scope he had denied his urbane, sensitive son. Indeed, during the late 1930s and early 1940s, when the service chief and Ford were together almost every day, Bennett became, in addition to lieutenant and crony, something of a substitute son to the industrialist.[8]

The designation of Bennett to direct labor relations distressed Edsel, who favored bargaining with the union. During the next few years Edsel and his father had long, heated wrangles over labor matters. On one occasion the younger Ford told Sorenson that he could no longer stomach Bennett and his handling of labor affairs, and that he intended to resign. Sorensen dissuaded him. But as Sorensen notes in his memoirs, "a feud between father and son was now on in earnest."[9]

The UAW-CIO launched its organizing drive at the Ford Company on May 26, 1937. A group of union officials, including Vice President Richard Frankensteen and Walter Reuther, attempted to distribute pamphlets to Ford workers as they walked over and down a street overpass leading from the Rouge. The unionists were attacked by members of Ford Service in full view of a corps of reporters and photographers. A number of the organizers were severely mauled, including Frankensteen and Reuther. Frankensteen's beating was "scientific." His attackers skinned his coat up his back and drew it forward over his face. Two men locked his arms, while the others slugged and kicked him in the head, groin, and kidneys. When prostrate, he was gored in the abdomen by the heels of his assailants. Company men also attacked the press corps. Three reporters had their notes wrenched from their hands. Films were forcibly removed from the cameras of every photographer who was slow on his feet. One photographer, who was pursued at seventy to eighty miles an hour for five miles, finally took refuge in a police station.[10]

In abusing the newsmen, Ford made a tactical blunder. The reporters and their incensed editors outdid themselves in describing the viciousness of the attack. The pictures which were salvaged, including one of Frankensteen's beating, were even more damaging. Reproduced by newspapers and magazines all over the country immediately following the riot (*Newsweek* illustrated its cover with one of the photographs), they also were widely reprinted in the labor and leftist press during the next four strife-torn years. The newsmen, furthermore, repeated their eye-witness reports of the battle when testifying against Ford at NLRB hearings during the summer of 1937. They proved, according to *Time,* the board's "best witnesses."[11]

After the "Battle of the Overpass," the NLRB filed a complaint which accused the company of violating virtually every unfair labor practice defined by the Wagner Act. At the subsequent hearings, held in Detroit, the UAW sought to prove that Henry Ford was not the enlightened industrialist he was thought to be and that the Ford Service Department threatened workers with physical injury and loss of their jobs if they showed interest in union membership. Ford's policy was to deny every charge; assert that employees involved in the fracas were acting in self-defense; and insist that UAW members went to Dearborn for the express purpose of promoting a riot. In the words of William J. Cameron, the company also claimed that the melee was a question of "Ford against the 'Reds,' " and that "only timid citizens . . . stand aside when amateur revolutionaries say 'boo.' " The company later dropped the charge that the battle was Communist-inspired, but continued to insist that its men were fighting only in self-defense.[12]

Newspapers, especially those in Detroit, carried scores of stories on the hearings, and Ford took a shellacking in most of them. Cameron admitted as much in a speech before the National Editorial Association. "Organized labor," he grumbled, "today has better connections with the press than any corporation or big business in the country." Adding that newspapers had "unwittingly grossly misinterpreted labor events in recent months," Cameron expressed hope there might be "at least one man in every newspaper office who understands the facts about the present labor difficulties.'' As for the May 26 fight, the Ford spokesman complained that ''the news of that event and the pictures displayed by the papers all played readily into the hands of those who planned it for that specific purpose.''[13]

The NLRB on December 23, in its ''most-publicized decision to date,'' found the company guilty of violating the Wagner Act and ordered it to cease interfering with employees' organization rights and to reinstate with back pay twenty-three employees who had been fired for union activity earlier in the year. Ford officials denounced the board's decision, saying they would not comply with it and would appeal. The NLRB thereupon took the case to the Sixth U.S. Circuit Court of Appeals in Cincinnati.[14]

A number of publications were critical of Ford as the appeal got under way. ''We believe he will lose if he wins,'' commented the *Washington News* in a widely-reprinted editorial, ''for we think he is bucking a tide too strong. . . . Ford's general policy of resistance to the right of labor to organize is as out of step with the times as the oxcart.'' But a greater number of papers extended their sympathy to the manufacturer. ''The attack of labor on the man who led the nation's employers in paying high wages is mysterious,'' said the *Harrisburg* (Pennsylvania) *News*. ''It may be assumed that the thoughtful automobile rider is not ready to join in such an attack for the very simple reason that Mr. Ford has made it possible for the automobile to become the property of the average man.'' Many small papers carried a syndicated editorial which said: ''We have no sympathy with the persecution of Henry Ford. Let persecution be confined to the men who have not done as much for working men as he has. Ford has kept his money at work making more and more jobs instead of hoarding it as he might have done.'' A syndicated cartoon titled, ''Our Memories Are So Short,'' summed up the pro-Ford sentiment by showing sequences of the Dearbornite as a young man in humble surroundings; making the first ''poor man's car''; providing factory employment; announcing the five-dollar day; thumbing his nose at Wall Street; and finally being hounded by characters labeled ''NLRB,'' ''labor,'' ''mob law,'' and ''Ickes.'' (Secretary of the Interior Ickes had, after the NLRB's decision was announced, caustically called Ford ''Henry Ford the Beneficent,'' adding that if the charges against him were true he ''is not entitled to the respect of the decent, law abiding citizens of America.'')[15]

Ford could find comfort in the public opinion surveys that invariably named him and his firm as ''labor's best friend.'' A survey by the Curtis Publishing Company in May 1937 found that 59.1 percent of Americans believed the Ford Company treated its labor better than any other firm did. A poll conducted for *Fortune* in the fall of 1937 found that Ford was the ''most popular'' industrial figure in America. The auto magnate was selected by 60.6 percent of the respondents, a figure twelve times greater than the next most popular businessman, Walter P. Chrysler. In January 1938 the American Institute of Public Opinion found that the sympathies of 66 percent of Americans of voting age were with Ford in his dispute with the UAW. Seventy-three percent of car-owning respondents lined up with the manufacturer. In addition, an estimated 700,000 persons from all over the country petitioned the President in mid-1938 to stop the administration's attacks on Ford.[16]

In mid-1938 Ford's nemesis, the NLRB, turned its sights on a number of the company's branch plants. The board's hearings on antiunion activities in these plants received little attention in the general press, although a few of the reports by NLRB trial examiners were carried by the wire services. Perhaps the most damaging of these reports, released in April 1940 by the examiner in Dallas, accused Ford of "gathering together the most brutal, vicious and conscienceless thugs in its employ" to block unionization of Ford workers in that city. The examiner added that the company's "strong-arm squad . . . employed blackjacks, loaded hose and a cat-o'-nine tails, made of rubber stripping and electric light wire" as weapons to intimidate its workmen. Testimony also showed that between June and November 1937, there were more than thirty instances in which Ford Service assaulted persons on the streets of Dallas or took them into the outskirts where they were "beaten, flogged, or tarred and feathered." By November 1940, the NLRB had adjudged the Ford Company guilty of unfair labor practices in nine of its plants.[17]

Meanwhile, Ford gained support from the press over an issue involving freedom of speech. On various occasions between 1937 and 1940 the NLRB objected to the manufacturer's antiunion outbursts and the Ford Company's distribution of antiunion literature on the grounds that these actions interfered with employees in the exercise of their rights under the Wagner Act. The American Civil Liberties Union twice filed briefs with the NLRB on Ford's behalf, declaring that the rights of an employer to express antiunion opinions were not sufficiently protected. Company attorneys seized on the issue as a means of justifying resistance to the board's orders, and charged that Ford was being deprived of the rights of free speech, "although this right is accorded advocates of communism and other isms." Publications, concerned lest the board's ruling threaten rights accorded by the First Amendment, followed the case with considerable interest. "The NLRB," *Newsweek* noted apprehensively, "in the Ford decision serves notice on all employers that they can't question the virtues of unionism by public statement, newspaper interviews, leaflet distribution in their plants, or any other means." Many publications ran editorials in Ford's defense, and the *Savannah News* was so indignant about the board's complaints that it ran a *news* story on an NLRB complaint under the headline, "Still Picking on Henry Ford." In late 1940 the U.S. Circuit Court of Appeals in Cincinnati refused to uphold a board order directing Ford to cease distribution of antiunion literature, and thus the free speech issue was concluded in Ford's favor.[18]

The UAW's organizing drive at Ford bogged down in 1938–39, mostly because of a divisive power struggle within the union. The upshot of the strife was the replacement of Martin as president by R.J. Thomas in January 1939. Martin and his followers formed a new union for auto workers which soon affiliated with the AFL. First through the UAW-AFL, then through federal local unions (locals affiliated directly with the parent federation), the AFL sought simultaneously with the UAW-CIO to organize the Rouge and Lincoln plants. The AFL organizing drive was abetted on and off by Bennett, who recognized it as significantly weaker than the CIO campaign and hoped to capitalize on its "nuisance value."[19]

The UAW-CIO was also handicapped by an ordinance enacted in December 1937, by the Dearborn City Council which, in effect, made it illegal for the union to distribute circulars near the Rouge. Thereafter, until the statute was declared unconstitutional by a Dearborn municipal judge in November 1940, organizers were powerless to circularize Ford employees. When the ban was lifted, the UAW-CIO immediately began distributing handbills at the Rouge. Later, 50,000 copies of its newspaper, *Ford Facts,* were handed out biweekly at the plant's gates. The screws were also tightened on the Ford Company by the court decision which grew out of the NLRB's original indictment of Ford in 1937. In October 1940, the U.S. Circuit Court of Appeals in Cincinnati upheld the board's directive that Ford must reinstate twenty-three employees with back pay and post notices stating that it would discontinue interfering with union organization. The company immediately announced it would carry an appeal to the U.S. Supreme Court.[20]

A week before the Circuit Court decision was announced, the UAW-CIO revealed plans for a "renewed" organization drive against Ford. Michael F. Widman, Jr., assistant organization director of the CIO, assumed direction of the campaign. A war chest of $100,000, jointly furnished by the UAW and CIO, was made available to Widman and a staff of fifty-four trained organizers. The Widman group published *Ford Facts,* issued multitudinous press releases, produced a series of foreign-language radio broadcasts for the various ethnic groups within the Ford work force, and "took particular pains to tell Ford's 10,000 black workers that without their help the job of organizing the Ford Motor Co. would be out of the question."[21]

Blacks were, in fact, courted assiduously by both Ford and the UAW-CIO. Along with the "large numbers" of handicapped employees and graduates of the Henry Ford Trade School, blacks were the least receptive of the company's workers to the union's organizing drive. Hundreds of Ford's black employees were participants on the company's side in the Battle of the Overpass, and Detroit's black community applauded their role. (A Detroit black newspaper referred to one Ford black, who had knocked down four unionists, as the "uncrowned hero of the pitched battle.") Martin, six weeks after the fight, told a black reporter that his union sought "to unite . . . occupations, without regard to race, creed, or color." He was immediately rebuked by leading members of the Detroit Interdenominational Ministers' Alliance (black), who wrote Henry Ford and Sorensen to affirm their belief that blacks were best served by Ford's labor policies. The ministers also promised resistance to the UAW-CIO "menace to American ideals" and assurance that Ford could "count on our group almost one hundred percent." The reference to Ford's labor policies was a telling blow, for the union obviously could not convince black workers that it would be able to improve their lot at Ford as long as the company employed almost twice as many blacks as General Motors, Chrysler, and Briggs combined. All of these companies which, after Ford, were the biggest employers in the Detroit area, had contracts with the UAW-CIO. Ford, moreover, offered its black employees opportunities for skilled employment and advancement that were not available to them anywhere else in the auto industry.[22]

In addition, most blacks feared the UAW-CIO and were reluctant to place themselves at the mercy of its white officials. Leaders of the black workers, nearly all of whom were clergymen, voiced their suspicion of the unions from the pulpit and in the press, telling their parishioners not to "bite the hand which had fed them." Black clergymen, themselves, had long been in debt to Ford, for gifts ranging from coal

A poignant scene in front of the
Lincoln Motor Company's Administration Building on February 4,
1922, the day Henry Ford bought
the faltering Lincoln enterprise.
Left to right are Lincoln's president, Henry M. Leland, his
daughter-in-law, Mrs. Wilfred C.
Leland, Wilfred C. Leland, Mrs.
Edsel Ford, Edsel Ford, Mrs.
Henry Ford, and Henry Ford.

Driven across the country for pub-
licity purposes, the ten millionth
Ford is welcomed in Hollywood by
Douglas Fairbanks, Sr., his wife,
Mary Pickford, front seat, and a
pint-sized cop. Ex-Ford racing star
Frank Kulick, the car's driver, is
seated behind Fairbanks.

Henry and Edsel Ford with the auto
king's 1896 quadricycle and the fifteen millionth Ford outside the
Dearborn Engineering Laboratory
on May 26, 1927, announcement
day of the Model T's discontinuance.

One of scores of cartoons which mourned the passing of the Model T in 1927.

During the last half of 1927 the press speculated endlessly about the Model T's successor.

The Model A's introduction in 1927 generated more public interest than any other new product in American history. Henry Ford was credited with having engineered the publicity campaign.

In the Higher Brackets of Publicity

New York Governor Franklin D. Roosevelt and his son, Elliott, pose proudly in
their new 1929 Model A cabriolet. Roosevelt autographed the picture for Edsel
Ford.

In 1923 Henry Ford advised customers to buy a Tin Lizzie and *spend*,
not save, the difference.

Henry Ford wielding a hammer and die, stamps ''A1'' on the motor block of the
first Model A. Released on November 26, this photo was published in virtually
every daily newspaper in the country.

Henry Ford shone at press conferences. Here he talks with reporters at a V-8 press
preview in December 1934.

Henry Ford clowns as Thomas A. Edison beams during a 1923 camping trip in Northern Michigan.

Shaving time in the Great Smokies, 1921. Left to right, Henry Ford, Methodist Bishop William F. Anderson, Harvey Firestone, Sr. (stooping), Thomas A. Edison, and President Warren G. Harding.

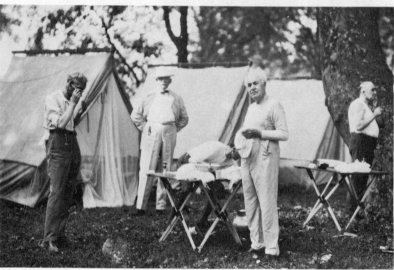

Henry Ford, left, Thomas A. Edison, center, and President Warren G. Harding camping in the Great Smokies in 1921.

Costumed early American dancers pose in the tiny ballroom of Henry Ford's Wayside Inn, South Sudbury, Massachusetts in 1928. Henry and Clara Ford are seated fourth and fifth from right.

Henry Ford in 1925 looks benignly upon his favorite fiddler, seventy-two-year-old Mellie Dunham, a Maine snowshoe maker. (*Detroit News* photo.)

"OH, FIDDLESTICKS"

A nation smiled when Henry Ford revived old-fashioned dancing in the mid-1920s.

Prelude to the "Battle of the Overpass," May 26, 1937. Ford thugs approach unsuspecting UAW-CIO officials, left to right, Robert Kanter, organizer; Walter Reuther, president of the union's west side local; Richard T. Frankensteen, organization director; and J. J. Kennedy, assistant to Frankensteen. (*Detroit News* photo.)

Richard T. Frankensteen, UAW-CIO organization director, coat pulled over his head, being beaten by Ford Company toughs on a Rouge plant footbridge. (*Detroit News* photo.)

UAW-CIO goons beat a non-striking Rouge employee in 1941. (*Courtesy of Mrs. Thomas D. Curtin.*)

deliveries to their churches to the hiring of thousands of men whom they had sent to Ford's employment offices with letters of recommendation. Ford did not let the clergymen forget their debts. Donald J. Marshall, for many years the company's leading black spokesman, frankly told 100 black religious and civic leaders in early 1941 that their future depended "on whether or not the union would be allowed to take over the employment problems of the Ford plant."[23]

The all-out drive to organize Ford held considerable promise for success. Widman found only 900 union members at the Rouge upon his arrival, but by the end of December some 14,000 employees had been enrolled. "At no time since the UAW became an important labor factor, nearly four years ago," commented the *New York Times* in late December, "has the Ford Motor Company faced a union organizing drive as intensive as that which is currently being waged against it." The *Times* cited two developments which gave the union a greater advantage than it had had in the past: the ruling that the Dearborn handbill ordinance was unconstitutional and the growing public concern lest disputes between labor and industry over compliance with labor laws adversely affect rearmament of the nation.[24]

The defense issue insofar as Ford was concerned centered around protests by Sidney Hillman, labor's representative in the Office of Production Management, that contracts should not be signed with firms accused of violating the Wagner Act. Hillman's first protest, in mid-December, against a War Department award of $2,000,000 for 1,500 Ford reconnaissance cars, was to no avail. Later in the month, however, the War Department announced that no additional contracts would be awarded firms found to be in violation of the act. In late January 1941, the department refused to buy 11,781 trucks from Ford, even though the company's bid was lower than that of any other. At this point, William S. Knudsen, head of the Office of Production Management, ruled that Ford's compliance with the provisions of the Wagner Act was a matter for court decision and that the defense program must not be impeded by legal settlements. Hillman again protested, but agreed that if the government could not obtain supplies from contractors who obeyed labor laws, it could award contracts to "law violators," in other words, Henry Ford.[25]

From 1937 until late 1940, the Ford Company, perhaps because it was reassured by the support it received in the conservative press and from the findings of public opinion surveys (and possibly also because it did not wish to "rock the boat") did little to acquaint the public with its views on labor-management relations. In late 1940 and early January 1941, however, as the UAW-CIO hurled its organizing forces against the company's Detroit area plants, Ford carried its case to the country in two full-page advertisements in newspapers (including many foreign-language papers) in every major industrial center. The first ad, entitled, "Does Ford Pay Good Wages?" indignantly asserted that Ford workers "need not depend on outsiders to get them benefits in wages, working hours, or working conditions." The second, headed, "What's This about Labor Trouble in Ford Plants?" denied that there was any friction between Ford labor and management. The ads were cordially received by a large segment of the press and the public. A justice of the peace in Hoboken, New Jersey, not untypically wrote the company that he believed Henry and Edsel Ford were "the greatest manufacturers the country had ever seen," especially Henry, "who came up from the ranks and knows what it is to work for wages and as a result appreciates a good employee.'' Several correspondents wrote that they were ''going right out to buy a Ford.'' Many newspapers ran the advertising copy in their news columns and numerous others praised Ford's labor policies and backed his antiunion stand in editorials. While lauding Ford, several publications also took a whack at the UAW and Hillman.[26]

Ford branch managers and dealers, especially those in plant communities, were delighted with the advertisements and predicted that they ''will do much to clear the atmosphere locally.'' A number of managers requested and received permission for dealers in smaller communities to run the ads in their local papers. Other regional executives furnished their dealers with thousands of tear sheets for displays on show windows and for the use of salesmen. Some dealers mailed reprints of the tear sheets to all post office box holders in their territory. Later, the company distributed pamphlets containing the advertising copy to dealers, who mailed them by the tens of thousands to large fleet buyers, business and professional people, and other potential customers.[27]

Ford reached a dead end in the courts on February 10, 1941, when the United States Supreme Court refused to review the October 1940 ruling of the Sixth U.S. Circuit Court of Appeals. As a consequence, the company reinstated ten employees who had been fired for union activity in 1937 (twelve had already been re-employed; one had died) and posted notices to the effect it would not interfere with workers' right to organize. The company continued to discharge men for union activity, however, and obdurately refused to heed the UAW's persistent clamor for elections to determine employee representation. On February 27 the UAW announced that it intended to strike Ford's Detroit area plants unless the company bowed to fifteen demands for higher wages and improved working conditions. The threat was ignored. ''Unions are losing ground,'' Henry Ford announced from his Georgia plantation, ''and haven't a leg to stand on.'' He added that his competitors were ''behind the unions,'' and left little doubt that he considered the Du Pont family, which owned a large share of General Motors' stock, as his main antagonist.[28]

At this point the company launched its branch managers on a nationwide campaign to enlist support for its cause from every leading editor and publisher in the country. The following letter of instruction from H. C. Doss, the company's general sales manager, to the managers reveals the Ford Company's assessment of its press relationships and its hope that it might yet roll back the inexorable tide of unionism:

> The friendly relationships we have enjoyed with the press of the country have been a great influence in the growth of the Ford Motor Company. Mr. Ford himself has always had a great interest in newspapers and newspaper men, and numbers many of the latter among his closest personal friends. There is scarcely a newspaper man in the country who does not admire Mr. Ford and the things he stands for. Most of the press is generous and friendly in its present editorial and news comments concerning the Ford Motor Company.
>
> As you know, however, there is a great deal of propaganda being spread at the present time against Mr. Ford and the Ford Motor Company. It converges on the papers from a number of different angles and is in most cases unfair, untrue and unfriendly. . . .

We . . . sincerely believe that if every important newspaper man in the country could have first-hand a story of all the things Mr. Ford is trying to do in the best interests of labor and in the best interests of the country through its national defense program, much of the effect of this vicious propaganda would be quickly dissipated.

Such information, however, cannot be given out effectively through correspondence or newspaper releases. It can be conveyed to the newspaper people only through friendly personal contacts. . . . We, therefore, are asking that you. . . personally make calls on the publishers and editors of each of the leading newspapers in your own territory.

It is not enough to talk to some newspaper writer or the automobile editor. Those who control the policies of the paper should be seen. . . .

Since the purpose of your visit is entirely to promote good will and to establish friendly relationships, you must be extremely tactful and bring no pressure whatever to bear. What we want is increased good will with the papers which in turn is bound to be reflected quickly in the attitude of the public toward our company.

. . . get going on this project immediately.

The regional managers were instructed to call Ford's defense activities to the attention of the news executives and, if an opportunity presented itself, to leave with them a summation of the company's contributions to defense.[29]

The branch managers immediately set out on their visits. Within a month they had called on more than 200 newspapers. They found a tremendous reservoir of goodwill toward Henry Ford and received scores of promises of support in the company's struggle with unions. The following excerpts from the report of the New Orleans branch manager indicate the response of small-town editors and publishers, some of whom said they were being visited for the first time by a "public relations man": "Anything to help Mr. Ford"; "No one like Mr. Ford. Anything we want"; "Says Ford is greatest man in America—full support"; "Says Ford can depend on his paper—asked for all publicity"; "Says Ford must win on labor. Full support"; "Never used anything but Fords. Running special editorial."

Expressions of support from metropolitan newspaper executives were little less effusive, especially in those cities where publications had been through the "ANG mill" (American Newspaper Guild, a CIO-affiliated union of editorial employees). In New York, E. L. James, executive of the *Times,* extended only "courteous neutrality" to the company, but Keats Speed of the *Sun* was "100% with Ford"; R. E. Clarke, managing editor of the *Daily News,* offered "utmost cooperation"; William A. Curley of the *Journal-American* said he would "print no 'smear Ford' stuff whatever"; and F. D. Schroth, publisher of the *Brooklyn Eagle,* said he was "very strongly behind Ford . . . but found the old man a little difficult." At the same time many newspapers took advantage of the visits to complain about the slowness with which Ford and other companies presented their side of the story in labor-management disputes. Others complained that the company gave an advantage to one or another of the wire services. Eight of the newspapers visited by the branch managers were classified as hostile. A "very cool" David Stern, owner of the *Philadelphia Record,* was found to be "much opposed to Henry Ford personally," and during the course of a two-and-a-half-hour conversation made numerous references to Ford's anti-Semitism and his negative attitude toward organized charities. The *Louisville Courier-Journal* and *Louisville Times* (both owned by the same company), which "do not pass up an opportunity to express their dislike for Mr. Ford and our Company in a most vicious manner," refused to discuss the source of their long-standing antipathy to Ford.

The visits of the branch managers resulted in a whirlwind of favorable editorials and news stories in support of Ford. Typically, the *Bridgeport* (Connect-icut) *Life* told its readers: "Our type of real American is Henry Ford. . . . He has done more for honest American labor than all the labor organizers combined. . . . When men can no longer applaud Henry Ford, then they are no longer Americans." Much of the defense literature left with newspapers was carried verbatim, some of it on the first page of the smaller publications. To a man, the branch managers were unanimous about the wisdom of undertaking the campaign. The New Orleans manager spoke for his colleagues: "Mr. Doss, we at this branch are firmly convinced that this public relations activity is one of the most important steps taken by our Company. . . . We will continue to keep in close touch with these newspapermen." But on April 2, as the UAW and Ford moved toward a showdown, the company abruptly terminated the visits.[30]

The efforts of state and federal mediators helped to keep Ford's Detroit area plants in operation through March 1941. The UAW, meanwhile, petitioned the NLRB for elections. Bennett's reply was characteristically blunt: "If the NLRB orders an election, of course we will hold one, because Mr. Ford will observe the law. CIO will win it, of course, because it always wins these farcical elections, and we will bargain with it because the law says so. We will bargain until Hell freezes over, but they won't get anything." In late March, as noted earlier, the American Institute of Public Opinion reported that Americans by a two-to-one margin upheld Ford's refusal to recognize unions in his plants (58 percent for Ford's point of view, 29 percent against it, 13 percent no opinion). In April 1937 the same polling agency had reported that only 47 percent of its respondents endorsed Ford's refusal to recognize unions; 41 percent had disagreed; and 12 percent had no opinion.[31]

In late March, in an effort to halt an epidemic of work stoppages in the Rouge, the company agreed to meet "unofficially" with an eight-man grievance committee of the UAW. But these men were fired on April 1 when Ford, apparently wishing to scrap the grievance machinery, accused them of being overzealous in their efforts to organize employees "not in sympathy with unionists." Upon hearing of the dis-missals, most of the workers in the huge plant (an exception being foundry workers, most of whom were blacks) walked off the job. The UAW immediately surrounded the factory with pickets and declared a strike.[32]

The UAW piously assured the public that "the strike will be maintained with complete discipline and effectiveness . . . despite the provocation of which . . . the Ford Motor Co. and its minions are capable." Bennett fired off an "open" telegram to President Roosevelt, protesting seizure of approaches to the plant "in a communis-tic demonstration of violence and terrorism" and asking for troops to help quell the strike. The Ford Service head added that nonstriking employees attempting to return to work had been brutally assaulted in attacks directed by Communist leaders and that saboteurs were committing "wanton destruction" within the plant. Roosevelt refused assistance.[33]

Taking note of Bennett's wire to the President (and a similar telegram to Michigan's governor, Murray D. Van Wagoner), the *Louisville Courier-Journal* commented: "It is strange to see Henry Ford call frantically for Government help, because no American industrialist has so often defied the Government in connection with labor disputes. . . . Now—in dismal danger—he yelps. . . . [He] has asked for what he is getting." But the vast majority of the press supported Ford throughout the strike. Some papers ran only photographs of nonstrikers being beaten by strikers as they attempted to enter the Rouge, giving the impression, as Keith Sward complained, that "lawlessness" and "CIO" were synonymous. Nothing indeed hurt the UAW's cause more than these syndicated photographs. One, captioned, "Ford Worker Pleads for Mercy," showed a battered and blood-smeared black worker pleading with club-swinging pickets as he sought entrance to the factory. The workman's car, a shambles, is in the background. Another picture showed a man, doubled over with his coat pulled over his head, vainly trying to shield himself from an unmerciful pounding by four toughs, one of whom, with tongue clenched between his teeth, prepared to swing on the man with a ball bat. Commenting on this photograph, Senator Arthur H. Vandenberg of Michigan remarked, "This poor chap with his overcoat thrown over his head is about 22 years old. I believe he is still in a hospital, fighting for his life." None of the assailants, who were readily identified from the photograph, was a Ford employee.[34]

In addition to members of Ford Service, several thousand blacks—some estimates run as high as 5,000—remained inside the plant, some out of loyalty to Ford, others fearful of venturing outside the plant gates once the strike was under way. As discipline crumbled, the garrison became a mob. Armed with steel bars and knives, blacks assaulted picket lines on several occasions. After the first assault, 150 unionists were treated at the UAW's "field hospital." Race relations were strained to the point where the UAW felt compelled to announce that it *too* had many black adherents. The union sought to allay the fears of the occupation forces through appeals over a public address system set up outside the plant. Walter White, president of the National Association for the Advancement of Colored People, was among those who addressed the blacks and promised safe conduct to those who would quit the plant. Only 200 to 300 of the black workers left.[35]

During the strike, Governor Van Wagoner served as a mediator. He was aided by Edsel Ford, who pleaded with his father to negotiate with the union, and by a NLRB announcement on April 7 that elections would be held within forty-five days to determine bargaining agents for the Rouge and Lincoln plants. On April 10 Ford accepted a settlement on terms proposed by Van Wagoner. The terms included reinstatement of five of the eight discharged committeemen; initiation of a grievance procedure; referral of unresolved disputes to a mediation board; suspension of pending NLRB hearings; and Ford consent to a speedy NLRB election. The labor and leftist press was jubilant. "The success achieved by the United Automobile Workers," observed the *Nation,* "is a historic victory for the American working class."[36]

Six weeks later, on May 21, after feverish canvassing in which Bennett worked for the AFL against the CIO, the NLRB elections were held at the Rouge and Lincoln plants. At the Rouge 51,886 voted for the CIO-affiliated union; 20,364 for the AFL; and 1,958 for no union. At Lincoln, 2,008 voted for the UAW-CIO; 587 for the AFL; and 146 for no union. The nonunion vote, only 2.6 percent at the Rouge and 5.3 percent at Lincoln, was, according to Charles Sorensen, "perhaps the greatest disappointment [Ford] had in all his business experience."[37]

The UAW-CIO held out an olive branch. "[We are] ready to draw the curtain on the past," said President R. J. Thomas. "We hope the Ford Motor Co. will do likewise. We are anxious to erase all bitterness." The answer to Thomas came from Bennett: "It's a great victory for the Communist Party, Gov. Murray Van Wagoner and the National Labor Relations Board. The law provides that we must live with them and we never violate the law." Bennett was seconded by Ford's attorney, who said that Ford "must now deal with a Communist-influenced and led organization . . . whose ultimate objective is, through strikes and turmoil, to produce that public confusion and bewilderment which is essential to a Communist seizure of government power in the United States."[38]

Nonetheless, the company negotiated with the union, and by June 18 a formal contract had been drawn up. Bennett showed the document to Ford who, after getting the "sense" of it, walked away. The next morning the auto magnate told Edsel and Sorensen that he would close the plant before he would sign a contract with the union. "Let the union take over." Sorensen pointed out that the company had large contracts with the government, and that if Ford closed his plants the government would reopen them under its management. "Well," replied Ford, "if the government steps in, it will be in the motorcar business and it won't be me." The next day, however, "Hell froze over in Dearborn," and newspapers announced in their biggest, blackest type that Ford and the UAW had signed an agreement.[39]

The UAW had asked for wage increases, abolition of Ford Service, a seniority system governing layoffs and rehiring, reinstatement of employees fired for union activity, overtime pay, a shop steward system and other features of standard UAW contracts. Although prepared to make concessions, the union obtained virtually everything it asked for; indeed "just about everything a union man dreams about." In addition to offering pay scales equal to the highest prevailing in the industry, Ford volunteered—to the astonishment of the union and the consternation of the auto industry—to operate his plants as a union shop (i.e., all employees would be required to join the union as a condition of employment) and to "check-off" union dues from the wages of each employee and transmit them to the UAW treasury. No other auto firm had agreed to such provisions. "Henry Ford," asserted *Business Week*, ". . . has made the CIO a full partner in the largest privately owned company in the world." Executives of other auto firms took a slightly different view. "Ford," one executive exclaimed in disgust, "has made a present of the whole goddamn industry to the UAW." In return for the concessions, the union agreed to withdraw all its charges pending before the NLRB and gave the company permission to stamp its products with the "union label." Edsel Ford explained the company's position: "No half-measures will be effective. We cannot work out one scheme of things for some of our workmen and another for the remainder. So we have decided to go the whole way."

"By giving the men everything they have asked for," Bennett added, "the company hopes it has eliminated every possible source of friction."[40]

Front-page news throughout the country, the agreement, according to *Newsweek,* "probably provoked as many gasps across the breakfast table as Ford's . . . $5-a-day wage." To the Associated Press the pact was "one of the greatest reversals of policy in industrial history"; to the *Cleveland Press* "one of the great milestones" in labor history; to *Christian Century* "one of the great landmarks in the history of organized labor"; to the *Christian Science Monitor* "one of the most sweeping events in the whole range of American labor history"; to the *Detroit News* "one of the biggest sensations in the history of American labor relations." Nearly all editorial comment was highly favorable to Ford. Many publications, in declaring that Ford "was smart in going all the way," compared the pact with other Ford announcements such as the five-dollar and seven-dollar days and the five-day week. All commentators agreed that "Henry had tossed another bombshell toward his rival motorcar manufacturers," and most felt that he had left his competitors in the ruck. "Once Ford passed 'em," a Nevada paper stated, "he passed at 90 mph."[41]

The company found, however, that it had bought a "fictitious labor peace." The UAW proved unable to control much of its Ford membership, and wildcat strikes, unauthorized slowdowns, and other labor disturbances halted production at one or another of Ford's plants almost every working day between July and December 1941. The situation was not greatly improved during World War II, for undisciplined employees, often antagonized by Bennett's heavy-handed tactics, provoked 733 work stoppages between 1941 and 1945.[42]

During the war, opinion surveys showed that the public, which undoubtedly was influenced by the publicity accompanying the 1941 pact, regarded Ford as the auto firm which "treats its workers best." *Workers* who were polled by Elmo Roper in 1944 shared this view, but, significantly, *unionists* who were surveyed did not.[43]

A number of reasons have been advanced as to why Ford "capitulated." Some observers felt that he could not stand to see his plants idle, and had decided that if the men really wanted a union they could have one. Others reasoned that the manufacturer could not afford the public censure that would result if he closed his plants just as the nation's rearmament program was getting into high gear. Still others suggest that Ford gave in because he realized that he could no longer fight off the NLRB and the union and that he feared that publicity from subsequent hearings would damage his prestige. This last view gains substance from the fact that an NLRB examination which would "dwarf all previous hearings" was scheduled to begin in Detroit in the summer of 1941 and it undoubtedly would have injured Ford's reputation. It has also been suggested that Ford was concerned about his squabbles with the War Department and his share of the auto market, which had fallen from 22.9 percent in 1939 to 19.8 percent in 1940. Supporters of this view reason that the industrialist, who over the years had alienated a number of important car-buying groups, including Jews, fervent New Dealers, tobacco manufacturers and their agents, and breweries, and who in the late 1930s was the target of a boycott by the CIO, no longer could afford the luxury of complete independence. It has also been said that Ford thought he could steal a march on his competitors, especially General

Motors, by "joining forces" with the union. Bennett expressed this view shortly after the contract was signed, remarking, "They're [the UAW] damn near partners in this thing now." In 1942 Ford told Reuther that "it was one of the most sensible things Harry Bennett ever did when he got the UAW into this plant."

"Well, I think so but I didn't think you did, Mr. Ford," smiled Reuther. "How do you figure it?"

"Well," said Ford, "you've been fighting General Motors and the Wall Street crowd. Now you're in here and we've given you a union shop and more than you got out of them. That puts you on our side, doesn't it? We can fight General Motors and Wall Street together, eh?"[44]

Perhaps the real reason for the capitulation (according to Sorensen) was that Ford's wife threatened to leave him if he did not give ground. About six weeks after the settlement was announced, Ford told Sorensen that he had informed his wife on June 19 that he had decided to close the plant. Clara Ford, who shared her son's, not her husband's, views regarding labor strife, was "horrified." She told her husband that if he did not sign with the union there would be riots and bloodshed and that he would have to choose between closing the plants and keeping the woman to whom he had been married for fifty-three years.

"What," Ford told Sorensen, "could I do?"[45]

Chapter 16
Isolationism

Just as prescient observers might have predicted that individualist Henry Ford would oppose the New Deal and organized labor, they might also have predicted that pacifist Henry Ford would support efforts in the 1930s and early 1940s to promote peace and to keep America out of war. When the League of Nations imposed economic sanctions on Italy, after Mussolini's attack on Ethiopia in 1935, the industrialist halted delivery of 800 Ford trucks for which the invaders had already made payment. Ford maintained his stand even after the League backed down on its sanctions, prompting General Rudolfo Graziani to tell his countrymen that his drive on Addis Ababa had been held up because the auto manufacturer was a "private sanctionist." Ford paid a price for his pacifism. Mussolini, who in 1932 had commanded King Victor Emmanuel III to award Ford the Degree of Grand Official of the Order of the Crown of Italy, the highest decoration his country could confer on a foreigner, imposed such stringent restrictions on the Ford Company's Italian operations that they were all but wiped out.[1]

As war clouds gathered in Europe in 1939, Ford issued a statement on pacifism for use in the "moral rearmament" drive of the Oxford group, which, under the leadership of Dr. Frank N. D. Buchman, made peace and understanding among nations a prime objective. Shortly before World War II began, Ford also endorsed America's "Neutrality Act." "Why should we go over there and help out their mess," he declared, "when it's just created by financiers?" The manufacturer refused to believe that war was imminent. On August 29 he told reporters that the European countries "don't dare have a war, and they know it. It's all a big bluff." Three days later German tanks rolled into Poland.[2]

With Europe at war, Ford spoke out vigorously against America's participation in the conflict. On a number of occasions he reaffirmed his strong support of the Neutrality Act, and in late September 1939 he helped to dramatize the American Legion's "Keep the United States Out of War" theme by attending the organization's national convention in Chicago. As the industrialist made a theatrical entrance on the convention floor, flanked by members of the company's Dearborn American Legion Post, the audience rose and applauded enthusiastically for ten minutes (the longest ovation of the convention). On one of his rare appearances as a speaker, Ford told the legionnaires, "I think it is my greatest honor to be here with you today," and sat down to more thunderous applause. Later, he told reporters that "this so-called war is nothing but about 25 people and propaganda—get them and you have the whole thing." When newsmen asked Ford what he thought of war production in Ford's Canadian plants, the magnate laughed and replied, "I'll tell you what I think about Canada. Canada should belong to us. They'd be much better off."[3]

Continuing to support pacifism and neutrality and to press his attack on "war profiteers" during the remainder of 1939 and into 1940–41, Ford also expressed the hope that neither the Allies nor the Axis would win. The United States, he suggested at one point, should give the Allies and the Axis "the tools to keep on fighting until they both collapse." In the fall of 1940 the manufacturer became a member of the America First Committee, which had been launched in the summer of 1940 in answer to the Committee to Defend America by Aiding the Allies. Headed by General Robert E. Wood, chairman of the board of Sears, Roebuck and Company, America First included among its influential membership Charles A. Lindbergh, Hugh S. Johnson, Mrs. Alice Roosevelt Longworth, Eddie Rickenbacker, Chester B. Bowles, Norman M. Thomas, Lillian Gish, John T. Flynn, Kathleen Norris, Irwin S. Cobb, and John P. Marquand. The Committee deliberately announced the memberships of Ford and Lessing J. Rosenwald, a director of Sears, Roebuck and a leader in the Chicago Jewish community, on the same day—to indicate that persons with opposing views regarding Germany could unite under the America First banner (Ford frequently expressed pro-German sentiments during the prewar era; Rosenwald shared Jewish antipathy toward the Reich). Rosenwald's identification with Ford was bitterly resented by many Jews. As a result of pressure applied by members of his faith, he resigned from the committee in December 1940. Ford himself was dropped from America First in January 1941. "He let us use his name in the beginning," said General Wood, "but he never contributed to the organization nor has he communicated with us." Wood added that his own attempts to reach Ford had been in vain.[4]

In the spring of 1940, as Nazi forces invaded Denmark, Norway, the Low Countries, and France, President Roosevelt called for an intensification of defense activities. Henry Ford, up to this point, had scoffed at the "phony war"; but in the late spring of 1940 it apparently was obvious to him as well as to others that the German conquests threatened the security of the United States. On May 28, twelve days after President Roosevelt had proposed to increase aircraft production to 50,000 planes a year, the manufacturer told one of his favorite newsmen, David J. Wilkie, of the Associated Press, that "if it becomes necessary the Ford Motor Company could—with the counsel of men like Lindbergh and Rickenbacker, under our own supervision and without meddling by government agencies—swing into the production of a thousand airplanes of standard design a day." When Wilkie suggested that such a figure was unheard of, Ford replied, "So was 10,000 motor-cars a day, but we did it; so was the production of one eagle boat a day during the World War, but we did it." Ford added that it would take about six months to reach this level of production. There was no mention of Ford's oft-repeated insistence that he would produce war materials only for the defense of America.[5]

The interview was flashed around the world. In France, government officials made plans to distribute thousands of reprints of Ford's statements throughout their beleaguered country "to bolster morale" and to drop thousands more over the Reich "to scare the devil" out of the enemy. In Britain, the Ministry of Aircraft Production instructed its representatives in America to investigate the possibility of purchasing planes from Ford. In America, Eddie Rickenbacker, when asked by reporters whether Ford could build 1,000 planes a day, replied, "I'm sure Henry Ford didn't exaggerate." Responding to the same question, William S. Knudsen, ex-president of

General Motors, who had assumed responsibility for production on the National Defense Advisory Committee, stated, ''If Mr. Ford says he can, I guess he can.'' When asked if General Motors could also produce 1,000 planes a day, Knudsen replied, ''I guess we could if we had plans for it.'' Carl Heine, the ex-manager of the Ford Company's German operations, also expressed faith in Ford's statement. ''There is no doubt,'' he informed the German government in a report which contributed to his conviction in 1941 on espionage charges, ''that Henry Ford can make good his promise.''[6]

Aircraft manufacturers, who scoffed at the idea of mass-producing planes and who looked upon the auto industry as interlopers in their own field, expressed incredulity at Ford's offer. Their retort that Ford's—or anybody else's—promise to build 1,000 planes per day amounted to ''sheer fantasy'' was, in fact, borne out in World War II by the experience of airplane manufacturers, Ford included. In 1940, however, the press gave Ford the benefit of any doubt. Indeed, many newspapers, as they noted the air strength of the Axis, looked to Ford as a ''national savior.'' ''Henry Can Save Us,'' ''Ford Can Make 'Em,'' ''Why Not Take Henry at His Word?,'' and ''Planes While You Wait'' sang out the headlines, and the copy which followed assured readers that ''Henry isn't talking through his hat'' and recommended that the government ''ought to give Henry Ford his own way.'' ''The American people,'' stated the *Port Huron* (Michigan) *Times-Herald* in an editorial typical of many, ''want this offer taken up now—immediately—at once. All government officialdom should be thrown into the discard. This is a time when people who don't know anything about mass production should keep their hands off and their fingers out.''[7]

The Ford announcement produced a swift response from the American government. At the request of Secretary of the Treasury Henry Morgenthau, Jr., Edsel Ford met with government officials in Washington on May 29 to discuss plane production. The group also discussed the possibility that Ford might build aircraft engines. The following week Henry Ford expressed interest in examining a pursuit plane of the kind the country would need in an emergency. Delighted with the industrialist's show of interest, the government sent a plane to Dearborn—and another wave of news stories and editorials about Ford's grandiose production plans swept the country. The plane arrived on June 10 and was immediately examined by Henry, Edsel, and manufacturing executive Charles E. Sorensen. After the inspection, the elder Ford told newsmen that ''the Rouge can turn out at least one thousand such air fighters a day.'' Newspapers throughout the country again publicized the manufacturer's words, hundreds of them running photographs of the ''genius of mass production'' examining the craft. Some papers, however, expressed concern over a possible shortage of pilots to man Ford's planes. Noting that only 7,000 pilots were to be trained annually by the Army Air Corps, the *Binghamton* (New York) *Sun* typically snorted, ''That's fine. It will take Henry Ford just seven days to furnish planes for all of them.'' The press also noted that Ford had repeatedly emphasized that his planes ''are to be for defense only; that's the bargain all the way through.'' The *Windsor* (Ontario) *Daily Star* tarried over the words ''defense only,'' then in a burst of wishful thinking concluded that Ford meant that ''Ford planes with Allied pilots over the German areas would be for 'defense only' of the United States.''[8]

At Knudsen's request, the younger Ford went to Washington on June 11 to confer about plane production. Shelving the idea of producing a complete plane, Knudsen proposed instead that Ford build 9,000 Rolls-Royce aircraft engines, 6,000 for the British government, 3,000 for the American government. Sorensen, who was summoned from a Florida vacation to examine the Rolls-Royce engine, and Edsel viewed the assignment with enthusiasm. They discussed the proposal with the elder Ford, pointing out that most of the order was for the British government. The magnate, notwithstanding his pronouncements against producing war materials for other nations, agreed to go ahead with the project.[9]

On June 19 Lord Beaverbrook, Britain's aircraft minister for aircraft production, proclaimed that the Ford Company had agreed to produce 6,000 airplane engines for his country. Henry Ford, when informed of Beaverbrook's announcement, huffed: "We are not doing business with the British Government," adding that any engines he made would have to be on order from the American government. Knudsen, when questioned, said that it had been made clear to the Ford Company that 6,000 of the engines were for the Allies, and that Edsel Ford had agreed to such an arrangement. Edsel himself was stunned by his father's reversal. "We wouldn't have made these commitments," he remonstrated during a lengthy and heated discussion with his father, "if you hadn't expressed yourself in favor." On June 24 the elder Ford summoned Knudsen, Sorensen, and Edsel. The magnate was cordial toward Knudsen, but warned him that he was "mixed up with some bad people in Washington" and was heading for trouble. He then told the government official that he wouldn't make any engines for Britain. Knudsen replied that he had Ford's word that he would make them. "I told the President of your decision, and he was very happy about it." The mention of Roosevelt was unfortunate, inasmuch as Ford had an almost "psychopathic" dislike for the chief executive. "We won't build the engine at all," Ford snapped. "Withdraw the whole order. Take it to someone else." Knudsen left Ford "purple with rage," and later informed the press that "co-operation in the production of this important military equipment will be sought elsewhere."[10]

Press comment on Ford's decision not to build engines for Britain reflected several points of view. Many newspapers reasoned that the magnate's pacifistic attitude was "unfortunate" and that he should recognize that "the first line of defense is across the sea." "What Mr. Ford does not appear to grasp," stated the *Brunswick* (Georgia) *News,* in an editorial typical of those critical of the industrialist, "is that U.S. help for England is the best possible way of defending this country against invasion by a foreign power." An even greater number of newspapers commented on both sides of the question. After congratulating Ford on being "more scrupulous in his neutrality than are most of the rest of us, including the government," these publications went on to question whether Ford "would not in time regret that he did not help a gallant country maintain a barrier to a threat to our security." But perhaps the majority of the press approved of the auto magnate's decision. "A lot of Americans . . . sympathize with Great Britain," declared the *Detroit News,* ". . . but they want—above everything else—to keep the United States out [of war]." "Mr. Ford," echoed the *Lansing* (Michigan) *State Journal,* "has always been pretty much for America, first, last and always . . . . And in that statement of creed he has a lot of company."[11]

Canadians and Britons, who of course were more directly affected by Ford's decision than were Americans, vehemently denounced the Dearbornite. In Canada, M. J. Coldwell, acting leader of the Co-operative Commonwealth Federation (CCF party), advocated the seizure of the Canadian properties of "this highly-placed saboteur." F. B. Black, a Conservative member of the Canadian Senate, said the government should cancel all purchases of Ford cars and forbid their sale in Canada. T. L. Church, a House Conservative, stated that Ford was "a menace to freedom and civilization" who should be kept out of Canada for all time. The Toronto Retail Fuel Dealers Association passed a resolution calling on members to boycott Ford vehicles and to refuse to handle Ford coke. Munitions Minister C. D. Howe, of the governing Liberal Party, informed his countrymen that "Henry Ford has taken an attitude that is distinctly unfriendly to the British empire and every part of it." At the same time Howe pointed out that Ford Motor Company of Canada was "beyond criticism" in cooperating with the government. The munitions minister having led the way, many prominent Canadians, including the Liberal and Conservative leaders in the Senate, stepped forward to commend Ford of Canada for its contribution to the war effort. Also, they pointed out that while a boycott of Ford products would hurt Henry Ford but little, it would prove very harmful to those Canadian citizens who owned Ford of Canada stock or owned or worked in Ford dealerships. The House of Commons dropped debate on the subject on a note sounded by Conservative Leader R. B. Hanson: "Public opinion in Canada . . . will deal with Mr. Henry Ford." Ford himself was unmoved by threats from Canada to boycott his car. "Anyone who would do that," he retorted, "is a sugar tit" (sugar tied up in a nipple-shaped cloth for a child to suck). Nonetheless, shortly thereafter, Ford of Canada felt compelled to substitute another name for the Ford car."[12]

In Britain the *London Daily Mirror* called Ford a "crab apple" and said that his claims regarding the manufacture of 1,000 planes a day was "balderdash" anyway. The *London Daily Mail* cabled Ford that the general feeling toward him among Britons was one of consternation and distress. Prompted by Sir Percival Perry, the managing director of Ford of England, the industrialist replied that the Ford plants in Canada and England were using their facilities to the utmost for the defense of the British Empire and would continue to serve their countries "as they should." Ford might have added that his British plant already had a contract to build the same Rolls-Royce engines that he would not permit his American factories to produce, a point generally overlooked in the press.[13]

At the same time that Ford's message was carried in the *Daily Mail,* Ford of England, in a further effort to repair the public relations damage, placed advertisements in London dailies stating that "the vast resources, human and mechanical, of the great Dagenham factory are engaged on urgent national work to the utmost." When Perry suggested to Henry and Edsel that they might help in the Battle of Britain by furnishing a fleet of fully equipped food vans for bombed areas, they agreed. During 1941 the Fords gave 450 "blitz canteens," worth approximately $770,000, to the British people.[14]

On August 12, 1940, Knudsen offered the company a second opportunity in defense production: the building of 4,000 Pratt & Whitney eighteen-cylinder air-cooled aircraft engines. Henry Ford, after some wavering, since he preferred to design his own motors, accepted the assignment. An aircraft engine factory was built within the Rouge complex "so as to be indistinguishable from other buildings in the event it becomes a military objective." By August 1941, completed engines were being produced. By year's end 323 motors had been built and shipped to the Glenn L. Martin Company, of Baltimore, for the B-26 bomber. At the time America entered the war the company held contracts for $328,275,690 worth of engines and the facilities with which to manufacture them.[15]

Ford also undertook a number of other defense assignments during 1940–41. In the fall of 1940 the company erected at its own expense a naval training station at the Rouge. On January 15, 1941, Henry and Edsel, speaking over two national radio networks, formally presented the installation to Rear Admiral Chester W. Nimitz, chief of the Navy Department's Bureau of Navigation. By November 1941, two thousand men were in training at the facility. In addition, the company assisted in the development of the Jeep and produced 1,500 of these vehicles; designed a "swamp buggy"; built 1,500 reconnaissance vehicles; and assisted in the design and manufacture of the M-4 medium tank. The M-4's engine, an adaptation of a motor the company began to build in June 1940 for use in Henry Ford's hypothetical 1,000-a-day pursuit plane, soon became the standard power unit for all of the nation's medium tanks. The company also investigated the possibility of mass producing an antiaircraft gun director, and was awarded a contract for 400 such devices in October 1941.[16]

By far the biggest military assignment that Ford was to undertake during the prewar and war period—and the one with which it would be most closely identified in the public mind—was the production of B-24 bombers (also called the Liberator). This project was begun in December 1940, when government officials asked the company if it would build 1,200 B-24's (the bomber already was being produced by its designer, Consolidated Aircraft, and Douglas Aircraft Company). Henry Ford agreed to consider the proposal and dispatched Edsel, Sorensen, and two grandsons, Henry, twenty-three, and Benson, twenty-one, who were working in the company's Engineering Department, to Consolidated's San Diego plant. Officials of Consolidated told the Ford group that they had set as a goal the production of one bomber a day. Sorensen, after examining the plant, expressed doubt that the production methods employed would permit attainment of this quota. When asked by Consolidated executives "how would you do it," the Rouge boss, who had to "put-up or shut-up," worked all night on a unique plan to produce bombers on assembly lines. At breakfast, Sorensen showed a penciled sketch of his plan to Edsel, won his approval, and then told government and Consolidated officials that the Ford Company would build a factory capable of turning out one B-24 an hour, if the Air Force would provide $200,000,000 for plant and equipment. The government accepted the proposal, and Consolidated agreed to give Ford a license to produce the plane. Later, Henry Ford endorsed the project.[17]

Ford was to undertake production of planes in three stages. Certain parts were to be made at first for "educational" purposes; then all parts of the plane were to be made, and these were to be supplied to Consolidated and Douglas for assembly in new plants to be erected in Tulsa and Fort Worth. The third step called for Ford to build entire planes. The company received formal authorization to build a bomber factory in February 1941. In April it broke ground for the famed Willow Run bomber plant (named for the tiny stream that flows through the property), located four miles southeast of Ypsilanti, Michigan, twenty-one miles from the Rouge. Limited parts production started at the plant in November. The first schedule of 100 "knockdown" sets of bombers a month, fixed on May 20, 1941, was raised in September to 205 units per month (sixty-five each for Consolidated and Douglas—and seventy-five flyaways). But when the Japanese struck Pearl Harbor, no part of the plant was completed; the landing field was unfinished; most of the necessary machine tools were undelivered; and the work force was almost nonexistent.[18]

All told, the Ford Company had completed or held government contracts worth $975,146,107 at the time of the attack on Pearl Harbor. Within a week of America's declaration of war, the company had adopted a continuous work schedule for all activities associated with defense production and construction. In January 1942 the firm was, according to R. J. Thomas, president of the UAW-CIO, further advanced on its war-production program than any of the other large auto companies. Civilian car production, sharply curtailed during the last half of 1941, ground to a halt at the Rouge on February 10, 1942. An Army Jeep followed the last passenger car off the line.[19]

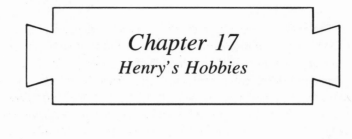

Chapter 17
Henry's Hobbies

1

In the 1930s Henry Ford, while embroiled in events of national importance and still supervising the Ford Motor Company, devoted more and more of his time to his hobbies. His business interests were focused mainly on engineering activities. But even in this sphere most of the ideas came from the Ford organization, not the founder. In all company matters Ford still had the last word, of course, but many decisions were reached without his participation. Meanwhile Edsel had achieved a position of considerable strength in the firm, had virtually a free hand in styling, sales, and advertising, and, in general, administered the business. His septuagenarian father therefore had more leisure for extracurricular activities.[1]

Ford's lessening interest in the company was reflected in the firm's lackluster performance as compared with the golden years of the 'teens and the 'twenties. The V-8 outsold the Chevrolet in 1935 and came within a few thousand units of outselling its principal rival in 1934 and 1937. But after the mid-1930s the Ford Company took a declining share of the auto market and consistently ran behind the Chrysler Corporation, as well as General Motors, in unit sales.[2]

In an effort to compete more successfully, Ford introduced several new cars during the 1930s. The first of the new models was the Lincoln Zephyr, unveiled in November 1935 to fill a gap in the medium-price field. The Zephyr contributed importantly to a seven-fold increase in Lincoln sales in 1936 and a high water mark of Lincoln registrations in 1937 (25,243). Then the model declined in popularity. Meanwhile, the Zephyrs hurt the sale of the "regular" Lincoln which dwindled to hundreds.[3]

Lincoln's models were supplemented in late 1939 by the luxurious Lincoln Continental. Designed to the specifications of Edsel Ford, who wanted an American-built car which would "suggest something of the low, slender effect which leading stylists of the foreign field had achieved," the Continental was too expensive to attract a wide market. In fact, only 5,322 of the cars were produced between 1939 and 1948, when the model was discontinued. The car won many admirers, however, and there was general agreement among dealers, designers, and automobile collectors that it had a striking design. Today, the 1940–48 Continentals are among the most prestigious of motordom's "classic cars" and, as such, are avidly sought by classic-car enthusiasts.[4]

At the opposite end of the Ford price scale was another new product, the sixty-horsepower "standard" V-8, introduced in November 1936. The "thrifty sixty," as it was advertised, accounted for almost one-third of the V-8's sales in 1937. But the newer model's popularity sagged, and in 1940 it accounted for only 3.6 percent of all V-8 sales and was discontinued.[5]

The most important of Ford's new entries in the automotive market was the Mercury, designed to fill a gap between the deluxe Ford and the Zephyr. Introduced in October 1938, the ninety-five-horsepower Mercury resembled the V-8 in general design (its larger frame and more powerful motor were, in fact, adapted from the V-8). The new car was well received by the public, and although called "an over-grown Ford" by some, it achieved a respectable 65,884 sales in 1939.[6]

Despite the introduction of four new models between 1935–39 (a greater number than during the quarter-century preceding 1935) and the creditable sale of the "original" V-8, the Ford Company made a poor financial showing during the prewar decade. Between 1933–41, in fact, it earned an estimated profit of only $32,000,000. Its assets in 1941 were $23,000,000 less than in 1927 (when Hornblower and Weeks offered to buy the company for $1,000,000,000).[7]

Inevitably, as the company drifted into third rank in the auto industry, people cast about for an explanation. Many factors contributed to the company's decline; but perhaps none was more important than Henry Ford's failure to create a system of administration which could guide the company efficiently through style changes, the labor problems of the 1930s, the growth of government controls, and the conversion to war production. No man had done more than Henry Ford to concentrate industrial power and accelerate production. Yet no leader in manufacturing had clung more stubbornly to an antiquated administrative system totally unequal to the demands of the new era. Thus, in a sense, the Ford Company had to fight not only its competitors but also its own leader's outdated ways of doing business. Henry Ford's vitality during most of this period was extraordinary, despite a mild stroke which he suffered in 1938 at age seventy-five. But the industrialist channeled only part of his energies into business affairs. Had he always given his company priority over his hobbies, his firm might have competed more successfully. (It can also be argued that the company would have been better off if Old Henry had completely retired from the business at about age seventy, and permitted Edsel and others to run it.) In any event, from the early 1930s onward, Ford was far more interested in the Edison Institute, his "village industries," farming, soybean and plastics experimentation, schools, and the development of a new tractor than he was in administering the Ford Motor Company.[8]

In a lengthy article, entitled, "Mr. Ford Doesn't Care," *Fortune* told of a typical day in Henry Ford's life in 1933. It bears repeating in some detail because it was typical of Ford's days for a decade to follow. The auto magnate, the magazine noted, had "no set program [and] does whatever may come into his head." His "headquarters," insofar as he had one, was W. J. Cameron's office in the Engineering Laboratory, adjacent to the Edison Institute (in later years it would be in Harry Bennett's office in the Administration building). If Ford had a visitor, he was much more likely to show him through the institute, rather than the Rouge, formerly his favorite haunt. Even visitorless, the industrialist was wont to wander over to the museum, where he might listen to a tune from a music box; or stroll through Greenfield Village to listen to children singing in the village school; or call for a fiddler to play "while he skips through the measures of an old-time waltz, all by himself." Then, according to the magazine, he might summon a V-8 (Ford usually rode in Lincolns only when with distinguished guests) and "go tearing down state at sixty miles an hour'' to Macon, Michigan, where he had some 7,400 acres of soybeans. After "talking farming with farmers" and provided he didn't wander off to one of his rural schools or village plants, Ford returned to the Engineering Laboratory for a late lunch, at which he would often discuss business with Edsel, Sorensen, and other executives. After lunch, he was likely to repeat several of his morning's activities. In the evening, at his nearby estate, Fair Lane, he perhaps would stroll around the premises, "from time to time chinning himself from some handy low-hanging branch, then striding on briskly." Friday evenings, the magazine added, were reserved for Ford's square dances. His typical day, *Fortune* might have concluded, was heavily weighted in favor of nonautomotive activities.[9]

Ford's outside interests had several common characteristics. They served as a drain on the Ford Company's none-too-robust exchequer. They could trace their origins to the predepression years—to Ford's extraordinarily creative phase in the 'teens and the 'twenties. They also were far removed from the large-scale manufacturing which for so many years had been at the vortex of Ford's life. Finally, they were closely related to rural America except for the Edison Institute; and even the institute had strong rural and small-town threads.

2

Each of the magnate's hobbies was well publicized, and the Edison Institute—for years commonly called "Greenfield Village"—was the best publicized of all. Of all Ford's outside activities, Greenfield Village was the closest to his heart. It memorialized his most treasured friend, Edison, and it symbolized much of what Ford valued most in life. He spent freely on it—more than $30,000,000. "It will never pay for itself," Ford told an aide during the early 1930s. "But," he added, with a twinkle in his eye, "you can't beat it as indirect advertising." About this time the auto magnate also informed a reporter that he "wouldn't be surprised" if as many as 300,000 people a year visited the village. The village was the subject of hundreds of newspaper stories and at least a dozen full-length magazine articles during the prewar decade. Much of the publicity centered around the historical importance and vastness of the institute. J. G. de Roulhac Hamilton, who investigated the still incomplete facility in 1931 at the request of the *American Historical Review,* said the institute had "every promise of becoming one of the most notable collections in the world of relics." *The Rotarian* declared in 1934 that the village was "probably the most complete and interesting visual presentation of America's social and industrial development," while *Etude* in 1936 expressed certainty that it would become "a great shrine of America." In 1936 the *New Republic* noted that "this extraordinary enterprise" was more complete in many departments than the famous Deutsches Museum in Munich, and the following year the *Saturday Evening Post* reported that Ford had "recaptured the nineteenth century." Taking a slightly different tack, *House and Garden* in 1941 concluded, "Henry Ford is at once an ideal collector and a collectors' ideal. His collection is all-inclusive yet never complete, and he has the means to acquire what most collectors can't—a place big enough to display it."[10]

Throughout the 1930s, Ford continued to make important acquisitions. Several of them focused nationwide attention on the historical center. In 1934 Ford bought a house in Pittsburgh in which Stephen Collins Foster allegedly had lived. As the industrialist was preparing to move the dwelling to Dearborn, the mayor of Pittsburgh declared that Ford had bought the wrong house. His statement was seconded by Foster's biographer, John Tasker Howard, who, while conceding the land on which the house stood had been owned by Foster's father, pointed out that there was "little documentary evidence" to support the claim that the homestead was ever occupied by Stephen Foster himself. Ford's agents, the biographer suggested "had been misled and failed to exercise due caution in examining evidence" (which consisted mostly of the recollections of elderly Pittsburghers, who, themselves, could only repeat what their parents had told them about the house). To judge for himself, Ford, who perhaps was pleased with the furore, made two well publicized trips to Pittsburgh; expressed his faith in the house and ordered it removed to Dearborn. On July 4, 1935, the house—in the presence of seventy of Foster's descendants and a sizable press corps—was formally added to the Greenfield Village collection. One of Foster's granddaughters lit "a perpetual monument of fire" in a stove inside the house and a sign, "The Birthplace of Stephen Foster," was hung above the front door.[11]

Just as stubborn as Ford, Mrs. Evelyn Foster Morneweck, a niece of Stephen Foster, returned to the attack in 1937. In a pamphlet, *The Birthplace of Stephen C. Foster As Recorded by His Father, Mother and Brother, and Other Contemporary Authorities,* she castigated the industrialist for "ruthlessly" setting aside her father's memories "of the actual Foster house." Mr. Ford, she added, might have displayed the house as a memorial to Foster: "But no, Mr. Ford's radio announcer, Mr. Truman Bradley [the dedication ceremony was broadcast nationwide], declared that it was 'not a reproduction but the actual little White Cottage in which Stephen C. Foster was born.' " Ford ignored the blast. Two years later, movie producer Darryl F. Zanuck, apparently unaware of the controversy, asked Ford if he could shoot pictures of the house for a movie, *Suwanee River,* based on the life of the composer. Ford agreed. In Pittsburgh, however, Zanuck's agents, while gathering biographical information, were told by the Foster Memorial Library that Ford's house "was just another house"; that "Foster was not born in it, never lived in it and probably never saw it." Zanuck retreated, shooting the entire film on location in Sacramento, California. Undaunted, Ford kept his sign.

A few years after the auto magnate's death, the trustees of Greenfield Village, wishing to clear up the controversy, engaged a professional historian, Milo M. Quaife, secretary of Detroit's Burton Historical Collection, to determine whether Foster had or had not been born in the house. Quaife sided with Mrs. Morneweck, concluding that the Foster birthplace had been torn down in 1865 and that Henry Ford's agents either "ignored or could not properly interpret the available documentary evidence" when they purchased the building. Deferring to Quaife's report, for years after 1953 the cottage was referred to as the "Stephen C. Foster Memorial." In 1963, however, a village spokesman indicated that the question of Foster's birthplace, while dormant, may not be dead. "We are not saying that we accept either side [in the dispute] absolutely," he declared. "We don't know what further historical research will reveal." In 1971, the village installed a new sign in front of the house declaring that the structure was Foster's birthplace.[12]

Perhaps the best publicized single event identified with Greenfield Village during the 1930s was the dedication of the house and cycle shop in which Wilbur and Orville Wright had lived and built their first airplane. For the ceremony, held on April 16, 1938, more than 200 airplane designers and manufacturers, explorers, army air force officers, and pioneer aviators were assembled, among them Orville Wright, Igor Sikorsky, Alexander P. de Seversky, Glenn L. Martin, Sir Hubert Wilkins, Vilhjalmur Stefansson, and Major James H. Doolittle. Broadcast nationally, the event was reported in newspapers throughout the country. Photographs appeared showing Henry Ford and Orville Wright inspecting the shop together.[13]

Between 1935 and 1942, the village also was publicized by a weekly fifteen-minute radio program originating from its chapel. The program, which broadcast the chapel service held for children who attended Ford's Village School, was presented without charge by more than fifty stations of the Columbia Broadcasting System. It was discontinued after the outbreak of war.[14]

Aided by publicity, Greenfield Village rapidly became a leading tourist attraction. Paid attendance totaled 243,000 in 1934 (the first year a count was made) and increased steadily to 633,000 in 1940, dropping to 621,000 in 1941. The village remained open during the war, but drew an average of only 178,000 visitors per year between 1942–45. Attendance showed a steady increase during the postwar era, exceeding the million mark for the first time in 1960. Among Detroit area tourist attractions, only the admission-free Ford Rotunda (destroyed by fire in 1962) drew more visitors than the village during the postwar years. Attendance was 1,651,464 in 1975, slightly below the all-time attendance record set in 1973—1,701,559.[15]

Today, Greenfield Village—described by John Gunther as "one of the most singular sights in the United States"—contains the world's largest collection of Americana. Its museum features a gallery that traces the development of American furniture and decorations from the settlement of the country to the present; five blocks of American shops of the eighteenth and nineteenth century; a mechanical arts section featuring exhibits related to transportation, agriculture, crafts, industrial machinery, steam and electric power, communications, and lighting; and a section containing the memorabilia of Henry Ford's life. The museum's automobile collection is world famous, its pottery and porcelain collection is one of the most comprehensive in the country, its clock and watch collection is one of the largest in the world, and its early American glass collection is more extensive than any other museum's. The "out-door" museum contains more than 100 historic buildings on a 200-acre site. Visitors can tour the area in a horse-drawn carriage (or a sleigh in the winter); have their tintype taken; see a glass blower, a blacksmith, a candle-maker, and a silkworm farmer at work; and take a ride on the stern-wheeler *Suwanee* or on a 1913 merry-go-round.

The village has been justly criticized for lacking coherence and for reflecting Ford's and his chief assistants lack of historical knowledge and perspective. Keith Sward, while praising some details of the exhibit, suggests that the "striving for sheer mass and for something of everything" produced a "hodge-podge" with "the appearance of an Old Curiosity Shop, magnified 10,000-fold." Nevins and Hill agree with this assessment, adding that the exhibit suffers because "the tremendously varied exhibits were not related to any clear central idea."[16]

3

If Greenfield Village was the "hobby" dearest to Ford's heart, his rural activities during the 1920s and 1930s were almost equally absorbing.

His village industries, which kept Ford in close touch with rural America during the 1920s, were not a financial success. But between 1935 and 1941, the auto magnate, in support of his one-foot-in-industry, one-foot-in-agriculture, America-is-safe theory, added a dozen rural hydroelectric plants to the ten already in operation. Aside from Ford's oft-quoted public statements on the village industry idea, the plants were discussed in numerous technical, business, and general magazines during the decade after 1935. Several of the publications shared Ford's own optimistic appraisal of his small factories. The *Reader's Digest* stated in 1938 that "beyond all room for argument, Ford has proved that the decentralization program is practical, that many kinds of work are done better in small plants where everybody from manager to sweeper can concentrate on specialized problems. . . . If other manufacturers learn this lesson, in a few years there will be hundreds of village industries scattered through the industrial states." The following year the *Christian Science Monitor Magazine* offered the "bright, shining faces" of the plants' employees as "proof of the success of Henry Ford's experiments," while the *Saturday Evening Post* in 1944 cited low overhead, a minimum of labor turnover, and first-rate workmanship as reasons for the "success" of the plants.[17] Despite these glowing accounts, village industries did not proliferate throughout the land. Indeed, Henry Ford's own rural plants were steadily phased out after the founder's retirement in 1945. All of the village plants are still standing in 1976, however, and nearly all of them are in active use—as manufacturing units, antique shops, community/youth centers, and county maintenance facilities. Most of the factories-in-the-meadows remain astride their picturesque dams, spillways, headraces, tailraces, and millponds. Some of the plants are still equipped with their original waterwheels and generators, while others retain two additional Ford plant hallmarks—pipe-filled tunnels (to facilitate pipe maintenance) and wooden block floors, which Ford believed were easier on his workers' feet than concrete or other rigid surfaces. Old Henry's plants may have died, but they have not faded into oblivion.[18]

In most of the communities in which he had small plants Ford also built and operated a one-room school. "His fifteen schools and the country around them," observed *School and Society* in 1934, "are his playground." Noting that the manufacturer had visited his Macon school six times in one month, the magazine added that it was "hard to see how a man with so many worldwide interests (though he says he has nothing to do) can take the time, but he does not hesitate to put off a group of officials in order to visit one of his schools."[19]

Ford hoped to develop schools which would "make for invention and for leadership." He believed that the student who saw and worked with "actual objects and machines" would be better able to invent and create than the student who only read about them. He also believed strongly in the vocational-school concept of learning by doing. The industrialist's rural schools combined the old-fashioned and the modern. They had one room and one teacher for all twelve grades (after 1938, however, ninth through twelfth grade students of several of the schools attended a Ford-operated "country high school"). No foreign languages, "no art but the utilitarian, and no literature for its own sake" were taught. Yet specialists were regularly sent to the schools to teach music, dancing, nature studies, telegraphy, and agriculture. Each student was furnished a hoe and a rake and expected to tend a preplowed and planted garden plot. Proceeds from the crop were kept by the student.[20]

Ford's unorthodox ideas about education and his quaint schools naturally attracted considerable attention. Between 1932 and 1944, ten national magazines and twenty-two educational publications carried articles on the industrialist's educational activities, and there was also a steady stream of newspaper articles about them. However, after his retirement, the schools fared worse than even his village plants. All of them, except the Greenfield Village school, were closed and/or turned over to the school districts in which they were located in 1946–47. The high school unit within the Greenfield Village school was abandoned in 1952, the elementary unit in 1969.[21]

4

Ford's interest in relating scientific technology to agriculture, which led to his extensive soybean experimentation and research into plastics, was keyed to his lifelong efforts to improve the lot of the farmer. As early as 1907 the industrialist experimented with an "automobile plow," hoping to ease the farmer's burden. During the 'teens and 'twenties he designed and built the Fordson. In early 1928, Ford became interested in a new agricultural concept, farm chemurgy; that is, putting chemistry and allied sciences to work for agriculture. The industrialist was chiefly interested in finding new industrial uses for farm crops, although he also hoped to find new ways to use crops for food. In 1929 he established a laboratory in Dearborn and began experiments to determine which plants or legumes offered the most promise. After extensive research, he decided in 1931 to focus attention on the soybean, rich in versatile oil, high in protein content, and with a residual fiber amenable to many uses.[22]

Ford planted 300 varieties of the soybean on some 8,000 acres of his farms in 1932 and 1933. He also urged Michigan farmers to plant the beans with the assurance that the Ford Company would provide a market for them. By 1933 his experimentation, which cost $1,250,000, had been rewarded with the discovery of a soybean oil which made a superior enamel for painting automobiles and for oiling casting molds, plus a soybean meal which was molded into the horn button. The discoveries excited Ford. "By now," Fortune reported in late 1933, "he is as much interested in the soya bean as he is in the V-8." Two years later, a bushel of soybeans went into the paint, horn button, gearshift knob, door handles, accelerator pedal, and timing gears of every Ford car. Numerous other small parts of the Ford car eventually were made of soybean-derived materials.[23]

By late 1937, Ford's research laboratory, under the direction of youthful, self-trained Robert Boyer, had developed a curved plastic sheet which Ford hoped would replace steel in automobile bodies. A few weeks later the magnate called in reporters, jumped up and down on the unbending sheet, and triumphantly exclaimed, "If that was steel, it would have caved in." He added, "almost all new cars will soon be made of such things as soybeans" and that the most prosperous era in American history was "just around the corner" because industry was opening up a "whole new field for agricultural by-products." In 1940 Boyer installed a plastic trunk lid on one of Ford's personal cars. The industrialist delighted in walloping the lid with an ax for the benefit of skeptics who questioned its dent-resistance; then he would invite them to swing the ax on their own cars. Again calling in the press, in November 1940, Ford startled reporters with his ax demonstration, then predicted that his company would be mass-producing "plastic-bodied" automobiles within one to three years. "I wouldn't be surprised," he declared, "if our [soybean research] laboratory comes to be the most important building of our entire plant." A picture of Ford's ax demonstration and accompanying wire service stories appeared in most of the nation's newspapers, but elicited little editorial comment.[24]

Carrying his dream a step further, on August 13, 1941, at the climax of Dearborn's annual community festival, Ford dramatically unveiled a handmade car with a complete plastic body. This event occurred at a time when Americans were just becoming aware of plastics. Moreover, the nation was being alerted to a metal shortage. The new car generated great publicity and stirred the imagination of editorial writers as had few other Ford-related events for some years. Many newspapers regarded the experimental Ford vehicle as revolutionary. The *New York Times* thought it "may have a great influence on the automobile industry"; the *Wheeling* (West Virginia) *Intelligencer* predicted it "will revolutionize the automobile industry"; and the *San Diego Union* said that it "may well bring about something in the nature of a highly desirable and peaceful agricultural revolution"; while the *Indianapolis Star* looked upon it as "an outstanding industrial achievement ... an artistic triumph, no matter what the future may bring." Other papers, noting that William S. Knudsen, of the National Defense Advisory Committee, had expressed "intense interest" in the vehicle, emphasized the possibility that Ford's plastic might be substituted for steel and other metals used in cars. "Obviously," stated the *Decatur* (Illinois) *Herald Review,* "here is something an America on wheels has been waiting for. Please hurry it, Mr. Ford; hurry, hurry!" The *Saginaw* (Michigan) *News* dismissed Ford's statement that the car was "purely experimental." "Shucks," it drawled, "who doubts that our motorists, or some of them at least, will soon be riding around in plastic car bodies?"[25]

Observing that Ford's plastic was molded from several common crops (including, in addition to soybeans, wheat, hemp, flax, and ramie—and that other commodities also could be used to make plastics), dozens of newspapers speculated on what large-scale plastics production could mean to the economy of their sections. Newspapers throughout the South anticipated a new market for cotton. The *Tampa Times* happily observed that "many of the products that Ford plans to put into automobiles are produced in Florida . . . including sugar cane, beeswax, tung oil, pine pitch, jute, and ramie''; the *Tacoma Sunday Ledger and News Tribune* hoped for the sake of the Northwest that a process might soon be found to turn sawdust into plastic; the *Tupelo* (Mississippi) *Journal* assumed this had already been done, and assured readers that ''the forest and woodlots of the South will be worth more than any single resource that we have''; and the *Elmira* (New York) *Star-Gazette* longed for the day when casein, a plastic derived from milk, might find its way into cars. A few papers, alas, had to pass on the depressing news that their areas could contribute little to the cars of the future. ''It is hard to get soybeans to mature here,'' mourned the far north *Cheboygan* (Michigan) *News*. ''Planting earlier might prove the solution.'' The *News,* however, offered a ray of hope: ''Resin for plastics is made from pine pitch, and Cheboygan county might produce some of that.''

A few newspapers were less interested in growing the ingredients for Ford's plastic than in putting the new substance to better use than motor cars. The *Bristol* (Connecticut) *Press,* noting that the plastic was ''dent resistant,'' suggested that it might be used for battleship armor, while the *Spartanburg* (South Carolina) *Herald* suggested that Ford ''might find greater profit in the manufacture of coffins than in automobile bodies.'' ''Plastic coffins,'' the paper declared, ''would be lighter, more durable and as attractive as the present metal things, and they could be made at far less cost.''[26]

A humorous vein, most of it related to the vegetable content in the Ford car, appeared in many editorials. The *Cleveland Press* wondered why Ford didn't strengthen his plastic by adding spinach; the *Cedar Rapids* (Iowa) *Gazette* suggested that the auto slogan of the future might be ''ask the man who grows one''; and the *St. Louis Globe-Democrat* stated that the new vehicle, ''part salad and part automobile,'' marked the triumph of the vegetable over the steel industry. Jokes about edible cars sprang up on all sides. *PM* reprinted a few of them:

> *Mother* (to recalcitrant small son): Now eat your succotash, Freddy, like a good boy.
> *Freddy:* I say it's a flivver and I say the hell with it!
>
> *Farmer Corntassel:* What crops ye growing this year, Zeke—Fords or Chryslers?
> *Farmer Hayseed:* Wall, if this corn don't git some rain pretty soon, the best I'll be able to do will be a crop of Baby Austins.

The new car would not need gas. Just sprinkle a little salt, pepper, and vinegar on it, and it will go to beat hell; a man need not buy a new car every year; he could have last year's car warmed over; a man could eat his car and have it too; ad infinitum. In 1943, several of these jokes were dusted off when a goat actually ate an Illinois license plate made of a soybean-derived fiberboard.[27]

Henry Ford was heavily praised for his vision and achievement in building a ''plastic'' car. The unveiling of the vehicle was one of the last occasions on which concerted praise would be heaped upon him by the nation's press. Many newspapers compared Ford's research into plastics favorably to his past achievements. The *San*

Diego Union regarded Ford's intention to convert farm products to industrial uses as "more revolutionary than that which gave birth to the flivver," while the *Detroit Legal Courier* felt that "when history is written and the achievements of Henry Ford are chronicled, the Soy Bean victory will stand out as his foremost contribution to mankind." "While it may seem funny to say 'let's take a ride in our new vegetable car,' " summed up the *Arkansas City* (Kansas) *Tribune,* "the world has only admiration and respect for Henry Ford, who like Edison, will leave so many testimonies of greatness and gifts to the masses by having put within their reach pleasures that otherwise would have been denied them."[28]

The outbreak of World War II and the suspension of automobile production forced Ford to abandon his efforts to mass produce plastic car bodies. Until 1943, however, he maintained that he would build them as soon as the war was over. In any event others carried forward his work, and in 1953 the first mass-produced car with a plastic body, the Corvette, was introduced by Chevrolet. A second mass-produced car with a plastic body, Studebaker's Avanti, made its appearance in 1962. By 1962 the Ford Company was using an average of twenty-nine pounds of plastic in its cars, by 1968, fifty pounds, by 1972, 120 pounds; and the firm expects to use an average of 200 pounds of plastic per car by 1980.[29]

During the same period in which Ford's laboratory developed plastic panels for cars, it also developed a fiber from soybean protein. The fiber resembled a soft wool. Because of a high degree of resilience and a natural crimp it could be used for upholstery in cars, in filling for hats, and for clothing. By 1938 Ford often sported a tie made from soybean fiber. Three years later he made a public appearance in a "soybean suit," with which, reported the *Detroit Times,* "he is as delighted as a boy with his first pair of long pants." Early in World War II the manufacturer tried, without success, to interest the armed forces in making uniforms out of soybean fabric. Ford persisted in his research until mid-1943, hoping to develop a textile which could sell at prices competitive with wool. Unable to do so, he sold his fabrication process and machinery to the Drackett Company, of Cincinnati, in November 1943. Neither the Drackett Company nor any other firm has been commercially successful in producing textile fibers from soybean protein.[30]

The auto magnate's efforts to develop palatable foods and popularize recipes based on soybeans met with even less success than his experiments with fabrics. To develop the nutritional possibilities of the bean, Ford set to work his boyhood friend, Dr. Edsel Ruddiman, formerly dean of the School of Pharmacy at Vanderbilt University. Ruddiman prepared a soybean biscuit, described by one of Ford's secretaries as "the most vile thing ever put into human mouths" (but which white rats did like and the auto magnate professed to like), and a wide variety of other recipes. On at least three occasions between 1934 and 1943 Ford, seeking to publicize his soybean experimentation, summoned wary reporters to a soybean luncheon. Every course was partially or wholly composed of the legume. The chief items were tomato juice with soybean sauce, celery stuffed with soybean cheese, puree of soybean, soybean croquettes with green soybeans, soybean bread and butter, apple pie with soybean sauce, soybean coffee, soybean milk, soybean ice cream, and soybean cookies and candy. "Nothing we newsmen ate that day," a guest wrote years later, "led us to foresee that soybeans were destined to become an ingredient in many popular food products. . . . We accepted as reasonable the possibility that the bean might become a leading cattle feed or industrial material." Yet after the war, soybean oil became a leading source of cooking fats, margarine, and salad oils.[31]

Ford also encouraged the great black scientist, George Washington Carver, to utilize edible weeds in what one Ford employee called "grass sandwiches." They were no more popular than the soybean biscuit: "It was just like eating hay." One youngster, asked if he would like to make a trip with Ford and others, replied staunchly: "Not if I have to eat another of those sandwiches!"[32]

Ford also advanced his ideas about the soybean and chemurgy with exhibits and a film. In 1934, he planted a small plot of soybeans and exhibited soybean processing machinery (in a barn built by Ford's father in 1863) in the company's exhibit area at the Chicago World's Fair. Similar exhibits were shown at various state, regional, and world's fairs during the 1930s. In 1935 the Ford Company produced and distributed *Farm of the Future,* a sound-slide film which illustrated Henry Ford's views on the importance of chemurgy.[33]

Although Ford's free-ranging predictions were often wide of the mark, his frequent assertion that "soybeans will make millions of dollars of added income for farmers . . . and provide industry with materials to make needed things nobody even knows about now" was proved correct by the passage of time. In addition to their uses in cooking, soybeans are used in plastics, in varnishes and enamels, in adhesives, coatings, and sizings, as additives in lubricants, and as industrial resins. By 1959, American soybean production—only 1,000,000 bushels in 1920—had grown to 538,000,000 bushels, making it fifth in importance of all our crops. By 1973 American farmers were devoting one acre in seven to soybean cultivation, growing $1.5 billion bushels of beans, and converting the legume into the country's No. 2 cash crop, which sold for $8.8 billion. Soybeans outpaced jet aircraft, computers, and all other products and crops to become the nation's most valuable export in the early 1970s. Treasury Secretary George P. Shultz facetiously suggested at a businessmen's conference in 1973 that soybeans might replace gold as a standard of international wealth if its price (45 cents per bushel in the 1930s, $2.60 in the mid-1960s and $12.12 in 1973) continued to climb. "When the price of soybeans reaches the price of gold, we'll be set," said Shultz. "We could go over to the soybean standard."[34]

Through his experimentation, and the publicity he gave it, Henry Ford made a substantial contribution to the increased utilization of the soybean. His work in this field, started when he was in his late sixties and carried forward until he was eighty years of age, is perhaps the outstanding achievement of his declining years. Of all of Ford's accomplishments, it is possible that none pleased him more than in helping to prove that there was industrial magic in a beanstalk.[35]

Ford's farm-related activities—unlike his attitudes toward the government and organized labor—were generally enlightened, progressive, and sometimes far ahead of his times. He helped to set in motion the whole chemurgic movement, not only by the example of his laboratories, but by playing host to 300 leading agriculturists, scientists, and industrialists who met in Dearborn to organize the National

Farm Chemurgic Council in 1935. Twenty-seven years later, Wheeler McMillen, ex-chairman of the council, regarded Ford's invitation to the charter members of the organization as "the outstanding single thing Mr. Ford did in behalf of chemurgy." The council and other groups subsequently induced the government to establish four large regional crop-utilization laboratories. By 1961 more than 8,000 new processes and scores of entirely new industries had resulted from their efforts.[36]

5

Ford embarked on yet another nonautomotive venture—tractors—which was to occupy much of his attention in the late 1930s and early 1940s. Production of the Fordson tractor had been shifted from Dearborn to Ford's plant in Cork, Ireland, in 1928, and again in 1933 to the Dagenham plant in England. Although a few Fordsons were imported into the United States during the 1930s, Ford executives seemed to have forgotten the machine. Thus Ford's associates were startled when the magnate proclaimed in the fall of 1937 that "what the country [and the Ford Company] needs right now is a good tractor that will sell for around two hundred and fifty dollars." Shortly thereafter, Ford was furiously at work on a "new low-priced tractor of unusual design." In January 1938, he showed newsmen a three-wheeled machine resembling a "lop-sided triangle." "As pleased as a small boy with a fire engine," Ford brushed aside questions as to whether his unorthodox tractor ("the likes of which," reported *Time*, "no one had ever seen") would be merchandisable: "I don't care if we don't make a cent of profit. The main thing is to get something started."[37]

Soon setting aside his three-wheeled tractor, Ford turned to a four-wheeled type. But this model was also rejected. At this point, October 1938, Henry George (Harry) Ferguson, of Ulster, who had developed a new method for attaching and hydraulically controlling plows and other implements to tractors (thus eliminating the need for wheeled instruments), demonstrated the advantages of his inventions to Ford. The auto king was particularly impressed with the hydraulic lift, which automatically set the implement at any desired depth or raised it above the ground for speedy transport. Soon after the demonstration, Ford and Ferguson entered into a "gentlemen's agreement": Ferguson was to place his inventions and his own services at Ford's disposal; Ford, in return, was to manufacture a machine incorporating the Ferguson System, as Ferguson's contribution was called. Either party on notice could terminate the agreement. In the months to come Ford fairly effervesced about the Ferguson System and its inventor, hailing the former as "the most revolutionary step that mechanical farming has taken" and declaring that Ferguson's "name will go down in history, along with those of Thomas Edison, Graham Bell, the Wright Brothers, and other famous inventors."[38]

In June 1939, Ford and Ferguson introduced their new machine at a quasi-public demonstration attended by 450 newsmen, agricultural and business leaders, and representatives of foreign governments. The visitors were impressed by the tractor's "appearance, flexibility, and performance" (plus a Fordian touch, a plastic seat, made partly out of field grass). Tractor manufacturers in attendance, aware of the "romance of the Ford name in agricultural circles," were relieved to learn that the new product would sell for $585, not $300 as some of them had feared. Ford and Ferguson evaded all questions about advertising the tractor, and a rumor swept the crowd that Ford was so thoroughly convinced of the revolutionary nature of the machine that he believed he could sell it without benefit of advertising. Acknowledging that "Ford's name alone will help sell a great many of his tractors," an alarmed *Printers' Ink* editorialized that "even the Ford name, great as it is," could not substitute for conventional merchandising practices. A few weeks later, the Ferguson-Sherman Manufacturing Corporation, which Ferguson had organized to distribute the tractor, announced that N. W. Ayer & Son, Inc., the Ford Company's agency, would handle its advertising. In April 1940, Ayer, plagued by troubles with Ford that would soon lead to the agency's dismissal, was replaced by Fuller & Smith & Ross, Inc., of New York. In addition to advertising placed by the Ferguson-Sherman organization (renamed Harry Ferguson, Inc., in 1942), the Ford Company displayed the tractor at its exhibits at various fairs. At the New York World's Fair, in July 1939, the machine was driven and demonstrated to the press by Edsel Ford, Grover Whalen, president of the fair, and Ferguson.[39]

The Ford Company produced 88,933 tractors during 1939–41, taking 20 percent of the market and moving from nowhere to second rank in the tractor industry. (International Harvester Company was the leader with 40 percent of sales.) Actually, Ford made every machine at a loss. After the outbreak of war, Edsel suggested that tractor production be discontinued. He was overruled by his father. During the war years, the company made 98,826 machines, still at a loss. In 1946, the Ford Company's new president, Henry Ford II—after several unsuccessful attempts to reach agreement with Ferguson on a better definition of the hazy Ford-Ferguson relationship and to resolve complicated misunderstandings between the two— severed relations between his company and the Ferguson interests. Before making the decision, Henry II talked with his grandfather. After the situation had been explained to him, the elder Ford replied: "Well, use your judgment. Ferguson is a hog anyway, and just keep on building the tractor."[40]

Agreeing to supply Ferguson with tractors until mid-1947, when Ferguson expected to have a new model and presumably would be ready to manufacture for himself, Ford executives organized an independent tractor distributing company, Dearborn Motors Corporation, in late 1946. In January 1948, Ferguson, now the head of his own tractor company, sued the Ford Company, Dearborn Motors, and the chief officers of both companies for $251,000,000. Ferguson alleged that Ford had infringed his patents, sought the destruction of his business, and engaged in unfair acts of competition. In a sharp rejoinder, Henry Ford II termed the charges "ridiculous," adding that "the blunt truth about this relationship is that it made Mr. Ferguson a multi-millionaire and cost the Ford Motor Company $25,000,000 in the process." After four years of expensive litigation, the Ford Company settled the suit out of court, giving Ferguson $9,250,000 "in full satisfaction of all claims for patent royalties." In return, Ferguson's charges against the Ford Company, Dearborn Motors, and their executives were dismissed.[41]

Henry Ford, had he lived to see it, would have been distressed by the Ferguson litigation and settlement. But he would have been pleased that his tractor hobby (for in the late 1930s the machine was less a business than a hobby) had turned a profit and made his company a major factor in the postwar tractor market. The firm was second only to International Harvester in tractor production during the late 1940s and 1950s, having captured from 17.3 to 23.4 percent of the market. In the peak sales year, 1948, Dearborn Motors (which was acquired by Ford in 1953) sold 103,462 tractors in America, another 50,561 abroad. Domestic deliveries gradually declined, as the market for tractors deteriorated. Ford's unit sales dipped to 23,718 in 1961, and stood at 41,090 in 1974. Foreign sales increased to a highwater mark of 85,198 units in 1963, and stood at 68,202 units in 1974. Ford's share of the market has remained constant over the past quarter-century, the firm making approximately a fifth of industry sales over this period.[42]

6

As we have seen, Henry Ford's "hobbies" and his embroilment in the swirl of current affairs kept him in the public eye throughout the prewar decade. Indeed, if the number of listings in the *New York Times Index* and the *Readers' Guide to Periodical Literature* can be used as measuring devices, only twenty-seven persons received more newspaper publicity and only nineteen persons received more attention in general magazines than did Ford between 1933–41. Among these people, who included the President and his wife, most (but not all) of the members of the President's cabinet, a handful of Congressmen, and several kings and dictators, only three persons, like Ford, were private citizens: Charles F. Lindbergh and labor leaders William Green and John L. Lewis. Among businessmen, only John D. Rockefeller, Jr. came close to receiving as much attention as Ford in the *New York Times* between 1933–41. In the general periodical press, the auto magnate was the subject of more than twice as many articles as the second best publicized businessman, Charles F. Kettering, director of General Motors Research Laboratory. Publications surveyed by the *Industrial Arts Index* gave Ford more than three times as much attention as either of the next most publicized businessmen, Kettering and Rockefeller.

Even so, Ford was far less newsworthy during this period than he had been during his heyday. The extent to which his post-1932 career was anticlimactic is apparent from a comparison of the amount of publicity that the motor magnate received before and after 1932. Whereas the *New York Times* ran an average of 134 stories per year about the industrialist between 1921–32, it did not carry half this number of stories about him during any one year of the 1930s and averaged only forty-one Ford items per year during the period 1933–41. The general periodical press ran an average of nineteen articles a year about him between 1921–32, but carried an average of only nine Ford articles per year during 1933–41. Nineteen full-length Ford biographies were published during the ten years before 1932; only four full-length books about the industrialist appeared during the ten years after 1932. Abroad, Ford received only one-sixth as much attention in periodicals during the decade after 1932 as he had in the decade before 1932.

As Ford's personal publicity waned, relatively more attention was focused on his company. Between 1933–41 the *New York Times* ran almost three times as many stories on the firm as on the founder. In the general periodical press, there were 119 articles on the company during the 1933–41 period; ninety-two on the magnate.[43]

Ford's reputation and prestige were more durable than his newsworthiness. In 1934, at a "choosing-a-career" conference attended by 4,500 students from 103 eastern colleges and universities, the auto magnate was voted the "most admired American businessman." A 1937 *Fortune* survey found that the nation's "poor people" rated only Senator William E. Borah and James Farley ahead of Ford when asked to name whom they would prefer (aside from Roosevelt) as president. The same year students at the Stout Institute, Menomonie, Wisconsin, ranked the manufacturer with Lincoln, Washington, Edison, and Franklin as one of the five greatest Americans of all time. Princeton students, when asked in 1939, "What famous person would you like to know?" placed only Hitler, President Roosevelt, and Anthony Eden ahead of Ford, who was followed by Lindbergh, Cordell Hull, Hedy Lamarr, George Bernard Shaw, Farley, Arturo Toscanini, and Thomas E. Dewey.[44]

The continual references in the press throughout the 1930s to what Ford *had done* for his fellowmen—in addition to what he was doing or thinking of doing—helps to explain why the industrialist retained much of his prestige in his declining years. Many commentators, while discussing Ford's attitude toward the NRA or his soybean experimentation, also reminisced about the Model T, the five-dollar day, and the magnate's pricing policies and his contribution to mass production. Some writers, observing that the Ford car had become "just another trade name" and noting Ford's recalcitrant attitude toward the government and organized labor, concluded that he had become "a symbol of reaction, rather than of the progress so vital to his legend." But most commentators and publications appraised him in a more kindly light. The *New York Sun* described Ford in 1934 as a "supernatural being who somehow or other achieved the colossal, the impossible"; in 1935 the author of *Men Who Run America* looked upon him as one of the two persons (Edison being the other) who had "most profoundly influenced American life in the social-economic field"; a syndicated columnist viewed him in 1939 as the "living American who had contributed most to making life more comfortable and attractive for the people of his country"; and a small-town Washington newspaper in 1941 called him a "modern miracle," who, by following "a pattern of hard-earned and deserved success. . . had had a life far surpassing anything that Horatio Alger ever even dreamed of." These and many similar observations about Ford's rise from "rags to riches," his efforts in behalf of mankind, and his heroic qualities, as symbolized by his "rugged individualism," evidently made an impression on readers. "Many Americans," the *Literary Digest* solemnly asserted in 1935, after reciting Ford's achievements, "would rather be Ford than President. To them Henry Ford typifies the national ideal." The *Literary Digest*'s appraisal of the motor magnate came, of course, before Ford's involvement in controversial labor and defense issues during the late 1930s and early 1940s. But in spite of the mixed publicity arising from these issues, Ford's reputation and achievements in 1941 were such that *Time*'s editors had agreed to name him ''Man of the Year for 1941''—until the attack on Pearl Harbor ''made a radical change in Mr. Roosevelt's position.'' The award, *Time*'s publisher wrote Ford, was to have been made ''both in your own right and as a symbol of the American businessman of 1941.''[45]

In August 1941, Ford suffered a second and more serious stroke. By late October he had recovered sufficiently to appear in public. Afterwards, however, it was apparent to associates that he spent less time on business and his hobbies, that he sometimes was slower in gait, and that he occasionally had mental lapses. He also became increasingly unreasonable, apprehensive, irritable; in Sorensen's words, ''a querulous, suspicious old man [whose] . . . previously set opinions about Wall Street and international bankers, the Roosevelt New Deal, scheming motorcar competitors, foreign wars, and his son Edsel's quiet determination to live his own life hardened into an obsession which occasionally flared in hallucination.''[46]

After the second stroke, Ford's star—bright now and then, but slowly waning throughout the prewar decade—began a more rapid descent. Epochal changes in the aging auto king's life and the destiny of his industrial empire lay just ahead.

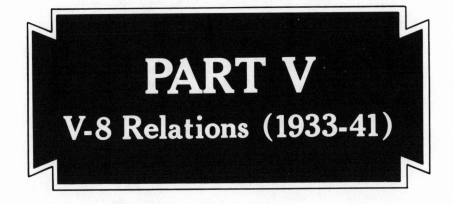

PART V
V-8 Relations (1933-41)

Chapter 18
Henry Ford, Showman

As his personal publicity waned and as competitive pressures mounted during the 1930s, Henry Ford found it increasingly necessary to resort to "conventional" public relations activities to publicize his company and bolster its sales. He did not establish a public relations department or designate an executive to coordinate public relations (as did General Motors in 1931). But from 1933 until the start of World War II, his company's public relations activities were more extensive and more costly than at any time in the past. During this period, in fact, the Ford Company probably devoted more attention and money to public relations than any firm in the country except General Motors.

Most of Ford's major prewar-decade public relations activities were started between late 1933 and late 1934. Some had been discontinued by the company in prior years and now were being drawn out of retirement; others broke new ground.

On December 6, 1933, as part of what the trade press called the "greatest merchandising drive" and "most aggressive sales campaign" in the Ford Company's history, Henry Ford held one of the best publicized new-model press previews in the history of the automobile industry. The event was noteworthy in several ways. It was only the second preview of its kind in the company's history, the first occurring in 1927 when newsmen were permitted to see the Model A two days in advance of its public showing. The preview also was held a month in advance of other auto manufacturers' press and public showings; previously, Ford's public showings had followed competitive showings by several weeks. Finally, it marked the first time that Henry Ford served an alcoholic beverage at a company function. This gesture, so incompatible with the industrialist's "notorious and violent objection to alcohol," created a sensation and received more attention in some news stories than the new models themselves. Ford's ploy received additional attention when a controversy developed over whether the motor magnate actually did serve beer to the 200 newsmen in attendance. *Business Week,* which did not have a representative at the preview and based its story on a report from one of the guests, declared that "the [beer] yarn was utterly untrue." The newsmen who had sipped beer and smoked in Ford's presence (while asking the Dearbornite if he recalled his earlier tirades against alcohol and tobacco), held to their original reports.[1]

Whatever he may have thought of serving beer, cigars, and cigarettes, Ford had his mind on selling cars. "He appeared," said *Advertising Age,* "as interested in the new-model demonstrations as any of his visitors," and, according to the *Business Week* report, "chatted with pretty nearly every guest at one time or another." Ford's personal interest in the preview and his charm paid dividends. His statement, "this is the best car we ever built'' (the 1934 model, with a few improvements, was similar to its predecessor), appeared with descriptions and photographs of the new vehicle in newspapers throughout the country. In addition, several publications spoke favorably of the "beautifully managed" preview itself.[2]

The day after the preview the industrialist again broke precedent by talking simultaneously to his 7,000 American and Canadian dealers and their 17,000 salesmen on "the greatest telephone hookup in history." "Hello, everybody," said the industrialist, "you know I don't make speeches; I make cars. . . . We have all got to pitch in and do all the business we can to help the President pull the country out of the hole." The statement, made when Ford was embattled with the President and General Johnson over the NRA's automobile code, was reported on the front pages of newspapers throughout the country. At the same time Ford, "by linking his product to the Presidential office," also obtained considerable publicity for his new model. While acknowledging that "Ford's genius as a gratuitous advertiser is without parallel," the *New York Financial World* nonetheless marveled at the manufacturer's audacity. "Not an eyelash flickers; not a lip is parched," mused the publication. "It takes genius of a sort to do such a *volte-face.*"[3]

Encouraged by the success of the 1933 press preview and "telephone conference," the industrialist participated in similar events in December 1934. But perhaps because each was staged for the second time around, and also because Ford said nothing which could be related to the national scene, neither attracted more than routine publicity. There were no full-scale new-model press previews in Dearborn from 1935 until 1938, although formal showings for newsmen were held during the years 1935 through 1939 in advance of the company's "independent" auto shows at the Hotel Astor and at its New York headquarters on Broadway. Henry Ford did not attend any of the New York previews; his son attended only one, in 1935. Conducted by the company's general sales manager or Edgewater, New Jersey branch manager, these previews also received only routine news coverage.[4]

At the 1938 press preview in Dearborn, the medium-price Mercury was unveiled. As the first new passenger car introduced in America since 1931, the Mercury attracted more than ordinary interest. But it was upstaged at its debut by Henry Ford, who took the occasion to comment on a variety of topics. The most newsworthy of Ford's remarks, "I'll bet anyone even money there will never be another war," was headlined on the front page of most of the nation's newspapers; descriptions and pictures of the Mercury and Ford's other 1939 models usually were carried on inside pages.[5]

Press previews for new models were also held in Dearborn in 1939, 1940, and 1941. Coverage of the 1939 and 1940 previews was ordinary, Henry Ford having almost nothing to say at them. But the 1941 event, which attracted a record 500 newspaper and radio representatives on the strength of the company's promise that Henry Ford would escort the press party through his defense plants—then much in the news—was heavily publicized. Even so, the industrialist's statement that his firm would build airplanes after World War II was given greater prominence in news stories than the new models.[6]

Although Ford's interest in showing his cars to newsmen waxed and waned, his enthusiasm for showing the public his products and "how we do things" was constant through the years. The magnate repeatedly said that the inspiration to build his first gasoline engine had come from an exhibit he had seen at the World's Columbian Exposition in Chicago in 1893. His firm belief in the "practical educational value" of exhibits, coupled with his awareness of their sales value, led him to present one of the major exhibits at the Panama-Pacific Exposition in San Francisco in 1915; to display his products and describe his company's integrated operations at fairs, exhibition halls and branch buildings throughout the 1920s; and to send road shows designed to acquaint people with the Ford organization through the U.S., Mexico, and Cuba in 1930–31. But it was between 1934 and 1940, when six American cities held huge regional or world's fairs, that Ford's ideas about educational exhibits flowered. During these years the company spent almost $12,000,000 on exhibits, which were visited by 56,619,000 people. With the exception of General Motors, no other company came close to matching these figures.[7]

Ford had intended to be a major exhibitor at the first of the great fairs of the 1930s, Chicago's A Century of Progress Exposition, which opened in 1933. He had planned to duplicate the highly popular assembly line exhibit he had presented in San Francisco eighteen years earlier. But in July 1931, before the "father" of the automobile moving assembly line had informed fair officials of his plans, General Motors announced that its Chicago exhibit would feature a Chevrolet assembly line. Ford was furious. Grumbling that Chevrolet had "stolen my idea," he announced that he would boycott the fair. His decision stunned and angered fair officials and many other Chicagoans, who had looked to the Ford Company for one of the exposition's major attractions.[8]

Partly, some said, because he wanted to upstage the Chicago fair, but also to call attention to his company's thirtieth anniversary, Ford held his own "industrial fair," the Ford Exposition of Progress, in Detroit and New York City in late 1933. Described by *Business Week* as "the greatest industrial show ever held," it traced the evolution of the motor car and showed how raw materials were transformed into auto parts. Its displays were prepared not only by the Ford Company, but also by 175 of its suppliers. The principal Ford exhibits were a replica of the workshop (including the original tools) in which Henry Ford had built his first car and a large collection of "historic" cars, including Ford's first "quadricycle," the 999 racing car, a 1903 Model A, and successive Ford models through the V-8. Most supplier companies' displays consisted of actual manufacturing operations, most notably an assembly line on which bodies for Ford cars were built by the Briggs Manufacturing Company.

The suppliers installed and staffed their displays; Ford paid charges for exhibit space, electricity, and incidentals. Records in the Ford Archives do not indicate whether any of Ford's suppliers balked at or rejected invitations to participate in the exposition. Many of them, beholden to Ford for much of their business, probably regarded the invitation as a command. At the same time, most companies, after considering the favorable financial arrangements and the opportunity to coexhibit with one of the nation's most highly regarded firms, probably welcomed the chance to participate. In any event, as Clarence W. Olmstead, an official of the exposition, remarked years later, "there were never any complaints by the co-exhibitors."[9]

The Ford Exposition of Progress opened in Detroit's Convention Hall on October 21 and was visited by an estimated 1,200,000 people during a ten-day stand (the widely acclaimed Ford Industrial Exposition, held in Madison Square Garden in 1928, attracted 1,052,842 visitors in one week). Henry Ford had originally planned to stage the exposition only in Detroit. But noting the impressive attendance figures and the excellent press coverage, he told associates, "this is too good to drop; let's take it on to New York."

"Always the showman," the industrialist insured a well publicized debut for his New York show by contracting to be the first exhibitor in the newly-completed, but yet-to-be-dedicated Port of New York Authority Commerce Building. "To no one's surprise," the building was dedicated, amid great fanfare, on the same day, December 9, that Ford swung open the gates to his show. The New York exposition, at which Ford publicly displayed his 1934 cars several weeks in advance of the industry's traditional January introductions, was generously publicized and well-attended throughout its two-week stand. Noting the "truly remarkable mass turn-out," the *New York Times,* which carried eleven articles and an editorial on the show, wondered whether the impressive crowds presaged improved economic conditions or simply meant that any free event would draw large crowds with so many people out of work. The total attendance figure, 2,298,000, almost twice that of the Detroit exposition, was claimed by the Port of New York Authority to be a "world's record for a single event." Moreover, the show (which cost "several hundred thousand dollars") was regarded as a sound investment. "In drama and glamor," reported *Advertising and Selling,* "the exposition has outdone the regular auto shows." Added *Tide,* "what the exposition netted Ford in sales, goodwill, publicity and the like isn't on record, but no one has put it at less than a great deal."[10]

Flushed with the success of the Ford Exposition of Progress and probably aware that General Motors and Chrysler had entertained an estimated 10,200,000 and 10,000,000 people, respectively, at the Chicago fair in 1933, Henry Ford decided in late 1933 to exhibit at the Chicago exposition in 1934. Calling in Fred L. Black, ex-head of the Advertising Department, who was to manage the company's exhibit buildings at the Chicago and other fairs of the 1930s, the industrialist said that his exhibit should show people "how we do things" and "provide places for visitors to rest." All of Ford's exhibits were subsequently built around these fundamental concepts.[11]

Ford's change of heart delighted Chicagoans, especially fair officials who, discouraged by the exposition's deficit in 1933, desperately hoped for a major new attraction to revitalize the fair in its second year. In fact, according to *Automotive Industries,* "it wasn't until after the announcement of Ford's entry that it became certain there would be a Fair" in 1934. "As THE exhibitor for 1934," reported the *Detroit Free Press,* "the Detroit man [is] a very popular figure in Chicago. He can pretty well have the keys of the city, the mayoralty or anything else he likes."[12]

Ford's exhibit building matched Chicagoans' hopes. The largest structure erected by any of the fair's individual exhibitors (indeed the "largest single exhibit of any World's Fair,'' according to the *Chicago Herald and Examiner*), the hastily constructed building was 900 feet long, 213 feet wide, and rose to a height of twelve stories in a gear-shaped rotunda section. A torch of light, 200 feet broad at its base, sprang from the parapet of the rotunda's open court and could be seen for more than twenty miles on clear nights. As strikingly attractive as it was huge, the building, in the opinion of *Printed Salesmanship*, was "the architectural sensation of the Fair." This same publication also was ecstatic about the structure's interior, describing it as "so perfect it makes the other buildings look like something that Balaban and Katz dragged in."[13]

Staffed by 800 employees, the Ford exhibit contained five major sections: the Ford museum, the Ford industrialized barn, the Ford drama of transportation, the industrial hall, and the Ford gardens. Displays in the museum (among them the replica of Ford's early workshop) traced the evolution of machine tools from the 1830s to the 1890s. The industrialized barn contained a soybean processing exhibit. The drama of transportation held the collection of historic vehicles shown at the Ford Exposition of Progress and the company's 1934 models. In this section a circular mural 600 feet long and twenty feet wide, billed as the "largest photo panorama ever made," pictured the company's manufacturing and assembly operations. The mural vividly impressed viewers. "Its effect," reported *New Outlook,* "is that of Gilbraltar giving voice to a battery of guns." *Printed Salesmanship* declared that the mural "set a new standard in the use of photography" [and] "is worth coming to Chicago to see."[14]

The industrial hall comprised the largest display section in the Ford building. In this area, twenty-one of the company's suppliers maintained exhibits similar to those shown at the Ford Exposition of Progress. The Ford Gardens encompassed a five-acre park between the Ford exhibit and Lake Michigan. In the gardens, Ford built a "roads of the world" exhibit, after overcoming Chrysler's vigorous protest to the fair management that a roads exhibit would infringe upon one of its principal attractions, a test track. The roads of the world exhibit comprised 100-foot-long replicas of nineteen famous highways, among them the Appian Way, the North American Wilderness Highway, and the Lincoln Highway. Visitors could walk or be driven in V-8's over a service path alongside the roads. Conceived by Fred L. Black, the roads idea was used in varying form at Ford exhibits at three later expositions.[15]

A bandshell and an amphitheater seating 2,300 people were built at the south end of the Ford Gardens. Here, under Ford sponsorship, concerts were presented throughout the summer by the Detroit Symphony Orchestra (which performed for thirteen weeks), the Chicago Women's Symphony Orchestra, the Mormon Tabernacle Choir, and lesser musical groups. Many of the performances were broadcast as a public service by the country's two major networks, the Columbia Broadcasting System and the National Broadcasting Company. Often the broadcasts were heard by audiences exceeding 10,000,000 people. Since the networks announced that the concerts originated from the "Ford Symphony Gardens," many listeners assumed that Ford sponsored them. Thousands of persons wrote to the company, expressing appreciation for the programs.[16]

Ford's exhibit—thanks to its newness, a generous publicity and advertising budget ($106,622), and the alertness of the press relations staff provided by Ayer—was easily the best publicized pavilion at the fair during 1934. Articles devoted exclusively to the Ford exhibit, for example, appeared in thirteen of the periodicals examined by the *Industrial Arts Index;* no other display was publicized in more than one of the magazines examined by this *Index.* [17]

Ford urged its 8,000 dealers to encourage as many home folks as possible to visit its exhibit. To assist dealers in their promotion, the company supplied literature on its exhibit, the exposition, and Chicago. Dealers also were furnished "courtesy cards," to be given to "persons of unusual prominence, good prospects and others entitled to special consideration." Bearers of such cards, if they arrived in Chicago by train, were met at the railroad station by a Ford chauffeur and driven to their hotel, or the company's headquarters at the Congress Hotel, or, if they wished, to the Ford exhibit building. At the building they were interviewed and photographed, the stories and pictures being sent to hometown newspapers. Holders of courtesy cards were also entitled to free guided tours of Chicago. In addition, Ford dealers in half a dozen large cities in the Midwest and South banded together and chartered special trains to take salesmen and guests to the fair. Other dealers organized motorcades, some of which provided transportation for as many as 2,000 fair-goers. [18]

The Ford exposition drew praise from all sides. A General Electric publicist reported to his superiors that the "Ford exhibit is the finest on the grounds—bar none," and an employee of the Studebaker display said that "Ford has the most marvelous exhibit of its kind" he had ever seen. The *Olympia* (Washington) *Olympian* and *Printed Salesmanship* told their readers that the Ford exposition "has stolen the fair," the latter publication adding that "if you have only a little time to spend at the exposition, and you saw it last year, you should go to the Ford Building and spend half your time there." "Here," continued the publication, "is a fair within a fair." [19]

Many visitors were impressed with the noncommercial and relaxed atmosphere of the Ford exhibit. "Contrary to all of the time-honored practices of World's Fair commercial shows," said *New Outlook,* "the usual ballyhoo of salesmanship is strangely and satisfyingly missing." "Attendants stand with arms folded and make no approaches," added *Sales Management.* "When asked questions they reply courteously. The technique is to make every visitor . . . feel that Ford considers him its guest. The idea behind the entire $2,000,000 Ford exhibit [actual cost $2,563,203] is good-will, friendliness, taste. Ford prefers to pass up the sales he might get at the Fair. Perhaps he is very wise." In contrast many of the other 650 manufacturers which exhibited at the fair, including General Motors, Chrysler, and several other auto manufacturers, followed the more conventional practice of exerting every effort to sell their products on the premises. General Motors, in fact, reported sales of 3,000 cars at its building in 1933, and also sent the names and addresses of 50,000 "prospects" to its dealers that year. [20]

Perhaps the most telling praise for the Ford exhibit was to be found in the attendance figures. Of the fair's 16,314,480 visitors in 1934, 12,539,319 or 76.9 percent—an exceptionally high ratio of attendance compared to other displays at the Chicago fair and at other expositions—were guests of the Ford exhibit. The 1934 runner-up in attendance, General Motors, drew less than half as many visitors as Ford. In 1933, General Motors, which was first in attendance and had the largest and most outstanding display during the fair's first season, drew only 10,200,000 or 45.7 percent of the 22,320,456 visitors.[21]

Among the millions who visited the Ford exhibit, perhaps none found more pleasure in it than Henry Ford himself. He visited the exposition on thirteen occasions. Hatless, coatless, and often surrounded by reporters and photographers, he strolled around the Ford building, explaining the displays to youthful guests. Once, as several adults waited for him to conclude such a tour, an aide pleaded with him to leave the youngsters, saying that they could get information about the displays from folders. "I'll give the statistics myself; the boys come first," retorted Ford. Perhaps he thought he might inspire a boy as he himself had been inspired at the World's Columbian Exposition in 1893.[22]

As the Chicago fair drew to a close, Ford toyed with the idea of moving his exhibit building, or at least a part of it, to Greenfield Village. Instead, after an appeal by Edsel, who for several years had wanted to erect a reception center for the tens of thousands of people who annually visited the Rouge, the elder Ford decided to move the rotunda section and a 110-foot by 80-foot wing to a site adjacent to the factory. Dismantling and rebuilding of the structure (replacing the sheet rock walls used in Chicago with limestone walls) took eighteen months and cost $2,500,000.[23]

Upon completion in May 1936, the building, named the Ford Rotunda, housed a display area for new cars in its center court, an exhibition hall in one wing, and a 388-seat theater in a second wing, also 110 feet by 80 feet. The courtyard featured a new-car display and a huge globe in relief. On the wall around the courtyard a gigantic photo mural (identical in size to the mural shown in Chicago) described manufacturing and assembly processes in the Rouge. Animated exhibits, showing how raw materials were brought to the Rouge, were on display in the exhibition hall. The company's motion pictures were shown at regular intervals in the theater. Adjacent to the building, a roads-of-the-world exhibit, similar to the company's Chicago fair exhibit, was opened in mid-1937 in the presence of the Detroit consuls of Great Britain, France, Germany, Italy, Belgium, and Mexico.[24]

The largest permanent industrial exhibit building in the country, the Rotunda was opened to the public on May 16, 1936. It quickly proved popular with tourists and Detroit area residents, attracting 900,976 visitors by the end of the year. Annual attendance averaged 757,308 during 1937–39, increasing in 1940 to 951,558, the record prewar figure. Benefiting from interest in the Rotunda, the number of Rouge visitors rose from 91,091 in 1935 to 132,507 in 1936, an all-time high for the factory. The Rouge set new attendance records in 1938, 1939, and 1940, the figure for the latter year, 166,519, being the high-water mark until 1954. Guests came from every state in the country and from more than seventy-five foreign nations. An average of 4,150 foreigners annually visited the Rotunda (and in most instances the Rouge as well) between 1936–39. Canadians were the most frequent visitors, followed by Germans, Britons, and Russians. The outbreak of World War II virtually halted the flow of foreign visitors, except for several hundred Latin Americans. The Ford

Company sought—much as it had at its exhibit at the Chicago fair—to publicize the Rotunda by issuing news releases about distinguished visitors. But the releases generated little publicity outside of the Detroit area.[25]

When America entered World War II, the Rouge and other Ford plants engaged in war production were closed to visitors. The company announced that the Rotunda would remain open and that its military products and films of its defense activities would be shown to guests. This policy was rescinded early in 1942, however, when the display space was converted into offices for military personnel assigned to Ford's war plants. For eight years after the war, the Rotunda, although used as the point of departure for Rouge tours, remained an office building. In 1953, as part of the observance of the company's fiftieth anniversary, the structure was redecorated, outfitted with new exhibits, and reopened to the public. Between 1953 and 1962, when it was destroyed by fire, the Rotunda was one of the Midwest's principal tourist attractions, annually drawing more than 1,500,000 visitors.[26]

With his triumph at the Chicago fair fresh in mind, Henry Ford decided late in 1934 to exhibit at San Diego's California Pacific International Exposition in 1935. The company was, in fact, one of only two industrial firms—the other being Standard Oil Company (California)—which erected exhibit buildings at the San Diego fair. Much larger than Standard's building and of permanent construction, the circular Ford structure contained 60,000 square feet of floor space (about one-third the footage of Ford's Chicago exhibit) and boasted a tower rising to a height of 221 feet. Displays inside the building explained how the company's vehicles were designed, manufactured, and tested. A series of dioramas showed how raw materials were processed into parts for Ford cars; another series of dioramas depicted the use of motor vehicles in twelve nations bordering the Pacific Ocean. The company also displayed several historic Ford cars and, of course, its new models. Visitors were driven over the "roads of the Pacific," replicas of fourteen highways (among them the Chinese Summer Palace road, the Oregon trail, and the Inca highway) which had played an important part in the history of nations rimming the Pacific Ocean.[27]

As at the Chicago fair, music was a feature of the exhibit. Walter Flandorf, of Chicago, one of the country's leading organists, and José Manzanares and his Latin American orchestra entertained visitors in the building's patio. In the nearby Ford Bowl, a 3,000-seat amphitheater built by the Ford Company and the Works Progress Administration, the symphony orchestras of San Diego, Los Angeles, San Francisco, Portland, and Seattle and the Mormon Tabernacle Choir performed. Just as the Ford-sponsored musical programs at the Chicago fair had been broadcast free of charge by the major radio networks, many of the San Diego concerts and recitals also were beamed throughout the country.[28]

The Ford building, which was under the company's auspices only during the first year of the two-year exposition, drew more visitors in 1935 than any other exhibit. Of the fair's 4,784,811 opening-season guests, 2,722,765 visited the Ford building. The California State Building ranked second in attendance with 1,719,836 visitors. Thousands of Ford's guests had been encouraged to visit the company's exhibit by dealers, many of whom regularly presented slide films on the fair in their showrooms. Ayer's publicists placed hundreds of news and photo-feature stories on the exhibit and its visitors in West Coast newspapers. In San Diego their efforts were rewarded with a weekly average of 600 column inches of publicity in the city's three daily newspapers during the opening weeks of the fair.[29]

The San Diego fair originally was scheduled to remain open only during 1935. Its officials, however, jubilant over the success of the 1935 season, decided to reopen the gates in 1936. The Ford Company, as the sponsor of the fair's most popular exhibit, was asked to maintain its display for the second year. But believing that fair attendance would drop sharply in 1936 and busy with preparations for a major exhibit at the Texas Centennial Central Exposition in 1936, it refused. In accordance with its prefair plan, Ford donated its exhibit to the exposition company. At the same time the auto firm agreed to replace its 1935 displays with the collection of historic vehicles it had shown at the Chicago fair, if the fair corporation would staff the exhibit. Ford also offered to furnish cars and drivers for the roads exhibit and to sponsor four- and two-week appearances in the Ford Bowl by the San Diego and San Francisco symphony orchestras, respectively. The proposal was accepted by grateful officials. As a result of its reduced commitment, Ford, which had spent $1,325,047 on its exhibit in 1935 (including the cost of the building), spent only $66,944 on the revamped 1936 display.

As Ford had surmised, the fair drew far fewer visitors in 1936 than in 1935; in fact, only 2,192,622. Of this number, 1,208,498 visited the Ford building.[30]

Still standing in the former fair grounds, Balboa Park, the Ford pavilion was used as a classroom building by the San Diego Vocational School from World War II until 1956. Since 1956 the structure, in a state of disrepair, has been used for storage. In 1970 and 1973 San Diego voters rejected bond proposals which would have transformed the building into an aerospace museum. Meanwhile, the amphitheater, renamed the Balboa Park Bowl in 1948, continues to be used for outdoor musical productions, including the summer series of San Diego's Starlight Opera and the Summer Symphony Series.[31]

In addition to its participation in the San Diego fair, the Ford Company also maintained a display on Atlantic City's Steel Pier during the summers of 1935 and 1936. Commercial in tone, the exhibit was billed by Ford as "the largest automotive show in the East." The company's cars and trucks were the featured attraction, but in 1935 training classes for auto mechanics were also conducted in full view of visitors, and in 1936 a model service station was operated on the premises. The 1936 exhibit also presented a "car in the clouds" display which, through an optical illusion, made it appear as if a V-8 were being driven through clouds. For six weeks during the exhibit's second year, José Manzanares and his orchestra entertained. Company salesmen stationed at the exhibit referred more than 14,000 visitors to dealers, 439 sales resulting from the referrals. The exhibit entertained 2,465,635 visitors during the two summers.[32]

By 1936, on the strength of his exhibits at the Chicago and San Diego fairs, Henry Ford had acquired a reputation as "America's No. 1 automobile exhibitor." Thus, when the magnate announced his intention to participate in the Texas Centennial Central Exposition in Dallas in 1936, the press correctly assumed that he would be one of the fair's largest exhibitors. *Advertising & Selling* reported that Ford would spend $2,000,000 on his display; *Time* and *Collier's* set the figure at $2,250,000, the latter adding that the building and exhibit would be "more elaborate than any predecessor." Actually, the company spent only two-fifths of what it had spent in Chicago, less than it had spent in San Diego. Still, among the scores of industrial firms which had displays at the Dallas fair, the Ford Company was the leading exhibitor.[33]

At Edsel Ford's suggestion, Ford's exhibit area featured displays which showed how the agricultural and natural resources of the Southwest were transformed into parts for cars and trucks. An outdoor court, where the company's vehicles were displayed, provided a rest area for guests. Adjacent to the building, the company operated a "roads of the Southwest" exhibit, with replicas of the Santa Fe trail, the Chisholm trail, the old San Antonio road, the Pan American highway, and so on. Musical entertainment was provided by the José Manzanares and Tommy Dorsey orchestras. Both bands broadcast Ford-sponsored network radio programs from the building, Manzanares in behalf of Lincoln dealers and Dorsey, a summer replacement for Fred Waring's orchestra, in behalf of Ford dealers.[34]

Of the 5,482,945 people who visited the fair, 3,198,000 were guests of the Ford exhibit. Although the fair did not release attendance figures for individual exhibitors, and contemporary news accounts made no mention of exhibitor attendance claims, it is certain that the Ford exhibit, as one of the largest on the grounds, was also one of the best attended.[35]

The Ford Company also exhibited at the Great Lakes Exposition of 1936, held in commemoration of the centennial anniversary of Cleveland. Neither Ford nor any of the other automobile companies erected buildings in Cleveland, since fair officials decreed that all automotive exhibitors be grouped together in the exposition's Automotive Building. Virtually all of the firms placed emphasis on product displays. Ford was no exception, although it supplemented its vehicle display with its "car in the clouds" exhibit, demonstrations of tools and machines by Henry Ford Trade School students, and a model of the company's wood distillation plant at Iron Mountain, Michigan.[36]

The Cleveland fair was visited by 3,700,000 people, of whom 1,750,000 entered the Automotive Building. Most of the building's visitors, Ford officials presumed, saw the company's exhibit. To reach these people, the company spent $82,142. The exhibit received few press mentions outside of the Cleveland area. However, dealers reported that 348 sales had resulted from the 3,778 customer referrals they had received.[37]

In November 1936, at the close of the Texas Centennial Exposition, the manager of Ford's Jacksonville, Florida branch induced the company to ship most of its Dallas displays to Miami to publicize the Ford organization and its products among Floridians and tourists. An exhibit building was hastily constructed and opened with a flourish in mid-January, the wife of Miami's mayor cutting a ribbon at the ceremony. As the "largest industrial exhibit ever staged in Florida by a manufacturer," the Ford Florida Exposition, as the exhibit was called, appealed to local pride and was generously publicized in newspapers throughout the state.

The exhibit's displays showed how Florida's products were used in the manufacture of automobiles. Musical entertainment was once again provided by José Manzanares and his orchestra. Open until April 11, 1937, the exhibit drew 529,117 visitors. Of this number, 180 purchased Ford cars or trucks as a result of referrals to dealers. The company paid a high price—$204,670—for these sales and the presumably favorable impression that the exhibit made upon visitors. Weighing the investment (the $87,000 building, of temporary construction, was sold for only $5,000), Ford did not repeat its Miami venture elsewhere.[38]

Befitting his reputation as one of America's foremost exhibitors, Henry Ford was a major participant in the 1939–40 world's fairs in San Francisco and New York which brought to a close the country's "big fair era." The industrialist wanted to build another large exhibit building at San Francisco's Golden Gate International Exposition. But his plans were blocked by a policy of the fair corporation requiring all exhibitors to use buildings or space provided by the exposition. The Ford Company thereupon took possession of a 42,000 square-foot building favorably located opposite the ferry entrance to the grounds. The company's chief rivals, General Motors and Chrysler, each occupied 14,000 square feet of floor space in the exposition's Vacationland Building in 1939, General Motors moving to a separate building in 1940. Among the fair's 350 commercial exhibitors, only General Motors, which in 1940 also occupied 42,000 square feet of floor space, had a display area as large as that of the Ford Company.[39]

In 1939 Ford's exhibit featured a score of displays which showed, primarily through laboratory tests and working and scale models of plants, how the firm conducted its research, engineering, and manufacturing operations. Otherwise, the exhibit followed a familiar format. Products were shown; a model service station was exhibited; and four supplier firms demonstrated how they made parts for Ford cars. At the close of the fair in 1939—acting on the assumption that the exposition's financial troubles would not permit its resumption in 1940—the company dismantled its exhibit. When exposition officials announced that there would be a second season, Edsel Ford was unenthusiastic. Recognizing, however, that the company had a moral commitment to the fair and that his father would wish to participate in 1940, he instructed Fred L. Black and Clarence W. Olmstead, who managed the exhibit in Black's absence, to prepare a new display. Its principal attractions were a quarter-size replica of the company's Dearborn weather tunnel and a 250-seat theater in which Ford films were shown continuously.[40]

McCann-Erickson, Inc., which handled all of Ford's West Coast branch advertising, promoted the San Francisco exhibit. Given only $33,000 for promotion, the agency did not send news releases and photographs to papers throughout the country; rather it "tried to place them in strategic points in the West where it is felt they will have a good chance of being used." The climax of the three-man staff's efforts came on July 24, 1940, Ford Day at the fair (each major exhibitor was honored with a "day"), when it entertained a sizable contingent of California newsmen and placed photo-features on the exhibit in newspapers throughout the West.[41]

Of the 10,496,203 people who attended the fair in 1939, 3,663,175 visited the

Ford exhibit. As Ford officials anticipated, second-season attendance dropped sharply to 6,545,796, Ford's exhibit attracting 2,336,849.[42] Although the Golden Gate International Exposition was one of the largest and best attended fairs in the country's history, it was dwarfed by the mammoth New York World's Fair of 1939-40, the largest exposition ever held. In keeping with the magnitude of the New York fair, Henry Ford's exhibit was the most elaborate, best publicized, and best attended of any in his firm's history.

Ford was the first auto manufacturer to announce plans to participate in the New York exposition. Aware that he had boycotted the Chicago fair in 1933 because General Motors had "stolen" his assembly line idea, Grover Whalen, president of the New York fair, decided early in 1937 to approach the magnate before seeking commitments from other auto companies. But Ford, who abhorred making appointments, rebuffed Whalen's repeated requests for an interview. Undaunted, Whalen went to Dearborn, managed to waylay Ford as he was entering the Rouge, was granted a hearing, and, after a few hours of discussion, had Ford's promise to participate in the fair.[43]

Ford's New York exhibit building, 520 feet long, 420 feet wide, and 88 feet high, enclosed more space—approximately 218,000 square feet—than the floor areas of his San Diego, Dallas, and Cleveland exhibits combined and was slightly larger than his huge building at the Chicago fair. Of the 1,600 commercial exhibitors at the New York exposition, only one company, the pacesetter of the auto industry, General Motors, had a larger structure. Ford spent $5,528,246 to build and maintain his exhibit over the fair's two-year span, almost half of what he had spent on displays between 1934 and 1940. Again, only General Motors' exhibit, which cost more than $7,000,000, was more expensive.[44]

Erected on the highest point within the fairgrounds, the Ford building was outwardly dominated by a half-mile-long "road of tomorrow" which wound around the company's exhibit area and rose in circling ramps to pass through the nave of the structure and emerge above the roof. From this vantage point Ford's guests, while riding over the road in V-8's, Mercurys, and Lincoln Zephyrs, had an unexcelled view of the fairgrounds.

Inside the Ford building were two large halls. The circular entrance hall, ninety-four feet in diameter, contained Henry Ford's "quadricycle," a 1903 Model A, the company's new lines of cars, and a series of displays which depicted the Ford Company's contributions to automotive progress and the changes the auto had made in American life. The entrance hall also contained a huge animated mural which showed how industry made use of scientific research. Beyond the entrance hall was the semicircular industrial hall, 250 feet wide, dominated by a massive inverted cone called the "Ford cycle of production." Described by *Advertising & Selling* as "the largest animated display ever produced" and by *Architectural Forum* as "unquestionably the most impressive display at the fair," the 152-ton cone measured 100 feet at its base and 30 feet in height. On the cone, which revolved slowly and resembled a huge wedding cake with many tiers, 87 working models and 142 animated figures showed how raw material (on the bottom tier of the cone) were progressively transformed into automobile parts. Atop the cone, on a platform, were mounted three finished products, a V-8, a Mercury, and a Lincoln-Zephyr. On the wall in back of the turntable was a 30- by 112-foot photo mural which described various Ford manufacturing operations. The company publicized this mural as "the largest of its kind in the world," apparently forgetting that the murals used in its Chicago exhibit and at the Rotunda, in Dearborn, were almost three times as large.

Just as the "cycle of production" was based on a familiar Ford exhibit theme, so were the other displays in the industrial hall. The company and four of its suppliers manufactured half a dozen small parts for the V-8; an "industrialized farm" processed soybeans into plastics; a model service station serviced the cars used on the road of tomorrow; Greenfield Village students made reproductions from Thomas A. Edison's original blueprints; and a scaled-down weather tunnel was shown in operation. Adjacent to the industrial hall was a garden court, where foot-weary guests rested at umbrella-shaded tables. Music, also a feature of every Ford exhibit, was provided by Ferde Grofé and his New World Ensemble, which performed on novachords, a newly developed instrument which simulated the tones of the piano, harpsichord, banjo, steel guitar, and various reed and string instruments.[45]

Between the 1939 and 1940 fair seasons the company added to its building a glass entrance facade seventy feet high and a wing containing a 420-seat theater. Inside the theater were shown a film fantasy, "Symphony in F," based on the animated models and figures in the "cycle of production," and a fifteen-minute musical comedy, "A Thousand Times Neigh." Although a Ford news release hailed "Symphony in F" as a "masterpiece of industrial photography," company executives privately were less enthusiastic. "It sounds like a puzzling combination of 'Snow White' and an educational, industrial reel," publicist George F. Pierrot confided to Fred L. Black. "I think we ought to pick one or the other." Pierrot was no happier with "A Thousand Times Neigh." "The whole show seems somewhat confused," he informed Black. "It's as though we hadn't decided whether to appeal to the intelligentsia or the proletariat and, consequently, we fall somewhere in between." Pierrot voted for appealing to the proletariat, and the show, revamped with the "average audience" in mind, subsequently was presented before 1,700,000 people.

Lauded for its treatment of guests at previous expositions, the Ford Company was also complimented on the way its 920-member staff welcomed New York visitors. "Guests were never hurried through the building," noted *Business Week,* "and there was always an attendant who could explain technical matters in layman's language." Ford, concluded the magazine, "did a particularly good reception job."[46]

Although mainly concerned with the people who visited their exhibit, Ford executives—mindful that only one in five Americans would visit the fair, and even fewer the company's building—made a special and highly successful effort to acquaint stay-at-homes with what Ford was doing at the exposition. A total of $325,198 was spent on publicity, almost ten times the amount spent to publicize the San Francisco exhibit, more than three times the publicity outlay at the Chicago fair. The exhibit's Press Department was headed by George F. Pierrot, a former editor of *American Boy-Youth's Companion* and president of Detroit's World Adventure [lecture] Series. Accurately described by Black as "one of the best publicity men in the U.S.," Pierrot directed a staff (most of whom, including Pierrot, were on Ayer's payroll) ranging in size from fifteen to twenty-six, including five photographers. Each week the publicists distributed photographs of the exhibit to seventy-four metropolitan dailies with circulations of 50,000 or more; to the sixty-four dailies with a rotogravure section; and to fifty-eight automotive publications. Photo mats were sent twice weekly to 1,500 smaller daily newspapers and biweekly to 2,035 weekly newspapers and eighty foreign-language publications. In addition, photographs or mats of every prominent visitor were sent to all newspapers in the guest's home state. [47]

Pierrot's staff also publicized the exhibit through scores of parties held in the Ford building, whose dining room was more suitable for large meetings than that of any other commercial exhibitor. During 1939–40 almost 50,000 persons dined free of charge in the Ford building, in groups ranging from curators of museums and Brooklyn orphans to county agricultural agents and French mayors. Virtually all of the events generated some publicity for the host, and some of them attracted nationwide attention. Perhaps the best publicized party was New York's official farewell banquet for Rear Admiral Richard E. Byrd, who in the fall of 1939 made a third trip to the Antarctic. The event was mentioned in virtually every newspaper in the country and, in addition, was described over a national radio broadcast by Lowell Thomas, cotoastmaster of the affair. Other nationally publicized parties included a meeting in May 1939 of the country's leading lecturers, among them Burton Holmes and Major George Fielding Eliot, and a "trade relations good-will" dinner in July 1939 for leading foreign government officials stationed in New York City. [48]

Ford's publicists also did their utmost to "inspire" publicity. "The first step," according to a 1939 report of the Press Department, "was to generate an idea and work it out. The second step was to interest a city editor or magazine editor. The third step was to meet the reporter here, accompany him on his rounds, and dig up any supplementary material he might want. Our clipping books are full of three, four, five, and six-column stories in New York papers and others which originated in this manner." Additional publicity was generated by special events, notably the dedication of the road of tomorrow and Ford Days in 1939 and 1940 (Henry Ford spoke briefly at the "day" in 1939, thus assuring national coverage).

> At most of these events [the Press Department reported] we issued in advance lengthy "handouts" telling the full story to all city editors, news services, photo services, and wire services. We followed these up by telephone, making sure that everyone would cover. On the day of the event we issued a new handout, and passed it to every reporter and photographer in attendance. Meanwhile, we made our own pictures and sent them out, with stories, both locally and nationally. Thus, we took no chances on being ignored.

As a result of the Press Department's initiative and diligence, more than 1,000 newsmen visited the Ford exhibit in 1939 alone. That year, the company filled "four large books with 375,000 square inches of press clippings devoted entirely or in part to ... the Ford Exposition." The Press Department estimated that these clippings represented only a fraction of the total "since it is unlikely that any clipping service supplies a client with more than 15 percent of his clippings." Averring that "our total volume in the newspaper and magazine press must be enormous," Pierrot, after the close of the 1939 season, informed his superiors that Ford had received more press play than any other exhibitor at the fair. His contention was corroborated in a nationwide press analysis conducted by the American Telephone & Telegraph Company throughout the summer of 1939. According to this "painstaking analysis," the Ford exhibit received "far more newspaper mentions" than any of its rivals. George Welbaun, director of general information for A.T. & T., which ranked second in its own poll (General Motors ranked third), acknowledged that Ford was doing "the best publicity job on the grounds." A similar view was expressed in the fall of 1939 by a member of the World's Fair publicity staff.[49]

Although the Ford Company had the best publicized exhibit at the fair, it did not have the most popular display on the grounds. The fair's outstanding attraction, by common consent, was the General Motors exhibit, which featured a ride through the "Futurama," a huge, realistic scale model of America as designer Norman Bel Geddes thought it would look in 1960. Ford officials conceded that GM's exhibit was more popular than their own. "Newspapermen tell us so," Pierrot ruefully reported to an Ayer associate, " and we hear it constantly from the general public also." At the same time Pierrot—perhaps whistling in the dark—insisted that the Ford show did a better job of selling Ford products and policies than did the GM exhibit, "which while an excellent 'stunt' show does not directly sell General Motors products."[50]

As far as popularity, not attendance, was concerned, several exhibitors, in fact, vied with Ford for the No. 2 position. The Dearborn company ranked fourth in a popularity poll conducted outside the fair's gates by the American Institute of Public Opinion (the Gallup poll) in May 1939, the month the exposition opened. Rated between first-ranked General Motors and Ford were the fair's theme center, the Perisphere, and American Telephone & Telegraph's exhibit, which daily permitted 150 visitors to telephone any point in the country while other visitors listened in.[51]

Of the 44,932,978 persons who visited the fair in 1939–40, General Motors entertained an estimated 24,000,000, Ford 15,148,684. All other exhibitors lagged far behind. General Motors' figures were later vigorously disputed by George F. Pierrot.[52]

Ford's exhibit, although it did not dominate its setting as had most of the company's prewar displays, nonetheless was a source of much satisfaction to the man who paid its bills, Henry Ford. Taking up temporary residence in a twenty-five-room house a few miles from the fairgrounds, the industrialist and his wife visited the company's exhibit many times, often mingling with the crowds. At times Ford announced his presence and permitted reporters to trail at his heels; at other times he instructed his staff to keep his presence a secret so that he could casually stroll around the grounds.

The New York fair was the last exposition attended by the manufacturer (he did not visit the San Francisco fair) and thus closed a chapter in his career. In 1940 he could look back on a six-year period in which his company had entertained tens of millions of people and vied with General Motors, now selling more than twice as many cars as his own firm, as the country's No. 1 exhibitor. The magnate's exhibits unquestionably paid dividends in the forms of goodwill and new-car sales, although it is probable that a comparable investment in print and radio advertising would have proved more productive as a sales tool. Moreover, the pavilions probably provided inspiration to many youngsters, as Ford fervently hoped. To the auto king, in any event, it perhaps was enough that he had tried to kindle a fire in young minds, and in so doing had repaid a debt contracted in Chicago more than four decades before.[53]

Chapter 19
Henry Ford on the Air

Although Henry Ford was usually the first automobile manufacturer to announce plans to participate in expositions (the Chicago fair was the exception), he was the last of the major auto makers to make continuing use of another and perhaps even more important advertising and public relations medium—network radio.

The magnate was, of course, no stranger to radio when he launched his first sustained network program in January 1934. During the 1920s his firm led all others in the use of intracompany radio communications, and between 1922 and 1926 he owned and operated a radio station in Dearborn; he abandoned the venture when broadcasting became less of a hobby than a business. He also arranged for his old-fashioned dance orchestra to perform over network radio at new-model introduction time in January 1926 and January 1927; but on these occasions he appeared more interested in popularizing early American dance music than in publicizing his cars.

For half-a-dozen years after 1927 the manufacturer turned his back on radio. During this period the broadcasting industry moved ahead rapidly. The National Broadcasting Company (NBC), after organizing the Red network in 1926, established a second chain of stations, the Blue network, in 1927. In 1928 a third "hook-up" of stations was formed by the Columbia Broadcasting System, Inc. (CBS). Between 1927 and 1932 the number of receiving sets in use in the United States increased from 6,500,000 to 16,679,000; by 1932, 55.7 percent of all American families owned a radio. By the early 1930s radio also had become an important advertising medium. [It] "has almost ceased to be an advertising sensation," declared *Fortune* in September 1932. "It has settled down to being an advertising success."[1]

In tune with the emergence of radio as an advertising medium, many large companies, including eight auto manufacturers, embarked on network advertising in the late 1920s and early 1930s. In 1927 auto makers spent $133,506 on time charges for network advertising. Six years later, in spite of the depression, this outlay had increased to $1,863,436. General Motors was the perennial leader among auto advertisers; it spent $751,138 on network time charges in 1933, more than twice the sum disbursed that year by runner-up Hudson Motor Car Company.[2]

Noting the swing to radio advertising, many Ford dealers (who received from the company a $3.00 allotment per car sold for local advertising) pooled their resources in the summer of 1933 and began sponsoring regional network radio programs. The most important of these programs, "Lum & Abner," which featured country store humor, was presented over nineteen eastern and midwestern stations of the Red network. Other leading dealer programs were "The Ford Merrymakers," a musical sponsored by Pacific Coast dealers on the Don Lee network, and "The Ford Revue," a variety show "starring Miss Nancy Garner, niece of Vice President Garner, a blackface comedy team, and a twenty-two piece orchestra," presented by Texas and Oklahoma dealers on a southwestern chain of stations. During the last half of 1933 Ford dealers pumped "several hundred thousand dollars" into these regional programs (abandoned in December 1933) and various local shows.[3]

As the number of receiving sets rapidly increased, as an increasing number of business firms advertised on radio—and as his own dealers surged into the medium—Henry Ford almost perforce had to take radio into consideration when mapping plans in late 1933 for what the trade press called the "greatest merchandising drive" in the Ford Company's history. Informed that Ford was considering sponsorship of a national radio show, network executives were jubilant, for "no single advertiser had been so much sought after since network broadcasting began." For years the rumor had circulated in the broadcasting industry that the CBS salesman who brought Ford "into the fold" would be rewarded with a $10,000 bonus ("Ford dealer programs didn't count," said *Tide*. "They were nice, but they were not Henry Ford"). CBS repeatedly denied that it had authorized such a bonus, but as *Broadcasting* pointed out, "the fact that the report gained such widespread credence was proof of the importance attached to this one piece of business." In any event, when Ford announced in early December 1933 that he would sponsor a program over both NBC and CBS networks, broadcasting officials were reported as having the "same sense of elation that General Johnson would have felt if Henry Ford had given his blessing to the NRA."[4]

Technically sponsored by the Ford Dealers of America, Inc., and financed by a $2.00 per vehicle charge levied on dealers at the time cars and trucks were wholesaled to them, Ford's first national network radio program was a musical variety show featuring Fred Waring and his Pennsylvanians. Organized in 1921 while Waring was a student at Pennsylvania State College, the Waring band, outfitted in knickers, loud striped sweaters, and big flowing ties, gained national recognition in 1924 with its rendition of the song, "Collegiate." The orchestra set box office records in numerous theaters and appeared in several motion pictures between 1924 and 1932 including Harold Lloyd's *The Freshman* (in which the Pennsylvanians started a fad for bell-bottomed trousers), and one of the first big screen musicals, *Syncopation*. By 1933 Waring's orchestra was the "pride and joy" of tobacco manufacturer P. Lorillard Co. Broadcasting in behalf of Lorillard's Old Gold cigarettes, the orchestra was rated as the "best musical program" and "third favorite program" on the air in a 1933 poll of radio editors conducted by the *New York World-Telegram*.[5]

Although Waring renewed his contract with Lorillard in November 1933, Ford, who was determined to sponsor the Pennsylvanians, "offered so much money" ($10,000 per week) that the orchestra leader negotiated a release from the tobacco company. Like Waring's Old Gold program, which had been broadcast over a greater number of stations (eighty) than any other regular program, the new Ford program was also presented over the "largest network in the history of regular commercial-program broadcasting"—eighty-six American and Canadian CBS stations.[6]

Launched on February 2, the twice-weekly Waring show was designed to "interest every type of listener." For several months, in addition to presenting popular musical selections and "novelty acts," the program featured such guest artists as Soprano Marion Talley, baritone Ezio Pinza, and composer-pianist George Gershwin. But noting that young people and women of all ages had requested "hundreds of thousands" of autographed pictures of the handsome thirty-three-year-old Waring, N. W. Ayer & Son, which supervised the program, abandoned the guest-star format and the effort to appeal to all musical tastes in favor of spotlighting the band leader and "aiming exclusively at young listeners and women Ford buyers."[7]

In deference to Henry Ford's lifelong aversion to blatant advertising, commercial messages on the Waring show were restrained compared to those of most other sponsors. In the first of Waring's broadcasts, Edsel Ford, who shared his father's distaste for "hard-sell" advertising, informed the audience that "our dealers do not intend to spoil this program by intrusive advertising. I know they will be glad enough to talk Ford V-8 to you whenever you wish, but they don't expect me to press on that subject while you are their guests on this program." Several publications commended the company for its low-pressure advertising. *Radio Stars* expressed its appreciation by awarding the Waring show its monthly "distinguished service award" for May 1934.[8]

The Pennsylvanians' shows ranked among the top ten radio programs in both the listenership and sponsor-identification surveys conducted by Clark-Hooper, Inc., one of the nation's leading radio audience measurement organizations. The shows also were acclaimed by radio editors and critics.[9]

Although Ayer and Ford executives were gratified by the Waring show's popular and critical success, a cutback in the company's radio advertising budget for 1937 forced cancellation of the program after three years of Ford sponsorship. Buoyed by Henry and Edsel Ford's enthusiasm for sponsorship of radio programs, the Ford organization by 1936 had become the third largest advertiser on radio, spending $2,082,664 on network air time alone that year (almost twice as much as fourteenth-ranked General Motors). The company spent an additional $1,500,000 on talent, advertising, agency commissions, and miscellaneous items for its four major radio programs: the Waring show, the Ford Sunday Evening Hour, the José Manzanares program, and World Series broadcasts.[10]

In early 1937 the company engaged comedian Al Pearce (who had been sponsored on network radio by Lever Brothers in 1936) to fill one of Waring's half-hour time slots, Rex Chandler and his orchestra the other. Both of these shows were sponsored by the Ford, Lincoln, and Lincoln Zephyr Dealers of America, Inc., the Lincoln dealers' year-old program, José Manzanares and his Latin American orchestra, having also been dropped for economy reasons at the close of 1936.[11]

Pearce's show, called "Watch the Fun Go By," toured the country for many months, broadcasting before groups of dealers and their friends. Neither the Pearce nor the Chandler program had as many listeners as Waring, although the Pearce show managed a midway position (sixth to tenth place) in listenership and sponsor-identification surveys of network radio's fifteen top comedy variety programs. Chandler's show, "Universal Rhythm," never achieved high listenership or sponsor identification, and was on the air only eight months. The decision to drop Chandler, together with the abandonment of the Waring and Manzanares shows in late 1936 (and World Series broadcasts in the fall of 1937), enabled the company to reduce its annual commitment to radio advertising by more than $700,000 in 1937. The Pearce program was discontinued in June 1938, when the Ford Company, in the midst of its poorest sales year since 1933, further reduced advertising expenditures.[12]

The Ford Company (technically, the Ford Dealers of America, Inc.) vied with the Buick Motor Division of General Motors as radio's leading sponsor of sports events during the mid-1930s. Buick sponsored broadcasts of most of the heavyweight championship boxing matches of the period, including those between Joe Louis and Max Baer, Max Schmeling, Jim Braddock, and Tommy Farr; Ford sponsored broadcasts of baseball's World Series.

By winning their first American League championship in twenty-five years in 1934, the Detroit Tigers set the stage for Ford sponsorship of the series. In August 1934, as "pennant fever" swept the Motor City, the auto company engaged Tiger manager Gordon S. (Mickey) Cochrane to present seven weekly broadcasts on the major league pennant races. Beamed over twenty-two stations of the CBS network, Cochrane's program had heavy listenership and, in turn, paved the way for company sponsorship of the October classic.[13]

Broadcasts of the series had not been commercially sponsored before 1934; the networks had presented the games as a public service. In 1934, however, Baseball Commissioner Judge Kenesaw Mountain Landis offered to sell broadcast rights to the series for $100,000. Edsel Ford—so enthusiastic about baseball that he once had planned to buy a National League franchise and transfer it to Detroit—persuaded his father to meet the commissioner's price.

The series was broadcast over the "greatest commercial hook-up of radio stations ever attempted"—180 outlets of the CBS and Red networks and two regional chains in Michigan and Missouri, the home states of the competing Tigers and St. Louis Cardinals. Announcing the games were several of the country's leading sportscasters: Ted Husing, Frances Laux, and Ford Bond for CBS; Graham McNamee, Tom Manning, and Pat Flanagan for NBC; and Ty Tyson for the regional networks.[14]

Ford advertising on the series broadcasts was as unobtrusive as that on the Waring show. "The Series [belongs] to the entire American public," Edsel Ford announced on the eve of the event, "and . . . will not be interrupted by unwarranted comment concerning the sponsor of the broadcast or its products." This restraint did not, however, prevent the company from urging its dealers to invite the public to listen to broadcasts in their showrooms or used car lots. Most of the company's dealers responded to this appeal, and millions of Americans listened to blaring radios on dealers' premises.[15]

In 1935 the Tigers repeated as American League champions, meeting the Chicago Cubs in the World Series. Ford again sponsored broadcasts of the classic, this time over the CBS, NBC (Red), and Michigan chains, plus the newly organized Mutual Broadcasting System network. In 1936 the series was contested by two New York teams, the Yankees and the Giants. But because the intramural contests attracted less national interest than the games between Detroit and St. Louis and Detroit and Chicago, listenership fell sharply.

In 1937 the Ford Company again bought, for $100,000, commercial rights to World Series broadcasts. At the same time the company, which had decided not to invest another $250,000 in air time if the all-powerful Yankees and Giants repeated as contestants, reserved the privilege of waiving its broadcast rights. When the two New York teams again won league championships, Ford exercised its waiver, thereby forfeiting the $100,000 paid to Commissioner Landis's office. With this decision the company discontinued sponsorship of sports broadcasts for the remainder of the prewar period.[16]

During the very week in which the Ford Company sponsored its first World Series broadcasts in 1934, it also launched another and vastly more important radio venture, the Ford Sunday Evening Hour.

The Sunday Evening Hour was an outgrowth of the Ford-financed Detroit Symphony Orchestra concerts at the Chicago World's Fair. These concerts, broadcast as a public service by the leading networks, prompted thousands of letters from appreciative listeners. Many of the letters were shown by Exhibit Manager Fred L. Black to Henry and Edsel Ford, William J. Cameron, and N. W. Ayer executives. Impressed by the enthusiastic response, Ayer recommended to Edsel that the Ford Company sponsor the Detroit orchestra on network radio during the 1934–35 season. The younger Ford endorsed the idea, telling his father in the late summer of 1934, "this thing is too good to pass up." Agreeing, Henry Ford instructed his son to "work out" a radio program.[17]

Like the Waring show, the Sunday Evening Hour was broadcast over the complete CBS network—eighty-six stations. But unlike the Waring show and other Ford programs, the Ford Hour was financed by the company rather than the Ford Dealers of America, Inc. As a result the company's dealers, many of whom looked askance at sponsorship of a symphony orchestra, had little direct association with the program during its eight-year run.

The musical format of the Sunday Evening Hour was "music of familiar theme, with majestic rendition." Each program was opened and closed with "The Children's Prayer" from Humperdinck's "Hänsel und Gretel." The music presented on the Ford Hour, although regarded as "light" by the sophisticated listener, probably was considered "heavy" by the average American and buyer of Ford cars. On the first program the orchestra performed works of Wagner, Bach, Sibelius, Mendelssohn—and in deference to Henry Ford's tastes—MacDowell ("Uncle Remus" and "To a Wild Rose"). The soloist, Maria Jeritza, a former soprano of the Metropolitan Opera, sang selections by Tchaikovsky, Joyce, Grieg, and Romberg. Most programs of later years followed a similar format, mixing symphonic classics and great concertos with numbers from operettas and such favorites of Henry Ford as "Turkey in the Straw" and "Home Sweet Home."[18]

Madame Jeritza was but the first of many internationally known artists who appeared on the Sunday Evening Hour. Jascha Heifetz, Albert Spaulding, José Iturbi, Rosa Ponselle, Ezio Pinza, Grace Moore, Jan Peerce, and Nelson Eddy were presented on the program during its first season. During subsequent seasons the Ford Hour also presented Mischa Elman, Yehudi and Hephziba Menuhin, Myra Hess, Kirsten Flagstad, Lucrezia Bori, Lauritz Melchior, Richard Crooks, Lily Pons, Lawrence Tibbett, John Charles Thomas, Gladys Swarthout, Marian Anderson, Helen Traubel, Oscar Levant, Bidu Sayao, and Risë Stevens. Many of these artists appeared on half a dozen or more of the Ford broadcasts.

The orchestra was conducted by Victor Kolar, associate director of the Detroit Symphony Orchestra, during the first two seasons. In later years it was directed by guest conductors, among them Eugene Ormandy, Sir Thomas Beecham, Wilfred Pelletier, Artur Rodzinski, George Szell, Reginald Stewart, Fritz Reiner, and André Kostelanetz.

The soloists and conductors were paid handsomely. During the 1934–35 season artists' fees per concert ranged from $350 for comparative "unknowns" to $5,000 for Heifetz and $5,250 for Ponselle. In 1937–38 fees ranged from $1,000 for lesser performers to $6,000 for Heifetz and Eddy and $10,000 for the Menuhins. In 1939 the company set a maximum fee of $5,000 per performance, and this ceiling was retained through the hour's last three seasons. Conductors were paid from $600 (Kolar) to $1,500 (Ormandy) per appearance. Orchestra costs ranged from $74,431 during the 1934–35 season to approximately $100,000 for each of the last several seasons.[19]

The admission-free broadcasts attracted capacity audiences to the halls in which they were presented. The broadcasts emanated from Detroit's 2,000-seat Orchestra Hall during 1934–36, thereafter from the Motor City's 5,000-seat Masonic Temple, the largest auditorium in Michigan. Between 1934 and 1942 more than 1,300,000 people attended the concerts; an additional 300,000 people applied for tickets but could not be accommodated.[20]

As a "long-hair" program, the Sunday Evening Hour could not hope to achieve as wide a listenership as the better comedy, variety, and dramatic programs. The Ford Hour, in fact, was never ranked higher than twenty-eighth in listenership surveys conducted by Clark-Hooper (becoming C. E. Hooper in 1938) and the Cooperative Analysis of Broadcasting (Crossley ratings), and usually was ranked much lower—from fiftieth to sixtieth—among the eighty-five to 100 programs surveyed. Moreover, the Ford Hour was never the most popular program in its time slot, lagging behind Dr. Lyon's "Manhattan Merry-Go-Round" during its first half-hour on the air and behind Jergen's "Walter Winchell" and Woodbury's "Hollywood Playhouse" during its second half-hour. On the average only 9 percent of the nation's radio sets were tuned to the Ford program, less than a fourth as many as to radio's most popular shows.

On the other hand the Sunday Evening Hour, whose audience was variously estimated at from 10,000,000 to 13,000,000, had almost twice as many listeners as any other symphonic program, including the General Motors Concert Hour (which featured the New York Philharmonic Orchestra). Moreover, the Ford Hour was consistently ranked among the top five programs of all kinds in sponsor-identification polls, with never less than 75 percent and as high as 96.5 percent of its listeners identifying it with the Ford Motor Company.[21]

Although not a favorite of the average listener, the Sunday Evening Hour was repeatedly acclaimed by radio editors and critics. The nation's radio editors, polled annually by the *New York World-Telegram,* rated the show as one of their ten favorite programs in 1936, 1937, and 1940. The crusading Woman's National Radio Committee cited the Ford Hour as the best commercially sponsored program of "serious music" in 1937, 1938, and 1939; and the National Federation of Press Women selected it as the outstanding program of "cultural music" in 1938, 1939, and 1940. No other commercially sponsored symphonic program received as much critical acclaim as the Sunday Evening Hour during the years it was on the air.[22]

If the Detroit Symphony Orchestra's music was responsible for the Ford Hour's critical acclaim, it was the six-minute "intermission talk" by William J. Cameron which set the program apart from all others of its era and made it the Ford Company's most important public relations activity during 1934–42.

Cameron himself conceived the program's "commercial" format. Asked by Edsel to recommend the kind of message that might be presented on the program in lieu of car and truck advertising, he suggested that "something interesting, informative, and general" should be discussed midway through the concert. Intrigued, Edsel asked Cameron to write four or five messages of the kind he had in mind. Cameron complied, preparing several essays reminiscent of articles he had written for "Mr. Ford's Own Page" in the *Dearborn Independent* and talks he had read over the Ford radio station, WWI. Several of the country's leading radio announcers read these essays before Edsel and other company executives. But none of the announcers was found suitable. After expressing his disappointment to his father, Edsel was directed by the elder Ford to audition Cameron. The publicist, after reading his essays in a "folksy style reminiscent of an earnest village parson," was named program commentator.

Both Edsel and Cameron spoke on the Sunday Evening Hour's first broadcast. Edsel introduced the series, assuring listeners, as he had on the Waring show, that "our program will not be interrupted by irritating sales talks." Cameron, during the intermission, announced that the Sunday Hour, in lieu of commercial messages, would offer comment on "certain matters of national interest and importance." In doing so, he added, "we shall sometimes have to sound the personal note . . . about Mr. Ford and what he stands for." In point of fact, Cameron discussed the elder Ford and his views—on such topics as wages, profits, the length of the work day, village industries, schools, and McGuffey readers—in nineteen of the 1934–35 season's thirty-nine talks. In subsequent seasons, however, the talks seldom mentioned Ford by name, although the magnate's philosophy pervaded nearly all of the essays.[23]

Cameron had a free hand in writing his talks. "I worked in a vacuum," he

Henry Ford samples a weed tidbit prepared by George Washington Carver, 1942.

The Henry Ford Museum, the entrance of which features a replica of Independence Hall.

On the day of Greenfield Village's dedication, October 21, 1929, President Herbert Hoover starts a "perpetual fire" in the courthouse in which Abraham Lincoln practiced law. Henry Ford looks on.

The Ford Company's pavilion at Chicago's A Century of Progress Exposition in 1934.

Touring the Ford exhibit at Chicago's A Century of Progress Exposition in 1934: left to right, Fred L. Black, pavilion manager, Colonel Bell of the fair's management, and three generations of Fords, Henry, Edsel, Benson, fourteen, and Henry II, sixteen.

The Ford Rotunda, "gateway to the Rouge" from 1936–62. The building originally was a part of Ford's exhibit at Chicago's A Century of Progress Exposition.

The gutted Ford Rotunda, enveloped in smoke, November 9, 1962. The building's north wing, upper left, which housed the Ford Archives, was spared, thanks to a fire wall.

Ford's pavilion at San Diego's California
Pacific International Exposition of 1935–36, as
it looks today.

The animated "Ford cycle of production," a
principal attraction of the Ford pavilion at the
New York World's Fair of 1939–40. The exhibit showed how raw materials were transformed into automobile parts.

The "road of tomorrow," atop Ford's pavilion
at the New York World's Fair of 1939–40.

Dedication ceremony for the "road of tomorrow," part of Ford's exhibit at the New York World's Fair of 1939–40. Left to right, Grover Whalen, New York City's official greeter, Henry Ford II, Edsel Ford, Henry Ford, former New York Governor Alfred E. Smith, and New York Mayor Fiorello H. La Guardia.

Adm. Richard E. Byrd, left, Fred L. Black, manager of Ford's pavilion at the New York World's Fair of 1939–40, and unidentified guest at a party given in advance of Byrd's third trip to the Antarctic, 1939.

Henry Ford swings an ax on the dent-resistant plastic trunk lid of a 1941 Ford.

Left to right, Capt. Edward V. "Eddie" Rickenbacker, Henry Ford, Edsel Ford, seated in
car, Harvey Firestone, Jr., Henry Ford II, Benson Ford, and Harvey Firestone, Sr., at Indianapolis Speedway in 1932.

Henry Ford, in a rare radio broadcast, supports
President Herbert Hoover's 1932 re-election
bid.

Henry Ford and his chief spokesman, William
J. Cameron, in Cameron's office, 1937.

Fred Waring, front center, Ford sales executive J. R. Davis, to Waring's right, and the Lane sisters, Rosemary, left, and Priscilla, standing behind the car, in Detroit, 1934.

A 1934 broadcast of the Ford Sunday Evening Hour.

A 1935 V-8 advertisement which resurrects Ford's 1907 advertising slogan, ''Watch the Fords Go By.''

FORD V-8

A 1943 Ford advertisement tieing in Ford's B-24 ''Liberator'' and the company's first popular slogan, ''Watch the Fords Go By.''

Ford-Built Consolidated Liberator Bomber

Watch The Fords Go By!

Ford manufacturing boss Charles E. Sorensen, left, and Henry Ford confer in June 1940 on plans to mass produce warplanes. They are standing in front of an army observation plane. (*Detroit Free Press* photo.)

Henry Ford watches grandson Henry II add his signature to Willow Run's 5,000th bomber in 1944. (Associated Press photo.)

Henry Ford, seated at left, guides French Gen. Henri Giraud through the Willow Run bomber plant in 1943. Behind Giraud is Ford manufacturing executive Charles E. Sorensen. (U.S. Army Signal Corps photo; courtesy of Acme.)

recalled later. "There was nobody to consult with, nobody to advise me." Twice the commentator asked Henry Ford about the content of the messages. Ford waved him away with "you know what's best." Cameron complained that preparation for the hour was "killing . . . like having a baby every week." He also insisted that he was not a "natural speaker"; but as a broadcaster, he excelled. "His voice," according to one writer, "had such calm and righteousness and certainty in it that one wondered why all the clashing elements were not immediately drawn into brotherhood, so clearly had [he] switched his road lights on the only path."

At times a heavy drinker, Cameron sometimes delivered his remarks while drunk. Ayer and Ford officials, concerned lest the commentator might not be sober enough to get from his home to the auditorium, assigned an escort to him the afternoon and evening of each broadcast, and also had Fred L. Black stand by to read the message if Cameron appeared too tipsy to go on the air. "My Sundays," Black moaned later, "were ruined for years." But Cameron was extraordinarily constant. He missed only one broadcast, because of an attack of influenza, during the eight years he was on the air. Moreover, he performed as well drunk as sober; only a huskiness in his voice betrayed his inebriation.[24]

Cameron's "sermonettes," as they were called by some of his critics, ranged widely. His favorite topics were morals, holidays, history, the lives of great Americans, economics, business practices, and politics. An analysis of the 1937–38 talks (which, except perhaps for the 1934–35 season, may be considered typical of those presented in other years as well) showed that one-third of the discussions concerned business-government relations. Most of these speeches either flogged the Roosevelt administration or lauded free enterprise, to Cameron "the spinal cord of every period of progress." The commentator, in fact, as Ford's spokesman, probably did more to publicize the merits of free enterprise than any other person during the prewar decade. Moreover, his talks, in the opinion of one competent observer, had "an accumulated effectiveness which only Roosevelt's Fireside Chats surpassed."[25]

As several propaganda analysts have pointed out, Cameron had one important advantage over the President or almost anyone else trying to influence public opinion: the setting. By the time Cameron had stepped to the microphone, his listeners had been lulled by almost half an hour of pleasing, usually relaxing, music; and they were in a "friendly, unguarded, and receptive" state of mind. As if this were not enough, the commentator occasionally further disarmed his audience with assurances that the Ford Company "had no theories to propagate," "no political ax to grind," "no partisan purpose of interest whatever," "no wish to be a professional reformer," and so on. The purpose of the Hour's talks, purred Cameron, was "to give effective help in banishing certain fallacies from public thinking . . . to make, if possible, a modest contribution to straight thinking and common sense."[26]

Cameron's protests to the contrary, the talks were "gems of propaganda." Many of them adroitly created a "plain folks" atmosphere in which Henry Ford was pictured as a "common, ordinary, simple, kindly, generous, democratic man . . . just like us." Many others used the "cloak of virtue" propaganda technique, associating such words as freedom, independence, initiative, truth, and loyalty with the idea being advocated, while still others used the "identification" approach, linking the names of Washington, Lincoln, Jefferson, and Lee, with Ford, and the "endorsement of the people" technique ("the people do not believe . . . are convinced . . . have been persuaded . . . do not want . . . finally realize," and so on). They also abounded in biblical references and slogans commanding universal homage.[27]

Although ignored by its prime target, the administration, Cameron's propaganda-larded talks could not be ignored by the two networks which carried the Ford Hour, the Canadian Broadcasting Company (serving stations in Montreal and Toronto) and CBS. After warning the Ford Company several times that "broadcasts of opinion on current controversial affairs are not eligible for commercial sponsorship," the Canadian company banned Cameron from its airwaves. Insisting that "Mr. Cameron's talks are a vital part of the Sunday Evening Hour," Ford stopped broadcasting over the Canadian stations. CBS twice protested that Cameron's talks had violated its policy of not permitting commercial time to be used for the discussion of controversial issues, threatening the second time to censor the speeches if the company did not "set up effective arrangements to prevent recurrence of these lapses." Thereafter, the commentaries were sufficiently restrained to avoid further censorship.[28]

Many of Cameron's talks, especially those which attacked the administration or commented on current affairs, were widely reported in the press. Several newspapers either ran the speeches verbatim or based an editorial on them, and *Vital Speeches* published twenty-nine of the 285 talks in the series. Moreover, 45,000,000 copies of the talks were distributed, upon request, to listeners. No other radio show of the prewar decade, except for Father Coughlin's highly controversial program, generated so much listener response.[29]

"Thousands of listeners," as *Time* pointed out, "regarded Cameron as an oracle; others made a household game of seeing who could be the first to dial him down." Among the thousands of persons expressing an opinion of Cameron and his talks in letters to the Ford Company, the great majority were complimentary. A California listener wrote that "Mr. Cameron's talk alone is worth the hour," while a Nebraskan felt that the speeches "contain truths and facts as fixed as the law of gravitation." A Baltimore admirer, after congratulating Cameron on his "God gift of being able to express thoughts in beautiful language," said he considered the talks "on a level with President Roosevelt's which I consider the best in the country." Many people wrote that they had saved Cameron's speeches so they could read them "again and again."[30]

Cameron's critics, although outnumbered, were no less extreme in their views. "During the intermission at 9:30," said *PM* in its review of the opening concert of the 1940–41 season, "William J. Cameron, the Ford front man, resumed his 'institutional' talks. This is a good time to go mix a drink." A Schenectady listener inquired whether it was necessary for Cameron to speak. "Your musical portion is one of the best on the air," he remarked, "but when it comes to the sermon, well it's a good thing we can tune to another station." A Texas woman complained that "the inevitable speech . . . gives the effect of a small-town editorial on the status of the cotton crops inserted in a book of classic poetry,'' while a Wisconsinite expressed regret that Ford was ''going out of the 'car' business and entering the propaganda field.'' The *United Auto Worker* vented its wrath in verse:

> Now the music dies out in the distance,
> They announced a lovely old hymn,
> Giving all glory to God
> And singing their praises to Him.
> Do you think, Henry Ford, you exploiter,
> You can buy with this kind of stuff
> The thanks and goodwill of thousands
> Who haven't nearly enough?
> So you might as well keep your music
> And shut old Cameron's yap
> For while we enjoy your music
> We haven't time for your crap.

Writer Dorothy Parker expressed a similar view, albeit more politely:

> Why is it that Gotterdamerung
> Is always followed by William J. Cameron?[31]

Unlike any other Ford-sponsored radio program, Henry and Edsel Ford both favored the Sunday Evening Hour throughout the prewar decade. The outbreak of World War II, however, signaled its downfall. On January 16, 1942, the Ford Company, invoking the ''war clause'' in its contract with CBS, announced that the program would be suspended on March 1. Hundreds of listeners expressed their regret. One person wrote of the ''inspiration'' he had received from the ''beautiful and magnificent'' music; another of the ''refreshing break in the dull round of radio 'jazz' and nostrum advertising''; and still another of the ''most pleasant experience'' and ''greatest cultural high light'' of her life. Acknowledging that the Ford Company should not be expected to sponsor the Sunday Evening Hour when it did not have consumer products for sale, several persons suggested that listeners would gladly contribute funds to keep the program alive. Many letters expressed a hope that the program would be resumed at the end of the war. Publications also expressed regret over the cancellation. Perhaps the finest of these tributes was paid by *Printers' Ink:*

> When the Ford Sunday Evening Hour was broadcast for the last time on March 1, more than a great advertising feature became only a memory; the American people lost an hour of delightful music which, for more than seven years, had been one of the bright spots of their lives. William J. Cameron, who has been a regular feature of the Hour since its inception, made his usual speech—a brave one. We thought we could detect in his voice a note of heartache. Maybe we were wrong, but it sounded that way. If Mr. Cameron did feel regret it can be readily understood. For there was being scrapped something that belonged in the upper brackets of the many high accomplishments of Henry Ford.

Cameron, although he had often asked to be relieved of his weekly task, did indeed regret the cancellation. ''As a musical program,'' he wrote a friend, ''it was, beyond all question, good." Asked what he would do in the future, he replied, "about as usual—the talks were only an extra chore."

At least one person, Harry Bennett, was not sorry to see the Ford Hour discontinued. He believed (as did many Ford dealers) that symphonic music had little appeal to Ford owners and prospective customers and furthermore he detested Cameron. Bennett had tried—unsuccessfully—for several years to persuade Henry Ford to discontinue or change the program.[32]

The average annual cost of the Sunday Evening Hour was $918,000, of which from $500,000 to $600,000 was paid annually to CBS, and a yearly average of $327,000 for talent, exclusive of conductors. In return for its $7,344,000 outlay, the Ford Company reached radio audiences totaling more than 5,000,000,000 and entertained studio audiences aggregating 1,300,000. Unquestionably the company looked upon the investment as sound; in fact, in June 1945—months before World War II was expected to end and full-scale civilian car production could be permitted—the firm announced that the program would be revived in September of that year.[33]

During the summers of 1939, 1940, and 1941, the Ford Company presented the Ford Summer Hour, a lighter musical program, as a replacement for the Sunday Evening Hour. Broadcast over CBS from 8 to 9 P.M. (EST), the Summer Hour featured currently popular songs and selections from musical comedies and operettas. The 1939 series presented singers James Melton and Francia White; the 1940 program Jessica Dragonette and James Newill; and the 1940 hour presented more than a dozen performers including Bob Hannon, Dennis Day, and Lanny Ross. Don Voorhees conducted the 1939 series; Leith Stevens the 1940 programs; and Meredith Willson, Percy Faith, and Harry Horlick the 1940 broadcasts. During the intermission a "Rouge Reporter" discussed Ford-related subjects ranging from the firm's interest in traffic safety and soybean research to its rubber plantations in Brazil and employee training programs. The Hour, one of the most popular of summertime programs, reached an average audience of 9,000,000 people per broadcast. Its average annual cost was $336,000.[34]

The $16,392,385 which the Ford Company spent on major prewar network programs—half again as much as on exhibits, the company's next most expensive public relations activity—kept the firm among the nation's leading radio advertisers throughout the 1934–42 period. Furthermore, Ford, although the last major automobile firm to turn to radio, quickly became the No. 1 advertiser in its industry. Indeed, between 1934–42 it spent more than twice as much money on the medium as the combined amounts spent by General Motors and Chrysler, the industry's next two biggest users of radio.[35] Although it is impossible to measure the effectiveness of Ford's radio advertising, it can be said with certainty that it acquainted millions of Americans with Henry Ford's views and the virtues of the Ford Company and its products. At the same time, it undoubtedly helped Ford dealers sell a great many vehicles.

Chapter 20
V-8 PR and Advertising

1

Henry Ford's company, a leading exhibitor and radio advertiser during the pre-World War II decade, was also heavily engaged during this period in a variety of other public relations and advertising activities.

Between 1933–41, the Ford Company was more active in the motion picture field than any other company except General Motors. Ford had abandoned its film studio as an economy measure in 1932, after having been a leading producer of motion pictures in the 'teens and 'twenties. Late in 1933 it returned to the film medium, using outside agencies rather than its own personnel.

The company's new film program was launched with the distribution of "These Thirty Years," a full-length feature commemorating the firm's thirtieth anniversary. The most expensive film ($105,464) produced by Ford between 1914 and the 1950s, "These Thirty Years" traced the life of a young farmer, who, after losing his land to a greedy mortgage holder, started an automobile dealership. The dealership prospered through the years, until the dealer's son lost much of his father's money in the stock market. By film's end, however, the "wastrel" had seen the error of his ways and "becomes the man his Dad would like him to be." Although accurately described as "naive and full of lengthy sales talk," the picture pleased both ex-farmer Henry Ford and his dealers. The auto magnate directed his sales organization to show the film admission-free for one to two weeks in rented theaters in thirty-two branch cities and other metropolitan areas. Most Ford dealers presented the picture in their showrooms six days a week between December 1933 and February 1934. Within three months of its December 8, 1933 premiere, the film was seen by 3,693,954 people.[1]

In 1934 the company produced two films, "Rhapsody in Steel," and "Ford and A Century of Progress." "Rhapsody in Steel," a musical fantasy which traced the processing of steel through the various stages of automobile manufacture, was described by *Film Daily* as "the best industrial picture we have ever viewed," and was rated by *Sales Management* as "the No. 1 film show" at the Chicago World's Fair. At the fair it was seen by capacity audiences—6,000 people each week. Both "Rhapsody in Steel" and "Ford and A Century of Progress," a documentary on the Chicago fair (about one-fifth of which dealt with the Ford exhibit), were also presented in dealer showrooms throughout America and Europe. In 1935 the company produced two films on the San Diego exposition, "Fair in the West" and "The Honeymoon V-8." The latter picture, a travelogue about newlyweds en route to the fair, was rated by *Sales Management* as one of the "three or four important industrial films of 1935."[2]

In the mid-1930s, Ford also produced more than a score of sound-slide films on such subjects as the Rouge, Greenfield Village, and the San Diego fair in order to attract potential customers to dealers' showrooms. Proving no match for the more exciting motion pictures, the slides were abandoned in 1937 in favor of an all-motion picture library featuring films on travel and Rouge operations. Recognizing that fewer and fewer Americans could be expected to visit dealerships to see Ford films, the company urged dealers to place less emphasis on showroom presentations and to step up their efforts to get the pictures before school, church, service club, and fraternal audiences.[3]

By 1938 Ford's film library included four travel pictures and five Rouge films. During the next two years, four more pictures were produced, among them "Symphony in F," the firm's second most expensive prewar film ($86,327). In 1940, the last prewar year for which attendance figures are available, the thirteen films in Ford's library were shown to 9,923,562 people, of whom 2,096,761 were guests at the Rotunda or the company's exhibit at the New York or San Francisco fairs. Among industrial exhibitors, only General Motors, which showed its library of thirteen films to 9,899,600 people in 1940, came close to matching Ford's figures.[4]

To attract film audiences, the Ford Company spent approximately $500,000 on motion pictures between 1937–41. The outlay, although far less than the $600,000 which the company spent annually on films in the late 'teens, was exceeded by only one industrial producer, General Motors, which devoted $925,000 to the medium between 1937–41. Film competition between the two auto makers was halted at the outbreak of war, when Ford suspended motion picture distribution. General Motors continued to produce and distribute films during 1942–45, topping its prewar attendance record in both 1942 and 1943.[5]

2

Another promotional venture resumed by Henry Ford during the 1930s, after a lapse of two decades, was racing. The Ford Company did not enter cars in contests, as it had in previous years, nor, with one exception, did it finance the construction of racing vehicles. But it strongly endorsed a resumption of racing activities by its dealers and directed its advertising agencies to publicize all important victories of Ford cars.

Impressed by the V-8's quick acceleration, speed, and agile "cornering," many Ford dealers in 1933 challenged "any low or medium-priced car" in hill-climbing, acceleration-from-standing-start, and top-speed-in-second gear contests. Few of the challenges were accepted, since Chevrolet, Plymouth, Essex, and other auto makers warned their dealers to "steer clear" of the Fords. Their reluctance to engage the V-8 was justified, for, according to a *Printers' Ink* survey, Fords won handily in every "specialty" contest in which they participated. Ford products were almost as successful in road races. In 1933 V-8's won the first seven places in the Elgin [Illinois] National Stock Car Road Race, the first six places in the International Alpine Trial, and the first two places in the Laredo-Monterrey Road Race. The following year Fords won the first ten places in both the Gilmore Gold Cup Stock Car Race and the Targo Florio Hill Road Race, held in Southern California. Ford cars also took the first three places in the stock car class of the 1934 Pikes Peak Hill Climb. After each of these victories Ayer blanketed the press with news releases and also sent film clips to dealers, suggesting that they pay local theaters to show them. Many did.[6]

Encouraged by the V-8's victories, Henry Ford decided in February 1935 to cosponsor with Miller-Tucker, Inc., of Detroit, a builder of racing cars, ten entries in the Indianapolis Speedway's 500-mile Memorial Day race. Under the terms of their agreement, the Ford Company was to furnish V-8 engines, parts, and services not to exceed $25,000 in value; Miller-Tucker was to build the cars. In the event of success, Ford was to control publicity; Miller-Tucker was to get the prize money. Miller-Tucker was to take possession of the cars after the race.[7]

The venture held considerable promise for success. Harry Miller, senior partner of Miller-Tucker, Inc., was perhaps the nation's leading designer of racing cars. Miller-built cars had, in fact, won six Indianapolis "500's," including the last three contests. The combine also recruited a team of outstanding drivers for its "flying red squirrels," as its cars were called. "Never before," observed the *New York Times,* "has such a large group of racers been built for the task . . . of putting over a winner on the Speedway."[8]

The Miller-Tucker-Ford vehicles, described by *Motor* as the "best looking, best streamlined cars ever seen at the Speedway," attracted "unusual interest" among racing fans throughout the country. Unfortunately, there was insufficient time to prepare all the cars for the race. Only five of the ten vehicles were entered in the qualifying trials. Of this number, four qualified to start the "500"; the fifth qualified as an alternate—the thirty-fourth car in a field limited to thirty-three starters. Still, with four cars in the race, each of which had exceeded 130 miles per hour in practice sessions (the qualifying speeds for the "500" in 1935 ranged from 109.937 to 120.736 miles per hour), the Miller-Tucker-Ford combine entered the race with high hopes. These expectations were dashed, however, when one of the cars was forced to quit the contest because of grease leakage in the front drive and the other three were forced out because of steering gear trouble. Ted Horn's car went the longest distance, 144 laps (360 miles), for a sixteenth-place finish. Ironically, Miller-designed engines powered the first twelve cars across the finish line.[9]

The sequel to the race was equally unhappy for Miller-Tucker and Ford. Miller-Tucker, spending freely in its haste to ready the cars for the race, contracted for materials and services in the amount of $117,244. The bills were passed along to Ford. Legally responsible for only $25,000 of the indebtedness, Henry Ford, incensed over the cars' mechanical imperfections, refused to pay the bills or, at this juncture, to surrender the vehicles to his partner. A lawsuit loomed, but the industrialist, recognizing that litigation would only further publicize the failure of the "Ford" racers, paid the indebtedness and, in exchange for $5,000, kept the cars.[10]

After the Indianapolis fiasco, the Ford Company turned its back on racing for a decade and a half. During the early and mid-1950s, however, when dealer- and owner-sponsored Fords dominated stock car racing, the company again publicized its cars' major victories. For five years after 1957, when the Automobile Manufacturers

Association passed a "safety resolution" banning factory participation in or support of speed contests, Ford was not openly involved in racing. But in 1962, Henry Ford II, noting that several manufacturers, including the Ford Company were interpreting the resolution "more and more freely," declared that his firm intended to race its products. In 1963 Ford-powered Lotus cars finished second and seventh in the Indianapolis "500"; first through fourth in 1965. In 1966, Ford-powered cars swept Europe's most prestigious race, Le Mans. The company discontinued racing in 1970 with the explanation: "We believe racing activities have served their purpose."[11]

Although it remained aloof from speed contests during the half-dozen years prior to the outbreak of war, between 1938–41 the Ford Company lent its assistance to Ford dealers who entered cars in the annual economy run sponsored by the Gilmore Oil Company, of Los Angeles. Started in 1936, the Gilmore contest, which was run from Los Angeles to Yosemite National Park between 1936–40 and from Los Angeles to the Grand Canyon in 1941, was regarded as an important promotional vehicle by California Ford dealers. After dealer-sponsored V-8's and Lincolns made a poor showing in the first two runs, a group of California Ford dealers urged the parent firm to sponsor entries in the 1938 contest. The company refused, but agreed to service and publicize dealer-sponsored cars.

The cooperative effort paid dividends. In 1938 a V-8 and a Lincoln Zephyr won first place in their price divisions; the winning Zephyr also traveled the second greatest number of "ton miles" (determined by a weight-fuel consumption formula) in the race, thereby becoming runner-up in the overall or so-called "sweepstakes" competition. In 1939 a Zephyr again led entries in its division, and the following year a Zephyr and a Mercury won in their classifications. Ford entries scored their greatest triumphs in the final prewar contest. Not only did a V-8, a Zephyr, and a Lincoln Custom (commonly called the "big Lincoln") emerge victorious in their divisions, but the winning Custom and Zephyr won first and second in the sweepstakes competition. After the 1941 race, Ford's advertising agency deluged the nation's press with news releases, photographs, and advertisements heralding the performance of the Ford Company's cars.[12]

3

After a lapse of ten years, Henry Ford in 1937 resumed publication of a magazine for motorists. The magazine, the *Ford News*, an employee publication during the 1920s, was published in separate editions for employees and dealers during the early and mid-1930s. The company encouraged dealers to buy copies of their edition for mailings to Ford owners and prospective customers. But because the magazine had limited appeal to motorists, few did so. In 1936, in an effort to capture the motoring public's interest, William A. Simonds, who had edited the magazine since 1926, began carrying fewer articles on Ford products and more features on the company's activities. Although this was an improvement, the hybrid magazine still lacked appeal for both motorists and dealers. Acknowledging the difficulty of appealing to such diverse groups as employees, dealers, and car and truck owners, early in 1937 Edsel Ford directed Simonds to redesign the *Ford News* into a publication specifically for motorists. Henry Ford, believing the proposed format too ostentatious, at first opposed the change. But he finally assented, and the revamped *Ford News* made its debut in June 1937. Enlarged to twenty-four pages (becoming twenty-eight pages in 1941), the magazine added more color (including color covers in 1938) and carried a well-balanced assortment of articles on travel, fashions, health, sports, entertainment, and nontechnical discussions of Ford's scientific and manufacturing activities. Advertisements of Ford's cars were carried only on the back cover and inside back cover. Editorial content, except in the annual new-car announcement issue, seldom mentioned Ford products.

Editorially and typographically, the magazine showed constant improvement between 1937 and 1942. Its circulation also showed a steady increase. In June 1937, 110,338 copies were distributed; a year later, 176,542. In 1940 the magazine's circulation passed the 300,000 mark, overtaking the Pontiac and Buick owner publications; in July 1941, circulation reached 450,000. At the start of World War II, mailings neared the half-million mark, almost half the circulation of the industry's No. 1 magazine for motorists, Chevrolet's *Friends*. The publication was suspended in February 1942. Its successor was the postwar *Ford Times*. [13]

4

The last of the Ford Company's major prewar public relations activities, a youth program, broke new ground. The program grew out of the interest in an award-winning traffic safety advertising campaign which the company ran in youth magazines in 1938 and 1939. The advertisements drew high praise and requests for thousands of reprints from students, parents, teachers, and auto club and traffic association officials. Impressed by this response, Elmer P. Grierson, publisher of *American Boy-Youth's Companion,* one of the magazines in which the advertisements had appeared, urged the Ford Company to supplement its advertising campaign by sponsoring a driver-education contest for teen-age motorists. Grierson's suggestion appealed strongly to Edsel Ford, himself the father of four young drivers, and in March 1940, Edsel announced the establishment of the Ford Good Drivers League and sponsorship of a nationwide competition to promote safe driving among fourteen to eighteen-year-old boys. [14]

Edsel assumed the presidency of the league and named George F. Pierrot, publicity director of the company's New York fair exhibit, as secretary. Actual operation of the league fell to the assistant secretary, M. L. Darlington, Jr., formerly a member of the general sales staff. Budgeted at $159,030, the league had two levels of competition, state and national. State contestants were required to write an essay on accident prevention and take a twenty-five-mile daylight driving test. Each state winner was awarded a prize of $100 and a free trip to the national finals. National finalists were scored on their day and night driving ability, proficiency in parking, backing, braking, and so on, and physical reactions during moments of stress. The winner of the national competition received a $5,000 scholarship, the runner-up a $2,000 scholarship.

Sixty thousand boys participated in the league's 1940 contest. At the close of the national finals, held in New York, the forty-eight state winners were honored at a banquet (in Ford's pavilion at the New York World's Fair) attended by Edsel Ford, Eddie Rickenbacker, and a score of prominent athletes. At the banquet Edsel announced that the 1941 contest would be opened to Washington, D.C. students and include a separate competition for teen-age girls.

Budgeted at $250,000, the 1941 contest drew 170,000 participants. After completion of the national finals, held in Dearborn, the state winners were feted by Henry and Clara Ford at an old-fashioned dancing party. They also were honored at an awards banquet attended by Edsel Ford; William B. Stout, the noted designer of airplanes and automobiles; Wilbur Shaw, winner of the Indianapolis "500" in 1937, 1939, and 1940; and Alice Marble, women's singles tennis champion in 1936 and 1938–40. Later, the boy and girl driving champions were introduced to Vice President Henry A. Wallace in Washington and appeared on the Ford Summer Hour.[15]

The Good Drivers League received considerable attention from the press. In 1940, when league publicity was handled by Ayer and Ford's press relations staff at the New York World's Fair, most New York newspapers ran several pictures and four or five stories about the contest. Detroit and hometown newspapers of the contestants also were generous in their reporting of the competition. The following year an aggressive publicity campaign conducted by McCann-Erickson, Inc., Ayer's successor, sparked hundreds of newspaper stories and a dozen national magazine articles on the league's activities. In addition, a score of newspapers, including the *New York Times,* ran editorials lauding Ford for sponsoring a safe driving program for young people.[16]

Elated over the league's success, Ford officials in the late summer of 1941 made plans to expand the competition still further in 1942. However, defense-related cutbacks in auto production ordered by the government in the early fall of 1941 forced the company to reconsider the league's future. Edsel, who felt he could not justify the expense of a full-scale competition, yet did not want to abandon the league, decided in November in favor of a scaled-down version of the program. A budget of $67,800, $37,500 for magazine advertising and $30,300 for distribution of a driving booklet, was drawn up for 1942.[17]

America's entry into the war a few weeks after Edsel's decision spared the Ford Company any embarrassment in announcing the abandonment of the league's contests. In early January 1942, Edsel informed the press that "it does not seem feasible to attempt to hold contests under present conditions." Two months later the younger Ford announced the suspension of all league activities for the duration of the war. For several years after the war the scarcity of automobiles made impractical any thought of resuming the driver contests. In the late 1940s the company considered reviving the program, deciding not to do so after learning that many of its dealers were unenthusiastic about it. The league nonetheless left a substantial legacy. It inspired countless high schools to offer driver education courses. It also prompted the United

States Junior Chamber of Commerce in 1952 to launch the Jaycee Safe Driving Teen-age Road-e-o. The road-e-o was patterned after the league, the junior chamber having obtained permission from Ford to reactivate the program under another name. To this day some of the league's driving tests are a part of the road-e-o competition.[18]

In 1940–41, Henry and Edsel Ford lent their names, but not their financial support, to a second youth program, the National Farm Youth Foundation. Sponsored by the Ferguson-Sherman Manufacturing Corporation, distributor of the Ford-Ferguson tractor, the foundation's principal activity was a contest for farm youths between the ages of eighteen and twenty-five. Winners, fifty-eight of whom annually were offered jobs with Ferguson-Sherman and its distributors, were determined on the basis of a scoring system which provided points for proficiency in operating farm machinery and for arranging demonstrations and contributing to sales of tractors and implements. Approximately 10,000 youths competed in the contest each of the two years it was in operation. The foundation, like the Good Drivers League, was suspended shortly after the attack on Pearl Harbor. It did not reappear after the war.[19]

5

During this period the Ford Company also placed more emphasis than ever before on the function of press relations. The majority of news stories about the Ford organization during the 1930s and early 1940s (as during the 'teens and 1920s) continued to originate independently of the firm's publicists. But an analysis of the company's monthly publicity reports shows that a great amount of publicity, virtually all of it favorable to Ford, can be traced to the firm's press relations representatives.

N. W. Ayer, which had handled the company's advertising and press relations activities since 1927, continued to provide publicity services for the company until 1940 when it was replaced by McCann-Erickson, Inc. and Maxon, Inc. In addition to handling product publicity (including press previews, auto shows, and so on), Ayer publicized all of Ford's major public relations programs and activities: exhibits at fairs, radio broadcasts, racing, the Rouge, Greenfield Village, "milestone" cars, etc. The agency's work was first-rate: its releases were newsworthy and well-written; its distribution system orderly; and its approach to editors sensible (all news releases were accompanied by a notation advising editors to judge copy "solely on the basis of its general interest, without relation to any advertising we may have placed in your publication"). Ayer's staff, headed by H. G. McCoy, could have been of even greater service to the Ford Company had it been asked to handle *all* of the firm's press relations, particularly publicity dealing with labor turmoil and controversial issues involving Henry Ford. However, except for distributing an occasional statement about labor matters and arranging new-car press previews at which Henry Ford sometimes appeared, the agency had no connection with labor publicity or the industrialist's personal press relations.[20]

During the last months of 1940 McCann-Erickson and Maxon assumed responsibility for the company's publicity as well as advertising. McCann-Erickson, which had serviced most of Ford's branch offices since 1933, directed all company accounts except Lincoln and Mercury. Maxon handled the lesser car lines. In addition to its work with the branches, McCann-Erickson conducted a "special news undertaking" for the Ford Company between November 1939 and late 1941. This semisecretive venture, usually referred to in Ford-McCann-Erickson correspondence as the "Curtin arrangement," was the brainchild of Harry Bennett. It called for McCann-Erickson to set up within its organization a special group of publicists and lobbyists, headed by D. Thomas Curtin, to "get in solid with media in major cities" and "give them additional insight regarding the Ford Motor Company." McCann-Erickson originally planned to base Curtin, a writer and lecturer with a wide acquaintance in press and radio circles, in Detroit and to assign men to him in Washington, New York, Chicago, San Francisco, and other key cities. But only the Detroit and Washington offices materialized.

For two years Curtin flitted about the country, buttering up and exchanging favors with newsmen and politicians. Detailed reports of his activities, preserved in the Ford Archives, show that his duties covered a wide range: attending meetings of editors to "sell them on the human side" of the Ford Company; attempting "to correct the *New York Post*'s views on [racketeer] Joe Adonis's alleged Ford connections"; trying to get the *Louisville Courier-Journal* to "take a less extreme view of Henry Ford's non-cooperation with government"; persuading Congressman George A. Dondero of Michigan to comment favorably on the 28,000,000th Ford car and asking friends to obtain Secretary of State Cordell Hull's cooperation in "welcoming" the 28,000,000th car to Mexico City and Ottawa; assisting Henry Ford in the preparation of a tribute to Thomas Edison for the *Port Huron* (Michigan) *Times-Herald;* arranging for the Maid of Cotton to be photographed in a Mercury, etc. In addition, Curtin made regular "press rounds in Detroit, New York, and Washington," and, especially in late 1940 and 1941, devoted considerable attention to "special good will work" among politicians in Washington.[21]

While Curtin and two assistants hired in mid-1940 were cultivating newspaper and radio people and performing special duties, McCann-Erickson's regular Detroit publicity office handled product publicity and all of the other press relations activities formerly managed by Ayer. McCann-Erickson's five-man publicity staff, headed by Robert Strother, was fully as competent as its predecessor. Indeed an appraisal of the stories and detailed weekly reports that it filed with A. R. Barbier, Ford's advertising manager, indicate that it was technically as competent and versatile as almost any present-day industrial press relations staff.

In part, the quality of the agencies' work could be attributed to Ford's generous publicity appropriations during the prewar decade. But three weeks after the attack on Pearl Harbor both McCann-Erickson and Maxon were notified by the company that their services were no longer needed. Until June 1942, when publicist Steve Hannagan was asked to establish and operate a Ford News Bureau, the company's publicity was handled by C. C. "Doc" Cheadle who, under Barbier's supervision, had been assigned the company's "publicity activity, including agency supervision," during the late 1930s and early 1940s.[22]

6

One of the foremost exponents of public relations during the 1930s and early 1940s, the Ford Company also was one of the nation's leading advertisers during this era. It virtually had to start its product advertising from scratch in late 1933. Nagged by poor sales and frightened by the Detroit banking crisis, Henry Ford had cancelled all advertising, eliminated his Advertising Department, and dismissed Ayer in February 1933. Except for a series of institutional "personal messages" pertaining to the fundamentals of the Ford organization and a few Lincoln advertisements, the industrialist did no advertising for ten months. But in late 1933, as the nation's economy and his company's sales picked up, he re-established the Advertising Department, rehired Ayer, and launched "the greatest and most aggressive sales campaign ever to be attempted by the Ford Company." Its most important features were the hiring of Fred Waring, the large-scale resumption of newspaper, magazine, billboard, and direct mail advertising, and an improved plan for coordinating branch-dealer and national advertising.[23]

During the advertising "interregnum" of 1933, many dealers had banded together and, under the direction of branch offices, advertised in local newspapers and on radio. A dozen agencies handled the branch-dealer accounts. Some of the agencies turned out mediocre advertising; others, notably McCann-Erickson and Ayer, did first-rate work. McCann-Erickson, founded in 1930 with the merger of the twenty-nine-year-old Erickson Company and the eighteen-year-old H. K. McCann Company, was more aggressive than its leading rival, which—since it already serviced the much larger company account—was not encouraged by Ford to press for branch-dealer business. Unfettered McCann-Erickson, on the other hand, prepared and submitted to the Ford Company in the fall of 1933 a 1,500-page study of the sales potential of the firm's passenger cars and trucks for each of the nation's 3,053 counties. Favorably impressed by the enterprising newcomer, Ford—when announcing in December 1933 that it would coordinate all future advertising—instructed its branches to dismiss all agencies except McCann-Erickson and Ayer, then choose one or the other to handle their business. McCann-Erickson, largely on the strength of its detailed market analysis, was selected by twenty-seven branches, Ayer by only five. Establishing fourteen new regional offices and staffing them with thirty-five "field men," McCann-Erickson within a few months had developed for Ford "the most thorough localized program of advertising and dealer helps any manufacturer had ever known." Continuing its outstanding work with branch accounts throughout the 1930s, the agency, which had repeatedly sought to take over Ayer's branch accounts, was awarded all of the branch business on January 1, 1940.[24]

In 1934 branch advertising was financed by a $6.00 per unit charge levied against dealers at the time cars were wholesaled to them, two-thirds of this amount being used for local advertising, the remainder for the Waring show. In 1935 the per unit charge was reduced to $5.00 and in late 1937 it was eliminated, the company assuming all advertising expenses. Under the assessment policy, the amount of money spent by or in behalf of dealers was directly tied to sales and thus varied from year to year. Company appropriations for branch advertising were more stable (averaging slightly more than $2,000,000 per year between 1938–41), but were less than half of the average annual amount ($5,400,000) obtained from dealer assessments during the previous four years.[25]

Although the branches were responsible for $29,000,000 worth of advertising expenditures during the years 1934–41, the company spent an even greater amount, $50,800,000, on national advertising during this period. About 35 percent of this sum was spent on V-8 advertising; about 25 percent of it on institutional advertising, of which the Sunday Evening Hour was the principal expenditure. Until 1940, national advertising was handled almost exclusively by Ayer. The largest and perhaps leading advertising agency in the country when retained by Ford in 1927, Ayer did highly creditable work for its Dearborn client throughout the 1930s. Ayer produced advertising which the trade regarded as "a bit on the conservative side." The fact was, however, that the agency could have produced no other kind of advertising for the Ford Company. Henry and Edsel Ford strongly preferred conservative advertising; so did Advertising Manager A. R. Barbier and William J. Cameron, both of whom were frequent participants in campaign planning sessions. Moreover, the elder Ford insisted that his company's advertising, irrespective of any claims advanced by rival auto makers, not be too "competitive." "Don't exaggerate," the magnate admonished his admen, "the truth is big enough." Ford would not permit Ayer and its successors to describe his cars as the best, the most economical, or the lowest-priced car (although they could refer to it as the best automobile that the Ford Company had ever made). Other taboos prohibited the agencies from making number-of-miles-per-gallon claims for its cars; using pictures with people smoking—or even describing the cigarette lighter as anything more than a "lighter"; or showing white sidewall tires in illustrations of the standard V-8. But whether because of or despite the conservatism and taboos, Ayer consistently won awards for its advertising campaigns and for the excellence of its copy, layout, art, and typography. Indeed in 1938 and 1939 the agency won ten of *Advertising & Selling*'s coveted awards for advertising excellence, a greater number than any other advertising agency.[26]

Despite the high quality of its work, Ayer, after many years of leadership in its field, was on the decline during most of the 1930s. Ayer could trace a considerable portion of its troubles to its largest client, the Ford Company. During this period, Henry Ford, usually through his chief satrap, Harry Bennett, constantly harassed the agency, which at times hardly knew from one week to the next whether it would continue handling the Ford account. Ayer's difficulties with Ford, according to A. R. Barbier, began in 1932, when the agency's president, George H. Thornley, misadvised Henry Ford on the outcome of the presidential election of that year. Thornley told Ford that Hoover would win, and the auto magnate, later claiming that he had acted on Thornley's prediction, came out in strong public support of the Republican nominee. Embarrassed and angered by Hoover's overwhelming defeat, Ford never forgave Thornley (or his agency). At times the industrialist made no effort to conceal his contempt.

"How many Ayer men have you got with you today?," Ford once asked Barbier in the presence of an Ayer executive.

"Just one, Mr. Ford," replied Barbier.

"That," said Ford belligerently, "is one too many!"[27]

Bennett was also derisive of the Ayer organization and, acting in Ford's name, on various occasions had insisted that the agency hire at least five of the magnate's relatives and friends. The last of these demands led to an abrupt termination of the thirteen-year-old Ford-Ayer relationship. Neither Ford nor Ayer formally announced the break which, according to *Business Week,* "titillated the advertising world as perhaps it could have been by no other news," nor did either offer any explanation for it. Rumors about the severance of relations swept through the advertising field like wildfire. One story had it that pacifist Henry Ford was disgruntled with Ayer because it was handling advertising for army recruitment; another held that Ford was angered with the discovery that Ayer had Jewish employees working on his account; while still another suggested that the magnate believed that Ayer's advertising was largely responsible for his company's perennial third-place ranking in the automobile industry. It also was rumored that the agency, unhappy with the "somewhat patrician style of advertising followed by the company," had voluntarily dropped the account.

A more plausible explanation for the break appeared in the 1949 edition of Ralph M. Hower's history of N. W. Ayer & Son. Fear of losing the Ford account, said Hower "weighed heavily upon the entire [Ayer] organization. . . . It hampered objective thinking in the client's interest." The agency, Hower added, had gone to "extreme lengths" to satisfy the whims of Ford and Bennett; ". . . it felt that its professional status was in jeopardy." Finally, in October 1940, according to Hower, the industrialist and his lieutenant forced Ayer's hand.

> A Ford executive asked the Ayer firm to put a man on its payroll. The man knew nothing about advertising, and indeed there was no expectation that he would even appear; the agency was simply to pay him! Batten [Ayer's president] and his associates felt that the time had come to draw the line. With full knowledge that it meant the severing of the relationship, they refused the request point blank and immediately lost the account.

Acquainted with this explanation, Barbier years later said that Ayer's usefulness had indeed been impaired by Ford's and Bennett's harassment—and that he had told as much to Edsel Ford. The younger Ford expressed doubt that his father either disapproved or wanted to get rid of Ayer, but agreed to question him. The elder Ford denied such intent, yet a few weeks later, for reasons known only to himself—and possibly Bennett—forced Ayer to its knees. The letter of dismissal, according to Barbier, "shocked the agency," which, in his opinion, "would have made any sacrifice—and it already had made many—to keep the account."[28]

Ayer's financial loss was McCann-Erickson's and Maxon's gain. McCann-Erickson, given all of Ayer's Ford business except the Mercury account, handled 65 percent of the company's advertising in 1940–41. Fast-rising Maxon, adding the $1,000,000 Mercury account to the $500,000 Lincoln account it had plucked from Ayer in August 1940, directed the remainder of the company's national advertising.[29]

Detroit-based Maxon could attribute its share of Ford business partly to the talents of an exceptionally aggressive management, headed by "tireless, ball-of-fire" Lou R. Maxon, and partly to nepotism. There can be little question that Maxon,

Inc., which since its founding in 1928 had become the Midwest's largest agency and numbered among its clients General Electric, H. J. Heinz, Pittsburgh Plate Glass, and Gillette Safety Razor, was fully capable of handling Ford's advertising. But there can also be little question that the agency was awarded the Ford business less for its capabilities than because Henry Ford wished to provide a financial cushion for his favorite niece, Mary Elizabeth Bryant, and her husband, Harry Wismer. Married in May 1940, the Wismers moved shortly afterward to Philadelphia, where Harry was employed by Ivey & Ellington, Inc., a small advertising agency. Reasoning that the best way to help the newlyweds was to give Wismer "a million dollars worth of advertising business," the elder Ford told Bennett to make the necessary arrangements. Bennett relayed Ford's mandate to Advertising Manager A. R. Barbier who immediately set out for Philadelphia to gauge Ivey & Ellington's ability to handle the $500,000 Lincoln account. Discovering that the Philadelphia agency was inadequately staffed to service Lincoln's business, Barbier informed Wismer that the account could be given to Lou Maxon—who "had been gunning" for Ford business for several years—if Wismer could make "satisfactory arrangements" with the Detroiter. Acting on this information, Wismer "worked out a deal with Maxon," who shortly afterward was given the Lincoln plum. The twenty-seven-year-old Wismer, named a vice-president of Maxon, became the "key contact man" on the Lincoln account. "His main contribution to the business," Barbier recalled years later, "was to come out to Dearborn now and then and ask, 'How are our men coming along?' " Wismer also served as "key contact man" on the Mercury account and on the truck, by-products, and service, parts, and accessories accounts which he successfully solicited for Maxon in the last half of 1941. The acquisition of these accounts was a hollow triumph, however, for the outbreak of war a few months later prompted the Ford Company to cancel all advertising and dismiss the agency. A similar fate befell McCann-Erickson.[30]

A few weeks before the war began, Bennett, next to Henry Ford the supreme arbiter of company personnel, fired the capable Barbier, an "Edsel man." Barbier was replaced by E. D. Bottom, former manager of the company's Alexandria, Louisiana and Louisville branches, whose chief recommendation for the advertising post was his subservience to Bennett. In February 1942, Bennett also fired another of the company's most competent advertising-public relations men, Fred L. Black, long one of Edsel's key assistants. These callous dismissals added to Edsel's embitterment toward his father and led to a heated exchange between the two men. When the elder Ford early in the war informed his son that Chevrolet was engaged in various advertising activities and suggested that the Ford Company should follow suit, Edsel—who seldom reproached his father, however frustrated or sickened he was by his and Bennett's actions—retorted, "We can't do anything, because *you* busted up our Advertising Department!" The younger Ford's remarks perhaps found their mark. In July 1942, Henry Ford, who many times in the past had discontinued, then resumed advertising, rehired Maxon and began to advertise again.[31]

Although the Ford Company was one of the country's ten leading advertisers between 1934–41, its advertising expenditures trailed considerably behind those of General Motors and Chrysler during this period. Ford's smaller volume can, of course, be partly attributed to its position within the industry; the company was outsold by its leading rivals, therefore it was not inconsistent that it should spend less than they did. But Ford's smaller appropriations also reflected its founder's continuing reluctance to advertise, except to introduce products. "Mr. Ford," A. R. Barbier observed years later, " ridiculed advertising—saw it as an economic waste. He made the subject of advertising unpopular at the company." Barbier almost dreaded his meetings with Ford. "I'd always try to get in the first word," related the adman, "because I knew what was coming. He'd start right out, 'How much money are we spending on advertising this year?' I'd tell him and he would say, 'It's too much.' Then he'd add up the amounts the car makers were spending on advertising and say, 'Look at all the money wasted before the first car is even sold!' " The motor magnate put less faith in advertising than in the "better mousetrap" theory. For years the Model T and, briefly, the Model A were the "best cars," and Ford's only concern was being able to meet the demand for them. But the V-8 was merely *one* of the best cars, and the magnate, however reluctant, was forced to advertise to keep it competitive. In fact, he advertised continuously between 1933 and 1941,. the longest uninterrupted stretch of advertising in his company's history. [32]

Even though its V-8 was not as popular as its predecessors and its sales, assets, and prestige declined after 1930, the Ford Company remained the best publicized and one of the most highly regarded firms in the country throughout the prewar decade. Ford received more attention in the *New York Times* between 1933–41 than any other company except the New York Central Railroad. Hinterland newspapers, which did not share the *Times*'s interest in the operational reports and lesser activities of the New York City-based railroad, undoubtedly gave the Dearborn company a greater amount of publicity than the rail organization. In the general periodicals surveyed by the *Readers' Guide to Periodical Literature* and the specialized magazines analyzed by the *Industrial Arts Index,* the Ford Company received more than twice as much publicity between 1933–41 as the next most publicized firm, General Motors, and almost three times as much attention as the third-ranked company, United States Steel Corporation (and more than eight times as much publicity as fourteenth-ranked New York Central).

In the shadow of Henry Ford between 1914 and 1930, the Ford Company received considerably more attention in the daily and periodical press during the 1930s and 1940s than its founder. But because Henry Ford's name appeared in the press far less after 1932, the name "Ford" was not in the public prints as much in the 1930s and 1940s as during the earlier "golden years." Moreover, unlike the 1914–30 period, part of the company's post-1932 publicity, particularly that part which appeared in the labor, Jewish, liberal, and leftist press, was unfavorable, some of it extremely so. [33]

Although the Ford Company's prestige declined during the 1930s, the firm was rated among the nation's three or four leading firms in prewar surveys to determine the relative public relations standing of companies. The public, as noted in chapter 13, thought more highly of only General Electric and the Bell Telephone Company in a 1937 public opinion study conducted by the Curtis Publishing Company. The Dearborn company's labor and pricing policies were judged head and shoulders above those of any other firm; only Bell was believed by more people to be operating in the public interest than Ford. These survey findings were largely corroborated by The Psychological Corporation's Link Audit, which, starting in November 1937, semiannually measured the public's favorable and unfavorable attitudes toward eight major companies. Between 1937 and 1942, 65 percent of the audit's respondents expressed a favorable attitude toward Ford, which was rated ahead of Du Pont, Standard Oil of New Jersey, United States Steel, and United States Rubber, but behind General Electric, General Motors, and Westinghouse. But Ford consistently led the field in unfavorable responses—with one out of every eight interviewees expressing a negative attitude toward the company. Ford's unfavorable response rate, probably fed by the antipathy of Jews, unionists, liberals, and New Dealers toward Henry Ford and his firm, was almost three times higher than the combined average of the other seven companies. In a third nationwide public opinion survey, conducted among the male population in August 1941 by Maxon, 84.7 percent of the respondents thought "favorably" of the Dearborn company, as compared to 94 percent for General Motors and 91.8 percent for General Electric, the firms with which Maxon compared Ford.

If the Ford Company was less prestigious than in the past, the name Ford was still a powerful word in 1941, commanding the respect and loyalty of millions of people. These sentiments were, however, based far less on the firm's achievements in the 1930s and early 1940s than on the reputation it had acquired during the 'teens and 'twenties. Like Henry Ford, the Ford Motor Company was living on its reputation to a considerable extent; and the portent for its future was not promising.[34]

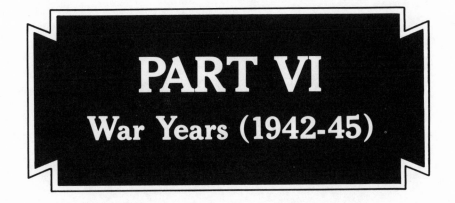

PART VI
War Years (1942-45)

1

Two days after the attack on Pearl Harbor the President declared in a radio address to the nation that the fate of the United States and its Allies would depend largely on America's industrial strength and capacity. From that moment the spotlight was focused on the industrial scene, particularly on the biggest defense contractors. Of these firms, the Ford Motor Company, the nation's fourth largest defense contractor, at the outbreak of war, was destined to be the best publicized.[1]

During the first eight months of the war virtually all the publicity about the Ford Company and Henry Ford (most Americans continued to think of the firm and its founder as being as indissoluble as Chang and Eng, the Siamese twins) was favorable, much of it extremely so. The press glowed with accounts of Henry Ford's World War I record; his transformation from a pre-World War II pacifist to a producer for war; and his "foresight" in gearing his company for military production before America's entry into World War II. The *Chicago Daily News* reported that Ford had built an Eagle boat a day between July and November 1918 (actually he had built only seven of the vessels before the Armistice). Several publications revived the hoary myth that Ford had "turned back every cent of profit to the Government" after World War I. "Ford has always been a lover of peace, goodwill, and justice," typically declared the *Madison* (Wisconsin) *State Journal,* "but today we have another Ford, literally a Ford with hands of steel . . . turning the tremendous power of the world's greatest factory into the world's most powerful engine of production warfare." The pragmatic Ford, perhaps with an eye to the press gallery, had a simple explanation for his transformation from pacifist to "fighting" pacifist. When asked to reconcile his hatred of war with the production of war machines, the industrialist, who during the previous decade had repeatedly defied the government, replied, "it's the law of the land, isn't it?" "That's exactly the right attitude," gushed the *Port Huron* (Michigan) *Times-Herald,* "and Mr. Ford's attitude is an example to every American who really loves his country."[2]

— Many publications commended the magnate for conducting pre-World War II defense research using "his own money . . . without asking the Government for a cent." Ford, *Time* asserted in its March 23 cover story on the auto king, "was always three jumps ahead of the OPM's [Office of Production Management] tapeworm," designing and building aircraft engines before he had an order for them and putting up huge plants "on the sole basis of relatively small orders for sub-assemblies." Several publications also exonerated Ford for refusing in 1940 to make Rolls-Royce engines for Britain. "He had a good mechanic's reason," explained *Time.* "Grief and headaches in other plants . . . proved what Ford knew or had guessed—that the British blueprints were informal to the point of helter-skelter." Ford's 1,000-planes-a-day statement of 1940 was similarly glossed over: "It was neither an idle boast nor a positive promise. It was just good American cockiness."[3]

If the press warmly applauded Ford's earlier stance on military production, it almost ran out of superlatives in discussing his contribution to the World War II defense effort. From early 1942 most of this discussion centered around the Willow Run bomber plant which, in the minds of many Americans, quickly symbolized both the Ford war effort and America's "intent to fill the skies with flying battleships."

Several factors contributed to the dramatization of Willow Run. At a time when leaders of the aircraft industry were highly skeptical of plans to mass-produce airplanes, the plant embodied a daring attempt, the first, to produce aircraft on a full-blown assembly line system. Moreover, the factory was operated by America's premier manufacturer, the man popularly credited with having invented mass production and universally regarded as its foremost exponent. Many people took it for granted that Ford's newest plant, like his Highland Park and Rouge factories, would blaze new methods of manufacture and set new production records, for as *Business Week* pointed out, "the nation had come to expect production miracles from Ford as routine. When Henry went to war," added the magazine, "—well, Berlin was the next stop." In addition, the plant had special appeal to many Americans because, in concept, size, and singleness of purpose, it seemed, in the words of the *Detroit Free Press*, "so typically American and particularly typical of Detroit [the highly publicized "arsenal of Democracy"], and of Henry Ford."[4]

Willow Run impressed everyone by its size. The main building was 3,200 feet long, 1,280 feet wide, and had 2,547,000 square feet of floor space—more floor area than the prewar factories of Consolidated Aircraft Corporation, Douglas Aircraft Company, and Boeing Aircraft Company combined. "There seems to be no end to anything," observed one journalist. "Like infinity, it stretches everywhere into the distance of man's vision." The plant was by far the largest factory in the world under a single roof, until the completion in 1943 of Chrysler's mammoth but less publicized Chicago aircraft engine plant.[5]

Finally, Willow Run was assigned one of the glamor products of the war, the four-engine, long-range B-24 (often called the "Liberator"), which in the early 1940s was one of the biggest, fastest, and most destructive bombers in the world. Amid the gloom of 1942 the nation looked to the B-24 and its predecessor, the B-17, with anxious hope. "They represent our supreme bid to regain the initiative," a national magazine declared in April 1942. "They may save our honor, our hopes—and our necks."[6]

Willow Run had begun limited parts production in November 1941; yet at the start of the war no part of the factory was complete. In early 1942 the main building and the flying field were pushed to a conclusion. But the plant, except for the relatively small area where parts production was under way, was in a state of turmoil as tools were received, fixtures set up, and officials and untrained employees tried to cope with the countless aspects of an alien undertaking. The task was complicated by a housing shortage in the Willow Run vicinity and the amount of time required (an hour or more each way) for Detroit workers to get to and from their jobs.[7]

Willow Run's problems were ignored or glossed over in the hundreds of news stories and editorials on the huge plant in early 1942. Instead, the press dwelt on the size of the factory and the scope of its operations, referring to it in such terms as the "greatest single-story structure in the world," the "largest workroom in the world," the "most enormous room in the history of man," the "largest building in the history of the world," and the "mightiest war-time effort ever made by industry." The plant was described as a "marvelous factory" by the *Boston American;* an "amazing bomber plant" by the *New York Sun;* a "U.S. miracle" by the nineteen newspapers of the Scripps-Howard chain; "Henry Ford's miracle" and "one of the wonders of the world" by the *Greenwood* (South Carolina) *Index-Journal;* "one of the seven wonders of the world" by the *Erie* (Pennsylvania) *Times;* "the greatest show on earth" by the *Baltimore Sun;* and "the damndest colossus the industrial world has ever known" by columnist Westbrook Pegler. Dozens of newspapers declared that Willow Run spelled ruin for the Axis. "It is a promise of revenge for Pearl Harbor," reported the *Detroit Free Press.* "You know when you see Willow Run that in the end we will give it to them [the Japanese] good." "If Hitler could just take a peek at the plant," averred the *Connellsville* (Pennsylvania) *Courier,* "he'd shiver in his boots."[8]

Seven members of the Senate's Special Committee Investigating the National Defense Program, who toured Willow Run in mid-April 1942, were no less effusive than the press in their praise of the facility. "The Willow Run plant is incomparable," Senator Harry S. Truman, the committee's chairman, told reporters after the visit. "They [the Fords] are doing a marvelous job. . . . We were very pleased with what we saw." Another member of the committee, Senator James M. Meade, of New York, predicted that Willow Run would make Detroit "the bomber capital of the world," adding that "this remarkable job . . . is one that perhaps could be expected from the efficient Ford organization and its personnel."[9]

If praise of the plant itself indicated that "the MacArthur of the assembly line" had wrought yet another miracle, statements and forecasts about how soon and how many bombers would flow from the facility confirmed this impression a hundredfold. Most press reports stated that B-24's would be rolling off the assembly line "before June 1"; others said that production of completed bombers would begin "shortly," "soon," "this spring," "next month," "in a few months," or, at the latest "early in the summer." A radio broadcast beamed to Manila Bay in February 1942 reported that Ford was already producing "astronomical" numbers of planes for the army. The broadcast spurred embattled American and Filipino troops on the Bataan Peninsula and Corregidor Island to start a "Bomber for Bataan" fund, some servicemen pledging a month's pay to the futile enterprise.[10]

Many of the stories about Willow Run reported that the plant, once production began, would build bombers at the "unprecedented" and "unbelievable" rate of "one every two hours," "one per hour," "two per hour," "dozens daily," "en masse," and "one every few minutes" (compared to the 169 B-24's built in one year, 1941, by the plane's designer, Consolidated Aircraft). Several publications, under the impression that Henry Ford's statement about building 1,000 fighter planes per day applied to bomber production at Willow Run, reported that 1,000 B-24's would emerge from the factory every twenty-four hours. The most exaggerated estimate of the plant's future production appeared in the usually conservative *New York Herald Tribune:* "Willow Run," stated the newspaper, annually "will produce planes by the tens of thousands and eventually, if required, by the hundreds of thousands." Dozens of newspapers also compared Ford's bomber production schedule with other plane-building programs. "Willow Run's performance," sniffed the *Champaign-Urbana* (Illinois) *Courier,* "will make Germany's performance look rather horse-and-buggy." Ford's projected production, exuded the Scripps-Howard Newspaper Alliance, "could easily add up to more bombers of this type in a year than there are now in the whole world."[11]

The plant's "build-up" was accelerated beginning May 14, 1942, when Major General Alexander D. Surles, director of the Department of War's Bureau of Public Relations, announced in Washington that Willow Run had begun the "actual production of bombers." He added that the facility eventually would produce as many heavy bombers as all of the factories of the Axis powers combined. Maintaining that "the army will not . . . reveal any production schedules . . . [nor] say when the first plane was produced in the plant or how many have been made so far," General Surles did not specifically state that *complete* planes were being *mass-produced*. But newspapers throughout the country *assumed* that mass-produced bombers were rolling off the assembly line, and many of them hailed the "industrial miracle" with their biggest, blackest headlines. "In the future," observed the *Detroit Free Press,* "it will be written that the shadows cast by the flight of Willow Run's bombers in the spring of 1942 portended the coming doom of the enemies of humanity."[12]

Only one individual, J. H. (Dutch) Kindelberger, the blunt-spoken president of North American Aviation, and one newspaper, the *Ann Arbor* (Michigan) *News,* questioned General Surles's announcement at the time it was made. Kindelberger, a severe critic of the government's decision to permit the auto industry to build planes, scoffed that "the only contribution the 'great and god-fearing' automobile makers have made so far to the war effort is the assembling of parts which the airplane producers sent to them" and that the industry "has not delivered a single aircraft part in 16 months." "You cannot expect blacksmiths," added the aviation executive, "to learn how to make watches overnight." Kindelberger's statements were vigorously rebutted by Detroit's auto makers, and were played down in the press.

The *Ann Arbor News,* in an editorial entitled, "What Is: 'In Operation'?," said it was disturbed by the official announcement that the plant was in operation. The newspaper explained that it was concerned "because the announcement may have been misinterpreted with the result that a good many persons are now burdened with false expectations. Acknowledging that Willow Run had been producing bomber parts for some months, the *News* cautioned the public "not to get excited with the false prospect of a stream of bombers sailing from the assembly lines in the near future. The public must, in fact, be patient. . . . Yes, the bomber plant is 'in operation.' But it most certainly is not in full operation, and will not be in full operation for some months to come."

Puzzled as to why the "deliberately misleading" report had been issued, the *News* suggested that the Department of War made the announcement because it "was forced to'' by an administration eager to pass along heartening news to the public. This view was lent credence by Steve Hannagan, the Ford Company's newly appointed publicist, and by *Newsweek*. Hannagan, who met with General Surles a month after the announcement, reported to aides that the officer had complained of the administration's "clamor for all-out information to the public." *Newsweek* declared that the government issued the statement because it "felt that the news would be a big boost to the morale of Allied and occupied countries and would correspondingly depress the Axis countries." [13] In any event, since army air force personnel was stationed at Willow Run, the Department of War was aware of the status of the plant's production.

Whatever the Department of War's reasoning, General Surles's announcement, considering the state of production at Willow Run, was decidedly premature and, in the light of the plant's future public relations, unfortunate. In truth, the Ford Company—although it was making bomber parts and subassemblies—had not mass-produced a single B-24. It had, in fact, turned out a single hand-built prototype, constructed for "educational" purposes, at the old Ford Airport in Dearborn. Furthermore, most of the parts and subassemblies used in this plane had been shipped to Dearborn from Consolidated's plant in San Diego. Actually, Ford had committed itself in February 1942 to produce two bombers in May, one a "knockdown" (parts for a complete plane) to be sent to Douglas's plant in Tulsa, the other a "flyaway." But it could not meet the commitment. The first knockdown did not leave for Tulsa until July and the first flyaway was not turned over to the army until September 10. [14]

In view of these circumstances, the Ford Company should have speedily denied General Surles's statement or at least cautioned against overoptimism. But the company did neither for several possible reasons: it would have been impolitic to refute the Department of War; it was reluctant to dampen enthusiasm generated by the government's claims; and at the time it lacked public relations direction. Thus "peacock-proud" Charles E. Sorensen, less than a week after General Surles's announcement, informed twenty-eight newsmen on a National Association of Manufacturers-sponsored tour that the first B-24 bomber had rolled off the assembly line and that Willow Run would be producing one bomber an hour by late summer. "Bring the Germans and Japs in to see it," exuded Sorensen, "hell, they'd blow their brains out." For the second time within five days the plant and the "assembly line that is a miracle of speed and precision" were publicized throughout the world by the major press associations. The importance which newspapers attached to Sorensen's remarks was shown in the *New York Times*'s treatment of the story. Running a four-column photograph of the plant, under the caption, "One of the Seven Wonders of the World of War," and a three-column picture of the B-24, the *Times* headlined its story, "Willow Run a Wonder of War," with a subhead, "A Bid for 'Hitler Suicide.' " "There she stood," the *Times*'s lengthy article led off, "one of the seven wonders of the world of war; vast enough to swallow up an entire city; awesome enough to reduce man, her creator, to a lost speck in a jungle of giant machines. The name," the account continued, "is Willow Run. Mark it. If America's coming offensive depends on her power to blast, and blast hard, from the air, the news learned here yesterday may presage one of the turning points of the battle of production. For Willow Run, the big bomber factory which 'Charlie' Sorensen described as 'the invitation for Hitler to commit suicide,' is just about on the edge of turning over and becoming a real plant.'' Two days later the *Times* predicted that ''with the Ford Motor Company's mass-production genius at work, the huge bombers will be rolling off the line at a rate of speed which will be accelerated almost daily until the plant is turning out a substantial portion of the 185,000 combat planes which the country is to build in 1942 and 1943.''[15]

On May 23, Sorensen's comments were repeated by company publicist William A. Simonds, ex-editor of the *Ford News,* during a tour of Willow Run by 200 Michigan editors and publishers. Again, paeans for the bomber plant resounded in the press. In the weeks that followed, Sorensen, Simonds, and other Ford executives gave equally optimistic reports on Willow Run's progress to several dozen American and Allied government officials and military officers who toured the facility.

Many of the starry-eyed visitors issued public statements immediately after their tour. The president of Peru, Manuel Prado, told reporters, ''This [the plant] is wonderful. . . . It will bring quick victory.'' Captain Randolph Churchill, son of the British prime minister, perhaps taking his cue from Sorensen, assured the press that ''if Adolf Hitler could see Willow Run, he'd cut his throat right now.'' Sir Norman Birkett, a prominent British jurist, described the plant as ''magnificent, tremendous, monumental, colossal.'' Returning to London, he told the Overseas Club on August 24 that the plant ''staggered the imagination'' and that its ''endless miles of machinery were turning out a Liberator every hour.'' Sir Oliver Lyttelton, Britain's minister of production, declared that his visit was ''a day I will remember all my life. I would like to have Hitler and Goering with me. If they had seen what I have seen, they would have thrown in their hands, or blown out their brains.'' Added Sir Oliver, ''Five men with the imagination of Henry Ford would end this war within a period of six months.'' The production chief, upon his return to London, expressed similar views in a broadcast to the people of occupied Europe. ''This was beautiful propaganda,'' declared *Flying* in 1943, ''and no doubt effective propaganda for the Continent and even the 'tight little isle.' '' But as the magazine noted, it contributed substantially to ''the curse of Willow Run . . . the idea that it was a kind of Superplant that could perform miracles.''[16]

2

The myth that production miracles were being performed at Willow Run was exploded in August 1942. Meantime, in June, Edsel Ford, dismayed by the company's uncoordinated press relations activities and the ''loose talk'' about Willow Run production, appointed Steve Hannagan ''to be responsible for the dissemination of all Ford news and be in all instances the one and only initial liaison with the press.''[17]

Launching his career as the Indianapolis Speedway's publicist in 1919 and founding his own publicity organization in 1924, the ebullient, forty-three-year-old

Hannagan had served a varied clientele. But the Ford account, as revealed in Hannagan's memoranda to assistants, was regarded by the publicist as the most exciting and challenging of his career. Hannagan-the-press-agent reveled in the belief that "next to the President, Henry Ford can reach page 1 faster than any man in the country." He also believed that the Ford organization, once Willow Run swung into production, had "the elements of the best industrial story of the war." In addition, Hannagan-the-public-relations-statesman saw in the Ford account "a great responsibility" to America's economic system. "It is the first time," he told his aides, "that the Fords have agreed to such a liaison between themselves and the press and it is my evangelistic belief that as the fortunes of the Ford organization ebb and flow so does the plight of all free enterprise."[18]

The announcement that Ford had engaged a "loud-shouting, belligerent, whip-smart press agent" whose specialty had been described as "peddling photos of pretty legs in mid-winter" raised many eyebrows and provoked considerable speculation as to the nature of Hannagan's new assignment. One columnist, while acknowledging that the publicist was a "master of mass emotion," wondered what need Henry Ford had of Hannagan's "genius." "This looks like carrying coals to Newcastle," declared the journalist, "for in sensing the mood of the public, Henry Ford is a genius in his own right. Giving Henry Ford advice on public relations strikes me like trying to teach P.T. Barnum the art of show business or Franklin Roosevelt the art of politics." The *Detroit News*, noting that publicist Ivy Lee had enhanced John D. Rockefeller, Sr.'s reputation by suggesting that the oil billionaire distribute dimes among schoolchildren, observed, "America will expect a lot from Steve Hannagan and Henry Ford." This view was echoed by William L. Stidger, a Ford biographer, who during the 1920s and 1930s had written many of the "as told to" articles signed by Henry Ford.[19]

To carry out his publicity plans, Hannagan and his chief assistant, Joe Copps, organized a news bureau in late June. John W. Thompson, who had worked for Hannagan in Puerto Rico and at Consolidated Aircraft in San Diego during the 1930s, was named director of the bureau. Four men were recruited from eastern and midwestern newspapers to round out the staff. One of them, Charles E. (Charlie) Carll, a former Indianapolis, Cleveland, and New Bedford, Massachusetts newspaperman, was to become the company's director of public relations in 1947. One of Hannagan's first recommendations—and one that undoubtedly had the strong endorsement of Edsel Ford—was that nothing more be said about Willow Run's production "until bombers actually are rolling off the line in quantity." "There have been too many leaks on this story," Hannagan wrote the Fords, Sorensen, Bennett, and other executives. "Today, the nation has the general impression that bombers are running off the line at the rate of one an hour. This is not yet true. When it is, we will tell the story with newsreels, radio, press associations' stories and pictures, in its full bloom." Hannagan added that in lieu of publicizing Willow Run the news bureau should focus attention on other aspects of the company's war work. Hannagan's recommendations were accepted, and during the last half of 1942 the bureau prepared and distributed dozens of news stories on all of the company's war-related activities including, in November and December, stories about the bomber plant.[20]

A few weeks after Hannagan was retained, the Ford Company—following the lead of General Motors, which resumed institutional radio advertising in June 1942—assumed sponsorship of a fifteen-minute daily newscast. The company hoped that its new program, "Watch the World Go By," would "improve public morale by creating a better understanding of Ford's war effort, maintain the prestige of the Ford name, keep alive public acceptance for Ford products, and provide dealers with continuous advertising support to enable them to obtain a larger share of service volume."[21]

Each of the major networks bid for the newscast, but the Blue network, which was able to offer prime time in the East (8 P.M.) was awarded the show—billed as radio's first seven-day-a-week wartime news program. Maxon, Inc. (sans Harry Wismer until June 1943) was re-engaged to supervise the program. Earl Godwin, dean of the White House Correspondents' Association and twice its president, whose homespun delivery appealed to Henry Ford, was named news analyst. A "conservative with anti-New Deal tendencies," Godwin directed his remarks to "the ordinary, common guy, the Model T American." His talks, most of which he wrote himself, were sprinkled, like those of Cameron on the Ford Sunday Evening Hour, with homilies on rural life, God, motherhood, and country. Like Cameron, Godwin never received any broadcast instructions from the Ford organization. He read the news twice each evening Monday through Friday (including a rebroadcast for West Coast audiences); on weekends he was relieved by Roy Porter, a Blue network newscaster. Launched on July 12, the program was presented over 108 stations. It comprised Ford's sole advertising effort during the last half of 1942, except for a print advertisement in November on the company's war work.[22]

3

For two months after Hannagan's appointment and for a month after Godwin's debut, there was little public criticism of Willow Run's productive effort. The transportation problem remained acute, and received an unfavorable press throughout 1942, abating in the spring of 1943 when an express highway was completed between Detroit and Willow Run. But even after the completion of the express route, many Detroiters, because of gasoline and tire rationing and also because they still had to spend forty to fifty minutes getting to and from the plant, quit jobs at Willow Run to take work nearer their homes. The Willow Run housing shortage, which continued throughout 1942 and 1943, generated even more unfavorable publicity about the plant than the transportation problem, and contributed more than any other factor to the high employee turnover which plagued the factory during this period.[23]

In mid-August 1942, Willow Run's production problems were rudely shoved into the limelight by Ford's aviation nemesis, "Dutch" Kindelberger, a nationwide radio broadcast, and *Life* magazine. Kindelberger, still smarting from the government's decision to let the auto industry build planes, fired the opening salvo. In an August 13 interview, the "purple-talking" aircraft executive—while attacking the "political cowards who are withholding from the American people the full true facts'' about the auto industry's aircraft production problems—zeroed in on Willow Run. Ford's bomber plant, he told a startled group of reporters, had yet to manufacture an airplane. Ascribing Willow Run's difficulties to material shortages, a "lack of know how," and not taking into consideration "the length of time it takes to build a plane," Kindelberger added that the bomber shown by Ford executives to newsmen in May had been shipped to the plant "by Steve Hannagan for the benefit of photographers."[24]

Only a few hours after Kindelberger's charges were flashed around the country, "The March of Time," a *Time*-sponsored national newscast, also lambasted Willow Run. Devoting most of its August 13 broadcast to "the truth about mismanagement and lack of morale in Detroit that is slowing U.S. war production to the danger point," the program briefly mentioned production and morale problems in various Motor City plants, then focused on the status of production at Willow Run. Noting that Henry Ford's recent interviews "had not once referred to Willow Run, his most ambitious war project," narrator Westbrook Van Voorhis surmised that the industrialist had maintained his silence because his plant, "heralded as a symbol of U.S. industrial might, is now operating at a fraction of capacity . . . and has not completed one plane on its assembly lines." Following this statement, a "hillbilly" voice, purported to be that of a Willow Run employee, drawled: "The company isn't getting anything done over at the plant. I'm going to stay home and go fishing."

A few days later, *Time*'s sister publication, *Life,* which had access to the same research data on Detroit as "The March of Time," described the Motor City's production and morale problems in a lengthy article, "Detroit is Dynamite." Although critical of nearly every major defense contractor in the city, the article, like the radio program, made Willow Run the chief target of its attack. Repeating almost word for word "The March of Time" accusation that Willow Run had not completed a single plane on its assembly lines and was working at a fraction of capacity, the magazine also stated that the morale of the factory's employees was "the worst in Detroit." *Life*'s charges were repeated in dozens of newspapers throughout the country.[25]

Angered by *Life*'s attack, Detroiters lashed back at the magazine and declared that Washington, not Detroit, was responsible for such industrial problems as existed in the Motor City. Mayor Edward J. Jeffries denounced *Life* as a "yellow magazine" and its article on Detroit as "scurrilous, with just enough half truths to impress anyone who doesn't know the facts." Staunchly defending Willow Run, Jeffries maintained that the plant was not scheduled to go into mass production of bombers until mid-1943; that it was six to eight months ahead of schedule; that it would be producing complete planes before the end of the year. The *Detroit News* sneered that the *Life* reporter who wrote on Detroit "doesn't understand Detroit any more than the middle-westerner who spends a few weeks in Moscow understands Russia, or a New Yorker, after a week-end in some squalid section of the South, knows his oats on the share-cropper problem." R. J. Thomas, president of the UAW-CIO, insisted that Detroit's industrialists were "stymied all too frequently by all the red tape and confusion in Washington," while the *Detroit Times* added that the Detroit-related "mess in Washington is sickeningly evident to reporters."[26]

Although pressed by newsmen to deny or confirm the charges made by Kindelberger, "The March of Time," and *Life*, inexplicably neither the Ford Company nor the Department of War offered immediate comment. As a result, the press, which had been led to believe that Willow Run was building complete bombers—at the rate of one per hour, according to some reports—was baffled. Finally, on August 28, Sorensen, in answer to questions by newswomen touring the plant under the auspices of the National Association of Manufacturers, admitted that the plant had yet to produce its first B-24. "That first plane," the executive informed the group, "will be along—well, say tomorrow, maybe. But let's not worry about it until next year when we'll be going full tilt." Referring to the mid-August criticism, Sorensen protested, "They're all trying to needle us. But our planes will be the best answer to that kind of talk." The attitude of the press toward Sorensen's explanation was summed up by *Newsweek:* "disappointing."[27]

Following Sorensen's talk to the newswomen and dedication ceremonies for a new system of approach highways to Willow Run on September 11, the Ford Company virtually closed the plant to reporters until November, at the same time declining to comment publicly on bomber production. The government, apparently recognizing that it had made a tactical error in declaring that Willow Run was in full operation and wishing neither to reaffirm nor correct its prevarication, also withheld public comment on the plant from May until January 1943—with the exception of President Roosevelt's visit to the factory on September 18. As a consequence, save for the presidential inspection, Willow Run received little publicity during the last four months of 1942.

By government directive, the President's visit, part of a two-week, nation-wide inspection of war plants, was not publicized until the Chief Executive's return to Washington on October 1. On that date newspapers and airwaves throughout America were filled with accounts of the tour. In virtually all of these reports the President's ninety-minute visit to Willow Run—and with Henry Ford—was naturally mentioned.

Traveling by train, the presidential party had arrived at Willow Run two hours behind schedule. Meanwhile, Henry Ford, bored with the delay—and perhaps to show his disdain for Roosevelt—had slipped away, unnoticed, from the four-man welcoming group, and was wandering in the plant when the train pulled in. After a frantic search by Bennett's men, the magnate was found talking with workmen about a new machine tool. Rejoining the other welcomers, Edsel, Sorensen, and Bennett, the founder greeted the President, Mrs. Roosevelt, and Donald M. Nelson, chairman of the War Production Board. This group, except for Bennett, entered an open limousine and rode through the factory, where Roosevelt received a "deafening" welcome from employees. Ford, according to Sorensen, bitterly resented the cheers. For one of the few times in his life, the manufacturer, who was seated between the "good-sized" Roosevelts and almost hidden from his workers' view, was at the edge of the spotlight. Never, noted Sorensen in his memoirs, had he seen the auto king as "gloomy or mean" as during his tour of Willow Run with the President.[28]

News dispatches on the President's visit to Willow Run, all of which were approved for publication by the Chief Executive, stated that he "saw sheet aluminum going into one end of quarter-mile-long assembly lines and four-motored B-24 bombers ready to fly away at the other,'' thus creating the impression that airplanes were being produced in quantity. But at a press conference upon his return to Washington, the President said "off the record" that "Willow Run is not yet in production, although nearly so." These conflicting statements—fueled by an Office of Censorship directive expressly forbidding the transmission of the President's remark about Willow Run to Great Britain— touched off more "hearsay and whispers," including an unfounded story that B-24's had been flown to Willow Run from other plants to convey the impression that the Ford facility was in production.[29]

Actually, at the time of the President's visit, bombers were trickling from the giant factory's assembly lines. The first Ford-built B-24 was produced on September 10, and was accepted by the Army Air Forces on September 30. By October 1 parts for four planes had been sent to Tulsa and eighteen "flyaways" had been built. By the end of the year 107 bombers had been shipped in parts to Dallas or Fort Worth or turned over to the Army Air Forces at the factory. Unfortunately, many of these planes had to be modified after year's end, and the net production for 1942 was only fifty-six. But even this figure, because of government censorship of production statistics, could not be released to the public. The best that Hannagan and Ford officials could do was to inform visiting newsmen on both November 4 and December 4 that "completed bombers are being delivered to the government at Willow Run." The company emphasized that peak production at the plant could not be expected until "the latter half of 1943." These statements provoked mixed press reaction. "The cocky, indomitable, wonderful Ford organization," typically reported the *New York Sun,* "has been set back on its heels temporarily and thrown for a loss of time, but it has not fumbled the ball or sacrificed a scoring position." The visiting newsmen, although no longer dazzled by mythical production figures, continued to express amazement at the plant itself—"a crazy, miraculous, beautiful thing," in the words of the *Sun,* "that resembles more than anything else a Hollywood conception of a Ford airplane factory."[30]

On January 30, 1943, the War Production Board, in a report on the status of military production in the Detroit area, further lifted the veil on the bomber plant's operations. "There have been many disappointments in connection with Willow Run," said the board, "and the plant, even now, is far from peak production. Discussions about the reasons for its long lag have been many, but bombers are being turned out, and production is increasing.' The report cited a shortage of manpower as the factory's No. 1 problem, noting that the plant found it difficult to hire competent workers and to keep those hired. The manpower problem, according to the board, was aggravated by inadequate housing near Willow Run and the length of time required for employees to travel between the Detroit area and the plant.

The board's report, unfortunately, raised more questions than it answered and, in fact, generated considerable speculation about Willow Run's production. Across the country people began calling the plant "Willit Run?," a name said to have been coined by rival aircraft manufacturers. On February 13, the Office of War Information, "because of widespread, conflicting stories reporting [Willow Run's] output all the way from ridiculously small to fantastically large numbers," felt constrained to issue a special statement on the plant. The information agency, like the

WPB, "for reasons of military secrecy," withheld Willow Run's production figures, thereby doing little to end the speculation which had prompted its statement. But its report, while reiterating that the factory "was slow in getting underway" and that "production is running at only a small fraction of the plant's ultimate potential," emphasized the WPB's one positive statement—that Willow Run's production had been increasing steadily for some months. It also presented a sympathetic analysis of the factors responsible for the plant's poor performance: the difficulty of employing, training, and keeping competent workers; housing and transportation problems; materials shortages; the length of time it had taken to tool the plant for production; and unforeseen changes in bomber design which had played havoc with the plant's "comparatively permanent and inflexible methods of tooling."[31]

On the same day the OWI released its report, Hannagan's news bureau, with the concurrence if not the encouragement of the OWI, bombarded the press with news stories and photographs of Willow Run's operations. Hundreds of newspapers ran stories and pictures of bombers on the assembly line and of employees, many of them attractive girls, working on the aircraft. But neither the OWI's report nor Hannagan's publicity offensive deterred Senator Truman from announcing on February 15 that a subcommittee of his Special Committee Investigating the National Defense Program would conduct an immediate inquiry into production at Willow Run (and also Curtiss-Wright Corporation's lagging aircraft plant in Columbus, Ohio). "There has been so little production at either plant," snapped the senator, "as to amount to virtually none." Many newspapers, surveying the maze of conflicting statements issued by Ford and government officials during the previous eight months, applauded Truman's announcement. "The committee's visit," typically observed the *Monroe* (Michigan) *News*, "should help clear up some misunderstandings and mysteries."[32]

On February 19, Truman, Senator Monrad C. Wallgren, the subcommittee's chairman, and four other members of the subcommittee discussed Willow Run's problems with Edsel Ford and other Ford executives, conferred with UAW-CIO officials, then inspected the plant. Truman declined comment on the factory pending publication of his committee's findings. Wallgren, however, expressed guarded optimism about what he had heard and seen. "If we can solve the manpower problem," he told reporters, "we can get the production. On actual work being done, Willow Run compares very favorably with any plant in the country."[33]

While awaiting the Truman committee's report, Ford officials could note with satisfaction Willow Run's mounting production. In January 1943, the plant had turned out 31 bombers. In February this number was increased to 75; in April, 148; and in June, 190. To be sure, these figures fell far short of the 405 airplanes per month the army had set as a goal in 1942 and the new goal of 535 aircraft per month, established in February 1943. But it was progressive accomplishment, and the Ford Company, bursting to make public the figures and hopeful that they would blunt criticism of the plant, requested the government's permission to release them. Although the appeal was rejected by the Office of Censorship, Ford executives could take heart in words of praise—the first concerning production in six months— from the press and a key government production official.

Welcoming Senator Truman's decision to investigate Willow Run, the *Detroit Free Press*, on February 17, asserted that the committee, "despite the whispers and hearsay," would find that "the facts are good." *Business Week* expressed a similar conviction in mid-February. "At long last," the magazine declared, "America is finding its faith in Henry Ford and Willow Run re-established. And this time it rests on the solid fact of bomber production." That same month, *Machinery*, in a twenty-three page article on the bomber factory, insisted that "production miracles are about to be achieved here." In late February, a widely-syndicated editorial assured Americans that their "faith in mass production and its father, Henry Ford" would soon be justified at Willow Run. In March, the *Manchester* (New Hampshire) *Leader and Evening Union* said that "old-timers" had never been discouraged by reports or production delays at the bomber plant. Recalling Ford's Herculean and, ultimately, successful efforts to get the Model A into mass production, the publication reminded its readers that "when Ford tools up he tools up . . . and the old fox has never failed to have the last laugh."

In April, Charles E. Wilson, vice-chairman of the War Production Board, after touring Willow Run, told reporters that the plant was "on the beam. We're truly surprised," he added, "at the fine progress that is being made. . . . The Willow Run plant will be turning out 500 planes a month by the time the next snow flies." The day after Wilson's visit snow fell in Detroit. "Once again," reported *Time*, "the joke was on Willow Run. But this might very well be the last laugh at Willow Run's expense," the magazine added. "Willow Run finally seems to be really underway . . . [it] may yet achieve the miracle of a bomber an hour." In May, two magazines, *Popular Science* and *Flying*, ran articles highly favorable to the factory. "Willow Run is running," led off *Popular Science*'s piece. "The river is rising, Mr. Hitler, here comes the flood!" *Flying* took a similar tack: "The glamor girl of the automotive industry's warplane production program has . . . gone to work. Henceforth her accomplishments will be written up in the German newspaper obituary columns."

In assessing Willow Run's achievements, Wilson and the publications took into account an important decision, made in February, to subcontract a substantial part of the factory's work to other Ford and non-Ford plants. Within a few months subcontractors (which were extensively employed by almost all aircraft manufacturers) were contributing significantly to the factory's burgeoning output.[34]

On July 10 the Truman committee issued its long-awaited findings on Willow Run. The report acknowledged that "some delay had to be expected" in building a large number of "huge and complicated" airplanes such as the B-24. It also stated that the Ford plant had made "great progress" and was producing "substantial numbers of bombers." On several counts, however, the findings were critical of Willow Run. "The production line was set up similar to an automobile assembly line," ran one passage, "despite the warnings of experienced airmen. . . . This probably was a mistake." Another passage noted that Willow Run's production difficulties had prevented Consolidated's Fort Worth plant from meeting its delivery schedule and had forced the army to switch Douglas's Tulsa plant to other work. In addition, the report asserted that until recent months Ford "had not produced a plane which was capable of use at the front'' and that the army had permitted ''freezing'' of the design to get out such bombers as had been completed.

Actually, several of the committee's criticisms were false or distorted. Veteran aircraft manufacturers were violently prejudiced against the idea of building planes on a moving assembly line, and their ''warnings'' should have been judged in the light of their prejudice. No evidence whatever exists that Ford bombers could not have been used for combat. All bombers were subject to modification for front-line use, and eventually the Air Forces set up twenty-eight centers for such work. Moreover, ''freezing'' of bomber designs had thus far affected only small blocks of planes, and in the end it applied to all aircraft producers.[35]

The report of the Truman committee marked both the climax and the end of responsible public criticism of Willow Run. Rumblings of dissatisfaction over the plant's production continued within the government, however, until the fall of 1943. Indeed in September the Army Material Command, despairing of the company's ability to meet production schedules, suggested to the Department of War that the government unhorse Henry Ford and take over the management of the factory. But during the last few months of 1943, as the giant plant began to live up to its press notices of 1941 and the first half of 1942, the threat of a government take-over faded. Bomber production, which stood at 190 in June 1943, increased to 231 in August, 308 in October, and 365 in December. In October a WPB report on the aircraft industry revealed that ''whereas Willow Run was one of the poorest producers last Fall it is now one of the best.'' The report added that ''production per man at Willow Run has risen about forty times in the last year.'' In November the Ford Company, for the first time, was permitted by the government to release ''generalized'' figures on Willow Run's production. The company proudly announced that ''more than 1,000'' bombers had been flown from the plant and that a ''substantial number'' of B-24's had been assembled at other plants from parts made at Willow Run. Ford added that its next 1,000 planes would come ''awfully fast.''[36]

Subsequent production reports, as the plant entered a period of glory, were impressive. In January 1944, the Ford Company declared that it was ''the largest supplier of B-24's''; in March the firm—using specific figures for the first time—reported that it had produced its 3,000th bomber; and on April 16 it announced that Willow Run, starting in February, had achieved its long-sought goal, the production of ''approximately one bomber an hour.'' On July 1, announcement was made that Willow Run had built 5,000 bombers, half of them in the first six months of 1944. At the same time it was reported that ''the automotive type precision tooling at Willow Run had resulted in such uniformity of production that more than half of all the Ford-built Liberators were accepted for delivery on their maiden flights,'' an unusually high percentage.[37]

As many of the early production boasts of Ford spokesmen and the press began to come true, the plant and company officials were lauded to the skies. On March 3, Charles E. Wilson of the Aircraft Production Board telegraphed: ''The APB notes with pride that our confidence in your company's ability to maintain a fine sustained production record has again been proven . . . our sincerest congratulations.'' On March 29, the Detroit News, commenting on the announcement of the 3,000th bomber, declared that "the present facts sum up into a clinching vindication [of Willow Run] at a critical stage of the war." The following month, Senator Truman, after a visit to the bomber plant, called Henry Ford "the production genius of these United States." In mid-April, upon announcement of the bomber-per-hour production rate, dozens of newspapers hailed Willow Run as "the war production miracle that has been wrought in Detroit" and as the plant that has furnished "a sky-full of bombers to wreck the Nazi war machine." Henry Ford was accorded similar praise. "His achievement is tremendous," declared the *Asheville* (North Carolina) *Citizen* in a representative editorial. "He symbolizes the remarkable industrial techniques which have made this nation one vast armory."[38]

During the remainder of 1944 and in 1945 hundreds of news and feature stories on Willow Run appeared in newspapers and magazines. Many of the phrases used to describe the plant were as effusive as, and reminiscent of, those published during the first half of 1942—"a symbol of American ingenuity," a "magnificently-tooled colossus," a "product of inventive genius," "one of the world's great monuments of production genius," a "production miracle," the "miracle production story of the war." The following account by a *Christian Science Monitor* reporter typifies much of the writing about Willow Run during this period:

> The Pyramid of the Cheops or the hanging gardens of Babylon may have satisfied the ancients. Such structures may have been worldbeaters in their day. But for me, I'll take a today's phenomenon to top my list of wonders. Willow Run is a name that fascinates, enthralls, and—I discover—convinces. It is tomorrow's plant built today—for which we have the war to thank. It is, horizontally, what the Empire State Building is, vertically, to American industry and architecture. It seals Hitler's doom. It is a promise of American greatness. . . . Willow Run has to be seen to be believed.

The plant also was extolled in an OWI battle-of-the-production-line film, *Three Cities,* which was shown to servicemen throughout the world in 1944–45. The huzzas for Willow Run were capped in the spring of 1945, when the plant was awarded an Army-Navy "E" for "superior performance."[39]

In 1944, Willow Run made 48.5 percent of all of the B-24's produced; in 1945, 70 percent. In its peak production year, 1944, the plant built 92,568,000 pounds of airframes, far more poundage than had ever poured out of any one plant in one year and 4.6 percent of all U.S. airframe production during 1940–44. Willow Run's 1944 airframe production, in fact, almost equalled Japan's total airframe poundage for that year—and was approximately half that of Germany, Great Britain, and the U.S.S.R. Moreover, the factory's assembly-line production methods permitted Ford to deliver Liberators to the government for $137,000 each in 1944, compared to $238,000 two years before.[40]

The plant's highest monthly bomber output, 428, was attained in August 1944. After September, when the plant was geared to make 650 bombers a month, or 9,000 planes per year, it did not produce to its fullest capacity, the Department of War having ordered cutbacks in B-24 production in favor of building B-29's and B-32's at other factories. Including 1,894 knockdowns, the total number of B-24's built at Willow Run was 8,685. The last of the bombers, named the "Henry Ford," moved off the assembly line on June 28, 1945. A few minutes before the plane was to be towed from the plant, the founder requested that his name be removed from the nose of the ship and that employees sign their names in its place. This done, Henry Ford II, then executive vice-president of the company, climbed aboard a tractor and towed the plane to the airfield.[41]

The wartime Willow Run experiment was beyond question successful. The obstacles which the plant had to overcome were many and varied: the delay in the delivery of tools and fixtures, labor problems, the isolation of the site with its twin problems of housing and transportation, and, perhaps as important as any other, the extravagant and premature buildup. The Department of War's misleading announcement in May 1942 and the unwarranted statements by Ford officials in mid-1942 both hastened and sharpened the criticism.

Only one of the principals in Willow Run's buildup, Sorensen, commented publicly on it and the problem it created. Years later, in his autobiography, the manufacturing executive grumbled that "extravagant government-inspired publicity" had produced "flarebacks." He ignored his own contribution to the fiasco. Actually, Sorensen, whose enthusiasm for Willow Run and its potential led him to exaggerate the factory's production on several occasions, was perhaps more responsible than any other person for its buildup and letdown. At the same time, this production genius must be given major credit for the final swing of the public relations pendulum in Willow Run's favor.[42]

4

Although the public identified Ford's war record almost exclusively with Willow Run and the B-24, the company was engaged in more than a dozen other kinds of military production. It led in the production of high-power aircraft engines (57,852) and gliders (4,290). The firm's efficiency in producing the Pratt & Whitney aircraft engine enabled it to manufacture, with only 26,000 employees, more than its principal rival, Curtiss-Wright, which employed 40,000 workers. Ford's gliders, according to Major General James M. Gavin, shared honors with the British glider, the Horsa, as the most successful motorless craft used in the war. The company also supplied 26,954 engines of its own design for the M-4 medium tanks made by Chrysler and General Motors and built 277,896 jeeps, 93,217 military trucks, 2,728 tanks and tank destroyers, 12,777 amphibian jeeps, 12,314 armored cars, 13,893 universal carriers, and 2,400 jet bomb engines. Only General Motors, among auto makers, compiled a more impressive record.[43]

Army-Navy "E" citations for "exceptional" war work were presented to eight Ford plants. The first of the awards, conferred in October 1942, went to the former assembly plant at Chester, Pennsylvania, a tank modification center. Citations were also awarded to plants in Richmond, California (tank modification and jeep assembly); Minneapolis-St. Paul (parts for aircraft engines); Somerville, Massachusetts (universal carriers); Ypsilanti, Michigan (generators); the Rouge (aircraft engine plant); and, of course, Willow Run. Two of the plants, Chester and Richmond, also received a second Army-Navy citation, the "star" award, while the Ypsilanti facility received two star awards. Recognizing the citations' public relations and morale-building value, the company dramatized each acceptance ceremony. Two-and-a-half months prior to his death, Edsel Ford accepted two of the citations on the company's behalf, including the "E" awarded the aircraft engine plant on March 12, 1943. Henry Ford II accepted five of the awards; J. R. Davis, the company's Western regional manager, one.[44]

Measured by the value of prime war supply contracts awarded between June 1940 and September 1944 (the government is unable to provide these data through the end of the conflict), the Ford Company was the nation's third largest defense contractor during the World War II era. Ford's prime war supply contracts totaled $5,269,600,000 between 1940–44, compared with $13,812,700,000 for top-ranked General Motors, $7,091,000,000 for second-ranked Curtiss-Wright, and $3,394,800,000 for eighth-ranked Chrysler. Measured by the expansion of facilities during the war, Ford ranked eighth among companies contributing to the armed forces, with $371,657,000 expended ($355,473,000 advanced by the government). Du Pont led all companies in war-related expansion with an expenditure of $915,985,000, while General Motors was a close second with $911,704,000 worth of defense plants; Chrysler stood ninth with an outlay of $313,293,000.[45]

Despite General Motors' far greater contribution to the war effort, the American public, according to two public opinion polls conducted in July 1944, felt that the Ford Company was doing more to win the war than its leading competitor. A national sample of public opinion by Elmo Roper showed that 31 percent of the American people believed that Ford was contributing more to the war effort than any other automobile company, as against 21 percent citing General Motors. A thirty-five-city survey of male motorists by J. Walter Thompson, Ford's advertising agency, found that 28.1 percent of the respondents—who were divided almost equally among Ford, Chevrolet, and Plymouth owners—thought that Ford was "doing most to aid the war effort"; 25.1 percent and 11.6 percent of the interviewees gave the nod to General Motors and Chrysler, respectively. In addition, Roper, in the spring of 1945, found that Henry Ford ranked second only to shipbuilder Henry Kaiser as the man believed to have done more to win the war than any other American (Presidents Roosevelt and Truman and military figures were excluded from the poll). The auto magnate, in fact, received approximately twice as many votes as the men ranked third and fourth in the poll, Donald M. Nelson, chairman of the War Production Board, and James F. Byrnes, director of war mobilization.[46]

Henry Ford's contribution to his company's war effort was, in fact, limited. Sorensen, in 1956, said it was nil; and his view, he added, was shared during the war by highly-placed Washington officials including Charles E. Wilson, chairman of the Aircraft Production Board, and President Roosevelt. The magnate's chief war-related interest undoubtedly was Willow Run. But even his contribution to the bomber plant is debatable. Edsel said in 1943 that his father "put a lot of his ideas" into the project. Sorensen, on the other hand, declared that the octogenarian was simply "the glorified leader'' and ''had nothing to do with this program. . . . He would have a look at how things were going at Willow Run... but talk about its problems went in one ear and out the other.''

What is certain, in any event, is that Ford approved the idea of building the plant, passed on major policy decisions affecting it, and had a keen interest in its construction and efforts to move into production. He was a frequent, almost daily, visitor to the factory during the first two years of the war. Numerous photographs show him inspecting assembly lines and scrambling under and around B-24's. He also fretted incessantly over the delays in bomber production. The statement by the head of a California aircraft plant that ''Ford would drop $100 million to get his bombers out'' probably was a correct assessment of the magnate's attitude toward the B-24 program. Ford's pride was hurt when the press referred to his plant as ''Willit Run?''; he was vastly pleased when in late 1943 the factory refuted its critics. In Willow Run's banner year, 1944, when the industrialist's physical and mental health perceptibly deteriorated, he was less frequently seen at the plant; the following year his precarious health prevented him from attending the ceremony marking the end of bomber production.[47] All factors considered, Sorensen's negative evaluation of the founder's contribution to the bomber effort seems harsh, but not unjust.

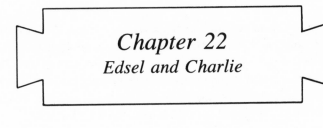

Chapter 22
Edsel and Charlie

1

Edsel Ford and Charles E. Sorensen, the two executives most responsible for the Ford Company's wartime achievements, were not on hand at war's end to share in the plaudits for a job well done. The younger Ford died on May 26, 1943; Sorensen left the company in March 1944.

Thwarted and opposed for years by his father and Harry Bennett, Edsel underwent an operation for stomach ulcers in January 1942. Although able to resume his duties after a short rest, he fell ill again—of stomach cancer—later in the year. To friends who suggested that he slow his pace, he merely shook his head and replied, "The war won't wait." Wan and haggard, and further weakened by an attack of undulant fever contracted from unpasteurized milk from his father's cows, Edsel managed to carry on his work until mid-April 1943. Almost to the end, his father refused to believe him in danger: if Edsel would only change his diet and mode of life to that which his father had found best, if he would stop worrying and listening to men of the wrong type, he would soon get well. Nonetheless, at age forty-nine, Edsel died, not only of stomach cancer and undulant fever, but of a broken heart as well. Edsel's death dealt Henry Ford the severest blow of his life, a blow from which he never recovered.[1]

Dissimilar in so many ways, Edsel and Henry Ford were particularly unlike in their desire for publicity and in the extent to which each was publicized. Throughout his life Edsel shunned publicity as much as his father sought it; and was no less successful in avoiding the spotlight than his father was in bathing in it. The younger Ford usually turned down requests for biographical data; almost always refused requests for written expressions of opinion; granted interviews only for compelling business reasons; even banned the use of the pronoun "I" in company statements in which his name appeared. When asked by company publicists to pose for pictures at business functions, his usual reply was, "See if you can't get father to do that. He likes that sort of thing. I don't." His reputation for shunting newsmen to the elder Ford provoked the *Philadelphia Inquirer* to grumble in 1942 that his longest statement to the press had been, "See father." During interviews, Edsel was pleasant, but said very little. "When he spoke," stated the *Detroit News*, "it was not with the picturesque flourish that would make a tale to be told and retold, but with quiet understanding and reserve." Edsel, although president of the world's most-publicized company for a quarter-century, never conducted a business press conference.[2]

The younger Ford remained in the background for several reasons. Perhaps foremost among them was one cited by the noted industrial designer, Walter Dorwin

Teague, who worked closely with Edsel during the 1930s: "An unselfconscious modesty that left no need for the kind of compensations publicity has to offer." Edsel also valued privacy. "I don't want to be in the position that father's in," he told an associate, ". . . to be set upon by autograph hunters and people trying to sell me some idea." Finally, Edsel surely knew that his father resented sharing the limelight with anyone—including his son. Edsel sought anonymity and he achieved it. In 1933, as he stood in front of the Senate Office Building with members of the Senate Banking and Currency Committee, before which he had just testified, he was waved out of camera range by a press photographer: "Bud, would you mind—this is just for big shots." In 1935, to his delight he was able to visit San Diego's California-Pacific Exposition nineteen times without being recognized by newsmen or any other visitors.[3]

In death, as in life, the younger Ford was overshadowed by his father. "When word was flashed that Edsel Ford had died," stated the *Detroit News,* "editors emptied their files of Ford lore and turned up only the countless anecdotes that have studded the life of the inventor-father." Many of Edsel's obituaries, consequently, devoted almost as much, if not more, attention to the auto king than to his son. Ironically, some of the articles described Henry as a nearly perfect father, attributing Edsel's finer qualities to his father's benign influence. "In all of [Henry's] worldly triumphs," observed a *Detroit Free Press* editorial typical of many, "there can be found nothing to match his achievement in the rearing of Edsel." The fact was, Edsel became an admirable figure in spite of, not because of, his father's treatment. As a father, Henry was a failure.[4]

Not one of the newsmen who wrote Edsel's obituaries was well acquainted with the younger Ford. Indeed, some of the writers admitted that they had seen him only at public meetings, if at all. Thus, unlike the "Henry Ford said to me" stories which filled newspaper columns after the auto king's death, Edsel's obituaries reflected the distance that Edsel had kept between himself and the press corps. Still Edsel's obituaries, sprinkled with moving tributes from Detroit's elite, were the most complete accounts of his life that had appeared in print. Virtually every obituary and editorial emphasized his modesty, gentility, and goodness, civic-mindedness, and exemplary family life. "His reputation," marveled one editor, "has never been blemished, even by a lying slander." Most articles also credited Edsel with having interested his father in aviation; having helped to persuade the elder Ford to replace the outmoded Model T; being responsible for the styling improvements in the company's post-1927 cars; and having contributed importantly to the firm's war effort. At the same time many publications acknowledged that Edsel, despite his title, had never exercised full control over the family enterprise.[5]

These publications might have added, but did not, that Edsel had been an island of stability in a sea of administrative confusion throughout the 1930s and early 1940s. His performance and the testimony of his associates leave little doubt that he was capable of managing the Ford Company on his own. Indeed, the firm would have fared better if the elder Ford, from about the time of his seventieth year, had devoted himself completely to his hobbies and relinquished control of the business to Edsel.

In retrospect, Edsel emerges as one of the most tragic figures in American business history. He was more than talented; he was creative. He was more than hard-working; he had an extraordinary sense of responsibility to his company and community. He was an excellent administrator, and he commanded the affection, respect, and loyalty of his associates. Unfortunately, his father, far from rejoicing in and making constructive use of these qualities, restricted and nullified them in his unceasing effort to remold his son into a tough, hard-hitting executive. Clara Ford watched fearfully as the tension mounted between father and son, and, unable to change Henry's course, sensed that it ultimately would become unbearable for both. Edsel, for his part, although often frustrated and sometimes heartsick over the harsh treatment he received from the elder Ford, had too much filial loyalty to fight back. "Father built this business," he would say when in disagreement with a parental decision, "and if that's the way father wants it, that's the way it's going to be." But the gulf between the two men and the years of persecution took their toll, eventually wearing down not only Edsel's body, but his spirit as well.[6]

Throughout his lifetime, except for a few articles criticizing him for refusing to "stand up" to his father, Edsel enjoyed a consistently good press. Since his death his reputation, particularly as a designer, has grown. Walter Dorwin Teague, writing in the foreword of a 1963 book about the Lincoln Continental, described Edsel as "a great soul ... wise, generous, strong and simple ... [and] a great designer." In similar vein, David J. Wilkie, former automotive editor of the Associated Press, writing in *Automotive News* on the twentieth anniversary of Edsel's death, referred to him as "a man with a great soul, a creative mind and one who undoubtedly would have become one of the industry's outstanding figures had he been afforded opportunity to alone direct the destinies of Ford Motor Co." Also in 1963, *Continental Comments,* magazine of the Lincoln Continental Owners Club, in an article commemorating the centennial anniversary of Henry Ford's birth, emphasized that one of the industrialist's more notable contributions to our times was "siring the son who gave us the Lincoln Continental." The *Detroit Free Press* in 1965 described Edsel as "exceptionally perceptive and artistically gifted ... ahead of his time in his understanding of industrial relations, social justice, civic responsibility, and aesthetic values." In 1973 the authoritative *Dictionary of American Biography* cited Edsel as "a man of diligence, poise, and discrimination who, in the opinion of many Ford executives, would have succeeded in rejuvenating the Ford Motor Company had he lived."[7]

Numerous efforts have been made to honor Edsel's memory. Detroit aviation pioneers tried unsuccessfully in 1944 to name Willow Run's airport (Detroit's major airport from 1946–66) the "Edsel B. Ford Memorial Airport." A B-24 from Willow Run's assembly line was enshrined near the bomber plant in 1946 as a peace memorial to the late executive. But in 1950, upon termination of the Edsel B. Ford American Legion Post 379, of Willow Run Village, which had installed and maintained the memorial, the plane was dismantled for scrap. In 1946 the younger Ford's name was given to a proposed East-West expressway in Detroit. Opened to traffic in 1955, the Edsel Ford Expressway has since been incorporated into Interstate Highway 94. Signs and Detroit area motorists, however, still refer to the expressway as "the Edsel Ford." The Edsel B. Ford Institute for Medical Research was established by Henry Ford Hospital in 1951; and a new Dearborn high school was named for the younger Ford in 1955. That same year, the Harvard Corporation named a Ford Foundation endowed chair the Edsel Bryant Ford Professorship of Business Administration. Edsel's name was lent to the Henry and Edsel Ford Auditorium, a handsome addition to Detroit's riverfront Civic Center, in 1956.[8]

Also in 1956 the federal government's Board of Geographic Names confirmed Admiral Richard E. Byrd's earlier designation of mountain ranges in Antarctica's Marie Byrd Land as the Edsel Ford Ranges. Byrd named the ranges for Edsel because the latter was the largest contributor to the explorer's Arctic and early Antarctic expeditions. Byrd also designated other Antarctic landmarks Ford Island, Ford Massif, Ford Nunataks, and Ford Peak. The explorer christened the Fokker plane used on his Arctic expeditions the "Josephine Ford," for Edsel's daughter; and in this plane the naval officer became the first to fly over the North Pole, on May 9, 1926. This plane, bought by Edsel for $30,000 to help meet Byrd's debts, is on display in the Henry Ford Museum. Byrd gave the name Mount Josephine to a 1,600-foot-high peak in the Alexandra Mountains of Antarctica's Edward VII Peninsula.[9]

In 1956 Edsel's name also was given to a Ford-built medium-priced car. Ironically, when the company began considering nameplates for the new car, Edsel's three sons ruled out their father's name, believing that he would not have wished to have it spinning on hubcaps. More than 18,000 names were suggested for the car, including Mustang, Zoom, Zip, Henry, Benson, and Drof (Ford spelled backwards). Responsibility for naming the vehicle fell to the company's executive committee, which, as it happened, dealt with the question at a time when the Ford brothers (each a member of the committee) were away from Dearborn. Failing to reach agreement on any of ten favored names, winnowed from the thousands, the group reviewed a list of "favored rejects." Among the rejects was the name Edsel, which, in spite of the Ford brothers' directive, had been kept alive as an anchor to windward. The committee's selection? Edsel. Henry Ford II, reached by telephone, said he would abide by the committee's decision, provided he could get his family's approval. He obtained it. "We have chosen a name," an Edsel Division executive wrote shortly afterwards. "It fails somewhat of the resonance, gaiety, and zest we are seeking. But it has a personal dignity and meaning to many of us here."

Introduced in September 1957, when both an economic recession and a shift in the market from medium-priced to low-priced cars were getting underway, the Edsel line failed. In November 1959, production of the vehicle was discontinued—at an estimated net loss of $350,000,000, the greatest single-product financial loss in the history of business until that year.[10] While pained by the financial reverse, the Ford brothers perhaps also regretted that the Edsel venture, far from honoring their father's memory, identified it with a business fiasco of unprecedented proportions.

For years, in fact, the Edsel car has been a staple of comedians' patter—the biggest boon to gag writers since the Murphy bed. Compared with the Edsel, Custer's Last Stand was a victory. The car was Detroit's version of baseball's hapless New

York Mets. It was a bigger loser than Harold Stassen. When Jackie Gleason bragged about stealing someone's "great idea," Art Carney, his sidekick, retorted, "yeah, it's just like stealing the patent rights to the Edsel." On the "Carol Burnett Show," Carol's long-suffering husband bellowed to his wife, "1958 was a beautiful year. I married you and bought an Edsel."

The Edsel car has become a synonym for a colossal mistake; and every "loser" or potential loser is apt to be tagged "an Edsel." The National Aeronautics and Space Administration's ill-starred Centaur rocket was described as "Edsel of the Missile Industry"; the TFX fighter-bomber "the flying Edsel"; General Electric's computer business "GE's Edsel"; Volkswagen's Model 411 "VW's Edsel"; and Du Pont's leather substitute, Corfam, "Du Pont's Edsel." In a single debate over funding of the supersonic transport plane (SST), Senator Edward M. Kennedy referred to the craft as "a fast-flying Edsel"; Senator Hubert H. Humphrey, a "national Edsel"; and Senator Charles H. Percy as a "federal flying Edsel." As a *Detroit News* columnist observed in 1973, "the Edsel endures today as a symbol of everything in life that flops." It seems only a matter of time before the standard dictionaries define the word "Edsel" as a failure of monumental proportions.[11]

In the late 1960s Edsel owners formed two organizations, the Edsel Owners of America and the International Edsel Club, both dedicated to the preservation and restoration of the vehicle. By 1974 the Edsel Owners of America, whose cofounder was Edsel Henry Ford (no relation to *the* Fords), had 1,500 members; the International Edsel Club, 700 members. The Ford Company ignored the Edsel owner groups for several years, but in 1972 formally welcomed the Edsel Owners of America to its fourth annual convention in Greenfield Village.[12]

2

A few days after Edsel's death Henry Ford, then almost eighty years of age, informed subordinates that he would resume the company's presidency, a post he had vacated in 1919. Sorensen, who felt that the founder was "mentally and physically . . . unable to handle the job," was flabbergasted; and he threatened to resign if the magnate did not change his mind. But Ford was adamant. On June 1 he and his grandsons, Henry II and Benson, held a stockholders' meeting at which they reelected themselves and Sorensen as directors and named Mrs. Edsel Ford, Harry Bennett, B. J. Craig (the company's secretary), Mead L. Bricker and Ray R. Rausch (both manufacturing executives) as new members of the board. Later that day the board formally elected Henry Ford president; Sorensen, vice-president; Craig, vice-president and treasurer, and Herman L. Moekle, formerly assistant secretary, assistant treasurer and secretary.[13]

Ford's decision to resume the presidency was applauded by the press. Congratulating the founder on his "pluck" and "courage," many editorials emphasized a "life begins at eighty" theme, praising Ford for "rolling up his sleeves," "shouldering the yoke of responsibility," and "grasping the reins firmly and carrying on the company's monumental work." "He has responded to the call of duty as a soldier would," typically declared the *Detroit News;* "neither grief nor fear of consequences to his own health could deter him. It is very admirable." "Ford's decision," echoed a Colorado weekly, "is a great picture, a great story, one of the sagas of modern times. Every American can well afford to applaud this patriotic American genius." Reciting Ford's past achievements, many of the editorials expressed confidence in his ability to keep the Ford Company "humming" and "moving forward"; no one, like Sorensen, who was aware of the magnate's diminishing—sometimes even negative— contribution to the firm, questioned this ability. Only one publication, the *New York Times,* suggested that Ford's resumption of the presidency would have little effect on the founder's business activities or on the operation of the Ford organization. "The affairs of the great company," the newspaper correctly predicted, "will be carried on much as in the past with the elder Ford sidestepping as much executive routine as possible."[14]

The death of the crown prince, so long the center of hope for an improvement in the Ford regime, plus the board's June 1 action, did, however, have an important bearing on the power alignment within the Ford Company. "Like all palace shifts," commented *Time,* "this one had backstairs significance. Greatly increased was the already great influence of Bennett [who, as he reached for enhanced power, could count on the support of the elder Ford, Rausch, and Craig]. Lessened was the influence of Sorensen, long nourished by the late Edsel Ford." Actually, Sorensen's influence with Henry Ford had been on the wane for perhaps a decade-and-a-half, while that of Bennett's was growing. Still, until the early 1940s, when Bennett adroitly began to manipulate the elder Ford's senile resentments and Sorensen began to get too much publicity for Ford's comfort, the production chief had been one of the few persons to whom the founder would listen.[15]

Virtually unpublicized before late 1940 (and unlisted in *Who's Who in America* until that year), Sorensen, like Edsel, knew that Henry Ford's jealousy was aroused when others received personal credit for the achievements of the Ford Company. "Henry Ford did not want his staff to receive publicity," Sorensen observes in his autobiography; "no one else in the organization could stand out and above him. My ability to keep out of the public eye was one reason why I stayed as long as I did at Ford while others left." Knowing that the auto king insisted on hogging the spotlight, it is all the more surprising that Sorensen in the early 1940s allowed himself to become the best publicized and most highly praised executive (except for Henry Ford) in the company's history.

Sorensen's buildup grew out of his involvement with Ford's defense activities, and it gathered momentum as the firm's military commitments increased. *Time,* in an article on Ford's aircraft engine plant in November 1940, perhaps quarried the first stone of Sorensen's sepulcher, heralding him as the company's "tough, brilliant Production Manager" and as a "wizard" of mass production. In mid-1941 the *Detroit Times* and the *New York Herald Tribune* referred to him as the Ford Company's "general manager"—a title which, as Henry Ford was later to make clear, was reserved solely for Henry Ford. Nonetheless, the "general managership" was bestowed on Sorensen by dozens of publications during the years 1941–44. Actually, Sorensen, like almost all other Ford executives, was titleless until July 1941, when he and A. M. Wibel, who had charge of purchasing, were named vice-presidents and directors of the company.[16]

In mid-1941 Sorensen began serving as a spokesman for the Ford Company on defense matters. Even in Henry Ford's presence, he occasionally did *all* of the talking during press interviews. With increasing frequency he served as the firm's host when newsmen and distinguished visitors toured the Rouge and Willow Run plants. Following many of the tours, the production executive was mentioned in news stories, often quoted. On a score of occasions in hundreds of newspapers, he was also pictured with prominent visitors including the Duke of Windsor, Senator Truman, President Manuel Prado of Peru, King Peter of Yugoslavia, Randolph Churchill, General H. H. Arnold, Rubber Director William M. Jeffers, and Charles E. Wilson.[17]

As Sorensen became a public figure, the press began to show an interest in his personal affairs, running stories on such matters as his birthday plans, his racing yacht, and his salary ($220,005 in 1942, in Detroit exceeded only by the salaries of Charles E. Wilson, then president of General Motors, and Edsel Ford). Praise was heaped upon the veteran executive by such diverse figures as R. J. Thomas, president of the UAW-CIO, and Harry Bennett. Thomas, in singling out the Ford Company in January 1942 as having a more advanced arms production program than any other large auto firm, gave Sorensen, not Henry Ford, credit for the firm's progress. A week later Bennett publicly cited Sorensen as "the man who knows most about Ford production."[18]

The most flattering of all of the articles about Sorensen appeared in *Fortune* in April 1942 and in hundreds of newspapers serviced by the Associated Press in June 1942. *Fortune*'s eight-page article, entitled, "Sorensen of the Rouge," with a subtitle, "Besides Making Engines, Tanks, and Guns, He Is Running the Biggest Bomber Factory in the World," included a full-page color picture of the executive and described him as "the creator of Willow Run," "a master of the metals," and "labor's candidate for high Washington posts." "Sorensen," the article added, "has the drive, the toughness, and the imagination for planning, for pushing through big things . . . and a profile that might have earned him a smashing salary in Hollywood." The Associated Press story, written by David J. Wilkie, described Sorensen as the "manufacturing genius of the Ford Motor Company" and as "one of the world's greatest production experts." Wilkie also lauded the production chief for the way he "supervised the expenditure of the Ford millions" and gave him major credit for developing the moving assembly line. "The Sorensen influence in the development of the Ford empire," rhapsodized Wilkie, "may be seen on all sides of the assembly plants, blast furnaces, the steel mills, the forging departments, and Ford factories scattered throughout the world, but nowhere is the evidence more tangible than at Willow Run, where in just little more than a year an industrial miracle has been wrought."[19]

The *Fortune* and Associated Press stories were followed by a rash of news and feature articles which made pleasant, albeit dangerous, reading for Sorensen. Many of these stories described him as a "production genius." Some of the articles credited him with "evolving the idea of the moving assembly line." Others said "his name is on many of the fundamental Ford patents''; ''he initiated many of the basic changes in the Ford engines''; and his ingenuity in casting motor blocks, crankshafts, and gears had ''helped bring the price of cars within range of the average American's pocketbook.'' Still other stories, commenting on Sorensen's contribution to the war effort, declared that he had ''launched the Ford magnesium foundry, aircraft engine plant and Willow Run'' and that he had ''built and equipped the bomber plant.'' ''Thirty-five years and two generations of men built the Ford Motor Company,'' noted the *Toledo Blade*. ''Thirteen months and Charles Sorensen driving the Ford organization built this incredible war machine'' [Willow Run]. The tributes were capped by newscaster Lowell Thomas, who, addressing Willow Run workers in the presence of Sorensen and Henry Ford, referred to the production executive as the ''legendary Charlie Sorensen.''[20]

As Sorensen's acclaim mounted, the founder, who long had considered himself the company's only production genius and legendary figure—as well as general manager—became more abrupt and waspish toward his lieutenant. He also became less attentive to Sorensen's recommendations.

For years before Edsel's death, Sorensen and Bennett, although tacitly antagonistic, had worked together in an uneasy partnership. But upon Edsel's death, when the actual administration of the Ford Company was at stake, their jealousy was transformed into enmity. It was quickly apparent that Bennett had the upper hand. Playing upon Henry Ford's senile spitefulness, he got rid of Steve Hannagan, whose retention by Edsel had had the strong support of Sorensen, and who had engineered much of the production executive's publicity. The service chief admits to having furnished information to the elder Ford about a Washington cocktail party in Edsel's honor at which Hannagan—along with James A. Farley, J. Edgar Hoover, Donald M. Nelson, and others—jestingly planned a reorganization of the Ford Company: Farley was to be made sales manager, Nelson production manager, and so on. Upon learning of these ''plans,'' Ford, according to Bennett, became convinced that ''ear-piddlers'' and ''high living'' had contributed to Edsel's illness and he was determined to sweep away the ''evil'' influences that surrounded his son. On June 1, 1943, only four days after Edsel's funeral, the magnate fired Hannagan; Sorensen was powerless to intervene. John W. Thompson, the head of Hannagan's News Bureau, who had kept Bennett's goodwill, remained at his post. Thereafter, Bennett, through Thompson, controlled the News Bureau.[21]

Sorensen's powers were sharply curtailed on June 18, when Bennett had himself appointed as the production chief's assistant for administrative problems; and he saw to it that his crony, Ray R. Rausch, was made Sorensen's assistant for production. From this point onward Sorensen's authority was largely confined to Willow Run. Four days later Henry Ford, in a slap at newsmen who had identified Sorensen as the company's general manager, announced that although ''the Ford Motor Company has never created a general managership . . . the duties of this position are being taken over by Henry Ford in addition to his duties as president.'' The statement added that Frank C. Campsall, Ford's personal secretary (and a Bennett confidant), had been appointed assistant general manager, a newly created post.

By the autumn of 1943, Sorensen—who had seen Ford and Bennett remove A. M. Wibel, John Crawford, Edsel's right-hand man in office affairs, Laurence Sheldrick, head of the company's engineering activities, and Eugene Gregorie, codesigner of the Lincoln Continental—knew that his own days were numbered. In November 1943, according to his account, he told an uncomprehending Henry Ford that he wished to be relieved of his responsibilities on January 1 to reside in Florida. When after New Year's Day Sorensen said goodbye, Ford's only comment was, "I guess there's something in life besides work." Still seeming not to understand what was happening, the founder left for his Georgia plantation. Sorensen had not resigned, and it can only be guessed whether he really wished to step out. From his winter home in Miami, he declares, he kept asking Ford through Campsall for "release"; and in March 1944 he got his answer. Ford, said Campsall, wished him to resign because he had been angling for the company presidency. Furious, Sorensen instantly offered his resignation. Whether Sorensen's exit was brought about by the publicity he had received between 1940–43; represented an impulse of the failing Henry Ford; or was the result of Bennett's machinations, nobody knows. But both Bennett and Fred L. Black believed the publicity Sorensen received contributed importantly to his ouster. Sorensen, perhaps unwittingly, implied as much in several sections of his autobiography.[22]

In June 1944, Sorensen accepted the presidency of Willys-Overland, Inc., of Toledo. But his Ford years were difficult to put behind. Asked after his resignation how he felt about leaving Ford, he replied by tapping his chest and saying, "it hurts here." "I never quite met anything of this sort before," observed Samuel Crowther, Henry Ford's former ghostwriter, after visiting Sorensen. "After all these years of almost dog-like service and loyalty, [he is] trying to find his own soul." His chagrin notwithstanding, Sorensen vigorously directed Willys's reconversion program. He persuaded a skeptical board of directors to offer a new utility line of civilian vehicles, and he produced the first civilian Jeep only ten days after V-J Day. In 1946, Sorensen, then sixty-four, resigned Willys's presidency, serving as the company's vice-chairman until his retirement in 1950. He died in Bethesda, Maryland, at age eighty-six, in 1968 and is buried in Miami.[23]

At the Ford Company, from mid-1943—with Edsel gone, Sorensen's arms pinioned, and Henry Ford's physical and mental powers on the wane—Bennett assumed increasing control. Indeed, until the rise of Henry Ford II in 1945, the service chief virtually ruled the firm. Nobody was sure whether the orders he gave were as Henry Ford's deputy or in his own right. Everyone wondered, "just how powerful is Harry Bennett alone?" One Ford executive had the answer. "Mr. Bennett is just so powerful that nobody around here wants to risk finding out."

Subject to the elder Ford's directives, Bennett began supervising labor matters and labor press relations in 1937. Expanding his press relations powers, the service chief by 1940 was at Ford's side during most interviews. Like Cameron before him, Bennett became Ford's "interpreter," rephrasing the founder's oft-enigmatic and sometimes "unprintable" statements so as "to keep Mr. Ford happy . . . and the company out of trouble." Most newsmen got along well with Bennett, appreciating his breeziness and willingness to provide background material on important stories.

They knew, moreover, that they had to maintain good relations with the service chief if they expected to remain on the Ford beat. Two ingratiating reporters went so far as to prepare a flattering biography of the "little fella." Upon finishing their draft, they submitted it to Bennett for his approval. He expressed disappointment, saying that no one would recognize him from what had been written.

"In what way, Harry?," asked one of the authors.

"Well," he responded, "you don't say I'm a son of a bitch." The manuscript was handed back; it never appeared in print.[24]

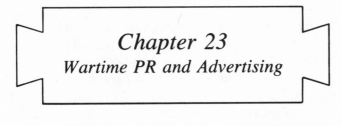

Chapter 23
Wartime PR and Advertising

1

The Ford Company paid scant attention to public relations and advertising in early 1942, and for many months afterward its programming in these spheres was sporadic and often erratic and ineffectual. Yet the firm's public relations work and advertising improved and gathered momentum as the war years went by, and by 1945 it had laid the foundation for its successful postwar public relations activities and advertising.

After Edsel's death and Hannagan's dismissal, the company's News Bureau was headed by Bennett. The service chief, although friendly with newsmen and helpful to Henry Ford in his personal interviews, had little conception of how to administer a public or press relations department; he therefore delegated responsibility for the bureau to John Thompson. Thompson, however, was handicapped by a lack of direction from higher management, a siphoning of his efforts into other activities, and the resignation of his most valuable assistant, Charles E. Carll, in August 1943. By September the News Bureau's floundering led *Steel* to report that Ford had "virtually no public relations policy or staff. It is extremely difficult," added the magazine, "to obtain any news data on what the company is doing." *Life* went further: "Trying to find out what goes on in Ford is like trying to find out what goes on in Russia."[1]

The News Bureau's performance remained lackluster for months, although the company—chiefly because of Willow Run's rapidly improving production record—enjoyed a fair press in late 1943 and a good press in 1944. In April 1944, Bennett rewarded a friend, J. Russell Gnau, Sorensen's ex-secretary, with the directorship of public relations. Lacking experience, Gnau contributed virtually nothing to the company's public relations effort. He was shifted to the company's office managership in October 1944. That month, Carll, at the invitation of Henry Ford II, reassumed active direction of the News Bureau. Highly popular with newsmen (he had been with the *Detroit Free Press* between jobs with Ford) and given a free hand by Henry II, Carll transformed the unit into an aggressive and efficient news-handling organization and improved relations with the press. Even so, the bureau, which was responsible for virtually all the company's public as well as press relations, was understaffed and unable to expand its activities. Visiting the company in 1945, John Gunther was amazed to find that "in this public-relations-choked era . . . Ford's public relations department employs exactly five men. Any comparable corporation," he noted, "has a staff of hundreds." Ford's erratic wartime press relations and its lack of a balanced public relations program were reflected in the findings of a *Tide*-sponsored poll of 1,000 public relations and business executives in late 1944 and early 1945. In reply to the question: "Which [American] organizations have the best public relations program?" none of the sample's 250 respondents named Ford. The company's arch-rival, General Motors, led the field with forty-one mentions.[2]

While the News Bureau floundered through 1943 and pre-Carll 1944, Thompson was devoting most of his time to Henry Ford's personal press relations and to advertising campaigns and radio programs in which the magnate was personally interested. The publicist spent considerable time with Ford during 1943–44, often, like Bennett, seeing him daily. From these meetings emerged many of the industrialist's more important wartime statements: his company would build cargo planes after the war; he would give job preferences to ex-servicemen after the war; he would raise the pay of all Ford workers "as soon as the government will let me," and so on.[3]

At his office in the Engineering Laboratory, William J. Cameron, reporting as always to Henry Ford, but occasionally working through the News Bureau, also prepared statements and letters for the founder. Ford instructed Cameron to draft some of this material; most of it, however, was initiated by Cameron and sent to Ford's secretary, Frank Campsall, or the News Bureau. Cameron's writings, with few exceptions, were less significant and newsworthy than those of Thompson's: a Christmas greeting for Greenfield Village students and a year-end statement for the *Detroit News* in 1942; a birthday greeting to President Roosevelt and a statement for the *Toronto Globe & Mail* expressing admiration for Canadian workmen in 1943; a birthday note to an old friend and fellow bird-lover in 1944; a New Year's message in 1945. In addition to writing for Henry Ford, Cameron also wrote several of Henry Ford II's speeches in 1944–45 and prepared copy for advertisements in the company's "Henry Ford" and "Famous Ford 'Firsts' " institutional advertising campaigns of 1944–46. Between January 1943 and June 1945, Cameron also gave biweekly talks—many of them similar in style and content to the homilies presented on the Sunday Evening Hour—at chapel services for Greenfield Village students.[4]

Cameron had far less influence with Henry Ford during the war years than he had had during the 1920s and 1930s. By 1940, Bennett had largely superseded him as Ford's press interpreter; from mid-1942 until mid-1943 the Hannagan organization controlled the dissemination of company news; and after mid-1943, Bennett, Thompson, and the News Bureau had primary responsibility for Henry Ford's and the company's press relations. By mid-1944, Cameron had dropped so far out of sight that *Fortune* did not even mention his name in a detailed article on the firm and its executives. Still, he continued to write for Henry Ford until 1945, when the auto magnate became inactive.[5]

Despite some habits which Ford abhorred and a streak of independence which the founder tolerated in no other executive, Cameron remained in Ford's good graces throughout his career. When the publicist ignored an edict requiring *Dearborn Independent* employees to start work at 8:30 A.M. and, in fact, often delayed his arrival at the office until early afternoon, Ford merely remarked, "Well, he's all here when he gets here." When Cameron drank excessively, the manufacturer, for years an uncompromising prohibitionist, told associates, "This is due to sickness. We're going to cure him. We'll never give up." When Cameron spurned invitations to attend Ford's weekly old-fashioned dances (summonses which Sorensen and other executives dared not refuse), the founder did not censure him. Alone among company officials, Cameron was immune from Bennett's machinations. For years the service chief, who hated Cameron, entreated Ford to say the word that would send the publicist packing. But Bennett himself was the first to go. [6]

Why was Ford loyal to Cameron? Fred L. Black believed that it was partly related to Cameron's acceptance of full responsibility for the *Dearborn Independent*'s anti-Semitic articles at the Sapiro trial in 1927 (thereby lessening the magnate's culpability) —and to Ford's awareness that Cameron had avoided alcohol for several years before the trial, resuming heavy drinking only immediately after testifying. Black also suggested that Ford's attitude toward Cameron was colored by the magnate's view—advanced for the day—that alcoholism was a curable disease.

Moreover, Ford undoubtedly respected Cameron's ability and judgment and was keenly aware of the publicist's value. Ford himself wrote with great difficulty, often spoke in contradictory terms, and was helpless in front of a sizable audience. Cameron, on the other hand, wrote exceptionally well, was a facile conversationalist and an accomplished orator. Above all, as his master's voice, he interpreted Ford's half-articulate remarks to perfection. "Cameron drunk," Ford once declared, "is still a better writer [and interpreter] than anyone else I know." [7]

Ford's respect for and loyalty to Cameron was returned manyfold. If Emperor Henry occasionally wore no clothes, Cameron was unaware of it. If Ford was "the most inconsistent man alive," as Cameron once admitted, he was "gloriously inconsistent." To the end of his company career, Cameron maintained that "other men dwindled in size when Ford entered a room." In April 1946, the publicist retired. "My services," he explained in his memoirs, "were with Mr. Henry Ford, and he was no longer there." With pride, Cameron noted that he had remained with the company two-and-a-half years beyond the normal retirement age of sixty-five. Few Ford executives of his generation could say the same. [8]

2

The confused state of the Ford Company's press relations in the wake of Edsel's death and Hannagan's departure in mid-1943 was paralleled in the radio and advertising media. In July 1943, the company's year-old newscast, "Watch the World Go By," came up for renewal. In early June, Maxon, Inc., strongly recommended the program's continuance, claiming that its listenership had exceeded original estimates and that it deserved "complete credit" for a marked improvement (according to the agency's surveys) in public attitudes toward Ford's defense contributions. In point of fact, the newscast's listenership—while slightly better than original forecasts—was mediocre. "Watch the World Go By" was never among the fifty leading radio programs in audience ratings. Moreover, any improvement in public attitudes toward the Ford organization probably could be attributed as much to Hannagan's efforts (and even more to the company's gains in military production) as to the newscast. [9]

As Maxon's recommendation was being weighed by the Ford Company, the agency—only two days after Hannagan's dismissal—announced the appointment of Harry Wismer as manager of its Radio Department. Wismer, who, as Henry Ford's nephew-in-law and Harry Bennett's friend, had "carte blanche" at Maxon's, wanted the newscast to be replaced by a musical show featuring Paul Whiteman and his orchestra. Aided by Bennett and John Thompson, Wismer laid careful plans to make the Whiteman proposal acceptable to Henry Ford. First he concocted a program schedule combining Whiteman and the magnate's old-fashioned dance orchestra. Then he approached his uncle-in-law, suggesting that the Ford Company sponsor Whiteman four days each week, the old-fashioned orchestra a fifth day. Wismer also recommended that Cameron should speak on one of the Whiteman broadcasts each week. At this point the receptive auto king agreed to listen to a "sample" recording of Whiteman's orchestra. The recording was made by a ninety-piece orchestra—twice the usual size of Whiteman's band—at the very considerable cost of $6,000. "The orchestration was beautiful," John Thompson recalled in 1952. "I doubt if it has ever been equalled." For extra insurance, the recording featured several of Ford's favorite songs, including "Camp Town Races" and "Jeanie with the Light Brown Hair."

After the record was made, but before it was auditioned, Ford informed Cameron that he was thinking of sponsoring Whiteman on radio and of putting the publicist on the air with him. Upon hearing the news, Cameron, according to Bennett, "worked real tears into his eyes." "I never thought I'd see the day," the publicist mourned to his employer, "when the Ford Motor Company would sponsor the King of Jazz." Ford, who hated jazz, said nothing. Later, the magnate, a dozen of his executives, and a sales representative of the Blue network gathered at the Engineering Laboratory to hear the Whiteman recording. After it had been played, the network salesman, who smoked cigars (which Ford despised) and wore a loud, checkered coat, rushed over to Ford. "How did you like that? How did you like that?" he shouted. Ford, who had had difficulty keeping time to the music with his foot, calmly replied: "I didn't like it at all." Plans to sponsor Whiteman were immediately scrapped. "We learned," drily observed Thompson, "never to make an experimental record for Henry Ford and spend any money on it."[10]

After rejecting Whiteman, the auto magnate ordered a renewal of the "Watch the World Go By" contract. Earl Godwin continued to present the program on weekdays; Roy Porter broadcast on week-ends and was also assigned Godwin's weekday rebroadcasts to the West Coast. But on December 7, 1943, for reasons never publicly explained, the company abruptly cancelled the newscast, effective in thirty days. The cancellation undoubtedly was related to Ford's simultaneous dismissal of Maxon, Inc., in favor of the J. Walter Thompson Company.[11]

The Ford Company, however, was still under contract with the Blue network (which had been purchased by the American Broadcasting System, Inc., in October 1943) for fifteen minutes of prime time each evening. Bennett and Thompson, joined by Henry Ford II, now a vice-president, suggested to Henry Ford that the company sponsor a program featuring popular (as opposed to jazz) music. Ford was agreeable. The trio had hoped to engage Fred Waring's orchestra but Waring was under firm contract to Owens-Illinois Glass Company, so the threesome recommended Tommy

Dorsey and his orchestra. Dorsey, like Waring, was known to Henry Ford, having served as Waring's replacement on network radio while performing at the company's exhibit at the Texas Centennial Exposition in 1936. He also had performed at several dances at Edsel's home in the late 1930s and early 1940s. Upon the assurance that Dorsey did not play jazz, the elder Ford consented to sponsor him. In mid-December, the band leader signed a thirteen-week contract at $10,000 per week; his broadcasts were to start on January 6. But during the first week of January Henry Ford had a change of mind. Through the company's attorney, I. A. Capizzi, he informed Thompson that he no longer wanted to sponsor Dorsey and that his contract should be cancelled. Thompson protested that a cancellation could cost the company $130,000. Capizzi replied that Ford was aware of the possible cost, but wanted Dorsey "unsigned and paid off." The band leader, whose orchestra had not rehearsed a note for the proposed program, accepted a $75,000 settlement.[12]

With Dorsey unacceptable to Henry Ford, company officials decided to continue broadcasts of "Watch the World Go By" on Monday through Saturday evenings and to present Greenfield Village's chapel services on Sunday nights; on January 22 the Saturday newscast was replaced by a program featuring Henry Ford's old-fashioned dance orchestra. Ray Henle, who in early December 1943 had succeeded Roy Porter as "Watch the World Go By"'s' alternate newscaster, was temporarily shifted to the weekday newscasts starting January 6. He was replaced on January 24 by Paul Neilson, who was regarded as a stopgap commentator. Neilson continued to broadcast on "Watch the World Go By" until August 5, 1944, when the network again assigned Henle to the program. In October, Ford officials pressured the network to replace Henle with Clifford A. Prevost, a veteran Washington correspondent, who, since April 1944, had served as the company's Washington public relations representative.[13]

A combination of circumstances—Prevost's ragged radio delivery, the newscast's low listenership, Henry Ford's virtual retirement, and, finally, an acceptable idea for a new program—brought "Watch the World Go By" to a close on December 7, 1944. The new program, a half-hour musical, "Stars of the Future," was launched the following evening over 167 ABC stations. The Ford Company had high hopes for the show, assuring its dealers that it would convey "the distinctive forward looking character which you will find in keeping with the stature and spirit of our company today." Featuring singers Frances Greer and Lawrence Brooks and an orchestra and chorus under the direction of Robert Russell Bennett, "Stars of the Future" presented six to eight promising young musicians on each show. The program was artistically successful (the *New York Times* called it "unpretentious yet polished"), but—chiefly because it was presented at the same time as the highly popular "Aldrich Family"—was unable to attain high listener ratings.[14]

In an effort to gain ground, the company in late March dropped the stars-of-the-future format and—after moving Brooks and the Bennett orchestra to a new Sunday afternoon program on NBC—built the show around Frances Greer and the Raymond Paige orchestra. The "Frances Greer Show," however, proved no more successful in competing against the "Aldrich Family" than "Stars of the Future," and was cancelled on June 1, 1945. Brooks and Bennett, joined by singer Jo

Stafford, languished in the Sunday afternoon radio doldrums through September. In October the "Ford Show," as it was called, was moved to 10 P.M. Tuesdays on CBS. But opposite the highly popular Bob Hope, it could make little headway. The program was replaced on January 1, 1946 by the "Bob Crosby Show."[15]

The company also cancelled its two other network radio programs, "Greenfield Village Chapel Service" and "Early American Dance Music," during the summer of 1945. For many months after their debut in January 1944, Henry Ford took a personal interest in these shows, often commenting on their quality and making suggestions for their improvement. Both programs were essentially noncommercial. The chapel service was broadcast from Ford chapels at the Wayside Inn, Richmond Hill, Georgia, and Macon, Michigan, as well as Greenfield Village. *Variety* lampooned the program, calling it "a folksy-religious stanza by the kid choir of Greenfield Village." The magazine added that "since it obviously pleases the sponsor, it probably doesn't matter that many people who find it boring, or who regard all commercialized religion askance, will string along with Edgar Bergen." The Ford program was tuned in by only 3 percent of the 8 to 8:15 P.M. Sunday listening audience, while Edgar Bergen's "Charlie McCarthy Show," the third most popular program on radio, drew 67 percent of listeners at that time. Noting these figures, the ABC network, which wanted to schedule a strong program opposite Bergen, pleaded with the Ford Company in the spring of 1944 to switch the chapel service to Sunday afternoons. The company refused. In March 1945, however, the network made the switch over Ford's objection. The program died a "natural death" in July 1945, as the company turned to a radio schedule offering greater commercial promise.[16]

"Early American Dance Music," a half-hour program featuring Henry Ford's old-fashioned dance orchestra (consisting at this time of a dulcimer player, a cymbalist, a violinist, and a bass violinist) and with Benjamin B. Lovett calling, was broadcast from the company's recording studio in the Engineering Laboratory. The only reference to Ford on the show was the opening statement: "Mr. and Mrs. Henry Ford present early American dance music." In January 1945, the Fords asked that their names no longer be associated with the program; the opening line was then changed to: "The Ford Motor Company, builder of cars and trucks, presents early American dance music by the Ford Early American Dance Orchestra." The program attained a fair audience rating, having almost twice as many listeners in early 1944 as "Stars of the Future" and ranking fourteenth among the twenty orchestras on network radio during the 1944–45 season. But most of its listeners, according to its fan mail, were retired or inactive people, many of them hospitalized—scarcely a car-buying audience. Acknowledging that the program was "not suitable for advertising automobiles," the company dropped it upon resuming civilian vehicle production in July 1945.[17]

The Ford Company, which had been the auto industry's leading radio advertiser since 1934, maintained this position throughout the war years. In fact, the Dearborn firm spent more money on radio advertising during 1942–45 than the industry's next two biggest radio sponsors (General Motors and Chrysler) combined.[18]

3

The Ford Company did not resume print advertising until November 1942. The first advertisement, which appeared in national magazines and leading newspapers throughout the country, described the production of jeeps, Pratt & Whitney engines, operations at Willow Run and the Ford Navy School, and other wartime activities. It was followed by four similar advertisements in 1943. Conforming to the pattern of industrial wartime advertising, the advertisements were lavish in their praise of Ford products and the company's contribution to the war effort. Ford's M-Y tank was described as "the answer to a tankman's prayer"; the M-10 tank destroyer as "the toughest Ford ever built"; and Ford-made jeeps as "sweethearts of the A.E.F." "Our men," declared one advertisement, "have speeded the war effort by millions of work days and saved the nation millions of dollars." Another advertisement boasted that "measured by any yardstick the wartime achievements of the Ford organization would be considered great."

Consistent with his lifelong aversion to boastful advertising, Henry Ford thought his firm's "war effort" advertisements were in poor taste. Slipping into John Thompson's office in November 1943, he declared, "that's not the right thing to do. . . . I don't see why we should blow our horn like that. It sounds like without the Ford Motor Company we couldn't win this thing [the war]." Thompson agreed, but pointed out that almost every other company's advertisements sounded the same. Ford cut him short: "John, I'd like for you to take over the advertising." Thompson, a public relations specialist, protested that he knew almost nothing about advertising. Brushing the objection aside, Ford ordered the publicist to tell H. C. Doss, the company's sales and advertising manager, who had worked with Maxon, Inc., on the advertisements, that he was being relieved of his responsibilities. The magnate also ordered Thompson to replace Maxon, Inc., with another advertising agency.[19]

The industrialist virtually gave Thompson a free hand in selecting Maxon's successor, suggesting only that the new agency be large and that it be equipped to handle the company's postwar foreign advertising. Thompson's thoughts turned to the J. Walter Thompson Company (JWT), of New York, which vied with Young & Rubicam as the nation's No. 1 agency in billings, had a worldwide network of offices, and employed two men with whom the publicist was personally acquainted, Daniel Danker, Jr., of the agency's Hollywood office, and O'Neill Ryan, Jr., the firm's vice-president in charge of new business. Shortly before Thanksgiving, Thompson and Henry Ford II invited Danker and Ryan, plus Henry T. Stanton, a part owner of JWT and head of its Chicago office, to Dearborn to meet with them, Harry Bennett, and the senior Ford. There was no presentation; but in late November Henry Ford, who thought that the JWT executives were "nice people," offered the agency his company's advertising account.[20]

Since the elder Ford had all but vetoed advertisements dealing with the company's war work, and there were no civilian products to advertise, John Thompson and JWT at first were at a loss. Pondering the problem for several weeks, they decided to develop a campaign, based on events in Henry Ford's life, which would "point up the sources from which sprang the genius and success of the Ford Motor Company." Working with Irving Bacon, a company artist, Thompson and the agency prepared a series of advertisements showing Ford as a youthful watch repairer; at his first meeting with Thomas A. Edison in 1896; demonstrating one of his early cars to a reporter in 1900 (the advertisement's headline, SWIFTER THAN A RACE HORSE IT FLEW OVER THE ICY STREETS, was identical to the original *Detroit News-Tribune* banner); participating in the New York-to-Seattle race of 1909, and so on. The advertisements delighted the auto king. In the early stages of the campaign, launched in April 1944, he often discussed Bacon's paintings with his wife, and made suggestions for improving their authenticity.

The "Henry Ford" series was discontinued in late 1944 in favor of a "Famous Ford 'Firsts' " campaign, started in January 1945. The new series recalled Ford's pioneering in research and manufacturing; and typical advertisements described the company's role in developing a radio beacon for airplanes, synthetic paints for cars, mass production methods for building bombers, and improved methods for making plate glass. All of the advertisements featured the headline, "Expect the 'Firsts' from Ford!" and promised that the company's postwar products "will reflect all of the ingenuity and precision engineering which are traditional with Ford." The "Famous Ford 'Firsts' " campaign ran until January 1946. Upon termination, it was hailed by the *New York World-Telegram* as "one of the brightest ideas for institutional copy during the war . . . [because] it leaned away from the obvious institutional copy of other industrial manufacturers who tooted their own horns."[21]

The company ran one other institutional campaign during the war—a series of advertisements signed by Henry Ford and Henry Ford II during the first four months of 1945. Under such headlines as "What Star Shall Guide Our Country?" and "No Wage Is 'Too High' That Is Earned!," they dealt with possible postwar problems (job shortages, inflation, excessive public indebtedness) and worthy postwar objectives (nurturing youth and family life, eliminating racial and religious prejudices). The advertisement on wages, which stressed that "fifty dollars a day *earned* is none too high, but a dollar a day *unearned* is much too high," was quoted in the news and editorial columns of many newspapers throughout 1945.[22]

Three product advertising campaigns also were introduced in 1944. The first of the campaigns, the "Sure Glad I've Got a Ford" series, was started in April. Its advertisements supported dealers in their efforts to persuade Ford owners to use dealer service facilities. A second campaign, begun in the fall of 1944, whetted readers' interest in postwar Lincolns and Mercurys by showing the 1942 models in picturesque rural settings and suggesting that their newer counterparts would be even more attractive and better engineered. These advertisements, the first in the industry to place emphasis solely on postwar cars, drew hundreds of letters from prospective buyers.[23]

The third campaign, featuring the slogan, "There's a Ford in Your Future," was launched in November and became the immediate postwar era's best-known automobile slogan. It was prompted by an article, "Lay That Crystal Down," which appeared in the July 1944 issue of the revived *Ford Times*. Featuring an illustration of a woman gazing into a crystal ball, the article pointed out that postwar cars would bear a close resemblance to prewar vehicles rather than the plastic, bubble-top, and autogyro-type "dream" cars envisioned by some journalists. At the time the story appeared, the newly appointed J. Walter Thompson agency was reviewing Ford literature in the hope of uncovering a suitable theme. Inspired by the article's title, illustration, and references to postwar cars, the agency came up with the "Ford in Your Future" campaign.[24]

The campaign's first advertisements simply showed a crystal ball, across which was written the slogan, plus the statement, "Ford has built more than 30,000,000 cars and trucks," and the company's signature. Later advertisements superimposed on the crystal ball illustrations of a man and a boy fishing, a young couple picnicking, beaming families looking at or seated in new Fords, and so on. Prior to the start of car production in July 1945, copy typically promised that "a smart, new peacetime Ford will be waiting to make those trips more fun. . . . We're going to start production plans as soon as we receive the necessary 'go ahead.' " In the latter half of 1945, copy reported that limited production had begun and that "next month and the month after there'll be more new Ford cars available . . . and still more in 1946. So hold to your plan—don't settle for less. There *is* a Ford in your future."[25]

When the company introduced a new slogan, "Ford's Out Front," in March 1946, the "Ford in Your Future" slogan and crystal ball illustration—although still used—were de-emphasized. The new slogan, which led into copy asserting that Ford was out front with an 100-horsepower engine, in styling, in extra values, and finally, "in everything," also caught on quickly. By mid-1946, Ford's Advertising Department could claim with considerable justification that both "Ford's Out Front" and "There's a Ford in Your Future" were "public by-words." The "Out Front" slogan was used until early 1949; the "Ford in Your Future" slogan—with variations in copy such as "There's a Ford in Your Future—with a Future Built in!"—until the fall of 1950.[26]

Of the many slogans used by the Ford Company, only "Watch the Fords Go By" has enjoyed as much public currency as "There's a Ford in Your Future." During the past two decades the "Future" slogan has given rise to countless variations on its theme. In 1946, when the Ford Company was hiring scores of men from other auto companies, *Business Week* reported that when one auto executive met another he opened the conversation by inquiring, "Is Ford in your future?" The following year, *Forbes,* in an article on business leaders, noted that Henry Ford II "has made America aware that there is a Ford in its future." In 1955, after signing a labor contract with Ford and announcing that he would seek a similar settlement with General Motors, Walter P. Reuther, president of the UAW-CIO, quipped: "You might say there's a Ford in General Motors' future." A year later, *Saturday Review* entitled an article about Greenfield Village, "A Ford in Your Past."

In 1963, when Michigan Congressman Gerald R. Ford was elected chairman of the House Republican Conference (Caucus), the *Detroit News* observed that "there is now a Ford in the Republican Party's future." Later that year, when Henry Ford II, after separating from his wife, was linked romantically with an Italian beauty, Maria Cristina Vettore Austin, *Newsweek* ran a picture of Mrs. Austin and inquired, "is there a Ford in her future?" In May 1964, when Henry Ford II announced that he would support President Lyndon B. Johnson's bid for re-election, a *Chicago Sun-Times*'s headline blazoned, "There's a Big Ford in Johnson's Future."

In 1965, the *New Republic* headlined an unfavorable review of a film directed by Director John Ford, "No Ford in Our Future." The same year, *Time* announced that "the company that fathered the tin lizzie sees a [LTD] limousine in its future" and headlined an article on a Ford Foundation grant to U.S. orchestras, "A Ford in Their Future"; while the society editor of the *New York World-Telegram,* in rating Henry Ford II's daughters, Charlotte and Anne, as Manhattan's "most marriageable maidens," declared that "any red-blooded guy would be lucky to have such a Ford in his future."

Cheered by agreement on a labor settlement with Chrysler, Walter Reuther in 1967 predicted that "there is a Chrysler in both Ford and GM's futures." In 1970 Ford's discussion of truck production with the Soviet Union evoked a chorus of such headlines as "Ford in Ivan's Future?" and "Is There a Ford in Russia's Future?" Similarly, when Ford's Chilean assembly plant was being subjected to nationalist pressure in 1971, many publications echoed *Business Week* in wondering "whether there was a Ford in Chile's future"; and when Ford announced in 1973 that it would build a plant in Spain, journalists duly noted that there would be "a Ford plant in Spain's future."

After Gerald Ford became vice-president, the *Detroit Free Press* declared that "it is splendid to have another Ford in our future"; while a *Detroit News* cartoon showed a palm reader telling her client, an elephant labeled GOP, that there's "a Ford in your future." After Ford became President, the *New York Daily News* pictured the President looking into a crystal ball under the caption, "The Future in Our Ford." When speculation centered around Nelson Rockefeller as a vice-presidential candidate, the Associated Press distributed nationwide a photo of the ex-governor seated in his Model A Ford under the caption, "Ford in His Future?" The "Ford in Your Future" slogan thus seems destined neither to die nor to fade away.[27]

During the war years, 1942–45, the Ford Company spent $11,212,734—60 percent of its advertising budget—on print advertising. Like radio advertising, expenditures for print advertising increased steadily during the war—from $409,563 in 1942 to $7,586,714 in 1945. The company's total expenditure for advertising during 1942–45 was $19,355,456, an amount slightly greater than that of General Motors' wartime advertising. Of Ford's total outlay, $4,394,733—less than half of the prewar expenditure—was spent in 1944, the last full year of the conflict; $11,496,514 was spent in 1945.[28]

4

In addition to its activities in the press relations and advertising spheres, the Ford Company paid special attention during the war years to the youth and serviceman-veteran publics. The company identified itself with a major youth activity, the American Legion Junior Baseball program, in the spring of 1943. Launched in 1926, the Junior Baseball competition offered league play for boys under seventeen years of age. From the start of competition a handful of Ford dealers had cosponsored teams with legion posts. The company itself expressed an interest in the activity in late 1941, when Advertising Manager H.C. Doss proposed to legion officials that the firm annually award a plaque to the team winning the national championship. But the offer was withdrawn with the outbreak of war.

Eighteen months later, at the urging of James F. O'Neil, chairman of the Legion's Americanism Commission, the company renewed its proposal, offering a plaque to the national championship team and a $50 war bond to each member of the winning club. The door was opened to further company participation in August 1943, when O'Neil, in Dearborn to accept the plaque in behalf of the winning team, met Henry Ford. The magnate expressed an interest in the program's effort to make better citizens of boys and asked a leading question: "Is there something more we can do for you?" O'Neil, knowing that financial difficulties had forced scores of legion posts to discontinue sponsorship of teams during the war years, suggested that the company encourage its dealers to assist posts with the program. Ford agreed to do so.[29]

During the summer of 1943, as the company spread word of its decision to participate in the Junior Baseball program, Ford and Lincoln-Mercury dealers aided 123 of the competition's 1,600 teams, generally limiting their support to providing trophies and banquets for local winners. In 1944 dealers cosponsored 264 teams, many providing equipment and transportation for the clubs. The following year, dealers cosponsored 1,232 of the legion's 4,000 teams, in many instances assuming complete financial responsibility for clubs. In a few cities, including Detroit, the Ford organization virtually financed the entire program. In 1945 the company offered trophies to teams winning state championships and cosponsored with dealers the first annual Junior Baseball all-star game in Detroit's Briggs Stadium.[30]

In 1946, as Ford braced for postwar competition, the company's interest in Junior Baseball took on a commercial tone. "Being a part of this national program," a General Sales Department memorandum informed branch managers, " . . . affords an excellent opportunity for the Ford dealer to become a civic leader in his neighborhood with all of the resultant benefits . . . publicity, goodwill, and sales contacts. The young men participating," the memorandum added, "are approaching manhood; they will become buyers; they will [influence] . . . other people's views with regard to preference in purchasing. . . . Most of a dealer's investment in this program will be returned with but a single car sale as a result of his participation." Branch managers were told, "When the umpire shouts, 'Play Ball!,' we're counting on your territory to have a full complement of teams on the diamond." Thus exhorted, each of the thirty-three branches appointed a full-time representative to encourage and assist dealers and legion posts in organizing teams and leagues. Hundreds of dealers extended their cooperation; in 1946 the Ford organization cosponsored 2,200 of the program's 5,891 teams.[31]

Junior Baseball received additional impetus in 1947, when Ford hired Babe Ruth as a consultant for the program. Operated on for cancer in January 1947, the former home run king, although noted for his hijinks as a player, took his new assignment seriously. "They call me a consultant," he told a press conference at the time of his appointment, "but I want to tell you that I plan to work hard at this job—just as hard as my health permits. The possibilities are unlimited and I won't be happy until we have every boy in America between the ages of 6 and 16 wearing a glove and swinging a bat.'' In 1947, the fifty-three-year-old baseball idol—enjoying greater popularity than at any time since his salad days with the New York Yankees two decades earlier—logged more than 40,000 miles in behalf of the program, appearing on diamonds before hundreds of thousands of youths. That year, Ford dealers cosponsored 3,987 of Junior Baseball's 8,000 clubs. The company renewed Ruth's contract early in 1948, ''not only because he serves as an inspiration to every American boy but because of the excellent results of his efforts last season.'' The ex-slugger's salary was not revealed, but the company announced that it ''ranks him high on the list of baseball's top money-earners.'' As long as his strength permitted, Ruth made appearances in behalf of the Junior Baseball program. At his last appearance, in June 1948, before 16,000 youngsters in St. Louis, he was too weak to wave a bat for photographers. Two months later he was dead of cancer. Meantime, dealers' cosponsorship of teams reached an all-time high in 1948—4,678.[32]

Sponsorship of legion baseball proved expensive. In 1947 alone, the Ford organization spent $1,250,000 on the activity, the company contributing approximately $175,000 of this amount, the dealers the remainder. Although the return on investment cannot be measured in dollars and cents, it undoubtedly was (and still is) judged worthwhile by the firm and many of its dealers, for the Ford organization has participated in the Legion Junior Baseball program for more than three decades. The Ford Division assumed responsibility for the program in the late 1960s, and its dealers annually sponsor more than 200 teams, award plaques and trophies to winners and runners-up in the several layers of competition, and stage a banquet for national finals' participants.

Ford's participation in the program has been as gratifying to the legion as to the company and its dealers. In 1957 the organization's national magazine extolled the Legion-Ford relationship as ''one of the finest 'partnerships' in the history of American sports.'' In 1964, James F. O'Neil, national commander of the legion in 1948 and still a high-ranking legionnaire, called Ford's participation ''the greatest continuing asset in the whole history of the Junior Baseball program.''[33]

During the war years the Ford Company extended its cooperation to legionnaires and other veterans in several other ways. Cooperation with the legion was, of course, not new to Ford. During the depression year 1933, while skirmishing with the National Recovery Administration, the firm offered 5,000 jobs to members of the Wayne County [Michigan] Council of the American Legion. In 1939 Henry Ford, because he admired the legion's antiinterventionist attitude, delivered one of the sixteen ''public addresses'' of his career before the organization's national convention. In early 1942, the magnate helped to publicize the legion's national defense bond sales campaign by buying the first bond from National Commander Lynn U. Stambaugh. The company did not launch a sustained bid for the goodwill of veterans, however, until it began participating in the legion's baseball program in 1943 and implemented two programs for ex-servicemen in April 1944.[34]

On April 9 Henry Ford announced that he would immediately convert Dearborn's Camp Legion—since 1938 a Ford-operated farm camp for underprivileged boys, most of whom were sons of deceased or disabled veterans—into an occupational rehabilitation center for handicapped ex-servicemen. The camp, the industrialist explained, would be operated by the Henry Ford Trade School, with the cooperation of the legion's Dearborn post. It would teach disabled veterans farming and mechanical skills, while providing them with room and board and $3.00 pay per week.

Announcement of the center, "the first privately-financed facility of its kind," was greeted with enthusiasm by the American Legion. "Mr. Ford's public-spirited action," declared National Commander Warren H. Atherton, "is a splendid contribution to the welfare of our handicapped ex-servicemen. . . . The American Legion salutes him for his understanding, foresight, and generosity." Among the scores of newspapers which publicized the announcement, many were no less effusive in their praise. "Out of the love, generosity, and patriotism of his kind heart," typically observed a Mississippi publication, "Mr. Ford is giving another chance to men who entered the ring with Mars and took a cruel K.O."[35]

Throughout the summer of 1944, Camp Legion was the subject of hundreds of news stories favorable to Henry Ford. In September of that year, the magnate, in recognition of the establishment of the Camp Legion School of Vocational Guidance (as the center became known), was awarded the American Legion's Distinguished Service Medal.

Hundreds of ex-servicemen received training in Camp Legion between 1944 and March 1946, when it was closed for economy reasons. "Graduates" of the center were free to accept any kind of employment. But most of them, familiar with Ford's unsurpassed record as an employer of the handicapped, accepted job offers extended by the company.[36]

Less than a week after announcing plans for the conversion of Camp Legion, Henry Ford pledged in a letter to Brigadier General Frank T. Hines, director of retraining and re-employment for the U.S. Veterans Bureau, to give job preferences to veterans in the postwar era. "Other people have made a lot of money out of this war," said Ford, "and the servicemen have made nothing. They deserve the first call." The magnate's pledge, coupled with an appeal for other employers to take a similar stand, "delighted" Office of War Mobilization officials and was hailed throughout the nation. An editorial in the *Atlanta Journal*, entitled, "When Johnny Comes Home," expressed a view shared by many newspapers: "Despite his age, Henry Ford is able to visualize the needs and desires of folks in the years ahead, and he gets into print first with a clear statement of a method to meet these wants. . . . In taking this patriotic and practical stand, Mr. Ford is the spearhead of concrete planning for the afterwar period." By year's end, more than 4,000 World War II veterans were in the company's employ. In the spring of 1945, Ford was cited by *Time* as one of the five business organizations which had done the most to assist veterans in obtaining employment.[37]

The Ford Company also publicly encouraged its dealers to give employment preferences to veterans. A booklet, *An Opportunity for World War Veterans,* endorsed by the American Legion and the Veterans of Foreign Wars, was sent to dealers in December 1944 for redistribution to ex-servicemen. It promised veterans not only a chance to learn about the retail automobile business, but also "an ultimate hope for a dealership." By November 1945, 4,460 veterans of World War II were employed in dealers' "earn-while-you-learn" training programs; by January 1946, their number had increased to more than 9,441.[38]

In July 1945, shortly after the company produced its first postwar car, announcement was made in Henry Ford's name that the firm would provide and install free of charge special equipment and controls which would enable amputee veterans to drive cars. "No man who lost a limb in the armed services," declared Ford, "is going to have to pay anything extra to drive a Ford automobile." The "humanitarian step" was lauded in the press. "A thoughtful gesture indeed," typically observed the *Boston Post*. "Many people have said they want to help these men, to whom we owe so much, but Mr. Ford is one of the first to do something about it at considerable cost to himself." The Ford Company was, in fact, the only auto firm to provide special equipment for disabled veterans without charge, although several other companies furnished and installed the devices at cost. Ford maintained its generous policy until the government, in August 1946, appropriated funds to provide a specially equipped auto for every amputee veteran.[39]

In addition, the company recommended to its dealers in December 1945 that as long as the nation remained car-starved at least 25 percent of their new cars should be sold to ex-servicemen. In many instances, as Ford later admitted, dealers ignored the recommendation, but some appear to have honored it. Ford dealers of metropolitan Detroit, in fact, publicly announced in March 1946 that 31.2 percent of their new car sales had been made to veterans.

General Motors, Westinghouse, Bethlehem Steel, Bulova, Standard Oil (New Jersey), and Botany Mills, to name a few firms, also received press recognition for making special concessions to ex-servicemen. But in the range and depth of its programs, no other firm in the country did as much for veterans during the mid-1940s as Ford.[40]

5

Ford's programs for youth and veterans were important. But they had less impact upon the company's future than the wartime findings of the firm's first comprehensive public opinion study, which significantly influenced Ford policies during the remainder of the 1940s and beyond. This study was originated in April 1944 by Henry Ford II, who, as he struggled to alter the firm's course, realized that an appraisal of public attitudes toward auto makers and their products was a necessary prelude to intelligent planning. To conduct this appraisal, young Henry, newly appointed as executive vice-president, engaged Elmo Roper, one of the country's leading pollsters and marketing research consultants. Roper's findings, based on interviews conducted during July 5–9, 1944, were made known to the company in October of that year. They indicated that revisions in Ford policies and improvements in its products were essential if the company were to prosper in the postwar era.

Certain conclusions drawn from the Roper study were affirmative. "One of the most obvious findings," the pollster reported, "is that the Ford Motor Company and Mr. Henry Ford both have a large reservoir of good will. The Ford Motor Company is still, in the minds of most Americans, our No. 1 corporation, the standard of comparison by which other corporations are judged." Roper also found that Americans thought that Ford had done more to advance industrial progress, had contributed more to the war effort, and had treated its employees better than any other motor car manufacturer. These favorable findings were, however, outweighed by others which sounded a warning note for the future:

> It would not be too much of an oversimplification to say that the "best friends" of the Ford Motor Company and its products are the poor, including the Negroes, the farmers, and the people in the older age brackets. On the other hand, the best friends of General Motors might be described as the well-to-do and the young and the city dwellers. Since it is the young rather than the old who normally set long-term purchasing trends, since it is the well-to-do rather than the poor who are usually the "style leaders" in purchasing, and since city dwellers rather than farmers normally set trends, the outlook for Ford is less bright than it would be if Ford's strong support came from the more progressive elements. We are concerned by the showing among young people. On practically all issues the youngsters were found to be less favorably impressed with, or inclined toward, Ford than were the older people.

The study also revealed that Jews, who had been so alienated by Henry Ford that they had almost stopped buying Ford products before the war, continued to harbor strong resentments against the magnate, his firm, and its vehicles. The study showed, too, that many members of organized labor, recalling the Ford Company's prewar antagonism toward the UAW-CIO, looked with disfavor upon the company and its products. Most significantly, Roper's survey of the general public indicated that "a substantially larger number of people would buy an $800 [postwar] car produced by General Motors rather than one produced by Ford." Roper explained why:

> The answer certainly does not lie in any appraisal of relative citizenship or even dollar value. The figures show that the answer can be largely found in the fact that it is General Motors as a company, not Ford, which is regarded as the company with the best styling and as being the most alert to the adoption of mechanical improvements. It is General Motors which has succeeded— particularly with the young—in surrounding itself with an aura of modernity and receptivity toward progress . . . the importance of being forward-looking as to style and progressive as to accepting improvements is manifest . . . we would suggest that the problem of Ford styling of cars, the problem of Ford pioneering in mechanical improvements—especially with the younger generation in mind—be considered with the idea of securing for Ford a reputation for modern design and modern improvements.

Roper's car-preference findings were corroborated by a thirty-five city survey of male Ford, Chevrolet, and Plymouth owners conducted by the J. Walter Thompson Company in July 1944. Thompson found Chevrolet and Plymouth owners to be far more enthusiastic about their cars' styling, performance, and overall value than were

Ford owners. The agency also discovered that more Chevrolet than Ford owners favored, as their first postwar purchase, the make of car they then drove. Among respondents who contemplated switching brands within the low-price field, the Thompson study revealed that Chevrolet stood to gain at Ford's expense.

The Roper and Thompson surveys showed, in summary, that while the public loved Ford, it preferred General Motors products. Henry Ford II and his associates, as they prepared for postwar competition, took to heart the surveys' findings, particularly those of the comprehensive Roper study. Indeed many of the Ford Company's most important policies and activities of the postwar period—its closer attention to product design and styling, its attempts to improve relations with employees, its efforts to win back the Jewish public, and its appeals to youth through radio programs and print advertising—may be traced to its wartime surveys. [41]

Chapter 24
Pacesetter for Reconversion

Henry Ford II had been released from the navy to assist in the administration of the Ford Company's war work. But from the time the twenty-six-year-old scion joined the family firm in August 1943, he was looking toward the postwar automobile market and devoting most of his thought and energy to preparations for civilian production.

In late 1943, Henry II assumed responsibility for the company's sales and advertising, helping fill a vacuum created by the abolishment of the central sales staff in October of that year. He closely supervised the firm's sales activities (confined mostly to dealer relations during wartime) until May 1944. At that time, following J. R. Davis's appointment as director of sales and advertising, he assumed broader management responsibilities. He had a free hand in directing the company's reconversion effort, but kept his grandfather informed of major developments. Old Henry's involvement with reconversion was limited to pronouncements that his firm would be making cars "in no time at all" or "within a month" after the government authorized civilian production.[1]

As the tide of the war shifted in the Allies' favor in 1943, the press, reflecting the reading interests of the car-starved public, endlessly discussed and speculated about postwar vehicles. Much of the speculation bordered on the fantastic: cars would be transparent, they would be shaped like teardrops, they would have a bulbous nose for housing luggage, they would run fifty to sixty miles an hour on a gallon of gasoline. Young Henry, in his first speech as a Ford official, delivered on January 25, 1944, before the National Automobile Dealers Association, debunked such ideas, adding that his firm's postwar cars "will be pretty much like our 1942 models." Although Henry II's statement was borne out, his company hedged his bet. Through the first half of 1944, Ford quietly worked on plans for a low-price, light-weight car. In July 1944, "an indiscreet Ford dealer, who learned about the car at a company sales meeting, talked out of turn and let [news of] the jalopy out of the bag." The disclosure prompted hundreds of publications to report that Ford had built "experimental models of a four-cylinder job, stripped to essentials and destined for the $500 price range." The company, pressed for a confirmation or denial of the reports, remained silent. In late September, however—one week after the War Production Board (WPB) had authorized auto manufacturers to spend the miniscule sum of $25,000 per month on the development of postwar models—Henry Ford II announced that his company did intend to produce "a lower-priced car than has been offered the public since the days of my grandfather's famous Model A. What the car will sell for, what it will look like," he added, "are matters of conjecture. We are not thinking in terms of a miniature 'doodlebug' type of automobile. We are thinking of a more economical utilization of space and weight.''[2]

At a time when an auto maker's pronouncement on postwar cars made page 1 news, Henry II's statement electrified the press. ''Within 24 hours,'' reported the *Ford Times,* ''every important newspaper and magazine in the United States had contacted the company to get further details.'' Many of the ''columns and pages'' of news stories about the car commended young Ford for ''carrying on the low-price tradition of his grandfather.'' Others, stretching Henry II's remarks, said that the new vehicle would be the ''lowest-priced car of all time.'' The news stories, in turn, unleashed ''a flood'' of unsolicited orders for the vehicle.[3]

On October 20, young Henry, at a meeting of the company's regional sales managers, was more specific about the price of the car: ''20 to 25 percent below the price of the regular Ford De Luxe model'' [which sold for $895 in late 1941]. Again the projected car was widely discussed in the press. Typically, *Fortune* applauded Ford for ''considering a new $500 car if not in the image of the old Model T at least as rugged and serviceable as the Model A. Mr. Ford,'' added the magazine, ''may have something. Even before the war what many Americans wanted was . . . more simplicity and economy in their automobile. . . . Here is a heartening reassertion of the philosophy of more for less, lower prices and bigger volume.'' Much of the press comment was in a humorous vein. The *Dearborn Press* saw advantages ''in having a car which could be tossed away after being used, like a drinking cup or a paper handkerchief.'' Syndicated columnist H. I. Phillips expressed delight that the new vehicle would be ''just a plain, efficient, low-priced car with a lot of Lizzie's character. Bring her out boys! and never mind the colors! Black will do. All we ask is that she run without oil, keep her health even if left out all night, operate with the tank dry and give 1,000 miles to the dollar.'' Phillips then launched into verse:

> Oh for the tender, bygone days
>   When life was not so dizzy
> And no one greater questions had
>   Than this one: How is Lizzie?
> When all the world was light and gay
>   And full of simple glories—
> And life seemed just a matter of
>   The latest Ford car stories.[4]

The Ford Company worked on designs for a light-weight, lower-priced car throughout the remainder of the war, provoking an announcement by General Motors in May 1945 that it too would produce a ''lighter weight and more economical'' car during the postwar era. In April 1946, Ford established a Light Car Division, declaring that its new automobile would make its debut in 1947. But in September 1946, faced with huge backlogs of unfilled orders and plagued by materials shortages, both Ford and General Motors abandoned plans to produce a light car for the domestic market. Ford's car was nevertheless designed, and appeared in 1948 as the French Ford company's Vedette.[5]

Meantime, through late 1944 and the first four months of 1945, the auto industry eagerly awaited the green light for the resumption of civilian production. On May 11, three days after V-E (victory in Europe) Day, the WPB authorized automobile manufacturers to start passenger car production on July 1. Two weeks later the government agency gave the industry permission to make 200,000 units (expanded on June 20 to 241,916 cars) in 1945. Ford's production quota, based on its 1941 output, was 39,910 vehicles. But there was no guarantee that this figure could be attained. Each manufacturer had the responsibility of finding the steel and other crucial materials—nearly all in short supply—with which to build its cars.[6]

The green light to build cars touched off frenzied activity among car builders as each company vied to be the first to start production. As the race began, Ford had several advantages over its competitors. Because of sizable cancellations and cutbacks in its war production program during the spring of 1945, the company was in a position to reconvert many of its plants to civilian production. Most other auto makers, on the other hand, held contracts which committed them to continued military production. Moreover, unlike its rivals, Ford owned several plants essential to an early startup of vehicle production, including "one of the most complete tool rooms in the country," a steel mill, a foundry, and a glass plant. The company also had a large and virtually complete bank of auto parts, kept in storage since the cessation of production in February 1942. A fourth ace in Ford's hand was, in the words of *Automobile News,* a "pronounced 'first urge.' "[7]

With the auto-building race under way, the press besieged manufacturers with requests for photographs and descriptions of their cars. Most of the companies, not wishing to "tip their hands" to the competition, decided to withhold information until production was imminent. But the Ford Company, planning to resume production within a month and intent on gaining a publicity advantage over its rivals, released photographs and details of its "1946 model" on June 2.

The postwar Ford, as Henry II had predicted eighteen months earlier, was a "warmed over" version of the 1942 model, with a 100-horsepower rather than a 90-horsepower engine, better springs and brakes, and a "face-lift." Publicity on the car was nevertheless snapped up by the press; virtually every news publication in the country splashed at least one photograph of the new model across its columns; some, including the *New York Times,* carried two prints. Many publications also congratulated Ford on its "moral victory in the reconversion race" and its "publicity scoop." Much of the credit redounded to the virtually inactive elder Ford. "It is just like Henry Ford," typically observed the *Kansas City* (Missouri) *Times,* "to be the first under the wire with something to show in picture and story." The publicity delighted Ford's dealers, dozens of whom expressed their gratitude in telegrams to the company. The publicity logjam broken, a second auto maker, Nash, released photographs of its postwar model on June 10. Many stories about the Nash rehashed details about the Ford.[8]

The Ford Company again led the reconversion parade on June 29, when it became the first auto manufacturer to display its postwar cars before an "outside" group. The unveiling followed a luncheon at the Dearborn Inn for thirty-nine state and two territorial governors, guests of the company while en route to Michigan's

Mackinac Island for the annual Governors Conference. At the close of the meeting, Henry Ford II casually mentioned that handmade models of the postwar Ford, Mercury, and Lincoln could be seen on the lawn outside. The governors rushed out to the cars, where the company had stationed ten photographers. After examining them, nearly all the politicians slid behind the steering wheel of a car for news photographs. The pictures, with prints and details of the hitherto unpublicized Mercury and Lincoln, were immediately sent to "home-state" newspapers throughout the country. This barrage of publicity, supplemented by stories filed by the sizable contingent of newsmen attending the luncheon, produced press coverage for the three cars almost equal to that of the June 2 Ford car announcement.[9]

At the governors' luncheon, Ford officials announced that Mercury production would begin within thirty to ninety days and that Lincoln's startup would occur "in several months." The officials sidestepped inquiries about when car production would begin. Meantime, as the WPB's July 1 production startup date approached, press speculation was rampant as to which of the auto makers would produce the first car. Most accounts, including a widely published story by the Associated Press's automobile editor, David J. Wilkie, credited Ford and General Motors' Pontiac and Oldsmobile divisions with leading the pack. General Motors, however, was far from ready to begin production. It did not assemble its first car, a Chevrolet, until October 3. Ford, on the other hand, while maintaining silence on its plans, was about to "pull a rabbit out of the hat."[10]

On July 3, Ford summoned "the entire Detroit industrial news-writing corps" to Dearborn for the first postwar automobile press preview. Henry Ford II and J. R. Davis briefly addressed the group, announcing plans to build four new assembly plants as part of the company's $150,000,000 postwar expansion program. Then, "in a blaze of klieg lights . . . for the Hollywood-size battery of photographers," Henry II drove America's first postwar car, a gray, two-door sedan, off the assembly line. For the third time within a month, Ford cars were publicized throughout the country—in virtually every daily newspaper, on hundreds of radio stations, in newsreels in thousands of theaters, in dozens of business publications, and in national news magazines. The company's early startup caught everyone outside of the Ford Company by surprise. Even the WPB's first reaction to the news was "Holy Smoke!" Several publications believed it necessary to reassure their readers that the startup "was no phony." "There were," declared *Automotive News,* "23 Ford cars in various stages of assembly." Many publications congratulated Henry Ford for "beating them all" and lauded the Ford Company for "winning the race" and for its "aggressive spirit." *Steel* and *Life* declared that the publicity was worth "millions of dollars" to the firm, the latter magazine noting that it "neatly complemented the organization's "Famous Ford 'Firsts' " advertising campaign.[11]

By July 13, the company had produced 58 cars; by the end of the month, 359 cars; by the end of August, 1,740. None could be sold, however, pending price-setting by the Office of Price Administration (OPA). In August Ford started building cars at its Edgewater, New Jersey, Louisville, and Dallas assembly plants. As the sole producer of passenger cars until August 30, when the Hudson Motor Car Company got under way, the company continued to exploit its front-running position. At

Edgewater, in the presence of dozens of newspapermen and newscasters, Captain Eddie Rickenbacker—with film star Carole Landis, then billed as the "G.I. Sweetheart," at his side—drove the first car off the assembly line. Louisville's Mayor Wilson Wyatt performed the same function for the press's benefit in Louisville. Harry A. Mack, the company's Southwest Regional Manager, drove the first car off Dallas's assembly line before 100 Texas newsmen and newscasters. Each of the ceremonies received widespread regional publicity. Most of the stories played up "the first postwar cars" produced in the East, in the South, and in the Southwest. But several articles also congratulated the Ford Company for averting mass layoffs while reconverting its plants from military to civilian production. "The Ford organization," typically observed the *Cliffside Park* (New Jersey) *Press,* "prepared for the changeover gradually and with great managerial skill."[12]

On August 29 the company again upstaged its competitors, giving its first postwar car to President Truman. A gift from Henry Ford, the car was presented to the Chief Executive by Henry Ford II in front of the White House. As a sizable contingent of reporters, photographers, and newsreel cameramen recorded the ceremony, the President, who cheerfully posed with the car, was brimful of quotable remarks: "I've waited years for one of these," he said as he twiddled the spotlight. "When I was a judge in Missouri, the sheriff never would let me have one." "With this car," he added with a smile, "I won't have any trouble getting Margaret [his daughter] back." Ford's gift was widely reported and generally applauded by the press. But some publications criticized the gift, sarcastically observing that "thousands of people who actually need new cars can't get them." "It was kindly and thoughtful of young Henry Ford to present President Truman with a shiny new car," noted one newspaper. "Nothing could be more neighborly or considerate . . . it takes a Ford to ferret out the unfortunates who have to walk to work and do something about it."[13]

With the Japanese surrender and the lifting of production quotas by the WPB in mid-August, auto industry leaders hoped to turn out 500,000 rather than the previously allocated 241,916 cars by the end of the year. The Ford Company's goal, remarked Henry Ford II on August 15, was between 75,000 and 85,000 passenger cars. By prewar standards this objective was small, representing a yearly rate of approximately 250,000 units, a figure which the company often had exceeded in a month. But with the scarcity of materials and labor's aggressive demands for higher wages, conditions were exceedingly difficult. The effect of these conditions was felt only a few days after young Ford's hopeful statement: the Kelsey-Hayes Wheel Company, a vital supplier, was struck. Deprived of wheels, Ford's assembly plants were forced to shut down. On September 5, J. R. Davis announced that plans for the scheduled September 21 national public showing of the Ford car were "postponed indefinitely." The following day the company laid off 25,000 men, and on September 15, 50,000 more, virtually halting all its production operations. Henry Ford II was disgusted. "In two and one-half months," he declared, "we have produced fewer automobiles [2,312] than we could in three hours of normal production, and the major reason is that these continued outbreaks by irresponsible labor groups are impeding the regular process of reconversion." The Kelsey-Hayes strike was settled on October 8, but the company struggled against a continued rash of strikes and stoppages (none in its own plants) which by November 27 included fifteen Ford suppliers, covering products from ball bearings and plate glass to crankshafts and transmissions.[14] The resumption of production after the Kelsey-Hayes settlement nevertheless encouraged the company to reschedule the national public showing of the Ford car for October 26. On ''V-8 Day,'' as the company termed the event, millions of ''businessmen, housewives, stenographers, eager servicemen, and curious kids'' flocked to Ford dealers' showrooms for their first look at a postwar car. Some dealers reported that the new model drew more people to their agencies than the introduction of the Model A. More than 300,000 persons, including three state governors, placed orders for the cars which had yet to be priced by the OPA. The public showing of the 1946 models once again splashed the name ''Ford'' across the nation's news columns.[15]

The Ford Company also received widespread publicity from sales of its first cars. Two days in advance of the national public showing, the firm, with an eye on potential press coverage, delivered the ''first purchased postwar automobile'' to a Congressional Medal of Honor winner, Lieutenant John C. Sjogren, of Rockford, Michigan. The car, a gift from Sjogren's fellow townsmen, was presented with fanfare; and the delivery was publicized nationally. Many Ford dealers, taking their cue from this sale, also sold their first cars to ex-servicemen. Unfortunately, from a public relations standpoint, the first sales in New York, the nation's communications capital, were made to a ''select group of buyers'' including municipal and state officials, business and labor leaders, and entertainers Edgar Bergen, Fred Waring, Morton Downey, Phil Baker, and Fay Bainter. The purchasers were to have taken possession of their cars in Central Park. But at the last minute the city's Department of Parks refused to allow the grounds to be used for the transaction. The buyers and a bevy of newsmen thereupon adjourned to the Bronx County Court House where the sales were completed. Each purchaser paid $1,150 for his car, agreeing to adjust his payment to conform to the OPA's future price list. The highly publicized New York ceremony generated considerable resentment. ''The sale of the new Fords to a group of politicians and radio and stage stars wouldn't hurt us and John Q. Public so much,'' typically editorialized the *New York Sun*, ''if there had been as much as a reply to letters to Henry months ago asking when we could get one, cash on the line. But our claim for a new car was based merely on the fact that the old one was minus a rear wheel, two fenders, both doors and parts of the engine. We didn't say a word about being able to croon, dance, or sing.''[16]

The Ford car's higher-priced stablemates, the Mercury and the Lincoln, were not produced until late 1945. The first postwar Mercury, with Henry Ford II behind the wheel, was driven off the Rouge assembly line on October 31; the initial Lincoln was built on November 26. Startups of the two cars generated only routine publicity, the Mercury being the twelfth nameplate to go into production, the Lincoln the fourteenth. Similarly, the public showings of the Mercury on December 13 and the Lincoln on January 10, 1946, attracted only nominal interest.[17]

Hopeful in August of producing between 75,000 and 85,000 passenger cars in 1945, the Ford Company—because of materials and parts shortages arising from repeated shutdowns in suppliers' plants—built only 34,439 Fords, 2,848 Mercurys, and 569 Lincolns by year's end. Although Henry Ford II publicly apologized in December for falling short of his production goal, his company could take pride in its limited achievement. Throughout 1945 it had paced the auto industry's reconversion effort, winning much valuable publicity in the process. More importantly, it had won the passenger car production race. Ford accounted for 41 percent of the industry's 1945 automobile output (83,786 units); General Motors, strike-bound after November 21, 30.5 percent; Chrysler only 7 percent.

Beset with reconversion problems common to all automobile firms, lacking volume production, and still inefficient in some spheres, the Ford Company—after earning substantial sums during the war years—lost heavily in 1945. But its prospects offered mild encouragement. By the end of 1945 the company had already demonstrated a capacity, not generally conceded by wartime observers, to hold its own amid the uncertainties of the immediate postwar era. Moreover the pent-up demand for cars assured Ford and all other auto manufacturers of a seller's market for several years. Finally, in Henry Ford II, the company had a new president, who, having resolved to rebuild the family firm, was vigorously pursuing a course destined to "turn the company around" before the sellers' market came to a close.[18]

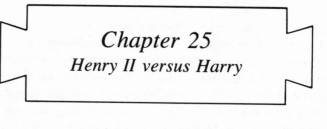

Chapter 25
Henry II versus Harry

1

At the time Henry II rejoined the Ford Company in August 1943, the company's administration was chaotic. Eighty-year-old Henry Ford was president, and Harry Bennett and Charles E. Sorensen jockeyed for power. Authority, never clearly defined at Ford, was so obscure that many minor officials and workers would obey "any superior person." Fear and uncertainty hovered paralyzingly over many operations. Financial management, because of Henry Ford's hostility to systematic accounting, was confused. Profits were measured by the amount of cash on deposit. Nobody knew what it cost to make steel in the Rouge; the cost figures of foundry and timber operations were scrambled with those for growing soybeans and staging square dances. Ford figured that he paid for all of these things anyway; why bother to spend money separating the accounts? Henry II later swore that costs in one department were determined by weighing stacks of invoices.[1]

There was not much in Henry II's background to suggest that he could successfully direct one of the world's largest firms. A quiet, pleasant, blue-eyed, apple-cheeked, 190-pound, twenty-six-year-old six-footer, he had been named a director of the company in December 1938, while a third-year student at Yale. As a collegian he took engineering courses, then switched to sociology. "I had flunked in engineering," he explained later. "The other guys said sociology was a snap course so I figured that was for me. I flunked *it*, too." Lacking sufficient credits, young Ford did not graduate with his class in 1940.[2]

In July 1940, Henry II married Anne McDonnell, daughter of a wealthy New York stockbroker, granddaughter of inventor and utilities magnate Thomas E. Murray. The nuptials were covered by more than fifty news photographers, and generated almost as much publicity for one of the guests, grandfather Ford, as for the bride and groom. If, as was reported later, the elder Ford was vexed by his grandson's conversion to Miss McDonnell's Roman Catholic faith the day before the wedding, he gave no hint of his displeasure on the day of the marriage. On the contrary, the seventy-seven-year-old magnate beamed happily throughout the festivities and danced vigorously with the bride.

Shortly after the wedding, Henry II and his twenty-one-year-old brother, Benson, who had left Princeton after two years "to get a practical education," joined the company's engineering staff, working in the company garage, in the dynamometer rooms and experimental shops. In October they were assigned to the firm's defense operations; and in this capacity visited Consolidated Aircraft's San Diego plant with their father and Sorensen in January 1941.[3]

In April 1941, Henry II was given an ensign's commission and assigned to administrative work at the Great Lakes Naval Training Station near Chicago. While there, he kept abreast of the company's activities by means of reports sent to him. After Edsel's death in May 1943, young Henry's uncle, Ernest C. Kanzler, former director general of the War Production Board, and high government officials who shared Kanzler's concern about the chaotic administration of the Ford organization, prevailed upon Secretary of the Navy Frank Knox to release Henry II from active naval service "to assist in managing the company's business." It was hoped that young Henry might soon rise to a position of importance within the firm, put an end to its incessant in-fighting, and help it to realize its full war-production potential. Actually, Henry II devoted most of his attention to preparing the company for the postwar market.[4]

When young Ford reported for work his grandfather was on vacation. Sorensen, whom Henry II disliked, and Bennett, whom he detested, were the Ford scion's nominal supervisors, although both had been instructed by the elder Ford to let "the boy" find his own way. "Nobody had any suggestions as to what I might do," young Henry said later, "so I just moseyed around on my own, visited the plants, talked with fellows—trying to find out how things operated." Wherever he went, his movements and even his questions were relayed to Bennett by the service chief's spies. Some employees avoided young Ford or were uncommunicative in his presence. "It was the damndest situation," Henry II recalled later. "People just weren't talking." These people sensed that Bennett regarded the Ford scion as an intruder, and they sensed correctly. Yet young Ford, cheerful, democratic, and observant, talked with hundreds of employees, and won the respect of most of them.[5]

In late 1943, young Henry found a niche for himself—sales and advertising. Fortified by his election to a vice-presidency in December 1943 and to the executive vice-presidency—the post next in rank to the presidency—in April 1944, he closely supervised the company's sales (dealer relations) and advertising activities until May 1944. After mid-1944 he devoted less time to merchandising activities and more effort to general management, seeking to establish sound policies, eliminate administrative confusion, and find capable, honest aides to prepare the company for postwar competition.[6]

As he gained in self-confidence, young Ford began to make public appearances and to get acquainted with members of the press. He wrote his first speeches himself, and gave his initial talk as a company executive before 5,000 persons on October 7, 1943, when, in his grandfather's behalf, he accepted Igor Sikorsky's first helicopter as a gift for the Edison Institute. His second speech, and first policy address—a discussion of the postwar auto market—was given before the National Automotive Dealers Association in January 1944. "It was no more profound than most convention speeches," *Life* accurately reported, "but it was not bad." The text, in point of fact, reflected young Ford's greatest handicap—immaturity—and several of his chief assets, forthrightness, earnestness, and sincerity.

Shortly after speaking to the dealer group, Henry II appeared before the Off the Record Club, composed of Detroit newsmen. He replied with candor to all of the journalists' questions, at times admitting, "I don't know." Finally he said, "Now I want to ask you a question." Permission was granted.

"Where's the men's room?"

The question brought down the house.[7]

Throughout 1944 and 1945, young Henry "wowed the working press" during his visits with dealer groups around the country. During press parties held at these meetings, Henry II strolled around, extending a friendly hand and the cheerful greeting, "My name is Ford." His alertness and frankness, combined with an affable, engaging manner, earned him high praise from newsmen. "Henry II underwent a barrage of questioning," observed a Scripps-Howard reporter of a September 1944 press conference, "and came out with an enhanced reputation." "No sharp-witted reporter has been able to trip him yet, although a lot of them have tried," noted *Motor* in January 1945. "Self-possessed and 'fast on his feet,' but modest withal, he answers questions 'on the record' with a surprising degree of candor." *Life,* while commenting in October 1945 on the Ford Company's previous "notorious press relations," pointed out that since Henry II's ascent to power the firm had handled reporters "with honest cordiality and candor."[8]

The press's attitude toward young Ford was reflected in an ever-growing number of favorable newspaper and magazine articles about him in 1944–45. The first of these stories, written by one of Henry Ford's press favorites, James Sweinhart, and syndicated by the News Enterprise Association in March 1944, set the tone for the many biographical sketches which followed. "Although an heir-presumptive," Sweinhart stated, "Henry the Second is no presumptuous heir. He isn't talking, he's working as his father and grandfather did." Young Ford, said the article, shared his grandfather's desire to pay high wages and his concern over employees' welfare and security. Moreover, the article stated, Henry II lacked "all sense of pride in money, thinking of it only as an essential for industrial production and human welfare." Much of the early comment about the Ford scion's character was summed up by *Fortune* in June 1944: "Everybody likes twenty-six-year-old Henry Ford II. The unanimity in praise of his modesty, earnestness and simple human likeability is almost alarming. It would be so except . . . for the comforting fact that Mr. Ford seems to be what everyone says he is." Henry II's publicity gradually began to make an impression upon the general public. Virtually unknown upon joining the Ford Company in August 1943, he was correctly identified by 9.5 percent of the population in July 1944. By the spring of 1945, as his star continued to rise, he was receiving an average of 100 speaking invitations a month from organizations throughout the country.[9]

Except for arranging press conferences at dealer meetings which Henry II attended, the Ford Company made no effort to publicize the young executive during 1944. Similarly, Henry II displayed no overt interest in personal publicity. In mid-year he declined an offer by one of his grandfather's ghostwriters, Samuel Crowther, to provide assistance in "getting started out right with the public," by preparing flattering articles on young Ford for national magazines. But by early 1945 a low-key "buildup" of Henry II was discernible. During the first four months of the year, the young scion cosigned, with his grandfather, a series of institutional advertisements on postwar problems and worthy postwar objectives. He also stepped up his speaking schedule, delivering a series of talks accurately described by John Gunther as "somewhat guarded, very much on the proper side, and conventionally well written." Several of the speeches were, in fact, written by Henry Ford's aging interpreter, William J. Cameron, then in his final year of Ford employment. Cameron's best effort, which had Henry stress that "fifty dollars a day *earned* is none too high, but a dollar a day *unearned* is much too high," was widely publicized in January 1945. The theme of the speech was later transferred to an advertisement in the Henry Ford–Henry II institutional advertising campaign.[10]

Noting young Ford's buildup, two of the company's advertising agencies, J. Walter Thompson, and Kenyon & Eckhardt, Inc., retained in July 1945, also advanced proposals for publicizing the young executive. In May 1945 JWT suggested that the company produce a film on its postwar plans which would serve as "a national vehicle to introduce Mr. Henry Ford II to a large cross-section of the public. The names of the Ford Motor Company and Henry Ford are practically synonymous," argued the agency, "and since the company is so highly personalized . . . it seems advisable to mildly publicize Mr. Henry Ford II who someday must assume the mantle." The agency probably was unaware that young Henry's grandfather had never shared the spotlight; the founder, in any event, knew nothing of the proposal, and even if he had, was so far removed from the company scene that he undoubtedly would not have resisted it. The film proposal reached the script stage, but was not carried out. In August 1945, Kenyon & Eckhardt suggested that young Henry appear on the revived Ford Sunday Evening Hour "when there is something concrete to demonstrate the Ford Motor Company's interest in the industrial problems of today and tomorrow." This proposal met with partial acceptance, Henry II serving as the intermission speaker on the first three shows of the program's 1945–46 season.[11]

Meanwhile, young Henry, by paying careful attention to detail and by avoiding conflict with Bennett while maintaining cordial relations with his grandfather, had steadily gained ground in the struggle for power within the Ford Company. In the spring of 1944 his improved status was noted in the press. "Henry Ford II, recently boosted into the executive vice president's saddle," observed a *Detroit News* columnist in May 1944, "is holding that saddle very well." By late 1944, young Henry's increasing influence could be defined in more precise terms. "Next to the founder of the company," declared James Dalton, editor of *Motor,* in November 1944, "Henry Ford II is the dominant figure in the Ford organization." Two months later, Dalton, by now aware that the elder Ford had virtually dropped from sight, was even more precise: "Henry Ford II now is the accepted spokesman for the great company." Dalton's view of the youthful executive's dominance was corroborated by a power play at the Rouge in June 1945, when Mead L. Bricker, backed by Henry II, displaced Ray R. Rausch, backed by Bennett, as production head. The significance of the shift was not lost upon Rouge employees, many of whom, reported *Newsweek,* were "perking up at the brighter atmosphere."[12]

For a time in the undeclared war between Henry II and Bennett, the service chief had appeared to have the edge. He commanded the allegiance of many well-placed executives as well as the strong-armed Service Department—so strong-armed that Henry II felt obliged to carry a gun for self-protection. Under terms of a codicil to Henry Ford's will, secretly drawn up after Edsel's death in May 1943, Bennett was to be the secretary of a board which would control the Ford Company for ten years after the founder's death. None of the elder Ford's grandchildren was to serve on this board. It was plain that Bennett completely dominated Henry Ford's faltering mind.

Although the service chief held a strong poker hand, Henry II held all the aces, if he had the insight and nerve to play them. From the moment he was elected a vice-president in December 1943, many employees regarded him as the heir-apparent. He also had the firm support of his grandmother, Clara, his mother, Eleanor—both of whom controlled large blocks of company stock—and of his brothers, Benson and William Clay.

In mid-1944 young Henry learned of the secret alteration to his grandfather's will. In his dismay he turned to John Bugas, who had recently joined the company's labor relations staff. "If this is true," he told Bugas, "I'm resigning from the company, and I'm writing every Ford dealer to tell them what they're up against." Bugas calmed Henry II, then went to Bennett's office to ask about the document. The service chief, in a state of agitation, told Bugas to "come in here tomorrow, and we'll straighten the whole thing out." The next day, Bennett burned the codicil in Bugas's presence. Later, Ford's lawyer, I. A. Capizzi, who had prepared the codicil at Bennett's request, concluded that old Henry, although once intent upon sidetracking his grandson, may not have signed the document. If true, Bennett's gesture cost him nothing.[13]

Behind the scenes, Clara Ford, convinced that Henry II was capable of managing the company, pleaded for months with her husband to transfer the presidency to his grandson. Old Henry was peevishly reluctant. Finally, in September 1945, Mrs. Edsel Ford forced the issue. Confronting her father-in-law with an ultimatum not unlike the one he had given his minority partners a quarter-century earlier, she threatened to sell her family's stock holdings (41.6 percent of the total) unless the old man yielded to her son. The founder yielded.

Summoned to Fair Lane by his grandfather on September 20, 1945, Henry II declared that he would take the presidency only if he had a "completely free hand" to make any changes he wished. "We argued about that," young Henry said later, "but he didn't withdraw his offer." After leaving the estate Henry II instructed Frank Campsall to prepare his grandfather's letter of resignation and to call a meeting of the board of directors the following day to act upon it. Shortly afterward, young Ford's phone rang. Bennett was on the line. "Henry," he said, "I've got wonderful news for you. I've just talked your grandfather into making you president of the company."[14]

On September 21, the board held one of the most important sessions in its history. Present were Henry Ford, Henry II, Mrs. Edsel Ford, Bennett, Campsall, Bricker, and B. J. Craig. As Craig read the first sentence of the letter of resignation, Bennett, anticipating his dismissal, hurled an angry word of congratulation at the younger Ford, then bolted for the door. Others prevailed upon him to stay. Immediately after the brief meeting, Henry II told Bennett that he was through at the Ford Motor Company. The new president added that the ex-service chief could have a month-long face-saving directorship and would be kept on the payroll for eighteen months, after which he would be pensioned. Bennett's reaction, Henry II recalled later, "was not very good." Snarling, Henry Ford's "personal man" told young Henry, "You're taking over a billion dollar organization here that you haven't contributed a thing to!" He could have offered no better revelation of his character and aims.[15]

The following day, after delivering a monologue to Henry II and Bugas on work that old Henry wanted completed, Bennett left for California. Five days later, the company announced that Bennett's future duties would be limited to "a consulting and advisory capacity." This statement triggered a wave of news and feature stories about the ex-service chief, none of them favorable. "If Harry Bennett had passed off the stage 10 years ago," typically observed the *Dayton News,* "the threat to labor peace in Detroit today might be a little less ugly than it is." A Detroit columnist, in debunking some of the legends surrounding Bennett's career, also spoke for many publications: "Bennett [was] about as romantic as a chicken-coop doorknob and about as glamorous as a castiron Charlie McCarthy . . . a little tough guy who did as he was told—and promptly." The columnist added that Bennett had been "canned" just as he had booted out others before him.

Returning to Michigan in mid-October, Bennett, with a former subordinate, Stanley Fay, and an attorney, Byron Geller, formed the B-F-G Manufacturers' Representatives Co., a partnership which fell apart in February 1946. Meanwhile, Bennett resigned on schedule from Ford's board in late October 1945.

Bennett and his wife, Esther, retired to their winter home in the foothills of Mt. Jacinto, twelve miles from Desert Hot Springs, California. In 1969, as a concession to Mrs. Bennett's precarious health, they moved to a ranch-style house in Las Vegas. In recent years Bennett's step has been slowed by arthritis and his eyesight has dimmed. But in 1973 at age eighty-one, when I visited him, he still possessed a great deal of restless energy, his voice was strong and his memory good. He has devoted most of his time to his favorite hobby, painting, and to home maintenance, including roof repairs. "Thank God for his poor eyesight," sighed his daughter, Billie. "If it weren't for that, there'd be no stopping him from doing anything and everything." Bennett has returned to Detroit only once since 1946—in 1951, when he was a reluctant witness at a Senate investigation of Detroit's underworld. "There is nothing in Michigan which interests me," he told a Detroit reporter in 1964.[16]

At the time of Bennett's departure from the Ford Company, in September 1945, one last scene was enacted in the Harry Bennett drama: Henry Ford had to be told that his "personal man" had been fired. Henry II broke the news to his grandfather, then braced himself for an explosion. It never came. After sitting in silence for a long while, the old man merely said, "Well, now Harry is back where he started from." At last, Henry Ford II ruled the Ford empire.

After firing Bennett, Henry II cleared the decks of the ex-sailor's chief mates. Rausch, exiled to California, resigned his job on October 12, and his board seat effective as of October 26. Stanley Fay, Bennett's assistant, and Office Manager Russell Gnau, a Bennett spy, ceased to be Ford employees. Harry Mack, head of the Dearborn sales branch for fourteen years, who had been banished to Dallas by young Henry in August 1945, was fired. John W. Thompson, whom Henry II had relieved of his duties, then given a face-saving leave of absence in July, was also dismissed. Clifford Prevost, the company's Washington representative, was given an "indefinite leave of absence." Thompson, after operating a short-lived public relations firm in Detroit, became vice-president and director of the Air Transport Association in Washington, in May 1946. The purge of Bennett's men continued through 1945 and into 1946. By July 1946, Henry Ford II was reported to have fired, demoted, or transferred more than 1,000 employees, most of them former Bennett men.[17]

As young Henry, in *Steel*'s words, "swept through the administrative ranks with the effectiveness of a new vacuum cleaner," he also announced promotions and confirmed assignments. Bugas was designated to head a new activity, industrial relations. Bricker was named vice-president in charge of manufacturing, and C. L. Martindale, former head of the Accounting Department, was appointed controller. In contrast to his grandfather's refusal to establish lines of authority, Henry II delegated responsibility to men who headed company activities: J. R. Davis, sales and advertising; C. H. Carroll, purchasing; R. H. McCarroll, engineering; and R. I. Roberge, foreign operations. B. J. Craig remained as treasurer and vice-president; Herman L. Moekle as secretary and assistant treasurer. On October 26 Davis and Moekle were elected to the board, joining Henry Ford, Henry II, Benson Ford, Bricker, Craig, and Frank Campsall. Campsall died in March 1946; Craig, who was shunted into the managership of the firm's nonprofit enterprises in 1946, was removed from the board in 1948.

Among his executives, Henry II had only three men of the highest ability: Bricker, Davis, and Bugas. But he was forced to work with what he had, and his realignment represented a step toward order.[18]

2

The Ford Company's "changing of the guard" was publicized throughout the country, not only by business and trade journals, but by the general press as well. Most news stories placed emphasis on the new president; most editorials on the founder. Almost all of the accounts were friendly toward Henry II; in fact, as *Newsweek* pointed out, "probably no head of a major industry took on a tough job with as much public support." Many publications saw in Henry a "worthy scion of his distinguished grandfather," acknowledged that he had "added immeasurably to the strength of the Ford Company," and predicted that he would "measure up to the responsibilities of running the world's biggest privately owned firm." Several publications also gave young Ford major credit for the company's "flying start" in the reconversion race, and said that he had, with J. R. Davis, "strengthened sales policies, improved relations with the company's dealers, and added punch to Ford advertising." A few articles noted that Henry II had capably directed the company when his grandfather was "away from Dearborn." But not a single publication went so far as to suggest that the twenty-eight-year-old president would rule the family business with a free hand.[19]

Until it became evident on September 27 that Bennett was *out* and that Henry II was giving the company "a shaking that rattled its teeth," many publications assumed that Henry Ford would continue to influence the firm's destiny. The *Hartford* (Connecticut) *Times* predicted that the elder Ford "will keep a watchful eye on how the young fellow makes out"; the *Indianapolis News* suggested that Ford's "hand will still be felt at the River Rouge and Highland Park"; the *Bridgeport* (Connecticut) *Life* said the founder's retirement was "more apparent than real"; and the *Detroit Times* observed that Detroiters "might be excused an amiable skepticism concerning the complete retirement of Henry Ford. . . . There will be many future chats between grandfather and grandson. Some of them will even concern Ford Motor policy." *Time* went further, stating that the change in presidents "was more in title than in fact. The Master of the Rouge," said the magazine, "at 82 will still keep his fingers on the controls of his company as an 'adviser.' He showed no signs of retiring [and] was once more dog-trotting through his plants last week, keeping a sharp blue eye on everything." In a wild burst of imagination, *Popular Science Monthly* declared that Ford "at 82 views his work as just beginning."

Actually, after the board's September 21 session, Henry II had full charge of the company's destiny; and, shortly thereafter, when Bennett was publicly consigned to an "advisory capacity," everyone knew it. The new president's grandfather, the broken old man who was led from the directors' meeting, all his glories behind him, was in complete retirement.[20]

As Ford tottered off the Rouge scene, dozens of editorials, most of them in small-town newspapers, summed up his career. He was hailed for "putting cheap transportation into the hands of nearly everybody," for raising wages and lowering prices, for "inventing" mass production, for "outwitting the bankers," for building the Rouge plant and the village industries, for his "unbelievable record" during two world wars, and for many other achievements. "Seldom," said the *Reno* (Nevada) *Gazette,* in summing up Ford's career, "have such all-around abilities been demonstrated to such an extent by a national figure." In Ford, the *Cumberland* (Maryland) *News* saw the "noblest Roman of all the industrialists of a great generation"; the *Boston Traveler* an "admired rugged individualist"; the *Marshfield* (Wisconsin) *Herald* a "splendid example" to his countrymen; the *McKeesport* (Pennsylvania) *News* "one of the greatest success stories of all time"; the *Prescott* (Arizona) *Courier* "one of the most fascinating Americans"; and the *Astoria* (Oregon) *Astorian-Budget* "one of our greatest men." "His contribution to American life ranks well up with those of Washington and Lincoln," declared the *Astorian-Budget*. "He deserves the highest honor we can give him."[21]

Chapter 26
Lengthening Shadows

1

If the war years saw a dramatic change in the life of Henry Ford II, they witnessed an even greater change in the life of Henry Ford. Physically active and mentally alert in 1941, the auto pioneer was, by the time of his retirement, a mere shadow of his former self.

Ford had suffered two strokes, one in 1938, the second in mid-1941; neither was reported in the press. His recovery from the first attack was rapid and, from all outward appearances, complete. He never fully recovered from the second stroke, although he regained much of his vigor and at times displayed astonishing vitality for an octogenarian. "I took one walk with him," said thirty-year-old John Thompson, "and that was enough. He walked too fast." In July 1943, shortly before his eightieth birthday, Ford outsprinted several colleagues in a seventy-five-yard dash, leaping the last "eight or ten" feet onto the running board of his parked car. In the fall of 1944 he vaulted over the railing on his yacht onto the dock at Munising, Michigan, repeating the leap several times to show his disdain for the portable steps which had been arranged for his disembarkation. Even in the spring of 1945, by which time his physical powers had greatly deteriorated, he briskly walked the mile from his home to Camp Legion, tiring his companion, Harry Bennett, who suggested that they get into a car.[1]

The industrialist repeatedly boasted that he was in excellent health. Asked how it felt to reach the age of eighty, he replied, "if I felt any better I'd have to run." On his eighty-first birthday he declared that he had "never felt better" in his life. Long a food faddist, Ford often attributed his physical condition to his diet, which in 1943–44 included warm "pollen water" from Maine and consisted largely of wheat—"the divine food." By drinking warm water, the Dearbornite explained, his body could retain healthful "heat and energy" ordinarily expended in heating cool water to body temperature. Wheat (but not flour), he insisted, contained all the ingredients needed to maintain good health. Some of Ford's meals consisted solely of wheat kernels that he had soaked until they were almost ready to sprout. Between meals the industrialist popped the kernels into his mouth like peanuts. His predilection for wheat came to an end only when an experiment showed that hogs wasted away on a diet of the "divine food." Ford himself was told by a medical specialist in early 1945 that he had been "starving to death" on his wheat diet.[2]

Unaware of Ford's strokes, the press during 1942–44 made continual references to his "perfect health," "quick step and firm handclasp," and "spryness." When, for example, Ford resumed his firm's presidency in June 1943, *Motor* reported that he was "amazingly vigorous mentally and physically," *Newsweek* stated that he was "alert and energetic," *Steel* said that he was "ageless," and the *Times* (London) declared that he was in "excellent health" and had "more energy and keenness than many men younger than he." Among press commentators, only Drew Pearson reported (in August 1943) that Ford's health had slipped during the war years. After making the statement, Pearson was castigated by Ford, the magnate's physician, and dozens of newspapers. Confronted with this barrage, Pearson retracted his statement. [3]

While Ford remained physically active until 1945, his mental powers slowly deteriorated between his second stroke in mid-1941 and Edsel's death in May 1943, then failed more rapidly after the loss of his son. Until Edsel's death, only members of Ford's family and domestic staff, a handful of close friends, and a few business associates such as Sorensen and Bennett were aware of the magnate's waning faculties. Ford continued to make his rounds of Greenfield Village, the village industries and farms, and Willow Run, occasionally showing political and military figures through the bomber plant. But he was aware that his mind was failing, and for this reason, and also because he no longer "made" much news, he granted fewer press interviews during 1942–45 than he had in previous years. His last full-blown press conference was a breakfast meeting with three wire service reporters and three Detroit newsmen on his seventy-ninth birthday, July 30, 1942. At this gathering, arranged by Hannagan's News Bureau, the industrialist spoke on many subjects: he advocated free trade; predicted that plastics eventually would have "universal use," and that postwar cars and tractors would be lighter in weight; he suggested that cargo planes would do much to solve the postwar distribution problem, and that "family airplanes" were unlikely to replace the family car. His comments were reported in hundreds of newspapers throughout the country. Dozens of editorials, most of them reflecting the magnate's optimism about the postwar era, followed in the wake of the news stories. [4]

After Edsel's death, almost everyone who knew Ford observed that a profound change had come over him. "It seems impossible," Bennett said later, "to describe how deeply the loss of his son hit him. After that, he wasn't anti-Semitic or anti-Catholic or anything else. He was just a tired old man who wanted to live in peace."

Ford's desolation was compounded by his belief that his mistreatment of Edsel had contributed to his son's death. Returning to his former residence at 66 Edison, where Edsel had spent seven boyhood years, Ford mused to the owner, "Maybe I worked Edsel too hard." For weeks after the funeral the auto king tramped for hours through Fair Lane's woods, mulling the past. His wife, who also believed that her husband's behavior had hastened Edsel's death, sat at home. The old couple, after fifty-five years of marriage, scarcely spoke to one another; they could not discuss Edsel at all. But in late June, Clara, realizing that her husband had to be rescued from his island of loneliness, handed him a basket and garden shears.

"Henry," she said, "the peonies are in bloom. We need a big jar of them for the front hall. Let's go and see what we can find."

Though they did not speak much, by the end of the morning they were together again.

The aging industrialist could not, however, keep his mind off his relationship with his son. Again and again he discussed the subject with his crony, Harry Bennett.

"Harry," he once asked, "do you honestly think I was ever cruel to Edsel?"

"Well," Bennett temporized, "if that had been me you'd treated that way, it wouldn't have been cruelty."

Ford was not satisfied: "Why don't you give me an honest answer?"

"Cruel, no," replied Bennett, "but unfair yes. If that had been me, I'd have got mad."

Ford seized on the statement: "That's what I wanted him to do—get mad."

At times Edsel *was* angered by his father- But unwilling and temperamentally unable to do battle with his parent, he simply turned the other cheek.[5]

Despite his grief, by July 1943 the elder Ford had virtually resumed his earlier pattern of life. He made several public appearances that month, mingling with 1,000 spectators at a threshing bee and showing General H. H. Arnold, commander of the Army Air Forces, then French General Henri Honoré Giraud, and later, Vice President Henry A. Wallace, through Willow Run. He also submitted to an interview by a *New York Times* writer—his first press interview since Edsel's death—and briefly parried reporters' questions at a prebirthday party on July 28 at the Ford Naval Training School. Ford's mind remained clear during most of the summer and fall of 1943. At times, however, he experienced the neurological disturbances usually identified with a stroke—irritability, suspiciousness, disordered memory, confusion, and lack of orientation.

These symptoms steadily worsened during the winter of 1943–44. By this time Ford was suspicious of virtually everyone. At one point he was convinced that the Du Ponts had "planted" a young member of their family in Detroit to influence Henry Ford II. Neither Bennett, Sorensen, nor Henry II could persuade the old man that his grandson's acquaintance with young Du Pont was harmless. The magnate also came to regard the military officers stationed at Willow Run as spies and potential assassins. To protect himself from them, he armed his chauffeur and fitted another gun under the cowl of his car. Liebold's later reference to these Mad Hatter years was apt: "I wouldn't have held Mr. Ford responsible for a great many things that he might have said."

The extent of Ford's uncertain memory and confusion during the winter of 1943–44 is revealed in Liebold's and Bennett's memoirs. "He would come into the office in the morning to ask me to do something," recalled Liebold, "and then not remember what it was. After he had concentrated three or four minutes, he'd remember. In the afternoon I'd see him and he did not know what we had talked about." "There were times," wrote Bennett, "when he'd tell me he was going someplace when he'd just come from there." By 1944 it often was an ordeal for Ford to meet and talk with persons other than members of his family and his confidants. When talking with "outsiders," his mind would occasionally wander. Sensing his dilemma, he would blurt out, "I'll be back again," then disappear.[6]

In spite of this deterioration, there were times when Ford's mind appeared normal. A United Press reporter, after interviewing him in February 1944, described him as "keen and alert." Two *Fortune* representatives, after talking with him for two hours in the spring of 1944, declared that "his conversation is alert to every nuance, and he can turn questions as deftly as ever." Ford chatted comfortably with Rear Admiral Arthur S. Carpenter during a tour of the Dearborn Naval Training Base in April 1944. In early July the industrialist appeared at a wheat-cutting attended by 2,000 people, and later that month he participated in a threshing bee attended by 2,500 persons; on both occasions he had full control of his faculties. That same month, columnist Marquis Childs, after lunching with the auto pioneer, wrote that Ford "looks as well preserved, as canny, as shrewd as he did 20 years ago. The flicker of his genius, his aliveness, is in his eyes, which move quickly, piercingly, when they are not veiled in contemplation." In September the old man readily autographed program cards at a ship launching and in October, in the presence of friends, he easily discussed the use of plastics, recalled his ill-fated peace ship, and mimicked Winston Churchill's speech.[7]

After November 1944, however, as his mental powers faded more rapidly, Ford seldom met with persons outside of his family. During the last ten months of his presidency, he attended only two public functions: a dinner in honor of veteran Ford employees at the Dearborn Inn on December 19, 1944, and a matinee performance of an Olsen and Johnson comedy, "Laffing Room Only," on September 6, 1945. On neither occasion was he interviewed. After November 1944, Ford's visits to his plants and his haunts in Dearborn and the surrounding countryside became infrequent. In April 1945, he inspected Camp Legion. The following month, he showed General Joseph W. "Vinegar Joe" Stilwell and Chairman Irving Olds and President Benjamin Fairless of the United States Steel Corporation through the Willow Run plant. He occasionally visited Greenfield Village and the Dearborn Engineering Laboratory. At times, however, he did not know where he was. "He stood in the middle of the Laboratory floor," recalled Irving Bacon, a veteran employee, "with a wan smile on his lips, like a lost child, with a faraway expression in his eyes . . . not noticing any person or thing in particular, and not knowing which way to turn."[8]

By 1945, the magnate, who years before had lost much of his interest in business affairs, no longer cared about his cherished hobbies. He abandoned the religion-oriented wheat growing experiment which had so intrigued him in 1943–44 and which he had promised to carry forward into 1945. He permitted his "personal" radio programs, "Greenfield Village Chapel Service" and "Early American Dance Music," to lapse. He disbanded the old-fashioned dance orchestra which had given him so much pleasure (his dancing master, Benjamin B. Lovett, was not remembered when he paid a farewell call at Fair Lane). He even stopped reading his favorite comic strip, "Little Orphan Annie." For months after mid-November 1944, employees and newsmen looked for the old man and wondered whether he would resume his regular rounds. By the summer of 1945 it was clear that he would not.[9]

Meantime, Ford's growing senility remained one of Dearborn's best-kept secrets. Henry II repeatedly insisted that his grandfather was "in excellent health" and "very chipper." Other company executives said the same. The press accepted the Ford-is-fine theme at face value. Thus when Ford retired in September 1945, the *New York Times* reported that the old man's health "was 'all right' and was not a factor in his decision again to relinquish the company presidency." *Motor* declared that the industrialist was "in excellent physical condition and appears frequently at the administration building." The careful concealment of Ford's diminishing mental powers was a dubious boon to the magnate, for many people, unaware of the erosion of his faculties, failed to make due allowance for his actions.[10]

Despite his waning activity, Ford's public statements continued to make news. The newsmen who interviewed Ford knew that the old man, more often than not, would have nothing new or important to say to them and that he would rehash familiar themes: there can be no lasting peace as long as hatreds exist; hatreds will exist until those who cause war—munitions makers—"are rooted out and exposed"; nations should establish free trade, a universal currency, and a world federation; "wheat is the divine food"; plastics will eventually have "universal use"; everyone should go to work "including people who have lived by cashing dividend checks"; by producing to the fullest in its factories and on its farms, America can lead the way to an improved standard of living throughout the world. But knowing that millions of people still valued Ford's opinions and hoping that he might make an important announcement or a startling statement, the press still jumped at any chance to interview Ford. It did not matter if the Dearbornite's pronouncements were repetitious or inconsequential. Newsmen filed stories on whatever he said; editors published them.[11]

Not all of Ford's wartime statements were conventional. Occasionally the auto maker revealed flashes of "his genius for anticipating events." On April 17, 1944, a few hours in advance of House passage of a bill to give preferences on postwar government jobs to veterans and their wives and widows, Ford pledged to give all ex-Ford employees in the armed forces first call on jobs in his plants. On September 17, 1944, in the midst of nationwide debate on whether the government should "unfreeze" wage ceilings, Ford announced, "I am going to raise wages as soon as the Government will let me. The wages of all Ford workers already are higher than those of the rest of the industry, but I would like to pay them more." Dozens of newspapers, regarding wage increases as a foregone conclusion, congratulated Ford on his "sound economics" and on "stealing the show." "He is the greatest master of his age in the art of timing," declared the *Detroit Free Press.*[12]

Ford's sense of timing, however, sadly failed him on March 20, 1944, when, in Atlanta, he declared that the war "will be over in two months." Ford was asked by his interviewer, Lee Fuhrman, city editor of the *Atlanta Constitution,* to explain why he believed the war would end so soon. "No reason for believing it," Ford grinned. A moment later he grinned again and said: "I can't tell my reasons. I have them of course. That's all I care to say on the subject." The prediction was immediately flashed around the world.

Ford's prediction was given credence in some quarters. It precipitated a price decline on the New York Stock Exchange, according to the United Press. The *Syracuse Herald-Journal,* after analyzing "the advance of the Russian armies, the disruption of German war production by Anglo-American bombing, the chaos in Bulgaria and Rumania, and the near-withdrawal of Finland," reasoned that Ford might prove prophetic at least with respect to the European war. Journalist Cornelius Vanderbilt, writing in the *New York Post* about rumored German peace proposals, suggested that Ford might know what he's talking about. "His factories in Russia, Germany, China, England, and Italy," said Vanderbilt, "are good 'listening posts.' "Vanderbilt's view was echoed by the *Canonsburg* (Pennsylvania) *Notes.* "Ford ought to know as much about the matter as anybody outside of Washington," observed the weekly, "because he is making war materials on an enormous scale and has sources of information not available to most people. But he says he 'can't tell his reasons' for thinking so. That might mean either that whatever he knows about the matter is a deep secret, or merely that he has a hunch. Ford has often seemed to operate more on hunches than on logic, and has certainly been right oftener than wrong."

Most observers, on the other hand, seeing no prospect of the end of the war in two months' time, did not take Ford's prediction seriously; and many of them were critical of the magnate for "talking loosely on a vital topic." Lord Halifax, Britain's ambassador to the United States, warned Ford that "any man who adopts the role of a prophet is taking a great risk with his reputation," while Winston Churchill, in a sarcastic reference to Ford's statement, railed at "those 'clever people' who always know just what is going to happen and when." Some newspapers based their criticism of Ford's prediction on the adverse effects it might have "on Allied troops, on the draft process, the zeal of war production in industry, and the manner in which hardships are borne in civil life." "Ford," declared the *Detroit News,* "should have remembered the large public he reaches and, for fear he might be mistaken, have kept to himself his opinions that 'the war will be over in two months.' If he is wrong, he may have given thousands who read everything he says a terribly misleading impression."

Other publications, while acknowledging the Dearbornite's "genius in the building of cars," said that, when it came to prognostications, Ford was "a jackass" and "all wet" and knew no more than "a schoolboy in the fourth or fifth grade," or a "rabbit." "As a prophet," declared the *Hartford* (Connecticut) *Times,* "Henry Ford is a very remarkable industrialist." The *Madison* (Wisconsin) *State Journal,* in an editorial entitled, "Watch the Fords Go By," reminded its readers that "this is the same old Henry who predicted the same thing about the first World War every few months, announced in 1931 that 'prosperity is here, but only a few realize it,' and that Herbert Hoover would be reelected in 1932." Although Ford's prediction riled some journalists, others saw only humor in it. An Alabama newspaper suggested that the auto maker was trying to revive the Ford joke. A Mississippi editor professed mock concern over Ford because "I do not know YET what ails him."[13]

The press kept close watch on Ford's prediction. A flurry of editorials appeared when half of the prediction time had elapsed. "The Allies will have to hurry up with that invasion," typically observed the *Northampton* (Massachusetts) *Gazette,* "if the war is to end when Henry Ford said it would." Two months to the day after making his prediction, Ford issued a brief statement: "I had information that led me to believe the war could or could be over within two months. I am sorry, as a lot of other people must be, that it is not over."

If Ford hoped that admission of his error would soften press criticism, his hopes were well founded. By not engaging in "argumentative acrobatics to justify his prognostication," he took much of the sting out of what might otherwise have been a devastating press attack. A few of the dozens of editorials which commented on his statement called him "a prophet without honor" and flailed him for "adding to the burdens of those with loved ones in the battle areas." But most of the editorials were uncritical. Many of them pointed out that "practically every American had done his share of bad guessing on the end of the war," and that "the only difference between others' predictions and Mr. Ford's is that Mr. Ford's made headlines." At least a dozen editors commended the old man for "doing the handsome thing" in admitting his error and for not whining—as other wrong guessers had done—that "bungling by army generals had upset his war strategy plans." "Ford," as one newspaper observed, "is in a class by himself in the frankness with which he comments on his wrong guess." Several publications continued to regard the whole affair as a joke: "Now," said one newspaper, "if Henry Ford will only predict that the war WON'T be over in two months!"[14]

After the furore created by Ford's prediction, the Ford family—which for months had fretted about the old man's statements to the press—discouraged him from granting additional interviews. With five exceptions, they were successful. Ford talked with *Fortune* reporters shortly after his return from Atlanta in March 1944. In July he lunched with columnist Marquis Childs, then was interviewed by several newsmen before leaving for a vacation in northern Michigan. On August 11, at his northern Michigan retreat, he was *formally* interviewed for the last time by David J. Wilkie, automotive editor of the Associated Press. On none of these occasions did Ford make "wild-eyed" statements. The old man's final interview occurred on February 2, 1945 in Knoxville, Tennessee. Passing through that city en route to his Georgia plantation, he was spotted by a Knoxville reporter, who asked him, "What will insure prosperity after the war?" Ford replied, "all we need is for everybody to get down to work," then commented no further. Such was the magic of an "interview" with Ford, however, that that one statement was dispatched throughout the country by the Associated Press; and it was printed in scores of newspapers.[15]

Aside from the impromptu interview in Knoxville, the motor magnate's final wartime contacts with the press came in the fall of 1944. On October 31, after hearing a speech by Ohio Governor John W. Bricker, Republican candidate for vice-president, he permitted news photographers to take pictures of himself with the nominee. On November 9, at the dedication of a historic generator at Greenfield Village's power plant, he chatted with reporters about the equipment. On November 10, he and General H. H. Arnold were photographed by news cameramen at Willow Run and at the Romulus (Michigan) Air Base. During the remaining two and a half years of his life, Ford was seldom seen by newsmen.[16]

Ford's personal news releases, which had been issued in a steady stream during the first three years of the war, virtually ceased by the fall of 1944. After November 5, in fact, Ford issued only four statements to the press: an announcement on July 11, 1945 that the Ford Company would provide free equipment for disabled veterans' cars; a July 30, 1945 birthday statement, advocating more competition in industry and predicting higher living standards throughout the world; the letter of resignation from the company's presidency, dated September 21, 1945; and a final birthday statement in 1946, calling for young Americans to rid the nation of "greed, selfishness, and narrow thinking" and to lead their country and the world to "unprecedented peace and prosperity."

After the issuance of Ford's final birthday statement, there was not a whisper from Fair Lane—not one reminder that cigarette smoking led to prison, that milk was poisonous, that salt was good for the hair, that charity resulted from misguided impulses, that roads would be paved with coffee beans, that cars would be made from soybeans. The master of the house, after four decades of sermonizing his countrymen on virtually every subject, had fallen silent.[17]

2

Although far past his prime during 1942–45, Ford was one of the country's best publicized businessmen during the war years. Among businessmen who did not enter government service, only Eric A. Johnston, president of the Chamber of Commerce of the United States, shipbuilder Henry J. Kaiser, and New Yorkers Winthrop W. Aldrich, John D. Rockefeller, Jr., and J. P. Morgan, Jr., received more publicity than Ford in the *New York Times* during 1942–45; it is almost certain that only Johnston and Kaiser received more attention than the auto king in the non-New York press. In periodicals surveyed by the *Readers' Guide to Periodical Literature* and the *Industrial Arts Index,* only Johnston and Kaiser—among businessmen—were more publicized than Ford during the war.[18]

Ford's reputation, although on the decline since the early 1930s, was more durable than his newsworthiness. The findings of public opinion polls reflect the extent of Ford's wartime popularity. In the spring of 1942, when *Fortune* asked a representative sample of Americans which of eleven prominent figures they "would like to see given an important position in Roosevelt's war administration," 30.9 percent named Ford. In this study the auto maker was outpolled only by General Douglas A. MacArthur, who was much in the news following his escape from The Philippines and appointment as supreme commander of the Allied forces in the southwest Pacific, and Wendell L. Wilkie, but Wilkie's margin over the industrialist was slight. Ford, in turn, received far more support in the survey than Thomas E. Dewey, Herbert Hoover, Fiorello H. La Guardia, Bernard M. Baruch, Alfred M. Landon, William O. Douglas, Charles A. Lindbergh, and John L. Lewis.

In the fall of 1942, the nation's newspaper editors, surveyed by Pearl S. Buck, president of the East and West Association, rated Ford second among "Americans, now living or alive since 1900, who [are] typical of our best" and about whom the peoples of Asia should know. Members of the East and West Association, also asked to list those post-1900 Americans about whom Asians should know, rated Ford fifteenth. In November 1942, a national public opinion study by Maxon, Inc., showed not only that Ford's name was familiar to every person interviewed, but that his actions were approved by 93.3 percent of the respondents as well. The Maxon survey also reaffirmed Americans' favorable opinion of Ford's labor policies. The man who announced the five-dollar day was regarded as "helpful to labor" by 82.6

percent of the interviewees, as compared to 51.6 percent for William Green, president of the American Federation of Labor; 41.5 percent for Senator Robert F. Wagner, coauthor of the prolabor Wagner Act; 25.1 percent for Secretary of Labor Frances Perkins; and 22.1 percent for John L. Lewis, president of the United Mine Workers of America.[19]

In February 1943, 500 members of the United Steel Workers of America (CIO), employees of the Irving Subway Grating Company's Long Island City, New York plant, voted only Kaiser ahead of Ford as the "nation's top business and industrial leader." A survey of the same workers in February 1944 rated only Kaiser and William S. Jack, president of Jack & Heintz, Inc., of Cleveland, ahead of the auto maker. In the spring of 1945, 10,000 boys, when asked by Optimist International, a men's service club, to name "the greatest persons now living," ranked Ford sixth, behind President Roosevelt, "my mother," "my father," Babe Ruth, and General MacArthur, but ahead of Winston Churchill. In July 1945, Americans, when asked: "In all of the history of the United States, whom do you regard as two or three of the greatest men who have ever lived in this country?" ranked Ford in a tenth-place tie with Benjamin Franklin. Only one private citizen, Thomas A. Edison, was rated higher than Ford in this poll, conducted by the National Opinion Research Center of America.[20]

The old man, in short, retained the respect of many Americans during the war years. At least one of his countrymen thought that he should be elected president in 1944. "Ford is a good and a very serious-minded man," declared a letter writer to the *Chicago Daily News*. "We would have another Abe Lincoln for the people of our nation." Ford also had at least one prominent wartime admirer overseas. Joseph Stalin, when asked by Eric Johnston to name the Americans he liked best, put at the head of his list Ford—"the greatest industrialist in the world." With fervor, the atheistic dictator exclaimed, "May God preserve him!"

The aging industrialist was honored by several institutions and organizations during the war years. In early 1942 he received a medal from La Salle College, of Philadelphia, for his "monumental contributions to national defense." In October 1943 he was awarded a scroll by the Chicago Executives Club for his "industrial genius." In June 1944 he was awarded the Migel Medal by the American Foundation for the Blind for his employment of the blind." Three months later he received the American Legion's distinguished service medal for his assistance to disabled servicemen. In January 1945, Rollins College, of Winter Park, Florida, added a stone from Ford's birthplace to its Walk of Fame, created to memorialize the world's "immortals."[21]

During World War II the Ford Company continued to be the nation's best publicized firm, as it had been since 1914. But it was not as well publicized as in earlier years. The company's wartime reputation was not as good as during the 'teens and 'twenties, but stayed at about the level of the 1930s, and was sufficiently good to rate it among the best-regarded concerns in the nation.[22]

Henry Ford, left, and his son, Edsel, in the Rouge plant, 1938.

Henry Ford and his right-hand man, Harry Bennett, in Bennett's office, about 1943.

Two good actors, Henry Ford II, left, and Harry Bennett, each of whom despised the other, in Bennett's office in 1944.

Twenty-eight men mooring Ford's post-World War II advertising blimp.

James Meigs, left, Henry Ford, and Hearst executive Merrill C. Meigs, inspect a steam engine given to Ford by the Meigs brothers. The setting is a wheat harvest near Tecumseh, Michigan in 1944. (Courtesy of Merrill C. Meigs.)

Octogenarian Henry Ford harvests wheat near Tecumseh, Michigan, in 1944.

Henry and Clara Ford seated in the magnate's first car in Greenfield Village in 1946.

Henry Ford's funeral procession arrives at Ford Cemetery, Joy near Greenfield roads, Detroit, April 10, 1947.

Greenfield Village schoolchildren placing wreaths on the graves of Henry and Clara Ford in 1964; the auto king's ledger stone is at right. (*Detroit Free Press* photo.)

A life-size statue of Henry Ford at Ford of England's Dagenham factory. (Courtesy of Ford of Britain.)

Henry Ford was honored in the Prominent American stamp series in 1968. (Courtesy of the Ford Motor Company.)

The square or "honeymoon" house as it looked during the Ford's occupancy, 1889–91. The structure was moved from Dearborn to Garden City, Michigan, in 1952.

The Fords' home in 1891–92 at 4420 John R Street, Detroit, as it looked in 1976.

Fair Lane, the Fords' home from 1915 until the end of their lives. The mansion is now a University of Michigan-Dearborn conference and cultural center.

PART VII
New Company (1945-47)

1

Upon assuming the Ford Company's presidency in September 1945, Henry Ford II inherited a firm with important assets and liabilities. One plus factor, as *Fortune* observed, was the "priceless luster" of the Ford name. But the firm had other, more tangible, resources. Thanks in large part to its energetic defense program, its assets stood at $815,515,214 in 1945, compared to a prewar high of $781,964,571 in 1930 and a prewar decade low of $673,496,284 in 1938. Thanks in large part, too, to substantial wartime earnings, it had an immense cash balance of $697,298,372 on June 30, a figure higher than that of any other automotive company except General Motors. It had strong, well-equipped plants in the Rouge, Highland Park, the Lincoln factory in Detroit, and its assembly facilities. As the war had proved, it still had "one of the world's greatest production machines," and its manufacturing staff remained intact. Moreover, a $150,000,000 postwar expansion and modernization program, announced in October 1944 and reaffirmed in July 1945, already was under way. The central sales organization had been revived and strengthened. The dealer organization, which came through the war 93 percent intact, had "fared exceptionally well" during 1942–45. In fact, by greatly increasing their service business and buying and selling used cars, some dealers made more money during the war than they had in peacetime.[1]

On the other side of the balance sheet, wartime deaths, resignations, and discharges had further weakened the company's thin managerial fabric. Moreover, several of the principal staffs were weak or inefficient. The engineering staff, which had the all-important responsibility of designing future products, had never been so depleted. The automotive engineering staff numbered only 550 in 1945, compared to more than 1,000 in 1940. The alpha and omega of the public relations organization was the undermanned News Bureau, whose activities were limited to press relations. Financial management was muddled. Tractors, production of which was continued during the war, had never shown a profit, and did not promise one in the immediate future. Various nonautomotive activities started by the founder continued to operate at losses. Moreover, the company's postwar cars—slightly altered versions of prewar models which had captured less than 19 percent of the market—were not noteworthy. But with sales orders for 680,000 cars and trucks in December 1945 and a seller's market of several years' duration almost a certainty, the appeal of the firm's first offerings was of secondary importance. What really counted was the popularity of the products the company would have on the market when all-out competition was resumed.[2]

On balance, the Ford Company's resources far outweighed its handicaps in 1945. In later years, many publications, in recalling the company's position in 1945–46, would exaggerate the precariousness of its situation. *Newsweek* in 1947 and *Look* in 1953 declared that the empire was "falling apart" in the immediate postwar era; *Forbes* said in 1957 that it was "fast sliding into ruins" and added in 1961 that it was a "gigantic shambles"; *Business Week* in 1961 called it a "stumbling giant"; *Fortune* reported in 1954 that it was "nearly broke" and in 1962 said that it was "almost moribund." Author Arnold R. Weber in 1961 declared in *The Structure of Collective Bargaining,* that it was on the "brink of disaster"; and Allan Nevins and Frank Ernest Hill, in their 1963 book, *Ford: Decline and Rebirth 1933–62,* described the organization as "tottering" and "resembling the famed one-hoss shay at the moment before its collapse." John R. Davis told Nevins and Hill that the company was in even worse shape than that. "You've got to remember," he insisted in 1960, "that when young Henry came in here the Company was not only dying, it was already dead, and *rigor mortis* was setting in." Significantly, few if any publications made such statements about the Ford Company in 1945, the first year of Henry II's reign, although some discerning journals correctly pointed out that the firm was thin in the top ranks of management and would have to undergo "a considerable period of consolidation and readjustment" before it could function efficiently.

Actually, the retrospective crepe-hangers, in assessing Ford's fortunes in 1945, overdramatized its weaknesses and understated its strengths. Although it had experienced a significant decline since 1930, the company was not moribund when Henry II assumed the presidency. An enterprise that had recently achieved such an outstanding war record, that was leading the automotive pack through the early stages of reconversion, that commanded so much goodwill, and could call upon important financial and other resources could not accurately be described as falling apart. But ominous warning signals were fluttering above Dearborn. If Henry II's native ability and common sense had failed him, if he and his associates had not put their house in better order during the breathing spell provided by the seller's market, death rattles might well have been heard along the banks of the Rouge during the late 1940s or early 1950s.[3]

Some of Ford's postwar problems were, of course, common to all automotive firms. Every management in that frenetic era was exasperated by a myriad of reconversion difficulties and taxed to the limit to resolve them; and every auto company sustained losses during several quarters of 1945–46. Even General Motors Chairman Alfred P. Sloan, Jr., later described his company's reconversion effort as "a mess." The smaller, so-called "independent" auto makers, in addition, could call upon only a fraction of the Big Three's resources in dealing with their problems. Yet all car manufacturers, as they licked their chops over the public's huge appetite for cars, not only expected to survive but to prosper. The Ford Company had similar expectations; indeed its goals, announced by young Henry in 1944, were more ambitious than those of any other car manufacturer: to wrest first place in the low-price field from Chevrolet and to surpass the Chrysler Corporation in the total number of cars sold. Both objectives were realistic, as subsequent events were to prove.

In the fall of 1945, however, the attainment of either objective must have seemed a light year away. Higher costs, parts and materials shortages, labor negotiations, and a pricing controversy nagged the company. Young Ford and his associates had to work like men in a leaking ship to keep the firm afloat.[4]

2

Henry II recognized that his personal public relations would influence his company's future. When he became president, public awareness of him was limited. He was known as Henry Ford's eldest grandson, therefore a rising star within the Ford organization; he was said to be modest, earnest, forthright, hardworking, likable; he had never been embroiled in a public controversy, never been the subject of unfavorable commentary in the press. In short, he had public relations assets, and no public relations liabilities.

Attitudes toward young Ford had yet to harden, as they had hardened years before, favorably and otherwise, toward his grandfather. If the new president performed well, his business reputation would continue to unfold along positive lines. But if he were to stumble, there would always be some to make the most of it. Long-term public attitudes toward Henry II were, in fact, to be shaped within five months of September 1945, determined by the executive's personal involvement in two national issues: labor negotiations with the UAW-CIO and the fixing of auto prices by the Office of Price Administration. By the time these two issues had been fought out—and six key statements related to them had been trumpeted across the land—Henry II would emerge as the most dynamic figure in the automobile industry.[5]

Young Henry was keenly aware of the importance of public attitudes toward himself and his company. In the summer of 1945, wanting "someone I could consult on such matters," he tried, on the recommendation of Elmo Roper, to engage a New York public relations consultant, Earl Newsom. But Newsom was wary. Recalling that Edsel Ford's public relations man, Steve Hannagan, had been scuttled by Bennett two years earlier, the New Yorker was reluctant to serve Edsel's son while Henry II lacked complete power; he pleaded too full a schedule. Shortly after young Henry became president, however, Newsom agreed to work with him. "With a sense of relief," Roper later recalled, "I walked Henry over to Newsom's office to cement the relationship."[6]

Head of his own public relations firm since 1935, Newsom by 1945 was one of the country's most highly respected public relations consultants. An Iowan educated at Oberlin, he had, before organizing his own business, worked for the *Literary Digest*, Oil Heating Institute, John Day Publishing Company, Distributors Group, Inc. (an investment house), and been a partner of Norman Bel Geddes & Company (an industrial design firm). Between 1935 and 1945, he had counseled Atlantic Refining Company, the Tea Association of the U.S.A., the International Wool Secretariat, American Locomotive Company, and Standard Oil Company of New Jersey. His reputation as a top-flight public relations man was established by his work for

Standard Oil. That company in 1942 had been lambasted at a Congressional hearing for dividing prewar markets with I. G. Farben, the German chemical trust. Newsom, hired to aid Standard's management in preparation for a second round of hearings, drafted a brilliant presentation which did much to improve Standard's public relations. Afterward, the consultant assisted the oil firm in organizing its own public relations department.[7]

Tall and lean, with a craggy, lined face that "suggests a resemblance to Lincoln," the forty-eight-year-old Newsom, at the time of his first meeting with Henry II, had both the qualifications and the visage to impress a troubled client. By 1945, too, he had risen above mere press agentry; his services consisted almost entirely of "pure consultation" and "statesmanlike writing." In Dearborn, in 1945, his counsel and his writing skills were to be put to a severe test. "You have two strikes on you before you start," Henry II cheerily informed him, "because you come from New York and are looked upon as an expert." Actually, with young Henry's backing, Newsom and his associates, unlike Hannagan and his men, were to play a highly creative role in shaping the Ford Company's public relations, and Henry II's reputation as well.[8]

The first important issue on which Newsom and Henry II collaborated was labor relations. Even before assuming the presidency, young Ford had made improved labor relations "a No. 1 objective on our list of postwar goals." Through the summer of 1945, talking over Bennett's head, he declared that "the majority of union men are reasonable and anxious to cooperate for our mutual good" and expressed confidence that the company and the UAW-CIO "can work out our postwar problems amicably." In October, a few weeks in advance of contract negotiations between the UAW-CIO and the auto industry, Henry II repeated these views to Secretary of Labor Lewis B. Schwellenbach, adding that he strongly supported the principle of collective bargaining. More accustomed to hearing denunciations of labor by businessmen, Schwellenbach, according to Drew Pearson, had "to pinch himself to be sure that his conference with Henry II . . . wasn't just a dream."[9]

Henry II's friendly attitude toward labor unions spawned a series of rumors in October and November to the effect that he was about to drop an "atomic bomb" on the forthcoming UAW auto industry talks. The "extremely social conscious" young executive planned, according to reports, to sell stock to his workers, permit employees to share in company profits, introduce a plantwide incentive system favored by the union, and offer his employees a 15 or a 23 percent increase in wages. Taking stock of these rumors and noting that Henry II had already improved working conditions in his plants, the UAW looked to young Ford as "an innocent glamor boy who would come through quickly with a generous new contract." A liberal agreement with Ford, in turn, was expected to set a pattern for the industry. Instead, "the white hope of the union," on November 15, "socked the UAW on the jaw."[10]

The "sock on the jaw," a four-page letter drafted and polished by Newsom "with the attentive care that a poet might lavish on a sonnet sequence," was the Ford Company's reply to a union demand that all auto makers raise wages by 30 percent. The letter stated that Ford would not discuss wage demands until the UAW had agreed to give the company "the same degree of security as we have given the union." It pointed out that the union shop and checkoff provisions of the company's 1941 contract had helped to stabilize the UAW's membership and finances; and that through the checkoff the firm had collected $7,779,924.25 for the union's treasury. In return for this generous agreement, declared Ford, the union had assured the company "that disturbances of the type then prevalent in other plants would be avoided." Instead, said the company, it had been victimized by 733 unauthorized work stoppages since 1941. "Peaceful relations have not materialized," the letter continued. "The experiment [no other auto maker as yet offered the union shop and checkoff] has been an unhappy one." These points made, Ford, following the tactical principle that the best defense is a good offense, reinforced its complaints with thirty-one specific demands for redress.[11]

Audacious, jolting, the letter's demands took everyone outside the Ford Company by surprise. Management actually demanding guarantees of labor? It was an almost unheard-of procedure. The letter was page-one news in most of the nation's newspapers; it also was discussed in scores of editorials. Almost all publications agreed that "in a nation where there is a growing demand for legislation to make unions responsible for carrying out their contracts," Ford's "bombshell" was a "logical request" and "smart bargaining." Although the letter had been signed by Mel B. Lindquist, the company's newly hired superintendent of labor relations, almost everyone ascribed the "adroit counterattack" to Henry II. Dozens of editorials commended the young man for his "thought-provoking contribution" to labor-management relations; for "stepping out as the champion of industry"; and for "throwing the whole book at the UAW." Thus Henry II, in the first of the six statements which focused national attention on him during his first months as president, was cast in a highly favorable light—imaginative, smart, bold.[12]

UAW leaders, on the other hand, having looked to young Ford as their "ace in the hole," were pictured as "shocked and shaken" by their "sharpest comeuppance yet" and a "new kind of problem." But their answer to Ford's letter was swift—and predictable: [it] "is a union-busting, irresponsible and strife-provoking document . . . an act of treason to the great bulk of the American people." "There is a very simple way to avoid work stoppages," declared the UAW's spokesman, Richard T. Leonard, director of the union's Ford Department. "That is to stop provoking them." But this retort, which would have had validity during Bennett's heyday, lacked conviction now that the service chief and his cronies were gone. Conversely, Ford's contention that the UAW had failed to maintain discipline among its rank and file touched upon a sensitive nerve. Leonard did not concede the point, but he did not deny it either. The union, then devoting scant thought to its obligations and a great deal of attention to its needs, was also infuriated by Ford's refusal to discuss its demand for higher wages—a demand justified in principle, for the cost of living had been mounting steadily. Rising to this point, Leonard, in the first public blast against the company since Henry II became president, excoriated the firm for joining "the conspiracy of profit-swollen corporations to perpetuate present starvation wages."[13]

The UAW and Ford opened formal contract negotiations on November 20. On the following day, however, the union—under pressure from a restive rank and file and urged on by Walter Reuther and other leaders—struck the biggest of the Big

Three, General Motors. Meantime, negotiations continued between the UAW and Ford. For the first time in the history of auto bargaining, both the union and Ford, as well as the UAW and General Motors, designated press relations representatives as accredited negotiators. After each bargaining session, press briefings were conducted. As a consequence, the 1945–46 auto negotiations received far more publicity than any previous auto talks.[14]

The Ford Company, riding a wave of favorable publicity, maintained the initiative in its negotiations with the UAW, insisting with force and cogency that the union offer a plan which would provide guarantees against unauthorized work stoppages. Otherwise, the company declared, it would not extend the union shop and checkoff provisions of earlier contracts. Since a satisfactory plan for company security was not offered, the firm, on November 28, proposed that the union pay the firm $5.00 a day for each of its members who participated in an illegal shutdown. Leonard immediately labeled the proposal "unrealistic," adding the "financial responsibility [for unauthorized work stoppages] would be a serious menace to the life of the union. We cannot put that weapon in anyone's hands." Yet Ford, by raising the crucial question of whether the UAW did or did not have authority over its members, compelled a response to its demands. The UAW did, after all, claim full authority over its members. It also had to go on record as wanting, no less than the company, to avoid unauthorized strikes. Besides, the union, like Ford, was getting its fill of wildcat walkouts, which too often revealed the union leaders' lack of power.[15]

Leonard's next move, also unprecedented in labor relations, surprised everyone outside the UAW. On December 10, the union leader, acknowledging that it was "not humanly possible to guarantee that there never will be a wildcat strike," proposed "pocketbook punishment" for instigators of and participants in unauthorized work stoppages. Fomentors of such strikes were to be fired; participants were to be fined $3.00 per day for a first offense, $5.00 per day for a second. The fines, suggested Leonard (in response to the company's recommendation that moneys collected be donated to charity), were to go to the National Foundation for Infantile Paralysis.[16]

Leonard's "admirable proposal" was hailed by newspapers throughout the country as "a great step forward in the evolution of industrial relations," a portent of "a revolutionary change in labor relations," a "heartening, far-visioned move," and "a breath of cleansing air out of the sorry mess of [America's] labor-management relations." The Ford Company termed Leonard's offer "encouraging" and worthy of study. Two days later the company made its first wage proposal: a conditional offer to raise wages fifteen cents an hour (12.4 percent). The increase was to take effect only when Ford vehicle production reached 80,000 units a month; it also was contingent on a satisfactory agreement on company security and was to stand for two years. The union rejected the offer, alleging that it was insufficient to meet the rising cost of living, that it would block further wage increases for too long a period, and that it was little better than the thirteen-and-a-half cent offer recently made by GM.[17]

Although the UAW and Ford had failed to reach an agreement, their talks, in contrast to the "violent language" and "throwing of brickbats" at the UAW-GM sessions, were virtually devoid of recriminations or bitterness. Henry II and his negotiators, Bugas and Lindquist, were far more friendly and fair-minded toward labor than Bennett and his cohorts. The UAW, for its part, seemed a shade friendlier toward Ford than toward General Motors and Chrysler. Ford had given the union an excellent contract in 1941; it had purged itself of the Bennett regime; and its new administration's spirit of decency promised a better day. Moreover, Ford's unionists were not walking cold picket lines as were their counterparts at General Motors; and it was generally believed that Leonard was under instructions to "lean over backward" to avoid a crisis at Ford that might dissipate UAW pressure on GM.[18]

Dozens of newspapers, while noting the "stubborn temper" of most labor-management disputes, praised the UAW and Ford for their "conciliatory attitude" and "correct spirit." Eleanor Roosevelt described the Dearborn talks as the "one bright spot" in the domestic labor picture. The *Detroit News* declared that "the Labor Department should have got out long ago a model contract containing the [company security] plan." Leonard was commended for his "reasonable bearing" and "statesmanlike qualities"; Henry II was lauded for his "modern, progressive ideas and ideals . . . in human relations" and his "liberal-minded and unfettered conceptions of labor-management relations."[19]

As the UAW and Ford exchanged proposals during the first half of December, the press ground out rumors that the company was about to reach agreement with the union by offering a guaranteed annual wage, a profit-sharing plan, a 30 percent wage increase, or "something equally spectacular." Actually, the company and the union were not near a settlement. The company talked mainly of security, worker efficiency, and mounting losses; the union tried to disassociate these matters from the wage issue and to paint the financial future of the firm as assuredly bright. On this note the parties adjourned on December 20 for the holidays.[20]

Negotiations were resumed on January 8, 1946. The following day Henry II, while delivering his first public address since assuming the presidency, participated indirectly in the contract talks. The occasion was the annual dinner of the Society of Automotive Engineers in Detroit; the topic, "The Challenge of Human Engineering." The speech, the second of the six messages which significantly shaped young Ford's postwar reputation, was prepared with meticulous care. It went through a dozen drafts in Newsom's office; it was revised many more times by Henry II and other Ford executives. The new president rehearsed the speech before his associates several times. When he stumbled over a word, it was changed on the spot. Practice made nearly perfect. The address, given before a jam-packed "who's-who-in-the-auto-industry" audience of 4,000, half of which stood, was not only delivered without a hitch but with feeling. "Ford," observed the *Detroit News*, "spoke with a sincerity that held his huge audience . . . several times during his speech there was barely a sound from it."

The address itself was timed perfectly. At a time when both labor and management had qualms about government intervention in labor negotiations—and government itself was reluctant to intervene in them—it called for a unified attack by labor and capital on common problems. "If we cannot succeed by cooperation," declared Ford, "it doesn't seem likely that we can succeed by any exercise of force. We cannot expect legislation to solve our problems."

At a time when many unions felt threatened by tough-minded employers, the speech assured unionists that "all of us agree that Labor Unions are here to stay. Certainly, we of the Ford Motor Company have no desire to 'break the unions,' to turn back the clock." Acknowledging that unions had arisen out of human problems inherent in mass production, Ford urged that their leaders be strengthened so that they might "help in solving the human equation in mass-production . . . and accept the social obligations that go with leadership."

At a time when many managers were at wits' end in trying to placate labor, the speech held out the hope that "industrial statesmanship—from both labor and management"—could replace an existing tradition of industrial antagonism. Ford warmed to this theme:

> Men who in their private lives would not think of entering into a brawl on the street have over the years found themselves blasting each other in the public press by colorful name-calling. This tradition has given rise in some circles to the theory that open conflict is inevitable. . . . We will always have some honest differences of opinion. But we can certainly deal with these controversies more wisely and efficiently. . . . There is no reason why a grievance case should not be handled with the same dispatch as a claim for insurance benefits. There is no reason why a union contract could not be written and agreed upon with the same efficiency and good temper that marks the negotiation of a commercial contract between two companies.

At a time when the public was fed up with labor-management strife and the shortages that it brought about, the speech declared that "the Public is the boss" and that "the public interest requires that we find ways to eliminate industrial warfare." Finally, Ford laid down a six-point program for common effort to attain a common goal—"to make at lower and lower cost more and better products to sell for lower and lower prices"; then he called for an attack on industrial problems "by giving the same hardheaded attention to human factors that we have given so successfully in the past to mechanical factors."[21]

Ford's speech, containing something for everybody, appealed to everybody. One employer called it "the best speech I've heard in ten years." Henry J. Kaiser described it as "a stirring address, beautifully phrased. . . . I think he had a great deal of courage to tell the world he understood we had to adapt ourselves to a modern way of living—that we couldn't go backward, we had to go forward." A spokesman for one of Ford's competitors agreed: "Someone should have said it just that way long ago." UAW Secretary-Treasurer George F. Addes praised the speech and called Ford "one of the greatest industrial statesman of the auto industry." At CIO headquarters in Washington, a UAW spokesman excitedly told a reporter, "Why Ford stole a page right out of Walter Reuther's book. Did you notice he said that the country could not afford to 'turn back the clock?' That was Walter's phrase. I wish you'd say that this exactly parallels the union's demand that both sides exhibit industrial statesmanship." [The UAW spokesman might have added that Henry II also "stole" the phrase, "human engineering," from Reuther, who on October 19, 1945, had said, "It is time management realized that human engineering is just as important as mechanical engineering."][22]

The government was just as pleased with Ford's remarks as were labor and management. "No expression by an American industrialist within recent memory," noted Blair Moody of the *Detroit News*'s Washington office, "has made a more instantaneous or powerful impression on official Washington." At the White House, where officials were trying to avert a steel strike and about to receive a presidential fact-finding board's report on the General Motors strike, a spokesman gleefully told reporters that Ford's insistence that labor and management rise to industrial statesmanship "was our idea. We've been saying it all along." The official then quoted a statement by John W. Snyder, director of War Mobilization and Reconversion, noting that "better human relationships" were the country's paramount need. The government also noted with satisfaction that young Ford, "whom everyone had been watching," had lined up with "progressive" industrialists (and the administration) in declaring that legislation could not be expected to solve labor-management problems.[23]

Ford's speech was the most publicized of his career. The youthful executive was shown in newsreels from coast to coast; his comments were reported on the front page of almost every newspaper in the country. Dozens of editorials, under such titles as "Horse Sense," "Common Sense," "Industrial Statesman," and "Ford Finds Key to Door of Industrial Progress," offered lavish praise. Winning high marks for his "courage," "refreshing candor," and "refreshingly different approach," as well as for his "industrial statesmanship" and "good sense," Henry II saw his prestige zoom to an all-time high. Four months earlier he had been a young man of little experience and unproven talents. He now had advanced to leadership in an important sphere within his industry and had gained national recognition in the labor field.[24]

On January 10, the day after young Ford's speech, a presidential fact-finding board recommended a nineteen-and-a-half-cent an hour wage boost as a formula for ending the UAW's strike against General Motors. The Ford Company responded to the recommendation on January 15 by offering to raise wages seventeen-and-a-half cents. The union rejected the offer, then compromised with Ford at eighteen cents, a 15.1 percent advance over the 1945 wage level. Meanwhile, Chrysler had settled with the UAW on the basis of an eighteen-and-a-half-cent per hour raise, the No. 2 auto maker conceding that its pay scale had not been as high as Ford's. After reaching agreement with the UAW, Ford and Chrysler ran a "breathless race" for the distinction of being the first auto company to break the industry's wage deadlock. The Dearborn firm, after learning on January 25 that Chrysler planned to sign a wage agreement at 2 P.M. the next day, secretly called a meeting of UAW-Ford negotiators for 11 A.M. on January 26. Ford's contract was signed at 1:25 P.M., the Chrysler document at 4 P.M., the Dearborn company thus winning a "valuable publicity break." The Ford and Chrysler agreements dealt with wages only. But both were hailed as "the first major rift in the nation's industrial storm clouds." Several newspapers, while rapping the "powerhouse tactics" of other labor-management negotiators, congratulated the UAW, Ford, and Chrysler bargainers for acting as "sensible men" and "negotiators without ulterior motives."

The final Ford agreement, with provisions for company security, was signed on February 26. The new contract continued the union shop and checkoff; it provided that any employee found guilty of fomenting or participating in illegal work stoppages would be subject to discharge without resort to the grievance machinery otherwise used in disciplining employees. Penalties were invoked for employees failing to meet production standards. The contract was to run until May 30, 1947. Again, the company and the union were commended for "keeping their tempers under control," for "remaining aware of their public responsibilities," and for reaching a settlement without a strike. Many newspapers also commended the parties for incorporating the "trail-blazing" company security provisions into their contract, and expressed the hope that they would be included in other contracts as well.[25]

The Ford Company had reason to feel satisfied. It had weathered the labor crisis without a strike. It had increased its labor costs less than Chrysler or General Motors (the 113-day GM strike was settled on March 13 with an eighteen-and-a-half-cent wage increase and other benefits that union officials believed worth more than another cent). It also had won some less tangible but immensely valuable gains. The company's entire labor-management atmosphere had been improved. The UAW was assured that Ford did not wish to destroy the union. This fact, together with the better attitude of foremen and superintendents toward those under them, paved the way for improved morale and greater working efficiency. The union had acted on the company security issue, and had agreed that better pay demanded better effort. It was disposed to provide its members with stronger, more constructive leadership. Both the union and the company had, in short, acted in accordance with the spirit advocated in Ford's January 9 speech.

The effectiveness of the security provisions in the new contract was mirrored in a significant decrease in unauthorized work stoppages and employee grievances. Wildcat strikes dropped from ninety-four in 1945 to twenty-seven in 1946 and thirty in 1947. Man-days lost from illegal strikes declined from 78,418 in 1945 to 3,532 in 1948. Grievances, which averaged 2,387 per month during the last nine months of 1945 (there were no reliable records before that time), dropped almost 50 percent to an average of 1,188 per month in 1946, and to 1,130 per month in 1947. Productivity, on the other hand, increased "perceptibly."[26]

Meantime, Henry II moved on a wide front to gain the confidence and support of his employees—in his words, to make the company "a fine place to work." In October 1946, for the first time in its history, the firm asked, via mail questionnaires, its 124,700 employees what they "really thought" about the organization. The survey's findings revealed the depth of the employees' frustrations and the dimensions of the employee relations job ahead. Among the 22,461 persons who completed and returned the anonymous mail questionnaires, more than 70 percent believed that company policies had not been explained satisfactorily, if at all, to them, and that little or no effort had been made to make them feel a part of the organization. Almost half of the respondents said that they had "never had any real chance" or only an occasional chance to talk with their supervisors, and 18.5 percent thought that it was "dangerous for a man to express his honest opinion here." Ninety percent of the interviewees, on the other hand, expressed gratification that the company was concerned about their opinions and 86 percent said that the firm's vehicles, when compared with those of competitors, offered "as good or better value for the money.'' The survey's findings were mailed to all employees with a letter from Henry II: "Critical or complimentary, your opinions are going to be most helpful in planning for better relationships."[27]

In response to the findings, the company accelerated or introduced several employee programs designed to provide a two-way flow of communications between employees and management. The firm's seven existing plant newspapers were supplemented by publications established in all factories employing more than 1,000 persons. By October 1948 Ford was publishing twenty-one plant newspapers with a combined circulation of 143,000. In offering guidelines for editorial content, the parent organization stressed that "no effort should be made to substitute loyalty to the company in opposition to loyalty to the union. The two can and must exist side by side." The purpose of newspapers, it was explained, was to develop "a spirit of teamwork, of pride in the job, the product and the Company" . . . and to inform employees of "management's problems and plans." In 1947 the firm introduced newsletters for management and started a "management meetings" program to keep all levels of supervision abreast of the organization's activities and objectives. Foremen were encouraged to relay information to those whom they supervised and, in turn, to solicit ideas, complaints, and comments from workers. Also in 1947, the company established a suggestion program to compensate hourly-rated employees for worthwhile ideas; eligible workers were paid up to $1,500 for adaptable suggestions. In 1948 the company issued a handbook which explained the firm's personnel policies to employees.[28]

Rules and procedures which had long vexed the personnel were also changed. The 23,000 salaried employees no longer had to punch time clocks after July 31, 1947. For the first time in company history male employees were permitted to smoke on Ford property, starting November 15, 1947. Tobacco firms, at odds with the Ford Company since Henry Ford published *The Case Against the Little White Slaver* in 1914, were jubilant. One of them, the Philip Morris Company, posted its living trademark, Johnny, a midget dressed as a bellhop, at the Rouge gates to pass out cigarettes to workers. Although Henry Ford had predicted dire consequences for companies which permitted their employees to smoke, the only apparent adversity suffered by the Ford Company as a result of its new policy was a wastepaper fire started by a janitor unaccustomed to emptying ashtrays.[29]

Ford also paid special attention to its foremen who, traditionally, identified themselves with management rather than labor. But many of them, whose power and status had been reduced by the UAW-company agreement of 1941, subsequently joined a supervisors' union, the Foremen's Association of America (FAA). The company recognized the association as a bargaining agent in 1942, and dealt with its foremen through the union after that year. Ford was dissatisfied with the arrangement, however; the firm resented the union's insistence that foremen be advanced on the basis of seniority rather than ability; it felt that foremen often favored the UAW at the firm's expense.

In 1946 Ford made a bid to win back the allegiance of its foremen, shifting them from an hourly to a salaried pay basis. The following year, on April 8, the company notified the association of its intention to terminate the agreement between them. In response, the union struck Ford on May 21. But a minority of the foremen remained on the job, and the company continued to produce. The association, in a weak position, desperately appealed to unionists throughout the country to boycott Ford vehicles. The appeal, issued at a time when millions of Americans were queueing up for new cars and trucks, had no effect whatever. Then on June 23 the Senate passed over the President's veto the Labor Management Relations Act (Taft-Hartley Act), which freed employers from the compulsion to bargain with supervisory unions. With the scales tipped decisively in favor of the company, the FAA voted on July 6 to end its strike, having won none of its demands.[30]

Aware that the Foremen's Association had grown "out of past injustices and the failures of past managements," Henry II redoubled his efforts to treat front-line supervisors as members of management. By late 1947, foremen, who earlier had been excused from punching time clocks and wearing badges, were provided with desks and locker rooms, special parking lots and eating places, and distinctive work apparel. Those who earned less than the skilled employees under their supervision were given pay raises in February 1948. Meantime, all supervisory employees were deluged with literature bearing on their management status and responsibilities. "Each step may seem small in itself," explained Henry Ford II, "but all of them are long overdue . . . and necessary." After 1947, most Ford foremen, convinced that the company was giving them a square deal, allowed their FAA membership to lapse.[31]

The company negotiated its second postwar contract with the UAW in mid-1947. It offered the union a choice of contracts—one providing a seven-cent per hour wage increase and a pension plan, and the other an eleven-and-a-half-cent per hour pay hike, plus six paid holidays, but no pension. The pension plan, the first offered hourly employees by an auto firm, was widely hailed as "heavy industry's . . . finest retirement plan for production workers" and as being "as revolutionary as Henry Ford's $5-a-day wage." But Ford's workers, preferring a "bird in the hand," voted three to one in favor of the higher cash offer. Two years later the union's leadership demanded and won a $100 per month pension for hourly Ford workers, setting a pattern which quickly spread throughout the auto industry and beyond.[32]

While striving to improve union and employee relations, Henry II and his associates also gave much thought to "human engineering" research during the mid-1940s. What was human engineering? In young Henry's words, it was "an approach to creating conditions under which the average man will not only increase his capacity to produce and earn, but with far less wear and tear on his physical and psychological equipment." In 1946 the company considered building a "laboratory" for testing and experimental work in human relations, but the plan never materialized. Henry II's discussion of human relations, however, gave employees and the public the correct impression that the "new" Ford Company was concerned about labor relations problems and hoped to find improved ways of dealing with them.[33]

The new administration's concern with human relations and, more importantly, its fair treatment of employees and honest dealings with the union, sharply reduced the savage tensions which marked labor-management relations of the Bennett era. By mid-1947, as *Fortune* noted, there was general agreement that Ford was "doing a labor-relations job second to none in the tense Detroit area." UAW leaders also expressed grudging admiration for the company: "While serving no tea and crumpets, [Ford] at least wears no brass knuckles." No unionist could have said the same of the pre-1945 Ford Company.

Because of Henry II's interest in human engineering and his firm's novel demands and offers during contract talks, Ford's labor relations program was "the most publicized in the nation" during the mid- and late 1940s. Much of the publicity on the company's labor relations was favorable; none of it, except in the labor press, was critical. As a consequence, Ford's reputation for good labor relations was enhanced during the immediate postwar years. In mid-1946, Elmo Roper, in the second of his Ford-sponsored public opinion studies, found that 41.8 percent of the respondents thought that Ford "treated its employees better" than any other auto firm, up from a figure of 31.8 percent in mid-1944. Roper's 1946 study also showed that 29.6 percent of the public thought that Ford had "the right attitude toward labor unions," as compared to 16.9 percent in 1944.[34]

The improved climate of the company's employee and labor relations was recognized by three awards presented to Henry II in 1948: a citation by Junior Achievement, Inc., in recognition of young Ford's "initiative and leadership in the field of human engineering"; a National Civic Service Award from the Fraternal Order of Eagles for his "promotion of better understanding between labor and management"; and a Human Relations Medal from the Society for the Advancement of Management for his efforts in "creating a feeling of understanding and co-operation throughout [his] organization."[35]

3

Henry II not only received nationwide publicity for his forthright stand on labor, he also won headlines with his outspoken views on price controls.

The government's price-fixing authority had been accepted by most Americans during the war. But the administration's refusal to abandon price ceilings after V-J Day, when it terminated many other controls, was highly controversial. Government critics blamed labor-management disputes, black markets, and shortages of critical goods on price controls, and demanded an end to them. The administration and its backers maintained that price ceilings were the sole guarantee against runaway inflation.

In late November 1945, after prolonged deliberation, the Office of Price Administration fixed factory and retail prices for most 1946 cars. On the average, retail prices, apart from increases which reflected improvements in new models over their 1942 counterparts, were no higher than those of January 1942. The OPA acknowledged that costs of labor and materials had soared since 1942; but it weighed this fact against the large sums that auto firms had earned during the war and the rosy prediction that car production would zoom to 500,000 units a month by June 1946, a 45 percent increase over the 1941 output. "This higher volume," declared the OPA, "means lower unit costs and the opportunity for higher profits and higher wages." Proceeding on this assumption, the agency permitted Ford, which was credited with several engineering improvements on its Ford line, a 2 percent retail price hike on Ford models. Chrysler was allowed a 1 percent price increase on its cars, while General Motors' prices were reduced 2.5 percent.[36]

The OPA's edict dismayed auto manufacturers. It meant that none could expect to operate profitably until its unit volume exceeded the prewar level. No auto executive, as he surveyed strike-torn and materials-short America in the fall of 1945, expected to attain that kind of volume for months. General Motors and Chrysler, when asked by the press for their reaction to the OPA announcement, offered a terse "no comment." Henry II's first impulse was to "launch a nationwide campaign blasting OPA." But after simmering down he issued a mild statement: "The prices . . . do not properly reflect the changed economic circumstances in which a motorcar manufacturer must operate today. . . . We will have to sell our cars at a loss. . . . This situation does not, however, alter our program in the slightest. Our first objective is still to get the greatest number of cars and trucks to the greatest number of people in the shortest possible time."[37]

But after two-and-a-half months of money-losing production, young Henry's hackles rose again. On January 29, 1946, he telegraphed John W. Snyder, director of War Mobilization and Reconversion, bemoaning his company's pitiful output during the previous six months and explaining why production had been so low. "Time and again," said Ford, in the third of the six statements which had an important bearing on his postwar public relations, "we have been forced to shut down operations because suppliers could not get us parts and materials for our cars and trucks. Some of them have stopped making our parts because they lost money at their ceiling prices. Some are slowed down in their production by strikes or are losing their employees because they cannot raise wages." Ford added that his company was losing $300 on each car it built, chiefly because it could not achieve quantity production, but partly because its prices were unrealistic. He conceded that there might be good reasons for continuing price controls on rent and food. But he demanded the prompt removal of all price controls affecting the auto industry. Such a step, he insisted, would stimulate production, which, in turn, would soon end the threat of inflation.[38]

Ford' s proposal, the first public demand for removal of price controls by an auto executive, was discussed in dozens of editorials. About two-thirds of them supported Henry II. "He is right," declared the *Bridgeport* (Connecticut) *Post*. "OPA . . . is becoming the greatest single factor tending toward inflation in this country because it is keeping production down." Many newspapers, in echoing this view, also maintained that increased production and competition in the motor industry would "automatically" keep prices down. Pro-OPA editorials, while agreeing that young Ford "has a real grievance with the Administration," insisted that "his remedy would make matters worse for everyone, including himself." With the removal of price controls, these newspapers insisted, "the inflationary spiral . . . would zoom upward—completely out of hand." But even those editors who disagreed with Ford acknowledged that he was an "important witness." "He has shown so many evidences of liberal and progressive thought and practice during the present industrial strife," typically observed the *Brooklyn Eagle*, "that his opinions on its causes and cures are deserving of respect."[39]

President Truman, holding fast to administration policy, rebuffed Ford's demands on January 31, saying that price controls could not be lifted "without wild inflation." A day later, Snyder, in reply to Ford's wire, also staunchly defended the continuance of price ceilings. He did, however, suggest that the company's prices could be adjusted upward, if the firm did not attain its prewar production level within an unspecified length of time.

Henry II thought he knew the government too well to hope for relief. On February 8, in San Francisco, while denying that he would take his case to the people over the heads of government agencies, he nonetheless did so. Before a Commonwealth Club luncheon audience of 1,650—a number exceeded only when presidential candidate Franklin D. Roosevelt addressed the group in 1932—the twenty-eight-year-old executive gave a detailed comparison of his firm's manufacturing costs with prices allowed by the OPA. Pointing out that his company had built its most popular model for $681 in 1941, he declared that this same car had cost $962 to produce in November 1945. After adding sales and distribution expenses, but allowing nothing for profit, the total cost of each model produced in November had been $1,046.26. Yet the OPA authorized the company to sell this car for only $728! Reiterating information sent to Snyder, Henry II emphasized that many of his company's suppliers faced a similar cost-price dilemma; and that some of them, rather than accept mounting losses, had switched to lines of manufacture for which there were no price controls. The cost-price squeeze could be solved, declared Ford, only when wage and price ceilings stop "playing havoc with production efforts."

Although his firm was losing $300 on each car it produced and sold, said Henry II, the Ford Company would "stick it out and do its utmost to produce." He expressed the hope that the firm could achieve a higher rate of production and that "the price ceiling problem can be solved." Until one or both of these developments occurred, he added, "we may lose very substantially in 1946." In his peroration, Henry II, borrowing from his grandfather's philosophy on work, appealed for everyone "to pitch in and work. . . . We must popularize the notion of work—and the best way to popularize it, that I know of, is to *do* it. . . . The reconversion battle is not going to be won by speeches—mine or anyone else's. It is not going to be achieved by recriminations, newspaper battles, memoranda or essays, but by hard work."[40]

Ford received a standing ovation from the business-oriented audience. His speech, the fourth in the series of his image-building postwar statements, was reported in news columns and discussed in editorials throughout the country. Anti-OPA publications again applauded the young man's "sensible views," "sound judgment," and "common sense." Pro-OPA publications, while crediting Henry II with being "a serious-minded young man with good intentions," again suggested that he had "pulled a boner" in demanding the abandonment of all price controls on vehicles. Nearly all editorials were unanimous, however, in praise of young Ford's advocacy of hard work. "We believe with Henry Ford II," typically stated the *Keokuk* (Iowa) *Gate City,* "that work can be a cure for the ills of the world." The *Holyoke* (Massachusetts) *Transcript & Telegram* added, "Those of us who are complaining that we don't know the way out [of the reconversion mess] might cut out this Fordism and put it in the inside pockets where men keep their favorite quotations and the children's pictures."[41]

Hammering away at his do-away-with-the-OPA theme, Henry II, at a press conference in Los Angeles on February 14, stated that "if price ceilings were taken off, our workers would again swing into full production and the resulting competition would soon drive the prices for cars down." His third attack on the OPA within two weeks triggered a sharp retort from Price Administrator Chester Bowles on February 15. The auto executive, said Bowles, has united himself with "the few selfish groups which have worked continuously to undermine the American people's bulwark against economic disaster" (the OPA). He added that Ford "should know very well that on August 31, 1945, ceilings were taken off most parts used as original equipment in passenger cars." Shortages of parts, stated the price chief, "can't possibly be due to difficulties with price ceilings as Mr. Ford claims."[42]

Bowles continued to counterattack Henry II in testimony before the House Banking and Currency Committee on February 19. Conceding that the Ford Company was losing $300 on each car it produced, he asserted that the loss was attributable to the lack of volume production, a failure that was no fault of the OPA. He added that during the previous summer Henry II had asked for a 55 percent increase in prices (a request which previously had been unpublicized). The request, he said, was "an outrageous increase to ask, much less to allow. I have no idea what Ford would ask if there was no price control." Noting that young Henry had based his costs on a fraction of prewar production, Bowles added, "I don't think any intelligent manufacturer would ask for pricing based on such low production." Bowles then observed that the Ford Company traditionally had led the way in offering high wages and lowering prices. "I am sorry," he said, "that young Ford seems to have departed from the tradition." When Bowles's allegations were questioned by several members of the committee, Chairman Brent Spence announced that he would invite Henry II to appear before the group.[43]

Henry II was in Los Angeles on February 19, the day Bowles testified. That same day an alarmed Newsom—who had drafted the Commonwealth Club speech—and Dearborn executives conferred on the crisis. Newsom reasoned that Henry II, having taken a public stand on the removal of price controls, had to defend his position; that the response to Bowles's counterattacks could cause "a great many people to gain or lose confidence" in Henry II; and that "the newspaper boys would . . . take Mr. Ford's part." The consultant recommended that a Dearborn official immediately rebut Bowles "to draw the fire away from Mr. Ford," the rebuttal to be followed by preparation of a "very good factual presentation" which Newsom hoped could be discussed "in private conference with the OPA." This recommendation was telephoned to Henry II.[44]

Young Ford, however, chose to meet Bowles head-on. On the very evening of the price administrator's appearance before the Banking and Currency Committee, he sent a long telegram to Chairman Spence—the fifth of Henry II's widely publicized postwar statements. Bowles's testimony, said Ford, did "not reflect all the facts." Specifically, he declared, the price chief had not made it clear that "manufacturers who supply our suppliers with parts do have price ceilings," that "parts for trucks and all automotive replacement parts are still subject to ceiling prices," and that tires, radios, batteries, and castings had not been freed from price controls. The executive also complained that Bowles had hit below the belt in giving the impression that the company had "secretly" applied for a 55 percent increase in price ceilings.[45]

Two days after wiring Spence, Henry II sent a blistering telegram to Bowles—the sixth and last of the statements which largely shaped young Ford's immediate postwar business reputation. "Your public statement," Henry II said, "leaves me no other course but to make public certain facts which you either do not know or refuse to reveal." The application for a 55 percent increase in car prices, he pointed out, had been made while the nation was at war and the company's production quota for the last six months of 1945 had been set at 39,910 units. "Low cost depends on volume production," Ford asserted, "so when the Government—not the Ford Motor Company—fixed production volume it thus determined cost and selling price." Henry II added that the application for prices on "low-volume, high-cost, wartime cars" had been submitted six weeks before the OPA had announced any peacetime price regulations on new autos and that the company had not applied for any price relief since OPA ceilings had been established. The auto executive also noted that, because postwar production had been near the quota imposed during wartime, his company's costs were "almost exactly what we estimated." This fact, said Ford, illustrated the point he had been trying to make: "High costs and high prices of automobiles are caused by low-volume production." High volume had thus far been impossible to attain, and, Ford implied, would not be attained while price controls remained. In a parting blast, Ford questioned "the propriety of a Government official's calling 'outrageous' actions taken in strict accordance with wartime government regulations."[46]

Under such headlines as "Bowles Blasts Ford Again," "Ford Blasts Bowles Again," and "Ford-Bowles Dispute Flares in Full Fury," the squabble between the auto executive and price official raged in the nation's press for a week. Among dozens of editorials, seven out of every eight castigated Bowles. To many newspapers the price administrator was a "plain ordinary garden liar," "the capital's most constant gallery player," "a magician whose bag of tricks had failed," "a busybody and a bit of a demagogue," and an "irresponsible, patronizing bureaucrat" who had "got out of line," "hit below the belt," and "wanted to ride roughshod over all critics." These publications, on the other hand, found young Ford "convincing."[47]

Criticism of Henry II centered on his company's request for the 55 percent price increase. "That kind of talk," editorialized the *Chicago Times,* "isn't good public relations." The *Detroit News* suggested that Henry II was "clearly in error . . . in launching a drive to wipe out controls entirely, like the fellow who burned down his house to get some roast pig." Declaring that Ford's problems stemmed from "molasses in the price control machinery," the *News* added that Bowles was "by all odds the most courageous, intelligent and valuable public servant now handling domestic problems in Washington. He has not had enough time to devote to administrative matters, because those lobbyists and their stooges in Congress who have been out to make an inflationary killing have kept him busy trying to keep from getting his throat cut."

A few newspapers, perhaps like much of the public, found the whole affair "confusing." Speaking for such publications, the *Highmore* (South Dakota) *Herald,* while admitting that it did not know whom to believe, contented itself by presenting the opposing statements and advising readers, "you can take the one that suits you best."[48]

Ford undoubtedly emerged the moral victor in the controversy with Bowles, enjoying not only overwhelming press support but considerable congressional backing as well. Many publications congratulated the young executive—a virtual "lone operator within his industry"—on showing the alertness and ability to speak out strongly for a cause which all auto companies and most businessmen embraced. Several publications also lauded Ford for the "surprising frankness," "courage," and public relations acumen which he displayed during the pricing crisis. "He certainly made a great hit with the members of the Fourth Estate," typically commented the *Los Angeles Examiner,* following Henry II's Los Angeles press conference, "as he has with the American people. He answered all questions in a straightforward, honest manner and did not try to evade any of them." "The refreshing candor about him," echoed the *Detroit Times,* "has won him amazing popularity in a short time . . . and is a welcome contrast to the stuffiness exhibited by some of the high officials in the industry." "Young Ford," said the *Chicago Times,* "has more public relations savvy than most of the Old Guard businessmen put together."[49]

Following Ford's telegram to Bowles, the auto executive and the price official held their fire. On March 11, two weeks after Ford and Chrysler increased the pay of their workers, all auto manufacturers were informed that their prices would soon be adjusted upward. On March 30, price ceilings on the Ford line's eleven models were increased from $10 to $16, on Mercurys from $15 to $21, and on Lincolns from $26 to $50. In May the OPA allowed auto makers a second price increase, the hike on Ford cars ranging from $42 to $62. But plagued with rising manufacturing costs and shutdowns caused by parts shortages, the industry nonetheless continued to lose an average of $200 on each car sold. In August, at the rate it was then producing, Ford estimated that it needed an $136-per-car increase in order to show a profit. At the same time, however, the company figured that it would break even on a $60 rise, if production schedules for September could be met. Some increase was imperative. The firm had lost $50,000,000 during the first seven months of the year, and would plunge into further loss unless output increased. Ford applied to the OPA for an $80 increase, and was permitted a rise of $62.50 in mid-September. That month, thanks as much to rising output as to the price increase, the company made a profit of $5,000,000, its first since the war. With additional gains during the remainder of the year, it wiped out the deficit incurred during the first eight months and registered a profit of $2,000 for 1946.[50]

After November 9, 1946, when almost all price and wage controls were abolished, auto manufacturers were free to adjust vehicle prices as they saw fit. General Motors, Willys-Overland, and Crosley quickly raised their prices, and between late November and early January all other auto makers, except Ford, followed suit. General Motors, in extenuation of its $100-per-vehicle price hike, justifiably stated that its cars had been priced lower than those of its competitors by the OPA. In mid-November, while insisting that it would be justified in raising prices "to give the company a fair and reasonable profit," Ford declared that it hoped to "hold the line" in the interest of wage-price stabilization.[51]

During late 1946 and early 1947, the Truman Administration pleaded with industrialists to reduce their prices in order to stabilize the economy and maintain public purchasing power. But the administration's pleas, rejected by nine of the ten auto makers, were also disregarded by most other manufacturers. In the wake of decontrols, prices on most commodities spiraled upward; prices were reduced only on small radios and a few overstocked food and clothing items. Wholesale price averages increased 24 percent between the lifting of controls in 1946 and January, 1947; food prices alone rose 36 percent.[52]

In this setting Henry II invited thirty reporters to attend a press conference in Dearborn on January 15. The newsmen expected to hear a routine disclosure of a price hike on Ford cars. Instead, the youthful president announced, in the words of several newspapers and radio commentators, "the biggest news since V-J Day"—a price cut on all nine models of the Ford line.

Noting that the company had a backlog of more than one million car orders, Henry II explained that the price reductions were his firm's "down payment" toward a continued high level of production and employment in the months ahead. "We believe," he added, "that the 'shock treatment' of prompt action is needed to halt the insane spiral of mounting costs and rising prices." Ford continued:

> Already, millions of American families are unable to buy the things which, in normal times, make up their standard of living. In the short view, we can see inflation. In the long view, there is danger of depression. . . . The American economy now stands at a turning point. . . . We have decided that now is the time for us to make an investment in the future.

Henry II added that Ford's lowest-priced car, a six-cylinder, two-door sedan, was priced $2.00 lower than its Chevrolet counterpart. Other Ford models, however, were still priced above comparable Chevrolet products.[53]

The Ford Company's decision to reduce car prices was acclaimed by everyone—except other manufacturers. Government officials were especially jubilant. "It has been a long time," reported the *Detroit News*'s Washington correspondent, "since any action by a business organization, or for that matter by a labor union, has stirred such a white heat at the White House as the Ford price cut. It was exactly the sort of leadership that the President and his associates have been hoping would be produced." John R. Steelman, assistant to the President, immediately wired Henry II that Ford's act was "good news for the country." Edwin G. Nourse, chairman of the President's Council of Economic Advisers, termed the Ford decision a "crucial" contribution to sustained high production and high employment and an "encouraging start toward general price reductions." The chairmen of the House and Senate Banking Committees congratulated Ford officials on their "marked perspicacity and business acumen" and "very valuable contribution to the stabilization of our economy." Michigan labor leaders described Ford's move as "a step in the right direction" and "very sound economic policy," although Richard T. Leonard, director of the UAW-CIO's Ford Department, added that Ford's price cuts would have no bearing on the demand of the union for a wage increase.[54]

Several Ford suppliers pledged themselves to hold the line on prices; one vendor promised to reduce its prices. Ford's dealers applauded the price cuts, and many of them ran advertisements saying so. A few dealers also advertised reductions in their service and repair charges. More than 1,500 dealers sent congratulatory wires to the company. "This morning's headlines are reminiscent of old times," chortled a veteran Pittsburgh dealer. "The new Ford team clicked again," wired a Cincinnati dealer, while a Kentuckian declared that the price cut was "a major step upwards for us to regain the No. 1 position. I see the greatest future with Ford that ever appeared on the horizon." The public responded to the price announcement with a "flood of orders" for Ford cars.[55]

Scores of publications throughout the nation praised Henry II and his company for their "common sense" and "industrial statesmanship," for "cutting the ground from under the price raisers," and for "squarely accepting the responsibility laid on private business by the President." To *Time,* Ford's decision was a "down payment toward stable prosperity"; to *Newsweek,* a "dramatic blow at high prices"; to the *Detroit Free Press,* a "concrete effort . . . to counteract dangerous inflation; to the *Boston Herald,* "the kind of enterprise the country needs"; and to dozens of publications a "challenge to the rest of industry." "Everybody talks about the need for lower prices," observed the *St. Louis Post-Dispatch.* "Henry Ford II has done something about it." Many publications, recalling Henry Ford's price cuts in the midst of the 1920 depression, described young Henry's act as being "in the best Ford tradition" and "worthy of the Old Master."[56]

Ford's price reduction, in the opinion of many editors, was "deftly timed." "If it is followed up elsewhere," stated the *New York Times,* [it] "has come at just the right psychological moment to keep the country out of a runaway boom-bust cycle." Economists, as well as editors, believed that Ford's announcement could have "widespread reverberations in industry, especially in the auto industry." "They've got to act now," said Nourse of the nation's large companies, "or state why they don't."[57]

Ford's competitors either withheld immediate comment on their pricing policies or "leaked" word that they did not intend to reduce prices. On January 21—after the *Detroit Times* reported that General Motors had informed dealers of $17 to $193 price hikes on eight-cylinder Pontiacs and on Oldsmobile, Buick, and Cadillac convertibles—Charles E. Wilson, president of the big auto maker, bared his company's position. Vigorously defending GM's latest price increases, the blunt-spoken Wilson explained that his company's $100-per-vehicle price hike in November 1946 had only "partly corrected" the price disparity between GM and other manufacturers' cars; he emphasized that the Chevrolet, notwithstanding Ford's price cuts, was still the lowest-priced car in its field. Wilson expressed "surprise" that the White House and newspapers had praised Ford. The Dearborn company's price cut, he insisted, was a "publicity stunt" and "a maneuver Ford was forced to make to restore its competitive position." Wilson went on to say that his company had no intention of reducing prices since "sales are not yet meeting any consumer price resistance."[58]

Wilson's assertion that the Chevrolet undersold the Ford was backed by a barrage of advertising proclaiming that Chevrolet had both the lowest-priced line of cars and, in its six-cylinder, three-passenger business coupe (a model which Ford had discontinued in October 1946), the lowest-priced model in the low-priced field.

General Motors' claims were valid, as was Ford's claim that its lowest-priced model (a six-cylinder, two-door sedan) was priced under its Chevrolet counterpart. The "battle of low prices" raged for months in the rivals' press releases and advertisements. In April 1947, Ford, after reintroducing its six-cylinder, three-passenger business coupe and shaving $20 from its previous listed price, triumphantly announced that it marketed the lowest-price car, as well as the lowest-priced sedan, in its field. Chevrolet continued to claim that its full range of cars was priced under Ford's.[59]

Pricing semantics aside, Ford's much-heralded price reduction of January 1947—to the great disappointment of the government and antiinflationists—was emulated by few manufacturers. In March 1947 International Harvester, whose chairman said that he had been "tremendously impressed" by Ford's act, announced price cuts of $50 to $300 on its trucks, tractors, farm machinery, and industrial power equipment. The following month, Chrysler reduced prices $25 to $55 on its Plymouths, which, compared with its major rivals, Chevrolet and Ford, had been overpriced. No other large firms reduced their prices during 1947. On the contrary, throughout the year, prices—and wages—spiraled upward in virtually all industries. Among auto makers, Hudson raised prices on its cars in April, followed by Packard in May. Ford itself hiked prices on its station wagons in June and on its trucks in July, when Chevrolet truck prices also were raised. In the face of soaring operating costs, General Motors increased prices on all of its cars in August, a move which triggered price boosts that month by all the other auto makers. Ford, the last to take action, except for Studebaker, raised prices on its high-volume models from $20 to $97, thus more than wiping out its January reductions. Despite the increases, Ford indefatigably declared that it still offered the lowest-priced coupe and sedan on the market. Chevrolet persistently retorted that its cars, across the line, were less expensive than Ford's.[60]

Ford's dramatic price cut of January 1947 was one of the company's most successful postwar public relations moves. The extent to which the price decrease was "shrewd public relations," as *Time* put it, was revealed in several public opinion surveys. These studies showed that the Ford Company, even though its full line of cars sold for more than Chevrolet's throughout 1947, was more highly esteemed in the pricing sphere than General Motors or any other manufacturer. A Psychological Corporation poll in late January 1947 revealed that 59.5 percent of the public believed that Ford "is the lowest priced car today," as against figures of 25.2 percent for Chevrolet and 6.6 percent for Plymouth. Among those expressing an intent to buy a car in 1947, a surprising 55.8 percent said they planned to buy a Ford, against 35.7 percent for Chevrolet and 6.5 percent for Plymouth. In May, when the Psychological Corporation asked respondents to compare "things you like about GM and Ford," 30 percent of the interviewees mentioned Ford's prices; only 4 percent mentioned General Motors' prices. In October, another Psychological Corporation survey revealed that 37.7 percent of the public thought that Ford had done a "good" job of keeping prices down, as compared with 28.5 percent for runner-up Eastman Kodak, 28.1 percent for General Electric, 24.2 percent for Standard Oil of New Jersey, and 17.7 percent for General Motors.[61]

There is no evidence to suggest that Ford reduced prices in January 1947 solely to curry public favor, although Henry II and his associates undoubtedly knew that their economic "shock treatment" would receive, in the words of the *Detroit News,* "virtually universal backing by enlightened public opinion." In any event, the price reduction received a press that even the elder Ford, in his heyday, would have found highly gratifying. Moreover, not a single publication suggested—as not a few did when the "Old Master" sprang some of his surprises—that the company's price reduction was a publicity scheme. Quite the contrary, the press and all commentators—Charles E. Wilson excepted—seemed to say that any company willing to sacrifice immediate profit in behalf of economic stabilization deserved all of the favorable publicity that came its way.

Henry Ford seems to have concerned himself little with Henry II's activities. But he received sporadic visits from his grandson and must have noted with satisfaction that the young man had taken charge of the family firm, and that it was making headway.

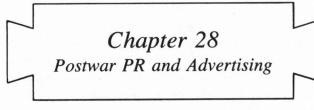

Chapter 28
Postwar PR and Advertising

1

Although the Ford Company's labor and pricing policies were the key determinants in shaping the firm's immediate postwar public relations, the company's formal public relations and advertising activities also played an important part in forming public attitudes toward the organization and its products.

When Henry II assumed the presidency, the firm's public relations organization was vest-pocket size. It included, in fact, only the five-man News Bureau, headed by Charles E. Carll, and a public relations representative in New York. In contrast, General Motors' Public Relations Department in 1945 employed scores of persons in a dozen units and eleven field offices. Twenty of GM's divisions also had public relations personnel.[1]

After becoming president, Henry II began a slow buildup of Ford's public relations organization. The appointment of Newsom in early October provided a much-needed policy adviser. A news bureau was established at the Lincoln plant in November to handle press relations for Lincoln and Mercury cars and personnel. Public relations representatives were appointed in Chicago and Los Angeles in January 1946.[2]

Although Ford had the nucleus of a public relations field organization in 1946, the three regional managers "almost died a natural death for lack of attention." In late January the trio had discussed operational procedures with Newsom, Carll, J. R. Davis, and William D. Kennedy, director of publications. Following this session, the field men were virtually ignored by Dearborn.[3]

While the regional offices went their separate ways, in early 1946 Carll added photographic and printing, information services, and guest relations units to the News Bureau. The News Bureau, in turn, came under the direction of William D. Kennedy in mid-September 1946, when the publications chief was named director of public relations. Before being named editor of the *Ford Times* in late 1945, Kennedy had been an assistant dean of Harvard's Business School, an account executive with J. Walter Thompson Company, and an officer in the Army Air Forces. His excellent work on the magazine attracted Newsom's attention, and led the consultant to recommend Kennedy for the directorship of public relations. Kennedy did not think he was suited for the job. "At the time," he wrote later, "press relations was of top importance; in this I had had little experience." During the six months that Kennedy served as public relations director, the organization remained static. In late 1946, however, the Sales and Advertising Division doubled the number of its public relations field representatives, assigning men to sales offices in Kansas City, Dearborn, and Chester, Pennsylvania.[4]

In early 1947, Kennedy asked—"before I was fired"—to be relieved of his public relations duties. On March 1, he was succeeded by James W. Irwin. Hired on Newsom's recommendation, Irwin had directed public relations for the Frigidaire and Dayton divisions of General Motors between 1931–38 and served as assistant to the president and chairman of Monsanto Chemical Company between 1938–41. Since 1944 he had been a senior partner in a New York and Chicago public relations firm bearing his name.[5]

Named assistant to the president, director of public relations, and made a member of Ford's Policy Committee in April 1947, Irwin was in a strong position to shape the company's public relations policies and further expand its public relations organization. He did organize a well-conceived Community Relations Department in April 1947. But the flamboyant publicist's pontifical mannerisms scuttled chances for an additional buildup of the public relations organization. J. R. Davis, an easy man to work with, got so fed up with the public relations chief that he "refused to have anything more to do with him." Newsom and Henry II also became increasingly disgusted with Irwin, and, finally, on November 7, 1947, young Ford dismissed the publicist.[6]

Irwin's successor as director of public relations was the highly popular Carll. The appointment was greeted with undisguised enthusiasm by the Detroit press, which regarded Carll as "the best public relations and press agent in the business." The enthusiasm for the modest Carll was heightened by the satisfaction that newshawks found in Irwin's departure. "My guess," said columnist Anthony Weitzel of the *Detroit News,* "is that he'll [Carll] do better than any of the fancy-pants guys imported from what is laughingly known as the Big Time."[7]

At the close of 1947 the company's Public Relations Division consisted of three departments: News Bureau, Guest Relations, and Graphic Arts. The Community Relations Department had been abolished in the wake of Irwin's departure. The News Bureau continued to be the heart of the division. Its new head was John L. Rose, a former Iowa newspaperman and United Press staffer, who had joined the company's Publications Department in 1946 and had served as assistant manager of the News Bureau since early 1947. Kennedy's Publications Department, previously a part of the Public Relations Division, was transferred to the Sales and Advertising Division.[8]

Carll recognized that his division, when compared with its counterparts at General Motors and other large companies, was weak and disorganized. In January 1948, almost apologetically, he admitted to a group of company dealers that his staff had devoted most of its attention to publicity and product promotion and that his organization had yet to reach "a high state of development—to relate its program to all aspects of company operations." Promising to reorganize his staff, Carll, as a first step, gained direct control over the six public relations field offices. He also reactivated the Community Relations Department in mid-1948 and assumed responsibility for the Motion Picture Department, previously a part of Sales and Advertising, in early 1949.[9]

Beyond these reorganizational moves, however, Carll did nothing more to reshape or build his division. He continued to focus his attention on the News Bureau, which maintained its vaunted reputation among newsmen. But he began to lose favor with Ford executives, particularly with Executive Vice President Ernest R. Breech, in the late 1940s. Grounded in newspapering, he found it difficult to think of public relations in terms other than press relations; he was unable, as the cliché has it, "to grasp the big picture." Invited to attend Policy Committee meetings, he tried to squirm out of them. After a time he no longer was invited. In the spring of 1952, the forty-five-year-old Carll, by then beset with health and drinking problems, was relieved of his job.[10]

Carll's successor at Ford was Charles F. Moore, Jr., an account executive with the Newsom organization. Under Moore, the company's public relations organization quickly came of age. Moore himself was named to the company's Administration Committee in 1952 and elected to a vice-presidency in 1955. In 1952–53 he established Speech Services, Educational Relations, Radio and TV Relations, Research, and Institutional Advertising departments and absorbed the Office of Information on Government Affairs. By the end of 1952 the Office of Public Relations had 165 employees; and twenty-three more (mostly guides) were added when the Rotunda Building was re-opened to the public in mid-1953. Among industrial firms, only General Motors' Department of Public Relations, consisting of 185 employees in 1952, was larger than Ford's.[11]

Moore's expanded organization successfully met its first crucial test in 1953, the year of Ford's fiftieth anniversary. His staff planned and executed a year-long celebration, the most elaborate observance of its kind in business history. It also proved to be the best publicized and most successful of business anniversary celebrations, one that impressed the name of Ford on the minds of tens of millions in America and abroad. As Moore noted in 1957, it also "broke down the last ramparts of resistance to public relations [within the company] and settled once and for all the status of our activity." By the close of 1953 the firm's public relations organization, after spending decades in the wilderness, had "arrived."[12]

Ford's film program, suspended at the outbreak of World War II, was resumed in August 1945. At that time, twenty-three titles were made available for showings to schools, churches, service clubs, and fraternal organizations. Fifteen of the films were of prewar vintage, including five travel pictures, four Rouge films, and two pictures based on the New York World's Fair. The remaining eight films, produced in 1944–45, dealt with Ford's war work. The company produced five motion pictures between 1946 and 1948: a film on the American Legion Junior Baseball program and four color travelogues. To maintain an adequate film library, however, the firm found it necessary to keep ten of its prewar pictures in circulation until 1949.[13]

Ford's film program took on new life with its transfer from Sales and Advertising to Public Relations in January 1949. Four films produced that year were released in 1950; a dozen others followed during the early 1950s. Since the early 1950s Ford has been one of the nation's largest industrial film producers and distributors; its films have helped appreciably to improve the company's public image and sales.[14]

Ford's publications program, like its film program, was suspended after the outbreak of World War II. In late 1942, however, Edsel Ford and the Hannagan organization decided that the company needed an employee newspaper. Edsel suggested that the publication be called the *Ford Times,* after the pioneer employee-dealer-consumer magazine of the same name.[15]

The first issue of the revived *Ford Times* appeared on April 2, 1943. An eight-page biweekly tabloid printed by the rotogravure process, the publication was filled with stories and pictures of employees at work and at play, of the company's defense activities and products, and of distinguished visitors to Ford plants. Henry Ford liked the publication but not its size. Noting that many employees glanced at the paper, then tossed it aside, he reasoned that more of them would take it home to read if it "was something you could put into your pocket." An admirer of the *Reader's Digest,* he decreed that the dimensions of the *Ford Times* should be *Digest*-size. But upon finding that a copy of the *Digest* would not fit into his pocket, he had a dummy of the *Ford Times* tailored to fit the pockets of his suit. His pockets measured 6-⅞ inches by 5 inches.[16]

The *Ford Times* was last published as a tabloid on May 12, 1944; and the first edition of the *Digest*-size publication was scheduled for June. But because all magazines had agreed to display a facsimile of a war bond on their covers in June and Henry Ford did not wish to conform to the agreement, the debut of the revived publication was rescheduled for July. That month, all magazines had agreed to illustrate the American flag on their covers. Ford also disliked this idea, and accepted it with reluctance. Prickling over the edict, he rejected the first three cover illustrations shown to him for approval. "He doesn't like the flag's colors," Thompson drily remarked at one point. Finally the auto king approved an illustration which, as discovered later, hung Old Glory in violation of the flag code. After the first several hundred copies of the magazine came off the press, Thompson rushed a copy to Ford. The old man tried to put it into his pocket. It would not fit. The suit he was wearing had smaller pockets than the one which he had worn when measured for the *Times*. Thompson therefore had to trim a fraction of an inch off thousands of copies of the magazine. That issue of the *Ford Times,* after trimming, measures 6-13/16 by 5 inches; all subsequent editions, reverting to the originally planned size, measure 6-⅞ by 5 inches.[17]

The pocket-size *Ford Times* was published monthly in sixty-four pages. In contrast to its black-and-white predecessor, it ran two- to four-color front covers and two colors inside. The magazine continued to feature news of Ford employees and operations. But it also carried entertainment features. Most of the articles were written by News Bureau members and Detroit newsmen, the outsiders being paid $25.00 to $100 for their contributions. After Kennedy assumed direction of the *Ford Times,* the magazine devoted less attention to employees and company operations and more emphasis to travel articles and general features. Kennedy also made the publication available to dealers, who, by March 1946, financed mailings to 350,000 Ford owners and potential customers. In April 1946, the magazine announced that future issues would be directed toward the motoring public, as well as employees. After November 1946, the *Ford Times* was sent only to employees who made a written request to remain on the mailing list.[18]

The change in editorial direction was accompanied by additional physical improvements in the magazine. Paintings were first used for cover art in June 1946, and inside the magazine in September 1947. By 1965 the magazine had published more than 8,000 paintings (by 1972, about 9,000), and its collection was valued at $1,000,000. Since 1949, *Ford Times* color photographs and paintings, mostly watercolors, have been displayed in hundreds of art galleries, libraries, schools, and Ford dealerships in America, and, under the auspices of the United States Information Agency, in dozens of foreign countries. In 1965 the *Times* began donating sets of fifty watercolors to selected school systems, and has given away more than 2,000 paintings with an appraised value exceeding $500,000.[19]

Starting with the publication of five poems by Berton Braley in the May 1947 issue, the magazine invited contributions from "name" writers. John P. Marquand contributed an article on Newburyport, Massachusetts, and Philip Wylie submitted a piece on fishing in Florida in 1947. Fulton Oursler and radio-film humorist Bob Burns contributed stories in 1948. Since that year the *Ford Times* has carried articles by Stewart Holbrook, Lucius Beebe, Bernard De Voto, Aldous Huxley, William Faulkner, William Saroyan, John Steinbeck, William O. Douglas, Eleanor Roosevelt, Ogden Nash, Earle Stanley Gardner, and E. B. White. This talent was willing to write for the publication, said Kennedy, because "its short articles take very little research and are a pleasure to write." The average payment for a story approximated $350 in 1972; contributors have been paid up to $1,500 for an article.[20]

Ford Times's circulation, benefiting from the editorial and format changes introduced in April 1946, more than doubled within six months, and doubled again to 1,400,000 in 1949, then leveled off. In 1974 the *Ford Times*'s circulation exceeded 2,000,000; and the magazine claimed a readership of 8,000,000. Among America's general magazines, about thirty have a circulation larger than that of the *Ford Times*. Among the nation's company publications, only nine have a greater circulation than the Ford magazine. Numbers aside, the *Ford Times*—in terms of editorial content, appearance, and subtlety in advertising—has consistently excelled. A description of the magazine by the *Detroit Free Press* in 1962 remains apt: "one of the finest company publications . . . in the whole wide world."[21]

2

Although Ford's public relations activities were limited at war's end, its advertising program at that time was "the most aggressive in the company's history." Making use of all the major media, the firm conducted six campaigns in August 1945, advertising Ford, Mercury, and Lincoln cars, Ford trucks, dealers' service facilities, and "Ford Firsts." Three advertising agencies served the company during the mid-1940s: Maxon, Inc., J. Walter Thompson Company, and Kenyon & Eckhardt, Inc.[22] Ford exhorted these agencies to develop "unusual—even spectacular [techniques] . . . to get people to talk about Ford and Ford products favorably." The agencies responded, as *Printers' Ink* noted, with "striking billboards, singing commercials, sky writing, and blimp spectaculars.'' The most novel and spectacular of these techniques was the use of an airship for advertising.[23]

J. Walter Thompson proposed the idea of blimp advertising after being approached in the spring of 1946 by Douglas Leigh, Inc., of New York. Before the war Leigh had designed many of the large illuminated signs which had given Broadway its sobriquet as the ''Great White Way.'' For Ford, Leigh proposed to convert a 265-foot surplus Navy blimp into a flying ''adship.'' It was to cruise at 2,500 feet, day and night, over the Atlantic seaboard, ranging from Washington on the south to Hartford, Connecticut, on the north. Ford agreed to the proposal in July, announcing that it would make ''automotive advertising history . . . with a dirigible which will carry 'super-spectacular' electric signs into the sky.''

Leigh decorated one side of Ford's blimp with the slogan, ''Ford's Out Front''; the other side with the message, ''There's a Ford in Your Future.'' At night, the ''Ford's Out Front'' side of the airship flashed the slogan and the alternating words ''in style'' and ''in safety.'' The ''Ford in Your Future'' message was supplemented by weather reports and news bulletins. The messages, averaging 25 feet in height and ranging from 170 feet to 200 feet in length, were legible from a distance of three miles at night, five miles during the day.[24]

Ford's adship did not take to the air until mid-October, five weeks after Leigh had launched a similar craft for Metro-Goldwyn-Mayer; Ford therefore could not claim a ''Ford First'' for its blimp advertisements. But, in announcing its flight plans, it could declare that it was the ''first manufacturer'' to advertise by dirigible. The Ford airship's maiden flights were heavily publicized up and down the eastern seaboard. Later flights frequently were mentioned in newspapers and on radio stations in the communities over which the blimp flew.[25]

Ford's dirigible flew over the eastern seaboard in late 1946 and through the spring of 1947, then spent the remainder of the year touring upstate New York, lower Ontario, New England, and the Midwest. The craft spent the early part of 1948 in Florida, the summer and fall of 1948 in the Midwest. The subject of hundreds of newspaper stories, it was also described and pictured in more than a dozen national magazines and shown in syndicated newsreels. To the delight of Ford dealers, tens of millions of people saw the airship. Moreover, the majority of viewers remembered having seen it. After the Ford dirigible had hovered for about 100 hours over Philadelphia, 64.8 percent of the residents interviewed by Alfred Politz Research, Inc., recalled seeing the blimp and could name the product it advertised. ''No advertising medium survey I have conducted,'' said Alfred Politz, ''has approached this high percentage of remembrance.''[26]

By 1948, however, the novelty of blimp ''spectaculars'' had worn thin. In 1947 Leigh had put dirigibles into the air for Ringling Bros. and Barnum & Bailey Circus, Tide Water Associated Oil Company, Mobilgas, and Wonder Bread; and by the end of that year there were few cities in the East and Midwest and on the West Coast that had not been exposed to at least one of the aircraft. Consequently, Ford was content to let its two-year contract with Leigh expire on October 15, 1948. The expenditure for the service—$496,000—probably was the auto maker's soundest advertising investment during the immediate postwar period.[27]

3

A major part of Ford's advertising outlay was devoted to electronics media. During the immediate post-World War II period, network radio reached its peak and commercial television made its debut. As one of the nation's largest consumer firms and advertisers, Ford was a leading sponsor of radio programs; as a company seeking to project a forward-looking image, it was a pioneer sponsor of televised events.

In May 1945, Henry II, looking ahead to the resumption of civilian auto production after July 1, requested J. Walter Thompson to submit plans for a postwar Ford Sunday Evening Hour. The next month, however, for reasons never made public, the youthful executive decided to turn the show over to another agency. Perhaps young Henry's faith in JWT's radio capabilities had been shaken by the failure of its "Stars-of-the-Future" and "Frances Greer" programs. Certainly Henry II's feathers had been ruffled by JWT's suggestion that "The Children's Prayer," the closing theme of the "Ford Show," be replaced by "something more in keeping with the dash and style of the program." Young Ford liked "The Children's Prayer," which had been played at the start and close of the prewar Sunday Evening Hour. "JWT's suggestion," he grumbled to an aide, "certainly doesn't show much thought on the agency's part." In any event, for these or better reasons, Henry II, to JWT's chagrin, handed the Sunday Hour plum to Kenyon & Eckhardt, which had recently joined the list of the nation's ten top agencies and was fast gaining a reputation for astute radio programming.[28]

K & E made elaborate preparations for the resumption of the Ford Hour. A first step was a survey of Syracuse residents to determine how many people recalled the prewar program. The findings were gratifying. Thirty-three percent of the respondents, when asked if they remembered having listened to a Ford radio program before the war, identified the Sunday Evening Hour by name; another 10 percent mentioned a program with "good music." Among those who claimed familiarity with the Hour, 11 percent, when asked if they recalled someone talking about "business and things in general," identified William J. Cameron by name, and another 38 percent said they remembered the program's commentaries.

The Syracuse findings strengthened Ford's resolve to retain the Sunday Evening Hour's original format: "The Children's Prayer" musical theme, fifty-four minutes of "familiar music, majestically rendered," spliced by an institutional message. Music would be provided, as before the war, by members of the Detroit Symphony Orchestra and outstanding soloists under the baton of distinguished conductors. The agency, however, after appraising the findings of Roper's 1944 public opinion study—which noted that the public thought Ford had not kept pace with its competitors in styling and engineering innovations and that younger people regarded the company less favorably than their seniors—recommended a change in the program's "commercial format." Instead of offering talks on "matters of national interest and concern," as did the prewar Hour, the postwar program, suggested the agency, should "present the company as a progressive, forward-thinking maker of automobiles—and particularly one attuned to the younger market." Ford agreed. The agency also acknowledged the need to deal, in some manner, with ''two lesser weaknesses disclosed by the Roper survey—one with members of organized labor and the other with the Jews. But these need not concern us for the moment,'' observed K & E, ''because the Jewish problem is not one that can be dealt with directly on the Sunday Evening Hour, and . . . labor is too deeply involved in questions of company policy for us to recommend a course of action.''[29]

K & E also recommended that Henry II occasionally serve as the Hour's intermission speaker, addressing himself to ''the industrial problems of today and tomorrow.'' Neither the agency nor the company wanted the prewar intermission speaker, William J. Cameron, to return to the program. The sixty-six-year-old ex-commentator, it was felt, was too old, too conservative, and too closely identified with prewar controversies to serve as a spokesman for a ''progressive'' postwar company. Thus K & E conducted an extensive search for an intermission speaker who could write appropriate talks and deliver them effectively. After screening a bevy of radio announcers, newspapermen, professors, and lecturers, the agency offered the intermission assignment to Carl Carmer, a New York writer-lecturer. But Carmer could not accept the invitation because of speaking commitments. Consequently, Henry II, who had intended to speak only on the opening program, found himself appearing on the first three shows. Young Henry found his own successor. Attending a meeting in New York in early October, he heard William I. Nichols, editor of *This Week* magazine, give an eyewitness report on Nazi concentration camps. Favorably impressed by Nichols's speaking ability and treatment of a difficult subject, Ford instructed K & E to offer the editor a ten-week contract as the Ford Hour's commentator. Nichols accepted the offer.[30]

K & E and Ford had hoped to present the Sunday Evening Hour on one of the two leading radio networks—CBS, which had carried the prewar program, or NBC. But with network time at a premium in the fall of 1945 and the networks more conscious of audience ratings than ever before, neither of the top networks was willing to devote an hour of prime Sunday evening time to a program so limited in appeal as the Ford Hour. Consequently, arrangements were made to broadcast the Sunday Hour over the No. 3 network, ABC, at 8 P.M. (EST). Meanwhile, K & E engaged distinguished guest artists and conductors many of whom had appeared on the prewar Ford Hour including Gladys Swarthout, Jascha Heifetz, Mischa Elman, Helen Traubel, Lauritz Melchior, Risë Stevens, José Iturbi, Jan Peerce, and Bidu Sayao. Among the newcomers who were engaged were Robert Casadesus, Dorothy Kirsten, Jussi Bjoerling, and Jeannette MacDonald. The Hour's conductors included Fritz Reiner, Eugene Ormandy, Reginald Stewart, Thomas Beecham, Victor Kolar, Wilfred Pelletier, and George Szell, all of whom had appeared on the prewar program, and Dimitri Mitropoulos, Eugene Goossens, Leonard Bernstein, and Iturbi. Talent fees were slightly higher than those on the prewar hour, with maximums of $6,000 per performance for Heifetz and pianist-conductor Iturbi and $1,500 for Ormandy. Many of the guest artists and conductors requested and received payment in difficult-to-obtain new cars in lieu of cash, as did guest stars on other Ford-sponsored programs during the immediate postwar period. Iturbi, for example, accepted a Lincoln and two Fords in payment for his April 7, 1946, appearance on the Ford Hour; while Helen Traubel exchanged the $2,500 fee for her May 5 performance for a Lincoln. Ford was delighted to pay entertainers in cars, despite its continuing production problems, because it found that "such payment," in the words of its sales and advertising executives, "was substantially to the advantage of the Ford Motor Company," the cost of the car to Ford always being less than the cash fee.[31]

The resumption of the Ford Hour was formally announced on September 14, 1945. Observing that the prewar program had "achieved the highest listener ratings of any symphonic program ever broadcast," the company declared that the program was being resumed "as a result of thousands of letters from the audience and numerous, repeated requests from Ford dealers." "The demand for the return of the program," added Henry II, "is another manifestation of the public's desire to get back to the good things of life—and it is our intention to perpetuate the high standards of entertainment that made the Ford Sunday Evening Hour so much an American family institution."

The postwar Ford Hour, broadcast from Detroit's Music Hall, had an auspicious beginning. "With a hustle and glitter reminiscent of prewar first nights," reported the *Detroit Free Press,* "the Ford Sunday Evening Hour returned to the air and to the hearts of Detroit last night [September 30]. Local society flocked to the opening, eager to give to the program its rightful place as a leading social event as well as a first-class musical evening." Among those in attendance were the entire Ford clan, headed by old Henry, Clara, and Mrs. Edsel. The program itself, featuring Gladys Swarthout, an "excellent chorus," and the Ford Symphony Orchestra under the direction of Fritz Reiner, conductor of the Pittsburgh Symphony Orchestra, was acclaimed by the Detroit press. A "plenty scared" Henry II, delivered his intermission remarks—on postwar opportunities awaiting young Americans—without a hitch. Young Ford made no mention of the Sunday Hour's commercial policy; he merely promised that future intermission talks would "review the personal opportunities that our postwar world will hold for young Americans." Henry II also expressed the hope that future commentaries "will be as memorable as the fine music I am sure you will hear."[32]

The Ford Hour's first three broadcasts, featuring talks by Henry II on the postwar-youth theme, generated 10,000 telegrams, letters, and postal cards from listeners. Hundreds of the messages expressed gratitude for the resumption of the program. "It truly was wonderful to hear the Sunday Evening Hour once again," ran a typical letter from Springfield, Ohio. "Everything was perfect, just as it used to be." "May I express our delight in welcoming back the Ford Hour on Sunday evenings," echoed a Pennsylvanian. "For so many years it gave us rich pleasure, and it is certainly good to find it unchanged from lovely theme song to closing hymn." Hundreds of letters were in praise of young Henry and his talks. "Your message," wrote a Virginian, "was inspiring. I know that there must be literally millions of people in this country who, like myself, are grateful that a man of your calibre will direct the Ford Motor Company and maintain the principles set by your grandfather." A Pennsylvania Ford dealer said that he was glad that Henry II had appeared on the program, "because our company has been lacking such a touch with the public and I feel it is needed." The dealer added, "this is the first time I have felt free to write direct to the head of our company." Many of the letters were from listeners—among them a young Congressman, Mike Mansfield, of Montana—requesting copies of young Ford's "opportunity talks" for themselves, or friends, or sons, husbands, and sweethearts in the service. Scores of letters linked Henry II to old Henry. "I hope that your President, Henry Ford," wrote a naval officer stationed in Seattle, "carries on in the footsteps of his grandfather, Henry Ford, Founder, whom I regard as one of the greatest living Americans." A St. Louisan, addressing old Henry, said that the automotive pioneer "should feel proud of your grandson, who from reports here, has conducted himself in a manner that would make you proud of him." Finally, scores of letters, to the Ford Company's probable annoyance, asked, "Where is Mr. Cameron?" "We do hope that Mr. Cameron is going to speak again," ran a typical "Cameron letter." "While we enjoy listening to young Mr. Ford, we always greatly profited from Mr. Cameron's quiet but sane and helpful talks from week to week."[33]

Although the mail response to the first three Ford Hour programs was highly gratifying to the company, subsequent shows, on which Nichols discussed such topics as "What Makes America Great" and "Armistice Day," drew only a few hundred "fan" letters. Nichols himself found the weekly commuting from New York to Detroit arduous. Since he could not catch the overnight train to New York on Sunday evenings, he had to lay over until Monday evening. "During the wait," he said later, "I think I got to know every animal in the Belle Isle Zoo by name." Nichols also grew weary of spending "two sleepless nights over the square wheels of The Detroiter" each week. In December the commentator requested permission to broadcast his message from New York. Despite Ford's "passion for seeing its talent on the hoof," permission was granted. Unfortunately, Nichols recalled, "after the second or third Sunday some genius at Rockefeller Center forgot to pull the right switch and my part of the program went dead . . . end[ing] my career in this area."[34]

K & E had hoped to replace Nichols with a Michiganian. But since none of the local newspapermen, radio announcers, professors, and sports personalities considered for the assignment was deemed suitable, the agency engaged another New Yorker, news commentator Gordon Fraser, to serve as intermission speaker. Fraser got off to a fast start. Four of his early talks were based on excerpts from Henry Ford II's address on "human engineering" before the Society of Automotive Engineers on January 9, 1946, and generated 5,300 requests for reprints of the commentaries or copies of the complete text of Ford's speech. The remainder of Fraser's messages—in contrast to Nichols's talks, which had soft-pedaled references to the company—focused squarely on "the Ford Motor Company, its people, its achievements, its aims, and its products." Fraser's messages evoked only token response. At times there was not a single request for a reprint; and during the five months Fraser was on the air only fifty reprints of his talks (aside from the "human engineering" excerpts) were requested. To a company accustomed to receiving thousands of requests for reprints of Cameron's prewar talks, this was a major disappointment.[35]

The company was also disappointed in the Sunday Evening Hour's audience ratings. The postwar Ford Hour—unlike the prewar program which had only run-of-the-mill competition—was placed opposite two of the most popular programs on the air, NBC's "Charlie McCarthy Show" and the "Fred Allen Show." During the 1945–46 season, from 25 to 28 percent of the nation's radio sets were tuned to the

McCarthy program, which was on the air during the first half of the Ford Hour; from 21 to 24 percent were tuned to the Allen show, which followed McCarthy. Only 3.1 to 5.3 percent of the nation's radios were tuned to the Sunday Evening Hour, compared to an average of 9 percent for the prewar program.

Against such stiff competition, the Ford Hour, according to audience surveys, barely held its own against classical music programs, most of which were broadcast at less competitive hours. Broadcasts of the New York Philharmonic consistently reached a larger audience than the Ford Hour; the NBC Symphony, sponsored by General Motors, usually reached more listeners.[36]

In addition to losing ground in audience surveys, the Ford Hour was criticized by scores of the company's dealers. While acknowledging that the program was artistically good and was appreciated by some of their customers, many dealers argued with logic that the program appealed chiefly to "a class of people who buy relatively few cars in the Ford price range." Some of them added that the Ford Hour did not sell as many cars as would a "good variety program."[37]

By April 1946, the cumulative effect of poor listenership and dealer complaints, plus the program's considerable expense—$992,456 over the nine-month season—raised doubts among Ford executives as to whether the company should present the Ford Hour during the 1946–47 radio season. Between January and August 1946 the company also debated whether it should sponsor one or two major radio programs during the following year. During the first six months of 1946 the company, working through K & E and J. Walter Thompson—whose radio department had been restored to Ford's good graces and was hungering for Dearborn business—weighed a variety of program possibilities for the 1946–47 season. Among these, in addition to the Sunday Evening Hour, were the hour's summer replacement, the Ford Festival of American Music, programs featuring Bing Crosby and Dinah Shore, musical shows centering around the orchestras of Fred Waring, André Kostelanetz, and Leigh Harline, and two theater presentations. In June K & E made a fervent appeal for the "early fall return of the best radio program on the air, the Sunday Evening Hour." Responding to this appeal, Ford tried in the early summer of 1946 to switch the Sunday Evening Hour from ABC to the more prestigious NBC network; but many NBC stations refused to broadcast the audience-poor program. As the possibility of renewing the Ford Hour waned, nimble K & E enthusiastically recommended the continuance of the Ford Festival of American Music into the 1946–47 season. The Ford Company, mulling over the alternatives suggested by K & E and JWT, delayed making a decision until early August. At that point, with time running out, the company contracted for a JWT-packaged musical comedy show starring vocalist Dinah Shore. K & E was left out in the cold.[38]

The Sunday Evening Hour's final broadcast was presented on June 23, 1946, with Benson Ford serving as the intermission speaker. Benson's remarks, however, were not heard in the East and much of the Midwest. Sixty-eight stations, because of damaged transmission lines, found themselves simultaneously broadcasting Ford's voice and a conversation between two women. ABC cut off both Ford and the females, filling the void with recorded music—but not before the women had exchanged a series of "hellos" and one had asked, "Where's Myrtle?" The conversation titillated millions of listeners, according to newspaper reports. "Imagine," said the *Cincinnati Post* in one of many humorous articles on the incident, "the number of places Myrtle might have been!"

The Ford Company made no public announcement, as it had in 1942, of the cancellation of the Sunday Evening Hour. Consequently, neither the press nor listeners echoed the prewar expressions of regret over the suspension of the program. The Ford Hour, after a promising start, failed to excite radio listeners. Its music was pleasant and artistically sound, although perhaps no more so than the music on the nine other programs which regularly presented symphonic orchestras in 1945–46. But the Ford Hour's intermission messages, which had distinguished its predecessor from all other radio shows, contributed little to the Hour's appeal. The talks were generally bland and dull, and evoked no strong listener feelings.[39]

The Ford Hour's summer replacement, the Ford Festival of American Music, made its debut from Hollywood on June 30, 1946. Patterned after the prewar Ford Summer Hour, the festival featured popular ballads, film and stage comedy melodies, and the lighter classics. Music for the program was furnished by the Leigh Harline orchestra. Alfred Drake, "Curley" in the original cast of "Oklahoma," served as the singing master of ceremonies. A feminine singer, furnished by a Hollywood film studio, also appeared on each program. The intermission talks, delivered by Knox Manning, were similar to those presented on the Sunday Evening Hour. Upon finding that the festival's audience ratings were no better than those of the Ford Hour, the firm allowed the program to lapse with its September 22 broadcast.[40]

The company and its dealers also sponsored two other radio programs during the 1945–46 radio season. One of these, the "Ford Show," was a carry-over from April 1945. Languishing in the Sunday afternoon doldrums on NBC for six months, the "Ford Show" was shifted to Tuesday evenings on CBS in October. But singers Lawrence Brooks and Jo Stafford and the Robert Russell Bennett orchestra proved no match for the competition on NBC, the highly popular "Bob Hope Show." In early November, Henry II instructed J. Walter Thompson to find a replacement for the Ford program; in early December the agency signed band leader-singer Bob Crosby and his orchestra, the "Bobcats."[41]

The Crosby show's audience ratings never approached the "first fifteen" list to which networks, advertising agencies, and sponsors attached so much importance. Ford and JWT, acknowledging that Bob Crosby had but a fraction of older brother Bing's singing and comedy talents, hoped to bolster the show with guest stars, particularly comedians. Starting in April, Bob Hope, Victor Borge, Cass Daley, Judy Garland, and Gracie Fields made appearances on the program. The guest-star format perked up the show. But it proved expensive. In June, when strikes in other industries had forced a six-week shutdown of Ford operations, the guest-star policy was abandoned, and the show immediately slumped. In early July, the company cancelled its option to sponsor the program through September; it died with its July 17 broadcast.[42]

During the 1946–47 radio season, Ford was represented by only one network program, the "Ford Show," starring Dinah Shore and featuring comedian Peter Lind Hayes and Robert Emmett Dolan's orchestra. Miss Shore, judged America's "most popular female vocalist'' by the nation's radio editors in 1944–45, also presented a guest star on each broadcast. Among the guests were many of the nation's leading singers, actors, and entertainers including Lily Pons, Jo Stafford, Ginny Simms, Dick Haymes, Dick Powell, Henry Fonda, Van Johnson, George Montgomery, William Bendix, John Garfield, Jimmy Durante, Eddie Cantor, and Jack Benny.[43]

The "Ford Show" was built around music and comedy. Almost everyone identified with the program, including the dealers who paid for it, were pleased with Miss Shore's singing. But they felt that she was miscast as a comedienne, and that Hayes, a young unknown, "does not help the program in any way." The "Ford Show" failed to generate enthusiasm among Ford people or radio listeners. "The show is not very good," a Wichita dealer lamented in January. "I am unable to get anyone in my own household to listen to it." In listener surveys, the "Ford Show" consistently trailed its competition. By April 1947, after months of fruitless tinkering with the program, the company decided to drop the series at the end of the season, June 11.[44]

The decision to drop J. Walter Thompson's "Ford Show" was accompanied by a decision to place all of the company's national radio advertising with Kenyon & Eckhardt. Although K & E had been shelved by Ford in the summer of 1946, the agency continued to pelt the company with recommendations for new radio programs throughout the 1946–47 season. Threaded through these recommendations was a recurrent theme: Ford could hope to attain "maximum radio advertising effectiveness only . . . by placing all of its radio advertising with a single agency"—K & E. The agency's proselytizing—abetted by the failure of the Dinah Shore program, which K & E had predicted in July 1946 would prove unsuitable—paid off in May 1947, when Ford switched agencies. "J. Walter Thompson," Henry II told his aides and K & E executives, "has done an excellent job with print advertising, and . . . a good radio job for other accounts. But the Ford account may have been a jinx. A change is necessary."[45]

As the summer replacement for and possible successor to the Dinah Shore program, K & E proposed a fast-rising comedy show, "My Friend Irma," starring Marie Wilson. But Henry II vetoed the recommendation, saying that the zany "My Friend Irma" was "somewhat below the standard of taste which the company should maintain in its radio programming." Then K & E proposed, and the company accepted, a program built around Iowan Meredith Willson, a first-rate musician with a flair for Will Rogers-type comedy. During the 1946–47 radio season, Willson had served as writer, producer, and star of "Sparkle Time," a program sponsored by Canada Dry Ginger Ale, Inc. His stature as a musician had earned him an invitation to direct the Ford Sunday Evening Hour orchestra in March 1942; an invitation that could not be kept because of the program's wartime suspension. In 1947, however, Willson's appeal to Ford lay less in his musical talents than in his "showmanship" and his promise of becoming "one of the next great personalities on the air."[46]

Willson described in cornpone prose the kind of entertainment his "Ford Showroom" would offer. "I'm going to talk about Iowa," he informed dealers in advance of his program's June 18 debut, "and the memories that everyone has, and the commonplace gripes, hopes, and plans. And I'm going to play melodic music on account of I think people may be tired of bands and singing groups that all sound exactly alike.'' Willson also proposed to have his ''talking people''—five vocalists chanting as one—do the commercials. Introduced by Willson on the Canada Dry show, the talking people had been voted the ''best advertising gimmick in radio'' by New York City College students in April 1947.[47]

The first few broadcasts of the ''Ford Showroom'' elicited mixed reviews. The company's dealers, who financed the ''Ford Showroom,'' were not overly enthusiastic about the program. The dealers enjoyed Willson's music, and wanted more of it but they were cool toward ''the attempts at comedy and the talking part of the program.'' Many eastern and metropolitan dealers declared that they were not interested in Willson's subject matter.

Kenyon & Eckhardt and Ford, which had agreed in May 1947 to present the Willson show through the 1947–48 radio season, were enthusiastic about the program. ''We think you have an awfully good property here,'' an agency executive wrote J. R. Davis in July, ''and one that you could live with for a long time.'' Davis concurred. Writing his dealers, he conceded that ''some'' of their number did not like the show, but emphasized that Willson was ''an immensely valuable property . . . and a most effective, hard-hitting salesman.'' But Davis's defense of the ''Ford Showroom'' fell on deaf ears. ''Widespread dealer opposition or apathy toward the Willson program,'' as an agency-client conference report put it, continued throughout the summer of 1947. Most of the dealers, wailed the report, unfairly compared the show with the long-established and highly successful Bob Hope, Fred Allen, Charlie McCarthy, and Fibber McGee and Molly programs.[48]

In mid-August, the company, bowing to dealer opinion, decided to close the show on September 24. Willson, for whom Ford and K & E executives had a high personal regard, was let down easily, the company placing advertisements in radio trade papers explaining that his show had been ''suspended because of materials shortages and a failure to secure a satisfactory time for his show.'' Willson went on to greater triumphs, writing the popular song, ''May the Good Lord Bless and Keep You'' in 1950 and the hit stage show, *The Music Man,* in 1957.[49]

As Ford and K & E were signing up Willson in May 1947, they were also concocting plans for a far more ambitious program, the ''Ford Theater.'' This program was designed to fulfill two company objectives: ''to get a program in the top fifteen as soon as possible,'' in Henry II's words, ''and certainly by 1949'' (the year the auto industry's sellers' market was expected to end); and to develop a program ''which would serve the company economically in the medium for the next twenty years.'' To attain these goals, K & E informed Ford, the company would have to buy a top-ranked program—and only rarely was one available for purchase— or build its own top-rated show, usually a time-consuming process. K & E added that a ''good dramatic program'' offered Ford its ''one best bet'' for developing a program which would provide ''both prestige and big audiences.'' The agency further assured the company that a Ford-sponsored dramatic program ''might'' reach radio's top fifteen list in its second year and that it ''would'' reach the list in its third year. Young Ford, fed up with his company's skipping from program to program during the previous two years and grasping at K & E's optimistic prediction, agreed to give the "Ford Theater" a three-year trial.[50]

Plans for the dramatic program were publicly announced in July. The show was to feature adaptations of "great plays, classic motion pictures, best-selling novels, prize-winning short stories, and an occasional musical." It also was to present six original plays, written by prominent dramatists commissioned by the company. Its cast, contrary to the policy of radio's leading dramatic programs, "Lux Radio Theater" and "Theater Guild on the Air," was to be comprised of "unknown" radio actors and actresses. The decision to "discard the venerated star system" stirred up "an unusual flurry of comment" within the broadcasting industry. Some publications applauded the "refreshing policy in casting" and predicted that it would give the show unexpected sparkle. But other publications questioned whether the "Ford Theater" could develop strong appeal without "name" actors and actresses. Actually, the company's decision to employ "unknowns" was prompted by one consideration: "star talent is more costly than is justified by the Sunday afternoon time."[51]

Kenyon & Eckhardt tried to engage Clifton Fadiman, moderator of the "Quiz Kids" program, as master of ceremonies for the "Ford Theater." But Fadiman wanted $1,500 for each appearance, and Ford was willing to pay only $1,000. The assignment subsequently went to playwright-producer-actor Howard Lindsay, star of the stage play, *Life With Father*. Since Ford, rather than its dealers, paid for the show, the company planned to divide the program's commercial time between institutional messages and product selling. After the opening show, however, a decision was made to devote almost all of the commercial time to selling. The program was scheduled on NBC from 5 to 6 P.M. (EST) Sundays, a "totally undesirable" time, but the best the agency could obtain in the intensely competitive scramble for network air time.[52]

Henry II welcomed listeners to the program's debut on October 5. Expressing the hope that the new series would "live up to the standard of entertainment set by the Sunday Evening Hour," young Henry explained that his company was offering a "dramatic show [rather than a musical program] because it seems that is what most people like best." The play itself, vying for listeners' attention with a crucial game of the World Series, was an adaptation of Mark Twain's "A Connecticut Yankee at King Arthur's Court." The show was panned by professional critics. "Twain," ran a typical review in the *New York Times,* "was subjected to a soap-opera rewrite . . . sounding a great deal more like a Norman Corwin script starring the Lone Ranger than 'A Connecticut Yankee in King Arthur's Court.'" Press reviews of subsequent broadcasts, according to reports forwarded to Ford by Kenyon & Eckhardt, were generally favorable; and the program, said the agency, "won kudos from many clubs, organizations, and educational institutions." But the Ford Company and its dealers were critical of the show. Both were highly dissatisfied with the Sunday afternoon broadcast time, and from December onward the company repeatedly tried to obtain a prime evening hour for the series. But its efforts were unavailing. The Ford organization also was keenly disappointed in the program's poor listenership. Despite these shortcomings, the sponsor maintained a stiff upper lip during the 1947–48 radio season, reiterating in January its intention to develop the "Ford Theater" into a show which would successfully project the firm on network radio for the next two decades. "Short of catastrophe," Henry II told Ford and K & E executives, "the Ford Theater will be given two years [he had originally said three] to prove itself."[53]

The program's lackluster first season called for a major overhaul for the 1948–49 season. The company, in fact, replaced the original "Ford Theater" with a rival dramatic program, "Studio One," which, sans sponsorship, had made a successful debut on the CBS network in 1947–48. Upon assuming sponsorship of "Studio One," immediately renamed the "Ford Theater," the auto maker was awarded prime CBS time for the program, 9 P.M. (EST) Fridays. Abandoning a nonstar policy for its shows, the company signed up Ingrid Bergman, Greer Garson, Bing Crosby, Ray Milland, Gregory Peck, and Lucille Ball. Many of the stars, like those on other Ford-sponsored programs, were paid with new cars.[54]

Ford officials started the 1948–49 season full of hope. Henry II, speaking to dealers in early October, admitted that the 1947–48 season "wasn't successful," but vowed to "make the Ford Theater one of the leading programs on the air, now that we're in a choice time spot." The first broadcast, in contrast to the program's debut in 1947, was greeted with rave reviews. "The performance" [of Madame Bovary], *Variety* typically observed, "made for an exciting hour of listening. The cast was excellent, notably Marlene Dietrich, Van Heflin and Claude Rains in the lead roles. The 'Ford Theater' has finally hit its stride and after a year's valiant but vain struggle to project itself into a big-time production gives every indication of shaping up as a definite click." Reviews of subsequent broadcasts, according to K & E's reports to the company, were equally favorable.[55]

The program's audience numbered approximately seven million early in the 1948–49 season, reached ten million within a few weeks, and levelled off at fifteen million at mid-season. Despite these impressive figures—and the fact that one of the program's broadcasts cracked the magic first fifteen ratings list (the show usually hovered around fortieth place in the standings)—the Ford Theater still had fewer listeners than "Lux Radio Theater" and "Theater Guild on the Air," to say nothing of its highly formidable broadcast-time competition on NBC, the Eddie Cantor and Red Skelton shows. The Ford organization, nonetheless, was pleased with the program's achievements during its second season and permitted K & E to tell its dealers, in December 1948, that the program "is an outstanding and recognized factor in radio . . . and is progressing, even beyond expectations, along the basic plans that were laid down for it over two years ago."[56]

Even as K & E was preening itself over the attainments of the revamped "Ford Theater," the agency was looking over its shoulder at a rapidly emerging competitor to radio—television. "In the years to come," K & E told the Ford organization, "the Ford Theater in radio will become the Ford Theater in television. But that is *in years to come,* and millions of automobiles must be sold by Ford Dealers before that time." "Big-time" radio during the 1948–49 season, however, was facing the beginning of the end. Milton Berle, appearing on television screens in June 1948, had quickly caught on with viewers in the thirteen cities served by the new NBC-TV network, and was prompting hundreds of thousands of Americans to stop at radio stores to be placed on the waiting list for a television receiver. Berle's success, the skyrocketing sales of television sets, and the rapid increase in television programming prompted K & E, in the summer of 1948, to recommend that Ford "enter television this year on a unified basis, rather than the hit or miss of sports events" (which the auto maker had sponsored on TV since 1946). Ford accepted the recommendation, introducing its first regular television show, the "Ford Television Theater," in October 1948. The hour-long video program, patterned after its radio counterpart, featured "name" entertainers and was telecast once a month in the seven cities linked by CBS's East Coast network; it was also shown on kinescope in Detroit, Chicago, and Los Angeles. Although the program was critically acclaimed, K & E—aware that television reached only a handful of people as compared to radio—played down the "Ford Television Theater" throughout the 1948–49 season, while continuing to advocate long-term sponsorship of the company's dramatic radio program. Ford, however, impressed by the success of its new video show and dazzled by television's potential, decided in May 1949 to cancel its radio show on July 1, and to expand its video counterpart. Thus the "Ford Theater," which was to have blasted its way into radio's "first fifteen" within two or three years and to have "carried the Ford banner on radio for twenty years," was phased out.[57]

In retrospect, K & E and Ford may be faulted for failing to foresee in 1947 that network radio was approaching its end. In 1947, however, virtually no one identified with radio—networks, stations, advertising agencies, sponsors, or entertainers— foresaw the onrush of television. In 1947 more than 18,000,000 radios were sold, fewer than a quarter-million television sets; and in March of that year there were only twenty-three sponsors of television shows. Not surprisingly, almost everyone thought that network radio, then enjoying its greatest prosperity and peak listenership, would endure for decades. K & E and Ford, until television began coming of age in 1948, thought so too. To the credit of the Ford organization, it did sponsor a continuing television network program a year or two ahead of the pack.[58]

As it discontinued the "Ford Theater" at the end of the 1948–49 season, the Ford organization also ended a more celebrated program—the "Fred Allen Show," sponsored by the company's dealers since January 1948.

In October 1947, when J. Walter Thompson informed Ford that it could acquire the highly popular Allen show for the company, the Ford organization regarded the news as almost too good to be true. As Kenyon & Eckhardt had told Henry II only six months before, programs of the Allen show's caliber were seldom available for sponsorship. But Allen's sponsor, Standard Brands, Inc., caught in a financial squeeze in the fall of 1947, was willing to give up the comedian's contract at the end of the year. If young Henry recalled that in May 1947 he had declared that he "no longer wanted J. Walter Thompson to handle Ford radio," he no longer felt bound by that statement. He had also said that he wanted a program among "the first fifteen as soon as possible," and Allen was almost at the head of the class. With Allen, JWT was thrice welcome to handle a Ford radio account. Kenyon & Eckhardt, swallowing hard, congratulated Ford's dealers for "bringing off one of the scoops of the radio business," adding that "no other show of Allen's calibre that also carried with it a premium broadcast time had been available for years."[59]

Fred Allen had been in radio since 1932, and had been one of the medium's most popular comedians since 1935. Specializing in satirizing events and foibles of the day, and endowed with a distinctive nasal twang, Allen was widely regarded as a "comedian's comedian." Jack Benny described him as "the best wit, the best extemporaneous comedian I know," and Edgar Bergen called him "the greatest living comedian." Novelist John Steinbeck considered him "unquestionably the best humorist of our time . . . a brilliant critic of manners and morals." Radio editors, who also admired his literate, acerbic wit, frequently rated Allen as their "favorite comedian" and his show as their "favorite program, the one you really hate to miss." Radio fans were vastly amused by his "feud" with Jack Benny, his very real feud with network officials, to whom Allen's nonconformism was galling.[60]

In 1947, Allen's program, which for a decade had been on or near radio's "first fifteen" list, was at the height of its popularity. On six occasions, including the week that Allen was signed by Ford, the show was rated No. 1 in Hooper's audience surveys.[61]

Allen's program, technically sponsored by the Ford Dealers of America, Inc., got off to a running start on January 4, 1948; and scores of dealers wired Dearborn in praise of the comedian's first broadcast. For months the Allen show rollicked along with high ratings, often being heard on more than 25 percent of the nation's radios. Allen's bubble burst, however, on May 23, 1948, when ABC lined up opposite the comedian the first of radio's spectacular giveaway programs, "Stop the Music." The new program had a simple format for winning a huge audience. Its musicians played a melody. At a signal, the master of ceremonies bellowed, "stop the music!" As the music was stopped, the announcer started talking by telephone with a listener. If he could name the song that had been interrupted, he was awarded cash and merchandise often valued at more than $100,000. The show quickly became the talk of the country. Tens of thousands of people refused to leave their homes between 8 and 9 P.M. Sundays, for fear that they would miss a telephone call from the program.

Allen's program, rated ninth by Hooper the week before "Stop the Music" went on the air, lost half of its audience and plunged to thirty-sixth place in the ratings in its initial encounter with the heavily publicized giveaway show. Four weeks later, pulling only 7.7 percent of the listening audience, the Allen show was accorded thirty-eighth place in the "Hooperatings." Meanwhile, "Stop the Music," opening with a nineteenth place rating, moved to second place by the time Allen went off the air in late June.[62]

During the summer of 1948, "Stop the Music" gathered momentum. NBC and Ford, worried about Allen's ability to compete with the giveaway during the 1948–49 season, tried to persuade the comedian to change his program's time. But Allen, a proud, stubborn man, said, " no!" On his first broadcast of the new season, the radio veteran "declared war" on his nemesis, offering to reimburse any of his listeners to the amount of $5,000 for any prize money or merchandise they might lose by tuning in the Allen show. On a subsequent program the comedian presented an "uproarious spoof of radio's Santa Claus Mania." Meantime, "Stop the Music" continued to flourish, attracting huge audiences by giving $30,000 worth of prizes, for example, to an Indiana beer salesman who correctly identified "Turkeys in the Treetop."

In the ''impossible position of trying to outdraw someone handing out dollar bills,'' the ''Fred Allen Show'' trailed ''Stop the Music'' in audience polls throughout the fall of 1948. In December, frustrated and embittered over the fact that listeners preferred a giveaway program to his literate humor, Allen announced that he would quit radio at the end of the 1948–49 season. ''It's a silly business to be in anyway,'' he added. ''Let the giveaway shows fight it out among themselves.''[63]

In early January 1949, NBC and Ford, in an effort to resuscitate Allen's show, moved the program up half an hour, to 8 P.M. Sundays. But this proved futile. ''Stop the Music'' continued to dominate its time slot; and Allen even fell behind his CBS competition, ''Adventures of Sam Spade.'' Ford, despairing of obtaining an adequate return on its huge investment ($877,500 annually for talent, $670,134 for network charges) and excited by the promise of television, allowed Allen's contract to lapse at the end of the 1948–49 season. When the program's demise was announced, NBC, to Allen's chagrin, received ''exactly fifteen'' letters of protest.[64]

With the demise of the ''Fred Allen Show'' and the ''Ford Theater,'' both within the same week, the Ford Company bowed out of ''big-time'' radio. The firm had spared no effort and little expense to succeed in the medium. It had, in fact, outspent its chief rival, General Motors, $4,709,342 to $4,298,342, during the 1945–47 period. Yet Ford's postwar experience with radio proved less than satisfactory. Except for Allen's show during the first half of 1948, the company had never backed a ''winner''—a show which Henry Ford and his associates considered worthy of the ''new'' Ford Company. General Motors' radio programming, Ford executives could note with cold comfort, fared no better than that of the Dearbornites.[65]

4

Although Ford's postwar reputation was not enhanced by its radio programming, the company's early entry into television gained the firm recognition as a video pioneer among sponsors of the infant medium.

At J. Walter Thompson's urging, Ford began mulling over the possibility of ''some kind of experimentation'' with television in September 1945. At that time there were only 5,800 television receiving sets in America, all but 800 of them in the New York area. In May 1946, the company and the agency began negotiating for telecasting rights for sports events in New York City, including activities in Madison Square Garden, professional and college football games, and boxing matches. Sponsorship of sports telecasts, B. R. Donaldson enthusiastically informed J. R. Davis, would bring the company ''leadership in the field of commercial television—another 'Ford First,' [an] opportunity to gain experience in the use of television and a knowledge of its value as an advertising medium at a time when costs are relatively low and there is no competition, [and] priority rights in Madison Square Garden television, as well as for outstanding athletic events.''[66]

On August 12, 1946, when the country still had fewer than 8,000 television receivers, Henry II and a phalanx of Ford, CBS, JWT, and Madison Square Garden executives, announced at a New York press conference that the Ford Company would sponsor telecasts of all Garden sports events, except boxing, during the ensuing year. These events, fifty-eight in all, included professional and collegiate basketball games, hockey games, track meets, horse and dog shows, and a rodeo. "It is the first time that any advertiser has signed to televise such a series of related events on an exclusive basis," announced the firm, "and makes Ford the leading advertiser in the commercial television field." Added Davis, "We are merely adding to a long list of 'Ford Firsts' in selling as well as engineering and manufacturing."[67]

Telecasting of Garden events under Ford sponsorship began over CBS's New York outlet, WCBS-TV, in September. That month, the company also contracted to sponsor telecasts of home football games of Columbia University and of the New York Yankees of the All-America Football Conference. The Yankees's contests were shown over WABD, a DuMont Television Company station. The company also arranged in September to sponsor telecasts of Northwestern University's home football games over Chicago's WBKB.[68]

Appraising its television activities at the close of 1946, Ford expressed itself as "most satisfied" with its "pioneering." Sponsorship of sports telecasts, declared a General Sales Department report, had furnished the company "considerable trade press publicity," established it as a leader in the video industry, and enabled it to obtain valuable television franchises. Seeking to build on its success, Ford authorized JWT to negotiate video rights for "sports packages" in each of the nation's six television markets (New York, Chicago, Philadelphia, Washington, Schenectady, and Los Angeles) and in "other television markets as they become active." The company left open the question of which kinds of sports telecasts to sponsor. "Out here" [in Detroit], explained advertising executive Frank J. McGinnis to a television executive, "we haven't even seen a television presentation, so we can't say what's good or bad."[69]

In 1947 Ford widened its lead as television's No. 1 sponsor of sports telecasts. In July the firm renewed its twelve-month Madison Square Garden commitment on a split-sponsorship basis, agreeing to sponsor thirty-five events, Maxwell House Coffee an equal number, and Knox Hats twelve. Ford also sponsored telecasts of wrestling and boxing matches in Los Angeles and cosponsored telecasts of the home games of four major league baseball clubs. The company was frustrated in its efforts to sponsor telecasts of important sports events in its home state, since the Detroit Tigers [baseball] and Detroit Lions [football] had sold their video rights to a Detroit brewery and the University of Michigan had offered television rights for football to Oldsmobile. Still, by mid-1947, in the vernacular of *Billboard,* the company had become "the first regular sponsor of full-time [sports] scanning on a multi-market basis."[70]

In late September and early October 1947, Ford cosponsored the "biggest show in television to date," the World Series. The company had considered sponsoring telecasts of the classic the year before, but backed away from the idea when sputtering auto production forced advertising cutbacks. Organized baseball, in any event, decided not to permit telecasting of the 1946 series. In early September 1947, however, Baseball Commissioner A. B. (Happy) Chandler announced that sponsorship rights for telecasts of the 1947 series could be bought for the "right price"—$100,000. Video executives promptly labeled the asking price as "very high," pointing out that the series' radio rights, which enabled a sponsor to reach an audience many times larger than that of television, sold for $175,000.

Only three companies expressed an interest in sponsoring telecasts of the series. Ford and the Gillette Safety Razor Company offered Chandler $60,000, each firm to pay half of the total amount. Ford also offered organized baseball $1,000,000 for rights to telecast the series over the next ten years. Both offers were rejected. Liebmann Breweries, Inc., of Brooklyn, then expressed willingness to meet Chandler's $100,000 asking price. But the commissioner, moving to high ground, rejected the Liebmann offer with the assertion that "it would not be good public relations for baseball to have the series sponsored by the producer of an alcoholic beverage." Finally, on September 26, four days before the series was to begin, Chandler sold the telecasting rights for $65,000 to "respectable sponsors," Ford and Gillette.[71]

The series was telecast by CBS, NBC, and DuMont over all eight television stations in New York, Philadelphia, Washington, and Schenectady, the only cities then connected by coaxial cable. Although there were only about 50,000 television sets in the four cities, an estimated 3,000,000 people jammed taverns and other public places and neighbors' homes to watch the seven-game classic. In addition, almost every daily newspaper in the transmitting areas publicized Ford's and Gillette's sponsorship of the games. Both of the sponsors were highly pleased with their series investment. Ford and JWT also congratulated themselves on having used canned (previously filmed) commercials, which were believed to have "come off" better than Gillette's "mikeside plugs."[72]

The company continued to sponsor sports telecasts throughout the country in 1948, a year in which sports events, because they were "both ready made and had proved box-office appeal," dominated video programming. The immediate success of Milton Berle's show in mid-1948, however, had convinced Ford (as well as other sponsors) as early as August that it should sponsor a continuing program rather than "hit-or-miss" sports events.[73]

Ford's first television program, "Ford's Television Theater," was introduced in October 1948 on a one-a-month basis. The Sunday evening programs were telecast "live" over CBS's seven-city East Coast network and by kinescope in three other cities. The first productions were condensed stage plays and motion pictures. Reviewing the third show, a play, "Night Must Fall," critic John Crosby, while praising Ford for a "fine job," typically observed that "a good deal of the suspense was drained away" when the production was chopped from two-and-a-half hours to one hour. Crosby also noted another chronic calamity of live shows: "one of the actors wasn't helped much by a stagehand (or somebody) who got in the way of the cameras in the climactic scene when he murdered the old lady." The first of Ford's television theater programs featured Lincoln as well as Ford or Mercury advertising in the belief that television sets "reside mostly in the homes of the mighty." "This point of view," noted Crosby, "would be disputed by a good many barkeeps." Considered a good investment by its sponsor, "Ford Television Theater" was presented twice monthly starting in October 1949, and was continued into the early 1950s.[74]

The company also sponsored telecasts of the United Nations' proceedings at

Flushing Meadow and Lake Success, New York, in late 1949. Henry II sounded an idealistic note in announcing plans to sponsor the telecasts: "Underwriting such a series is underwriting better understanding of the great role the United Nations is playing. . . . Better understanding cannot but advance the all-important cause of world peace and world cooperation. We are grateful for the opportunity of helping." Young Ford, in deference to the UN's wishes, eschewed commercials on the telecasts. "We want this program to be just right," he told the press, "and our definition of just right is for it to be precisely the way the UN wants it." Thus, mentions of Ford were limited to brief opening and closing statements, merely noting that the day's proceedings had been transmitted as a "public service project" of the company.[75]

The telecasts were carried by CBS into twelve cities in the East and Midwest between 11 A.M.–1 P.M. and 3–4 P.M. (EST) Mondays through Fridays—fifteen hours per week in all. In addition to covering proceedings of the General Assembly, the program also provided glimpses of Security Council and lesser committee meetings and presented interviews with delegates. Sponsorship of the telecasts, described by the *New York Times* as "the most extensive series yet undertaken by video," cost Ford $100,000, second only to the $175,000 paid by Gillette to sponsor baseball's 1948 World Series.

Ford's decision to sponsor telecasts of UN sessions was lauded by the press. "Not even the most exacerbated critics of commercial broadcasting," said *Broadcasting-Telecasting*, "can greet Ford's action with less than acclaim." The *New York Times*, noting that two-hour-long kinescopes of each week's telecast would be made available without cost to television outlets abroad, envisioned the televised series as the beginning of a "world town meeting, each listener hearing his own tongue and each seeing the same picture at the same time."[76]

The first few telecasts of "United Nations in Action," as the program was called, elicited favorable comment. "As entertainment," reported *Time*, which found "high drama, tense comedy, and a touch of slapstick" in the telecasts, "the United Nations was shaping up as better than anything else on daytime television." But as the sessions droned on, most viewers found the "long speeches and static drama . . . neither so funny as Milton Berle nor so exciting as baseball." Some set owners complained about "the tendency of opposing orators to repeat their arguments over and over again." Other viewers grumbled that "once a delegate finishes talking, he goes to sleep." Almost everyone eventually agreed with the *New York Time*'s assessment of telecasting at the UN: "the nature of the UN's business does not often provide lively looking."

The program nonetheless was continued until General Assembly's adjournment on December 2. Although "United Nations in Action" was anything but a hit with television audiences, Ford's $100,000 expenditure was worthwhile from a publicity standpoint alone. Moreover, in 1950, as frosting on the cake, the show was awarded a prestigious George Foster Peabody citation for "outstanding service and excellence" by the University of Georgia's Henry W. Grady School of Journalism and the National Association of Broadcasters.[77]

Ford's "experimentation" and trailblazing in television was historically significant. The firm was among the first dozen or so sponsors of telecasts. During

1946–47, it pumped more money into the new medium—$75,584.24 in 1946, $212,207.68 in 1947—than any other advertiser. Its investment was fully in keeping with Henry II's promise to project his firm as one of the most forward-looking companies in the land.[78]

The company spent a growing amount on advertising during the immediate postwar period, ranging from $8,131,322 in 1945 to $13,647,377 during the first nine months of 1948.[79] Ford's advertising and postwar public relations activities did not immediately affect sales, for the company readily marketed all of the vehicles it produced in the sellers' market which prevailed until late 1948. But the firm's promotional efforts revealed a flair and drive found in few other industrial concerns, created goodwill, a better understanding of corporate goals, and improved the company's position for the competitive race ahead.

Chapter 29
Twilight for Henry

During the last two years of his life Henry Ford resembled a blurred and faded photograph of his former self. Lights and shadows played over his mind. Alert one moment, he was bewildered the next. Occasionally he did not recognize relatives, friends, and employees. At a garden party he panicked when an old friend, Mrs. Henry B. Joy, waved from a distance and began to walk toward him. Turning to his chauffeur, Robert Rankin, he said, "I don't know that woman. Get Mrs. Ford and let's go." "Of course you know her," replied Rankin. "That's Mrs. Joy. She's been sick lately. Ask her how she is, and about her children." A few seconds later Ford chatted easily with Mrs. Joy. In October 1946, Henry and Clara were asked by a photographer to pose next to the Greenfield Village gates. Two pictures were taken less than thirty seconds apart. The first shows two smiling, interested people. The second depicts Henry as incredibly old and tired. The light was gone from his eyes, his face drooped; even his light gray hat seemed to have sagged. Ford was uncommunicative much of the time. He spent hours in the study with Clara, she writing letters, he sitting quietly. On a pleasure drive with Clara and the Fords' pastor, the Reverend Hedley G. Stacey, he said not a word, instead giving Stacey digs in the ribs to indicate that he caught the drift of the conversation. "It was very pathetic to see his faculties slipping away," Stacey said later.

More and more Ford clung to his wife, following her about like a troubled child. He accompanied her on her walks in the gardens and on her drives about Dearborn. When going by car, he repeatedly reminded the chauffeur of the scheduled departure time, and could not rest until settled into the rear seat beside his wife. Clara tried to keep her husband under constant surveillance. When he wandered out of sight, she would tell her servants, "We must find Mr. Ford!"

Physically as well as mentally, Henry Ford failed perceptibly during his final two years. He tired easily and often did not feel well. Sometimes he wore a shawl, and increasingly appeared to be an enfeebled old man. The foot racing at which he was so adept, the bicycle rides he so enjoyed, were things of the past.[1]

During the year-and-a-half of his retirement Ford rarely went to the company's administration building, and only occasionally visited a favored haunt, the Dearborn Engineering Laboratory. Henry Ford II, busily reorganizing the company, addressing dealers, and trying to get more steel out of Pittsburgh, did not visit his grandfather for weeks at a time. If the elder Ford had any foggy misgivings about what was going on inside the company, they never surfaced in public print.

470

Ford's outside interests, to the extent he had any, were handled by Clara; a longtime secretary, Rex Waddell; and the Ford News Bureau. The bureau prepared Ford's 1946 birthday statement, which was approved by Clara with the words, "We both think this will do." The bureau also screened media requests to interview and photograph Ford, none of which was granted. The media knew so little of Ford's failing health that CBS invited the old man in August 1946 to debate H. L. Mencken on the subject, "Are We on the Road to Permanent Recovery?" Waddell wrote back, "Thank you, but Mr. Ford has other commitments." In May 1946 the News Bureau did manage, however, to pose Henry and Clara in the 1896 quadricycle, with Henry Ford II standing nearby. The elder Ford, "pushed into place by Clara," appeared alert and happy in the photograph, one of the most widely published of the thousands of pictures taken of him.[2]

Old Henry generated little news during his retirement. But he remained of interest to his countrymen. John Gunther's 1947 edition of *Inside U.S.A.* devoted twelve pages exclusively to the motor magnate, and mentioned him on ten additional pages. Gunther gave Ford more attention than any other private citizen and all other Americans except for Presidents Roosevelt and Truman and politicians Thomas E. Dewey, Harold Stassen, and Robert A. Taft. In November 1945, a cross section of the *Woman's Home Companion* readership, when asked, "What five American men and women now living do you admire most?" rated only General Dwight D. Eisenhower, President Truman, Eleanor Roosevelt, and General Douglas MacArthur ahead of Ford. Two months later representative voters, invited by the American Institute of Public Opinion (Gallup Poll) to select the nonpolitical figure best qualified for the Presidency, gave only MacArthur, Eisenhower, and industrialist Henry J. Kaiser more support than the auto maker. In June 1946, a sample of Americans, when asked by Gallup, "What person living today in any part of the world do you admire most?," ranked Ford eighteenth. The motor king was the only businessman cited among the top twenty figures named in the survey.[3]

Ford took rides around Greenfield Village and the Dearborn area for as long as he lived, but made few formal appearances between 1945–47. He attended the Sunday Evening Hour's first concert of the 1945–46 season at Detroit's Masonic Temple on September 30, 1945, and went to a banquet at the Dearborn Inn on December 21, 1945, in honor of veteran Ford employees. Pictures taken of him at the banquet suggest that he was not alert. In Grosse Pointe, Michigan, on November 24, 1945, he attended the funeral of one of the Ford Company's twelve charter stockholders, John W. Anderson. Photographs taken of him outside the church depict a white-haired, wizened man who might not have known where he was. On May 26, 1946, fuller of face than in previous pictures, he attended a ceremony near the Willow Run plant at which a B-24 bomber was enshrined to the memory of Edsel. On June 15, in the Masonic Temple, he and thirteen other auto pioneers were honored by the Automotive Golden Jubilee Committee. Photos show the Dearbornite standing quietly next to Charles B. King and Ransom E. Olds. On June 23, he and Clara attended a wedding of a Grosse Pointe couple. As Clara talked with friends outside the church, her husband simply looked into space. On August 2,

Ford attended a party honoring his birthday at Dearborn's Ford Field, where he heard Edgar A. Guest read a poem, listened to 50,000 people sing "Happy Birthday," and accepted a silver plaque with a whispered "thank you." The honoree also visited one of the city's playgrounds, at which he was presented a cake. In early November the Fords watched the razing of the mooring mast for dirigibles at the former Ford airport; and two weeks later the couple observed the demolition of a company water tower in Dearborn. At the razing of the mast, a photographer snapped a picture of Clara and a disinterested Henry, a blanket over his legs. On December 19, Henry and Clara attended yet another Dearborn Inn banquet honoring old-time company employees. Pictures of Henry suggest he looked "lost." In early 1947 the Fords inspected a clay mock-up of the 1949 Ford car at the Dearborn Engineering Laboratory. Clara broke the door handle of the model when she tried to turn it. "It looked so real," she explained.[4]

Living quietly, the Fords spent the late summer at their Huron Mountain Club lodge in northern Michigan and most of February and March on their Richmond Hill, Georgia, plantation. En route to or from the plantation, they invariably visited Berry College, near Rome, Georgia, an institution which they had generously supported since 1924. At Berry on March 31, Henry Ford made his last public appearance. After Clara had been granted an honorary doctor's degree, Henry participated in a tree-planting ceremony in front of the Ford buildings. "He appeared to be well and quite enthusiastic," a college official later noted. "I said that I hoped his tree would grow to be the most beautiful on the campus. He looked at me, smiled in his natural way, and said, 'Well, Inez, it is off to a good start.' " Insisting that the tree be planted straight, Ford instructed his youthful helpers to reset the sapling before tossing in the first spadeful of soil. The slow-growing tree, marked by a metal plaque at its base, still graces the campus.[5]

Returning from Georgia in early April, Ford seemed in good physical condition. On April 7, his last day, his mind was clear, and he appeared interested in his surroundings. At the time the Rouge River was in flood, and while the rising waters did not touch Fair Lane, which was thirty feet above the normal level of the stream, they did partly cover the powerhouse a short distance downstream, and deprived the residents of telephone, heat, and electricity. Since Fair Lane's kitchen was without electricity, Ford ate his breakfast—for him an unusually hearty meal of oatmeal, prunes, bacon, toast, and coffee—in his chauffeur's cottage, supplied with power from outside the estate. "This is the best oatmeal I ever ate," Ford told the chauffeur's wife. "Please fix some more for my breakfast tomorrow."

In the early afternoon of a "pretty day," Ford called for his driver and set out on a tour of familiar scenes. The first stop was the powerhouse behind the Dearborn Engineering Laboratory, followed by a visit to Ray Dahlinger's former office in the laboratory. There Ford directed Rankin to telephone his grandson, Benson, who was out-of-town and could not be reached. Then Ford asked to be taken into Greenfield Village to inspect flood damage to the old riverboat, *Suwanee*. Finding the boat virtually covered by water, the magnate, sensing a challenge, chuckled and said, "We'll soon put it back on an even keel again." Leaving the village, Ford instructed Rankin to take him to the administration building; he wanted to see Henry II. Rankin absentmindedly began to enter the building's underground garage on an exit lane. Stopping, he told his passenger, "we're going the wrong way." "Let's go anyway and see what will happen," replied Ford, in a pixieish mood. The maverick vehicle created a commotion and yells of "Where are you going?"—until Ford was discovered in the car. Once in the garage, Ford changed his mind about seeing Henry II, and asked Rankin to drive him to the Greenfield Congregational Church, on the west bank of the Rouge River on Rotunda Drive. There Ford, without leaving the car, chatted with the pastor about flood damage.

Ford's next stop was the boat slip within the Rouge plant, where the founder looked over the twin iron ore carriers, *Henry Ford II* and *Benson Ford*. Pointing to the *Henry Ford II,* on which he and his wife had taken many trips to and from northern Michigan, he told Rankin, "That's my yacht." Ford then asked to be taken to the St. Alphonsus Catholic Cemetery at Schaefer Road and Warren Avenue. The auto king, wearing the bedroom slippers he called "clodhoppers," strolled amid the tombstones of old friends, and reminisced. Leaving this cemetery, he asked to be taken to the Ford family burying ground on Joy Road, west of Greenfield Road. "Well," he told Rankin upon arrival, "this is where they're going to bury me when I die. In among the rest of my folks." On the return to Fair Lane, via Greenfield Road, Ford was in good spirits. Delayed by a long freight train laboring on an up-grade, he said eagerly, "Let's see if this fellow is going to make it."

Swinging into the estate, Ford went directly to the malfunctioning powerhouse. As electrician Charlie Voorhees labored on the generators, the power snapped on. "Well," Ford chuckled to the electrician, "I'm going up and tell Mrs. Ford that I've been here and fixed it. That won't make you sore, will it?" Later he mentioned to the chauffeur, "You don't think Charlie will be thinking we're taking credit for fixing the lights, do you?" Rankin said he didn't think so. Soon thereafter the power failed again, and the mansion was without electricity, steam heat, and telephones as evening came on. Powerhouse engineer John McIntyre waded through twenty-eight inches of water in an effort to get steam up. Ford himself went into the mansion's basement to see what could be done. That evening, Clara read to Henry by candlelight before a wood-burning grate fire. The couple retired about 9 P.M., their bedroom illuminated by an oil lamp and flickering candles. At 11:15, Clara heard her husband call. He complained of a headache and a "dry throat." Clara called her maid, Rosa Buhler, and, saying, "I'm afraid Mr. Ford seems very ill," asked her to have the chauffeur summon her husband's physician, Dr. John G. Mateer.

"When I came into the bedroom I saw that Mr. Ford was dying," said the maid. "We propped him up and he put his head on Mrs. Ford's shoulder just like a tired child. He tried to fold his hands, as if in prayer. She kept saying, 'Henry, please speak to me.' I said to her, 'I think Mr. Ford is leaving us.' She seemed paralyzed. I felt his pulse and listened to his heart. I told Mrs. Ford, 'I think he has passed away.'" "The time was 11:40. Dr. Mateer, arriving about twenty minutes later, pronounced the cause of death a cerebral hemorrhage. Ford's body was removed from the estate at 4 A.M. In the pockets of the millionaire's suit were only a comb, a pocketknife, and a Jew's harp.[6]

In accordance with plans made two years earlier, Dr. Mateer immediately issued instructions for Henry II to be notified of his grandfather's death. Young Henry, according to the prearranged plan, was to be the sole person to inform the News Bureau of the elder Ford's death, and the bureau was to break the news to the press. Detroit's newspapers and the three wire services were informed of the arrangement, and were told that, if feasible, announcement of Ford's death would be made on a conference call so that no paper or agency would get a news break. Henry II's call to Charles E. Carll of the News Bureau was made at 12:55 A.M., April 8, at which time young Ford could only say, "My grandfather died at 11:40." Young Henry and Carll agreed that the publicist should call Fair Lane within the hour, by which time Henry II would have driven from his Grosse Pointe home through Detroit to Dearborn. Carll telephoned James W. Irwin, the company's public relations director, then set out for his office. Within thirty-seven minutes of having heard from young Henry, Carll had completed a conference call to the morning *Detroit Free Press* and two of the three wire services, and also communicated with Detroit's all-night radio stations. After contacting the media, Carll unsuccessfully tried to telephone Fair Lane. About 2 A.M., when he learned that Fair Lane's phones were out of order, he and Irwin set off for the residence, where they talked with young Henry and members of the household staff. Returning to the office, Carll and Irwin dictated and transmitted a memorandum on the circumstance of Ford's death. At the same time a press room was readied for the newsmen who would begin pouring in for the wake.

The Detroit offices of the wire services dispatched bulletins on Ford's death, followed by lengthy obituaries. The Associated Press's 20,000-word obituary, written and updated through the years by David J. Wilkie, was the longest and most widely used. Wilkie, long one of Henry Ford's favorite newsmen, was reporting on state election results when the death flash reached his office. He ground out Ford copy through the night and the following morning. Throughout the country Ford's death was the top news story of April 8. Newscasters blared the story throughout the day. Newspapers, under banner headlines, ran lengthy articles which focused on the setting of Ford's death, as well as the highlights of his life.[7]

Editorial tributes to Ford were overwhelmingly favorable, probably more favorable than for any other tycoon in the nation's history. Business publications spared few laudatory adjectives in eulogy of Ford; and newspapers, public opinion magazines, and the black press were almost as effusive in their praise. Ford was pictured as a patriot, philanthropist, philosopher, sociologist, reformer, economist, teacher, and, above all, as a man of simple tastes, a homebody. He was depicted as an inspiration to youth, as an "authentic" American, and as a symbol of individualism, of America's productive genius, of free enterprise, of America itself. Editorial opinion, moreover, almost unanimously agreed that Ford's career not only benefited the public, but that public service was the compelling motive which dictated the magnate's acts and decisions. Since Ford was said to be a man of the people, despite his greatness, many publications sprinkled their editorials with his maxims, making use of quotations which conformed closely to the favorable image they had chosen to present: "I have tried to live as my mother would have wanted me to," "Profits are a public trust," and "Competition is the great teacher." There was no mention of "It is pretty well understood that a man in the Ford plant works," "It's a good thing the recovery is prolonged," and "The cow must go."

Ford's errors of judgment and prejudices were glossed over by the general media; these were simply "traits that he shared with the rest of us." Along with the lavish praise, however, were a few sour notes sounded by the liberal, labor, and Jewish press. New York's *PM* stated that Ford's mind was a "jungle of fear and ignorance and prejudice in social affairs"; *New Republic* took the magnate to task for his production speedups, hiring of stoolpigeons, and having his "servicemen beat the ears off the organizers"; and the Communist *Daily People's World* ran a photograph of Ford receiving the Grand Cross of the German Eagle. A syndicated labor news service noted that "there was little mourning for the individualist antiunion auto maker in the Detroit area," and the *Detroit Jewish News*, recalling the "black marks" on Ford's record, observed that he had been "on the top list of the world's anti-Semites." Yet some labor and Jewish leaders had kind words for Ford. Thomas Thompson, president of the Rouge plant's huge Local 600, declared that Ford "stood out as a friendly beacon in a stormy sea" and that "a great man died on the banks of the River Rouge." Richard E. Gutstadt of B'nai B'rith expressed "deep admiration" for Ford's "great contribution to the American economy and to social relations." Black editorial opinion was summed up by the *Journal of Negro History*: "He endeavored to help humanity by offering men work at living wages and making it comfortable for them in his employment. In this respect he was a great benefactor of the Negro race, probably the greatest that ever lived."[8]

Scores of individuals, including six senators and congressmen, spoke out in praise of Ford. The remarks of Michigan's Senator Arthur Vandenberg typify those of his colleagues: "Mr. Henry Ford's death ends one of the greatest and most thrilling careers in the life of his country. It is the vivid epitome of what a man can do for himself and for his fellow men under our system of American freedom through his own irresistible genius and courage. He probably had as great an impact on his time as if he had been president of the United States." Alfred P. Sloan, Jr., chairman of General Motors, spoke for many businessmen: "The impact of Henry Ford's inventive and productive genius on the well-being of America was incalculable."

The *Ford Times*, as Sigmund Diamond notes in *The Reputation of the American Businessman*, had no need to scratch around for favorable quotations in presenting a postmortem "symposium" of comments on the motor maker's life. In contrast to the laudatory remarks about Ford, Diamond observed that the press had described John D. Rockefeller as "Old Skull and Bones," and said that the Reverend Harry Emerson Fosdick would be hard put to "think up a snappy funeral oration"; declared that publisher Frank Munsey had "contributed to the journalism of his day the great talent of a meat packer, the morals of a money changer, and the meanness of an undertaker, may he rest in trust"; insisted that J. P. Morgan "has done more harm in the world than any man who ever lived in it"; and expressed gratitude that "mankind is mortal, and that nature wisely provided that Cornelius Vanderbilt should not live longer."[9]

Abroad, Ford's death also generated an outpouring of editorial and individual comment, most of it favorable. "In Britain," reported *Time*, "they still gaped at the facts & fable of his wealth and power." The *Times* of London described Ford as a "great man" and predicted that he would be remembered as the "outstanding symbol of the age of growing American industry." A Hungarian businessman declared that Ford "would have made a great partner"; an Italian bricklayer said "If all owners had poured back the profits in their company like Ford, there would be no need for nationalization"; and a Swedish union leader stated that Ford would "find a credit account in heaven for the magnificence of his achievements." But not all foreigners praised the auto king. A Parisian biology teacher said his "system marks the beginning of modern slavery," and a Viennese Socialist newspaper said that his "production line . . . showed the ridiculous and tragic power of Fordismus over man." The Russians delivered perhaps the unkindest cut of all—they virtually ignored Ford's death. Of the end of the father of *Fordzonishko* [dear little Fordson Tractor], *Pravda* and *Izvestia* merely said, "A correspondent of Reuters Agency reports the death of the well-known owner of automobile plants, Henry Ford."[10]

Ford's death evoked a considerable display of public appreciation and affection in Michigan and throughout the auto industry. Members of the Michigan legislature paused "in commemoration of the passing of a great man," and Governor Kim Sigler ordered flags on state buildings to fly at half-mast until the funeral on April 10. Detroit's common council directed that a large portrait of Ford, draped in mourning colors, be displayed on the front of the city hall for thirty days, and that mourning posters be displayed on buses. All motorists in Detroit were requested by the council to come to a complete halt as Ford's body was lowered into the grave. The mayor of Dearborn proclaimed thirty days of official mourning. Ford plants were closed the day of Ford's funeral, and all other auto manufacturers ordered their assembly lines shut down for one minute on that day. Ford dealers nationwide closed their establishments the afternoon of April 10. About 7,000,000 workers participated in the demonstration of sympathy, according to the Automobile Manufacturers Association.[11]

Ford's body lay in state on the first floor of Greenfield Village's Recreation Building. Irving Bacon, the company artist who had studied Ford's face for more than three decades, examined the magnate's features for a final time. "He did not resemble the Henry Ford I had known," the artist concluded, "the iron-gray hair having bleached to white, the muscular cheek and jaw covered with soft-puffy flesh, and the chiseled nose more shapeless." Factory workers in overalls, fashionably dressed businessmen, and others stood in a mile-long queue to view Ford's body. Estimates of the mourners ranged from the *Montgomery Advertiser*'s 30,000 and the *New York Times*'s 70,000 to *Newsweek*'s 100,000 and *Time*'s 105,000.[12]

Ford's body, placed aboard a Packard hearse, was transported under leaden skies to St. Paul's Cathedral in Detroit. Hours before the funeral umbrellas bobbed along the sidewalks in front of the cathedral; and the curious hung out of windows, perched on roofs, and climbed trees to get a better view. More than 30,000 persons were milling around the cathedral as limousines dropped off the Ford family and Michigan's auto elite. Inside, Ford's $14,935 bronze casket sealed, Dean Kirk B. O'Ferrall bade the industrialist Godspeed on his journey. The service over, the

Packard carried Henry's body to the family cemetery. The coffin was lowered into a hole in the wet, clayey mud, and a heavy rain poured down while the police hustled 20,000 sightseers on their way and opened nearby streets to traffic. Cars sped within fifty-five feet of Henry's grave, charging the night air with the odor of vehicle emissions. The funeral was front-page news around the country, but was over-shadowed by an Oklahoma tornado which killed 154 persons.[13]

At the time of Ford's burial, the Ford cemetery, although within the city of Detroit, was surrounded on the east, west, and south by a ninety-acre parcel of Ford Company-owned land. This land had been zoned for heavy industrial use since 1940. In December 1947, however, an effort was made by Ford, the Chesapeake & Ohio Railway Company, and the Detroit Creamery Company to rezone fifteen acres for "limited industrial use." This move prompted area residents to advocate rezoning for residential use. During the ensuing squabble, construction man George Frischkorn declared that Henry Ford, when buying the property, had told him that he wanted to "retain the property around this cemetery. It is where my mother and father were laid to rest, and I expect to lie there too. I hope that some day it will be made into a memorial park." Frischkorn's claims were challenged by Ford attorney, Charles J. Fellrath, who said he had been told that "Mr. Ford did agree to sell the land for industrial use." Chiming in, the Chesapeake & Ohio declared that the fifty-five train movements daily through the area made it suitable for factory sites, but not for homes. The controversy simmered down only after the Ford Company announced in 1948 that it had no immediate plans to sell or improve the property; but when it did it would prevent its use by "steel mills, foundries, slaughter houses or other 'harmful' industries."

Concerned over the land's future use, Clara Ford, who for many years had deliberated with her husband as to how the cemetery might be protected from the onward march of urbanism, decided in 1949 to surround the burying ground with the ecclesiastical buildings of a living parish. Mrs. Ford set aside eight-and-a-half acres of land and donated $1,000,000 for the construction of St. Martha's Episcopal Church, complete with parish house, rectory, sexton's residence, and garage. Before her death in 1950, Clara participated in the planning of St. Martha's, which was dedicated in 1954. Mrs. Ford also provided for the remainder of the ninety-acre holding to be given to other religious institutions; and today the "church corner," as it is called, encloses the Islamic Center of Detroit, Rosary High School, Saint Vartan Armenian Roman Catholic Church, and Lutheran High School, plus an Episcopal-sponsored child society and home for boys. One religious group, however, after obtaining a parcel of land southwest of the Joy and Greenfield intersection, sold it in 1946 to a supermarket chain. In addition to the store built by the chain, apartment buildings and more than a dozen small business establishments have sprung up across from the cemetery on Joy Road. These businesses range from a nursing home and drugstore to a car wash, beer and wine distributor, and a service station, the night lights of which illuminate the cemetery's tombstones.[14]

The Ford burying ground, located on St. Martha's front lawn, is only eight steps from busy Joy Road. Measuring thirty-three yards along the highway, it is twenty yards in width. The plot is surrounded by a green cast iron fence, about three and a half feet high by the road, two to three feet high elsewhere. The three gates in the fence usually are locked, but visitors can step over the iron work without difficulty. Once inside, they can stroll amid the tombstones, find shade under evergreens, or rest on one of four wooden benches. Atop Henry Ford's grave, located near the center of the cemetery, is a low-slung white marble ledger stone, three and a half by seven feet, upon which is engraved a large cross and a simple inscription:

HENRY FORD

July 30, 1863

April 7, 1947

Henry's and Clara's graves initially were guarded around the clock to prevent desecration. "People," said Ford's niece, Catherine Ruddiman, a cemetery trustee, "were taking grass, dirt, branches, anything that could be moved." To eliminate the need for a guard and guardhouse and to provide permanent protection against vandalism, the Fords' bodies were exhumed, then reburied in a concrete vault to which a metal grille rising eighteen inches above the ground was anchored. The grille is unlocked only for grass cutting as well as on the anniversary of Ford's death. For more than two decades, children from Greenfield Village schools placed flowers on the Fords' graves on or near the anniversary of Henry's death. After the last of the schools closed in 1969, officials of the village continued the tradition.

Ford's grave is visited by only a handful of people, probably no more than ten a week, according to St. Martha's rector, the Reverend Edwin A. Griswold. By contrast, Ford's birthplace, removed from its original site, the southeast corner of Greenfield and Ford roads, to Greenfield Village in 1944, is visited by most of the 1,700,000 persons who annually troop through that tourist shrine. Few people, especially tourists, seem to know where Henry Ford is buried. For years the author has posed the question to his students at the University of Michigan. They invariably reply, "Greenfield Village," "Fair Lane," or, in giving up, "in Dearborn," or "somewhere around Detroit." It is probable, in fact, that not one out of 1,000 Detroiters can identify Ford's burial place, and that only a small percentage of those who reside in the vicinity of Joy and Greenfield roads are aware that one of the great figures of world history lies buried within a few hundred yards of them.

Ford's grave is probably much as the motor magnate would have wanted it. He might have preferred a more rustic setting, with a less busy street and fewer commercial establishments nearby. But as a person who looked back on his boyhood and early manhood with much fondness, his earthly remains probably rest comfortably in the tidy Ford burying ground, surrounded by family and oldest friends.[15]

Henry Ford's will was brief. He left his voting stock in the Ford Company to his daughter-in-law and four grandchildren, his nonvoting stock to the Ford Foundation. The family thus retained control of the firm. Estimates of Ford's estate (which some publications equated with the worth of the Ford Company) ranged to $700,000,000. But the government valued the firm at the time of Ford's death at $466,141,500, and the magnate's estate was reckoned at $80,319,445. The estate included a $26,500,000 personal bank account and $20.00 "due from the sale of hay" from a Ford farm.[16]

Clara Ford survived her husband by three years. Much of her time was devoted to charitable interests, receiving relatives and old friends at Fair Lane, and caring for her gardens. She also maintained an interest in Greenfield Village and Henry II's work. "Young Henry," she wrote a friend in late 1947, "is doing a good job." Although occupied, Clara was lonely. "I shall miss my companion this Christmas," she said in 1947, "as we have spent so many of them together." She gave to Dearborn's Christ Church the prayer book that Henry had given her on their wedding day. "I could not bear to think that it might be treated carelessly after my death," she told the rector. Suffering from a heart ailment, she entered Henry Ford Hospital a few days before her death on September 27, 1950. The day of her funeral Ford's world-wide empire paused for three minutes in tribute. In Detroit flags flew at half-mast, for the first time in honor of a woman. "The Believer" was laid to rest beside a dreamer who had once said of his mate, "If I were to die and come back to another life, I would want the same wife."[17]

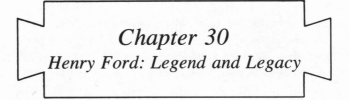

Chapter 30
Henry Ford: Legend and Legacy

Idolized by many Americans during his lifetime, Henry Ford remains a folk hero, his name constantly paraded before the public. Millions drive vehicles bearing his name; additional millions see the word "Ford" daily on cars and trucks and in advertisements. Local and syndicated news and feature stories related to the founder are so numerous that years ago the company's News Department, unwilling to pay for large numbers of clippings about him, instructed its press service to stop forwarding them. Many of these stories are published independently of the Ford Company; others are inspired by the firm, especially during anniversary years. Because of the company's drum-beating, Henry Ford received more publicity than any living businessman in 1953, the fiftieth anniversary of the firm's founding, and in 1963, the centennial anniversary of his birth. The founder has become a public relations asset to the company in the way that Robert E. Lee is to the South, Thomas Jefferson to the Democrats, Abraham Lincoln to the Republicans, and Martin Luther King, Jr., to the blacks; his words and deeds can be advantageously publicized as need arises. Ford undoubtedly will trot out old Henry during its seventy-fifth anniversary in 1978 and all future company/founder milestone years, despite mutterings of a few executives that "ancient history and Model T talk don't sell cars." Indeed, the company can scarcely act otherwise, so closely are the company's history and Ford's life intertwined.[1]

If Ford is generously mentioned in the daily and periodical press, he is publicized infinitely more in old-car and special-interest auto club and trade publications. These journals, few of which are cited in major literature indexes, are read by millions. A dozen Ford-related club publications are devoted exclusively to Ford topics; and two magazines have been published solely for Fordophiles. Multiple-make car clubs and old-car trade press journals try to run at least one story per issue on Henry Ford, his company, and its products since about 35 percent of their subscribers own Ford-made vehicles.[2]

Ford's image and legend are also enhanced by favorable treatment in major American and foreign reference works. An analysis of nine of America's leading encyclopedias shows that among all those listed an average of only sixty-eight individuals are accorded more space than Ford. These and a half-dozen other American encyclopedias consistently emphasize the positive aspects of Ford's career, while playing down or ignoring the negative features. They also have one other common characteristic: inaccuracy. Eight of the reference works, for example, state that Ford built his first car in 1892 or 1893 rather than 1896; another six, including *Encyclopedia Britannica,* erroneously report that all Model T's were painted black. The leading encyclopedias of Great Britain, France, Germany, Switzerland, and Indonesia, also analyzed quantitatively, on the average give more space to eighty-three persons (all deceased) than to Ford. Most reference works of non-Communist nations accentuate the brighter side of Ford's life. The British are told that Ford was a "strong pacifist . . . an anti-Semite . . . and an "inveterate enemy of trade unions," but more typically, Swedes are informed that the auto king "doubled his workers' pay" and that "nothing seemed impossible to him"; Spaniards, that he "spent large sums for welfare and learning"; Taiwanese that he "gave large bonuses to his workers"; and Koreans that he "advocated mass production through high wages, high efficiency, and lowering of prices." Encyclopedias published in Communist nations say nothing good about Ford, and exaggerate or fabricate "facts" about him. The Soviet Union's leading reference work emphasizes Ford's "introduction of the sweat-shop system of production." Hungary's major encyclopedia declares that the magnate was a "demagogue" and an "active sponsor of Fascist organization." The main thrust of Communist China's leading encyclopedia is that Ford headed a family which "controls forty-two percent of all of the capital in America."[3]

Ironically, Ford's reputation probably would have been enhanced if, like Pope John XXIII and John F. Kennedy, he had died after having set in motion sweeping changes. Had he passed on in late 1914, with his moving assembly lines humming, his Model T running away with the market, and his Selden patent fight, five-dollar day, and price cuts behind him, his star might now be brighter. Through the years the press and public would have speculated endlessly on the additional production and socioeconomic thunderbolts the man might have thrown; and such speculation undoubtedly would have improved Ford's image. Ford's reputation similarly would have been better served had he retired in 1929, at age sixty-six, leaving behind a mixed bag of additional accomplishments—the building of a great vertically-integrated company, the launching of the Model A, and the start of Greenfield Village/Henry Ford Museum, to name a few, while revealing his ignorance, anti-Semitism, and other assorted deficiencies. But rather than move offstage and permit Edsel, Sorensen, and others to run the company, he hung on until 1945, occasionally displaying visionary flashes and intuitive inspiration, but progressively falling out of step with the times and acquiring a "Model T image."

Still, Henry Ford maintains a reputation for greatness. In 1967, a nationwide sample of business executives, when asked by the University of Michigan to name the greatest businessmen in American history, rated Ford first, followed by Andrew Carnegie and Thomas A. Edison. In 1971, readers of *Nation's Business,* published by the Chamber of Commerce of the United States, ranked Ford as the greatest businessman in American history, followed by Alexander Graham Bell and Thomas A. Edison. In 1969, the auto maker was one of only 104 persons (and one of only two businessmen) cited in a University of Michigan poll of daily newspaper editors to determine the five "most admired" figures in all of world history.[4]

Numerous other indicators also suggest the esteem in which Ford is held. He is the only businessman, and one of only sixteen persons honored in the "Prominent American" stamp series. The twelve-cent Ford stamp, issued in 1968, features a portrait of the industrialist superimposed on the silhouette of a 1909 Model T. Ford has been memorialized in four halls of fame: the Automotive Organization Team Hall of Fame, Midland, Michigan; the Automobile Hall of Fame, Sebring, Florida; the Racing Hall of Fame, Los Angeles; and *Fortune*'s Business Hall of Fame. *Fortune,* in naming Ford a charter member of its hall in 1975, noted that the magnate's reputation "has gone up and down with the years and it is due for a rise; his great feat of reducing car prices looks even more miraculous now than it did [earlier]. He was the first to find a mass market for what we would now call a 'big-ticket' item. All over the world his name came to stand for the ability of industrial capitalism to lift workers and consumers to higher levels of prosperity." Ford probably will be elected, in time, to the Aviation Hall of Fame, Dayton, Ohio, and the Hall of Fame for Great Americans at New York University, although the latter body has admitted only two businessmen since its founding in 1900.[5]

The auto maker is one of five entrepreneurs honored in the Hall of Historic Americans at the Smithsonian Institution's Museum of History and Technology, in Washington. In addition, Ford's effigy is displayed in Washington's National Historical Wax Museum and in Potter's International Hall of Fame, the nation's oldest wax emporium. At first glance, the inclusion of the industrialist's figure may seem beside the point. But wax museums, for business reasons, must display effigies of familiar persons; and Ford's inclusion is a tribute to his fame. Similarly, a stone from Ford's birthplace has been placed in Rollins College's Walk of Fame in Orlando, Florida. The first step in Ford's "deification" occurred in 1964, when San Francisco's Grace [Episcopal] Cathedral installed a stained glass window bearing the magnate's likeness. Newly elected officers of the Dearborn chapter of the Early Ford V-8 Club of America, standing over Ford's grave in 1974, took an oath "to have the best V-8 chapter in the country, so help us Henry!" The anniversary of Ford's death summons Greenfield Village/Henry Ford Museum officials to his grave for wreath-laying; the anniversary of his birth draws the faithful to Fair Lane for a dinner program. If Ford is canonized, relics can be turned up on all sides. Six light brownish hair swatches from the octogenarian's head, swept up by Henry's barber in 1943, are carefully preserved by the barber's daughter, Helene Pierce, Dearborn, and are not for sale at any price. Conversely, the chair in which Ford was barbered while wintering at his Georgia plantation can be had from owner Wiley Carpenter "for the right price." The Henry Ford Room of the Henry Ford Museum abounds with Ford relics, among them four Jew's harps, bicycle pants clips, and patent leather dancing slippers; all will probably be displayed in perpetuity.[6]

Ford's greatness also may be gauged by the continuous references to industrial leaders and others as "the Henry Ford of their nation or sphere of activity." Thus Louis Renault has been called the "Henry Ford of France," Yen Tjing-ling "Free China's Henry Ford"; Konosuke Matsushita the "Henry Ford of Japan's appliance industry"; William R. Morris (Lord Nuffield), the founder of Morris Motors, the "Henry Ford of Britain"; Milton S. Hershey the "Henry Ford of the candy business"; William T. Piper the builder of the Piper Cub, the "Henry Ford of aviation"; Henry J. Kaiser the "Henry Ford of shipbuilding"; and Theodore Presser the "Henry Ford of music." It has even been predicted that there will be a "Henry Ford in space."[7]

Unlike Frank Woolworth or Walter P. Chrysler, Ford made no attempt to memorialize himself by building and naming for himself the world's tallest structure. But his Fair Lane mansion, given by the Ford Company to the University of Michigan in 1957, was open to the public from 1963 to 1966. The tours were discontinued following a disagreement between the university and the Women of Fair Lane—volunteer Dearbornites who conducted the tours—over whether funds raised should be used for restoration (the women's preference), or for heat, light, and other routine expenses. After an eight-year lapse, the tours were resumed by the university. Meanwhile, in 1966 the mansion was designated as a national registered historic landmark by the U.S. Department of the Interior. The house, now a conference and cultural center, interprets Ford's life only minimally. Devoid of the Fords' furnishings and other belongings, which were auctioned in 1951, it lacks the shrine-like atmosphere of Franklin D. Roosevelt's home at Hyde Park, New York, or Thomas A. Edison's residence in West Orange, New Jersey, which retain original furnishings and memorabilia and are dedicated to the glorification of the former occupants. Fair Lane does not even memorialize Ford in the manner that George Eastman's Rochester, New York home, now a photography and art museum, honors the camera king; or that Jay Gould's Tarrytown, New York castle, administered by the National Trust for Historic Preservation, memorializes one of America's leading robber barons.[8]

Henry Ford's greatest tangible monument is the Ford Motor Company, for years the world's third largest industrial company in terms of sales; America's fourth largest and the world's fifth biggest firm in terms of assets. The Dearborn enterprise usually ranks fifth in net income and in stockholders' net equity among American industrial companies, sixth worldwide, and is perennially the world's second largest industrial employer. Of the company's worldwide properties, the River Rouge plant, built by Henry Ford during the 'teens and 1920s, remains the most impressive. To this day the factory has been challenged in size only by the Volkswagen Works in Wolfsburg, Germany. Much of Henry Ford's older and second largest industrial complex, the Highland Park plant, remains standing. But production there has been virtually phased out, and most of the buildings are scheduled to be razed.[9] Henry Ford's third great factory, the Willow Run bomber plant, is intact, and, as a General Motors manufacturing facility, will probably remain in production for many years to come.

Many other company structures built during Henry Ford's reign remain in use, including the former Administration Building at Schaefer and Rotunda, Dearborn, now headquarters of the Lincoln-Mercury Division, and the Dearborn Engineering Laboratory, in which the Model A was designed, now the Triple E (Engine and Electrical Engineering) Building. Inside the Triple E Building, located behind the Henry Ford Museum, is a pencil-marked pillar against which the heights of Henry and Edsel Ford, Charles E. Sorensen, and several other company executives were measured in 1938. The former Lincoln factory, built at Warren and Livernois in Detroit in 1917–18 by Henry Leland and acquired by Ford in 1922, has been a Detroit Edison Company [electric utility] service center since 1956.[10] As noted in chapter 17, all of Ford's former village industries on the Rouge, Saline, Raisin, Huron, and Clinton

Ford Country

1. Site of Henry Ford's birthplace, Ford and Greenfield roads, Dearborn.
2. Fair Lane, the Fords' Dearborn estate from 1916 until their deaths. The estate originally was bounded by Michigan Avenue on south, Rouge River on west, Ford Road on north, and Southfield Freeway on east. The mansion is on a thoroughfare named Fair Lane.
3. The Fords' graves (Ford Cemetery), 15801 Joy Road, Detroit.
4. Dearborn Engineering Laboratory (now Engine and Electrical Engineering Building), facing Oakwood Boulevard, behind the Henry Ford Museum.
5. Henry Ford Museum and Greenfield Village, Dearborn; bounded by Village Road on south, Oakaood Boulevard on west, Penn Central tracks on north, and Southfield Freeway on east.
6. Ford Airport (now Ford's Dearborn Proving Grounds); bounded by Rotunda Drive on south, Oakwood Boulevard on west, Village Road on north, and Southfield Freeway on east.
7. Dearborn Inn, 20301 Oakwood Boulevard, Dearborn.
8. Rouge plant, Dearborn; bounded by Rouge River on south, Schaefer Road on east, I-94 on north, and Miller Road on east.
9. Ford Motor Company Administration Building, 1928–56 (now headquarters, Lincoln-Mercury Division), 3000 Schaefer Road, Dearborn.
10. Site of Ford Rotunda, across from 3000 Schaefer Road, Dearborn.
11. Henry Ford Centennial Library (also statue of Henry Ford), 16301 Michigan Avenue, Dearborn.
12. Ford World Headquarters Building, The American Road (Michigan Avenue at Southfield Freeway), Dearborn.
13. Lincoln plant (now Detroit Edison Company service center), 6200 W. Warren Avenue, Detroit.
14. Site of Mack Avenue plant (1903–4), Mack Avenue at Belt Line Railroad (697 Mack), Detroit.
15. Site of Piquette plant (1904–11), Piquette and Beaubien avenues, Detroit.
16. The Fords' home in 1891–92, at 4420 John R Street (formerly 618), Detroit.
17. Site of the Fords' home from 1893–97, originally 58 Bagley Avenue (now covered by Michigan Building).
18. The Fords' home from 1905–8, at 417 Harper Avenue (formerly 145), Detroit.
19. The Fords' home from 1908–15, 140 Edison Avenue (formerly 66), Detroit.
20. Henry Ford Hospital, 2799 W. Grand Boulevard, Detroit.
21. Highland Park plant; bounded by Manchester Avenue on south, Woodward Avenue on east, Detroit Terminal Railroad tracks on north, and Oakland Avenue on east.
22. Edsel Ford's grave (Woodlawn Cemetery), 19975 Woodward Avenue, Detroit.
23. Botsford Inn, 28000 Grand River Avenue, Farmington.

Map, courtesy of the Automobile Club of Michigan

rivers in southeastern Michigan are still standing. Most are in use as antique shops and community centers, highway maintenance facilities, or for non-Ford manufacturing (the Northville plant is the sole factory still operated by Ford).

In addition to Fair Lane, four dwellings in which the Fords lived remain. The square house, or "honeymoon house," which Clara designed and for which Henry cut the timber and helped build, was the couple's home from 1889–91. Ford always kept a watchful eye on the place, and in 1937 installed a young company chemist, Robert Smith, and his family in it. When the structure was threatened by highway expansion in 1952, the Smiths removed it a few miles west to 29835 Beechwood, Garden City. The house, now surrounded on three sides by two supermarkets and a launderette, was put up for sale in 1975 (asking price $40,000). Some of its furniture, including a desk, rocking chair, bookcase, couch, bed, and dining room set, dates to the Fords' occupancy. A vacant dilapidated duplex at 4420 (formerly 618) John R Street, Detroit, in which the Fords resided in 1891–92, likely will be torn down to make way for the Motor City's burgeoning medical center. An apartment house at 417 (formerly 145) Harper, Detroit, in which the Fords lived in 1905–8, has been well maintained. The residence which the Fords built at 66 (now 140) Edison Avenue, Detroit, in 1908, and in which they lived until 1915, is owned and occupied by the Temple of Light, a nondenominational sect which combines the teachings of Christianity and astrology.[11]

There are also other substantial monuments. The Ford Foundation, which Henry, Clara, and Edsel established in 1936, is the giant of foundation philanthropy. The Henry Ford Museum and Greenfield Village are among the nation's leading tourist attractions. The museum devotes three rooms to memorabilia related to the manufacturer's life. The crown jewel of these is Ford's first car, his 1896 "quadricycle." Detroit's Henry Ford Hospital, to which the Ford family gave $14,628,799 from 1914 to 1936 and to which the Ford Foundation pledged $100,000,000 in 1973, was rated as the nation's sixth best hospital by leading health authorities in 1967. The Dearborn Inn, one of the nation's first airport hotels, retains the charm that has made it a pleasant hostelry ever since it was opened by Henry Ford in 1931.[12]

Several institutions have been named for Ford, notably Henry Ford Community College and the Henry Ford Centennial Library, Dearborn's public library. The community college, founded as Fordson Junior College in 1938, adopted Ford's name in 1952. The institution moved its campus onto seventy-five acres of Fair Lane donated by the Ford Company in the mid-1950s. The library, at 16301 Michigan Avenue, owes its existence to a 15.3-acre land grant by the Ford Company and two gifts totaling $3,500,000 from the Ford Foundation. The library commemorates the 100th anniversary of Henry Ford's birth (1963), but was not opened until 1969. A life-size statue of Ford, financed by $50,000 in private gifts, mostly from Dearbornites, was installed in front of the library in 1975. Seven high, junior high, and elementary schools in the Detroit area also have been named for Ford: two each in Dearborn and Detroit and one each in Highland Park, Westland, and Willow Run Village. Dearborn schools also have been named for Clara, Edsel, and Ford's brother, William.[13]

In addition to the Dearborn Inn, two other notable inns associated with Henry Ford remain in operation: the Botsford Inn, Farmington, Michigan, where Henry and Clara danced in the 1880s, and the Wayside Inn, South Sudbury, Massachusetts, the nation's oldest inn. Both hostelries were restored by the Fords in 1924. Wayside's picturesque gristmill, built by Ford in 1929, still grinds flour; and its Martha-Mary Chapel, dedicated by Henry and Clara in 1940 as a memorial to their respective mothers, has been preserved. Similar memorial chapels still stand in Greenfield Village, Richmond Hill, Georgia (one for blacks, one for whites), and in Trenton and Brighton, Michigan. The Trenton structure originally stood in Macon, Michigan; the Brighton chapel initially was a part of Dearborn's Camp Legion.[14]

The Fords' home in Fort Myers, Florida, occupied during the late winter months from the 'teens until 1934, was sold in 1945. It is now a private residence. Between the house and Edison's winter home is Friendship Walk, made up of stones etched with the names of Edison's and Ford's friends. The stone representing Ford is flat, smooth, and nameless—the way Ford wanted it. The Richmond Hill, Georgia, plantation home visited regularly by the Fords from the mid-1930s until shortly before their deaths, was sold by Ford interests in 1951. The mansion was allowed to deteriorate in the 1960s and 1970s, but its owner, a Long Island, New York realtor, has announced plans to restore the house and convert its grounds into the home course of the Ladies Professional Golf Association. Summer "cottages" leased by the Fords in Harbor Beach, Michigan, on Lake Huron, during the 'teens and 1920s, and at Big Bay, Michigan's Huron Mountain Club, on Lake Superior, during the 1930s and 1940s are occupied by successor families. The Big Bay Hotel, restored by Ford at a cost of $550,000 in 1944, and in which the Fords maintained a seldom-used suite, still stands. Sold by Ford interests in 1951, the hostelry, locale of part of the motion picture, *Anatomy of a Murder,* was renamed Thunder Bay Inn in 1959. One of the largest hotels in northern Michigan, the inn has been vacant since 1963. Ford's mid-nineteenth century Greek Revival farmhouse in Macon, once the capital of Ford's southeastern Michigan rural empire, has been well maintained by its private owners. Ford often stayed overnight in the house, rather than drive fifty miles back to Dearborn.[15]

Henry Ford's native community has a plethora of minor reminders of the auto king's life. Major streets leading into Dearborn are marked with signs of welcome, identifying the community as the "Home Town of Henry Ford." Three of the State of Michigan's five Ford-related historical markers are located in Dearborn. One is at Ford and Greenfield roads, the site of Henry Ford's birth (the house in which Ford was born was removed to Greenfield Village by the auto maker in 1944); a second, in front of the Henry Ford Museum, discusses Ford's interest in education and history; and a third, in front of the Dearborn Inn, across from the old Ford Airport, recalls Ford's contribution to aviation. Ford Field, site of the huge parties given for the auto king by Dearbornites on his seventy-fifth and eighty-third birthdays, serves as one of the community's major recreation facilities. A four-feet-high stone memorial to Henry and Edsel Ford, erected in 1948 by residents of Springwells Park subdivision, popularly known as the Foundation [the Ford Foundation developed the residential-commercial complex] stands near Rotunda Drive and Greenfield Road. Atop the monument is a metal strip which reads, "The Shadow Passes—Light Remains."[16]

Outside of Dearborn, in southeastern Michigan, Ford's name has been memorialized in several ways. Detroit's Henry and Edsel Ford Auditorium, financed by Ford and Mercury dealers, the Ford family, and the City of Detroit in 1956, is part of the Civic Center, and is the home of the Detroit Symphony Orchestra. State of Michigan markers call attention to the Highland Park plant and the Botsford Inn. A City of Detroit plaque marks 58 Bagley Avenue, where Ford built his first car. Since 1926, the site has been covered by a huge office edifice, the Michigan Building. The site of the Ford Company's first plant, on Mack Avenue, is unmarked; a scaled-down reconstructed version of the factory stands in Greenfield Village. In northern Michigan, Michigan Technological University created the Ford Forestry Center in 1954, after the Ford Company donated the village of Alberta with its sawmill and 1,703 acres of adjacent timberland to the institution. Roads have been named for Ford in Dearborn; Detroit; Highland Park; Richmond Hill, Georgia; Sidnaw, in northern Michigan; and Garnet, California.[17]

Abroad, one of three buildings of the Uberaba unit of Brazil's National Service of Industrial Training has borne Ford's name since 1928. Fordlandia, Ford's former rubber-growing community on the Tapajós River in Brazil's state of Para, is now administered by the Brazilian government. The community is the only one ever named for Ford, except for Fordson, which was incorporated into Dearborn in 1929. Since 1948, a life-size statue of the auto king has stood on the banks of the Thames River, in front of Ford of England's Dagenham factory. The Henry Ford Bau, so named despite objection from the Ford Foundation, which financed the structure, has been a part of the Free University of Berlin since 1948.[18]

Other tangible reminders of Henry Ford are an estimated 300,000 surviving Model T's, much larger numbers of Model A's and early V-8's, and lesser numbers of Mercurys, Lincolns, Lincoln Zephyrs, and Lincoln Continentals produced during the auto magnate's reign. Many of these cars have been viewed by millions of people in museums; many others are constantly on display in parades and tours and at old-car meets. Most of these carefully preserved vehicles, whether owned by individuals or museums, seem likely to outlast the massive plants in which they were built.

How will Ford be regarded in the twenty-first century or 1,000 years from now? Niven Busch, Jr., writing in 1930, suggested that "if it were possible to preserve alive, for the interests of history, one man from each century and country— not, of course, the best or wisest, but the one who represented most thoroughly the hopes, crudities, background, and achievements of his place—no one could better represent this time and the United States than Henry Ford." General Motors' great inventor, Charles F. Kettering, observed in 1943 that "a thousand years from now, when the Churchills and the Roosevelts are but footnotes in history, Henry Ford will loom as the most significant figure of our age."[19] Ford's future reputation rests, of course, not only on his achievements, but on future value systems as well. The auto king played a key role in putting the nation on wheels and providing greater abundance for millions. But have these millions become too dependent on spinning vehicle and factory wheels, and, if so, what will be the consequences? Time, as the cliché has it, will tell; and Ford, perhaps more than any other mortal, will be judged accordingly.

The auto maker, in any event, will probably continue to receive major attention in encyclopedias and history texts. As the years pass and perspective is gained, his faults will seem a part of the general ignorance and gullibility of an adolescent civilization. His blunders and misdeeds will arouse less interest; they already have. The best-remembered fact of his life will be his great achievement. By preaching high-volume production, low prices, and universal consumption, he became the key figure in a far-reaching revolution. He actually did help remold the world according to his vision.

Of his great company, he said to Edsel one day, "Well, we'll build this as well as we know how, and if we don't use it, somebody will use it. Anything that is good enough will be used." Because of its founder, the Ford Company has today as rich and valuable a heritage as any commercial organization on earth, perhaps richer than any other. With the exception of Coca-Cola, the Ford brand name and trademark are the best known in the world today.[20] Henry Ford built well.

As for Ford's public image, it undoubtedly will rise and fall through the years. His legend and legacy will live on.

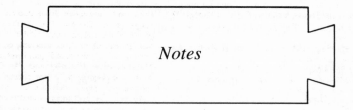

Notes

The names of four newspapers which are cited repeatedly in the notes are abbreviated as follows: *Detroit Free Press* (DFP), *Detroit News* (DN), *Detroit Times* (DT), and *New York Times* (NYT). Ford Motor Company is referred to as FMC; General Motors Corporation as GM. Two advertising agencies, J. Walter Thompson and Kenyon & Eckhardt, are cited as JWT and K & E. Full facts of publication are presented once for books and articles cited ten or more times, these references are abbreviated thereafter. For all other books and articles, full facts of publication are furnished the first time the entry appears in a chapter. All correspondence, documents, clip books, and other data cited by accession and box number are in the Ford Archives, a part of Dearborn's Henry Ford Museum. The clip books comprise Acc. 7.

Books cited ten or more times, by order of appearance, are: chapter 1, Keith Sward, *The Legend of Henry Ford* (New York: Rinehart & Company, Inc., 1948); M. M. Musselman, *Get a Horse! The Story of the Automobile in America* (Philadelphia: J. B. Lippincott Company, 1950); E. D. Kennedy, *The Automobile Industry: The Coming of Age of Capitalism's Favorite Child* (New York: Reynal & Hitchcock, 1941); Allan Nevins and Frank Ernest Hill, *Ford: The Times, the Man, the Company* (New York: Charles Scribner's Sons, 1954); William A. Simonds, *Henry Ford: His Life–His Work–His Genius* (Indianapolis: The Bobbs-Merrill Company, 1943); chapter 2, Harry Barnard, *Independent Man: The Life of Senator James Couzens* (New York: Charles Scribner's Sons, 1958); Roger Burlingame, *Henry Ford* (New York: The New American Library, 1954); Philip Van Doren Stern, *The Story of the Fabulous Model T Ford Tin Lizzie* (New York: Simon and Schuster, 1955); Allan Nevins and Frank Ernest Hill, *Ford: Expansion and Challenge 1915–1933* (New York: Charles Scribner's Sons, 1957; chapter 3, Charles E. Sorenson with Samuel T. Williamson, *My Forty Years with Ford* (New York: W. W. Norton & Company, Inc., 1956); Charles Merz, *And Then Came Ford* (Garden City, N.Y.: Doubleday, Doran & Company, Inc., 1929); Allan L. Benson, *The New Henry Ford* (New York: Funk & Wagnalls Company, 1923); chapter 4, Mark Sullivan, *Our Times The United States 1900–1925*, 4, *The War Begins 1909–1914* (New York: Charles Scribner's Sons, 1937); Samuel S. Marquis, *Henry Ford: An Interpretation* (Boston: Little, Brown, and Company, 1923); William C. Richards, *The Last Billionaire* (New York: Charles Scribner's Sons, 1948); chapter 5, Garet Garrett, *The Wild Wheel* (New York: Pantheon Books, 1952); Harry Bennett, as told to Paul Marcus, *We Never Called Him Henry* (New York: Fawcett Publications, Inc., 1951); chapter 14, Allan Nevins and Frank Ernest Hill, *Ford: Decline and Rebirth 1933–1962* (New York: Charles Scribner's Sons, 1962); chapter 15, *The Army Air Forces in World War II*, Office of Air Force History (eds., Wesley Frank Craven and James Lee Cate) 6 vols., Chicago, 1948–58, 6 (*Men and Planes*).

Articles cited more than ten times are: chapter 6, "The Ford Heritage," *Fortune* 29 (June 1944); chapter 13, Sidney Fine, "The Ford Motor Company and the N.R.A.," *Business History Review* 32 (Winter 1958).

Chapter 1

1. N.S.B. Gras, "Shifts in Public Relations," *Bulletin of the Business Historical Society* 19 (Oct. 1945), 113–14. Vanderbilt denied having made the statement which was carried in the press all over the world. In any event, the quotation was generally regarded as an accurate reflection of the magnate's attitude toward the public. Fred L. Black, "History and Growth of Public Relations in America," *Michigan Business Review* 6 (May 1954), 1.

2. Eric F. Goldman, *Two-Way Street: The Emergence of Public Relations Counsel* (Boston: Bellman Publishing Company, Inc., 1948), 3.

3. National Automobile Chamber of Commerce, *Facts and Figures of the Automobile Industry* (New York: National Automobile Chamber of Commerce, 1926), p. 11 (size of auto industry). Early volumes of *Horseless Age*, America's first automobile publication, which was introduced in November 1895, contain hundreds of automobile advertisements and references to automotive contests, exhibitions, press functions, and promotional literature. The best single volume dealing with the auto industry's early sales-

promotion and advertising activities is Rudolph E. Anderson's *The Story of the American Automobile* (Washington: Public Affairs Press, 1950).

4. Lawrence H. Seltzer, *A Financial History of the American Automobile Industry: A Study of the Ways in Which the Leading American Producers of Automobiles Have Met Their Capital Requirements* (Boston: Houghton Mifflin Company, 1928), p. 3; Henry Ford, in collaboration with Samuel Crowther, *My Life and Work* (Garden City, N.Y.: Garden City Publishing Co., Inc., 1922), p. 36.

5. Seltzer, *Automobile Industry*, pp. 3, 91; Keith Sward, *The Legend of Henry Ford* (New York: Rinehart & Company, Inc., 1948), p. 14; C.G. Sinsabaugh, "The Melting Pot of Design," *Automobile Trade Journal* 29 (Dec. 1, 1924), 230; M.M. Musselman, *Get a Horse! The Story of the Automobile in America* (Philadelphia: J.B. Lippincott Company, 1950), p. 200.

6. *Horseless Age* 1 (Jan. 1896), 29–33. On the strength of the victory, the Duryea vehicle toured the country in 1896 as the feature attraction of Barnum and

Bailey's "Greatest Show on Earth." *Ibid.*, p. 35; Arthur Pound, *The Turning Wheel* (Garden City, N.Y.: Doubleday, Doran & Company, Inc., 1934), p. 36 called the race "the first red-hot automotive news."

7. *Horseless Age* 1 (June 1896), 12; 1 (Sept. 1896), 6–7; Musselman, *Get a Horse!*, pp. 38–39.

8. *Horseless Age* 4 (Apr. 5, 1899), 34; 11 (Apr. 1897), 4–7; E.D. Kennedy, *The Automobile Industry: The Coming of Age of Capitalism's Favorite Child* (New York: Reynal & Hitchcock, 1941), p. 12.

9. Musselman, *Get a Horse!*, p. 44; *Horseless Age* 1 (Nov. 1896), 17; 11 (Feb. 1897), 12.

10. *Horseless Age* 2 (May 1897), 7 (speed record for the mile); Musselman, *Get a Horse!*, p. 44; Merril Denison, *The Power To Go* (New York: Doubleday, 1956), pp. 97, 111; Chris [C.G.] Sinsabaugh, *Who, Me? Forty Years of Automobile History* (Detroit: Arnold-Powers, Inc., 1940), p. 228. Winton, incidentally did not regard himself as a professional racer, but as a manufacturer. *Horseless Age* 8 (Nov. 13, 1901), 708.

11. Allan Nevins, in collaboration with Frank Ernest Hill, *Ford: The Times, the Man, the Company* (New York: Charles Scribner's Sons, 1954), pp. 149, 156–57.

12. Nevins and Hill, *Ford: The Times*, p. 167; *Horseless Age* 3 (Nov. 1898), 23.

13. Nevins and Hill, *Ford: The Times*, pp. 172–76.

14. The secretary, Frank R. Alderman, was frequently quoted in news stories. The mention of Ford was in the *Detroit Free Press*, Aug. 19, 1899, which simply referred to him as "superintendent of the works."

15. Ford's shyness, initial modesty, and difficulty in speaking in public will be discussed in a later connection. The interview appears in the *Detroit News-Tribune*, Feb. 4, 1900.

16. Nevins and Hill, *Ford: The Times*, pp. 190–91.

17. Nevins and Hill, *Ford: The Times*, pp. 191–94, 199, 202, 204. Ford seems to have entertained no illusions regarding his racing prowess, saying after the event "Put Winton in my car and it will beat anything in the country." *Ibid.*, p. 205; Anderson, *Story of American Automobile*, p. 145.

18. DN, Oct. 11, 1901.

19. Malcolm W. Bingay, "Get a Horse," *Saturday Evening Post* 212 (June 29, 1940), 72.

20. Nevins and Hill, *Ford: The Times*, pp. 206, 210.

21. *Ibid.*, pp. 209–11, 213. The Henry Ford Company was reorganized into the Cadillac Automobile Company. John B. Rae, *American Automobile Manufacturers The First Forty Years* (Philadelphia: Chilton Company, 1959), pp. 33–34.

22. William A. Simonds, *Henry Ford: His Life—His Work—His Genius* (Indianapolis: Bobbs-Merrill Company, 1943), pp. 73–76; Ford and Crowther, *Life and Work*, pp. 50–51.

23. *Automobile and Motor Review* 7 (Nov. 1, 1902), 12; Simonds, *Henry Ford*, p. 76 (amount of publicity received by the race); William F. Nolan, "You Knew Him...Barney Oldfield," *Automobile Quarterly* 1 (Spring 1962), 23–24; Nevins and Hill, *Ford: The Times*, pp. 217–18.

24. Nevins and Hill, *Ford: The Times*, pp. 225–27, 229, 237–39.

Chapter 2

1. DN, *Detroit Journal*, and DFP, June 19, 1903; *Horseless Age* 11 (Jan. 17, 1903), 712; *Motor Age* 3 (June 25, 1903), 11; F.M. Dampman, "Detroit—the Largest Producer of Automobiles in the World," *Cycle and Automobile Trade Journal* 7 (June 1, 1903), 56–57. The Model A was the only car displayed in the United States exhibit at the Brussels World's Fair of 1958. Considerable criticism of the administration's choice of display items, including the Model A, was expressed by various American visitors to the fair. George V. Allen, director of the U.S. Information Agency, defended the selection of the antique car over contemporary models on the grounds "you can go out on the streets anytime and see plenty of our new ones." NYT, June 18 and 25, 1958.

2. Automobile Club of Michigan, "Tallyho": Being the Roll Call of the Horseless Carriages (Detroit: Automobile Club of Michigan, n.d. [1946]); C. B. Glascock, *Motor History of America; or, The Gasoline Age* (Los Angeles: F. Clymer, 1937), pp. 296–342.

3. James Rood Doolittle, *The Romance of the Automobile Industry,* (New York: Klebold Press, 1916), pp. 37–38; Kennedy, *Automobile Industry*, p. 11; Nevins and Hill, *Ford: The Times*, pp. 250, 284; Ralph C. Epstein, *The Automobile Industry Its Economic and Commercial Development* (Chicago: A.W. Shaw and Co., 1928), p. 353; Musselman, *Get a Horse!*, pp. 24–25. The excellent treatment of the Selden patent suit in *Ford: The Times* which is cited extensively in the following discussion, was based on research conducted by William Greenleaf, a research associate of Nevins and Hill. Greenleaf's definitive study was published under the title, *Monopoly on Wheels: Henry Ford and the Selden Automobile Patent* (Detroit: Wayne State University Press, 1961).

4. Nevins and Hill, *Ford: The Times*, pp. 284, 98–100, 157, 289–94.

5. *Ibid.*, pp. 295–96. Ford was told that his concern was nothing but an "assemblage plant"—anathema to the licensed group. Actually many of the ALAM's members still had that character, and none made machines without drawing for some elements on parts dealers. Ford also was informed that when he obtained his own plant and became a factor in the industry he would be welcome to join the ALAM, inasmuch as the type of car he was then making was not being turned out by any of the association's members.

6. *Ibid.*, p. 298; DFP, July 28, 1903.

7. Nevins and Hill, *Ford: The Times*, pp. 299–301.

8. Lawrence H. Seltzer, *A Financial History of the American Automobile Industry: A Study of the Ways in Which the Leading American Producers of Automobiles Have Met Their Capital Requirements* (Boston: Houghton Mifflin Company, 1928), p. 41; Eric F. Goldman, *Two-Way Street: The Emergence of Public Relations Counsel* (Boston: Bellman Publishing Company, Inc., 1948), p. 4.

9. Nevins and Hill, *Ford: The Times*, pp. 284–85; *Detroit Journal*, Oct. 24, 1903.

10. Musselman, *Get a Horse!*, pp. 24–25, 126–31.

11. Harry Barnard, *Independent Man: The Life of Senator James Couzens* (New York: Charles Scribner's Sons, 1958), p. 57; *Ford Times* 1 (May 15, 1908), 16; Nevins and Hill, *Ford: The Times*, pp. 293, 646. On an $850 Ford—the cost of the Model A runabout in 1903 and of the Model T touring car in 1908—the patent fee would have been $10.63 prior to June 1908 and $6.80 after that month, when the royalty percentage was reduced from 1.25 percent to .80 percent of the sales price.

12. Frederick C. Russel, "When Advertising Turned the Tide in the Automobile Industry," *Advertising & Selling* 9 (July 13, 1927), 52.

13. *Wall Street Journal*, Oct. 10, 1925; Roger Burlin-

game, *Henry Ford* (New York: The New American Library, 1954), p. 38.

14. Nevins and Hill, *Ford: The Times*, p. 303. Detroit newspapers, which probably had more interest in the Selden suit than any other metropolitan press, did not give the case front-page treatment until its conclusion. The vast nonauto-buying public was probably not overly aware of the litigation.

15. Ralzemond A. Parker to FMC, Jan. 2, 1906, Acc. 2, Box 37, Ford Motor Company Archives, Dearborn, Mich.; (hereafter all correspondence, documents, and other data cited by accession and box number are in the Ford Archives); DFP, Jan. 13, 1907.

16. Nevins and Hill, *Ford: The Times*, p. 319; *Motor Age* 9 (June 14, 1906), 5. The AMCMA also arranged public exhibitions of its members' cars and promoted races. Nevins and Hill, *Ford: The Times*, p. 319.

17. DFP, Jan. 13, 1907.

18. Nevins and Hill, *Ford: The Times*, pp. 307, 313; *Motor Age* 12 (Sept. 12, 1907), 7.

19. Nevins and Hill, *Ford: The Times*, pp. 321, 420–24, 426–28; Musselman, *Get a Horse!*, p. 131.

20. Nevins and Hill, *Ford: The Times*, pp. 429–30; *Motor Age* 17 (Mar. 3, 1910), 7.

21. Nevins and Hill, *Ford: The Times*, pp. 424, 430. Ford said later that fewer than fifty buyers asked for bonds. Henry Ford, in collaboration with Samuel Crowther, *My Life and Work* (Garden City, N.Y.: Garden City Publishing Co., Inc., 1922), pp. 62–63. However, Ford's sales manager, Norval A. Hawkins, later testified that the Selden suit greatly increased sales resistance and that some dealers were so discouraged that they left the company. DN, Feb. 2, 1927. Hawkins testified in connection with a tax appeal made in 1926–28 by James Couzens and other former Ford stockholders, hereafter cited as "Stockholders' Tax Case."

22. DFP, Mar. 1, 1910.

23. Nevins and Hill, *Ford: The Times*, p. 437; *Horseless Age* 27 (Jan. 18, 1911), 145; Hawkins's testimony in Stockholders' Tax Case, DN, Feb. 2, 1927.

24. Nevins and Hill, *Ford: The Times*, pp. 437–38; DN, Jan. 10, 1911; DFP, Jan. 10, 1911; *Horseless Age* 27 (Jan. 11, 1911), 120–26; *Motor World* 26 (Jan. 12, 1911), 1–3.

25. Ford and Crowther, *Life and Work*, p. 63; Barnard, *Independent Man*, p. 57; Hawkins's testimony in Stockholders' Tax Case, DN, Feb. 2, 1927.

26. Burlingame, *Henry Ford*, p. 39. The Selden suit was among the aspects of Ford's life treated in an institutional advertising campaign conducted in 1944. Proofs of the advertisement are in Acc. 44, Box 13. Ford Motor Company, *A Series of Talks on the Ford Sunday Evening Hour* (Dearborn: Ford Motor Company, 1935), pp. 56–58.

27. Nevins and Hill, *Ford: The Times*, pp. 296, 298–300; Barnard, *Independent Man*, pp. 55–58.

28. John B. Rae, *American Automobile Manufacturers The First Forty Years* (Philadelphia: Chilton Company, 1959), pp. 50, 108; Kennedy, *Automobile Industry*, pp. 30, 73–74; Nevins and Hill, *Ford: The Times*, pp. 237–40, 488.

29. Nevins and Hill, *Ford: The Times*, pp. 219, 347. Although racing was the company's most important sales-promotion activity, the firm in one year, at least, spent more money on space advertising than on racing. The only comparative figures available on spending for racing and space advertising are for the fiscal year ending Sept. 30, 1905, when $14,309.44 was spent on the sport and $39,513.07 for space. (Exhibition costs totaled $4,164.39.) Minute Books, FMC of Michigan, Stockholders' meeting, Oct. 16, 1905,

Acc. 85, Box 1; (hereafter cited as "Stockholders' Minutes" or "Directors' Minutes").

30. Nevins and Hill, *Ford: The Times*, p. 218; DFP, July 28, 1903; *Horseless Age* 11 (June 24, 1903), 744; 12 (July 15, 1903), 81; 12 (July 29, 1903), 124–25; 12 (Sept. 16, 1903), 310; *Scientific American* 89 (Aug. 8, 1903), 96. Oldfield began driving for Winton in September 1903. Virtually every book or article which deals with the Ford-Oldfield relationship comments on Oldfield's habit, years later, of telling people that he and Ford had made each other, "but I did much the best job of it."

31. *Scientific American* 88 (Jan. 17, 1903), 42–43.

32. Nevins and Hill, *Ford: The Times*, p. 260; *Detroit Tribune*, Jan. 13, 1904.

33. Ford and Crowther, *Life and Work*, pp. 57–58.

34. DN, Jan. 15, 1904; *Detroit Tribune*, Jan. 16, 1904; DFP, Jan. 22, 1904.

35. *Detroit Tribune*, Jan. 17, 1904; DN, Jan. 15, 1904.

36. *Detroit Tribune*, Jan. 21, 1914; *Horseless Age* 13 (Feb. 3, 1904), 141.

37. Chris Sinsabaugh, *Who, Me? Forty Years of Automobile History* (Detroit: Arnold-Powers, Inc., 1940), p. 120; *Detroit Tribune*, Jan. 19, 1904; *Detroit Journal*, Feb. 4, 1904.

38. DN, Aug. 28, 1905; DFP, Jan. 27, 1906.

39. *Horseless Age* 14 (Aug. 31, 1904), 214; 14 (Sept. 14, 1904), 267; 14 (Oct. 5, 1904), 347; 14 (Nov. 9, 1904), 485; *Ford Times* 4 (Nov. 1, 1910), 88.

40. *Ford Times* 1 (May 15, 1908), 12–13. The publication said that the home office, branches, dealers, and owners had entered every important contest in the U.S. and had won "hundreds of prizes." Trade publications of the period tend to bear out the *Ford Times*'s assertion.

41. *Motor Age*, for example, devoted a highly flattering newsfeature article and an editorial to the achievement. *Motor Age* 11 (June 27, 1907), 10–11, 13; DFP, June 25, 1907.

42. *Motor Age* 11 (Apr. 18, 1907), 6; 11 (May 23, 1907), 29.

43. *Horseless Age* 15 (May 31, 1905), 599; 14 (Aug. 17, 1904), 146 (multiple winners); *Motor Age* 9 (May 10, 1906), 6; 12 (Oct. 3, 1907), 9 (deaths); "Automobile Racing," *Nation* 84 (Feb. 14, 1907), 148.

44. *Motor Age* 9 (May 10, 1906), 6; 11 (Feb. 21, 1907), 20; *Horseless Age* 15 (May 31, 1905), 599; "Automobile Racing," *Nation*, p. 148.

45. *Cleveland Plain Dealer*, Oct. 6, 1907; NYT, Oct. 13, 1907. The cylinder displacement of Ford's Model T racers was 176.7 cubic inches. Philip Van Doren Stern, *The Story of the Fabulous Model T Ford Tin Lizzie* (New York: Simon and Schuster, 1955), p. 164. Motors of earlier Ford models probably were smaller than the Model T's. Of course Ford's special racing cars the 999, Arrow, and the vehicles used at Cape May and Ormond Beach, were among the largest built.

46. *Ford Times* 3 (Oct. 1, 1909), 8; Locomobile Company of America, *The Car of 1911* (Bridgeport, Conn.: Locomobile Company of America, 1910), p. 39; NYT, Oct. 13, 1907. In a letter to *Motor Age* Oldfield stated that he was selling his racing gear and wanted to find an accident-free position with an auto company. *Motor Age* 12 (Sept. 26, 1907), 32. However, the following year Oldfield bought two Stearns cars and was seeking exhibition engagements. *Motor Age* 13 (June 11, 1908), 33.

47. *Ford Times* 3 (Oct. 1, 1909), 8.

48. *Ibid.*, 1 (July 1, 1908), 40; 2 (Apr. 15, 1909), 2.

49. *Ford Times* 1 (July 1, 1908), 41; 1 (June 1, 1908), 4.

50. Barnard, *Independent Man*, pp. 39, 45–46; Theodore

F. MacManus and Norman Beasley, *Men, Money, and Motors* (New York: Harper & Brothers, 1930), p. 28.

51. Philip Van Doren Stern, *A Pictorial History of the Automobile As Seen in Motor Magazine 1903–1953* (New York: Viking Press, 1953), p. 148. The slogan, "Not an Experiment!," was actually used by National Motor Carriage Co. and Locomobile Company of America at the turn of the century. *Horseless Age* 4 (Apr. 5, 1899), 34; 4 (Aug. 23, 1899), 26. *Horseless Age* 3 (Sept. 1898), 1, carried a Haynes-Apperson ad, typical of many, stating, "We can fill orders promptly and guarantee results." The Racine, Oakman, and Locomobile ads are in *Horseless Age* 1 (Nov. 1895), 2; 4 (Apr. 5, 1899), 31; 4 (Aug. 23, 1899), 26.

52. Musselman, *Get a Horse!*, p. 110. *Motor Age* and *Saturday Evening Post* ran Cadillac's slogan, "The Car That Climbs," from 1904 to 1907, and *Horseless Age* and *Motor* carried Marmon's "A Mechanical Masterpiece" from 1905 to 1909. Musselman, *Get a Horse!*, p. 110, noted that only the 1901 Packard slogan had survived to the date of his book's publication (1950). Arthur W. Einstein, Jr., "The Advertising of the Packard Motor Car Company 1899–1956," (Unpublished M.A. thesis, Dept. of Journalism, Michigan State University, 1959), pp. 37, 262. The Packard nameplate was discontinued in 1958. *Horseless Age* 23 (Jan. 13, 1909), 53; 24 (Dec. 29, 1909), 766–68.

53. Nevins and Hill, *Ford: The Times*, pp. 243, 342; *Saturday Evening Post* 176 (July 11, 1903), 17.

54. This observation is based on an analysis of advertisements in three Detroit newspapers, the *Free Press*, *Journal*, and *News*, and in *Horseless Age*, *Motor Age*, and *Saturday Evening Post* between 1903 and 1908.

55. So much emphasis was placed on vanadium that the company often was asked if it were "the product of an advertising man who has seized upon a new steel as a means for securing additional publicity for the car he represents." *Ford Times* 2 (Nov. 1, 1908), 11. Floyd Clymer, *Henry's Wonderful Model T, 1908–1927* (New York: Bonanza Books, 1955), p. 19, reproduces a 1916 advertisement which emphasizes vanadium steel.

56. FMC Accounts Journal, Acc. 85, Box 7 (hereafter cited as "Accounts Journal"). The *Detroit News-Tribune*, Sept. 20, 1908, reported the Mulford agency was founded in the 1880s and had placed "millions in successful advertising."

57. Many direct payments to Detroit and New York newspapers and to trade and general magazines are listed in the Accounts Journal, which covers the period Aug. 18, 1903–Sept. 24, 1904, Acc. 85, Box 7. There is no evidence that Mulford was retained by the company after September 1904. *Ford Times* 5 (Oct. 1911), 18.

58. Accounts Journal, Acc. 85, Box 7; Stockholders' Minutes, Oct. 16, 1905, Acc. 85, Box 1. An examination of the trade, periodical, and daily press between 1905 and 1910 shows that the largest advertisers were Winton, Olds, Packard, Jeffery, Cadillac, Franklin, Maxwell-Briscoe, Reo, Chalmers-Detroit, Stearns, Peerless, Adams-Farwell, Knox, Northern, and Elmore.

59. The Ford appropriation was $25,000 in 1908. Helen Woodward, *It's an Art* (New York: Harcourt, Brace and Company, 1938), p. 120.

60. *Motor World* 33 (Dec. 12, 1912), 20.

61. DFP, Sept. 6, 1938; DN, Sept. 6, 1938 (obituaries of Pelletier).

62. Pelletier discussed the transition from engineer to publicist in a speech, "Henry Ford As I Know Him,"

before the Detroit Vortex Club, July 23, 1930. DN, July 24, 1930. Contemporary data contain no mention of Pelletier's advertising-promotional activities prior to the spring of 1907.

63. DFP, Apr. 21, 1907.

64. *Motor Age* 11 (Apr. 18, 1907), 6; *Ford Times* 1 (June 1, 1908), 16. Mrs. Pelletier, living in Detroit in the 1950s, credited the slogan to her husband. Nevins and Hill, *Ford: The Times*, p. 623. In 1941 the company requested its advertising agencies "to keep this slogan alive and use it in advertising when the opportunity presents itself." STANDARDS AND INFORMATION for the Guidance of Advertising Agencies of the FMC in Writing Copy and Preparing Art Work, Mar. 24, 1941, Acc. 149, Box 102.

65. DFP, Aug. 11, 1907.

66. Rudolph E. Anderson, *The Story of the American Automobile* (Washington: Public Affairs Press, 1950), p. 100; *Ford Times* 1 (July 1, 1908), 19; 1 (June 15, 1908), 4. "High Priced Quality in a Low Priced Car" was used in 1909 and "Ford—The Quality Car" in 1910. *Detroit News-Tribune*, July 18, 1909; DN, July 2, 1910.

67. DFP, Sept. 6, 1938, reported that "advertising men agree" that the "Watch the Fords" slogan "is the greatest of all time." The slogan is also cited in Isaac E. Lambert, *The Public Accepts: Stories Behind Famous Trade-Marks, Names, and Slogans* (Albuquerque, N.M.: University of New Mexico Press, 1941), p. 151, as one of the most effective slogans in business history. J.T. Flynn, "Watch the Ford Myths Go By," *New Republic* 91 (Aug. 4, 1937); *Grand Rapids Press*, Apr. 12, 1940; *Madison* (Wis.) *Journal*, Apr. 13, 1944; *Broadcasting-Telecasting* 37 (Nov. 14, 1949), 38; "Watch the Fords Go By," *Newsweek* 61 (Apr. 22, 1963), 78; "Watch the Fords Go Back," *Business Week* (Apr. 29, 1972), 26.

68. *Motor Age* 12 (Dec. 26, 1907), 23. Pelletier became advertising manager of Maxwell-Briscoe Co. early in 1908. *Horseless Age* 2 (Jan. 13, 1908), 79. In later years Pelletier served as advertising manager for the E-M-F, Studebaker, Reo, and Rickenbacker companies. DN, Sept. 6, 1938.

69 DN, July 24, 1930. Pelletier claimed "the honor of being the first man fired from the Ford organization." DN, July 24, 1930. He was, however, a great admirer of Ford and was working on a biography, which was to be entitled "My Henry Ford," when he died at the age of 70 in 1938. DFP, Sept. 6, 1938.

70. *Horseless Age* 20 (Dec. 25, 1907), 906. Harper's name is on the masthead of the first edition of the *Ford Times*, Apr. 15, 1908. Walsh is cited as Harper's assistant in *Ford Times* 1 (July 1, 1908), 36.

71. Anderson, *Story of American Automobile*, pp. 174–76, 178; *Horseless Age* 2 (Apr. 1897), 4–7; Pound, *Turning Wheel*, p. 61; Musselman, *Get a Horse!*, p. 83.

72. Edwin Emery, *History of the American Newspaper Publishers Association* (Minneapolis: University of Minnesota Press, 1950), p. 127; *San Francisco Chronicle*, Sept. 7, 1912.

73. *Motor Age* 19 (Feb. 2, 1911), 22. Automotive news and advertising usually were printed in newspapers' sports sections during the first decade of the century. Emery, *History of ANPA*, p. 128; J.C. Long, *Roy D. Chapin*, ([Bethlehem, Pa.: privately printed], 1945), p. 95. MacManus and Beasley, *Men, Money, and Motors*, p. 163.

74. The above observations are based on an analysis of three Detroit newspapers, the *Free Press*, *News*, and *Journal*, during 1903–8.

75. Statements sent to FMC in 1908 by several Detroit photographers are in Acc. 2, Box 37.
76. The Ford Company established "branch stores"—which replaced mere dealerships—in seven major Eastern and Midwestern cities in 1905. Within a few years all important cities were served by company branches. Nevins and Hill, *Ford: The Times*, pp. 265, 346–47. The quote is in Ernest G. Liebold, *Reminiscences*, p. 1073, Ford Archives, Dearborn, Mich.; (hereafter all *Reminiscences* cited are in the Ford Archives). *Ford Times* 1 (May 15, 1908), 10, describes Plantiff as a "good mixer."
77. Pound, *Turning Wheel*, p. 416; Locomobile Company of America, *Car of 1911*, p. 41.
78. Nevins and Hill, *Ford: The Times*, p. 249; Burlingame, *Henry Ford*, pp. 40–41. The company's first cars, according to Burlingame, were unable to climb hills.
79. Nevins and Hill, *Ford: The Times*, pp. 260, 344; Norval A. Hawkins to branch managers, Feb. 11, 1913, Acc. 509, Box 1.
80. Hawkins's testimony in Stockholders' Tax Case, DN, Feb. 2, 1927; Nevins and Hill, *Ford: The Times*, p. 402; Hawkins to branch managers, Apr. 9 and Aug. 5, 1913, Acc. 509, Box 1.
81. Hawkins to dealers, Dec. 8, 1912, Acc. 509, Box 1; *Ford Times* 2 (Feb. 1, 1909), 9; 3 (Dec. 15, 1909), 106–7; 4 (Mar. 1911), 201; 5 (Feb. 1912), 164.
82. *Ford Times* 3 (Jan. 15, 1910), 159–60; 4 (Apr. 1911), 212; Hawkins to branch managers, Jan. 8, 1912, Acc. 509, Box 1.
83. Hawkins's testimony in Stockholders' Tax Case, *Printers' Ink* 138 (Feb. 10, 1927), 94–96.
84. *Horseless Age* 2 (Feb. 1897), 12, 16; Nevins and Hill, *Ford: The Times*, pp. 196–97; Sinsabaugh, *Who, Me?*, pp. 54, 58.
85. Directors' Minutes, Oct. 24, 1903, Acc. 85, Box 1.
86. Nevins and Hill, *Ford: The Times*, pp. 319–20; *Motor Age* 19 (Jan. 5, 1911), 66; 21 (Jan. 25, 1912), 17; 21 (Feb. 1, 1912), 62; 21 (Mar. 7, 1912), 2; DT, Apr. 30, 1940.
87. Simonds, *Henry Ford*, pp. 94–95; *Ford Times* 3 (July 1, 1910), 421; 4 (Dec. 1910), 122.
88. *Ford Times* 3 (Oct. 1, 1909), 15; G.H. Perrine & Sons, Centralia, Ill., to Henry Ford, Dec. 20, 1909, Acc. 2, Box 31; Saskatchewan Motor Company, Ltd. to Henry Ford, Apr. 12, 1911, Acc. 2, Box 35; *Ford Times* 5 (Dec. 1911), 69; *New York Morning Telegraph*, Oct. 10, 1912. The *Telegraph* called the Ford Company's participation in the Land Show "a progressive move," adding that Ford was the only auto manufacturer with enough foresight to go after the farm market.
89. Nevins and Hill, *Ford: The Times*, pp. 644, 647. Other members of the "Big Four" were Buick, Reo, and Maxwell-Briscoe. *Ibid.*, p. 354. Buick was the largest producer in 1908, manufacturing and selling 8,487 cars. Cadillac was the biggest money-maker in 1908, earning $1,936,382; Packard was second with earnings of $1,412,832. Kennedy, *Automobile Industry*, pp. 25–27; Seltzer, *Automobile Industry*, p. 250. Buick's 1908 profits are unknown. They probably exceeded Ford's earnings inasmuch as Buick outsold Ford in 1908 and its product sold for a higher price, and presumably at a higher profit margin, than the Ford. Ford's advertising at this time bragged about the low profit made on each car. *Ford Times* 1 (May 15, 1908), 16.
90. FMC's sales figures from 1903 to 1921 and net income figures from 1903 to 1921 may be found in Nevins and Hill, *Ford: The Times*, p. 647. Sales figures from 1918 to 1934 are listed in Allan Nevins

and Frank Ernest Hill, *Ford: Expansion and Challenge, 1915–1933* (New York: Charles Scribner's Sons, 1957), p. 685. Production of the American automobile industry from 1903 to 1927, net income of the industry from 1910 to 1926, and Ford profits from 1903 to 1921 are cited in Epstein, *Automobile Industry*, pp. 341, 353, 356.

Chapter 3

1. *Ford Times* 1 (Apr. 15, 1908), 14–15; Stern, *Tin Lizzie*, p. 53.
2. Stern, *Tin Lizzie*, p. 53; Nevins and Hills, *Ford: The Times*, pp. 388, 414, 646. In 1908 the average automobile price is estimated to have been between $2,800 to $3,000. The Model T, at $825 and up, was in the low-price class. In 1908 Ford also sold the Model N for $600, the Model S for $700, the Model R for $750, and the Model K for $2,800. Kennedy, *Automobile Industry*, pp. 41, 73.
3. Merrill Denison, in *The Power To Go* (New York: Doubleday, 1956) p. 148, states unequivocally, "Never in previous marketing experience had a new product been launched with more fanfare."
4. *Horseless Age* 22 (Sept. 30, 1908), 470–72; *Motor Age* 14 (Sept. 24, 1908), 30–33; *Motor World* 19 (Oct. 8, 1908), 65–66. Daily newspapers, which during this period devoted virtually no space to the introduction of new cars, gave the Model T only minimal attention. Among the Detroit newspapers, only the *News* of Oct. 4, 1908, noted the debut of the T.
5. *Ford Times* 2 (Oct. 15, 1908), 10.
6. Nevins and Hill, *Ford: The Times*, p. 388; *Ford Times* 2 (Jan. 15, 1909), 3.
7. *Ford Times* 2 (Oct. 15, 1908), 14; Barnard, *Independent Man*, 66; Nevins and Hill, *Ford: The Times*, pp. 396, 644; Nevins and Hill, *Expansion and Challenge*, pp. 686–88.
8. Nevins and Hill, *Ford: The Times*, pp. 510, 644; *Indianapolis Star*, Jan. 4, 1914.
9. *Ford Times* 5 (Mar. 1912), front cover; 7 (Nov. 1913), 65; *Pittsburgh Dispatch*, Sept. 1913.
10. *Ford Times* 7 (July 1914), 434. The Model T "was its own best publicity agent, advertisement, and topnotch salesman," according to Denison, *Power To Go*, p. 148; and it was "a leaping, rattling billboard," in the view of Jonathan Norton Leonard, *The Tragedy of Henry Ford* (New York: G.P. Putnam's Sons, 1932), p. 23.
11. Nevins and Hill, *Ford: The Times*, p. 491.
12. *Newton* (Mo.) *Chronicle*, June 5, 1913; *Winterset* (Iowa) *Madisonian*, July 2, 1913; *Jackson* (Ohio) *Sun*, June 5, 1913; *Eldon* (Mo.) *Advertiser*, May 29, 1913; *Elgin* (Ill.) *Courier*, July 3, 1914.
13. *San Antonio Light*, Dec. 13, 1913; *Philadelphia Record*, July 19, 1913; *St. Louis Republic*, Oct. 10, 1912; *Ford Times* 7 (Aug.-Sept. 1914), 499; 6 (Oct. 1912), 13; 6 (Apr. 1913), 308; 3 (Mar. 15, 1910), 259.
14. Burlingame, *Henry Ford*, p. 62. The precise year in which Ford issued the "multitude" statement is not known (the earliest source I have found is the *Ford Times* 6 [June 1913], 366). It probably was made during the period 1903–6, when Ford frequently expressed similar views to business associates and the press. Nevins and Hill, *Ford: The Times*, pp. 276–77, 282–83, 332; *Detroit Journal*, May 9, 1905; DFP, May 10, 1905. Couzens also made analogous state-

ments, declaring in early 1906 that the future of the automobile industry was dependent upon the production of cars "in large quantities and at a low price...in reach of the ordinary man." Charles E. Sorensen with Samuel T. Williamson, *My Forty Years with Ford* (New York: W.W. Norton & Company, Inc., 1956), p. 84.

15. Stern, *Tin Lizzie*, p. 11. Many Model T owners were proud of the car's utility, and used it to "saw wood, pump water, store grain, run stock shears, generate electricity, plow on week days and go riding on Sundays." Floyd Clymer, *Henry's Wonderful Model T, 1908-1927* (New York: Bonanza Books, 1955), p. 11.

16. Charles Merz, *And Then Came Ford* (Garden City, N.Y.: Doubleday, Doran & Company, Inc., 1929), pp. 131, 134. The obvious incompatibility of the two policies—price-cutting and prestige-building—did not deter the company from espousing both at the same time.

17. Barnard, *Independent Man*, p. 80; Clayton Sedgwick Cooper, "Advertising Values in the Ford Business," *Editor & Publisher* (May 20, 1916), 1583.

18. From 1911 to 1920, the company did not concern itself with estimating market requirements for the year ahead; it simply built all the Model T's it could, knowing there would be a demand for them. Nevins and Hill, *Ford: The Times*, p. 532. There are no accurate Ford sales figures for the *calendar* years between 1903 and 1918 since the Ford Company kept figures only for its fiscal years (many historians, incidentally, have mistakenly used the fiscal and calendar years interchangeably). Prices of the Ford cars and the company's sales figures between 1903 and 1916 are in Nevins and Hill, *Ford: The Times*, pp. 644, 646–47.

19. *Chicago Post*, Sept. 30, 1912; *Atlanta Constitution*, Aug. 17, 1913; Gerald Stanley Lee, "Is Ford an Inspired Millionaire?," *Harper's Weekly* 58 (Mar. 14, 1914), 9.

20. *Ford Times* 2 (Apr. 15, 1909), 2. The publication remarked: "Can you see in your mind's eye any but a reliable, honest, well-built substantial car finishing that [the New York-to-Seattle] contest? Few manufacturers will have sufficient confidence in their own product to even make an entry, but that contest is the sort of one the Model T is built for." Ford was never more inconsistent than in his racing views. Writing in *My Life and Work* of the events which led him to build his first racer in 1901, he said that he could "hardly imagine any test that would tell less" about the merits of a car than racing. In 1907, as he was pleading for a reduction in the size of engines, he told the *Cleveland Plain Dealer* that "track racing is of inestimable value to the trade and to the development of the art of automobile building." A few months before he re-entered racing in 1909 he was quoted by *Horseless Age* to the effect that "automobile racing is a thing of the past, and it is a good thing for the industry that this is so. It takes time and money...that could be better spent in improving the car as a commercial, not a sporting proposition." In 1911 Ford told the *New York World*, "The question of automobile racing has become the subject of criticism by some manufacturers who seemingly overlook the possible benefits that may be derived by successful competitors....There was never inaugurated an enterprise that did not carry with it its portion of those who sacrificed their lives in contribution of its glory and ultimate success." Ford's policy was dictated by expediency.

21. *Ford Times* 2 (Apr. 15, 1909), 2; 2 (May 1, 1909), 13; 2 (June 15, 1909), 1–3; 2 (July 1, 1909), 2; 2 (July 15, 1909), 1–10.

22. Nevins and Hill, *Ford: The Times*, p. 406. A copy of the booklet is in Acc. 292, Box 5. A typical advertisement in the *Detroit News-Tribune*, July 11, 1909, declares, "Of course we are proud of the victory—so can every owner of a Model "T" Ford.... We Don't Blame Other Manufacturers for staying out of the race. It was a hard one—probably the hardest test ever proposed."

23. *Ford Times* 2 (Aug. 15, 1909), 7; 3 (Oct. 1, 1909), 3.

24. Stern, *Tin Lizzie*, p. 74.

25. FMC news releases, May 1959 (*sic*) and June 23, 1959 (in the possession of the author); *Editor & Publisher* 92 (Oct. 10, 1959), 36.

26. Every issue of the *Ford Times* during the summer and fall of 1910 carries a considerable amount of racing news.

27. *Ford Times* 3 (Sept. 1, 1910), 534; *Motor Age* 19 (May 25, 1911), 4; 20 (Dec. 14, 1911), 2–3.

28. *Ford Times* 3 (Apr. 15, 1910), 306; 3 (June 1, 1910), 371; 3 (June 15, 1910), 409; 3 (July 15, 1910), 440; 5 (Nov. 1911), 34–35; 2 (Sept. 1912), 391.

29. *Motor Age* 18 (Sept. 1, 1910), 15–16; *Ford Times* 3 (Oct. 1, 1909), 8. The Model T touring car was priced at $780 in the fiscal year 1909–10 and at $690 in the fiscal year 1910–11.

30. See *Ford Times* 3 (Aug. 15, 1910), 494; 4 (Sept. 15, 1910), 544; 4 (Oct. 1, 1910), 5; 4 (Oct. 15, 1910), 51–52; 4 (Mar. 1911), 192–93; *Motor Age* 19 (Mar. 2, 1911), 34; *Detroit Journal*, Sept. 27, 1911.

31. *Ford Times* 4 (Oct. 1, 1910), 7.

32. DFP, Sept. 27, 1911.

33. *Ford Times* 5 (Mar. 1912), 183–84. The performance was among "the top sporting events of the year." *Motor Age* 22 (Dec. 26, 1912), 10.

34. The quote is in a feature story on Kulick in the *Buffalo Courier*, Jan. 12, 1913. A good contemporary account of the victory may be found in *Motor Age* 21 (June 27, 1912), 16; Chris Sinsabaugh, *Who, Me? Forty Years of Automobile History* (Detroit: Arnold-Powers, Inc., 1940), p. 87.

35. Nevins and Hill, *Expansion and Challenge*, p. 593; DT, May 5, 1946.

36. Only a few races are reported in vol. 6 (Oct. 1912-Sept. 1913) of the *Ford Times;* vol. 3 (Oct. 1913-Aug.-Sept. 1914) reports none. Large-scale Model T racing was resumed about 1915 when all-Ford races became a vogue at fairs and carnivals throughout the country. The cars in these races usually were entered and driven by private Ford owners rather than dealers. *Ford Times* 9 (Dec. 1915), 228. Model T races were held annually in Calgary, Alta. until 1951. Stern, *Tin Lizzie*, pp. 134–35. T races were revived in southern California in 1962; and were being held anually in northern California in the 1970s. Lee Chase, "Model T Races," *Timer* 9 (July-Aug. 1963), 18; Tom Rohner, "Dirt Track Race," *Vintage Ford* 8 (Sept.-Oct. 1973), 31–33.

37. Dan R. Post Publications, *Model T Ford in Speed and Sport* (Arcadia, Calif.: D.R. Post Publications, 1956), pp. 10, 12–13, 31, 81, 102–3, 105, 109; P.W. Cornelius, *The Ford As a Racing Car: A Comprehensive Illustrated Treatise on the Design, Construction and Operation of Dirt Track Racing Fords* (Indianapolis: P.W. Cornelius, 1924), p. 1; Norman E. Isaacs, "Indianapolis Speedway... Casualty of War," *Ford Times* 2 (July 1945), 40; Al Bloemker, *500 Miles to Go: The Story of the Indianapolis Speedway* (New York: Coward-McCann, 1961), pp. 164, 166. Two of the Fronty-Fords did not run the full distance in the 1923 Indianapolis 500, being waved off the track after twelve machines had completed the race. During the 1920s most Indianapolis-type racing cars cost from

$10,000 to $20,000; Fronty-Fords usually cost less than $1,000. According to the Feb. 25, 1962 edition of DN, the Fronty-Ford "practically faded from existence when the Ford V-8 was introduced at 65 horsepower in 1932." The 20-horsepower Model T, even with special equipment, obviously could not out-race the V-8.

38. DFP, June 22, 1907; *Motor Age* 12 (Oct. 31, 1907), 68–69; *Ford Times* 1 (May 1, 1908), 11; 1 (June 1, 1908), 16; 1 (June 15, 1908), 16; 1 (July 1, 1908), 36–37; 1 (Aug. 1, 1908), 9–11. Of course, Ford dealers and owners probably did not report contest results unless they made a good showing.

39. *Ford Times* 2 (Mar. 1, 1909), 15; 2 (Jan. 15, 1909), 14; 2 (Oct. 1, 1909), 8; 3 (Oct. 15, 1909), 33; 3 (July 1, 1910), 420.

40. Kennedy, *Automobile Industry*, p. 65; Musselman, *Get a Horse!*, p. 202; *Ford Times* 4 (Oct. 1, 1910), 16; *Motor Age* 19 (June 15, 1911), 1; 21 (June 27, 1912), 16. Vols. 1–4 (Apr. 15, 1908-Sept. 15, 1911) of the *Ford Times* report a great many contests in which dealers and owners participated.

41. *Ford Times* 2 (Sept. 15, 1909), 15. These stunts perhaps gave rise to the popular saying, "A Ford can go anywhere except in society."

42. The story was important enough to be relayed with foreign news on the trans-Atlantic cable. DFP, June 11, 1911. A half-holiday was declared in Fort William, at the base of the peak, on the day of the T's descent. "A score of photographers and cinematograph operators bearing ponderous cameras" were on hand to record the event. *Ford Times* 4 (July 1911), 300–2; 4 (Aug. 1911), 333.

43. *Ford Times* 5 (Oct. 1911), 10–11; 5 (Aug. 1912), 358; 7 (May 1914), 345.

44. *Denver Post*, Sept. 5, 1922; "The Junk Flivver That Won the Pikes Peak Climb," *Literary Digest* 75 (Oct. 7, 1922), 57–59. A Model T finished first in the *stock car* class of the 1921 Pikes Peak Hill Climb, but did not win the championship or open class as did Bullock in 1922. *Ford News* 1 (Oct. 15, 1921), 3. A hill climb for Model T's has been sponsored annually since 1956 at Signal Hill, Calif. by the Long Beach (Calif.) Model T Club. A limit of 100 entries was imposed in 1973 because the event had been attracting too many entries. "California Model T Drivers Tackle Annual Hill Climb," *Old Cars* 2 (Aug. 1–15, 1973), 25.

45. *Ford Times* 1 (June 15, 1908), 6–7; 2 (Apr. 15, 1909), 2.

46. Vols. 1–5 (Apr. 15, 1908-Sept. 1912) of the *Ford Times* report many victories. The 1907 wins are recorded in *Ford Times* 1 (July 1, 1908), 35.

47. *Motor Age* 18 (Sept. 1, 1910), 20; 20 (Nov. 2, 1911), 2; *Ford Times* 6 (Dec. 1912), 117–19. The annual Glidden Tour, from 1905 to 1911 (when the Indianapolis "500" began), was the greatest prize an auto manufacturer could win for his car. The Pierce-Arrow won the Glidden four consecutive years, and the resultant publicity made that car almost an automatic choice for people of wealth and for funeral directors. Kennedy, *Automobile Industry*, p. 65; Musselman, *Get a Horse!*, p. 202. An annual 100-mile Model T endurance run for speedsters was instituted by the Santa Clara (Calif.) Model "T" Ford Club in 1968. "1973 Santa Clara Run," *Ford Life* 3 (Sept.-Oct. 1973), 24.

48. *Ford Times* 5 (Feb. 1912), 144–45; 6 (Feb. 13, 1913), 199–202.

49. *Ford Times* 5 (Nov. 1911), 60. In Dallas fifteen adults were loaded on a T; in Paris, Tenn., nineteen. *Ford Times* 5 (June 1912), 275.

50. *Ford Times* 5 (Sept. 1912), 406–10; *Boston American*, Dec. 5, 1912.

51. James Rood Doolittle, *The Romance of the Automobile Industry* (New York: Klebold Press, 1916), p. 331; *Motor Age* 9 (May 10, 1906), 6; *Ford Times* 3 (Oct. 1, 1909), 9. Probably the most noteworthy victory of a Ford in an economy run was the Model S's triumph in the 1908 Chicago-to-Valparaiso (Ind.) contest. *Ford Times* 1 (May 1, 1908), 14. The annual Pikes Peak Hill Climb, started in 1916, is the major auto climb in the country today. A victory in this event continues to have considerable promotional value.

52. Norval A. Hawkins's testimony in Stockholders' Tax Case, *Printers' Ink* 137 (Feb. 10, 1927), 105; Pound, *Turning Wheel*, p. 61; *Motor Age* 14 (Aug. 27, 1908), 33.

53. Nevins and Hill, *Expansion and Challenge*, p. 17. In October 1909, Harper complained that since the magazine's inception the branch managers had not supplied enough news to fill an eight-page issue. He added that only about thirty dealers had been cooperative. *Ford Times* 3 (Oct. 1, 1909), 12–13.

54. DFP, Mar. 10, 1910.

55. The magazine accepted advertising for only one year.

56. Source of the quotation is the *Ford Times* 8 (Oct. 1914), back cover.

57. Special Report, Chicago Investigator No. 22, Nov. 14, 1913, Acc. 62, Box 4 (citing the biographical data on Buck). The investigator was assigned by E.G. Liebold, Henry Ford's secretary, to obtain information that might be used against Buck were he to carry out a threat—made after his resignation—to sue the Ford Company. The first four pages of the January 1913 edition of the *Ford Times* were devoted to "Glen Buck-Isms." Among them were such statements as: "The one thing we need most to fear is fear"; "Business may be good—but you and I are here to make it better"; and "Some day we shall class incompetency among the crimes."

58. *Detroit Journal*, Aug. 1, 1914. Brownell's relationship with Henry Ford is described in Samuel S. Marquis, *Henry Ford: An Interpretation* (Boston: Little, Brown, and Company, 1923), p. 126.

59. The pacifist articles greatly antagonized Couzens, who was Canadian-born and vigorously pro-Ally. In his letter of resignation, Oct. 12, 1915, Couzens stated, "I could not agree with Mr. Ford's utterances on peace, and the Allies' war loan, and national unpreparedness. This has been brewing for more than a week. For some time I have disapproved of the manner in which Mr. Ford has been giving statements to the press. His statements on these and other matters disgusted me. I told him so and we had it out." Simonds, *Henry Ford*, pp. 148–49.

60. *Ford Times* 9 (Jan. 1916), 275; Minute Books, FMC Executive Committee, Feb. 14, 1917, Acc. 85, Box 5; *Ford Times* 10 (Mar. 1917), 339. The company offered no explanation of its decision to suspend the *Ford Times* other than to inform its branches that it "has been decided to discontinue publication of the 'Ford Times' with the issue of April, 1917." Undoubtedly the firm assumed—correctly as it turned out—that it would have to devote much of its productive capacity to military needs for the duration of the war. Advertising Department to branches, Apr. 21, 1917, Acc. 78, Box 44. Complete files of the *Ford Times* are in the reference room of the Ford Archives and in the National Automotive History Collection of the Detroit

Public Library. The company did not resume publication of a magazine for the motoring public until June 1937, when the *Ford News,* formerly an employee publication, was recast for the outside public. General Sales Department to branch managers, Aug. 18, 1937, Acc. 509, Box 19.

61. *Ford Times* 1 (Apr. 15, 1908), 11. Nearly all auto companies prepared sales-promotional literature. As early as 1897 and 1898 the Riker Electric Motor Company, Winton, Pope, the Haynes-Apperson Motor Co., and the Pittsburgh Vehicle Company distributed descriptive catalogs to prospective customers. *Horseless Age* 2 (Oct. 1897), 7; 2 (Feb. 1897), 12; 3 (Aug. 1898), 4.

62. *Ford Times* 2 (Mar. 1, 1909), 16; 3 (July 1, 1910), 17; 5 (Dec. 1912), 82; 5 (June 1912), 283; 5 (Jan. 1912), 130; Irvin S. Cobb, *Exit Laughing* (Indianapolis: Bobbs-Merrill Company, 1941), p. 468. Cobb said he wrote the six "light tracts" in three days.

63. *Ford Times* 3 (May 15, 1910), 358; 4 (Apr. 1911), 222; 5 (June 1912), 283; 6 (Jan. 1913), 165.

64. *Ford Times* 3 (Nov. 15, 1909), 73; 3 (Sept. 15, 1910), 27.

65. Most copies of the *Fordowner* are in Acc. 170, Box 1. The masthead of early editions read, "The *Fordowner* is an independent monthly journal having no connection with the Ford Motor Company or any other organization."

66. At the time of the name change, May 1920, the readership was divided "about equally between car owners and the trade." *Ford Owner and Dealer* 13 (May 1920), 33.

67. By 1926 virtually the entire readership was composed of "dealers, authorized Ford service stations, individual Ford repair shops, and others in the trade." *Ford Dealer and Service Field* 24 (Jan. 1926), 1. The magazine's name was changed again, to *Ford Field,* in September 1939. In 1955, the publication was merged with *Ford Dealers News,* which had been prepared exclusively for Ford dealers since 1917. Nearly complete files of the magazines are in Acc. 170.

68. Hawkins's testimony in the Stockholders' Tax Case, *Printers' Ink* 138 (Feb. 10, 1927), 108; Edwin Emery, *History of the American Newspaper Publishers Association* (Minneapolis: University of Minnesota Press, 1950), p. 127. The Ford Company's clipbooks, which comprise Acc. 7, contain thousands of stories on Ford which do much to corroborate Hawkins's recollections. For example, many articles which ran simultaneously in newspapers all over the country had identical wording except for the name of the branch manager or dealer who served as the "source" of the information.

69. See Clipbook 1.

70. Directors' Minutes, Nov. 20, 1913, Acc. 85, Box 1. The appointee was David Gray, an heir of John S. Gray, FMC's first president.

71. Musselman, *Get a Horse!,* pp. 149, 75; Larry Freeman, *The Merry Old Mobiles* (Watkins Glen, N.Y.: Century House, 1949), p. 219. "In My Merry Oldsmobile" is the only auto song which is familiar to the present generation. The Oldsmobile Division of GM plays it as background music during certain of its radio and television commercials. The history of the song from 1905 through Oldsmobile's fortieth anniversary in 1937 and a 1939 film based on the life of Gus Edwards is traced in Rudolph E. Anderson, *The Story of the American Automobile* (Washington: Public Affairs Press, 1950), pp. 225–29. "In My Merry

Oldsmobile" was banned by the British Broadcasting Corporation in 1962. "We have nothing against the song," a BBC official explained, "but one has to consider where this sort of thing will stop. Next you could have the Rolls-Royce concerto or the Mini-Minor waltz." *New York Herald Tribune,* July 24, 1962. The only song about automobiles which has achieved "hit" status in recent years is "Beep Beep," which in 1958 ranked fourth in nationwide record sales for several weeks. The song described how a "Nash Rambler" passed a Cadillac at 120 miles per hour in "second gear." The tune was banned by many radio stations because of its commercial overtones. American Motors Corporation did not commission the song or attempt to promote it. Thomas Mahoney, *The Story of George Romney* (New York: Harper, 1960), p. 206; John R. Pichurski, press relations manager, American Motors Corporation, to David L. Lewis, May 31, 1962.

72. *Ford Times* 1 (Apr. 15, 1908), 10; 1 (May 1, 1908), 14; 1 (July 15, 1908), 12; 2 (Nov. 15, 1908), 4; 2 (Mar. 15, 1909), 12.

73. Anderson, *Story of American Automobile,* pp. 231, 238. In 1947, the Ford Company's New York public relations representative, John Weld, commissioned a song, "I Can Afford a Ford But I Can't Afford Frieda," which he sought to have recorded by Johnny Mercer and the Pied Pipers on a Capitol label. Report of the Eastern Public Relations Field Office for Oct. 1947, Acc. 452, Box 4. If the recording was made, there is no evidence that it was a success.

74. Stern, *Tin Lizzie,* p. 160. "The Little Ford Rambled Right Along" was as popular at the time of its introduction as "In My Merry Oldsmobile" had been in 1905–6, according to Anderson, *Story of American Automobile,* p. 230. In 1947, the Ford Company considered distributing recordings of "The Little Ford Rambled Right Along" to disc jockeys throughout the country. Report of the Eastern Public Relations Field Office for Oct. 1947, Acc. 452, Box 4.

75. Clymer, *Henry's Model T,* pp. 182–85. Sheet music for a number of Ford songs can be found in Acc. 163, Box 1.

76. *Windsor* (Ont.) *Star,* Apr. 25, 1927, which quotes verbatim the *Boston Transcript*'s review; *San Francisco Call-Post,* May 27, 1927; DFP, July 12, 1927; NYT, July 17, 1927.

77. Stern, *Tin Lizzie,* p. 160.

78. Simonds, *Henry Ford,* pp. 113–14; Nevins and Hill, *Ford: The Times,* p. 451; Nevins and Hill, *Expansion and Challenge,* p. 619. The plant, according to *Motor Age* 14 (Dec. 24, 1908), 33, also was the largest concrete building erected to date. Upon its completion in 1910, the Ford factory replaced the Buick plant as the world's largest automobile manufactory. Pound, *Turning Wheel,* p. 90. The Highland Park population figure is for 1910.

79. *Boston Transcript,* Oct. 12, 1912; *Horseless Age* 31 (May 28, 1913), 966; *New York Sun,* Sept. 7, 1913; *Pasadena News,* Nov. 5, 1913.

80. *Boston News Bureau,* Jan. 10, 1914. An unidentified, undated [1911] clipping on page seven of Clipbook 1 states, "Doubting Thomases have been wondering how the Ford Motor Co. could possibly build 75,000 cars for 1912. Some have even gone on record as saying that such an enormous output was impossible for one automobile factory." (Some of the press items in Clipbook 1, especially those dealing with events in 1911 and 1912, are undated and unidentified. Identification practices were instituted in 1913, when Henry

Romeike, Inc., New York, Consolidated Press Clipping Company, Chicago, and the MacManus Company, Detroit, were employed to furnish clippings.)

81. Nevins and Hill, *Ford: The Times*, p. 504; Paul Lacroix, of Renault Frères Selling Branch, Inc., to Henry Ford, Apr. 29, 1911, Acc. 2, Box 35.

82. The headline cited appeared in the *Jackson* (Mich.) *Press*, Oct. 18, 1913. See Clipbook 1 for clippings based on the Ford news release.

83. *Peoria* (Ill.) *Transcript*, May 16, 1913.

84. *Boston American*, June 1, 1913.

85. Allan L. Benson, *The New Henry Ford* (New York: Funk & Wagnalls Company, 1923), p. 155; John Kenneth Galbraith, "The Mystery of Henry Ford," *Atlantic* 210 (Mar. 1958), 41; Denison, *Power to Go*, p. 167; unnumbered clipbook. Most of the newspapers datelined the story Mar. 1, 1914.

86. Nevins and Hill, *Ford: The Times*, p. 372; Mark Sullivan, *Our Times The United States 1900–1925, Pre-War America*, 6 vols. (New York: Charles Scribner's Sons, 1930), 3; 58; Nevins and Hill, *Expansion and Challenge*, p. 599. The largest single role in developing mass production was played by a former supervisor of manual training at the Detroit University School, Clarence W. Avery, who had joined the Ford Company as a production man in 1912. Nevins and Hill, *Ford: The Times*, p. 474. Avery's contribution was never publicized by the company.

87. An excellent discussion of Ford as a symbol of mass production is in Nevins and Hill, *Expansion and Challenge*, pp. 598–607.

88. *Ford Times* 5 (Aug. 1912), 341–42. When visitors first began going through the plant, the superintendent complained that they were a nuisance because they diverted the attention of the workers. Ford's answer was to shuttle so many persons through the factory "that they ceased to be a novelty." Benson, *New Henry Ford*, p. 155.

89. *Christian Science Monitor*, Jan. 8, 1913. "The policy of the Ford Motor Company is rather unique in one respect," reported the *Fort Worth Star-Telegram* of Mar. 8, 1914, "in that every effort is made to welcome and encourage visitors. In Europe, and in some of the Eastern automobile factories, it is impossible to gain entrance under any pretext."

90. *Fort Worth Star-Telegram*, Mar. 8, 1914.

91. Merz, *Then Came Ford*, p. 126; *Ford Times* 8 (Jan. 1915), 158; 8 (Feb. 1915), 209; 9 (June 1916), 496; *New York Evening Post*, Mar. 11, 1916; *Ford Man* 3 (Nov. 3, 1919), 2.

92. Nevins and Hill, *Ford: The Times*, pp. 407, 501.

93. *Oklahoma City Daily Oklahoman*, Aug. 11, 1916; *Ford Times* 10 (Sept. 1916), 65.

94. *Ford Times* 10 (Dec. 1916), 195.

95. *Ford Times* 1 (July 1, 1908), 32.

96. Every volume of the *Ford Times* contains numerous articles and photographs about Ford owners' clubs. Although Ford owners were the first automobile enthusiasts to form ownership organizations, possessors of other makes of cars soon followed suit. By 1910, owners' clubs were quite common. *Motor Age* 18 (Oct. 13, 1910), 30.

97. *Ford Times* 7 (Aug.-Sept. 1914), 509–11; 10 (Sept. 1916), 80.

98. *Ford Times* 5 (July 1912), 322; *Printers' Ink* 88 (Sept. 19, 1914), 93.

99. Directors' Minutes, Dec. 1, 1908, Acc. 85, Box 1; Norval A. Hawkins to Fred D. Clark, Plattsburg, N.Y., Mar. 12, 1913, Acc. 509, Box 1.

100. DFP, June 11, 1912; Nevins and Hill, *Ford: The Times*, p. 584. According to a later statement by H.B. Harper, Ford, just prior to this time, was even toying with the idea of writing a book on birds. Barnard, *Independent Man*, p. 76.

101. A lengthy account of Buck's and Ford's activities in support of the Weeks-McLean Bill is in the *Detroit News-Tribune*, Mar. 23, 1913. Numerous wires in Clipbook 1 substantiate the *News-Tribune*'s articles and provide additional information on the "string-pulling" activities in which the Ford forces were engaged on behalf of the bill.

102. *Detroit Journal*, Apr. 21 and 26, 1913; *St. Paul Pioneer*, Aug. 24, 1913; *New York World*, Jan. 10, 1914; *Tacoma Tribune*, Jan. 10, 1914; *New York Herald*, Jan. 11, 1914; *New York Sun*, Nov. 22, 1918. The *San Francisco Bulletin*, Jan. 17, 1914, not untypically pointed out that "Henry Ford spends more on birds than on himself."

103. DFP, Mar. 31, 1912; Commercial Department sample questionnaire, Acc. 509, Box 1.

104. Norval A. Hawkins to branch managers, July 30, 1914.

105. Stern, *Tin Lizzie*, p. 61; Pound, *Turning Wheel*, p. 427; Nevins and Hill, *Expansion and Challenge*, pp. 397, 400.

106. *Motor Age* 17 (Mar. 24, 1910), 35 (GM figure); Norval A. Hawkins to dealers, Jan. 31, 1912; *Ford Times* 6 (Mar. 1913), 236; 6 (Nov. 1912), 72–73. Some dealers apparently did buy space for goodwill purposes. The *Atchison* (Kan.) *Globe*, Dec. 2, 1912, congratulated the local Ford agent for "advertising every day in the newspaper, despite not having a car in stock."

107. *Ford Times* 3 (Mar. 15, 1910), 273.

108. Special Report, Chicago Investigator No. 22, Nov. 14, 1913, Acc. 62, Box 4.

109. Helen Woodward, *It's an Art* (New York: Harcourt, Brace and Company, 1938), p. 120; G.A. Nichols, "What Will Take the Place of Advertising in Ford's Marketing Scheme?," *Printers' Ink* 135 (June 17, 1926), 18. Nichols states that from 1911 to 1913, inclusive, the Ford Company spent $1,000,000 on advertising. The NYT reported on Aug. 1, 1914, that Ford "is an advertiser who cuts a respectable, but by no means impressive, figure. He spends a good deal of money that way, but by no means as much as many other men in his own and other businesses."

110. *Printers' Ink* 98 (Feb. 1, 1917), 33. Model T advertising was resumed in August 1923. Edsel Ford to branch managers, Aug. 10, 1923, Acc. 572, Box 10. Anderson, *Story of American Automobile*, p. 281.

111. Representative small-space ads are in *Motor Age* 21 (June 27, 1912), 108 and *Horseless Age* 31 (June 25, 1913), 40. *New York Daily News*, Nov. 17, 1917 (Brownell).

112. One competent survey of automobile advertising suggested in 1913 that the Ford Company should, for maximum appeal, concentrate entirely on price advertising. Charles Coolidge Parlin and Henry Sherwood Youker, Report on Gasoline Cars, Curtis Publishing Company, Division of Commercial Research, 1913, Acc. 96, Box 3.

113. Norval A. Hawkins to branches, dealers, and subdealers, Mar. 30, May 22, 1912, Acc. 509, Box 1; *Ford Times* 5 (Mar. 1912), back cover; 5 (July 1912), 316; for examples of ads which devote more than half their space to the trademark, see *Saturday Evening Post* 184 (Apr. 6, 1912), 64, and *Motor Age* 21 (June 27, 1912), 108; *Ford Times* 6 (Oct. 12,

1912), 29; Stockholders' Tax Case, Petitioners' Brief, pp. 130–31, Acc. 96, Box 15; Minute Books, FMC Operating Committee, Dec. 14, 1916, Acc. 85, Box 5; Liebold, *Reminiscences,* p. 51.

114. *Ford Times* 2 (Mar. 1, 1909), 16; 3 (June 1, 1910), 372. Harper resigned his position with Ford in February 1911 to become export manager for the Willys-Overland Company. *Ford Times* 4 (Feb. 1911), 179; *Chicago Post,* Nov. 18, 1912.

115. *Detroit Journal,* Dec. 31, 1920; *Horseless Age* 31 (Feb. 26, 1913), 421.

116. *Detroit News-Tribune,* Sept. 13, 1908. Brownell had been an advertising man in Detroit since 1886, and at one time handled the Oldsmobile account. *Detroit Journal,* Dec. 31, 1920; Pound, *Turning Wheel,* p. 61.

117. *Ford Times* 5 (Oct. 1911), 18; 5 (Nov. 1911), 11; Morris J. White, Michigan News and Advertising Service, Detroit, to Henry Ford, Apr. 15, 1911, Acc. 2, Box 35.

118. *Horseless Age* 31 (Feb. 26, 1913), 421; Liebold, *Reminiscences,* pp. 50–51. Ford was also much impressed with an advertising volume, *The Glen Buck Book,* which John Burroughs had presented to him with the comment, "It's full of wit and wisdom." John Burroughs to Glen Buck (copy), Dec. 9, 1912, Acc. 62, Box 4.

119. Liebold, *Reminiscences,* p. 52; Special Report, Chicago Investigator No. 22, Nov. 14, 1913, and Special Report, Chicago Investigator No. 130, Nov. 8, 1913, Acc. 62, Box 4. When Buck resigned, according to the source last cited, he told Couzens he had earned a bonus of several thousand dollars and asked for a check for the full amount. Couzens's reply was, "We do not give bonuses to people who resign or leave our employ, so consequently, Mr. Buck, you have nothing coming." Buck returned to Chicago, where for many years he was a successful advertising man. In 1918, he and Liebold patched up their argument, and as late as 1936 were exchanging friendly correspondence. Acc. 62, Box 4, Acc. 285, Box 1865. In an undated [1913] letter to A. V. Ingham, an applicant for Buck's job, Couzens wrote: "Just at the present time we are not going to do anything with the Advertising Department. We are going to let it run along with the men that were under Mr. Buck." Acc. 62, Box 4.

Chapter 4

1. For typical evaluations, see Merz, *Then Came Ford,* pp. 109–13, and Mark Sullivan, *Our Times The United States 1900–1925,* 4, *The War Begins 1909–1914* (New York: Charles Scribner's Sons, 1937), p. 48.

2. *Who's Who in America,* 1900–1 and 1912–13 eds. Chalmers, in 1907, at the age of twenty-eight, received a salary of $72,000 from the National Cash Register Company. Kennedy, *Auto Industry,* p. 89.

3. *San Antonio Light,* Oct. 19, 1913; *Roanoke News,* Jan. 17, 1914.

4. For typical views on the amount of publicity Ford received up to 1913, see Merz, *Then Came Ford,* pp. 109–10, Sullivan, *Our Times,* 4, p. 48, and Simonds, *Henry Ford,* p. 135. For pre-1913 articles on Ford in the NYT, see the editions of Jan. 13, 1904, Oct. 13, 1907, and Jan. 10, 1911. For pre-1914 syndicated

stories on Ford, see Clipbook 1 and the unnumbered clipbooks in Acc. 7. *Industrial Arts Index,* 1913 ed.

5. This view is based on an analysis of the Ford Company's press clipbooks.

6. *Horseless Age* 16 (Dec. 13, 1905), 2; *Boston News Bureau,* Jan. 10, 1914; Stockholders' Tax Case, Opinion Rendered by United States Board of Tax Appeals in the Appeal of James Couzens vs. Commissioner of Internal Revenue Docket No. 10438, May 5, 1928, p. 112, Acc. 96, Box 13. "During the period from 1910 to 1913," according to this opinion, "articles on Ford were numerous in all trade periodicals, not only in this country, but in Germany and England as well. There were many more Ford articles than those descriptive of other machines or other motor companies."

7. For evidence of skepticism as to Ford's ability to fulfill its production schedules, see n. 80 in chap. 3. Sources of Ford rumors include the *New York Journal of Commerce,* Jan. 6, 1913; *Los Angeles Express,* Jan. 14, 1913; and *Holland* (Mich.) *Sentinel,* Aug. 11, 1914. The California Standard rumor also is mentioned in Gerald T. White, *Formative Years in the Far West: A History of Standard Oil Company of California and Predecessors Through 1919* (New York: Appleton-Century-Crofts, 1962), p. 402. In response to a 1910 query concerning Ford's possible sale to Studebaker, the company angrily wired: "A lie out of the whole cloth. Not a word of truth in the published statements. . . . We are not for sale. Please publish this." *Ford Times* 3 (Apr. 1, 1910), 286.

8. *New York Herald,* Jan. 4, 1914; Stockholders' Tax Case, Opinion Rendered by United States Board of Tax Appeals in the Appeal of James Couzens vs. Commissioner of Internal Revenue Docket No. 10438, May 5, 1928, p. 112, Acc. 96, Box 13. Stockholders' Tax Case, [Stockholders] vs. Commissioner of Internal Revenue, Before the United States Board of Tax Appeals, Petitioners' Brief and Argument, p. 129, Apr. 18, 1927, Acc. 96, Box 15; R. L. Bruckberger, *Image of America,* trans., C. G. Paulding and Virgilia Peterson (New York: Viking Press, 1959), p. 181; DT, June 16, 1913.

9. *San Francisco Chronicle,* Jan. 10, 1913; *Los Angeles Express,* Dec. 14, 1914; DN, June 19, 1903; Benson, *New Henry Ford,* pp. 132–33. Benson states that in 1903 he was editor of a Detroit newspaper and that he had never heard of Ford. DFP, July 9, 1905; Floyd Clymer, *Treasury of Early American Automobiles, 1877–1925* (New York: McGraw-Hill Book Company, Inc., 1950), p. 49; *Motor Age* 9 (Jan. 18, 1906), [New York Show Number—pages are unnumbered].

10. H. U. Palmer intended to discuss Ford "in a deluxe book on automobiling in which a very few pioneers will be treated and their names handed down as the fathers of the American automobile industry." J. H. Gerrie to Henry Ford, Nov. 15, 1909, Acc. 2, Box 31. *Motor Times* regarded Ford as one of the six "veterans in the industry." F. Ed Spooner, editor, *Motor Times,* to Henry Ford, Mar. 8, 1911. On May 5, 1911, the Bancroft Company of New York asked Ford to join J. J. Hill, George Westinghouse, Judge Gary, Henry C. Frick, Washington Roebling, J. Ogden Armour, and Levi P. Morton in contributing to a revision of H. H. Bancroft's *Wealth and the Achievements of Civilization.* Each of the above letters is in Acc. 35, Box 2.

11. Illustrated Press Bureau to Henry Ford, Apr. 8, 1910. Acc. 2, Box 32; Pack Brothers to Henry Ford, May 5, 1911, Acc. 2, Box 35; Oliver Lippincott to Henry Ford, Feb. 4, 1910, Acc. 2, Box 32; *San Francisco*

Chronicle, Jan. 10, 1913; New Britain (Conn.) Herald, n.d. [1912]; Grand Rapids (Mich.) Herald, Jan. 4, 1914.

12. According to Samuel S. Marquis, Henry Ford: An Interpretation (Boston: Little, Brown, and Company, 1923), p. 134, Couzens, after each of the company's major accomplishments, "joined with the bleachers" in shouting, " 'Henry did it.' " In his 1915 letter of resignation, Couzens stated, "It was largely through my efforts that the Ford Motor Company was built up around one man—Henry Ford." Simonds, Henry Ford, pp. 148–49.

13. Keith Sward, The Legend of Henry Ford, p. 20; Musselman, Get a Horse!, pp. 46–47; DFP, July 28, 1903. In the early 1930s, Ford dumbfounded his advertising staff by telling them that he had built his first car in 1896, not 1893, as the manufacturer's official biographies and company publicity had steadfastly maintained for thirty years. William C. Richards, The Last Billionaire: Henry Ford (New York: Charles Scribner's Sons, 1948), p. 326.

14. Nevins and Hill, Ford: The Times, p. 448; J.C. Long, Roy D. Chapin ([Bethlehem, Pa.: privately printed], 1945), pp. 109–13. When Hudson ads proclaimed Coffin as the foremost designer in the automobile industry, Couzens wrote Roy D. Chapin, Hudson's president, that Ford, not Coffin, was America's leading auto designer, and demanded that Chapin admit it. Chapin replied that the question was a "matter of opinion," after which Couzens again insisted that Ford's accomplishments were much greater than those of Coffin. The exchange of correspondence is revealing in that it indicates the lengths to which Couzens went in upholding Ford's reputation.

15. Ford's election followed the death of John S. Gray, the company's first president, on July 6, 1906. During the same year, four of the original twelve stockholders, including Alexander Malcomson, sold their shares to Ford and Couzens. Ford owned 58.5 percent of the stock from 1906 until 1919, when he acquired 100 percent ownership. Couzens held 10.1 percent of the stock during this period. Directors' Minutes, July 14, 1906, Acc. 85, Box 1; Nevins and Hill, Ford: The Times, pp. 330–31.

16. Horseless Age 16 (Oct. 8, 1905), xxi; Motor Age 20 (Aug. 17, 1911), 51; 21 (June 27, 1912), 84. George Romney and Henry Ford II are the only auto executives in recent years who have signed their firms' advertisements. Romney and American Motors Corporation's Public Relations Department at first objected to this advertising approach, but were won over by the firm's advertising agency, which produced evidence that such ads would be more widely read. The ads, of course, put the emphasis on AMC's products, not Romney. AMC also centered its publicity effort on Romney during the late 1950s and early 1960s. This policy, according to a company spokesman, was "deliberate" but not contrived—it simply made sense and developed naturally from Romney's "articulateness, his extraordinary news sense, his persuasiveness, his willingness to speak out, and the generally appealing nature of his personality." John R. Pichurski, press relations manager, American Motors Corporation to David L. Lewis, May 31, 1962. Romney went on to become governor of Michigan in 1962, and was named secretary of the U.S. Department of Housing and Urban Development in 1969. Henry Ford II signed introductory newspaper and magazine advertisements for the Pinto car in 1970. For representative ads see DFP, May 18, 1970, and Newsweek 75 (May 25, 1970), 96.

17. Motor 3 (Feb. 1905), 16; Simonds, Henry Ford, p. 107; DFP, Mar. 20 and 27, 1910.

18. Ford Times 1 (July 1, 1908), 8; 5 (Nov. 1911), 160. For laudatory articles on Couzens, see Ford Times 1 (July 1, 1908), 9; 6 (Oct. 1912), 37; and 6 (June 1913), 372–73.

19. Charles B. Sawyer to Frank L. Klingensmith, July 14, 1909, Acc. 2, Box 31; Accounting Department to Farm Implement News, June 12, 1908; H. B. Waldron, Fowler, Kan., to Henry Ford, Oct. 9, 1909; and Frank L. Klingensmith to Gas Power Age, Mar. 8, 1910; all in Acc. 2, Box 27.

20. Nevins and Hill, Ford: The Times, p. 352; DN, Dec. 27, 1908; Milwaukee Free Press, Aug. 10, 1913; San Francisco Chronicle, Oct. 1, 1912; Chicago Post, n.d. [1911], Clipbook 1.

21. Motor Age 23 (Jan. 15, 1914), 16. Ford's modest behavior as the guest of honor at an ALAM banquet immediately following the Selden patent victory was reported in glowing terms by the trade press, which, incidentally, viewed Ford's refusal to make a speech as a reflection of his modesty rather than of any fear of the public rostrum. Motor Age 25 (Jan. 19, 1911), 27; Horseless Age 27 (Jan. 18, 1911), 172. According to Elbert Hubbard, Ford was "very seldom in the limelight, and then not of his own choosing." Elbert Hubbard, "A Little Journey to the Workshop of Henry Ford," Ford Times 5 (June 1912), 244. DT, June 16, 1913; New York Sun, Sept. 7, 1913.

22. Frank L. Klingensmith to Horace P. Dix, Nov. 18, 1909, Acc. 2, Box 31; Fred L. Black, Reminiscences, p. 174; Sorensen, Forty Years, p. 29.

23. The figure "sixteen" is based on an analysis of the company's clipbooks and all the other sources I have examined. When Ford spoke, even informally to schoolchildren, it was such a newsworthy occasion that it seems doubtful that he ever gave a talk which was not reported. Ford told the story about Sing Sing at a Dearborn (Mich.) high school banquet in 1916. Dearborn Independent, Feb. 4, 1916. Harvey Firestone later denied that Ford had addressed the prisoners, stating that he had merely bowed to them. Simonds, Henry Ford, p. 150. Chicago American, July 2, 1934; Louis P. Lochner, Henry Ford—America's Don Quixote (New York: International Publishers, 1925), pp. 41–42.

24. DFP, Sept. 24, 1934 and April 12, 1928; NYT, Apr. 29, 1938; Acc. 285, Box 2367 (for a copy of the World's Fair speech).

25. DT, Feb. 5, 1906; Henry Ford, "Special Automobile Steels," Harper's Weekly 51 (Mar. 16, 1907), 386G.

26. Ford Times 3 (Feb. 1, 1910), 14 [reprint of article in Detroit Saturday Night]; unidentified, undated [1911] item on p. 10 of Clipbook 1; Los Angeles Record, July 7, 1914. The quotation is in the Memphis (Tenn.) Scimitar, Feb. 8, 1913.

Chapter 5

1. Nevins and Hill, Ford: The Times, pp. 527, 647–48. The Ford Company was one of relatively few firms which provided incentive bonuses to employees before World War I. Ford's "efficiency" bonuses were introduced in 1911. Many companies adopted incentive compensation plans during the war, including Studebaker (1914) and GM (1918). Daniel Bloomfield, ed., Financial Incentive for Employers and Executives (New York: H. W. Wilson Company, 1923), 1, pp. 115, 298; 2, p. 367.

2. Ibid., pp. 529–30.

3. Sorensen, Forty Years, p. 139; E.G. Pipp, Henry Ford: Both Sides of Him (Detroit: Pipp's Magazine, 1926), p. 48. Couzens wrote a friend in 1916: "It was

quite natural that Mr. Ford should be credited with this project because he was the head of the company, a majority stockholder, and it was to the benefit of the Ford Motor Company that he should be credited with it; because it gave it a personal touch which was greatly beneficial in an advertising way and kept the name Ford much more before the public...." Barnard, *Independent Man*, p. 94. Nevins and Hill make the point that the plan "would probably have been vetoed had Couzens violently opposed it, and could certainly never have been approved without Ford's hearty support." Nevins and Hill, *Ford: The Times*, pp. 533, 539–40.

4. Garet Garrett, "Henry Ford's Experiment in Good-Will," *Everybody's Magazine* 30 (Apr. 1914), 463; *Detroit Journal*, Jan. 5, 1941.

5. Shepard Bancroft Clough and Charles Woolsey Cole, *Economic History of Europe* (3rd ed., Boston: Heath, 1952), p. 665. Nevins and Hill, *Expansion and Challenge*, p. 601; R.L. Bruckberger, *Image of America*, trans., C.G. Paulding and Virgilia Peterson (New York: Viking Press, 1950), pp. 195–97. The American automobile industry—and particularly the Ford Company, which made record profits of $25,046,000 in 1913 and $30,338,000 in 1914—remained prosperous throughout the depression of 1913–14. Consequently, at the time the profit-sharing plan was announced there were no fears that Ford might not earn enough money in 1914 to pay its employees a minimum of $5.00 a day. Nevins and Hill, *ibid.*, p. 542; Kennedy, *Automobile Industry*, pp. 75, 85.

6. *Detroit Journal*, Jan. 5, 1914; Merrill Denison, *The Power To Go* (New York: Doubleday, 1956), p. 193; Garrett, "Experiment in Good-Will," pp. 462–63.

7. Musselman, *Get a Horse!*, p. 232. Detroit newspapers sold "like war extras," according to *Detroit Saturday Night* 7 (Jan. 10, 1914), 2.

8. Theodore F. MacManus and Norman Beasley, *Men, Money, and Motors* (New York: Harper & Brothers, 1930), p. 163; *Boston Commercial*, Jan. 17, 1914; Musselman, *Get a Horse!*, p. 232; Merz, *Then Came Ford*, pp. 118, 122; Mark Sullivan, *Our Times The United States 1900–1925*, 6 vols. (New York: Charles Scribner's Sons, 1932), 4, p. 40; *Motor Age* 25 (Jan. 15, 1914), 26–27. The Brownell quotation was made in a speech before the Birmingham (Ala.) Exchange and Advertising clubs and reported in the *Birmingham News* of Jan. 7, 1924. See Clipbooks 1 through 5 for press items on the five-dollar day.

9. *Cleveland Plain Dealer*, Jan. 11, 1914; Merz, *Then Came Ford*, p. 118 (quoting *New York Sun, New York Herald, New York Evening Post*, and *New York World*); *Toledo Blade*, Jan. 9, 1914; *Algonac* (Mich.) *Courier*, Jan. 9, 1914.

10. Five-dollar day cartoons, many of them unidentified as to source, abound in Clipbooks 2 and 3. The Mutt and Jeff cartoon appears in the *South Bend* (Ind.) *Tribune*, n.d. [Jan. 1914], Clipbook 2; the farm boy in the *Cincinnati Times-Star*, Jan. 9, 1914; the Webster cartoon in the *New York Globe*, Jan. 10, 1914. Women actually did dress as men in an attempt to get jobs at Ford. *Detroit Tribune*, Feb. 26, 1914.

11. *Wall Street Journal*, Jan. 8, 1914; Merz, *Then Came Ford*, p. 118 (quoting NYT); *St. Louis Post-Dispatch*, Jan. 11, 1914 (quoting *Pittsburgh Gazette-Times*).

12. *Syracuse Journal*, Jan. 13, 1914; *Kittanning* (Pa.) *Times*, Jan. 13, 1914; *Washington Times*, Jan. 9, 1914. In 1913 Detroit's auto workers were among the nation's highest paid industrial employees. Sweepers, paid a daily minimum of $2.34 by Ford and a comparable figure by other auto makers, received only $1.00 to $1.50 a day in New York. Nevins and Hill, *Ford: The Times*, p. 535; Merz, *Then Came Ford*, p. 116.

13. *Everett* (Wash.) *Tribune*, Jan. 10, 1914; Jan. 8, 1914; *Boston News Bureau*, Jan. 8, 1914; *Printers' Ink* 86 (Jan. 22, 1914), 190; *Syracuse Journal*, Jan. 8, 1914; *Philadelphia Telegram*, Jan. 9, 1914; *Menominee* (Wis.) *Herald-Leader*, Jan. 17, 1914; Gerald Stanley Lee, "Is Ford an Inspired Millionaire?," *Harper's Weekly* 58 (Mar. 14, 1914), 10.

14. *Burlington* (Iowa) *Hawkeye*, Jan. 18, 1914; *Marshalltown* (Iowa) *Republican*, Jan. 9, 1914. The only company in the automobile industry which followed Ford's example was the Timken Axle Company of Akron. Its profit-sharing plan was abandoned after one year. Nevins and Hill, *Ford: The Times*, p. 550. American Motors Corporation, which signed a profit-sharing agreement with the United Auto Workers in 1961, acknowledged that its plan was partly inspired by the five-dollar day. Vice-president Edward L. Cushman, the "architect" of the 1961 agreement, was fond of showing reporters the "screaming 47-year-old newspaper headlines" which heralded the Ford announcement. *Christian Science Monitor*, Aug. 14, 1961; *Wall Street Journal*, Feb. 15, 1962.

15. *East Boston* (Mass.) *Free Press*, n.d. [Jan. 1914], Clipbook 3; *Cleveland News*, Jan. 14, 1914; Nevins and Hill, *Ford: The Times*, pp. 548–49.

16. Nevins and Hill, *Ford: The Times*, pp. 434–35; Dixon Wecter, *The Hero in America: A Chronicle of Hero-Worship* (New York: Charles Scribner's Sons, 1941), p. 420; Marshall W. Fishwick, *American Heroes: Myth and Reality* (Washington: Public Affairs Press, 1954), p. 121; United Press dispatch of Jan. 6, 1914; *Detroit Journal*, Jan. 12, 1914; see Clipbook 1 for news stories and editorials on the riot.

17. *Ford Times* 7 (Mar. 1914), 253; Nevins and Hill, *Ford: The Times*, p. 544. The letters apparently were discarded; they are not in the Ford Archives.

18. See Clipbook 1 for news stories and editorials crediting Ford with responsibility for the five-dollar day; Burlingame, *Henry Ford*, p. 79; *New York Sun*, Jan. 5, 1914; Barnard, *Independent Man*, pp. 76–77; Malcolm W. Bingay, "Get a Horse," *Saturday Evening Post* 212 (June 29, 1940), 74. Although Bingay, a member of the editorial staff of the *Detroit News* for many years, states that Couzens actually did write this statement to the newspaper, Barnard says that the story is apocryphal.

19. *Horseless Age* 33 (Jan. 14, 1914), 63; *Detroit Journal*, Jan. 14, 1914. The article that referred to Couzens's office was Garrett's "Experiment in Good-Will," p. 463. Other major articles on the five-dollar day are "Henry Ford," *Independent* 77 (Jan. 19, 1914), 99; "Sensationalism in Profit-Sharing," *Living Age* 280 (Feb. 28, 1914), 568–71; Lee, "Inspired Millionaire," pp. 9–11; Julian Street, "Detroit the Dynamic," *Collier's* 53 (July 4, 1914), 10; "Henry Ford; Or, How to Be Happy on a Million a Month," *Current Opinion* 57 (Aug. 1914), 95–96.

20. *Detroit Journal*, Jan. 7, 1914; *Rochester* (N.Y.) *Union and Advertiser*, Jan. 9, 1914; *New York Herald*, Jan. 11, 1914; *New York World*, Jan. 10, 1914; Sullivan, *Our Times*, 4, p. 59.

21. *Washington Times-Herald*, Jan. 9, 1914; *New York Herald*, Jan. 9, 1914; *Philadelphia North American*, Jan. 9, 1914. The statement, "I think it is a disgrace to die rich," did of course reflect a view expressed earlier by Andrew Carnegie. Walter Wilson Jennings, *Twenty Giants of American Business* (New York: Exposition Press, 1953), p. 102.

22. Merz, *Then Came Ford*, pp. 122–24.

23. *New York Times Index*, Jan.-Mar. 1914 ed.; *Reader's Guide to Periodical Literature*, 1910–1914 ed.; Clipbooks 1–5; *Tacoma Tribune*, Jan. 10, 1914; *New York*

Herald, Jan. 11, 1914; Merz, *Then Came Ford,* p. 118; *Cleveland Press,* Jan. 13, 1914; *Tacoma Times,* Jan. 15, 1914.

24. Street, "Detroit the Dynamic," p. 24; *East Boston* (Mass.) *Free Press,* Jan. 10, 1914.

25. Sward, *Legend of Henry Ford,* p. 279; W.M. Cunningham, *"J8": A Chronicle of the Neglected Truth about Henry Ford D. E. and the Ford Motor Company* (Detroit: North American Publishing Co. [1930]), pp. 5–6, 103; Black, *Reminiscences,* p. 158; Wilbur Forrest, *Behind the Front Page* (London: Appleton-Century Company, 1934), p. 267; Samuel S. Marquis, *Henry Ford: An Interpretation* (Boston: Little, Brown, and Company, 1923), p. 72; *Ford Times* 7 (Feb. 1914), 197; *Detroit News-Tribune,* Oct. 27, 1914.

26. *Detroit Journal,* Dec. 18, 1916; "Henry Ford," *Current Opinion,* p. 95; Stewart H. Holbrook, *The Age of the Moguls* (Garden City, N.Y.: Doubleday & Company, Inc., 1953), pp. ix, 213; Arthur Train, "The Billionaire Era," *Forum* 72 (Dec. 1924), 749; *Chicago Record-Herald,* Feb. 1, 1914.

27. *Toledo Blade,* Jan. 9, 1914; Sward, *Legend of Henry Ford,* p. 342.

28. *What the Public Thinks of Big Business,* Curtis Publishing Company, Division of Commercial Research, May 1937, Acc. 454, Box 9; Sward, *Legend of Henry Ford,* p. 370; "Ten Men and a Woman," *Fortune* 21 (June 1940), 163; *Boston Globe,* Mar. 29, 1941. The *Fortune* survey, conducted for the magazine by Elmo Roper, is believed to have been the first nationwide representative sample of labor ever taken. Respondents were shown a list containing the names of eleven prominent labor leaders, industrialists, and political figures, then asked, "Which of these people do you feel have been on the whole helpful to labor and which harmful?"

29. Richards, *Last Billionaire,* pp. 1, 7; Sullivan, *Our Times* 4, p. 48; Sward, *Legend of Henry Ford,* p. 63; Nevins and Hill, *Expansion and Challenge,* p. 20; Merz, *Then Came Ford,* pp. 124–25; *New York Telegraph,* May 8, 1914; "What Detroit Thinks of Henry Ford's Farce," *Detroit Saturday Night* 9 (Dec. 18, 1915), 1.

30. *Detroit Journal,* July 9, 1914; *Detroit Tribune,* Jan. 23, 1915; *Gloversville* (N.Y.) *Republican,* n.d. [Jan. 1915], p. 134 of Clipbook 5.

31. Garet Garrett, *The Wild Wheel* (New York: Pantheon Books, 1952), p. 152; Nevins and Hill, *Expansion and Challenge,* p. 617; *Chicago Examiner,* Mar. 21, 1921; Arthur Pound, "The Ford Myth," *Atlantic Monthly* 133 (Jan. 1924), 44; Sorensen, *Forty Years,* p. 27.

32. Harry Bennett, as told to Paul Marcus, *We Never Called Him Henry* (New York: Fawcett Publications, Inc., 1951), p. 156; Richards, *Last Billionaire,* pp. 220, 224; Marquis, *Henry Ford,* p. 163.

Chapter 6

1. *Detroit News-Tribune,* Mar. 23, 1913; *The Case of the Little White Slaver* (Detroit: Henry Ford, 1914), p. 5; *Dearborn Independent,* May 22, 1920; Nevins and Hill, *Expansion and Challenge,* pp. 311–16; DFP, July 12, 1925; *Cincinnati Times-Star,* July 15, 1925; DN, July 28, 1944.

2. *Ford Times* 8 (Feb. 1915), inside front cover; Nevins and Hill, *Expansion and Challenge,* p. 23; *Detroit Journal,* Nov. 29, 1915.

3. See Clipbook 6 for antipreparedness articles under Ford's signature; *New York American,* Aug. 16, 1915; DFP, Aug. 22, 1915; DFP, Sept. 5, 1915.

4. *Detroit Journal,* Sept. 13, 1915 (quoting the *Army and Navy Journal*); *Ford Times* 9 (Oct. 1915), 103–7.

5. Barnard, *Independent Man,* pp. 4–5; Nevins and Hill, *Expansion and Challenge,* pp. 23–24; Richards, *Last Billionaire,* p. 70.

6. Louis P. Lochner, *Henry Ford—America's Don Quixote* (New York: International Publishers, 1925), pp. 10–14, 17–20; Nevins and Hill, *Expansion and Challenge,* pp. 26–28.

7. Oswald Garrison Villard, "Unveiling of Henry Ford," *Nation* 106 (July 26, 1919), 102; Nevins and Hill, *Expansion and Challenge,* pp. 28–30.

8. Merz, *Then Came Ford,* p. 158; *Tampa Tribune,* Dec. 5, 1915; *New York American,* Dec. 6, 1915. Representative stories and editorials appear in the *Atlantic City Review,* Dec. 3, 1915; *Austin Statesman,* Dec. 15, 1915; *Goshen* (N.Y.) *Democrat,* Dec. 16, 1915; *San Francisco Chronicle,* Dec. 23, 1915, and the *Phoenix Republican,* Dec. 26, 1915. These and hundreds of other articles on the peace ship are in Clipbook 6.

9. Nevins and Hill, *Expansion and Challenge,* pp. 36, 40; NYT, Jan. 31, 1915; *New York American,* Jan. 3, 1916; "Henry Ford," *Nation* 102 (Jan. 13, 1916), 45; *Elmira Advertiser,* Dec. 7, 1915; Simonds, *Henry Ford,* pp. 153, 155.

10. *Philadelphia North American,* Dec. 5, 1915; Jonathan Norton Leonard, *The Tragedy of Henry Ford* (New York: G.P. Putnam's Sons, 1933), p. 83; *Times* (London), Dec. 6, 1915; *New York Telegraph,* Dec. 6, 1915.

11. *New York World,* Jan. 16, 1916; *New York Telegram,* Dec. 5, 1915; *New York American,* Dec. 6, 1915. The *Los Angeles Times,* Dec. 18, 1915, ran a full page of the cartoons.

12. *New York World,* Dec. 21, 1915; "Aboard the *Oscar II,*" *Survey* 35 (Jan. 15, 1916), 458–59.

13. Nevins and Hill, *Expansion and Challenge,* p. 42; *Duluth* (Minn.) *Tribune,* Dec. 26, 1915; *New York American,* Dec. 19, 1915; *Troy* (N.Y.) *Record,* Dec. 28, 1915.

14. *Boston Post,* Jan. 10, 1916; DN, Feb. 1, 1916; *Detroit Journal,* Jan. 6, 1916. When the *Oscar II* entered European waters its radio was silenced. Reporters had to mail their dispatches to America, which accounts for the delayed publication dates.

15. DT, Jan. 1, 1916; DN, Jan. 15, 1916; *New York Sun,* Jan. 25, 1916.

16. "Aboard *Oscar II,*" *Survey,* p. 458; *Quincy* (Mass.) *Journal,* Feb. 5, 1916; *New York Tribune,* Jan. 9, 1916.

17. Nevins and Hill, *Expansion and Challenge,* pp. 44–46, 50–52; Lochner, *Henry Ford,* p. 89; DN, Dec. 24, 1915; NYT, Mar. 12, 1916 and Feb. 15, 1917. The *Oscar II* was dismantled in 1933 by a British ship-breaking company which paid $67,500 for the ex-peace ark. *Time* 22 (Sept. 11, 1933), 36.

18. *Saginaw* (Mich.) *Herald,* Jan. 6, 1916; *New York American,* Jan. 3, 1916.

19. *New York Tribune,* Dec. 30, 1915.

20. Benson, *New Henry Ford,* p. 298; Archibald Henderson, *Contemporary Immortals* (New York: D. Appleton and Company, 1930), p. 193; Simonds, *Henry Ford,* pp. 156–57; "The Ford Heritage," *Fortune* 29 (June 1944), 140; Nevins and Hill, *Expansion and Challenge,* p. 53.

21. Leonard, *Tragedy of Henry Ford,* p. 47; Liebold, *Reminiscences,* p. 273. Ford felt that it would have cost him $10,000,000 to "break in cold" into the European market after the war; and that the expendi-

ture of this sum was made unnecessary by the publicity he obtained from his $465,000 peace venture. Richards, *Last Billionaire*, p. 48.

22. DT, Feb. 14, 1916; *Editor & Publisher* 84 (Feb. 26, 1916), 1139; *Fourth Estate*, no. 1148 (Feb. 26, 1916), 2; Merz, *Then Came Ford*, p. 171; NYT, Feb. 22, 1916; DN, Apr. 9, 1916.

23. DN, May 6, 1916; *Mankato* (Minn.) *Free Press*, May 26, 1916; *New York Journal of Commerce*, Aug. 22, 1916; DN, Aug. 22, 1916; *Evansville* (Ind.) *Courier*, May 10, 1916; DT, Feb. 5, 1917; *New York Telegraph*, July 10, 1917.

Chapter 7

1. DT and DN, Feb. 5, 1917; Nevins and Hill, *Expansion and Challenge*, p. 76.

2. Nevins and Hill, *Expansion and Challenge*, pp. 64–65; Merz, *Then Came Ford*, p. 172. Jonathan Daniels, in *The End of Innocence* (New York: J.B. Lippincott Co., 1954), p. 176, quotes Franklin D. Roosevelt, then Assistant Secretary of the Navy, to the effect that Ford, "until he saw a chance for publicity free of charge, thought a submarine was something to eat."

3. *New York World*, Mar. 25, 1918; *New York Tribune*, Aug. 23, 1918; *Chicago Tribune*, Feb. 9, 1919.

4. Nevins and Hill, *Expansion and Challenge*, pp. 69–70, 72, 74; Sward, *Legend of Henry Ford*, p. 95.

5. Nevins and Hill, *Expansion and Challenge*, pp. 74–75; *Ford Man* 3 (May 3, 1919), 1; NYT, Jan. 4, 5, 15, 1919.

6. Directors' Minutes, June 21, 1917, Acc. 85, Box 1; *Printers' Ink* 102 (June 3, 1918), 17; NYT, Nov. 19, 1915, Nov. 25, 1915; Merz, *Then Came Ford*, p. 156; Nevins and Hill, *Expansion and Challenge*, pp. 76, 80.

7. Nevins and Hill, *Expansion and Challenge*, pp. 66–68, 80.

8. William Yorke Stevenson, *At the Front in a Flivver* (Boston: Houghton Mifflin Company, 1917), pp. xvi, 1–2. *Detroit Journal*, July 26, 1918; DN, June 29, 1919; Benson, *New Henry Ford*, p. 222; Nevins and Hill, *Expansion and Challenge*, p. 80; *Printers' Ink* 101 (Dec. 27, 1917), 112; *American Field Service Bulletin*, no. 12 (Sept. 22, 1917), 4–6. The poem also can be found in a May 31 letter from Percival Perry, head of Ford activities in Great Britain, to Edsel Ford, Acc. 6, Box 260.

9. George S. Anderson, assistant secretary to Henry Ford, to H.A. Oldham, Mitchell, S.D., Oct. 18, 1917, Acc. 2, Box 40; Directors' Minutes, June 21–22, 1917, Acc. 85, Box 1; DT, Apr. 3, 1918; Ambrose B. Jewett, head of Department of Photography, to branch managers, Jan. 30, 1918, Acc. 78, Box 45; Film List, Acc. 6, Box 31.

10. DN, Nov. 16, 1917; E.G. Liebold to Herbert Hoover, Sept. 21, 1917, Acc. 2, Box 40; Liebold, *Reminiscences*, p. 354; NYT, Nov. 10, 1917; DFP, Sept. 12, 1918.

11. *Passaic* (N.J.) *News*, Jan. 22, 1918; "Mr. Henry Ford," *World's Work* 36 (Aug. 1918), 340; *Illustrated London News*, Sept. 24, 1918; DT, July 24, 1918; *Automobile Dealer and Repairer* (Mar. 1918), p. 63 of Clipbook 12; *Philadelphia North American*, July 24, 1919; John B. Rae, *American Automobile Manufacturers The First Forty Years* (Philadelphia: Chilton Company, 1959), pp. 124–26; Bernard M. Baruch, *The Public Years* (New York: Holt, Rinehart,

and Winston, 1960), pp. 59–61. The Aug. 26, 1918 edition of the *New York Times*, while reporting the terms of an agreement between the auto manufacturers and the War Industries Board, makes no mention of Baruch's behind-the-scenes power play.

12. Sward, *Legend of Henry Ford*, p. 98; Sarah T. Bushnell, *The Truth about Henry Ford* (Chicago: The Reilly & Lee Co., 1922), p. 96; *Coldwater* (Mich.) *Reporter*, Mar. 28, 1922; *Brooklyn Eagle*, July 26, 1923; Nevins and Hill, *Expansion and Challenge*, pp. 83–84.

13. A.G. Gardiner, *Portraits and Portents* (London: Harper & Brothers, 1926), p. 153; Sward, *Legend of Henry Ford*, pp. 98–99; *Ford News* 18 (Nov. 1938), inside back cover; B. W. Burroughs, Cincinnati branch manager, to H.C. Doss, Mar. 17, 1941, Acc. 450, Box 7; Burlingame, *Henry Ford*, pp. 93–94.

14. Merz, *Then Came Ford*, p. 127; "Henry Ford; Or, How to Be Happy on a Million a Month," *Current Opinion* 57 (Aug. 1914), 95; *Lansing Journal*, May 19, 1914.

15. DN, Apr. 17, 1915 (citing editorials in the *Pasadena News* and *New York Herald*); *Bemidji* (Minn.) *Herald*, Dec. 16, 1915.

16. *Grand Rapids Press*, Apr. 6, 1916; *New York Sun*, Apr. 25, 1916; "The Latest Ford Joke," *Literary Digest* 52 (May 6, 1916), 1267–68; DN, Apr. 24, 1916; Nevins and Hill, *Expansion and Challenge*, pp. 114–15 (citing *St. Louis Times*); *Detroit Journal*, June 10, 1916.

17. DT, July 11, 1916; Nevins and Hill, *Expansion and Challenge*, pp. 116–17; *New York Sun*, Oct. 31, 1916; DFP, Nov. 25, 1916; *Macon* (Ga.) *Telegraph*, Nov. 5, 1916; *Elmira* (N.Y.) *Herald*, Nov. 1, 1916. Ford's advertising campaign, Henry Morgenthau said later, was offered in exchange for a guarantee that the industrialist could personally present to Wilson a plan whereby Ford women employees would be added to the list of eligibles for the five-dollar day. Ford, according to Morgenthau, wanted Wilson to receive credit for "advising" him to take the step, thus giving a publicity fillip to the announcement. *Boston American*, Dec. 4, 1921.

18. Nevins and Hill, *Expansion and Challenge*, p. 118; NYT, June 17, 1918; *Grand Rapids* (Mich.) *Herald*, June 22, 1918; *Detroit Saturday Night* 12 (June 22, 1918), 13; DT, June 14, 1918.

19. Nevins and Hill, *Expansion and Challenge*, pp. 119–20; E.G. Pipp, *The Real Henry Ford* (Detroit: Pipp's Weekly, 1922), p. 31; Sward, *Legend of Henry Ford*, p. 118; *Grand Rapids Press*, Nov. 4, 1918.

20. DFP, Nov. 3, 1918; Simonds, *Henry Ford*, p. 176; Nevins and Hill, *Expansion and Challenge*, p. 79; Bushnell, *Truth about Henry Ford*, pp. 112, 125. Litigation involving Newberry's alleged violation of the Federal Corrupt Practices Act and repeated demands for the senator's expulsion from the upper chamber so embarrassed Newberry that he resigned from the Senate on Nov. 18, 1922. Although Ford had not won a senate seat, neither, in the end, had his rival. Nevins and Hill, *Expansion and Challenge*, pp. 300–1. Ford was elected to the Dearborn Board of Education from 1911 onward. He simply lent his name to the board; he did not attend meetings. *Ibid.*, p. 496.

21. Nevins and Hill, *Expansion and Challenge*, pp. 88, 90, 93–94, 97; DN, Nov. 4, 1916; Burlingame, *Henry Ford*, p. 92; Garrett, *Wild Wheel*, p. 107. The gist of the *Detroit News* article was reprinted in many newspapers; see Clipbook 9.

22. John F. Dodge and Horace E. Dodge *v.* Ford Motor Company, Henry Ford, *et al.*, 204 Michigan Records and Briefs, January term, 1919, pp. 168–69, 215;

Nevins and Hill, *Expansion and Challenge,* p. 97; Richards, *Last Billionaire,* p. 55.

23. DN, Oct. 31, 1917; Nevins and Hill, *Expansion and Challenge,* pp. 103–4; Richards, *Last Billionaire,* p. 55. See Clipbooks 9 and 10 for dozens of articles quoting Ford's testimony at the trial.

24. R.L. Bruckberger, *Image of America,* trans., C.G. Paulding and Virgilia Peterson (New York: Viking Press, 1959), p. 207; Archibald Henderson, *Contemporary Immortals* (New York: D. Appleton and Company, 1930), pp. 182–83; Dixon Wecter, *The Hero in America: A Chronicle of Hero-Worship* (New York: Charles Scribner's Sons, 1941), p. 419; *Detroit Journal,* Dec. 18, 1916.

25. Among newspapers which have carried articles and columns on Ford's testimony are: *Chicago Examiner,* Apr. 14, 1925; *Washington News,* Sept. 6, 1933; *Jones City* (Okla.) *News,* Feb. 18, 1938; *Dearborn Independent,* Feb. 18, 1938 (reprinting *Des Moines Register* cartoon); *Chicago Daily News,* Feb. 23, 1940; and *New York Daily Mirror,* Apr. 22, 1962. Most of the biographies of Ford have devoted attention to the philosophy expressed by Ford during the suit, if not to the suit itself. Bruckberger, *Image of America,* pp. 207, 216–17.

26. Nevins and Hill, *Expansion and Challenge,* pp. 88–89. After Couzens's resignation in 1915, Ford was the only stockholder who was active in the company's management,

27. Stewart H. Holbrook, *The Age of the Moguls* (Garden City, N.Y.: Doubleday & Company, Inc., 1953), p. 208; Nevins and Hill, *Expansion and Challenge,* pp. 105–6; *Los Angeles Examiner,* Mar. 5, 1919. See Clipbook 14 for stories on Ford's plan to build a new car.

28. *Baltimore Evening Sun,* Mar. 11, 1919; *Sacramento Bee,* Mar. 6, 1919; *Automobile Topics* 53 (Mar. 8, 1919), 539. See Acc. 2, Box 42 for the telegrams from chambers of commerce. Clipbook 14 contains newspaper editorials which describe various cities as being ideal as a Ford plant site.

29. *Kansas City Star,* Apr. 18, 1918; DT, Mar. 11, 1919; *Printers' Ink* 106 (Mar. 12, 1919), 138; *Washington Herald,* Mar. 25, 1919; Edsel B. Ford to dealers, Mar. 21, 1919, Acc. 78, Box 1.

30. *Boston Traveler,* Mar. 11, 1919; Nevins and Hill, *Expansion and Challenge,* pp. 107, 109–10, 159.

31. *New York World,* July 16, 1919; Burlingame, *Henry Ford,* p. 98; Holbrook, *Age of Moguls,* p. 208. Shortly after acquiring full ownership of the company, Ford expanded the firm's capitalization to $100,000,000. He turned over 41.652 percent of the stock to Edsel and 3.136 percent to his wife, Clara, and retained the remaining 55.212 percent in his own name. Nevins and Hill, *Expansion and Challenge,* p. 113.

32. *Chicago Tribune,* June 23, 1916; Nevins and Hill, *Expansion and Challenge,* pp. 129–30.

33. *Fall River* (Mass.) *Globe,* Sept. 9, 1916; *Philadelphia Public Ledger,* Sept. 10, 1916; *Sheridan* (Wyo.) *Enterprise* and *Lowell* (Mass.) *Courier,* Sept. 11, 1916; *New York Evening Post,* n.d. [Sept. 1916]; *Washington* (Ind.) *Herald,* Sept. 8, 1916. Pertinent clippings from these newspapers can be found in Acc. 44, Box 14. See Clipbook 8 for general press reaction to Ford's suit.

34. Nevins and Hill, *Expansion and Challenge,* pp. 130–31; Black, *Reminiscences,* pp. 8–9; "Henry Ford at Bay," *Forum* 62 (Aug. 1919), 142; Mt. Clemens News Bureau to editors, May 19, 1920, Acc. 53, Box 17.

35. Black, *Reminiscences,* pp. 8–9; Liebold, *Reminiscences,* p. 299; Mt. Clemens News Bureau Bulletin No. 6, May 26, 1919, Acc. 62, Box 102. Black, a keen young salesman, had joined the *Independent's* staff in November 1918, after being asked to collect information on the cost of publishing the type of newspaper that Ford had in mind. Black, *Reminiscences,* p. 4. For the next twenty-four years he was to play a leading role in Ford's publication, advertising, and public relations activities.

36. "Henry Ford at Bay," *Forum,* p. 142; Black, *Reminiscences,* p. 8; Liebold, *Reminiscences,* p. 432; William J. Cameron, *Reminiscences,* p. 17; DFP, May 22, 1919.

37. Richards, *Last Billionaire,* p. 254; State of Michigan. On the Circuit Court for the County of Macomb, Henry Ford *vs.* The Tribune Company, *et al.* Transcript of Court Record, May 13, 1919-Aug. 14, 1919, p. 7997 (a copy can be found in Acc. 53, Box 6); hereafter cited as Tribune Suit Record. Fred L. Black to D.J. Hutchins, Sales Department, Dec. 8, 1936, Acc. 554, Box 2; DN to Fred L. Black, Oct. 1, 1936, Oct. 30, 1936, Acc. 554, Box 2; DN to FMC, Dec. 12, 1945, Acc. 44, Box 5; Nevins and Hill, *Expansion and Challenge,* p. 125.

38. "Henry Ford at Bay," *Forum,* pp. 135–36; DFP, July 21, 191; D.D. Martin to E.G. Liebold, Aug. 8, 1919, Acc. 62, Box 104; *Detroit Journal,* July 21, 1919; D.D. Martin to O.O. Buck, secretary of the Nebraska Press Association, Aug. 5, 1919, Acc. 53, Box 17; DFP, July 21, 1919; Independent News Bureau to editors, Oct. 21, 1919, Acc. 284, Box 17; Mt. Clemens News Bureau, Detailed Statement of Expenses, Acc. 62, Box 104.

39. Mt. Clemens News Bureau to editors, May 19, 1919, Acc. 53, Box 17. See the Bureau's Bulletins, Acc. 62, Box 104.

40. "Henry Ford at Bay," *Forum,* p. 141; Nevins and Hill, *Expansion and Challenge,* pp. 133, 136–38; Tribune Suit Record, 5747, 5868–5872; Niven Busch, Jr., *Twenty-One Americans* (Garden City, N.Y.: Doubleday, Doran & Company, Inc., 1930), p. 6 (cartoons); "Grilling of Henry Ford," *Literary Digest* 62 (Aug. 9, 1919), 44–46 (citing *Cincinnati Times-Star*); Burlingame, *Henry Ford,* p. 7.

41. *Chicago Tribune,* Aug. 21, 1919 (citing NYT and *Sioux City Journal*); "Grilling of Henry Ford," *Literary Digest,* p. 44 (citing *New York Tribune*); "Unveiling of Henry Ford," *Nation* 109 (July 26, 1919), 102.

42. Sward, *Legend of Henry Ford,* p. 106; Kenneth M. Goode and Harford Powel, Jr., *What about Advertising?* (New York: Harper & Brothers, 1927), p. 211; Garrett, *Wild Wheel,* p. 185; *Baltimore News,* July 29, 1919; *Baltimore Evening Sun,* Feb. 4, 1927; Nevins and Hill, *Expansion and Challenge,* p. 140. Box 4 of Acc. 62 is filled with signed coupons. "Grilling of Henry Ford," *Literary Digest,* p. 46 (citing *Ohio State Journal*); *Cleveland Plain Dealer,* Aug. 24, 1919.

43. *Detroit Journal,* July 21, 1919. Ford mentioned the first objective in conversation with Joseph J. O'Neill, a member of the News Bureau's staff, in late July 1919, according to O'Neill's letter of resignation to Ford, Dec. 22, 1919, Acc. 62, Box 1. Suggestions for attaining the second objective are set forth in a five-page memorandum from D.D. Martin to E.G. Liebold, Aug. 8, 1919, Acc. 62, Box 104.

44. *Detroit Journal,* Aug. 16, 1919. O'Neill, who was president of the peace ship's Viking Press Club, was cited in Stanley Walker's book, *City Editor* (New York: Blue Ribbon Books, Inc., 1934), pp. 282–87 as

one of New York's twelve best reporters. D.D. Martin to E.G. Liebold, Aug. 25, 1919, Sept. 4, 1919, Acc. 62, Box 104; Independent News Bureau to editors, Oct. 21, 1919, Acc. 284, Box 17; Mt. Clemens News Bureau, Detailed Statement of Expenses, Acc. 62, Box 104.

45. Independent News Bureau to editors, Oct. 21, 1919, and D.D. Martin to E.G. Liebold, Nov. 28, 1919, Nov. 29, 1919, Acc. 284, Box 17.

46. D.D. Martin to E.G. Liebold, Jan. 3, 1920, Acc. 284, Box 17, and Feb. 11, 1920, Acc. 284, Box 1; Farnham F. Dudgeon, editor and publisher, Community and Suburban Press Service, Frankfort, Ky., to David L. Lewis, July 13, 1962; Fred R. Dolsen, assistant secretary to Henry Ford, to D.D. Martin, Feb. 13, 1920, Acc. 284, Box 1.

47. D.D. Martin to E.G. Liebold, Aug. 8, 1919, Acc. 62, Box 104; Edsel Ford to FMC Department Heads, July 2, 1942, Acc. 285, Box 2495; Steve Hannagan to Joe Copps and John Thompson (Hannagan subordinates), June 26, 1942, Acc. 7, Box 376. Martin left Ford's employ to become editor of the *Detroit Free Press,* and during the 1950s was head of the Department of Journalism at the University of Arizona. D.D. Martin, Tucson, Ariz., to David L. Lewis, Aug. 24, 1962.

48. Lawrence H. Seltzer, *A Financial History of the American Automobile Industry: A Study of the Ways in Which the Leading American Producers of Automobiles Have Met Their Capital Requirements* (Boston: Houghton Mifflin Company, 1928), pp. 75, 109; Nevins and Hill, *Expansion and Challenge,* pp. 148–50.

49. Nevins and Hill, *Expansion and Challenge,* pp. 152–53, 159; *San Francisco Bulletin,* Sept. 21, 1920; *Chicago Examiner,* Sept. 22, 1920.

50. See Clipbook 20 and Acc. 284, Boxes 10, 14 for scores of front-page news stories (and editorials) on Ford's announcement. *San Francisco Call,* Sept. 21, 1920; *Sidney* (Del.) *Record,* Sept. 25, 1920; *Utah Times,* Sept. 25, 1920; *Pratt* (Kan.) *Republican,* Sept. 25, 1920; *San Diego Sun,* n.d. [Sept. 1920]; *Kerrville* (Texas) *Sun,* n.d. [Sept. 1920]; *Denver Post,* Sept. 22, 1920.

51. *Baltimore Manufacturers Record,* Sept. 30, 1920; *San Francisco Commercial News,* n.d. [Sept. 1920]; *Arkansas Democrat,* n.d. [Sept. 1920], all in Acc. 284, Box 10.

52. *Michigan Manufacturer and Financial Record* 26 (Oct. 2, 1920), 7; Nevins and Hill, *Expansion and Challenge,* pp. 153–54; *Automobile Topics* 59 (Oct. 2, 1920), 782; Henry Ford, in collaboration with Samuel Crowther, *My Life and Work* (Garden City, N.Y.: Garden City Publishing Co., Inc., 1922), p. 171.

53. *Motor Age* 38 (Sept. 30, 1920), 3; Kennedy, *Automobile Industry,* p. 120; Nevins and Hill, *Expansion and Challenge,* pp. 154–55, 157–59.

54. Garrett, *Wild Wheel,* p. 121; *Philadelphia Public Ledger,* n.d. [Jan. 1921]; NYT, Jan. 21, 1921; *Oil City* (Pa.) *Blizzard,* Jan. 31, 1921; *Denver Post,* Feb. 5, 1921; Robert Littell, "Henry Ford," *New Republic* 36 (Nov. 14, 1923), 302; *Columbus* (Ohio) *Citizen,* Feb. 4, 1921; *New York Sun,* Feb. 9, 1921.

55. Nevins and Hill, *Expansion and Challenge,* pp. 160, 164–66; DN, July 22, 1921. The *Springfield* (Mass.) *Union,* of July 17, 1921, reported that 125,000 "surplus cars" were forwarded to agents.

56. DN, July 22, 1921; Jonathan Norton Leonard, *The Tragedy of Henry Ford* (New York: G.P. Putnam's Sons, 1932), p. 191; "How Henry Ford Did It," *Literary Digest* 70 (July 30, 1921), 42; Sward, *Legend*

of Henry Ford, p. 77; Benson, *New Henry Ford,* p. 183; Oswald Garrison Villard, *Prophets True and False* (New York: A.A. Knopf, 1928), p. 297; Nevins and Hill, *Expansion and Challenge,* p. 167.

Chapter 8

1. Simonds, *Henry Ford,* p. 141; Merrill Denison, *The Power To Go* (New York: Doubleday, 1956), p. 194; *Ford Times* 7 (Aug.-Sept. 1914), 483; NYT, July 31, 1914.

2. Denison, *Power To Go,* p. 194; NYT, July 31, Aug. 1, 1914.

3. *Jackson* (Mich.) *Press,* Aug. 1, 1914; *New Castle* (Pa.) *Herald,* Aug. 1, 1914; *San Antonio Light,* Aug. 16, 1914; DFP, Aug. 16, 1914; *Butte* (Mont.) *Miner,* Aug. 6, 1914; Liebold, *Reminiscences,* p. 1110; *Ford Times* 9 (Nov. 1915), 187. See Clipbook 5 for clippings on the announcement of the rebate plan and on the rebate itself.

4. *Ford Times* 9 (Aug. 1915), 3; 9 (Sept. 1915), 66; 9 (Nov. 1915), 172, 187; *St. Louis Republic,* Aug. 5, 1915; "A New Yardstick," *Sales Management and Advertisers' Weekly* 16 (Nov. 17, 1928), 444. In late 1960 American Motors Corporation announced a "rebate" plan which was widely compared with the Ford scheme. Under the AMC plan, buyers of the corporation's cars during the Dec. 1960-Mar. 1961 period were given a $25.00 U.S. savings bond for each 10 percent increase in unit sales for the comparable month of the previous year. AMC's December sales were up 13.8 percent and each customer was sent a $25.00 bond. However, sales declined throughout the auto industry in early 1961, and the AMC plan fizzled. DN, Dec. 15, 16, 21, 1960; NYT, Dec. 16, 1960; DFP, Dec. 19, 1960 and Jan. 6, 1961; AMC news release, Feb. 2, 1961, GM Public Relations Library, Detroit.

5. *Ford Times* 9 (July 1916), 540; "New Yardstick," *Sales Management and Advertisers' Weekly,* p. 444. Commonwealth Edison Company, of Chicago, and General Electric were perhaps the first firms to use film for sales-promotion purposes. Commonwealth Edison showed film on powerhouse operations and on the use of electricity in the home at Chicago's White City Amusement Park in 1909; and the Essanay Corporation, of Chicago, produced an appliance film, *Every Husband's Opportunity,* for General Electric in 1909. General Electric itself produced a film on railroad electrification in 1912. The same year United States Steel made a nontheatrical film, *An American in the Making*: the following year the National Association of Manufacturers produced three films on industrial safety, fire prevention, and the need for a formal education. Splitdorf Electrical Company and Thomas B. Jeffery had sales-promotion films produced for their use in 1913 and 1914. Other pioneer sponsors of films included International Harvester, Swift and Company, American Telephone & Telegraph, Caterpillar Tractor, the Lackawanna Railroad, and the Great Northern Railway. "Central Station Publicity By the Use of Moving Pictures," *Electrical World* 60 (Apr. 28, 1910), 1068–69; D.E. Wretlind, Audio-Visual Communications Section, General Electric Company, to David L. Lewis, May 25, 1962; William H. McGaughey, vice-president, National Association of Manufacturers, to Milton Fairman, editor, *Public*

Relations Journal, June 23, 1971 (copy to David L. Lewis); Robert O. Dunn, "Ford Motor Company Captures Annual Film Audience of 64,000,000," *Public Relations Journal* 18 (Dec. 1961), 11; *Horseless Age* 31 (June 18, 1913), 1095; DFP, Sept. 13, 1914; L.L.L. Golden, "Public Relations," *Saturday Review* (Dec. 9, 1961), 65.

6. *Boston American,* June 1, 1913; *New York Sun,* Sept. 7, 1913; *New York World,* Jan. 11, 1914; *Akron Times,* Jan. 13, 1914; DN, Apr. 15, 1918; *Belvidere* (Ill.) *Republican,* July 15, 1914.

7. *St. Louis Republic,* Nov. 20, 1914; *Ford Times* 9 (July 1916), 535, 537. The company also bought film from free-lance motion-picture cameramen. King Vidor, in *A Tree Is a Tree* (New York: Harcourt, Brace, 1952), p. 55, tells how he and a few friends in 1915 staged a mock bank robbery in hopes of selling film footage to Ford. The company recognized the scene as a farce, but did buy some "travel" film which Vidor had taken between Galveston and Hollywood the same year.

8. DN, Feb. 26, 1916; *Ford Times* 9 (May 1916), 459; 9 (July 1916), 535; Vidor, *Tree Is a Tree,* p. 47; Clayton Sedgwick Cooper, "Advertising Values in the Ford Business," *Editor & Publisher* (May 20, 1916), 1583.

9. *Ford Times* 10 (Feb. 1917), 302; DN, April 15, 1918; *Advertising & Selling* 30 (July 10, 1920), 40. A list of the 190 Ford Educational Weeklies produced between 1916 and 1920 can be found in Acc. 6, Box 31.

10. *New York Telegraph,* Dec. 7, 1918; *Ford Times* 10 (Feb. 2, 1917), 313; *Ford Man* 1 (Sept. 20, 1917), 3; 4 (Dec. 31, 1919), 2; *Butte* (Mont.) *Post,* June 19, 1920; "Why Henry Ford Wants to Be Senator," *World's Work* 36 (Sept. 1918), 527; DN, Dec. 8, 1918. In 1952, for example, GM spent $330,000 on films. Ford spent $450,000 in 1952, $407,000 in 1954. The Public Relations Program of General Motors Corporation with Marginal Notes on the Ford Motor Company Public Relations Program, prepared by Research Department, FMC, Jan. 12, 1953; Ford Motor Company Office of Public Relations 1955 Budget Presentation. Both manuscripts are in the possession of the author.

11. *New York Telegraph,* Dec. 7, 1918; *Ford Man* 4 (Dec. 31, 1919), 2; *Advertising & Selling* 30 (July 10, 1920), 40; Ambrose B. Jewett to branch managers, June 5, 1919, Acc. 78, Box 1; Taylor M. Mills, Motion Picture Association of America, Inc., New York, to David L. Lewis, July 27, 1962; W. "Bill" Watmough, Warner Brothers Pictures Distributing Corporation, Los Angeles, to Lewis, July 27, 1962. Irving R. Bacon to Henry Ford, Feb. 11, 1921, Acc. 285, Box 1.

12. *Motion Picture World* (Apr. 25, 1921), see Clipbook 24; Liebold, *Reminiscences,* p. 517; Irving R. Bacon to Henry Ford, Feb. 11, 1921, Acc. 285, Box 1; *Ford News* 2 (Jan. 1, 1922), 1.

13. *Exhibitors Trade Review* 8 (July 31, 1920), 926; *Ford News* 2 (Jan. 1, 1922), 1; 1 (Jan. 15, 1921), 2; 5 (June 15, 1925), 5; FMC news release, [Ford fillers], n.d. [1925], Acc. 541, Box 1. There were 750 feet of film in the average Library production; thus the cost per reel was $37.50. *Ford News* 1 (Jan. 15, 1921), 2.

14. Department of Photography to branch managers, Jan. 10, 1922, Feb. 16, 1922, Dec. 18, 1922, Acc. 78, Box 84; *Ford News* 1 (Nov. 15, 1920), 5 (quotes several newspaper reviews); *Advertising & Selling* 30 (July 10, 1920), 40; *Appleton* (Wis.) *Crescent,* Mar. 24, 1922; DT, May 30, 1923.

15. *Ford News* 3 (Jan. 15, 1923), 1; Department of Photography to branch managers, Feb. 3, 1923, Acc. 78,

Box 48; Nov. 2, 1922, Dec. 18, 1922, Apr. 23, 1923, Acc. 78, Box 84; Bacon, *Reminiscences,* pp. 43, 45, 227; Department of Photography to branch managers, Nov. 1, 1923, Acc. 78, Box 90; *Ford News* 5 (June 15, 1925), 5; List of Ford Films Loaned on Free Rental Basis, June 15, 1927, Acc. 509, Box 4; FMC Sales Promotion Films and Educational Subjects, Sept. 3, 1930, Acc. 61, Box 4.

16. Operating Committee Minutes, Dec. 14, 1916, and Executive Committee Minutes, Feb. 14, 1917, Acc. 85, Box 5; C.R. Frede to branch managers, June 16, 1920, Acc. 78, Box 46; Irving R. Bacon to Henry Ford, Feb. 11, 1921, and P.E. Martin to E.G. Liebold, Feb. 25, 1921, Acc. 285, Box 1.

17. General Sales Letter No. 830, July 21, 1920, Acc. 78, Box 89; FMC Sales Promotion Films and Educational Subjects, Sept. 3, 1930, Acc. 61, Box 4 (citing 1921–30 films on the company's activities, except for *Romance of Making a Modern Magazine,* which is cited in List of Ford Films Loaned on a Free Rental Basis, June 15, 1927, Acc. 509, Box 4); *Ford News* 3 (June 15, 1923), 4.

18. Department of Photography to branch managers, Dec. 21, 1925, Acc. 78, Box 52, and Branch Film Activities Report, Dec. 29, 1924, Acc. 78, Box 50 (attendance figures); Department of Photography to branch managers, Aug. 26, 1924, Acc. 78, Box 50.

19. Branch Film Activities Report, Dec. 29, 1924; J.J. Callan, Ford sales representative, to C.R. Frede, Aug. 11, 1924; Department of Photography to branch managers, July 1, 1924, all in Acc. 78, Box 50; *Ford News* 6 (Feb. 15, 1926), 4.

20. Bacon, *Reminiscences,* pp. 80–81, 89, 96; C.C. Cheadle, Advertising Department, to John Crawford, assistant to Edsel Ford, Feb. 16, 1931, Acc. 6, Box 394; speech by Charles F. Moore, vice-president-public relations and advertising, FMC, at annual meeting of the Public Relations Society of America, Philadelphia, Nov. 1957.

21. *New Britain* (Conn.) *Record,* n.d. [July 1914], p. 102 of Clipbook 5; *New York Herald,* May 6, 1915; *Ford Times* 8 (July 1915), 455; Black, *Reminiscences,* p. 192; Frank Vivian, *Reminiscences,* p. 27; *Ford Times* 9 (Aug. 1915), 24–25. See Clipbook 5 for clippings on the Ford exhibit.

22. *Detroit News-Tribune,* May 2, 1915; *New York Herald,* May 2, 1915; *Ford Times* 8 (July 1915), 455; Black, *Reminiscences,* pp. 45, 193, 198. The *Ford News* 19 (July 1939), 145, DN, June 16, 1939, and *San Francisco Chronicle,* Jan. 15, 1939 carry stories on Ford's belief that exhibits should be used to educate people, particularly the young.

23. *Ford Times* 6 (May 1913), 338; 6 (Sept. 1913), 494; *Ford Man* 2 (Feb. 18, 1918), 2; 3 (July 3, 1919), 1; 3 (Aug. 16, 1919), 3; 4 (Aug. 17, 1920), 3; *Ford Times* 9 (Sept. 1915), 75–79; *Ford Man* 3 (Oct. 3, 1919), 4; *Ford News* 1 (Nov. 1, 1920), 3; 1 (Aug. 1, 1921), 4; 2 (Oct. 15, 1922), 4; 5 (Dec. 1, 1924), 8; 6 (Nov. 15, 1925), 1; DN, Sept. 15, 1925.

24. *Ford Times* 9 (Aug. 1915), 43; 9 (Jan. 1916), 297; 9 (Apr. 1916), 427; 9 (May 1916), 447; George S. Anderson to Grove Park Inn, Asheville, N.C., Jan. 16, 1919, E.G. Liebold to E.C. Van Huson, May 1, 1917, Acc. 62, Box 12; *Fordson Worker* 1 (Dec. 15, 1919), 4; *Ford Man* 4 (Aug. 17, 1920), 3; Nevins and Hill, *Expansion and Challenge,* p. 591.

25. Cooper, "Advertising Values," p. 1583; Charles A. Brownell to branch managers, Apr. 5, 1915, Acc. 509, Box 2; Nevins and Hill, *Ford: The Times,* p. 575; Nevins and Hill, *Expansion and Challenge,* p. 493; Directors' Minutes, May 1, 1912, Dec. 31, 1918, Acc. 85, Box 1.

26. Nevins and Hill, *Expansion and Challenge*, p. 493; Nevins and Hill, *Ford: The Times*, pp. 561–63; Bacon, *Reminiscences*, p. 33.

27. Nevins and Hill, *Ford: The Times*, pp. 561–63, 567; Nevins and Hill, *Expansion and Challenge*, p. 324; *Chicago Examiner*, Apr. 18, 1914; DFP, *New York Sun*, *New York World*, Jan. 23, 1915; *San Francisco Star*, Jan. 30, 1915; Burlingame, *Henry Ford*, p. 173.

28. *Ford Times* 9 (Apr. 1916), 407; 9 (June 1916), 524; *Ford News* 9 (Feb. 15, 1929), 43; Nevins and Hill, *Ford: The Times*, p. 549. News stories on the English Language School are scattered throughout Clipbooks 5–10; stories on the Henry Ford Trade School are scattered throughout all of the clipbooks, beginning with Clipbook 8.

29. Nevins and Hill, *Expansion and Challenge*, pp. 494–95; Benson, *New Henry Ford*, p. 312.

30. Liebold, *Reminiscences*, p. 118; Benson, *New Henry Ford*, p. 312; Richards, *Last Billionaire*, pp. 243–44 (citing news releases and amount of publicity received by the hospital); Sward, *Legend of Henry Ford*, p. 140. Nevins and Hill, *Expansion and Challenge*, p. 507.

31. *Boston News Bureau*, Mar. 30, 1926; DN, Feb. 9, 1927; Musselman, *Get a Horse!*, pp. 10, 105–6, 109–10.

32. *Printers' Ink* 92 (Sept. 22, 1915), 102; *Ft. Atkinson* (Wis.) *Union*, Feb. 18, 1921; DFP, Apr. 28, 1907; *Motor Age* 11 (June 27, 1907), 99; Simonds, *Henry Ford*, p. 118.

33. B.A. Botkin, "The Lore of the Lizzie Label," *American Speech* 6 (Dec. 1930), 84–85; William P. Young, *A Ford Dealer's Twenty Year Ride The Joy Ride The Sleigh Ride and Rough Ride with Old and New Model Ford Policies Through Changing Scenery from Company Profits to Dealer Losses* (Hempstead, N.Y.: Twenty Year Ride Publishing Co., 1932), pp. 45, 53, 59–60.

34. Cooper, "Advertising Values," p. 1583; Merz, *Then Came Ford*, p. 132; *Ford Times* 9 (Feb. 1916), 321; 9 (Dec. 1915), 237; 10 (Sept. 1916), 95; *Ford News* 2 (Apr. 15, 1922), 5.

35. *Ford Times* 8 (July 1915), 434.

36. *Printers' Ink* 95 (June 22, 1916), 33; Floyd Clymer, *Henry's Wonderful Model T, 1908–1927* (New York: Bonanza Books, 1955), pp. 7, 15; Stern, *Tin Lizzie*, pp. 151–52. Ford accessory manufacturers, which did an annual business of about $60,000,000 for many years, spent many millions of dollars on advertising. Whole sections of popular automobile magazines frequently were printed on yellow or red paper to set apart the advertisements of the Ford accessory group. Stern, *Tin Lizzie*, p. 153.

37. Merz, *Then Came Ford*, p. 133; *New York Tribune*, Mar. 18, 1917; Mark Sullivan, *Our Times The United States 1900–1925*, 6 vols. (New York: Charles Scribner's Sons, 1930), 4, p. 61; *Latrobe* (Pa.) *Bulletin*, Feb. 10, 1927. Merz, p. 131, erroneously says that the Ford joke was born in 1914; Sullivan, p. 61, states that it was at its height between 1914–18.

38. Sullivan, *Our Times*, 4, p. 62; *Dayton News*, May 31, 1927; *Illustrated World* 24 (Chicago), Feb. 16, 1916, 813–14; *Funny Stories about the Ford*, 2 (Baltimore: Presto Publishing Company, 1915), p. 47. Six joke books can be found on the book shelves at the Ford Archives.

39. *Ford Smiles: Best Jokes about a Rattling Good Car* (Chicago: Shrewsbury Publishing Co., 1917), p. 148; Sullivan, *Our Times*, 4, pp. 63–65.

40. *Funny Stories about the Ford*, 2, p. 24; *Grand Rapids* (Mich.) *Herald*, Aug. 25, 1922; *Jackson* (Mich.) *Patriot*, Aug. 12, 1914; *Elizabethtown* (Ky.) *News*, Jan. 16, 1923; *Chicago Herald Examiner*, Feb. 2, 1926.

41. *Asheville* (N.C.) *Citizen*, May 6, 1914; Merz, *Then Came Ford*, p. 134; Simonds, *Henry Ford*, p. 132; Sullivan, *Our Times*, 4, pp. 63–65; Marshall W. Fishwick, *American Heroes: Myth and Reality* (Washington: Public Affairs Press, 1954), p. 122.

42. *Funny Stories about the Ford*, 1 (Baltimore: Presto Publishing Company, 1915), p. 5; *Printers' Ink* 112 (July 1, 1920), 121; *Wenatchee* (Wash.) *World*, Aug. 21, 1920.

43. B.A. Botkin, "Lore of Lizzie Label," pp. 81–84, 86–87, 93; B.A. Botkin, "An Anthology of Lizzie Labels," *American Speech* 7 (Oct. 1931), 32–39. Many magazines and newspapers also printed sentimental or humorous verse about the Model T, and drugstores all over the country sold post cards and valentines with witticisms about the vehicle. Clymer, *Henry's Model T*, pp. 11, 68; Floyd Clymer, *Those Wonderful Old Automobiles* (New York: Bonanza Books, 1953), p. 152.

44. *Printers' Ink* 92 (Sept. 23, 1915), 102; DN and *Wall Street Journal*, Feb. 9, 1927; *New Bedford* (Mass.) *Standard* and *Pittsburgh Sun*, Feb. 11, 1927; *Springfield* (Mass.) *Republican*, Nov. 30, 1927; *New York Sun*, Dec. 2, 1937; NYT, Feb. 10, 1927; *Cincinnati Star*, June 1, 1915; *Edmonton* (Alta.) *Western Veteran*, May 7, 1921; Clymer, *Henry's Model T*, p. 11.

45. *Brooklyn Eagle*, June 6, 1926; Sward, *Legend of Henry Ford*, p. 196; George Burton Hotchkiss, *Advertising Copy* (New York: Harper & Brothers, 1939), p. 12; *Iron Mountain* (Mich.) *News*, Feb. 16, 1926; *New York American*, Sept. 19, 1926; *Printers' Ink* 112 (July 1, 1920), 121; General Letter No. 1425, Sept. 7, 1923, No. 1556, Dec. 11, 1924, and No. 1637, Dec. 5, 1925, Acc. 572, Box 10.

46. *Brooklyn Eagle*, Apr. 25, 1927; *New York Sun*, Dec. 2, 1927; Fishwick, *American Heroes*, p. 123. In 1945, "jeep jokes" were the rage, and the former Ford manufacturing executive, Charles E. Sorensen, then president of Willys, emulated Henry Ford by repeating them to reporters. "I hope they don't stop," Sorensen was quoted. "It's a sign of popularity." DN, July 15, 1945. During the late 1950s, jokes about the Rambler and Volkswagen were widely circulated. Owners of these cars reacted to the jokes much as did Model T owners forty years earlier. *Time* 73 (Apr. 6, 1959), 84–85; Baron K. Bates, Public Relations Department, Volkswagen of America, Inc., to David L. Lewis, May 23, 1962; John R. Pichurski, press relations manager, American Motors Corporation, to David L. Lewis, May 31, 1962.

47. Charles A. Brownell to branch managers, Feb. 13, 1915, May 3, 1915, Acc. 509, Box 2; *Detroit Motorist* 4 (Nov. 1915), see Clipbook 6; *Detroit News-Tribune*, June 20, 1915; Operating Committee Minutes, Dec. 14, 1916, Acc. 85, Box 5; Cooper, "Advertising Values," p. 1583.

48. *Printers' Ink* 131 (June 25, 1925), 174; Theodore F. MacManus, *The Sword-Arm of Business* (New York: The Devin-Adair Company, 1927), p. 149; Judson C. Welliver, "Henry Ford, Dreamer and Worker," *American Review of Reviews* 64 (Nov. 1921), 494; Black, *Reminiscences*, pp. 158, 181; Liebold, *Reminiscences*, p. 1246; Cameron, *Reminiscences*, pp. 86, 196; G.A. Nichols, "What Will Take the Place of Advertising in Ford's Marketing Scheme?," *Printers' Ink* 135 (June 17, 1926), 17–18; Cooper, "Advertising Values," p. 1583; Garrett, *Wild Wheel*, p. 67; NYT, Jan. 9, 1927; Archibald Henderson, *Contemporary Immortals* (New York: D. Appleton and Com-

pany, 1930), pp. 178–79; *Staunton* (Va.) *Leader,* Dec. 2, 1927.

49. *Omaha News,* Jan. 14, 1914; *Elmira* (N.Y.) *Advertiser,* Dec. 7, 1915; *New York Tribune,* Oct. 26, 1916; DT, Apr. 13, 1925.

50. Nevins and Hill, *Expansion and Challenge,* pp. 150, 261, 264; Charles A. Brownell to branch managers, Apr. 23, 1919, Acc. 78, Box 1; *Springfield* (Mass.) *Union,* July 17, 1919; Franklin Russell, "So Ford Is Advertising," *Printers' Ink* 128 (July 17, 1924), 42.

51. D.D. Martin to O.O. Buck, Aug. 5, 1919, Acc. 53, Box 19; Operating Committee Minutes, Dec. 14, 1916, Acc. 85, Box 5; *Printers' Ink* 98 (Feb. 1, 1917), 33; Nevins and Hill, *Expansion and Challenge,* pp. 262–63; Charles A. Brownell to branch managers, Apr. 23, 1919, Acc. 78, Box 1.

52. Charles A. Brownell to branch managers, Mar. 7, 1919, Oct. 15, 1919, Acc. 78, Box 1.

53. Theodore F. MacManus and Norman Beasley, *Men, Money, and Motors* (New York: Harper & Brothers, 1930), pp. 175–76, 256; Charles A. Brownell to branch managers, Sept. 2, 1914, Acc. 509, Box 2; *Fourth Estate,* no. 1148 (Feb. 26, 1916), 2; Brownell to Roberts-Toledo Auto Company, Toledo, Feb. 26, 1915, Acc. 509, Box 2; *Wichita Beacon,* Jan. 7, 1916; Brownell to E.G. Liebold, Aug. 28, 1920, Acc. 284, Box 10; *Detroit Journal,* Dec. 31, 1920; *Motor World* 66 (Jan. 5, 1921), 35. Among the Ford executives fired during this period were Frank L. Klingensmith, treasurer; William S. Knudsen, who had charge of all branch operations; Dean Marquis, head of the Sociological Department; Hubert E. Hartman, assistant secretary and general attorney; Louis H. Turrell, chief auditor; and Warren C. Anderson, the company's European representative. Nevins and Hill, *Expansion and Challenge,* pp. 167–68.

54. Young, *Twenty Year Ride,* p. 124; Samuel S. Marquis, *Henry Ford: An Interpretation* (Boston: Little, Brown, and Company, 1923), p. 126. Liebold, in his *Reminiscences,* p. 1106, suggests that Brownell was dismissed "because he was well up in years." Brownell's age in 1920 is unknown. According to the *Detroit Journal,* Dec. 31, 1920, he was an advertising man in Detroit as early as 1886. The *Boston American,* Feb. 2, 1921, reported that he was fired "because he dared to issue a favorable statement that 1921 would see a bigger output than ever of Ford machines." Brownell served as vice-president of Wildman Rubber Company, Bay City, Mich., from August 1921 until 1923. The firm, which made "Daddy Brownell" cord tires and "Daddy Brownell" pure gum floating inner tubes for Ford cars, apparently sought to capitalize on Brownell's popularity with Ford dealers. DFP, Aug. 7, 1921; Brownell to E.G. Liebold, Apr. 13, 1923, Acc. 285, Box 119; Brownell to Liebold, Nov. 15, 1923, Acc. 285, Box 160. In 1931 Brownell, who still regarded Ford as "the foremost man ... in the world," was living in Birmingham, Ala., gathering material for a biography of Ford. Brownell to C.E. Sorensen, June 22, 1931, Acc. 572, Box 20. Apparently Brownell died before the projected book materialized.

55. Nevins and Hill, *Expansion and Challenge,* p. 146. Hawkins, after serving in the Army Ordnance Department in 1918, returned to the company only to find that his assistant, Ryan, had been appointed to the sales managership, and that he had been named a special sales representative for Europe and South America. Hawkins's salary was not reduced, but he was offended and left the company. DN, Jan. 2, 1919; DFP, Jan. 12, 1919. From 1921 to 1924 Hawkins served GM in a sales and advertising advisory capac-

ity, at a salary of $150,000 a year. He lost $500,000 in promoting a baby buggy business, and in 1935 filed a bankruptcy petition listing liabilities of $350,000. Hawkins also lost a great amount of money in the 1933 bank failures. He died in 1936 at the age of sixty-nine. DN, Feb. 2, 1927; DT and DN, Aug. 18, 1936.

56. See *Readers' Guide to Periodical Literature, Industrial Arts Index,* and *New York Times Index* for the years 1914–19; *Philadelphia Public Ledger,* Aug. 12, 1920; Nevins and Hill, *Ford: The Times,* p. 590.

57. *Philadelphia Public Ledger,* May 5, 1916; B.C. Forbes, *Men Who Are Making America* (New York: B.C. Forbes Publishing Co., 1919), p. 115; *Denver Post,* Dec. 29, 1919; *Cleveland Press,* Nov. 20, 1919; *New York Sun,* Nov. 22, 1918 Statements in this and subsequent chapters on the relative amounts of publicity received by Henry Ford and other prominent persons and by FMC and other leading firms are based on a year-by-year count of entries in the *New York Times Index, Readers' Guide to Periodical Literature, Industrial Arts Index,* and *International Index to Periodicals.* For the paragraph which this note documents, the *New York Times Index* 2–7 (1914–19) and the *Readers' Guide to Periodical Literature* 3–5 (1910–14, 1915–18, 1919–21) were consulted.

58. Richards, *Last Billionaire,* p. 9; Burlingame, *Henry Ford,* p. 177; "W. Forrest Tells Just How He Got to Ford," *Fourth Estate,* no. 1409 (Feb. 26, 1921), 6, 12; DT, July 1, 1923; John Gunther, *Inside U.S.A.* (New York: Harper & Brothers, 1947), p. 398; MacManus and Beasley, *Men, Money, and Motors,* pp. 203–4; *New York Tribune,* Feb. 20, 1921; *Literary Digest* 68 (Feb. 26, 1921), 38; Judson C. Welliver, "Mr. Ford Is Interviewed," *American Review of Reviews* 72 (Sept. 1925), 264; *New Orleans Times-Picayune,* July 22, 1934. Of course, Ford was even more inaccessible to the general public than he was to newsmen. "The approach to him is, I believe, the most guarded and most difficult of that of any man alive," said Dean Marquis, who added that in view of the cranks, promoters, and dreamers who were constantly trying to see the industrialist, the latter could not altogether be blamed for his aloofness. Marquis, *Henry Ford,* pp. 72–74.

59. *Detroit News-Tribune,* Oct. 27, 1914; *Chicago Record-Herald,* Feb. 1, 1914; Richards, *Last Billionaire,* pp. 159, 242; Julian Street, "Detroit the Dynamic," *Collier's* 53 (July 1914), 24; *Pipp's Weekly* 1 (May 15, 1920), 8; E.G. Liebold to Frank P. Stockbridge, Sept. 7, 1918, Acc. 2, Box 39; Liebold to *Denver Post,* Apr. 24, 1919, Acc. 2, Box 42; Liebold to *Yazoo City* (Miss.) *Daily Sentinel,* Aug. 13, 1921, Acc. 285, Box 20. Black, *Reminiscences,* p. 132; Bennett, *Never Called Henry,* p. 48; E.G. Liebold to Fred R. Schmalzriedt, Feb. 2, 1921, Acc. 572, Box 20.

60. Cameron, *Reminiscences,* p. 38; Bennett, *Never Called Henry,* p. 89; Richards, *Last Billionaire,* p. 159; Marquis, *Henry Ford,* p. 72.

61. Nevins and Hill, *Expansion and Challenge,* pp. 218, 223, 273, 348; Richards, *Last Billionaire,* p. 241; Harold M. Cordell, *Reminiscences,* p. 14; Cameron, *Reminiscences,* p. 38; Wilbur Forrest, *Behind the Front Page* (London: Appleton-Century Company, 1934), p. 270.

62. Black, *Reminiscences,* pp. 155, 157–58; Richards, *Last Billionaire,* pp. 36–37, 39; *Detroit Journal,* Nov. 29, 1915. Yonker inexplicably lost favor with Ford and eventually became a public relations man. Delavigne left Ford's employ in 1917 to serve in the armed forces. After the war he became city editor of

the *Detroit Times,* then worked for Hearst Universal Services, and was a reporter on the *Detroit Times* at the time of his death in 1937. Richards, *Last Billionaire,* pp. 36–37; DT, Dec. 21, 1937.

63. Edward A. Rumely to Henry Ford, Nov. 20, 1916, Nov. 17, 1917, n.d. [Dec. 1918], Acc. 284, Box 25; *New York Evening Mail,* Nov. 18, 1917. Rumely, a German sympathizer before America's entry into World War I, lost control of the *Mail* in 1918, after he was indicted by a federal grand jury for failing to report German ownership of the *Mail* to the Alien Property Custodian. NYT, July 9 and Dec. 3, 1918.

64. Edward A. Rumely to Henry Ford, Aug. 19, 1943, Acc. 285, Box 2751; Liebold, *Reminiscences,* p. 1243; *Tulsa Tribune,* Jan. 2, 1927; *Buffalo Enquirer,* Jan. 17, 1920; *Boston Advertiser,* June 20, 1920; *Indianapolis Star,* Aug. 1, 1928; *Syracuse Journal,* Nov. 13, 1933; Arthur Brisbane to Frank Campsall, secretary to Henry Ford, Jan. 10, 1927, Acc. 285, Box 690; DT, Apr. 20, 1931; Brisbane to Charles E. Sorensen, Mar. 21, 1933, Acc. 572, Box 10; Brisbane to Edsel Ford, Sept. 26, 1935, Acc. 285, Box 1728.

65. *Capper's Weekly* 51 (May 1, 1926), 3; Henry Ford to Arthur Brisbane, Jan. 27, 1936, Acc. 285, Box 1846; DT, Apr. 19, 1931; Black, *Reminiscences,* p. 157; *New York American,* July 8, 1928; Milton Bradley Company, *Famous Fortunes: Intimate Stories of Financial Success* (Boston, Mass.: Milton Bradley Company, 1931), p. 53; *New Orleans Times-Picayune,* July 22, 1934; Brisbane to Frank Campsall, Nov. 30, 1934, Acc. 285, Box 1846; Vehicle Gift List, Acc. 292, Box 1; E.G. Liebold to Charles E. Sorensen, July 24, 1919, Acc. 62, Box 80.

66. Richards, *Last Billionaire,* pp. 1–2, 36–37; DFP, May 16, 1941; Liebold, *Reminiscences,* p. 1266; Black, *Reminiscences,* p. 157; Bennett, *Never Called Henry,* p. 133; C.E. Sorensen to William J. Cameron, Sept. 13, 1934, Acc. 44, Box 15; D.C. Hight, vice-president, McCann-Erickson, Inc., to A. R. Barbier, Feb. 4, 1941, Acc. 149, Box 147; Robert LaBlonde, McCann-Erickson publicity representative, to James Sweinhart, July 29, 1942, Acc. 285, Box 2351.

67. Bennett, *Never Called Henry,* p. 87; E.G. Liebold to Karl Bickel, Sept. 16, 1925, June 28, 1921, Jan. 2, 1923, Acc. 285, Boxes 347, 41, and 121, respectively. For Bickel's correspondence with Henry Ford's office, see Acc. 285, Boxes 1, 41, 45–46, 79, 121, 159, 201, 210, 347; Associated Press dispatch in the *Savannah News,* May 29, 1940; Arthur S. Hatch, Ford Chicago branch manager, to H.C. Doss, general sales manager, Mar. 14, 1941, Acc. 450, Box 7; DN, July 28, 1941.

68. NYT, May 22 and May 29, 1932; Henry Ford to Anne O'Hare McCormick, Sept. 30, 1943; Nevins and Hill, *Expansion and Challenge,* pp. 608–9; DT, Apr. 19, 1931; *Rochester* (N.Y.) *Democrat & Chronicle,* Oct. 18, 1939; Merrill C. Meigs to Henry Ford, Oct. 14, 1939, Acc. 285, Box 2251; John Thompson, director, Ford News Bureau, *Reminiscences,* p. 57.

Chapter 9

1. Circulation figures can be found in Acc. 285, Boxes 1, 3, 4, 91, 126, 219, 609.

2. Nevins and Hill, *Expansion and Challenge,* pp. 124–25; DN, Nov. 22, 1918; History of the *Dearborn Independent,* n.d., Acc. 44, Box 14.

3. *Bridgeport* (Conn.) *Telegram,* Dec. 16, 1918; *New York Evening Mail,* Nov. 22, 1918; NYT, Nov. 26, 1918; *New York World,* Dec. 14, 1918; DT, Nov. 22, 1918; *Advertising & Selling* 28 (Nov. 30, 1918), 1; *Printers' Ink* 105 (Dec. 26, 1918), 160.

4. *Dearborn Independent,* Jan. 11, 1919; DT, Jan. 14, 1919; E.G. Pipp to E.G. Liebold, Oct. 10, 1919, Acc. 62, Box 81. Liebold, *Reminiscences,* p. 448; Fred Black, Walter Blanchard, and Ben R. Donaldson, *Joint Reminiscences* (Black speaking), p. 15.

5. *Printers' Ink* 105 (Dec. 26, 1918), 160; *Editor & Publisher* 51 (Jan. 18, 1919), 8; *New York Sun,* Jan. 4, 1919; *New York World* and *New York Tribune,* Jan. 10, 1919; DT, Jan. 14, 1919. See Clipbook 14 for favorable and unfavorable reviews of the *Independent'*s first issue. The statement that most reviewers described the *Independent* as dull is based on an analysis of these reviews.

6. *New York World,* Dec. 14, 1918; *New York Herald,* Jan. 12, 1919; DT, Jan. 14, 1919; *Detroit Saturday Night* 13 (Jan. 11, 1919), 3.

7. *New York American,* Jan. 10, 1914; *New York Herald,* Jan. 12, 1919; "Mr. Ford's Own Page," *Life* 73 (Jan. 30, 1919), 180. Among the newspapers which published Ford's epigrams were the *Baltimore Sun* and the *New York American.* See Clipbook 14 for the reactions of editors to "Mr. Ford's Own Page."

8. Black, Blanchard, and Donaldson, *Reminiscences* (Donaldson speaking), p. 8; Fred L. Black to E.G. Liebold, Dec. 18, 1918 and Feb. 21, 1919, Acc. 62, Box 81; Frank Campsall to P.E. Martin, Nov. 18, 1919, Acc. 62, Box 81; E.B. Sinclair to Liebold, Jan. 29, 1919, Acc. 62, Box 81; H.W. Roland to Liebold, Sept. 4, 1920, Acc. 284, Box 1. Circulation figures for 1919 can be found in Acc. 62, Box 81.

9. E.G. Pipp to E.G. Liebold, Dec. 29, 1919, Liebold to Pipp, Dec. 5, 1919, and *Dearborn Independent* staff to Liebold, Dec. 29, 1919, Acc. 62, Box 81.

10. J.J. O'Neill to E.G. Liebold, Nov. 26, 1919, Acc. 62, Box 81.

11. Nevins and Hill, *Expansion and Challenge,* p. 312; Black, *Reminiscences,* p. 132. Letters in which Liebold expresses anti-Semitic views can be found in Acc. 62, Box 100 and Acc. 285, Boxes 2, 18, 609.

12. Nevins and Hill, *Expansion and Challenge,* pp. 312–13. The British Israelites based an esoteric interpretation of history and eternity on data derived from the Great Pyramid. Cameron served as president of the sect and as editor of its magazine, *Destiny,* during the 1930s. DN, Nov. 20, 1933; Harold Lavine, "Fifth Column Literature," *Saturday Review of Literature* 22 (Sept. 14, 1940), 16.

13. Nevins and Hill, *Expansion and Challenge,* pp. 313, 323; Benjamin R. Epstein and Arnold Forster, *Some of My Best Friends...* (New York: Farrar, Straus and Cudahy, 1962), p. 6; Oswald Garrison Villard, *Prophets True and False* (New York: A.A. Knopf, 1928), p. 297; Benson, *New Henry Ford,* pp. 356–57; Judson C. Welliver, "Henry Ford, Dreamer and Worker," *American Review of Reviews* 64 (Nov. 1921), 492–93 (quoting Ford); Charles Reznikoff, ed., *Louis Marshall Champion of Liberty: Selected Papers and Addresses,* 1 (Philadelphia: Jewish Publication Society of America, 1957), p. 371; Frank Campsall to Irving M. Robitshek, June 21, 1920, Acc. 62, Box 100. Ford permitted Jewish employees to absent themselves from work on Jewish holidays during the 'teens; this decision was termed "a gracious act" by the *Detroit Jewish Chronicle,* n.d. [Sept. 1916].

14. NYT, June 20, 1921; *Chicago Examiner,* Mar. 21, 1921; Nevins and Hill, *Expansion and Challenge,* p. 314; Richards, *Last Billionaire,* p. 91; Black, Blan-

chard, and Donaldson, *Reminiscences* (Blanchard speaking), p. 39; Black, *Reminiscences*, p. 143. Cameron later maintained that he was in "total disagreement" with plans to launch the anti-Semitic campaign. Cameron, *Reminiscences*, p. 10.

15. *The Universal Jewish Encyclopedia*, 1939 ed., s.v. "Anti-Semitism" (quoting first systematic anti-Jewish agitation); Oscar I. Janowsky, *The American Jew A Composite Portrait* (New York: Harper & Brothers, 1942), pp. 189–90; Rabbi Lee J. Levinger, *A History of Jews in the United States* (Cincinnati: Union of American Hebrew Congregations, 1935), pp. 361–62; Garrett, *Wild Wheel*, p. 147. See copies of the *Dearborn Independent* from May 1920 to January 1922. Bound copies of the *Independent* are in Acc. 8; Bernard M. Baruch, *The Public Years* (New York: Holt, Rinehart, and Winston, 1960), p. 162. Starting in 1920 the Ku Klux Klan, which espoused "native, white Protestant supremacy," also attacked Jews, along with blacks, Catholics, and immigrants. Although the Klan had an estimated membership of between 4,000,000 and 5,000,000 in the mid-1920s and controlled politics not only in the South but also in Oregon, Indiana, and Maine, its propaganda was of less concern to Jews than the anti-Semitic campaign waged by Ford. The industrialist, unlike the Klan, concentrated his fire on the Jews; in addition, he had much greater influence among the majority of Americans than did the Klan. *The Columbia Encyclopedia*, 1950 ed., s.v. "Ku Klux Klan"; Rufus Learsi (pseud.), *The Jews in America: A History* (Cleveland: World Publishing Co., 1954), pp. 289–91.

16. Charles H. Joseph, editor, *Jewish Criterion* (Pittsburgh), to E.G. Liebold, June 26, 1920; Liebold to Joseph, June 30, 1920; M.M. Barnet, editor, *Jewish Times* (San Francisco), to Liebold, July 28, 1920; Liebold to Barnet, Aug. 4, 1920; S. Dingol, editor of *The Day* (New York), to Henry Ford, Oct. 30, 1920; *The Day*, Oct. 14, 1920; Liebold to J.A. Baer, Aug. 17, 1920; all in Acc. 62, Box 100.

17. *New York American*, n.d. [July 1920], Acc. 62, Box 100; Arthur Brisbane to Frank Campsall, Sept. 7, 1933, Acc. 285, Box 1533; H.W. Roland to E.G. Liebold, Sept. 4, 1920, Acc. 284, Box 1; *Redford* (Mich.) *Record*, June 3, 1920. For newspaper comment on the *Independent* see Clipbook 18.

18. Reznikoff, *Marshall*, pp. xxxix, 315; Ismar Elbogen, *A Century of Jewish Life* (Philadelphia: Jewish Publication Society of America, 1944), pp. 262, 562–63; Nevins and Hill, *Expansion and Challenge*, p. 315; *Hartford Times*, Feb. 25, 1921; *Escanaba* (Mich.) *Press*, Mar. 2, 1921 (regarding the Patterson, N.J. library); *Cleveland Plain Dealer*, Jan. 17, 1921; *New York World*, May 24, 1921.

19. *Providence News*, Jan. 24, 1921; Richards, *Last Billionaire*, p. 94; Attitude of New York Dealers Toward the *Dearborn Independent*, Nov. 10, 1920, Acc. 6, Box 35; E.G. Liebold to E.C. Lindsay, Virginia, Minn., Oct. 22, 1920, Acc. 62, Box 100 (see this box for a number of other letters between Liebold and dealers regarding the economic pressure that some Jews applied to agents); Black, Blanchard, and Donaldson, *Reminiscences* (Donaldson speaking), p. 33.

20. Richards, *Last Billionaire*, p. 94; Black, Blanchard, and Donaldson, *Reminiscences* (Donaldson speaking), p. 33; *Detroit Saturday Night* 16 (June 17, 1922), 8 (quoting Rogers).

21. E.G. Pipp, *The Real Henry Ford* (Detroit: Pipp's Weekly, 1922), p. 23; Nevins and Hill, *Expansion and Challenge*, pp. 316–17; Reznikoff, *Marshall*, pp. 361–64; Fred Dolsen to Arthur Brisbane, Sept. 21,

1920, Acc. 62, Box 100; Brisbane to Frank Campsall, Sept. 7, 1933, Acc. 285, Box 1533; Upton Sinclair, *The Flivver King: A Story of Ford-America* (Pasadena, Calif.: The Author, 1937), p. 58; *Wall Street Journal*, Jan. 26, 1926. Although Ford stopped his anti-Semitic series, his attitude toward the campaign continued to trouble Jews. In 1923 a Yiddish-language biography of Ford warned that Jews had much to fear from the industrialist because he continued to be both "the most popular man in America" and "the Jews' worst enemy." David Louis Mekler, *Der emes vegen Henri Ford* (New York: Verlag PNKM, 1924), n.p.

22. Pipp, *Real Henry Ford*, p. 34; Black, Blanchard, and Donaldson, *Reminiscences* (Black speaking), pp. 26–27; H.W. Roland to E.G. Liebold, Sept. 4, 1920, Acc. 284, Box 1. The *Independent*'s circulation stood at 29,620 on April 1, 1920, but, on the strength of a subscription campaign among agents, rocketed to 158,251 by May 15, 1920 (one week before the anti-Semitic series began). Circulation stood at 297,312 as of January 28, 1921, but skidded to 148,000 as dealer-inspired subscriptions ran out during the following three-and-a-half months. On January 2, 1923, the magazine had a circulation of 271,675; by June 30, 1923, 472,501; by January 2, 1924, 641,143. These circulation figures can be found in Acc. 285, Boxes 4, 126, 219.

23. William P. Young, *A Ford Dealer's Twenty Year Ride The Joy Ride The Sleigh Ride and Rough Ride with Old and New Model Ford Policies Through Changing Scenery from Company Profits to Dealer Losses* (Hempstead, N.Y.: Twenty Year Ride Publishing Co., 1932), p. 117; Attitude of New York Dealers Toward the *Dearborn Independent*, Nov. 10, 1920, Acc. 6, Box 35; Charles T. Lathers, Detroit branch manager, to dealers, July 14, 1926, Acc. 509, Box 3; W.A. Ryan to branch managers, July 3, 1922, Acc. 78, Box 84; Jesse Rainsford Sprague, "Confessions of a Ford Dealer," *Harper's Monthly Magazine* 155 (June 1927), 30–31; Black, *Reminiscences*, p. 21; E.G. Liebold to John J. Wright, May 27, 1920, Acc. 284, Box 10; Liebold, *Reminiscences*, p. 449; Black, Blanchard, and Donaldson, *Reminiscences* (each speaking), pp. 8–12. Young and Sprague, both Ford dealers, and Black, Blanchard, and Donaldson, all employees of the *Independent*, state that most Ford dealers bitterly resented having to solicit subscriptions for the publication.

24. Charles T. Lathers, Detroit branch manager, to dealers, June 15, 1927, Acc. 509, Box 4; Department of Photography to branch managers, Dec. 21 and 31, 1925, Acc. 78, Box 52; B.R. Donaldson to E.G. Liebold, Aug. 21, 1922, Acc. 285, Box 91; *Ford News* 1 (Sept. 8, 1921), 1; 1 (Oct. 8, 1921), 4; Department of Photography to branch managers, Nov. 2, 1922, Mar. 30, 1923, Acc. 78, Box 84; Walter Blanchard to Liebold, Jan. 26, 1927, June 20, 1927, Acc. 285, Box 91.

25. Liebold, *Reminiscences*, p. 449; Nevins and Hill, *Expansion and Challenge*, p. 311; FMC news release, Feb. 25, 1925, Acc. 78, Box 52; *Ford News* 5 (Sept. 1, 1925), 1; Black, Blanchard, and Donaldson, *Reminiscences* (Black and Donaldson speaking), pp. 56–59; see ledgers in Acc. 43, Box 11, for payments to contributors. The *Independent*'s page size was reduced to standard magazine dimensions, 8 ¾ inches by 12 inches, in May 1925. *Ford News* 5 (Feb. 15, 1925), 1.

26. Nevins and Hill, *Expansion and Challenge*, pp. 316–17; Carey McWilliams, *A Mask for Privilege: Anti-Semitism in America* (Boston: Little, Brown & Co.,

1948), p. 34; Elbogen, *Century of Jewish Life,* p. 566; Abram Leon Sacher, *The Jew in the Contemporary World: Sufferance Is the Badge* (New York: A.A. Knopf, 1939), p. 535; William L. Shirer, *The Rise and Fall of the Third Reich: A History of Nazi Germany* (New York: Simon and Schuster, 1960), p. 149, and *PM* (New York), Apr. 9, 1947 (von Schirach); Gustavus Myers, *History of Bigotry in the United States* (New York: Random House, 1943), pp. 336, 365–66. Of course anti-Semitism was so rife in the Germany of the 1920s and 1930s that von Schirach and those like him probably were exposed to much anti-Jewish propaganda that had no relationship to Ford.

27. DT, May 16, 1922, and *Spokane Press,* Aug. 10, 1922 (quoting *Hearst's International Magazine*); *Grand Rapids* (Mich.) *Press,* Dec. 19, 1922; *Philadelphia Public Ledger,* July 6, 1923; Kurt G.W. Ludecke, *I Knew Hitler: The Story of a Nazi Who Escaped the Blood Purge* (New York: Charles Scribner's Sons, 1937), p. 197; Oswald Garrison Villard, *The German Phoenix: The Story of the Republic* (New York: H. Smith & R. Haas, 1933), pp. 132, 140. Reports on the number of brochures which Ford distributed can be found in Acc. 284, Box 1. Correspondence between Liebold and persons requesting copies of the booklets is in Acc. 285, Box 2. Adolf Hitler, *Mein Kampf,* unabridged American ed. (New York: Reynal & Hitchcock, 1939), pp. 929–30.

28. Richards, *Last Billionaire,* p. 97; Nevins and Hill, *Expansion and Challenge,* pp. 317–18; Allan Nevins, "Henry Ford—a Complex Man," *American Heritage* 6 (Dec. 1954), 58. The trial was fully covered by the NYT, *New York World,* DN, and DT, Mar. 15-Apr. 22, 1927. Louis Marshall, president of the American Jewish Committee, regretted that Sapiro had brought suit against Ford, "because it gives Ford the publicity which he has craved ever since he embarked upon his attack of the Jews." Sapiro, however, sought neither advice nor financial aid from Jewish groups in taking action against Ford. Reznikoff, *Marshall,* p. 372. The Sapiro suit was one of the most widely publicized libel suits of the twentieth century, according to Stanley Walker, *City Editor* (New York: Blue Ribbon Books, Inc., 1934), p. 200.

29. Nevins and Hill, *Expansion and Challenge,* p. 319; NYT, June 10, 1921; Liebold, *Reminiscences,* pp. 492–93; A Personal Letter from the Editor of The Dearborn Independent to the Ford Dealer, n.d. [June 1921], Acc. 572, Box 13; *Ford News* 4 (Oct. 1, 1924), 3.

30. Nevins and Hill, *Expansion and Challenge,* pp. 319–20; DN, Mar. 30, 1927. The only witnesses to the accident were two youngsters walking nearby. They gave no dependable account of the mishap, and the full circumstances were never publicly clarified by Ford. Before the auto accident and the juror's blunder, attempts by Sapiro's counsel to get Ford on the stand were frustrated by "some of the most adroit maneuvering in the history of American court trials," according to Baruch, *Public Years,* p. 163.

31. *Boston Traveler,* Mar. 30, 1927; *Grand Rapids* (Mich.) *Herald,* Mar. 31, 1927; *Chicago Herald-Examiner,* Mar. 31, 1927; *New York Graphic,* Apr. 1, 1927; DT, Apr. 1, 1927.

32. Nevins and Hill, *Expansion and Challenge,* pp. 320–22; Liebold, *Reminiscences,* p. 504; Bennett, *Never Called Henry,* pp. 55–56. Ford's chief attorney, Senator James A. Reed, of Missouri, learned of the retraction through the press. He telephoned from Texas to inquire of his Detroit colleagues, "What in hell is this I see in the Dallas paper?," Richards, *Last Billionaire,* p. 101. Cameron was "stunned" by the

retraction. "The whole thing is a mystery to me," he told one of Hitler's fund-raisers, Kurt G.W. Ludecke, who visited the editor shortly after Ford's apology. Ludecke, *I Knew Hitler,* pp. 313–15.

33. Nevins and Hill, *Expansion and Challenge,* p. 320; Reznikoff, *Marshall,* pp. 376–78; Bennett, *Never Called Henry,* p. 56; Richards, *Last Billionaire,* p. 101 (citing *American Hebrew*); Arthur Brisbane to Henry Ford, July 8, 1927, Acc. 292, Box 31; *New York American,* July 8, 1927.

34. NYT, Nov. 14, 1927; Black, *Reminiscences,* p. 177; Charles T. Lathers, Detroit branch manager, to dealers, July 26, 1927, Acc. 509, Box 4; *New York American,* July 8, 1927; *New York World,* Dec. 3, 1927.

35. Letters for and against Ford's retraction can be found in Acc. 292, Boxes 31–32. The letter from Rabbi A.B. Reines, dated July 8, 1927, is in Box 31.

36. *New York Herald Tribune,* July 9, 1927; NYT, July 9, 1927; *New York American,* July 8, 1927; *New Republic* 51 (July 29, 1927), 212. "Henry Ford's Apology to the Jews," *Outlook* 146 (July 20, 1927), 372–74, recapitulates press comment on the retraction. Sheet music for Rose's song is in the National Automotive History Collection, Detroit Public Library.

37. DFP, Dec. 7, 1927; DFP, May 24, 1929; Reznikoff, *Marshall,* pp. 388–89. Not every Jewish newspaper accepted Ford's advertising—*The Day* (New York) being a notable example. Some Jewish newspapers which accepted the advertising were subject to "considerable agitation" from the Jewish community. *The Forward* (New York) sometimes was called the "Fordward" because it ran Ford advertisements. Philip Slomovitz, editor and publisher, *Detroit Jewish News,* to David L. Lewis, May 16, 1963 (based on data furnished to Slomovitz by Bernard G. Richards of the Jewish Information Bureau, May 14, 1963.

38. *Detroit Jewish Chronicle,* April 1, 1932; *New York Sun,* May 15, 1934; DN, June 6, 1934.

39. Livraria do Globo of Pôrto Alegre, Brazil, to Henry Ford, Dec. 10, 1932; E.G. Liebold to Livraria do Globo, Jan. 28, 1933; Rabbi Leo M. Franklin to Henry Ford, May 16, 1933; Liebold to H. Steagall, manager, FMC, Pôrto Alegre, Brazil, June 13, 1933; Steagall to Liebold, July 13, 1933; Liebold to Franklin, Aug. 22, 1933; Liebold to Steagall, Aug. 22, 1933; Livraria do Globo to Steagall, Oct. 5, 1933; all in Acc. 285, Box 1769. Rabbi Franklin and Ford were close friends during the 'teens. Rabbi Franklin reluctantly terminated the friendship shortly after the *Independent* launched its first anti-Semitic campaign in 1920. Following Ford's retraction in 1927, Rabbi Franklin congratulated the magnate on his "courageous stand" and expressed the hope that he might resume "those fine friendly relationships which through so many years it was mine to enjoy." Franklin to Ford, July 8, 1927 (copy), Ford file, *Detroit Jewish News.*

40. E.C. Heine to E.G. Liebold, Nov. 7, 1933; Hammer-Verlag Publishing Company to Heine, Nov. 2, 1933; Liebold to Heine, Nov. 27, 1933; Rabbi Leo M. Franklin to Liebold, Oct. 4, 1933; all in Acc. 285, Box 1769. *New York Sun,* May 15, 1934.

41. Rabbi Leo M. Franklin to Henry Ford, May 16, 1933; E.G. Liebold to Franklin, Oct. 2, 1933; Franklin to Liebold, Oct. 4, 1933; Ford to Franklin, n.d. [Aug. 1933]; all in Acc. 285, Box 1769. J.H. Schakue, *Detroit Jewish Chronicle,* to Ford, Jan. 14, 1937, Acc. 285, Box 2001 (regarding article in *Jewish Chronicle*). Philip Slomovitz, editor of the *Jewish Chronicle,* urged Ford in 1940—when the leftist press repeatedly charged the magnate with anti-

Semitism—to reaffirm his 1937 stand. Ford instructed Harry Bennett to meet with Slomovitz to deny the charges orally. Slomovitz to Bennett, Aug. 29, 1940, Ford file, *Detroit Jewish News;* Slomovitz interview, May 7, 1963.

42. *New York Daily News,* July 23, Sept. 5, 1933; *Detroit Jewish Chronicle,* July 28, 1933; E.G. Liebold to Philip Slomovitz, editor, *Detroit Jewish Chronicle,* July 28, 1933, Ford file, *Detroit Jewish News; New York Journal,* Dec. 18, 1933; DFP, Dec. 6, 1939; DN, June 6, 1934. In 1934 Prince Louis Ferdinand was a "free-lance salesman" for Ford in Berlin. DN, July 29, 1934. Louis Ferdinand looked favorably on the Nazi regime in 1933–34, according to Nevins and Hill, *Expansion and Challenge,* p. 561. The prince later turned against the Nazis; and becoming a personal friend of President Roosevelt in the late 1930s, stayed in the White House during his honeymoon in 1938. Plotters against Hitler's life during World War II agreed to offer the German throne to Louis Ferdinand, if successful in eliminating Hitler. Shirer, *Third Reich,* p. 907. General Motors and J.P. Morgan also were accused of providing funds for the Hitler movement. Both denied the charges. *Detroit Jewish Chronicle,* July 28, 1933.

43. DN, July 31, 1938; DFP, July 31, 1938; *New York Herald Tribune,* July 31, 1938. N. Dencker, consul (Detroit), Federal Republic of West Germany, to David L. Lewis, July 2, 1962.

44. E.G. Liebold to Lewis J. Miller, Nov. 20, 1939, Acc. 285, Box 2357; Bennett, *Never Called Henry,* pp. 120–21; *Akron Beacon-Journal,* Aug. 13, 1938.

45. The DN, July 31, 1938 and NYT, Aug. 1, 1938, were among newspapers which carried Ford's photograph.

46. *Lansing* (Mich.) *State Journal,* Aug. 4, 1938; *Akron Beacon-Journal,* Aug. 13, 1938; DN, Aug. 6, 1938.

47. NYT, Nov. 28, 1938; *Cleveland Plain Dealer,* Dec. 19, 1938; NYT, Dec. 22, 1938; Emil Zoerlein (FMC engineer, 1926–50), *Reminiscences,* p. 232. William Guggenheim, an official of the American Defense Society, who had been decorated by the Italian government in 1920, and Thomas J. Watson, president of International Business Machines Corporation and president of the International Chamber of Commerce, who had received a medal from the German government in 1937 for his efforts in behalf of world trade and peace, returned the donors' militarism. NYT, June 7, 12, 1940.

48. DFP, Dec. 1, 1938.

49. DT and DN, Dec. 2, 1938 (quoting the Jewish press and liberal organizations); DN, Dec. 4, 1938.

50. DFP, Dec. 5, 1938; *Look* 4 (Apr. 9, 1940), 19–21; DT, Dec. 5, 1938.

51. FMC Personnel Department to William J. Cameron, Apr. 7, 1937, Acc. 44, Box 17; NYT, Dec. 7, 1939; *PM* (New York), Sept. 20, 1940; *Detroit Labor News,* Apr. 4, 1916; clips of *Friday* magazine for Sept. 27 and Oct. 24, 1940, and a copy of the purported letter can be found in Acc. 44, Box 17. The DFP, Sept. 24, 1940, the *Seattle Jewish Times,* Oct. 11, 1940, and Walter Winchell's broadcast of Jan. 26, 1941 also discussed Kuhn in connection with Ford and Cameron. Maurice A. Neenberg, America's foremost handwriting expert, said the alleged Cameron letter was "a clumsy forgery." *Pittsburgh American Jewish Outlook,* Sept. 27, 1940.

52. DN, Sept. 19, 1941; *New York Sun,* Sept. 22, 1941; NYT, Dec. 13, 1941; DFP, Mar. 6, 1941; DN, May 27, 1940; *New York Daily News,* Nov. 23, 1940; NYT, May 17, 1942; *Atlanta Constitution,* Mar. 30, 1940; DFP, Feb. 1, 1942; NYT, Aug. 26, 1941. The

UAW-CIO for three years had been thwarted in its efforts to organize Ford employees. In seeking support from Ford workers and the public, the union took advantage of every opportunity to discredit and embarrass the company.

53. DN, May 10, 1940; DN, Aug. 29, 1939; Philip Slomovitz to Dr. Jacob Billikopf, June 23, 1940 (Ford file), *Detroit Jewish News; Winnipeg* (Man.) *Free Press,* May 26, 1941.

54. Bennett, *Never Called Henry,* p. 121; W.K. Edmunds, eastern branch manager, to John W. Thompson, Mar. 11, 1944, Acc. 149, Box 147; FMC Advertising and Sales Promotion Expense Sheet for 1941 Car Year, Acc. 149, Box 119 (citing the $50,000 fund); Report of Wallace A. Scotten, of McCann-Erickson, Inc., to William A. Simonds, Aug. 16, 1939, Acc. 285, Box 2287.

55. A Review of the First Year of "Watch the World Go By," submitted to FMC by Maxon, Inc., n.d. [June 1943], Acc. 149, Box 94; *Jackson* (Miss.) *News,* Aug. 28, 1941; A Survey of Attitudes Toward and Opinions about Ford Motor Company (photostatic copy), submitted to FMC by Elmo Roper, Oct. 1944, Acc. 134, Box 17.

56. Bennett, *Never Called Henry,* p. 121; *Chicago News,* Jan. 12, 1942; *Newsweek* 19 (Jan. 19, 1942), 28; Myers, *History of Bigotry,* pp. 366–67.

57. *Chicago News,* Jan. 12, 1942; DFP, Feb. 1, 1942; *Savannah News,* Feb. 1, 1942; *Brooklyn Jewish Examiner,* Mar. 20, 1942; "Dear Mr. Henry Ford," *The Propaganda Battlefront* 20 (Aug.-Sept. 1944), 1–2; Richard E. Gutstadt, national director, Anti-Defamation League of B'nai B'rith, to editors of Anglo-Jewish press, Dec. 27, 1945 (copy), Ford file, *Detroit Jewish News.* Gutstadt names Panama, Chile, Mexico, Peru, Columbia, Honduras, Guatemala, Costa Rica, El Salvador, and Nicaragua as the countries surveyed by the League.

58. FMC advertising and sales promotion expense sheets for the years 1935–37 are in Acc. 454, Box 1, and for the years 1938–41 in Acc. 149, Box 119; Radio and General Advertising Expenses, Oct. 14, 1943, Acc. 149, Box 119 (citing 1943 expenditure); Leonard Hyde, of JWT to B.R. Donaldson, Aug. 20, 1946, Acc. 149, Box 113 (discusses Ford advertising in Yiddish and Anglo-Jewish newspapers in connection with Rosh Hashanah (Jewish New Year); JWT Client Confirmation Report, Mar. 28, 1947, Acc. 149, Box 114 (citing cost of the one Ford advertisement and number of newspapers in which it appeared). Seidman's role in selecting newspapers for Ford advertisements is discussed in JWT Client Confirmation Report, Mar. 28, 1947, Acc. 149, Box 114. Letters from Seidman to the *Detroit Jewish News* for the years 1941–48 can be found in the Ford file, *Detroit Jewish News.* The requests for publication of Ford press releases cover a wide range of topics, from announcement of the Ford Good Drivers League and settlement with the UAW-CIO in 1941 to a feature story on Henry Ford's eightieth birthday in 1943 and an article by Henry Ford II in the December 1948 issue of *Atlantic Monthly.* Seidman, who sometimes presented bound volumes of clippings from Jewish newspapers to Henry Ford, counted "as one of my greatest achievements my success in contributing to the establishment of cordial relations between Henry Ford and the Jewish press." Seidman to the *Detroit Jewish News,* July 15, 1943.

59. DN, May 22, 1946; NYT, Nov. 19, 1948, Feb. 14–15, 1951; DFP, Feb. 14, 1951; Thomas B. Morgan, "The Fight Against Prejudice," *Look* 27 (June 4, 1963), pp. 66, 72.

60. FMC biographical sketch of Benson Ford, Dec. 3, 1962 (available from the Ford News Department); NYT, June 16, 1951, Nov. 10, 1952, Jan. 24, 1953, Nov. 12, 1953, Dec. 10, 1953, Nov. 13, 1954, Nov. 12, 1955; DN, Nov. 5, 1947; interview with Isidore Soboloff, executive vice-president, Detroit Jewish Welfare Federation, May 10, 1963; interview with George Barnetson, financial director of the Detroit Roundtable of Catholics, Jews and Protestants, Inc. (the Detroit branch of the NCCJ), May 29, 1963. Ford Motor Company Notice of Meeting and Proxy Statement, Apr. 26, 1963 (available from the Ford Shareholder Relations Department). Ford's '$1,000,000 gift to the NCCJ was the largest received by the organization in its thirty-three-year history.

61. DN, June 6, 1945, and June 27, 1959; Slomovitz interview, May 7, 1963; interview with Rabbi Julius Weinberg, of Beth Israel Congregation, Ann Arbor, Mich., May 17, 1962. May is well qualified for his role as Ford's "Jewish advisor," having served as a director of the National Conference of Christians and Jews and president of its Detroit branch.

62. Anti-Defamation League of B'nai B'rith, *Anti-Semitism in the United States in 1947* (New York, n.d. [1948]), pp. 16–17. A copy of Henry Ford II's disavowal, which is in the form of a March 12, 1947, letter to Nathan H. Seidman, president, the Inter-Racial Press of America, Inc., is in the Ford file, *Detroit Jewish News; Canadian Jewish Review,* May 16, 1947 (a copy is in Acc. 378, Box 2); FMC Research Department Review and Evaluation of the Link Audit, Oct. 11, 1953, p. 23, Acc. 465, Box 1 (citing the Roper survey); interview with Christopher Whittle, ex-member of FMC's New York public relations staff, Apr. 22, 1966.

63. "The International Jew by Henry Ford of the Ford Motor Company" was serialized in the *Thunderbolt* starting with the April 1964 issue. Each of the articles serialized in 1966 by the monthly *Cross and the Flag* was entitled, "The International Jew: Originally Published by Henry Ford I"; the articles were published throughout the year starting in January; Gary Allen, *None Dare Call It Conspiracy* (Seal Beach, Calif.: Concord Press, 1972); *Detroit Jewish News,* Aug. 21, 1964, Aug. 25, Sept. 8, and Nov. 17, 1967, Jan. 26, Apr. 19, and June 14, 1968, and June 30, 1972; DN, Mar. 14, 1972; *Universal Jewish Encyclopedia in Ten Volumes,* 1948 ed., s.v. "Ford, Henry"; *New Standard Jewish Encyclopedia,* 1970 ed., s.v. "Ford, Henry"; *Encyclopedia Hebraica,* 1959 ed., s.v. "Anti-Semitism"; *Encyclopedia Judaica,* 1971 ed., s.v. "Anti-Semitism." Ford and the *Dearborn Independent* also are cited under the year 1920 in *Encyclopedia Judaica*'s "Chronological Chart of Jewish History."

64. *Detroit Jewish News,* July 12 and 19, 1963; copy of Jewish Telegraphic Agency dispatch, July 25, 1963 (in *Detroit Jewish News*'s Ford file); *Jersey City* (N.J.) *Jewish Standard,* Sept. 13, 1963.

65. Interview with Isidore Soboloff, May 10, 1963; "Ford at Fifty: A Case Study of One of the Great Comebacks in All Business History," *Tide* 27 (May 9, 1953), 60; *Detroit Jewish News,* Dec. 18, 1964.

66. "Ford át Fifty," *Tide,* p. 60; NYT, Oct. 7, 1963; *New York World-Telegram,* Oct. 7, 1963; *New York Journal-American,* Oct. 7, 1963; DFP, Oct. 8, 1963; *Ann Arbor* (Mich.) *News,* Oct. 8, 1963; *Detroit Jewish News,* Oct. 11, 1963. The League maintained that only 146 of Ford's 17,500 white-collar employees were Jews. In reply, Ford said that it recognized that "there may be fewer persons of the Jewish faith in our organization than one might expect from a statistical

point of view . . . [but] your report underestimates the number. In any case, there are a variety of reasons for this. Our policies, and more importantly, our intentions are not contributing factors."

67. "Israel on Wheels," *Time* 54 (Aug. 8, 1949), 62; Graeme K. Howard, vice-president-International Division, FMC, to Robert Nathan, Jewish Agency for Palestine, New York, Apr. 20, 1950 (copy), and Alfred A. May to Philip Slomovitz, May 2, 1950, both in Ford file, *Detroit Jewish News.* Slomovitz, editor of the *Detroit Jewish News,* after a visit to Israel in 1949, wrote May, "I am confident that the Ford organization will find an echo of appreciation not only in Israel but also in the United States from the great Jewish community." Slomovitz to May, Dec. 20, 1949, Ford file, *Detroit Jewish News.* Interview with Eric R. Eyebe, former Ford Mideast representative, Jan. 23, 1969; interview with two executives of Ford OAO who prefer to remain anonymous, Jan. 2, 1966, May 1 and Nov. 6, 1967; Anne Kalessis, administrative assistant, UNRWA Liaison Office, to David L. Lewis, Jan. 11, 1966; NYT, June 2, 1966; "Business in Mideast Walks on Shifting Sands," *Business Week* (July 2, 1966), 26; "Arabs Step Up Israeli Boycott," *Business Week* (Aug. 23, 1969), 82 (regarding Brooklyn market); *Detroit Jewish News,* June 10, 1966.

68. DN, Sept. 25, 1966; "Arabs Ban Coke, Ford," *Business Week* (Nov. 26, 1966), 52; "Boomerang Boycott," *Time* 88 (Dec. 2, 1966), 94; *Detroit Jewish News,* Oct. 21, 1966. Arab League countries in 1966 were Algeria, Iraq, Jordan, Kuwait, Lebanon, Libya, Morocco, Saudi Arabia, Sudan, Syria, Egypt, and Yemen; Tunisia was "half in" at the time. In March 1966 Henry II discussed with President Habib Bourguiba the possibility of opening a plant in Tunisia. *Ann Arbor* (Mich.) *News,* Mar. 10, 1966.

69. *Detroit Jewish News,* Nov. 25, 1966; "Ban Ford," *Business Week,* p. 52; "Israeli Boycott," *Business Week,* p. 82; DFP, Nov. 26, 1966; *New York World Journal Tribune,* Dec. 4, 1966. Ford and its dealers had 6,000 Arab employees, of whom 350 worked in the Alexandria plant, which was valued at $3,000,000. Seven hundred firms had been blacklisted by the Arab League as of 1966, 200 of them American. "Boomerang Boycott," *Time,* p. 94. Interview with Charles McCabe, manager, news relations, GM Overseas Operations, Apr. 10, 1975; GM news release, Sept. 17, 1974 (in possession of author).

70. *Detroit Jewish News,* Feb. 17, 1967, Apr. 10, 1970, Mar. 3, 1972; interview with Ford OAO executive, May 21, 1967; DFP, Mar. 15, 1975.

71. Slomovitz interview, May 7, 1963; *London Jewish Chronicle,* Sept. 6, 1963; *Jersey City* (N.J.) *Jewish Standard,* Sept. 13, 1963; Ben Shapiro, of Philadelphia, to Philip Slomovitz, Aug. 4, 1963; interview with Anti-Defamation League representative who prefers to remain anonymous, Mar. 10, 1965; Mark Harris, *Freedman & Son* (New York: Macmillan, 1963), p. 39; interview with Harold Kellman, University of Michigan student, Mar. 31, 1967; letter to Jerome Hesch, University of Michigan student, from his father, Apr. 2, 1967 (copy in author's possession). Some Israeli and North American Jews also can not bear to ride in, much less buy, a German Volkswagen because of its early identification with Hitler. "Should an Israeli Buy a Volkswagen?" *Time* 93 (Apr. 11, 1969), 92.

72. Soboloff interview, May 10, 1963; *Detroit Jewish News,* July 19, 1963, Apr. 10, 1970; interview with Anti-Defamation League representative, Mar. 10, 1965.

Chapter 10

1. *Escanaba* (Mich.) *Press*, Apr. 24, 1925; *Wall Street Journal*, July 21, 1926; DFP, Feb. 17, 1925; Nevins and Hill, *Expansion and Challenge*, pp. 230, 248.
2. DFP, Dec. 28, 1924; Highland Park Plant Visitors Sheet, 1922–27, Acc. 162, Box 3; DFP, Jan. 29, 1928. Even General Electric's "House of Magic," one of industry's leading showplaces during the 1930s, did not receive as many visitors annually as Highland Park (and, later on, the Rouge). "The Public Is Not Damned," *Fortune* 19 (Mar. 1939), 109.
3. *Ford News* 7 (Oct. 1, 1927), 1; *Miami Herald*, Oct. 7, 1928; DT, Feb. 3, 1929; DFP, Jan. 26, 1928; DN, Mar. 28, 1929.
4. Nevins and Hill, *Expansion and Challenge*, pp. 69, 72, 209–10; DN, May 18, 1920, Apr. 17, 1921.
5. Judson C. Welliver, "Mr. Ford Is Interviewed," *American Review of Reviews* 72 (Sept. 1925), 273; DN, Mar. 28, 1929; DFP, May 9, 1938, Mar. 14, 1926; *Kansas City Post*, Feb. 25, 1923; Nevins and Hill, *Expansion and Challenge*, pp. 279, 288, 293.
6. There are hundreds of clippings on the Rouge plant in Clipbooks 23 through 72 (1921–29); see Ford news releases on the factory in Acc. 78, Boxes 51, 53; Acc. 450, Box 3; Acc. 447, Boxes 3, 7; and Acc. 545, Box 1, in which the quoted release, dated May 17, 1923, can be found.
7. *Ford News* 5 (Sept. 15, 1925), 1; 7 (Nov. 1, 1927), 1; and 16 (Feb. 1936), 23; FMC news release, Jan. 16, 1926, Acc. 78, Box 53; *Ford Man* 3 (Nov. 3, 1919), 2 (citing Highland Park attendance figure for 1917); Ford Rotunda Activities for 1940, Acc. 629, Box 3 (citing Rouge attendance figures for 1936, 1939, 1940); J. Alfred Spender, "Impressions of Post-War America 1927–28," *America Through British Eyes*, ed. by Allan Nevins (New York: Oxford University Press, 1948), Part 5, 421. Sward, *Legend of Henry Ford*, pp. 277, 361–62.
8. Benson, *New Henry Ford*, p. 166; Nevins and Hill, *Expansion and Challenge*, pp. 226–27; *Automotive Daily News*, June 11, 1932.
9. *New York Tribune*, Feb. 20, 1921; *Christian Science Monitor*, Feb. 14, 1921; *Philadelphia Public Ledger*, May 30, 1932; Paul Sklar and S.H. Walker, *Business Finds Its Voice: Management's Effort to Sell the Business Idea to the Public* (New York: Harper & Brothers, 1938), pp. 60–67; NYT, Aug. 21, 1938; H.G. McCoy, of McCann-Erickson, Inc., to A.R. Barbier, Ford advertising manager, July 16, 1940, Acc. 285, Box 2230.
10. *Elyria* (Ohio) *Telegram*, May 25, 1921; *Marshfield* (Wis.) *News*, Sept. 29, 1922; *Buffalo Courier*, June 18, 1922; *Walden* (N.Y.) *Citizen Herald*, Jan. 2, 1922; *Noblesville* (Ind.) *Ledger*, Mar. 13, 1922; DT, Dec. 6, 1922; *Indianapolis News*, July 27, 1922; *Vienna* (Ill.) *Times*, Jan. 2, 1923.
11. Roscoe Smith (head of village industries) to Fred L. Black, April 20, 1939, Acc. 554, Box 31; FMC news release, Sept. 21, 1939, Acc. 450, Box 7.
12. NYT, Jan. 7, 1934; *Jackson* (Mich.) *Tribune*, Apr. 5, 1935 (quoting *Le Temps*); DN, Jan. 30, 1934; DFP, June 25, 1934. The United States government founded a community, Roosevelt, N.J. (originally called Jersey Homesteads), in 1936, to test its theory "that a man could work on the farm in the summer and in the local factory during the rest of the year." The project, supported by the federal government for almost a decade, "didn't work very well." *New Yorker* 38 (Sept. 29, 1962), 32.
13. *Detroit Journal*, July 12, 1920; Nevins and Hill, *Expansion and Challenge*, pp. 218–21; DT, Dec. 28, 1922, Mar. 23, 1923.
14. Nevins and Hill, *Expansion and Challenge*, pp. 220–21; *San Antonio Express*, Aug. 31, 1922; *Bartlesville* (Okla.) *Enterprise*, Aug. 27, 1922; *Pueblo* (Colo.) *Star-Journal*, Aug. 3, 1922; DT, Sept. 24, 1922.
15. Sward, *Legend of Henry Ford*, p. 134; *Sacramento Leader*, Sept. 1, 1922; *Modesto* (Calif.) *Herald*, Sept. 2, 1922; DT, Sept. 24, 1922; *Pipp's Weekly* 3 (Sept. 23, 1922), 7; *Detroit Saturday Night* 16 (Sept. 9, 1922), 7.
16. DT, Nov. 23, 1922; NYT, Mar. 29, 1928; *Providence News*, Mar. 30, 1928.
17. Nevins and Hill, *Expansion and Challenge*, pp. 231, 233–35, 237–38; DT, Apr. 24, 1923; DN, Oct. 11, 1927; *Christian Science Monitor*, Jan. 21, 1942; DT, Mar. 22, 1942; NYT, Feb. 1, 1942, Nov. 29, 1945.
18. *Detroit Journal*, July 10, 1920; Sorensen, *Forty Years*, p. 185.
19. *Railway Age* 69 (July 16, 1920), 90; Nevins and Hill, *Expansion and Challenge*, pp. 221–24.
20. *La Crosse* (Wis.) *Tribune*, July 26, 1921; Nevins and Hill, *Expansion and Challenge*, p. 224; *East Liverpool* (Ohio) *Review*, Aug. 1, 1921; *Rochester* (N.Y.) *Times-Union*, Sept. 1, 1921; Sward, *Legend of Henry Ford*, p. 131. See Clipbook 24 for numerous clippings praising Ford for his desire to reduce freight rates.
21. Oswald Garrison Villard, *Prophets True and False* (New York: A.A. Knopf, 1928), p. 295; Nevins and Hill, *Expansion and Challenge*, pp. 224–25.
22. NYT, July 20, 1928; Nevins and Hill, *Expansion and Challenge*, p. 225; interview with Fred L. Black, April 4, 1959.
23. DT, Mar. 2, 1924; DFP, Apr. 27, 1924; DT, June 20, 1925; Nevins and Hill, *Expansion and Challenge*, pp. 225–26; Oliver T. Burnham, vice-president, Lake Carriers' Association, Cleveland, to David L. Lewis, July 26, 1962, and May 31, 1963; "Ford Motor Company Fleet Adds Life to River Rouge," *Lake Carriers' Association Bulletin* 49 (June 1960), 3–4; Janet Coe Sanborn, vice-president, Great Lakes Historical Society, Cleveland, to David L. Lewis, Aug. 9, 1962.
24. "Ford's Plan to Double Jack's Pay," *Literary Digest* 86 (July 18, 1925), 14; *New York American*, June 25, 1925; Nevins and Hill, *Expansion and Challenge*, p. 226. Ford had thirty lake vessels and five ocean ships in service at the start of World War II. During the war all of the vessels except the *Henry* and the *Benson* and one tug were requisitioned by the War Shipping Board. After the war Ford disposed of all of its ships except the *Henry* and the *Benson*. "Ford Fleet," *Lake Carriers' Association Bulletin*, p. 4. Clare J. Snider, "Marine Operations—Ford Motor Company Steel Division," *Dearborn Historian* 15 (Winter 1975), 3–5.
25. NYT, Aug. 5, 1925; *Chicago Herald Examiner*, Oct. 3, 1926.
26. Nevins and Hill, *Ford: The Times*, p. 239; DT, June 17, 1920; *Ellwood City* (Pa.) *Ledger*, July 26, 1920.
27. *Dallas News*, Oct. 21, 1928; Nevins and Hill, *Expansion and Challenge*, pp. 239–41. Rumrunners, flying from nearby Canada, used the Ford airport—until they were apprehended. DN, Nov. 19, 1926.
28. DN, Aug. 7, 1925; DT, Apr. 13, 1925; DFP, Apr. 14, 1925; *Milwaukee Journal*, May 4, 1925; DT, Apr. 13, 1925.
29. *New York Telegram and Mail*, Feb. 12, 1926; DN, Sept. 28, 1925; DT, Oct. 5, 1925; DFP, Oct. 5, 1925; *New York Sun*, Oct. 8, 1925; *Wall Street Journal*, Oct. 10, 1925. See Clipbook 40 for scores of articles on the National Air Reliability Tour.

30. DT, June 27, 1927, Oct. 27, 1929; *Ford News* 6 (Sept. 1, 1926), 1; 11 (Aug. 1931), 2. The tour was combined with the annual Gordon Bennett International Balloon Race and the finals of the Boys' National Model Airplane Contest during the late 1920s. DT, Sept. 10, 1927, July 1, 1928; *Ford News* 8 (July 16, 1928), 1.

31. *New York Post*, Jan. 30, 1926, Apr. 5, 1926; NYT, May 10, 1926; DFP, Aug. 2, 1927; Richard E. Byrd, *Little America* (New York: G.P. Putnam's Sons, 1930), p. 357. In recognition of Edsel's backing, Byrd and Bennett named the Fokker taken on the 1926 trip, "Miss Josephine Ford," after Ford's daughter. Byrd also named an escarpment in Antarctica the "Edsel Ford Range." Byrd, *ibid.*

32. Nevins and Hill, *Expansion and Challenge*, pp. 244–45; DFP, Aug. 6, 1926; DT, Feb. 26, 1928; *Chicago Journal*, Dec. 14, 1928; DN, Apr. 10, 1932; John H. Frederick, *Commercial Air Transportation* (3rd ed. (Chicago: Richard D. Irwin, Inc., 1951), p. 4. *Atlanta Journal*, July 26, 1931.

33. Ralph Merle Hower, *The History of an Advertising Agency: N.W. Ayer & Son at Work, 1869–1949* (Cambridge, Mass.: Harvard University Press, 1949), p. 315; E.S. Turner, *Shocking History of Advertising!* (New York: Dutton, 1953), pp. 233–34; *Printers' Ink* 140 (Sept. 29, 1927), 10; Black, *Reminiscences*, p. 188; DN, Mar. 9, 1929; *Ford News* 10 (Apr. 1, 1930), 81. (The bound ad series has been quoted at $7.50 in rare book catalogs. Black, *ibid.*) Julian Lewis Watkins, *The 100 Greatest Advertisements: Who Wrote Them and What They Did* (New York: Moore Publishing Co., 1949), pp. 64–65. A number of $1,000 Bok awards, established by E.W. Bok, were granted annually by the Harvard Graduate School of Business Administration for outstanding achievement in various areas of advertising. DN, Mar. 9, 1929.

34. Nevins and Hill, *Expansion and Challenge*, pp. 246–47. The Ford Company lost $70,900,000 in 1932, a deficit second only to the 1928 loss of $72,000,000. Eleven Ford trimotor airplanes still exist, and one is flown daily by Island Airlines between Port Clinton, Ohio and the Lake Erie islands. *Cars & Parts* 17 (Nov. 1974), 123.

35. Black, *Reminiscences*, pp. 15–16; Fred L. Black to E.G. Liebold, Sept. 27 and 30, 1919, Acc. 62, Box 108.

36. *Ford News* 2 (Feb. 1, 1922), 1; DN, Jan. 25, 1925.

37. *New York Telegram*, Mar. 26, 1922; *Albion* (Mich.) *Recorder*, Mar. 28, 1922; NYT, Oct. 22, 1922; DT, Oct. 23, 1922.

38. *Ford News* 2 (June 1, 1922), 1; Black, *Reminiscences*, pp. 170–71. WWI programs for the year 1922 can be found in Acc. 285, Boxes 75, 114. Ford appeared before a WWI microphone only once. In 1923 he was asked, along with other prominent men, to speak during the National Association of Broadcasters' annual attempt to establish two-way radio communication between Great Britain and the United States. His speech never left the broadcasting studio, however, for in switching over from the KDEN to the WWI wave length, the technicians temporarily silenced the station. Black and other WWI employees were spared the ordeal of explaining the matter to Ford when an inexplicable cable of congratulations arrived from a British ship, the S.S. *Berengaria*. DT, Dec. 2, 1923; Black, *Reminiscences*, pp. 172, 173.

39. Black, *Reminiscences*, pp. 175–76; A.J. Tyvier, acting commissioner of the Federal Bureau of Navigation, to FMC, Mar. 18, 1926, Acc. 285, Box 561; DN, Aug. 1, 1926. Although WWI made only a minor contribution to the radio industry, the station's en-

gineers contributed significantly to the field of aviation. They worked out the first good system of airplane directional control, and their patent was shared with all who wished to take advantage of it. Black, *Reminiscences*, p. 17; *Ford News* 7 (Mar. 15, 1927), 1.

40. Nevins and Hill, *Expansion and Challenge*, pp. 20, 59; DN, July 6, 1915; DT, Aug. 28, 1915; Fred Albert Shannon, *America's Economic Growth* (3rd ed.; New York: Macmillan, 1951), pp. 712–13; Stewart H. Holbrook, *Machines of Plenty: Pioneering in American Agriculture* (New York: Alfred A. Knopf, 1955), pp. 169–70. *Motor Age* 18 (Aug. 25, 1910), 19; *Popular Science* 87 (Dec. 1915), 780.

41. *Omaha News*, Aug. 7, 1916; E.G. Liebold to P.C. Van Vleet, Ontario Department of Agriculture, Oct. 21, 1916, and Liebold to C.E. Sorensen, Nov. 3, 1916, Acc. 2, Box 39.

42. Nevins and Hill, *Expansion and Challenge*, pp. 58, 60–61, 63; U.S. Department of Agriculture, *The Manufacture and Sale of Farm Equipment in 1920* (Washington: United States Government Printing Office, 1922), pp. 2–3.

43. *Printers' Ink* 102 (June 3, 1918), 17; The Editors of *Fortune, Understanding the Big Corporations* (New York: R.H. McBride & Company, 1934), p. 22.

44. Shannon, *America's Economic Growth*, p. 713; Theodore F. MacManus and Norman Beasley, *Men, Money, and Motors* (New York: Harper & Brothers, 1930), p. 247; Charles A. Brownell to branch managers, Mar. 11, 1920, Acc. 78, Box 46; Norton T. Brotherton to Edsel Ford, July 7, 1920, Acc. 6, Box 30. Fordson distributors' national advertising was placed by Seelye, Brotherton & Brown, Detroit, starting in early 1919. *Printers' Ink* 106 (Feb. 13, 1919), 20. This agency was replaced in 1920 by the Brotherton-Knoble Company, which in turn was superseded by the Brotherton Company in 1922. Brotherton to Edsel Ford, June 7, 1920, Acc. 6, Box 30; Brotherton to Edsel Ford, June 7, 1922, Acc. 6, Box 37. Brotherton was a boyhood friend of Edsel Ford. Interview with A.R. Barbier, Ford advertising executive, 1922–41, July 12, 1962.

45. Shannon, *America's Economic Growth*, pp. 719–22; Charles A. Brownell to branch managers, Aug. 20, 1920, Acc. 78, Box 89; Brownell to branch managers, Aug. 30, 1920. Acc. 78, Box 46; *Columbia* (Tenn.) *Herald*, Aug. 30, 1920; General Sales Letter No. 830, July 21, 1920, Acc. 78, Box 89; *Ford Man* 4 (Sept. 3, 1920), 1; *Ford Worker* 1 (Sept. 1, 1920), 1 and 1 (Oct. 1, 1920), 1; *Ford News* 2 (Nov. 1, 1920), 1; DT, Jan. 26, 1921; *Motor Age* 39 (June 16, 1921), 20.

46. FMC news release, Dec. 23, 1925, Acc. 545, Box 1; E.G. Liebold to Grant Wright, editor of the *Eastern Dealer*, July 3, 1922, Acc. 285, Box 117; Sward, *Legend of Henry Ford*, p. 212; *Pipp's Weekly* 3 (Aug. 26, 1922), 7–10; Arthur Brisbane to Liebold, May 13, 1919, and Liebold to Brisbane, May 21, 1919, Acc. 62, Box 5; William P. Young, *A Ford Dealer's Twenty Year Ride The Joy Ride The Sleigh Ride and Rough Ride with Old and New Model Ford Policies Through Changing Scenery from Company Profits to Dealer Losses* (Hempstead, N.Y.: Twenty Year Ride Publishing Co., 1932), pp. 70, 72.

47. General Sales Letter No. 1221, Feb. 1, 1922, Acc. 78, Box 89; Editors of *Fortune, Understanding Big Corporations*, p. 22; R.E. Bryan, Public Relations Department, International Harvester Company, Chicago, to David L. Lewis, July 26, 1962; William A. Ryan to branch managers, May 10, 1922, Acc. 78, Box 84; *Ford News* 2 (Aug. 1, 1922), 6.

48. William A. Ryan to branch managers, Mar. 10, 1922,

Acc. 78, Box 84; *Ford News* 3 (Nov. 15, 1922), 8; *Grants Pass* (Ore.) *Courier*, July 11, 1922.

49. *Ford News* 2 (Aug. 15, 1922), 1; 2 (Sept. 1, 1922), 3; 2 (Sept. 15, 1922), 3; 2 (Oct. 15, 1922), 3; and 3 (Nov. 1, 1922), 3; William A. Ryan to branch managers, May 10, 1922, Acc. 78, Box 84; *Palo Alto* (Calif.) *Times*, June 6, 1922.

50. Nevins and Hill, *Expansion and Challenge*, p. 255; Advertising Department to branch managers, Nov. 2, 1923, Acc. 78, Box 84, Mar. 9, 1925, Acc. 78, Box 51, Oct. 15, 1926, Acc. 78, Box 53, and Aug. 4, 1927, Acc. 509, Box 4; General Sales Letter No. 1421, Sept. 5, 1923, Acc. 572, Box 10; William A. Ryan to branch managers, July 20, 1926, Acc. 235, Box 16; *Ford News* 4 (Jan. 15, 1924), 5. The price of the Fordson was raised to $420 in the fall of 1923. DN, Oct. 2, 1923. *Fordson Magazine* was discontinued in December 1925. General Sales Letter No. 1637, Dec. 5, 1925, Acc. 572, Box 10.

51. *Fortune, Understanding Big Corporations*, p. 22; Sales Department to branch managers, Feb. 20, 1928, Acc. 509, Box 5; Nevins and Hill, *Expansion and Challenge*, p. 255. More than 300,000 Fordson tractors were still in operation in the United States in 1939. "Sigh of Relief Comes As Ford's New Tractor Is Shown, But Drama Is in the Making," *Printers' Ink* 188 (July 14, 1939), 14.

52. Nevins and Hill, *Expansion and Challenge*, pp. 172–76, 179, 181–82; DN, Jan. 5, Feb. 4 and 6, 1922.

53. Nevins and Hill, *Expansion and Challenge*, pp. 184–89; DT, June 19, 1922. The Lelands' departure received little attention outside of automotive circles and the Detroit press.

54. *Pipp's Weekly* 3 (Mar. 10, 1923), 1; Associated Press story in *Wall Street Journal*, Mar. 10, 1923; DT, Mar. 9, 1923; *Automotive Industries* 48 (Mar. 15, 1923), 643; William L. Stidger, *Henry Ford: The Man and His Motives* (New York: George H. Doran Company, 1923), pp. 75–76. See clippings in Acc. 44, Box 16 regarding Ford's press in connection with the payment of the Lincoln creditors.

55. DFP, Nov. 16, 1927; Nevins and Hill, *Expansion and Challenge*, pp. 196–97.

56. Nevins and Hill, *Expansion and Challenge*, pp. 193–94; *Ford News* 2 (Apr. 8, 1923), 5; 3 (Aug. 15, 1923), 1. The Lincoln, unlike the Model T, was shown at the National Auto Show in New York's Grand Central Palace, since Lincoln was a member of the National Automobile Chamber of Commerce. *New York Post*, Jan. 8, 1927.

57. General Sales Letter No. 1304, Oct. 13, 1922, Acc. 78, Box 84, and No. 1333, Jan. 4, 1923, Acc. 78, Box 90; Advertising Department to branch managers, Nov. 20, 1923, Acc. 78, Box 84.

58. Lincoln Advertising Expense Sheet 1923–32, Acc. 454, Box 1; General Sales Letter No. 1325, Acc. 78, Box 90, No. 1556, Dec. 11, 1924, Acc. 572, Box 10, and No. 1637, Dec. 5, 1925, Acc. 78, Box 53; Advertising Department to branch managers, Apr. 10, 1924, Acc. 78, Box 85; *Hastings* (Mich.) *Banner*, Apr. 28, 1926. Agents were assessed $25.00 at the time of each Lincoln delivery, and the company added a similar amount to the Lincoln fund. It may be recalled that starting in September 1923, Ford dealers were assessed $3.00 at the time of delivery of each Ford car and truck, Lincoln, and Fordson.

59. General Sales Letter No. 1436, Oct. 12, 1923, Acc. 572, Box 10; *Ford News* 4 (Jan. 15, 1924), 5; Lawrence H. Seltzer, *A Financial History of the American Automobile Industry: A Study of the Ways in Which the Leading American Producers of Automobiles Have Met Their Capital Requirements* (Boston: Houghton

Mifflin Company, 1928), pp. 137, 250; Kennedy, *Automobile Industry*, pp. 159, 176, 199, 209, 228.

60. Merz, *Then Came Ford*, pp. 205–6; DN, Oct. 22, 1928; DFP, Jan. 5, 1923, Oct. 20, 1925; *Glendale* (Calif.) *News*, n.d. [July 1925], Clipbook 38.

61. *Christian Science Monitor*, Sept. 16, 1926; *Dearborn Press*, Jan. 7, 1921; *Muncie* (Ind.) *Press*, Jan. 13, 1926; DT, May 12, 1923; *Brooklyn Eagle*, Aug. 26, 1921; *Winnipeg Free Press*, Dec. 31, 1921; *Cleveland Plain Dealer*, Apr. 11, 1920; *St. Louis Democrat*, Aug. 22, 1921; DT, Oct. 22, 1922; *Chicago American*, Nov. 3, 1922; *Paragould* (Ark.) *Press*, Oct. 6, 1922; *New Orleans Item*, May 16, 1922; *Chicago Journal of Commerce*, Nov. 14, 1922.

62. *Philadelphia Public Ledger*, Aug. 12, 1920; Arthur Pound, "The Ford Myth," *Atlantic Monthly* 133 (Jan. 1924), 47; NYT, Dec. 18, 1927. For other favorable comment on Ford's industrial empire see Welliver, "Ford Is Interviewed," p. 272; Franklin Russell, "So Ford Is Advertising," *Printers' Ink* 128 (July 17, 1924), 41; *Wall Street Journal*, July 21, 1926; *Philadelphia Record*, Feb. 5, 1927.

63. The quotation appears in Edsel Ford to Wetmore Hodges, secretary, American Radiator Company, Apr. 30, 1924; DFP, Dec. 28, 1924; *Ford News* 3 (June 15, 1923), 4; 3 (July 15, 1923), 1; 5 (Jan. 1, 1925), 5. See pertinent press releases in Acc. 545, Boxes 1–2.

64. *Ford News* 3 (Sept. 15, 1923), 1; 4 (Feb. 1, 1924), 1; FMC news release, Jan. 4, 1928, Acc. 544, Box 2; *New York World*, Jan. 8, 1928; NYT, Jan. 14, 1928; DN, Oct. 29, 1962.

65. *New York American*, Jan. 11, 1927; Black, *Reminiscences*, p. 184; *Detroit Saturday Night* 22 (Jan. 28, 1928), 2 of sec. 2; *Ford News* 8 (Feb. 15, 1928), pp. 25–26.

66. *New York American*, Jan. 10, 1926, Jan. 9, 1927; *New York World*, Jan. 8, 1927; *Ford News* 7 (Feb. 1, 1927), 1; 10 (May 1, 1930), 105; C.C. Cheadle, Advertising Department, to John Crawford, assistant to Edsel Ford, Oct. 23, 1931, Acc. 6, Box 394.

67. Wetmore Hodges to Edsel Ford, Apr. 12, 1924, and Ford to Hodges, Apr. 30, 1924, Acc. 572, Box 10; *Ford News* 4 (Aug. 1, 1924), 6; Russell, "So Ford Is Advertising," p. 41; *Printers' Ink Monthly* 23 (Nov. 1931), 38. The advertising agency which prepared the 1924–25 series was the Critchfield Company, of Chicago. N.W. Ayer & Son, Inc., of Philadelphia, prepared the 1931 campaign. The Ford Company also ran a "one profit" advertising campaign in 1938. "The only profit," said the first of the advertisements, "is on the finished result—the car or truck as it comes off the line. Some years there is no profit for us. But we see to it that the customers always profit." "Henry and Edsel," *Printers' Ink* 185 (Nov. 10, 1938), 12.

68. *Battle Creek* (Mich.) *Moon Journal*, July 18, 1925; *New York Herald Tribune*, Aug. 12, 1925; *Literary Digest* 86 (July 18, 1925), 14; *Philadelphia Record*, Feb. 5, 1927 (quoting the *New York World*); Villard, *Prophets*, p. 295.

69. Nevins and Hill, *Expansion and Challenge*, p. 248.

Chapter 11

1. Lawrence H. Seltzer, *A Financial History of the American Automobile Industry: A Study of the Ways in Which the Leading American Producers of Au-*

tomobiles Have Met Their Capital Requirements (Boston: Houghton Mifflin Company, 1928), pp. 121, 135; Nevins and Hill, *Expansion and Challenge*, pp. 394–97.

2. Arthur Pound, *The Turning Wheel* (Garden City, N.Y.: Doubleday, Doran & Company, Inc., 1934), p. 427; The Editors of *Fortune, Understanding the Big Corporations* (New York: R.H. McBride & Company, 1934), p. 102. See chapter 3 for a discussion of Ford's prewar market studies.

3. Nevins and Hill, *Expansion and Challenge*, pp. 405, 415; DT, Aug. 26, 1925; Kennedy, *Automobile Industry*, pp. 187–88.

4. E.G. Liebold to R. Marshall, of *Concrete* magazine, Oct. 17, 1922; D.D. Martin to O.O. Buck, Aug. 5, 1919, Acc. 53, Box 19; *Automotive Industries* 49 (Aug. 16, 1923), 344; Edsel Ford to branch managers, Aug. 10, 1923, Acc. 572, Box 10.

5. Edsel Ford to branch managers, Sept. 5, 1923; General Sales Letter No. 1425, Sept. 7, 1923, Acc. 572, Box 10.

6. Advertising Department to branch managers, Oct. 18, 1923, Acc. 78, Box 84, and Feb. 5, 1924, Acc. 78, Box 85; Report of O.L. Armour, district supervisor, to Edsel Ford, Jan. 28, 1924, Acc. 572, Box 10.

7. General Sales Letter No. 1481, Feb. 18, 1924, Acc. 572, Box 10; Advertising Department to branch managers, Mar. 9, 1925, Acc. 78, Box 51, and Mar. 1, 1926, Acc. 78, Box 53; W. Livingston Larned, "Ford and Douglas Drop Homely Layouts," *Printers' Ink* 125 (Dec. 13, 1923), 57.

8. Interview with Norton Brotherton, Mar. 10, 1967; Norton Brotherton to Frank Campsall, Apr. 25, 1939, Acc. 285, Box 2245; Edsel Ford to branch managers, Jan. 31, 1924, Acc. 78, Box 85; General Sales Letter No. 1556, Dec. 11, 1924, Acc. 572, Box 10; Barbier interview, July 12, 1962.

9. Recapitulation of FMC Advertising Expenditures, Sept. 1923 to Oct. 1926, inclusive, Dec. 8, 1926, Acc. 454, Box 1; *Wall Street Journal*, Mar. 31, 1925; NYT, Mar. 8, 1926; W.A. Ryan to branch managers, July 20, 1926, Acc. 235, Box 16. After the company abandoned advertising, Barbier "sat around the Highland Park plant for a year, doing next to nothing." Barbier interview, July 12, 1962.

10. General Sales Letter No. 1637, Dec. 5, 1925, Acc. 572, Box 10; W.M. Cunningham, *"J8": A Chronicle of the Neglected Truth about Henry Ford D.E. and the Ford Motor Company* (Detroit: North American Publishing Co. [1930]), pp. 101–2.

11. *Sales Management* (Oct. 30, 1926), 711, 774–75; *New York American*, Sept. 19, 1926; *Fourth Estate* (Nov. 13, 1926).

12. Nevins and Hill, *Expansion and Challenge*, p. 409; Cunningham, *Chronicle of Neglected Truth*, p. 76; *New York Sun*, May 12, 1926; *New York Post*, June 5, 1926; *Brooklyn Eagle*, June 6, 1926.

13. *New York Post*, May 29, 1926; *New York World*, Aug. 23, 1926; *Cleveland Press*, Sept. 14, 1926; *Boston Post*, Oct. 9, 1926; *New York American*, Sept. 11, 1926; DFP, Feb. 16, 1927; DT, Mar. 20, 1927; *New York Post*, Aug. 7, 1926; *New York Sun*, Sept. 8, 1926; *Chicago Journal of Commerce*, Dec. 16 and 20, 1926; DFP, Dec. 3, 1926.

14. Nevins and Hill, *Expansion and Challenge*, pp. 428–29; *Advertising & Selling* 36 (July 28, 1926), 50; NYT, Dec. 26, 1926.

15. DT, Feb. 15, 1927; DFP, Feb. 16, 1927; *Aurora* (Ill.) *News*, Feb. 20, 1927; *New York Sun*, Feb. 23, 1927; *New York Journal*, Mar. 22, 1927; *Flint* (Mich.) *Journal*, Apr. 1, 1927; *Ironton* (Ohio) *Tribune*, Apr. 14, 1927.

16. DT, May 18, 1927; *Windsor* (Ont.) *Star*, May 19, 1922; *Baltimore Sun*, May 22, 1927.

17. *Pittsburgh Sun*, May 27, 1927; *Milwaukee Journal*, May 26, 1927; FMC to branch managers, May 25, 1927, Acc. 78, Box 54; Edsel Ford to Ford dealers, May 25, 1927, Acc. 78, Box 54.

18. DN, May 26, 1927; *Ford News* 7 (June 1, 1927), 1; DFP, June 5, 1927.

19. *Louisville Times*, May 28, 1927; *Baltimore Sun*, May 26, 1927; *New York Herald Tribune*, May 30, 1927; *Dayton News*, May 31, 1927; *Roanoke News*, May 31, 1927.

20. Nevins and Hill, *Expansion and Challenge*, p. 432; *Automotive Daily News* 5 (July 22, 1927), 6; DN, Oct. 22, 1971.

21. Merz, *Then Came Ford*, p. 304; Archibald Henderson, *Contemporary Immortals* (New York: D. Appleton and Company, 1930), p. 183; Lee Strout White (pseud.), "Farewell, My Lovely," *New Yorker* 12 (May 16, 1936), 20; Stern, *Tin Lizzie*, p. 13; "The 100 'Best Designed' Products," *Fortune* 59 (Apr. 1959), 135–40; "Motor Trend's Hall of Fame," *Motor Trend* 25 (Apr. 1974), 127; Nevins and Hill, *Expansion and Challenge*, p. 435. "Farewell, My Lovely" was published in book form by its authors, E. B. White and L. S. Strout, in 1936, with the title, *Farewell to Model T*, and has been reprinted in chapter form in at least three anthologies: E. B. White and L. S. Strout, eds., *A Subtreasury of Humor* (New York: Coward-McCann, Inc., 1941), pp. 747–53; W. H. Stone and R. Hoopes, eds., *Form and Thought in Prose* (New York: Ronald Press, 1954), pp. 542–48; and Harlow O. Waite and Benjamin P. Atkinson, eds., *Literature for Our Time: an Anthology for College Students*, 3rd ed. (New York: Holt, Reinhart, & Winston, 1948), pp. 866–70.

22. FMC news release, Oct. 24, 1958 (in author's possession); Nevins and Hill, *Expansion and Challenge*, p. 434; DN, Feb. 6, 1972; *Ann Arbor* (Mich.) *News*, Feb. 17, 1972; Herbert W. Williamson, manager, public relations, Volkswagen of America, Inc., to David L. Lewis, Apr. 18, 1975; G. N. Georgano, *The Complete Encyclopedia of Motorcars* (New York: E. P. Dutton and Company, Inc., 1968), pp. 487, 590–91, 130, 222–23.

23. Nevins and Hill, *Expansion and Challenge*, p. 435; *Restorer* 9 (July–Aug. 1963), 11; *Cleveland Plain Dealer*, Oct. 11, 1931; DFP, Mar. 28, 1942; Stern, *Tin Lizzie*, pp. 8–9; "The Story of the Model T," *Antique Automobile* 17 (June 1953), 11; "Henry Reads Lizzies, Collectors Read Henry," *Ford World* 8 (Feb. 10, 1971), 4; "Collectors Won't Part with 'T's,'" *Ford World* 8 (Feb. 10, 1971), 4; Sears, Roebuck and Co. 1975 Spring Summer Catalog, p. 641. Sears acknowledges that "parts for very old cars are best left to specialty auto parts houses ... since today's 'T' owner is more likely to be a collector or hobbyist, rather than one who operates his 'T' for average daily needs as so many of our customers did in the past." Richard G. Williford, public relations manager-automotive, Sears, Roebuck and Co., to David L. Lewis, Apr. 24, 1975. "Ancient Model T Keeps Truckin," *Ford World* 11 (Apr. 1974), 4; DN, Mar. 17 and Apr. 22, 1974; *Washington Post*, Nov. 19, 1972. Scores of advertisements for Model T parts and accessories appear in every issue of *Hemmings Motor News, Cars & Parts*, and *Old Cars*. Ford was selling $20,000,000 worth of Model T parts each month as late as 1948, most of the items going to Latin America, Africa, and Arabia. "Antiques," *News-*

week (Mar. 22, 1948), 48. In 1975, excellently re-stored T's had a price range of $3,250 for a 1922–23 coupe to $16,500 for a 1909 towncar. "Old Cars Price Guide . . . Fords," *Old Cars* 4 (Mar. 11, 1975), 6.

24. *Model T Times* no. 155 (Jan.–Feb. 1975), inside back cover; *Vintage Ford* 10 (Jan.–Feb. 1975), 34. The Model T Ford Club International's membership was 5,700 in 1971, according to Mary Moline, "The Clubs for the Model 'T' Enthusiast," *Ford Life* 1 (May–June 1971), 32. The club prefers not to release membership data. Arthur R. Bergstrom, president, MTFCI, to David L. Lewis, Apr. 14, 1974. Its membership was estimated at 1,700 in 1975 by its rival organization. Ray Miller, executive secretary, Model T Ford Club of America, to David L. Lewis, Apr. 27, 1975. T.R. Nicholson, *The World's Motor Museums*, (Philadelphia: J.B. Lippincott Company, 1970); Harrah's Automobile Collection (Reno: Harrah's Automobile Collection, 1973); "Automobile Museums of the World," *Car Classics 1975 Yearbook*, pp. 57–62. Skip Goodale, "Church Collection in Illinois Shows Fords and Nostalgia," *Old Cars* 3 (Jan. 1–15, 1974), 3.

25. Most of the chapters and all of the books on the Model T may be found in the Ford Archives; Irwin Ross, *The Image Merchants: The Fabulous World of Public Relations* (Garden City, N.Y.: Doubleday & Company, Inc., 1959), pp. 179–80; David L. Lewis, "The Rise of the Model T," *Public Relations Journal* 14 (Nov. 1958), 12; interview with William Goodell, manager, FMC News Department, Oct. 8, 1968.

26. *Life* 53 (July 20, 1962), 43 (Autolite advertisement); FMC news release, May 14, 1970 (in author's possession); DFP, May 18, 1970, and *Life* 68 (May 29, 1970), 52A (Pinto advertisements); Joseph G. Schulte, account executive, Grey Advertising Inc. to David L. Lewis, Mar. 28, 1972; *Life* 55 (Sept. 13, 1963), 2 (Volkswagen-Model T advertisement); *Time* 100 (Sept. 11, 1972), 30; *Bulb Horn* 20 (July–Aug. 1969), 1 (Mennen Company-Model T advertisement); *Business Week* (July 11, 1964), inside back cover (Universal Oil Products Company-Model T advertisement).

27. Paul Mandel, "What Must Have Happened Under Massive Pressures," *Life* 54 (Apr. 19, 1963), 40; *New York Journal-American*, Aug. 25, 1963; DN, Feb. 16, 1963 and Mar. 10, 1971; "A Man for Vassar," *Time* 81 (June 28, 1963), 63; *Detroit Emergency Press*, Aug. 20, 1964; "Mustang Kicks Up Its Heels for Ford," *Advertising Age* 35 (Nov. 16, 1964), 135; "High Life Down on Animal Farm," *Insider's Newsletter* 6 (June 22, 1964), 6; "High Flying Buckeyes," *Newsweek* 52 (Nov. 25, 1968), 62; DFP, Dec. 7, 1973. The author has a thick file of cartoons and comments relating President Ford to a Model T and other Ford cars.

28. "One Dozen Classic Furs," *Holiday* 30 (Dec. 1961), 159; *Newsweek* 33 (Feb. 7, 1949), 33; "The New Douglas," *Forbes* 95 (June 15, 1965), 24; Samuel Eliot Morison, *The Oxford History of the American People* (New York: Oxford University Press, 1965), 896; "Tin Lizzie of Aviation," *Model "A" News* 21 (Nov.–Dec. 1974), 18; Ford trimotor exhibit placard, Ontario Science Museum, July 25, 1974; *Time* 84 (July 24, 1965), 81 (Caterpillar); NYT, July 7, 1963 (Trieste); Detroit Historical Museum placard, Jan. 19, 1968 (Birney car); *Ann Arbor* (Mich.) *News*, Jan. 22, 1968 (Atwater-Kent); Gay 90's Melody Museum placard, Dec. 23, 1970 (Coinola Style A); Bernard A. Weisberger, "You Press the Button, We Do the Rest," *American Heritage* 23 (Oct. 1972), 87.

Chapter 12

1. *Utica Observer-Dispatch*, Dec. 1, 1927; F.L. Smith, Jr., "The Greatest Show on Earth," *Independent* 119 (Dec. 31, 1927), 650; *Staunton* (Va.) *Leader*, Dec. 2, 1927; DFP, Dec. 11, 1927; Frederick Lewis Allen, *Only Yesterday* (New York: Harper & Brothers, 1931), p. 162. Most authorities agree that Lindbergh's flight was the decade's biggest story.

2. "Strut, Miss Lizzie!," *Nation* 125 (Dec. 14, 1927), 627; *Sales Management & Advertisers' Weekly* 16 (Nov. 17, 1928), 444; *Rochester* (N.Y.) *Times-Union*, Oct. 14, 1927; *Elyria* (Ohio) *Telegram*, Aug. 15, 1927; Garrett, *Wild Wheel*, p. 69.

3. FMC to branch managers, May 25, 1927, Acc. 78, Box 54; NYT, June 22 and June 23, 1927; DN, June 23, 1927; *New York Journal of Commerce*, June 23, 1927; *Chillicothe* (Ohio) *Advertiser*, June 23, 1927.

4. *Marietta* (Ohio) *Times*, June 23, 1927; NYT, Nov. 29, 1927; Nevins and Hill, *Expansion and Challenge*, pp. 447–48, 450.

5. *Duluth Herald*, Nov. 20, 1927; *Danville* (Va.) *Bee*, Oct. 28, 1929; Merrill Denison, *The Power To Go* (New York: Doubleday, 1956), p. 213; Nevins and Hill, *Expansion and Challenge*, p. 438; *New York Graphic*, Nov. 16, 1927; DT, Nov. 29, 1927. See p. 125 of Clipbook 62 for five cartoons by Franklin Collier.

6. DFP, Nov. 17, 1927; E.S. Turner, *Shocking History of Advertising!* (New York: Dutton, 1953), p. 233; Chris Sinsabaugh, *Who, Me? Forty Years of Automobile History* (Detroit: Arnold-Powers, Inc., 1940), pp. 113–14; *New York Graphic*, Nov. 16, 1927; *Westward* (serving suburban Detroit communities), Nov. 16, 1927; "A Country Editor's 'Scoop' on the New Ford Car," *Literary Digest* 95 (Dec. 3, 1927), 54 (quoting *New York World*). William Randolph Hearst sent wires to all of his newspapers, ordering them to publish the *Brighton* (Mich.) *Argus*'s Model A photograph on the front page. Arthur Brisbane to E.G. Liebold, Oct. 24, 1927, Acc. 285, Box 690.

7. *Danville* (Va.) *Bee*, Oct. 25, 1927; *Royal Oak* (Mich.) *Tribune*, Aug. 11, 1927; *Toledo Times*, Oct. 27, 1927; *Washington Post*, July 27, 1927; *Elyria* (Ohio) *Telegram*, Aug. 15, 1927.

8. DT, Oct. 11, 1927; *Rochester* (N.Y.) *Times-Union*, Oct. 14, 1927; *Lynn* (Mass.) *Telegram-News*, Oct. 17, 1927.

9. DN, Nov. 25, 1927; DT, Nov. 26, 1927. See Clipbook 65 for photographs of Ford stamping the first engine block.

10. Merz, *Then Came Ford*, p. 292; Nevins and Hill, *Expansion and Challenge*, pp. 437, 451, 453.

11. DT, Aug. 28, 1927; *New York Sun*, Sept. 21, 1927; Advertising Department to branch managers, June 24, 1927, Acc. 78, Box 54; FMC news release, Oct. 11, 1927, Acc. 544, Box 2; Nevins and Hill, *Expansion and Challenge*, pp. 450, 463.

12. Kennedy, *Automobile Industry*, pp. 196–97; *Cleveland News*, Oct. 7, 1927; Maurice Coates, "Henry Ford Shows Us a Trick or Two about Marketing," *Advertising & Selling* 10 (Dec. 14, 1927), 38; Nevins and Hill, *Expansion and Challenge*, p. 454; Burlingame, *Henry Ford*, p. 120.

13. Garrett, *Wild Wheel*, p. 67; Black, *Reminiscences*, pp. 177–78, 182.

14. *Printers' Ink* 139 (June 2, 1927), 33–34; *Business Week* (Oct. 19, 1940), 16; Fred L. Black to E.G. Liebold, May 20, 1927, Acc. 285, Box 609; Black,

Reminiscences, pp. 177, 182. The Advertising Department had always reported to the sales manager before 1927; this chain of command was reinstated in 1933.

15. *Editor & Publisher* 60 (Dec. 3, 1927), 5; *Automotive Industries* 57 (Dec. 10, 1927), 853; *Printers' Ink* 141 (Dec. 1, 1927), 20; *Morgantown* (W.Va.) *New Dominion,* Dec. 8, 1927; "Henry Ford as Super-Showman and Salesman," *Literary Digest* 115 (Dec. 17, 1957), 10; Earnest Elmo Calkins, "The Triumph of Paid Advertising," *Advertising & Selling* 10 (Dec. 14, 1927), 20; Coates, "Trick about Marketing," p. 38. As mentioned previously, 12 percent of the introductory campaign's budget was spent in Hebrew language newspapers, DFP, Dec. 7, 1927, Allen Churchill, *The Year the World Went Mad* (New York: Crowell, 1960), p. 281.

16. *New York Advertising Club News* 12 (Dec. 12, 1927), 6; Allen, *Only Yesterday,* p. 163; *Sales Management* 13 (Dec. 10, 1927), 1009; Calkins, "Triumph of Paid Advertising," p. 20; Smith, "Greatest Show on Earth," p. 650; Oliver Gramling, *AP: The Story of News* (New York: Farrar and Rinehart, 1940), p. 506; *Motor West* (Los Angeles), Dec. 1, 1927; *Ford News* 8 (Dec. 15, 1927), 1. One of the Ford ads, entitled "Important Facts about the New Ford Car," was awarded a $1,000 Bok Award by Harvard after its selection as the "advertisement most effective in typography" for the year 1927. DN, Feb. 18, 1928. The first ad, two decades later, was named by a leading advertising executive as one of the "100 greatest advertisements." Watkins, *100 Greatest Advertisements,* pp. 98–99.

17. DN, Nov. 30, 1927; *New York Telegram,* Dec. 2, 1927; *Ford News* 8 (Dec. 15, 1927), 1.

18. DN, Dec. 2, 1927; *New York World,* Dec. 2 and 4, 1927; *New York Sun,* Dec. 2, 1927.

19. NYT, Dec. 3, 1927; *New Orleans States,* Dec. 2, 1927; Sales Department to branch managers, Dec. 8, 1927, Acc. 509, Box 4; *Sales Management* 13 (Dec. 10, 1927), 1009; *Ford News* 8 (Dec. 15, 1927), 1; DN, Dec. 2, 1927; Nevins and Hill, *Expansion and Challenge,* p. 459; Calkins, "Triumph of Paid Advertising," p. 20. "When All America Wondered," *The Ford Dealer Story* (Dearborn: Ford Division, Ford Motor Company, 1953), p. 81.

20. *New York World,* Dec. 4, 1927; NYT, Dec. 2, 1927.

21. Nevins and Hill, *Expansion and Challenge,* pp. 455–57.

22. DN, Jan. 10, 1928; Nevins and Hill, *Expansion and Challenge,* pp. 460, 466–67, 469. Twenty years after introducing the Model A, Ford unveiled another new car, the medium-priced Edsel. Although the company allocated $50,000,000 for the initial advertising and promotion of the Edsel (and undoubtedly spent a large part, if not all, of that amount), the car drew only 2,850,000 to dealers' showrooms on the day of its introduction and was ordered by fewer than 13,000 persons during the first month it was on sale. John Brooks, *The Age of the Edsel and Other Business Ventures* (New York: Harper & Row, 1963), pp. 41, 46–48, 50, 60–61, 67. Brooks suggested (p. 50) that the Edsel reached its high-water mark in public acceptance on September 7, 1957—three days after its introduction—when one of the new models was stolen in north Philadelphia. "Only a few months later," he observed, "any but the least fastidious of car thieves might not have bothered."

23. *Danville* (Va.) *Bee,* Oct. 25, 1927; *Charleston* (W. Va.) *Gazette,* Nov. 26, 1927; "A Country Editor's 'Scoop' on the New Ford Car," *Literary Digest* 95 (Dec. 3, 1927), 54 (quoting the *New York World*); *Newark News,* Nov. 30, 1927; "Super-Showman," *Literary Digest,* p. 10 (quoting the *Springfield* [Mass.] *Union*); *Staunton* (Va.) *Leader,* Dec. 2, 1927.

24. *Duluth Herald,* Nov. 10, 1927; *Baltimore Manufacturers Record,* Dec. 22, 1927; Smith, "Greatest Show on Earth," p. 650; *Lexington* (Mass.) *Times,* Dec. 30, 1927 (quoting *Norwood* [Mass.] *Messenger*); "The Nation's Honor Roll for 1927," *Nation* 126 (Jan. 4, 1928), 4.

25. *Asheville* (N.C.) *Citizen,* Dec. 1, 1927; William C. Richards in the DFP, Dec. 11, 1927.

26. Black, *Reminiscences,* pp. 182, 189; Nevins and Hill, *Expansion and Challenge,* p. 464; James E. Adams, *More Power to Advertising* (New York: Harper & Brothers, 1927), p. 66; Arthur Brisbane to Frank Campsall, Oct. 4, 1928, Acc. 285, Box 748. The Ford Company heavily advertised the Model A during the four-year period the car was on the market. Appropriations for advertising from 1928 through 1932 totaled $29,000,000, ranging from a low of $4,981,445 in 1928 to a high of $10,144,011 in 1930. The entire amount came from the company, a complete reversal of the dealer-assessment policy established during the mid-1920s. In contributing nothing to national advertising between 1927 and 1934, Ford dealers were virtually unique among automobile agents. Chevrolet assessed its dealers $10.00 per car; Nash, an average of $13.97 per unit; Studebaker, from $10.00 to $25.00; and Hudson, from $15.00 to $20.00. FMC Advertising Expense Sheet 1928–36, Aug. 8, 1937, Acc. 44, Box 13; Federal Trade Commission, *Report on Motor Vehicle Industry* (Washington: United States Government Printing Office, 1939), pp. 684, 714–15, 815–16; G.A. Nichols, "Why Chevrolet and Ford Won't Run an Advertising Race," *Printers' Ink* 142 (Feb. 9, 1928), 49–52; Kenneth M. Goode and Carroll Rheinstrom, *More Profits from Advertising* (New York: Harper & Brothers, 1931), p. 55. Many Ford dealers did advertise locally on their own initiative. *Ford News* 9 (Apr. 15, 1929), 93.

27. Nevins and Hill, *Expansion and Challenge,* pp. 477, 570–73, 578; Black, *Reminiscences,* p. 186. Although Ford reduced prices on its Model A coupe by $10.00 in 1930–31 (two $5.00 cuts), Plymouth and Chevrolet reduced prices on their coupes by $90.00 and $50.00, respectively, during these two years. Comparable price reductions were made on other Plymouth and Chevrolet models. Kennedy, *Automobile Industry,* pp. 225, 233–35, 238.

28. DN, Aug. 15, 1973; Ray Miller, *Henry's Lady* (Oceanside, Calif.: Evergreen Press, 1972), p. 319; Murray Fahnestock, "Why Model A Endures," *Restorer* 8 (July-Aug. 1963), 11; *Model "A" News* 22 (Jan.-Feb. 1975), inside front cover; *Restorer* 19 (Jan.-Feb. 1975), 2; Annabelle Pope, executive secretary, Model A Ford Club of America, to David L. Lewis, Apr. 21, 1975; *Automotive News* 34 (Aug. 17, 1959), 72; William D. Tyler, "Top Ad Puts Pinto on Offense Against Foreign Models," *Advertising Age* 43 (Mar. 6, 1972), 42 (Pinto-Model A advertising); *Life* 54 (Apr. 12, 1963), inside front cover (Volkswagen-Model A advertisement); see any issue of *Hemmings Motor News, Cars & Parts,* or *Old Cars* for advertisements of Model A parts houses; "That Other A," *Special-Interest Autos* 4 (Aug.-Oct. 1973), 20–21. As late as 1966 Sears, Roebuck advertised that "you can overhaul a Model A engine with the parts Sears keeps in stock." *Life* 61 (Nov. 11, 1966), 96–97. But the company's 1975 Spring Sum-

mer Catalog advertises only engine gaskets and pistons for the A.

29. DN, Feb. 11, 1932.

30. *New York Post*, Jan. 2, 1932; Sinsabaugh, *Who, Me?*, p. 115. Among those publications speculating on the new car were *Advertising & Selling* 18 (Mar. 31, 1932), 25; *Dearborn Independent*, Dec. 11, 1931; DT, Dec. 20, 1931; NYT, Dec. 22, 1931; *Newark News*, Jan. 2, 1932; *Cincinnati Enquirer*, Jan. 3, 1932; DN, Mar. 17, 1963 (citing Hollywood Theater). The V-8 attracted "tremendous crowds" to the theater. "The police had to be called to keep order," Tom McGuire, the theater's manager recalled years later.

31. DN, Feb. 11, 1932; *Rock Springs* (Wyo.) *Rocket*, Feb. 25, 1932; *Cleveland Plain Dealer*, Feb. 12, 1932. See Clipbooks 77–78 for reprints of Sweinhart's story.

32. DN, Feb. 27, 1932; *Toronto* (Ont.) *Financial Post*, Mar. 5, 1932; *Stoughton* (Mass.) *Sentinel*, Mar. 1, 1932.

33. *New York Post*, Mar. 5, 1932; DN, Apr. 3, 1932; *Advertising & Selling* 18 (Mar. 31, 1932), 25; *Variety* 106 (Apr. 5, 1932), 1.

34. Garrett, *Wild Wheel*, p. 171; *Ford News* 12 (May 1932), 3–4; [University of Illinois] *Daily Illini*, Apr. 12, 1932; *New York Sun*, Mar. 30, 1932; DFP, Mar. 31, 1932; Musselman, *Get a Horse!*, p. 274; DFP, Aug. 19, 1934; *Time* 91 (Apr. 5, 1968), 12 (Barrow letter); N.W. Ayer & Son, Inc., National Ford V-8 Owners Survey, Mar. 2, 1934, Acc. 572, Box 14; Clem Davis, FMC engineer, *Reminiscences*, p. 35.

35. Nevins and Hill, *Expansion and Challenge*, p. 596; *New York City East Side News*, Nov. 2, 1935.

36. W.A. Ryan to branch managers, Jan. 18, 1921, Apr. 6, Dec. 16, 1922, Acc. 78, Box 48, and Mar. 13, 1923, Apr. 14, 1923, Acc. 78, Box 84. See news release in Acc. 545, Boxes 1–2 and Clipbooks 20 through 72.

37. General Sales Letter No. 1481, Feb. 18, 1924, Acc. 572, Box 10; Advertising Department to branch managers, Nov. 19, 1925, Acc. 78, Box 52, and Feb. 2, 1926, Acc. 78, Box 53.

38. General Sales Letter No. 1425, Sept. 7, 1923, Acc. 78, Box 90; W.M. Cunningham, *"J8": A Chronicle of the Neglected Truth about Henry Ford D.E. and the Ford Motor Company* (Detroit: North American Publishing Co. [1930]), p. 104; *Detroit Saturday Night* (Ford Industries Number), (June 15, 1935), 22, 26 of sec. 2. The company followed no established policy in attributing data in the news release to any one person. Henry Ford and Edsel Ford each were cited singly and together, and at other times neither name appeared in stories. Henry Ford usually was identified in highly complimentary terms, i.e., "the most striking figure in the world today," and "the genius who has developed this great industry." In contrast, Edsel Ford was simply "the president of the Ford Motor Company." N.W. Ayer was asked to handle most of Ford's press relations activities when it obtained the company's advertising account in mid-1927. The agency employed publicists in its Detroit office and received liberal annual appropriations of about $40,000 for Ford car, Lincoln, aviation, and general company publicity. In addition to handling routine news releases, Ayer also was charged with much of the responsibility for new-car and other publicity campaigns. During the early 1930s the agency's chief publicity representative in Detroit was Marvin Murphy, who served as vice-president of Ayer's Public Relations Department from 1941 to 1962. The agency's efforts were supervised by Fred L. Black, head of the company's Advertising Department. See news releases in Acc. 545, Boxes 1–2 for years 1923–26 and in Acc. 545, Boxes 366–68 and Acc. 509, Box 10 for the years after 1926; *Printers' Ink* 139 (June 2, 1927), 33–34; Report on 1929 Advertising Placed through N.W. Ayer & Son, Inc., Acc. 6, Box 287 (citing publicity appropriations for 1928 and 1929); Charles O. Herb, of *Machinery* magazine, to Marvin Murphy, Jan. 2, 1931; Glenn I. Tucker to Fred L. Black, May 21, 1929, Acc. 545, Box 368.

39. *Ford Times* 9 (Nov. 1915), 150; *Philadelphia Public Ledger*, June 2, 1921; *Ford News* 4 (June 15, 1924), 1; 4 (Aug. 1, 1924), 1; 5 (Dec. 15, 1924), 1; Department of Photography to branch managers, Nov. 28, 1924, Acc. 78, Box 50. Frank Kulick, the company's racing star of the 1904–12 period, drove the ten millionth Ford around the country.

40. DN, Oct. 14, 1924; *New York Journal*, May 22, 1931; *Ford News* 11 (July 1931), 3; 12 (Jan. 1932), 5.

41. An average of 35,500 persons attended the open houses, with 105,000 visiting the Somerville (Mass.) plant and 107,000 touring the Twin City operation. Open houses were again held in the assembly plants in 1930 and 1931, with attendance averaging 28,000 per installation. *Ford News* 6 (July 15, 1926), 1; 7 (Dec. 1, 1926), 1; 7 (Apr. 1, 1927), 1; 7 (May 1, 1927), 1; 10 (May 1, 1930), 98; 11 (July 31, 1931), 17; 11 (Sept. 1931), 5.

42. *La Crosse* (Wis.) *Tribune and Leader-Press*, Oct. 11, 1921; *Nebraska City* (Neb.) *Press*, Oct. 27, 1921; *Excelsior Springs* (Mo.) *Sun*, July 23, 1922; *Grand Rapids* (Mich.) *Herald*, Aug. 25, 1922; *Ford News* 2 (Oct. 1, 1922), 7; 2 (Oct. 15, 1922), 6; 4 (Nov. 15, 1923), 5; Sales Department to branch managers, n.d. [Summer 1961], Acc. 509, Box 8.

43. *Ford News* 11 (May 1931), 4; 11 (June 1931), 12–13; 11 (July 1931), 4; Sales Department to branch managers, n.d. [Summer 1931], Acc. 509, Box 8.

Chapter 13

1. *Wall Street Journal*, Feb. 28, 1927; NYT, Mar. 27, 1927; Samuel Crowther to E. G. Liebold, Sept. 12, 1924, Acc. 285, Box 117; Wetmore Hodges to Edsel Ford, Apr. 12, 1924, Acc. 572, Box 10; Murray Godwin, "The Case Against Henry Ford," *American Mercury* 23 (July 1931), 264. In 1926, three corporations employed more people than Ford, four showed bigger net profits, seven had higher market valuations, and nine listed greater assets.

2. What the Public Thinks of Big Business, Curtis Publishing Company, Division of Commercial Research, May 1937, Acc. 454, Box 9.

3. The Link Audit: a Review and Evaluation, FMC Research Department, Oct. 11, 1953, Acc. 465, Box 1.

4. *Detroit Journal*, Nov. 14, 1921; Roger Babson to Henry Ford, May 16, 1922, Acc. 285, Box 47; B. C. Forbes to Henry Ford, Sept. 18, 1941, Acc. 285, Box 2480; *Wall Street Journal*, July 1, 1926; *Portland* (Maine) *Express*, Jan. 17, 1927; NYT, Jan. 23, 1927; *New York Sun*, DN, and *Detroit World*, Feb. 2, 1927; DT and *Brooklyn Times*, Feb. 3, 1927; *New York Herald Tribune*, Feb. 19, 1927; Simonds, *Henry Ford*, p. 209.

5. See editions of *Readers' Guide to Periodical Literature*, *Industrial Arts Index*, *New York Times Index*, and *International Index to Periodicals* for the years 1920–30. The three major railroads serving New York

City were the New York Central, the Pennsylvania, and the New York, New Haven & Hartford.

6. "The Public Is Not Damned." *Fortune* 19 (Mar. 1939), 144; Sward, *Legend of Henry Ford*, p. 270; Gerald Stanley Lee, "The Clue to Mr. Ford," *Everybody's Magazine* 34 (Jan. 1916), 92; *Manchester* (N.H.) *Leader*, Dec. 2, 1927; Milton Bradley Company, *Famous Fortunes: Intimate Stories of Financial Success* (Boston: Milton Bradley Company, 1931), p. 53.

7. See editions of *New York Times Index, Readers' Guide to Periodical Literature, Industrial Arts Index,* and *International Index to Periodicals* for the years 1920–30; *Philadelphia Public Ledger*, May 31, 1923; DT, June 17, 1922 (Ford index); see Acc. 285, Box 23 for reports prepared by M.T. Woodruff on the amount of publicity Henry Ford received each month in 1922 in the DFP. E.G. Pipp, who took it upon himself to analyze the amount of Ford publicity in the three Detroit daily newspapers on a typical day in 1923 (Dec. 2), discovered that the name "Ford" appeared more than 100 times in each publication. The DT, a Hearst newspaper, ran two stories under eight-column headlines, four lesser items, a full-page editorial, an eight-column illustration, and a cartoon; the DN ran two front-page stories and two additional articles; the DFP ran six stories. *Pipp's Weekly* 4 (Dec. 15, 1923), 1–4.

8. Arthur Pound, "The Ford Myth," *Atlantic Monthly* 133 (Jan. 1924), 41; "Why They Love Henry," *New Republic* 35 (June 27, 1923), 111; *Huntington* (W. Va.) *Advertiser*, n.d. [June 1923], Clipbook 33; *Staunton* (Va.) *Ledger*, Dec. 2, 1927.

9. Lee, "Clue to Ford," p. 92; *Newspaperdom* (New York City), Nov. 10, 1921; *Huntington* (W. Va.) *Advertiser*, n.d. [June 1923], Clipbook 33; *Brockton* (Mass.) *Times*, June 24, 1927; *La Follette* (Tenn.) *Press*, n.d. [Nov. 1921], Clipbook 27.

10. "Have You a Case of Ford-osis?," *Detroit Saturday Night* 22 (Jan. 28, 1928), 2 of sec. 2; DN, Nov. 13, 1922; James Martin Miller, *The Amazing Story of Henry Ford, the Ideal American and the World's Most Famous Private Citizen* (n.p., M.A. Donohue & Co., 1922), p. 1; Bradley, *Famous Fortunes*, p. 53; *Manchester* (N.H.) *Leader*, Dec. 2, 1927; *New York American*, July 8, 1928.

11. Elbert Hubbard, *One of the World-Makers* (East Aurora, N.Y.: The Roycrofters, 1913); Rose Wilder Lane, *Henry Ford's Own Story* (New York: Ellis O. Jones, 1917); Frank Bonville, *What Henry Ford Is Doing* (Seattle: Priv. printed, 1920).

12. Edward A. Rumely to E. G. Liebold, Nov. 20 and 27, 1916, and Liebold to Rumely, Nov. 25 and 30, 1916, Acc. 284, Box 25; Liebold to Ellis O. Jones, New York publisher, Jan. 3, 1917, and Gaston Plantiff to Liebold, Apr. 16, 1917; Acc. 62, Box 17; Liebold, *Reminiscences*, p. 1253. Both Henry and Clara Ford were angered by the inaccuracies in Miss Lane's book, of which only the first two chapters had been read and approved by Liebold; see Liebold's letter to Jones above.

13. "Two More Biographies of Henry Ford," *Detroit Saturday Night* 16 (Nov. 25, 1922), 9.

14. All of the books mentioned have been cited except William L. Stidger's *Henry Ford: The Man and His Motives* (New York: George H. Doran Company, 1923). According to Nevins and Hill, *Expansion and Challenge*, p. 613, Dean Marquis's book pained Henry Ford and led him to direct his organization to buy up and suppress the volume. Richards, *Last Billionaire*, p. 381, states that so many copies of the Marquis book were borrowed from the Detroit Public Library and never returned that the library concluded that Ford representatives were seeking to eliminate the volume from its shelves. The library was forced to discontinue circulation of the work. Pipp, speaking of his book on Ford in an article, "Ford's Far-Flung Organization," *Pipp's Weekly* 3 (Jan. 20, 1923), 4, said that Ford dealers in some cities had "created a scene to the point where sellers felt it easier to quit selling the book."

15. NYT, Feb. 10, 1924, Mar. 6, 1927; Cameron, *Reminiscences*, p. 157; Black, Blanchard, Donaldson, *Reminiscences* (Black and Donaldson speaking), pp. 19–20; Samuel Crowther to E. G. Liebold, Feb. 27, 1924, Acc. 285, Box 117; Crowther to Liebold, Sept. 14, 1923, Acc. 285, Box 164; Maurice Hindus, "Henry Ford Conquers Russia," *Outlook* 118 (Mar. 26, 1924), 282.

16. Samuel Crowther to E. G. Liebold, Apr. 9, 1926; *New York American*, Apr. 8, 1931.

17. Henry Ford, *Ford Ideals: Being a Selection from "Mr. Ford's Page"* in the *Dearborn Independent* (Dearborn: The Dearborn Publishing Company, 1926); Henry Ford, *My Philosophy of Industry* (New York: Coward-McCann, Inc., 1929); Henry Ford and Clara Bryant Ford, *Good Morning: After a Sleep of 25 Years, Old Fashioned Dancing Is Being Revived by Mr. and Mrs. Henry Ford* (Dearborn: The Dearborn Publishing Company, 1926); Richards, *Last Billionaire*, p. 106; NYT, Jan. 13, 1941; E. G. Liebold to Otto Zimmerman, a Cincinnati publisher, Mar. 30, 1943, Acc. 285, Box 2786.

18. *Life* 93 (May 3, 1929), 38; Nevins and Hill, *Expansion and Challenge*, p. 611; E. G. Pipp, *Henry Ford: Both Sides of Him* (Detroit: Pipp's Magazine, 1926); J. G. de Roulhac Hamilton, *Henry Ford: The Man, the Worker, the Citizen* (New York: Henry Holt and Co., 1927); William A. Simonds, *Henry Ford, Motor Genius* (Garden City, N.Y.: Doubleday, Doran & Company, Inc., 1929); Ralph Waldo Trine, *The Power That Wins* (Indianapolis: Bobbs-Merrill Company, 1920); Cunningham's book has been cited in chapter 5.

19. See entries in the *Cumulative Book Index* for the years 1921–29 and the *Essay and General Literature Index 1900–1933*.

20. John Kenneth Galbraith, "The Mystery of Henry Ford," *Atlantic Monthly* 210 (Mar. 1958), 47; Black, *Reminiscences*, p. 158.

21. NYT, Aug. 1, 1914. Ford announced a five-day week for his employees in 1922, and, after quietly rescinding it, announced it anew in 1926. Although a number of smaller industries had begun a five-day week in the early 1920s, Ford was perhaps the first large manufacturing company to institute it. Ford's announcement received very favorable nationwide publicity. See, for example, the *St. Louis Post-Dispatch*, Sept. 27, 1926; *Dayton News*, Sept. 27, 1926; *New York Herald Tribune*, Oct. 10, 1926; NYT, Oct. 17, 1926.

22. Richards, *Last Billionaire*, pp. 145–47; *Boston American*, Jan. 9, 1926, and Clipbook 44 which contains hundreds of photographs and stories on Ford's "flivver skates." *Chicago Tribune*, Jan. 28, 1920; Harold Hicks, FMC engineer, *Reminiscences*, p. 28 (Hicks states that Ford's challenge was a publicity stunt); *Ford News* 8 (Oct. 15, 1928), 218. The concrete block, complete with signature, footprints, and spade, can be seen today in the lobby of the Henry Ford Museum.

23. Samuel S. Marquis, *Henry Ford: An Interpretation* (Boston: Little, Brown, and Company, 1923), pp. 15–16; *Winnipeg* (Man.) *Free Press*, May 26, 1941; Richards, *Last Billionaire*, pp. 145, 149, 372; *Battle*

Creek News, Dec. 16, 1928; *New York World,* Jan. 10, 1926; DT, May 8, 1928; DN, May 2, 1932; *Cleveland News,* Oct. 8, 1921; *Akron Beacon-Journal,* Dec. 29, 1927; DFP, June 5, 1930.

24. DN, Aug. 9, 1919; *New York Tribune,* Feb. 9, 1921; *Baltimore Sun,* Feb. 10, 1921; *Minneapolis Journal,* Mar. 18, 1921; "Henry Ford Wants Cowless Milk and Crowdless Cities," *Literary Digest* 68 (Feb. 26, 1921), 38–42.

25. *New York World,* Aug. 26, 1925; *New York Sun,* Aug. 28, 1925; *Van Wert* (Ohio) *Times,* Dec. 23, 1925; *Auburn* (N.Y.) *Citizen,* Feb. 14, 1927; DFP, Feb. 15, 1927; *Butchers' Merchandiser* (New York City), May 31, 1919; *Savannah Evening News,* Mar. 22, 1944; "Cracking the Secret Riddle of Flavor," *Life* 53 (Nov. 23, 1962), 120.

26. *Ft. Wayne* (Ind.) *Journal-Gazette,* Jan. 28, 1919; *Santa Barbara* (Calif.) *News,* June 1, 1922; *Pipp's Weekly* 4 (Aug. 25, 1923), 7; "Henry Ford's Gospel of Spending," *Literary Digest* 99 (Dec. 29, 1928), 10; DT, Feb. 10, 1929.

27. *Hillsdale* (Mich.) *News,* July 12, 1929; DT, Aug. 2, 1929; *Brooklyn Times-Union,* May 26, 1934; NYT, Mar. 26, 1933; DFP, May 26, 1934; *New York Herald Tribune,* Aug. 26, 1939.

28. Marquis, *Henry Ford,* p. 7; Harold M. Cordell, assistant secretary to Henry Ford, 1921–29, *Reminiscences,* p. 43; *Detroit Saturday Night* 17 (Apr. 28, 1923), 1; DT, July 1, 1923.

29. DFP, July 16, 1933; see the NYT, Aug. 30 and Nov. 25, 1933, and the *Washington Herald,* Sept. 6, 1933 for Johnson's statements; see the DT, Aug. 17, 1933 and the *Washington Herald,* Oct. 28, 1933 for company statements; see the DN, July 30, 1933 and the NYT, Jan. 11, 1934 for Ford's interviews; *Louisville Times,* Aug. 23, 1933; see Clipbooks 85 through 88 for speculative stories on Ford and the NIRA; Sidney Fine, "The Ford Motor Company and the N.R.A.," *Business History Review* 32 (Winter 1958), 364–68.

30. William J. Cameron, *The Why and Wherefore of the Ford International Weekly The Dearborn Independent* (pamphlet), circa 1924, Acc. 43, Box 9; *St. Catherine* (Ont.) *Standard,* Aug. 28, 1924; *New York Journal,* Dec. 18, 1933.

31. Black, *Reminiscences,* pp. 137, 147–48, 152–53; DT, Sept. 14, 1930; Ben Donaldson to Judge Henry Neil, New York City, Mar. 22, 1926, Acc. 572, Box 4; Cameron, *Reminiscences,* p. 38.

32. C. A. M. Vining, of the *Toronto Star,* to Henry Ford, Sept. 7, 1922, Acc. 285, Box 79; Robert Littell, "Henry Ford," *New Republic* 36 (Nov. 14, 1923), 303–4; Black, *Reminiscences,* pp. 26, 149; Liebold, *Reminiscences,* pp. 1260–63; Richards, *Last Billionaire,* pp. 150, 261; Cordell, *Reminiscences,* pp. 27–29.

33. Black, *Reminiscences,* p. 150; *Boston Post,* Aug. 18, 1928.

34. DT, Aug. 14, 1924; DFP, Apr. 28, 1925; *Boston Advertiser,* Nov. 11, 1932; *New York World-Telegram,* Apr. 21, 1938; DN, Aug. 29, 1939; NYT, Feb. 16, 1941; *Savannah Evening News,* Mar. 22, 1944; Bennett, *Never Called Henry,* p. 163.

35. "Ford Party Takes Universal Cameraman," *Motion Picture News* 18 (Aug. 31, 1918), 1364; DT and *Connellsville* (Pa.) *Courier,* Aug. 21, 1918; *Harrisburg* (Pa.) *News,* Sept. 3, 1918; DT, Nov. 18, 1920; *Chicago Tribune,* Aug. 4, 1921.

36. Henry Ford, in collaboration with Samuel Crowther, *My Life and Work* (Garden City, N.Y.: Garden City Publishing Co., Inc., 1922), p. 240; Garrett, *Wild Wheel,* p. 136; the typewritten report for which Ford asked can be found in Acc. 62, Box 80; Sorensen, *Forty Years,* p. 18. Edison, the publicist, is discussed in John C. Long, *Public Relations: A Handbook of*

Publicity (New York: McGraw-Hill, 1924), p. 137. A caravan of six cars and a truck loaded with beds, stoves, iceboxes, chairs, and tables accompanied the vagabonds. A member of the camp's staff regularly had to return to town for Ford's bread. Louise B. Clancy and Florence Davies, *The Believer: The Life Story of Mrs. Henry Ford* (New York: Coward-McCann, Inc., 1960), p. 132.

37. *Chicago Journal,* Feb. 19, 1926; Liebold, *Reminiscences,* pp. 499, 501; Nevins and Hill, *Expansion and Challenge,* pp. 501–2; *Pipp's Weekly* 5 (Jan. 17, 1925), 9; *New York Telegraph,* May 16, 1926; *Boston Herald,* Jan. 4, 1927; DN, July 25, 1928; NYT, Feb. 22, 1931, Feb. 8, 1933; *Syracuse Herald,* Dec. 2, 1934.

38. *Fordson* (Mich.) *Independent,* Jan. 7, 1927; DT, Aug. 31, 1928; Nevins and Hill, *Expansion and Challenge,* p. 500; *Ford News* 9 (Nov. 1, 1929), 242–43. The village and museum were opened to the public in 1933. During the next eight years, as Detroit's principal tourist attractions, the institutions were visited annually by more than half a million people. FMC news release, June 10, 1943, Acc. 44, Box 5.

39. Liebold, *Reminiscences,* pp. 1262–63; Cameron, *Reminiscences,* p. 124; Laurence R. Campbell, *Exploring Journalism* (New York: Prentice-Hall, Inc., 1946), p. 424; Leonard W. Doob, *Propaganda: Its Psychology and Technique* (New York: Henry Holt and Company, 1935), p. 195; George L. Bird and Frederic E. Merwin, *The Newspaper and Society* (New York: Prentice-Hall, Inc., 1942), pp. 517–20; Stanley Walker, *City Editor* (New York: Blue Ribbon Books, Inc., 1934), p. 144; Richard S. Lambert, *Propaganda* (London: T. Nelson and Son, 1938), pp. 98–99; Black, *Reminiscences,* p. 64; interview with Black, June 30, 1958. Bernays, who has devoted a good deal of attention to his own public relations (and who has done more to upgrade the reputation of public relations work than any other person), cites twenty references to his participation in the Jubilee in *Public Relations, Edward L. Bernays and the American Scene* (Concord, N.H.: F.W. Faxon Company, 1951), an eighty-six page bibliography and guide to writings by and about Bernays. Among those helping to perpetuate the Bernays-Jubilee myth are the DN, Mar. 20, 1955; Robert L. Heilbroner, "Public Relations—the Invisible Sell," *Harper's Magazine* 214 (June 1957), 25–26; and "PR's Edward L. Bernays: Creating Acts That Make News That Raise Sales," *Printers' Ink* 269 (Dec. 4, 1959), 64.

40. *Boston Post,* July 11, 1923; DFP, Aug. 27, 1924; NYT, Jan. 9, 1926; Apr. 25, 1927; *Boston Traveler,* Jan. 8, 1926; *Brooklyn Eagle,* Oct. 16, 1928.

41. DT, Jan. 18, 1927; Nevins and Hill, *Expansion and Challenge,* p. 499; NYT, Jan. 18, 1927.

42. See *New York Times Index* for 1925 and 1926 and Clipbooks 38 through 55; Nevins and Hill, *Expansion and Challenge,* pp. 491–92; DFP, July 12, 1925; *Boston Post,* Aug. 2, 1925; *Cincinnati Times-Star,* July 15, 1925.

43. DT, Nov. 3, 1925; *New York Post,* Jan. 9, 1926; *Ford News* 7 (Jan. 12, 1927), 1; DT, Dec. 16, 1926; *Boston Traveler,* Dec. 17, 1926. The radio programs were the first sponsored by the Ford Company. In 1926, the programs were presented over the sixteen stations of the WEAF network; in 1927, over the twenty-two stations of the National Broadcasting Company's Red network. "The Biggest Success Story of 1934," *Broadcasting* 7 (Oct. 15, 1934), 11.

44. *Buffalo Courier,* July 29, 1925; DFP, Oct. 18, 1925; DT and *Cleveland News,* Dec. 27, 1925; *New York Post,* Jan. 9, 1926; *Cleveland News,* Jan. 27, 1926; Richards, *Last Billionaire,* pp. 108–9; *New York World,* Sept. 24, 1926.

45. Davis, *Reminiscences,* p. 21; DN, Jan. 5, 1923; *Cadillac* (Mich.) *News,* Sept. 21, 1923; DFP, Nov. 22, 1923, Dec. 5, 1925; *Big Rapids* (Mich.) *Pioneer,* Feb. 17, 1924; DT, Apr. 8, 1925, Jan. 10, 1926; *New York Herald Tribune,* Dec. 9, 1925.

46. *Norway* (Maine) *Advertiser,* Nov. 18, 1925; *New York World,* Nov. 19, 1925; DN, Nov. 25, 1925; *Vaudeville* (Jan. 1926).

47. DT, Dec. 4, 7, 8, and 9, 1925; *New York Herald Tribune,* Dec. 5, 1925; *New York American,* Dec. 7, 1925; DN, Dec. 9, 1925. Dunham had made the snowshoes which Peary's men used on their trip to the North Pole in 1909. *New York World,* Nov. 19, 1925.

48. DT, Dec. 12, 1925; "Fiddling to Henry Ford," *Literary Digest* 88 (Jan. 2, 1926), 33–38; *New York Telegram & Mail,* Dec. 10, 1925; *Boston Globe,* Dec. 13, 1925; *Atlanta Constitution,* Dec. 16, 1925; DFP, Mar. 15, 1926; DN, May 8, 1927.

49. DFP, Dec. 11, 1925, Jan. 2, 10, 1926; *Boston Globe,* Dec. 9, 1925; *Music Trade* (New York City), Jan. 6, 1926; *New York World,* Jan. 7, 1926; DN, Jan. 10, 1926; *Greater Minneapolis Amusement,* Feb. 6, 1926; *Boston Herald,* Feb. 21, 1926. Lists of all persons invited to Ford's dancing parties during the 1930s and 1940s can be found in Acc. 292, Boxes 2–3. The manufacturer once invited the great dancer, Ruth St. Denis, to one of his square dances, thinking it would be a treat for her. "But," according to another guest, "she just sat there sighing, 'How awful!'" DN, Jan. 6, 1963.

50. Nevins and Hill, *Expansion and Challenge,* p. 489; DN, Oct. 29, 1947, Aug. 22, 1929; *Cleveland Town Topics,* Aug. 31, 1929; *Asbury Park* (N.J.) *Press,* Sept. 1, 1929; *New York World,* Mar. 11, 1930; *New York World-Telegram,* Dec. 6, 1933; *New York Mirror,* Dec. 7, 1933.

51. C. J. Smith, FMC "Experimental" Department employee, 1906–49, *Reminiscences,* p. 46; Benson, *New Henry Ford,* p. 265; DT, May 1, 1925, Mar. 29, 1926; *Boston Advertiser,* Jan. 10, 1926; *Wichita Eagle,* Feb. 20, 1929; Cordell, *Reminiscences,* p. 31; *Ford News* 19 (Feb. 1939), 20; DN, July 28, 1944; Bennett, *Never Called Henry,* p. 164; John W. Thompson, FMC public relations representative, 1942–45, *Reminiscences,* p. 82.

52. DT, Aug. 14, 1924, July 15, 1936, Aug. 29, 1943; Benson, *New Henry Ford,* pp. 263–64; DFP, Nov. 27, 1932; DN, May 24, 1928; Marquis, *Henry Ford,* p. 33; *Washington News,* Aug. 25, 1943; *PM* (New York), Aug. 26, 1943. Notwithstanding Ford's continued prowess at racing and Dr. McClure's statement. the magnate's physical and mental health was failing rapidly in 1943.

53. *Washington News,* Aug. 25, 1943; *Newsweek* 22 (Sept. 6, 1943), 10; *Akron Beacon-Journal,* Aug. 26, 1943; *Pittsburg* (Kan.) *Headlight,* Aug. 26, 1943; *Abilene* (Kan.) *Chronicle,* Sept. 6, 1943; *Wausau* (Wis.) *Record-Herald,* Aug. 28, 1943; DT, Aug. 29, 1943; DFP, Aug. 25 and 30, 1943; *Philadelphia Record,* Aug. 26, 1943.

54. DT, Aug. 26, 1928; *Chicago Examiner,* Apr. 26, 1938; Benson, *New Henry Ford,* p. 110; Bennett, *Never Called Henry,* p. 47; *Our Sunday Visitor* (Huntington, Ind.), Sept. 1, 1929.

55. *New York Mirror,* June 2, 1927; NYT, Aug. 14, 1926; DFP, Jan. 7, 1929, July 19, 1935. Richards, *Last Billionaire,* p. 324; Simonds, *Henry Ford,* p. 147.

56. *Akron Beacon-Journal,* Dec. 29, 1927; Mark Sullivan in the *New York Tribune,* Aug. 21, 1926; *Tacoma Tribune,* n.d. [Jan. 1914], Acc. 53, Box 17.

57. *San Francisco Examiner,* Mar. 24, 1918; *Syracuse Herald,* Feb. 20, 1921; *New York American,* Sept. 10, 1926; *Washington Herald,* Feb. 7, 1927; DN, Sept. 22, 1922; *Neenah* (Wis.) *News,* Nov. 2, 1922;

Arthur D. Smith, *Men Who Run America* (Indianapolis: Bobbs-Merrill Company, 1935) pp. 167–68; "Henry Ford; Or, How to Be Happy on a Million a Month," *Current Opinion* 57 (Aug. 1914), 95; *Milwaukee News,* Jan. 6, 1922; NYT, May 20, 1923; *New York Journal of Commerce,* May 7, 1925; *Courtland* (N.Y.) *Standard,* Feb. 19, 1925; *Boston Post,* Sept. 10, 1926; *Brooklyn Times,* Nov. 28, 1926; *Milwaukee Journal,* Apr. 28, 1927; *Chicago Herald-Examiner,* Apr. 12, 1926; DFP, May 8, 1927.

58. NYT, Feb. 13, 1927; Marquis, *Henry Ford,* p. 31; Bradley, *Famous Fortunes,* p. 53; *Chicago Examiner,* Apr. 14, 1925; Stewart H. Holbrook, *The Age of the Moguls* (Garden City, N.Y.: Doubleday & Company, Inc., 1953), pp. 210–11; *Cleveland Press,* Feb. 7, 1927; *Philadelphia Record,* Feb. 5, 1927; Sullivan, *Our Times,* 4, p. 57; *New Duluth* (Minn.) *Steel Plant News,* Oct. 2, 1920.

59. DN, Mar. 4, 1914, Feb. 24, 1924; *Denver News,* Aug. 11, 1922; *Ann Arbor* (Mich.) *News,* Oct. 15, 1923; NYT, Feb. 17, 1924; *Brooklyn Eagle,* Aug. 15, 1926; *Pittsburgh Press,* July 22, 1926; *Philadelphia Public Ledger* (quoting *System* magazine), Jan. 11, 1926.

60. *Sioux City* (Iowa) *Journal,* May 29, 1927; DN, Nov. 17, 1927; *New York American,* Jan. 19 and July 8, 1928.

61. B.C. Forbes, *Men Who Are Making America* (New York: B.C. Forbes Publishing Co., 1919), p. 115; Nevins and Hill, *Expansion and Challenge,* p. 373; *New York World,* Jan. 6, 1924; Marshall W. Fishwick, *American Heroes: Myth and Reality* (Washington: Public Affairs Press, 1954), pp. 114, 137; Dixon Wecter, *The Hero in America: A Chronicle of Hero-Worship* (New York: Charles Scribner's Sons, 1941), pp. 420–21; *Springfield* (Mass.) *Union,* Apr. 13, 1928; Stuart Chase, *Men and Machines* (New York: Macmillan Co., 1929), p. 331; Maurice Hindus, "Henry Ford Conquers Russia," p. 280.

62. John Kenneth Galbraith, *The Great Crash 1929* (London: Houghton Mifflin, 1955), p. 127; DN and NYT, Nov. 22, 1929.

63. DN and DT, Nov. 22, 1929; Nevins and Hill, *Expansion and Challenge,* p. 529. In contrast to news of the five-dollar day, the announcement of the seven-dollar day did not make a lasting impact on Ford's public relations status.

64. DT, Oct. 30, 1931; Kennedy, *Automobile Industry,* p. 219. The minimum wage fell to $4.00 a day in 1933, and, as business conditions improved, was raised to $5.00 in 1934 and to $6.00 in 1935. DN, Mar. 13, 1934; NYT, May 21, 1935.

65. Kennedy, *Automobile Industry,* p. 227; Burlingame, *Henry Ford,* p. 135; DN, Aug. 17, 1930; *New York Post,* Oct. 20, 1931; *Tampa Tribune,* Mar. 15, 1931; "Interview, Model 1931," *Outlook and Independent* 157 (Mar. 25, 1931), 421.

66. DN, May 30, 31 and June 1, 1932; *Printers' Ink* 159 (June 2, 1932), 10; *Buffalo News,* May 7, 1932.

67. *Automotive Daily News* 13 (June 11, 1932), 4; *Toledo Times,* Apr. 30, 1932; *Philadelphia Record,* May 30, 1932; Wecter, *Hero in America,* p. 422; NYT, May 9, 1932; Garrett, *Wild Wheel,* p. 17.

Chapter 14

1. Marshall W. Fishwick, *American Heroes: Myth and Reality* (Washington: Public Affairs Press, 1954), p. 116; Dixon Wecter, *The Hero in America: A Chronicle of Hero-Worship* (New York: Charles Scribner's

Sons, 1941), p. 422; Garrett, *Wild Wheel*, p. 17; NYT, May 29, 1932; Black, *Reminiscences*, p. 191; Edsel Ford to George H. Thornley, vice-president, N.W. Ayer, Inc., Mar. 1, 1933, Acc. 572, Box 10; *Printers' Ink* 165 (Dec. 14, 1922), 17; Nevins and Hill, *Expansion and Challenge*, p. 247.

2. Kennedy, *Automobile Industry*, pp. 234–35, 285–86; *Ward's Automotive 1950 Yearbook*, pp. 86–87, and *Ward's Automotive 1956 Yearbook*, p. 155.

3. Sorensen, *Forty Years*, p. 225; Garrett, *Wild Wheel*, p. 171.

4. For a favorable discussion of Ford's role in the banking crisis, see Simonds, *Henry Ford*, pp. 233–36; for critical accounts of his activities, see Barnard, *Independent Man*, pp. 214–46, 288–90, and Sward, *Legend of Henry Ford*, pp. 242–56.

5. Howard Ralph Neville, *The Detroit Banking Collapse of 1933* (East Lansing, Mich.: Michigan State University, 1960), pp. 19, 51; F. Clever Bald, *Michigan in Four Centuries* (New York: Harper & Brothers, 1954), p. 407; Allan Nevins and Frank Ernest Hill, *Ford: Decline and Rebirth 1933–1962* (New York: Charles Scribner's Sons, 1962), p. 12. For data on the evolution of the complex Detroit banking structure, see G. Walter Woodworth, *The Detroit Money Market* (Ann Arbor, Mich.: University of Michigan, 1932). Howard Ralph Neville and John T. Flynn, "Michigan Magic: The Detroit Banking Scandal," *Harpers* 168 (Dec. 1933), 1–11 provides a detailed discussion of the abuses which contributed to the Detroit banking crisis.

6. Patricia O'Donnell McKenzie, "Banking, Economics, and Politics: the Detroit Bank Crisis of 1933" (unpublished Ph.D. dissertation, Department of Economics, Wayne State University, 1963), chapter 2, pp. 7–11; Barnard, *Independent Man*, pp. 221–27. The Union Guardian Trust Company borrowed $15,000,000 from the RFC in 1932 and $6,000,000 from Edsel Ford in 1930–31. It also borrowed $3,500,000 from FMC in 1932 under an agreement whereby all major decisions would be subject to FMC approval. In addition, Edsel and another Guardian group director, Charles S. Mott, aided the trust company by guaranteeing a $5,000,000 loan in 1931. McKenzie (Ph.D. diss.), "Banking," chapter 2, pp. 8–9.

7. McKenzie, "Banking," chapter 1, pp. 8–9; Frank B. Woodford, *Alex J. Groesbeck Portrait of a Public Man* (Detroit: Wayne State University Press, 1962), p. 277; Barnard, *Independent Man*, pp. 229, 233; *Boston Herald*, Feb. 14, 1933; DFP, Feb. 15, 1933; Ford Motor Company, *The Truth About Henry Ford and the Banking Situation* (Detroit: Ford Motor Company, 1933), p. 1.

8. Barnard, *Independent Man*, pp. 235–37, 288–89; J.C. Long, *Roy D. Chapin* ([Bethlehem, Pa.: privately printed], 1945), p. 249; Sward, *Legend of Henry Ford*, pp. 254–56.

9. Barnard, *Independent Man*, p. 241; DFP, Feb. 27, 1933; NYT, Feb. 27, 1933; *Washington Herald*, Feb. 28, 1933; "Banks," *Time* 21 (Mar. 6, 1933), 18. Ford's $11,000,000 offer was reduced to $8,250,000 after the RFC reduced its own offer of aid to the new ventures from $135,000,000 to $78,000,000. *Ibid.*

10. See Clipbook 83 for newspaper headlines, news stories, and editorials on the Ford announcement. DFP, Mar. 27, 1933; DT, Mar. 27, 1933; *Monessen (Pa.) Independent*, Mar. 27, 1933; NYT, Feb. 27, Mar. 2 and Mar. 26, 1933; Sward, *Legend of Henry Ford* (quoting the *Christian Science Monitor*); DN, Mar. 2, 1933.

11. DN, Feb. 27, 1933; DFP, Mar. 2 and 5, 1933; Simonds, *Henry Ford*, p. 235.

12. "Detroit Gets a Bank," *Business Week* (Apr. 5, 1933), 5; Pound, *Turning Wheel*, p. 422; Barnard, *Independent Man*, pp. 241–42. The *Business Week* article attributed the bankers' decision to self-interested financiers who "didn't want to be rescued. They knew," stated the magazine, "that the Fords' first move would be to wipe clean the slate of officers and directors, and start over with a new personnel. They knew that both the First National and the Guardian would go into receivership, with offsets of deposits against loans, and stockholders and directors held liable for losses. So the Ford move was blocked." The amount of capital subscribed in the Manufacturers National Bank by Ford was $3,000,000. McKenzie, "Banking," chapter 7, p. 16.

13. *Washington Times*, Jan. 11, 1934; *Christian Science Monitor*, Jan. 12, 1934; Barnard, *Independent Man*, pp. 275–85, 287–90.

14. *The Truth About Henry Ford and the Banking Situation*, p. 2. When the twenty-year receivership of the Guardian Detroit Union Group, Inc. ended in 1953, most of the group's $9,000,000 in unpaid debts were owed to the Edsel Ford estate, the Ford Foundation, and the Ford Motor Company. The end of the receivership cancelled this debt. The Ford Company had $32,500,000 on deposit with the group when it failed. DN, Aug. 9, 1953.

15. Nevins and Hill, *Decline and Rebirth*, p. 16; Fine, "Ford and N.R.A.," p. 354.

16. Nevins and Hill, *Decline and Rebirth*, pp. 17–18; DN, July 30, 1933; Fine, "Ford and N.R.A.," pp. 360–61.

17. Fine, "Ford and N.R.A.," p. 361; DN, July 30, 1933.

18. *Louisville Times*, Aug. 23, 1933; *Springfield* (Ill.) *State-Journal*, Sept. 2, 1933; *New York Daily News*, Sept. 2, 1933; *Brooklyn Times-Union*, Aug. 20, 1933; "Ford Vs. Blue Eagle: A Nation Uniting for Recovery Waited to Hear from One 'Rugged Individualist,'" *News-Week* 2 (Sept. 9, 1933), 4, NYT, Sept. 2, 1933. It also was rumored in late September that Ford's answer to the Blue Eagle would be a vastly improved model which he would sell at cost for a year. *Washington Times*, Sept. 25, 1933.

19. NYT, Sept. 1, 2, 1933; *Christian Science Monitor*, Aug. 30, 1933; *Brooklyn Eagle*, Sept. 6, 1933; "Ford VS. Blue Eagle," *News-Week*, p. 3; Arthur Brisbane to Frank Campsall, Sept. 7, 1933, Acc. 285, Box 1533; *Philadelphia Record*, Aug. 20, 1933.

20. *New York Journal*, Aug. 30, 1933; *New York Post*, n.d. [Sept. 7, 1933]; Fine, "Ford and N.R.A.," p. 362; *Advertising & Selling* 21 (Sept. 14, 1933), 48.

21. *Boston Transcript*, Aug. 29, 1933; *Syracuse Journal*, Nov. 13, 1933; Fine, "Ford and N.R.A.," p. 363; *New York World-Telegram*, Sept. 8, 1933; NYT, Nov. 4, 1933.

22. Fine, "Ford and N.R.A.," pp. 363–64; NYT, Oct. 27, 1933; *New York Herald Tribune*, Nov. 8, 1933; NYT, Nov. 25, 1933.

23. Fine, "Ford and N.R.A.," pp. 363–64; DN, Sept. 15, 1933; *Baltimore Sun*, Nov. 4, 1933; NYT, Nov. 5, 1933; *Washington News*, Nov. 6, 1933; *Durham* (N.C.) *Herald*, Nov. 7, 1933; *Akron Beacon-Journal*, Nov. 7, 1933. Ford returned to a five-day forty-hour week on Aug. 6, 1933. *New York American*, Aug. 6, 1933.

24. *Brooklyn Times-Union*, Oct. 27, 1933; Cameron statements, Acc. 44, Box 17; *Washington Herald*, Oct. 28, 1933; NYT, Oct. 28, 1933.

25. NYT, Oct. 27, 1933; *Brooklyn Eagle*, Oct. 29, 1933; *Washington Herald*, Oct. 30, 1933; *New York Sun*, Nov. 11, 1933; *Cleveland Plain Dealer*, Dec. 3, 1933; Fine, "Ford and N.R.A.," pp. 365–66.

26. Fine, "Ford and N.R.A.," pp. 366–68.
27. *Business Week* (Oct. 14, 1933), 20; NYT, Nov. 4, 1933. A United Press story by Raymond Clapper reported that the administration, sensing the danger of stirring up sympathy for a manufacturer "whose high wages and short hours have been a trade-mark in industry for 20 years," did not wish to make a martyr of Ford. The strategy was to encourage the public to pass by salesmen whose cars did not bear a Blue Eagle. *Washington News*, Sept. 6, 1933.
28. *Wheeling* (W. Va.)*News*, July 27, 1934; Fine, "Ford and N.R.A.," pp. 368–69.
29. *Washington News*, Aug. 19, Sept. 6, 1933; *Toledo News-Bee*, Sept. 19, 1933; *New York American*, Sept. 19, 1933; Garrett, *Wild Wheel*, p. 153; DN, May 27, 1935.

Chapter 15

1. The labor disturbances at Chester and Edgewater are treated in detail in Fine, "Ford and N.R.A.," pp. 371–85. An AFL federal local union had been organized at Edgewater in August 1933, and an AFL charter was granted to Chester employees after their strike had begun. *Ibid.*, pp. 372, 376. The Rouge was the scene of one of the Communists' "hunger marches" on Mar. 7, 1932. Four marchers were killed and twenty wounded by Dearborn police. Harry Bennett, in seeking to quell the disorder, was knocked unconscious and barely averted losing his life. A grand jury investigation absolved Ford of any responsibility for the disturbance. DN and *St. Louis Post-Dispatch*, Mar. 7, 1932; DT, Mar. 8, 1932; Sward, *Legend of Henry Ford*, p. 238.
2. Kennedy, *Automobile Industry*, pp. 252–56; Edward Levinson, *Labor on the March* (New York: Harper & Brothers, 1956), p. 57; Sidney Fine, "The Origins of the United Automobile Workers, 1933–1935," *Journal of Economic History* 18 (Sept. 1958), 256, 259–60.
3. Walter Galenson, *The CIO Challenge to the AFL: A History of the American Labor Movement 1935–1941* (Cambridge, Mass.: Harvard University Press, 1960), pp. 3, 99, 131–33, 148–49; Fine, "Origins of U.A.W.," pp. 281–82.
4. Galenson, *CIO Challenge*, p. 643; Joel Seidman, *American Labor from Defense to Reconversion* (Chicago: University of Chicago Press, 1953), pp. 6–7.
5. Galenson, *CIO Challenge*, pp. 178–90; John H. O'Brien, "Henry Ford's Commander in Chief Harry Bennett and His Private Army," *Forum* 99 (Feb. 1938), 67; "Board on Ford," *Time* 31 (Jan. 3, 1938), 10; John McCarten, "The Little Man in Henry Ford's Basement," *American Mercury* 50 (May 1940), 10.
6. Sward, *Legend of Henry Ford*, pp. 342–43; Oswald Garrison Villard, "Issues and Men," *Nation* 144 (Apr. 24, 1937), 467. Henry Ford evidently was much impressed with the Service Department's competence. He once told an Englishman that Bennett and six of his men could "get rid of Hitler for you in no time." Bennett, *Never Called Henry*, p. 122.
7. *Dearborn Independent*, Feb. 26, 1937; DT, Apr. 14, 1937; Sorensen, *Forty Years*, p. 260. A poll by the American Institute of Public Opinion in 1937 showed that more than two-thirds of the people queried hoped that the Supreme Court would declare sit-down strikes illegal. DT, Sept. 27, 1937.
8. Bennett, *Never Called Henry*, pp. 5, 33; Nevins and Hill, *Expansion and Challenge*, pp. 211, 591–93;

Liebold, *Reminiscenses*, p. 1203; Nevins and Hill, *Decline and Rebirth*, pp. 232–39.
9. Sorensen, *Forty Years*, pp. 260–62.
10. DN, DT, May 27, 1937; Sward, *Legend of Henry Ford*, p. 392; "Ford: Frankensteen Gets a Beating, U.A.W. Gets 'Tremendous Impetus,' " *News-Week* 9 (June 5, 1937), front cover.
11. Sward, *Legend of Henry Ford*, p. 394; "Fordism Versus Unionism," *Time* 30 (July 26, 1937), 13. The issue of *News-Week* cited is June 5, 1937.
12. "Fordism Versus Unionism," *Time*, p. 13; NYT, July 1, 1937; Sward, *Legend of Henry Ford*, p. 396.
13. DT and DN, July 21, 1937.
14. "Board on Ford," *Time*, p. 10; DN, Dec. 24, 1937; DFP, Dec. 25, 1937.
15. *Washington News*, Dec. 27, 1937; *Harrisburg* (Pa.) *News*, Jan. 3, 1938; *Jones City* (Okla.)*News*, Feb. 18, 1938 (for syndicated editorial); *Dearborn Independent*, Feb. 18, 1938 (for syndicated cartoon); DFP, Dec. 31, 1937.
16. What the Public Thinks of Big Business, Curtis Publishing Company, Division of Commercial Research, May 1937, Acc. 454, Box 9; *Fortune* 16 (Oct. 1937), 167; DN, Jan. 19, 1938; DT, Mar. 13, 1938; *Traverse City* (Mich.) *Record-Eagle*, Apr. 12, 1938.
17. Sward, *Legend of Henry Ford*, pp. 370–418; DT and *British Columbia Enquirer and Evening News*, Apr. 20, 1940. In mid-1940, a *Fortune* survey of laboring men and women found that 73.6 percent of the respondents believed that Henry Ford was among those Americans who were "helpful to labor." Senator Wagner received a 51.8 percent response. Among persons considered "harmful to labor," Ford's 12.3 percent vote was topped by John L. Lewis's 44.6 percent. *Fortune* 21 (June 1940), 163. Although the hearings received little attention in the general press, they were well publicized in the labor press, which had more than 6,000,000 readers. Sward, *Legend of Henry Ford*, p. 418.
18. DN, Apr. 24, 1939; "Ford," *Newsweek* 11 (Jan. 3, 1938), 41; *Savannah News*, Jan. 23, 1940; *Jackson Citizen Patriot*, Oct. 8, 1940; DFP, Oct. 9, 1940. Among newspapers which ran editorials in Ford's defense were the *Marion* (Ohio) *Star*, *Altoona* (Pa.) *Mirror*, *Buffalo News*, and *Jackson* (Mich.) *Citizen Patriot*, Aug. 21, 1939.
19. Sward, *Legend of Henry Ford*, pp. 381–84; DT, Jan. 25, 1939; DFP, Mar. 8, 1939, Mar. 13, 1939, and Feb. 3, 1941; *PM* (New York), Feb. 3, 1941. Martin retired from the UAW-AFL in Apr. 1940 and in June 1940 became a manufacturer's agent, working for a parts company which supplied the Ford Company. DN, June 28, 1940.
20. NYT, Jan. 23, 1938; *Dearborn Press*, Nov. 7, 1940; DT, Dec. 8, 1940; Sward, *Legend of Henry Ford*, p. 401; *Jackson* (Mich.) *Citizen Patriot*, Oct. 8, 1940; DFP, Oct. 9, 1940; DT, Dec. 3, 1940.
21. DFP, Oct. 2, 1940; Sward, *Legend of Henry Ford*, pp. 400–1; Galenson, *CIO Challenge*, p. 180.
22. *PM* (New York), Jan. 5, 1941 (citing least receptive employees to unionism); Lloyd H. Bailer, "Negro Labor in the Automobile Industry," (unpublished Ph.D. diss., University of Michigan, 1942), pp. 201–2; *Detroit Tribune*, June 12, July 10, 1937; Rev. R. L. Bradby, pastor, Second Baptist Church, Detroit, to Charles E. Sorensen, May 28, 1937, and William W. Jason, secretary, Men's Club, St. Matthew's Episcopal Church, Detroit, to Sorensen, June 3, 1937, Acc. 38, Box 84; Herbert R. Northrup, *Organized Labor and the Negro* (New York: Harper & Brothers, 1944), p. 186; Irving Howe and B. J. Widick, *The UAW and Walter Reuther* (New York: Random House, 1949), pp. 207–8. Only four mem-

bers of the Interdenominational Ministers' Alliance supported the UAW in its struggle against Ford. *Detroit Tribune,* Aug. 21, 1939.

23. *Detroit Tribune,* Aug. 21, 1937 and Apr. 12, 1941; Charles E. Sorensen to Edsel Ford, Sept. 15, 1930, Selected Documents File, Ford Archives; interview with Rev. Charles Hill, assistant to Rev. Bradby, June 9, 1954.

24. NYT, Dec. 22, 1940.

25. DFP, Dec. 14, 1940; NYT, Dec. 22, 1940 and Feb. 1, 1941; *Milwaukee Journal,* Dec. 26, 1940; *New York Herald Tribune,* Dec. 28, 1940; DN, Dec. 27, 1940 and Jan. 31, 1941; *New York Journal-American,* Feb. 20, 1941.

26. See Acc. 450, Box 9 for copies of the advertisements; letters supporting Ford's position; and editorials on his labor policies.

27. See Acc. 450, Box 9 for correspondence concerning the advertisements between the General Sales Department and branch managers.

28. *New York Sun,* Feb. 10, 1941; DFP, Feb. 11, 1941; DN, Feb. 17, 20, 1941; NYT, Mar. 9, 1941.

29. H. C. Doss, general sales manager, to branch managers, Feb. 28, 1941, Acc. 450, Box 7.

30. See Acc. 450, Box 7 and Acc. 285, Box 2341 for correspondence between the General Sales Department and branch managers concerning the visits; for the reports of the branch managers; and for newspaper stories and editorials published after the visits.

31. "Model T Tycoon," *Time* 37 (Mar. 17, 1941), 17; *Boston Globe,* Mar. 29, 1941 (citing the public opinion surveys).

32. DT and DFP, Apr. 2, 1941.

33. DFP, Apr. 2, 5, 1941; DT, Apr. 3, 1941.

34. *Louisville Courier-Journal,* Apr. 4, 1941; see Clipbook 117 for the press's treatment of the strike; Sward, *Legend of Henry Ford,* p. 415. The *New York World-Telegram,* Apr. 4, 1941, *Marquette* (Mich.) *Daily Mining Journal,* Apr. 7, 1941, and *Time* 37 (Apr. 14, 1941), 21, are only three of many publications which carried one or both of the photographs mentioned in the text; *New York Sun,* June 14, 1941. The picture of the black pleading for mercy won a prize in a photo contest and was reprinted in this connection in the DN, Dec. 28, 1941. The picture of the youth being beaten also has been reprinted on various occasions. It appeared in *Time* 81 (Mar. 1, 1963), 15.

35. DN, Apr. 2, 4, 1941; DFP, Apr. 7, 1941; Galenson, *CIO Challenge,* p. 182.

36. DN, Apr. 7, 10, 1941; Bennett, *Never Called Henry,* p. 136; NYT, Apr. 12, 1941. Henry Ford had little respect for Van Wagoner. After receiving the governor at his estate, Ford told Bennett, "I'd give him six dollars a day—but not any more." Bennett, *Never Called Henry,* p. 137. "Ford Knuckles Under," *Nation* 152 (Apr. 19, 1941), 460–61.

37. DFP, May 23, 1941; Sorensen, *Forty Years,* p. 268.

38. DFP and DT, May 23, 1941.

39. Sorensen, *Forty Years,* pp. 268–69.

40. DN, June 20, 1941; NYT, June 21, 1941; Galenson, *CIO Challenge,* p. 183; "A Car with a Union Label," *Time* 37 (June 30, 1941), 14; "Ford's Partner," *Business Week* (June 28, 1941), 40. In a burst of enthusiasm the UAW and Ford ordered 200,000 union labels (small steel ovals) without deciding who would pay for them. When the labels arrived each tried to "outfumble" the other; and the UAW ended up signing the check—for $2,000. The labels were installed only when requested by customers. *Flint* (Mich.) *Journal,* Aug. 31, 1941.

41. "Union Milestone," *Newsweek* 17 (June 30, 1941), 34; *Boston Post,* July 6, 1941 (Associated Press);

Cleveland Press, June 21, 1941; "Ford Goes the Whole Way in Unionizing Shops," *Christian Century* 58 (July 2, 1941), 851; *Christian Science Monitor,* June 27, 1941; DN, June 20, 1941; *Las Vegas* (Nev.) *Journal,* June 28, 1941. Representative stories and editorials appear in Clipbook 120.

42. NYT, Nov. 30, 1941; *New York Sun,* Nov. 30, 1945.

43. A Survey of Attitudes Towards and Opinions About Ford Motor Company (photostatic copy), submitted to FMC by Elmo Roper, Oct. 1944, Acc. 134, Box 17; A Review of the First Year of "Watch the World Go By," submitted to FMC by Maxon, Inc., n.d. [June 1943], Acc. 149, Box 44; The Ford Sunday Evening Hour Plan for Commercial Policy; Advertising, Publicity, submitted to FMC by K & E, Aug. 23, 1945, Acc. 149, Box 21.

44. Galenson, *CIO Challenge,* pp. 182–83; Sward, *Legend of Henry Ford,* p. 418; Richards, *Last Billionaire,* pp. 390–92; W. A. Scotten, reporter, *Ford News,* to W. A. Simonds, editor, *Ford News,* June 22, 1939, Acc. 285, Box 2287; *New York Daily News,* Nov. 18, 1938 (regarding CIO boycott); *St. Louis Globe-Democrat,* June 27, 1941. Antipathy toward Henry Ford was so strong among brewers that in 1933, when Prince Louis Ferdinand, a FMC employee, was introduced to Adolphus Busch, Jr., head of the famous St. Louis family of brewmasters, he was greeted with the words, "As a grandson of dear Kaiser Wilhelm you are welcome to me and my family. But please don't mention the name Ford in my presence." Louis Ferdinand, *The Rebel Prince* (Chicago: Henry Regnery Company, 1952), p. 245.

45. Sorensen, *Forty Years,* p. 271. In 1962 Upton Sinclair claimed that he was responsible for settlement of the Ford strike since he had convinced Mrs. Ford of the wisdom of coming to terms with organized labor during one of her visits to California. NYT, Apr. 22, 1962.

Chapter 16

1. NYT, Dec. 16, 1935; DFP, Sept. 22, 1932; Nevins and Hill, *Decline and Rebirth,* pp. 103–4. The Ford Company's Italian plant was taken over by the Italian government in 1940. *Times* (London), Oct. 7, 1940.

2. DFP, July 20, 1939; DN, Aug. 29, 1939.

3. *Lansing* (Mich.) *State Journal,* Sept. 3, 1939; NYT, Sept. 21, 1939; *Kalamazoo* (Mich.) *Gazette,* Sept. 24, 1939; DN, Sept. 25, 1939; *Chicago Herald-American,* Sept. 25, 1939; *Chicago Tribune,* Sept. 26, 1939.

4. *New York Herald Tribune,* Oct. 4, 1939; NYT, Dec. 31, 1939; DT, Nov. 16, 1940; NYT, Feb. 16, 1941; *Chicago Herald-American,* Sept. 24, 1940; Louis Ferdinand, *The Rebel Prince* (Chicago: Henry Regnery Company, 1952), p. 155; Kenneth S. Davis, *The Hero Charles A. Lindbergh and the American Dream* (Garden City, N.Y.: Doubleday & Company, Inc., 1959), pp. 399–400, 410; DN, Aug. 29, 1939; *New York Post,* Jan. 3, 1941.

5. *New York Herald Tribune,* Oct. 4, 1939 (citing Ford's views on the "phony war"); NYT, May 17, 1940 (citing Roosevelt's proposal); *Savannah News,* May 29, 1940. Adolf Hitler, as well as many leaders of the American aircraft industry, regarded the President's plan to produce 50,000 airplanes a year as "fantastic." Norman Beasley, *Knudsen a Biography* (New York: McGraw-Hill Book Company, Inc., 1947), p. 229.

6. DFP, Jan. 16, 1941; *New York World-Telegram,* June 5, 1940; NYT, May 30, 1940; Chris Sinsabaugh, "Sparks," *Automotive Daily News* 15 (June 17, 1940), 1; "People," *Time* 35 (June 10, 1940), 70; DT, Sept. 22, 1941. Beasley, *Knudsen,* p. 229, states that newsmen quoted Knudsen as saying "there was a possibility that General Motors could turn out 1,000 warplanes a month."

7. *The Army Air Forces in World War II,* eds. Wesley Frank Craven and James Lee Cate, 6 vols. (Chicago: University of Chicago Press, 1948–58), *Men and Planes,* 6:320, 322. *Providence Bulletin,* June 14, 1940; *Portland* (Maine) *Press-Herald,* June 17, 1940; *Marshalltown* (Iowa) *Times,* June 1, 1940; *La Crosse* (Wis.) *Tribune,* June 15, 1940; *Portland* (Ore.) *Journal,* June 7, 1940; *Kansas City* (Mo.) *Drovers Telegram,* June 20, 1940; *Baltimore News-Post,* June 7, 1940; *Port Huron* (Mich.) *Times-Herald,* June 14, 1940. See Clipbook 108 for hundreds of news stories and editorials on Ford's statement about building 1,000 planes per day.

8. DT, June 10 and 11, 1940; *Pittsburgh Sun-Telegraph,* June 10, 1940; *New York Sun,* June 11, 1940; *Dayton News,* June 16, 1940; *Binghamton* (N.Y.) *Sun,* June 21, 1940; *Windsor* (Ont.) *Daily Star,* June 12, 1940. A retired army major suggested that Ford could resolve a pilot shortage by building pilotless planes. *Pontiac* (Mich.) *Daily Press,* June 21, 1940.

9. NYT and *Washington Post,* June 12, 1940; *Mt. Clemens* (Mich.) *Daily Leader,* June 13, 1940; Sorensen, *Forty Years,* pp. 274–75; Black, *Reminiscences,* p. 90.

10. DN and *New York Sun,* June 19, 1940; DFP, June 20, 1940; Black, *Reminiscences,* p. 90; Sorensen, *Forty Years,* p. 275; DT, June 24, 1940; *New York Mirror* and DN, June 26, 1940. The Packard Motor Car Company was offered the Rolls-Royce engine contract, and subsequently built a fine engine. *Grand Rapids Press,* July 13, 1940; Sorensen, *Forty Years,* p. 274.

11. *Greensboro* (N.C.) *News,* June 28, 1940; *Cumberland* (Md.) *Times,* June 30, 1940; *Brunswick* (Ga.) *News,* June 27, 1940; *Sandusky* (Ohio) *Register,* July 2, 1940; *Dallas Morning News,* June 27, 1940; DN, June 28, 1940; *Lansing* (Mich.) *State Journal,* June 30, 1940. See Clipbook 109 for hundreds of newspaper stories and editorials on Ford's decision not to build the Rolls-Royce engines for Britain.

12. "Ford's Rolls-Royces," *Time* 36 (July 8, 1940), 60; "Battle of Detroit," *Time* 39 (July 23, 1942), 42; *New York Daily News,* June 27, 1940; *Columbus* (Ohio) *Dispatch,* June 27, 1940; *Windsor* (Ont.) *Daily Star,* June 24, 27, and 28, 1940; *Mt. Clemens* (Mich.) *Daily Leader,* June 27, 1940; *Monroe* (Mich.) *News,* June 27, 1940; *Ludington* (Mich.) *Daily News,* June 27, 1940; NYT, June 26 and 28, 1940; Liebold, *Reminiscences,* p. 1182. The *Windsor Daily Star,* June 28, 1940, suggested that Coldwell's attack on Ford was motivated by the "well-known C.C.F. yen to confiscate private industry." The publication also recalled that Coldwell at one time protested against sending Canadian troops to Britain.

13. DT, June 27, 1940 (quoting *London Daily Mirror*); E.G. Liebold to Editor, *London Daily Mail,* Acc. 285, Box 2258; "Ford and Aircraft," *Time* 36 (July 15, 1940), 60.

14. *Columbus* (Ohio) *Dispatch,* June 27, 1940; DT, Aug. 13, 1941; DN, Sept. 18, 1941. The King and Queen inspected the food vans on Sept. 16, 1941 and expressed their gratitude for the Fords' "magnificent gesture," *Times* (London), Sept. 17, 1941.

15. DT, Sept. 17, 1940; Paul Burton, public relations associate, Pratt & Whitney Aircraft Division of United Aircraft Corporation, East Hartford, Conn., to David L. Lewis, June 28, 1963. Government Contracts As of Dec. 9, 1941, Acc. 149, Box 102.

16. *Grand Rapids* (Mich.) *Press,* Sept. 28, 1940; NYT, Jan. 16, 1941; *Ford News* 21 (Nov. 1941), 283; Nevins and Hill, *Decline and Rebirth,* pp. 193–95; DFP, Sept. 25, 1941; Government Contracts As of Dec. 9, 1941, Acc. 149, Box 102. Admiral Nimitz, in his acceptance speech, said that Harry Bennett "was tireless in his efforts to perfect plans for the school." By Feb. 1941, Bennett was a lieutenant commander in the U.S. Naval Reserve. *Ford News* 21 (Feb. 1941), 39.

17. DN and *Ann Arbor* (Mich.) *News,* Jan. 8, 1941; Sorenson, *Forty Years,* pp. 279–84; "Sorensen of the Rouge," *Fortune* 25 (Apr. 1942), 79; Automobile Manufacturers Association, *Freedom's Arsenal The Story of the Automotive Council for War Production* (Detroit: Automobile Manufacturers Association, 1950), p. 44; *Army Air Forces,* 6, pp. 332–33.

18. *New York Sun,* Feb. 5, 1941; *Ann Arbor* (Mich.) *News,* May 1, 1941; *New York Sun,* May 21, 1941; *New York Journal of Commerce,* Dec. 31, 1941; Nevins and Hill, *Decline and Rebirth,* pp. 192–93.

19. Government Contracts As of Dec. 9, 1941, Acc. 149, Box 102; NYT, Dec. 13, 1941; DFP, Jan. 10, 1942; NYT, Feb. 11, 1942. Until the attack on Pearl Harbor, the automobile industry maintained a cautious, go-slow attitude toward rearmament. "No industrial manager," declared the Automobile Manufacturers Association, "could be blamed for undertaking arms production with caution. Time had not yet healed the scars left by the phrases, 'war-monger' and 'merchant of death,' which had been hurled at those industrialists who had helped arm the nation in World War I." Automobile Manufacturers Association, *Freedom's Arsenal,* p. 53.

Chapter 17

1. Nevins and Hill, *Decline and Rebirth,* pp. 115, 131; Garrett, *Wild Wheel,* p. 171.

2. *Automotive News 1938 Almanac,* p. 50; *Automotive News 1948 Almanac,* p. 52. In 1935, the Ford Company's best year during the prewar decade, 826,519 Fords and 2,370 Lincolns were sold. Ford captured 30 percent of the market in 1935, less than 19 percent in 1941. GM pushed its market share from 43 percent in 1933 to 47.3 percent in 1941; Chrysler from 17.5 to 24 percent during the same period.

3. NYT, Oct. 29, 1935; Nevins and Hill, *Decline and Rebirth,* p. 129. The Zephyr in 1951 was described by the [New York] Museum of Modern Art as "the first successfully designed streamlined car in America" and by *Motor Trend* as "one of the most revolutionary automobiles of the Thirties." 8 Automobiles (folder) [New York] Museum of Modern Art, 1951; "The Lincoln Continental," *Motor Trend* 4 (July 1952). The regular Lincoln was called the Lincoln Custom beginning with the 1941 model year. In 1944 the Ford Company announced that the Zephyr nameplate would not reappear after the war, and the regular Lincoln subsequently won back some of the ground it had lost.

4. *Automotive News 1940 Almanac,* p. 28. The Continental sold for $2,840. In 1951 the Continental was among eight "automobile aristocrats" exhibited as "works of art" at the Museum of Modern Art. In 1959, 100 of the world's leading designers, architects, and design teachers surveyed by the Illinois Institute

of Technology ranked the 1940 Continental as the "sixth best-designed mass-produced product of modern times." Among all domestic and foreign cars ever built, only the 1953 Studebaker hard-top coupe was ranked higher in this survey. "Parking Space for 8 Automobiles," *Exhibition Record* (Sept. 1951), 126; "The 100 'Best Designed' Products," *Fortune* 59 (Apr. 1959), 137. The eight cars featured in the Museum's 1951 exhibit were the Bentley, Cisitalia, M.G., Talbot-Lago, Mercedes, Cord, Lincoln Continental, and Jeep. Completely restyled, the Continental "Mark II" was reintroduced in 1955. A "Mark III" was offered in 1968, a "Mark IV" in 1971. FMC Annual Report, 1955, p. 9; NYT, Feb. 13, 1968; FMC Annual Report, 1971, p. 5.

5. DN, Nov. 7, 1936; R.L. Polk Company Calendar Year Registrations (typescript), GM Public Relations Library, Detroit. The "standard" V-8 was almost identical to the eighty-five-horsepower "de luxe" V-8, except for the smaller engine.

6. DN and DT, Oct. 6, 1938; "Henry and Edsel," *Printers' Ink* 85 (Nov. 10, 1938), 12; *Automotive News 1948 Almanac*, p. 52. The *Gaffney* (S.C.) *Ledger*, Nov. 3, 1938, described the Mercury as a "half-sister to the Lincoln Zephyr." Mercury sales totaled 81,874 in quota-ridden 1941, giving the new car 2.19 percent of the passenger car market.

7. Nevins and Hill, *Decline and Rebirth*, p. 295; see GM and Chrysler Corporation annual reports for the years 1931–41; "The Ford Heritage," *Fortune* 29 (June 1944), 249. Between 1933–41 GM netted $1,454,279,000 and Chrysler $303,070,000; GM's assets increased by 60 percent. Chrysler's more than doubled.

8. Nevins and Hill, *Decline and Rebirth*, pp. 131, 230, 242. Ford's stroke occurred shortly after his seventy-fifth birthday. The magnate made a rapid recovery and within a month was "more aggressive than ever." News of Ford's stroke was withheld from the press. Sorensen, *Forty Years*, pp. 266–67.

9. "Mr. Ford Doesn't Care," *Fortune* 8 (Dec. 1933), 63–64. The title of this article was inspired by Ford's reply to a question about Chevrolet by a *Fortune* representative: "I don't know how many cars Chevrolet sold last year. I don't know how many they're selling this year. I don't know how many they may sell next year. And—I don't care." *Ibid.*, p. 65. *Fortune* added that the business lunches lasted from one to five hours, and that "Henry Ford [was] in command."

10. "Henry Ford—Social Philosopher," *Printers' Ink* 159 (June 2, 1932), 10 (regarding the financial drain of Ford's "non-profit work"); William Greenleaf, *From Tiny Beginnings: The Early Philanthropies of Henry and Edsel Ford* (Detroit: Wayne State University Press, 1964), p. 107; E.J. Cutler, *Reminiscenses*, p. 121 (Cutler had charge of reconstruction of buildings at Greenfield Village); Mary Augusta Rodgers, "Henry Ford, Collector Extraordinary." *Ford Times* 56 (July 1963), 34. Clipbooks 70 through 123, which cover the years 1929 through 1941, contain hundreds of newspaper stories about the village. See editions of the *Readers' Guide for Periodical Literature* for the years 1932–41 for listings of magazine articles on the village. J.G. de Roulhac Hamilton, "The Ford Museum," *American Historical Review* 36 (July 1931), 773; "History Lives at Greenfield," *Rotarian* 44 (May 1934), 53; "Start the Day with a Song," *Etude* 54 (April 1936), 203; Bruce Bliven, "Mr. Ford Collects," *New Republic* 90 (Apr. 28, 1937); "Grandpa Town," *Saturday Evening Post* 211 (Nov. 19, 1938), 22; "Henry Ford Is the Country's First Collector of Americana," *House and Garden* 80 (July 1941), 29.

11. DFP, May 19 and 24, 1934; NYT, May 29 and 30, 1934, and July 5, 1935; *Ford News* 15 (Aug. 1935), 143; Richards, *Last Billionaire*, p. 184.

12. Stark Young, "Massa's in Cold, Cold Ground," *New Republic* 91 (May 29, 1937), 46–47; DFP, Aug. 30, 1939; Spyros P. Skouras, chairman, 20th Century-Fox Film Corporation, to David L. Lewis, Sept. 11, 1962; interview with William Toohey, director of public relations, The Edison Institute, Aug. 30, 1962; DN, July 7, 1963; Greenleaf, *Beginnings*, p. 110. The rewording of the Foster sign was first noted by the author—who visits Greenfield Village at least thrice annually—on Oct. 12, 1971.

13. DN, Apr. 16 and 17, 1938; see Clipbook 94 for scores of articles on the dedication of the Wright house and shop.

14. General Sales Department to branch managers, Dec. 11, 1935 and Oct. 1, 1936, Acc. 509, Box 12; DT, Sept. 29, 1937; Report on Greenfield Village Choir Program, 1941–42 Season, Feb. 3, 1942, Acc. 149, Box 102.

15. Interview with William Toohey, Aug. 30, 1962; interview with J. Robert Dawson, director of public relations, The Edison Institute, Jan. 12, 1976.

16. John Gunther, *Inside U.S.A.* (New York: Harper & Brothers, 1947), p. 401; Rodgers, "Collector Extraordinary," pp. 34, 36; *Dearborn Guide*, July 25, 1963; Sward, *Legend of Henry Ford*, p. 264; Nevins and Hill, *Expansion and Challenge*, p. 504.

17. Nevins and Hill, *Decline and Rebirth*, pp. 72–73; Roscoe Smith, head of village industries, to Fred L. Black, Apr. 20, 1939, Acc. 554, Box 31; FMC news release, Sept. 9, 1939, Acc. 450, Box 7; *Ford News* 21 (July 1941), 171; see 1937 edition of the *Industrial Arts Index* for a listing of seven articles on the village industries; Arthur Van Vlissingen, "Ford's Little Plants in the Country," *Reader's Digest* 33 (July 1938), 62; Ralph W. Cessna, "Down by the New Mill Stream," *Christian Science Monitor Magazine* 32 (Dec. 30, 1939), 8–9; John Bird, "One Foot on the Land," *Saturday Evening Post* 216 (Mar. 18, 1944), 46.

18. Nevins and Hill, *Decline and Rebirth*, pp. 73–74; Reynold Millard Wik, "Henry Ford's Science and Technology for Rural America," *Technology and Culture* 3 (Summer 1962), 256; FMC 1958 Annual Report, p. 15; Bob Boelio, "Henry's Loves," *Motor News* 45 (June 1963), 15. Only eight of the village factories were operated by Ford in 1947; five in the mid-1950s, three in the early 1960s, and one—the Northville valve plant—in 1976. The Northville factory for years has obtained all of its power from an electric utility. David L. Lewis, "Ford Village Industries: A History and a Tour Route," *Horseless Carriage Gazette* 35 (July-Aug. 1973), 14–19.

19. Henry S. Curtis, "The Pennington, a Ford School," *School and Society* 40 (Oct. 6, 1934), 450–1. Christy Borth, in "Henry Ford, Schoolmaster," *Forum* 100 (Sept. 1938), 120, states that "the best place to hunt [for Ford] is not in the shops or offices of the great River Rouge plant but among his school children."

20. Samuel Crowther, "Educating for Leadership," *Ladies' Home Journal* 47 (Aug. 1930), 12; Henry Ford as told to James C. Derieux, "The Making of an American Citizen," *Good Housekeeping* 99 (Oct. 1934), 20; interview with Donald Currie, superintendent of schools, Royal Oak, Mich. (a member of the administrative staff of Ford's schools during the 1930s and 1940s), June 4, 1963; "Ford Schools," *Time* 31 (June 27, 1938), 47. In addition to his schools in Greenfield Village and in rural Michigan, during the 1930s Ford also operated three one-room schools at Sudbury, Mass.; seven one-room schools in Georgia;

an agricultural institute in England; a school in Fordlandia, Brazil; and the Henry Ford Trade School, Apprentice School, and Training School for High School Graduates at the Rouge. In 1938 about 20,000 students attended these schools. Ford also contributed liberally to the Martha Berry Schools in Georgia. *Ibid.*

21. See editions of the *Readers' Guide to Periodical Literature* for the years 1932–39 and of the *Education Index* for the years 1932–41 for listings of articles on Ford's schools. Newspaper stories on the schools are scattered throughout Clipbooks 77 through 123, which cover the years 1932–41. Currie interview, June 4, 1963; interview with Mark Stroebel, principal, Greenfield Village school, June 3, 1963; DN, June 13, 1969.

22. Nevins and Hill, *Ford: The Times*, p. 272; Wheeler McMillen, chairman of the board, National Farm Chemurgic Council, to David L. Lewis, Oct. 1, 1962; Nevins and Hill, *Expansion and Challenge*, p. 490; *Chambersburg* (Pa.) *Opinion*, Dec. 15, 1931. McMillen states that he "first discussed the idea of new uses for farm products, and new crops, with him [Ford] early in 1928." There are no articles in the Ford clipbooks concerning Ford's interest in the chemurgic concept prior to 1931.

23. *Toledo Times*, Apr. 30, 1932; DT, Dec. 2, 1932; "Ford Doesn't Care," *Fortune*, pp. 65, 134; "Plastic Molding at the Ford Plant," *Automotive Industries* 69 (Sept. 30, 1933), 390–2; "Ford's Soy Bean Requirement 1,000,000 Bushels Yearly for Million Car Output," *Automotive Industries* 73 (Oct. 26, 1935), 541.

24. "Old Gentleman in Detroit," *Time* 31 (Jan. 17, 1938), 53; "Plastics in 1940," *Fortune* 22 (Oct. 1940), 108; "Plastic Fords," *Time* 36 (Nov. 11, 1940), 65; DN, Nov. 21 and 24, 1940; see Clipbook 113 for newspaper stories on Ford's ax demonstration. The steel industry, alarmed by reports that cars with plastic bodies might become universal within a few years, sent a research committee to Dearborn in October 1940, to investigate the potential of Ford's plastic; it did not issue a public statement on its findings. "Plastic Fords," *Time*, p. 65.

25. NYT, Aug. 14 and 17, 1941; *Wheeling* (W. Va.) *Intelligencer*, Aug. 18, 1941; *San Diego Union*, Aug. 25, 1941; *Indianapolis Star*, Aug. 17, 1941; *Decatur* (Ill.) *Herald-Review*, Aug. 17, 1941; *Saginaw* (Mich.) *News*, Aug. 17, 1941. Clipbook 121 contains scores of editorials and hundreds of news stories on Ford's plastic car.

26. The *Troy* (Ala.) *Messenger*, Aug. 14, 1941 and *Spartanburg* (S.C.) *Journal & Spartan*, Aug. 16, 1941, ran typical editorials on the potential market for cotton; *Tampa Times*, Aug. 28, 1941; *Tacoma Sunday Ledger and News Tribune*, Aug. 23, 1941; *Tupelo* (Miss.) *Journal*, Aug. 14, 1941; *Elmira* (N.Y.) *Star-Gazette*, Aug. 27, 1941; *Cheboygan* (Mich.) *News*, Aug. 14, 1941; *Bristol* (Conn.) *Press*, Aug. 18, 1941; *Spartanburg* (S.C.) *Herald*, Aug. 30, 1941.

27. *Cleveland Press*, Aug. 15, 1941; *Cedar Rapids* (Iowa) *Gazette*, Aug. 21, 1941; *St. Louis Globe-Democrat*, Aug. 18, 1941; *PM* (New York), Aug. 26, 1941; Charles F. Carpentier, "History of Motor Vehicle License Plates, State of Illinois," *Model T Times*, no. 75 (Sept.-Oct. 1961), 13.

28. *San Diego Union*, Aug. 25, 1941; *Detroit Legal Courier*, Aug. 22, 1941; *Arkansas City* (Ark.) *Tribune*, Aug. 21, 1941.

29. Joseph L. Nicholson and George R. Leighton, "Plastics Come of Age," *Harper's Magazine* 185 (Aug. 1942), 300; William L. Stidger, "Henry Ford on Plastics," *Rotarian* 62 (Feb. 1943), 58; P.J. Passon, Chevrolet Motor Division, GM, "The Corvette Story," (paper read at summer meeting of Society of

Automotive Engineers, St. Louis, June 8, 1961). The fiber glass reinforced plastic bodies for the Corvette and Avanti are rust and corrosion proof and weigh about half as much as would a steel body of comparable size. "Would the Public Pay a Premium for Fiber Glass Family Car?," *Steel* 51 (Sept. 10, 1962), 160. Although the soybean has not been an ingredient of the Corvette or Avanti body, it is used in many plastics. Wheeler McMillen, "Chemurgy," *The Encyclopedia Americana*, 1962 ed., p. 410a.

30. Wik, "Henry Ford's Science," p. 252; NYT, Dec. 25, 1941 and Nov. 25, 1943; "Henry Ford, 75," *Newsweek* 12 (Aug. 8, 1938), 11; DT, Dec. 21, 1941; DFP, June 1, 1943; Mildred Lager, *The Useful Soybean: A Plus Factor in Modern Living* (New York: McGraw-Hill Book Company, Inc., 1945), pp. 36–37; McMillen, "Chemurgy," p. 410a. Ford's soybean processing plant and most of his farmland were sold in 1946. Nevins and Hill, *Decline and Rebirth*, p. 323.

31. *Chicago Herald and Examiner*, Aug. 24, 1934; Robert S. Strother, "Mr. Ford and the Magic Beanstalk," *Reader's Digest* 79 (Nov. 1961), 188–90; DFP, Sept. 20, 1943; McMillen, "Chemurgy," p. 410a.

32. Nevins and Hill, *Expansion and Challenge*, p. 491.

33. "The Schoolmaster of Dearborn," *New Outlook* 164 (Sept. 1934), 62; NYT, Apr. 4, 1934; *Escanaba* (Mich.) *Press*, June 27, 1940; DFP, Aug. 29, 1941; *Automotive Industries* 75 (Oct. 10, 1936), 470.

34. McMillen, "Chemurgy," p. 410a; Strother, "Magic Beanstalk," p. 190; "Can Agriculture Save the Dollar?," *Forbes* 111 (Mar. 15, 1973), 38; United States Department of Agriculture, *Agricultural Statistics 1974* (Washington: U.S. Government Printing Office, 1974), p. 437; *Ann Arbor* (Mich.) *News*, Mar. 11 and Apr. 29, 1973. America's corn crop was valued at $13.3 billion in 1973, according to the Department of Agriculture.

35. "Through his research studies at Dearborn," stated the *Kalamazoo* (Mich.) *Gazette* of Dec. 14, 1939, "Ford has done more to promote the soybean industry in the United States than perhaps any one person in the nation." Ford also tried, but failed, between 1934 and 1938 to propagate silk culture. Like everyone who has tried to process silk in the United States, he found that labor costs were prohibitive compared to those in the Far East. *Muskegon* (Mich.) *Chronicle*, Aug. 14, 1941.

36. Wik, "Henry Ford's Science," p. 257; McMillen to Lewis, Oct. 1, 1962; McMillen, "Chemurgy," p. 410b; Strother, "Magic Beanstalk," pp. 190, 192; *Automobile Bodies That Farmers Help to Build*, FMC brochure (dated 1941), Acc. 692, Box 2.

37. Nevins and Hill, *Decline and Rebirth*, p. 124; "Old Gentleman in Detroit," *Time*, p. 53.

38. Nevins and Hill, *Decline and Rebirth*, pp. 124–26; NYT, July 29, 1939; DT, Apr. 27, 1939.

39. DT, June 29 and 30, 1939; Andrew M. Howe, "Sigh of Relief Comes As Ford's New Tractor Is Shown, But Drama Is in the Making," *Printers' Ink* 188 (July 14, 1939), 11–14, and "Ford and Advertising" (editorial), 72; "Ford Will Advertise," *Printers' Ink* 188 (July 28, 1939), 79–80; NYT, Apr. 19, 1940 and July 29, 1939; DT, June 8, 1942.

40. "Mr. Ford's Only Partner," *Fortune* 25 (Jan. 1942), 67; Report by H.J. Robinson, superintendent, FMC Tractor Division, Mar. 26, 1946, Acc. 378, Box 1; Nevins and Hill, *Decline and Rebirth*, pp. 346–47.

41. FMC news release, Nov. 25, 1946; DFP, Jan. 9, 1948 and Apr. 10, 1952. Dearborn Motors Corporation was not a subsidiary of the Ford Company, which did not invest funds in its tractor distributor.

42. Nevins and Hill, *Decline and Rebirth,* p. 383; FMC 1958 Annual Report, p. 14; 1959 Annual Report, inside back cover; 1974 Annual Report, p. 36.

43. See editions of the *New York Times Index, Readers' Guide to Periodical Literature, Industrial Arts Index, Cumulative Book Index,* and *International Index to Periodicals* for the years 1921–41.

44. NYT, July 2, 1934; *New York Post,* Dec. 24, 1937; *Menomonie* (Wis.) *Stoutonia,* Dec. 10, 1937; *Nassau Sovereign,* n.d. [Spring 1939].

45. Arthur D. Howden, *Men Who Run America* (Indianapolis: Bobbs-Merrill Company, 1935), pp. 163, 170; DN, Apr. 12, 1938; Marshall W. Fishwick, *American Heroes: Myth and Reality* (Washington: Public Affairs Press, 1954), p. 116; Dixon Wecter, *The Hero in America: A Chronicle of Hero-Worship* (New York: Charles Scribner's Sons, 1941), p. 422; *New York Sun,* Jan. 6, 1934; *Omaha Bee-News,* Aug. 20, 1939; *Wenatchee* (Wash.) *World,* Aug. 1, 1941; "Like a Dream," *Time* 31 (May 9, 1938), 9; "Henry Ford, Jim James, and Taxes," *Literary Digest* 122 (Aug. 17, 1935), 5; P. I. Prentice, publisher of *Time,* to Henry Ford, Dec. 30, 1941 (a copy of the letter is in the Henry Ford file of the DFP library). Peter F. Drucker believes that Ford became "just another automobile manufacturer" when he adopted the annual model change in the early 1930s. Peter F. Drucker, "Henry Ford: Success and Failure," *Harper's Magazine* 195 (July 1947), 7.

46. Nevins and Hill, *Decline and Rebirth,* p. 242; Sorensen, *Forty Years,* pp. 271–72, 313.

Chapter 18

1. "General Motors: a Unit in Society," *Fortune* 19 (Mar. 1939), 48–49, 150; "Business Finds Its Voice: Motion Pictures and Combined Efforts," *Harper's Magazine* 176 (Feb. 1938), 326–27; NYT, Dec. 7, 1933; "Here Come the Cars," *Business Week* (Dec. 9, 1933), 7; *New York Sun,* Jan. 6, 1933; "Ford Precedents," *Time* 22 (Dec. 18, 1933), 51; *Business Week* (Dec. 16, 1933), 1; *New York Mirror,* Dec. 7, 1933. Henry Ford did not attend the 1927 press preview; Edsel Ford put the new model through its paces for cameramen. DN, Nov. 30, 1927. Ford also offered cigars and cigarettes at the Dearborn preview. "Ford Precedents," *Time,* p. 51. See Clipbook 87 for news stories on the press showing.

2. "Advertising at All Dealer Points Will Back Up 1934 Fords," *Advertising Age* 4 (Dec. 9, 1933), 1; DT, Dec. 6, 1933; *Business Week* (Dec. 16, 1933), 1.

3. "Ford Precedents," *Time,* pp. 51–52; *New York Herald Tribune,* Dec. 8, 1933; *New York Financial World,* Dec. 27, 1933. Dealers gathered in forty-one cities, thirty-two in the U.S., nine in Canada. Two thousand attended the Boston meeting; eight amplifiers were used. *Boston Globe,* Dec. 8, 1933. See Clipbook 86 for news stories on Ford's statement.

4. See Clipbook 89 for 1934 telephone conference publicity; NYT, Dec. 28, 1934, Oct. 28 and 29, 1935, Nov. 11, 1936, Nov. 2, 1937, and Nov. 11, 1938. Edsel Ford spoke at a breakfast for newsmen in advance of the Ford Company's participation in New York's 35th annual auto show. The occasion marked Ford's first participation in the show since 1910. In 1935 the show was sponsored by dealers rather than the Association of Automobile Manufacturers of which Ford was not a member. NYT, Jan. 7, 1935; *Automotive Industries* 71 (Oct. 6, 1934), 397.

5. DT, Oct. 25, 1938; *Boston Globe,* Oct. 25, 1938;

NYT, Oct. 25, 1938. See Clipbook 99 for news stories on the Mercury's debut and Henry Ford's statement.

6. DN, Oct. 2, 1939; Clipbook 104 for 1939 publicity; NYT, Sept. 12, 1940; Clipbook 111 for 1940 publicity; DN, Sept. 11, 1941; NYT, Sept. 12, 1941; Clipbook 121 for 1941 publicity. Seventy-five newsmen attended the 1939 preview. *Ford News* 19 (Nov. 1939), 244–45. Two hundred fifty journalists attended the 1940 showing. DFP, Sept. 12, 1940.

7. *Ford News* 19 (July 1939), 145; DN, June 16, 1939; *San Francisco Chronicle,* Jan. 15, 1939 (quoting Edsel Ford's speech). Summary of Charges in Connection with Various Motor Company Exhibits, July 11, 1946, Acc. 6, Box 363. Attendance figures for all the fairs can be found in a folder marked "Costs" in Acc. 554, Box 4. "General Motors," *Fortune,* p. 49.

8. Pound, *Turning Wheel,* p. 455; Black, *Reminiscences,* p. 197; interview with Clarence Olmstead, Ford exhibit employee, Sept. 24, 1962.

9. "Ford Is Out," *Time* 22 (Nov. 6, 1933), 20; "Here Come the Cars," *Business Week* (Dec. 9, 1933), 7; "Ford Staging Big Working Display of Products and Processes Starting October 21," *Automotive Industries* 69 (Oct. 21, 1933), 495; Olmstead interview, Sept. 24, 1962.

10. See Clipbooks 86 and 87 for press coverage of Detroit and New York expositions, respectively. Olmstead interview, Sept. 24, 1962; "Ford Precedents," *Time,* p. 52; "Ford Jumps the Gun in Race to Regain Lost Leadership," *Advertising & Selling* 22 (Dec. 21, 1933), 50; "Foxy Ford," *Tide* 8 (June 1934), 18. The opening of the New York exposition was covered on network radio throughout the East. "Ford Advertising Plans," *Printers' Ink* 165 (Dec. 14, 1933), 18. The average daily attendance at the New York show, 109,333, compared favorably with the Chicago fair's average daily attendance of 130,000.

11. J. Parker Van Zandt and L. Rohe Walton, "The People's Choice," *Advertising & Selling* 22 (Dec. 21, 1933), 15; *Dearborn Press,* Jan. 15, 1934; GM news release, May 5, 1934, GM Public Relations Library, Detroit; Athel F. Denham, "Automotive Industries Again Will Dominate Century of Progress," *Automotive Industries* 70 (June 2, 1934), 686; Black, *Reminiscences,* p. 193. Edsel Ford, Fred L. Black, and Walter Dorwin Teague were the key figures in Ford's expositions. After designing only the interior and exhibits for the Chicago exposition, Teague designed all of the other buildings. Albert Kahn designed the Chicago building and carried out the architectural engineering on the other structures. Black, *Reminiscences,* p. 204. Henry Ford, according to Teague, did not concern himself with design treatment and colors. Ocee Ritch, *The Lincoln Continental* (Los Angeles: Floyd Clymer, 1963), p. 89.

12. Denham, "Automotive Industries," p. 684; DFP, May 16, 1934.

13. *Chicago Herald and Examiner,* May 27, 1934; Valentino Sarra, "A Camera's-Eye View of a Century of Progress," *Printed Salesmanship* 63 (June 1934), 180; Constance Moran, "A Personally Conducted Tour of the Fair Grounds," *Printed Salesmanship* 63 (June 1934), 172. The fair was described as "one of the greatest structures ever built in the world for exposition purposes" in a May 9, 1934 Century of Progress news release, GM Public Relations Library. GM's rectangular building, with rounded corners, was 490 feet long, 306 feet wide, and had a tower 177 feet high. GM news release, Apr. 26, 1934, GM Public Relations Library. Ford's exhibit structure, built around the clock by three shifts of workers, was constructed in three months' time. "101 Years of Progress," *Business Week* (May 5, 1934), 18.

14. "Ford at the Fair," *System and Business Management* 63 (Aug. 1934), 371; "The Schoolmaster of Dearborn," *New Outlook* 164 (Sept. 1934), 56; Eugene Whitmore, "What the Fair Has Taught Us About Selling," *Printed Salesmanship* 63 (June 1934), 175.

15. "Ford Exposition Gates Open," *Ford News* 14 (June 1934), 103–4; Black, *Reminiscences*, pp. 194–96. Barney Oldfield supervised Ford's roads of the world exhibit. *Automotive Industries* 70 (June 2, 1934), 686. There were no roads of the world at Cleveland's Great Lakes Exposition in 1936 or at San Francisco's Golden Gate Exposition of 1939–40 because Ford did not build its exposition buildings, and therefore had neither the space nor an appropriate layout for such an exhibit. Black, *Reminiscences*, p. 194.

16. *Ford News* 14 (July 1934), 124; Black, *Reminiscences*, p. 199. The 1,500 concerts and recitals at the Ford pavilion were attended by 1,192,000 people. DN, Sept. 9, 1934. According to Black, the two networks offered Ford air time they were unable to sell during the summer of 1934.

17. Chicago World's Fair Costs, Acc. 554, Box 4; Clipbook 88; daily press reports of N.W. Ayer's Press Department, Acc. 545, Box 371, and *Industrial Arts Index* for 1934, p. 278.

18. Your Part in the Ford Exposition, Acc. 450, Box 2; *Ford News* 14 (July 1934), 123. Ford provided more services for special guests than any other auto maker. Most companies chartered trains to take employees to the fair. A Century of Progress news release, May 9, 1934, GM Public Relations Library, Detroit.

19. Report of C.M. Ripley of General Electric Publicity Department, Acc. 285, Box 1675; *Olympia* (Wash.) *Olympian*, Aug. 19, 1934 (quoting Studebaker employee); Moran, "Tour of Fair Grounds," p. 173.

20. "Schoolmaster of Dearborn," *New Outlook*, p. 56; "World's Fair Reveals New Strength of Films as Advertising Media," *Sales Management* 34 (Aug. 15, 1934), 147; Summary of Charges in Connection with Various Ford Motor Company Exhibits, July 11, 1946, Acc. 6, Box 363; Van Zandt and Walton, "People's Choice," p. 15; *Automotive Industries* 70 (June 2, 1934), 685–87. All of Ford's guides, lecturers, and exhibit operators were carefully trained college students; none was an auto salesman. Black, *Reminiscences*, pp. 193–94. GM's exhibit represented an investment of $3,000,000 over a two-year period; Chrysler's $500,000. GM news release, Apr. 26, 1934, GM Public Relations Library. The Big Three's exhibit expenditures were much larger than those of Studebaker, Nash, Hupp, Hudson, Packard, Cord, Mack, and other vehicle manufacturers. *Automotive Industries* 70 (June 6, 1934), 685–87.

21. NYT, Nov. 4, 1934; Van Zandt and Walton, "People's Choice," p. 15; Chicago World's Fair Attendance Figures, n.d. [Dec. 1, 1934], Acc. 554, Box 1.

22. Black, *Reminiscences*, p. 203 (Ford visiting the fair thirteen times); *New York American*, May 27, 1934; NYT, May 27, 1934.

23. Black, *Reminiscences*, pp. 204–5; "Preserve Ford Fair Rotunda at Dearborn," *Automotive Industries* 71 (Dec. 1, 1934), 669; *Ford News* 16 (July 1936), 138.

24. Rotunda Building Statistics, Acc. 629, Box 3; "Preserve Rotunda," *Automotive Industries*, p. 669; "Ford Opens a Gateway," *Business Week* (May 16, 1936), 15; *Ford News* 16 (June 1936), 103–4; NYT, July 22, 1937; *Ford News* 17 (Sept. 1937), 74. The globe, twenty feet in diameter, had been displayed in Ford's exhibits at the Chicago and San Diego fairs.

25. DT, May 29, 1936; *Ford News* 16 (July 1936), 138; A.G. Coulton to Frank Campsall, July 1, 1936, Acc. 285, Box 1903; Lawrence Vail Coleman, *Company Museums* (Washington: American Association of Museums, 1943), pp. 117–18 (Rotunda attendance figures for 1936–41); Ford Rotunda Activities for 1940, Acc. 629, Box 3; *Ford News* 16 (Feb. 1936), 23; *Ford News* 17 (Mar. 1937), 2; 21 (July 1941), 181. Prewar Rotunda attendance by year was: 1936, 900,976; 1937, 793,059; 1938, 770,541; 1939, 708,323; 1940, 951, 558; 1941, 686,017. Prewar Rouge attendance by year was: 1929, 121,811 (record until 1936); 1934, 63,603; 1935, 91,091; 1936, 132,507; 1937, 131,437; 1938, 133,030; 1939, 163,188; 1940, 166,519; 1941, 123,266. FMC news release, Oct. 10, 1957 (in author's possession); semimonthly reports on Rotunda publicity, Acc. 447, Box 7.

26. DFP, Dec. 13, 1941; H.K. Turner to Dearborn branch dealers, Dec. 18, 1941, Acc. 509, Box 23; FMC news release, Oct. 15, 1957 (in author's possession); NYT, Nov. 11, 1962; "Fire Destroys Ford Rotunda," *Rouge News* 17 (Nov. 12, 1962), 1, 4.

27. *Ford News* 15 (Mar. 1935), 43; Walter Dorwin Teague and Richard S. Requa, "Ford Building California-Pacific-International Exposition," *Architectural Forum* 63 (Aug. 1945), 123; "President and 2 Orphans Open California Exposition," *Newsweek* 5 (June 8, 1935), 19; Lucille Mortimer, director, Research & Information Department, San Diego Chamber of Commerce, to David L. Lewis, July 31, 1962.

28. Mortimer to Lewis, Sept. 21, 1962; *Ford News* 15 (Dec. 1935), 227. The symphony orchestras presented 132 concerts, the choir fourteen recitals, before audiences totaling 560,000 people in 1935.

29. The Palace of Electricity and Varied Industries Building drew 1,640,000 guests, the Federal Building 1,588,071, and Standard Oil of California's Tower to the Sun 1,552,295. California Pacific International Exposition folder, Acc. 555, Box 2; General Sales Department to branch managers, Jan. 17, 1935, Acc. 509, Box 12; Fred L. Black to Edsel Ford, July 23, 1935, Acc. 285, Box 1631. A total of $70,000 was spent on exhibit promotion.

30. Frank Belcher (president of Exposition) to Edsel Ford, Apr. 17 and May 10, 1936; Fred L. Black to A.J. Lepine, Aug. 20, 21, and 25, 1936, Acc. 6, Box 337; *Ford News* 16 (Sept. 1936), 178; Summary of Charges in Connection with the Ford Motor Company Exhibits at San Diego, Acc. 554, Box 4; R.L. Rutherford, Accounting Department, to Fred L. Black, Sept. 15, 1936, Acc. 554, Box 1. Black told the author on May 1, 1963 that Ford saved $20,000—the cost of demolition—by giving its building to the San Diego Exposition. Fair officials asked the company to sponsor the San Francisco orchestra for a third week, the company demurring, feeling that the San Diegans were "riding a willing horse to death." Black to Lepine, Aug. 20, 1936, Acc. 6, Box 337.

31. Mortimer to Lewis, July 31 and Sept. 21, 1962, Apr. 18, 1973, Jan. 9, 1975. "Undoubtedly," notes Mrs. Mortimer, "the fact that the Bowl was not solely constructed by the Ford Motor Company was behind the Council's decision to rename the Bowl. The renaming was opposed by a number of substantial citizens." Mortimer to Lewis, Sept. 21, 1962.

32. NYT, July 21, 1935; General Sales Department to branch managers, July 30, 1935, Acc. 509, Box 12; *Ford News* 15 (Aug. 1935), 152; Report of Activities at Steel Pier, Atlantic City, Dec. 2, 1935, Acc. 450, Box 1; "Ford Exhibit Reopened on Atlantic City Pier," *Automotive Industries* 74 (Apr. 11, 1936), 548; Report of Activities at Steel Pier, Atlantic City, Oct. 6, 1936, Acc. 554, Box 1. The Atlantic City exhibit cost $126,818. Summary of Charges in Connection

with the FMC Exhibit at Steel Pier, Atlantic City, Nov. 18, 1936, Acc. 554, Box 4.

33. "National Advertisers at the Texas Centennial," *Advertising & Selling* 27 (June 4, 1936), 26; "Bluebonnet Boldness," *Time* 27 (June 8, 1936), 12; Owen P. White, "Texas Roundup," *Collier's* 97 (May 30, 1936), 21; NYT, Apr. 16, 1936; Summary of Charges in Connection with the Ford Motor Company Exhibit at Dallas, Sept. 13, 1937, Acc. 554, Box 4. Ford's 65,655 square-foot air-conditioned building was by far the largest erected for the exposition. Only General Motors occupied more space, 68,864 square feet, located in a renovated auditorium on the fairgrounds. Chrysler's building was the exposition's third largest: 54,852 square feet. Virginia Leddy Gambrell, Dallas Historical Society Museum, to David L. Lewis, Aug. 17, 1962. The Texas Centennial Exposition was held on the grounds of the State Fair of Texas.

34. Edsel Ford to Fred L. Black, Sept. 23, 1935, Acc. 6, Box 332; *Ford News* 16 (Feb. 1936), 24 and 16 (July 1936), 129. Texas fair officials, familiar with Ford's sponsorship of symphonic concerts at the San Diego fair, asked the company to finance a concert series by the Dallas Symphony Orchestra. But Ford, reasoning that the cost would outweigh the possible benefit, turned down the request. Black to Edsel Ford, Sept. 1, 1936, Acc. 6, Box 339.

35. Attendance Figures, Dallas Fair, Acc. 554, Box 1; Andrew DeShong, vice-president, Dallas Chamber of Commerce, to David L. Lewis, July 27, 1962; Joseph P. Rucker, Jr., assistant general manager, State Fair of Texas, to David L. Lewis, Aug. 13, 1962.

36. NYT, June 28, 1936; "Organizing the Cleveland Fair," *Review of Reviews* 94 (Aug. 1936), 41–43; *Ford News* 16 (Aug. 1936), 143. Among the automotive exhibitors were GM, Chrysler, Studebaker, and White. Agnes O. Hanson, Cleveland Public Library, to David L. Lewis, Aug. 3, 1962.

37. Hanson to Lewis, Aug. 3, 1962; Estimated Attendance Figures, Cleveland, n.d. [Oct. 12, 1936], Acc. 554, Box 1. Only $677 was spent on publicity. Summary of Charges in Connection with the FMC Exhibit at Cleveland, Sept. 28, 1936, Acc. 450, Box 2. Report of Activities at the Ford Exhibit, Cleveland, Oct. 21, 1936, Acc. 554, Box 1.

38. *Miami News*, Jan. 11, 14, 15, 1937; Black interview, Sept. 21, 1962; Olmstead interview, Sept. 21, 1962; Walter J. Cooper, exhibit employee, to David L. Lewis, Oct. 2, 1962; *Ford News* 17 (Feb. 1937), 25; Albin P. Dearing, exhibit manager to C.C. Cheadle, Mar. 36, 1937, Acc. 450, Box 3; Report of Activities at Ford Florida Exposition, Apr. 12, 1937, Acc. 450, Box 5; Summary of Charges in Connection with FMC Exhibit at Miami, Aug. 24, 1937, Acc. 450, Box 3.

39. Black interview, Sept. 21, 1962; *Architectural Forum* 70 (June 1939), 490; GM news releases of Mar. 7, May 19, 1940, GM Public Relations Library; "Automotive Progress on Parade at the Golden Gate Exposition," *Automotive Industries* 80 (Feb. 25, 1939), 254; "Business Shines at Golden Gate," *Business Week* (Apr. 15, 1939), 40; "Coast Fair's Plans and Postmortems," *Business Week* (Nov. 25, 1939), 32.

40. *Ford News* 19 (Feb. 1939), 29; 20 (Apr. 1940), 78; *San Francisco Chronicle*, Mar. 5, 1939; NYT, Feb. 28, 1940; Olmstead interview, Sept. 24, 1962.

41. Summary of Charges in Connection with the FMC Exhibit at San Francisco, Feb. 11, 1941, Acc. 554, Box 3; C.A. Bullwinkle, Richmond branch manager, to Fred L. Black, May 11, June 7, 1939, Acc. 554, Box 3. Total cost of Ford's San Francisco exhibit was $723,600.

42. Statistical Record, San Francisco Fair, Oct. 29, 1939, Acc. 554, Box 2; Fred L. Black to Edsel Ford, Oct. 3, 1940, Acc. 554, Box 8. Attendance figures for the fair

were not released by the fair or exhibitors themselves. But a *Business Week* report on industrial exhibits at the close of the 1939 season noted that "the top exhibitors drew around 40 percent of the general attendance." Among the best attended commercial exhibits, according to this source, were those sponsored by Ford, General Motors, General Electric Company, American Telephone & Telegraph Company, Radio Corporation of America, Westinghouse, and Du Pont. "$100,000,000 Treasure Island," *Business Week* (Oct. 14, 1939), 26. GM claimed that it played host to 5,000,000 visitors in 1939. Larry Lieurance, librarian, *San Francisco Examiner*, to David L. Lewis, Sept. 25, 1962. Because the fair ran only 126 days in 1940, as against 253 days in 1939, the Ford exhibit's average daily attendance in 1940—18,546—was markedly higher than the comparable figure for 1939—14,478.

43. Ed Tyng, *Making a World's Fair Organization, Promotion, Financing, and Problems with Particular Reference to the New York World's Fair of 1939-40* (New York: Vantage Press, 1958), pp. 36–37; NYT, Dec. 8, 1937.

44. New York Fair Exhibit Pictures Ford Role in American Life, n.d. [1939], Acc. 450, Box 1; Summary of Charges in Connection with the Ford Company Exhibit at New York, Feb. 17, 1941, Acc. 554, Box 22; "What Shows Pulled at the Fair," *Business Week* (Nov. 4, 1939), 22–28.

45. New York Fair Exhibit Pictures Ford Role in American Life, n.d. [1939], Acc. 450, Box 1; "Display," *Advertising & Selling* 32 (Feb. 1939), 22; *Architectural Forum* 70 (June 1939), 413; NYT, Jan. 6, Apr. 6, 1939. *Architectural Forum*'s opinion of the Ford exhibit was virtually unique inasmuch as almost every other publication regarded GM's Futurama as the fair's outstanding exhibit. NYT, Feb. 12, 1939; "The Pianoless Piano: Hammond Electrical Novachord Mystifies Musicians," *Newsweek* 13 (Feb. 20, 1939), 36. Henry Ford Trade School students also maintained the Ford building's equipment. Olmstead interview, Jan. 18, 1964.

46. NYT, Feb. 21, 1940; *Ford News* 20 (Apr. 1940), 78; 20 (May 1940), 99; 21 (Jan. 1941), 5 (theater attendance); FMC news release, July 30, 1940, Acc. 447, Box 1; George Pierrot to Fred L. Black, May 28, 1940, Acc. 56, Box 10; "Shows Pulled at Fair," *Business Week*, p. 27. A total of 320 members of the staff were collegians. Black, *Reminiscences*, p. 205.

47. Summary of Charges in Connection with the Ford Company Exhibit at the New York Fair, Feb. 17, 1951, Acc. 554, Box 22; Black, *Reminiscences*, p. 206; Ford Exhibit Organization Chart, Acc. 554, Box 21; Press Department Report to Fred L. Black, Oct. 31, 1939, Acc. 56, Box 5.

48. Press Department Report to Fred L. Black, June 5, 1939, Acc. 554, Box 14; Press Department Report to Black, Oct. 31, 1939, Acc. 554, Box 5; Black, *Reminiscences*, pp. 206–7; Benefits Received from Participation in the New York World's Fair, n.d. [Oct. 1939], Acc. 554, Box 3; NYT, July 21, Oct. 28, 1939; *New York Herald Tribune*, July 21, 1939.

49. Press Department Report to Fred L. Black, Oct. 31, 1939, Acc. 56, Box 5; Fred L. Black to Frank Campsall, Aug. 14, 1939, Acc. 285, Box 2367 (A.T. & T. poll and view of fair publicist).

50. "Shows Pulled at Fair," *Business Week*, p. 22. "Even blasé New Yorkers, most entertainment-conscious citizens in America, call the GM show a knock-out," reported *Sales Management* 45 (July 1, 1939), 25–26. [The show] "is by far the most popular exhibit at the World's Fair," echoed the NYT, Sept. 10, 1939. George Pierrot to H.G. McCoy, May 18, 1939, Acc. 56, Box 3; Press Department

Report to Fred L. Black, Oct. 31, 1939, Acc. 56, Box 5.

51. NYT, May 17, 1939; H.G. McCoy to George Pierrot, May 18, 1939, Acc. 56, Box 3. A 1939 survey conducted by Ross Federal Research Corporation showed that 39.4 percent of the fair's visitors rated General Motors' exhibit as the "most interesting large exhibit" at the fair, compared to 8.5 percent for second-ranked Ford and 7.6 percent for General Electric's third-ranked exhibit, which attracted attention through a spectacular lighting display and a magic show. In both 1939 and 1940, surveys conducted by Market Analysts, Inc. ranked General Motors, General Electric, and Ford in that order as the fair's "most popular exhibits." "New York World's Fair Great Success to Favored Commercial Exhibits," *Sales Management* 45 (July 1, 1939), 25; Ratings of Most Popular Exhibits, New York World's Fair 1939–40, compiled by Market Analysts, Inc., GM Public Relations Library.

52. NYT, Nov. 5 and Dec. 28, 1939; *New York Herald Tribune,* Dec. 1, 1939; *Ford News* 21 (Jan. 1941), 5; New York Fair Attendance Report, Oct. 20, 1940, Acc. 285, Box 2367. In 1939, GM informed fair officials that 13,000,000 or 50.4 percent of the exposition's 25,817,265 visitors were received at its display; Ford reported 8,181,067 visitors or 31.7 percent of the total. The Railroad Presidents' Conference (an organization composed of the heads of twenty-seven eastern railroads), American Telephone & Telegraph, and General Electric each claimed it had played host to 8,000,000 guests. Chrysler, whose exhibit featured a three-dimensional film, a "frozen forest," a talking car, and a rocketport, reported 7,000,000 visitors. In 1940, the fair issued an attendance figure of 19,115,713, but did not compile figures for individual exhibitors. General Motors claimed it had 11,000,000 visitors or 57.5 percent of the fair's total, while Ford reported its attendance at 6,967,617 or 36.4 percent. Tyng, *World's Fair,* p. 100; William Berns, New York World's Fair 1964–65 Corporation, to David L. Lewis, Aug. 14, 1962; Mark Hopkins, Jr., supervisor—publicity programs, General Electric Company, to David L. Lewis, Nov. 19, 1964; Joseph L. Knapp, of Corporate Shows and Exhibits, Chrysler Corporation, to David L. Lewis, Aug. 14, 1964. Interview with William Horton, display supervisor, A.T. & T., Aug. 26, 1964; interview with George Pierrot, Aug. 2, 1962. Ford, Pierrot insisted, was the "only exhibitor which actually counted its visitors—and counted them but once. The others didn't have sufficient capacity to handle crowds of the size they claimed, and their attendance estimates are inflated." Pierrot's convictions are borne out, at least in part, by the fact that the attendance figures claimed by all exhibitors except Ford were rounded off and labeled "estimates." Ford had an independent bonded agency count its guests every day; many other exhibitors apparently did not even count guests themselves. In any event, Ford's pavilion, as Pierrot admitted, did not dominate the fair. The "Futurama," the heart of GM's exhibit, could not accommodate the number of people who wished to view it. As many as 12,000 to 15,000 persons often queued up to see it. *Highways and Horizons The World's Fair in New York 1939–40 Where 24,000,000 People Saw the Future with General Motors* (Detroit: General Motors Corporation, n.d. [1940]), pp. 23, 92–93.

53. NYT, Apr. 6, 23, May 23, June 17, Oct. 25, 1939; Sept. 20, 1940. GM had 1,624,677 passenger car registrations in 1940, Chrysler 809,405, Ford 644,177. *Ward's Automotive 1950 Yearbook,* p. 86. "I don't know of a better place [than the fair] for young people to gain inspiration for what they have to do," declared Henry Ford typically in late 1939. NYT, Dec. 1, 1939. The Ford Company was one of the two leading commercial exhibitors (the other being the "Bell System") at the Seattle World's Fair in 1962, attracting 4,077,300 visitors to its pavilion. J. Rockey, director, Public Relations Division, Seattle World's Fair, to David L. Lewis, Dec. 12, 1962. Ford drew 14,908,983 visitors to its building at the New York World's Fair of 1964–65, at which GM was the No. 1 draw, followed by Vatican Pavilion, New York State Pavilion, Chrysler, and General Electric. *New York Herald Tribune,* Oct. 19, 1965.

Chapter 19

1. See chapter 10 for a detailed discussion of Ford's intracompany radio communications and the operation of radio station WWI and chapter 13 for comment on the old-fashioned dance orchestra. Herman S. Hettinger, *A Decade of Radio Advertising* (Chicago: University of Chicago Press, 1933), pp. 42, 80–81; Neal Midgley, *The Advertising and Business Side of Radio* (New York: Prentice-Hall, Inc., 1948), pp. 50, 67–68; "An Appraisal," *Fortune* 6 (Sept. 1932), 98. NBC solicited the Ford Company in 1930, but was turned down by Edsel Ford. Fred L. Black to M. H. Aylesworth, of NBC, Nov. 13, 1920, Acc. 285, Box 1142.

2. Hettinger, *Radio Advertising,* p. 131; *Broadcasting* 5 (Dec. 15, 1933), 13; 6 (Feb. 1, 1934), 15.

3. *New York Daily News,* June 27, 1933; *Boston Record,* July 3, 1933; *Broadcasting* 5 (July 15, 1933), 6; 5 (Sept. 15, 1933), 13; 5 (Dec. 15, 1933), 12–13; 7 (Oct. 15, 1934), 11; "Ford Dealers Carry the Flag," *Printers' Ink* 164 (Aug. 24, 1933), 36. The dealers' advertising agencies billed the company's branches which, in turn, obtained payments from dealers on a pro rata sales basis. "Ford Dealers," *Printers' Ink,* p. 36. "Lum & Abner" was not sponsored by Ford after Jan. 1, 1934. *Broadcasting* 6 (Jan. 1, 1934), 35.

4. *Tide* 7 (Dec. 1933), 12; *Broadcasting* 5 (Dec. 15, 1933), 12. Ford sponsored broadcasts by Lowell Thomas, John B. Kennedy, and D. Thomas Curtin from its Detroit and New York Expositions of Progress in late 1933.

5. General Sales Department to branch managers, Jan. 17, 1934, Feb. 15, 1934, Acc. 509, Box 11; *Ford News* 14 (Jan. 1934), 4; *Washington Star,* Jan. 22, 1934; *Current Biography,* s.v. "Waring, Fred"; "81 Melodious Madcaps," *Newsweek* 13 (June 19, 1939), 40; *Broadcasting* 6 (Feb. 15, 1934), 18.

6. *Broadcasting* 5 (Dec. 1, 1933), 16; 6 (Jan. 15, 1934), 6; 7 (Oct. 15, 1934), 11; *Tide* 7 (Dec. 1933), 12; "Ford in Biggest Hook-Up," *Printers' Ink* 166 (Feb. 8, 1934), 26.

7. "Biggest Hook-Up," *Printers' Ink,* p. 26; *Broadcasting* 7 (Oct. 15, 1934), 11; "Flivver Week: Ford Hires Bands, Soloists, Announcers," *News-Week* 4 (Oct. 6, 1934), 24. Waring's singing trio was composed of Rosemary and Priscilla Lane (sisters) and Babs Ryan; his chief novelty entertainer was frog-voiced drummer Poley McClintock. Each of the Waring musicians had one or more specialty acts, such as "crowing, hog-calling, whistling, imitating Katherine Hepburn, making queer faces, or odd sub-human noises." NYT, Aug. 29, 1937.

8. Interviews with Hay L. McClinton, Ayer executive,

and A. R. Barbier, July 12, 1962; "Biggest Hook-Up," *Printers' Ink,* p. 26; Kenneth M. Goode, *What About Radio?* (New York: Harper & Brothers, 1937), p. 192. Henry Ford regarded much of radio advertising as "insolent." DT, Dec. 26, 1937.

9. Clark-Hooper, Inc., Co-Incidental Radio Advertising Summaries for 1934, 1935, 1936 (obtained from C.E. Hooper, Inc., New York, and in possession of author). In 1934 and 1935 the Waring program was voted the "best musical program" in the *New York World-Telegram*'s radio polls; and in 1934 it was named as the "fifth favorite program" in the survey. In 1936 it was given a rating of "honorable mention" (the equivalent of second place) in the "light music" award classification of the Woman's National Radio Committee, a group dedicated to "holding sponsors, networks and entertainers in line by crusading against the objectionable and placing a premium on excellence." *Broadcasting* 8 (Feb. 15, 1935), 6; 10 (Feb. 1, 1936), 12; *Printers' Ink* 170 (Feb. 7, 1935), 81; *Literary Digest* 121 (May 2, 1936), 34. Yale students rated the Waring show as one of their three favorite programs. NYT, Jan. 20, 1935. One of Waring's CBS shows was transferred to NBC's Blue network in 1936; the NBC program lagged in popularity.

10. McClinton to Barbier, Sept. 24, 1936, Acc. 44, Box 16; McClinton and Barbier interviews, July 12, 1962; *Automotive News 1938 Almanac,* p. 48; Costs, Waring Program, and 16 Leading Advertisers 1926–36, Acc. 454, Box 1.

11. *Ford News* 17 (Feb. 1937), 29; Chandler's orchestra replaced the Ford Sunday Evening Hour during the summer of 1937. *Ford News* 17 (June 1937), 21.

12. General Sales Department to branch managers, May 10, 1937, Acc. 509, Box 17; *Ford News* 17 (June 1937), 21; Clark-Hooper, Inc., Co-Incidental Radio Advertising Summaries for 1937 and 1938 (becoming C. E. Hooper, Inc., Reports in 1938); "Car Radio Program," *Automotive Industries* 77 (Sept. 4, 1937), 300; Barbier to Ayer, Apr. 28, 1938, Acc. 149, Box 147; Advertising Cost Comparisons—1936–1945, n.d. [1945], Acc. 149, Box 106.

13. Programs Sponsored by Automobile Manufacturers, *Automotive News 1938 Almanac,* pp. 38–49; "Mickey Cochrane on the Pennant Race," *Broadcasting* 7 (Oct. 1, 1934), 15; *Automotive Industries* 71 (Aug. 18, 1934), 190. The Cochrane show cost $22,462. 1934 Advertising Costs, Oct. 15, 1934, Acc. 454, Box 1.

14. *Chicago Tribune,* Sept. 27, 1934; DN, Nov. 6, 1938 (Edsel Ford's enthusiasm for baseball); *Broadcasting* 7 (Oct. 1, 1934), 15; *Ford News* 14 (Oct. 1934), 184–86; 14 (Nov. 1934), 212–13; "Flivver Week," *News-Week* pp. 23–24. Ford dealers also sponsored thirteen-week programs over Philadelphia and Detroit stations featuring football coaches Glenn (Pop) Warner, of Temple University, and Harry Kipke, of the University of Michigan, in the fall of 1934. "Flivver Week," *News-Week,* pp. 23–24. Henry Ford attended one series game and met St. Louis Cardinals pitching stars Dizzy and Paul Dean in Greenfield Village. DT, Oct. 5, 1934.

15. FMC news release, Oct. 3, 1934, Acc. 6, Box 323; *Jasper* (Ala.) *Eagle,* Sept. 26, 1934; General Sales Department to branch managers, Sept. 18, 1936, Acc. 509, Box 14; Kenneth M. Goode and M. Zenn Kaufman, *Showmanship in Business* (New York: Harper & Brothers, 1936), p. 209; *Ford News* 16 (Nov. 1934), 212.

16. *Ford News* 15 (Oct. 1935), 186; 16 (Nov. 1936), 218; DN and NYT, Nov. 4, 1937.

17. Black, *Reminiscences,* p. 199; *Ford News* 14 (July 1934), 124.

18. General Sales Department to branch managers, Sept. 27, 1934, Acc. 572, Box 10; DFP, Oct. 8, 1934; DN, Oct. 8, 1934. The Sunday Evening Hour was broadcast over ninety-five stations in 1937–38; over seventy-six stations in 1938–39. Ford saved $52,462 in time charges as a consequence of the cutback. Analysis of 1937–38 Sunday Evening Hour, Acc. 451, Box 7. As a young man, Henry Ford heard many of the lighter songs played on the organ in his home. Sidney Olson, *Young Henry Ford: A Picture History of the First Forty Years* (Detroit: Wayne State University Press, 1963), p. 13. Iturbi was dropped after the 1938–39 season because he "could not conduct some of the music acceptably." McClintock to Barbier, Aug. 4, 1939, Acc. 44, Box 15.

19. Lists of the guest artists and conductors and their fees are in Acc. 454, Box 1 (1934–38 seasons), Acc. 45, Box 8 (1939–41 seasons), and Acc. 149, Box 102 (1941–42 season). Sunday Evening Hour cost figures can be found in Acc. 45, Box 8, and Acc. 454, Box 1.

20. DFP, Oct. 8, 1934; Ford Sunday Evening Hour (traces history of program), n.d. [1942], Acc. 44, Box 15; DFP, Feb. 27, 1942. The first concert of each season was a social event, attended by many of the Motor City's leading figures including Henry, Clara, Edsel, and Eleanor Ford. See DFP, Oct. 8, 1934, DT, Nov. 7, 1937, and "Four Hundred Fords," *Newsweek* 26 (Dec. 31, 1945), 85, for representative press comment on first broadcast of the season. Ford also mailed a seasonal average of 26,000 concert programs to persons requesting them. *Ford News* 19 (Jan. 1939), 22.

21. See Clark-Hooper, Inc., Co-Incidental Radio Advertising Summaries for 1934–38; and C. E. Hooper Reports for 1938–39 (1936 Report, Acc. 44, Box 15; 1939 Report, Acc. 451, Box 7; others in possession of author); Cooperative Analysis of Broadcasting Program Reports for 1940–42, Acc. 149, Box 21. The Sunday Evening Hour was rated a radio favorite by a sizable segment of the public on at least one occasion. Radio owners polled by *Fortune* in late 1937 ranked the hour fifth in popularity, behind only the Jack Benny, Major Bowes, and Charlie McCarthy shows and newscasts. "Radio Favorites," *Fortune* 17 (Jan. 1938), 91.

22. "Awards," *News-Week* 9 (Apr. 10, 1937), 25; *Broadcasting* 14 (Feb. 1, 1938), 74; 20 (Feb. 3, 1941), 14; NYT, Apr. 1, 1937, May 5, 1938, Apr. 20, June 27, 1939; "More Radio Awards," *Printers' Ink* 183 (June 2, 1938), 20; Barbier File, June 4, 1940, Acc. 285, Box 2378. Newspaper radio editors polled by Hearst Publications in early 1937 also rated the Sunday Evening Hour as the "Best Program of Classical Music" on the air. *Broadcasting* 12 (Feb. 15, 1937), 76.

23. Cameron, *Reminiscences,* p. 221; *Ford News* 14 (Nov. 1934), 203; "He Plays the Jew's Harp," *Printers' Ink* 169 (Dec. 27, 1934), 272–74; *A Series of Talks Given on the Ford Sunday Evening Hour by W. J. Cameron 1934–1935* (Dearborn: Ford Motor Company, 1935), p. 7. Cameron's talks of the 1934–38 seasons are in Acc. 44, Box 15; of the 1939–42 seasons in Acc. 44, Box 16.

24. Cameron, *Reminiscences,* pp. 58, 223–24; Richards, *Last Billionaire,* p. 239; Black interview, June 30, 1958; *Dearborn Press,* Apr. 27, 1939 (missed performance).

25. Thomas S. Green, Jr., "Mr. Cameron and the Ford Hour," *Public Opinion Quarterly* 3 (Oct. 1939), 669–75; Fishwick, *American Heroes,* p. 127.

26. Sward, *Legend of Henry Ford*, p. 282; Richards, *Last Billionaire*, p. 266; Harvey Pinney, "The Radio Pastor of Dearborn," *Nation* 145 (Oct. 9, 1937), 374–75; *A Series of Talks Given on the Ford Sunday Evening Hour by W. J. Cameron 1935–36* (Dearborn: Ford Motor Company, 1936), p. 129; Paul Hutchinson, "Heretics of the Air: Mr. Ford's Mr. Cameron," *Christian Century* 52 (Apr. 17, 1935), 508–10.

27. Green, "Mr. Cameron," pp. 669–75; Hutchinson, "Heretics of the Air," p. 508; "The Ford Sunday Evening Hour," *Propaganda Analysis* 1 (July 1938), 1–4.

28. NYT, Oct. 25, 1939; *Broadcasting* 17 (Nov. 1, 1939), 76; 17 (Nov. 15, 1939), 71; Edward L. Kluber, executive vice-president, CBS, to Barbier, Dec. 14, 1939, Acc. 44, Box 15.

29. Goode, *What About Radio?*, p. 109. Four of Cameron's talks were reprinted in *Vital Speeches* during the 1935–36 season, three during 1936–37, six 1937–38, three 1938–39, five 1939–40, four 1940–41, and three 1941–42; see *Readers' Guide to Periodical Literature* for the years 1935–42. Irving Settel, *A Pictorial History of Radio* (New York: Bonanza Books, 1965), p. 77. Figures on the number of talks distributed are in Acc. 44, Box 15.

30. "Farewell, Ford," *Time* 39 (Feb. 2, 1942), 53; Summary of Weekly Analysis of Symphony Mail, Nov. 23, 1941, Acc. 447, Box 1.

31. *PM* (New York), Sept. 29, 1940; Summary of Weekly Analysis of Symphony Mail, Nov. 23, 1941, Acc. 447, Box 1; Sigmund Diamond, *The Reputation of the American Businessman* (Cambridge, Mass.: Harvard University Press, 1955), p. 167 (UAW verse); William I. Nichols, publisher, *This Week Magazine*, to David L. Lewis, Nov. 22, 1965 (Parker couplet).

32. NYT, Jan. 17, 1942; "Farewell, Ford," *Time*, p. 53. Letters from Sunday Hour listeners are in Acc. 274, Box 2. "Mr. Ford's Hour," *Printers' Ink* 198 (Mar. 27, 1942), 66. William J. Cameron to William L. Stidger, Feb. 8, 1942, Acc. 44, Box 2. Bennett, *Never Called Henry*, p. 154. Among the publications which editorially mourned the cancellation of the Sunday Hour were the *Cleveland News*, Jan. 22, 1942; *Syracuse Herald-American*, Jan. 25, 1942; *Plymouth* (Mich.) *Mail*, Jan. 23, 1942, and DFP, Feb. 28, 1942. The *Free Press*'s editorial was transmitted by the United Press on Mar. 2, 1942.

33. Cost figures for the Sunday Hour are in Acc. 6, Box 354 and Acc. 45, Box 8; DFP, Feb. 27, 1942; NYT, June 3, 1945.

34. General Sales Department to branch managers, June 6, 1939, Acc. 509, Box 21; "Ford Stays on the Air with a Summer Program," *Newsweek* 13 (June 12, 1939), 46; *Ford News* 20 (June 1940), 135–42; 21 (June 1941), 144; Ford Summer Hour Soloist Schedule 1941, Acc. 45, Box 8; Ford Summer Hour Expenditures, Dec. 12, 1941, Acc. 45, Box 48; C. E. Hooper, Inc., Reports for 1939–41, Acc. 451, Box 7.

35. Ford Advertising Costs for Years 1934–42, Acc. 454, Box 1; Advertising Disbursements for Years 1935–45, Aug. 14, 1946, Acc. 134, Box 17. Ford paid $10,595,269 to radio networks during 1934–42; GM $4,826,030, Chrysler $4,675,835. "Network Expenditure of Individual Passenger Car Advertisers, '34–'38," *Automotive News 1938 Almanac*, p. 43; "Network Expenditure of Individual Passenger Car Advertisers, '37–'47," *Automotive News 1948 Almanac*, p. 96. Chrysler's "Major Bowes Amateur Hour" was commonly regarded as the most successful pre-World War II radio program. Presentation to Lincoln-Mercury dealers by William B. Lewis, K & E vice-president and radio director, n.d. [Dec. 1948], Acc. 149, Box 51.

Chapter 20

1. " 'These Thirty Years' Has Première Showing," *Automotive Industries* 69 (Dec. 16, 1933), 743; *Ford News* 13 (Dec. 1933), 229; *Philadelphia Record*, Dec. 11, 1933; *New York Post*, Dec. 14, 1933; General Sales Department to A.R. Barbier, Oct. 4, 1934. Acc. 454, Box 4; What They Say About "These Thirty Years" (booklet), Acc. 454, Box 6.

2. FMC news release, Sept. 4, 1934, Acc. 545, Box 374; Milton Wright, *Public Relations for Business* (New York: Whittlesey House, 1939), p. 116 (quoting *Film Daily*); "World's Fair Reveals New Strength of Films As Advertising Media," *Sales Management* 35 (Aug. 15, 1934), 146–47; "Ford Rhapsody," *Printers' Ink* 168 (Aug. 9, 1934), 53–54; "How Ford Uses Films on a Year Around Basis," *Sales Management* 37 (Oct. 10, 1935), 400.

3. "Ford Films," *Sales Management*, p. 400; Paul Sklar and S.H. Walker, *Business Finds Its Voice: Management's Effort to Sell the Business Idea to the Public* (New York: Harper & Brothers, 1938), p. 33; General Sales Department to branch managers, Feb. 12, 1937, Acc. 509, Box 16; Jan. 1, 1939, Acc. 509, Box 21.

4. Ford Films, n.d. [1938], Acc. 149, Box 97; FMC news release, July 18, 1940, Acc. 450, Box 5; Mass Selling Motion Picture Activity Report, Jan. 15, 1941, Acc. 149, Box 97; Film Library Distribution Report 1962, GM Public Relations Library.

5. Ford Advertising Costs for Years 1934–42, Acc. 454, Box 1; GM Public Relations Planning Committee Minutes, Apr. 23, 1946, Exhibit H, GM Public Relations Library.

6. General Sales Department to branch managers, Sept. 5, 1933; "Ford Dealers Carry the Flag," *Printers' Ink* 164 (Aug. 1933), 36–37; *Automotive Trade Journal* 38 (Sept. 1933), 30–31; DFP, Feb. 25 and Apr. 28, 1934; *Ford News* 14 (Mar. 1934), 46; DN, Sept. 30, 1934. Ayer's news releases on V-8's racing victories are in Acc. 545, Box 372. The Pikes Peak Hill Climb was not held in 1935; Ford won second place in the championship or open class in 1936. Official Souvenir Program, Pikes Peak Auto Hill Climb July 4, 1964. During the late 1930s Henry Ford told A.R. Barbier that "the way to beat Chevy is to compete with it in hill climbing contests," and instructed his advertising manager to have branch managers issue challenges. Barbier asked the San Francisco, Denver, and Pittsburgh managers to arrange for competitive climbs, but they refused to do so. "They knew by this time," said Barbier, "that while the V-8 might have more horsepower, the Chevy had more torque and could beat the V-8 in climbing." Barbier interview, July 17, 1962.

7. The agreement between Miller-Tucker and Ayer, acting in behalf of Ford dealers, was signed on Feb. 2, 1935. All of the Miller-Tucker-Ford correspondence is in Acc. 454, Box 9.

8. Charles T. Pearson, *The Indomitable Tin Goose: The True Story of Preston Tucker and His Car* (New York: Abelard-Schuman, 1960), pp. 45–46; NYT, May 5, 1935. Among Ford's drivers were Pete De Paolo, winner of the Indianapolis race in 1925 and national racing champion in 1925 and 1927; Dave

Evans, who was credited with more speed and endurance records than any other driver; and Ted Horn, who had broken several eastern track records in 1934 and was to become national racing champion from 1946 through 1948. Ayer news release, May 13, 1935, Acc. 545, Box 372.

9. "Kelly Petrillo Wins Indianapolis Race," *Motor* 63 (June 1935), 81–82; "Ford Engines in New Millers," *Motor* 63 (June 1935), 88, 90; DFP, May 31, 1935.

10. Accounting Department to Auditing Department, June 14, July 2, Sept. 3, 1935; A. R. Barbier to George Crimmins, Sales Department, Apr. 4, June 24, 1935; Status of Dealer Radio Account & Expenditures 1935, Jan. 22, 1936, Acc. 454, Box 4; Barbier interview, July 12, 1962.

11. Leo Levine, *Ford: The Dust and the Glory* (New York: The Macmillan Company, 1968), pp. 167–68. FMC news release, June 11, 1962 (in possession of author); *Atlanta Journal*, June 12, 1962; *Washington Daily News*, May 31, 1963; "The Day the Fords Won at Indy," *Ford Times* 58 (Aug. 1965), 12–15; "Le Mans Adds Fuel to Ford's Future," *Business Week* (June 25, 1966), 34–36; "Ford Pulls Off the Track," *Business Week* (Nov. 28, 1970), 22.

12. J. S. Moffat, of Graves & Moffat, Long Beach, Calif. dealer, to General Sales Department, Nov. 19, 1937; J. R. Davis, General Sales Department, to Moffat, Dec. 14, 1937, Acc. 450, Box 4; *Ford News* 18 (Feb. 1938), 46; 21 (Mar. 1941), 65; General Sales Department to branch managers, Jan. 20, 1939; McCann-Erickson, Inc. news releases, photographs, and advertising proofs for all years are in Acc. 450, Box 4, and Acc. 477, Boxes 3, 6.

13. A complete set of the *Ford News* is in the reference room of the Ford Archives. William A. Simonds to David L. Lewis, July 16, 1962. General Sales Department to branch managers, Aug. 18, 1937, July 15, 1938, Acc. 509, Box 19; Report by W. A. Scotten to W. A. Simonds, Aug. 16, 1939, Acc. 285, Box 2287; Dearborn Branch to dealers, Mar. 18 and July 31, 1941, Acc. 509, Box 23; Feb. 16, 1942, Acc. 509, Box 24.

14. Pierrot interview, Aug. 8, 1962; interview with James W. McCandless, Ayer publicist, July 11, 1962; Black interview, Sept. 21, 1962; DT, Nov. 12, 1939, Mar. 11, 1940; *Ford News* 20 (Apr. 1940), 94. The traffic safety advertising campaign was awarded a prize in *Advertising & Selling*'s annual advertising awards competition in 1938–39. "Annual Advertising Awards 1938," *Advertising & Selling* 32 (Feb. 15, 1939); "Annual Advertising Awards 1939," *Advertising & Selling* 33 (Feb. 15, 1940).

15. Pierrot interview, Aug. 8, 1962; Ford Good Drivers League (brochure), Acc. 450, Box 4; Ford Good Drivers League Costs, 1940, Apr. 10, 1940, Acc. 45, Box 8; NYT, Aug. 27, 1940, Aug. 26, 1941; DFP and DN, Aug. 26, 1941; A. R. Barbier to Accounting Department, Dec. 10, 1940, Acc. 149, Box 147.

16. Newspaper and magazine publicity on the league is in Clipbook 121; Ayer's and McCann's news releases, Acc. 450, Box 4. *Ford News* 20 (Nov. 1940), 254; 20 (Oct. 1941), 265; NYT, Sept. 2, 1941. Among the periodicals which ran articles on the league in 1941 were *Life, Scholastic, Boy's Life, American Legion Magazine, Public Safety,* and *Safety Education.* McCann-Erickson Report, Nov. 6, 1941, Acc. 454, Box 7.

17. Ford Good Drivers League Report, Nov. 7, 1941, Acc. 454, Box 7; FMC Advertising Appropriations—1942 Model Year, Oct. 17, 1942, Acc. 149, Box 102 (scheduled budget).

18. DFP, Jan. 4, 1942; NYT, Mar. 8, 1942; M. L. Darlington, Jr., managing director, Auto Industries Highway Safety Committee, Inc., to David L. Lewis, Sept. 25, 1962; Paul Lehman, United States Junior Chamber of Commerce, Tulsa, Okla., to David L. Lewis, Oct. 3, 1962; United States Junior Chamber of Commerce to David L. Lewis, Apr. 21, 1975. The league never had the wholehearted support of dealers; some worked at it, others did not. Interview with B. R. Donaldson, Ford sales/advertising executive, Oct. 7, 1962.

19. Interview with Roger M. Keyes, July 12, 1962; DT, May 13, 1940; "Chance for Farm Boys," *Printers' Ink* 191 (May 17, 1940), 26; "Henry Ford Lends Support to Farm Youth Foundation," *Automotive Industries* 82 (June 1, 1940), 531.

20. Ayer's monthly reports to the Ford Company for Aug. 2, 1936 to Jan. 16, 1938 are in Acc. 545, Box 368; news releases for 1938–41 are in Acc. 447, Boxes 1–8, Acc. 545, Boxes 370 and 372, Acc. 450, Boxes 2–3, 5; and Acc. 6, Box 323. Ayer's news releases for Latin American countries are in Acc. 450, Box 5. McCann-Erickson handled labor publicity starting in April 1941. Harry Bennett to all departments, Apr. 7, 1941, Acc. 285, Box 2495.

21. H. K. McCann to A. R. Barbier, Nov. 3, 1939; Reports of D. Thomas Curtin to Barbier [with copies to Bennett], Dec. 6, 1939 to July 7, 1941, Acc. 447, Box 7. The notorious Adonis was credited by the Kefauver Crime Commission with control of a company which received a car-hauling contract from Ford's Edgewater, N.J. plant. Nevins and Hill, *Decline and Rebirth,* pp. 238–39.

22. McCann-Erickson's news stories and weekly reports to Barbier are in Acc. 285, Box 2341. Ayer's payment for publicity services averaged $65,000 annually between 1934–39. McCann-Erickson received $104,000 in 1940 and $112,000 in 1941, of which about half was earmarked for the "Curtin arrangement." A budget of $110,000 was approved in the fall of 1941 for press relations activities in 1942. FMC Expenditures for Car Year [all years], Acc. 149, Box 119; E.D. Bottom, advertising manager, to D.C. Hight, vice-president, McCann-Erickson, and to M.F. Mahoney, vice-president, Maxon, Dec. 30, 1941, Acc. 149, Box 102; Barbier to H. C. Doss, Nov. 7, 1941, Acc. 149, Box 102; Publicity and Public Relations Activity Report by C.C. Cheadle [dated Jan. 30, 1942], Acc. 451, Box 8. Cheadle died on Oct. 6, 1942. DN, Oct. 6, 1942. Curtin was released effective Jan. 1, 1942. Hight to Bottom, Dec. 18, 1941, Acc. 149, Box 102. By late 1941 Maxon was handling the truck, by-products, and parts, service, and accessories accounts, as well as Lincoln and Mercury.

23. Black, *Reminiscences,* p. 191; Edsel Ford to George H. Thornley, Ayer president, Feb. 21, 1933, Acc. 572, Box 10 (institutional advertisements, copies of which are in Acc. 44, Box 13); "Ford's Advertising Plans," *Printers' Ink* 165 (Dec. 14, 1933), 17; "Million Ford Prospects to Get Mailings," *Advertising Age* 4 (Nov. 18, 1933), 17; "Ford Jumps Gun in Race to Regain Lost Leadership," *Advertising & Selling* 22 (Dec. 21, 1933), 50. The late 1933 campaign also included a press preview of new models, a mammoth exhibit in New York, and multiple showings of "These Thirty Years."

24. "Ford Dealers Carry Flag," *Printers' Ink,* pp. 35–38; "Dealers' Own?," *Tide* 7 (Sept. 1, 1933), 42–43; "Highlights of the Ford Against-the-Field Fight," *Advertising & Selling* 21 (Sept. 14, 1933), 48; General Sales Department to branch managers, Sept. 5, Dec. 1 and Dec. 15, 1933, Acc. 509, Box 10; Barbier interview, Jan. 17, 1964; "Bridge Between Maker

and Buyer,'' *Printers' Ink* 283 (June 14, 1963), 80 (McCann-Erickson history). Lawrence M. Hughes, ''Custom Built Local Advertising Helps Ford Double Sales,'' *Sales Management* 35 (Oct. 1, 1934), 298; H. K. McCann to A. R. Barbier, Nov. 3, 1939, Acc. 149, Box 147; ''Ford Account Shifts,'' *Business Week* (Oct. 19, 1940), 16.

25. General Sales Department to branch managers, Oct. 14, 1935, Acc. 509, Box 12; R. C. Russell, Auditing Department to A. R. Barbier, Mar. 23, 1937, and Barbier to R. C. Siple, General Sales Department, Jan. 5, 1938, Acc. 149, Box 147. For the Lincoln Zephyr, the per unit charge levied against dealers was $10.00. General Sales Department to branch managers, Jan. 10, 1936, Acc. 509, Box 14.

26. Analysis of Advertising Expense 1934–39, n.d. [1939], Acc. 454, Box 1; Advertising and Sales Promotion Expense 1940, Dec. 30, 1940, and Advertising and Sales Promotion Expense, Dec. 30, 1941, Acc. 149, Box 119; ''Early Failure to Stress Ads Nearly Engulfed Ford, Recalls Roy Barbier,'' *Advertising Age* 29 (Nov. 3, 1958), 104; Cameron, *Reminiscences*, p. 232; ''Do's and Don'ts'' for Ford, Mercury, Lincoln and Lincoln Zephyr Advertising, Aug. 4, 1939, Acc. 149, Box 102; Standards and Information for the Guidance of the Advertising Agencies of the Ford Motor Company in Writing Copy and Preparing Art Work, Mar. 24, 1941, Acc. 149, Box 102; ''Annual Advertising Awards 1938,'' *Advertising & Selling*, p. 76; ''Annual Advertising Awards, 1939,'' *Advertising & Selling*, pp. 34–35.

27. Ralph Merle Hower, *The History of an Advertising Agency: N.W. Ayer & Son at Work, 1869–1949* (Cambridge, Mass.: Harvard University Press, 1949), pp. 178, 182; Barbier interview, Aug. 5, 1963. Ayer had serious internal dissension between 1933–36. A change of management in 1936 alleviated the situation, but the agency continued to lose business, suspending dividends between 1938 and 1942. Hower, *Advertising Agency*, pp. 156–57, 181.

28. Hower, *Advertising Agency*, pp. 181–82; NYT, Oct. 12, 1940; ''Ford Account Shifts,'' *Business Week*, p. 16; interview with Hay L. McClinton, July 12, 1962; Barbier interviews, July 17, 1962 and Jan. 17, 1964.

29. NYT, Oct. 17, 1940; ''Ford Account Shifts,'' *Business Week*, p. 16; National and Branch Advertising, Oct. 13, 1941, Acc. 149, Box 119. Maxon's first Ford assignment was a minor direct mailing in 1935. *Dearborn Press*, Aug. 15, 1940.

30. ''Detroit Fireball,'' *Time* 36 (Aug. 12, 1940), 59–60; DT, May 12, 1940; Black interview, Sept. 21, 1962; Barbier interview, July 17, 1962; W. H. Pessefall, of Advertising Department, to Barbier, Aug. 23, 1940, Acc. 149, Box 147; DFP, Sept. 3, 1941; *Port Huron* (Mich.) *Times-Herald*, Sept. 4, 1941; ''Auto Advertising,'' *Business Week* (Dec. 20, 1941), 37. Maxon billed $9,000,000 worth of advertising in 1939, ''enough to rank [it] in the first flight of U.S. agencies.'' ''Fireball,'' *Time*, p. 59. The Wismers were divorced in July 1959; and Mrs. Wismer married ex-U.S. Senator Charles E. Potter in 1960. NYT, May 8, 1960. Wismer and Bennett were close and spent a lot of time together. Black interview, Sept. 21, 1962, and interview with William D. Laurie, Maxon executive, Aug. 20, 1963. ''Bennett was Wismer's benevolent protector,'' added Laurie.

31. Barbier was told of the exchange between Edsel and Henry Ford by William J. Cameron. Barbier interview, July 12, 1962; Black, *Reminiscences*, p. 130. GM introduced a nationwide advertising campaign on dealer servicing in January 1942; and launched an institutional campaign on the company's war work in April 1942. P. H. Erbes, Jr., *Printers' Ink* 198 (Jan.

16, 1942), 15–16; Harvard Business School Case Study of General Motors Corporation Institutional Advertising, 1957, pp. 18–19.

32. Lists of the nation's leading advertisers from 1934–41, furnished to Barbier by members of his staff, are in Acc. 454, Box 1. During this period *Advertising Age* published annual lists of the expenditures of the 100 largest national advertisers. Edsel Ford was a strong believer in advertising, and helped to maintain advertising budgets. ''Recalls Barbier,'' *Advertising Age*, p. 104.

33. At the end of 1941, Ford's assets were $23,000,000 less than they had been in 1927. During this same period, GM's assets increased 60 percent, and those of Chrysler more than doubled. ''Ford Heritage,'' *Fortune* 29 (June 1944), 249. *New York Times Index, Readers' Guide to Periodical Literature*, and *Industrial Arts Index* for the pertinent years; author's analysis of Ford Archives clipbooks.

34. What the Public Thinks of Big Business, Curtis Publishing Company, Division of Commercial Research, May 1937, Acc. 454, Box 9; The Link Audit: a Review and Evaluation, FMC Research Department, Oct. 11, 1953, Acc. 465, Box 1; A Review of the First Year of ''Watch the World Go By'' [June 1943] (citing Aug. 1941 survey), Acc. 149, Box 94; Nevins and Hill, *Decline and Rebirth*, p. 131.

Chapter 21

1. NYT, Dec. 12, 1941. At the start of the war the aircraft industry had $6,000,000,000 worth of defense orders, the automobile industry $5,000,000,000, of which nearly half was related to aircraft production. The largest defense contractors were Bethlehem Steel, GM, and Curtiss-Wright, respectively. ''Boom, Shortages, Taxes, War,'' *Time* 39 (Jan. 5, 1942), 58–59.

2. ''Man of the Year,'' *Time* 39 (Jan. 5, 1942), 14; ''Boom,'' *Time*, pp. 58–59; *Chicago Daily News*, Feb. 18, 1942; *Greenwood* (S.C.) *Index-Journal*, Mar. 24, 1942; *San Francisco News*, Dec. 26, 1941; DFP, Jan. 17, 1942; *Albany* (N.Y.) *Knickerbocker*, May 1, 1942; *Madison* (Wis.) *State Journal*, Feb. 6, 1942; *Iron Age*, 149 (Jan. 14, 1942), 218; *Port Huron* (Mich.) *Times-Herald*, Dec. 8, 1941. The DT, Feb. 13, 1942 commended Ford on his soybean fiber research and predicted that many Americans would be wearing soybean suits, while *Newsweek* 19 (Apr. 27, 1942), 50, reported that Ford was reputedly working on a tire containing only one-sixteenth of the amount of rubber ordinarily used.

3. *San Francisco News*, Dec. 26, 1941; ''Battle of Detroit,'' *Time* 39 (Mar. 23, 1942), 10–14; see Clipbook 124 for news stories and editorials on Ford's pre-World War II defense research and on his refusal to make Rolls-Royce engines for Britain.

4. See Clipbook 124 for news stories and editorials on the Willow Run plant in early 1942. *The Army Air Forces in World War II*, eds. Wesley Frank Craven and James Lee Cate, 6 vols. (Chicago: University of Chicago Press, 1948–58), *Men and Planes*, 6: 329; *Lansing* (Mich.) *State Journal*, Jan. 13, 1942; *Business Week* (Feb. 20, 1942), 17; DFP, Feb. 1, 1942.

5. ''Sorensen of the Rouge: Besides Making Engines, Tanks, and Guns, He Is Running the Biggest Bomber Factory in the World,'' *Fortune* 25 (Apr. 1942), 79; Simonds, *Henry Ford*, 332. Chrysler's plant had 6,430,000 square feet of floor space. *Army Air For-*

ces, p. 315. The biggest aircraft factory under one roof now is Lockheed–Georgia's Marietta, Ga. plant, which has 3,345,754 square feet of floor space. Chess Abernathy to David L. Lewis, Jan. 16, 1965.

6. Called the B-24 by the United States Air Force, it was known as the Liberator in Britain's Royal Air Force. Larger than the B-17, the plane had a wing spread of 110 feet, a speed of 300 miles per hour, a cruising range of 2,850 miles, and a bomb capacity of 8,800 pounds. It carried a ten-man crew. *Jane's All the World's Aircraft 1942*, comp. and ed. Leonard Bridgman (London: S. Low, Marston & Co., 1943), p. 161c. *Army Air Forces*, pp. 206–8. "Sorensen," *Fortune*, p. 79.

7. Nevins and Hill, *Decline and Rebirth*, pp. 211, 214; Special Committee Investigating the National Defense Program, Aircraft Report, July 10, 1943, Report 10, Part 10, 78th Congress, 1st session.

8. See Clipbook 124 for early 1942 news stories and editorials on Willow Run. *Boston American*, May 18, 1942; *New York Sun*, Apr. 10, 1942; *San Francisco News*, Mar. 26, 1942 (Scripps-Howard); *Greenwood (S.C.) Index-Journal*, Mar. 24, 1942; *Erie (Pa.) Times*, Mar. 24, 1942; *Baltimore Sun*, May 3, 1942; *New York World-Telegram*, Feb. 4, 1942 (quoting Pegler); *DFP*, Feb. 1, 1942; *Connellsville (Pa.) Courier*, Mar. 24, 1942.

9. DFP, DT, and DN, Apr. 14, 1942.

10. *Oxnard (Calif.) Press-Courier*, Apr. 7, 1942; *Boston Traveler*, Feb. 13, 1942; *St. Louis Post-Dispatch*, Feb. 6, 1942; *New York World-Telegram*, Feb. 24, 1942. The President expressed regret that it was impossible to get airplanes to Bataan. *Glens Falls (N.Y.) Post-Star*, Feb. 24, 1942.

11. See Clipbook 124 for news stories and editorials on Willow Run's projected production. *Tupelo (Miss.) Journal*, Mar. 19, 1942; *Portland (Maine) Press-Herald*, Apr. 10, 1942; *New York World-Telegram*, Feb. 13, 1942; *Shreveport (La.) Journal*, Mar. 30, 1942; *Plattsburgh (N.Y.) Republican*, Feb. 3, 1942; *Oklahoma City Oklahoman*, Jan. 1, 1942; *Madison (Wis.) State Journal*, Feb. 6, 1942; *New York Herald Tribune*, Apr. 9, 1942; *Champaign-Urbana (Ill.) Courier*, Mar. 5, 1942; *New York World-Telegram*, Feb. 13, 1942 (Scripps-Howard).

12. DFP, DN, *New York Mirror*, and DT, May 16, 1942; *Fayetteville (N.C.) Observer*, May 21, 1942; *Salt Lake City Tribune*, May 20, 1942; *St. Louis Post-Dispatch*, May 17, 1942; DFP, May 18, 1942. See Clipbook 124 for articles on Willow Run's alleged production miracle. General Surles, a 1911 graduate of the United States Military Academy, served with cavalry units until 1927. He became an intelligence officer in 1927, a public relations officer in 1935. *Who's Who in America* 23rd ed., s.v. "Surles, Alexander D."

13. NYT, Aug. 14, 1942; DFP, Aug. 16, 1942; *Ann Arbor (Mich.) News*, May 21, 1942; "Morale By Ford," *Newsweek* 19 (June 1, 1942), 12. General Surles's announcement did stir the hopes of America's allies. It answered inquiries such as that of a Yugoslav guerilla, made to a press correspondent in the mountain hideout of General Mihailovich: "When will Ford start turning out bombers?" In Egypt, according to NBC's Cairo correspondent, "everyone was talking about the big bomber plant 'where pots and pans were pushed in at one end, and big warbirds came out at the other.'" "Morale By Ford," *Newsweek*, p. 12; Simonds, *Henry Ford*, p. 329.

14. "The '43 Ford," *Fortune* 27 (Feb. 1943), 113; "Tom Girdler's Truce," *Fortune* 26 (Sept. 1942), 162; Christy Borth, *Masters of Mass Production* (Indianapolis: Bobbs-Merrill Company, 1945), p. 277;

Louisville Courier-Journal, Feb. 17, 1943; Sorensen, *Forty Years*, p. 286; Bennett, *Never Called Henry*, p. 155; *Jane's All the World's Aircraft 1945*, comp. and ed., Leonard Bridgman (London: S. Low, Marston & Co., 1946), p. 257c.

15. *Columbus (Ohio) Dispatch*, May 21, 1942 (Associated Press story); *Savannah News*, May 22, 1942 (International News Service story). The Savannah newspaper quoted Sorensen as saying, "This fellow Hitler is going to get such a volume of stuff poured over there that he will wonder where it came from." Raymond Moley, "Ford Does It Again," *Newsweek* 19 (May 25, 1942), 72; NYT, May 22, 24, 1942; "Dutch vs. Charlie," *Time* 39 (June 1, 1942), 68. See Clipbook 124 for scores of news stories on journalists' tours of Willow Run and Sorensen's statement. A total of 133,734 military aircraft were built in 1942–43. *Army Air Forces*, p. 350.

16. DN, May 23, 1942. News stories and editorials on the May 23 Simonds-led tour are quoted in the Ford News Departmental Newsletter, June 1, 1942, Acc. 44, Box 15; and press reports on Willow Run tours may be found in Clipbook 124, DFP, May 13, 1942 (Prado); DT, July 25, 1942 (Randolph Churchill); DT, May 29, 1942 (Birkett); NYT, Aug. 15, 1942 (Birkett); DFP, June 7, 1942 (Lyttelton); Borth, *Masters of Mass Production*, p. 277 (Lyttelton); Robert Stewart, "'Will It Run?' An Enigma From the Start, Henry Ford's Gargantua Has Puzzled Laymen and Experts Alike," *Flying* 32 (May 1943), 22.

17. DFP, June 13, 1942. Hannagan, sometimes referred to as "the prince of press agents," was no stranger to the Ford organization. He had been a friend of Sorensen's for many years, and the two were frequent companions in Miami, Sorensen's winter home. In 1934, Hannagan earned both Sorensen's and Henry Ford's gratitude by arranging for Harold Gray, the creator of "Little Orphan Annie," Ford's favorite comic strip, to have lunch with the auto king (a meeting which never materialized). He also had met Henry Ford at least once and Edsel Ford on several occasions at the Indianapolis Speedway, a Hannagan account. Steve Hannagan to Charles E. Sorensen, June 6, 1934, Acc. 285, Box 1611; Bennett, *Never Called Henry*, p. 155. Harold Gray to David L. Lewis, Mar. 8, 1965.

18. Al Bloemker, *500 Miles To Go: The Story of the Indianapolis Speedway* (New York: Coward-McCann, 1961), p. 1. Steve Hannagan to Joe Copps and John Thompson, June 26, 1942, Acc. 6, Box 376. Hannagan had publicized Gene Tunney as "the prize fighter who reads Shakespeare" and had helped to change the image of financier Samuel Insull (who was tried on charges of fraud and embezzlement in 1934–35) from that of a reprehensive swindler and fugitive to that of a "gentle misunderstood old man persecuted for the sins of his generation." He had successfully promoted Miami Beach, Sun Valley, and Puerto Rico as resort areas and had handled press relations for several large industrial firms, notably the Coca-Cola Company and the Union Pacific Railroad Company. "Prince of Press Agents," *Collier's* 120 (Nov. 22, 1947), 5; "Public Not Damned," *Fortune* 19 (Mar. 1939), 86; "Steve Hannagan," *Scribner's Magazine* 103 (May 1938), 9–13.

19. DFP, June 15, 1942 (quoting columnist Malcolm W. Bingay) and June 13, 1942 (Rockefeller); William L. Stidger to William J. Cameron, Aug. 4, 1942, Acc. 44, Box 2. "I suppose the next thing I will see," wrote Stidger to Cameron, "will be a picture of you, Clay Doss [the company's general sales manager], and Ben [Donaldson, a member of Doss's staff] all dressed up in Johnny Weissmuller or Superman or Tarzan suits, swinging from jungle ropes and landing in the arms of

Dorothy Lamour on some South Sea Island with a Ford car in the distance waiting to carry you to security and safety."

20. Steve Hannagan to Joe Copps and John Thompson, June 26, 1942, Acc. 6, Box 376; Edsel Ford to all department heads, July 2, 1942, Acc. 285, Box 2495; André Fontaine, "The Paper That Nobody Sees," *Nation's Business* 36 (Oct. 1948), 55–56; John W. Thompson, *Reminiscences,* pp. 5–6, 10; Steve Hannagan to Ford executives, July 7, 1942, Acc. 6, Box 376. See Ford News Bureau reports for last half of 1942, Acc. 285, Box 2351. Copps had worked with Hannagan since 1924, principally on the Miami Beach and Indianapolis Speedway accounts, Bloemker, *500 Miles,* p. 186.

21. GM news release, June 1, 1942, GM Public Relations Library; A Review of the First Year of "Watch the World Go By," submitted to FMC by Maxon, Inc., n.d. [June 1943], Acc. 149, Box 44.

22. DT, June 28, 1942; DN, July 1, 1942; C.R. Allen, Purchasing Department, to L.C. Disser, Purchasing Department, July 8, 1942, Acc. 454, Box 1; NYT, June 27, 1942 (Maxon reinstated); correspondence between Maxon, Inc. and Godwin and Porter is in Acc. 149, Box 103; Donaldson interview, Sept. 10, 1962; "Ford Going on Air," *Business Week* (July 4, 1942), 69; "Model T Newscaster," *Newsweek* 28 (Aug. 16, 1942), 86; "Godwin to Broadcast for National Board," *Eastern Underwriter* 46 (June 22, 1945), 18. One of the print advertisements appears in *Saturday Evening Post* 215 (Nov. 14, 1942), 52–53.

23. DN, Feb. 1, 1942; DFP, Mar. 14 and June 24, 1942; DT, Apr. 26, 1942 (all dealing with transportation problems); "Ford Bucks FPHA Housing Development in Backyard of His Willow Run Plant," *Engineering News* 129 (July 9, 1942), 58; "What Housing for Willow Run," *Architectural Record* 92 (Sept. 1942), 51; DN, Feb. 16, 1943. Henry Ford was opposed to housing development near Willow Run, saying it was "unnecessary, wasteful, and extravagant." "Ford Bucks Housing," *Engineering News,* p. 58.

24. Kindelberger had been publicly critical of the auto industry's plane making for months. "Dutch vs. Charlie," *Time,* p. 67; DFP, Aug. 14, 1942; NYT, Aug. 14, 1942. Kindelberger's accusation that Hannagan had imported a B-24 for the press's benefit was half-correct; the plane had been brought in for photographic reasons, but not by Hannagan, who was not working for Ford at that time.

25. "The March of Time on the Air," Aug. 13, 1942, script furnished the author by Andrew Heiskell, chairman, Time, Inc., Nov. 5, 1962; "Detroit Is Dynamite," *Life* 13 (Aug. 17, 1942), 20–23. Only one newspaper, Ford's longtime nemesis, the *Louisville Courier-Journal,* Aug. 17, 1942, commented on the "March of Time" broadcast, if clipbooks in the Ford Archives may be used as a yardstick. See Clipbook 125 for articles repeating *Life's* charges; representative articles are those in *Eastport* (Maine) *Sentinel,* Sept. 2, 1942, and *New Kensington* (Pa.) *Dispatch,* Sept. 11, 1942.

26. DFP, Aug. 17, 1942; DN, Aug. 30, 1942; DT, Aug. 19, 1942.

27. See Clipbook 125 for news stories and editorials reflecting press's confusion over Willow Run in August 1942 (typical stories in *Battle Creek* (Mich.) *Inquirer-News,* Aug. 30, 1942; NYT, Aug. 29, 1942; "Aviation Notes," *Newsweek* 20 (Sept. 7, 1942), 67. GM, taking heed of Ford's unfavorable publicity, did not publicize the first "flyaway" plane produced by its Allison Division in September 1942. Public Relations Policy Group Presentation, Oct. 20, 1942, GM Public Relations Library.

28. The new approach highway to Willow Run was the first of three links in the Detroit-Willow Run roadway system. At the dedication ceremony Edsel Ford, in paying tribute to Willow Run's workers, acknowledged that "premature publicity has led the public to expect too much ahead of time." DN, Sept. 12, 1942. See Clipbook 126 for news stories on the President's visit to Willow Run. DT, Oct. 1, 1942; NYT, Oct. 2, 1942; "The Story of a Trip," *Time* 40 (Oct. 12, 1942), 16; "President's Hush-Hush Tour Brings Repercussions," *Newsweek* 20 (Oct. 12, 1942), 45; Sorensen, *Forty Years,* pp. 296–97. An unidentified article on page 95 of Clipbook 126 reports on Henry Ford having slipped away from the welcoming group. Ford took special pride in showing the Roosevelts Willow Run's Martha-Mary Chapel, named in honor of the mothers of Clara and Henry Ford, respectively. DN, Oct. 2, 1942; Simonds, *Henry Ford,* p. 334. The Roosevelts and Henry and Edsel Ford sipped orangeade aboard the presidential train following the visit. DT, Oct. 1, 1942.

29. NYT, Oct. 2, 1942; *Louisville Courier-Journal*, Feb. 17, 1943; Oswald Garrison Villard, *The Disappearing Daily: Chapters in American Newspaper Evolution* (New York: Alfred A. Knopf, 1944), p. 43. The President could offer no explanation as to why the Office of Censorship would not allow the transmission of his remarks to Great Britain, and added that he thought everyone knew what he knew about the plant's production problems. DN, Oct. 6, 1942.

30. Nevins and Hill, *Decline and Rebirth,* p. 216; *Jane's Aircraft,* 1946 ed., p. 257c; Lowell Julliard Carr and James Edson Stermer, *Willow Run A Study of Industrialization and Cultural Inadequacy* (New York: Harper, 1952), p. 4; DFP, Apr. 7, 1943; NYT, Nov. 5, 1942; DT, Dec. 4, 1942; "Willow Runs," *Newsweek* 20 (Dec. 14, 1942), 88; *New York Sun,* Nov. 4, 1942; see Clipbooks 125–26 for press comment on Willow Run during late November and December, 1942.

31. NYT, Jan. 31, 1943; "The '43 Ford," *Fortune* 27 (Feb. 1943), 209; DN, Feb. 14, 1943; "What's with Willow Run?," *Time* 40 (Feb. 8, 1943), 19; "Output and Lag," *Newsweek* 21 (Feb. 15, 1943), 60; "Production with Apologies," *Time* 41 (Feb. 22, 1943), 19. Willow Run's rate of absenteeism was reported at 17 percent. DN, Mar. 8, 1944. "Willow Run Production Up to Schedule But Not Up to Capacity," *Automotive and Aviation Industries,* 88 (Mar. 1, 1943), 39. An average of 500 design changes were made daily in the B-24. DT, Dec. 4, 1942. The Liberator had 1,250,000 parts including 400,000 rivets. DN, Aug. 27, 1944.

32. See Clipbook 127 for stories and photographs of Willow Run's operations. DN, Feb. 14, 16, 1943; *Newsweek* 21 (Feb. 22, 1943), 60; DFP, Feb. 17, 1943; *Louisville Courier-Journal,* Feb. 17, 1943; NYT, Feb. 20, 1943; *Monroe* (Mich.)*News,* Feb. 16, 1943.

33. DFP, DN, and NYT, Feb. 20, 1943. In addition to Truman and Wallgren (Wash.), senators visiting Willow Run were: Homer Ferguson (Mich.), Harley M. Kilgore (W. Va.), Joseph H. Ball (Minn.), and Harold H. Burton (Ohio).

34. Nevins and Hill, *Decline and Rebirth,* pp. 218–19; "Over the Hump at Willow Run," *Time* 41 (Apr. 19, 1943), 25; DFP, Feb. 17, 1943; "Willow Run Runs," *Business Week* (Feb. 20, 1943), 17; Charles O. Herb, "Willow Run: Ford's Bomber Plant," *Machinery* 49 (Feb. 1943), pp. 121–24. Among newspapers carrying the syndicated editorial were the *Perry* (Iowa) *Chief,* Feb. 25, 1943; *Ashland* (Pa.) *News,* Feb. 25, 1943; *Houghton* (Mich.) *Sunday Mining Gazette,*

Feb. 28, 1943; and *Owosso* (Mich.) *Press,* Mar. 1, 1943. *Manchester* (N.H.) *Leader and Evening Union,* Mar. 9, 1943; "Over Hump," *Time,* p. 25 (Wilson visit); Harrison Powell, "Look Out Hitler—Here Comes the Flood," *Popular Science* 142 (May 1943), 78; "Will It Run," *Flying,* p. 21; DN, Feb. 22, 1943 (subcontracting); *Army Air Forces,* p. 339. The best article on Willow Run's decentralization is E.L. Warner, Jr., "Decentralization of Willow Run," *Automotive and Aviation Industries* 90 (Apr. 15, 1944): 18–20, 85–86, 88.

35. Special Committee Investigating the National Defense Program, Aircraft Report, July 10, 1943, Report 10, Part 10, 78th Congress, 1st session; Nevins and Hill, *Decline and Rebirth,* pp. 219–20; DFP, July 11, 1943; *Grand Rapids* (Mich.) *Press,* July 12, 1943; *Army Air Forces,* pp. 320, 322,, 328–29, 332–33.

36. *Army Air Forces,* p. 329; Nevins and Hill, *Decline and Rebirth,* p. 221; NYT, Oct. 26, 1943; *Grand Rapids* (Mich.) *Herald,* Nov. 21, 1943; "Ford's Bombers," *Newsweek* 22 (Nov. 29, 1943), 66. Two UAW officials charged in October 1943 that Willow Run was "the outstanding failure of the war." Their chief complaint was that small parts work was being moved away from the plant. Ford tartly replied that the charges were "verbal sabotage," and questioned whether the election of the complainants to union office "suddenly transformed these gentlemen into production experts." "Willow Run Set-to," *Business Week* (Oct. 9, 1943), 17–18. Sorensen maintains that the President and Charles E. Wilson wanted Henry Ford to remove himself from Willow Run, and for the government and Sorensen to take over. Sorensen, *Forty Years,* p. 322.

37. DFP, Jan. 16, 1944; DT, Mar. 26, 1944; NYT, Apr. 17 and July 2, 1944; DFP, July 3, 1944. Willow Run eventually turned out a complete plane for every fifty-five minutes of working time. *Wall Street Journal,* May 22, 1945. Willow Run also produced 80 percent of emergency spare parts for the B-24 and 50 percent of all spare parts. *Ford Times* 2 (Apr. 28, 1944), 5.

38. Charles E. Wilson to FMC, Mar. 3, 1944, Acc. 38, Box 99; DN, Mar. 29, 1944; DT, Apr. 14, 1944; DFP, Apr. 18, 1944; *Asheville* (N.C.) *Citizen,* Apr. 4, 1944; see Clipbook 131 for praise of Willow Run and Henry Ford.

39. *Decatur* (Ill.) *Herald,* June 30, 1945; DT, May 7, 1945; DN, Aug. 27, 1944; *Washington Post,* July 8, 1944; *Dearborn Press,* June 28, 1945; *Christian Science Monitor,* Nov. 25, 1944; Carr and Stermer, *Willow Run,* p. xiii; DFP, July 17, 1945. A list of the Ford Company's "E" awards is in Acc. 452, Box 2.

40. *Army Air Forces,* pp. 318, 350, 354–55; G.R. Simonson, "The Demand for Aircraft and the Aircraft Industry, 1907–1958," *Journal of Economic History* 20 (Sept. 1960), 375; Automobile Manufacturers Association, *Freedom's Arsenal The Story of the Automotive Council for War Production* (Detroit: Automobile Manufacturers Association, 1950), p. 160.

41. NYT, Aug. 11, 1944; *Army Air Forces,* pp. 329–30; DN, June 29, 1945; "Last 'Lib' Gets Bon Voyage Party," *Ford Times* 2 (Aug. 1945), 15. Willow Run produced its last "knockdown" plane in July 1944, at which time 40 percent of the planes built had been knockdowns. DFP, July 9, 1944. A total of 18,190 B-24's were built between 1940–45, of which Consolidated made 9,468. Consolidated's main factory at San Diego produced 6,725 of the planes. Foster Adams, director, Directorate for Statistical Services, Office of the Assistant Secretary of Defense, to David L. Lewis, July 17, 1963. The Ford Company had an option to buy Willow Run from the government after the war, and throughout 1943–44 Henry Ford and Henry II talked of future production of commercial airplanes or farm equipment. But the option was not exercised, and in September 1945 the factory was leased by the Reconstruction Finance Corporation to a newly organized automobile firm, the Kaiser-Frazer Corporation. Kaiser-Frazer bought the building in 1948, then, as sales of its cars dwindled, sold it to General Motors in 1953. The structure, although now partitioned, still awes visitors by its vastness. Willow Run's airfield and a hangar adjacent to it were sold by the RFC for $1.00 to the University of Michigan in 1946, on the condition that the facilities be made available to airlines serving Detroit. The field served as the Motor City's major airport until 1966, and since then has bustled with flights of company- and individually-owned aircraft. DT, Nov. 12, 1943, July 11 and Sept. 29, 1944, May 4, 1945; "Plane Talk," *Time* 42 (Nov. 22, 1943), 77; "Ford Heritage," *Fortune,* p. 141; "Planes into Plowshares," *Newsweek* 24 (Sept. 11, 1944), 72; NYT, Dec. 7, 1944; DFP, Sept. 22, 1945; GM Annual Report 1953, p. 20; *Ann Arbor* (Mich.) *News,* June 24, 1966, Aug. 20, 1973.

42. *Army Air Forces,* p. 330; Automobile Manufacturers Association, *Freedom's Arsenal,* p. 52. Sorensen, *Forty Years,* p. 290. Willow Run's production record has yet to be equalled by any other aircraft plant. The bomber factory also served as the setting of two wartime novels. Dan E. Patch, *Moon Over Willow Run* (Grand Rapids, Mich.: Zondervan Publishing House, 1943), and Glendon Swartout, *Willow Run* (New York: Crowell, 1943).

43. *Army Air Forces,* pp. 207–8 (B-24's success); Nevins and Hill, *Decline and Rebirth,* p. 226; "Ford and the War Years," *Ford Times* 2 (Sept. 1945), special insert. Ford's Pratt & Whitney engines powered Martin B-26 medium bombers, Republic Thunderbolt pursuit planes, and Curtiss Commando cargo transports. Ford Motor Company. *Forty Years 1903–1943* (Dearborn, Mich.: Ford Motor Company, 1943), p. 41. The company designed the amphibian and reconnaissance truck and assisted in the redesigning of the medium tank, according to the *Ford Times.* Automobile Manufacturers Association, *Freedom's Arsenal,* pp. 199–201.

44. *Philadelphia Inquirer,* Oct. 1, 1942 (Chester); *Ford Times* 1 (July 1944), 20 (Ypsilanti and Richmond); 1 (Aug. 1944), 28 (Iron Mountain and Somerville); 2 (June 1945), 40 (Minneapolis-St. Paul and Ypsilanti); NYT, July 4, 1945 (Minneapolis-St. Paul, Chester, Richmond); DN, July 13, 1945 (Ypsilanti). Edsel looked thin and drawn at the March 12, 1943 ceremony. DN, May 26, 1943. Foster Adams to David L. Lewis, Feb. 18, 1964.

45. "One Hundred Corporations Ranked by Volume of Prime War Supply Contracts Cumulative June 1940 Through September 1944," furnished author by Foster Adams, Sept. 21, 1964; Nevins and Hill, *Decline and Rebirth,* p. 226.

46. A Survey of Attitudes Toward and Opinions About Ford Motor Company (photostatic copy), submitted to FMC by Elmo Roper, Oct. 1944, Acc. 134, Box 17; Relative Standing of Ford Among Owners of Lower Price Automobiles, submitted to Ford by JWT, July 1944, Acc. 149, Box 98; *Louisville Times,* May 24, 1945.

47. Sorensen, *Forty Years,* pp. 313, 317, 332–33; NYT, May 22, 1943 (quoting Edsel); " '43 Ford," *Fortune,* p. 113; "Sorensen," *Fortune,* p. 120; Simonds, *Henry Ford,* pp. 332–33.

Chapter 22

1. Nevins and Hill, *Decline and Rebirth,* pp. 228, 246–48; DN, Jan. 18, 1942; Sorensen, *Forty Years,* pp. 317–20, 323; *Bergen* (N.J.) *Evening Record,* May 26, 1943 (Associated Press obituary); *Philadelphia News,* May 26, 1943 (United Press obituary); *Atlanta Journal,* May 26, 1943 (International News Service obituary); NYT, May 26, 1943; Louise B. Clancy and Florence Davies, *The Believer: The Life Story of Mrs. Henry Ford* (New York: Coward-McCann, Inc., 1960), p. 207. Ford's worldwide factories stopped work for five minutes in tribute to Edsel; Detroit's 319 schools observed a moment of silence. DT, May 28, 1943. Edsel is buried in Woodlawn Cemetery, 19975 Woodlawn, Detroit.
2. Black, *Reminiscences,* p. 94; A.J. Lepine, secretary to Edsel Ford, *Reminiscences,* p. 30; Leon Pinkson, automotive editor, *San Francisco Chronicle, Reminiscences,* p. 11; Steve Hannagan to Edsel Ford, July 21, 1942, Acc. 6, Box 376 (non-use of "I" in news releases); *Philadelphia Inquirer,* Aug. 8, 1942; DN, May 26, 1943. Edsel "dreads publicity," declared DN, Nov. 6, 1938.
3. Ocee Ritch, *The Lincoln Continental* (Los Angeles: Floyd Clymer, 1963), p. 89; Richards, *Last Billionaire,* p. 200; DN, May 26, 1943 (quoting Fred L. Black on Edsel's anonymous visits to the San Diego fair). Characteristically, Edsel agreed to underwrite any deficit incurred by the U.S. Olympic team of 1936 on the condition that his gift remain anonymous. DN, Nov. 6, 1938.
4. DN, May 26, 1943; *Atlanta Journal,* May 26, 1943; *Pueblo* (Colo.) *Star-Journal,* May 26, 1943; DFP, May 27, 1943. Edsel's death was rated by Michigan newspaper editors surveyed by the Associated Press as the third most important Michigan news story of 1943, behind Detroit's race riot and a grand jury investigation of the state legislature. DN, Dec. 31, 1943. [Henry Ford's] "greatest failure was his treatment of his only son Edsel," wrote Sorensen, "and this treatment may have hastened his son's death." Sorensen, *Forty Years,* p. 301.
5. The most complete articles on Edsel Ford's life prior to his death were David J. Wilkie's Dec. 31, 1939 Associated Press biography (see *Buffalo Courier-Express,* Dec. 31, 1939, Clipbook 106) and Edward Thierry's syndicated July 28, 1921 article (see *Sault Ste. Marie* (Mich.) *News,* Clipbook 24). The most complete article on Edsel to 1975 is Patricia Barbara Smith's two-part biography in the DFP Sunday magazine, *Detroit,* Oct. 17, 24, 1965. There is no book-length biography of Edsel. Edsel was viciously attacked in 1918 by his father's political enemies for having avoided military service. Nevins and Hill, *Expansion and Challenge,* p. 119.
6. Nevins and Hill, *Decline and Rebirth,* pp. 115, 246; Black, *Reminiscences,* pp. 83, 94; Sorensen, *Forty Years,* chapters 18–20; Clancy and Davies, *The Believer,* pp. 122, 198–99. At times Edsel rebelled against his father; as a seven-year-old in 1901 he bested him. Entries from his mother's diary tell the story: January 13: "Henry fixed Edsel's old sleigh to take him coasting, but Edsel would not go, said sleigh was no good. He was sent up stairs for punishment for his pride. He was sorry." January 19: "Henry bought Edsel new coaster." January 20: "Henry and Edsel went coasting on the boulevard." January 23, 1901: "Edsel had big time coasting." Sidney Olson, *Young Henry Ford: A Picture History of the First Forty Years* (Detroit: Wayne State University Press, 1963), pp. 130–31.

7. Ritch, *Lincoln Continental,* p. 89; *Automotive News* (June 3, 1963), 24; "Henry Ford," *Continental Comments* 11 (July–Aug. 1963), 18; DFP, Oct. 24, 1965; *Dictionary of American Biography,* s.v. "Ford, Edsel Bryant."
8. DN, Aug. 5, 1944; DN, May 27, 1946. The *Ypsilanti* (Mich.) *Press,* Nov. 9, 1964, reported the bomber was the 139th produced at Willow Run. William S. Knudsen, ex-president of GM, presented petitions to Detroit's Common Council requesting that the Motor City's proposed expressway be named for Edsel Ford; Council approval was granted on Apr. 30, 1946. Thomas D. Leadbetter, city clerk, City of Detroit, to David L. Lewis, Dec. 31, 1964. William S. Haubrick and Enisse Chimes, eds., *Henry Ford Hospital Graduate Medical Education* (Detroit: Henry Ford Hospital, 1970), p. 34. The Detroit telephone directory for 1965 places the Edsel Ford High School at 20601 Rotunda Drive. *Harvard Business School Bulletin* 46 (Nov.-Dec. 1970), 27; "Ford Auditorium Opened in Detroit," *Musical America* 86 (Nov. 1, 1956), 5. The auditorium seats 2,926 and is the home of the Detroit Symphony Orchestra. The Ford family contributed $1,000,000 of the auditorium's cost; Ford and Mercury dealers, $1,500,000; and the City of Detroit, $2,500,000. DN, Oct. 10, 1956.
9. *Antarctica Official Name Decisions of the United States Board on Geographic Names,* Gazetteer No. 14, 3rd ed. (Washington: Geographic Names Division, U.S. Army Topographic Command, 1969), pp. 56, 65, 98. Interview with Meredith F. Burrill, executive secretary, United States Board on Geographic Names, June 9, 1971. See William Greenleaf, *From These Beginnings: The Early Philanthropies of Henry and Edsel Ford* (Detroit: Wayne State University Press, 1964), pp. 157–61 for an excellent discussion of Edsel's support of Antarctic expeditions.
10. William T. Noble, "What If They Had Named It 'Utopian Turtletopper?,' " *Detroit News Magazine,* p. 18, DN, Dec. 25, 1966; John Brooks, *The Fate of the Edsel and Other Business Adventures* (New York: Harper & Row, 1963), pp. 32–36, 67. Martin Mayer, *Madison Avenue, U.S.A.* (New York: Harper & Brothers, 1958), pp. 107–18. The Edsel no longer ranks as American industry's most costly mistake. The failure of General Dynamics Corporation's Convair 880 and 990 airplanes led to a 1960–62 loss estimated from $425,000,000 to $475,000,000. Antony Jay, *Management and Machiavelli: An Inquiry into the Politics of Corporate Life* (New York: Holt, Rinehart and Dinston, 1968), p. 37; "Aerospace: New Growth Vistas," *Business Week* (June 3, 1972), 74. RCA wrote off $490,000,000 in getting out of the computer business in 1971. "RCA After the Bath," *Fortune* 76 (Sept. 1972), 123. Estimates of the Penn-Central Company's losses between 1970–72 range up to $1,100,000,000. *Business Week* (Oct. 7, 1972), 38. The name "Edsel" may figure anew in Ford Company history. Henry Ford II's only son, Edsel Bryant Ford II, after graduating from Babson Institute of Business Administration, joined the firm in 1974 as a product planning analyst in the North American Car Strategy Office of the Product Planning and Research Staff. Upon joining the company, Edsel, twenty-five, said, "I hope someday to run the company. But if I can't, I can't." DFP, Jan. 10, 1974.
11. *Wall Street Journal,* Apr. 17, 1968 (Custer's Stand, New York Mets, Stassen); "Jackie Gleason Show," Feb. 4, 1967; "Carol Burnett Show," Apr. 22, 1968; "Flight of the Hangar Queen." *Time* 86 (Aug. 20, 1965), 62 (rocket); "The Troubled Hybrid," *Time* 88 (Aug. 19, 1966), 19 (fighter-bomber); "GE's Edsel,"

Forbes 99 (Apr. 1, 1967), 21; "The Beetle's Spider Web," *Newsweek* 74 (July 21, 1969), 81; "Du Pont's Edsel," *Newsweek* 77 (Mar. 29, 1971), 84; DN, Mar. 25, 1971 (three senators); DN, Mar. 26, 1973 (symbol of flop).

12. George T. Waterman, national executive secretary, Edsel Owners of America, to David L. Lewis, May 6, 1974; J.R. Leonard, founder, International Edsel Club, to David L. Lewis, May 10, 1974.

13. NYT, May 30, 1945; Sorensen, *Forty Years*, p. 224; DFP, June 2, 1943. After Edsel's death, the Associated Press said Sorensen was the company's "key man," and predicted that either he or Henry Ford would fill the presidency. *New York Journal-American*, May 26, 1942.

14. *Los Angeles Herald and Express*, June 3, 1943; *Kinston* (N.C.) *Free Press*, June 2, 1943; *Boise* (Idaho) *Morning Statesman*, June 3, 1943; *Martins Ferry* (Ohio) *Times*, June 2, 1943; *Tampa Daily Times*, June 2, 1943; *Richmond* (Ind.) *Palladium*, June 8, 1943; DN, June 21, 1943; *Crested Butte* (Colo.) *Pilot*, June 17, 1943; *Spring Valley* (Wis.) *Sun*, June 24, 1943; *Anoka* (Minn.) *Union*, June 23, 1943; *Farmville* (Va.) *Herald*, June 18, 1943; *Milwaukee Journal*, June 8, 1943; *Charleston* (S.C.) *News & Courier*, June 8, 1943; *Cortland* (N.Y.) *Democrat*, June 11, 1943; *Scranton* (Pa.) *Tribune*, June 2, 1943; *Watertown* (N.Y.) *Times*, June 8, 1943. The *Times* (London) even reported that Henry Ford was "in excellent health, and is said by his associates to have more energy and keeness than many men younger than he."

15. Nevins and Hill, *Decline and Rebirth*, pp. 116–17; "Ford's War Cabinet," *Time* 41 (June 14, 1943), 87. By 1940, according to Nevins and Hill, *Decline and Rebirth*, p. 232, Henry Ford listened only to Sorensen, P.E. Martin, and Harry Bennett. Edsel, of course, could also obtain a hearing from his father.

16. *Who's Who in America*, 21st ed., s.v. "Sorensen, Charles E."; Sorensen, *Forty Years*, pp. 27–28, 296; "Production," *Time* 36 (Nov. 18, 1940), 23; DT, May 7, 1941; *New York Herald Tribune*, June 9, 1941; *Flint* (Mich.) *Journal*, July 17, 1941. Among publications which cite Sorensen as "general manager" are Frank J. Oliver, "Ford Ready for Mass Production of Equipment for U.S. Defense," *Iron Age* 145 (June 20, 1940), 86; *Adrian* (Mich.) *Telegram*, Feb. 3, 1942; *Madison* (Wis.) *State Journal*, Apr. 11, 1942; DN, May 23, 1942; DT, June 7, 1942; DFP, Dec. 4, 1942.

17. DN, Jan. 17, 1942 (Sorensen doing all of talking while in Henry Ford's and Harry Bennett's presence); DN, Oct. 31, 1941 (Windsor); DT, Apr. 14, 1942 (Truman); DT, May 12, 1942 (Prado); DN, July 2, 1942 (King Peter); DT, July 24, 1942 (Churchill); DFP, Aug. 1, 1942 (Arnold); DN, Mar. 17, 1943 (Jeffers); DFP, Apr. 7, 1943 (Wilson). Wilson, vice-chairman of the War Production Board, formerly head of General Electric, is not to be confused with Charles E. Wilson, president of GM. One Wilson was called "Electric Charlie"; the other "Engine Charlie."

18. DFP, Sept. 7, 1941 (birthday); DN, July 11, 14, 1942 (yacht); "Sorensen," *Fortune* 25 (Apr. 1942), 120 (salary); DT, July 17, 1944 (salary); DFP, Jan. 10, 1942; DT, Jan. 17, 1942.

19. "Sorensen," *Fortune*, pp. 78–81, 119; DFP, June 14, 1942, and other Associated Press stories in Clipbook 125. Wilkie praised Sorensen no less highly in a 1962 biographical sketch. "Profiles of Auto Greats," *Automotive News* 37 (Aug. 6, 1962), 1, 49.

20. See Clipbook 125 for news and feature stories inspired by *Fortune* and the Associated Press. *Wall Street Journal*, Apr. 11, 1942; DFP, June 14, 1942; "Edsel Ford, 1893–1943," *Newsweek* 21 (June 7, 1943), 73; *New York Sun*, May 26, 1943; *Ypsilanti* (Mich.) *Press*, Apr. 21, 1942; *New Haven* (Conn.) *Journal-Courier and Times*, June 10, 1943; Richards, *Last Billionaire*, pp. 224–25; DT, Dec. 28, 1942; Christy Borth, "Automotive Merlins," *Coronet* 13 (Jan. 1943), 82; *Toledo Blade*, May 23, 1942. Copies of Thomas's address, delivered on Oct. 18, 1943, are in Acc. 285, Box 2764.

21. Nevins and Hill, *Decline and Rebirth*, pp. 257–59; DFP, Mar. 5, 1944; Bennett, *Never Called Henry*, pp. 164–65; *New York Journal-American*, June 2, 1943; *New York Journal of Commerce*, June 3, 1943; "Ford's Cabinet," *Time*, p. 87; interview with John W. Thompson, Sept. 25, 1962. Another version of Hannagan's dismissal was reported by *Steel* in October 1943. The firing, according to this source, was precipitated by Henry Ford's anger with the publicist over newspaper reports that Willow Run recruiters were "raiding" mechanics from Ford dealers. The dealers were said to have complained to the company, whereupon Hannagan was "called upon the carpet" for permitting the stories to be published. "Although there obviously was not much he could do about it," observed *Steel*," ... this marked the end of Hannagan's association with Ford." A.H. Allen, "Mirrors of Motordom," *Steel* 113 (Oct. 25, 1943), 58. Bennett was happy to see Hannagan fired. Thompson interview, Sept. 25, 1962; interview with Fred Collins, DT reporter in 1942, later a member of GM's News Department, Feb. 19, 1964. Hannagan died at age fifty-three in 1953. His firm was bought by Hill and Knowlton, Inc. in 1955. L.L.L. Golden, "Public Relations: The Survival Rate," *Saturday Review* 48 (Mar. 13, 1965), 149.

22. NYT, June 19, 1943; DN, June 22, 1943; "Ford on the Road Back," *Time* 42 (Oct. 11, 1943), 83; Nevins and Hill, *Decline and Rebirth*, pp. 257–60; Sorensen, *Forty Years*, p. 331; DT and NYT, Mar. 5, 1944; DFP, Mar. 5, 6, 1944; "The Winner," *Time* 43 (Mar. 13, 1944), 85; Black, *Reminiscences*, p. 130; Bennett, *Never Called Henry*, pp. 156, 170. Bennett correctly observed that "There wasn't room in the Ford Motor Company for two 'geniuses.' "

23. DN, June 13, 1944; "Henry's Boy Gets a Job," *Time* 43 (June 19, 1944), 84; "Profiles," *Automotive News*, pp. 1, 49 (departure from Ford "hurts"); Samuel Crowther to William J. Cameron, n.d. [last half of 1944], Acc. 44, Box 1; "Willys-Overland," *Fortune* 24 (Aug. 1946), 83, 86–87; DT, Jan. 16, 1946; "Capt. Mooney Takes Helm at Willys," *Motor* 85 (Feb. 1944), 68; Sorensen's ten-year contract with Willys called for an annual salary of $52,000, plus an option to buy 100,000 shares of stock at $3.00 per share at a time when the stock was selling for $12.50 (by mid-1946 Willys's stock was selling for $26.75). A post-D-Day bull market, talk of a Sorensen-built, low-price, postwar car, and rumors of a postwar Willys combine of small automotive companies resulted in a trebling in the value of Willys's stock within two weeks of Sorensen's appointment. "Bull Market," *Time* 43 (June 26, 1944), 86; DT, July 21, 1944; *Time* 92 (Aug. 23, 1968), 57.

24. Nevins and Hill, *Decline and Rebirth*, p. 240; "Ford Heritage," *Fortune*, pp. 139–40; Thompson, *Reminiscences*, p. 77; " '43 Ford," *Fortune* 27 (Feb. 1943), 113; "The Little Giant Goes," *Time* 46 (Oct. 8, 1945), 81; Bennett, *Never Called Henry*, pp. 88, 120; Collins interview, Feb. 19, 1964; interview with Anthony G. De Lorenzo, United Press automotive editor, later vice-president in charge of public relations staff, GM, Nov. 8, 1965; Richards, *Last Billionaire*, p. 236.

Chapter 23

1. A.H. Allen, "Mirrors of Motordom," *Steel* 113 (Sept. 27, 1943), 59; Gilbert Burck, "Henry Ford II," *Life* 19 (Oct. 1, 1945), 109–10. "Bennett," Charles E. Carll told the author on Sept. 21, 1962, "did not think like a newspaper guy." "Before Charlie Carll took over," News Bureau staffer Ross Mac-Naughton informed the author on May 12, 1962, "the Bureau was all hodgepodge." The *Steel* article observed "that to a lesser degree, the public relations effort of Chrysler is a negative sort of thing, certainly well behind the aggressive policy of GM."

2. DN, Apr. 28, 1944; DFP, Oct. 15, 1944; John Gunther, *Inside U.S.A.* (New York: Harper & Brothers, 1947), 400; André Fontaine, "The Paper That Nobody Sees," *Nation's Business* 36 (Oct. 1948), 55; Gnau, while Sorensen's secretary, was Bennett's spy. Nevins and Hill, *Decline and Rebirth*, p. 245. Carll, who reported to John Thompson and John Bugas, was greatly admired by members of his staff. John Rose, Carll's successor, described him as "the best press relations man I've ever known." Scott Wigle told the author on Nov. 23, 1965 that Carll was an "absolutely terrific press relations man . . . and was the first man I ever remember or saw who could read things in blocks of copy . . . he was so goddamn fast it was frightening." GM received forty-one votes in *Tide*'s survey; A.T. & T. thirty-seven, American Red Cross thirty, Association of American Railroads twenty-eight, CIO's Political Action Committee fourteen, and United States Steel Corporation thirteen. GM's public relations head, Paul Garrett, was named the top "public relations counselor" with twenty-four votes. "Public Relations," *Tide* 19 (June 15, 1945), 19–21.

3. Thompson interview, Sept. 25, 1962; Thompson, *Reminiscences*, pp. 18–20, 26, 37–38; DT, Nov. 12, 1943 (cargo planes); NYT, Apr. 18, 1944 (jobs for veterans); DT, Sept. 16, 1948 (raise wages).

4. Both Cameron and Liebold believed Henry Ford to be less newsworthy and less interested in press interviews during World War II than previously. Cameron, *Reminiscences*, pp. 251, 286, 290; Liebold, *Reminiscences*, p. 1248. Drafts of letters, statements, speeches, and advertisements written by Cameron for Henry Ford, Henry Ford II, and the company are in Acc. 44, Boxes 5, 14–15. Titles and dates of Cameron's Greenfield Village talks are listed in Acc. 274, Box 3.

5. Thompson, *Reminiscences*, pp. 16–17, 89–90; "Ford Heritage," *Fortune*, pp. 139–44, 245–46, 249–50, 252, 254, 256.

6. Cameron, *Reminiscences*, pp. 227, 277 (late for work); Black, *Reminiscences*, p. 144 (cure Cameron); Liebold, *Reminiscences*, p. 1263. During February 1920, Cameron reported late for work on six days. Tardiness reports from Fred L. Black to E. G. Liebold, Acc. 284, Box 1.

7. Black, *Reminiscences*, pp. 143–44; Cordell, *Reminiscences*, pp. 22, 27, 41; Richards, *Last Billionaire*, p. 259.

8. Richards, *Last Billionaire*, p. 252; *Canonsburg* (Pa.) *Daily News*, Apr. 29, 1932; Cameron, *Reminiscences*, p. 290. At times, however, Cameron, upon hearing Henry Ford harangue a reporter on a subject such as Wall Street or diets, would express amazement that "so much chaff could come out of what you know to be really a fine mill." Garrett, *Wild Wheel*, p. 14. Cameron continued to eat lunch at the Roundtable (for top executives) when Henry Ford II was head of the company. Cameron, *Reminiscences*, p. 290. The publicist received a pension from Ford at a time when most of its executives did not. Liebold, *Reminiscences*, p. 1263. Cameron died on Aug. 1, 1955. *Time* 66 (Aug. 15, 1955), 73.

9. A Review of the First Year of "Watch the World Go By," submitted to FMC by Maxon, Inc., n.d. [June 1943], Acc. 149, Box 94; Earl Godwin—Ford Motor Company–Hooperating History July 12, 1942—Jan. 9, 1944, Acc. 149, Box 2. Ford gained slightly in public favor between May 1942 and May 1943, according to the Link Audits conducted by the Psychological Corporation, of Princeton, N.J. GM Public Relations Policy Group Minutes, Aug. 7, 1945, GM Public Relations Library.

10. DFP, June 4, 1943; *Pittsburgh Press*, June 18, 1943; Thompson, *Reminiscences*, pp. 45–48; Bennett, *Reminiscences*, p. 154; "Model T Newscaster," *Newsweek* 23 (Aug. 16, 1943), 86. A.H. Allen, "Mirrors of Motordom," *Steel* 113 (Oct. 25, 1943), 58. After leaving Maxon in late 1941, when the agency lost its Ford accounts, Ford's nephew-in-law became one of the nation's leading sportscasters. He combined sportscasting and management of Maxon's Radio Department. DFP, June 4, 1943. There were rumors that Henry Ford planned to sponsor Phil Spitalny's "Hour of Charm" featuring an all-girl orchestra. Maxon, which had put Spitalny on the air in behalf of General Electric, figured "the soft, sweet old songs and hymns on the Hour will make a hit with Henry Ford when Phil auditions for him in the near future." *New York Mirror*, Aug. 8, 1943. Correspondence among Wismer and Blue network and Ford officials regarding the Whiteman fiasco is in Acc. 149, Box 109.

11. "Model T Newscaster," *Newsweek*, p. 86; B.J. Craig, vice-president and treasurer, FMC, to Maxon, Inc., Dec. 7, 1943, Acc. 149, Box 94. Additional "Watch the World" correspondence among Maxon, Blue network, and Ford officials is in Acc. 149, Box 103. The nimble Wismer jumped from Maxon to Ford's new advertising agency, J. Walter Thompson. He later became chairman of the American Football League. *Who's Who in America*, 32nd ed., s.v. "Wismer, Harry." Godwin, although at odds with the company over speaking engagements arranged for him by the firm, was stunned by the notice of termination. "Never," he wrote Bennett, "will I ever cease to wonder what happened." Earl Godwin to Harry Bennett, Jan. 7, 1944, Acc. 149, Box 94.

12. Thompson, *Reminiscences*, pp. 45–47; interview with O'Neill Ryan, JWT executive, Sept. 12, 1962; *Broadcasting* 25 (Dec. 13, 1943), 16; 26 (Jan. 10, 1944), 14; *Variety* 153 (Jan. 12, 1944), 37. The Ford Company made no statement about buying up Dorsey's contract. *Time* reported that Henry Ford was said "to have objected to the way modern dance bands go to town." "Tune Callers," *Time* 43 (Feb. 7, 1944), 37.

13. *Broadcasting* 26 (Jan. 17, 1944), 65; 26 (Jan. 31, 1944), 14; Ray Henle to David L. Lewis, Oct. 3, 1963; John Thompson to Chester J. LaRoche, Blue network official, Oct. 16, 1944, Acc. 149, Box 109 (hiring Prevost); Prevost had been a newsman with the *Detroit Free Press* for twenty-five years, the Knight Newspapers' Washington bureau chief for ten years. He was Ford's first Washington public relations representative. *Motor* 81 (June 1974), 164; *Ford Times* 1 (July 1944), 47. Letters of complaint regarding Prevost's performance are in Acc. 149, Box 109.

14. "Shades of Cameron," *Broadcasting* 27 (Nov. 20, 1944), 38; J.R. Davis to all dealers, Dec. 1, 1944, Acc. 149, Box 29; *Automotive News* 20 (Feb. 19, 1945), 35 (Ford advertisement); NYT, Dec. 24, 1944. Hooper and CAB ratings of the "Stars of the Future,"

"Frances Greer Show," and "Ford Show" are in General Motors Corporation Public Relations Policy Group Minutes, Mar. 6, 1945, GM Public Relations Library.

15. "Advertisers Using ABC Network During 1945," *Broadcasting-Telecasting 1946 Yearbook,* p. 224; Harry T. Mitchell to B. R. Donaldson, Aug. 9, 1945, Acc. 149, Box 10 (program shifts and listener ratings); NYT, Dec. 9, 1945. Scripts for the "Stars of the Future," "Frances Greer Show," and "Ford Show" are in Acc. 149, Boxes 28–30.

16. Ryan interview, Sept. 14, 1962; Thompson, *Reminiscences,* p. 84; see correspondence between B.R. Donaldson and JWT executives regarding the chapel service in Acc. 149, Boxes 109–10; programs are in Acc. 44, Box 5. "Ford Shuffle Starts in July," *Variety* 159 (June 20, 1945), 25.

17. *Radio Daily* (Feb. 23, 1944) clipping in Acc. 149, Box 109; Donaldson to Harry Mitchell, JWT, Jan. 4, 1945; Donaldson to Earl Mullin, Blue network, Jan. 4, 1945, and Donaldson to Mitchell, Jan. 4, 1945, Acc. 149, Box 110; "8 Months Ork Ratings Tabbed," *Billboard* 57 (May 26, 1945), 14; "Ford Shuffle," *Variety,* p. 25. After Lovett returned to New England, the square dances were called by one of his former students, Francis L. Brancheau. C.A. Perry, director of old-fashioned dance orchestra, to Donaldson, July 18, 1945, Acc. 149, Box 45. See Acc. 149, Box 45 for fan mail of "Early American Dance Music." Programs for each of the broadcasts are in Acc. 149, Box 43.

18. During the years 1942–45, the Ford Company spent $5,564,629 on radio programs—20 percent of its advertising budget. The expenditures increased steadily throughout the war years: $713,047 in 1942, $1,426,094 in 1943, $1,679,123 in 1944, and $1,736,363 in 1945. The greatest commitment was to "Watch the World Go By," which was on the air for two-and-a-half years at a cost of $3,277,608. "Early American Dance Music" cost $485,190; "Greenfield Village Chapel Service," $377,435; other programs, including the Ford Sunday Evening Hour, resumed in September 1945, the remaining amount. FMC Advertising Breakdown, n.d. [1945], Acc. 149, Box 124. GM spent $3,427,229 on radio advertising during World War II, having sponsored a symphonic broadcast for two years, a newscast for one year. Neil H. Borden, *Advertising Text and Cases* (Chicago: Richard D. Irwin, Inc., 1950), pp. 502–3.

19. "Business at War," *Fortune* 26 (Nov. 1942), 60. The first of Ford's wartime advertisements appeared in *Saturday Evening Post* 215 (Nov. 14, 1942), 52–53. The other four can be found in *Business Week* (Apr. 24, 1943), 68–69 (tanks and wartime achievements great); (June 12, 1943), 54–55 (Pratt & Whitney engines); (Aug. 21, 1943), 66–67 (jeeps); and *Saturday Evening Post* 216 (Nov. 20, 1943), 88–89 (speeded war effort). Thompson, *Reminiscences,* pp. 66–67; Thompson interview, Sept. 25, 1962.

20. Thompson, *Reminiscences,* pp. 48–49, 66; Ryan interview, Sept. 14, 1962; Donaldson interview, Sept. 10, 1962; *New York World-Telegram,* Dec. 3, 1943; "Boom at Thompson," *Tide* 17 (Dec. 15, 1943), 30; John Thompson to David L. Lewis, Oct. 12, 1962. Lou R. Maxon had no comment about his agency's dismissal. DFP, Dec. 3, 1943. Founded in 1864, JWT had placed advertising for more than fifty automobile manufacturers since the turn of the century, including the Ford Company between 1910–12. From 1927 until the early 1930s it served General Motors Export Division; from 1933–37, the Nash Division of Nash-Kelvinator; and in 1942–43, Chrysler (institutional advertising only). By 1943 the

agency's domestic staff numbered 817; its billings totaled $55,000,000. Within a year, fast-growing JWT's employees would number 1,026; its billings would achieve $67,000,000, far more than Young & Rubicam's $51,000,000 and third-ranking Ayer's $33,000,000. Not having a Detroit office, JWT initially serviced the Ford account out of its Chicago office, appointing Harry Mitchell, a veteran automobile advertising specialist, as account executive. In 1944 a Detroit office assumed responsibility for Ford advertising. "Architects of 'Mad Av,' " *News Front* 8 (Mar. 1964), 40; Automotive Clients Serviced by JWT (photocopy), furnished the author by Edward Royal, of JWT, to David L. Lewis, May 26, 1964; James Webb Young, "Mister J. Walter Thompson," *Saturday Review* 47 (Apr. 11, 1964), 71; Joseph E. Boyle, vice-president, JWT, to David L. Lewis, Sept. 4, 1962 (JWT's size during 1943–44); *Advertising Age* 16 (Jan. 8, 1945), 1 (agencies' billings); "Boom at Thompson," *Tide,* p. 30.

21. Thompson, *Reminiscences,* pp. 49–51; Ford Motor Company Wartime Advertising Policy 1942–1945, n.d. [1944], Acc. 149, Box 105. *New York World-Telegram,* Jan. 25, 1946. Proofs of advertisements in the "Henry Ford" and "Famous Ford 'First' " campaigns are in Acc. 44, Box 13. Advertisements in the "Henry Ford" series appeared in *Automotive News* 19 (Aug. 7, 1944), 23 (repairing watch); 20 (Sept. 4, 1944), 11 (Edison meeting); 19 (May 5, 1944), 17 (swifter than a race horse); 19 (June 12, 1944), 23 (New York-to-Seattle race). Advertisements in the "Famous Ford 'Firsts' " campaign may be found in *Saturday Evening Post* 217 (Jan. 6, 1945), 50 (radio beacon); 218 (Nov. 24, 1945), 40 (paints); 218 (July 21, 1945), 48 (bombers); 218 (Sept. 29, 1945), inside front cover (glass); *Ford Times* 3 (Jan. 1946), inside back cover (soybeans). *New York World-Telegram,* Jan. 25, 1946.

22. Advertisements in the series signed by Henry Ford and Henry Ford II are in Acc. 44, Box 13. Representative advertisements appeared in the *Los Angeles Times,* Jan. 21, 1945 ("What Star Shall Guide"), *St. Louis Post-Dispatch,* Apr. 21, 1945 ("No Wage"), *Chicago Tribune,* Mar. 12, 1945 (disabled veterans). News stories and editorials on the wage advertisement appeared in the *St. Louis Post-Dispatch,* Apr. 21, 1945, *Vandergrift* (Pa.) *News,* May 7, 1945, *La Grange* (Ill.) *Citizen,* May 17, 1945, *Lincoln* (Calif.) *Messenger,* May 31, 1945, *New Haven Register,* Sept. 22, 1945, *Boston News Bureau,* Sept. 22, 1945, *San Angelo* (Tex.) *Standard-Times,* Sept. 23, 1945, *Pensacola News,* Sept. 28, 1945, and *Orange* (Calif.) *News,* Oct. 4, 1945.

23. Ford Motor Company Wartime Advertising Policy 1942–45, n.d. [1944], Acc. 149, Box 105. "Ford Kicks Postwar Fable Out Window," *Motor* 82 (Sept. 1944), 150. Typical "Sure Glad I've Got a Ford" advertisements appear in the DN, Apr. 10 and 12 and Sept. 12, 1944; a representative Lincoln-Mercury advertisement appears in the DT, Nov. 26, 1944.

24. James Pooler, "Lay That Crystal Down," *Ford Times* 1 (July 1944), 11–14; Thompson, *Reminiscences,* p. 106; Donaldson interview, Sept. 10, 1962; Ryan interview, Sept. 14, 1962. Pooler was one of five *Detroit Free Press* reporters who won a Pulitzer prize for general reporting in 1932. Gerald O.T. Erdalh, later director of the North Carolina State College Union, claimed that he coined the "Ford in Your Future" slogan by winning a national advertising contest while an undergraduate at the University of Wisconsin. DN, Nov. 5, 1961.

25. The first "Ford in Your Future" advertisement appeared in the DT, Nov. 6, 1944. Other representative

advertisements in the series were published in the *Saturday Evening Post* 217 (Mar. 24, 1945), 45 (boy fishing); 217 (May 19, 1945), 52 (couple picnicking); 218 (Aug. 11, 1945), 48 (families looking); 218 (Dec. 1, 1945), 31 (family seated); 218 (Oct. 6, 1945), 58–59. The *Christian Science Monitor* apologized for not running ads in the series, saying that it had "interdicts on the subject of crystal gazing and fortune telling."

26. The first "Ford's Out Front" advertisement appeared in *Time* 47 (Mar. 18, 1946), 40. Representative "Ford's Out Front" advertisements include those in *Time* 47 (May 13, 1946), 40 (styling); 47 (May 27, 1946), 41 (extra values); 47 (June 10, 1946), 42 (everything). The last "Out Front" advertisement appeared in the *Saturday Evening Post* 221 (Jan. 29, 1949), 38; the last "Ford in Your Future" advertisement appeared in the *Saturday Evening Post* 223 (Sept. 30, 1950), 42. J.R. Davis to B. R. Donaldson, July 10, 1946, Acc. 149, Box 106 (slogans "public by-words"). The *New York World-Telegram,* June 6, 1945 reported that the most recent Index of Public Opinion poll, conducted by the Psychological Corporation of Princeton, N.J., showed that Ford's advertising had been seen or heard by a higher percentage of people than that of any other company.

27. *Business Week* (Dec. 21, 1946), 24; B.C. Forbes, "Today's 50 Foremost Leaders," *Forbes* 60 (Nov. 15, 1947), 42; NYT, June 7, 1955; "A Ford in Your Past," *Saturday Review* 39 (Sept. 15, 1956), 38; DN, Jan. 10, 1963; "Girl on the Grill," *Newsweek* 42 (Aug. 19, 1963), 49; *Chicago Sun Times,* May 23, 1964; "No Ford in Our Future," *New Republic* 152 (Jan. 23, 1965), 36; "A Limousine in Your Future," *Time* 85 (Apr. 16, 1965), 45; "A Ford in Their Future," *Time* 86 (Oct. 29, 1965), 71; *New York World-Telegram,* May 8, 1965; "And Now for GM," *Time* 89 (Nov. 17, 1967), 96; *Wall Street Journal,* Mar. 26, 1970 (Ivan's Future); *Business Week* (Apr. 18, 1970), 41 (Russia's Future); "Weeding Out Auto Plants," *Business Week* (May 22, 1971), 36 (Chile); "Ford's in Its Future," *Newsweek* 81 (Jan. 17, 1973), 62 (Spain); DFP, Dec. 10, 1973; DN, Apr. 13, 1974; *New York Daily News,* Aug. 13, 1974; *Utica* (N.Y.) *Observer-Dispatch,* Aug. 16, 1974.

28. Advertising Disbursements 1935–1945, Acc. 134, Box 17; Automobile Industry Comparative Advertising 1942, n.d., Acc. 149, Box 119; 1943 Radio and General Advertising, Oct. 14, 1943, Acc. 149, Box 119; 1944 Advertising Budget, n.d., Acc. 149, Box 119; Ford Motor Company 1945 Advertising Breakdown, n.d. [1945], Acc. 149, Box 124; Advertising Cost Comparisons 1944–1945, n.d., Acc. 149, Box 106. B.R. Donaldson to J.C. Roberts, Sales Department, Nov. 12, 1946, Acc. 148, Box 106. Borden, *Advertising,* pp. 501–3 (exhibits on GM's advertising expenditures, 1923–27). Advertising figures in these manuscripts lack complete consistency inasmuch as advertising and sales promotion budgets and expenses are not always charged to the same budgets and/or departments over a period of time. Twenty-nine percent of Ford's advertising budget was spent on radio, 11 percent on literature, displays and exhibits, and motion pictures. Ford spent $915,504 on print advertising in 1943; $2,713,514 in 1944.

29. Interview with James F. O'Neil, ex-chairman of American Legion Americanism Commission, Feb. 24, 1964; Clint D. Mahlke, ex-coordinator, Junior Baseball program, later display and exhibit manager, Ford Division, to David L. Lewis, Feb. 12, 1964; Virgil Cory, "Baseball's Biggest Backer," *American Legion Magazine* 63 (July 1957), 26–27; Clint D. Mahlke, "Industry Aids Baseball's Fastest Growing Program," *Physical Educator* 5 (Mar. 1948), 13. The plaque, declared the *Ford Times,* "is in line with Henry Ford's long interest in and high regard for the American Legion." "Winners of Junior World Series Will Get Ford Plaque," *Ford Times* 1 (Aug. 6, 1943), 6.

30. Clem Davis, manager, Dearborn branch, to Dearborn and Cleveland branch dealers, July 12, 1943, Acc. 509, Box 24; J.R. Davis to dealers, Sept. 17, 1943, Acc. 509, Box 24; "Jr. Baseballers Keep Eye on Ford Trophy, Big Time," *Ford Times* 2 (Apr. 1945), 43; General Sales Department to branch managers, Mar. 1, 1946, Acc. 454, Box 147; FMC news release, Mar. 28, 1946, Acc. 454, Box 11; Cory, "Baseball's Backer," pp. 26–27; J.G. Taylor Spink, "New Teamwork in Behalf of Junior Ball," *Sporting Goods Dealer* (Apr. 1947), 122; Mahlke, "Fastest Growing Program," p. 13. In 1945, Ford dealers sponsored forty-two of Detroit's forty-six teams.

31. General Sales Department to branch managers, Mar. 1, 1946, Acc. 149, Box 147; FMC news release, Mar. 28, 1964, Acc. 454, Box 11; DFP, Apr. 22, 1947.

32. FMC news release, Apr. 7, 1947, Acc. 285, Box 2935; NYT, Apr. 8, 1947; Advertising Department to district managers, Apr. 25, 1947, Acc. 285, Box 2954; DFP, Nov. 25, 1947; DT, Mar. 8, 1948; FMC news release, May 7, 1948, Acc. 285, Box 2953. Cory, "Baseball's Backer," p. 42; Mahlke to Lewis, Feb. 12, 1964. "The Ford Company's act," said Ruth, "is to my mind the finest kind of public service and I'm proud to be a part of it." Babe Ruth, as told to Bob Considine, *The Babe Ruth Story* (New York: E.P. Dutton & Co., Inc., 1948), p. 235.

33. Mahlke to Lewis, Feb. 12, 1964, May 8, 1973; interview with Gregory Nezark, Ford Division, FMC, Nov. 27, 1972; George W. Rulon, national director, American Legion Baseball, The American Legion, to David L. Lewis, Dec. 27, 1972; Cory, "Baseball's Backer," p. 26; O'Neil interview, Feb. 24, 1964. The first and second plaques awarded by Ford are in the Baseball Hall of Fame, Cooperstown, N.Y. *Automotive News* (July 20, 1964), 20. The Ford Company spent $85,808.53 on Junior Baseball in 1948. Report on Advertising Budget Expenditures Jan. 1, 1948–Dec. 31, 1948, Feb. 9, 1949, Acc. 149, Box 51.

34. DN, Sept. 15, 1933; *Chicago Herald-American,* Sept. 25, 1939; DT, Feb. 6, 1942; Doss, *Reminiscences,* pp. 81–82. Doss adds that Henry Ford gave a new car each year to the legion's national commander.

35. FMC news release, Apr. 9, 1944, Acc. 454, Box 9; DFP, Apr. 9, 1944, *Dubois* (Pa.) *Courier-Express,* Apr. 24, 1944 (Atherton statement). The editorial in the unidentified Mississippi newspaper appears on p. 7 of Clipbook 132 which contains scores of news stories and editorials on Ford's announced support of handicapped ex-servicemen. Representative articles appeared in the *New York News,* Apr. 25, 1944; *Chicago Sun,* May 14, 1944; *Virginia* (Minn.) *Sun,* May 5, 1944; *Orange* (Calif.) *News,* May 5, 1944. Camp Legion is described in detail in "Young Partners with Henry Ford," *Nation's Business* 28 (Feb. 1940), 30.

36. See Clipbook 132 for news stories on Ford's support of disabled veterans during the summer of 1932. DN, Mar. 29, 1946; *Sault Ste. Marie* (Mich.) *News,* Aug. 17, 1944 (Associated Press story). Irene Cornell, "Peace in Wartime," *Ford Times* 2 (Jan. 1945), 21–23. The medal had previously been awarded only to sixteen persons. *Chicago Sun,* Sept. 20, 1944. In 1946, the national commander of the Disabled American Veterans declared that the Ford Company had led the way in making productive citizens out of handicapped servicemen. NYT, Oct. 27, 1946. For information on Ford's record as an employer of the hand-

icapped, see "Case Material in Rehabilitation," *Factory Management and Maintenance* 102 (Feb. 1944), 88. Ford employed more than 8,000 handicapped workers in 1944. DN, Apr. 9, 1944.

37. Henry Ford to General Hines, Apr. 14, 1944 (copy), and Hines to Ford, Apr. 19, 1944, Acc. 285, Box 2771; *Atlanta Journal,* Apr. 22, 1944; NYT, Dec. 7, 1944; "Jobs Preferred," *Time* 45 (Apr. 9, 1945), 85. See Clipbook 132 for stories and editorials on Ford's announcement on job preferences to veterans. Among representative stories and editorials are those which appeared in *Newport News* (Va.) *Press,* Apr. 18, 1944, *Philadelphia Bulletin,* Apr. 19, 1944, DN, Apr. 24, 1944, and *Homestead* (Pa.) *Messenger,* Apr. 26, 1944.

38. FMC news release, Dec. 29, 1944, Acc. 454, Box 9; Welcome (booklet), n.d. [1944], Acc. 454, Box 3; NYT, Nov. 11, 1945; DT, Jan. 18, 1946. The majority of the trainees were enrolled in auto mechanics courses. "Ford Dealers Offer Veterans an 'Earn While You Learn' Training Program," *Machinery* 52 (Feb. 1944), 248.

39. DN, July 11, 1945; *Boston Post,* July 14, 1945; NYT, July 28, 1946 (Ford only company to provide equipment free), Aug. 2, 1946; Kirby Katz, "They Drive Again," *Leatherneck* 29 (Sept. 1946), 30–32. See Clipbook 134 for news stories and editorials on Ford's assistance to disabled veterans.

40. DT, Dec. 23, 1945; General Sales Department to all branches and offices, Feb. 6, 1946, Acc. 149, Box 147; DN, Mar. 12 1946; "Jobs Preferred," *Time,* p. 85; *Washington Post,* June 27, 1945.

41. A Survey of Attitudes Towards and Opinions About Ford Motor Company (photostatic copy), submitted to FMC by Elmo Roper, Oct. 1944, Acc. 134, Box 17; Relative Standing of Ford Among Owners of Low Price Automobiles, submitted to FMC by JWT, n.d. [Fall 1944], Acc. 149, Box 98. "Young King Henry Ford II," *Newsweek* 29 (Apr. 21, 1947), 75. Roper's initial survey for Ford cost $40,000. 1944 Advertising Budget, Aug. 30, 1944, Acc. 149, Box 19. Henry II sought out Roper, and the pair was introduced by Hank Flower of JWT. Roper to David L. Lewis, Jan. 26, 1965.

Chapter 24

1. DN, Jan. 23, 1944; "All Quiet on the River Rouge," *Business Week* (June 24, 1944), 20–21; "Ford Heritage," *Fortune,* p. 246; Gilbert Burck, "Henry Ford II," *Life* 19 (Oct. 1, 1945), 117–18; *Automotive News* 19 (Feb. 21, 1944), 2; "Needed: Nine Million New Cars," *Fortune* 30 (July 1944), 164. In October 1943 responsibility for Ford's sales and service policies was delegated to six regional managers reporting directly to the board of directors—"an experiment unique in factory merchandising," according to "Six Regional Managers to Direct Ford Sales," *Motor* 80 (Dec. 1943), 33. Henry II worked with this committee and soon assumed its powers.

2. DT, Jan. 25, 1944; NYT, Jan. 26 and Feb. 6, 1944; "A New Model A?," *Business Week* (July 29, 1944), 20; "Stripped Tease," *Newsweek* 24 (July 31, 1944), 52 (indiscreet dealer); "Talk of a Low-Priced Ford," *Motor* 82 (Aug. 1944), 148; DFP, Sept. 20 and 27, 1944. See Clipbook 132 for hundreds of July 1944 news stories on Ford's light-weight car.

3. "Small Car Plans Cause Sensation Throughout Country," *Ford Times* 1 (Dec. 1944), 50. See Clipbook 132 for publicity on Henry II's September and October 1944 comments on the light-weight car.

4. DN, Oct. 20, 1944; Representative List Prices 1908–1947, n.d., Acc. 378, Box 41; "Less Plush—Less Price," *Fortune* 30 (Nov. 1944), 103; *Dearborn Press,* n.d. [late 1944]; H.I. Phillips, "Lizzie's Comeback," *Ford Times* 1 (Dec. 1944), 51–52.

5. NYT, May 16, 1945; "The Race Is On," *Time* 47 (Apr. 22, 1946), 81; "Little Car, Where Now?," *Time* 48 (Sept. 23, 1946), 84; DFP, Apr. 14, 1946.

6. DFP, Sept. 20, 1944; NYT, May 25 and June 21, 1945.

7. DFP, Sept. 30, 1944; "Auto Notes," *Newsweek* 25 (Apr. 23, 1945), 22; Stanley H. Brams, "Assembly Line," *Iron Age* 156 (July 12, 1945), 66, 68; "First Ford Off Line Two Days After Production Was Authorized," *Automotive and Aviation Industries* 93 (July 15, 1945), 46; "Ford Begins New Car Output As Others Near Starting Line," *Automotive News* 20 (July 9, 1945), 1.

8. Thompson, *Reminiscences,* p. 107; "Ford—1946 Model," *Newsweek* 25 (June 11, 1945), 78; NYT, June 3, 1945; *Kansas City Times,* June 5, 1942; *Automotive News* 20 (June 11, 1945), 1 (Nash). News stories and editorials on Ford's new model announcement are in Clipbook 133; telegrams and letters from dealers, Acc. 454, Box 7. Oldsmobile on July 19 became the third manufacturer to release photos and data on its 1946 model. *Automotive News* 20 (July 23, 1945), 1.

9. DN and DT, June 30, 1945; *Time* 46 (July 9, 1945), 16. Thompson, *Reminiscences,* p. 108. See Clipbook 133 for photographs and news stories on the July 29 display of cars. The Mercury and Lincoln 1946 models also were face-lifted 1942 models. *Motor* 84 (Oct. 1945), 94, 120.

10. NYT, June 30, 1945; *Houghton* (Mich.) *Daily Mining Journal,* June 22, 1945 (Associated Press story). GM began producing Pontiacs on Oct. 4, Oldsmobiles and Buicks, Oct. 15, and Cadillac, Oct. 17. "Daily Automotive Chronology," *Ward's 1946 Automotive Yearbook,* p. 37. Alfred P. Sloan, Jr., noted with pride that GM built its first cars forty-five days after V-J Day. Alfred P. Sloan, Jr. *My Years with General Motors* (Garden City, N.Y.: Doubleday & Company, Inc., 1964), p. 385.

11. DT and NYT, July 4, 1945; Brams, "Assembly Line," *Iron Age,* p. 66; *Automotive News* 20 (July 9, 1945), 1 (WPB reaction); *Dawson* (Ga.) *News,* July 19, 1945; "Autos on the March," *Newsweek* 26 (July 9, 1945), 66; "First Fords Driven Off Rouge Assembly Line," *Steel* 117 (July 16, 1945), 99; Burck, "Henry Ford II," p. 108. Hundreds of news stories and editorials on Ford's July 3 production startup can be found in Clipbook 133.

12. *Automotive News* 20 (July 16, 1945), 1; NYT, Aug. 7, 1945; Comparative Vehicle Schedules and Actual Production 1945–1946 Models Not Including Lincoln, (Feb. 20, 1946), Acc. 454, Box 10; "Here They Come," *Time* 46 (Sept. 3, 1945), 77; *New York Sun,* Aug. 12, 1945 (Edgewater); *Louisville Courier-Journal,* Aug. 22, 1945; *Dallas Times Herald,* Aug. 28 and 29, 1945; "New Fords Are Spinning Off Branch Assembly Lines Too," *Ford Times* 2 (Oct. 1945), 54–55; *Automotive News* 21 (Sept. 3, 1945), 1 (Hudson); *Cliffside Park* (N.J.) *Press,* Aug. 23, 1945. Willys-Overland converted its jeep from military to civilian production on July 17. *Automotive News* 20 (July 23, 1945), 1.

13. "Picture of the Month," *Ford Times* 2 (Oct. 1945),

19; "The Presidency," *Time* 46 (Sept. 10, 1945), 20; *New York Herald Tribune* and *Big Rapids* (Mich.) *Press*, Aug. 30, 1945; *Houghton* (Mich.) *Daily Mining Journal*, Sept. 4, 1945; *Binghamton* (N.Y.) *Sun*, Sept. 19, 1945 (applaud gift); see p. 227 of Clipbook 134 for unidentified news story regarding Henry II ferreting out the unfortunate.

14. NYT, Aug. 13, 1945; Nevins and Hill, *Decline and Rebirth*, pp. 298–99; DT, Sept. 5, 1945; *New York Herald Tribune*, Sept. 15, 1945; Comparative Vehicle Schedules and Actual Production 1945–1946 Models Not Including Lincoln (Feb. 20, 1946), Acc. 454, Box 10.

15. "Ford Dealers Make V-8 Day Big Success," *Ford Times* 2 (Dec. 1945), 42; Reaction of Dealers to Presentation of 1946 Ford Car, n.d. [Nov. 1945], Acc. 454, Box 7; NYT, Nov. 2, 1945 (orders). See Clipbook 135 for press reaction to V-8 Day.

16. DFP, Oct. 24, 1945; *Washington Post*, Nov. 2, 1945; NYT, Nov. 3, 1945; *New York Sun*, Nov. 6, 1945. See Clipbook 135 for news stories and editorials on first sales of Ford cars.

17. NYT, Nov. 1, 1945; "Daily Automotive Chronology," *Ward's 1946 Automotive Yearbook*, p. 39 (Lincoln startup); NYT, Dec. 13, 1945; DFP, Jan. 10, 1946. See Clipbook 136 for nominal publicity on the Mercury and Lincoln public showings.

18. FMC Production Report (U.S.—Including Export), 1903–57 (Jan. 8, 1958), FMC News Department Library; "Art of Negotiation II," *Time* 46 (Dec. 24, 1945), 21; "Young Henry's $72,000,000 Gamble," *Newsweek* 31 (June 14, 1948), 68.

Chapter 25

1. Nevins and Hill, *Decline and Rebirth*, p. 294; *New York Journal-American*, Dec. 3, 1964; George Koether, "How Henry Ford II Saved the Empire," *Look* 17 (June 30, 1953), 48.

2. Gilbert Burck, "Henry Ford II," *Life* 19 (Oct. 1, 1945), 109 (description); DT, May 26, 1939 (directorship); André Fontaine, "Revolution on the Rouge," *Collier's* 120 (Nov. 15, 1947), 20; "Ford Heritage," *Fortune*, p. 245. [At first] there were few outside his family who had confidence in [Henry II], noted *Tide* 19 (Oct. 1, 1945), 25.

3. "Ford's Grandson Marries Anne McDonnell in Major 1940 Wedding," *Life* 9 (July 29, 1940), 26–27; Sorensen, *Forty Years*, p. 327 (Henry Ford's vexation over Henry II's conversion); see Clipbook 100 for press play on the wedding. DFP, Oct. 20, 1940; Sorensen, *Forty Years*, p. 279. Miss McDonnell was one of sixty-three grandchildren of inventor Thomas Murray, who was granted almost as many patents as Thomas A. Edison. "Ford Heritage," *Fortune*, p. 245.

4. Nevins and Hill, *Decline and Rebirth*, pp. 253–54; Burck, "Henry Ford II," pp. 117–18; DT, Aug. 13, 1943; "Ford Heritage," *Fortune*, p. 246. The director general of the War Production Board was second in command under the WPB's director, Donald M. Nelson. DFP, Jan. 19, 1943.

5. "Ford on the Road Back," *Time* 42 (Oct. 11, 1943), 84; "Ford Heritage," *Fortune*, p. 246; *New York Journal-American*, Nov. 29 and 30, 1964 (series of articles by Bob Considine); "Prince Henry," *Newsweek* 23 (Apr. 24, 1944), 70.

6. *New York Herald Tribune*, Aug. 31, 1951 (found niche); DT, Jan. 23, 1944 (vice-presidency an-

nounced); DFP, Apr. 11, 1944; "All Quiet on the River Rouge," *Business Week* (June 24, 1944), 20–21; Nevins and Hill, *Decline and Rebirth*, p. 264. *Current Biography*, 1946 ed., s.v. "Ford, Henry 2d." Young Henry's promotion to vice-president was the result of "pressure from Henry II's mother and grandmother," but Henry II knew Bennett still ruled. *New York Journal American*, Dec. 1, 1964.

7. "Sikorsky Presents Helicopter to Edison Institute Museum," *Ford Times* 1 (Oct. 15, 1943), 1; DT, Jan. 26, 1944; Burck, "Henry Ford II," p. 118.

8. DFP, Oct. 6, 1944 (wowed the press); "Ford Has a New Driving Force: He's Energetic, Young Henry II," *Newsweek* 25 (June 18, 1945), 70; unidentified clipping, datelined Detroit, Sept. 30, 1944 on p. 215 of Clipbook 132 (Scripps-Howard); "Ford Fast on Feet," *Motor* 83 (Jan. 1945), 35; Burck, "Henry Ford II," pp. 109–10.

9. *Jackson Patriot*, Mar. 29, 1944 (Sweinhart story); "Ford Heritage," *Fortune*, p. 29; A Survey of Attitudes Toward and Opinions About Ford Motor Company (photostatic copy), submitted to FMC by Elmo Roper, Oct. 1944, Acc. 134, Box 17; DN, Apr. 8, 1945. D.D. Martin, head of Ford's News Bureau during Henry Ford's suit against the *Chicago Tribune* in 1919, also wrote a story on Henry II that was widely syndicated in mid-1945; see *Chicago News*, June 16, 1945 and Clipbook 133. Henry II also found time to dine with Frank Sinatra at New York's Stork Club in late 1944. DT, Oct. 13, 1944.

10. "Bigger Job for Younger Ford," *Motor* 81 (May 1944), 84; Samuel Crowther to William J. Cameron, May 6 and Aug. 14, 1944, Acc. 44, Box 1; John Gunther, *Inside U.S.A.* (New York: Harper & Brothers, 1947), p. 408; "Detroit," speech given by Henry Ford II before the Beavers, Detroit Athletic Club, Dec. 21, 1944 (copy in author's possession). Copies of Cameron's speech drafts are in Acc. 44, Box 5; copies of the institutional advertisements are in Acc. 44, Box 13. News stories for 1945 on Henry II are in Clipbooks, 131–33.

11. Letter signed by Dwight Mills, executive vice-president, K & E and B.J. Craig, July 20, 1945, Acc. 149, Box 20 (retention date); William H. Wilson, JWT, to B.R. Donaldson, May 2, 1945, Acc. 149, Box 110; The Ford Sunday Evening Hour Plan for Commercial Policy, Advertising, Publicity, submitted to FMC by K & E, Aug. 23, 1945, Acc. 149, Box 21. Programs for the Hour's first three shows are in Acc. 44, Box 16.

12. Nevins and Hill, *Decline and Rebirth*, p. 268; DN, May 11, 1944; James Dalton, "Henry Ford II Speaks," *Motor* 82 (Nov. 1944), 37; "Fast on Feet," *Motor*, p. 35; "Driving Force," *Newsweek*, p. 70.

13. Nevins and Hill, *Decline and Rebirth*, pp. 248–50, 262–68; *New York Journal-American*, Nov. 30 and Dec. 1, 1964; Bennett, *Never Called Henry*, p. 174.

14. Nevins and Hill, *Decline and Rebirth*, pp. 268–69; David J. Wilkie, "Henry Ford—Man and Magnate," *Automotive News* 37 (July 29, 1963), 16; *New York Journal-American*, Dec. 2, 1964.

15. Nevins and Hill, *Decline and Rebirth*, p. 269; *New York Journal-American*, Dec. 2, 1964; Bennett, *Never Called Henry*, p. 178. Henry Ford's letter of resignation read as follows:

"I hereby resign the office of president of this company, to take effect upon acceptance. I feel free to take this step at this time because the critical period during which I again assumed office has passed. As you know, I have many personal interests to which I now desire to devote most of my time. I shall be glad to remain on the board, and to assist in an advisory way. May I recommend to the board that it consider the appointment of my grandson, Henry Ford II, as my successor. To the officers and director I extend my thanks for the cordial cooperation always given me and to which is due so greatly the success of the company." [FMC news release, Sept. 21, 1945, Acc. 149, Box 91.]

16. *New York Journal-American,* Dec. 2, 1964; DFP, Oct. 2, 13 and 19, 1945; *Dayton News,* Oct. 2, 1945; FMC news release, Sept. 27, 1945, Acc. 149, Box 91; DFP, Feb. 27, 1946, Oct. 26, 1945; DN, June 21, 1964; interview with Bennett, Apr. 14–15, 1973.

17. *New York Journal-American,* Dec. 2, 1964 (informing Henry Ford of Bennett's ouster); DT, Oct. 12 1945; DFP, Sept. 28 and 30, 1945; DN, Sept. 29, 1945; "Ford Runs Ford," *Business Week* (Oct. 6, 1945), 18–19; A. H. Allen, "Mirrors of Motordom," *Steel* 117 (Oct. 8, 1945), 91; "Henry Ford II Clears Out All Executives and Names New," *Motor* 84 (Nov. 1945), 92, 94; DT, Feb. 3 and May 23, 1946; DFP, July 13, 1946. Thompson's ouster was a "classic furniture firing," the office furniture from the publicist's office being carted from the Administration Building to the Rotunda Building across the street. MacNaughton interview, May 12, 1962. Following his dismissal Thompson tried to get into the Administration Building via the tunnel leading from the Rotunda, but found the exit blocked by Henry II's men. Interview with Jimmy Rooney, a former Sales and Advertising Department employee Feb. 26, 1958. In 1962, Thompson, when interviewed by the author, was a public relations consultant in California.

18. Allen, "Mirrors of Motordom," p. 91; FMC news releases, Sept. 27 and Oct. 26, 1945, Acc. 149, Box 91; Nevins and Hill, *Decline and Rebirth,* pp. 296, 319; DN, June 4, 1948.

19. See Clipbook 136 for news stories on Ford's "changing of the guard." "Auto Makers Bring in New Blood for Stiff Post-Strike Competition," *Newsweek* 26 (Oct. 8, 1945), 74; DN, Sept. 22, 1945; *Business Week* (Sept. 29, 1945), 18; Burck, "Henry Ford II," pp. 108–9; *Boston News Bureau,* Sept. 22, 1945; NYT, Sept. 22, 1945; *Tide* 19 (Oct. 1, 1945), 25.

20. "Little Giant Goes," *Time* 46 (Oct. 8, 1945), 81; *Hartford* (Conn.) *Times,* Sept. 22, 1945; *Indianapolis News,* Sept. 22, 1945; *Bridgeport* (Conn.) *Life,* Sept. 30, 1945; DT, Sept. 25, 1945; "The New Man," *Time* 46 (Oct. 1, 1945), 88; DT, Sept. 25, 1945 (*Popular Science* advertisement); FMC news release, Sept. 27, 1945, Acc. 149, Box 91. "The retirement of Harry Bennett from the post in administration of the Ford Company he has had in the past," observed the Associated Press, "will be taken as evidence that the presidency and direction of Henry Ford II is to be real in every sense of the word." *Houghton* (Mich.) *Daily Mining Journal,* Sept. 29, 1945.

21. See Clipbook 136 for dozens of editorials summing up Henry Ford's career especially *Lemmon* (S.D.) *Leader,* Sept. 27, 1945; *Indianapolis News,* Sept. 22, 1945; *Hartford* (Conn.) *Times,* Sept. 22, 1945; DT, Sept. 25, 1945; *Baton Rouge* (La.) *Times, New Castle* (Pa.) *News,* and *Reno Gazette,* Sept. 24, 1945; *Cumberland* (Md.) *News,* Sept. 26, 1945; *Indianapolis News, Boston Traveler, Marshfield* (Wis.) *Herald, McKeesport* (Pa.) *News, Prescott* (Ariz.) *Courier, Astoria* (Ore.) *Astorian-Budget,* Sept. 22, 1945.

Chapter 26

1. Nevins and Hill, *Decline and Rebirth,* p. 242; Thompson, *Reminiscences,* p. 87; *PM* (New York), Aug. 26, 1943; Nelson, *Reminiscences,* p. 100; DFP, Apr. 26, 1945.

2. DT, July 29, 1943; DT, July 30, 1944; *New York Sun,* July 28, 1944; Raymond J. Jeffreys, *God Is My Landlord* (Chicago: Van Kampen Press, 1947), pp. 81, 93.

3. "Henry Ford, at 80, Carries Staggering Burden," *Motor* 80 (July 1943), 56; "Edsel Ford, 1893–1943," *Newsweek* 21 (June 7, 1943), 75; A.H. Allen, "Mirrors of Motordom," *Steel* 112 (June 7, 1943), 85; *Times* (London), June 2, 1943; *Washington News,* Aug. 25, 1943; DFP, Aug. 25, 1943; *Wausau* (Wis.) *Record Herald,* Aug. 28, 1943; *Abilene* (Kan.) *Chronicle,* Sept. 6, 1943. See news stories and editorials on the Ford-Pearson flap in Clipbook 129.

4. C.J. Smith, employee of FMC Experimental Department, *Reminiscences,* p. 47; Cameron, *Reminiscences,* pp. 251, 286; DN, July 30, 1942. See Clipbook 125 for news stories and editorials based on Ford's breakfast press conference. Those attending the breakfast conference were David J. Wilkie, Associated Press; Anthony G. De Lorenzo, United Press; Clyde Reece, International News Service; Jack Manning, *Detroit Times;* Malcolm Bingay, *Detroit Free Press;* and James Sweinhart, *Detroit News.* After breakfast, Ford posed for newsreel and photo syndicate representatives. Ford News Bureau sheet on program details, n.d., Acc. 285, Box 2351.

5. Bennett, *Never Called Henry,* p. 168; Rufus Wilson, Henry Ford's chauffeur, 1932–45, *Reminiscences,* p. 35; Liebold, *Reminiscences,* pp. 1176, 1178–79; interview with the Rev. Florence B. Crews, pastor, Temple of Light, Mar. 12, 1973; Louise B. Clancy and Florence Davies, *The Believer: The Life Story of Mrs. Henry Ford* (New York: Coward-McCann, Inc., 1960), pp. 199–201; Nevins and Hill, *Decline and Rebirth,* p. 115.

6. Jeffreys, *Landlord,* p. 42; *New York Herald Tribune,* July 15, 1944 (Arnold); NYT, July 16, 1943 (Giraud); NYT, July 25, 1944 (Wallace); S.J. Woolf, "Ford, at 80, Expounds His Faith," *New York Times Magazine* (July 25, 1943), 6; DFP, July 27, 1944; Bennett, *Never Called Henry,* p. 170; Sorensen, *Forty Years,* p. 313; Nevins and Hill, *Decline and Rebirth,* p. 242; Liebold, *Reminiscences,* pp. 1191, 1220–21. For a discussion of neurological symptoms identified with stroke see Arthur P. Noyes, M.D. and Lawrence C. Kolb, M.D., *Modern Clinical Psychiatry,* 5th ed. (Philadelphia: W.B. Saunders Company, 1958), p. 227.

7. NYT, Feb. 6, 1944; "Ford Heritage," *Fortune,* p. 141; "Admiral Carpenter Calls Dearborn Naval Training Base 'Finest I Have Seen,'" *Ford Times* 2 (May 12, 1944), 3; NYT, July 10, 1944; DFP, July 11, 1944; DN, Sept. 18, 1944; Jeffreys, *Landlord,* pp. 81, 85–86.

8. DFP, Dec. 20, 1944, Sept. 7 and Apr. 26, 1945; DT, May 16, 1945; Bacon, *Reminiscences,* pp. 210–11.

9. Jeffreys, *Landlord,* p. 96; Richards, *Last Billionaire,* p. 3 (Lovett); Joe McCarthy, "The Amazing Mansion of Henry Ford," *Saturday Evening Post* 225 (May 16, 1953), 176 ("Little Orphan Annie"); Burlingame, *Henry Ford,* p. 163.

10. Nevins and Hill, *Decline and Rebirth,* pp. 256, 272; James Dalton, "Henry Ford II Speaks," *Motor* 82 (Nov. 1944), 37; NYT, Sept. 22, 1945; "Elder Ford 'Very Chipper,'" *Motor* 84 (Oct. 1945), 68.

11. See Clipbooks 131–32 covering the period Feb.-Oct. 1944, for evidence that Henry Ford's views were still

newsworthy. "Any interview with him or anything he said during the war years was still news around the world," as former United Press Automotive Editor Anthony G. De Lorenzo told the author in November 1965.

12. DFP, Sept. 19, 1944 (genius for anticipating events and master of timing); *New York Sun*, Apr. 17, 1944; DT, Sept. 17, 1944. See Clipbook 132 for news stories and editorials on Ford's promise of job preferences to veterans and on his promise to raise wages.

13. *Atlanta Constitution*, Mar. 20, 1944; *Savannah Press*, Mar. 21, 1944 (decline in value of stock); *Syracuse Herald-Journal*, Mar. 21, 1944; *New York Post*, Mar. 22, 1944; *Canonsburg* (Pa.) *Notes*, Mar. 23, 1944; *Savannah Press*, Mar. 22, 1944; *Cadillac* (Mich.) *News*, Mar. 21, 1944; *St. Charles* (Mo.) *Banner*, Mar. 30, 1944; *Marshall* (Tex.) *Messenger*, Apr. 2, 1944; *Tuscaloosa* (Ala.) *News*, Apr. 5, 1944; DN, Mar. 28, 1944; *Hartford* (Conn.) *Times*, Apr. 12, 1944; *Madison* (Wis.) *Journal*, Apr. 13, 1944; *Greenville* (Ala.) *Advocate*, Apr. 20, 1944; *Clarksdale* (Miss.) *Register*, n.d. [Apr. 2, 1944]. News stories and editorials on Ford's prediction are in Clipbooks 131–32.

14. *Northampton* (Mass.) *Gazette*, Apr. 21, 1944. Many of the news stories and editorials in Clipbooks 131–32 on Ford's expression of regret are undated and unidentified; see especially Clipbook 131 articles headlined, "Tip from the Wrong Feed Box," and "Ford Has No Alibi for Guess on War," p. 141; "Stick to Your Knitting," p. 241; "Ho Hum," p. 248; and "Henry's Bad Guess," p. 251. Other useful stories are in *Atlanta Constitution*, May 19, 1944; *Chicago Daily News*, May 19, 1941; and *Lincoln* (Neb.) *Star*, May 19, 1944. Many other notables also inaccurately predicted the end of the war. England's *Old Moor's Almanack*, which had been making predictions for almost 250 years, asserted in 1942 that Germany would be beaten in 1943, as did Czechoslovakian President Edward Benes and Senator Carter Glass. In early 1943 Admiral William F. Halsey and James A. Farley predicted Germany's defeat in 1943, while Eisenhower, General Henri Giraud, economist Leon Henderson, Rabbi Stephen S. Wise, and 54 percent of a Swedish sample in 1943 predicted victory over Germany in 1944. In July 1944, Marshall Bernard L. Montgomery declared that Germany would be beaten before the end of 1944; in August 1944, Undersecretary of War Robert Patterson gave Germany four more months and Lloyd's of London bet eight to five that the European war would be over by October. The best of the press's prognosticators was eighty-eight-year-old historian, Albert Bushnell Hart, who on Jan. 2, 1943 said "the United States and her Allies will be victorious over Germany in two years. Japan will give up soon afterward." *Miami Herald*, Jan. 30, 1943; *New York World-Telegram*, Apr. 4, 1945.

15. Cameron, *Reminiscences*, pp. 251, 286; Jeffreys, *Landlord*, p. 94; "Ford Heritage," *Fortune*, p. 141; DFP, July 11, 1944 (Childs); DFP, July 27, 1944; DN, Aug. 11, 1944; NYT, Feb. 3, 1945.

16. DN, Oct. 31, 1944; DT, Nov. 10, 1944; NYT, Nov. 11, 1944. Ford visited the Rouge plant's blood bank on Nov. 2, 1944, attended a party for veteran Ford employees at the Dearborn Inn on Dec. 19, 1944, and visited Camp Legion on Apr. 19, 1945, but was not interviewed by the press on these occasions. Statements on his activities were issued to the press, however. *Dearborn Press*, Nov. 2, 1944; DFP, Dec. 20, 1944; DT, Apr. 20, 1945.

17. DN, July 11, 1945; NYT, July 30, 1945; FMC news releases, Sept. 21, 1945, July 29, 1946, Acc. 149, Box 91; Burlingame, *Henry Ford*, p. 165.

18. Albeit one of the nation's best publicized businessmen between 1942–45, Ford was far less newsworthy during this period than he had been during the previous quarter-century. The *New York Times* ran an average of only fourteen items per year about him during 1942–45, compared with an average of 134 stories per year between 1921–32 and forty-one stories per year between 1933–41. The general periodical press ran an average of five articles per year about Ford between 1942–45, as against an average of nineteen per year between 1931–32 and nine between 1933–41. See *New York Times Index, Readers' Guide to Periodical Literature*, and *Industrial Arts Index* for years 1921–45.

19. "The Fortune Survey," *Fortune* 25 (May 1942), 43–44; "What Americans Should Asians Know?," *Asia and the Americas* 43 (Jan. 1943), 57; "These Are, By Your Votes, the Americans Asians Should Know," *Asia and the Americas* 43 (Apr. 1943), 55; A Review of the First Year of "Watch the World Go By," submitted by Maxon, n.d. [June 1943], Acc. 149, Box 94. In the *Fortune* survey, Ford had more support than Wilkie among blacks, farm laborers and owners, and in four of nine sections of the country: East North Central, West North Central, East South Central, and Mountain.

20. *Brooklyn Eagle*, Feb. 11, 1943; NYT, Feb. 3, 1944; *Riverside* (Calif.) *Enterprise*, Apr. 3, 1945; *New York Herald Tribune*, Jan. 31, 1946 (National Opinion Research Center of America). In addition to Edison, those rated higher than Ford in the National Opinion Research Center of America poll were Franklin D. Roosevelt, Lincoln, Washington, Wilson, Jefferson, Eisenhower, MacArthur, and Theodore Roosevelt.

21. *Chicago Daily News*, Aug. 4, 1943; "Journal About Town," *Ladies' Home Journal* 62 (Apr. 1945), 15 (Stalin); DT, Apr. 24, 1942; *Ford Times* 1 (Oct. 29, 1943), 3. Henry Ford pioneered in assigning industrial work to the blind; and his example led other manufacturing firms to employ blind people. Ford was the first recipient of the Migel Medal not actively identified with an agency for the blind. NYT, June 9, Sept. 20, 1944. Stones memorializing P.T. Barnum and Sir William Osler were added to the Walk of Fame at the same time as Ford's stone; the walk consisted of more than 600 stones. NYT, Jan. 18, 1945.

22. Four companies, General Electric, Pan American Airways, Westinghouse, and Montgomery Ward, received slightly more attention than Ford in the *New York Times*—and perhaps other newspapers as well—during 1942–45. But Ford received far more attention than these firms or any other companies both in general periodicals and in the trade press. Among its leading automotive rivals, Ford received four times as much publicity in general magazines as General Motors, almost ten times as much as Chrysler. The *New York Times* ran an annual average of seventy-eight Ford stories during the war years; the general and trade periodical press published an average of fifty-three Ford articles during this period. In a nationwide public opinion survey conducted by Maxon in November 1942, Ford (which was favorably regarded by 84.6 percent of the respondents) was rated slightly behind General Motors and General Electric, and substantially ahead of Chrysler. A public opinion study conducted by Elmo Roper in June 1944 concluded that "most Americans" still looked upon the Ford Company as the country's "No. 1 corporation." Respondents in the Link Audit's wartime surveys, which semiannually measured favorable and unfavorable at-

550 Notes, pages 425 to 431

titudes toward eight major firms, regarded Ford less favorably than General Electric, General Motors, Westinghouse, and Du Pont, but more favorably than Standard Oil Company of New Jersey, United States Steel, and United States Rubber (Ford received a more favorable vote than Du Pont in the November 1945 audit, however). Ford, along with all the other companies, achieved a higher percentage of favorable votes in the 1942–45 period (69 percent) than during the 1937–41 era (65 percent); and, in common with its rivals, was regarded *unfavorably* by fewer of the respondents in the years 1942–45 (9 percent) than during the previous four years (12 percent). See *New York Times Index, Readers' Guide to Periodical Literature,* and *Industrial Arts Index* for the years 1933–45; A Review of the First Year of "Watch the World Go By," submitted to FMC by Maxon, Inc., n.d. [June 1943], Acc. 149, Box 94; A Survey of Attitudes Towards and Opinions About Ford Motor Company (photostatic copy), submitted to FMC by Elmo Roper, n.d. [Oct. 1947], Acc. 134, Box 17; The Link Audit a Review and Evaluation, prepared by Public Relations Research Department, FMC, Oct. 10, 1953, Acc. 465, Box 1.

Chapter 27

1. "The Rebirth of Ford," *Fortune* 35 (May 1947), 83, 207, 211; *Moody's Manual of Investments American and Foreign* for period 1930–45; "Young Henry Takes a Risk," *Time* 47 (Feb. 4, 1946), 75; H.C. Doss, Ford sales manager during war years, *Reminiscences,* p. 94; William B. Harris, "Ford's Fight for First," *Fortune* 30 (Sept. 1944), p. 234; *Boston News Bureau,* July 5, 1945.

2. Nevins and Hill, *Decline and Rebirth,* pp. 294–95; A.H. Allen, "Mirrors of Motordom," *Steel* 118 (June 10, 1946), 74; *New York Journal-American,* Dec. 3, 1964; George Koether, "How Henry Ford II Saved the Empire," *Look* 17 (June 30, 1953), 48; *Buffalo News,* Mar. 25, 1946; Harris, "Ford's Fight," p. 123; DN, Dec. 8, 1945.

3. "Autos: Young King Henry Ford," *Newsweek* 29 (Apr. 21, 1947), 70; Koether, "Saved the Empire," *Look,* p. 48; "Heirs at the Helm," *Forbes* 80 (Nov. 15, 1957), 72; "Strong Hand at Ford's Wheel," *Forbes* 88 (Nov. 15, 1961), 19; "How Henry Ford II Reshaped His Company," *Business Week* (Sept. 30, 1961), 52; Harris, "Ford's Fight," p. 65; "It's a New Kind of Ford Motor Company," *Fortune* 65 (Feb. 1962), 114; Arnold R. Weber, *The Structure of Collective Bargaining* (New York: Free Press of Glencoe, 1961), p. 83; Nevins and Hill, *Decline and Rebirth,* pp. 294, 447; *Steel* 117 (Oct. 8, 1945), 92.

4. Leonard Westrate, "1946 a Year of Calamity," *Automotive and Aviation Industries* 95 (Dec. 15, 1946), 18; Leonard Westrate, "Prices, Production and Sales Possibilities," *Automotive and Aviation Industries* 95 (Dec. 1, 1946), 60; Alfred P. Sloan, Jr., *My Years with General Motors* (Garden City, N.Y.: Doubleday & Company, Inc., 1964), pp. 207–8, 385; "Ford Market Recapture," *Newsweek* 24 (Sept. 25, 1944), 20; *New York Journal-American,* Nov. 29, 1964; Nevins and Hill, *Decline and Rebirth,* p. 295.

5. Speech by Charles E. Carll, director of public relations, to FMC dealers, June 20, 1947, Acc. 234, Box 9; Irwin Ross, *The Image Merchants: the Fabulous World of Public Relations* (Garden City, N.Y.: Doubleday & Company, Inc., 1959), pp. 87–88; see

Clipbooks 129–35 for news stories and editorials on Henry Ford II's career between August 1943 and September 1945.

6. A.H. Allen, "Mirrors of Motordom," *Steel* 117 (Oct. 8, 1945), 91; Nevins and Hill, *Decline and Rebirth,* p. 296; "Ford's Public," *Business Week* (Mar. 30, 1946), 26, 28; Elmo Roper to David L. Lewis, Jan. 26, 1965.

7. Ross, *Image Merchants,* pp. 91–93; *Who's Who in America,* 32nd ed., s.v. "Newsom, Edwin Earl."

8. Ross, *Image Merchants,* p. 86; speech by Earl Newsom to Adcraft Club of Detroit and Detroit Chapter, Public Relations Society of America, Mar. 21, 1952, Acc. 234, Box 33; speech by Charles F. Moore, Jr., vice-president-public relations and advertising, FMC, to Public Relations Society of America, Philadelphia, Nov. 19, 1957. Newsom was retained by Ford until 1958.

9. "Ford Has a New Driving Force: He's Energetic, Young Henry II," *Newsweek* 25 (June 18, 1945), 70; Sward, *Legend of Henry Ford,* p. 471; DFP, Oct. 24 and 30, 1945.

10. DT, Oct. 29, Nov. 16, 1945; *New York Journal of Commerce,* Oct. 31, 1945; A.H. Allen, "Mirrors of Motordom," *Steel* 117 (Oct. 22, 1945), 94; DT, Oct. 29, Nov. 16, 1945; *New York Journal of Commerce,* Oct. 31, 1945; "That 23%," *Time* 46 (Oct. 15, 1945), 21; "Ford's Surprise Maneuver Upsets CIO Divide and Conquer Strategy," *Newsweek* 26 (Nov. 26, 1945), 70; "D-Day in Detroit," *Time* 46 (Nov. 26, 1945), 21.

11. Ross, *Image Merchants,* p. 87; DT, Nov. 16, 1945; NYT, Nov. 16, 1945; "Surprise Maneuver," *Newsweek,* p. 70; "Ford Asks Union for Work Guarantees," *Factory Management and Maintenance* 104 (Jan. 1946), 280. Henry II's letter also noted that employees' productivity had decreased about 34 percent since the company had signed its first contract with the union in 1941. "One Solution to Our Problems," speech by Henry Ford II to Commonwealth Club of California, San Francisco, Feb. 8, 1946 (copy in author's possession).

12. Joel Seidman, *American Labor From Defense to Reconversion* (Chicago: University of Chicago Press, 1953), p. 229; "Two-Way Bargaining Demand," *Business Week* (Nov. 24, 1945), 93; "Henry Ford II's Mr. Bugas," *Fortune* 34 (July 1946), 146; *Atlanta Constitution,* Nov. 17, 1945; DFP, Nov. 16 and 17, 1945; *Glens Falls* (N.Y.) *Post-Star,* Nov. 17, 1945; *Washington News,* Nov. 17, 1945; *Cincinnati Times-Star,* Nov. 21, 1945; *Astoria Astorian-Budget,* Nov. 27, 1945. News stories and editorials on Ford's letter are in Clipbook 136.

13. "D-Day in Detroit," *Time,* p. 21; NYT, Nov. 16, 1945; "Surprise Maneuver," *Newsweek,* p. 70.

14. Sward, *Legend of Henry Ford,* p. 472; "Art of Negotiation I," *Time* 46 (Dec. 24, 1945), 20; James Dalton, "Strike Is Heavy Blow at Reconversion," *Motor* 84 (Dec. 1945), 45, 188; "Ford Employs New Strategy," *Business Week* (Dec. 8, 1945), 96.

15. "Two-Way Bargaining," *Business Week,* p. 93; DFP, Nov. 17 and 29, 1945; "New Strategy," *Business Week,* p. 96.

16. DT, Dec. 10, 1945; *Chicago Tribune,* Dec. 11, 1945; "Sensational Union Offer," *Motor* 84 (Dec. 1945), 34; "Art of Negotiation," *Time,* p. 21.

17. *New York Post* and DFP, Dec. 12, 1945; DT and DN, Dec. 11, 1945; *Columbus Dispatch,* Dec. 18, 1945; *St. Louis Post-Dispatch,* Dec. 20, 1945. See Clipbook 136 for news stories and editorials on Leonard's proposal.

18. "Art of Negotiation," *Time,* p. 20; DN, Dec. 2 and 9,

1945; *New York Herald Tribune,* Dec. 11, 1945; *St. Louis Post-Dispatch,* Dec. 15, 1945; Stanley H. Brams, "Assembly Line," *Iron Age* 156 (Dec. 6, 1945), 86.

19. "Union Offer," *Motor,* p. 34; *Los Angeles Daily News,* Dec. 14, 1945 (Eleanor Roosevelt); DN, Dec. 11 and 12, 1945; DFP, Dec. 12, 1945; *New York Herald Tribune,* Dec. 11, 1945. See Clipbook 136 for press comment on Ford-UAW bargaining relations.

20. DN, Dec. 9, 1945; DT, Dec. 10, 1945; DFP, Dec. 16, 1945; *Los Angeles Times,* Dec. 18, 1945. The UAW at one point insisted that its members be given the right to buy Ford cars at cost. "Fine," said Henry II. But the union backed off upon learning that government price restrictions, coupled with the company's pitifully low volume of production, forced the firm to sell its cars for $300 less than they cost. George Koether, "How Henry Ford II Saved the Empire," *Look* 17 (June 30, 1953), 48.

21. "The Challenge of Human Engineering," speech by Henry Ford II to the Society of Automotive Engineers, Jan. 9, 1946, Acc. 454, Box 11; Ross, *Image Merchants,* p. 88; Booten Herndon, *Ford: An Unconventional Biography of the Men and Their Times* (New York: Weybright and Talley, 1969), pp. 192–93; DN, Jan. 9 and 10, 1946.

22. "Defining the Goal," *Time* 47 (Jan. 21, 1946), 19; DFP, Jan. 11, 1946 (quoting Kaiser); *Current Biography,* 1946 ed., s.v. "Ford, Henry 2d."; DN, Jan. 10, 1946; *St. Louis Post-Dispatch,* Oct. 19, 1945.

23. DN, Jan. 10 and 11, 1946; *New York Herald Tribune,* Jan. 10, 1946; DT, Jan. 11, 1946.

24. DFP, Jan. 18, 1946; Nevins and Hill, *Decline and Rebirth,* p. 307; see Clipbook 136 for news stories and editorials on Henry II's SAE speech.

25. DN, Jan. 15, 1946; *New York Herald Tribune,* Jan. 16, 1946; DT, Jan. 26 and 27, 1946; DFP, Jan. 27 and 28, 1946; *New York Sun,* Jan. 26 and 28, 1946.

26. Nevins and Hill, *Decline and Rebirth,* pp. 306–7; " 'Human Engineering' Program Pays Off For Ford," *Business Week* (Oct. 30, 1948), p. 89. R.J. Thomas claimed that General Motors hoped to destroy the UAW. *Louisville Courier-Journal,* Jan. 17, 1946.

27. Lawrence M. Hughes, "Ford Girds to Regain First Place in Motors," *Advertising Age* 18 (Mar. 3, 1947), 55; "The Rebirth of Ford," *Fortune* 35 (May 1947), 86–87; "Employee Opinion Survey Aids Ford in Policy Making," *Factory Management and Maintenance* 105 (June 1947), 132–33; "Human Engineering," *Business Week,* p. 94; "Ford at Fifty," *Tide* 27 (May 9, 1953), 60.

28. "Human Engineering," *Business Week,* p. 94; Employee Publications—Procedure No. 1, n.d. [May 1946], Acc. 44, Box 17; William D. Kennedy, director of publications, to Henry Ford II, May 24, 1946, Acc. 44, Box 17; Tom Lilley, "Henry Ford II Speaks Out," *Atlantic Monthly* 180 (Dec. 1947), 32; C. Wayne VanDerwill, supervisor, Suggestion Program Unit, Personnel and Organization Staff, FMC, to David L. Lewis, Dec. 28, 1965; DT, Dec. 12, 1948. The *Ford Times* was the company's sole postwar company publication until March 1946 when the *River Rouge News* was started. The *Rouge News* began publishing special editions for Highland Park and village industry employees beginning in April and May, 1946, respectively. Kennedy to Henry II, May 24, 1945, Acc. 44, Box 17. Employee communications were a responsibility of the Industrial Relations Division.

29. DFP, July 13, 1947 (time clocks); DN, Nov. 19, 1947; "Manners & Morals," *Time* 50 (Nov. 10, 1947), 29; "The New Ford," *Life* 24 (June 14, 1948),

112. Henry Ford II, in the manner of his grandfather years before at the Highland Park and Rouge plants, made the rounds of Ford factories during the early years of his presidency. News photographs show young Ford with veteran workers, who, overwhelmed by the presence of the boss and embarrassed by their greasy hands, proffered only a little finger for a handshake. "The Small Hello," *Time* 49 (June 16, 1947), 85.

30. Lilley, "Henry Ford Speaks," p. 30; Charles P. Larrowe, "A Meteor on the Industrial Relations Horizon: the Foreman's Association of America," *Labor History* 2 (Fall 1961), 270; Nevins and Hill, *Decline and Rebirth,* pp. 335–37; DT, Jan. 29, 1946; DFP, May 16 and July 7, 1947; "End of Experiment," *Time* 50 (July 14, 1947), 79.

31. Richards, *Last Billionaire,* p. 371; DN, Feb. 6, 1948; Lilley, "Henry Ford Speaks," pp. 30–31. The FAA deteriorated rapidly after failing to win its strike at Ford. Larrowe, "Meteor on Horizon," p. 290.

32. DN, June 27, 1947; "Rouge Revolution," *Time* 50 (July 7, 1947), 83; "Pension in Ford's Future," *Newsweek* 30 (July 7, 1947), 70; DFP, Oct. 1 and 10, 1947; "Wage Chronology No. 14: Ford Motor Co., 1941–50," *Monthly Labor Review* 72 (Apr. 1951), 400–1. The 1949 contract provided for $100 per month pensions for workers at age sixty-five who had thirty years of service. The $100 included the workers' social security benefits, but, except for social security payroll deductions, cost employees nothing. "Auto Peace," *Newsweek* 34 (Oct. 10, 1949), 21.

33. A.H. Allen, "Mirrors of Motordom," *Steel* 118 (June 10, 1946), 73; FMC news release, May 29, 1949 (speech by Henry Ford II at Harvard University Graduate School of Business Administration, May 20, 1949), FMC News Department Library; JWT Client Confirmation Report, Apr. 10, 1946, Acc. 149, Box 113.

34. "Mr. Bugas," *Fortune,* p. 148; "Rebirth of Ford," *Fortune,* p. 87; "Human Engineering," *Business Week,* p. 89; Hughes, "Ford Girds," p. 55 (Roper study).

35. DT, May 20, July 13, 1948; DFP, Oct. 20, 1948; "Human Engineering," *Business Week,* p. 89.

36. George H. Mayer and Walter O. Forster, *The United States and the Twentieth Century* (Boston: Houghton Mifflin Company, 1958), p. 652; DT, Nov. 19, 1945; NYT, Nov. 19, 1945; "New Car Prices Confusing and Incomplete," *Motor* 84 (Dec. 1945), 190, 194. The OPA reduced General Motors' prices because it was believed that GM's high volume of production would enable the big manufacturer to produce more cheaply than its competitors. "General Motors' Prices Lowest," *Motor* 85 (Mar. 1946), 33. Price Administrator Chester Bowles ordered dealers to cut their discounts by 2½ percent, saying that postwar profit margins would be higher than prewar because the heavy demand for cars eliminated the need for generous trade-in allowances. "At Last: Prices," *Time* 46 (Nov. 26, 1945), 8. Ford was permitted to raise prices on the Mercury by an average of 4 percent because of design changes. NYT, Dec. 15, 1945. Lincoln prices could be raised an average of 1 percent. *Automotive News* 21 (Jan. 14, 1946), 52.

37. DT, Nov. 20, 1945; *New York Herald Tribune,* Nov. 20, 1945; "Young Henry Takes a Risk," *Time* 47 (Feb. 4, 1946), 77. The Ford Company said in December 1945 that it had granted wage increases totaling 36.65 percent, exclusive of benefits in the form of vacation pay and shift differentials, between January 1941 and July 1945. The company also stated that, at present OPA ceilings, it would lose $35,000,000, or

an average of $27 per car and truck in 1946, even if producing at capacity with increased productivity of 16 percent and at the same wage rate. DT, Dec. 13, 1945.

38. See copy of Henry II's telegram to Snyder in Acc. 454, Box 10; *St. Louis Post-Dispatch*, Jan. 31, 1946. Ford produced 71,822 passenger cars in January 1946; its scheduled production was 180,416 units. Comparative Vehicle Schedules and Actual Production 1945–46 Models, Feb. 20, 1946, Acc. 454, Box 10.

39. See Clipbook 137 for editorial comment on Henry II's proposal to remove automotive price controls on the automotive industry. Pro-Ford editorials can be found in *Bridgeport* (Conn.) *Post*, Feb. 1, 1946; *Albion* (Mich.) *Recorder*, Jan. 31, 1946; *Wilmington Journal*, Feb. 1, 1946; *Lewiston* (Maine) *Journal*, Jan. 31, 1946; *Jersey City Jersey Journal*, Feb. 1, 1946; and *Albany* (N.Y.) *Knickerbocker*, Feb. 2, 1946. Editorials unfavorable to Ford are in *St. Louis Post-Dispatch*, Feb. 1, 1946; *St. Louis Star-Times*, Feb. 1, 1946; and *Brooklyn Eagle*, Feb. 3, 1946.

40. DFP, Feb. 1, 2, and 9, 1946; *St. Louis Post-Dispatch*, Feb. 2, 1946. "Young Henry's Plan," *Time* 47 (Feb. 18, 1946), 89–90; Ross, *Image Merchants*, p. 88; Elizabeth B. Drewry, director, Franklin D. Roosevelt Library, to David L. Lewis, Aug. 11, 1967. Roosevelt's Sept. 23, 1932 audience numbered 1,738. Durward S. Riggs, assistant executive secretary, Commonwealth Club of California, to David L. Lewis, Aug. 18, 1967. "One Solution to Our Problems," speech by Henry Ford II to Commonwealth Club of California, Feb. 8, 1946 (copy in author's possession).

41. See Clipbook 137 for news stories and editorials on Henry II's Commonwealth Club speech. Pro-Ford editorials can be found in *Lewiston* (Maine) *Sun*, Feb. 11, 1946; *Bridgeport* (Conn.) *Post*, Feb. 10, 1946; *Ironwood* (Mich.) *Globe*, Feb. 12, 1946; *Council Bluffs* (Iowa)*Nonpareil*, Feb. 13, 1946; *Cedar Rapids* (Iowa) *Gazette*, Feb. 14, 1946; *Richmond* (Ind.) *Palladium-Item*, Feb. 15, 1946; *Galax* (Va.) *Gazette*, Feb. 21, 1946; *Keokuk* (Iowa) *Gate City*, Feb. 11, 1946; *Holyoke* (Mass.) *Transcript & Telegram*, Feb. 14, 1946. A summation of anti-Ford sentiment appears in "Young Mr. Ford Is Wrong," *New Republic* 114 (Feb. 11, 1946), 174.

42. *Los Angeles Times*, Feb. 14, 1946; NYT and *Washington Star*, Feb. 16, 1946. A copy of Bowles's statement is in Acc. 454, Box 10. Bowles was named director of the Office of Economic Stabilization on Feb. 25, 1946. *Washington Post*, Feb. 25, 1946.

43. *New York Sun*, Feb. 19, 1946; NYT, Feb. 20, 1946. Henry II was never invited to appear before the House Banking and Currency Committee.

44. NYT, Feb. 20, 1946; Notes Taken During Telephone Conversation Between Messrs. Martindale, Crimmins and Newsom, 4 p.m., Feb. 19, 1946, Acc. 454, Box 10.

45. *Los Angeles Herald & Express*, Feb. 20, 1946. The text of Henry II's telegram to Spence is in a FMC news release, Feb. 20, 1946, Acc. 454, Box 10.

46. *New York Herald Tribune*, Feb. 22, 1946. The text of Henry II's telegram to Bowles is in a FMC news release, Feb. 21, 1946, Acc. 454, Box 10.

47. See Clipbook 137 for news stories and editorials on the debate between Henry II and Bowles. Pro-Ford newspapers include *Chattanooga News*, Feb. 23, 1946; *Worcester Telegram*, Feb. 22, 1946; *Waterloo* (Iowa) *Courier*, Feb. 22, 1946; *Marquette* (Mich.) *Daily Mining Journal*, Feb. 23, 1946; *Bridgeport* (Conn.) *Post*, Feb. 23, 1946; *Hudson* (N.Y.) *Star*,

Feb. 23, 1946; *Meriden* (Conn.) *Journal*, Feb. 22, 1946; *Waukegan* (Ill.) *News-Sun*, Feb. 23, 1945; *Cohoes* (N.Y.) *American*, Feb. 21, 1946; *Lewiston* (Maine) *Sun*, Feb. 20, 1946.

48. *Chicago Times*, Feb. 25, 1946; DN, Feb. 24, 1946. Newspapers taking a neutral position in the Ford-Bowles controversy include the *Chicago Times*, Feb. 25, 1946; *Newport News* (Va.) *Press*, Feb. 22, 1946; and *Highmore* (S.D.) *Herald*, n.d. [late Feb. 1946], Clipbook 137.

49. Nevins and Hill, *Expansion and Challenge*, p. 302; *New York Journal-American*, Dec. 4, 1964; *Los Angeles Examiner*, Feb. 17, 1946; DT, Feb. 10, 1946; *Chicago Times*, Feb. 25, 1946. See Clipbook 137 for other news articles and editorials which laud Henry II for his role during the pricing crisis.

50. NYT, Mar. 12, 1946; DFP, Mar. 30, 1946; DT, May 23, 1946; "Up Again," *Time* 47 (June 3, 1946), 81. Price increases on Ford products in mid-September averaged 6 percent. DN, Sept. 16, 1946. Ford's initial claim to have earned $2,000 in 1946 was discounted by the company in 1955, at which time the firm announced that it had lost $8,100,000 in 1946. The discrepancy is symptomatic of the financial confusion still existing at Ford in 1946. Nevins and Hill, *Decline and Rebirth*, pp. 322, 468.

51. "Prices Adjusted by GM, IHC, Willys, Crosley," *Automotive News* 22 (Nov. 18, 1946), 1; "Packard Price Boosted $62; K-F Up Again," *Automotive News* 22 (Jan. 13, 1947), 1. Price controls were suspended for twenty-six days in July 1946. Mayer and Forster, *Twentieth Century*, pp. 652–53.

52. Mayer and Forster, *Twentieth Century*, pp. 653–54; *St. Louis Post-Dispatch*, Jan. 16, 1947; NYT, Jan. 19, 1947; DN, Jan. 19, 1947.

53. The full text of Henry II's January 15 statement is in NYT, Jan. 16, 1947; also see DFP, Jan. 16, 1947; *Christian Science Monitor*, Jan. 16, 1947; "Prices," *Time* 49 (Jan. 27, 1947), 83; "Autos: Watch the Fords," *Newsweek* 29 (Jan. 27, 1947), 66.

54. DN, Jan. 19, 1947; *Washington Post*, Jan. 16, 1947 (Steelman wire); *Chicago Herald-American*, Jan. 16, 1947; NYT, Jan. 17 and 19, 1947; *St. Louis Post-Dispatch*, Jan. 16, 1947. The Ford Company announced that it would not pressure its suppliers to decrease their prices. "Rebirth of Ford," *Fortune*, p. 204.

55. DFP, Jan. 17, 1947; "Dealers Back Up Ford Price Cut: First Reduction in 6 Years," *Automotive News* 22 (Jan. 20, 1947), 1, 6; Hughes, "Ford Girds," p. 1.

56. See Acc. 246, Box 1 for editorials praising Ford's price reduction. "Prices," *Time*, p. 83; "Autos: Young King Henry Ford," *Newsweek* 29 (Apr. 21, 1947), 66. DFP, Jan. 16, 1947; *Boston Herald*, Jan. 17, 1947; *St. Louis Post-Dispatch*, Jan. 16, 1947; DN, Jan. 16, 1947.

57. NYT, Jan. 19, 1947; DN, Jan. 19, 1947 (quoting Nourse).

58. NYT, Jan. 17, 1947; DT, Jan. 21, 1947; DFP, DN, and *Boston Herald*, Jan. 22, 1947; Pete Wemhoff, "GM Luxury Car Prices Raised," *Automotive News* 22 (Jan. 27, 1947), 1.

59. See DN, Jan. 20, 1947 for Chevrolet advertisement; "Dealers Back Price Cut," *Automotive News* 22 (Jan. 20, 1947), 1; "Watch Fords," *Newsweek*, pp. 66–67; "Lowest Price Car Claimed by Ford with Coupe Cut," *Automotive News* 22 (Apr. 7, 1947), 1; "Fuel to the Fire," *Business Week* (Apr. 5, 1947), p. 43.

60. DFP, Mar. 9, 1947; "IHC Reduces Prices $50 to $300 on Trucks: Hits Wage-Price Spiral," *Automotive News* 22 (Mar. 17, 1947), 1; "Plymouth Cut Tightens 'Big 3' Price Lineup," *Automotive News* 22 (Apr. 14, 1947), 1; "Hudson Ups Prices $25–$69 As Cost Price

Pinch Tightens,'' *Automotive News* 22 (Apr. 7, 1947), 1; ''Packard Ups Prices: Others Likely to Hold,'' *Automotive News* 22 (May 19, 1947), 1; ''Ford Hikes Prices on Station Wagon; Cites Low Volume,'' *Automotive News* 22 (June 30, 1947), 8; ''Ford Truck Prices Revised,'' *Automotive News* 22 (July 14, 1947), 1; ''New Chevrolet Truck Prices Up $26–$162,'' *Automotive News* 22 (July 7, 1947), 1; DFP, Aug. 27, 1947. In August 1947, Ford increased prices on its convertibles by $199; on station wagons by $229; on regular Mercury models from $86 to $93; on Mercury convertibles and wagons by $226; and on Lincolns from $148 to $200. There had been no increase on Mercurys or Lincolns, except for an advance on Mercury wagons, since September 1946. ''Threat of New Boost in Prices Appears as the Old Round Ends,'' *Automotive News* 23 (Sept. 1, 1947), 1, 6.

61. ''Prices,'' *Time*, p. 83; Public Relations Policy Group Minutes, Mar. 26, July 23, 1947, Jan. 21, 1948, GM Public Relations Library; DN, Jan. 17, 1947. Ford's price cuts enabled Ford, alone among the eight companies rated by the Psychological Corporation, to improve its public standing in 1947, and for the first time gave Ford a rating equal to that of General Motors. More than seven times as many respondents said they liked Ford's pricing policy better than that of GM; although twice as many interviewees said they preferred GM's products over Ford's. Ford spent $164,000 to advertise its January 1947 price cut. B.R. Donaldson to J.R. Davis, Jan. 21, 1947, Acc. 149, Box 127.

Chapter 28

1. Carll interview, Sept. 21, 1962; GM Public Relations Policy Group Minutes, May 8, 1945, GM Public Relations Library. Members of the five-man News Bureau included Carll, Virgil La Marre, Robert O. Dunn, Ross E. MacNaughton, and Joseph R. Thomas. The company's New York representative, former *Ford Times* editor John Weld, had been appointed by Henry II in July 1945. He reported not to Carll, but to the manager of the company's eastern region; and was assigned to handle press relations and special events and to provide assistance to sales offices and dealers. John Weld to David L. Lewis, Feb. 24, 1965; DFP, Aug. 11, 1945.

2. Speech by Charles F. Moore, Jr., vice-president-public relations and advertising, FMC, before Public Relations Society of America, Philadelphia, Nov. 19, 1957; FMC news release, Nov. 27, 1945 (in possession of author); Ford Supervisory Bulletin, Feb. 18, 1946, Acc. 454, Box 9. In January 1946 Weld was transferred to the Los Angeles office, where, in addition to handling routine field office assignments, he promoted the use of Ford cars in motion pictures. John E. Sattler, a former advertising man and ex-Army Air Forces officer, succeeded Weld in New York. Mark J. Henehan, a former newspaperman and ex-director of publications for Bell Aircraft Corporation, was named head of the Chicago office. See Weekly Activity Reports of public relations field representatives, Acc. 454, Box 4; John Weld to David L. Lewis, Feb. 24, 1965; Mark J. Henehan to David L. Lewis, Dec. 20, 1965. In 1965 Weld was a lecturer and Henehan was with Sperry Rand Corporation; in 1976 Sattler was a Dearborn-based Ford public relations executive.

3. John E. Sattler, public relations representative, eastern region, to William D. Kennedy, Sept. 30, 1946. The public relations field offices were to remain un-

coordinated from Dearborn until August 1947. Sattler newsletter to eastern region dealers, Aug. 1947, Acc. 452, Box 4.

4. Charles E. Carll to William D. Kennedy, Sept. 18, 1946, Acc. 452, Box 4; DFP, Oct. 13, 1946; DT, Oct. 24, 1946; William D. Kennedy to David L. Lewis, Dec. 8, 1965; Rose interview, May 23, 1962; MacNaughton interview, May 12, 1962; Wigle interview, Nov. 23, 1965. Kennedy's career is summed up in a FMC news release, Jan. 8, 1960, the date of Kennedy's retirement from Ford. In 1946 the company had six sales regions, divided into thirty-three districts. Public relations field representatives for each region, as of December 1946, were John Sattler (eastern), John Weld (western), James Chapman (central), Jack Clarke (midwestern), A. Bruce Ewing (southwestern), and Bruce Felknor (southeastern). Weekly Activity Reports from the field men to the home office are in Acc. 452, Box 4. The eastern region added a second man, Russell M. Hart, to its office in March 1947. Sattler to C.J. Seyffer, Feb. 26, 1947, Acc. 452, Box 4. Kennedy, said Wigle, ''wandered around the halls and was unhappy in the public relations directorship.'' Wigle interview, Nov. 23, 1965.

5. William D. Kennedy to David L. Lewis, Dec. 8, 1965; FMC news release, Feb. 16, 1947, Acc. 285, Box 2953; NYT, Feb. 16, 1947.

6. DT, Apr. 10, 1947; FMC news release, Apr. 23, 1947, Acc. 285, Box 2953; DFP, Nov. 8, 1947. In 1947 Irwin was the only Ford employee, except for Executive Vice President Ernest R. Breech, who reported to Henry II. He changed the News Bureau's name to Press and Radio Relations Section; the name was changed back after his departure. Irwin was described by ex-associates as a ''complete extrovert,'' a ''fancy Dan,'' a ''blow-hard,'' a ''braggart,'' a ''poseur extraordinary,'' and ''the biggest name-dropper I ever heard.'' He enjoyed reclining in his special ''posture chair'' while pontificating to office visitors. Interview with Robert O. Dunn, Nov. 23, 1965; MacNaughton interview, May 12, 1962; Rose interview, May 23, 1962; Wigle interview, Nov. 23, 1965. Coincident with Irwin's ''resignation,'' the company announced that he had formed a firm which would sell Ford buses in the Cleveland-Buffalo-Pittsburgh area. The publicist's valedictory speech to his staff was ''pure Irwin''; ''I don't know anything about buses, but I'll sell them until they come out of my ears.'' ''Ford, James Irwin & Buses,''*Tide* 21 (Nov. 14, 1947), 21. Actually, after a short time in the bus field, Irwin was soon back in Chicago, dispensing public relations counsel. He was living in retirement at Northfield, Illinois, near Chicago, in 1975. *Who's Who in America*, 37th ed., s.v. ''Irwin, James W.''

7. DN, Nov. 26, Dec. 4, 1947; DT, Nov. 30, Dec. 7, 1947.

8. Dunn interview, Nov. 23, 1965; DFP, Nov. 26, 1947; *Who's Who in Public Relations (International)*, 1st ed., s.v. ''Rose, John L.''; FMC news release, Apr. 23, 1947, Acc. 285, Box 2953. Kennedy retained jurisdiction over customer and dealer publications, but relinquished control of employee publications to the Employee Relations Department, newly established by the Industrial Relations Division. The public relations field representatives continued to report to regional managers until 1948. FMC Executive Committee Minutes, June 4, 1947, Acc. 452, Box 3. Rose was named assistant director of public relations in 1949.

9. Speech by Charles E. Carll before Ford dealers at Ford Merchandising School, Jan. 7, 1948, Acc. 234, Box 9; Dunn interview, Nov. 23, 1965.

10. Rose interview, May 23, 1962; MacNaughton interview, May 12, 1962; Wigle interview, May 23, 1965; Dunn interview, Nov. 23, 1965. Carll, said Dunn, could have remained at Ford as a press relations man, but "his pride would not let him do it." Carll was granted a Lincoln-Mercury franchise in La Jolla, Calif., but soon went broke. After working for an advertising agency and operating his own public relations consulting firm, he became director of press relations for Litton Industries, Inc., in Beverly Hills, Calif., in 1960. He remained in this post until his death in September 1965. Litton Industries, Inc. news release, Mar. 16, 1960. "Charlie was a wonderful associate and a hell of a fine public relations man." J.R. Lewis, corporate director, advertising and public relations, Litton Industries, Inc., to David L. Lewis, Nov. 23, 1965.

11. Speech by Charles F. Moore, Jr. before Public Relations Society of America, Philadelphia, Nov. 19, 1957; "Top Goal of Ford's News Management: to Outsell Chevrolet," *Business Week* (June 13, 1953), 95. Ford's expenditure for public relations—$2,545,000 in 1952—was among the largest in the country, although it fell far short of General Motors' public relations outlay for that year, $7,350,000. The Public Relations Program of General Motors Corporation with Marginal Notes on the Ford Motor Company Public Relations Program, prepared by the Research Department of FMC's Public Relations Staff, Jan. 12, 1953 (in possession of author).

12. Ross, *Image Merchants*, pp. 176–78; see summary of press activity and other events during the fiftieth anniversary year in the library of the Ford Company's News Department; speech by Charles F. Moore, Jr. before Public Relations Society of America, Philadelphia, Nov. 19, 1957.

13. See Acc. 452, Box 4, and Acc. 149, Box 147 for lists of postwar film titles; monthly film reports, Jan. 1, 1946–Jan. 31, 1947, Acc. 149, Box 97; General Sales Department to branches, May 7, 1946, Acc. 149, Box 147; Dunn interview, Nov. 23, 1965; Robert O. Dunn to David L. Lewis, Nov. 24, 1965. Ford's postwar film attendance was not tabulated until 1949. That year, only 2,200,000 people saw the company's motion pictures; 9,923,562 viewers had seen them in 1940. By contrast, General Motors, which continued to produce and distribute films throughout the war, showed its forty-eight titles to 8,950,000 people in 1947. The two companies' film expenditures tell the story. General Motors spent $2,239,955 on its program during 1942–47; Ford only $358,226. In 1947, the No. 1 auto maker, although well stocked with new titles, spent $278,519 on films; Ford $97,626. Mass Selling Motion Picture Advertising Report—All Branches, Dec. 1940, Acc. 149, Box 97; GM Policy Group Minutes, Nov. 19, 1947, GM Public Relations Library; 1944 Advertising Budget, Aug. 30, 1944, Acc. 149, Box 119; 1945 Advertising Breakdown (Revised), n.d. [1945], Acc. 149, Box 124; Advertising Budget—1946, Jan. 1–Dec. 1946, n.d., Acc. 149, Box 127; Report on Advertising Budget Expenditures, Feb. 20, 1948, Acc. 149, Box 126.

14. Dunn interview, Nov. 23, 1965; Dunn to Lewis, Nov. 24, 1965; The Public Relations Program of General Motors Corporation with Marginal Notes on the Ford Motor Company Public Relations Program, prepared by the Research Department of FMC's Public Relations Staff, Jan. 12, 1953 (in possession of author); Robert O. Dunn, "Ford Motor Company Captures Annual Film Audience of 64,000,000," *Public Relations Journal* (Dec. 1961), 11; *London Financial Times*, June 19, 1962. In 1972, Ford Motor Company showed fifteen films to approximately 20,000,000 people; and General Motors showed thirty-nine titles to more than 29,000,000 viewers. R.J. Haynes, supervisor, film distribution, FMC, to David L. Lewis, May 31, 1973; Joseph McKeon, Public Relations Staff, GM, to David L. Lewis, May 31, 1973.

15. *Ford News* 22 (Feb. 1942), 31; Thompson, *Reminiscences*, pp. 98–99. Maxon, Inc., the company's advertising agency, initially produced the *Ford News*. The agency hired as editor B. Mark Mulcahy, an ex-newspaperman who had worked for John Thompson at Consolidated Vultee. Mulcahy soon was switched to the Ford payroll, upon finding that his news-gathering was hampered by wartime security restrictions on the movement of non-Ford personnel within company plants. B. Mark Mulcahy to David L. Lewis, Feb. 8, 1964.

16. See volumes 1 and 2 of the *Ford Times* (Apr. 2, 1943 through May 12, 1944); B. Mark Mulcahy to David L. Lewis, Feb. 8, 1964; John Weld to David L. Lewis, Feb. 24, 1965; Thompson, *Reminiscences*, p. 99. Mulcahy resigned effective June 30 to take a job with the Office of War Information.

17. B. Mark Mulcahy to David L. Lewis, Feb. 8, 1964; Thompson, *Reminiscences*, p. 98; see first and subsequent copies of the pocket-size *Ford Times* in the reference room of the Ford Archives and Automotive History Collection of the Detroit Public Library. The *Ford Times* was supplemented on Mar. 12, 1946 by the tabloid *Ford River Rouge News*, the name of which was changed to *Ford Rouge News* on May 1, 1946 (see copies in Ford Archives). John Weld, who also had worked for Thompson at Consolidated Vultee, succeeded Mulcahy as editor of the *Ford Times*. Weld remained in this post until July 1945, when "caught in the middle of a battle between Bennett and Henry II," he was fired by Bennett, only to be immediately rehired by young Henry as the company's eastern region public relations representative. Weld's successor as editor of the *Ford Times* was Irene Cornell, who, after William D. Kennedy was named editor in late 1945, remained as managing editor until June 1947. Cornell was succeeded by C. H. Dykeman, who became editor-in-chief of Ford publications upon Kennedy's retirement in 1960. Dykeman headed Ford publications until his death in 1965. John Weld to David L. Lewis, Feb. 24 and Dec. 18, 1965; interview with Nancy Kennedy, *Ford Times* staff member, Feb. 3, 1964; DT, Oct. 24, 1946. Dykeman worked with Kennedy on *Air Operations*, an Army Air Forces magazine, during World War II. "Ford Press: 23 Titles and Growing," *Printers' Ink* 278 (Jan. 26, 1962), 57. *Ann Arbor* (Mich.) *News*, July 4, 1966. Kennedy was living in Zurich in 1965. William D. Kennedy to David L. Lewis, Dec. 5, 1965. Robert O. Dunn has been Ford's publication manager since 1972. Dunn to David L. Lewis, Aug. 8, 1974.

18. See volumes 2 and 3 of the *Ford Times* in the Ford Archives and Detroit Public Library; Thompson, *Reminiscences*, p. 105; *Business Week* (Mar. 30, 1946), 28; *Ford Times* 3 (Apr. 1946), 63; 3 (Nov. 1946), back cover; F.W. Fairfield, manager, consumer publications, to David L. Lewis, Dec. 14, 1965. Typical features included quizzes, articles on games for children, and stories on movie stars and such subjects as the Burma Road, salt mining in Michigan, sea elephants off Guadalupe, the future of synthetic tires, and postwar highways.

19. See copies of *Ford Times* in the Ford Archives and .Detroit Public Library; Robert Wells, "The Industry's Top Communicator," *Ward's Quarterly* 1

(Summer 1965), 116; F.W. Fairfield to David L. Lewis, Dec. 14, 1965; Roland W. Williams, manager, consumer publications, FMC, Mar. 21, 1972.

20. See copies of the *Ford Times* in the Ford Archives and Detroit Public Library; "Pocket-Size America," *Newsweek* 51 (Apr. 14, 1958), 68; F.W. Fairfield to David L. Lewis, Dec. 14, 1965; William D. Kennedy to David L. Lewis, Dec. 5, 1965; Roland W. Williams, editor-in-chief, *Ford Times,* to David L. Lewis, June 26, 1972.

21. F.W. Fairfield to David L. Lewis, Dec. 14, 1965; DN, Dec. 19, 1974; interview with Roland W. Williams, editor-in-chief, *Ford Times,* June 26, 1972; David W. Krupp, "Ford Times: Continuing Link with Customers," *Journal of Organizational Communications* 1 (Winter 1972), 3–4; Robert O. Dunn, publications manager, North American Automotive Operations, Ford Motor Company, to David L. Lewis, Aug. 8, 1974. DFP, Sept. 2, 1962. The *Ford Times* may be found at many "multiple readership points" including doctors' and dentists' offices and barbershops and beauty salons. In recent years the magazine has emphasized articles on recreation, auto travel, and adventure. It also includes recipe pages which reveal the culinary secrets of the nation's best restaurants.

22. Advertising Plans for Dealers, Aug. 31, 1945, Acc. 149, Box 166. In 1945 the company spent $8,131,322 on advertising, almost twice its highest prewar advertising outlay. FMC Advertising Disbursements, 1935–45, Aug. 14, 1946, Acc. 134, Box 17. During the mid-1940s the company's advertising effort was directed by three men, J.R. Davis, Ben R. Donaldson, and Frank J. McGinnis. Davis headed the trio, serving as director of sales and advertising until December 1946, thereafter as vice-president of sales and advertising. Donaldson, a twenty-five-year veteran of Ford's advertising staff, was named assistant director of advertising in January 1946, and was advanced to the directorship at the time of Davis's promotion. McGinnis was assigned responsibility for the Ford passenger car advertising, the company's key account, in January 1946. Before that time, while a vice-president of Campbell-Ewald Company (Chevrolet's advertising agency), he had had charge of the Chevrolet account. FMC news release, Dec. 6, 1946, Acc. 149, Box 1; DFP, Jan. 4, 1946. McGinnis was succeeded by Gordon C. Eldredge in April 1947. DFP, Apr. 18, 1947. William G. Licht was named advertising manager of Lincoln-Mercury Division in November 1946. FMC news release, Nov. 11, 1946, Acc. 149, Box 91. Maxon had had Ford accounts both before and during the war, losing them in 1941 and 1943. In early 1945, however, the Detroit-based agency—after Ford instructed its thirty-three sales districts to select either Maxon or JWT to service districtwide dealer advertising—landed twenty-three district accounts; Thompson was awarded ten. Maxon's return to the Ford fold proved of typically short duration. In September 1946, because of the difficulty in coordinating dealer advertising with national campaigns, the agency's district business was transferred to Thompson, which handled Ford's postwar national advertising except for four radio programs. The third agency, K & E, of New York, supervised the four "non-JWT" radio programs, after being retained on July 20, 1945 to oversee the postwar Ford Sunday Evening Hour. See chapters 20 and 23 for discussion of Ford's prewar and wartime retention of Maxon, Inc.; DT, Feb. 15, Mar. 16, 1945; Hughes, "Ford Girds," p. 57; DN, Aug. 27, 1946; see Acc. 149, Box 113 for file on transfer of Maxon's accounts to JWT; "Ford Dealers Relinquish Maxon, Inc.," *Broad-

casting-Telecasting* 31 (Sept. 2, 1946), 28; DN, July 25, 1945.

23. "7 Musts for Public Relations in Advertising and Selling," *Printers' Ink* 220 (July 25, 1947), 29.

24. Norman H. Strouse, JWT, to B.R. Donaldson, May 7, 1946, Acc. 149, Box 56; JWT Blimp Estimate, May 22, 1946, Acc. 149, Box 56; "Leigh's Most Spectacular 'Spectaculars,' " *Business Week* (Apr. 26, 1947), 30; FMC news release, July 14, 1946, Acc. 149, Box 91; Statistical Data on Ford Dirigible, Oct. 15, 1946, Acc. 149, Box 56. During New York's wartime dim-out, Leigh designed the famous Camel cigarette billboard which blew continuous smoke rings over Times Square.

25. FMC news release, Oct. 15, 1946, Acc. 452, Box 4; John E. Sattler to eastern region dealers, Oct. 29, 1946, Acc. 452, Box 4; John E. Sattler to C.J. Seyffer, Feb. 27, 1947 (copy), Acc. 452, Box 4.

26. JWT Client Confirmation Report, June 16, 1947, Acc. 149, Box 114; Special Promotion and Publicity Log of the Ford Flying Spectacular 1946–1948, Sept. 7, 1948, Acc. 149, Box 57; "See the Blimp?," *Newsweek* 30 (Dec. 22, 1947), 66.

27. "Leigh's Spectaculars," *Business Week,* p. 30; "See the Blimp?," *Newsweek,* p. 66; B.R. Donaldson to S.V. MacArthur, vice-president of Douglas Leigh Sky Advertising Corporation, Aug. 30, 1948, Acc. 149, Box 57; Norman H. Strouse to Donaldson, Sept. 23, 1948, Acc. 149, Box 57; Advertising Budget—Jan. 1–Dec. 31, 1946, Acc. 149, Box 127; Report on Advertising Budget Expectations, January Through December 1947, Feb. 20, 1948, Acc. 149, Box 126. Henry II was a blimp passenger in May 1947. DT, May 20, 1947. As a joke he had his craft provide an "honor guard" for General Motors' Train of Tomorrow when the train transported members of the Associated Press Managing Editors Association from Detroit to Ann Arbor, Mich. for a football game. DT, Oct. 28, 1947.

28. E.F. Seehafer and J.W. Laemmar, *Successful Radio and Television Advertising* (New York: McGraw-Hill Book Company, 1951), p. 9; W.E. Blanchard to J.R. Davis, May 23, 1945, Acc. 149, Box 10; NYT, June 3, 1945; marginal note by Henry Ford II on letter from C.P. Tyler, JWT executive, to B.R. Donaldson, June 6, 1945, Acc. 149, Box 110; FMC news release, July 24, 1945, Acc. 149, Box 91; DN, July 25, 1945.

29. Survey Report for Ford Sunday Evening Hour, prepared by Kenyon Research Corporation, Acc. 149, Box 21, n.d. [Aug. 1946]; FMC news release, Sept. 14, 1945; The Ford Sunday Evening Hour Plan for Commercial Policy, Advertising, Publicity, prepared for FMC by K & E, Aug. 23, 1945, Acc. 149, Box 21.

30. Plan for Commercial Policy, Advertising, Publicity, Aug. 23, 1945, Acc. 149, Box 21; K & E Conference Report, Aug. 29–30, Sept. 18, and Oct. 10, 1945, Acc. 149, Box 20; DFP, Oct. 18, 1945.

31. Interview with B.R. Donaldson, Sept. 10, 1962; *Broadcasting* 29 (Sept. 3, 1945), 81; Ford Sunday Evening Hour 1945–1946 Season—Talent, Apr. 30, 1946, Acc. 149, Box 111; K & E Conference Report, Mar. 18, Apr. 24, May 6, and May 16–17, 1946.

32. FMC news release, Sept. 14, 1945, Acc. 148, Box 21; DFP, DN, and DT, Oct. 1, 1945; copies of Henry II's first two talks are in Acc. 149, Box 20. A total of $68,976.50 was spent to publicize the resumption of the Sunday Evening Hour. Plan for Commercial Policy, Advertising, Publicity, Aug. 23, 1945, Acc. 149, Box 21.

33. Condensed Analysis of Comments on Talks of Mr. Henry Ford II on Ford Sunday Evening Hour, compiled by Advertising Services, n.d. [Oct. 1945], Acc.

149, Box 20; Ford Sunday Evening Hour Complete Analysis, prepared by Advertising Services, Oct. 14, 1945, Acc. 149, Box 23.

34. Ford Sunday Evening Hour Complete Analysis, prepared by Advertising Services, Nov. 25, 1945, Acc. 149, Box 23; William B. Lewis, vice-president and radio director, K & E to B.R. Donaldson, Dec. 26, 1945, Acc. 149, Box 24; William I. Nichols to David L. Lewis, Nov. 22, 1965. Nichols's last broadcast was on Jan. 6, 1946.

35. Survey Report for Ford Sunday Evening Hour Commentator, n.d. [Dec. 1945], Acc. 149, Box 20; Edwin Cox, vice-president, K & E, to John Bugas, Jan. 11, 1946, Acc. 149, Box 20; *New York City Enquirer,* Mar. 18, 1946, and *Lawrence* (Mass.) *Daily Eagle,* Apr. 12, 1946 (stories on Fraser); Year's Analysis of Ford Sunday Evening Hour from Sept. 30, 1945 Through June 23, 1946, n.d., Acc. 149, Box 20; Ford Sunday Evening Hour Comments on Henry Ford II Talk Before S.A.E., Jan. 9, 1946, Acc. 149, Box 20; K & E Conference Report, Mar. 18, June 16 and 24, 1946, Acc. 149, Box 20; Ford Motor Company Copy Platform for Radio Talks, prepared by K & E, July 1946, Acc. 149, Box 98. Titles of Fraser's talks are cited in K & E Conference Report, Apr. 25, 1946, Acc. 149, Box 20. Nichols wrote his talks, as did Fraser until Mar. 1946, when Henry II and J.R. Davis expressed dissatisfaction with them. Thereafter Fraser's talks were prepared with the aid of a K & E writer. K & E Conference Report, Mar. 8, 1946, Acc. 149, Box 20.

36. See chapter 19 for a detailed discussion of the prewar Ford Sunday Evening Hour. "Four Hundred Fords," *Newsweek* 26 (Dec. 31, 1945), 85; K & E informed Ford of audience ratings in weekly memos which can be found in Acc. 149, Boxes 20, 21, and 111. During 1945–46, broadcasts of the New York Philharmonic were sponsored by United States Rubber; broadcasts of the Boston Symphony, which had fewer listeners than the Ford Hour, by Allis-Chalmers. The Hour was rated highly in sponsor identification surveys. More than 70 percent of its audience could correctly identify the show, a figure topped by only eight other programs. The intermission talks, although more commercial than the prewar sermonettes, also won high praise. Readers of *Woman's Day* rated the commercials, along with those of General Electric's "Hour of Charm," as the most "inoffensive" and "dignified" on the air. The nation's radio editors, in *Billboard*'s annual poll, ranked the Ford messages second only to the Johnson's Wax commercials on "Fibber McGee and Molly" as radio's "most effective commercials in good taste." The program itself fared less well in polls. *Billboard*'s radio editors placed the New York Philharmonic, the NBC Symphony, and the Boston Symphony programs ahead of the postwar Ford Hour; as did 500 music editors surveyed by *Musical America.* The music editors did, however, rate the Ford Hour second only to the Telephone Hour as the program which presented "the most outstanding orchestra with featured soloists." The Ford Hour's time-slot rivals on CBS—"Beulah" and "Crime Doctor"—were heard on approximately 10 percent of the country's radios; Mutual Broadcasting Systems's "Mediation Board" and "Gabriel Heatter" by approximately 5 percent. Dwight Mills, executive vice-president, K & E, to B.R. Donaldson, Jan. 3, 1946, Acc. 149, Box 114; Jack Cluett, "Listen Here," *Woman's Day* 9 (July 1946), 18; *New Bedford* (Mass.) *Standard Times,* Mar. 10, 1946 (quoting *Billboard*); *PM* (New York), May 27, 1946 (quoting *Musical America*). *Billboard*'s poll was a continuation of prewar surveys of radio editors conducted by the *New York Journal-American.*

37. J.L. Roberts to B.R. Donaldson, June 12, 1946, Acc. 149, Box 33 (summarizing regional managers' reports for May 1946).

38. Ford Sunday Evening Hour Costs, May 16, 1946, Acc. 149, Box 124; K & E Conference Report, Apr. 17, May 6 and 22, June 13, 24, and 30, July 25 and Aug. 8, 1946, Acc. 149, Box 20. William B. Lewis to Everett Crosby, Feb. 1 and May 15, 1946, Acc. 149, Box 111; Year's Analysis of Ford Sunday Evening Hour from Sept. 30, 1945 Through June 30, 1946, n.d., Acc. 149, Box 20; Fred C. Foy, of JWT, to B.R. Donaldson, July 22, 1946, Acc. 149, Box 111. K & E recommended that the Ford Hour in 1946–47 employ one conductor for the entire season, sign four singers for ten appearances each, and have "simple routines." K & E Conference Report, May 16–17, 1946, Acc. 149, Box 20.

39. Thomas K. Carpenter, Jr., of K & E, to B.R. Donaldson, June 27, 1946, Acc. 149, Box 111; *New York Post,* June 24, 1946; *Cincinnati Post,* June 26, 1946; Ford Sunday Evening Hour Quarterly Publicity Summary (Second Quarter 1946), Acc. 149, Box 21.

40. *Mobile Register,* Apr. 26, 1946; "Promotion Planned for Ford Program," *Broadcasting-Telecasting* 30 (June 3, 1946), 79; William B. Lewis to J.R. Davis, July 17, 1946, Acc. 149, Box 27; K & E Conference Report, Apr. 17, June 27, Aug. 6, 1946, Acc. 149, Box 20; Proposal of Continuation of Ford Festival in 1946–47, prepared by K & E, n.d., Acc. 149, Box 20; "Ford Drops ABC," *Broadcasting-Telecasting* 31 (Sept. 9, 1946), 14.

41. DN, Nov. 4, 1945; *Chicago Times,* Nov. 18, 1945; NYT, Dec. 9, 1945.

42. General Sales Department to branch managers, Feb. 4, Mar. 18, 1946, Acc. 149, Box 147; Fred C. Foy, vice-president, JWT, to B.R. Donaldson, Mar. 25, 1946, Acc. 149, Box 33; J.R. Davis to branch managers, Apr. 30, 1946, Acc. 149, Box 35; J.L. Roberts to Donaldson, June 12, 1946 (summarizing regional managers' reports for May 1946), Acc. 149, Box 33; Foy to FMC, July 2, 1946, Acc. 149, Box 114. Scripts for the Crosby show are in Acc. 149, Box 35. Hooper reported on the top fifteen radio shows; CAB (Crossley Co-operative Analysis of Broadcasters) on the top ten programs.

43. NYT, Feb. 20, 1944 (1944 radio editors poll); Fred C. Foy to J.R. Davis, Nov. 26, 1946 (1945 radio editors poll); Guest Stars, The Ford Show, June 11, 1947, Acc. 149, Box 39.

44. J.L. Roberts to B.R. Donaldson, Nov. 8 and Dec. 13, 1946, Acc. 148, Box 40 (summarizing regional managers' reports of Oct. and Nov. 1946, respectively); Will G. Price, Jr., of Price Auto Service Co., to FMC, Kansas City, Jan. 16, 1947, Acc. 148, Box 20; Goodman Ace, CBS writer, to Paul de Fur, of JWT, Dec. 9, 1946, and Herschel Williams, CBS writer, to de Fur, Feb. 5, 1947, Acc. 149, Box 92; Fred C. Foy to J.R. Davis, Apr. 28, 1947, Acc. 149, Box 114; "Radio Notes," *Newsweek* 29 (May 12, 1947), 22.

45. William B. Lewis to J.R. Davis, July 17, 1946, Acc. 149, Box 27; K & E Conference Report, May 13, 1947 (for meeting held May 6), Acc. 149, Box 167; "Radio Agency of the Year," *Newsweek* 29 (June 2, 1947), 67 (quoting *Billboard*). JWT was to continue placing all other Ford Company advertising, according to DFP, May 8, 1946. JWT suggested that Ford, if it replaced Dinah Shore, should alternate dramatic shows and the hour-long Toscanini symphony hour over the full 1947–48 season. The suggestion was rejected. Fred C. Foy to Davis, Apr. 28, 1947, Acc. 149, Box 114.

46. K & E and FMC Conference Report, May 6, 1947, Acc. 149, Box 167 ("My Friend Irma"); Irving Settel, *A Pictorial History of Radio* (New York: Bonanza

Books, 1965), p. 148; "Ford and the People," *Newsweek* 29 (June 30, 1947), 50; *Mobile Register*, July 27, 1947 (Willson biography); Meredith Willson, *Eggs I Have Laid* (New York: Henry Holt and Company, 1955), p. 99. Ford Sunday Evening Hour Talent List 1941–1942 Season, Jan. 9, 1942, Acc. 139, Box 20; FMC Radio Plans, July 14, 1947, Acc. 149, Box 167. Willson had played the flute in John Philip Sousa's band and the New York Philharmonic orchestra, had been musical director of NBC's western division, and had conducted bands and acted as a comedy stooge on several national radio shows.

47. Meredith Willson to Ford and Lincoln-Mercury dealers, June 2, 1947, Acc. 149, Box 38; "People," *Newsweek*, p. 50 (New York City College students); *Denver Post*, June 10, 1947.

48. *Billboard* described the program as "a draggy affair which failed just about completely to sustain interest." But the *Charleston* (S.C.) *News-Courier* regarded the show as "unique and relaxing entertainment," the *Cincinnati Enquirer* looked upon it as "one of the most engaging things on the air," and the *Pasadena Independent* said it was "one show we never miss." Every reviewer praised Willson's "fine, imaginative music," and most critics clamored for more of it. A few reviews lauded Willson's down-home philosophy; but some publications panned it. Most reviews also gave high marks to the "talking people," although a few complained that they "didn't know when or where to stop," and two listeners wrote Henry II that they were "just talking nit-wits." "The Ford Showroom," *Billboard* 59 (June 28, 1947), 14; *Charleston* (S.C.) *News-Courier*, June 30, 1947; *Cincinnati Enquirer*, June 25, 1947; *Pasadena Independent*, July 30, 1947; *Newark News*, n.d. [June 20, 1947]; *New York World-Telegram*, June 20, 1947; *New York Herald Tribune*, June 20, 1947; *Cleveland Plain Dealer*, June 25, 1947; "People," *Newsweek*, p. 50; Mr. and Mrs. Wade McClay, of Ann Arbor, Mich., to Henry Ford II, June 18, 1947, Acc. 149, Box 38. The "Ford Showroom" generated 1,695 news stories and 113 press pictures during the eight weeks it was on the air. Publicity Report on Ford Showroom, n.d., Acc. 149, Box 93. The program was broadcast over CBS from 9:30 to 10 p.m. Wednesdays. Regional managers' and dealers' comments on the "Ford Showroom" are in Acc. 149, Box 38; Wilder Breckenridge to J.R. Davis, July 3, 1947, Acc. 149, Box 38; Davis to dealers, n.d., Acc. 149, Box 38, and July 14, 1947, Acc. 149, Box 167; K & E and FMC Conference Report, Aug. 12–13, 1947, Acc. 149, Box 167. Ford and K & E originally planned to put the Willson show on the road in support of dealer promotion during the 1947–48 season. *New Orleans Illustrated Press*, May 30, 1947.

49. K & E Conference Report, Aug. 12–13 and 22, 1947, Acc. 149, Box 167; Advertising Department, Sales and Advertising Division, to district managers, Sept. 24, 1947, Acc. 149, Box 106; *Current Biography*, 1958 ed., s.v. "Willson, Meredith." The "Ford Showroom" cost $312,021.18, of which $172,296.18 was for network time charges, $139,725 for talent. Ford Showroom Budget and Schedule, Nov. 11, 1947, Acc. 149, Box 126.

50. K & E and FMC Conference Report, May 6, 1947, and Jan. 25, 1948, Acc. 149, Box 167. K & E proposed as early as January 1946 that Ford sponsor a dramatic program in the summer of 1946. K & E Conference Report, Jan. 31, 1946, Acc. 149, Box 20.

51. NYT, July 14, Aug. 24, Dec. 12, 1947; B.R. Donaldson to Frank Stanton, president of CBS, Aug. 4, 1947, Acc. 149, Box 92; presentation by William B. Lewis to Lincoln-Mercury dealers, Dec. 1948, Acc. 149, Box 51.

52. K & E and FMC Conference Report, July 10, Oct. 6, 1947, Acc. 149, Box 167; NYT, Aug. 28, 1947; presentation by William B. Lewis before Ford dealers, Feb. 1949, Acc. 149, Box 51. Kenneth Banghart read the commercials.

53. See script of Henry II's "Ford Theater" welcoming remarks in Acc. 149, Box 8; NYT, Oct. 12, 1947, Feb. 22, 1948; "Current Listening," *Newsweek* 30 (Nov. 10, 1947), 52; "The Ford Pitch," *Tide* 21 (Dec. 5, 1947), 66; presentation by William A. Chalmers, of K & E, before Ford dealers, Dec. 9, 1947, Acc. 149, Box 7; Conference Report, Dec. 22, 1947, Acc. 149, Box 7, and Jan. 25, 1948, Acc. 149, Box 167; Lewis presentation to Lincoln-Mercury dealers, Dec. 1948, Acc. 149, Box 51. Ford tried to obtain prime time for the Ford Theater on CBS and ABC as well as NBC. K & E maintained that the show ended the year with an audience "equal to or better than" the first-season audiences of "Lux Radio Theater" and "Theater Guild on the Air."

54. The Ford Theater 1948–49 Season, n.d. [Fall 1948], Acc. 149, Box 7; *Variety* (Oct. 13, 1948), Acc. 149, Box 49; Conference Report, June 29, 1948, Acc. 149, Box 167; Chalmers presentation, Dec. 9, 1948, Acc. 149, Box 7. Twenty-six-year-old Fletcher Markle directed the revamped "Ford Theater"; Kenneth Banghart was retained as the announcer.

55. Speech by Henry Ford II to Ford dealers, n.d. [early Oct. 1948], Acc. 148, Box 48; *Variety* (Oct. 13, 1948), Acc. 149, Box 49; Dwight Mills, of K & E, to B.R. Donaldson, Dec. 17, 1948, Acc. 149, Box 49.

56. Chalmers presentation, Dec. 9, 1948, Acc. 149, Box 7; Dwight Mills to B.R. Donaldson, Dec. 17, 1948, Acc. 149, Box 49.

57. Dwight Mills to B.R. Donaldson, Dec. 17, 1948, Acc. 149, Box 49; Paul G. Gumbinner, "From Advertising a Stronger Voice," *Printers' Ink* 283 (June 14, 1963), 275; Richard A.R. Pinkham, "The Glamour Medium—and Some Men Who Made It," *Printers' Ink* 283 (June 14, 1963), 237; Donaldson to J.R. Davis, Aug. 4, 1948, Acc. 149, Box 49; Lewis presentation, Dec. 1948, Acc. 149, Box 51; Chalmers presentation, Dec. 9, 1948, Acc. 149, Box 7; Lewis presentation, Feb. 1949, Acc. 149, Box 51; NYT, May 26, 1949.

58. *Information Please Almanac*, 11th ed., p. 319; "Eyes of the Nation," *Newsweek* 30 (Aug. 4, 1947), 70; Settel, *History of Radio*, p. 157.

59. JWT Client Confirmation Report, Oct. 27, 1947 (regarding Oct. 23, 1947 meeting), Acc. 149, Box 114; NYT, Nov. 4, 1947; "Mr. Allen, Mr. Ford," *Newsweek* 30 (Nov. 10, 1947), 53; Chalmers presentation, Dec. 9, 1948, Acc. 149, Box 7.

60. NYT, June 2, 1947, and Mar. 19, 1956; "The World's Worst Juggler," *Time* 49 (Apr. 7, 1947), 71–72, 74; Settel, *History of Radio*, p. 82; "Comedian's Comedian," *Newsweek* 47 (Mar. 26, 1956), 62.

61. The *New York Times* and *Broadcasting-Telecasting* published Hooper's ratings each week. For "Hooperratings" the week Allen was signed by Ford, see NYT, Nov. 4, 1947 and "National Network Hoopers," *Broadcasting-Telecasting* 33 (Nov. 3, 1947), 16. Allen's show was presented on NBC at 8:30 p.m. Sundays.

62. Telegrams and letters on the Allen show from dealers are in Acc. 149, Box 167; Fred Allen, *Treadmill to Oblivion* (Boston: Little, Brown & Co., 1954), pp. 214–15; "'Stop Music' Stops Fred Allen Hooper," *Broadcasting-Telecasting* 35 (July 5, 1948), 22; NYT, July 2, 1948. Allen tried unsuccessfully to get Henry Ford II to appear as a guest star on his first Ford-sponsored program. DFP, Dec. 11, 1947.

63. "Forever Allen," *Newsweek* 32 (Sept. 6, 1948), 46–48; NYT, Oct. 4 and 10, 1948, and Mar. 25, 1962; "Oh, Mr. Allen!," *Broadcasting-Telecasting* 35 (Oct. 11, 1948), 26; Allen, *Treadmill*, pp. 214–15; "Mr. Allen Regrets," *Time* 52 (Dec. 13, 1948), 51. Allen had higher ratings in the fall of 1948 than he had had in May-June, 1948; see discussion of fall ratings in NYT, Oct. 12, 1948, and weekly Hooper ratings in NYT and *Broadcasting-Telecasting*.

64. NYT, Dec. 13, 1948, May 26, 1949, and Mar. 18 and 19, 1956; Desmond Smith, "American Radio Today the Listener Be Damned," *Harper's Magazine* 229 (Sept. 1964), 59; "What Do You Think of Television, Mr. Allen?," *Life* 27 (July 4, 1949), 69; "Back to the Mines," *Time* 56 (Oct. 2, 1950), 48; "Comedian's Comedian," *Newsweek*, p. 62; "Sad Farewell to a Very Funny Man," *Life* 40 (Apr. 2, 1956), 98. Bowing out of radio, Allen appeared on his own, unsuccessful television program in 1950–51. Afterwards he made frequent guest appearances on television; and was a regular member of a panel show, "What's My Line?," at the time of his death in 1956.

65. FMC Advertising Breakdown—1945, Acc. 149, Box 124; FMC Advertising Budget—Jan. 1–Dec. 31, 1946, Acc. 149, Box 127; Report on Advertising Budget Expenditures—1947, Feb. 20, 1948, Acc. 149, Box 126. General Motors had never sponsored a popular radio program, having discarded forty shows in rapid-fire order between 1927 and 1945. Some of the castaway programs, notably the Jack Benny and Al Jolson shows, later attained great popularity under other sponsors. General Motors' immediate postwar programs, "The Symphony of the Air," "Your Land and Mine" (the Henry J. Taylor newscast), "Hollywood Star Time," and "Man Called X," were no more popular than their numerous predecessors; but the corporation, in behalf of "economic education," continued to sponsor the Taylor program through 1956. Neil H. Borden, *Advertising Text and Cases* (Chicago: Richard D. Irwin, Inc., 1950), p. 502 (GM's advertising expenditures); GM Public Relations Policy Group Minutes, Mar. 7, 1944, Mar. 6, 1945, GM Public Relations Library; *New York Herald Tribune* [Summer 1947], Acc. 149, Box 167; General Motors Corporation Institutional Advertising, case study prepared by Harvard Business School, 1957, pp. 3, 33. Ford and its dealers sponsored one additional radio program during the immediate postwar period—"RFD America," a quiz show designed to promote the company's farm equipment. The program was presented over the Mutual Broadcasting System during the first three months of 1948. It was abandoned because dealers believed that the Allen show and spot announcements met their radio advertising needs. The show was handled by JWT. "Ford Pitch," *Tide*, p. 66; "Ford Dealers Not Picking Up Sponsorship Package," *Broadcasting-Telecasting* 34 (Mar. 8, 1948), 86.

66. Harry T. Mitchell, vice-president, JWT, to B.R. Donaldson, Sept. 4, 1945, Acc. 149, Box 49; JWT Client Confirmation Report, May 21, 1947, Acc. 149, Box 113; Report on Television, July 1945, prepared by Compton Advertising, Inc., n.d., Acc. 149, Box 49; Television Broadcasting in Metropolitan New York City, 1946–47, July 24, 1946, prepared by JWT, Acc. 149, Box 124; Donaldson to J.R. Davis, July 26, 1946, Acc. 149, Box 106.

67. *Information Please Almanac*, 11th ed., p. 319; FMC news release, Aug. 12, 1946; John E. Sattler to C.J. Seyffer, Weekly Activity Report for July 29–Aug. 14, 1946, Acc. 452, Box 4. Although black-and-white television was in its infancy, Davis stated in the Aug. 12 news release that Ford was looking ahead to color

television. "It is bound to be one of the greatest advertising and selling media for the automobile industry," he declared, "and Ford will be in the number one position to take advantage of it."

68. JWT Client Confirmation Report, Sept. 10 and 13, 1946, Acc. 149, Boxes 113 and 127, respectively; Norman H. Strouse to Frank J. McGinnis, Sept. 3, 1946, Acc. 149, Box 49; Mark J. Henehan to W.K. Edmunds, Midwest regional manager, Oct. 15, 1946, Acc. 452, Box 4. Strouse to B.R. Donaldson, Oct. 22, 1946, Acc. 149, Box 49.

69. Television Report, n.d. [late 1946], prepared by General Sales Department, Acc. 149, Box 49; Fred C. Foy to J.R. Davis, Sept. 12, 1947, Acc. 149, Box 114; Frank J. McGinnis to George L. Moskovics, WCBS-TV commercial manager, Dec. 10, 1946, Acc. 149, Box 49. When the district dealer committees agreed to finance half of the cost of sponsorship of the "packages," the company agreed to tap the Central Advertising Fund to finance the remaining half.

70. JWT Client Confirmation Report, July 3 and Dec. 2, 1947, Acc. 149, Box 114; Fred C. Foy to J.R. Davis, Sept. 12, 1947, Acc. 149, Box 114; Henry Krigner, Advertising Department, Sales and Advertising, to B.R. Donaldson, May 2, 1947, Acc. 149, Box 106; *Billboard* 59 (July 12, 1947), Acc. 149, Box 114. Ford rejected offers to sponsor sports telecasts in Philadelphia and Washington, refusing "to pay prices which don't represent reasonable investment." Foy to Davis, Sept. 12, 1947, Acc. 149, Box 114.

71. B.R. Donaldson to C.J. Seyffer, Eastern regional manager, Aug. 22, 1946, Acc. 149, Box 133; NYT, Sept. 4, 10, and 27, 1947; "Teleseries," *Newsweek* 30 (Oct. 6, 1947), 53.

72. *Famous First Facts*, 3d ed., p. 603; "Teleseries," *Newsweek*, p. 53; Fred C. Foy to B.R. Donaldson, Sept. 2, 1947, Acc. 149, Box 114; "Radio's Biggest Show," *Newsweek* 30 (Oct. 13, 1947), 57; George L. Moskovics to J.R. Davis, Oct. 6, 1947, Acc. 149, Box 92; *Variety* 168 (Oct. 1, 1947), Acc. 149, Box 50; Henry A. Houston, of JWT, to B.R. Donaldson, Oct. 20, 1947, Acc. 149, Box 50.

73. JWT Client Confirmation Report, Dec. 2, 1947, Acc. 149, Box 114; NYT, Nov. 13, 1948; B.R. Donaldson to J.R. Davis, Aug. 4, 1948, Acc. 149, Box 49.

74. Chalmers presentation, Dec. 9, 1948, Acc. 149, Box 7; Dwight Mills to B.R. Donaldson, Dec. 17, 1948, Acc. 149, Box 49; Lewis presentation, Dec. 1948, Acc. 149, Box 1; Ford Television Theater Estimated Costs, Feb. 10, 1949, Acc. 149, Box 1; DFP [Dec. 1948] (Crosby review); Charles C. La Croix to Donaldson, May 23, 1951, Acc. 149, Box 51.

75. NYT, Oct. 31 and Nov. 13, 1949; "As UN Wants It," *Newsweek* 34 (Nov. 14, 1949), 57; "Ford Sponsors UN on TV: Dealers Buy Kay Kyser," *Broadcasting-Telecasting* 37 (Oct. 31, 1949), 4.

76. NYT, Oct. 30 and 31, Nov. 1 and 13, 1949; "Watch the UN Go By!," *Broadcasting-Telecasting* 37 (Nov. 14, 1949), 38; "As UN Wants," *Newsweek*, p. 57. Telecasts of UN proceedings began on Nov. 7.

77. "Newer Than Baseball," *Time* 54 (Dec. 5, 1949), 72; NYT, Nov. 13, 1949 and May 5, 1950; *Broadcasting-Telecasting 1950 Yearbook Number*, p. 401. "Advertisers Using CBS Network During 1949," *Broadcasting-Telecasting 1950 Yearbook Number*, p. 401; NYT, May 8 and June 1, 1949; "Buy Kyser," *Broadcasting-Telecasting*, p. 4; "Advertisers Using NBC Network During 1949," *Broadcasting-Telecasting 1950 Yearbook Number*, p. 409; "Advertisers Using CBS Network During 1950," *Broadcasting-Telecasting 1950 Yearbook Number*, p. 402; "TV Hoopers," *Broadcasting-Telecasting* 37 (Nov. 28, 1949), 10.

78. Charles Hull Wolfe, *Modern Radio Advertising* (New York: Funk & Wagnalls, 1949), p. 679; FMC Advertising Budget—January 1–December 31, 1946, Acc. 149, Box 127; Report on Advertising Budget Expenditures January Through December 1947, Feb. 20, 1948, Acc. 149, Box 126. Approximately $500,000 was spent on television advertising in 1946; Ford's outlay thus was one-sixth of the total amount. Seehafer and Laemmar, *Radio and Television Advertising*, p. 9.

79. FMC Advertising Disbursements, 1935–45, Aug. 14, 1946, Acc. 134, Box 17; Comparative Expenditures, January Through September, 1948, n.d., Acc. 149, Box 129. Ford spent $8,886,677 on advertising in 1946; $11,311,832 in 1947. B.R. Donaldson to J.R. Davis, Jan. 21, 1947, Acc. 149, Box 127; Comparative Expenditures, January Through December, 1947, Feb. 2, 1948, Acc. 149, Box 129. Ford's advertising outlay during the immediate postwar period amounted to 60 percent of General Motors' advertising expense, twice that of Chrysler's.

Chapter 29

1. Louise B. Clancy and Florence Davies, *The Believer: The Life Story of Mrs. Henry Ford* (New York: Coward-McCann, Inc., 1960), pp. 205–8; Hedley G. Stacey, rector, Christ Episcopal Church, Dearborn, *Reminiscences*, p. 41; Joe McCarthy, "The Amazing Mansion of Henry Ford," *Saturday Evening Post*, 225 (May 16, 1953), 176. The "before and after" photos of Ford were taken on Oct. 26, 1946; the "before" photo was published in DN, Apr. 8, 1947. Slipping out of Clara's sight in the fall of 1945, Ford telephoned Bennett, asking him to shut down the Rouge plant, after which he began weeping and became incoherent. Bennett, *Never Called Henry*, p. 180.

2. Lawrence M. Hughes, "Ford Girds to Regain First Place in Motors," *Advertising Age* 18 (Mar. 3, 1947), 54; *New York Journal-American*, Dec. 4, 1964; Charles E. Carll to Rex Waddell, July 3, 1946, and Clara Ford to News Bureau, July 25, 1946, Acc. 285, Box 2829; A. Bruce Ewing, of News Bureau, to Waddell, Aug. 6, 1946, and Waddell to Ewing, Aug. 26, 1946, Acc. 378, Box 2; Helen J. Sioussat, director of CBS's Department of Radio Talks, Aug. 9, 1946, and Waddell to Sioussat, Aug. 21, 1946, Acc. 285, Box 2809; Carll interview, Sept. 21, 1962. The News Bureau's "quadricycle" photo appears in "Picture of the Week," *Life* 20 (June 3, 1946), 35, and on the cover of *Newsweek* 27 (June 10, 1946).

3. Ford was the subject of eight stories in the *New York Times* in 1945; nine in 1946; and seventeen in 1947 (see *New York Times Index* for these years); the *Readers' Guide to Periodical Literature* cites four articles on Ford in its 1945–47 edition; eighteen (almost all of them related to his death) in its 1947–49 edition. John Gunther, *Inside U.S.A.* (New York: Harper & Row, 1947), pp. 398–409, xiii, 131, 139, 274, 411–12, 417, 567, 569, 745; David L. Lewis, "The Stature of Henry Ford," *Ford Life* 1 (Nov.–Dec. 1970), 16–17; Nora M. Sanborn, editorial secretary, American Institute of Public Opinion, to David L. Lewis, Mar. 4, 1965.

4. Clancy and Davies, *The Believer*, p. 208; DFP, Oct. 1, 1945; NYT, Dec. 22, 1945; DN, Nov. 25, 1945, May 27, June 16, 1946; DT, June 23, Nov. 21, 1946; *Dearborn Independent*, Aug. 2, 1946; Nevins and Hill, *Decline and Rebirth*, p. 334.

5. Clancy and Davies, *The Believer*, p. 203; Inez Henry, assistant vice-president, Berry College, to David L. Lewis, June 8, 1972. The author photographed "Ford's tree" in March 1972 and July 1974. The Fords entertained Lady Astor at Richmond Hill in 1946. DFP, Mar. 15, 1946.

6. Clancy and Davies, *The Believer*, p. 208–10; Nevins and Hill, *Decline and Rebirth*, pp. 334–35; Robert Rankin, Henry Ford's chauffeur, *Reminiscenses*, pp. 66–73; "Detroit Dynast," *Time* 49 (Apr. 21, 1947), 28–29; DN, May 8, 1953; DT, May 11, 1953; McCarthy, "Amazing Mansion," p. 172.

7. Presentation by Charles E. Carll to dealers, Dearborn, June 20, 1947, Acc. 234, Box 1; Richards, *Last Billionaire*, p. 411; "He Wrote Ford's Obit," *Newsweek* 29 (Apr. 21, 1947), 66; see Acc. 292, Boxes 11–15 for press play on Ford's death. Carll made up for Clara a scrapbook containing news stories, editorials, and photographs on her husband's death. Waddell to Carll, Apr. 14, 1947, Acc. 285, Box 2953.

8. Sigmund Diamond, *The Reputation of the American Businessman* (Cambridge, Mass.: Harvard University Press, 1955), pp. 153, 156–57, 159–65, 168, 174; "Symbol," *New Republic* 116 (Apr. 21, 1947), 9; *Detroit Jewish News*, Apr. 11, 1947; "Henry Ford," *Journal of Negro History* 32 (July 1947), 400.

9. Diamond, *American Businessman*, pp. 66–67, 89, 133, 141–42, 144, 166; "Henry Ford A Symposium," *Ford Times* 39 (May 1947), 2–5.

10. "The Last of an American," *Time* 49 (Apr. 21, 1947), 31–32; Richards, *Last Billionaire*, p. 412; *Times* (London), Apr. 9, 1947.

11. Diamond, *American Businessman*, p. 158.

12. Bacon, *Reminiscences*, p. 215; Diamond, *American Businessman*, p. 159; "Young King Henry Ford II," *Newsweek* 29 (Apr. 21, 1947), 70; "Detroit Dynast," *Time*, p. 28.

13. "Detroit Dynast," *Time*, p. 28; "King Henry II," *Newsweek*, p. 70; DN and DT, Apr. 10, 1947; DFP, Jan. 17, 1948 (cost of casket).

14. DN and DT, Dec. 12, 1947; DN, May 31, 1948; Clancy and Davies, *The Believer*, pp. 211–12; DFP, May 27, 1964; Clara's original land gift of eight-and-one-half acres was supplemented by gifts which increased St. Martha's property holdings to approximately twenty-two acres. St. Martha's Episcopal Church (folder), St. Martha's Episcopal Church Archives.

15. Interview with Catherine Ruddiman, Henry Ford's niece, Dec. 11, 1974; interview with Rev. Edwin A. Griswold, rector, St. Martha's Episcopal Church, Sept. 1, 1970; David L. Lewis, "The Last Resting Place of the World's Greatest Industrialist," *Michigan Heritage* 13 (Spring 1972), 121–24. The author visits the Ford cemetery several times each year. "No Model Change," *Time* 49 (Apr. 28, 1947), 90; "What Ford Left," *Business Week* (Jan. 13, 1951), 85.

16. "Fortune," *Newsweek* 29 (Apr. 28, 1947), 58; "No Model Change," *Time* 49 (Apr. 28, 1947), 90, 92; "What Ford Left," *Business Week* (Jan. 13, 1951), 85; "Hay Hay," *Newsweek* 32 (July 5, 1948), 44.

17. Clancy and Davies, *The Believer*, pp. 211–14.

Chapter 30

1. Interview with William Goodell, manager, News Department, Mar. 3, 1965; see *New York Times Index* and *Readers' Guide to Periodical Literature* for the years 1947–75, especially 1953 and 1963.

2. The principal Ford-related club publications are the

Model T Ford Club of America's *Vintage Ford*, Model T Ford Club International's *Model T Times*, Model A Restorers Club's *Model "A" News*, Model A Ford Club of America's *Restorer*, Early Ford V-8 Club of America's *V-8 Times*, Lincoln Owners' Club's *Fork and Blade*, Lincoln-Zephyr Owners Club's *Way of the Zephyr*, Lincoln Continental Owners Club's *Continental Comments*, Classic Thunderbird Club's *Early Bird*, Ford and Mercury Restorers Club's *Ford-Mercury Historian*, Ford and Mercury Club of America's *Flathead*, Edsel Owner's Club *Big "E,"* International Edsel Club's *Edseletter*, Fabulous Fifties Ford Club of America's *Keystone Times*, and Pantera International's *Pantera International News*. The leading multimake old- and special-interest auto club publications are the Antique Automobile Club of America's *Antique Automobile*, Veteran Motor Car Club of America's *Bulb Horn*, Horseless Carriage Club of America's *Horseless Carriage Gazette*, Classic Car Club of America's *Classic Car*, Milestone Car Society's *Milestone Car*, and Contemporary Historical Vehicle Association's *Action Era Vehicle*. Major old-car trade publications include *Automobile Quarterly*, *Cars & Parts*, *Old Cars*, *Special-Interest Autos*, and *Classic Cars*. The Society of Automotive Historians publishes the *Automotive History Review*. The first of the nonclub magazines for Fordophiles was *Ford Life*, a California-based bimonthly with 6,000 subscribers, published between 1970–74. Its banner was picked up by the quarterly *Ford Illustrated*, published in Arizona.

3. The most recent editions of the following nine encyclopedias were analyzed to determine the amount of space accorded every important deceased world figure (the number of persons who received more space than Ford also is cited): *Encyclopedia Britannica*, 101, *Encyclopedia Americana*, fifty-four, *Collier's Encyclopedia*, thirty-five, *Columbia Encyclopedia*, sixty, *Compton's Pictorial Encyclopedia*, fifty-three, *Merit Students Encyclopedia*, 120, *Grolier Universal Encyclopedia*, ninety-three, *World Book Encyclopedia*, fifty-three, and *Encyclopedia International*, forty. Foreign encyclopedias examined in the same manner were *Chamber's Encyclopedia* (British), 149, *Ensiklopedia Indonesia*, three, *Grand Larousse Encyclopédique* (France), eighty-nine, *Der Grosse Brockhaus* (Germany), thirty, *Meyers Neues Lexikon* (Germany), 135, and *Schweizer Lexikon* (Switzerland), ninety-four. Biographies of Ford also were examined in the most recent editions of the following American encyclopedias: *Our Wonderful World: an Encyclopedia Anthology for the Entire Family*, *Golden Book Encyclopedia*, *Encyclopedic Dictionary of American History*, *Book of Knowledge*, and *American Peoples Encyclopedia*. Ford's biographies were examined in the most recent editions of the following foreign encyclopedias: *Svensk Uppslagsbok* (Sweden), *Enciclopedia Universal Ilustrada Europeo-Americana* (Spain), *Biographical Dictionary* (Taiwan), *Tong-A's New Encyclopedia* (Korea), *Soviet Union Encyclopedia*, *U J Magyar Lexikon* (Hungary), *World Knowledge Hand Book* (People's Republic of China), *Grande Enciclopédia Portuguesa e Brasilerira* (Portugal and Brazil), *Enciclopedia Italiana di Scienze, Lettere ed Arti* (Italy), *Winkler Prins Encyclopaedie* (Netherlands), *Hagerups Illustrerede Konversations Leksikon* (Denmark), and *Norsk Allkunnebok* (Norway).

4. *Wall Street Journal*, Sept. 20, 1967; "The 10 Greatest Men of American Business—As You Picked Them," *Nation's Business* 59 (Mar. 1971), 44–45; DFP, Dec. 21, 1970.

5. *Ann Arbor* (Mich.) *News*, July 28, 1968 (stamp); *Midland* (Mich.) *Daily News*, Jan. 18, 1973 (Automotive Organization Team Hall of Fame); Elmer W. Sherwood, president, Automotive Hall of Fame to David L. Lewis, Apr. 27, 1972; W.R. Schroeder, managing director, Helms Athletic Foundation to David L. Lewis, Aug. 10, 1970 (Racing Hall of Fame); "A Hall of Fame for Business Leadership," *Fortune* 91 (Jan. 1975), 67. The only businessmen elected to the Hall of Fame for Great Americans were Peter Cooper and George Peabody, both admitted in 1900. Among scores of other businessmen voted on, Andrew Carnegie has come closest to being elected. Before becoming eligible for nomination to the hall, candidates had to have been deceased for twenty-five years. Thus, Ford's first bid for election came in 1973.

6. The author has visited the Smithsonian's Hall of Historic Americans, the National Historical Wax Museum, International Hall of Fame, Walk of Fame, and Grace Cathedral; "Ford Country," *Cars & Parts* 17 (Sept. 1974), 107. Ford's birthday parties are organized by Helene Pierce and Iris Becker, of Dearborn. The author has photographed Ford's hair, barber chair, and Henry Ford Museum memorabilia. Windows of the clerestory of Grace Cathedral are dedicated to twelve personalities including Ford "in recognition of those Americans of the Twentieth Century whose outstanding achievements in the various fields of human endeavor have opened new avenues of progress and development." Ford represents industry; Jane Addams, social work and welfare; Luther Burbank, agriculture; John Dewey, education; Albert Einstein, natural sciences; Robert L. Frost, letters; John H. Glenn, exploration; John L. Lewis, labor; Thurgood Marshall, law; Franklin D. Roosevelt, politics; William H. Welch, medicine; and Frank Lloyd Wright, creative arts. The Ford and nine other windows were financed by a gift from W. Selby McCreery, a wealthy San Franciscan. Conservative members of the Episcopal hierarchy opposed the selection of Roosevelt and Lewis. Very Rev. C. Julian Bartlett, dean, Grace Cathedral, to David L. Lewis, Feb. 12, 1974.

7. Anthony Rhodes, *Louis Renault: A Biography* (New York: Harcourt, Brace & World, Inc., 1969), dust jacket; NYT, Oct. 8, 1972 (Yen Tjing-ling); "Meet Mr. Matsushita," *Life* 57 (Sept. 11, 1964), 108; DN, June 4, 1942 (Morris), and Aug. 25, 1974 (Hershey); *Ann Arbor* (Mich.) *News*, Jan. 16, 1970 (Piper); DFP, Mar. 29, 1943 (Kaiser); Francis Cooke, "Theodore Presser," *Etude* 67 (Mar. 1949), 141; *Time* 78 (Oct. 27, 1961), 94 (space).

8. Miriam Beard, *A History of Business*, vol. 2, *From the Monopolists to the Organization Men* (Ann Arbor: University of Michigan Press, 1963), p. 265 (businessmen's memorials); Visit Historic Fair Lane, brochure, University of Michigan-Dearborn Office of University Relations, Dearborn, 1974; DN, June 29, 1966, and June 21, 1974; DFP, Nov. 15, 1966 (landmark designation); Jane Wyeth, Customer Advisory Service, Sotheby Parke Bernet, to David L. Lewis, Sept. 12, 1973; the author has visited the Roosevelt, Edison, Eastman, and Gould homes.

9. See *Fortune's* "The Fortune Directory of the 500 Largest Industrial Corporations," annually published since 1955 in issues ranging from May to August. Ford, along with all other recession-hit auto firms, was ranked lower in 1974 in certain categories than in previous years; the company was

rated twentieth in net income, eighth in stock-holders' net equity. *Fortune* 91 (May 1975), 208, 210–11; Louise Huxtable, "The Mighty Rouge: Her Colossal Impact on America," *Detroit* (DFP Sunday magazine), Aug. 30, 1970; "Volkswagen Gets a Much-Needed Tune-Up," *Fortune* 85 (Mar. 1972), 85; DN, May 11, 1973 (Highland Park).

10. Henry Ford was measured at five feet, nine inches; Edsel, five feet, seven and one-half inches; and Sorensen, six feet, one inch. "How Tall Was Henry?," *Ford Life* 3 (Jan.–Feb. 1972), 38; Detroit Edison Company Service Center to David L. Lewis, Aug. 22, 1972.

11. Interviews with Robert Smith, Mar. 10, 1974, Roger Evans, owner of Harper house, May 16, 1974, and the Rev. Florence B. Crews, owner of Temple of Light, Mar. 12, 1973; DN, Jan. 22, 1975 (square house for sale).

12. "Society's Scouts: The New Role of Foundations," *Life* 66 (Mar. 7, 1969), 36; William Greenleaf, *From These Beginnings: The Early Philanthropies of Henry and Edsel Ford, 1911–1936* (Detroit: Wayne State University Press, 1964), p. 69; DN, Oct. 23, 1973; "America's 10 Best Hospitals," *Ladies' Home Journal* 84 (Feb. 1967), 34, 134. Henry Ford Hospital was the only nonteaching hospital named by the *Journal's* jury.

13. University of Michigan-Dearborn from 1959 to 1974, supplement to *Dearborn Times-Herald,* Sept. 11, 1974; *Dearborn Guide,* Nov. 26, 1969; *Dearborn Press,* June 12, 1975; addresses of schools named for the Fords may be found in telephone directories.

14. Willis F. Dunbar, ed., *Michigan Historical Markers* (Lansing: Michigan Historical Commission, 1967), p. 173 (Botsford); David L. Lewis, "The Flivver of Hostelries: Ford's Wayside Inn," *Cars & Parts* 17 (Apr. 1974), 126–30A; the author has photographed all of the Martha-Mary chapels as well as the Botsford and Wayside inns.

15. *Fort Myers Southwest Floridian,* Aug. 11, 1945; Thomas A. Edison's Winter Home, Laboratory, and Botanical Gardens, brochure in possession of author (Friendship Walk); DFP, Mar. 23, 1975 (Richmond Hill); Sally Redfield, leasor of Ford's former Harbor Beach cottage, to David L. Lewis, Sept. 27, 1973; interview with members of the John M. O'Boyle family, leasor of Ford's former Huron Mountain Club cottage, July 31, 1973; interview with I.B. Hutchison, owner of Thunder Bay Inn, July 31, 1973; David L. Lewis, "Macon, Michigan: A Ford Country Home," *Cars & Parts* 18 (Dec. 1974), 126–27.

16. Dunbar, *Michigan Markers,* pp. 136, 147–48, 62–63; Dearborn celebrated Ford's seventy-fifth birthday on July 28 rather than July 30, DN, July 28, 1938; *Dearborn Independent,* Aug. 2, 1946; DN, May 23, 1947 (stone memorial, which the author has photographed as recently as Jan. 10, 1975).

17. The Henry and Edsel Ford Auditorium was discussed in chapter 22; Dunbar, *Michigan Markers,* pp. 3, 173; Ford Forestry Center: A Research and Educational Facility of Michigan Technological University, brochure in possession of author (1973); the author has traveled each of the Ford roads except for the one in Garnet, Calif.

18. Paul D. Taylor, consul of the U.S.A., São Paulo, Brazil, to David L. Lewis, June 5, 1970; David L. Lewis, "A Monument for Henry," *Ford Life* 1 july–Aug. 1971), 16. Moselle Kimbler, Ford Foundation, to David L. Lewis, Aug. 22, 1968.

19. Niven Busch, Jr., *Twenty-One Americans* (Garden City, N.Y.: Doubleday, Doran & Company, Inc., 1930), pp. 44–45; DFP, May 8, 1953 (Kettering).

20. Coca-Cola's advertising proclaims that its name and trademark are better known than any other; Ford's advertising declares that Ford and Coca-Cola have the two best known names and trademarks on earth.

Index

David L. Lewis is professor of business history at the University of Michigan, from which he received his doctorate in economic history. He is also an award-winning journalist and public relations specialist. He is the author of more than 300 published articles, most of them concerning the life of Henry Ford and the history of the Ford Motor Company. *The Public Image of Henry Ford,* his first book-length study, is the result of nineteen years of research.

The manuscript was edited by Elaine P. Halperin. The book was designed by Richard Kinney. The typeface for the text is Times Roman, designed under the supervision of Stanley Morison in 1931. The display face is Cheltenham based on the original design by Bertram G. Goodhue in 1896.

The text is printed on Glatfelter's T & S Litho paper and the book is bound in Columbia Mill's Fictionette cloth over binders' board. Manufactured in the United States of America.

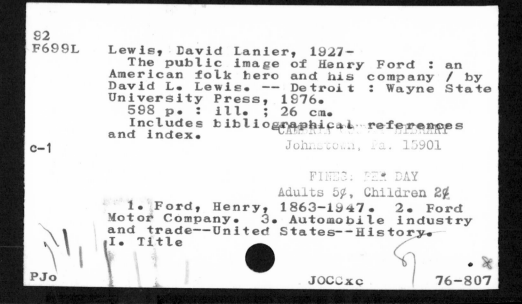